monitoring the future

questionnaire responses from the nation's high school seniors

1985

Lloyd D. Johnston, Jerald G. Bachman, and
Patrick M. O'Malley

Survey Research Center • Institute for Social Research
The University of Michigan
Ann Arbor, Michigan

ISR Code Number 4750
ISSN 0190-9185
ISBN 0-87944-313-8
Library of Congress Catalog Card Number 79-640937

Copyright 1986 by The University of Michigan,
All Rights Reserved

Published in 1986 by:
Institute for Social Research,
The University of Michigan, Ann Arbor, Michigan

6 5 4 3 2 1

Printed in the United States of America

Table of Contents

Preface vii
   Purposes of this Series of Publications vii
   A Guide for the Reader viii
   Availability of Archived Data ix
   Other Publications from the Study ix
   Acknowledgements x

Introduction 1
   The Need for Social Indicators 2
   Research Design and Procedures 2
      Reasons for Focusing on High School Seniors 2
      Sampling Procedures 3
      School Recruiting Procedures 4
      Advance Contact with Teachers and Students 4
      Questionnaire Administrations 4
      Procedures for Protecting Confidentiality 5
   Content Areas and Questionnaire Design 5
   Representativeness and Validity 5
      School Participation 5
      Student Participation 7
      Validity of Self-Report Data 7
      Accuracy of the Sample 7
      Consistency and the Measurements of Trends 8
   Caveats to Users of the Data 8
      Estimation of Sampling Errors 8
      Subgroup Definitions 8
      Missing Data Notes 8
      Characterizing Heroin Users 8
      Interpreting Racial Differences 9

Descriptive Results 13
   Introduction to the Table Format and Conventions 13
   Questionnaire Form 1-5 16
      Section C (all Forms): Demographic Variables, Family Background, etc. ... 16
      Section B (all Forms): Drug Use 25
   Questionnaire Form 1 33
      Section A 33
      Section B (Detailed Drug Use) 40
      Section D 82

Questionnaire Form 2   89
    Section A   89
    Section D   104
    Section E   111
Questionnaire Form 3   119
    Section A   119
    Section D   133
    Section E   136
Questionnaire Form 4   146
    Section A   146
    Section D   160
    Section E   166
Questionnaire Form 5   174
    Section A   174
    Section D   188
    Section E   194

Cross-Time Index of Questionnaire Items   205
Introduction to the Indexing Conventions   205
Question Index   211

Appendices

Appendix A: Sampling Error Estimates and Tables   247
Appendix B: Procedures Used to Derive Design Effects
            and Sampling Errors   257
Appendix C: Questionnaire Covers, Instructions, and
            Sample Page   271

References   275

Tables

Table 1: Sample Sizes and Student Response Rates   4
Table 2: Measurement Content Areas   6
Table 3: Subject Area Key   208
Table A-1: Confidence Intervals (95% Level) Around Percentage Values   251
Table A-2: Confidence Intervals for Differences Between Two Percentages
    (95% Confidence Level)   253
Table B-1: Sample Sizes (Unweighted and Weighted) in Subgroups by Year   265
Table B-2: Sample Sizes (Unweighted and Weighted) in Subgroups by Year
    for Questions on a Single Form   266
Table B-3: Guidelines for Computing Design Effects (DEFFs) for
    Percentages and Means Derived from Monitoring the Future Samples   268

Figures

Figure 1: Guide to Table Format   15
Figure 2: Guide to Cross-Time Index   207
Figure B-1: Design Effects for Single Percentages   261
Figure B-2: Design Effects for Differences Between Percentages   263

Preface

This volume is the latest in a series which presents descriptive statistical results from a national survey of young people entitled Monitoring the Future: A continuing Study of the Lifestyles and Values of Youth. Each year the study surveys a large sample of high school seniors, located in approximately 125 schools nationwide, and drawn to be representative of all seniors in the coterminous United States.

The first four volumes in this series, dealing with the high school classes of 1975, 1976, 1977, and 1978 were published simultaneously early in 1980. Additional volumes appear on an annual basis. The most important contribution of this series is likely to be the opportunity it provides for the exploration of trends, a process that obviously involves the use of several different volumes. With that in mind, we have kept the format highly consistent from one volume to another, and we have developed an index (described below) which should facilitate the process of matching data across years. It should be noted that the volume presenting 1975 data is different from the others in several respects.*

Although we designed the volumes to fit together as a series, we also saw distinct advantages in having each volume able to stand alone — to be usable without reference to any of the others. For that reason, the introductory material on research design and questionnaire content, the instructions for accessing the data tables, and the appendices on sampling errors are all included in each volume. Thus, the small price we pay for making each volume self-contained is that much of the text portion is repeated each year.

Purposes of this Series of Publications

Monitoring the Future, which is conducted by the University of Michigan's Institute for Social Research and receives its core funding from the National Institute on Drug Abuse, is an unusually comprehensive research project in several respects: surveys are conducted annually on an ongoing basis; the samples are large and nationally representative; and the subject matter is very broad, encompassing some 1,300 variables per year. Many people — scholars, policy makers, educators, and so on — will have an interest in the results.

The principal investigators are already writing for a number of these audiences and will continue to do so. Because of the limitations in our own time, interests, and expertise, however, there is an enormous amount of valuable information which may never be utilized if the initiative to digest and disseminate all of it must come from us alone. Further, since the project is in part a social indicator series, its value rests to a considerable degree on *timely* dissemination of the results. For these reasons, we wish to share the study's results with others in a number of fields on a rapid and regular basis. We have chosen to provide two major and complementary vehicles for doing this: (a) these annual reference volumes of descriptive results, and (b) machine-readable data archives for direct analysis by others.

We believe that many potential users who would not mount the effort required to conduct computer analyses of archived data will be able to get most of

*The 1975 volume does not include comparison data for black and white subgroups, nor does it include data for the subgroups who did and did not plan to complete four years of college. Also, somewhat fewer questionnaire items appear than in the other volumes. These restrictions are the result primarily of missing data problems that occurred only in the 1975 survey. In most respects, however, those seeking to compare different classes of high school seniors will find the 1975 data useful.

what they want from these volumes of descriptive results. The user of any one of these volumes can estimate – usually with considerable accuracy – a wide variety of characteristics of the high school class described in that volume. To take just one example, the user of the 1984 volume can ascertain that 40.0 percent of seniors in the high school class of 1984 reported using marijuana at least once during the preceding year. Further, by utilizing two or more of these volumes the reader can describe recent trends in any such characteristic. To continue with the same example, the volume describing the high school class of 1975 also indicates that 40.0 percent of these seniors reported marijuana use during the preceding year; and when that is combined with the data from the intervening years the reader is able to discern a steady increase between 1975 and 1979 (50.8 percent of that class reported having used marijuana at least once in the preceding year), and a subsequent steady decrease back down to the 1975 level. The figures for the years 1975 to 1984 are:

1975: 40.0	1980: 48.8
1976: 44.5	1981: 46.1
1977: 47.6	1982: 44.3
1978: 50.2	1983: 42.3
1979: 50.8	1984: 40.0

A similar examination of trends can be carried out for over 1,300 different variables dealing with a wide variety of subject areas (listed in Table 2 of the Introduction). A simple indexing system (described below) has been developed which makes it quite straightforward for the reader wishing to do trend analyses to locate the results for a given question for any year of the study. The index in the present volume lists the location of all items included in the surveys from 1976 onward, as well as most items included in 1975.

Analyses such as those illustrated above need not be limited to the total sample. The data provided in these volumes also permit examination of a variety of subgroups (e.g., males, females, those from different regions, those with different levels of drug use experience).

We recognize that providing ready access to essentially undigested data carries certain risks, particularly the risk of mistaken interpretations based on inadequate controls, lack of awareness of sample limitations, etc. More than offsetting the risks, in our view, are the advantages of prompt and widespread dissemination of these nationally representative survey indicator data. Although we are unable to eliminate the risks, we hope to reduce them by providing the reader with an extensive list of caveats presented at the end of the Introduction section. We ask all who use the data to read these caveats carefully and take them seriously.

A Guide for the Reader

This volume is divided into three main parts: (1) the introductory section, (2) the section giving the descriptive results from the current year's survey, and (3) the cross-time item reference index.

Introductory Section. The introduction contains a description of the study — its purposes, major content areas, design, field procedures, response rates, and methods of publication and data dissemination. Since most of this material remains unchanged from year to year, anyone having read another of the volumes may wish to skim this section. We do, however, suggest reviewing the caveats, located at the end of the introductory section, which deal with interpreting and extrapolating from these data.

Descriptive Results Section. In this section all questions contained in this year's survey are presented along with percentagized frequency distributions of answers for the entire sample and for selected subgroups. The questions in this section are organized according to the number of the questionnaire form in which they were contained (forms one through five) and according to the order in which the questions occurred. There is one important exception, however. A major segment of questions common to all five forms of the questionnaire (dealing with drug use, background characteristics, and some other subjects) is presented only once, at the beginning of the Descriptive Results section, using the data from respondents on all five forms.

The first portion of the descriptive results section contains detailed definitions of all subgroups for whom data are presented. It also describes the statistical conventions used in generating the tables.

Cross-Time Index of Questionnaire Items. Beginning with the 1982 volume, this index is ordered by subject area. (It was ordered by item reference number prior to 1982.) The index is intended to serve two purposes.

First, it should be useful in locating items dealing with a subject area of interest. The subject area key at the beginning of the cross-time item index shows the alphabetical code assigned to various subject areas (e.g., "politics" or "work and leisure"). Having selected a subject area of interest, one can then go to that section of the index to locate all questions in any of the surveys which deal with that subject. (The procedure is slightly different in volumes prior to 1982, as described in those volumes.) To locate the results for any given question in this volume, simply look in column two of the item index for its page location.

The cross-time index can also be used to determine in which other years an item was used and where to locate it. If, in reviewing the Descriptive Results section, one locates an interesting item and would like to know in which of the other annual surveys of seniors it has appeared, it may be found in the cross-time index by the unique "item reference number" within the relevant subject area. The index will indicate all years in which that same item appeared and show the questionnaire form, section, and item number for each year. This information thus can be used to decide which other volumes in this series might be of relevance; and the same item may be readily located by its reference number in the index of any other volume prior to the 1982 volume, and by its subject area and reference number in any volume from 1982 on.

Sampling Appendices. Appendix A is provided for those wishing to determine the confidence limits around a percentage estimate, or to test the statistical significance of an observed difference between two groups, or to test the significance of a change from one year to another. It gives the necessary procedures and tables for such tests and provides the appropriate factors by which to correct for the fact that the study makes use of a multi-stage probability sample clustered in a limited number of schools (usually about 125). Appendix B provides further detail on sample design effects and the procedures which were used to derive the sampling error estimates.

Availability of Archived Data

As was mentioned earlier, this series of volumes is complemented by an archiving of the raw data set for direct analysis by others not associated with the project. The present volumes should be a considerable help to those wishing to access the archived data since they provide a verbatim statement of items and answer categories, and also because they include basic univariate and bivariate frequency distributions for all items, as well as the missing data rates. The cross-time index of items contained in each of these volumes also provides an efficient way to identify the relevant variables in various content areas, as well as to determine when they were measured and their questionnaire locations. In fact, we hope that the availability of this series will not only facilitate the use of the archived data but actually stimulate interest in their use.

The individual level data which are summarized in this and previous volumes are available from:

The Interuniversity Consortium for Political and Social Research (ICPSR)
Institute for Social Research
P.O. Box 1248
Ann Arbor, Michigan 48106

The ICPSR archive makes individual-level data available to interested investigators for analysis. A few variables have been modified or deleted to ensure that the answers of an individual respondent cannot be located through pattern recognition (i.e., using various descriptor variables in combination to make a unique identification). The changed or deleted variables include month of birth, race, and the sampling weight, which adjusts for selection probability.

Other Publications from the Study

A number of different forms of publications based on Monitoring the Future data have been developed or are being planned. One series of reports, dealing with trends in drug use and drug-related attitudes and beliefs, is being published by the National Institute on Drug Abuse. The first report in that series, *Drug Use Among American High School Students 1975-1977* (Johnston, Bachman, and O'Malley), was published in late 1977. Subsequent reports have been issued annually.

An Occasional Paper series has been launched by the project. It includes papers on design and methodological issues as well as special substantive analyses and early, and sometimes more detailed, drafts of articles planned for journal publication. The first occasional paper, "The Monitoring the Future Project Design and Procedures" (Bachman and Johnston, 1978), provides a detailed description of the study and its underlying rationale.

The present series of reference volumes is being published by the Institute for Social Research. A new volume will be added to this series each year.

To request particular papers, reprints, or periodic notification of publications available from the study, write to Monitoring the Future, Room 2030, Institute for Social Research, The University of Michigan, Box 1248, Ann Arbor, Michigan 48106.

---

*Single copies of these reports may be ordered without cost from the National Clearinghouse for Drug Abuse Information, National Institute on Drug Abuse, 5600 Fishers Lane, Rockville, Maryland 20857. See References for a complete list of reports.

Acknowledgements

A great many people have contributed to the launching and development of this research effort. We are indebted to a number of officials of the National Institute on Drug Abuse and the Special Action Office for Drug Abuse Prevention for their encouragement and advice at the outset — in particular, Richard Bucher, Robert DuPont, William Pollin, and Louise Richards.

Our colleagues at the Institute for Social Research and elsewhere who shared their insights, and often their most cherished instrumentation, are too numerous to mention; but their contributions are greatly appreciated. To the former director of the Survey Research Center's Sampling Section, Irene Hess, and to her colleagues we owe a particular debt for the creativity of the sampling design for the study. The contributions of the SRC Field Section also have been very valuable.

Major contributions to the production of this particular volume were made by staff members Jerome Hiniker, Dawn Bare, and Ginger Maggio. We would also like to thank the staff of the Publishing Division of the Institute for Social Reserch for their work in arranging publication.

The present and former members of the project staff (listed below) have, of course, contributed greatly to the building of this large and complex research series.

Finally, we would like to acknowledge the tens of thousands of high school seniors, their teachers, and their principals, whose cooperation and generous contributions of time make the Monitoring the Future project possible.

LLOYD D. JOHNSTON
JERALD G. BACHMAN
PATRICK M. O'MALLEY

Present and Former Members of the Project Staff

Donna Ando	Michael Fisher	John Miller
Margaret Bailey	Henry Freeman	Marion Morse
Dawn Bare	Walter Gruhn	Jim Neveaux
Ellen Berger	Lana Harrison	Dorothy Paulette
Mary Lou Bewley	James Hersey	Susan Pauls
Katherine Blatt	A. Regula Herzog	Sharon Pietila
Mary Lea Bonucchi	Jerome Hiniker	Joseph Pleck
Katheryn Boris	Pamela Kittel	Deborah Poinier
Marcy Breslow	Mark Krell	Judith Redmond
Susan Burek	Zenon Kuzmyn	Barbara Renaud
Mary Danneffel-Mashruwala	Carol Larsen	Don Rubinstein
Mary Lou Davis	Sally Lawson	Maria Sanchez
Mary Dempsy	Ludmilla Litus	Tina Smith
William Diedrich	A. Kathryn Loker	Ann Taylor
Robert Doljanac	Regina Lumbard	Richard Taylor
Karen Donahue	Mary Lutz	Lynda Tolen
Leslie Eveland	Ginger Maggio	Sandra Wronski
Halford Fairchild	Oksana Malanchuk	Thelma Wurzelbacher
Maureen Ferrell	Wayne McCulloch	Daniel Zahs
Marjorie Fisher	Joan McGraw	

Introduction

The Monitoring the Future project is designed to explore changes in many important values, behaviors, and lifestyle orientations of contemporary American youth. Two general types of tasks may be distinguished. The first is to provide a systematic and accurate *description* of the youth population of interest in a given year, and to quantify the direction and rate of the changes taking place among them over time. The second task, more analytic than descriptive, involves the *explanation* of the relationships and trends observed to exist.

The task of description may be subdivided into three parts: (1) the description of static conditions (which may be accomplished through a single cross-sectional study); (2) the description of cross-cohort or, in longer time-spans, generational changes (usually accomplished using repeated cross sections of the same age groups); and (3) the description of changes with aging (usually accomplished by means of longitudinal studies). The Monitoring the Future project has the capacity to provide each of these three types of description, since it incorporates all three types of research design into a single study. (This complex design, in which multiple cohorts are followed longitudinally, has been referred to as a cohort-sequential design.)

The content of this volume exemplifies the first of these types of description in that it contains cross-sectional data on a single high school class. When the data in this volume are used in combination with data from other such volumes in the series, the nature, direction, and rates of change from one cohort of seniors to another also may be described — the type of reporting which is often labeled as the social indicator approach. The third class of description — dealing with the maturational changes which occur during the years after high school — will not be dealt with in this series of volumes but will be reported in other publications from the study.*

The accurate characterization of American young people and the description of important changes occurring among them is but one class of objectives for the study. The second class of objectives involves the development of a greater understanding of what causes these young people to be as they are, and why the changes being documented are occurring. Explanation will be sought through both the analysis of change at the aggregate level and at the individual level. The results of these explorations will be disseminated via the various publications discussed in the Preface.

The merging of the social indicator approach and the analysis of relationships (particularly longitudinal relations) into a single cohort-sequential design is, in our view, synergistic: the effectiveness of the two approaches combined is greater than if the two were undertaken separately. Because the present series of volumes deals with senior year data only, our remarks here focus primarily on the project's social indicator contributions — the accurate description of high

---

* Panels of students from each graduating class are being randomly selected and followed longitudinally for up to ten years. Thus it soon will be possible to characterize the changes which seem to take place consistently with aging during the early adult years. Not only will longitudinal development in the years after high school be studied, but once enough of these longitudinal panels have accumulated, it will also be possible to characterize cross-sectionally most American young people aged 18 to 28, (at least the major segment of the population who completed high school — roughly 80-85 percent), and to describe the changing characteristics of that age group each year.

school seniors and the documentation of trends over time. It is worth noting, however, that even the limited amount of bivariate data included in the present volumes will suggest promising directions for relational analyses, many of which can be carried out using the archived data tapes from the project.

The Need for Social Indicators

The fundamental argument for developing social indicators is that there are considerable scientific and practical benefits derived from having accurate information about current social realities and the way those realities have been changing. For the scientific community such indicators provide a rich set of information against which existing theory may be tested and from which new theory may be suggested. For the community at large, social indicators permit the "reality testing" of common perceptions and beliefs about the nation and its people. Past experience has demonstrated that widely held conceptions, which themselves may serve to create or exacerbate problems, can be most inaccurate. One example is the exaggerated popular conception of the size and nature of the "gap" between generations (see Adelson, 1970, 1979); another is the mistaken assumption that most young people condone the use of a variety of illegal drugs (Johnston, 1973; Johnston, Bachman, and O'Malley, 1977; 1979 a, b; 1981).

While deflating exaggerated perceptions, a continual monitoring of indicators on youth also can reveal the beginning of new problems and thus give rise to corrective efforts at a relatively early stage. For instance, most would view with concern the emergence of new types of drug use. Monitoring the Future has already documented and reported a sharp increase in regular marijuana use among high school seniors, and as a result more attention has been paid to the issue by policy makers, the media, and the general public. The discovery of such trends may trigger more intense efforts to discover the causes, consequences, and (when appropriate) preventatives of such behaviors.

Although social indicators seldom translate directly into specific policy decisions, the availability of descriptive information can substantially enhance the decision-making capabilities of policy makers. These data provide considerable insight into the size and nature of problems, the rate of change occurring nationally and in subgroups, and in some instances information about related factors and even the likely impacts of major social interventions (such as changed drug laws, or new incentives for recruitment into the military, to name but two). They also provide the possibility of feedback on the consequences of some social interventions as well as major historical events.

The particular topics included in our monitoring system are summarized later in this introduction and, of course, they are presented fully in the complete set of data tables. For present purposes, it is enough to indicate that the range of topics is very broad. This breadth is partly due to the wide interests of the principal investigators; but it also reflects our conviction that the concurrent examination of trends in a variety of areas is not only much more cost efficient but also more scientifically productive.

Research Design and Procedures*

The basic research design involves annual data collections from high school seniors during the spring of each year, beginning with the class of 1975. Each data collection takes place in approximately 125 public and private high schools selected to provide an accurate cross section of high school seniors throughout the coterminous United States. The design also provides for the longitudinal study of a subsample from each class of participating seniors; but since the focus of this series of volumes is exclusively on the data collected annually from seniors, the follow-up procedures will not be discussed here.

Reasons for Focusing on High School Seniors. There are several reasons for choosing the senior year of high school as an optimal point for monitoring the behaviors and attitudes of youth. One is that the completion of high school represents the end of an important developmental stage in this society, since it demarcates both the end of universal public education and, for many, the end of living in the parental home. Therefore, it is a logical point at which to take stock of the accumulated influences of these two environments on American youth.

Further, the completion of high school represents the jumping off point from which young people diverge into widely differing social environments, including college, business firms, military service, and homemaking. But these environmental transitions are not the only important changes which coincide with the end of high school. Most young men and women now reach the formal age of adulthood shortly before or after graduation; more significantly, they begin to assume adult roles, including financial self-support, marriage, and parenthood.

Finally, there are some important practical advantages to building a system of data collections around samples of high school seniors. The last year of high school constitutes the final point at which a reasonably good national sample of an age-specific cohort can be drawn and studied economically. The need for systematically repeated, large-scale samples from which to make reliable estimates of change requires

---

*A more extensive description of the research design and procedures may be found in Bachman and Johnston (1978).

that considerable stress be laid on efficiency and feasibility; the present design meets those requirements.

One limitation in the design is that it does not include in the target population those young men and women who drop out of high school before graduation (or before the last few months of the senior year, to be more precise). This excludes a relatively small proportion of each age cohort — between 15 and 20 percent (Dearman and Plisko, 1982) — though not an unimportant segment, since we know that certain behaviors such as illicit drug use (Johnston, 1973) and delinquency (Bachman, O'Malley, and Johnston, 1978) tend to be higher than average in this group. However, the addition of a representative sample of dropouts would increase the cost of the present research enormously, because of their dispersion and generally higher level of resistance to being located and interviewed.

For the purposes of estimating characteristics of the entire age group, the omission of high school dropouts does introduce certain biases; however, their small proportion sets outer limits on the bias (Johnston, O'Malley, and Bachman, 1985, Appendix). For the purposes of estimating *changes* from one cohort of high school seniors to another, the omission of dropouts represents a problem only if different cohorts have considerably different proportions who drop out. We have no reason to expect dramatic changes in those rates for the foreseeable future, and recently published government statistics indicate a great deal of stability in dropout rates since 1970 (Dearman and Plisko, 1982, p. 4).

Some may use our high school data to draw conclusions about changes for the entire age group. While we do not encourage such extrapolation, we suspect that the conclusions reached often would be valid, since over 80 percent of the age group is in the surveyed segment of the population *and* we expect that change among those not in school are very likely to parallel the changes among those who are. Nevertheless, for purposes of characterizing the entire age group we would urge the user to check the results emanating from the present monitoring system against those emerging from other data collection systems using different methods, such as household interviews. (It is encouraging to note that when we have compared drug use data for this age group from the present study with those from interview studies, the findings have shown a high degree of similarity.)

Sampling Procedures. The procedure for securing a nationwide sample of high school seniors is a multistage one. Stage 1 is the selection of particular geographic areas, Stage 2 is the selection of one or more high schools in each area, and Stage 3 is the selection of seniors within each high school.

Stage 1: Geographic Areas. The geographic areas used in this study are the primary sampling units (PSUs) developed by the Sampling Section of the Survey Research Center for use in the Center's nationwide interview studies. These consist of 74 primary areas throughout the coterminous United States — including the 12 largest metropolitan areas, which contain about 30 percent of the nation's population. Of the 62 other primary areas, 10 are in the Northeast, 18 in the North Central area, 24 in the South, and 10 in the West. Because these same PSUs are used for personal interview studies by the Survey Research Center (SRC), local field representatives can be assigned to administer the data collections in practically all schools.

Stage 2: Schools. In the major metropolitan areas more than one high school is often included in the sampling design; in most other sampling areas a single high school is sampled. In all cases, the selections of high schools are made such that the probability of drawing a school is proportionate to the size of its senior class. The larger the senior class (according to recent records), the higher the selection probability assigned to the high school. When a sampled school is unwilling to participate, a replacement school as similar to it as possible is selected from the same geographic area.

Stage 3: Students. Within each selected school, up to about 400 seniors may be included in the data collection. In schools with fewer than 400 seniors, the usual procedure is to include all of them in the data collection. In larger schools, a subset of seniors is selected either by randomly sampling classrooms or by some other random method that is convenient for the school and judged to be unbiased. Sample weights are assigned to each respondent so as to take account of variations in the sizes of samples from one school to another, as well as the (smaller) variations in selection probabilities occurring at the earlier stages of sampling.

The three-stage sampling procedure described above yielded the number of participating schools and students indicated in Table 1.

One other important feature of the base-year sampling procedure should be noted here. All schools (except for half of the initial 1975 sample) are asked to participate in two data collections, thereby permitting replacement of half of the total sample of schools each year. One motivation for requesting that schools participate for two years is administrative efficiency; it is a costly and time-consuming procedure to secure the cooperation of schools, and a two-year period of participation cuts down that effort substantially. Another important advantage is that whenever an appreciable shift in scores from one graduating class to the next is observed, it is possible to check whether the shift might be attributable to some differences in the newly sampled schools. This is done simply by repeating the analysis using only the 60 or so schools which participated both years. Thus far, the half-sample approach

Table 1

Sample Sizes and Student Response Rates

	1975	1976	1977	1978	1979	1980	1981	1982	1983	1984	1985
Number of Public Schools	111	108	108	111	111	107	109	116	112	117	115
Number of Private Schools	14	15	16	20	20	20	19	21	22	17	17
Total Number of Schools	125	123	124	131	131	127	128	137	134	134	132
Total Number of Students*	15791	16678	18436	18924	16662	16524	18267	18348	16947	16499	16502
Student Response Rate**	78%	77%	79%	83%	82%	82%	81%	83%	84%	83%	84%

* Sample weights are assigned to each respondent to correct for unequal probabilities of selection which arise in the multi-stage sampling procedure.

** The student response rate is derived by dividing the attained sample by the target sample (both based on weighted numbers of cases). The target sample is based upon listings provided by schools. Since such listings may fail to take account of recent student attrition, the actual response rate may be slightly underestimated.

has worked quite well; and examination of drug prevalance data from the "matched half-samples" showed that the half samples of repeat schools yielded drug prevalence trends which were virtually identical to trends based on all schools.

School Recruiting Procedures. Early during the fall semester an initial contact is made with each sampled school. First a letter is sent to the principal describing the study and requesting permission to survey seniors. The letter is followed by a telephone call from a project staff member, who attempts to deal with any questions or problems and (when necessary) makes arrangements to contact and seek permission from other school district officials. Basically the same procedures are followed for schools asked to participate for the second year.

Once the school's agreement to participate is obtained, arrangements are made by phone for administering the questionnaires. A specific date for the survey is mutually agreed upon and a local SRC representative is assigned to carry out the administration.

Advance Contact with Teachers and Students. The local SRC representative is instructed to visit the school two weeks ahead of the actual date of administration. This visit serves as an occasion to meet the teachers whose classes will be affected and to provide them with a brochure describing the study, a brief set of guidelines about the questionnaire administration, and a supply of flyers to be distributed to the students a week to 10 days in advance of the questionnaire administration. The guidelines to the teachers include

a suggested announcement to students at the time the flyers are distributed.

From the students' standpoint, the first information about the study usually consists of the teacher's announcement and the short descriptive flyer. In announcing the study, the teachers are asked to stress that the questionnaires used in the survey are not tests, and that there are no right or wrong answers. The flyer tells students that they will be invited to participate in the study, points out that their participation is strictly voluntary, and stresses confidentiality (including a reference to the fact that the Monitoring the Future project has a special government grant of confidentiality which allows their answers to be protected). The flyer also serves as an informative document which the students can show to their parents.

Questionnaire Administrations. The questionnaire administration in each school is carried out by the local SRC representatives and their assistants, following standardized procedures detailed in a project instruction manual. The questionnaires are administered in classrooms during normal class periods whenever possible, although circumstances in some schools require the use of larger group administrations. Teachers are not asked to do anything more than introduce the SRC staff members and (in most cases) remain in the classroom to help guarantee an orderly atmosphere for the survey. Teachers are urged to avoid walking around the room, so that students may feel free to write their answers without fear of being observed.

The actual process of completing the questionnaires is quite straightforward. Respondents are given sharpened pencils and asked to use them because the questionnaires are designed for automatic scanning. Most respondents can finish within a 45-minute class period; for those who cannot, an effort is made to provide a few minutes of additional time.

Procedures for Protecting Confidentiality. In any study that relies on voluntary reporting of drug use or other illegal acts, it is essential to develop procedures which guarantee the confidentiality of such reports. It is also desirable that these procedures be described adequately to respondents so that they are comfortable about providing honest answers.

We noted that the first information given to students about the survey consists of a descriptive flyer stressing confidentiality and voluntary participation. This theme is repeated at the start of the questionnaire administration. Each participating student is instructed to read the message on the cover of the questionnaire, which stresses the importance and value of the study, notes that answers will be kept strictly confidential, states that the study is completely voluntary, and tells the student "If there is any question you or your parents would find objectionable for any reason, just leave it blank." The instructions then point out that in a few months a summary of nationwide results will be mailed to all participants and also that a follow-up questionnaire will be sent to some students after a year. The cover message explains that these are the reasons for asking that name and address be written on a special form which will be removed from the questionnaire and handed in separately. The message also points out that the two different code numbers (one on the questionnaire and one on the tear-out form) cannot be matched except by a special computer tape at The University of Michigan. (The content of the inside and outside of the standard questionnaire cover, including the tear-out form, may be found in Appendix C.)

Content Areas and Questionnaire Design

Drug use and related attitudes are the topics which receive the most extensive coverage in the Monitoring the Future project; but the questionnaires also deal with a wide range of other subject areas, including attitudes about government, social institutions, race relations, changing roles for women, educational aspirations, occupational aims, and marital and family plans, as well as a variety of background and demographic factors.* (Table 2 provides an outline of the 20

general subject areas into which all items are categorized in the Question Index toward the end of this volume.) Given this breadth of content, the study is not presented to respondents as a "drug use study," nor do they tend to view it as such.

Because many questions are needed to cover all of these topic areas, much of the questionnaire content is divided into five different questionnaire forms which are distributed to participants in an ordered sequence that produces five virtually identical subsamples. About one-third of each questionnaire form consists of key or "core" variables which are common to all forms. All demographic variables and some measures of drug use are included in this "core" set of measures. This use of the full sample for drug and demographic measures provides a more accurate estimation on these dimensions and also makes it possible to link them statistically to all of the other measures which are included in a single form only.**

Representativeness and Validity

The samples for this study are intended to be representative of high school seniors throughout the 48 coterminous states. We have already discussed the fact that this definition of the sample excludes one important portion of the age cohort: those who have dropped out of high school before nearing the end of the senior year. But given the aim of representing high school seniors, it will now be useful to consider the extent to which the obtained samples of schools and students are likely to be representative of all seniors and the degree to which the data obtained are likely to be valid.

We can distinguish at least four ways in which survey data of this sort might fall short of being fully accurate. First, some sampled schools refuse to participate, which could introduce some bias. Second, the failure to obtain questionnaire data from 100 percent of the students sampled in participating schools would also introduce bias. Third, the answers provided by participating students are open to both conscious and unconscious distortions which could reduce validity. Finally, limitations in sample size and/or design could place limits on the accuracy of estimates. Each of these issues is treated extensively elsewhere (Johnston, Bachman, and O'Malley, 1979a, especially Appendices A and B), so in this section we will present only the highlights of each of those discussions.

School Participation. As noted in the description of the sampling design, schools are invited to participate

---

*An example of analyses relating background, demographic, and lifestyle factors to drug use is Bachman, Johnston, and O'Malley (1981); a much broader array of other subject areas included in the study is treated by Bachman and Johnston (1979).

**These core variables are the first ones on which data are presented in the Descriptive Results Section.

Table 2

Measurement Content Areas

A. **Drugs.** Drug use and related attitudes and beliefs, drug availability and exposure, surrounding conditions and social meanings of drug use. Views of significant others regarding drugs.

B. **Education.** Educational lifestyle, values, experiences, and environments.

C. **Work and Leisure.** Vocational values, meaning of work and leisure, work and leisure activities, preferences regarding occupational characteristics and type of work setting.

D. **Sex Roles and Family.** Values, attitudes, and expectations about marriage, family structure, sex roles, and sex discrimination.

E. **Population Concerns.** Values and attitudes about overpopulation and birth control.

F. **Conservation, Materialism, Equity, etc.** Values, attitudes, and expectations related to conservation, pollution, materialism, equity, and the sharing of resources. Preferences regarding type of dwelling and urbanicity.

G. **Religion.** Religious affiliation, practices, and views.

H. **Politics.** Political affiliation, activities, and views.

I. **Social Change.** Values, attitudes, and expectations about social change.

J. **Social Problems.** Concern with various social problems facing the nation and the world.

K. **Major Social Institutions.** Confidence in and commitment to various major social institutions (business, unions, branches of government, press, organized religion, military, etc.).

L. **Military.** Views about the armed services and the use of military force. Personal plans for military service.

M. **Interpersonal Relationships.** Qualitative and quantitative characteristics of cross-age and peer relationships. Interpersonal conflict.

N. **Race Relations.** Attitudes toward and experiences with other racial groups.

O. **Concern for Others.** Concern for others; voluntary and charitable activities.

P. **Happiness.** Happiness and life satisfaction, overall and in specific life domains.

Q. **Other Personality Variables.** Attitudes about self (including self-esteem), locus of control, loneliness, risk-taking, trust in others, importance placed on various life goals, counter-culture orientation, hostility.

R. **Background.** Demographic and family background characteristics, living arrangements.

S. **Deviant Behavior and Victimization.** Delinquent behaviors, driving violations and accidents (including those under the influence of drugs), victimization experiences.

T. **Health Habits and Symptoms.** Health habits, somatic symptoms, medical experiences.

in the study for a two-year period. With very few exceptions, each school which has participated for one data collection has agreed to participate for a second. Thus far, from 66 percent to 80 percent of the schools initially invited to participate have agreed to do so each year; for each school refusal, a similar school (in terms of size, geographic area, urbanicity, etc.) was recruited as a replacement. The selection of replacement schools almost entirely removes problems of bias in region, urbanicity, and the like that might result from certain schools refusing to participate. Other potential biases are more subtle, however. For example, if it turned out that most schools with "drug problems" refused to participate, that could seriously bias the drug estimates derived from the sample. And if any other single factor were dominant in most refusals, that also might suggest a source of serious bias. In fact, however, the reasons for schools' refusals to participate are varied and largely a function of happenstance events of the particular year. Thus, we feel fairly confident that school refusals have not seriously biased the surveys.

Student Participation. Completed questionnaires are obtained from three-fourths to four-fifths of all students sampled. The single most important reason that students are missed is that they are absent from class at the time of data collection, and in most cases it is not workable to schedule a special follow-up data collection for them. Students with fairly high rates of absenteeism also report above-average rates of drug use; therefore, there is some degree of bias introduced by missing the absentees. That bias could be largely corrected through the use of special weighting; however, this course was not chosen because the bias in estimates (for drug use, where the potential effect was hypothesized to be largest) was determined to be quite small and because the necessary weighting procedures would have introduced undesirable complications (see Johnston et al., 1977).

In addition to absenteeism, student nonparticipation occurs because of schedule conflicts with school trips and other activities which tend to be more frequent than usual during the final months of the senior year. Of course, some students refuse to complete or turn in a questionnaire. However, the SRC representatives in the field estimate this proportion to be only about one percent.

Validity of Self-Report Data. Survey measures of delinquency and of drug use depend upon respondents reporting what are, in many cases, illegal acts. Thus, a critical question is whether such self-reports are likely to be valid. Like most studies dealing with

these areas, we have no direct, objective validation of the present measures; however, the considerable amount of inferential evidence which exists strongly suggests that the self-report questions produce largely valid data. A number of factors have given us reasonable confidence about the validity of the responses to what are presumably among the most sensitive questions in the study: a low nonresponse on the drug questions; a large proportion admitting to some illicit drug use; the consistency of findings across several years of the present study; strong evidence of construct validity (based on relationships observed between variables); a close match between our data and the findings from other studies using other methods; and the findings from several methodological studies which have used objective validation methods.*

As for others of the measures, a few have a long and venerable history — as scholars of the relevant literatures will recognize — though some of these measures have been modified to fit the present questionnaire format. Many (probably most) questions, however, have been developed specifically for this project through a careful process of question writing, pilot testing, pretesting, and question revision or elimination. Some already have been included in other publications from the study, but many have not; therefore, there currently exists little *empirical* evidence of their validity and reliability. On the other hand, the fact that virtually all results presented in this volume are based on individual items, rather than indexes or abstract concepts, should make it easy for the reader to judge the degree to which each item has "face validity" and also the degree to which there is some evidence of construct validity in the bivariate results.

Accuracy of the Sample. A sample survey never can provide the same level of accuracy as would be obtained if the entire target population were to participate in the survey — in the case of the present study, about three million seniors per year. But perfect accuracy of this sort would be extremely expensive and certainly not worthwhile considering the fact that a high level of accuracy can be provided by a carefully designed probability sample. The accuracy of the sample in this study is affected both by the size of the student sample and by the number of schools in which they are clustered. Appendix B presents a discussion of the ways in which this clustering and other aspects of the sampling design are taken into account in computing the precision or accuracy of the samples. For the purposes of this introduction, it is sufficient to note that virtually all estimates based on the total sample have confidence intervals of ±1.5 percentage points or smaller — sometimes considerably smaller.

---

* A more detailed discussion of the evidence for validity of the measures of illicit drug use may be found in Johnston et al. (1977; 1979a), Appendix A. An analysis of inconsistencies in students' reports of monthly versus yearly drug use is provided by Bachman and O'Malley (1981).

This means that, had we been able to invite all schools and all seniors in the 48 coterminous states to participate, the results from such a massive survey would be within an estimated 1.5 percentage points of our present sample findings at least 95 times out of 100. We consider this to be a quite high level of accuracy, and one that permits the detection of fairly small trends from one year to the next.

Consistency and the Measurement of Trends. One other point is worth noting in a discussion of the validity of our findings. The Monitoring the Future project is, by intention, a study designed to be sensitive to changes from one time to another. Accordingly, the measures and procedures have been standardized and applied consistently across each data collection. To the extent that any biases remain because of limits in school and/or student participation, and to the extent that there are distortions (lack of validity) in the responses of some students, it seems very likely that such problems will exist in much the same way from one year to the next. In other words, biases in the survey estimates should tend to be consistent from one year to another, which means that the measurement of *trends* should be affected very little by any such biases.

Caveats to Users of the Data

In attempting to understand and interpret the statistical results contained in this volume, the reader should keep in mind the several considerations discussed below.

Estimation of Sampling Errors. Appendix A provides figures which allow the reader to determine the 95 percent confidence interval around any observed percentage for both the total sample and the several subgroups for which statistics are given. Appendix A also provides tables and guidelines for testing the statistical significance of observed differences between subgroups (e.g., males vs. females) and the significance of year-to-year changes for the entire sample and for the various subgroups on any given variable. Estimates based on subgroups containing relatively few cases (e.g., those who have used heroin) will have substantially larger margins of error than those subgroups with large numbers of cases.

Subgroup Definitions. At the beginning of the Descriptive Results section there is a careful definition of each of the subgroups analyzed in this series of volumes. It is important for the reader to read these definitions so as not to be misled by the necessarily abbreviated descriptions given in the column headings of the data tables. For example, the column labeled "4-year college plans" includes data only for seniors who expect to be graduated from a four-year college, which is only a subset of all who expect to receive some college training. To take another example, several column headings in the lifetime illicit drug use index use the term "pills"; however, these categories contain people who indicate that they used any of a number of drugs — including some which usually are not taken in pill form (e.g., cocaine and narcotics other than heroin).

Missing Data Notes. Each column of percentages for a given variable adds to 100 percent (with slight variations due to rounding), whether based on the entire sample or any one of the subgroups being described. Missing data were not included in computing these percentages, so it is up to the reader to determine whether an exceptional level of missing data exists on any given question. This can be done by comparing the weighted number of cases on which those percentages were based (given in italics under each percentage distribution) with the total number of weighted cases who took the questionnaire (given at the top of the same column). As would be expected, the missing data rate tends to rise modestly toward the end of each questionnaire. Occasionally there is an exceptional level of nonresponse for some other reason, the most common being that the respondent has been branched around a question or set of questions which are inappropriate for him or her. In this case the percentages are based only on those for whom the question was appropriate *and* who answered. A footnote has been entered to help call attention to the fact that completing a particular question is contingent upon the answer on a prior question. Most such cases are contained in Form 1 of the questionnaire, which has several sets of detailed questions about drug use which are answered only by those respondents who have used a particular class of drug during the past year.

Characterizing Heroin Users. Because this project places a special emphasis on the study of drug use, one set of columns distinguishes respondents according to the extent to which they have been involved with illicit drugs. The five drug use categories are based on an index of seriousness of involvement. The index has Guttman-like properties — that is, anyone classified at a given level is also very likely to have exhibited any drug-using behaviors which are associated with the lower levels in the index.

The most extreme category in the index is defined in terms of the respondent's ever having used heroin during his or her lifetime. However, any interpretations made about heroin users from these data must be tempered with extreme caution, not only because the small number of cases makes estimation in a given year relatively unreliable, but also because heroin users are probably the most selectively represented of all of the subgroups presented here. Heroin users — especially continuing users — are among those most likely to drop out of high school (Johnston, 1973). Therefore, we feel that heroin users are particularly underrepresented in a sample of high school seniors. Furthermore, most of those included in the study report only very occasional heroin use. Frequent users — addicts, if you will — are not well represented in these data.

Given these problems with the representation of heroin users, the readers may wonder why it was decided to present them as a separate category of drug users. There are two reasons for doing so. First, because even occasional heroin use represents such an extreme point on the continuum of drug involvement, it seems preferable that the heroin users not be mixed in with the next highest category of use (the "more pills" category). It remains quite possible, of course, for anyone to *combine* any two or more categories in the drug use continuum (by computing means of percentages weighted by the number of cases in each category); therefore, those wishing to incorporate heroin users with the next category can do so whenever they wish. The second reason for keeping them separate is that we suspect the data based on high school seniors provide some indication of the characteristics which might be found among heavier heroin users who dropped out of school. Some variables in the study are strongly correlated with the drug use continuum, and the present heroin user category provides both an end point for that continuum and an indication of the direction (further out on the continuum) in which heavier heroin users are likely to lie.

In sum, the reporting of separate percentages for heroin users among high school seniors permits greater clarity in analyzing other levels of drug use and provides data which may be suggestive about the larger population of young heroin users. But the particular data are clearly limited and should be interpreted with these cautions in mind.

Interpreting Racial Differences. Data are given for the two largest racial/ethnic subgroups in the population — those who identify themselves as white or Caucasian and those who identify themselves as black or Afro-American. Data are not given for the other ethnic categories (American Indians, Asian Americans, Mexican Americans, Puerto Ricans, or other Latin Americans) since each of these groups comprises less than three percent of the sample in any given year, which means that their small Ns (in combination with their clustered groupings in a limited number of schools) would yield estimates which would be too unreliable. In fact, even blacks — who constitute approximately 12 percent of each year's sample — are represented by only 350 to 425 respondents per year on any single questionnaire form. Further, because our sample is a stratified clustered sam-

ple, it yields less accuracy than would be yielded by a pure random sample of equal size (see Appendix B for details). Therefore, because of the limited number of cases, the margin of sampling error around any statistic describing blacks is larger than for most other subgroups described in this volume.

There exists, however, a quick way to determine the replicability of any finding involving racial comparisons. Since most questions are repeated from year to year, one can readily establish the degree to which a finding is replicated by looking at the results for the same question in prior or subsequent years. Given the relatively small Ns for blacks, the reader is urged to seek such replication before putting much faith in the reliability of any particular racial comparison.

There are factors in addition to unreliability, however, which could be misleading in the interpretation of racial differences. Given the social importance which has been placed on various racial differences reported in the social science literature, we would like to caution the reader to consider the various factors which could account for differences. These factors fall into three categories: differential representation in the sample, differential response tendencies, and the confounding of race with a number of other background and demographic characteristics.

Differential Representation. Census data characterizing American young people in the approximate age range of those in our sample show that somewhat lower proportions of blacks than whites remain in school through the end of twelfth grade (Dearman and Plisko, 1982, p. 23). Therefore, a slightly different segment of the black population than of the white population resides in our target population of high school seniors. Further, our samples appear to underrepresent slightly those black males who, according to census figures, *are* in high school at the twelfth grade level. Identified black males comprise about 6 percent of our sample, whereas census data suggest that they should comprise around 7 percent (U.S. Bureau of the Census, 1978). Therefore, it appears that we are losing more black males from our target population than white males or females of either race. This may be due to generally poorer attendance rates on the part of some black males and/or an unwillingness on the part of some to participate in data collections of this sort.

In sum, a smaller segment of the black population than of the white population of high school age is represented by the data contained here. Insofar as any characteristic is associated with being a school dropout or absentee, it is likely to be somewhat disproportionately underrepresented among blacks in our sample.

Differential Response Tendencies. In examining our full range of variables, we have noted certain racial differences in response tendencies. First, the tendency to state agreement in response to agree-disagree questions is generally somewhat greater among blacks than among whites. For example, blacks tend to agree more with the positively worded items in our index of self-esteem, but they also tend to agree more with the negatively worded items. As it happens, that particular index has an equal number of positively and negatively worded items, so that any overall "agreement bias" should be self-cancelling when the index score is computed. Since all data in this volume are based on single items, however, group differences in agreement bias are likely to affect results on questions employing the agree-disagree format. Fortunately, most of our questions are not of that type.

We have also observed a somewhat greater than average tendency for black respondents to select extreme answer categories on attitudinal scales. For example, even if the same proportion of blacks as whites felt positively (or negatively) about some subject, fewer of the whites are likely to say they feel very positively (or very negatively). We do not have any ready explanations for these differences in response styles, but what seems important for our present purposes is that, in the process of interpreting racial differences, the reader should be aware that differences in responses to particular questions may be related to these more general tendencies.

A somewhat separate issue in response tendency is a respondent's willingness to answer particular questions. The missing data rate, which can be determined by dividing the number responding to a question by the number taking the questionnaire (given at the top of each page), may reflect willingness to answer particular questions. If a particular question or set of questions has a missing data rate higher than is true for the prior or subsequent questions, then presumably more respondents than usual were unwilling (or perhaps unable) to answer it. We have observed such an exaggerated missing data rate for black males on the set of questions dealing with the respondent's own use of illicit drugs. Clearly a respondent's willingness to be candid on such questions depends on his or her trust of the research process and of the researchers themselves. We interpret the exaggerated missing data rates for black males in these sections as possibly reflecting, at least in part, less trust. The reader is advised to check for exceptional levels of missing data when making comparisons on any variable in which candor is likely to be reduced by lower system trust. One bit of additional evidence related to trust in the research process is that higher proportions of blacks than whites indicated that if they had used marijuana or heroin they would not have been willing to report it in the survey.

Covariance with Other Factors. Some characteristics such as race are highly confounded (correlated) with other variables — variables which may in fact explain some observed racial differences. Put another way, at the aggregate level we might observe a consid-

erable racial difference on some characteristic, but once we control for some background characteristics such as socio-economic level or region of the country — that is, once we compare the black respondents with whites who come from similar backgrounds — there may be no racial difference at all.

Race happens to be correlated with important background and demographic variables much more than some of the other variables dealt with here (like the respondent's sex). When we compare males and females in this sample we know that observed differences between them are not likely to be explained by differences in their family background (such as the socioeconomic level of their families, the region of the country, or the size of the cities in which they grew up) because males and females on the average come from extremely similar backgrounds. A perusal of Section C of Questionnaire Forms 1 through 5, however, will illustrate that on the average the black subgroup in this sample is quite different from the white subgroup in a number of such respects. A higher proportion of blacks live in the South and a higher proportion grew up in families with the father and/or mother absent, and more had mothers who worked while they were growing up. A substantially higher proportion of blacks are Baptists, and blacks tend to attribute more importance to religion in their lives than do whites. Fewer are enrolled in a college-preparatory curriculum (though a higher proportion say they plan to attend some type of college). A slightly higher proportion of black respondents are married and have children, and on the average they are slightly older than the white sample. As was mentioned earlier, black males are more underrepresented in our sample than black females, with the result that each year roughly 58 percent of our black sample is female versus roughly 51 percent of the white sample.

We note these differences in demographic, background, and ascriptive characteristics because, in any attempt to understand *why* a racial difference exists, one would want to be able to examine the role of these covarying characteristics. It is not possible, given the amount of data contained in this volume, to "factor out" the contribution of most of these covarying characteristics when interpreting racial differences. Therefore, while the data here may provide a relatively accurate *description* of racial differences (keeping in mind our earlier cautions about representativeness and response style), they do not by themselves yield a great deal by way of explanation.

However, since the full data sets now reside in an archive, described in the Preface, it is possible for the reader to conduct a more in depth exploration of observed differences—or nondifferences, for that matter. We particularly encourage readers interested in racial comparisons to make further explorations in the data in order to determine the possible role of the other variables discussed here.

Users of the data are also encouraged to contact the principal investigators for information on the most recent analyses of racial differences, some of which are already underway.

Given the long list of caveats about interpreting racial differences, one might ask why we chose to publish the statistics for racial subgroups at all. After considerable deliberation among ourselves as well as with colleagues more knowledgeable in the field of race relations, we concluded that the expected benefits of making these data available (along with this cautionary discussion) outweigh the potential costs of having them misused. Unfortunately, because blacks constitute a relatively small proportion of the American population, they constitute too small a number in most surveys to be characterized separately. Because the sample sizes in the present survey are large in comparison to most, we have at least sufficient numbers of cases to consider publishing data on blacks separately. Further, given the iterative nature of the series, we are also able to provide checks for replication of findings on different samples each year. While there may be some risk that findings will be taken out of context or used carelessly in ways that might tend to increase racial misunderstandings, there is substantially greater risk that valuable information concerning the races (and relative to their well-being) will be lost if it were not included here.

A note on the questions about amphetamine use. Prior to the 1982 survey, we discovered that some respondents' answers to questions on amphetamine use erroneously included use of over-the-counter stay-awake and diet pills, as well as some "look-alike" pills. In the 1982 survey, we introduced some new questions on the use of amphetamines in order to make more clear to the respondents that "look-alike" pills and over-the-counter products should be excluded. We also kept the old version of the questions in two questionnaire forms in the 1982 and 1983 surveys so that it would be possible to "splice" the trend lines resulting from the old and new questions.

As a result of these changes, the reader who uses these volumes to examine trends in amphetamine use must be careful not to make inappropriate comparisons. The response distributions shown in the combined Forms 1 to 5 section (pages 28–29) from 1975 to 1981 contain the responses for Forms 1 through 5. In 1982 and 1983, that section contains two sets of responses. The first set is for Forms 1, 2, and 4 (with Form 1 double-weighted); these provide what we believe to be the best estimates of current amphetamine use and of trends from 1982 on. The second set of responses are based on Forms 3 and 5, the old versions of the questions; thus, these questions provide the best comparisons for looking at trends over time from 1975 to 1983 (although there is reason to be cautious about these trends because of the erroneous inclusion of non-amphetamines, as described above). Beginning with 1984, all forms use the new versions of the questions.

---

* An exended analysis and discussion of black-white differences in response styles may be found in Bachman and O'Malley (1984).

Descriptive Results

Introduction to the Table Format and Conventions

Univariate and selected bivariate percentage distributions are given in this section for all questions asked of this year's senior class. The definitions of column headings and the source of the standard contents for each table are given below under the numbers indicated in Figure 1.

Definitions of Column Headings

① **Questionnaire Form.** The form from which all data on the page were derived is given here. When the designation "Forms 1-5" is used, it indicates that responses from students completing all five questionnaires have been combined; accordingly, the numbers of respondents in each column are five times as large for questions contained in a single form only.

② **Total Sample.** Univariate percentage distributions based on the total sample of respondents are given in this column.

③ **Sex.** Percentage distributions are given separately for males (M) and females (F). Respondents with missing data on the question asking the respondent's sex (Question C03) are omitted from both groupings.

④ **Race.** Percentage distributions are given separately for those describing themselves as "White or Caucasian" (W) and "Black or Afro-American" (B) in answer to Question C04. Comparable columns for the other racial or ethnic groups (Mexican Americans, Asian Americans, American Indians, etc.) are not shown because of the low number of cases in each group. *Note:* See the caveats regarding the interpretation of racial differences in the introduction section of this volume.

⑤ **Region.** Percentage distributions are given separately for respondents living in each of four mutually exclusive regions of the country. The regional classifications are based on Census categories and are defined as follows:

Northeast (NE): Census classifications of New England and Middle Atlantic states; includes Maine, New Hampshire, Vermont, Massachusetts, Rhode Island, Connecticut, New York, New Jersey, and Pennsylvania.

North Central (NC): Census classifications of East North Central and West North Central states; includes Ohio, Indiana, Illinois, Michigan, Wisconsin, Minnesota, Iowa, Missouri, North Dakota, South Dakota, Nebraska, and Kansas.

South (S): Census classifications of South Atlantic, East South Central, and West South Central states; includes Delaware, Maryland, District of Columbia, Virginia, West Virginia, North Carolina, South Carolina, Georgia, Florida, Kentucky, Tennessee, Alabama, Mississippi, Arkansas, Louisiana, Oklahoma, and Texas.

West (W): Census classifications of Mountain and Pacific states; includes Montana, Idaho, Wyoming, Colorado, New Mexico, Arizona, Utah, Nevada, Washington, Oregon, and California.

⑥ **Four-Year College Plans.** Percentage distributions are given separately for (1) respondents who indicate that they "definitely will" or "probably will" graduate from a four-year college program and (2) those who say that they "definitely won't" or "probably won't" graduate from a four-year college program, based on responses to Question C21d. Respondents not answering question C21d are omitted from both columns. (A number of those who do not expect to complete a four-year college program *do* expect to get some post-secondary education, as may be seen in

13

the tables for questions C21a and c.)

⑦ Illicit Drug Use: Lifetime. Percentage distributions are given separately for five mutually exclusive subgroups differentiated by their degree of involvement with illicit drugs. Eligibility for each category is defined below.

None. This column contains data from those respondents who indicated that they had not used marijuana at any time and did not report use of any of the following illicit drugs in their lifetime: LSD, other psychedelics, cocaine, amphetamines, tranquilizers, methaqualone, barbiturates, heroin, or other narcotics.*

Marijuana Only. This column contains data from other respondents who indicated that they had used marijuana (or hashish) but had never used any of the other illicit drugs just listed.

Few Pills. This column contains data from those respondents who indicated having used one or more of the above listed drugs (other than marijuana) but who had not used any one class of them on three or more occasions *and* who had not used heroin at all.

More Pills. This column contains data from respondents who had used any of the above listed drugs (other than marijuana) on three or more occasions but who had never used heroin.

Any Heroin. This column contains data from those respondents who indicated having used heroin on one or more occasions in their lifetime.

⑧ N(Weighted Number of Cases). This row contains the number of students who turned in questionnaires in each of the categories indicated by the column headings. The number of cases is stated in terms of the weighted number of respondents rather than the actual number, since all percentages in the tables have been calculated using weighted cases. The actual number of respondents generally is about 15 percent higher than the weighted number for data collected in 1975, 1976, and 1977. (A comparison of weighted and unweighted numbers is provided in Tables B-1 and B-2 in Appendix B.) For data collected in 1978 or later, the actual number of respondents is roughly equal to the weighted number. Weighting is used to improve the accuracy of estimates by correcting for unequal probabilities of selection which arise in the multi-stage sampling procedures.

⑨ Percentage of Weighted Total. This row indicates the percentage of the total number of respondents who fall into the category indicated by each column heading. Unlike all other percentages on the page, which can be summed vertically, these percentages sum horizontally. To the extent that the subcate-

gories in a column (e.g., Males and Females) fail to sum to 100 percent, cases have been eliminated because of missing data on the variable in question (e.g., Sex), or, in the case of Race, because several subcategories have been omitted intentionally.

Table Contents

⑩ Questions and Answers. Each question along with its accompanying answer alternatives is presented verbatim. The alphanumeric prefix to the question indicates the section of the questionnaire in which it is located and its sequence within that section. So, for example, a prefix of B12c indicates that the item was question 12c in the B Section of the questionnaire.

⑪ Item Reference Number. This is a unique identification number permanently assigned to each question. Any question may be located in the Question Index of the 1975–1981 volumes by using this number, and in the Question Index of all subsequent volumes by using this number in conjunction with the subject area code.

⑫ Subject Area Code. Every question has been classified into one or more subject areas; the alphanumeric code indicates the subject area (or areas) applicable to the question shown. The complete listing of subject areas is presented in Table 3 (at the beginning of the Question Index near the end of this volume). Starting with the 1982 volume, the Question Index is ordered first by subject area, and then (within areas) by item reference number.

⑬ Percentage Distribution. Each column of numbers beside a question gives the percentage of each group (defined by the column heading) who chose each answer alternative, rounded to the nearest tenth of a percent. These figures add vertically to 100 percent (with some rounding error). Nonrespondents to the question are excluded from the percentage calculations.

⑭ Number of Weighted Cases Answering (N). The number of students in the relevant group (defined by the column heading) who answered the question is given just below the percentage distribution. The number of nonrespondents may be determined by subtracting this weighted number answering from the weighted number taking the questionnaire, shown at the top of the same column. Nonresponse may be due to the subject not answering the question, even though it pertains to him or her, or to the subject skipping inappropriate questions as instructed on a prior item.

---

*Inhalants (including the amyl and butyl nitrites) are not included in this list of illicit drugs because the relevant questions are not contained in all questionnaire forms nor in all years of the study. Similarly, the use of PCP is counted only if it was reported under "other psychedelics" use, because specific questions about PCP are not included in all forms or years. This results in a few apparent inconsistencies in the tables relating the drug use index to specific questions about these drugs.

Figure 1
Guide to Table Format

	TOTAL	SEX		RACE		REGION				4YR COLLEGE PLANS		ILLICIT DRUG USE: LIFETIME				
QUESTIONNAIRE FORM 1-5 1982		M	F	White	Black	NE	NC	S	W	Yes	No	None	Mari- juana Only	Few Pills	More Pills	Any Her- oin
N (Weighted No. of Cases):	18348	8828	8788	13887	2080	4741	5383	5551	2672	9360	7507	6328	4040	2439	4839	210
% of Weighted Total:	100.0	48.1	47.9	75.7	11.3	25.8	29.3	30.3	14.6	51.0	40.9	34.5	22.0	13.3	26.4	1.1

These next questions ask for some background information about yourself.

C01: In what year were you born?

1. Before '62	.3	.3	.3	.1	.6	.2	.3	.4	.2	.2	.4	.4	.1	.3	.2	1.1
2. 1962	2.0	2.6	1.4	1.3	3.9	1.5	2.0	2.7	1.5	1.0	2.9	2.0	1.9	2.2	1.4	5.3
3. 1963	23.3	26.6	19.6	21.8	26.1	15.2	27.2	25.6	24.4	19.4	27.1	23.4	23.9	23.4	22.0	25.4
4. 1964	72.8	69.3	76.6	75.6	66.3	80.5	69.5	69.9	72.2	77.3	68.6	72.2	72.2	72.7	75.2	67.9
5. 1965	1.6	1.1	2.1	1.2	3.0	2.5	1.0	1.4	1.6	2.1	1.0	1.8	1.9	1.3	1.2	.2
6. 1966	*	*	*	*	*	*	*	*	*	*	*	.1				
7. 1967	-	-	-	-	-	-	-	-	-	-	-	-	-	-	-	-
8. After 1967	*	*	*	*	-	*	*	*	*	-	*	*	-	-	-	-
Item 10 Subject R01 N	17899	8816	8787	13882	2079	4572	5306	5428	2593	9324	7466	6259	3986	2408	4718	207

C02: In what month were you born?

01. January	8.0	8.0	8.3	7.7	10.0	8.4	8.0	8.4	6.9	8.2	7.9	8.2	7.3	9.1	7.5	11.6
02. February	7.3	7.3	7.5	7.2	7.8	7.4	7.2	7.8	6.6	7.4	7.4	7.4	7.6	7.1	7.2	7.0
03. March	7.8	8.2	7.5	7.8	7.7	8.4	7.6	7.0	8.8	8.0	7.6	7.2	8.3	7.2	8.7	4.3
04. April	7.7	7.7	7.7	7.8	7.3	8.1	7.5	7.4	8.1	7.8	7.7	7.5	7.8	7.7	7.6	12.1
05. May	8.2	8.2	8.1	8.4	7.2	8.6	8.5	7.4	8.4	8.4	8.0	8.3	8.2	7.8	8.6	8.4
06. June	8.2	8.7	7.9	8.6	7.4	7.3	8.9	8.2	8.5	7.9	8.8	7.8	8.0	8.1	9.0	6.1
07. July	9.0	9.1	8.9	9.1	9.2	8.6	9.2	8.9	9.3	9.1	8.8	8.9	9.1	9.2	8.7	13.4
08. August	9.1	9.5	8.6	9.1	9.1	9.3	8.9	9.4	8.9	8.9	9.5	9.7	9.4	8.9	8.5	8.4
09. September	9.2	8.7	9.8	9.2	10.0	9.3	9.2	9.5	8.3	8.9	9.5	9.5	8.4	9.8	9.4	4.9
10. October	8.9	8.6	9.0	8.9	8.0	8.6	8.8	9.6	8.5	9.0	8.8	9.2	9.0	9.0	8.5	7.4
11. November	8.1	8.0	7.9	8.2	7.3	7.8	8.0	8.4	8.2	8.0	8.4	8.0	8.2	8.4	8.2	5.4
12. December	8.3	8.0	8.7	8.0	8.8	8.1	8.3	8.0	9.0	8.6	7.8	8.4	8.5	7.8	8.1	11.0
Item 20 Subject R01 N	17871	8802	8779	13863	2079	4566	5294	5420	2591	9312	7455	6253	3986	2398	4706	207

C03: What is your sex?

1. Male	50.1	100.0	-	50.9	43.2	49.8	50.6	50.0	49.9	50.0	48.7	47.8	55.3	48.7	48.7	62.6
2. Female	49.9	-	100.0	49.1	56.8	50.2	49.4	50.0	50.1	50.0	51.3	52.2	44.7	51.3	51.3	37.4
Item 30 Subject R01 N	17616	8828	8788	13676	2047	4511	5214	5339	2552	9216	7324	6177	3913	2370	4650	202

C04: How do you describe yourself?

1. American Indian	1.4	1.5	1.2	-	-	.8	1.2	1.6	2.4	.6	2.2	.8	1.5	1.4	1.7	3.2
2. Black or Afro-American	11.7	10.1	13.3	-	100.0	10.2	5.1	21.9	6.3	11.3	10.5	13.7	16.1	11.4	4.3	13.1
3. Mexican American or Chicano	2.2	2.3	2.1	-	-	.2	1.0	.9	10.9	1.7	2.4	2.2	2.1	2.4	1.9	2.5
4. Puerto Rican or other Latin American	1.9	1.8	2.0	-	-	4.1	.5	1.4	1.6	2.1	1.3	2.2	2.0	1.3	1.6	1.5
5. Oriental or Asian American	1.8	1.9	1.7	-	-	2.4	1.3	.3	5.1	3.0	.4	3.4	1.0	.8	.8	1.6
6. White or Caucasian	78.1	79.4	76.9	100.0	-	78.9	87.7	72.4	69.3	78.7	80.0	74.7	74.3	79.8	87.3	68.5
7. Other	2.9	3.1	2.7	-	-	3.4	3.3	1.5	4.4	2.6	3.1	3.0	3.0	2.9	2.4	9.6
Item 40 Subject R01 N	17775	8763	8729	13887	2080	4534	5272	5406	2562	9286	7412	6215	3961	2392	4688	203

C05: Where did you grow up mostly?

1. On a farm	7.9	8.3	7.4	8.9	4.0	2.7	9.7	11.7	5.2	5.3	11.3	10.1	6.7	7.2	6.1	4.1
2. In the country, not on a farm		15.4	13.7	14.8	17.0	12.3	13.1	19.5	11.5	11.1	19.2	16.0	14.2	14.6	12.8	14.0
3. In a small					20.8	34.5	31.4	26.4	24.4	29.0	31.0	30.3	28.4	29.4	30.2	30.1
							12.1	11.4	21.8	13.2	13.4	12.0	14.1	13.2		
						9.8	8.5	7.7	9.6	7.7	7.5	8.5	9.2			
							9.7	12.4	10.0	7.3	8.6					

Numbered callouts: ① ② ③ ④ ⑤ ⑥ ⑦ ⑧ ⑨ ⑩ ⑪ ⑫ ⑬ ⑭

QUESTIONNAIRE FORM 1-5 1985	TOTAL	SEX		RACE		REGION				4YR COLLEGE PLANS		ILLICIT DRUG USE: LIFETIME				
		M	F	White	Black	NE	NC	S	W	Yes	No	None	Mari-juana Only	Few Pills	More Pills	Any Her-oin
N (Weighted No. of Cases):	16502	7776	8164	12291	1995	3878	4516	5028	3079	9448	5770	6412	3449	2264	3802	193
% of Weighted Total:	100.0	47.1	49.5	74.5	12.1	23.5	27.4	30.5	18.7	57.3	35.0	38.9	20.9	13.7	23.0	1.2

These next questions ask for some background information about yourself.

C01: In what year were you born?

	TOTAL	M	F	White	Black	NE	NC	S	W	Yes	No	None	Mari-juana Only	Few Pills	More Pills	Any Her-oin
1. Before '64	0.1	0.1	*	*	0.2	0.1	0.1	*	0.1	0.1	0.1	0.1	0.1	-	0.1	1.2
2. 1964	0.2	0.1	0.1	*	0.3	0.2	0.1	0.2	0.1	0.1	0.2	0.1	0.1	0.2	0.1	0.5
3. 1965	1.8	2.4	1.1	1.2	3.4	1.7	1.9	2.1	1.5	1.0	2.9	1.8	2.0	1.6	1.3	5.9
4. 1966	23.1	26.6	19.4	22.2	23.9	19.2	27.3	23.5	20.9	19.8	27.9	23.2	22.7	23.0	22.7	26.3
5. 1967	73.4	69.4	77.6	75.3	70.3	76.8	69.7	72.7	75.8	77.1	68.0	73.1	73.6	73.7	74.7	64.5
6. 1968	1.4	1.2	1.6	1.2	1.9	1.9	0.9	1.4	1.6	1.8	0.9	1.6	1.5	1.4	1.0	0.6
7. 1969	0.1	*	*	*	*	0.1	-	0.1	0.1	*	0.1	0.1	*	*	*	0.9
8. After 1969	-	-	-	-	-	-	-	-	-	-	-	-	-	-	-	-
Item 10 Subject R01 N	16165	7769	8158	12285	1989	3766	4462	4905	3032	9411	5741	6340	3405	2244	3732	191

C02: In what month were you born?

	TOTAL	M	F	White	Black	NE	NC	S	W	Yes	No	None	Mari-juana Only	Few Pills	More Pills	Any Her-oin
01. January	8.4	8.7	8.2	8.3	7.7	9.1	8.9	7.7	8.0	8.2	8.7	8.2	9.2	7.0	8.7	8.3
02. February	7.5	7.4	7.7	7.4	8.6	6.9	7.4	8.1	7.4	7.6	7.2	7.5	7.7	7.4	7.6	7.0
03. March	8.2	8.3	8.2	8.1	8.4	8.3	8.1	8.4	7.8	8.0	8.4	8.6	7.6	8.7	7.9	7.9
04. April	7.6	7.5	7.5	7.7	6.6	8.0	7.6	7.1	7.6	7.8	7.4	8.0	7.1	7.8	7.4	6.2
05. May	8.9	9.3	8.5	8.9	8.9	8.0	9.5	9.5	8.1	9.3	8.4	9.3	8.4	9.5	8.1	10.9
06. June	7.9	7.9	8.0	8.2	6.4	7.9	8.2	7.4	8.3	8.0	7.7	8.0	7.3	7.8	8.4	6.5
07. July	8.6	8.4	8.6	8.9	7.8	8.7	8.8	8.6	8.2	8.6	8.7	8.8	8.5	8.3	8.6	11.8
08. August	8.7	8.7	8.6	8.3	10.2	8.7	8.0	9.1	9.0	8.6	8.7	8.0	9.0	9.3	9.1	7.8
09. September	8.9	8.9	9.2	9.0	9.4	9.5	8.3	8.7	9.6	8.9	9.0	8.7	9.4	9.2	8.7	8.7
10. October	8.7	8.6	8.6	8.4	9.7	8.6	8.5	9.1	8.5	8.5	9.1	8.7	9.2	8.1	8.5	8.7
11. November	7.9	7.8	7.8	8.0	7.8	7.5	7.6	7.8	8.8	7.9	7.9	7.8	8.1	7.8	8.1	5.8
12. December	8.7	8.4	9.1	8.7	8.6	8.8	9.1	8.4	8.6	8.6	8.8	8.5	8.6	9.0	8.8	10.4
Item 20 Subject R01 N	16144	7756	8155	12271	1988	3760	4454	4901	3029	9404	5731	6339	3402	2240	3723	189

C03: What is your sex?

	TOTAL	M	F	White	Black	NE	NC	S	W	Yes	No	None	Mari-juana Only	Few Pills	More Pills	Any Her-oin
1. Male	48.8	100.0	-	49.1	45.4	53.5	46.9	46.1	50.1	47.5	49.4	47.0	53.1	46.1	48.8	61.9
2. Female	51.2	-	100.0	50.9	54.6	46.5	53.1	53.9	49.9	52.5	50.6	53.0	46.9	53.9	51.2	38.1
Item 30 Subject R01 N	15939	7776	8164	12141	1954	3712	4403	4833	2991	9322	5630	6271	3359	2208	3682	178

C04: How do you describe yourself?

	TOTAL	M	F	White	Black	NE	NC	S	W	Yes	No	None	Mari-juana Only	Few Pills	More Pills	Any Her-oin
1. American Indian	1.3	1.4	1.2	-	-	1.0	1.3	1.4	1.5	0.7	2.1	0.9	0.9	1.8	1.7	4.6
2. Black or Afro-American	12.4	11.5	13.2	-	100.0	8.1	8.8	23.0	6.1	11.5	12.5	13.9	18.5	9.9	4.6	10.3
3. Mexican American or Chicano	2.2	2.0	2.4	-	-	0.3	0.9	1.5	7.8	1.9	2.7	2.1	2.3	2.6	2.2	3.8
4. Puerto Rican or other Latin American	2.0	1.7	2.2	-	-	5.0	0.8	1.5	0.9	2.0	1.5	2.1	1.4	2.4	1.8	0.8
5. Oriental or Asian American	2.6	3.0	2.2	-	-	1.8	1.1	1.1	8.1	3.7	0.9	3.5	2.0	2.5	1.7	2.6
6. White or Caucasian	76.6	77.2	76.2	100.0	-	78.9	85.3	70.0	71.3	77.8	77.1	74.6	72.5	78.4	84.3	74.1
7. Other	2.9	3.2	2.5	-	-	5.0	1.8	1.5	4.4	2.4	3.3	2.9	2.4	2.3	3.6	3.8
Item 40 Subject R01 N	16055	7715	8109	12291	1995	3733	4441	4889	2992	9361	5693	6313	3383	2225	3700	186

C05: Where did you grow up mostly?

	TOTAL	M	F	White	Black	NE	NC	S	W	Yes	No	None	Mari-juana Only	Few Pills	More Pills	Any Her-oin
1. On a farm	6.2	7.2	5.4	7.0	3.2	2.7	8.4	8.3	4.0	4.5	9.0	8.4	4.7	4.0	5.0	8.3
2. In the country, not on a farm	14.1	14.4	13.7	14.6	15.7	15.1	12.9	18.7	7.1	11.1	19.3	16.1	13.3	13.3	12.3	8.6
3. In a small city or town (under 50,000 people)	30.1	29.9	30.6	32.0	23.9	33.1	35.0	26.4	25.1	28.8	32.1	29.2	29.9	31.5	31.7	26.4
4. In a medium-sized city (50,000 - 100,000)	13.9	12.7	15.0	13.1	15.4	11.5	10.2	14.4	21.5	14.4	13.1	13.2	13.8	15.3	14.3	11.7
5. In a suburb of a medium-sized city	8.6	8.0	9.1	8.9	7.1	9.1	8.0	9.3	7.6	9.7	6.9	7.5	9.0	8.7	9.5	7.6
6. In a large city (100,000 - 500,000)	9.2	8.5	9.8	7.1	16.1	8.4	9.4	7.1	13.3	9.7	8.1	8.4	9.6	9.4	9.8	11.5
7. In a suburb of a large city	7.6	7.7	7.4	8.4	3.7	7.5	9.0	7.1	6.2	9.5	4.8	7.3	7.9	7.8	7.7	7.8
8. In a very large city (over 500,000)	6.2	6.9	5.5	4.6	12.3	8.3	3.7	4.8	9.8	7.1	4.3	5.9	7.1	5.8	5.6	13.5
9. In a suburb of a very large city	4.1	4.8	3.5	4.3	2.5	4.3	3.5	3.9	5.3	5.3	2.3	3.9	4.5	4.1	4.1	4.6
Item 50 Subject R03 N	14891	7180	7474	11365	1810	3446	4174	4502	2771	8754	5246	5876	3133	2051	3444	158

C06: What is your present marital status?

	TOTAL	M	F	White	Black	NE	NC	S	W	Yes	No	None	Mari-juana Only	Few Pills	More Pills	Any Her-oin
1. Married	2.0	1.9	2.1	1.8	3.1	1.5	2.0	2.7	1.8	1.2	3.1	2.1	1.8	2.4	1.8	5.0
2. Engaged	6.3	3.9	8.6	6.3	7.1	5.7	5.8	7.5	6.2	3.6	10.8	5.1	5.7	6.3	8.9	12.8
3. Separated/divorced	0.7	0.7	0.6	0.5	1.3	0.9	0.6	0.6	0.5	0.6	0.7	0.5	0.9	0.2	0.9	3.4
4. Single	90.9	93.5	88.7	91.4	88.5	91.9	91.6	89.2	91.6	94.5	85.4	92.4	91.6	91.1	88.4	78.8
Item 60 Subject D01,R01 N	16131	7724	8140	12250	1976	3747	4453	4898	3034	9412	5733	6331	3402	2240	3722	187

*=less than .05 per cent.

QUESTIONNAIRE FORM 1-5 1985	TOTAL	SEX M	F	RACE White	Black	REGION NE	NC	S	W	4YR COLLEGE PLANS Yes	No	ILLICIT DRUG USE: LIFETIME None	Marijuana Only	Few Pills	More Pills	Any Heroin
N (Weighted No. of Cases):	16502	7776	8164	12291	1995	3878	4516	5028	3079	9448	5770	6412	3449	2264	3802	193
% of Weighted Total:	100.0	47.1	49.5	74.5	12.1	23.5	27.4	30.5	18.7	57.3	35.0	38.9	20.9	13.7	23.0	1.2

C07: How many brothers and sisters do you have? (Include step brothers and sisters and half-brothers and sisters.)

C07A: Older brothers and sisters

	TOTAL	M	F	White	Black	NE	NC	S	W	Yes	No	None	Mari only	Few	More	Heroin
0. None	28.2	28.6	27.8	29.2	21.9	28.3	25.6	29.6	29.4	31.5	23.7	31.3	26.0	28.3	25.0	22.8
1. One	26.8	27.5	26.2	28.2	21.5	27.4	26.5	26.6	26.9	27.3	25.9	26.2	26.6	27.4	27.8	25.8
2. Two	16.8	16.5	17.1	17.4	14.1	17.2	17.4	16.2	16.3	16.7	17.0	16.3	16.9	16.4	17.5	18.1
3. Three	10.9	10.5	11.2	10.6	11.6	11.4	11.8	10.3	9.9	10.0	12.3	10.7	10.6	11.0	11.4	10.6
4. Four	6.4	6.3	6.5	5.9	8.5	6.4	6.8	5.9	6.7	5.8	7.4	5.2	7.3	7.1	7.1	9.6
5. Five	4.1	3.9	4.4	3.7	7.0	3.6	4.1	4.6	4.0	3.3	5.3	3.9	4.8	3.7	4.2	3.7
6. Six or more	6.9	6.7	6.9	5.0	15.5	5.7	7.8	6.8	6.9	5.5	8.4	6.4	7.7	6.1	7.0	9.5
Item 75 Subject R02 N	14973	7159	7573	11328	1861	3458	4163	4547	2805	8729	5368	5863	3178	2086	3442	179

C07B: Younger brothers and sisters

0. None	29.4	30.0	29.0	31.0	22.1	32.2	30.3	27.9	27.3	30.1	29.2	27.6	30.5	28.8	32.4	31.2
1. One	35.6	35.5	35.8	37.0	30.8	36.8	34.6	36.1	34.8	36.1	34.9	36.8	33.3	36.5	35.3	33.2
2. Two	19.5	19.4	19.4	19.1	19.1	18.8	19.3	19.4	20.7	19.6	19.1	19.9	19.7	18.6	19.0	18.1
3. Three	8.3	7.9	8.5	7.1	12.3	6.8	8.7	8.3	9.3	7.9	8.7	8.6	8.4	8.8	7.1	6.5
4. Four	3.6	3.6	3.6	3.1	6.3	2.7	4.2	3.7	3.5	3.2	3.7	3.3	4.5	3.6	3.2	2.8
5. Five	1.8	1.9	1.8	1.4	4.4	1.1	1.7	2.2	2.1	1.5	2.2	1.7	2.1	1.6	1.7	3.1
6. Six or more	1.9	1.8	1.9	1.3	4.9	1.6	1.1	2.4	2.3	1.6	2.1	2.1	1.5	2.2	1.3	5.1
Item 76 Subject R02 N	14627	6980	7414	11101	1787	3342	4038	4429	2818	8645	5139	5794	3090	2046	3303	172

C07C: Which of the following people live in the same household with you? (Mark ALL that apply.)

A. I live alone	0.6	0.8	0.3	0.5	0.6	0.5	0.5	0.5	0.8	0.4	0.7	0.4	0.3	0.5	0.9	3.7
B. Father (or male guardian)	77.1	78.0	76.4	82.0	49.0	77.9	79.6	73.9	77.7	79.8	74.1	79.9	75.2	75.2	76.2	74.0
C. Mother (or female guardian)	91.3	90.4	92.2	92.8	85.2	92.2	91.7	90.1	91.3	93.5	88.7	92.9	91.0	91.6	89.3	83.9
D. Brother(s) and/or sister(s)	72.5	71.8	73.4	73.3	66.8	75.8	72.1	70.4	72.6	74.0	70.3	75.4	71.2	73.2	69.0	67.7
E. Grandparent(s)	5.1	5.4	4.9	4.2	9.2	6.0	4.0	6.0	4.3	4.6	5.6	4.9	5.6	4.7	5.2	7.8
F. My husband/wife	0.9	0.5	1.1	0.9	0.6	0.6	0.8	1.2	0.6	0.3	1.5	0.8	0.5	1.2	0.9	2.7
G. My children	1.0	0.4	1.5	0.6	3.4	0.8	1.0	1.3	0.6	0.5	1.8	0.9	0.8	0.5	1.2	6.0
H. Other relative(s)	4.4	3.8	4.9	3.0	10.1	4.1	3.2	5.5	4.5	3.8	4.9	4.1	4.6	3.8	4.7	7.2
I. Non-relative(s)	2.9	2.7	3.2	2.9	1.6	3.1	2.6	2.2	4.5	2.5	3.6	2.0	2.9	3.4	4.2	7.2
Item 80-160 Subject R03 N	16072	7680	8129	12223	1960	3719	4442	4881	3030	9387	5730	6314	3392	2231	3711	178

The next three questions ask about your parents. If you were raised mostly by foster parents, step-parents, or others, answer for them. For example, if you have both a step-father and a natural father, answer for the one that was most important in raising you.

C08: What is the highest level of schooling your father completed?

1. Completed grade school or less	5.3	4.9	5.6	3.9	8.2	5.3	4.1	6.9	4.3	3.5	8.0	5.7	4.7	5.4	4.6	6.9
2. Some high school	13.1	12.9	13.2	11.9	16.1	13.3	12.7	15.2	10.3	8.9	19.5	12.1	13.6	12.4	14.7	13.3
3. Completed high school	31.0	31.6	30.5	31.8	33.6	33.2	36.9	28.5	23.7	26.5	38.2	31.0	30.5	31.7	31.0	30.5
4. Some college	14.9	14.8	15.0	16.0	10.2	12.8	13.8	14.0	20.4	16.9	11.7	14.6	14.4	15.1	15.9	9.9
5. Completed college	18.4	18.4	18.5	20.1	11.1	17.7	16.7	17.5	23.2	23.1	11.2	18.2	19.0	19.4	18.0	21.0
6. Graduate or professional school after college	11.9	12.4	11.4	13.0	5.3	12.9	11.2	10.7	13.7	17.4	3.4	12.4	12.8	10.8	11.1	14.7
7. Don't know, or does not apply	5.4	5.0	5.9	3.3	15.6	4.8	4.6	7.3	4.4	3.7	8.0	6.0	5.0	5.1	4.6	3.8
Item 310 Subject R02 N	16033	7667	8103	12197	1947	3706	4430	4870	3027	9385	5736	6303	3381	2227	3695	182

C09: What is the highest level of schooling your mother completed?

1. Completed grade school or less	3.2	2.8	3.6	2.0	4.0	3.3	1.9	3.9	3.9	2.5	4.2	3.5	2.7	4.0	2.7	3.5
2. Some high school	13.3	12.4	13.8	11.2	21.8	12.1	12.8	16.5	10.2	8.8	20.0	12.0	13.6	14.2	14.1	14.1
3. Completed high school	39.9	42.0	38.1	42.1	35.9	44.3	44.8	38.4	29.8	35.2	47.5	40.4	39.0	38.4	41.3	36.8
4. Some college	17.3	15.6	19.0	18.5	13.4	13.6	16.0	16.7	24.5	21.0	11.6	16.3	17.1	17.7	18.8	22.9
5. Completed college	15.5	16.2	14.9	16.5	12.2	15.4	14.7	13.9	19.7	19.8	9.0	15.9	16.3	15.5	14.5	12.4
6. Graduate or professional school after college	7.8	7.8	7.9	7.8	7.2	8.7	7.0	7.0	9.4	10.9	3.0	8.5	8.4	7.4	6.6	6.6
7. Don't know, or does not apply	3.0	3.2	2.8	2.0	5.6	2.7	2.8	3.6	2.6	1.8	4.8	3.5	2.9	2.8	2.0	3.7
Item 320 Subject R02 N	16036	7667	8108	12199	1954	3698	4432	4878	3028	9394	5739	6301	3382	2231	3694	182

QUESTIONNAIRE FORM 1-5 1985	TOTAL	SEX		RACE		REGION				4YR COLLEGE PLANS		ILLICIT DRUG USE: LIFETIME				
		M	F	White	Black	NE	NC	S	W	Yes	No	None	Mari-juana Only	Few Pills	More Pills	Any Her-oin
N (Weighted No. of Cases):	16502	7776	8164	12291	1995	3878	4516	5028	3079	9448	5770	6412	3449	2264	3802	193
% of Weighted Total:	100.0	47.1	49.5	74.5	12.1	23.5	27.4	30.5	18.7	57.3	35.0	38.9	20.9	13.7	23.0	1.2

C10: Did your mother have a paid job (half-time or more) during the time you were growing up?

	TOTAL	M	F	White	Black	NE	NC	S	W	Yes	No	None	Mari-juana Only	Few Pills	More Pills	Any Her-oin
1. No	25.8	26.4	25.3	27.9	13.0	26.8	27.7	23.2	26.3	26.8	24.4	28.8	23.6	23.4	24.6	22.8
2. Yes, some of the time when I was growing up	30.2	30.6	29.9	32.3	18.9	32.0	30.9	27.2	31.5	30.2	30.6	30.3	29.9	30.8	30.0	27.9
3. Yes, most of the time	18.5	19.3	17.6	17.8	20.6	18.9	17.9	18.4	19.0	17.9	19.3	16.8	18.4	20.0	20.2	24.4
4. Yes, all or nearly all of the time	25.5	23.7	27.3	22.0	47.5	22.3	23.5	31.2	23.3	25.1	25.7	24.0	28.1	25.8	25.2	25.0
Item 330 Subject R02 N	15984	7645	8077	12172	1938	3694	4413	4853	3023	9383	5728	6279	3376	2230	3681	181

C11: How would you describe your political preference?

	TOTAL	M	F	White	Black	NE	NC	S	W	Yes	No	None	Mari-juana Only	Few Pills	More Pills	Any Her-oin
1. Strongly Republican	11.4	14.4	8.5	13.1	3.7	8.1	9.9	14.4	12.7	12.5	9.3	13.6	10.3	9.7	9.2	15.7
2. Mildly Republican	18.0	19.7	16.4	20.7	4.6	14.5	18.5	18.4	20.8	20.0	15.3	19.5	16.0	19.0	17.3	16.6
3. Mildly Democrat	11.8	10.6	12.8	10.7	17.1	10.8	10.8	12.7	12.8	12.7	10.1	11.8	12.9	11.3	11.2	7.0
4. Strongly Democrat	9.8	9.5	10.0	6.3	31.2	8.5	8.6	12.4	8.9	10.0	9.0	9.7	11.9	9.9	8.0	6.0
5. American Independent Party	1.5	1.6	1.3	1.3	1.7	1.8	1.1	1.7	1.5	1.2	2.0	1.4	1.4	1.5	1.7	3.0
6. No preference, independent	21.8	22.9	20.9	23.6	12.9	26.1	25.8	17.1	18.1	21.1	23.0	20.2	21.0	21.8	25.3	26.0
7. Other	1.6	2.3	1.0	1.5	1.1	2.2	1.4	1.2	2.0	1.7	1.4	1.2	1.5	1.3	2.4	7.0
8. Don't know, haven't decided	24.2	19.0	29.1	22.8	27.8	28.0	23.9	22.1	23.2	20.7	29.7	22.6	25.1	25.5	24.9	18.8
Item 340 Subject H01 N	15910	7623	8030	12133	1927	3663	4407	4835	3004	9349	5711	6254	3368	2216	3660	179

C12: How would you describe your political beliefs?

	TOTAL	M	F	White	Black	NE	NC	S	W	Yes	No	None	Mari-juana Only	Few Pills	More Pills	Any Her-oin
1. Very conservative	3.6	4.9	2.3	3.3	5.1	3.0	2.8	5.0	3.1	3.6	3.1	4.5	3.1	3.0	2.7	3.7
2. Conservative	14.8	17.7	12.3	15.4	11.2	12.6	14.8	15.8	16.1	16.7	12.0	17.3	13.9	13.4	12.6	10.4
3. Moderate	30.8	30.3	31.4	32.2	28.5	28.5	31.8	31.8	30.6	32.7	28.4	31.7	31.4	32.4	28.8	17.2
4. Liberal	16.0	14.9	17.0	15.3	17.8	16.5	14.5	14.9	19.2	18.4	12.2	14.1	16.5	17.8	17.6	20.7
5. Very liberal	3.1	3.3	2.9	2.8	4.4	3.8	2.9	3.0	2.9	3.4	2.5	2.4	2.8	2.9	4.5	5.9
6. Radical	3.0	4.6	1.5	2.9	3.0	3.7	2.5	2.5	3.6	2.7	3.2	1.8	2.4	2.7	5.1	13.0
8. None of the above, or don't know	28.7	24.4	32.7	28.1	29.9	32.0	30.8	27.0	24.5	22.5	38.7	28.2	29.9	27.8	28.7	29.3
Item 350 Subject H01 N	15868	7583	8027	12093	1929	3638	4408	4825	2998	9353	5691	6235	3357	2212	3653	177

C13: The next three questions are about religion.

C13A: What is your religious preference?

	TOTAL	M	F	White	Black	NE	NC	S	W	Yes	No	None	Mari-juana Only	Few Pills	More Pills	Any Her-oin
01. Baptist	21.8	21.2	22.2	17.1	60.6	7.9	15.4	44.1	11.9	18.5	26.7	24.6	22.8	19.6	17.1	14.3
02. Churches of Christ	6.0	6.7	5.4	5.5	7.0	5.9	6.5	4.5	7.7	4.5	8.0	5.4	5.8	5.7	7.3	6.4
03. Disciples of Christ	0.5	0.5	0.4	0.4	0.7	0.2	0.6	0.7	0.1	0.4	0.4	0.5	0.6	0.5	0.2	1.0
04. Episcopal	1.7	1.7	1.6	1.9	0.9	2.5	1.0	2.0	1.1	2.1	1.0	1.5	1.7	1.7	2.0	2.3
05. Lutheran	5.1	5.0	5.3	6.3	0.4	3.5	10.6	2.1	3.9	5.3	5.1	5.2	4.6	4.8	5.5	4.7
06. Methodist	7.9	7.3	8.4	8.7	7.5	6.4	9.5	10.1	3.4	8.2	7.6	9.4	7.7	7.3	6.0	6.0
07. Presbyterian	3.4	3.4	3.4	4.0	1.0	3.5	3.0	3.8	3.0	4.0	2.5	3.5	3.2	3.5	3.4	2.0
08. United Church of Christ	0.8	0.8	0.9	1.0	0.3	1.1	1.3	0.3	0.6	0.9	0.7	1.0	0.9	0.6	0.7	0.7
09. Other Protestant	4.4	4.4	4.3	5.1	1.3	6.6	5.1	1.5	5.3	4.2	4.5	4.6	4.1	4.4	4.5	3.0
10. Unitarian	0.2	0.2	0.1	0.2	0.1	0.3	0.1	0.2	0.1	0.2	0.1	0.2	0.3	0.1	0.1	0.2
11. Roman Catholic	28.5	27.0	30.0	29.9	4.9	41.7	28.7	17.4	30.2	31.3	24.2	25.7	29.8	31.5	30.7	25.8
12. Eastern Orthodox	0.3	0.3	0.3	0.4	-	0.8	0.4	0.1	*	0.4	0.2	0.3	0.2	0.5	0.3	0.1
13. Jewish	1.2	1.2	1.2	1.4	0.2	2.7	0.6	0.7	1.0	1.7	0.4	1.0	1.4	1.1	1.3	1.9
16. Latter Day Saints	1.7	1.6	1.8	2.1	0.1	0.2	0.3	0.5	7.5	1.9	1.4	2.2	1.5	1.9	1.1	1.0
14. Other religion	5.2	4.8	5.5	4.0	7.4	4.1	5.6	5.0	6.4	4.7	5.9	6.0	4.4	4.8	4.6	9.1
15. None	11.5	14.0	9.1	12.0	7.5	12.5	11.4	6.9	17.6	11.5	11.4	9.2	11.0	12.0	15.1	21.6
Item 360 Subject G N	15803	7549	8001	12037	1940	3620	4372	4839	2972	9336	5642	6228	3337	2196	3629	174

C13B: How often do you attend religious services?

	TOTAL	M	F	White	Black	NE	NC	S	W	Yes	No	None	Mari-juana Only	Few Pills	More Pills	Any Her-oin
1. Never	11.1	13.7	8.7	11.9	5.6	14.7	10.6	6.8	14.5	9.2	13.7	8.7	9.7	10.6	16.0	21.4
2. Rarely	37.0	39.0	35.3	37.2	33.9	43.1	35.9	33.1	37.7	33.7	42.1	28.4	41.5	40.0	46.2	39.5
3. Once or twice a month	16.6	15.7	17.2	15.3	24.2	14.9	16.4	19.3	14.3	17.2	15.5	15.8	18.6	19.2	14.6	8.2
4. About once a week or more	35.3	31.6	38.8	35.7	36.3	27.3	37.1	40.8	33.5	39.9	28.6	47.1	30.3	30.3	23.2	31.0
Item 370 Subject G N	15970	7616	8090	12163	1946	3670	4420	4862	3019	9404	5735	6284	3374	2221	3673	177

*=less than .05 per cent.

QUESTIONNAIRE FORM 1-5 1985	TOTAL	SEX		RACE		REGION				4YR COLLEGE PLANS		ILLICIT DRUG USE: LIFETIME				
		M	F	White	Black	NE	NC	S	W	Yes	No	None	Mari- juana Only	Few Pills	More Pills	Any Her- oin
N (Weighted No. of Cases):	16502	7776	8164	12291	1995	3878	4516	5028	3079	9448	5770	6412	3449	2264	3802	193
% of Weighted Total:	100.0	47.1	49.5	74.5	12.1	23.5	27.4	30.5	18.7	57.3	35.0	38.9	20.9	13.7	23.0	1.2

C13C: How important is religion in your life?

1. Not important	12.7	16.4	9.2	14.5	3.0	18.1	12.2	6.7	16.5	12.1	13.5	9.4	12.5	14.0	17.4	26.0
2. A little important	27.6	28.6	26.6	30.0	13.4	32.8	29.6	21.8	27.8	25.6	31.2	21.3	29.9	29.5	35.7	25.2
3. Pretty important	32.4	31.6	33.1	32.2	30.9	30.2	33.2	34.5	30.7	33.1	31.7	31.9	34.1	33.4	31.3	25.7
4. Very important	27.3	23.3	31.0	23.3	52.7	18.9	25.0	37.1	25.0	29.2	23.5	37.4	23.5	23.1	15.6	23.1
Item 380 Subject G　　N	*15951*	*7612*	*8076*	*12147*	*1943*	*3672*	*4408*	*4852*	*3018*	*9396*	*5726*	*6276*	*3373*	*2220*	*3663*	*177*

C14: When are you most likely to graduate from high school?

1. By this June	98.3	97.7	99.0	98.6	98.0	98.2	98.2	98.5	98.3	99.1	97.2	99.0	98.3	98.3	97.6	93.8
2. July to January	1.4	1.8	0.9	1.1	1.7	1.3	1.6	1.3	1.3	0.7	2.3	0.8	1.3	1.3	2.0	5.0
3. After next January	-	-	-	-	-	-	-	-	-	-	-	-	-	-	-	-
6. Don't expect to graduate	0.3	0.5	0.1	0.2	0.3	0.4	0.2	0.2	0.4	0.1	0.5	0.2	0.4	0.3	0.4	1.2
Item 390 Subject B01　　N	*15919*	*7588*	*8052*	*12134*	*1929*	*3663*	*4406*	*4839*	*3012*	*9436*	*5751*	*6264*	*3360*	*2215*	*3659*	*175*

C15: Which of the following best describes your present high school program?

1. Academic or college prep	49.7	47.2	52.6	53.1	38.7	58.2	46.9	47.6	46.6	70.3	18.0	56.2	49.5	48.9	41.0	33.2
2. General	30.0	30.1	29.7	28.4	32.8	22.3	30.6	31.2	36.6	21.3	43.3	26.0	30.3	30.7	35.9	34.4
3. Vocational, technical, or commercial	13.8	16.2	11.3	13.6	15.3	15.1	16.2	13.5	9.4	5.0	27.6	11.5	14.0	13.7	17.0	24.2
4. Other, or don't know	6.5	6.5	6.4	4.9	13.2	4.4	6.3	7.7	7.5	3.4	11.1	6.4	6.2	6.8	6.1	8.2
Item 400 Subject B01　　N	*15828*	*7542*	*8008*	*12078*	*1908*	*3646*	*4379*	*4808*	*2996*	*9404*	*5733*	*6226*	*3346*	*2202*	*3639*	*173*

C16: Compared with others your age through-out the country, how do you rate yourself on school ability?

1. Far below average	0.6	0.8	0.3	0.5	1.2	0.8	0.6	0.7	0.3	0.2	1.1	0.7	0.5	0.6	0.5	0.6
2. Below average	1.8	2.0	1.6	1.7	2.2	1.7	2.2	1.5	2.1	1.0	3.1	1.4	1.7	2.2	2.4	2.6
3. Slightly below average	5.1	5.8	4.3	4.6	6.5	5.6	5.1	4.4	5.5	3.4	7.6	3.7	5.2	5.5	6.8	7.3
4. Average	37.0	35.4	38.3	33.8	50.2	35.7	35.8	40.5	34.7	26.2	53.8	33.2	37.9	39.3	40.0	42.8
5. Slightly above average	24.2	23.4	24.9	25.1	21.4	23.6	24.7	23.2	26.0	26.5	20.9	23.7	25.0	24.2	25.2	18.3
6. Above average	25.7	25.4	26.3	28.3	16.0	26.9	26.3	24.7	24.8	34.6	11.9	30.3	24.5	23.7	21.3	17.2
7. Far above average	5.6	7.1	4.2	6.0	2.5	5.6	5.5	5.0	6.5	8.1	1.5	7.0	5.2	4.4	3.9	11.3
Item 410 Subject B01　　N	*15597*	*7445*	*7881*	*11937*	*1851*	*3566*	*4338*	*4726*	*2967*	*9297*	*5650*	*6133*	*3302*	*2172*	*3583*	*172*

C17: How intelligent do you think you are compared with others your age?

1. Far below average	0.5	0.6	0.3	0.3	0.6	0.7	0.5	0.4	0.2	0.2	0.9	0.4	0.5	0.4	0.5	0.9
2. Below average	1.4	1.5	1.3	1.3	0.9	1.4	1.4	1.2	1.6	0.8	2.3	1.2	1.2	2.0	1.5	1.8
3. Slightly below average	3.6	3.2	3.8	3.4	3.3	3.1	4.1	3.4	3.8	2.3	5.6	3.3	3.8	4.1	3.4	3.7
4. Average	35.8	31.9	39.4	34.2	40.7	34.8	35.8	38.4	32.8	25.2	52.9	33.2	35.3	39.1	38.2	37.1
5. Slightly above average	24.6	24.3	24.7	25.2	23.0	24.8	24.1	23.7	26.4	26.5	21.6	23.5	25.6	25.2	25.9	19.0
6. Above average	27.1	29.6	25.0	28.6	23.4	27.7	27.7	25.8	27.5	35.6	13.4	30.4	26.9	24.2	23.9	23.0
7. Far above average	7.1	8.9	5.4	7.0	8.1	7.5	6.5	7.0	7.7	9.5	3.3	8.1	6.6	4.9	6.6	14.5
Item 420 Subject B01　　N	*15629*	*7443*	*7919*	*11964*	*1858*	*3572*	*4342*	*4751*	*2964*	*9327*	*5664*	*6158*	*3293*	*2175*	*3599*	*173*

C18: During the LAST FOUR WEEKS, how many whole days of school have you missed . . .

C18A: Because of illness

1. None	58.8	65.2	53.0	59.4	57.9	58.0	58.8	60.9	56.6	61.0	56.1	65.5	58.2	55.9	50.5	55.3
2. 1 day	17.7	15.3	19.9	18.5	14.3	18.5	17.5	17.7	16.9	17.5	17.8	16.5	18.5	19.0	18.6	9.4
3. 2 days	10.5	8.9	12.0	10.3	11.0	10.5	10.4	9.6	12.1	10.1	10.8	8.4	11.0	11.4	13.0	10.9
4. 3 days	6.1	4.8	7.3	5.8	7.1	5.9	6.5	5.6	6.4	5.4	7.0	4.6	5.8	6.5	8.5	7.5
5. 4-5 days	4.2	3.4	4.8	3.8	5.5	4.3	4.0	3.9	4.7	3.6	5.0	3.1	3.7	4.2	6.0	8.4
6. 6-10 days	1.8	1.5	2.0	1.6	2.5	1.5	1.8	1.6	2.4	1.5	2.2	1.1	2.0	2.1	2.2	4.3
7. 11 or more	1.0	0.9	1.0	0.7	1.6	1.3	1.0	0.8	0.8	0.9	1.0	0.7	0.8	1.0	1.2	4.3
Item 430 Subject B06　　N	*15413*	*7325*	*7815*	*11800*	*1839*	*3516*	*4284*	*4688*	*2925*	*9213*	*5599*	*6072*	*3255*	*2150*	*3536*	*172*

QUESTIONNAIRE FORM 1-5 1985	TOTAL	SEX		RACE		REGION				4YR COLLEGE PLANS		ILLICIT DRUG USE: LIFETIME				
		M	F	White	Black	NE	NC	S	W	Yes	No	None	Mari- juana Only	Few Pills	More Pills	Any Her- oin
N (Weighted No. of Cases):	16502	7776	8164	12291	1995	3878	4516	5028	3079	9448	5770	6412	3449	2264	3802	193
% of Weighted Total:	100.0	47.1	49.5	74.5	12.1	23.5	27.4	30.5	18.7	57.3	35.0	38.9	20.9	13.7	23.0	1.2

C18B: Because you skipped or "cut"

1. None	70.9	68.0	73.7	69.8	80.1	69.2	74.4	74.9	61.4	73.2	67.6	83.6	69.2	66.5	55.1	41.9
2. 1 day	13.3	13.8	12.9	14.3	8.4	12.8	13.5	12.0	15.6	12.8	14.2	9.6	15.3	15.1	16.4	16.3
3. 2 days	6.4	7.2	5.7	6.7	4.7	7.5	5.3	5.7	8.0	5.9	7.2	3.6	6.6	8.3	9.8	10.0
4. 3 days	4.2	4.6	3.6	4.1	3.6	4.7	3.1	3.7	5.8	3.6	4.9	1.7	4.7	5.5	6.9	7.9
5. 4-5 days	3.1	3.5	2.6	3.0	1.8	3.4	1.9	2.3	5.6	2.8	3.4	0.7	2.5	2.9	7.3	10.8
6. 6-10 days	1.3	1.7	0.9	1.3	0.8	1.5	1.2	0.8	1.8	1.0	1.6	0.4	0.9	1.2	2.7	4.8
7. 11 or more	0.9	1.2	0.6	0.7	0.7	0.9	0.7	0.5	1.9	0.7	1.1	0.3	0.7	0.5	1.9	8.2
Item 440 Subject B06 N	14980	7148	7567	11506	1756	3408	4183	4536	2853	8982	5458	5856	3177	2092	3477	166

C18C: For other reasons

1. None	59.5	61.3	57.7	59.1	60.4	58.5	59.0	61.6	58.3	59.2	60.1	62.5	59.8	57.6	55.8	50.5
2. 1 day	19.2	18.0	20.3	19.9	16.8	19.8	18.9	19.2	18.7	19.6	18.7	18.9	18.7	20.5	19.6	16.8
3. 2 days	10.0	9.2	10.7	9.9	10.0	10.2	9.9	9.6	10.6	10.2	9.5	8.9	10.2	10.7	11.1	13.8
4. 3 days	5.2	5.2	5.3	5.3	4.9	5.0	5.8	4.6	5.8	5.0	5.6	4.7	5.1	5.1	6.2	4.2
5. 4-5 days	3.7	3.6	3.8	3.6	4.5	3.7	4.3	3.4	3.2	3.7	3.6	3.1	3.9	4.1	3.9	6.7
6. 6-10 days	1.5	1.6	1.4	1.4	2.2	1.7	1.5	1.1	2.1	1.5	1.5	1.2	1.3	1.4	2.1	1.8
7. 11 or more	0.9	1.0	0.8	0.8	1.2	1.1	0.7	0.6	1.4	0.8	1.0	0.6	1.0	0.5	1.3	6.2
Item 450 Subject B06 N	15113	7185	7669	11606	1782	3445	4203	4594	2872	9103	5468	5985	3191	2104	3447	169

C19: During the last four weeks, how often have you gone to school, but skipped a class when you weren't supposed to?

1. Not at all	66.4	63.1	69.6	67.0	68.4	67.4	73.3	73.7	43.1	66.9	66.0	78.8	62.7	61.7	52.5	34.3
2. 1 or 2 times	20.1	21.8	18.4	20.1	18.8	18.2	17.7	17.6	30.0	20.0	20.1	15.0	23.5	23.9	23.5	23.4
3. 3-5 times	8.7	9.5	7.8	8.4	7.3	8.6	6.0	5.5	17.7	8.6	8.9	3.9	9.3	9.8	15.2	16.9
4. 6-10 times	2.9	3.2	2.6	2.8	2.1	3.2	1.7	1.6	6.3	2.8	2.8	1.1	2.8	2.9	5.6	15.1
5. 11-20 times	1.1	1.3	0.8	0.9	1.8	1.3	0.8	0.6	2.0	1.0	1.2	0.6	0.9	1.0	2.0	4.0
6. More than 20 times	0.9	1.2	0.7	0.7	1.5	1.4	0.5	1.0	1.0	0.8	0.9	0.6	0.8	0.8	1.3	6.3
Item 460 Subject B06 N	15797	7520	8003	12085	1892	3617	4384	4804	2991	9422	5752	6227	3333	2196	3628	175

C20: Which of the following best describes your average grade so far in high school?

9. A (93-100)	8.8	7.3	10.3	10.0	3.4	6.6	9.2	10.8	7.5	12.7	2.7	13.3	7.1	5.8	4.5	7.0
8. A- (90-92)	10.6	8.9	12.4	11.8	5.8	9.5	11.1	11.7	9.4	13.9	5.7	14.0	8.8	9.7	7.5	6.9
7. B+ (87-89)	16.7	14.6	18.9	17.1	15.1	14.6	14.6	17.6	18.1	19.4	12.2	18.7	16.1	17.4	14.0	11.8
6. B (83-86)	20.6	19.6	21.5	21.1	17.6	22.5	19.2	20.0	21.2	21.9	18.6	20.0	21.3	21.3	20.7	17.2
5. B- (80-82)	15.1	16.2	14.1	14.7	16.4	17.5	15.0	13.0	16.0	13.8	17.1	13.0	16.2	17.0	16.7	12.6
4. C+ (77-79)	13.7	15.7	11.6	12.4	20.7	12.2	14.0	15.0	12.8	10.0	19.3	10.9	15.3	13.6	16.9	19.6
3. C (73-76)	9.6	11.4	7.7	8.6	13.4	9.6	11.0	7.7	10.5	6.1	15.0	7.3	9.3	9.9	12.8	14.7
2. C- (70-72)	3.7	4.7	2.8	3.4	5.9	3.8	4.3	3.4	3.3	1.7	7.0	2.4	4.4	4.3	4.8	6.5
1. D (69 or below)	1.2	1.6	0.7	1.0	1.8	1.4	1.6	0.8	1.0	0.4	2.4	0.5	1.5	1.0	2.0	3.7
Item 470 Subject B01 N	15719	7478	7972	12023	1892	3589	4351	4802	2977	9400	5721	6201	3325	2181	3602	175

C21: How likely is it that you will do each of the following things after high school?

C21A: Attend a technical or vocational school

1. Definitely won't	46.6	41.4	51.8	49.3	38.0	54.5	46.5	46.4	37.9	60.5	25.5	49.6	47.2	46.7	41.3	36.6
2. Probably won't	27.1	29.5	25.1	27.2	25.4	22.6	26.2	26.8	34.3	26.1	29.2	26.8	27.0	25.9	28.8	24.9
3. Probably will	17.2	19.4	14.9	15.0	25.7	13.4	17.5	18.6	19.2	9.3	29.4	15.2	16.5	18.4	20.3	22.6
4. Definitely will	9.0	9.7	8.2	8.4	10.9	9.5	9.7	8.2	8.6	4.1	15.9	8.4	9.2	9.0	9.6	15.9
Item 480 Subject B09,C03 N	14979	7046	7664	11467	1778	3366	4179	4578	2855	9074	5734	5969	3155	2067	3408	164

C21B: Serve in the armed forces

1. Definitely won't	60.9	44.0	76.9	64.1	42.1	62.6	61.8	57.9	62.4	64.5	55.9	61.8	58.1	61.7	62.5	53.9
2. Probably won't	23.0	30.7	15.8	23.6	19.4	23.3	22.7	22.9	23.2	23.2	23.0	23.3	23.5	21.2	23.2	21.5
3. Probably will	9.5	14.1	5.1	7.0	22.3	7.6	8.8	11.6	9.4	7.7	12.2	8.7	10.3	10.9	8.5	11.4
4. Definitely will	6.6	11.2	2.3	5.3	16.3	6.4	6.8	7.6	5.1	4.6	8.9	6.2	8.2	6.2	5.8	13.3
Item 490 Subject B09,L01 N	14596	6875	7470	11271	1690	3283	4077	4454	2782	8919	5516	5815	3080	2015	3340	153

QUESTIONNAIRE FORM 1-5 1985	TOTAL	SEX		RACE		REGION				4YR COLLEGE PLANS		ILLICIT DRUG USE: LIFETIME				
		M	F	White	Black	NE	NC	S	W	Yes	No	None	Mari- juana Only	Few Pills	More Pills	Any Her- oin
N (Weighted No. of Cases):	16502	7776	8164	12291	1995	3878	4516	5028	3079	9448	5770	6412	3449	2264	3802	193
% of Weighted Total:	100.0	47.1	49.5	74.5	12.1	23.5	27.4	30.5	18.7	57.3	35.0	38.9	20.9	13.7	23.0	1.2
C21C: Graduate from a two-year college program																
1. Definitely won't	38.5	38.1	38.9	40.5	30.9	46.1	40.4	38.1	27.0	44.2	30.5	41.2	37.9	37.9	34.6	37.1
2. Probably won't	27.9	31.4	24.8	28.7	27.6	23.3	30.5	29.5	26.9	27.8	29.0	28.4	28.9	28.1	26.3	26.8
3. Probably will	21.6	20.8	22.1	19.4	29.6	17.4	19.2	22.3	28.8	16.8	28.5	18.9	22.2	22.7	24.8	24.4
4. Definitely will	12.1	9.7	14.2	11.5	11.9	13.1	9.9	10.2	17.3	11.3	12.0	11.5	11.0	11.3	14.3	11.7
Item 500 Subject B09 N	14926	7016	7649	11461	1759	3368	4165	4554	2840	9010	5719	5964	3140	2040	3401	163
C21D: Graduate from college (four-year program)																
1. Definitely won't	21.1	21.0	20.8	21.4	19.0	23.3	23.8	20.3	15.7	-	55.6	17.6	19.4	22.9	26.3	33.8
2. Probably won't	16.8	17.6	16.0	16.3	20.8	14.7	16.2	18.8	17.2	-	44.4	15.3	16.7	17.0	19.4	18.9
3. Probably will	21.9	23.7	20.2	21.0	24.0	18.9	21.8	20.6	27.8	35.3	-	21.3	22.2	21.6	23.1	20.9
4. Definitely will	40.2	37.7	43.0	41.4	36.3	43.2	38.1	40.3	39.4	64.7	-	45.8	41.6	38.5	31.3	26.4
Item 510 Subject B09 N	15217	7206	7746	11673	1784	3446	4249	4628	2894	9448	5770	6053	3200	2099	3478	170
C21E: Attend graduate or professional school after college																
1. Definitely won't	29.4	29.6	28.9	29.9	28.1	31.6	32.4	28.6	23.9	11.3	58.4	25.2	28.0	31.7	35.7	35.5
2. Probably won't	32.6	34.6	30.7	33.3	32.0	28.5	34.1	33.2	34.4	33.3	32.1	33.3	33.5	32.5	31.0	30.4
3. Probably will	26.2	24.9	27.6	26.1	26.5	27.7	24.0	26.1	27.8	38.8	6.3	28.8	27.0	23.7	23.3	17.8
4. Definitely will	11.8	10.9	12.8	10.7	13.5	12.2	9.6	12.1	13.9	16.7	3.2	12.7	11.6	12.1	10.0	16.4
Item 520 Subject B09 N	14936	7035	7640	11441	1761	3381	4158	4556	2841	9074	5729	5943	3139	2054	3420	164
C22: Suppose you could do just what you'd like and nothing stood in your way. How many of the following things would you WANT to do? (Mark ALL that apply)																
A. Attend a technical or vocational school	23.1	26.6	19.6	21.7	28.1	20.0	24.1	23.3	25.2	11.1	43.1	21.2	22.7	24.5	25.7	31.8
B. Serve in the armed forces	15.2	21.7	9.1	12.7	30.2	13.6	15.2	18.1	12.6	12.7	19.2	14.8	17.0	15.5	13.9	17.3
C. Graduate from a two-year college program	24.3	19.2	28.9	23.3	26.3	22.5	22.7	23.1	30.6	16.2	37.2	22.4	22.1	25.3	28.5	29.0
D. Graduate from college (four year program)	64.1	62.5	66.2	65.2	61.5	61.7	63.0	63.8	69.0	89.4	24.8	68.1	66.8	63.2	57.1	47.9
E. Attend graduate or professional school after college	41.7	39.6	44.2	41.9	39.9	42.4	39.8	41.5	44.3	56.9	17.5	43.9	44.0	40.5	37.9	34.2
F. None of the above	8.0	8.9	7.1	8.5	5.1	9.9	8.4	7.8	5.6	2.6	16.9	7.1	6.6	7.6	10.6	14.9
Item 530-580 Subject B09,C03 N	15467	7331	7868	11838	1844	3498	4312	4710	2947	9363	5662	6120	3275	2135	3547	165
C23: On the average over the school year, how many hours per week do you work in a paid or unpaid job?																
1. None	24.5	22.5	26.6	21.0	42.2	21.5	23.6	29.2	21.8	25.3	23.1	28.1	25.2	21.0	19.9	15.3
2. 5 or less hours	10.2	10.0	10.2	10.2	9.7	8.4	11.2	10.0	11.1	11.8	7.4	12.2	9.6	9.1	7.8	6.4
3. 6 to 10 hours	9.8	9.6	10.0	10.2	8.4	9.6	10.1	9.1	10.7	10.5	8.5	10.8	9.5	9.9	8.4	8.9
4. 11 to 15 hours	10.5	9.8	11.2	11.3	6.6	10.9	11.7	9.2	10.1	11.4	9.2	11.2	10.1	9.8	9.9	11.1
5. 16 to 20 hours	15.4	14.8	16.0	16.3	10.5	17.2	16.6	12.9	15.3	15.5	15.2	14.4	15.6	17.3	15.5	19.4
6. 21 to 25 hours	12.4	12.2	12.6	13.4	8.8	14.4	11.7	11.8	12.1	11.8	13.3	9.8	12.4	15.5	15.2	16.7
7. 26 to 30 hours	8.3	9.5	7.0	8.5	5.7	8.8	7.2	8.3	9.2	7.3	9.7	6.6	8.1	9.7	10.1	13.3
8. More than 30 hours	9.1	11.7	6.4	9.0	8.2	9.2	7.9	9.5	9.8	6.2	13.6	7.0	9.3	7.6	13.1	9.0
Item 590 Subject C01 N	15515	7355	7887	11891	1832	3509	4320	4734	2952	9372	5683	6134	3270	2147	3565	170
C24: During an average week, how much money do you get from . . .																
C24A: A job or other work																
1. None	28.5	26.6	30.4	25.6	42.4	23.8	29.0	33.2	26.0	30.2	26.3	33.4	27.9	25.7	23.1	16.4
2. $1-5	3.4	3.2	3.5	3.7	2.2	2.3	4.7	2.8	3.6	3.6	2.8	3.8	3.2	3.9	2.8	0.6
3. $6-10	4.3	3.7	4.7	4.5	4.2	3.2	5.0	4.3	4.4	4.4	4.1	5.1	4.4	3.9	3.2	2.1
4. $11-20	5.0	4.5	5.6	5.1	5.0	4.3	5.3	4.8	5.9	5.6	4.2	5.8	4.3	5.3	4.1	9.0
5. $21-35	7.9	6.5	9.2	8.2	6.4	8.5	8.5	6.9	7.7	8.3	7.1	8.4	7.4	8.0	7.3	6.8
6. $36-50	11.5	10.8	12.2	12.2	8.0	12.3	13.0	9.3	11.8	12.1	10.5	11.3	11.9	10.7	11.8	15.5
7. $51-75	15.9	15.4	16.5	17.2	10.1	19.0	15.6	14.8	14.5	15.7	16.3	14.2	16.6	16.7	18.0	15.2
8. $76-125	16.9	19.5	14.3	17.2	13.9	19.6	14.0	17.0	17.9	15.1	19.7	13.1	17.9	19.9	20.7	18.5
9. $126+	6.6	9.7	3.5	6.2	7.9	6.9	4.9	6.8	8.2	5.0	8.9	5.0	6.4	5.8	9.1	15.9
Item 600 Subject C02 N	14931	7076	7592	11515	1706	3373	4161	4537	2859	9029	5487	5904	3143	2083	3415	168

QUESTIONNAIRE FORM 1-5 1985	TOTAL	SEX		RACE		REGION				4YR COLLEGE PLANS		ILLICIT DRUG USE: LIFETIME				
		M	F	White	Black	NE	NC	S	W	Yes	No	None	Mari- juana Only	Few Pills	More Pills	Any Her- oin
N (Weighted No. of Cases):	16502	7776	8164	12291	1995	3878	4516	5028	3079	9448	5770	6412	3449	2264	3802	193
% of Weighted Total:	100.0	47.1	49.5	74.5	12.1	23.5	27.4	30.5	18.7	57.3	35.0	38.9	20.9	13.7	23.0	1.2
C24B: Other sources (allowances, etc.)																
1. None	34.0	34.5	33.5	35.6	24.1	39.7	32.5	31.0	34.5	32.0	37.3	35.1	34.0	35.4	32.0	27.3
2. $1-5	15.9	14.4	17.3	16.9	12.4	14.6	19.2	14.8	14.5	16.5	15.2	18.2	15.4	15.5	13.4	12.0
3. $6-10	19.4	18.0	20.7	19.8	17.6	18.2	20.0	19.6	19.4	20.6	17.4	19.9	19.6	19.5	18.2	16.6
4. $11-20	15.8	16.1	15.6	15.1	20.0	13.4	15.6	17.3	16.2	16.3	14.7	15.0	15.9	14.8	17.4	12.7
5. $21-35	7.4	8.2	6.5	6.5	11.5	6.6	6.0	8.7	8.1	7.6	7.0	6.1	7.7	7.3	9.1	11.8
6. $36-50	3.3	3.5	3.1	2.8	6.1	3.1	2.9	4.1	2.8	3.3	3.4	2.5	3.7	3.8	3.9	4.4
7. $51-75	1.4	1.7	1.2	1.2	2.7	1.4	1.5	1.5	1.2	1.2	1.7	0.8	1.7	1.1	2.2	2.9
8. $76-125	1.1	1.2	1.0	0.8	2.2	0.9	1.0	1.3	1.2	1.0	1.3	1.0	0.9	1.1	1.3	2.6
9. $126+	1.7	2.5	1.1	1.3	3.4	2.0	1.3	1.7	2.2	1.6	1.9	1.4	1.0	1.5	2.6	9.8
Item 610　Subject C02　N	14635	6878	7515	11246	1715	3250	4102	4510	2772	8924	5344	5800	3077	2018	3382	158
C25: During a typical week, on how many evenings do you go out for fun and recreation?																
1. Less than one	7.8	6.3	9.1	6.4	12.6	7.7	6.8	8.6	7.9	7.7	7.8	11.2	5.9	6.6	4.3	4.6
2. One	13.5	11.9	15.0	12.7	16.5	12.6	12.5	15.4	13.0	13.5	13.4	18.3	11.9	11.3	8.7	4.7
3. Two	30.2	29.4	31.1	30.2	30.5	29.4	29.9	31.1	30.2	32.7	26.2	33.9	31.6	31.0	22.8	17.8
4. Three	26.1	26.7	25.6	27.2	22.8	25.0	26.4	25.5	27.6	26.9	24.8	22.7	28.6	27.6	28.7	22.7
5. Four or five	15.3	16.4	14.2	16.5	10.4	15.8	16.6	13.3	15.9	14.0	17.5	10.3	15.4	16.9	22.4	23.4
6. Six or seven	7.2	9.4	5.0	7.1	7.2	9.5	7.8	6.0	5.4	5.2	10.3	3.5	6.7	6.6	13.1	26.8
Item 620　Subject C07,M01　N	15480	7332	7876	11869	1828	3494	4307	4724	2955	9361	5665	6119	3267	2139	3556	169
C26: On the average, how often do you go out with a date (or your spouse, if you are married)?																
1. Never	12.8	13.2	12.4	10.5	18.7	13.3	11.8	11.8	15.0	12.7	12.9	19.1	9.3	9.8	6.4	10.1
2. Once a month or less	18.6	19.7	17.5	18.5	18.0	17.4	20.1	17.3	19.7	19.8	16.7	20.7	18.9	18.1	15.6	11.8
3. 2 or 3 times a month	17.9	19.4	16.6	17.9	20.5	16.0	17.9	19.0	18.4	18.9	16.5	17.4	18.9	18.1	18.4	17.0
4. Once a week	16.6	18.2	15.3	16.6	17.8	16.7	16.5	17.2	15.9	17.5	15.0	16.4	17.5	18.1	14.7	17.6
5. 2 or 3 times a week	22.4	20.8	24.0	23.9	18.5	22.0	22.6	24.4	19.6	21.9	23.2	19.4	24.2	23.2	25.5	22.2
6. Over 3 times a week	11.6	8.9	14.1	12.5	6.5	14.5	11.1	10.3	11.3	9.3	15.6	7.0	11.1	12.7	18.7	21.3
Item 630　Subject C07,M01　N	15305	7229	7808	11755	1784	3423	4271	4679	2933	9241	5590	6059	3214	2111	3525	172
C27: During an average week, how much do you usually drive a car, truck, or motorcycle?																
1. Not at all	14.8	10.1	19.0	10.6	31.9	24.9	10.7	11.6	14.2	13.7	16.6	16.3	13.8	13.3	13.3	14.0
2. 1 to 10 miles	11.5	8.7	14.2	9.9	20.3	12.5	12.1	10.9	10.5	10.9	12.6	12.7	11.5	11.5	9.7	9.5
3. 11 to 50 miles	30.2	25.8	34.4	31.2	27.0	26.3	34.3	29.8	29.3	32.3	26.8	33.6	31.0	30.0	24.2	23.5
4. 51 to 100 miles	21.3	25.0	18.1	23.5	12.5	18.4	22.4	22.1	22.0	22.1	20.3	19.8	21.1	22.5	23.8	21.4
5. 100 to 200 miles	13.8	18.5	9.4	15.9	4.6	10.8	13.4	15.9	14.6	13.9	13.7	11.5	14.1	15.0	17.1	12.3
6. More than 200 miles	8.3	12.0	4.9	8.9	3.8	7.1	7.0	9.7	9.4	7.1	10.1	6.1	8.5	7.7	11.8	19.2
Item 640　Subject F07　N	15449	7310	7862	11866	1800	3471	4304	4720	2955	9328	5628	6115	3246	2137	3551	172
C28: Within the LAST 12 MONTHS, how many times, if any, have you received a ticket (OR been stopped and warned) for moving violations such as speeding, running a stop light, or improper passing?																
0. None–GO TO Q.C30	72.3	62.6	81.5	69.8	86.7	78.6	71.9	71.9	66.4	73.2	71.4	80.3	70.6	71.8	61.2	49.4
1. Once	17.3	21.3	13.5	19.0	9.1	12.4	18.2	18.5	19.7	17.7	16.7	14.2	18.1	18.0	21.7	18.3
2. Twice	6.1	9.1	3.2	6.5	2.9	4.9	6.2	5.5	8.2	5.3	7.1	3.7	6.8	5.8	9.2	15.8
3. Three times	2.7	4.2	1.2	2.9	1.0	2.7	2.6	2.4	3.2	2.3	3.0	1.1	2.9	2.7	4.7	7.6
4. Four or more times	1.7	2.8	0.6	1.8	0.3	1.5	1.2	1.7	2.4	1.5	1.9	0.6	1.6	1.8	3.2	8.8
Item 650　Subject S02　N	15141	7145	7731	11706	1706	3393	4237	4619	2892	9208	5451	6030	3181	2088	3471	161
C29: How many of these tickets or warnings occurred after you were . . .																
C29A: Drinking alcoholic beverages?																
0. None	84.2	82.2	87.7	83.2	94.3	86.0	80.6	85.4	85.6	86.2	81.1	94.7	85.7	84.8	74.5	61.7
1. One	12.1	13.3	10.1	12.8	3.6	10.5	15.5	10.7	10.9	10.4	14.4	4.8	11.3	12.2	18.9	21.3
2. Two	2.2	2.7	1.5	2.4	1.3	1.6	2.9	2.1	2.1	1.9	3.1	0.3	2.2	1.7	3.9	8.9
3. Three	0.8	1.0	0.5	1.0	0.4	1.1	0.4	1.1	0.8	0.9	0.8	0.2	0.3	0.9	1.5	5.2
4. Four or more	0.6	0.8	0.2	0.5	0.3	0.7	0.5	0.7	0.5	0.7	0.6	0.1	0.5	0.3	1.2	2.9
Item 660　Subject A07a,S02　N★	4159	2644	1432	3515	228	717	1181	1295	967	2455	1546	1190	931	587	1328	76

★=excludes respondents for whom question was inappropriate.

QUESTIONNAIRE FORM 1-5 1985	TOTAL	SEX		RACE		REGION				4YR COLLEGE PLANS		ILLICIT DRUG USE: LIFETIME				
		M	F	White	Black	NE	NC	S	W	Yes	No	None	Mari-juana Only	Few Pills	More Pills	Any Her-oin
N (Weighted No. of Cases):	16502	7776	8164	12291	1995	3878	4516	5028	3079	9448	5770	6412	3449	2264	3802	193
% of Weighted Total:	100.0	47.1	49.5	74.5	12.1	23.5	27.4	30.5	18.7	57.3	35.0	38.9	20.9	13.7	23.0	1.2
C29B: Smoking marijuana or hashish?																
0. None	94.4	93.2	96.8	94.3	97.0	91.6	94.9	95.2	94.8	95.8	91.7	100.0	97.9	97.8	87.2	60.3
1. One	3.9	4.3	2.9	4.0	1.3	5.8	3.8	3.4	3.1	2.7	6.0	-	1.8	1.6	8.9	19.1
2. Two	1.0	1.5	0.1	1.0	1.2	1.1	0.9	0.8	1.2	0.6	1.7	1.7	0.1	0.6	2.1	8.9
3. Three	0.5	0.6	0.2	0.5	0.5	0.8	0.3	0.3	0.7	0.5	0.5	-	0.1	-	0.9	9.5
4. Four or more	0.3	0.5	*	0.2	-	0.8	0.2	0.3	0.1	0.4	0.2	-	-	-	0.8	2.2
Item 670 Subject A07a,S02 N★	4109	2615	1416	3470	224	708	1170	1271	959	2430	1526	1184	912	571	1321	76
C29C: Using other illegal drugs?																
0. None	97.8	97.4	98.7	98.1	98.0	95.3	98.2	98.5	98.2	98.2	97.0	100.0	100.0	99.7	95.0	74.7
1. One	1.3	1.4	1.1	1.2	0.7	2.9	1.3	0.5	0.9	0.9	1.8	-	-	0.2	3.4	7.2
2. Two	0.5	0.7	0.1	0.4	1.3	1.1	0.4	0.3	0.3	0.3	0.7	-	-	0.1	0.6	12.0
3. Three	0.3	0.3	0.1	0.3	-	0.1	0.2	0.2	0.5	0.3	0.2	-	-	-	0.6	3.9
4. Four or more	0.2	0.3	*	0.1	-	0.5	-	0.4	-	0.2	0.2	-	-	-	0.5	2.2
Item 680 Subject A07a,S02 N★	4097	2602	1417	3456	226	706	1162	1269	960	2427	1517	1183	914	574	1304	77
C30: We are interested in any accidents which occurred while you were driving a car, truck, or motorcycle. ("Accidents" means a collision involving property damage or personal injury– not bumps or scratches in parking lots.)																
During the LAST 12 MONTHS, how many accidents have you had while you were driving (whether or not you were responsible)?																
0. None–GO TO Q.C32	75.6	71.0	79.8	73.2	89.1	78.3	75.9	73.6	75.1	75.3	76.5	81.8	75.8	72.9	67.0	60.6
1. One	18.5	21.4	16.0	20.4	9.0	15.4	18.8	20.6	18.5	19.2	17.3	15.0	18.9	20.4	23.3	23.8
2. Two	4.5	5.7	3.5	5.0	1.5	5.2	3.9	4.4	4.9	4.2	4.9	2.7	4.3	5.4	6.9	9.7
3. Three	0.9	1.2	0.6	1.0	0.2	0.7	1.0	0.8	0.9	0.9	0.9	0.3	0.7	1.0	1.7	3.4
4. Four or more	0.5	0.7	0.2	0.4	0.2	0.4	0.3	0.6	0.6	0.4	0.4	0.2	0.3	0.3	1.0	2.5
Item 690 Subject S02 N	14939	7047	7632	11555	1680	3333	4176	4554	2876	9091	5377	5984	3141	2051	3415	161
C31: How many of these accidents occurred after you were . . .																
C31A: Drinking alcoholic beverages?																
0. None	89.0	87.2	91.1	88.6	94.9	89.6	87.3	89.9	89.1	90.2	87.1	96.8	90.0	91.3	80.8	64.7
1. One	9.4	10.6	8.1	10.0	3.5	9.2	10.8	8.2	9.9	8.4	11.0	3.0	8.5	7.5	16.4	27.3
2. Two	1.0	1.3	0.7	1.0	0.6	0.8	1.1	1.1	0.9	0.9	1.3	0.1	0.7	1.0	2.1	2.1
3. Three	0.1	0.2	-	0.1	-	0.1	0.1	0.1	-	0.1	0.1	-	0.2	-	0.2	-
4. Four or more	0.5	0.7	0.1	0.3	1.0	0.2	0.7	0.6	0.1	0.4	0.5	0.1	0.7	0.3	0.4	5.9
Item 700 Subject A07a,S02 N★	3639	2037	1541	3097	186	727	1002	1201	709	2231	1267	1098	763	556	1120	61
C31B: Smoking marijuana or hashish?																
0. None	95.4	94.0	97.4	95.8	92.7	93.4	94.9	96.7	96.1	96.0	94.2	100.0	98.3	97.2	89.1	76.1
1. One	3.8	4.9	2.3	3.5	6.3	5.1	4.3	2.7	3.7	3.3	4.9	-	1.3	2.8	9.2	14.0
2. Two	0.5	0.7	0.2	0.6	-	0.9	0.6	0.4	0.1	0.6	0.4	-	0.2	-	1.3	4.1
3. Three	*	0.1	-	0.1	-	0.2	-	-	-	-	0.1	-	0.1	-	0.1	-
4. Four or more	0.2	0.3	*	0.1	1.0	0.4	0.2	0.1	0.1	0.2	0.3	-	0.1	-	0.3	5.8
Item 710 Subject A07a,S02 N★	3587	2004	1524	3047	186	722	985	1175	705	2212	1243	1085	750	549	1101	62
C31C: Using other illegal drugs?																
0. None	98.5	98.1	99.1	98.8	97.0	98.0	99.0	98.4	98.4	98.5	98.4	100.0	100.0	99.3	96.8	82.0
1. One	1.0	1.1	0.9	0.9	1.2	1.0	0.5	1.3	1.3	1.1	0.9	-	-	0.4	2.5	10.8
2. Two	0.1	0.2	-	0.1	0.8	0.5	-	-	0.2	*	0.3	-	-	0.3	0.2	1.0
3. Three	0.1	0.2	-	0.1	-	0.2	0.3	-	-	0.1	0.2	-	-	-	0.3	-
4. Four or more	0.2	0.3	*	*	1.1	0.3	0.2	0.2	0.1	0.3	0.2	-	-	-	0.3	6.2
Item 720 Subject A07a,S02 N★	3556	1976	1521	3022	182	709	977	1171	698	2196	1229	1083	747	550	1077	58

*=less than .05 per cent.   ★=excludes respondents for whom question was inappropriate.

QUESTIONNAIRE FORM 1-5 1985	TOTAL	SEX		RACE		REGION				4YR COLLEGE PLANS		ILLICIT DRUG USE: LIFETIME				
		M	F	White	Black	NE	NC	S	W	Yes	No	None	Mari- juana Only	Few Pills	More Pills	Any Her- oin
N (Weighted No. of Cases):	16502	7776	8164	12291	1995	3878	4516	5028	3079	9448	5770	6412	3449	2264	3802	193
% of Weighted Total:	100.0	47.1	49.5	74.5	12.1	23.5	27.4	30.5	18.7	57.3	35.0	38.9	20.9	13.7	23.0	1.2

C32: If you have not entered military service, and do not expect to enter, GO TO PART D.

What is, or will be, your branch of service?

1. Army	27.4	27.3	27.6	23.7	37.6	21.9	29.1	30.9	24.0	25.8	28.7	29.3	28.2	24.1	23.1	39.3
2. Navy	14.6	15.7	11.7	17.3	9.2	14.9	12.9	14.0	18.0	13.7	15.2	14.8	13.7	15.0	15.5	14.8
3. Marine Corps	14.0	16.5	6.2	14.6	11.2	15.5	15.3	13.2	12.0	11.9	16.8	12.0	17.3	12.9	14.7	17.9
4. Air Force	30.9	28.4	39.0	30.6	31.2	33.1	30.5	28.8	33.4	35.3	26.5	31.8	29.4	31.5	32.3	17.4
5. Coast Guard	2.4	2.3	2.4	2.8	0.9	3.3	2.4	1.8	2.5	2.5	2.2	2.0	1.2	3.4	4.0	-
6. Uncertain	10.6	9.9	13.2	10.9	9.9	11.2	9.9	11.2	10.1	10.8	10.7	10.0	10.2	13.1	10.3	10.6
Item 730 Subject L01 N★	2612	1883	653	1633	632	521	700	938	452	1264	1219	955	636	368	551	40

C33: Do you expect to be an officer?

1. No	14.8	14.8	14.6	15.6	11.4	13.6	16.0	14.0	16.2	9.0	19.5	13.6	14.7	14.8	15.5	20.4
2. Uncertain	42.9	42.0	45.7	44.7	38.1	45.3	42.6	42.2	42.0	34.1	52.0	41.3	42.1	42.7	47.3	43.3
3. Yes	42.2	43.2	39.7	39.8	50.5	41.0	41.3	43.8	41.7	56.9	28.5	45.2	43.2	42.5	37.3	36.3
Item 740 Subject L01 N★	2640	1904	666	1643	648	525	707	951	457	1276	1232	959	646	381	553	40

C34: Do you expect to have a career in the Armed Forces?

1. No	24.2	24.9	21.5	26.9	17.3	26.1	24.6	22.1	25.6	25.5	21.9	24.7	23.4	25.4	24.5	13.4
2. Uncertain	48.1	49.5	44.4	50.7	41.6	51.9	48.6	45.1	49.1	47.4	50.0	43.2	50.1	49.0	54.1	58.8
3. Yes	27.8	25.5	34.1	22.4	41.0	22.0	26.8	32.8	25.3	27.1	28.1	32.2	26.5	25.6	21.4	27.8
Item 750 Subject L01 N★	2640	1898	671	1643	648	526	712	947	455	1271	1233	962	639	388	551	40

★=excludes respondents for whom question was inappropriate.

QUESTIONNAIRE FORM 1-5 1985	TOTAL	SEX		RACE		REGION				4YR COLLEGE PLANS		ILLICIT DRUG USE: LIFETIME				
		M	F	White	Black	NE	NC	S	W	Yes	No	None	Marijuana Only	Few Pills	More Pills	Any Heroin
N (Weighted No. of Cases):	16502	7776	8164	12291	1995	3878	4516	5028	3079	9448	5770	6412	3449	2264	3802	193
% of Weighted Total:	100.0	47.1	49.5	74.5	12.1	23.5	27.4	30.5	18.7	57.3	35.0	38.9	20.9	13.7	23.0	1.2

The following questions are about CIGARETTE SMOKING.

B01: Have you ever smoked cigarettes?

	TOTAL	M	F	White	Black	NE	NC	S	W	Yes	No	None	Mar. Only	Few Pills	More Pills	Any Her.
1. Never	31.2	32.6	30.3	29.8	39.2	28.6	28.4	34.9	32.6	36.3	24.1	57.8	15.6	17.4	10.1	10.5
2. Once or twice	29.8	32.0	27.7	28.4	38.4	27.4	28.4	31.7	31.5	31.4	27.1	28.5	40.3	35.6	19.9	11.1
3. Occasionally but not regularly	16.9	15.7	18.0	18.2	11.6	16.0	18.7	15.2	18.2	17.3	16.6	8.8	23.1	23.2	21.2	18.7
4. Regularly in the past	6.6	5.6	7.5	7.1	3.3	7.7	6.3	5.9	6.8	5.8	7.8	2.2	6.9	7.7	12.7	15.6
5. Regularly now	15.5	14.0	16.5	16.5	7.5	20.3	18.1	12.3	10.9	9.2	24.5	2.8	14.0	16.2	36.1	44.1
Item 760 Subject A01a N	16151	7643	8046	12145	1911	3786	4441	4897	3027	9323	5667	6310	3407	2231	3752	188

B02: How frequently have you smoked cigarettes during the past 30 days?

	TOTAL	M	F	White	Black	NE	NC	S	W	Yes	No	None	Mar. Only	Few Pills	More Pills	Any Her.
1. Not at all - incl. (1) in B01	69.9	71.8	68.6	68.3	81.3	65.8	65.9	74.4	73.7	77.2	59.5	90.2	68.7	65.3	41.8	30.7
2. Less than one cigarette per day	10.6	10.4	10.8	11.0	7.9	9.3	11.7	9.6	12.2	10.4	10.9	5.5	13.5	14.1	14.6	10.9
3. One to five cigarettes per day	7.0	5.5	8.5	7.1	6.7	7.9	7.5	6.3	6.6	5.9	8.9	2.5	8.1	8.4	12.3	15.5
4. About one-half pack per day	5.8	5.4	5.9	6.1	3.1	7.8	6.6	4.5	4.3	3.3	9.5	1.0	4.9	6.5	14.0	12.8
5. About one pack per day	5.2	5.3	4.9	6.0	0.7	6.9	6.6	4.0	2.8	2.6	8.8	0.7	3.8	4.7	13.5	15.3
6. About one and one-half packs per day	1.1	1.3	1.0	1.2	0.1	1.8	1.3	0.9	0.4	0.5	2.0	0.1	0.7	0.8	3.1	9.7
7. Two packs or more per day	0.3	0.4	0.3	0.3	0.2	0.5	0.4	0.2	0.1	0.2	0.6	*	0.3	0.2	0.6	5.2
Item 780 Subject A01c N	16131	7635	8038	12124	1918	3780	4439	4893	3019	9312	5663	6300	3404	2232	3743	189

B03: Next we want to ask you about drinking alcoholic beverages, including beer, wine, and liquor.

Have you ever had any beer, wine, or liquor to drink?

	TOTAL	M	F	White	Black	NE	NC	S	W	Yes	No	None	Mar. Only	Few Pills	More Pills	Any Her.
1. No	7.8	7.3	8.2	6.0	16.2	5.0	6.6	9.9	9.7	8.2	6.8	17.8	1.0	1.8	1.0	1.4
2. Yes	92.2	92.7	91.8	94.0	83.8	95.0	93.4	90.1	90.3	91.8	93.2	82.2	99.0	98.2	99.0	98.6
Item 790 Subject A01a N	12607	6016	6277	9619	1442	2966	3461	3809	2371	7392	4432	4949	2653	1750	2990	151

B04: On how many occasions have you had alcoholic beverages to drink . . .

B04A: . . . in your lifetime?

	TOTAL	M	F	White	Black	NE	NC	S	W	Yes	No	None	Mar. Only	Few Pills	More Pills	Any Her.
1. 0 occasions - incl. (1) in B03	7.8	7.4	8.1	6.0	16.6	5.0	6.5	10.3	9.4	8.1	7.0	17.7	0.9	1.9	0.9	1.2
2. 1-2	7.8	7.2	8.4	6.1	17.5	5.2	8.0	10.4	6.4	7.8	7.8	15.4	3.8	4.4	1.0	0.7
3. 3-5	8.7	7.0	10.4	7.8	14.4	7.1	8.5	10.8	7.6	8.9	8.6	15.0	6.6	6.6	1.7	1.1
4. 6-9	8.9	7.3	10.5	8.1	13.1	8.0	9.1	9.7	8.5	9.5	8.2	12.0	9.5	9.4	3.2	2.5
5. 10-19	12.2	10.6	13.6	12.0	12.7	12.2	12.2	12.2	12.2	12.6	11.5	13.3	15.3	14.7	6.4	6.2
6. 20-39	13.9	12.6	15.2	14.8	9.6	15.4	13.7	12.7	14.2	14.9	12.8	10.9	18.9	16.6	13.1	7.7
7. 40 or more	40.7	47.9	33.8	45.1	16.2	47.1	42.1	33.8	41.7	38.1	44.2	15.7	45.0	46.4	73.7	80.6
Item 810 Subject A01a N	15586	7396	7774	11858	1767	3685	4274	4665	2962	9096	5426	6110	3319	2159	3666	180

B04B: . . . during the last 12 months?

	TOTAL	M	F	White	Black	NE	NC	S	W	Yes	No	None	Mar. Only	Few Pills	More Pills	Any Her.
1. 0 occasions - incl. (1) in B03	14.4	13.8	15.0	11.2	30.9	9.4	13.3	18.8	15.4	14.5	14.0	29.0	5.3	6.5	3.1	5.1
2. 1-2	14.7	11.7	17.8	13.3	23.6	13.4	14.6	17.5	12.3	15.4	14.0	23.5	12.3	11.7	4.7	4.5
3. 3-5	12.7	10.8	14.6	12.1	15.4	13.1	12.3	13.2	12.1	13.2	12.0	15.6	13.6	14.3	6.8	5.9
4. 6-9	11.5	10.9	12.2	11.8	9.2	11.6	11.7	11.0	12.0	11.7	11.6	10.5	15.4	13.8	8.8	8.3
5. 10-19	15.8	15.9	15.8	17.1	9.5	17.1	15.8	13.8	17.2	16.2	15.3	10.9	19.9	20.6	17.6	9.9
6. 20-39	12.7	13.4	12.0	14.3	5.2	12.8	14.1	10.9	13.2	12.2	13.5	5.6	16.6	15.1	19.4	16.0
7. 40 or more	18.1	23.6	12.6	20.1	6.2	22.6	18.2	14.8	17.7	16.7	19.6	4.9	16.8	18.0	39.7	50.4
Item 820 Subject A01b N	15527	7352	7756	11839	1733	3675	4268	4643	2941	9058	5407	6063	3311	2147	3670	181

B04C: . . . during the last 30 days?

	TOTAL	M	F	White	Black	NE	NC	S	W	Yes	No	None	Mar. Only	Few Pills	More Pills	Any Her.
1. 0 occasions - incl. (1) in B03	34.1	30.2	37.9	29.8	56.4	27.7	33.2	40.0	33.8	35.4	32.1	56.7	23.3	25.4	12.3	13.7
2. 1-2	23.9	21.6	26.1	24.0	23.5	24.5	22.7	24.4	24.0	24.9	22.8	24.6	29.4	26.2	17.4	8.5
3. 3-5	17.5	18.2	16.8	19.1	9.8	18.8	18.5	14.2	19.6	17.6	17.3	10.7	22.1	22.3	22.0	12.6
4. 6-9	11.1	12.7	9.7	12.5	4.9	12.3	12.1	9.5	10.8	10.7	12.0	4.4	13.0	12.9	19.1	17.2
5. 10-19	8.4	10.2	6.5	9.3	3.0	10.2	9.0	6.8	7.8	7.3	9.4	2.3	8.2	9.4	17.4	19.3
6. 20-39	2.7	3.5	2.0	2.9	0.9	3.2	2.4	2.7	2.5	2.3	3.4	0.7	2.2	2.1	6.2	14.2
7. 40 or more	2.3	3.6	1.1	2.3	1.4	3.4	2.0	2.3	1.5	1.7	3.1	0.6	1.7	1.7	5.5	14.5
Item 830 Subject A01c N	15527	7359	7752	11847	1724	3675	4280	4625	2947	9070	5398	6039	3314	2150	3689	179

*=less than .05 per cent.

QUESTIONNAIRE FORM 1-5 1985	TOTAL	SEX		RACE		REGION				4YR COLLEGE PLANS		ILLICIT DRUG USE: LIFETIME				
		M	F	White	Black	NE	NC	S	W	Yes	No	None	Mari- juana Only	Few Pills	More Pills	Any Her- oin
N (Weighted No. of Cases):	16502	7776	8164	12291	1995	3878	4516	5028	3079	9448	5770	6412	3449	2264	3802	193
% of Weighted Total:	100.0	47.1	49.5	74.5	12.1	23.5	27.4	30.5	18.7	57.3	35.0	38.9	20.9	13.7	23.0	1.2

B05: On the occasions that you drink alcoholic beverages, how often do you drink enough to feel pretty high?

1. On none of the occasions	24.3	20.7	28.1	20.9	41.7	20.2	23.5	29.6	22.6	26.9	21.0	49.5	14.2	16.2	5.0	6.5
2. On few of the occasions	31.0	27.3	34.4	30.9	32.7	30.1	29.2	33.9	30.5	30.7	31.6	30.6	35.9	33.6	26.2	16.7
3. On about half of the occasions	16.7	18.4	15.1	18.1	10.6	18.8	17.1	14.2	17.6	16.0	18.0	9.1	20.3	20.7	21.7	17.0
4. On most of the occasions	18.1	20.4	16.1	19.8	9.3	19.5	19.7	14.4	19.8	17.8	18.5	7.2	21.0	19.2	29.3	28.1
5. On nearly all of the occasions	9.8	13.2	6.3	10.4	5.7	11.3	10.5	8.0	9.5	8.6	11.0	3.6	8.6	10.3	17.8	31.8
Item 840 Subject A01e N★	11799	5665	5851	9144	1258	2866	3281	3487	2165	6864	4222	4107	2679	1752	3019	153

B06: Think back over the LAST TWO WEEKS. How many times have you had five or more drinks in a row? (A "drink" is a glass of wine, a bottle of beer, a shot glass of liquor, or a mixed drink.)

1. None - incl. (1) in B03	63.3	54.7	71.8	59.9	83.3	57.6	60.3	70.3	63.9	67.0	58.4	84.9	58.2	57.6	36.9	24.6
2. Once	11.8	12.8	10.8	13.0	5.8	13.1	12.7	9.7	12.1	12.0	11.6	7.2	15.2	14.8	15.0	8.0
3. Twice	9.7	11.7	7.9	10.5	4.1	10.9	10.3	7.6	10.8	8.5	11.6	4.2	11.6	12.0	15.8	15.1
4. Three to five times	9.8	12.8	6.8	10.8	4.2	11.4	11.7	7.3	9.1	8.6	11.3	2.6	10.6	11.0	20.3	17.4
5. Six to nine times	3.2	4.6	1.8	3.6	1.4	4.3	3.2	2.9	2.3	2.4	4.3	0.5	2.8	3.4	7.2	17.2
6. Ten or more times	2.1	3.3	0.8	2.1	1.1	2.8	1.8	2.1	1.7	1.5	2.8	0.6	1.6	1.2	4.8	17.7
Item 850 Subject A01d N	15449	7300	7748	11787	1737	3638	4262	4605	2944	9055	5347	6078	3285	2127	3636	174

The next major section of this questionnaire deals with various other drugs. There is a lot of talk these days about this subject, but very little accurate information. Therefore, we still have a lot to learn about the actual experiences and attitudes of people your age.

We hope that you can answer all questions; but if you find one which you feel you cannot answer honestly, we would prefer that you leave it blank.

Remember that your answers will be kept strictly confidential: they are never connected with your name or your class.

B07: On how many occasions (if any) have you used marijuana (grass, pot) or hashish (hash, hash oil) . . .

B07A: . . . in your lifetime?

1. 0 occasions	45.8	43.4	48.5	44.8	50.6	37.8	46.2	55.5	39.6	49.8	40.9	100.0	-	25.7	8.7	3.5
2. 1-2	12.0	11.8	12.3	11.5	16.4	11.1	12.0	13.1	11.3	11.8	12.6	-	37.7	17.4	6.1	4.8
3. 3-5	7.7	7.3	8.2	7.8	7.6	8.1	7.5	6.6	9.4	8.0	7.6	-	20.6	12.5	6.5	5.3
4. 6-9	5.8	5.7	5.7	5.8	5.5	6.6	5.8	4.9	6.3	5.9	5.3	-	13.6	9.0	6.8	2.9
5. 10-19	6.9	6.4	7.5	7.4	5.1	7.4	7.0	5.7	8.2	6.9	6.8	-	12.0	12.0	11.3	4.0
6. 20-39	5.6	5.7	5.5	6.0	4.0	6.8	5.5	4.2	6.4	5.2	6.3	-	7.2	8.9	11.8	5.4
7. 40 or more	16.2	19.7	12.3	16.7	10.7	22.2	16.1	9.9	18.8	12.4	20.5	-	8.9	14.5	48.7	74.2
Item 860 Subject A01a N	15950	7581	7956	12063	1880	3719	4387	4834	3010	9275	5581	6412	3430	2202	3704	179

B07B: . . . during the last 12 months?

1. 0 occasions	59.4	56.9	62.2	57.8	67.6	51.8	59.2	69.0	53.8	62.5	56.0	100.0	36.0	45.8	20.6	16.9
2. 1-2	11.6	11.3	11.9	11.9	11.2	12.2	12.0	10.2	12.6	11.7	11.6	-	29.6	18.0	11.8	5.0
3. 3-5	7.2	6.5	7.9	7.4	5.0	8.6	6.9	5.6	8.4	6.7	7.7	-	13.7	11.3	11.2	6.1
4. 6-9	4.7	4.5	4.9	5.0	4.2	4.5	4.8	3.9	6.2	4.7	4.8	-	8.5	7.2	8.0	5.5
5. 10-19	5.0	5.3	4.6	5.4	3.3	6.1	4.6	3.8	6.1	4.9	4.9	-	6.2	6.9	11.3	7.1
6. 20-39	3.4	3.8	3.0	3.5	3.0	4.7	3.5	2.0	4.0	2.9	4.0	-	2.7	4.8	8.7	14.6
7. 40 or more	8.7	11.7	5.6	9.1	5.7	12.2	9.0	5.6	9.0	6.5	11.0	-	3.3	6.1	28.5	44.8
Item 870 Subject A01b N	15861	7528	7925	12013	1857	3697	4362	4802	3000	9236	5543	6412	3385	2186	3679	177

★=excludes respondents for whom question was inappropriate.

QUESTIONNAIRE FORM 1-5 1985	TOTAL	SEX		RACE		REGION				4YR COLLEGE PLANS		ILLICIT DRUG USE: LIFETIME				
		M	F	White	Black	NE	NC	S	W	Yes	No	None	Marijuana Only	Few Pills	More Pills	Any Heroin
N (Weighted No. of Cases):	16502	7776	8164	12291	1995	3878	4516	5028	3079	9448	5770	6412	3449	2264	3802	193
% of Weighted Total:	100.0	47.1	49.5	74.5	12.1	23.5	27.4	30.5	18.7	57.3	35.0	38.9	20.9	13.7	23.0	1.2

B07C: . . . during the last 30 days?

	TOTAL	M	F	White	Black	NE	NC	S	W	Yes	No	None	Marijuana Only	Few Pills	More Pills	Any Heroin
1. 0 occasions	74.3	71.3	77.6	73.6	78.3	68.0	73.9	82.0	70.3	77.3	71.0	100.0	69.1	68.2	40.5	26.7
2. 1-2	9.8	9.5	10.1	10.1	9.7	10.6	9.7	7.4	12.8	9.9	9.8	-	19.4	15.1	15.0	8.0
3. 3-5	4.6	5.0	4.3	4.9	3.7	5.8	4.3	3.3	5.6	4.3	5.0	-	5.9	7.5	9.6	6.7
4. 6-9	3.0	3.2	2.7	3.0	2.7	3.9	2.9	2.0	3.7	2.6	3.3	-	2.4	3.7	7.8	13.9
5. 10-19	3.4	4.1	2.6	3.5	2.1	4.8	3.6	2.3	3.1	2.6	4.2	-	1.6	3.2	10.6	14.5
6. 20-39	2.5	3.2	1.7	2.6	1.7	3.7	2.9	1.5	1.9	1.7	3.5	-	1.0	1.2	8.1	15.7
7. 40 or more	2.4	3.6	1.1	2.3	1.8	3.0	2.7	1.5	2.6	1.6	3.2	-	0.5	1.2	8.4	14.5
Item 880 Subject A01c N	15865	7534	7924	12019	1856	3695	4367	4803	3000	9241	5549	6412	3376	2187	3690	178

B08: On how many occasions (if any) have you used LSD ("acid") . . .

B08A: . . . in your lifetime?

	TOTAL	M	F	White	Black	NE	NC	S	W	Yes	No	None	Marijuana Only	Few Pills	More Pills	Any Heroin
1. 0 occasions	92.5	90.6	94.4	91.7	98.5	90.6	91.5	95.2	91.8	94.4	90.3	100.0	100.0	95.0	73.6	34.5
2. 1-2	3.7	4.3	3.2	4.1	0.8	4.5	3.9	2.6	4.4	2.9	4.7	-	-	5.0	12.3	16.8
3. 3-5	1.5	2.0	1.1	1.8	0.3	1.6	1.9	1.1	1.7	1.1	2.2	-	-	-	6.0	14.2
4. 6-9	0.9	1.2	0.6	1.0	0.2	1.3	0.9	0.4	1.3	0.7	1.1	-	-	-	3.5	9.2
5. 10-19	0.6	1.0	0.4	0.7	*	0.9	0.9	0.3	0.4	0.4	0.8	-	-	-	2.3	9.0
6. 20-39	0.3	0.5	0.2	0.3	*	0.5	0.5	0.2	0.2	0.2	0.4	-	-	-	1.2	4.2
7. 40 or more	0.4	0.6	0.2	0.4	0.2	0.5	0.6	0.2	0.2	0.3	0.5	-	-	-	1.1	12.2
Item 890 Subject A01a N	16123	7660	8052	12160	1930	3761	4428	4893	3040	9346	5670	6388	3428	2241	3743	178

B08B: . . . during the last 12 months?

	TOTAL	M	F	White	Black	NE	NC	S	W	Yes	No	None	Marijuana Only	Few Pills	More Pills	Any Heroin
1. 0 occasions	95.6	94.1	97.2	95.1	99.1	94.6	94.7	97.2	95.4	96.6	94.4	100.0	100.0	97.9	84.6	51.0
2. 1-2	2.7	3.4	2.0	3.0	0.6	3.0	3.0	1.8	3.3	2.2	3.3	-	-	2.1	9.3	21.7
3. 3-5	0.9	1.4	0.4	1.1	*	0.9	1.3	0.4	1.1	0.6	1.3	-	-	-	3.7	4.6
4. 6-9	0.4	0.5	0.2	0.4	0.1	0.8	0.4	0.2	*	0.3	0.5	-	-	-	1.2	9.1
5. 10-19	0.3	0.4	0.1	0.3	*	0.3	0.3	0.3	0.2	0.2	0.4	-	-	-	0.8	6.4
6. 20-39	0.1	0.1	*	0.1	0.1	0.2	0.2	*	*	0.1	0.1	-	-	-	0.3	2.2
7. 40 or more	0.1	0.2	*	0.1	0.1	0.2	0.1	0.1	-	0.1	0.1	-	-	-	0.2	5.1
Item 900 Subject A01b N	16116	7654	8051	12157	1930	3759	4427	4892	3039	9344	5671	6389	3431	2235	3737	180

B08C: . . . during the last 30 days?

	TOTAL	M	F	White	Black	NE	NC	S	W	Yes	No	None	Marijuana Only	Few Pills	More Pills	Any Heroin
1. 0 occasions	98.4	97.6	99.2	98.2	99.7	97.9	97.7	99.1	98.7	98.7	98.0	100.0	100.0	99.4	94.6	74.2
2. 1-2	1.2	1.7	0.7	1.3	0.1	1.5	1.7	0.5	1.1	0.9	1.4	-	-	0.6	4.2	10.7
3. 3-5	0.3	0.4	0.1	0.3	-	0.4	0.3	0.2	0.1	0.2	0.3	-	-	-	0.9	6.3
4. 6-9	0.1	0.2	*	0.1	0.1	*	0.2	0.1	-	0.1	0.1	-	-	-	0.3	3.3
5. 10-19	*	*	*	*	-	0.1	*	-	*	*	0.1	-	-	-	0.1	1.1
6. 20-39	*	*	*	*	-	-	*	*	-	*	*	-	-	-	*	0.3
7. 40 or more	0.1	0.1	*	*	0.1	0.1	0.1	-	-	*	*	-	-	-	*	4.2
Item 910 Subject A01c N	16111	7652	8049	12156	1927	3757	4424	4892	3039	9344	5666	6389	3430	2235	3734	179

B09: On how many occasions (if any) have you used psychedelics other than LSD (like mescaline, peyote, psilocybin, PCP) . . .

B09A: . . . in your lifetime?

	TOTAL	M	F	White	Black	NE	NC	S	W	Yes	No	None	Marijuana Only	Few Pills	More Pills	Any Heroin
1. 0 occasions	93.5	91.9	95.2	93.2	98.2	87.7	94.8	96.8	93.4	94.8	92.4	100.0	100.0	95.3	77.9	37.4
2. 1-2	3.1	3.7	2.6	3.4	1.1	5.1	2.7	1.8	3.5	2.7	3.5	-	-	4.7	9.7	22.1
3. 3-5	1.3	1.7	0.8	1.3	0.4	2.4	1.0	0.6	1.4	1.2	1.4	-	-	-	5.0	11.4
4. 6-9	0.7	1.0	0.5	0.7	0.1	1.3	0.6	0.3	0.9	0.5	0.8	-	-	-	2.8	7.7
5. 10-19	0.6	0.8	0.3	0.6	-	1.4	0.3	0.2	0.5	0.4	0.6	-	-	-	2.0	7.9
6. 20-39	0.3	0.4	0.3	0.3	0.1	1.0	0.1	0.1	0.2	0.2	0.6	-	-	-	1.2	4.2
7. 40 or more	0.4	0.5	0.3	0.4	0.2	1.1	0.4	0.1	0.1	0.2	0.6	-	-	-	1.3	9.4
Item 920 Subject A01a N	16099	7652	8043	12152	1931	3742	4437	4895	3025	9340	5665	6389	3418	2232	3734	182

B09B: . . . during the last 12 months?

	TOTAL	M	F	White	Black	NE	NC	S	W	Yes	No	None	Marijuana Only	Few Pills	More Pills	Any Heroin
1. 0 occasions	96.4	95.4	97.5	96.3	99.1	92.9	96.9	98.5	96.4	97.1	95.9	100.0	100.0	98.5	87.3	57.8
2. 1-2	2.1	2.5	1.7	2.2	0.5	3.5	2.0	0.8	2.7	2.0	2.2	-	-	1.5	7.4	18.7
3. 3-5	0.6	0.9	0.4	0.7	0.1	1.4	0.6	0.3	0.4	0.4	0.8	-	-	-	2.4	7.1
4. 6-9	0.5	0.7	0.2	0.4	0.1	1.1	0.3	0.3	0.2	0.3	0.5	-	-	-	1.6	8.5
5. 10-19	0.2	0.3	0.1	0.2	-	0.5	0.1	*	0.2	0.1	0.3	-	-	-	0.6	3.7
6. 20-39	0.1	0.2	0.1	0.1	0.2	0.5	0.1	*	-	0.1	0.2	-	-	-	0.5	1.0
7. 40 or more	0.1	0.1	*	0.1	-	0.1	0.1	0.1	-	*	0.1	-	-	-	0.1	3.0
Item 930 Subject A01b N	16087	7643	8043	12148	1931	3735	4438	4891	3022	9336	5664	6390	3419	2231	3717	185

*=less than .05 per cent.

QUESTIONNAIRE FORM 1-5 1985	TOTAL	SEX		RACE		REGION				4YR COLLEGE PLANS		ILLICIT DRUG USE: LIFETIME				
		M	F	White	Black	NE	NC	S	W	Yes	No	None	Mari- juana Only	Few Pills	More Pills	Any Her- oin
N (Weighted No. of Cases):	16502	7776	8164	12291	1995	3878	4516	5028	3079	9448	5770	6412	3449	2264	3802	193
% of Weighted Total:	100.0	47.1	49.5	74.5	12.1	23.5	27.4	30.5	18.7	57.3	35.0	38.9	20.9	13.7	23.0	1.2
B09C: . . . during the last 30 days?																
1. 0 occasions	98.7	98.3	99.2	98.7	99.6	97.0	98.9	99.4	99.2	99.0	98.5	100.0	100.0	99.6	95.6	75.7
2. 1-2	0.9	1.1	0.6	0.9	0.1	1.9	0.7	0.4	0.6	0.7	1.0	-	-	0.4	2.8	13.0
3. 3-5	0.3	0.4	0.2	0.2	0.1	0.7	0.2	0.2	0.1	0.2	0.3	-	-	-	0.8	7.2
4. 6-9	0.1	0.1	*	0.1	0.1	0.2	0.1	*	-	*	0.2	-	-	-	0.3	1.2
5. 10-19	0.1	0.2	*	0.1	0.1	0.1	0.1	*	0.1	0.1	0.1	-	-	-	0.3	1.6
6. 20-39	-	-	-	-	-	-	-	-	-	-	-	-	-	-	-	-
7. 40 or more	*	*	-	*	0.1	0.1	*	-	-	*	*	-	-	-	0.1	1.4
Item 940 Subject A01c N	16090	7645	8043	12150	1932	3737	4439	4891	3022	9337	5664	6390	3418	2234	3717	187
B10: On how many occasions (if any) have you use cocaine (sometimes called "coke") . . .																
B10A: . . . in your lifetime?																
1. 0 occasions	82.7	80.3	85.2	82.4	89.9	74.1	88.5	88.9	74.6	85.4	79.8	100.0	100.0	73.3	45.4	17.5
2. 1-2	7.0	7.7	6.3	6.9	5.8	8.6	6.1	5.3	9.2	6.2	7.8	-	-	26.7	13.1	21.9
3. 3-5	3.0	3.5	2.3	3.1	1.4	4.3	1.7	1.8	4.9	2.6	3.2	-	-	-	12.0	13.7
4. 6-9	2.1	2.4	1.7	2.2	1.1	3.4	1.1	1.3	3.1	1.9	2.2	-	-	-	8.5	7.6
5. 10-19	1.8	2.1	1.5	1.9	0.7	2.7	1.0	1.3	2.7	1.5	2.0	-	-	-	7.3	10.4
6. 20-39	1.5	1.5	1.4	1.5	0.5	3.1	0.5	0.6	2.1	0.9	2.2	-	-	-	5.7	10.6
7. 40 or more	2.0	2.5	1.5	2.0	0.6	3.9	0.9	0.8	3.3	1.3	2.8	-	-	-	7.9	18.2
Item 950 Subject A01a N	16090	7659	8058	12173	1925	3738	4437	4886	3030	9357	5663	6375	3406	2240	3740	183
B10B: . . . during the last 12 months?																
1. 0 occasions	86.9	85.2	88.8	86.3	94.1	79.2	91.8	92.5	80.3	88.6	85.3	100.0	100.0	86.7	54.8	34.3
2. 1-2	5.6	6.3	4.9	5.8	3.4	7.4	4.6	3.7	7.8	5.3	5.8	-	-	13.3	15.2	17.0
3. 3-5	2.4	2.7	1.9	2.5	0.8	3.9	1.0	1.5	4.0	2.2	2.4	-	-	-	9.5	15.8
4. 6-9	1.7	1.9	1.6	1.9	0.7	3.0	1.0	0.8	2.7	1.5	1.9	-	-	-	7.1	8.3
5. 10-19	1.6	1.9	1.4	1.7	0.6	3.2	0.7	0.8	2.4	1.3	2.1	-	-	-	6.7	8.9
6. 20-39	0.8	0.8	0.8	0.8	0.2	1.6	0.3	0.3	1.3	0.5	1.2	-	-	-	3.1	5.8
7. 40 or more	0.9	1.2	0.6	0.9	0.1	1.8	0.5	0.4	1.5	0.6	1.3	-	-	-	3.6	10.0
Item 960 Subject A01b N	16072	7651	8046	12155	1928	3732	4434	4880	3026	9343	5660	6378	3406	2233	3725	184
B10C: . . . during the last 30 days?																
1. 0 occasions	93.3	92.3	94.4	93.0	97.3	88.0	96.1	96.7	90.2	94.5	92.1	100.0	100.0	96.7	75.1	56.7
2. 1-2	3.8	4.3	3.2	4.2	1.6	6.1	2.4	2.0	5.6	3.3	4.0	-	-	3.3	13.4	17.8
3. 3-5	1.3	1.4	1.2	1.3	0.5	2.3	0.7	0.7	2.1	1.1	1.5	-	-	-	5.4	7.6
4. 6-9	0.8	0.9	0.6	0.7	0.4	1.8	0.4	0.3	0.8	0.6	1.0	-	-	-	2.9	8.4
5. 10-19	0.5	0.6	0.4	0.5	0.1	1.0	0.2	0.2	0.8	0.3	0.8	-	-	-	2.0	4.4
6. 20-39	0.2	0.2	0.2	0.2	0.1	0.4	0.1	*	0.3	0.1	0.3	-	-	-	0.8	1.3
7. 40 or more	0.2	0.2	0.1	0.1	0.1	0.4	0.1	0.1	0.1	0.1	0.2	-	-	-	0.5	3.8
Item 970 Subject A01c N	16063	7645	8043	12148	1925	3730	4430	4877	3025	9340	5654	6377	3406	2231	3719	183
B11: Amphetamines can be prescribed by doctors to help people lose weight or to give people more energy. They are sometimes called uppers, ups, speed, bennies, dexies, pep pills, and diet pills. Drugstores are not supposed to sell them without a prescription from a doctor. Amphetamines do NOT include any non-prescription drugs, such as over-the-counter diet pills (like Dexatrim) or stay-awake pills (like No-Doz), or any mail-order drugs. On how many occasions (if any) have you taken amphetamines on your own–that is, without a doctor telling you to take them...																
B11A: . . . in your lifetime?																
1. 0 occasions	73.8	75.4	72.4	70.8	91.4	72.4	72.3	77.9	70.9	77.4	68.1	100.0	100.0	49.3	21.5	19.9
2. 1-2	9.1	8.6	9.4	9.9	4.2	8.8	8.1	8.7	11.4	8.6	9.7	-	-	50.7	8.3	5.7
3. 3-5	4.4	4.0	4.8	5.0	1.4	4.1	4.7	3.6	5.9	4.0	5.3	-	-	-	18.6	10.6
4. 6-9	3.1	2.7	3.3	3.3	1.0	3.3	3.6	2.4	3.0	2.5	3.9	-	-	-	12.6	10.8
5. 10-19	3.1	3.1	3.2	3.6	0.9	3.5	3.8	2.4	2.9	2.6	4.1	-	-	-	13.0	10.1
6. 20-39	2.3	2.2	2.4	2.7	0.5	2.9	2.5	1.8	2.1	2.0	2.8	-	-	-	9.4	10.4
7. 40 or more	4.2	3.9	4.5	4.8	0.6	5.0	5.0	3.1	3.9	3.0	6.2	-	-	-	16.6	32.6
Item 980 Subject A01a N	16081	7665	8055	12172	1937	3751	4434	4870	3025	9353	5653	6344	3399	2236	3744	183

*=less than .05 per cent.

QUESTIONNAIRE FORM 1-5 1985	TOTAL	SEX		RACE		REGION				4YR COLLEGE PLANS		ILLICIT DRUG USE: LIFETIME				
		M	F	White	Black	NE	NC	S	W	Yes	No	None	Marijuana Only	Few Pills	More Pills	Any Heroin
N (Weighted No. of Cases):	16502	7776	8164	12291	1995	3878	4516	5028	3079	9448	5770	6412	3449	2264	3802	193
% of Weighted Total:	100.0	47.1	49.5	74.5	12.1	23.5	27.4	30.5	18.7	57.3	35.0	38.9	20.9	13.7	23.0	1.2

B11B: . . . during the last 12 months?

1. 0 occasions	84.2	85.1	83.6	82.3	95.7	83.2	82.7	87.2	82.7	86.7	80.3	100.0	100.0	83.5	44.9	37.6
2. 1-2	6.5	5.9	6.9	7.3	2.1	6.3	6.3	5.7	8.2	6.0	7.4	-	-	16.5	17.6	11.8
3. 3-5	3.0	3.0	3.1	3.4	1.0	3.6	3.3	2.3	3.1	2.5	3.8	-	-	-	12.4	14.4
4. 6-9	2.2	2.2	2.3	2.5	0.5	2.6	2.7	1.6	2.1	1.7	3.0	-	-	-	9.2	8.2
5. 10-19	1.8	1.8	1.9	2.1	0.5	2.0	2.3	1.4	1.6	1.4	2.5	-	-	-	7.6	4.9
6. 20-39	1.0	1.0	1.0	1.1	0.1	0.7	1.3	0.9	1.3	0.8	1.3	-	-	-	4.0	11.2
7. 40 or more	1.2	1.1	1.2	1.3	0.2	1.6	1.3	0.8	0.9	0.9	1.6	-	-	-	4.4	11.8
Item 990 Subject A01b N	16035	7636	8038	12142	1928	3739	4424	4857	3015	9330	5642	6344	3400	2210	3726	181

B11C: . . . during the last 30 days?

1. 0 occasions	93.2	93.5	92.9	92.4	98.2	92.7	92.3	94.6	92.7	94.7	90.8	100.0	100.0	96.1	75.1	55.3
2. 1-2	3.6	3.6	3.6	4.1	1.2	3.4	4.0	2.9	4.3	2.8	4.9	-	-	3.9	12.4	17.2
3. 3-5	1.3	1.2	1.5	1.5	0.2	1.8	1.3	1.0	1.4	1.0	1.8	-	-	-	5.5	6.1
4. 6-9	0.8	0.8	0.7	0.9	0.2	0.9	0.9	0.6	0.8	0.6	1.1	-	-	-	3.0	6.9
5. 10-19	0.7	0.6	0.7	0.7	0.1	0.7	0.9	0.7	0.4	0.6	0.7	-	-	-	2.6	7.3
6. 20-39	0.3	0.2	0.3	0.3	0.1	0.3	0.3	0.3	0.2	0.2	0.4	-	-	-	0.9	5.1
7. 40 or more	0.2	0.1	0.2	0.2	0.1	0.3	0.2	*	0.2	0.1	0.3	-	-	-	0.6	2.0
Item 1000 Subject A01c N	16027	7633	8032	12134	1928	3736	4422	4853	3016	9328	5635	6344	3400	2210	3715	182

B12: On how many occasions (if any) have you used quaaludes (quads, soapers, methaqualone) on your own–that is, without a doctor telling you to take them . . .

B12A: . . . in your lifetime?

1. 0 occasions	93.3	92.9	94.0	92.7	98.4	92.1	93.2	93.3	95.1	94.7	91.3	100.0	100.0	94.3	77.8	38.5
2. 1-2	3.4	3.2	3.4	3.7	0.9	3.9	3.3	3.4	2.9	2.8	4.2	-	-	5.7	10.4	13.6
3. 3-5	1.2	1.4	1.0	1.4	0.3	1.5	1.2	1.3	0.8	0.9	1.7	-	-	-	4.6	10.5
4. 6-9	0.8	0.9	0.6	0.8	0.2	0.9	0.6	0.8	0.6	0.5	1.2	-	-	-	2.8	9.7
5. 10-19	0.5	0.6	0.4	0.6	-	0.5	0.9	0.3	0.4	0.4	0.8	-	-	-	2.0	5.6
6. 20-39	0.4	0.6	0.3	0.4	0.2	0.7	0.4	0.4	0.1	0.4	0.4	-	-	-	1.3	10.7
7. 40 or more	0.4	0.4	0.3	0.4	0.1	0.4	0.5	0.4	0.1	0.3	0.5	-	-	-	1.1	11.5
Item 1010 Subject A01a N	16080	7665	8074	12186	1936	3734	4439	4881	3027	9359	5671	6341	3400	2240	3734	187

B12B: . . . during the last 12 months?

1. 0 occasions	97.2	96.5	97.9	96.9	99.6	96.4	97.2	97.2	98.1	97.7	96.4	100.0	100.0	99.1	90.4	58.2
2. 1-2	1.6	1.8	1.3	1.8	0.2	1.9	1.5	1.6	1.3	1.3	2.0	-	-	0.9	5.7	10.0
3. 3-5	0.6	0.7	0.4	0.6	0.2	0.9	0.5	0.5	0.4	0.5	0.7	-	-	-	2.0	12.4
4. 6-9	0.3	0.5	0.1	0.3	-	0.4	0.3	0.4	0.1	0.3	0.4	-	-	-	1.0	7.2
5. 10-19	0.2	0.3	0.1	0.2	*	0.3	0.3	0.2	*	0.1	0.2	-	-	-	0.5	6.1
6. 20-39	0.1	0.1	0.1	0.1	-	0.2	*	0.2	0.1	*	0.2	-	-	-	0.3	3.3
7. 40 or more	0.1	*	0.1	0.1	-	0.1	0.1	*	-	*	0.1	-	-	-	0.1	2.7
Item 1020 Subject A01b N	16065	7656	8069	12173	1934	3726	4437	4875	3027	9353	5670	6341	3400	2239	3722	183

B12C: . . . during the last 30 days?

1. 0 occasions	99.0	98.7	99.3	99.0	99.7	98.6	98.9	99.1	99.6	99.3	98.6	100.0	100.0	99.8	97.1	75.7
2. 1-2	0.6	0.9	0.4	0.7	0.3	0.9	0.7	0.6	0.3	0.4	0.9	-	-	0.2	1.9	13.2
3. 3-5	0.2	0.2	0.2	0.2	-	0.3	0.2	0.2	0.1	0.2	0.2	-	-	-	0.5	7.4
4. 6-9	0.1	0.1	0.1	0.1	-	0.1	0.1	0.1	0.1	*	0.2	-	-	-	0.3	1.6
5. 10-19	0.1	0.1	0.1	0.1	-	*	0.1	0.1	-	*	0.1	-	-	-	0.2	1.5
6. 20-39	*	*	*	*	-	*	*	*	-	-	-	-	-	-	*	0.7
7. 40 or more	*	*	-	*	-	*	*	*	-	-	*	-	-	-	-	-
Item 1030 Subject A01c N	16064	7654	8069	12173	1934	3726	4436	4875	3028	9354	5669	6341	3400	2240	3721	183

B13: Barbiturates are sometimes prescribed by doctors to help people relax or get to sleep. They are sometimes called downs, downers, goofballs, yellows, reds, blues, rainbows. On how many occasions (if any) have you taken barbiturates on your own–that is, without a doctor telling you to take them...

*=less than .05 per cent.

QUESTIONNAIRE FORM 1-5 1985	TOTAL	SEX		RACE		REGION				4YR COLLEGE PLANS		ILLICIT DRUG USE: LIFETIME				
		M	F	White	Black	NE	NC	S	W	Yes	No	None	Mari-juana Only	Few Pills	More Pills	Any Her-oin
N (Weighted No. of Cases):	16502	7776	8164	12291	1995	3878	4516	5028	3079	9448	5770	6412	3449	2264	3802	193
% of Weighted Total:	100.0	47.1	49.5	74.5	12.1	23.5	27.4	30.5	18.7	57.3	35.0	38.9	20.9	13.7	23.0	1.2

B13A: . . . in your lifetime?

	TOTAL	M	F	White	Black	NE	NC	S	W	Yes	No	None	Mari Only	Few Pills	More Pills	Any Heroin
1. 0 occasions	90.8	90.1	91.7	90.2	96.6	89.5	90.4	92.0	90.9	92.6	88.1	100.0	100.0	90.9	69.2	29.1
2. 1-2	4.1	4.3	3.8	4.2	2.0	4.4	4.1	3.5	4.7	3.7	4.6	-	-	9.1	11.3	17.1
3. 3-5	1.8	1.8	1.8	2.0	0.7	2.1	1.7	1.5	2.0	1.3	2.5	-	-	-	7.3	8.5
4. 6-9	1.2	1.4	0.9	1.3	0.2	1.3	1.4	0.9	1.0	0.8	1.8	-	-	-	4.6	9.8
5. 10-19	0.9	1.1	0.7	1.0	0.1	1.3	0.9	0.8	0.6	0.7	1.2	-	-	-	3.4	12.9
6. 20-39	0.5	0.5	0.5	0.5	0.2	0.6	0.5	0.5	0.4	0.4	0.7	-	-	-	1.7	9.0
7. 40 or more	0.7	0.9	0.6	0.8	0.2	0.8	0.9	0.8	0.4	0.5	1.1	-	-	-	2.5	13.5
Item 1040 Subject A01a N	16015	7634	8044	12145	1928	3716	4418	4869	3012	9342	5644	6325	3385	2230	3714	186

B13B: . . . during the last 12 months?

	TOTAL	M	F	White	Black	NE	NC	S	W	Yes	No	None	Mari Only	Few Pills	More Pills	Any Heroin
1. 0 occasions	95.4	94.8	96.1	95.2	98.5	94.7	95.1	95.8	95.9	96.4	93.8	100.0	100.0	97.3	84.2	51.0
2. 1-2	2.2	2.4	2.0	2.4	0.6	2.3	2.2	2.0	2.5	1.8	2.9	-	-	2.7	7.3	13.5
3. 3-5	1.0	1.3	0.8	1.1	0.4	1.5	1.1	0.9	0.7	0.8	1.4	-	-	-	4.0	10.5
4. 6-9	0.5	0.6	0.4	0.5	0.1	0.6	0.7	0.5	0.4	0.4	0.8	-	-	-	1.9	9.4
5. 10-19	0.4	0.5	0.3	0.5	0.2	0.5	0.5	0.4	0.2	0.3	0.5	-	-	-	1.6	5.7
6. 20-39	0.2	0.2	0.2	0.3	0.1	0.1	0.3	0.2	0.2	0.2	0.4	-	-	-	0.7	5.9
7. 40 or more	0.1	0.2	0.1	0.1	*	0.2	0.1	0.2	0.1	0.1	0.1	-	-	-	0.4	4.0
Item 1050 Subject A01b N	16012	7631	8044	12142	1928	3713	4419	4867	3013	9339	5644	6325	3386	2228	3714	184

B13C: . . . during the last 30 days?

	TOTAL	M	F	White	Black	NE	NC	S	W	Yes	No	None	Mari Only	Few Pills	More Pills	Any Heroin
1. 0 occasions	98.0	97.6	98.4	98.0	99.3	97.7	97.8	98.1	98.5	98.4	97.5	100.0	100.0	98.9	93.6	70.1
2. 1-2	1.2	1.4	1.0	1.2	0.5	1.5	1.2	1.1	1.0	1.0	1.4	-	-	1.1	3.7	14.9
3. 3-5	0.4	0.5	0.3	0.4	0.1	0.5	0.5	0.4	0.2	0.3	0.5	-	-	-	1.5	5.8
4. 6-9	0.2	0.2	0.2	0.2	*	0.1	0.3	0.2	0.2	0.2	0.3	-	-	-	0.6	5.0
5. 10-19	0.1	0.2	0.1	0.2	-	0.1	0.1	0.2	0.1	0.1	0.3	-	-	-	0.5	1.2
6. 20-39	*	0.1	*	*	0.1	0.1	*	0.1	-	*	0.1	-	-	-	0.1	3.0
7. 40 or more	*	-	*	*	*	0.1	-	*	-	-	-	-	-	-	*	-
Item 1060 Subject A01c N	16007	7629	8041	12138	1927	3713	4417	4866	3011	9338	5640	6325	3385	2228	3709	184

B14: Tranquilizers are sometimes prescribed by doctors to calm people down, quiet their nerves, or relax their muscles. Librium, Valium, and Miltown are all tranquilizers. On how many occasions (if any) have you taken tranquilizers on your own–that is, without a doctor telling you to take them...

B14A: . . . in your lifetime?

	TOTAL	M	F	White	Black	NE	NC	S	W	Yes	No	None	Mari Only	Few Pills	More Pills	Any Heroin
1. 0 occasions	88.1	88.3	88.3	87.1	95.2	86.0	88.5	88.9	88.8	89.2	86.6	100.0	100.0	78.4	64.8	37.8
2. 1-2	6.3	5.7	6.5	6.7	3.3	6.9	5.9	6.1	6.4	5.9	6.8	-	-	21.6	13.1	18.9
3. 3-5	2.2	2.2	2.3	2.4	0.6	3.1	2.0	1.7	2.3	2.1	2.3	-	-	-	9.3	5.7
4. 6-9	1.2	1.3	1.0	1.4	0.3	1.3	1.3	1.1	1.1	1.1	1.5	-	-	-	4.7	9.2
5. 10-19	0.9	1.0	0.8	1.1	0.2	1.2	1.1	0.7	0.5	0.7	1.2	-	-	-	3.6	4.9
6. 20-39	0.6	0.7	0.6	0.6	0.2	0.7	0.6	0.7	0.5	0.5	0.8	-	-	-	2.0	14.0
7. 40 or more	0.7	0.8	0.5	0.7	0.1	0.9	0.6	0.7	0.4	0.5	0.8	-	-	-	2.4	9.5
Item 1070 Subject A01a N	16036	7649	8063	12172	1935	3719	4430	4867	3019	9355	5667	6332	3388	2244	3711	185

B14B: . . . during the last 12 months?

	TOTAL	M	F	White	Black	NE	NC	S	W	Yes	No	None	Mari Only	Few Pills	More Pills	Any Heroin
1. 0 occasions	93.9	93.6	94.3	93.3	98.3	92.9	94.0	94.1	94.7	94.5	93.2	100.0	100.0	92.6	80.2	57.2
2. 1-2	3.6	3.4	3.6	3.9	1.3	3.9	3.4	3.4	3.6	3.3	3.8	-	-	7.4	10.2	15.5
3. 3-5	1.2	1.3	1.0	1.3	0.3	1.5	1.2	0.9	1.0	1.0	1.4	-	-	-	4.5	9.0
4. 6-9	0.6	0.7	0.5	0.6	0.1	0.7	0.7	0.5	0.4	0.5	0.7	-	-	-	2.2	6.2
5. 10-19	0.4	0.5	0.3	0.4	0.1	0.5	0.3	0.7	0.1	0.3	0.5	-	-	-	1.5	6.3
6. 20-39	0.2	0.3	0.2	0.2	-	0.3	0.2	0.2	0.2	0.3	0.2	-	-	-	0.9	3.0
7. 40 or more	0.1	0.1	0.1	0.2	-	0.2	0.1	0.2	*	0.1	0.2	-	-	-	0.4	3.0
Item 1080 Subject A01b N	16022	7645	8053	12160	1930	3715	4425	4865	3018	9345	5664	6334	3389	2239	3702	184

B14C: . . . during the last 30 days?

	TOTAL	M	F	White	Black	NE	NC	S	W	Yes	No	None	Mari Only	Few Pills	More Pills	Any Heroin
1. 0 occasions	97.9	97.8	98.1	97.8	99.2	97.4	97.9	97.9	98.7	98.2	97.7	100.0	100.0	98.7	93.0	75.6
2. 1-2	1.3	1.2	1.4	1.4	0.6	1.7	1.3	1.3	0.9	1.1	1.4	-	-	1.3	4.3	10.7
3. 3-5	0.4	0.4	0.3	0.4	0.1	0.4	0.4	0.4	0.3	0.3	0.5	-	-	-	1.4	5.3
4. 6-9	0.2	0.3	0.1	0.2	-	0.1	0.2	0.3	0.1	0.2	0.2	-	-	-	0.6	3.5
5. 10-19	0.2	0.2	0.1	0.2	*	0.3	0.2	0.2	0.1	0.2	0.2	-	-	-	0.6	3.6
6. 20-39	*	*	*	*	-	*	-	*	-	*	*	-	-	-	0.1	-
7. 40 or more	*	*	*	*	-	0.1	-	*	-	*	*	-	-	-	*	1.3
Item 1090 Subject A01c N	16006	7634	8048	12148	1930	3716	4421	4853	3016	9340	5655	6334	3390	2231	3695	182

*=less than .05 per cent.

QUESTIONNAIRE FORM 1-5 1985	TOTAL	SEX		RACE		REGION				4YR COLLEGE PLANS		ILLICIT DRUG USE: LIFETIME				
		M	F	White	Black	NE	NC	S	W	Yes	No	None	Mari-juana Only	Few Pills	More Pills	Any Her-oin
N (Weighted No. of Cases):	16502	7776	8164	12291	1995	3878	4516	5028	3079	9448	5770	6412	3449	2264	3802	193
% of Weighted Total:	100.0	47.1	49.5	74.5	12.1	23.5	27.4	30.5	18.7	57.3	35.0	38.9	20.9	13.7	23.0	1.2

B15: On how many occasions (if any) have you used heroin (smack, horse, skag) . . .

B15A: . . . in your lifetime?

	TOTAL	M	F	White	Black	NE	NC	S	W	Yes	No	None	Mari-juana Only	Few Pills	More Pills	Any Her-oin
1. 0 occasions	98.8	98.6	99.2	98.9	99.0	98.4	98.8	98.8	99.2	99.1	98.4	100.0	100.0	100.0	100.0	-
2. 1-2	0.7	0.8	0.6	0.7	0.5	1.1	0.6	0.6	0.5	0.5	0.9	-	-	-	-	57.3
3. 3-5	0.2	0.2	0.1	0.1	0.3	0.1	0.2	0.2	0.2	0.1	0.3	-	-	-	-	13.6
4. 6-9	0.1	0.1	*	0.1	-	0.1	0.1	*	0.1	0.1	0.1	-	-	-	-	7.0
5. 10-19	0.1	0.1	0.1	0.1	-	0.1	0.1	0.2	*	0.2	0.1	-	-	-	-	10.3
6. 20-39	*	*	0.1	*	-	*	0.1	*	-	*	0.1	-	-	-	-	3.9
7. 40 or more	0.1	0.1	*	0.1	0.3	0.1	0.1	0.1	-	0.1	0.1	-	-	-	-	7.9
Item 1100　Subject A01a　N	16033	7651	8068	12178	1928	3722	4428	4864	3019	9355	5663	6329	3390	2229	3718	193

B15B: . . . during the last 12 months?

	TOTAL	M	F	White	Black	NE	NC	S	W	Yes	No	None	Mari-juana Only	Few Pills	More Pills	Any Her-oin
1. 0 occasions	99.4	99.2	99.7	99.4	99.4	99.2	99.4	99.4	99.7	99.5	99.3	100.0	100.0	100.0	100.0	47.6
2. 1-2	0.3	0.4	0.2	0.3	0.4	0.5	0.4	0.2	0.2	0.2	0.6	-	-	-	-	30.2
3. 3-5	0.1	0.1	0.1	0.1	0.1	0.1	0.1	0.2	*	0.1	0.1	-	-	-	-	9.6
4. 6-9	*	0.1	*	*	-	0.1	*	0.1	*	0.1	*	-	-	-	-	4.1
5. 10-19	*	0.1	-	*	-	-	*	0.1	-	*	*	-	-	-	-	3.0
6. 20-39	*	0.1	-	*	0.2	-	0.1	*	-	*	*	-	-	-	-	2.5
7. 40 or more	*	*	-	*	-	0.1	-	*	-	*	*	-	-	-	-	3.0
Item 1110　Subject A01b　N	16030	7649	8068	12177	1926	3723	4427	4861	3020	9357	5659	6331	3390	2232	3718	186

B15C: . . . during the last 30 days?

	TOTAL	M	F	White	Black	NE	NC	S	W	Yes	No	None	Mari-juana Only	Few Pills	More Pills	Any Her-oin
1. 0 occasions	99.7	99.7	99.9	99.8	99.6	99.7	99.7	99.7	99.9	99.8	99.8	100.0	100.0	100.0	100.0	78.1
2. 1-2	0.1	0.1	0.1	0.1	0.2	0.2	0.1	0.1	0.1	0.1	0.1	-	-	-	-	11.3
3. 3-5	*	0.1	*	*	0.1	*	*	0.1	-	0.1	*	-	-	-	-	4.2
4. 6-9	*	0.1	-	*	0.1	*	0.1	-	*	*	*	-	-	-	-	2.8
5. 10-19	*	*	-	*	-	*	*	-	-	-	*	-	-	-	-	1.0
6. 20-39	-	-	-	-	-	-	-	-	-	-	-	-	-	-	-	-
7. 40 or more	*	*	-	*	-	0.1	-	*	-	*	-	-	-	-	-	2.6
Item 1120　Subject A01c　N	16029	7649	8067	12176	1926	3721	4426	4861	3021	9356	5659	6330	3390	2232	3718	186

B16: There are a number of narcotics other than heroin, such as methadone, opium, morphine, codeine, demerol, paregoric, talwin, and laudanum. These are sometimes prescribed by doctors. On how many occasions (if any) have you taken narcotics other than heroin on your own–that is, without a doctor telling you to take them...

B16A: . . . in your lifetime?

	TOTAL	M	F	White	Black	NE	NC	S	W	Yes	No	None	Mari-juana Only	Few Pills	More Pills	Any Her-oin
1. 0 occasions	89.8	88.7	90.9	88.7	96.3	88.0	89.6	92.8	87.3	90.7	88.5	100.0	100.0	86.6	67.7	23.9
2. 1-2	4.9	5.2	4.7	5.4	2.7	5.7	5.4	3.2	6.2	4.7	5.4	-	-	13.4	12.2	21.7
3. 3-5	2.0	2.3	1.8	2.2	0.5	2.0	2.0	1.4	2.9	1.8	2.3	-	-	-	8.0	12.8
4. 6-9	1.1	1.3	0.9	1.3	0.1	1.5	1.0	0.8	1.3	1.2	1.0	-	-	-	4.2	11.2
5. 10-19	0.9	0.9	0.8	1.0	-	1.2	0.8	0.7	1.0	0.7	1.1	-	-	-	3.2	13.0
6. 20-39	0.5	0.6	0.4	0.5	0.2	0.6	0.4	0.4	0.6	0.4	0.5	-	-	-	1.8	4.9
7. 40 or more	0.8	1.0	0.6	0.9	0.3	1.1	0.8	0.6	0.8	0.5	1.1	-	-	-	2.8	12.5
Item 1130　Subject A01a　N	15986	7648	8064	12169	1930	3699	4421	4861	3004	9350	5648	6318	3384	2234	3691	185

B16B: . . . during the last 12 months?

	TOTAL	M	F	White	Black	NE	NC	S	W	Yes	No	None	Mari-juana Only	Few Pills	More Pills	Any Her-oin
1. 0 occasions	94.1	93.2	94.9	93.3	98.3	92.7	93.7	96.2	92.9	94.6	93.4	100.0	100.0	94.6	80.2	46.9
2. 1-2	3.2	3.6	2.8	3.6	1.2	3.9	3.6	1.8	3.8	3.0	3.5	-	-	5.4	9.4	22.3
3. 3-5	1.2	1.3	1.1	1.4	0.1	1.4	1.3	0.8	1.6	1.1	1.4	-	-	-	4.7	11.6
4. 6-9	0.6	0.5	0.7	0.7	0.1	0.5	0.7	0.5	0.6	0.6	0.6	-	-	-	2.2	5.5
5. 10-19	0.4	0.6	0.3	0.5	0.1	0.5	0.4	0.4	0.5	0.4	0.5	-	-	-	1.6	6.9
6. 20-39	0.3	0.4	0.2	0.3	0.1	0.4	0.1	0.3	0.3	0.2	0.3	-	-	-	1.1	2.1
7. 40 or more	0.2	0.4	*	0.3	0.2	0.4	0.2	0.1	0.3	0.2	0.3	-	-	-	0.8	4.6
Item 1140　Subject A01b　N	15970	7640	8058	12157	1928	3695	4416	4858	3000	9343	5643	6318	3385	2231	3681	181

*=less than .05 per cent.

QUESTIONNAIRE FORM 1-5 1985	TOTAL	SEX		RACE		REGION				4YR COLLEGE PLANS		ILLICIT DRUG USE: LIFETIME				
		M	F	White	Black	NE	NC	S	W	Yes	No	None	Mari-juana Only	Few Pills	More Pills	Any Her-oin
N (Weighted No. of Cases):	16502	7776	8164	12291	1995	3878	4516	5028	3079	9448	5770	6412	3449	2264	3802	193
% of Weighted Total:	100.0	47.1	49.5	74.5	12.1	23.5	27.4	30.5	18.7	57.3	35.0	38.9	20.9	13.7	23.0	1.2

B16C: . . . during the last 30 days?

1. 0 occasions	97.7	97.4	98.0	97.4	99.3	96.9	98.2	98.1	97.0	97.7	97.6	100.0	100.0	98.1	92.3	74.0
2. 1-2	1.5	1.5	1.5	1.7	0.4	1.8	1.4	1.0	2.1	1.6	1.3	-	-	1.9	4.8	11.3
3. 3-5	0.3	0.4	0.3	0.4	0.1	0.5	0.1	0.4	0.3	0.3	0.5	-	-	-	1.2	5.1
4. 6-9	0.2	0.3	0.2	0.3	0.1	0.3	0.2	0.3	0.2	0.2	0.2	-	-	-	0.8	4.1
5. 10-19	0.2	0.3	0.1	0.2	-	0.2	0.1	0.2	0.2	0.1	0.3	-	-	-	0.6	3.1
6. 20-39	*	0.1	-	*	-	*	*	-	0.1	*	*	-	-	-	0.1	-
7. 40 or more	0.1	0.1	*	*	0.2	0.2	*	*	*	*	0.1	-	-	-	0.2	2.4
Item 1150 Subject A01c N	15963	7638	8054	12152	1928	3696	4413	4854	3000	9341	5637	6318	3384	2229	3676	183

B17: On how many occasions (if any) have you sniffed glue, or breathed the contents of aerosol spray cans, or inhaled any other gases or sprays in order to get high . . .

B17A: . . . in your lifetime?

1. 0 occasions	84.6	81.5	87.6	83.5	92.0	81.7	85.4	87.0	83.0	85.5	83.5	95.6	87.7	80.4	67.7	45.9
2. 1-2	8.8	10.2	7.4	9.5	4.7	9.8	8.4	7.6	10.2	8.4	9.4	3.3	8.7	12.9	15.1	17.6
3. 3-5	2.8	3.4	2.3	3.0	1.8	3.3	2.4	2.4	3.4	2.5	3.2	0.6	1.8	4.2	6.5	7.0
4. 6-9	1.4	1.8	1.0	1.5	0.3	2.0	1.4	0.8	1.7	1.3	1.5	0.2	0.9	0.8	4.1	7.7
5. 10-19	1.1	1.4	0.9	1.2	0.5	1.3	1.1	1.1	1.1	1.0	1.2	0.1	0.4	1.0	3.3	6.4
6. 20-39	0.4	0.6	0.3	0.5	0.1	0.6	0.5	0.4	0.1	0.4	0.4	0.1	0.1	0.4	1.2	4.0
7. 40 or more	0.8	1.1	0.5	0.8	0.4	1.3	0.8	0.6	0.5	0.8	0.8	0.1	0.3	0.3	2.1	11.4
Item 1160 Subject A01a N	12871	6210	6450	9817	1561	3004	3556	3906	2404	7555	4585	5043	2695	1806	3037	154

B17B: . . . during the last 12 months?

1. 0 occasions	94.3	93.1	95.5	93.7	98.5	92.0	94.2	95.8	94.6	94.3	94.2	98.6	95.8	93.6	87.2	67.8
2. 1-2	3.1	3.5	2.7	3.4	0.9	3.8	3.2	2.1	3.6	3.1	3.2	0.9	2.9	4.0	6.2	7.0
3. 3-5	1.0	1.3	0.7	1.1	0.4	1.4	1.0	0.8	0.9	0.9	1.1	0.2	0.5	1.0	2.5	8.4
4. 6-9	0.6	0.6	0.5	0.6	0.1	1.0	0.4	0.4	0.4	0.5	0.6	*	0.2	0.5	1.7	3.2
5. 10-19	0.5	0.7	0.3	0.6	0.2	0.5	0.7	0.5	0.2	0.5	0.5	0.1	0.3	0.6	1.0	5.3
6. 20-39	0.3	0.3	0.2	0.2	-	0.5	0.2	0.2	-	0.4	0.1	0.1	0.2	*	0.7	2.5
7. 40 or more	0.3	0.5	0.1	0.3	-	0.8	0.2	0.1	0.2	0.3	0.3	-	0.1	0.2	0.8	6.0
Item 1170 Subject A01b N	12848	6191	6444	9801	1555	3001	3556	3891	2400	7547	4582	5033	2693	1807	3023	155

B17C: . . . during the last 30 days?

1. 0 occasions	97.8	97.2	98.3	97.6	99.2	96.4	97.7	98.5	98.3	97.9	97.7	99.4	98.7	97.2	95.3	81.4
2. 1-2	1.2	1.5	0.9	1.3	0.5	1.6	1.3	0.8	1.2	1.1	1.3	0.4	0.9	1.9	2.3	2.9
3. 3-5	0.5	0.5	0.5	0.6	0.3	0.8	0.6	0.4	0.2	0.5	0.4	0.1	0.2	0.6	1.2	6.5
4. 6-9	0.2	0.1	0.2	0.2	0.1	0.3	0.2	0.1	*	0.1	0.2	0.1	*	*	0.3	1.7
5. 10-19	0.2	0.3	*	0.2	-	0.4	0.1	0.1	-	0.2	0.2	-	0.1	0.2	0.3	3.9
6. 20-39	0.1	0.2	0.1	0.1	-	0.2	0.1	-	0.1	0.1	0.1	-	0.1	0.1	0.3	-
7. 40 or more	0.1	0.2	*	0.1	-	0.3	0.1	*	*	0.1	0.1	-	*	0.1	0.2	3.7
Item 1180 Subject A01c N	12846	6192	6441	9799	1556	3000	3553	3892	2400	7546	4579	5033	2692	1807	3024	154

*=less than .05 per cent.

QUESTIONNAIRE FORM 1 1985	TOTAL	SEX		RACE		REGION				4YR COLLEGE PLANS		ILLICIT DRUG USE: LIFETIME				
		M	F	White	Black	NE	NC	S	W	Yes	No	None	Mari-juana Only	Few Pills	More Pills	Any Her-oin
N (Weighted No. of Cases):	3316	1505	1663	2415	400	783	902	1004	627	1822	1121	1307	719	444	716	29
% of Weighted Total:	100.0	45.4	50.2	72.8	12.1	23.6	27.2	30.3	18.9	55.0	33.8	39.4	21.7	13.4	21.6	0.9

A001: Taking all things together, how would you say things are these days–would you say you're very happy, pretty happy, or not too happy these days?

3. Very happy	19.8	18.6	21.1	21.1	13.6	16.8	19.4	19.8	24.3	22.5	16.8	22.1	20.4	17.5	16.6	19.4
2. Pretty happy	69.4	71.3	68.2	71.3	64.1	69.3	71.0	69.9	66.4	68.5	71.0	69.2	71.3	70.8	69.5	56.5
1. Not too happy	10.8	10.1	10.7	7.6	22.3	13.9	9.6	10.4	9.3	8.9	12.2	8.6	8.3	11.7	13.9	24.0
Item 1190 Subject P01,Q01 N	3304	1501	1658	2411	399	779	898	1002	625	1817	1118	1304	717	444	713	29

A002: How much do you agree or disagree with each of the following statements?

A002A: The nation needs much more long-range planning and coordination to be prepared for the future

1. Disagree	1.8	1.9	1.5	1.6	3.1	1.9	2.3	1.8	1.2	1.1	2.5	1.4	2.9	0.8	1.4	1.5
2. Mostly disagree	5.0	4.9	4.9	5.2	3.0	6.6	4.7	4.4	4.5	5.1	4.1	4.7	5.6	3.6	5.9	-
3. Neither	11.1	10.8	11.0	12.5	5.0	11.4	13.3	8.3	12.1	11.0	10.7	10.6	9.8	12.5	12.4	20.1
4. Mostly agree	44.0	42.5	46.0	44.8	38.8	44.6	44.3	41.1	47.7	44.8	44.7	43.1	43.5	46.9	44.1	55.6
5. Agree	38.1	40.0	36.7	36.0	50.1	35.6	35.5	44.5	34.5	38.0	37.9	40.2	38.2	36.2	36.2	22.8
Item 1200 Subject I01 N	3269	1496	1638	2395	393	764	891	996	618	1807	1104	1294	714	438	701	29

A002B: I enjoy the fast pace and changes of today's world

1. Disagree	12.2	12.3	11.9	10.0	20.2	12.9	11.5	13.5	10.4	9.8	15.8	11.0	14.5	10.6	11.7	3.7
2. Mostly disagree	14.2	13.5	15.0	13.9	19.4	12.5	13.6	16.4	13.8	12.5	17.5	14.9	13.2	18.6	11.5	16.4
3. Neither	16.1	18.1	14.6	17.0	12.8	16.5	17.1	14.2	17.1	15.4	16.9	14.7	16.5	17.2	18.2	16.3
4. Mostly agree	35.4	32.4	38.3	36.7	30.1	34.0	35.9	33.8	39.1	39.3	29.7	38.4	35.1	33.2	32.1	34.6
5. Agree	22.0	23.7	20.2	22.4	17.4	24.1	22.0	22.1	19.6	23.0	20.1	21.0	20.7	20.5	26.6	29.0
Item 1210 Subject I03,Q02 N	3277	1493	1646	2397	392	768	893	992	623	1812	1110	1296	712	440	706	29

A002C: Things change too quickly in today's world

1. Disagree	15.4	17.2	13.8	16.2	11.8	16.8	17.2	15.5	11.0	15.4	14.8	15.3	15.0	14.4	16.2	26.0
2. Mostly disagree	22.5	22.7	22.0	24.5	12.1	23.9	20.7	19.5	27.8	25.3	18.0	22.1	21.9	23.3	23.8	28.8
3. Neither	17.1	18.2	16.3	18.8	12.5	16.4	18.5	15.4	18.5	20.4	12.3	16.5	15.7	18.6	19.5	13.8
4. Mostly agree	22.6	20.6	24.5	21.8	27.8	20.5	23.0	23.8	22.9	20.6	25.4	23.5	24.7	22.1	20.0	8.1
5. Agree	22.4	21.2	23.4	18.8	35.7	22.4	20.5	25.8	19.7	18.2	29.6	22.6	22.7	21.6	20.4	23.3
Item 1220 Subject I03,Q02 N	3270	1489	1645	2396	388	770	893	986	622	1806	1111	1295	709	440	706	29

A002D: I think the times ahead for me will be tougher and less fun than things are now

1. Disagree	19.7	19.8	19.4	20.7	13.7	20.1	20.8	19.6	17.7	21.5	17.2	20.0	17.6	20.7	19.8	25.3
2. Mostly disagree	19.6	19.9	20.3	21.7	14.3	16.9	21.3	17.4	23.7	22.3	16.3	20.5	18.9	20.2	20.2	3.3
3. Neither	13.4	14.0	12.5	14.2	9.1	13.6	13.8	11.5	15.4	13.7	12.4	13.7	11.2	12.8	14.7	22.3
4. Mostly agree	22.8	22.7	22.9	22.8	23.4	22.7	23.0	23.0	22.4	21.2	25.2	22.4	26.6	20.8	21.2	21.0
5. Agree	24.6	23.6	24.9	20.6	39.5	26.7	21.1	28.5	20.8	21.4	28.9	23.5	26.6	23.3	24.1	28.1
Item 1230 Subject I01,J N	3271	1492	1646	2399	391	769	891	987	624	1809	1111	1290	713	443	706	29

A003: Of all the time you spend with other people, about how much is spent with people over 30?

1. Very little	23.1	26.3	19.7	19.3	36.8	25.7	22.0	22.2	23.1	19.6	28.3	20.2	25.3	24.2	23.5	29.7
2. Some	41.1	43.5	39.6	44.2	28.6	40.1	44.5	40.1	39.2	44.5	36.7	40.8	41.3	40.5	44.4	39.1
3. About half	29.1	24.3	33.5	30.9	23.5	28.1	28.1	29.2	31.7	30.4	27.2	32.2	27.1	29.5	26.2	28.2
4. Most	5.2	4.7	5.5	4.8	6.9	5.0	4.4	6.2	5.1	4.6	5.8	5.4	4.9	4.4	4.6	3.0
5. Nearly all	1.4	1.2	1.7	0.8	4.2	1.1	1.1	2.3	0.9	0.9	1.9	1.4	1.5	1.4	1.2	-
Item 1240 Subject M02 N	3310	1504	1662	2414	400	780	900	1003	627	1821	1121	1307	718	444	716	29

QUESTIONNAIRE FORM 1 1985	TOTAL	SEX		RACE		REGION				4YR COLLEGE PLANS		ILLICIT DRUG USE: LIFETIME				
		M	F	White	Black	NE	NC	S	W	Yes	No	None	Mari-juana Only	Few Pills	More Pills	Any Her-oin
N (Weighted No. of Cases):	3316	1505	1663	2415	400	783	902	1004	627	1822	1121	1307	719	444	716	29
% of Weighted Total:	100.0	45.4	50.2	72.8	12.1	23.6	27.2	30.3	18.9	55.0	33.8	39.4	21.7	13.4	21.6	0.9

A004: Would you like to spend more time, or less time, with people over 30 if you could?

	TOTAL	M	F	White	Black	NE	NC	S	W	Yes	No	None	Mari-juana Only	Few Pills	More Pills	Any Her-oin
1. Much less time	3.9	5.0	2.7	3.2	5.8	5.4	3.9	3.3	3.0	3.1	4.6	2.9	3.7	4.3	5.3	8.7
2. Somewhat less time	7.2	7.2	7.2	6.9	8.3	8.7	8.3	5.8	6.2	6.4	8.1	6.7	5.6	8.1	8.2	15.9
3. About the same as now	67.7	68.0	68.5	71.0	58.0	64.9	67.3	68.0	71.6	69.2	68.6	68.0	69.5	68.8	67.7	54.4
4. Somewhat more time	18.0	17.6	18.3	17.0	21.9	18.3	17.5	19.3	16.3	18.9	15.5	19.4	18.4	17.3	15.3	21.0
5. Much more time	3.1	2.3	3.3	1.8	6.1	2.6	3.0	3.7	2.9	2.4	3.2	3.1	2.8	1.5	3.5	-
Item 1250 Subject M02 N	3307	1504	1660	2412	399	782	899	1001	624	1820	1119	1304	719	444	714	29

A005: Would you like to spend more time, or less time, working with or helping younger children?

	TOTAL	M	F	White	Black	NE	NC	S	W	Yes	No	None	Mari-juana Only	Few Pills	More Pills	Any Her-oin
1. Much less time	5.5	8.7	2.3	5.6	2.8	7.8	6.0	3.7	4.7	4.8	6.5	4.5	5.9	3.1	6.4	26.9
2. Somewhat less time	6.1	8.4	3.9	6.1	4.7	8.2	6.7	4.7	4.8	6.2	5.5	4.7	7.3	7.4	6.2	7.3
3. About the same as now	35.1	44.2	25.9	37.2	27.7	35.2	33.1	36.5	35.6	34.2	36.2	34.2	33.4	40.0	37.5	34.4
4. Somewhat more time	33.8	30.0	38.6	35.1	29.8	33.2	35.1	31.1	37.3	36.6	30.2	34.2	31.7	34.5	37.0	13.8
5. Much more time	19.5	8.7	29.2	15.9	35.0	15.6	19.0	24.1	17.6	18.4	21.5	22.5	21.7	15.0	12.9	17.6
Item 1260 Subject M02 N	3305	1501	1663	2411	400	778	900	1001	626	1818	1121	1307	718	443	713	29

A006: The next questions ask how satisfied or dissatisfied you are with several aspects of your life. For each question, mark the circle that shows best how you feel. If you are neutral about something, or are just as satisfied as you are dissatisfied, mark the middle answer.

How satisfied are you with...

A006A: Your job? (If you have no job, leave blank)

	TOTAL	M	F	White	Black	NE	NC	S	W	Yes	No	None	Mari-juana Only	Few Pills	More Pills	Any Her-oin
7. Completely satisfied	22.3	22.7	21.6	21.8	21.3	24.0	20.5	23.8	20.5	19.9	26.1	25.2	19.9	24.2	19.1	25.6
6.	18.8	18.8	18.8	21.3	5.6	16.1	20.3	19.7	19.1	20.9	17.0	18.8	19.6	17.3	20.1	19.2
5.	12.0	13.6	10.9	12.8	8.8	11.8	14.2	8.6	14.0	14.5	8.6	14.1	11.2	11.4	10.4	10.2
4. Neutral	28.3	26.0	30.6	26.0	47.6	30.5	27.6	30.7	23.4	26.8	29.4	25.9	30.9	27.9	28.3	29.0
3.	6.9	7.5	6.4	7.3	3.5	7.1	6.9	4.9	9.3	7.2	6.0	6.9	7.9	7.6	5.7	6.6
2.	4.2	4.5	4.1	4.7	1.6	4.3	3.7	2.9	6.7	4.3	4.4	3.8	2.5	4.7	6.6	-
1. Completely dissatisfied	7.5	6.9	7.5	6.1	11.5	6.3	6.9	9.4	7.0	6.4	8.6	5.4	7.9	7.0	9.8	9.4
Item 1270 Subject C01,P02 N	2061	996	967	1606	167	529	571	559	402	1138	692	761	470	281	477	16

A006B: The neighborhood where you live?

	TOTAL	M	F	White	Black	NE	NC	S	W	Yes	No	None	Mari-juana Only	Few Pills	More Pills	Any Her-oin
7. Completely satisfied	33.7	34.8	33.1	34.8	34.7	26.1	34.5	38.7	34.1	33.1	36.0	36.7	35.3	33.2	29.0	19.7
6.	19.4	21.8	17.5	22.3	8.4	19.6	21.2	15.1	23.2	22.7	14.7	22.1	17.0	17.0	18.3	28.3
5.	8.8	10.3	7.4	9.4	5.9	8.4	11.3	6.5	9.5	10.0	6.8	7.4	9.7	10.9	9.1	9.6
4. Neutral	22.8	18.9	25.6	20.1	32.5	25.4	21.3	25.5	17.2	19.3	27.0	19.5	24.2	25.0	24.6	27.6
3.	5.3	5.0	5.6	5.6	1.9	7.3	3.6	4.4	6.7	5.8	4.2	5.4	4.8	2.7	7.1	-
2.	3.8	3.7	4.0	3.5	4.1	5.3	3.7	3.0	3.4	4.3	3.3	3.1	4.0	4.7	4.3	5.3
1. Completely dissatisfied	6.2	5.6	6.8	4.3	12.6	7.9	4.4	6.8	5.9	4.9	8.0	5.8	4.9	6.5	7.7	9.6
Item 1280 Subject P02 N	3304	1504	1658	2414	395	781	900	997	626	1821	1119	1303	718	444	716	29

A006C: Your personal safety in your neighborhood, on your job, and in your school–safety from being attacked and injured in some way?

	TOTAL	M	F	White	Black	NE	NC	S	W	Yes	No	None	Mari-juana Only	Few Pills	More Pills	Any Her-oin
7. Completely satisfied	40.4	46.3	35.2	42.7	31.8	37.3	41.8	40.5	41.8	42.0	37.8	40.4	41.3	41.5	40.0	38.4
6.	19.7	20.2	19.1	22.3	10.9	19.9	21.6	17.0	20.7	21.7	17.4	21.5	17.7	20.4	18.6	12.8
5.	9.1	8.2	10.2	9.9	5.9	8.2	9.4	7.6	12.2	9.6	9.4	9.2	9.1	8.9	9.8	2.9
4. Neutral	20.8	17.6	23.4	16.8	36.4	22.6	18.4	24.1	16.6	16.4	26.1	19.4	21.2	19.8	21.2	28.0
3.	4.0	3.6	4.5	4.1	3.5	4.3	3.5	3.8	4.8	4.5	3.2	3.6	4.4	3.7	4.7	1.5
2.	1.8	1.4	2.2	1.6	1.5	2.0	1.7	1.6	1.9	2.0	1.5	1.4	1.5	1.8	2.7	3.9
1. Completely dissatisfied	4.3	2.7	5.4	2.5	10.3	5.6	3.6	5.4	1.9	3.8	4.6	4.5	4.8	3.9	3.0	12.5
Item 1290 Subject P02 N	3301	1501	1660	2414	396	778	900	999	624	1820	1118	1306	716	443	714	29

QUESTIONNAIRE FORM 1 1985	TOTAL	SEX		RACE		REGION				4YR COLLEGE PLANS		ILLICIT DRUG USE: LIFETIME				
		M	F	White	Black	NE	NC	S	W	Yes	No	None	Marijuana Only	Few Pills	More Pills	Any Heroin
N (Weighted No. of Cases):	3316	1505	1663	2415	400	783	902	1004	627	1822	1121	1307	719	444	716	29
% of Weighted Total:	100.0	45.4	50.2	72.8	12.1	23.6	27.2	30.3	18.9	55.0	33.8	39.4	21.7	13.4	21.6	0.9

A006D: The safety of things you own from being stolen or destroyed in your neighborhood, on your job, and in your school?

7. Completely satisfied	21.5	22.6	20.5	21.4	24.8	20.1	20.9	24.3	19.7	21.0	21.7	22.7	21.9	18.6	20.9	16.6
6.	20.0	20.1	20.1	22.9	8.1	19.7	23.1	17.3	19.9	23.2	17.2	22.2	19.8	17.1	18.5	35.5
5.	13.4	14.2	13.5	15.1	5.8	13.2	13.4	10.4	18.6	15.1	12.1	13.5	13.7	12.8	14.7	5.7
4. Neutral	21.0	19.0	22.5	18.5	31.6	21.7	19.8	24.1	17.0	16.6	26.3	18.0	20.2	27.6	22.4	14.6
3.	9.2	9.1	9.2	9.9	7.1	7.7	11.2	7.8	10.3	10.3	7.0	9.7	9.2	10.1	8.4	3.9
2.	5.1	5.0	5.3	5.0	5.1	5.8	4.1	4.4	6.8	5.1	5.4	4.4	4.7	4.7	6.5	1.5
1. Completely dissatisfied	9.8	9.9	9.0	7.3	17.4	11.7	7.6	11.6	7.6	8.7	10.4	9.5	10.6	9.1	8.5	22.1
Item 1300 Subject P02 N	3293	1498	1655	2407	393	776	897	994	625	1819	1114	1301	715	443	712	29

A006E: Your educational experiences?

7. Completely satisfied	23.0	22.0	24.1	21.1	34.4	21.4	19.0	29.3	20.4	23.8	23.3	26.7	22.8	22.3	16.6	9.7
6.	23.1	22.4	24.5	25.9	14.2	22.9	27.0	20.0	22.7	28.2	17.3	27.9	22.4	21.0	17.8	30.2
5.	16.6	18.9	14.8	18.4	9.8	15.3	18.5	13.5	20.6	16.5	16.5	15.3	18.5	16.2	17.7	12.4
4. Neutral	24.6	22.9	25.2	23.0	30.4	26.9	23.2	25.6	22.1	19.4	29.7	20.4	23.7	27.9	30.1	30.1
3.	5.4	5.5	5.2	5.6	2.3	5.3	4.8	4.8	7.2	5.8	4.5	5.0	5.3	5.2	6.6	1.5
2.	3.1	3.7	2.6	3.1	1.7	3.2	3.2	2.7	3.4	3.8	2.5	2.5	3.0	3.1	4.5	4.1
1. Completely dissatisfied	4.2	4.6	3.6	3.0	7.2	5.0	4.3	4.0	3.5	2.5	6.1	2.3	4.3	4.4	6.6	12.0
Item 1310 Subject B01,P02 N	3282	1491	1655	2402	394	774	893	995	620	1810	1115	1296	715	442	710	28

A006F: Your friends and other people you spend time with?

7. Completely satisfied	49.2	45.9	52.6	49.2	54.0	48.8	49.1	53.5	42.9	45.1	56.8	50.7	49.6	47.6	46.5	59.3
6.	26.7	28.9	24.9	29.2	13.6	27.7	28.6	21.2	31.4	30.1	21.8	25.7	27.2	30.6	27.5	10.7
5.	9.1	10.5	7.8	9.7	6.9	8.4	9.4	8.0	11.4	10.9	6.9	10.0	8.6	8.3	8.4	12.7
4. Neutral	10.7	10.8	10.3	8.2	20.2	9.8	8.9	13.6	10.1	9.4	11.8	10.7	10.6	9.6	11.4	9.8
3.	2.0	1.6	2.4	2.0	2.0	2.2	2.0	1.8	2.3	2.5	1.2	1.2	2.3	1.7	3.2	-
2.	0.9	1.0	0.6	0.7	0.5	1.1	0.5	0.7	1.5	1.0	0.4	0.6	1.0	0.8	1.1	3.9
1. Completely dissatisfied	1.4	1.2	1.4	0.9	2.8	2.1	1.6	1.2	0.5	1.1	1.1	1.2	0.7	1.4	2.0	3.6
Item 1320 Subject M04,P02 N	3296	1498	1658	2407	397	776	896	999	625	1814	1119	1304	716	444	710	29

A006G: The way you get along with your parents?

7. Completely satisfied	35.5	36.4	34.1	32.9	53.0	34.4	32.8	41.2	31.4	33.9	37.9	40.6	35.5	32.6	27.8	31.1
6.	21.4	21.7	21.4	23.4	14.9	19.5	24.5	19.0	23.1	22.9	19.3	21.5	22.0	24.2	19.5	14.2
5.	11.4	13.7	9.3	12.9	3.8	11.3	12.5	8.7	14.1	12.9	9.2	10.5	12.2	11.5	12.4	5.3
4. Neutral	17.6	15.7	19.7	16.4	19.3	19.0	15.8	18.6	17.1	15.3	21.0	16.7	17.3	17.1	19.3	23.7
3.	5.4	5.5	5.7	6.2	2.4	4.8	5.5	5.2	6.4	6.6	3.9	4.9	6.1	6.6	5.4	8.0
2.	3.4	2.9	3.6	3.3	2.4	4.1	3.7	2.2	4.4	3.9	2.6	2.1	2.6	3.4	6.3	7.5
1. Completely dissatisfied	5.3	4.1	6.2	5.0	4.1	6.8	5.3	5.3	3.4	4.6	6.2	3.6	4.3	4.4	9.3	10.2
Item 1330 Subject M03,P02 N	3298	1501	1657	2410	396	779	897	998	624	1817	1119	1301	717	443	715	29

A006H: Yourself?

7. Completely satisfied	34.0	38.4	29.6	29.3	59.2	30.5	29.5	41.6	32.8	30.1	38.8	37.3	35.4	30.3	28.3	36.4
6.	26.4	27.6	26.3	29.2	15.6	27.3	28.9	21.0	30.6	29.0	23.4	26.7	26.3	27.1	26.9	17.8
5.	13.9	13.8	14.5	15.9	5.8	15.8	15.8	9.8	15.7	16.5	10.5	13.6	15.2	13.8	14.3	10.4
4. Neutral	17.7	13.9	20.7	17.5	14.2	18.2	16.3	21.0	14.0	15.2	21.4	15.0	17.4	21.0	20.2	21.3
3.	3.9	3.4	4.2	4.3	1.0	3.9	4.9	3.2	3.6	5.0	2.6	4.1	2.3	3.6	5.4	3.5
2.	1.9	1.2	2.6	1.9	1.3	1.9	2.0	1.3	2.8	2.2	1.5	1.8	1.8	1.8	2.7	-
1. Completely dissatisfied	2.0	1.6	2.1	1.8	2.8	2.3	2.7	2.1	0.4	2.0	1.7	1.5	1.7	2.4	2.2	10.5
Item 1340 Subject P01,Q01 N	3275	1488	1650	2395	390	771	894	990	621	1809	1108	1296	712	439	708	29

A006I: Your standard of living–the things you have like housing, car, furniture, recreation, and the like?

7. Completely satisfied	35.3	36.3	34.9	36.1	34.0	36.3	29.8	39.6	35.3	36.2	36.0	38.0	35.0	35.8	30.9	43.1
6.	25.5	26.8	24.8	27.8	17.2	21.3	31.5	20.6	29.7	28.5	21.4	25.9	23.9	29.2	24.7	20.1
5.	12.9	12.8	13.0	13.4	8.0	14.5	13.1	10.5	14.4	13.4	12.0	13.0	13.9	11.3	13.1	10.1
4. Neutral	16.5	14.4	17.7	13.7	29.3	18.0	14.6	19.4	12.8	12.0	22.2	15.8	15.9	12.0	19.9	17.3
3.	4.8	5.0	4.4	4.8	2.9	5.1	5.9	3.8	4.4	5.0	3.7	4.2	5.3	5.7	4.8	-
2.	2.5	2.4	2.5	2.3	3.5	2.6	2.3	2.8	1.9	2.9	1.7	1.4	3.9	2.4	3.1	4.1
1. Completely dissatisfied	2.6	2.4	2.6	1.8	5.2	2.1	2.9	3.4	1.5	2.1	3.0	1.7	2.1	3.6	3.6	5.4
Item 1350 Subject F01,P02 N	3301	1503	1660	2412	398	776	900	1000	624	1821	1118	1305	719	442	714	28

QUESTIONNAIRE FORM 1 1985	TOTAL	SEX		RACE		REGION				4YR COLLEGE PLANS		ILLICIT DRUG USE: LIFETIME				
		M	F	White	Black	NE	NC	S	W	Yes	No	None	Marijuana Only	Few Pills	More Pills	Any Heroin
N (Weighted No. of Cases):	3316	1505	1663	2415	400	783	902	1004	627	1822	1121	1307	719	444	716	29
% of Weighted Total:	100.0	45.4	50.2	72.8	12.1	23.6	27.2	30.3	18.9	55.0	33.8	39.4	21.7	13.4	21.6	0.9
A006J: The amount of time you have for doing things you want to do?																
7. Completely satisfied	16.3	18.1	14.1	14.5	24.3	13.6	16.9	18.9	14.5	14.7	18.4	16.9	17.7	15.9	13.8	12.8
6.	16.0	17.8	14.7	17.9	8.4	15.9	16.1	14.0	19.3	16.4	16.3	16.7	14.2	15.1	17.8	17.0
5.	17.4	18.3	16.9	18.6	11.9	16.8	19.9	14.1	19.8	20.0	13.4	18.2	19.0	16.5	16.2	18.5
4. Neutral	18.4	16.1	19.9	15.8	29.7	21.3	14.9	20.9	15.7	15.6	21.2	18.6	18.2	16.9	17.3	19.8
3.	11.6	10.6	12.7	12.6	6.2	10.4	13.1	9.4	14.6	13.6	9.4	10.9	12.9	12.2	12.1	14.1
2.	7.8	7.3	8.4	8.8	3.4	8.2	8.0	8.2	6.4	8.7	6.3	8.0	6.5	10.2	7.6	-
1. Completely dissatisfied	12.5	11.7	13.3	11.8	16.1	13.7	11.0	14.5	9.8	10.9	15.0	10.7	11.5	13.2	15.2	17.8
Item 1360 Subject P02 N	3302	1505	1660	2414	398	777	900	1000	625	1821	1121	1306	718	443	714	29
A006K: The way you spend your leisure time– recreation, relaxation, and so on?																
7. Completely satisfied	30.0	30.7	29.4	29.0	37.4	26.1	29.8	36.0	25.9	27.5	33.2	30.0	31.1	31.2	27.2	37.0
6.	22.1	22.8	21.6	23.8	14.3	23.2	22.8	18.2	25.8	23.8	20.0	23.2	22.8	19.0	22.3	27.1
5.	15.9	17.4	15.2	17.8	8.6	15.9	17.7	12.8	18.2	18.3	13.6	15.7	14.9	17.3	17.5	1.5
4. Neutral	17.0	15.3	17.7	15.4	21.8	17.2	16.3	19.4	13.8	14.5	20.2	17.2	15.5	17.8	16.7	23.3
3.	6.5	5.7	7.4	6.9	4.4	5.7	6.5	5.5	9.2	7.8	5.3	6.1	7.4	6.8	6.2	1.5
2.	3.6	3.5	3.6	3.2	3.2	5.3	3.2	2.3	3.9	3.6	3.1	3.5	3.4	3.3	4.0	5.9
1. Completely dissatisfied	4.9	4.7	5.1	3.8	10.3	6.5	3.7	5.8	3.2	4.5	4.6	4.3	4.9	4.5	6.0	3.7
Item 1370 Subject C08,P02 N	3301	1502	1661	2412	397	778	899	999	624	1819	1120	1304	717	443	713	29
A006L: Your life as a whole these days?																
7. Completely satisfied	22.4	22.0	23.0	21.4	30.6	19.3	18.5	29.2	21.0	21.3	25.5	25.4	22.6	20.1	18.9	13.2
6.	28.4	30.2	27.5	32.2	16.3	27.7	30.9	24.7	31.7	31.8	24.6	29.0	31.1	25.6	27.1	33.2
5.	16.4	18.5	14.4	17.3	10.1	16.6	17.2	13.3	20.0	18.2	14.4	15.0	16.8	19.3	17.8	8.0
4. Neutral	21.7	19.5	23.2	19.3	31.6	21.4	23.5	23.4	16.6	17.9	25.6	20.8	21.5	25.1	20.4	15.6
3.	5.5	5.6	5.3	5.2	2.9	7.6	5.3	3.9	5.8	5.6	4.7	5.2	3.4	4.1	8.0	24.8
2.	2.7	2.1	3.1	2.4	3.6	3.5	2.0	2.7	2.8	2.8	2.2	2.3	3.1	2.1	3.4	-
1. Completely dissatisfied	2.9	2.0	3.5	2.2	4.9	3.9	2.7	2.8	2.1	2.6	3.0	2.3	1.5	3.6	4.4	5.2
Item 1380 Subject P01 N	3287	1497	1653	2406	394	769	899	994	625	1817	1113	1300	715	441	709	29
A006M: The way our national government is operating?																
7. Completely satisfied	3.7	4.8	2.2	3.7	2.7	3.6	2.9	5.9	1.7	3.3	4.1	4.1	2.9	4.7	2.7	12.3
6.	7.8	9.7	6.3	9.0	1.8	7.5	8.9	7.3	7.5	9.2	5.2	9.5	7.1	5.8	6.9	1.3
5.	13.1	16.6	10.5	15.3	4.7	13.3	12.3	12.3	15.4	14.4	11.1	14.2	12.2	13.0	12.9	10.9
4. Neutral	40.0	34.2	45.2	40.5	40.8	41.1	38.6	42.2	37.0	37.0	45.1	37.7	43.1	42.0	41.2	41.1
3.	11.6	11.4	11.7	11.9	7.5	9.0	13.1	10.2	14.8	13.6	8.6	13.2	11.4	11.7	9.3	4.0
2.	8.0	7.2	8.8	8.2	6.7	8.8	9.4	6.0	8.1	8.8	6.6	8.2	6.6	8.1	9.0	1.5
1. Completely dissatisfied	15.8	16.1	15.3	11.6	35.8	16.7	14.9	16.0	15.5	13.6	19.3	13.2	16.7	14.7	18.1	28.8
Item 1390 Subject H02,K02 N	3291	1500	1656	2409	397	774	896	997	623	1817	1116	1301	717	441	711	29
A006N: The amount of fun you are having?																
7. Completely satisfied	26.5	25.7	27.2	26.5	30.2	22.2	25.7	32.6	23.6	23.9	29.9	27.6	27.5	27.2	23.0	24.6
6.	25.4	27.9	23.7	27.7	16.5	24.9	28.8	19.3	30.8	28.3	22.4	26.2	28.7	22.4	24.7	18.5
5.	16.4	17.6	15.5	18.3	8.6	17.8	16.7	14.1	17.8	18.3	13.9	15.9	14.9	19.8	16.8	25.7
4. Neutral	18.4	17.1	19.5	15.6	27.4	19.6	15.7	21.0	16.6	15.9	22.6	18.5	17.4	16.8	18.9	19.6
3.	5.3	4.6	5.9	5.7	4.3	5.3	6.9	4.1	5.0	6.0	4.1	5.2	4.5	6.1	6.4	3.9
2.	3.4	2.8	3.7	3.0	2.4	4.8	2.8	2.7	3.6	3.6	2.4	3.1	2.7	3.4	4.5	3.9
1. Completely dissatisfied	4.5	4.3	4.5	3.2	10.7	5.4	3.4	6.1	2.6	3.9	4.8	3.5	4.2	4.4	5.7	3.7
Item 1400 Subject P02,Q01 N	3301	1504	1661	2414	398	778	899	999	625	1820	1121	1306	717	443	714	29
A007: How important is each of the following to you in your life?																
A007A: Being successful in my line of work																
1. Not important	0.9	1.1	0.7	0.8	0.7	1.3	1.0	0.9	0.5	0.7	1.0	1.0	0.3	0.3	1.6	1.5
2. Somewhat important	8.1	8.1	7.9	7.9	8.8	7.7	9.2	8.6	6.1	5.3	12.4	6.7	7.6	10.4	9.2	16.0
3. Quite important	31.1	31.5	31.0	33.1	20.2	33.0	32.3	25.4	36.4	29.3	34.5	31.5	32.2	28.0	31.7	29.6
4. Extremely important	59.8	59.3	60.4	58.2	70.3	58.0	57.4	65.2	57.0	64.7	52.0	60.9	59.9	61.3	57.5	53.0
Item 1410 Subject C06,Q07 N	3278	1492	1648	2394	394	770	893	994	622	1806	1111	1299	717	437	702	29

QUESTIONNAIRE FORM 1 1985	TOTAL	SEX		RACE		REGION				4YR COLLEGE PLANS		ILLICIT DRUG USE: LIFETIME				
		M	F	White	Black	NE	NC	S	W	Yes	No	None	Mari- juana Only	Few Pills	More Pills	Any Her- oin
N (Weighted No. of Cases):	3316	1505	1663	2415	400	783	902	1004	627	1822	1121	1307	719	444	716	29
% of Weighted Total:	100.0	45.4	50.2	72.8	12.1	23.6	27.2	30.3	18.9	55.0	33.8	39.4	21.7	13.4	21.6	0.9
A007B: Having a good marriage and family life																
1. Not important	3.7	4.9	2.5	3.3	4.8	3.4	4.3	3.8	3.2	3.2	4.1	3.0	4.3	2.7	4.6	5.2
2. Somewhat important	6.8	9.1	4.3	6.5	7.5	9.6	5.7	5.8	6.5	6.0	7.3	5.1	7.1	5.2	9.0	15.5
3. Quite important	15.2	17.6	12.8	15.2	14.4	15.2	17.3	13.0	15.7	14.8	15.1	13.9	14.4	16.6	16.8	20.8
4. Extremely important	74.3	68.4	80.4	75.0	73.2	71.8	72.8	77.5	74.6	76.0	73.5	78.1	74.2	75.4	69.6	58.5
Item 1420 Subject D03,Q07　N	3265	1481	1649	2389	393	767	892	989	617	1802	1109	1293	717	435	701	29
A007C: Having lots of money																
1. Not important	5.6	5.0	6.0	5.7	4.8	4.2	4.8	6.1	7.5	5.9	5.7	6.9	4.6	4.0	5.1	6.7
2. Somewhat important	33.1	27.8	38.5	35.3	25.8	31.7	36.5	31.7	32.4	33.2	34.4	35.6	32.5	34.0	30.1	29.0
3. Quite important	35.2	35.0	35.9	35.9	33.1	35.1	34.0	34.2	38.8	36.2	33.4	33.9	38.4	37.2	34.2	14.8
4. Extremely important	26.1	32.2	19.6	23.1	36.2	29.0	24.7	28.1	21.2	24.7	26.5	23.6	24.6	24.8	30.6	49.5
Item 1430 Subject F01,Q07　N	3273	1491	1647	2393	397	768	892	993	619	1807	1113	1300	715	434	702	29
A007D: Having plenty of time for recreation and hobbies																
1. Not important	2.4	1.6	2.9	1.5	6.6	1.2	2.3	3.3	2.6	1.5	3.3	2.8	2.0	0.9	1.8	7.3
2. Somewhat important	28.9	23.1	33.9	28.2	36.7	26.1	31.1	31.1	25.8	25.6	33.1	29.3	27.7	31.0	28.5	5.6
3. Quite important	42.3	43.0	42.3	43.5	35.0	42.7	42.8	38.5	47.1	44.5	39.7	42.8	44.3	42.5	40.7	40.0
4. Extremely important	26.4	32.3	20.8	26.7	21.7	30.0	23.9	27.1	24.5	28.4	23.9	25.1	26.0	25.6	29.0	47.2
Item 1440 Subject C08,Q07　N	3278	1494	1646	2397	395	769	893	995	620	1810	1111	1302	716	437	702	29
A007E: Having strong friendships																
1. Not important	1.0	1.0	1.0	0.5	3.4	1.1	0.8	1.6	0.4	0.7	1.2	0.8	1.4	0.5	0.5	7.3
2. Somewhat important	7.7	7.8	6.8	5.1	18.6	6.7	6.8	8.9	8.4	6.3	9.4	6.9	7.5	8.3	8.0	3.6
3. Quite important	27.4	29.2	25.6	26.5	33.7	26.6	30.2	26.6	25.5	25.9	28.5	27.7	27.3	30.8	24.1	10.7
4. Extremely important	63.9	62.1	66.6	67.9	44.2	65.6	62.2	62.9	65.7	67.1	60.9	64.6	63.7	60.4	67.4	78.4
Item 1450 Subject M04,Q07　N	3280	1494	1649	2398	397	770	892	999	619	1808	1113	1298	719	436	704	29
A007F: Being able to find steady work																
1. Not important	0.7	0.9	0.5	0.6	0.1	0.7	0.3	1.2	0.5	0.7	0.4	0.5	0.6	1.1	0.9	-
2. Somewhat important	4.5	5.0	3.8	4.6	3.4	5.4	4.4	3.5	5.2	4.3	4.8	4.4	3.1	5.7	4.7	15.5
3. Quite important	22.4	21.1	23.7	23.8	18.3	24.5	21.2	20.5	24.5	23.5	21.4	21.9	23.5	23.6	21.5	18.6
4. Extremely important	72.4	73.0	72.0	71.0	78.2	69.4	74.1	74.8	69.8	71.6	73.4	73.2	72.8	69.6	72.9	65.9
Item 1460 Subject C04,Q07　N	3283	1496	1648	2397	398	769	894	999	621	1809	1115	1302	719	435	704	29
A007G: Making a contribution to society																
1. Not important	7.4	9.1	5.6	7.7	5.4	9.0	8.0	6.0	6.9	6.0	9.2	5.2	7.4	7.2	9.9	18.2
2. Somewhat important	37.8	37.1	38.2	38.4	39.5	37.5	40.0	37.2	36.2	32.7	45.1	35.8	38.5	42.3	38.7	37.4
3. Quite important	37.9	37.0	39.5	38.1	36.1	37.7	35.9	39.5	38.6	40.0	35.3	39.1	38.2	36.6	36.9	34.3
4. Extremely important	16.8	16.7	16.7	15.8	19.0	15.8	16.2	17.3	18.2	21.3	10.4	19.8	15.9	14.0	14.5	10.1
Item 1470 Subject O01,Q07　N	3268	1490	1643	2392	393	768	892	992	617	1801	1111	1297	715	433	702	29
A007H: Being a leader in my community																
1. Not important	32.8	31.9	33.3	33.5	28.5	38.8	36.9	27.4	28.3	27.0	41.6	29.4	33.3	31.7	38.4	39.2
2. Somewhat important	41.1	40.7	42.3	42.2	40.6	39.1	39.1	41.1	46.2	42.2	39.7	41.5	40.2	44.1	40.1	39.8
3. Quite important	18.3	19.3	17.3	17.6	20.7	16.0	15.9	22.4	18.1	21.4	13.5	19.3	19.2	19.0	15.0	15.3
4. Extremely important	7.8	8.1	7.1	6.7	10.3	6.1	8.0	9.1	7.4	9.5	5.2	9.8	7.3	5.2	6.5	5.7
Item 1480 Subject M05,Q07　N	3280	1494	1650	2398	396	770	894	998	618	1812	1110	1302	719	437	701	28
A007I: Being able to give my children better opportunities than I've had																
1. Not important	3.0	4.0	2.2	3.4	1.6	3.4	3.0	2.7	3.1	3.3	3.1	3.8	1.9	1.9	3.3	1.5
2. Somewhat important	10.4	10.6	10.5	12.4	3.4	10.8	12.8	7.0	11.8	12.2	8.8	8.9	12.3	12.9	9.5	7.0
3. Quite important	29.2	30.1	28.5	32.1	16.4	30.3	30.3	24.9	33.1	29.2	29.3	28.7	28.4	27.6	32.3	29.9
4. Extremely important	57.4	55.3	58.8	52.1	78.6	55.5	53.9	65.4	52.0	55.3	58.9	58.6	57.4	57.6	54.8	61.6
Item 1490 Subject Q07　N	3254	1477	1640	2378	390	762	890	986	616	1794	1103	1286	715	435	696	29

QUESTIONNAIRE FORM 1 1985	TOTAL	SEX		RACE		REGION				4YR COLLEGE PLANS		ILLICIT DRUG USE: LIFETIME				
		M	F	White	Black	NE	NC	S	W	Yes	No	None	Mari-juana Only	Few Pills	More Pills	Any Her-oin
N (Weighted No. of Cases):	3316	1505	1663	2415	400	783	902	1004	627	1822	1121	1307	719	444	716	29
% of Weighted Total:	100.0	45.4	50.2	72.8	12.1	23.6	27.2	30.3	18.9	55.0	33.8	39.4	21.7	13.4	21.6	0.9
A007J: Living close to parents and relatives																
1. Not important	25.8	27.6	24.1	26.5	27.5	27.7	27.5	25.6	21.3	27.2	24.5	23.7	25.5	24.8	30.0	30.4
2. Somewhat important	39.9	39.8	40.3	40.8	40.4	37.6	41.5	39.3	41.2	41.1	39.2	38.0	41.7	40.7	41.2	35.9
3. Quite important	22.9	22.1	23.6	23.1	17.3	22.4	20.6	24.2	24.7	21.0	24.9	24.5	23.3	23.2	19.9	18.1
4. Extremely important	11.5	10.6	12.0	9.6	14.8	12.3	10.3	11.0	12.8	10.7	11.4	13.7	9.5	11.3	8.8	15.6
Item 1500 Subject M03,Q07 N	3270	1487	1648	2390	396	768	891	994	618	1807	1106	1296	715	436	701	29
A007K: Getting away from this area of the country																
1. Not important	49.5	51.5	48.0	52.4	39.7	45.8	43.0	53.6	57.0	51.0	49.2	54.2	52.4	46.6	41.1	28.6
2. Somewhat important	24.1	21.6	26.2	23.8	27.2	23.8	27.1	23.9	20.4	22.6	25.6	23.7	22.0	27.2	25.1	30.1
3. Quite important	13.0	12.8	13.6	12.1	17.7	13.4	16.6	9.9	12.5	12.8	13.2	11.1	14.4	12.6	16.3	11.7
4. Extremely important	13.4	14.1	12.3	11.7	15.5	17.1	13.3	12.6	10.0	13.6	12.0	11.0	11.3	13.6	17.5	29.5
Item 1510 Subject Q07 N	3282	1493	1652	2399	395	771	893	999	619	1810	1113	1300	718	436	704	29
A007L: Working to correct social and economic inequalities																
1. Not important	21.0	25.1	17.5	23.5	13.0	24.9	22.5	17.9	19.0	19.7	24.7	19.7	18.8	22.4	25.5	29.4
2. Somewhat important	46.8	47.9	46.8	49.2	43.2	46.0	48.6	46.3	45.8	47.2	48.2	47.4	47.8	43.4	47.5	43.6
3. Quite important	23.1	18.7	26.8	20.4	30.4	21.3	21.8	25.1	24.1	23.5	20.0	22.9	25.3	25.4	18.9	23.6
4. Extremely important	9.1	8.3	8.9	6.8	13.4	7.8	7.1	10.7	11.0	9.6	7.1	10.0	8.1	8.9	8.1	3.5
Item 1520 Subject N02,O01,Q07 N	3269	1486	1646	2388	396	767	890	995	617	1807	1107	1295	717	435	701	29
A007M: Discovering new ways to experience things																
1. Not important	7.0	8.9	5.5	7.3	7.9	6.7	8.2	7.7	4.3	7.2	7.2	8.2	6.2	5.3	6.6	5.6
2. Somewhat important	34.8	35.5	33.8	36.2	32.4	35.0	36.7	36.7	28.8	32.4	39.3	38.9	33.8	34.5	28.6	26.6
3. Quite important	38.9	38.0	40.2	38.7	38.6	39.0	39.2	35.7	43.3	39.3	37.8	35.4	42.7	41.3	41.0	32.5
4. Extremely important	19.4	17.7	20.5	17.8	21.1	19.4	15.8	19.9	23.6	21.1	15.7	17.5	17.4	18.9	23.8	35.3
Item 1530 Subject Q07 N	3275	1490	1651	2396	396	768	892	998	617	1806	1114	1299	715	436	703	28
A007N: Finding purpose and meaning in my life																
1. Not important	3.3	5.3	1.4	3.7	1.8	3.8	4.2	2.9	2.4	4.0	2.2	2.8	3.6	1.4	5.1	5.5
2. Somewhat important	10.4	13.7	7.2	11.7	5.4	14.3	11.5	6.7	10.0	9.9	10.7	10.8	9.8	11.4	9.9	14.4
3. Quite important	27.3	32.7	22.1	28.7	22.2	24.9	27.4	27.3	30.3	25.7	30.1	26.1	29.5	26.4	28.6	3.4
4. Extremely important	58.9	48.2	69.4	55.8	70.7	57.0	56.9	63.2	57.3	60.4	56.9	60.2	57.1	60.9	56.4	76.7
Item 1540 Subject Q07 N	3278	1492	1652	2397	398	768	893	999	618	1809	1114	1297	718	437	704	29
A008: Generally speaking, would you say that most people can be trusted or that you can't be too careful in dealing with people?																
3. Most people can be trusted	28.6	29.3	28.8	33.5	9.5	24.9	32.6	26.0	31.5	33.2	24.5	33.5	28.6	26.2	23.2	21.9
2. Don't know, undecided	25.9	27.8	24.4	25.4	25.8	27.7	26.4	22.6	28.4	25.0	26.5	25.6	24.2	27.2	26.1	21.9
1. Can't be too careful	45.5	42.9	46.8	41.1	64.7	47.3	41.0	51.4	40.1	41.8	49.0	41.0	47.2	46.7	50.7	56.2
Item 1550 Subject Q05 N	3222	1466	1629	2367	390	753	886	977	607	1786	1086	1275	708	429	689	29
A009: Would you say that most of the time people try to be helpful or that they are mostly just looking out for themselves?																
3. Try to be helpful	34.4	30.9	38.0	36.0	26.2	30.6	38.1	33.6	35.0	37.3	31.9	38.7	33.5	33.0	29.5	20.5
2. Don't know, undecided	29.6	32.3	27.0	30.7	26.8	33.0	27.3	29.9	28.0	27.9	32.0	29.2	29.1	31.0	29.4	22.6
1. Just looking out for themselves	36.1	36.8	35.1	33.3	47.0	36.4	34.6	36.5	37.1	34.9	36.2	32.1	37.3	36.0	41.0	56.9
Item 1560 Subject Q05 N	3275	1492	1652	2395	398	767	891	999	618	1809	1110	1298	717	436	704	29
A010: Do you think most people would try to take advantage of you if they got a chance or would they try to be fair?																
3. Would try to be fair	27.6	27.8	28.0	30.5	15.0	25.3	29.2	25.5	31.3	29.5	26.6	29.9	26.7	28.5	24.4	19.7
2. Don't know, undecided	32.8	32.0	33.3	34.6	24.0	33.4	33.5	32.2	32.1	32.7	32.5	33.6	34.2	29.3	32.7	27.4
1. Would try to take advantage of you	39.6	40.2	38.7	34.9	61.0	41.3	37.3	42.3	36.6	37.8	40.9	36.5	39.1	42.2	42.8	52.9
Item 1570 Subject Q05 N	3277	1494	1652	2397	398	768	891	998	619	1810	1111	1298	717	437	705	29

QUESTIONNAIRE FORM 1 1985	TOTAL	SEX		RACE		REGION				4YR COLLEGE PLANS		ILLICIT DRUG USE: LIFETIME				
		M	F	White	Black	NE	NC	S	W	Yes	No	None	Marijuana Only	Few Pills	More Pills	Any Heroin
N (Weighted No. of Cases):	3316	1505	1663	2415	400	783	902	1004	627	1822	1121	1307	719	444	716	29
% of Weighted Total:	100.0	45.4	50.2	72.8	12.1	23.6	27.2	30.3	18.9	55.0	33.8	39.4	21.7	13.4	21.6	0.9

A011: These next questions ask your opinions about a number of different topics. How much do you agree or disagree with each statement below?

A011A: I feel that you can't be a good citizen unless you always obey the law

	TOTAL	M	F	White	Black	NE	NC	S	W	Yes	No	None	Marijuana Only	Few Pills	More Pills	Any Heroin
1. Disagree	19.6	22.7	17.0	18.9	23.2	22.2	19.0	18.8	18.3	19.5	18.9	15.7	21.9	17.2	25.4	26.6
2. Mostly disagree	18.2	17.5	18.7	19.4	14.0	19.2	17.0	16.8	20.8	18.6	17.0	16.8	18.1	18.3	21.9	24.5
3. Neither	19.7	19.0	20.9	20.5	15.1	21.0	23.0	14.3	22.0	19.2	21.3	18.1	19.9	18.8	23.3	20.2
4. Mostly agree	31.7	29.9	33.6	32.8	28.1	27.8	32.7	34.3	31.2	32.9	30.8	35.2	30.8	34.6	24.1	28.6
5. Agree	10.9	11.0	9.8	8.4	19.7	9.8	8.4	15.8	7.7	9.9	12.0	14.2	9.4	11.1	5.3	-
Item 1580 Subject H03 N	3281	1494	1652	2397	398	771	892	997	621	1809	1114	1300	716	436	706	29

A011B: I feel a good citizen should go along with whatever the government does even if he disagrees with it

	TOTAL	M	F	White	Black	NE	NC	S	W	Yes	No	None	Marijuana Only	Few Pills	More Pills	Any Heroin
1. Disagree	40.8	40.0	42.0	40.1	47.6	45.0	39.6	40.5	37.9	43.4	36.9	38.4	42.4	37.6	45.1	45.6
2. Mostly disagree	23.8	23.3	24.6	24.4	18.4	24.6	25.4	19.1	28.1	23.9	23.5	23.7	24.7	27.6	22.3	16.9
3. Neither	17.3	17.9	16.5	18.5	11.2	16.3	18.3	17.7	16.7	15.5	21.0	18.0	16.4	17.8	16.7	18.3
4. Mostly agree	13.3	13.5	12.8	12.7	14.9	11.1	12.9	15.2	13.6	13.0	13.6	14.2	12.8	12.6	12.2	16.4
5. Agree	4.7	5.3	4.1	4.4	7.9	3.0	3.9	7.5	3.7	4.2	5.0	5.8	3.7	4.4	3.7	2.9
Item 1590 Subject H03 N	3278	1492	1652	2396	397	769	891	996	622	1810	1111	1300	716	437	704	29

A011C: I feel a good citizen tries to change the government policies he disagrees with

	TOTAL	M	F	White	Black	NE	NC	S	W	Yes	No	None	Marijuana Only	Few Pills	More Pills	Any Heroin
1. Disagree	8.4	8.0	8.6	6.9	14.7	8.5	6.4	11.0	7.2	7.6	9.9	7.7	6.8	9.1	10.5	12.8
2. Mostly disagree	8.8	8.1	9.4	8.4	10.9	9.7	8.4	7.3	10.6	8.0	9.7	8.6	9.1	9.0	7.2	5.6
3. Neither	26.6	25.0	27.6	25.7	27.4	26.8	27.2	26.3	26.1	24.0	30.6	27.4	25.2	25.3	27.0	33.3
4. Mostly agree	30.5	30.1	31.5	32.3	24.1	28.1	34.0	30.0	29.4	31.4	29.8	28.9	30.3	37.5	30.3	33.5
5. Agree	25.6	28.7	22.8	26.7	22.9	26.9	24.0	25.4	26.7	29.0	20.0	27.4	28.6	19.2	25.0	14.8
Item 1600 Subject H03 N	3263	1489	1642	2389	393	764	890	993	616	1804	1107	1297	712	436	700	29

A011D: The way people vote has a major impact on how things are run in this country

	TOTAL	M	F	White	Black	NE	NC	S	W	Yes	No	None	Marijuana Only	Few Pills	More Pills	Any Heroin
1. Disagree	5.5	6.0	4.6	5.1	4.3	6.9	5.3	4.0	6.5	5.2	5.2	5.5	5.3	3.7	6.3	18.1
2. Mostly disagree	8.8	10.0	7.7	9.5	7.2	8.1	11.0	8.3	7.4	9.9	7.7	7.0	9.7	9.6	11.1	5.7
3. Neither	12.1	12.3	11.7	12.9	7.4	12.8	12.8	10.1	13.6	11.9	13.0	11.8	10.9	11.2	14.2	16.4
4. Mostly agree	34.0	31.9	36.5	34.4	32.2	34.7	32.9	32.3	37.4	34.1	34.7	33.8	35.4	36.3	32.8	25.3
5. Agree	39.6	39.7	39.5	38.0	49.0	37.5	38.0	45.3	35.2	39.0	39.4	41.8	38.7	39.1	35.7	34.6
Item 1610 Subject H05,I02 N	3266	1489	1647	2390	398	760	892	994	620	1806	1108	1296	716	437	699	29

A011E: People who get together in citizen action groups to influence government policies can have a real effect

	TOTAL	M	F	White	Black	NE	NC	S	W	Yes	No	None	Marijuana Only	Few Pills	More Pills	Any Heroin
1. Disagree	4.0	5.7	2.5	3.6	4.2	5.2	4.2	3.9	2.6	3.2	4.9	4.2	3.6	3.7	4.3	8.8
2. Mostly disagree	8.6	10.1	7.2	9.1	7.8	10.7	8.7	7.5	7.5	9.8	6.6	7.4	8.5	9.6	10.0	7.8
3. Neither	25.1	24.8	24.5	26.3	17.0	29.3	29.0	18.0	26.0	22.2	28.8	23.3	25.0	22.3	28.8	34.1
4. Mostly agree	38.8	36.5	41.8	39.8	37.4	34.6	36.7	43.6	39.3	38.9	39.6	38.0	38.9	45.0	38.0	32.3
5. Agree	23.5	22.9	23.9	21.2	33.7	20.3	21.4	27.0	24.6	25.8	20.0	27.1	24.0	19.4	19.0	17.0
Item 1620 Subject H03,I02 N	3259	1485	1643	2386	395	759	888	995	617	1801	1105	1295	714	435	693	29

A011F: Despite its many faults, our system of doing things is still the best in the world

	TOTAL	M	F	White	Black	NE	NC	S	W	Yes	No	None	Marijuana Only	Few Pills	More Pills	Any Heroin
1. Disagree	5.3	4.8	5.4	3.6	8.9	6.7	4.8	4.3	5.9	4.5	5.8	5.2	4.3	4.1	6.3	16.6
2. Mostly disagree	8.0	7.0	8.3	6.1	15.5	9.7	7.1	8.1	7.1	5.7	10.7	6.8	9.4	5.6	9.7	-
3. Neither	21.1	17.0	25.0	20.5	23.0	21.4	24.5	16.9	22.4	19.5	24.7	20.6	21.0	25.7	18.2	18.5
4. Mostly agree	31.2	30.6	32.3	31.8	30.8	30.3	29.9	32.9	31.4	31.7	31.7	30.5	32.0	33.1	32.5	12.9
5. Agree	34.4	40.6	29.1	37.9	21.8	31.9	33.7	37.8	33.1	38.6	27.2	36.9	33.2	31.5	33.2	51.9
Item 1630 Subject H04 N	3267	1489	1646	2391	394	761	892	996	619	1807	1107	1297	715	437	698	29

QUESTIONNAIRE FORM 1 1985	TOTAL	SEX		RACE		REGION				4YR COLLEGE PLANS		ILLICIT DRUG USE: LIFETIME				
		M	F	White	Black	NE	NC	S	W	Yes	No	None	Mari-juana Only	Few Pills	More Pills	Any Her-oin
N (Weighted No. of Cases):	3316	1505	1663	2415	400	783	902	1004	627	1822	1121	1307	719	444	716	29
% of Weighted Total:	100.0	45.4	50.2	72.8	12.1	23.6	27.2	30.3	18.9	55.0	33.8	39.4	21.7	13.4	21.6	0.9
A011G: America needs growth to survive, and that is going to require some increase in pollution																
1. Disagree	35.1	34.9	36.5	36.2	30.6	37.6	34.8	32.9	36.3	38.0	32.6	35.5	36.2	35.1	35.3	18.1
2. Mostly disagree	22.2	23.0	21.8	23.9	17.3	21.3	23.3	22.0	22.1	24.5	19.0	22.8	23.4	21.1	21.7	9.3
3. Neither	21.9	20.7	22.8	22.5	20.6	22.9	23.8	20.1	21.2	20.2	24.1	20.2	20.9	25.0	24.1	28.8
4. Mostly agree	13.2	13.6	12.1	11.4	17.2	12.1	11.6	14.3	14.8	11.0	15.9	13.4	13.0	12.5	12.3	18.8
5. Agree	7.5	7.8	6.8	6.0	14.3	6.1	6.6	10.6	5.6	6.3	8.4	8.0	6.6	6.4	6.6	25.0
Item 1640 Subject F04 N	3259	1485	1641	2385	395	760	890	995	614	1802	1105	1296	715	433	695	29
A011H: If we just leave things to God, they will turn out for the best																
1. Disagree	21.9	23.8	20.1	23.8	6.2	29.7	21.6	13.5	26.0	25.9	15.8	19.8	23.0	19.7	26.8	22.7
2. Mostly disagree	13.0	13.3	12.9	14.8	4.0	15.3	14.5	8.5	15.3	13.6	13.0	12.5	10.0	16.4	15.4	14.8
3. Neither	24.7	24.4	24.9	26.6	15.0	28.1	27.2	20.7	23.2	23.2	26.5	22.6	26.1	27.5	25.8	30.5
4. Mostly agree	19.0	18.6	19.6	18.1	24.6	15.4	19.4	22.1	17.8	17.9	21.0	19.0	18.4	21.5	16.8	15.2
5. Agree	21.5	19.8	22.6	16.6	50.3	11.5	17.3	35.3	17.7	19.4	23.8	26.2	22.5	14.9	15.3	16.8
Item 1650 Subject I02 N	3249	1480	1640	2374	394	754	888	988	619	1795	1102	1290	711	432	696	28
A011I: Going to school has been an enjoyable experience for me																
1. Disagree	6.7	8.3	5.2	6.5	5.7	8.6	7.0	7.1	3.5	3.9	10.8	5.0	6.6	6.1	9.3	21.8
2. Mostly disagree	8.1	8.6	7.2	8.6	6.1	9.8	9.1	7.1	6.3	6.8	9.6	6.3	5.5	10.5	12.5	5.9
3. Neither	14.0	16.0	11.9	15.0	10.3	14.2	14.2	12.3	16.1	12.7	16.8	12.4	14.2	14.2	17.1	11.7
4. Mostly agree	40.4	37.2	44.2	41.5	36.5	40.6	41.7	38.9	41.0	42.1	37.6	40.5	41.8	43.1	37.8	47.2
5. Agree	30.7	29.8	31.5	28.3	41.5	26.9	27.9	34.6	33.1	34.6	25.2	35.8	32.0	26.0	23.4	13.3
Item 1660 Subject B01 N	3259	1488	1642	2389	391	757	891	991	619	1807	1102	1293	714	436	697	28
A011J: Doing well in school is important for getting a good job																
1. Disagree	2.3	3.7	0.9	2.2	2.4	3.3	1.6	2.0	2.5	1.7	2.9	1.4	2.3	1.8	3.6	16.1
2. Mostly disagree	2.7	3.6	1.9	2.8	2.4	3.5	2.5	2.1	3.1	2.1	3.7	1.6	4.0	1.8	4.1	1.5
3. Neither	7.0	9.9	4.1	7.3	4.4	9.0	6.6	5.3	8.0	5.2	8.9	4.8	7.0	8.7	9.7	8.5
4. Mostly agree	30.9	32.3	29.9	32.1	27.4	31.7	30.5	29.5	32.4	30.5	32.4	29.4	31.1	33.9	33.2	22.9
5. Agree	57.1	50.5	63.2	55.6	63.3	52.5	58.6	61.1	54.1	60.6	52.0	62.8	55.6	53.8	49.4	51.0
Item 1670 Subject B01 N	3272	1491	1650	2394	395	764	892	996	620	1809	1108	1299	717	437	699	28

The following questions are about CIGARETTE SMOKING.

	TOTAL	M	F	White	Black	NE	NC	S	W	Yes	No	None	Mari-juana Only	Few Pills	More Pills	Any Her-oin
B001: Have you ever smoked cigarettes?																
1. Never-GO TO Q.B006	30.7	33.6	29.2	29.8	38.3	28.8	28.6	33.4	31.7	37.1	24.2	58.1	13.1	17.8	7.2	12.4
2. Once or twice	29.9	31.4	28.6	27.8	45.3	27.1	28.4	33.9	29.0	31.1	28.5	27.7	43.5	34.8	18.8	-
3. Occasionally but not regularly	17.1	15.5	18.3	19.1	8.2	16.7	17.9	15.1	19.7	18.3	15.3	8.3	24.7	23.2	22.6	8.4
4. Regularly in the past	6.4	5.0	7.3	6.6	2.9	7.3	7.1	5.0	6.2	5.0	7.1	2.1	6.7	7.0	12.2	11.6
5. Regularly now	16.0	14.5	16.5	16.8	5.4	20.1	17.9	12.6	13.3	8.5	24.9	3.7	11.9	17.3	39.1	67.6
Item 760 Subject A01a N	3237	1478	1631	2371	388	760	886	973	618	1790	1103	1277	710	433	706	28
B002: When did you first smoke cigarettes on a daily basis?																
0. Never smoked daily	51.8	56.7	49.0	51.9	62.1	47.4	52.7	53.6	53.5	61.6	42.3	68.5	59.2	55.9	32.4	3.2
1. Grade 6 or earlier	5.8	6.9	4.6	5.5	4.0	4.6	6.7	5.5	6.3	5.4	5.7	5.8	4.9	2.5	6.5	32.7
2. Grade 7 or 8	10.8	9.6	11.7	10.6	8.9	10.9	12.4	10.3	9.0	8.2	13.2	7.2	7.9	12.6	15.0	16.9
3. Grade 9 (Freshman)	9.2	7.8	9.8	9.2	7.6	12.2	9.2	7.9	7.3	6.0	12.5	3.6	9.6	8.1	12.9	19.6
4. Grade 10 (Sophomore)	8.9	7.0	10.2	8.7	7.2	11.6	5.8	9.5	9.0	7.4	10.6	4.9	6.3	8.6	14.1	20.8
5. Grade 11 (Junior)	8.4	8.0	8.8	8.9	6.7	9.3	7.9	8.5	8.1	6.6	11.1	6.0	6.8	8.5	12.3	6.7
6. Grade 12 (Senior)	5.1	4.0	5.9	5.3	3.6	4.0	5.4	4.7	6.8	4.9	4.5	4.0	5.3	3.8	6.9	-
Item 1680 Subject A01g N★	2224	967	1149	1644	242	541	626	642	415	1116	826	526	611	354	652	25

★=excludes respondents for whom question was inappropriate.

QUESTIONNAIRE FORM 1 1985	TOTAL	SEX		RACE		REGION				4YR COLLEGE PLANS		ILLICIT DRUG USE: LIFETIME				
		M	F	White	Black	NE	NC	S	W	Yes	No	None	Mari-juana Only	Few Pills	More Pills	Any Her-oin
N (Weighted No. of Cases):	3316	1505	1663	2415	400	783	902	1004	627	1822	1121	1307	719	444	716	29
% of Weighted Total:	100.0	45.4	50.2	72.8	12.1	23.6	27.2	30.3	18.9	55.0	33.8	39.4	21.7	13.4	21.6	0.9
B003: How frequently have you smoked cigarettes during the past 30 days?																
1. Not at all	56.8	57.4	56.9	54.2	80.2	54.4	52.7	61.2	59.4	66.5	47.1	76.3	64.9	59.6	34.2	4.7
2. Less than one cigarette per day	14.9	16.0	14.3	16.0	7.9	12.5	16.5	14.3	16.5	14.8	14.1	12.1	15.9	14.5	16.7	8.4
3. One to five cigarettes per day	10.7	9.0	12.6	11.3	9.2	9.5	11.8	10.0	11.6	10.2	12.3	5.2	10.7	13.2	13.5	12.2
4. About one-half pack per day	8.7	8.7	7.9	8.8	1.5	12.8	8.5	6.7	6.8	4.3	13.2	4.5	3.8	7.6	17.0	24.3
5. About one pack per day	7.2	6.9	7.3	8.2	1.2	9.5	8.7	5.8	4.1	3.6	10.7	1.8	3.8	4.6	15.3	24.0
6. About one and one-half packs per day	1.3	1.6	0.8	1.5	-	1.1	1.5	1.7	0.7	0.6	2.1	0.1	0.7	0.5	2.9	15.6
7. Two packs or more per day	0.4	0.4	0.2	0.1	-	0.2	0.4	0.3	0.8	0.1	0.6	-	0.2	-	0.4	10.8
Item 780 Subject A01c N★	*2229*	*972*	*1151*	*1649*	*242*	*539*	*630*	*646*	*415*	*1121*	*828*	*527*	*614*	*354*	*652*	*25*
B004: Have you ever tried to stop smoking and found that you could not?																
1. Yes	16.9	14.8	18.3	16.0	14.4	22.8	15.3	15.0	14.4	11.3	22.5	7.8	12.6	14.1	26.1	63.0
2. No	83.1	85.2	81.7	84.0	85.6	77.2	84.7	85.0	85.6	88.7	77.5	92.2	87.4	85.9	73.9	37.0
Item 1690 Subject A01i N★	*2130*	*926*	*1099*	*1580*	*227*	*514*	*604*	*609*	*403*	*1064*	*794*	*487*	*583*	*338*	*641*	*25*
B005: Do you want to stop smoking now?																
1. Yes	14.7	12.8	15.5	14.4	10.3	18.7	16.4	11.3	12.2	9.5	18.6	6.6	12.2	15.0	21.6	39.0
2. No	18.3	18.4	17.6	19.9	4.0	16.9	20.1	17.0	19.4	13.9	22.8	7.3	13.9	14.5	32.5	46.3
8. Don't smoke now	67.0	68.8	66.9	65.7	85.7	64.4	63.5	71.6	68.4	76.6	58.6	86.1	74.0	70.4	45.9	14.7
Item 1700 Subject A01i N★	*2193*	*955*	*1132*	*1622*	*236*	*525*	*622*	*634*	*411*	*1101*	*817*	*512*	*610*	*347*	*643*	*25*
B006: Do you think you will be smoking cigarettes five years from now?																
1. I definitely will	0.8	0.9	0.4	0.5	0.5	0.6	1.2	0.6	0.7	0.4	1.1	0.3	0.2	0.8	1.0	15.6
2. I probably will	13.7	11.7	15.0	14.3	7.4	16.0	14.6	13.3	10.1	9.0	19.7	4.5	11.7	12.4	31.5	50.7
3. I probably will not	24.7	24.8	24.2	24.2	22.7	25.2	28.2	22.2	23.0	21.0	27.8	17.2	29.1	33.0	29.1	21.9
4. I definitely will not	60.8	62.7	60.4	61.0	69.4	58.3	56.0	63.8	66.3	69.6	51.4	78.0	58.9	53.9	38.4	11.8
Item 1710 Subject A04a N	*3243*	*1475*	*1632*	*2366*	*393*	*754*	*886*	*983*	*619*	*1786*	*1103*	*1282*	*712*	*429*	*703*	*29*

The different questionnaire forms used in this study tend to emphasize somewhat different topics. The next major section in this form deals with alcohol and various other drugs. There is a lot of talk these days about these subjects, but very little accurate information. Therefore, we still have a lot to learn about the actual experiences and attitudes of people your age.

We hope that you can answer all questions; but if you find one which you feel you cannot answer honestly, we would prefer that you leave it blank.

Remember that your answers will be strictly confidential. We never connect them with your name or your class.

The next questions are about ALCOHOLIC BEVERAGES, including beer, wine, and liquor.

B007: On how many occasions (if any) have you had alcohol to drink . . .

B007A: . . . in your lifetime?

	TOTAL	M	F	White	Black	NE	NC	S	W	Yes	No	None	Mari-juana Only	Few Pills	More Pills	Any Her-oin
1. 0 occasions	7.4	7.4	7.0	5.7	16.4	4.7	5.8	10.9	7.8	7.4	7.5	16.1	0.7	1.7	0.6	-
2. 1-2	10.4	9.4	11.5	7.9	22.7	7.7	10.0	13.5	9.4	10.3	11.2	19.4	5.2	6.9	1.3	-
3. 3-5	9.4	8.5	10.8	8.5	17.1	7.9	9.4	12.1	7.3	9.6	9.7	14.8	7.6	9.4	2.0	-
4. 6-9	8.4	7.5	9.4	7.5	13.1	9.4	8.4	8.6	7.0	9.8	7.0	11.7	8.0	7.7	3.4	5.8
5. 10-19	12.3	10.4	14.2	12.4	11.2	10.9	12.6	12.0	14.2	12.9	12.6	12.8	16.0	13.9	7.1	13.0
6. 20-39	14.2	12.3	16.3	15.5	9.0	17.4	14.5	11.3	14.5	15.0	14.0	11.6	19.4	15.5	15.5	5.9
7. 40 or more	37.8	44.5	30.8	42.5	10.5	42.1	39.5	31.5	39.9	35.0	38.1	13.7	43.2	47.1	70.2	75.3
Item 810 Subject A01a N	*3125*	*1435*	*1567*	*2315*	*358*	*735*	*856*	*931*	*602*	*1740*	*1057*	*1252*	*689*	*413*	*676*	*29*

★=excludes respondents for whom question was inappropriate.

QUESTIONNAIRE FORM 1 1985	TOTAL	SEX		RACE		REGION				4YR COLLEGE PLANS		ILLICIT DRUG USE: LIFETIME				
		M	F	White	Black	NE	NC	S	W	Yes	No	None	Marijuana Only	Few Pills	More Pills	Any Heroin
N (Weighted No. of Cases):	3316	1505	1663	2415	400	783	902	1004	627	1822	1121	1307	719	444	716	29
% of Weighted Total:	100.0	45.4	50.2	72.8	12.1	23.6	27.2	30.3	18.9	55.0	33.8	39.4	21.7	13.4	21.6	0.9
B007B: ... during the last 12 months?																
1. 0 occasions	16.1	15.6	16.5	12.9	33.2	11.1	14.8	21.6	15.6	15.7	18.0	31.8	4.7	7.6	2.9	6.0
2. 1-2	15.2	13.2	17.5	13.3	27.6	14.3	14.5	18.4	12.4	16.5	14.3	22.7	13.7	12.7	4.6	9.8
3. 3-5	12.8	11.3	14.5	12.1	14.7	14.5	12.0	12.6	12.2	14.1	10.3	14.8	13.1	14.7	8.3	10.1
4. 6-9	12.3	10.7	14.1	12.7	8.2	12.6	12.0	11.6	13.3	12.6	13.0	11.3	16.2	15.7	8.8	8.6
5. 10-19	15.4	15.2	15.3	16.8	7.9	17.9	15.8	12.8	15.5	14.3	17.3	9.3	20.0	19.2	19.5	15.5
6. 20-39	12.6	13.4	11.9	14.6	3.4	10.9	14.1	10.0	16.4	12.6	11.6	5.8	15.6	15.7	20.0	14.1
7. 40 or more	15.7	20.6	10.3	17.7	4.9	18.7	16.9	13.1	14.5	14.2	15.5	4.1	16.9	14.4	36.0	36.0
Item 820 Subject A01b N	*3120*	*1432*	*1566*	*2317*	*349*	*736*	*858*	*925*	*600*	*1745*	*1046*	*1246*	*687*	*413*	*678*	*28*
B007C: ... during the last 30 days?																
1. 0 occasions	37.0	33.7	40.6	32.1	64.2	31.7	35.6	44.8	33.5	38.5	37.5	60.4	23.1	26.9	13.7	33.6
2. 1-2	23.4	21.5	25.0	23.8	22.0	24.4	22.8	22.1	25.1	24.8	21.7	22.4	30.7	26.2	18.0	4.1
3. 3-5	16.9	17.5	17.0	18.9	5.3	18.5	17.4	13.4	19.7	16.9	17.1	10.2	19.9	21.9	23.7	15.7
4. 6-9	10.6	11.2	9.8	11.9	5.0	11.1	11.2	8.7	11.9	9.8	10.5	3.6	13.6	14.3	17.8	10.4
5. 10-19	7.6	9.7	5.2	8.5	2.3	7.4	9.2	6.7	6.8	6.4	7.9	2.3	8.2	9.2	15.5	15.9
6. 20-39	2.3	3.2	1.3	2.6	0.2	3.1	2.3	2.2	1.7	1.5	3.0	0.6	3.0	0.6	5.2	9.4
7. 40 or more	2.2	3.3	1.1	2.2	1.0	3.8	1.6	2.2	1.3	2.1	2.3	0.6	1.6	1.0	6.2	11.0
Item 830 Subject A01c N	*3124*	*1434*	*1570*	*2325*	*348*	*738*	*859*	*922*	*604*	*1748*	*1045*	*1241*	*686*	*414*	*686*	*28*

IF YOU HAVE NOT HAD ANY BEER, WINE, OR LIQUOR IN THE LAST TWELVE MONTHS, GO TO Q.B017.

B008: When you used alcohol during the last year, how often did you use it in each of the following situations?

	TOTAL	M	F	White	Black	NE	NC	S	W	Yes	No	None	Marijuana Only	Few Pills	More Pills	Any Heroin
B008A: When you were alone																
1. Not at all	73.0	65.7	80.8	73.3	75.1	70.0	75.3	74.3	71.6	76.5	69.1	84.4	75.2	72.3	57.9	47.8
2. A few of the times	21.6	26.6	16.8	21.8	19.5	24.0	19.7	20.8	22.5	19.4	25.0	13.3	20.3	23.0	32.7	25.0
3. Some of the times	3.9	5.5	1.9	3.7	3.6	4.5	4.0	3.1	4.0	2.7	4.7	1.4	3.4	3.2	7.0	25.1
4. Most of the times	1.1	1.5	0.5	0.9	1.8	1.1	0.8	1.4	1.1	1.0	0.7	0.6	0.6	1.3	1.8	2.1
5. Every time	0.4	0.7	*	0.3	-	0.4	0.2	0.3	0.8	0.4	0.4	0.3	0.6	0.3	0.5	-
Item 1720 Subject A05a N★	*2622*	*1200*	*1318*	*2022*	*238*	*656*	*737*	*716*	*513*	*1458*	*867*	*826*	*655*	*390*	*674*	*25*
B008B: With just 1 or 2 other people																
1. Not at all	13.1	9.5	16.7	12.5	15.6	13.3	14.4	12.9	11.2	15.9	9.0	26.1	8.4	7.3	4.6	4.1
2. A few of the times	32.7	30.5	35.5	31.3	46.3	32.1	34.0	31.2	33.8	34.7	30.1	37.4	34.5	38.3	22.6	23.1
3. Some of the times	24.0	26.6	21.7	25.2	14.2	26.9	22.2	20.2	28.1	22.7	26.3	12.5	24.4	27.0	35.6	43.9
4. Most of the times	23.4	26.1	20.0	24.7	16.3	22.1	23.9	26.7	19.4	20.8	26.6	15.5	25.9	23.7	30.9	24.4
5. Every time	6.8	7.3	6.0	6.3	7.6	5.5	5.4	8.9	7.5	5.8	7.9	8.4	6.9	3.7	6.3	4.5
Item 1730 Subject A05b N★	*2627*	*1201*	*1322*	*2025*	*239*	*655*	*740*	*718*	*515*	*1461*	*870*	*831*	*654*	*391*	*674*	*25*
B008C: At a party																
1. Not at all	13.8	13.5	14.1	12.8	26.2	10.8	11.6	20.3	11.8	14.2	15.1	27.2	8.6	9.6	5.1	-
2. A few of the times	18.7	16.8	20.6	17.3	33.3	17.2	18.6	20.3	18.7	18.3	19.0	22.8	21.3	17.8	11.8	2.1
3. Some of the times	16.0	16.2	15.9	15.9	16.0	14.9	15.8	15.7	18.0	15.8	15.3	12.6	18.0	19.7	16.4	27.5
4. Most of the times	31.2	31.2	31.6	33.7	14.3	34.2	32.1	25.8	33.8	34.6	27.1	23.8	33.2	33.1	37.0	32.3
5. Every time	20.3	22.3	17.8	20.2	10.2	22.9	21.9	18.0	17.8	17.0	23.5	13.6	19.0	19.7	29.7	38.1
Item 1740 Subject A05c N★	*2619*	*1195*	*1320*	*2018*	*239*	*658*	*737*	*709*	*515*	*1459*	*863*	*826*	*652*	*391*	*672*	*25*
B008D: When your date or spouse was present																
1. Not at all	36.4	42.4	31.2	32.5	61.0	37.0	35.3	37.8	35.1	38.1	35.7	55.3	32.5	33.3	18.0	25.1
2. A few of the times	25.7	26.5	25.3	25.9	28.0	26.7	24.0	25.9	26.5	25.6	24.6	22.1	30.7	26.7	25.5	17.8
3. Some of the times	17.9	18.2	17.4	19.5	7.0	18.7	18.8	14.8	19.9	17.7	17.0	9.8	17.9	21.6	25.7	27.4
4. Most of the times	13.6	9.2	17.5	15.1	2.1	13.4	13.0	14.0	14.1	13.3	14.8	7.0	13.0	11.9	23.6	16.4
5. Every time	6.4	3.7	8.5	7.0	1.9	4.2	8.8	7.5	4.4	5.3	7.9	5.9	6.0	6.5	7.2	13.4
Item 1750 Subject A05b N★	*2604*	*1188*	*1312*	*2006*	*239*	*646*	*735*	*712*	*511*	*1446*	*863*	*820*	*650*	*390*	*669*	*25*

*=less than .05 per cent.   ★=excludes respondents for whom question was inappropriate.

QUESTIONNAIRE FORM 1 1985	TOTAL	SEX		RACE		REGION				4YR COLLEGE PLANS		ILLICIT DRUG USE: LIFETIME				
		M	F	White	Black	NE	NC	S	W	Yes	No	None	Marijuana Only	Few Pills	More Pills	Any Heroin
N (Weighted No. of Cases):	3316	1505	1663	2415	400	783	902	1004	627	1822	1121	1307	719	444	716	29
% of Weighted Total:	100.0	45.4	50.2	72.8	12.1	23.6	27.2	30.3	18.9	55.0	33.8	39.4	21.7	13.4	21.6	0.9
B008E: When people over age 30 were present																
1. Not at all	35.2	34.3	36.5	33.6	54.7	29.2	36.6	39.8	34.4	36.8	34.0	42.3	41.5	30.6	23.2	18.4
2. A few of the times	37.0	38.8	35.3	38.8	23.6	41.6	38.4	33.0	34.9	38.0	35.0	31.3	38.8	46.3	37.7	41.9
3. Some of the times	15.7	15.6	15.6	15.9	13.2	16.0	15.1	14.3	18.1	13.2	18.2	9.0	12.2	16.0	26.5	24.3
4. Most of the times	7.7	7.3	8.1	7.4	5.0	9.1	5.4	8.4	8.1	7.1	9.2	8.2	5.5	5.5	10.1	9.3
5. Every time	4.4	3.9	4.5	4.3	3.5	4.1	4.4	4.5	4.6	4.8	3.5	9.2	1.9	1.7	2.5	6.2
Item 1760 Subject A05b N★	2616	1197	1315	2016	237	653	738	713	513	1453	868	825	653	390	675	25
B008F: During the daytime (before 4:00 p.m.)																
1. Not at all	58.8	50.6	67.6	56.6	74.0	54.5	64.5	60.9	53.2	62.0	57.1	76.1	62.7	53.6	38.2	6.5
2. A few of the times	29.4	33.7	25.1	31.4	18.2	29.8	27.4	27.9	34.0	27.7	30.2	18.4	29.0	36.3	39.3	50.5
3. Some of the times	9.3	12.3	6.0	9.8	5.3	12.1	6.5	8.3	11.1	8.5	9.7	3.0	6.6	8.9	18.8	35.4
4. Most of the times	1.6	2.1	0.9	1.3	2.4	2.1	0.8	1.8	1.5	1.3	1.5	1.2	0.8	1.2	2.7	7.6
5. Every time	0.9	1.3	0.4	1.0	-	1.4	0.8	1.1	0.2	0.4	1.5	1.3	0.9	-	0.9	-
Item 1770 Subject A05c N★	2617	1197	1317	2017	239	656	737	711	513	1453	868	823	654	389	676	24
B008G: At your home (or apartment or dorm)																
1. Not at all	40.3	36.7	44.4	39.7	50.1	34.5	43.5	47.8	32.6	40.5	41.5	50.9	43.0	38.8	25.5	24.2
2. A few of the times	31.4	32.9	30.1	31.3	25.4	32.7	31.1	30.0	32.3	31.9	30.0	27.8	32.7	34.6	33.1	22.7
3. Some of the times	17.5	18.9	15.7	18.3	14.0	20.3	15.8	13.2	22.1	17.0	17.3	9.1	16.9	17.9	28.1	32.9
4. Most of the times	7.0	7.4	6.4	6.9	8.0	8.6	6.3	4.7	8.9	6.4	7.4	4.8	6.1	5.8	10.7	20.2
5. Every time	3.9	4.1	3.4	3.8	2.4	3.8	3.3	4.4	4.1	4.2	3.8	7.4	1.3	3.0	2.6	-
Item 1780 Subject A05c N★	2614	1199	1312	2014	239	653	737	711	514	1451	866	826	651	386	677	24
B008H: At school																
1. Not at all	86.6	82.3	91.5	87.3	87.2	83.5	90.6	89.7	80.6	88.8	86.3	97.9	86.9	86.6	73.4	65.6
2. A few of the times	10.0	13.1	6.7	10.0	7.0	12.5	7.2	7.5	14.5	8.7	10.7	1.9	9.2	9.9	20.4	22.5
3. Some of the times	2.4	3.2	1.4	2.1	3.6	2.7	1.6	1.8	3.7	2.1	1.9	0.2	2.5	3.3	4.5	1.8
4. Most of the times	0.4	0.6	0.2	0.2	1.4	0.5	0.1	0.4	0.7	0.1	0.5	-	1.0	0.2	0.4	2.1
5. Every time	0.6	0.8	0.2	0.4	0.8	0.7	0.5	0.6	0.6	0.4	0.6	-	0.5	-	1.3	7.9
Item 1790 Subject A05c N★	2619	1201	1315	2018	238	656	736	715	512	1456	868	825	654	389	677	24
B008I: In a car																
1. Not at all	40.2	34.5	46.0	38.2	54.0	49.9	35.6	35.0	41.6	45.2	34.5	59.3	36.1	35.9	23.7	19.4
2. A few of the times	24.8	24.8	24.7	25.0	21.9	21.1	23.9	28.1	26.5	23.0	27.2	20.4	27.2	26.6	27.2	22.9
3. Some of the times	20.4	22.9	17.8	21.8	13.1	19.5	24.4	19.2	17.7	19.0	21.7	10.8	20.6	22.2	30.6	25.1
4. Most of the times	11.8	14.1	9.6	12.1	9.3	7.9	13.1	14.5	11.1	10.8	12.7	8.4	12.5	13.2	14.7	15.1
5. Every time	2.8	3.7	1.9	2.9	1.7	1.6	3.1	3.3	3.1	2.0	3.8	1.2	3.6	2.0	3.7	17.5
Item 1810 Subject A05c N★	2619	1200	1317	2020	238	656	737	714	513	1455	869	825	654	391	676	24
B009: What have been the most important reasons for your drinking alcoholic beverages? (Mark all that apply.)																
A. To experiment–to see what it's like	44.5	43.2	46.3	41.8	65.2	39.2	44.4	49.4	44.3	46.2	43.6	54.2	48.3	41.2	31.5	39.3
B. To relax or relieve tension	38.8	38.9	38.4	40.8	21.2	41.9	40.6	34.1	38.9	36.8	41.3	26.1	39.2	45.9	49.5	51.3
C. To feel good or get high	48.5	52.5	43.6	49.9	32.7	54.1	48.0	41.5	52.0	45.7	48.4	23.0	51.7	54.9	70.7	81.3
D. To seek deeper insights and understanding	4.4	6.2	2.4	3.9	4.4	4.7	4.5	3.5	5.1	3.4	4.8	1.1	4.5	4.1	7.2	14.5
E. To have a good time with my friends	71.4	73.6	69.6	73.3	50.9	74.2	76.5	62.2	73.5	70.9	71.4	58.0	75.5	74.5	81.2	86.6
F. To fit in with a group I like	12.1	14.4	10.4	12.4	9.0	9.7	14.1	13.1	10.9	11.8	12.1	12.7	10.8	10.2	13.1	20.4
G. To get away from my problems or troubles	23.4	21.4	24.9	23.4	21.0	23.7	25.4	21.6	22.8	20.1	28.0	13.9	22.6	27.4	31.6	38.9
H. Because of boredom, nothing else to do	22.2	25.0	19.3	22.6	21.6	23.2	23.6	21.1	20.4	19.9	24.0	14.0	21.2	21.4	31.9	39.5
I. Because of anger or frustration	19.4	17.5	20.9	19.6	16.1	18.5	20.3	19.2	19.4	16.3	23.8	11.1	19.4	21.6	27.2	27.9
J. To get through the day	2.5	3.0	1.6	2.2	1.8	3.4	1.5	3.1	2.1	1.9	2.6	0.7	1.6	1.7	4.9	14.4
K. To increase the effects of some other drug(s)	6.6	8.1	4.6	6.0	5.4	7.4	6.5	5.3	7.6	5.0	7.9	0.2	2.0	6.8	16.5	53.6
L. To decrease (offset) the effects of some other drug(s)	1.4	2.0	0.4	1.0	2.0	2.4	0.7	1.0	1.7	0.7	1.6	0.2	0.4	0.7	3.0	18.9
M. To get to sleep	7.4	8.3	6.2	6.7	10.8	7.0	6.5	8.2	8.0	5.9	8.8	5.2	6.5	7.7	9.7	18.9
N. Because it tastes good	44.9	43.8	46.3	47.9	26.5	45.5	46.3	42.1	46.0	45.0	45.5	35.1	42.0	52.0	56.0	41.1
O. Because I am "hooked"–I feel I have to drink	1.8	2.2	1.1	1.4	0.9	3.0	1.8	0.9	1.3	0.9	2.2	0.2	1.0	1.3	4.2	4.0
Item 1820-1960 Subject A06a N★	2571	1185	1288	1991	231	642	728	701	501	1437	847	796	642	388	673	25

★=excludes respondents for whom question was inappropriate.

QUESTIONNAIRE FORM 1 1985	TOTAL	SEX		RACE		REGION				4YR COLLEGE PLANS		ILLICIT DRUG USE: LIFETIME				
		M	F	White	Black	NE	NC	S	W	Yes	No	None	Marijuana Only	Few Pills	More Pills	Any Heroin
N (Weighted No. of Cases):	3316	1505	1663	2415	400	783	902	1004	627	1822	1121	1307	719	444	716	29
% of Weighted Total:	100.0	45.4	50.2	72.8	12.1	23.6	27.2	30.3	18.9	55.0	33.8	39.4	21.7	13.4	21.6	0.9
B010: When you drink alcoholic beverages, how high do you usually get?																
1. Not at all high	19.7	18.8	20.5	17.6	33.2	16.0	19.0	26.0	16.6	21.3	19.2	43.1	11.3	12.3	4.0	2.4
2. A little high	34.8	29.8	39.4	33.1	41.0	36.0	32.8	35.1	35.5	35.4	34.5	35.7	41.8	36.6	25.4	42.6
3. Moderately high	38.5	42.1	35.4	42.1	20.7	41.8	39.3	33.2	40.3	37.1	39.0	19.0	41.5	44.1	57.0	35.7
4. Very high	7.1	9.2	4.7	7.2	5.1	6.1	8.8	5.7	7.6	6.2	7.3	2.2	5.4	6.9	13.6	19.3
Item 1970　Subject A01e　　N★	*2618*	*1198*	*1319*	*2020*	*235*	*653*	*742*	*709*	*514*	*1460*	*866*	*823*	*653*	*395*	*673*	*25*
B011: When you drink alcoholic beverages, how long do you usually stay high?																
1. Usually don't get high	21.5	20.6	22.5	19.6	37.4	17.3	21.1	28.2	18.2	23.2	20.8	46.1	13.8	12.8	5.1	2.4
2. One to two hours	41.5	37.0	45.5	41.0	40.8	43.5	39.9	40.6	42.5	41.9	42.0	35.2	49.6	46.6	37.7	52.8
3. Three to six hours	33.5	38.5	29.3	36.4	18.0	36.0	35.6	28.0	35.1	32.6	32.7	17.8	32.3	37.2	51.6	41.0
4. Seven to 24 hours	3.1	3.2	2.7	2.9	2.6	2.8	3.3	2.8	3.3	2.2	3.8	0.9	3.3	3.3	5.3	1.7
5. More than 24 hours	0.4	0.6	*	0.2	1.3	0.4	0.1	0.4	0.8	-	0.6	-	0.9	-	0.3	2.1
Item 1980　Subject A01f　　N★	*2608*	*1198*	*1308*	*2011*	*235*	*651*	*736*	*707*	*514*	*1455*	*863*	*815*	*652*	*394*	*674*	*25*

The following questions ask about how much you have to drink on the occasions when you drink alcoholic beverages. For these questions, a "drink" means any of the following: A 12-ounce can (or bottle) of beer, a 4-ounce glass of wine, a mixed drink or shot glass of liquor.

	TOTAL	M	F	White	Black	NE	NC	S	W	Yes	No	None	Marijuana Only	Few Pills	More Pills	Any Heroin
B012: Think back over the LAST TWO WEEKS. How many times have you had five or more drinks in a row?																
1. None	62.0	52.1	71.9	59.1	85.3	59.6	59.4	66.8	62.0	66.1	59.9	80.7	62.6	59.8	40.6	28.5
2. Once	12.5	13.4	11.7	13.4	6.5	12.6	12.6	12.0	12.7	12.5	12.0	9.2	12.8	13.4	15.9	10.9
3. Twice	10.3	12.9	8.5	11.6	2.3	11.9	11.5	7.5	10.4	9.4	12.1	5.9	11.1	12.7	14.0	11.6
4. 3 to 5 times	10.4	14.2	6.2	11.3	2.8	10.5	12.5	7.5	11.5	8.5	11.0	3.3	9.7	11.1	19.1	17.2
5. 6 to 9 times	3.0	4.9	1.1	3.1	2.0	2.8	2.7	4.3	2.0	2.2	3.0	0.2	2.7	2.1	6.3	23.1
6. 10 or more times	1.8	2.5	0.7	1.4	1.2	2.5	1.3	2.0	1.4	1.3	2.0	0.7	1.1	0.9	4.0	8.6
Item 850　Subject A01d　　N★	*2590*	*1190*	*1302*	*2003*	*235*	*649*	*735*	*701*	*505*	*1454*	*852*	*826*	*641*	*387*	*662*	*25*
B013: During the last two weeks, how many times have you had 3 or 4 drinks in a row (but no more than that)?																
1. None	60.1	55.1	65.8	57.8	82.7	60.0	59.1	63.2	57.5	64.4	58.5	80.0	59.3	58.3	38.8	39.0
2. Once	16.7	16.5	16.7	17.8	8.9	14.7	17.9	15.8	18.6	16.6	16.0	9.8	20.7	18.9	19.7	15.9
3. Twice	12.4	14.0	10.6	12.6	5.3	14.1	11.5	9.5	15.3	10.6	12.7	6.0	12.2	12.1	20.0	24.7
4. 3 to 5 times	8.0	10.5	5.4	9.0	1.0	7.7	8.4	9.0	6.7	6.7	9.8	3.0	5.6	9.4	15.4	14.1
5. 6 to 9 times	1.9	2.5	1.1	1.7	2.0	2.0	2.5	1.8	0.9	0.9	2.1	1.0	1.1	1.0	4.1	2.2
6. 10 or more times	1.0	1.3	0.4	1.1	-	1.5	0.6	0.7	1.1	0.8	0.9	0.2	1.1	0.3	1.9	4.1
Item 1990　Subject A01d　　N★	*2586*	*1184*	*1306*	*2001*	*236*	*647*	*737*	*696*	*506*	*1444*	*855*	*822*	*642*	*386*	*666*	*25*
B014: During the last two weeks, how many times have you had two drinks in a row (but no more than that)?																
1. None	58.5	56.2	60.9	56.8	70.6	58.4	60.6	58.7	55.3	61.6	55.2	73.6	55.2	57.4	44.0	71.9
2. Once	20.8	19.3	22.0	21.3	18.8	18.7	20.2	22.5	22.0	20.4	21.9	16.4	24.5	24.1	21.4	-
3. Twice	10.7	11.4	10.2	11.0	6.3	11.6	10.7	8.8	12.2	9.5	12.7	5.8	12.1	9.9	15.7	6.1
4. 3 to 5 times	6.3	7.6	5.1	6.8	3.0	6.6	4.1	7.4	7.4	5.7	6.0	3.1	4.9	6.0	11.1	19.8
5. 6 to 9 times	2.5	3.6	1.3	2.9	1.0	3.4	3.1	1.5	1.8	1.9	2.8	0.7	2.4	2.1	5.2	2.2
6. 10 to 19 times	0.7	1.0	0.3	0.7	0.3	0.7	0.7	0.5	0.7	0.6	0.5	-	0.5	0.5	1.7	-
7. 20 or more times	0.6	0.9	0.2	0.5	-	0.7	0.6	0.5	0.6	0.3	0.9	0.3	0.4	-	1.1	-
Item 2000　Subject A01d　　N★	*2547*	*1161*	*1293*	*1974*	*230*	*633*	*726*	*687*	*501*	*1430*	*837*	*810*	*633*	*380*	*654*	*25*

*=less than .05 per cent.　　★=excludes respondents for whom question was inappropriate.

QUESTIONNAIRE FORM 1 1985	TOTAL	SEX		RACE		REGION				4YR COLLEGE PLANS		ILLICIT DRUG USE: LIFETIME				
		M	F	White	Black	NE	NC	S	W	Yes	No	None	Mari- juana Only	Few Pills	More Pills	Any Her- oin
N (Weighted No. of Cases):	3316	1505	1663	2415	400	783	902	1004	627	1822	1121	1307	719	444	716	29
% of Weighted Total:	100.0	45.4	50.2	72.8	12.1	23.6	27.2	30.3	18.9	55.0	33.8	39.4	21.7	13.4	21.6	0.9

B015: During the last two weeks, how many times have you had just one drink?

1. None	56.9	56.2	57.7	55.8	64.9	58.2	60.5	56.3	50.9	58.1	56.0	64.2	52.5	60.4	50.3	69.4
2. Once	25.9	23.9	27.8	26.9	21.9	21.5	25.4	27.6	29.9	26.1	27.4	24.7	27.7	25.0	27.3	1.6
3. Twice	9.6	10.0	9.3	9.4	8.8	11.0	7.8	10.2	9.7	9.3	9.3	8.0	12.2	7.1	9.8	10.0
4. 3 to 5 times	5.5	7.0	4.2	5.7	3.7	6.8	4.8	4.0	7.0	5.0	5.0	2.7	5.2	6.4	8.5	16.8
5. 6 to 9 times	1.0	1.1	0.6	0.9	0.7	1.7	0.3	0.9	1.3	0.7	0.7	0.1	1.7	0.8	1.5	-
6. 10 to 19 times	0.7	1.1	0.3	0.8	-	0.8	0.8	0.5	0.5	0.5	1.0	0.1	0.3	0.4	1.8	2.3
7. 20 or more times	0.4	0.7	0.1	0.4	-	-	0.4	0.5	0.7	0.3	0.5	0.1	0.4	-	0.8	-
Item 2010　Subject A01d　N★	2484	1132	1261	1933	224	614	711	672	487	1383	827	784	617	373	642	24

B016: Have you ever tried to stop using alcoholic beverages and found that you couldn't stop?

1. Yes	4.5	4.7	4.2	3.5	10.4	3.7	3.6	5.4	5.4	3.1	6.2	2.5	4.0	4.7	6.3	9.8
2. No	95.5	95.3	95.8	96.5	89.6	96.3	96.4	94.6	94.6	96.9	93.8	97.5	96.0	95.3	93.7	90.2
Item 2020　Subject A01i　N★	2576	1180	1299	1998	225	645	729	696	506	1437	856	807	642	390	668	25

B017: Do you think you will be drinking alcoholic beverages five years from now?

1. I definitely will	17.2	19.7	14.6	20.3	4.3	23.2	18.7	11.9	16.0	19.1	12.0	7.9	17.8	19.3	32.0	33.1
2. I probably will	52.3	51.1	53.5	55.6	32.3	54.3	56.6	46.0	53.7	51.1	54.7	46.9	56.6	59.0	55.4	53.4
3. I probably will not	14.8	14.1	15.5	11.9	27.4	11.5	13.4	19.5	13.5	14.7	15.8	19.6	13.7	14.7	6.5	9.4
4. I definitely will not	15.7	15.2	16.4	12.2	35.9	11.0	11.3	22.7	16.9	15.1	17.5	25.6	11.9	7.0	6.1	4.1
Item 2030　Subject A04a　N	3264	1495	1640	2386	398	767	889	984	624	1804	1114	1294	712	438	710	28

The next questions are about MARIJUANA and HASHISH.

Marijuana is sometimes called: grass, pot, dope.

Hashish is sometimes called: hash, hash oil.

B018: On how many occasions (if any) have you used hashish . . .

B018A: . . . in your lifetime?

1. 0 occasions	79.5	75.5	84.1	77.7	89.7	71.3	78.2	87.7	78.5	83.7	77.2	100.0	81.7	74.2	45.5	19.5
2. 1-2	9.4	10.4	8.3	10.3	6.3	10.6	10.3	6.0	11.7	7.8	9.6	-	13.0	16.3	17.9	21.9
3. 3-5	3.3	4.0	2.6	3.9	0.6	5.1	3.1	1.8	3.7	3.2	3.2	-	1.6	4.8	10.3	-
4. 6-9	2.3	2.6	1.8	2.4	0.6	3.7	2.8	1.1	2.0	1.8	2.6	-	1.7	1.7	7.5	5.6
5. 10-19	2.4	2.9	1.9	2.8	0.7	4.7	1.9	1.0	2.2	1.6	3.3	-	1.1	1.9	8.0	14.4
6. 20-39	1.0	1.4	0.5	0.8	1.3	0.8	1.7	1.0	0.3	0.6	1.5	-	0.3	0.3	3.4	7.4
7. 40 or more	2.2	3.2	0.8	2.1	0.9	3.9	2.1	1.3	1.6	1.3	2.7	-	0.6	0.9	7.5	31.2
Item 2040　Subject A01a　N	3240	1487	1631	2390	383	760	884	973	622	1802	1103	1307	718	439	702	28

B018B: . . . during the last 12 months?

1. 0 occasions	88.5	85.6	91.7	87.3	96.6	83.3	87.7	94.1	87.0	90.9	87.3	100.0	92.7	88.0	65.3	31.8
2. 1-2	6.3	7.1	5.7	7.3	1.5	8.2	6.6	3.1	8.6	5.5	6.4	-	5.7	8.4	16.8	26.8
3. 3-5	2.0	2.6	1.3	2.3	0.5	3.3	1.8	0.8	2.5	1.3	2.6	-	0.5	1.5	7.2	10.9
4. 6-9	1.0	1.1	0.6	0.9	0.6	1.0	1.8	0.5	0.6	0.4	1.4	-	0.8	1.0	3.0	3.3
5. 10-19	1.2	2.0	0.4	1.4	0.3	2.7	0.7	0.8	0.8	1.1	1.1	-	-	0.4	4.7	8.0
6. 20-39	0.5	0.7	0.3	0.5	-	0.9	0.7	0.2	0.2	0.3	0.7	-	0.2	0.7	1.1	8.3
7. 40 or more	0.6	0.9	0.1	0.4	0.5	0.5	0.8	0.6	0.3	0.4	0.6	-	0.2	-	2.0	10.8
Item 2050　Subject A01b　N	3232	1477	1632	2384	382	759	881	972	620	1799	1096	1307	717	436	698	28

B018C: . . . during the last 30 days?

1. 0 occasions	95.4	93.5	97.9	95.3	98.3	92.7	95.4	97.1	96.3	96.5	95.6	100.0	98.1	96.8	85.1	62.5
2. 1-2	2.3	3.2	1.3	2.6	0.6	3.3	2.4	1.0	3.2	1.7	2.2	-	1.4	1.8	7.3	13.7
3. 3-5	1.0	1.3	0.5	1.1	0.3	2.4	0.6	0.5	0.5	0.8	0.8	-	0.1	0.9	3.6	6.1
4. 6-9	0.6	1.1	0.1	0.7	0.3	0.6	0.9	0.8	-	0.3	1.1	-	0.3	0.1	1.9	9.3
5. 10-19	0.5	0.7	0.2	0.3	-	0.6	0.5	0.7	-	0.4	0.4	-	-	0.4	1.7	1.5
6. 20-39	*	-	-	-	-	0.1	-	-	-	-	-	-	-	-	0.1	-
7. 40 or more	0.2	0.2	0.1	*	0.5	0.3	0.3	-	-	0.2	-	-	0.1	-	0.4	6.8
Item 2060　Subject A01c　N	3231	1479	1631	2385	381	758	881	972	620	1799	1097	1307	717	436	698	28

*=less than .05 per cent.　★=excludes respondents for whom question was inappropriate.

QUESTIONNAIRE FORM 1 1985	TOTAL	SEX		RACE		REGION				4YR COLLEGE PLANS		ILLICIT DRUG USE: LIFETIME				
		M	F	White	Black	NE	NC	S	W	Yes	No	None	Mari-juana Only	Few Pills	More Pills	Any Her-oin
N (Weighted No. of Cases):	3316	1505	1663	2415	400	783	902	1004	627	1822	1121	1307	719	444	716	29
% of Weighted Total:	100.0	45.4	50.2	72.8	12.1	23.6	27.2	30.3	18.9	55.0	33.8	39.4	21.7	13.4	21.6	0.9

B019: On how many occasions (if any) have you used marijuana . . .

B019A: . . . in your lifetime?

1. 0 occasions	45.8	43.5	48.8	44.6	50.5	39.6	46.8	54.5	38.2	51.1	42.4	100.0	0.9	20.6	8.7	-
2. 1-2	11.8	10.8	13.0	11.3	16.0	9.1	11.6	14.6	11.2	11.5	12.4	-	35.4	18.3	6.2	12.5
3. 3-5	7.0	7.1	7.3	7.6	7.1	7.8	6.3	7.0	7.0	7.6	6.6	-	19.4	11.0	5.3	1.9
4. 6-9	5.2	5.0	5.2	5.0	7.2	6.6	4.5	4.4	6.1	5.0	4.8	-	13.7	7.5	4.9	-
5. 10-19	7.5	6.2	8.7	8.1	5.0	7.0	7.4	6.2	10.2	7.7	6.9	-	11.8	14.9	12.6	-
6. 20-39	5.8	6.2	5.3	6.0	4.4	7.7	5.1	4.1	7.0	5.4	6.5	-	7.5	10.9	11.8	5.4
7. 40 or more	16.9	21.2	11.6	17.3	9.8	22.2	18.3	9.3	20.3	11.8	20.4	-	11.2	16.8	50.6	80.2
Item 2070 Subject A01a N	3205	1473	1612	2369	373	746	873	969	617	1787	1081	1307	717	427	702	28

B019B: . . . during the last 12 months?

1. 0 occasions	59.2	56.8	62.5	57.9	66.8	51.4	59.0	70.2	52.0	63.4	57.8	100.0	36.4	39.3	20.6	13.7
2. 1-2	10.5	10.6	10.5	10.6	10.8	10.5	10.2	9.8	11.6	10.6	10.1	-	29.2	14.9	8.7	8.7
3. 3-5	7.8	6.5	9.1	8.3	5.5	11.1	6.2	5.6	9.3	7.7	8.0	-	13.0	15.8	11.8	4.1
4. 6-9	5.1	4.3	5.7	5.0	4.6	5.4	5.9	3.0	6.7	4.8	5.3	-	8.0	10.0	8.6	5.5
5. 10-19	4.9	5.4	4.1	5.4	2.4	5.9	5.0	3.7	5.2	4.7	4.3	-	6.0	6.6	11.6	5.9
6. 20-39	3.4	3.6	3.2	3.5	3.6	3.7	4.2	2.0	4.3	2.1	4.7	-	2.4	4.0	9.7	23.8
7. 40 or more	9.2	12.9	4.9	9.4	6.2	12.0	9.5	5.7	10.9	6.8	9.9	-	5.0	9.4	28.9	38.3
Item 2080 Subject A01b N	3176	1458	1601	2353	367	740	866	958	612	1774	1069	1307	703	420	694	28

B019C: . . . during the last 30 days?

1. 0 occasions	74.2	72.0	77.6	73.8	77.9	69.4	73.2	83.1	67.4	77.9	73.0	100.0	69.8	61.8	40.2	34.1
2. 1-2	9.2	8.1	10.1	9.6	7.5	10.3	8.3	6.3	13.5	9.3	8.3	-	18.1	16.4	13.2	1.7
3. 3-5	4.7	4.4	5.0	4.7	5.1	5.7	5.3	2.6	5.9	4.4	5.1	-	5.8	9.4	9.3	4.2
4. 6-9	3.2	3.9	2.2	3.0	4.1	3.3	3.2	2.0	4.8	2.7	2.9	-	2.7	4.1	8.3	14.0
5. 10-19	4.0	5.1	2.8	4.4	2.2	5.3	5.0	2.9	2.8	2.4	5.3	-	1.7	5.0	13.0	18.2
6. 20-39	2.4	3.3	1.3	2.3	2.1	2.8	2.4	1.7	3.0	1.6	2.6	-	1.3	1.8	7.5	19.3
7. 40 or more	2.3	3.3	1.1	2.2	1.1	3.1	2.6	1.3	2.6	1.6	2.8	-	0.6	1.4	8.6	8.5
Item 2090 Subject A01c N	3177	1460	1600	2354	369	742	864	959	612	1775	1069	1307	703	423	692	28

IF YOU HAVE NOT USED MARIJUANA OR HASHISH IN THE LAST TWELVE MONTHS, GO TO Q.B028.

B020: When you used marijuana or hashish during the last year, how often did you use it in each of the following situations?

B020A: When you were alone

1. Not at all	64.9	56.4	75.4	67.1	61.0	59.7	65.5	69.5	65.9	71.1	60.2	-	83.0	69.1	50.4	25.3
2. A few of the times	21.4	24.3	18.0	19.9	27.6	23.0	21.2	20.9	20.0	18.6	24.6	-	14.5	23.9	25.3	29.7
3. Some of the times	10.0	13.8	5.5	10.4	2.8	12.5	9.1	6.6	11.2	8.5	10.2	-	1.3	5.0	17.6	40.5
4. Most of the times	2.6	3.7	1.0	2.0	5.0	3.3	2.5	2.3	2.2	1.0	4.0	-	0.8	1.1	4.7	4.5
5. Every time	1.2	1.8	0.2	0.7	3.6	1.5	1.6	0.7	0.7	0.7	1.0	-	0.5	0.9	2.0	-
Item 2100 Subject A05a N★	1296	624	605	986	123	358	355	288	295	651	454	-	445	261	546	24

B020B: With just 1 or 2 other people

1. Not at all	7.5	7.4	7.4	7.1	6.0	12.0	6.3	6.3	4.8	8.5	6.4	-	12.8	7.4	3.5	-
2. A few of the times	30.6	25.2	37.7	29.5	44.9	25.0	31.7	34.3	32.5	31.9	29.8	-	38.8	37.3	21.2	24.7
3. Some of the times	19.3	22.8	15.6	19.3	17.6	21.3	18.1	17.6	20.2	18.0	19.2	-	11.4	19.6	26.2	14.3
4. Most of the times	31.2	34.4	27.2	32.7	18.6	31.9	32.5	25.8	33.9	30.2	32.3	-	22.8	24.2	39.5	58.6
5. Every time	11.4	10.2	12.1	11.2	12.9	9.7	11.4	16.1	8.7	11.4	12.3	-	14.1	11.5	9.6	2.4
Item 2110 Subject A05b N★	1303	630	607	991	124	360	361	288	294	654	459	-	447	264	549	24

B020C: At a party

1. Not at all	25.1	21.5	29.6	24.9	37.9	19.5	22.8	37.4	22.5	26.2	24.7	-	39.5	28.2	12.8	3.5
2. A few of the times	24.3	24.4	24.3	24.0	19.9	22.7	26.7	20.2	27.2	25.1	23.0	-	26.5	29.3	21.3	9.7
3. Some of the times	21.4	21.8	21.1	21.4	18.5	25.0	18.2	19.2	22.8	25.0	17.6	-	17.6	20.1	25.0	20.2
4. Most of the times	17.3	18.2	15.9	18.0	11.8	19.7	16.9	13.0	19.0	14.9	19.9	-	10.1	14.9	24.1	23.4
5. Every time	12.0	14.1	9.0	11.7	11.9	13.1	15.3	10.2	8.5	8.8	14.5	-	6.4	7.5	16.8	43.3
Item 2120 Subject A05c N★	1293	622	605	986	120	359	357	285	292	652	450	-	444	258	548	24

★=excludes respondents for whom question was inappropriate.

QUESTIONNAIRE FORM 1 1985	TOTAL	SEX		RACE		REGION				4YR COLLEGE PLANS		ILLICIT DRUG USE: LIFETIME				
		M	F	White	Black	NE	NC	S	W	Yes	No	None	Mari-juana Only	Few Pills	More Pills	Any Her-oin
N (Weighted No. of Cases):	3316	1505	1663	2415	400	783	902	1004	627	1822	1121	1307	719	444	716	29
% of Weighted Total:	100.0	45.4	50.2	72.8	12.1	23.6	27.2	30.3	18.9	55.0	33.8	39.4	21.7	13.4	21.6	0.9

B020D: When your date or spouse was present

1. Not at all	49.5	58.5	41.2	48.1	62.7	45.7	47.6	53.7	52.4	51.1	47.2	-	66.6	53.2	35.2	25.4
2. A few of the times	22.4	20.1	24.8	23.1	17.0	25.0	22.5	20.9	20.6	22.9	21.4	-	16.8	26.2	24.2	35.2
3. Some of the times	12.8	12.0	14.0	13.8	8.2	14.3	12.2	10.8	13.9	13.5	12.5	-	7.0	8.2	19.8	8.8
4. Most of the times	9.9	6.5	12.7	10.2	6.6	9.4	11.9	7.4	10.3	8.5	11.9	-	5.5	7.2	14.1	30.7
5. Every time	5.3	2.9	7.4	4.8	5.5	5.6	5.8	7.2	2.8	4.0	7.0	-	4.0	5.2	6.7	-
Item 2130 Subject A05b N★	1290	624	602	982	124	353	358	285	293	653	449	-	444	259	545	24

B020E: When people over age 30 were present

1. Not at all	67.5	65.3	71.5	68.5	68.5	65.5	68.8	68.1	67.7	75.2	60.2	-	82.3	75.5	54.0	25.9
2. A few of the times	19.7	20.6	18.4	19.4	20.6	20.1	17.9	18.8	22.2	15.4	24.2	-	11.8	16.9	25.8	54.0
3. Some of the times	8.5	9.8	6.1	7.8	7.4	9.1	9.0	7.4	8.3	7.5	8.5	-	3.8	4.8	13.6	13.2
4. Most of the times	2.7	2.7	2.6	2.7	2.6	4.4	1.9	2.9	1.6	1.2	4.3	-	0.6	2.8	4.1	6.9
5. Every time	1.6	1.6	1.4	1.6	0.8	0.9	2.5	2.9	0.2	0.6	2.8	-	1.6	-	2.5	-
Item 2140 Subject A05b N★	1296	628	602	985	123	357	357	287	295	651	453	-	446	261	547	23

B020F: During the daytime (before 4:00 p.m.)

1. Not at all	42.4	37.9	48.6	42.1	60.2	36.7	47.2	47.8	38.0	50.0	37.8	-	63.0	45.9	25.4	16.6
2. A few of the times	23.7	23.4	24.8	24.6	19.2	23.5	20.5	26.5	25.0	23.3	23.6	-	21.4	33.6	20.5	26.3
3. Some of the times	20.1	23.5	16.7	20.9	14.5	22.4	21.9	13.3	21.6	17.3	22.3	-	9.6	13.4	31.5	32.0
4. Most of the times	10.3	11.3	7.3	9.0	4.5	13.1	7.4	7.3	13.4	7.1	12.0	-	3.6	5.8	16.8	22.8
5. Every time	3.6	3.9	2.5	3.4	1.5	4.3	2.9	5.1	2.1	2.3	4.2	-	2.3	1.3	5.7	2.3
Item 2150 Subject A05c N★	1303	630	607	993	124	359	359	290	296	654	457	-	448	262	550	24

B020G: At your home (or apartment or dorm)

1. Not at all	53.9	49.4	60.0	54.4	54.3	50.1	57.6	58.6	49.2	56.5	53.8	-	74.2	56.3	37.6	29.1
2. A few of the times	22.4	24.2	20.8	22.5	24.0	20.6	18.8	26.6	24.9	22.2	21.1	-	14.7	24.0	27.5	31.5
3. Some of the times	12.9	16.1	9.1	13.5	9.3	15.9	13.8	6.2	14.5	11.9	12.7	-	6.5	10.0	19.1	26.1
4. Most of the times	7.4	6.8	7.5	6.8	5.3	8.2	7.2	4.7	9.3	6.6	8.3	-	1.7	7.2	12.0	8.5
5. Every time	3.5	3.5	2.6	2.9	7.1	5.2	2.6	3.9	2.1	2.8	4.0	-	2.8	2.4	3.7	4.9
Item 2160 Subject A05c N★	1296	627	604	989	120	356	359	290	292	653	451	-	444	260	550	24

B020H: At school

1. Not at all	67.0	62.1	74.8	69.7	65.0	62.9	72.1	72.8	60.1	73.8	64.7	-	81.4	75.4	53.7	25.8
2. A few of the times	16.9	19.5	13.7	16.4	21.0	17.9	16.4	14.0	19.0	14.7	17.5	-	11.6	14.3	21.4	29.4
3. Some of the times	8.7	9.8	7.1	8.1	7.3	11.4	5.4	6.7	11.6	6.3	10.2	-	3.5	4.6	14.4	24.0
4. Most of the times	5.0	5.4	3.0	3.8	4.2	5.9	3.5	3.6	7.1	3.9	4.2	-	1.8	3.0	7.5	20.9
5. Every time	2.4	3.3	1.5	1.9	2.4	2.0	2.6	3.0	2.3	1.4	3.4	-	1.7	2.7	3.0	-
Item 2170 Subject A05c N★	1302	629	609	994	122	357	359	291	295	654	457	-	448	262	550	24

B020I: In a car

1. Not at all	27.2	24.0	32.0	28.1	28.1	27.5	20.5	29.0	33.4	33.6	20.6	-	40.0	33.6	15.4	1.6
2. A few of the times	25.2	23.4	27.1	24.4	33.0	22.3	25.3	30.9	23.1	26.2	24.7	-	30.6	25.7	21.0	12.0
3. Some of the times	20.4	24.7	16.9	22.7	15.8	24.1	21.9	13.1	21.3	19.2	21.2	-	13.2	15.8	28.2	36.2
4. Most of the times	21.1	21.5	18.9	19.5	16.9	21.3	23.8	19.4	19.2	16.3	25.2	-	11.8	18.6	27.9	43.0
5. Every time	6.1	6.3	5.0	5.3	6.3	4.8	8.6	7.5	3.0	4.7	8.3	-	4.3	6.2	7.5	7.1
Item 2190 Subject A05c N★	1301	630	607	993	122	356	361	291	294	655	456	-	449	260	550	24

B021: How many of the times when you used marijuana or hashish during the last year did you use it along with alcohol-that is, so that their effects overlapped?

1. Not at all	29.1	28.5	31.0	25.6	51.7	27.6	24.4	36.9	29.1	30.1	30.2	-	43.7	29.7	17.9	3.4
2. A few of the times	31.5	29.1	34.2	32.7	25.8	32.7	27.3	27.8	38.6	32.2	32.0	-	36.4	36.2	25.2	43.2
3. Some of the times	17.8	21.3	14.2	19.5	9.1	17.5	20.4	14.2	18.5	16.7	17.1	-	8.2	17.1	25.7	19.7
4. Most of the times	16.2	15.7	15.3	16.3	12.3	17.0	22.1	12.6	11.6	16.1	15.0	-	7.8	14.1	23.5	24.7
5. Every time	5.4	5.3	5.4	5.8	1.0	5.2	5.8	8.4	2.2	4.9	5.7	-	3.9	2.8	7.7	9.0
Item 2200 Subject A01h N★	1277	623	593	977	122	350	351	284	292	645	447	-	443	257	539	23

★=excludes respondents for whom question was inappropriate.

QUESTIONNAIRE FORM 1 1985	TOTAL	SEX		RACE		REGION				4YR COLLEGE PLANS		ILLICIT DRUG USE: LIFETIME				
		M	F	White	Black	NE	NC	S	W	Yes	No	None	Mari-juana Only	Few Pills	More Pills	Any Her-oin
N (Weighted No. of Cases):	3316	1505	1663	2415	400	783	902	1004	627	1822	1121	1307	719	444	716	29
% of Weighted Total:	100.0	45.4	50.2	72.8	12.1	23.6	27.2	30.3	18.9	55.0	33.8	39.4	21.7	13.4	21.6	0.9

B022: What have been the most important reasons for your using marijuana or hashish? (Mark all that apply.)

	TOTAL	M	F	White	Black	NE	NC	S	W	Yes	No	None	Mari-juana Only	Few Pills	More Pills	Any Her-oin
A. To experiment–to see what it's like	63.9	64.0	65.8	64.0	72.1	55.5	68.8	70.3	61.8	70.3	58.0	-	78.2	65.0	52.1	50.3
B. To relax or relieve tension	42.2	42.3	39.8	42.5	26.7	41.5	44.4	36.4	46.2	38.8	43.7	-	26.0	41.1	54.4	70.6
C. To feel good or get high	74.9	73.9	75.6	76.7	62.1	76.4	79.3	68.7	73.9	72.9	78.4	-	60.5	76.7	84.5	94.7
D. To seek deeper insights and understanding	15.0	19.2	10.2	14.8	12.9	16.1	14.9	13.8	14.8	15.3	13.3	-	7.9	11.5	21.2	38.5
E. To have a good time with my friends	65.7	66.2	64.7	66.0	59.7	69.9	66.3	58.9	66.5	65.6	64.9	-	56.8	63.4	73.8	65.8
F. To fit in with a group I like	11.8	13.7	10.2	12.3	13.1	12.4	13.7	12.6	8.2	10.1	14.8	-	12.7	10.6	11.3	9.1
G. To get away from my problems or troubles	22.4	22.6	22.3	21.5	21.2	20.5	20.1	21.6	28.4	19.3	27.2	-	14.4	22.4	27.4	32.3
H. Because of boredom, nothing else to do	27.0	26.8	26.1	25.9	29.5	27.4	25.9	24.8	29.9	24.2	30.5	-	18.2	20.0	36.0	52.2
I. Because of anger or frustration	16.4	15.7	16.8	15.4	19.5	17.6	17.3	14.6	15.6	13.3	20.5	-	9.7	18.9	19.3	23.5
J. To get through the day	8.4	8.1	7.5	6.6	8.6	9.4	8.5	5.3	10.1	5.7	11.0	-	2.3	2.6	13.6	32.8
K. To increase the effects of some other drug(s)	13.7	16.6	9.0	13.0	9.1	16.4	14.1	11.2	12.3	12.2	14.2	-	4.7	9.7	22.0	27.9
L. To decrease (offset) the effects of some other drug(s)	3.1	4.1	1.6	2.9	2.2	5.4	2.8	1.3	2.5	2.8	2.8	-	-	1.2	5.9	16.3
M. Because I am "hooked"–I have to have it	3.4	4.6	1.8	2.7	5.0	3.1	4.2	2.7	3.3	2.6	3.6	-	0.9	0.9	5.5	14.4
Item 2210-2330 Subject A06a N★	1302	631	606	994	122	359	361	288	295	652	458	-	448	262	549	24

B023: When you use marijuana or hashish how high do you usually get?

	TOTAL	M	F	White	Black	NE	NC	S	W	Yes	No	None	Mari-juana Only	Few Pills	More Pills	Any Her-oin
1. Not at all high	7.2	5.9	8.1	7.0	8.6	5.4	5.8	13.5	4.8	8.6	4.7	-	14.0	9.3	1.0	
2. A little high	27.2	24.4	31.3	27.0	36.0	26.4	26.0	29.1	27.6	28.5	27.7	-	37.4	28.7	18.7	21.5
3. Moderately high	41.8	44.1	40.3	42.9	38.7	46.5	39.0	35.9	45.5	43.0	40.0	-	37.0	44.5	45.3	34.4
4. Very high	23.8	25.6	20.4	23.1	16.8	21.6	29.2	21.6	22.1	19.9	27.6	-	11.6	17.5	35.0	44.0
Item 2340 Subject A01e N★	1298	624	611	993	123	355	361	290	291	648	459	-	447	262	546	24

B024: When you use marijuana or hashish, how long do you usually stay high?

	TOTAL	M	F	White	Black	NE	NC	S	W	Yes	No	None	Mari-juana Only	Few Pills	More Pills	Any Her-oin
1. Usually don't get high	9.3	8.0	10.4	9.0	12.8	7.8	9.9	14.3	5.6	10.6	7.0	-	18.6	10.2	1.8	2.0
2. One to two hours	52.4	50.1	54.6	52.2	50.5	52.5	55.6	48.9	51.8	52.6	53.0	-	53.2	48.1	54.4	44.0
3. Three to six hours	34.0	36.9	31.8	35.5	30.7	36.4	29.8	31.6	38.6	33.6	34.4	-	24.9	39.6	37.8	45.5
4. Seven to 24 hours	3.9	4.3	3.2	3.0	5.1	2.8	4.3	4.5	4.1	3.1	4.8	-	3.1	2.1	5.1	8.5
5. More than 24 hours	0.4	0.7	-	0.4	0.9	0.6	0.5	0.7	-	0.2	0.8	-	0.2	-	0.8	-
Item 2350 Subject A01f N★	1295	627	604	989	122	358	359	289	289	646	460	-	446	258	549	25

B025: During the LAST MONTH, about how many marijuana cigarettes (joints, reefers), or the equivalent, did you smoke a day, on the average? (If you shared them with other people, count only the amount YOU smoked.)

	TOTAL	M	F	White	Black	NE	NC	S	W	Yes	No	None	Mari-juana Only	Few Pills	More Pills	Any Her-oin
1. None	43.5	38.3	50.5	44.9	41.4	40.5	43.0	47.5	43.8	49.7	39.2	-	62.1	47.5	28.6	27.0
2. Less than 1 a day	34.2	35.4	33.9	36.6	27.6	35.6	31.4	32.3	38.1	35.4	33.9	-	27.6	34.8	40.1	16.4
3. 1 a day	7.7	8.9	5.9	7.4	5.2	9.2	7.1	5.8	8.3	6.4	7.7	-	3.9	6.1	11.4	6.4
4. 2 - 3 a day	9.1	10.4	7.1	7.4	15.2	7.5	11.8	9.4	7.5	5.2	12.4	-	4.4	7.3	12.8	25.5
5. 4 - 6 a day	3.6	4.2	2.2	2.6	7.1	4.9	4.6	2.4	1.9	1.8	4.6	-	1.8	2.7	4.4	15.3
6. 7 - 10 a day	1.4	2.1	0.4	0.9	1.4	1.5	0.9	2.7	0.4	0.9	2.0	-	0.2	0.8	2.3	1.7
7. 11 or more a day	0.5	0.8	0.1	0.2	2.2	0.6	1.2	-	0.1	0.5	0.2	-	-	0.8	0.4	7.7
Item 2360 Subject A01d N★	1214	578	574	930	112	335	339	267	272	616	421	-	401	242	529	25

B026: Do you know how much marijuana you have used (in ounces) during the LAST MONTH?

	TOTAL	M	F	White	Black	NE	NC	S	W	Yes	No	None	Mari-juana Only	Few Pills	More Pills	Any Her-oin
8. Don't know	20.7	14.2	26.9	20.7	20.8	16.7	23.6	22.3	20.3	19.4	22.2	-	20.0	21.5	21.2	10.8
1. None	39.4	36.3	44.4	40.4	38.1	39.2	38.2	44.9	35.6	44.0	36.2	-	57.3	38.1	27.5	20.8
2. Less than 1/2 ounce	22.0	26.7	16.4	22.7	20.2	22.6	18.9	18.1	28.9	22.9	19.2	-	16.0	26.5	25.1	8.9
3. About 1/2 ounce	7.2	8.9	5.7	6.9	7.7	7.0	5.9	5.4	11.0	6.2	9.3	-	2.9	7.4	10.2	16.2
4. About 1 ounce	5.9	6.5	5.2	5.6	6.6	7.6	7.0	5.2	3.0	4.4	7.5	-	1.6	3.2	9.8	16.0
5. About 2 ounces	2.5	3.8	0.9	1.8	2.4	3.7	3.2	2.2	0.7	1.6	2.7	-	0.8	2.3	3.3	16.3
6. 3 to 5 ounces	1.7	2.6	0.5	1.6	0.9	2.2	2.3	1.3	0.4	1.2	2.3	-	1.2	1.0	2.1	1.7
7. 6 or more ounces	0.7	1.1	-	0.2	3.2	1.1	0.9	0.5	-	0.3	0.6	-	0.3	-	0.9	9.3
Item 2370 Subject A01d N★	1212	577	574	930	110	334	340	266	272	616	422	-	402	242	528	25

★=excludes respondents for whom question was inappropriate.

QUESTIONNAIRE FORM 1 1985	TOTAL	SEX		RACE		REGION				4YR COLLEGE PLANS		ILLICIT DRUG USE: LIFETIME				
		M	F	White	Black	NE	NC	S	W	Yes	No	None	Marijuana Only	Few Pills	More Pills	Any Heroin
N (Weighted No. of Cases):	3316	1505	1663	2415	400	783	902	1004	627	1822	1121	1307	719	444	716	29
% of Weighted Total:	100.0	45.4	50.2	72.8	12.1	23.6	27.2	30.3	18.9	55.0	33.8	39.4	21.7	13.4	21.6	0.9
B027: Have you ever tried to stop using marijuana or hashish and found that you couldn't stop?																
1. Yes	5.9	6.8	4.2	4.1	12.5	6.4	5.0	3.9	8.4	4.1	6.2	-	3.9	3.8	7.9	7.1
2. No	94.1	93.2	95.8	95.9	87.5	93.6	95.0	96.1	91.6	95.9	93.8	-	96.1	96.2	92.1	92.9
Item 2380 Subject A01i N★	1281	619	602	986	117	352	355	284	290	638	457	-	439	257	545	25
B028: Thinking back over your whole life, has there ever been a period when you used marijuana or hashish on a daily, or almost daily, basis for at least a month?																
1. No–GO TO QUESTION B032.	84.5	82.4	88.0	84.6	91.4	79.3	83.8	91.2	81.5	89.5	80.4	100.0	90.7	82.7	55.0	29.6
2. Yes	15.5	17.6	12.0	15.4	8.6	20.7	16.2	8.8	18.5	10.5	19.6	-	9.3	17.3	45.0	70.4
Item 21180 Subject A01a N	3147	1441	1595	2329	372	737	869	940	600	1755	1067	1228	702	428	695	29
B029: How old were you when you first smoked marijuana or hashish that frequently?																
1. Grade 6 or earlier	7.7	9.9	3.9	7.2	4.0	10.0	9.4	7.8	2.5	6.8	7.0	-	5.1	4.7	7.0	33.8
2. Grade 7 or 8	23.0	25.3	21.2	22.5	17.5	20.2	22.8	20.0	29.7	20.9	25.7	-	13.4	25.1	25.5	28.7
3. Grade 9(Freshman)	23.7	21.1	25.3	21.9	27.9	30.7	20.1	23.7	18.7	23.8	23.9	-	24.5	21.4	24.7	16.9
4. Grade 10(Sophomore)	21.7	18.6	26.0	23.6	15.8	17.9	17.8	25.0	28.2	22.0	19.9	-	21.6	27.0	22.8	-
5. Grade 11(Junior)	18.0	19.4	18.2	19.5	24.0	19.6	22.0	13.4	15.6	19.1	18.3	-	24.4	15.0	16.4	20.6
6. Grade 12(Senior)	5.9	5.8	5.4	5.3	10.8	1.5	8.0	10.1	5.3	7.3	5.1	-	10.9	6.8	3.5	-
Item 21190 Subject A01g N★	595	286	249	405	57	177	158	127	133	217	257	-	117	93	337	21
B030: How recently did you use marijuana or hashish on a daily, or almost daily, basis for at least a month?																
1. During the past month	25.5	27.1	22.7	23.1	28.2	21.6	28.1	26.2	27.1	20.3	28.6	-	20.2	22.7	27.5	22.3
2. 2 months ago	9.7	12.5	7.3	10.9	10.7	7.7	12.7	11.9	7.1	8.6	11.5	-	7.2	8.5	10.3	21.2
3. 3 to 9 months ago	14.7	15.1	15.0	16.0	11.5	15.4	16.7	13.1	12.7	17.7	11.0	-	14.5	8.9	15.7	26.3
4. About 1 year ago	15.6	14.1	16.0	15.0	20.8	16.6	11.8	20.8	14.4	17.8	14.3	-	16.5	11.2	16.5	7.7
5. About 2 years ago	17.2	13.8	21.8	16.8	12.8	20.2	16.1	12.0	18.9	18.2	17.9	-	15.9	29.1	16.1	7.8
6. 3 or more years ago	17.2	17.4	17.2	18.2	16.0	18.6	14.6	15.9	19.8	17.6	16.6	-	25.6	19.7	14.0	14.6
Item 21200 Subject A01a N★	554	271	234	390	49	169	151	110	125	200	247	-	90	87	334	21
B031: Over your whole lifetime, during how many months have you used marijuana or hashish on a daily or near-daily basis?																
1. Less than 3 months	36.1	31.8	40.8	34.0	52.5	34.3	34.8	41.4	35.2	39.6	33.9	-	57.2	50.9	26.4	12.4
2. 3 to 9 months	19.5	19.5	20.6	21.6	11.4	22.9	19.1	15.7	18.7	18.7	20.3	-	11.2	17.2	23.9	14.0
3. About 1 year	13.0	12.5	13.3	13.2	1.1	11.7	14.9	8.3	16.6	13.0	13.4	-	12.3	6.1	14.2	24.1
4. About 1 and 1/2 years	6.7	7.9	5.3	7.6	8.4	4.8	8.0	6.2	8.1	4.9	7.3	-	3.2	5.6	8.1	5.4
5. About 2 years	11.3	11.7	11.3	11.5	6.6	11.2	8.8	12.9	13.1	11.8	11.6	-	5.7	12.0	12.7	17.5
6. About 3 to 5 years	10.0	11.7	7.1	9.1	14.1	12.0	8.0	12.9	7.2	11.0	8.4	-	6.1	3.4	12.3	20.9
7. 6 to 9 years	2.1	3.4	0.5	2.2	1.5	3.1	4.1	0.4	-	0.7	2.8	-	1.5	3.4	1.9	5.6
8. 10 or more years	1.3	1.5	1.1	0.8	4.3	-	2.4	2.2	1.1	0.3	2.1	-	2.9	1.4	0.4	-
Item 21210 Subject A01a N★	551	275	227	386	49	166	149	111	125	199	244	-	89	85	333	21
B032: Do you think you will be using marijuana or hashish five years from now?																
1. I definitely will	2.5	3.5	1.3	2.4	2.0	3.6	2.5	1.9	2.3	2.1	2.6	0.3	1.8	1.4	7.8	7.3
2. I probably will	12.6	12.6	11.9	12.4	10.0	17.4	12.7	7.9	14.0	10.2	14.8	0.5	10.9	19.7	31.0	56.8
3. I probably will not	21.4	21.0	21.6	22.0	18.6	25.5	16.8	18.7	27.2	21.7	19.3	6.9	33.2	31.8	30.2	16.7
4. I definitely will not	63.5	62.8	65.1	63.2	69.5	53.5	68.0	71.4	56.6	66.0	63.3	92.2	54.2	47.1	31.0	19.1
Item 2390 Subject A04a N	3204	1466	1627	2358	387	757	878	967	603	1772	1100	1281	701	434	689	27

The next questions are about LSD, the psychedelic drug which is sometimes called "acid".

B033: On how many occasions (if any) have you taken LSD . . .

★=excludes respondents for whom question was inappropriate.

QUESTIONNAIRE FORM 1 1985	TOTAL	SEX		RACE		REGION				4YR COLLEGE PLANS		ILLICIT DRUG USE: LIFETIME				
		M	F	White	Black	NE	NC	S	W	Yes	No	None	Mari-juana Only	Few Pills	More Pills	Any Heroin
N (Weighted No. of Cases):	3316	1505	1663	2415	400	783	902	1004	627	1822	1121	1307	719	444	716	29
% of Weighted Total:	100.0	45.4	50.2	72.8	12.1	23.6	27.2	30.3	18.9	55.0	33.8	39.4	21.7	13.4	21.6	0.9

B033A: ... in your lifetime?

1. 0 occasions	92.1	90.4	94.4	91.4	98.6	89.3	91.9	94.5	92.3	94.8	89.6	100.0	100.0	93.3	71.3	17.3
2. 1-2	3.5	3.7	3.2	3.9	0.6	3.7	3.5	3.4	3.8	2.3	4.6	-	-	6.7	11.5	15.7
3. 3-5	1.8	2.4	1.1	2.2	0.3	3.1	2.2	0.6	1.4	1.0	2.9	-	-	-	7.8	9.4
4. 6-9	1.0	1.2	0.7	1.0	-	1.9	0.6	0.2	1.5	0.8	1.0	-	-	-	3.8	17.2
5. 10-19	0.6	1.0	0.4	0.8	-	0.6	0.8	0.4	0.8	0.6	0.7	-	-	-	2.4	12.1
6. 20-39	0.3	0.5	0.1	0.4	-	0.5	0.6	0.2	0.1	0.2	0.5	-	-	-	1.5	2.9
7. 40 or more	0.6	0.9	0.1	0.4	0.5	0.9	0.5	0.7	0.2	0.4	0.6	-	-	-	1.6	25.3
Item 890 Subject A01a N	3184	1462	1618	2370	370	739	875	952	618	1785	1085	1294	704	432	689	28

B033B: ... during the last 12 months?

1. 0 occasions	95.3	93.6	97.4	95.1	99.0	93.9	95.0	97.0	94.9	96.6	94.4	100.0	100.0	97.4	82.4	40.6
2. 1-2	2.6	3.0	1.9	2.7	0.5	3.6	2.6	1.6	3.2	1.9	3.1	-	-	2.6	9.8	19.5
3. 3-5	1.0	1.9	0.2	1.2	-	1.0	1.4	0.3	1.4	0.8	1.5	-	-	-	4.4	2.9
4. 6-9	0.4	0.4	0.3	0.4	-	0.9	0.5	0.2	-	0.2	0.3	-	-	-	1.6	5.6
5. 10-19	0.3	0.6	0.1	0.4	-	0.1	0.2	0.5	0.5	0.2	0.5	-	-	-	0.9	15.0
6. 20-39	*	*		*	-	0.1	0.1	-	-	-	0.1	-	-	-	0.2	-
7. 40 or more	0.3	0.5	*	0.2	0.5	0.4	0.4	0.5	-	0.3	0.3	-	-	-	0.8	16.4
Item 900 Subject A01b N	3178	1458	1616	2365	371	737	874	951	616	1783	1083	1294	704	427	688	28

B033C: ... during the last 30 days?

1. 0 occasions	98.2	97.1	99.3	98.1	99.5	97.3	98.1	98.8	98.4	98.8	97.9	100.0	100.0	99.8	93.1	64.0
2. 1-2	1.2	1.9	0.5	1.4	-	1.9	1.0	0.6	1.5	0.9	1.3	-	-	0.2	5.1	7.3
3. 3-5	0.4	0.7	0.1	0.4	-	0.5	0.4	0.6	0.1	0.1	0.7	-	-	-	1.4	12.5
4. 6-9	0.1	0.2	-	0.1	-	-	0.3	-	-	0.1	-	-	-	-	0.2	3.9
5. 10-19	-	-	-	-	-	-	-	-	-	-	-	-	-	-	-	-
6. 20-39	*	-	*	*	-	-	-	0.1	-	-	0.1	-	-	-	-	1.9
7. 40 or more	0.1	0.1	-	*	0.5	0.4	0.2	-	-	0.1	-	-	-	-	0.2	10.4
Item 910 Subject A01c N	3177	1457	1616	2365	370	736	874	951	616	1783	1082	1294	704	427	687	28

IF YOU HAVE NOT TAKEN LSD IN THE LAST TWELVE MONTHS, GO TO Q.B041.

B034: When you used LSD during the last year, how often did you use it in each of the following situations?

B034A: When you were alone

1. Not at all	80.2	78.4	88.3	84.1	67.6	70.0	86.6	77.6	88.5	79.1	83.1	-	-	100.0	81.5	48.0
2. A few of the times	13.2	15.8	9.1	11.0	32.4	14.5	12.3	21.2	3.9	14.4	14.5	-	-	-	13.4	27.3
3. Some of the times	3.0	2.7	-	1.4	-	6.5	1.0	-	3.8	2.0	-	-	-	-	3.5	2.9
4. Most of the times	1.2	2.0	-	1.6	-	3.2	-	1.2	-	2.5	0.6	-	-	-	1.2	2.3
5. Every time	2.5	1.2	2.6	1.9	-	5.8	-	-	3.8	2.0	1.7	-	-	-	0.5	19.4
Item 2400 Subject A05a N★	156	95	44	117	6	46	46	33	31	58	63	-	-	14	119	17

B034B: With just 1 or 2 other people

1. Not at all	17.7	14.6	22.6	16.5	50.4	16.7	17.8	22.7	13.7	18.7	18.4	-	-	19.0	13.2	16.7
2. A few of the times	31.8	27.9	41.3	34.5	-	35.8	22.0	39.4	32.4	28.1	31.8	-	-	40.6	34.9	13.3
3. Some of the times	10.0	12.6	1.9	8.9	32.4	12.3	15.6	3.0	5.4	11.8	6.5	-	-	-	8.2	37.0
4. Most of the times	17.4	21.1	12.0	17.8	-	11.6	18.2	22.8	19.2	23.6	16.4	-	-	17.9	17.7	21.9
5. Every time	23.1	23.8	22.3	22.2	17.2	23.6	26.4	12.2	29.2	17.8	26.9	-	-	22.4	26.0	11.0
Item 2410 Subject A05b N★	158	98	44	119	6	46	47	33	31	60	64	-	-	14	122	16

B034C: At a party

1. Not at all	38.4	36.5	37.1	37.4	36.6	39.0	29.3	43.3	45.3	39.1	32.9	-	-	50.5	35.3	25.8
2. A few of the times	25.5	28.0	22.8	26.8	-	25.9	37.1	12.1	21.8	22.8	32.0	-	-	27.1	29.3	5.2
3. Some of the times	12.8	15.5	7.7	13.8	49.6	10.4	11.4	19.4	11.7	14.1	13.3	-	-	6.8	10.9	38.3
4. Most of the times	11.4	9.4	14.3	9.1	-	18.0	9.9	13.2	2.2	11.7	8.5	-	-	5.0	12.9	10.1
5. Every time	11.9	10.6	18.1	13.0	13.8	6.6	12.2	12.0	19.0	12.2	13.3	-	-	10.7	11.6	20.6
Item 2420 Subject A05c N★	158	98	44	119	6	47	46	32	33	62	63	-	-	14	121	16

*=less than .05 per cent.   ★=excludes respondents for whom question was inappropriate.

QUESTIONNAIRE FORM 1 1985	TOTAL	SEX		RACE		REGION				4YR COLLEGE PLANS		ILLICIT DRUG USE: LIFETIME				
		M	F	White	Black	NE	NC	S	W	Yes	No	None	Mari- juana Only	Few Pills	More Pills	Any Her- oin
N (Weighted No. of Cases):	3316	1505	1663	2415	400	783	902	1004	627	1822	1121	1307	719	444	716	29
% of Weighted Total:	100.0	45.4	50.2	72.8	12.1	23.6	27.2	30.3	18.9	55.0	33.8	39.4	21.7	13.4	21.6	0.9
B034D: When your date or spouse was present																
1. Not at all	70.4	86.2	45.0	73.4	82.8	59.4	77.7	83.2	62.1	81.2	70.3	-	-	74.0	69.4	65.8
2. A few of the times	14.4	5.1	27.2	11.8	-	19.9	11.7	7.9	17.0	8.8	14.5	-	-	10.7	15.6	10.7
3. Some of the times	5.1	4.7	6.2	6.1	-	4.2	5.4	3.4	7.9	8.1	0.7	-	-	-	5.3	10.7
4. Most of the times	3.3	2.2	4.7	1.8	-	6.5	-	-	6.9	-	3.7	-	-	-	4.3	-
5. Every time	6.9	1.8	16.8	6.8	17.2	10.0	5.3	5.4	6.0	1.9	10.8	-	-	15.3	5.4	12.8
Item 2430 Subject A05b N★	158	97	44	118	6	47	47	33	31	60	64	-	-	14	121	16
B034E: When people over age 30 were present																
1. Not at all	68.8	67.5	74.1	69.3	100.0	67.2	63.9	72.2	74.7	71.2	69.0	-	-	95.4	64.5	71.4
2. A few of the times	14.0	16.0	9.7	16.0	-	11.6	20.9	13.3	7.9	11.1	19.6	-	-	4.6	15.9	11.1
3. Some of the times	10.2	12.8	6.9	9.7	-	11.9	7.3	14.5	7.4	14.1	6.9	-	-	-	11.1	17.5
4. Most of the times	3.7	1.8	7.1	2.7	-	4.0	5.8	-	3.9	2.0	3.0	-	-	-	4.8	-
5. Every time	3.4	1.9	2.3	2.4	-	5.3	2.1	-	6.0	1.5	1.5	-	-	-	3.6	-
Item 2440 Subject A05b N★	159	98	44	119	6	47	47	33	32	60	64	-	-	14	121	16
B034F: During the daytime (before 4:00 p.m.)																
1. Not at all	50.1	43.1	64.0	50.7	50.4	31.9	49.7	68.7	58.5	48.7	52.6	-	-	81.5	46.4	30.7
2. A few of the times	27.1	32.2	18.6	28.2	32.4	39.0	25.7	15.5	23.6	25.3	28.8	-	-	13.5	28.0	43.0
3. Some of the times	13.0	14.7	8.0	12.1	-	14.8	16.7	8.7	9.1	18.7	9.6	-	-	-	15.5	10.4
4. Most of the times	4.3	5.9	2.5	4.9	-	7.0	4.3	1.7	3.1	4.6	4.9	-	-	-	4.3	10.4
5. Every time	5.5	4.1	6.9	4.1	17.2	7.4	3.5	5.4	5.6	2.7	4.1	-	-	5.0	5.8	5.5
Item 2450 Subject A05c N★	158	97	44	118	6	47	47	33	30	59	64	-	-	14	121	16
B034G: At your home (or apartment or dorm)																
1. Not at all	55.1	55.9	58.2	53.8	100.0	50.4	62.8	52.2	53.6	49.9	61.0	-	-	82.7	52.2	38.4
2. A few of the times	24.1	22.7	22.7	26.0	-	28.8	18.9	23.5	25.4	24.8	23.2	-	-	4.6	27.7	25.1
3. Some of the times	7.3	8.6	4.1	5.5	-	5.6	7.4	10.0	6.8	10.0	3.1	-	-	-	8.8	5.8
4. Most of the times	8.7	9.4	10.8	11.4	-	7.2	10.9	14.3	1.9	8.8	11.0	-	-	-	9.3	16.2
5. Every time	4.8	3.3	4.2	3.4	-	7.9	-	-	12.4	6.6	1.7	-	-	12.7	2.1	14.4
Item 2460 Subject A05c N★	159	97	44	118	6	47	47	33	31	59	64	-	-	14	121	16
B034H: At school																
1. Not at all	76.9	77.3	83.6	81.5	100.0	67.5	79.8	84.6	79.1	85.9	81.6	-	-	78.5	75.8	73.0
2. A few of the times	16.6	16.5	10.5	13.7	-	22.9	10.8	15.4	17.1	8.8	14.8	-	-	21.5	17.0	17.0
3. Some of the times	3.0	3.6	2.9	3.2	-	6.3	3.8	-	-	3.3	3.7	-	-	-	2.7	10.0
4. Most of the times	1.3	0.7	3.0	1.1	-	-	4.3	-	-	2.1	-	-	-	-	1.7	-
5. Every time	2.1	1.8	-	0.5	-	3.3	1.2	-	3.8	-	-	-	-	-	2.7	-
Item 2470 Subject A05c N★	159	97	45	118	6	49	47	33	30	59	65	-	-	14	121	16
B034I: In a car																
1. Not at all	54.1	53.8	53.8	52.1	100.0	54.8	45.8	44.7	75.3	59.2	49.0	-	-	74.6	50.2	45.9
2. A few of the times	24.6	28.5	18.0	25.0	-	22.8	34.6	24.5	12.3	14.0	34.8	-	-	18.7	27.3	22.1
3. Some of the times	8.8	7.4	13.2	11.1	-	12.8	8.5	8.2	3.8	11.1	7.5	-	-	-	9.4	17.5
4. Most of the times	5.1	3.9	8.1	6.3	-	4.1	4.2	7.7	5.5	7.8	3.2	-	-	-	4.9	14.4
5. Every time	7.4	6.4	6.9	5.5	-	5.5	7.0	14.9	3.1	7.8	5.5	-	-	6.8	8.2	-
Item 2490 Subject A05c N★	160	97	45	118	6	49	47	33	31	59	65	-	-	14	121	16
B035: How many of the times when you used LSD during the last year did you use it along with each of the following drugs–that is, so that their effects overlapped?																
B035A: With alcohol																
1. Not at all	26.1	21.8	32.7	24.2	50.4	23.4	20.3	37.1	26.8	23.3	24.5	-	-	61.6	19.5	17.8
2. A few of the times	22.3	28.2	15.2	25.2	-	21.5	23.1	13.1	31.9	24.5	24.0	-	-	16.4	25.1	16.6
3. Some of the times	10.8	15.1	4.2	12.2	32.4	12.6	11.1	11.2	7.2	17.5	7.1	-	-	6.8	9.8	25.7
4. Most of the times	12.2	11.6	10.4	12.8	-	12.6	19.1	8.0	6.1	6.1	17.4	-	-	-	12.4	26.5
5. Every time	28.6	23.3	37.5	25.7	17.2	30.0	26.4	30.6	28.0	28.5	27.0	-	-	15.3	33.2	13.2
Item 2500 Subject A01h N★	159	96	44	120	6	46	47	34	32	62	63	-	-	14	121	17

★=excludes respondents for whom question was inappropriate.

QUESTIONNAIRE FORM 1 1985	TOTAL	SEX		RACE		REGION				4YR COLLEGE PLANS		ILLICIT DRUG USE: LIFETIME				
		M	F	White	Black	NE	NC	S	W	Yes	No	None	Mari- juana Only	Few Pills	More Pills	Any Her- oin
N (Weighted No. of Cases):	3316	1505	1663	2415	400	783	902	1004	627	1822	1121	1307	719	444	716	29
% of Weighted Total:	100.0	45.4	50.2	72.8	12.1	23.6	27.2	30.3	18.9	55.0	33.8	39.4	21.7	13.4	21.6	0.9
B035B: With marijuana																
1. Not at all	21.6	17.4	25.2	19.3	62.4	16.9	15.1	38.6	20.0	17.4	21.7	-	-	56.2	14.3	13.0
2. A few of the times	19.5	21.8	16.5	21.0	-	20.8	14.8	12.3	31.2	22.0	18.0	-	-	27.1	21.9	3.8
3. Some of the times	10.7	11.9	10.4	12.1	37.6	13.9	13.7	6.1	6.7	14.5	9.8	-	-	-	10.3	27.4
4. Most of the times	13.9	11.7	15.5	13.5	-	15.7	17.6	13.2	7.2	6.2	22.6	-	-	11.4	13.3	26.6
5. Every time	34.4	37.3	32.4	34.0	-	32.7	38.8	29.9	34.8	39.8	27.9	-	-	5.3	40.2	29.3
Item 2510 Subject A01h N★	159	98	44	120	5	45	46	33	34	61	64	-	-	14	122	16
B036: What have been the most important reasons for your taking LSD? (Mark all that apply.)																
A. To experiment–to see what it's like	84.8	86.5	81.6	84.1	100.0	76.0	83.7	91.0	94.1	88.5	80.4	-	-	80.9	86.2	76.0
B. To relax or relieve tension	8.4	8.8	6.7	5.8	51.1	11.5	10.5	5.3	3.7	5.7	6.6	-	-	-	7.8	14.9
C. To feel good or get high	64.8	70.1	52.6	63.4	100.0	62.4	76.6	64.4	51.9	68.6	65.2	-	-	48.6	65.4	72.5
D. To seek deeper insights and understanding	33.0	40.4	22.0	33.1	78.2	25.5	38.8	50.0	21.3	43.6	29.9	-	-	9.6	34.0	42.6
E. To have a good time with my friends	57.9	58.4	58.4	54.0	48.9	59.2	65.9	60.6	41.9	57.0	59.6	-	-	44.5	60.2	49.9
F. To fit in with a group I like	5.6	5.4	4.1	4.4	-	7.9	4.9	6.4	2.3	3.2	3.6	-	-	5.0	5.6	-
G. To get away from my problems or troubles	14.4	8.2	27.6	13.6	-	19.7	9.6	13.0	14.6	9.9	13.9	-	-	-	14.7	20.5
H. Because of boredom, nothing else to do	22.4	24.1	18.5	19.3	21.8	22.3	22.9	23.6	20.8	19.7	24.2	-	-	17.4	20.3	37.9
I. Because of anger or frustration	5.7	6.1	2.9	3.9	-	11.2	2.8	3.1	3.7	5.0	1.4	-	-	-	6.0	2.8
J. To get through the day	2.9	1.8	2.5	2.4	-	3.3	1.3	7.9	-	-	1.9	-	-	5.0	2.2	-
K. To increase the effects of some other drug(s)	10.9	5.8	20.1	9.1	-	13.4	12.2	10.4	5.5	5.1	14.4	-	-	10.7	10.7	6.2
L. To decrease (offset) the effects of some other drug(s)	1.5	-	1.7	0.6	-	3.3	1.6	-	-	1.2	-	-	-	-	1.0	-
M. Because I am "hooked"–I have to have it	3.4	1.6	-	0.4	-	9.8	1.1	-	-	-	1.8	-	-	-	2.2	10.0
Item 2520-2640 Subject A06a N★	152	96	42	117	4	48	45	28	31	61	62	-	-	14	121	16
B037: When you take LSD how high do you usually get?																
1. Not at all high	1.2	0.8	-	-	4.8	1.9	-	2.8	0.6	-	-	-	-	-	0.7	-
2. A little high	3.7	3.6	2.8	2.9	-	11.9	-	-	-	5.5	2.0	-	-	8.8	3.7	-
3. Moderately high	16.2	9.5	30.5	15.6	48.7	16.2	13.2	16.0	20.7	15.9	12.2	-	-	7.5	14.7	37.2
4. Very high	78.9	86.1	66.8	81.5	46.5	70.1	86.8	81.2	78.6	78.6	85.7	-	-	83.7	80.9	62.8
Item 2650 Subject A01e N★	151	95	42	115	4	47	45	28	31	61	60	-	-	14	119	16
B038: When you take LSD how long do you usually stay high?																
1. Usually don't get high	1.2	0.8	-	-	4.8	1.9	-	2.6	0.6	-	-	-	-	-	0.7	-
2. One to two hours	3.3	2.6	2.5	3.0	-	6.3	-	6.8	-	2.6	-	-	-	21.7	0.5	-
3. Three to six hours	32.4	31.4	32.3	30.5	69.4	24.4	42.7	32.8	29.2	29.1	31.4	-	-	16.8	32.1	52.8
4. Seven to 24 hours	60.3	61.7	65.2	64.6	25.8	62.9	56.1	57.8	64.7	65.5	66.0	-	-	61.5	64.0	40.3
5. More than 24 hours	2.8	3.4	-	1.9	-	4.5	1.2	-	5.5	2.8	2.6	-	-	-	2.7	6.9
Item 2660 Subject A01f N★	153	97	42	117	4	47	45	30	31	61	62	-	-	14	121	16
B039: Have you ever had a "bad trip" on LSD?																
1. No	73.2	79.2	58.3	74.7	25.5	69.7	68.1	79.0	79.7	81.1	62.8	-	-	80.3	76.5	37.9
2. Yes, once	20.9	15.4	33.9	20.2	74.5	21.1	29.5	12.3	16.6	15.2	31.1	-	-	19.7	19.5	34.6
3. Yes, more than once	6.0	5.4	7.8	5.1	-	9.2	2.5	8.6	3.6	3.7	6.1	-	-	-	3.9	27.5
Item 2670 Subject A01k N★	153	98	42	118	4	46	45	31	32	62	62	-	-	14	122	16
B040: Have you ever tried to stop using LSD and found that you couldn't stop?																
1. Yes	2.0	1.7	-	0.5	-	5.4	1.2	-	-	-	2.6	-	-	-	1.6	6.9
2. No	98.0	98.3	100.0	99.5	100.0	94.6	98.8	100.0	100.0	100.0	97.4	-	-	100.0	98.4	93.1
Item 2680 Subject A01i N★	153	97	42	117	4	47	45	30	32	61	62	-	-	14	121	16

★=excludes respondents for whom question was inappropriate.

QUESTIONNAIRE FORM 1 1985	TOTAL	SEX		RACE		REGION				4YR COLLEGE PLANS		ILLICIT DRUG USE: LIFETIME				
		M	F	White	Black	NE	NC	S	W	Yes	No	None	Marijuana Only	Few Pills	More Pills	Any Heroin
N (Weighted No. of Cases):	3316	1505	1663	2415	400	783	902	1004	627	1822	1121	1307	719	444	716	29
% of Weighted Total:	100.0	45.4	50.2	72.8	12.1	23.6	27.2	30.3	18.9	55.0	33.8	39.4	21.7	13.4	21.6	0.9

B041: Do you think you will be using LSD five years from now?

1. I definitely will	1.1	1.5	0.6	0.9	0.9	1.5	1.3	0.8	0.9	0.7	1.5	0.4	1.4	1.2	1.9	4.1
2. I probably will	1.6	1.9	1.2	1.6	0.5	1.8	2.2	1.2	1.3	1.3	1.7	-	0.1	0.8	6.1	23.4
3. I probably will not	7.0	7.8	5.8	7.4	4.8	8.7	7.3	6.0	6.0	6.4	7.5	1.8	4.9	7.4	18.1	24.8
4. I definitely will not	90.3	88.8	92.4	90.0	93.7	88.0	89.3	92.0	91.7	91.6	89.3	97.8	93.5	90.6	73.9	47.7
Item 2690　Subject A04a　　N	3132	1437	1598	2323	378	722	864	956	591	1754	1075	1277	683	416	665	27

The next questions are about PSYCHEDELICS OTHER THAN LSD.

This group would include the following drugs: Mescaline, Peyote, Psilocybin, PCP.

B042: On how many occasions (if any) have you taken psychedelics other than LSD . . .

B042A: . . . in your lifetime?

1. 0 occasions	92.5	91.0	94.6	91.9	98.2	86.1	92.9	95.7	94.5	94.7	90.7	100.0	100.0	92.9	72.7	20.1
2. 1-2	3.8	4.7	3.0	4.4	0.9	7.0	3.4	2.4	2.9	2.9	5.3	-	-	7.1	12.2	29.6
3. 3-5	1.3	1.3	0.9	1.3	0.1	2.3	1.0	0.8	1.0	1.0	1.2	-	-	-	5.5	8.7
4. 6-9	0.9	1.0	0.6	1.0	-	1.7	1.1	0.3	0.7	0.6	0.5	-	-	-	3.7	13.7
5. 10-19	0.5	0.8	0.1	0.4	-	0.5	0.4	0.4	0.6	0.3	0.5	-	-	-	2.0	1.6
6. 20-39	0.3	0.3	0.4	0.4	0.3	0.7	0.4	0.1	0.1	0.1	0.6	-	-	-	1.2	7.1
7. 40 or more	0.7	0.9	0.4	0.7	0.5	1.7	0.8	0.3	0.2	0.4	1.1	-	-	-	2.7	19.2
Item 920　Subject A01a　　N	3143	1441	1603	2351	361	721	873	944	605	1773	1068	1289	692	420	679	27

B042B: . . . during the last 12 months?

1. 0 occasions	95.8	95.0	97.3	95.8	98.9	92.3	95.7	98.0	96.9	96.9	95.9	100.0	100.0	98.2	84.0	42.0
2. 1-2	2.2	2.3	1.8	2.4	0.3	4.2	2.1	1.0	2.0	1.8	2.2	-	-	1.8	8.1	30.6
3. 3-5	0.9	1.4	0.4	1.1	-	1.0	1.5	0.3	0.7	0.7	0.9	-	-	-	3.7	7.8
4. 6-9	0.5	0.7	0.1	0.3	-	0.9	0.4	0.5	0.1	0.3	0.1	-	-	-	1.8	10.4
5. 10-19	0.2	0.2	0.1	0.2	-	0.6	0.1	-	0.2	*	0.4	-	-	-	0.9	-
6. 20-39	0.3	0.3	0.2	0.1	0.8	0.9	0.2	-	-	0.2	0.4	-	-	-	1.0	7.2
7. 40 or more	0.1	0.1	*	0.1	-	0.2	-	0.3	-	0.1	0.1	-	-	-	0.5	2.1
Item 930　Subject A01b　　N	3139	1439	1604	2350	361	720	872	944	604	1774	1067	1289	692	420	675	27

B042C: . . . during the last 30 days?

1. 0 occasions	98.6	98.5	99.1	98.7	99.2	97.2	98.2	99.4	99.6	99.3	98.2	100.0	100.0	99.7	94.6	78.8
2. 1-2	0.7	0.8	0.6	0.8	-	1.5	0.9	0.2	0.2	0.3	1.1	-	-	0.3	2.8	7.9
3. 3-5	0.3	0.4	0.3	0.4	-	0.6	0.4	0.2	0.1	0.1	0.5	-	-	-	1.3	6.1
4. 6-9	0.2	0.1	*	*	0.3	0.5	0.2	-	-	-	0.2	-	-	-	0.7	-
5. 10-19	0.2	0.3	*	0.1	0.5	0.1	0.2	0.2	0.1	0.2	*	-	-	-	0.5	7.2
6. 20-39	-	-	-	-	-	-	-	-	-	-	-	-	-	-	-	-
7. 40 or more	*	-	-	-	-	0.1	-	-	-	-	-	-	-	-	0.1	-
Item 940　Subject A01c　　N	3142	1442	1605	2353	361	723	872	944	604	1774	1067	1289	692	423	675	27

IF YOU HAVE NOT TAKEN ANY PSYCHE-DELICS OTHER THAN LSD IN THE LAST TWELVE MONTHS, GO TO Q.B046.

B043: When you take psychedelics other than LSD how high do you usually get?

1. Not at all high	3.2	1.5	2.6	2.2	-	4.1	2.9	4.1	-	4.0	-	-	-	14.2	2.0	-
2. A little high	9.5	4.0	20.6	10.2	6.9	6.2	12.8	14.6	6.6	5.8	18.7	-	-	21.0	10.1	-
3. Moderately high	36.1	36.5	30.8	35.8	55.4	39.6	33.3	23.9	44.8	29.2	40.4	-	-	46.0	33.4	54.1
4. Very high	51.3	58.0	46.0	51.8	37.8	50.2	51.0	57.4	48.5	61.0	41.0	-	-	18.8	54.4	45.9
Item 2700　Subject A01e　　N★	134	71	44	101	5	55	40	21	19	55	44	-	-	8	109	15

*=less than .05 per cent.　　★=excludes respondents for whom question was inappropriate.

QUESTIONNAIRE FORM 1 1985	TOTAL	SEX		RACE		REGION				4YR COLLEGE PLANS		ILLICIT DRUG USE: LIFETIME				
		M	F	White	Black	NE	NC	S	W	Yes	No	None	Mari- juana Only	Few Pills	More Pills	Any Her- oin
N (Weighted No. of Cases):	3316	1505	1663	2415	400	783	902	1004	627	1822	1121	1307	719	444	716	29
% of Weighted Total:	100.0	45.4	50.2	72.8	12.1	23.6	27.2	30.3	18.9	55.0	33.8	39.4	21.7	13.4	21.6	0.9
B044: When you take psychedelics other than LSD how long do you usually stay high?																
1. Usually don't get high	0.9	-	2.7	1.2	-	-	2.9	-	-	2.1	-	-	-	17.0	-	-
2. One to two hours	12.9	9.7	19.8	14.0	24.0	13.4	10.4	16.8	12.7	10.2	18.8	-	-	-	13.2	11.0
3. Three to six hours	46.7	56.0	30.4	47.9	55.4	40.4	38.6	49.8	77.7	51.2	42.7	-	-	42.0	45.6	59.4
4. Seven to 24 hours	37.1	32.9	45.9	35.4	20.6	41.2	46.8	33.4	9.6	34.6	37.4	-	-	18.4	40.7	21.9
5. More than 24 hours	2.5	1.4	1.2	1.5	-	5.0	1.3	-	-	1.9	1.2	-	-	22.5	0.5	7.7
Item 2710 Subject A01f N★	132	71	42	100	5	54	40	18	19	54	43	-	-	7	109	15
B045: What psychedelics other than LSD have you taken during the last year? (Mark all that apply.)																
A. Mescaline	53.8	42.7	63.2	50.5	59.4	78.1	45.4	24.0	28.7	40.1	64.4	-	-	42.4	52.2	70.5
B. Peyote	10.9	10.6	12.6	9.8	56.0	7.1	12.6	8.9	21.7	14.5	6.3	-	-	-	6.0	39.9
C. Psilocybin	14.0	18.8	5.3	10.7	38.8	7.8	10.6	18.9	35.0	21.9	2.4	-	-	-	13.3	21.6
D. PCP	21.4	21.4	19.8	18.5	6.9	16.8	13.2	45.2	26.0	21.2	22.1	-	-	-	20.2	36.8
E. Concentrated THC	26.0	19.9	31.8	25.2	-	29.9	14.1	44.0	18.4	21.8	25.9	-	-	-	25.1	42.6
F. Other	30.9	34.6	29.2	27.6	55.4	18.5	39.0	60.1	20.6	34.8	29.9	-	-	32.5	27.2	53.2
G. Don't know the names of some I have used	24.4	29.2	23.8	26.2	55.4	12.0	45.9	23.1	20.0	23.1	34.6	-	-	44.5	19.3	45.8
Item 2720-2780 Subject A01l N★	132	69	44	99	5	56	38	20	18	55	41	-	-	8	107	16

The next questions are about some non-prescription drugs.

B046: Some types of diet pills (also called appetite suppressants) can be sold legally without a doctor's prescription by drugstores, through the mail, etc. These "over-the-counter" drugs include Dexatrim, Dietac, Prolamine, and others.

On how many occasions (if any) have you taken such non-prescription diet pills ...

B046A: . . . in your lifetime?	TOTAL	M	F	White	Black	NE	NC	S	W	Yes	No	None	Mari- juana Only	Few Pills	More Pills	Any Her- oin
1. 0 occasions	71.3	85.2	58.5	68.5	88.5	72.5	68.9	73.3	70.3	74.4	67.1	85.3	77.3	65.9	43.7	39.5
2. 1-2	10.8	6.1	15.3	11.3	5.9	9.5	11.1	10.2	12.6	10.4	11.1	7.2	11.3	16.3	13.3	10.8
3. 3-5	5.2	2.8	7.2	5.3	2.4	6.2	4.9	4.7	5.2	4.3	5.9	2.8	4.3	5.9	10.1	4.3
4. 6-9	3.4	1.8	4.9	3.9	0.9	3.3	4.4	3.1	2.5	2.5	5.0	1.9	2.2	3.0	7.9	1.9
5. 10-19	3.1	1.1	4.8	3.7	0.2	2.0	4.4	2.5	3.4	2.5	4.2	0.9	2.3	3.4	7.3	14.8
6. 20-39	2.5	0.8	4.0	2.9	0.8	2.5	2.4	2.8	2.0	2.4	2.6	0.7	1.2	3.0	6.6	4.4
7. 40 or more	3.8	2.2	5.3	4.5	1.3	4.0	3.9	3.4	4.1	3.5	4.1	1.2	1.5	2.5	11.1	24.1
Item 21220 Subject A01a N	3190	1471	1621	2379	374	742	876	955	616	1792	1086	1286	702	432	695	27

B046B: . . . during the last 12 months?																
1. 0 occasions	83.1	91.0	75.6	80.2	95.7	83.5	80.8	85.1	82.7	85.3	79.3	92.5	87.6	81.8	61.7	69.2
2. 1-2	6.4	4.0	8.8	7.4	1.1	7.6	6.7	4.9	7.0	5.7	7.3	3.5	6.5	8.0	11.4	-
3. 3-5	3.0	1.2	4.7	3.7	0.9	2.8	3.7	2.6	2.8	2.5	4.4	1.7	1.9	2.7	6.8	5.1
4. 6-9	2.5	1.5	3.4	2.9	0.7	2.2	3.2	2.3	2.2	1.8	3.8	0.5	1.6	3.7	6.8	-
5. 10-19	2.2	1.3	3.0	2.6	0.8	1.1	2.2	2.5	2.9	2.0	2.6	0.7	1.0	1.4	6.0	11.6
6. 20-39	1.5	0.7	2.4	1.7	0.8	1.5	2.1	1.4	0.9	1.5	1.4	0.6	0.8	1.5	4.0	1.6
7. 40 or more	1.2	0.2	2.2	1.5	-	1.3	1.3	1.0	1.4	1.1	1.3	0.5	0.5	0.9	3.2	12.5
Item 21230 Subject A01b N	3175	1466	1611	2371	371	740	871	953	612	1791	1077	1283	702	427	691	27

B046C: . . . during the last 30 days?																
1. 0 occasions	92.7	96.3	89.3	91.1	97.5	93.0	91.1	93.2	93.6	93.8	90.6	96.9	96.3	92.4	81.5	74.3
2. 1-2	3.2	1.9	4.4	4.0	0.8	3.7	3.2	3.0	2.9	2.4	4.8	1.7	1.7	4.1	7.3	-
3. 3-5	1.6	0.7	2.3	1.8	0.9	1.2	2.2	1.2	1.7	1.4	2.0	0.4	1.0	2.1	4.0	-
4. 6-9	1.0	0.6	1.3	1.1	0.7	0.4	1.9	0.9	0.7	1.1	0.8	0.2	0.5	0.6	2.6	17.5
5. 10-19	0.7	0.1	1.2	0.8	-	0.6	0.6	0.8	0.7	0.6	1.0	0.3	0.1	0.5	2.0	-
6. 20-39	0.7	0.3	1.2	0.9	0.1	0.7	0.9	0.8	0.4	0.7	0.6	0.4	0.4	0.2	1.7	8.2
7. 40 or more	0.2	-	0.2	0.1	-	0.5	0.1	*	-	0.1	0.2	-	-	-	0.7	-
Item 21240 Subject A01c N	3174	1464	1612	2371	371	739	870	954	612	1792	1075	1283	702	427	690	27

*=less than .05 per cent.   ★=excludes respondents for whom question was inappropriate.

QUESTIONNAIRE FORM 1 1985	TOTAL	SEX		RACE		REGION				4YR COLLEGE PLANS		ILLICIT DRUG USE: LIFETIME				
		M	F	White	Black	NE	NC	S	W	Yes	No	None	Marijuana Only	Few Pills	More Pills	Any Heroin
N (Weighted No. of Cases):	3316	1505	1663	2415	400	783	902	1004	627	1822	1121	1307	719	444	716	29
% of Weighted Total:	100.0	45.4	50.2	72.8	12.1	23.6	27.2	30.3	18.9	55.0	33.8	39.4	21.7	13.4	21.6	0.9

B047: Some stay-awake pills can be sold legally without a doctor's prescription by drugstores, through the mail, etc. These non-prescription or "over-the-counter" drugs include No-Doz, Vivarin, Wake, Caffedrine, and others.

On how many occasions (if any) have you taken such non-prescription stay-awake pills...

B047A: . . . in your lifetime?

	TOTAL	M	F	White	Black	NE	NC	S	W	Yes	No	None	Mari-juana Only	Few Pills	More Pills	Any Her-oin
1. 0 occasions	73.7	72.0	75.1	70.0	93.3	75.3	74.7	78.1	63.3	73.0	73.9	89.7	79.2	67.9	42.4	33.8
2. 1-2	10.8	12.2	9.6	12.1	3.8	10.9	10.0	9.3	14.4	10.4	12.1	5.9	12.0	14.9	16.1	24.3
3. 3-5	4.8	3.5	6.0	5.4	1.2	3.4	4.5	4.5	7.4	5.4	4.4	2.7	3.2	8.8	7.8	10.3
4. 6-9	2.5	2.5	2.3	2.7	0.3	2.5	2.6	1.8	3.3	2.6	2.1	0.8	1.9	2.0	6.6	4.5
5. 10-19	3.9	4.4	3.6	4.7	0.7	3.2	4.1	2.5	6.3	4.1	3.5	0.5	1.6	2.7	13.4	4.3
6. 20-39	1.6	2.1	1.3	2.1	-	1.4	1.6	1.5	2.3	1.9	1.1	0.2	0.5	1.9	5.4	4.6
7. 40 or more	2.7	3.2	2.2	3.1	0.8	3.3	2.5	2.4	2.9	2.5	2.9	0.3	1.6	1.9	8.3	18.1
Item 21250 Subject A01a N	3196	1463	1636	2379	379	747	875	960	614	1797	1087	1291	701	435	696	26

B047B: . . . during the last 12 months?

	TOTAL	M	F	White	Black	NE	NC	S	W	Yes	No	None	Mari-juana Only	Few Pills	More Pills	Any Her-oin
1. 0 occasions	81.8	80.3	83.0	78.6	96.0	81.8	81.6	86.7	74.4	79.6	84.5	92.6	85.9	80.1	57.9	74.9
2. 1-2	8.1	8.7	7.7	9.6	1.8	8.7	7.8	5.8	11.3	9.3	7.1	4.8	8.0	9.8	14.1	-
3. 3-5	3.3	3.3	3.4	3.9	1.2	2.7	4.0	2.3	4.6	3.7	2.8	1.4	2.3	5.0	7.1	-
4. 6-9	2.6	3.1	2.0	2.9	0.3	2.5	2.6	1.6	4.3	3.1	1.8	0.6	1.6	2.1	7.9	2.3
5. 10-19	1.8	1.9	1.7	2.3	0.3	1.9	1.4	1.4	2.8	2.2	1.1	0.3	1.0	1.1	5.7	7.6
6. 20-39	1.1	1.5	0.8	1.3	0.5	0.7	1.2	1.3	1.4	1.1	1.1	0.2	0.4	1.0	3.5	9.0
7. 40 or more	1.2	1.2	1.3	1.4	-	1.7	1.3	0.9	1.0	1.1	1.6	0.1	0.9	0.8	3.8	6.1
Item 21260 Subject A01b N	3182	1456	1630	2369	377	745	872	956	609	1792	1080	1290	699	428	690	26

B047C: . . . during the last 30 days?

	TOTAL	M	F	White	Black	NE	NC	S	W	Yes	No	None	Mari-juana Only	Few Pills	More Pills	Any Her-oin
1. 0 occasions	92.8	92.3	93.3	91.4	97.5	92.1	92.7	94.3	91.5	92.1	93.8	98.3	94.2	93.8	80.8	74.9
2. 1-2	3.5	3.7	3.5	4.2	1.7	3.6	3.7	2.6	4.7	4.4	2.7	1.3	4.1	3.8	7.2	2.3
3. 3-5	1.2	1.3	1.0	1.4	0.3	1.0	0.9	1.3	1.6	1.3	0.8	0.3	0.7	1.0	3.3	4.5
4. 6-9	1.1	1.5	0.7	1.2	-	1.4	1.4	1.0	0.7	0.9	1.1	*	0.7	1.0	3.4	10.8
5. 10-19	1.0	0.8	1.1	1.3	-	1.1	0.8	0.7	1.5	1.0	1.0	0.1	0.3	0.3	3.9	-
6. 20-39	0.2	0.2	0.3	0.2	0.5	0.3	0.4	0.1	0.1	0.2	0.3	-	-	-	0.8	7.5
7. 40 or more	0.2	0.2	0.2	0.2	-	0.5	0.1	0.1	-	0.1	0.2	-	0.1	0.1	0.6	-
Item 21270 Subject A01c N	3178	1453	1630	2365	377	743	872	955	608	1790	1078	1288	699	428	688	26

B048: In addition to non-prescription diet and stay-awake pills, there are other stimulants and pep pills which can be sold legally in most states without a prescription–usually by mail. These are sometimes called "fake pep pills," "imitation speed," or "look-alikes," because they look like prescription amphetamines and sometimes have similar names.

Other than diet pills and stay-awake pills you have already told us about, on how many occasions (if any) have you taken other non-prescription stimulants or pep pills ...

B048A: . . . in your lifetime?

	TOTAL	M	F	White	Black	NE	NC	S	W	Yes	No	None	Mari-juana Only	Few Pills	More Pills	Any Her-oin
1. 0 occasions	85.8	85.9	86.2	84.2	96.4	86.0	85.8	86.3	84.7	89.2	81.6	99.0	94.9	81.8	56.4	15.1
2. 1-2	5.3	5.3	5.2	5.5	2.6	4.2	4.1	6.1	7.2	5.2	5.9	0.7	4.2	11.8	10.5	23.6
3. 3-5	2.5	2.7	2.3	3.0	0.1	2.6	3.0	1.9	2.2	1.4	3.7	0.1	0.7	2.6	8.5	4.3
4. 6-9	1.9	1.4	2.2	2.1	0.4	1.7	2.3	1.6	1.7	1.0	2.7	*	0.1	1.1	7.2	15.1
5. 10-19	1.3	1.3	1.3	1.5	0.2	1.1	1.6	1.4	1.2	0.8	1.8	0.1	0.1	0.5	5.2	11.1
6. 20-39	1.1	0.9	1.3	1.3	-	1.2	0.7	0.7	2.1	1.0	1.1	-	0.1	1.0	3.7	14.7
7. 40 or more	2.2	2.5	1.6	2.3	0.3	3.1	2.4	2.0	0.9	1.3	3.2	0.1	-	1.2	8.5	16.0
Item 21280 Subject A01a N	3190	1466	1633	2381	375	741	877	959	613	1796	1086	1288	703	434	691	26

*=less than .05 per cent.

QUESTIONNAIRE FORM 1 1985	TOTAL	SEX		RACE		REGION				4YR COLLEGE PLANS		ILLICIT DRUG USE: LIFETIME				
		M	F	White	Black	NE	NC	S	W	Yes	No	None	Mari-juana Only	Few Pills	More Pills	Any Her-oin
N (Weighted No. of Cases):	3316	1505	1663	2415	400	783	902	1004	627	1822	1121	1307	719	444	716	29
% of Weighted Total:	100.0	45.4	50.2	72.8	12.1	23.6	27.2	30.3	18.9	55.0	33.8	39.4	21.7	13.4	21.6	0.9
B048B: . . . during the last 12 months?																
1. 0 occasions	91.8	91.7	92.2	90.8	98.5	91.1	91.0	92.7	92.3	93.5	90.0	99.6	98.4	91.2	71.9	46.2
2. 1-2	3.3	3.0	3.3	3.6	0.7	3.2	3.6	2.9	3.5	2.8	3.9	0.2	1.0	5.6	9.2	26.0
3. 3-5	1.3	1.3	1.4	1.5	0.1	1.5	1.3	1.0	1.8	0.9	1.7	*	0.5	0.8	5.1	-
4. 6-9	1.2	1.5	0.9	1.4	0.7	1.8	1.0	0.9	1.1	0.8	1.4	-	0.1	0.7	4.6	11.7
5. 10-19	1.1	1.1	1.1	1.3	-	0.7	1.3	1.5	0.8	1.0	1.3	0.1	-	0.4	4.6	6.2
6. 20-39	0.5	0.3	0.6	0.4	-	0.1	1.1	0.2	0.3	0.4	0.6	-	-	1.2	1.2	4.1
7. 40 or more	0.8	1.1	0.5	0.9	-	1.6	0.7	0.8	0.1	0.5	1.1	0.1	-	0.1	3.4	5.8
Item 21290 Subject A01b N	3182	1461	1630	2375	374	741	874	956	611	1796	1081	1288	701	432	688	26
B048C: . . . during the last 30 days?																
1. 0 occasions	96.4	96.2	96.9	96.1	99.5	95.4	96.0	96.5	98.0	97.5	95.2	99.9	99.6	97.6	86.6	73.8
2. 1-2	1.6	1.7	1.4	1.8	0.5	2.0	1.3	1.9	1.0	1.2	2.1	-	0.2	1.1	6.2	10.0
3. 3-5	0.4	0.4	0.4	0.4	-	0.3	0.4	0.6	0.1	0.1	0.8	0.1	0.3	-	1.3	1.6
4. 6-9	0.8	0.9	0.6	0.8	-	0.9	1.2	0.3	0.9	0.7	0.9	-	-	1.1	2.9	4.5
5. 10-19	0.4	0.2	0.4	0.4	-	0.6	0.7	0.1	-	0.3	0.3	0.1	-	-	1.4	4.1
6. 20-39	0.3	0.4	0.2	0.4	-	0.4	0.2	0.4	-	0.2	0.4	-	-	-	1.2	1.5
7. 40 or more	0.1	0.1	0.1	0.2	-	0.3	0.1	0.1	-	-	0.3	-	-	0.1	0.4	4.3
Item 21300 Subject A01c N	3181	1461	1629	2375	374	740	874	956	611	1795	1080	1288	701	432	686	26

The next questions are about AMPHETA-MINES, which doctors can prescribe to help people lose weight or to give people more en-ergy. Drugstores are not supposed to sell them without a prescription from a doctor.

Amphetamines are sometimes called: uppers, ups, speed, bennies, dexies, pep pills, diet pills. They include the following drugs: Ben-zedrine, Dexedrine, Methedrine, Ritalin, Pre-ludin, Dexamyl, Methamphetamine.

IN YOUR ANSWERS ABOUT AMPHETA-MINES, DO NOT INCLUDE ANY NON-PRESCRIPTION OR OVER-THE-COUNTER DRUGS.

B049: Have you ever taken amphetamines because a doctor told you to use them?

	TOTAL	M	F	White	Black	NE	NC	S	W	Yes	No	None	Mari-juana Only	Few Pills	More Pills	Any Her-oin
1. No	92.5	92.3	93.0	92.6	94.9	93.0	91.1	93.6	92.3	93.4	92.2	96.3	95.9	90.3	84.3	68.5
2. Yes, but I had already tried them on my own	2.5	2.5	2.2	2.7	1.1	3.0	3.3	1.6	2.1	1.5	3.2	0.1	0.3	1.0	9.5	21.6
3. Yes, and it was the first time I took any	5.0	5.2	4.8	4.7	4.0	4.1	5.7	4.8	5.5	5.1	4.6	3.6	3.8	8.8	6.2	9.9
Item 2790 Subject A01j N	3183	1460	1631	2382	370	744	876	951	612	1790	1086	1277	694	439	701	26

B050: On how many occasions (if any) have you taken amphetamines on your own–that is, without a doctor telling you to take them . . .

B050A: . . . in your lifetime?

	TOTAL	M	F	White	Black	NE	NC	S	W	Yes	No	None	Mari-juana Only	Few Pills	More Pills	Any Her-oin
1. 0 occasions	77.9	78.6	77.5	75.0	93.1	76.5	77.2	81.4	75.0	81.8	73.3	100.0	100.0	60.3	27.2	5.7
2. 1-2	7.2	7.3	7.0	7.6	4.3	6.6	6.2	8.5	7.4	6.9	7.0	-	-	39.7	8.0	9.5
3. 3-5	3.8	3.8	4.0	4.5	0.9	3.8	4.4	2.5	5.0	2.9	5.1	-	-	17.2	4.3	-
4. 6-9	2.3	2.0	2.3	2.6	0.4	2.1	2.8	1.8	2.4	1.8	2.8	-	-	-	9.9	10.7
5. 10-19	3.2	2.8	3.5	3.7	0.5	3.9	4.2	2.1	2.7	2.1	4.4	-	-	-	13.3	35.2
6. 20-39	2.1	1.5	2.4	2.4	-	2.1	2.4	0.8	3.6	1.6	2.6	-	-	-	9.0	9.4
7. 40 or more	3.6	4.0	3.3	4.3	0.8	4.9	2.9	2.9	3.9	2.8	4.8	-	-	-	15.3	25.2
Item 980 Subject A01a N	3173	1459	1622	2375	372	738	874	949	613	1790	1074	1282	695	431	697	25

B050B: . . . during the last 12 months?

	TOTAL	M	F	White	Black	NE	NC	S	W	Yes	No	None	Mari-juana Only	Few Pills	More Pills	Any Her-oin
1. 0 occasions	87.1	88.1	86.7	85.4	95.9	86.9	85.9	90.3	84.3	90.2	83.9	100.0	100.0	88.4	51.0	29.5
2. 1-2	4.9	4.1	5.4	5.3	2.5	5.3	4.0	4.5	6.4	4.3	5.7	-	-	11.6	14.7	18.2
3. 3-5	2.3	2.0	2.6	2.8	0.3	3.1	2.8	1.0	2.8	1.2	3.7	-	-	-	10.2	12.6
4. 6-9	2.1	2.0	1.9	2.4	0.5	1.3	3.3	1.3	2.5	1.1	3.0	-	-	-	8.7	19.6
5. 10-19	1.7	1.5	1.8	1.9	0.5	1.9	2.3	1.2	1.2	1.4	2.2	-	-	-	7.3	6.4
6. 20-39	0.9	1.0	0.8	1.1	0.1	0.5	0.8	0.5	2.1	0.9	0.7	-	-	-	4.0	3.0
7. 40 or more	1.0	1.2	0.8	1.1	0.1	1.1	0.9	1.2	0.7	1.0	0.9	-	-	-	4.1	10.6
Item 990 Subject A01b N	3157	1448	1616	2362	371	736	869	944	608	1782	1069	1282	695	418	694	25

*=less than .05 per cent.

QUESTIONNAIRE FORM 1 1985	TOTAL	SEX		RACE		REGION				4YR COLLEGE PLANS		ILLICIT DRUG USE: LIFETIME				
		M	F	White	Black	NE	NC	S	W	Yes	No	None	Marijuana Only	Few Pills	More Pills	Any Heroin
N (Weighted No. of Cases):	3316	1505	1663	2415	400	783	902	1004	627	1822	1121	1307	719	444	716	29
% of Weighted Total:	100.0	45.4	50.2	72.8	12.1	23.6	27.2	30.3	18.9	55.0	33.8	39.4	21.7	13.4	21.6	0.9

B050C: . . . during the last 30 days?

	TOTAL	M	F	White	Black	NE	NC	S	W	Yes	No	None	Marijuana Only	Few Pills	More Pills	Any Heroin
1. 0 occasions	94.3	94.1	94.5	93.4	97.9	94.5	92.9	95.9	93.4	95.9	92.6	100.0	100.0	98.2	76.4	61.7
2. 1-2	2.9	3.0	2.7	3.3	1.7	2.9	3.3	1.7	4.1	1.7	4.4	-	-	1.8	11.3	23.4
3. 3-5	1.1	1.1	1.1	1.3	0.3	1.4	1.2	0.9	0.7	0.6	1.6	-	-	-	4.8	1.7
4. 6-9	0.9	1.1	0.7	1.0	-	0.2	1.1	0.8	1.4	1.0	0.4	-	-	-	3.6	8.6
5. 10-19	0.7	0.6	0.8	0.8	-	0.7	1.3	0.4	0.4	0.7	0.6	-	-	-	3.1	4.6
6. 20-39	0.1	0.1	0.1	0.1	0.1	0.2	0.1	0.1	-	0.1	*	-	-	-	0.5	-
7. 40 or more	0.1	0.1	0.1	0.1	-	-	0.1	0.2	-	-	0.2	-	-	-	0.4	-
Item 1000 Subject A01c N	3158	1449	1616	2363	371	735	869	944	609	1782	1069	1282	695	419	693	25

IF YOU HAVE NOT TAKEN AMPHETAMINES IN THE LAST TWELVE MONTHS, GO TO Q.B059.

THE FOLLOWING QUESTIONS REFER ONLY TO TAKING AMPHETAMINES WITHOUT A DOCTOR'S ORDERS. IF YOU HAVE NOT DONE THIS IN THE LAST TWELVE MONTHS, GO TO Q.B059

B051: When you used amphetamines during the last year, how often did you use them in each of the following situations?

B051A: When you were alone

	TOTAL	M	F	White	Black	NE	NC	S	W	Yes	No	None	Marijuana Only	Few Pills	More Pills	Any Heroin
1. Not at all	43.3	50.3	38.3	44.4	35.9	48.9	31.4	49.4	46.1	46.3	39.0	-	-	62.7	41.7	5.4
2. A few of the times	27.4	24.5	29.2	26.6	39.4	23.3	35.4	26.2	23.0	24.0	30.1	-	-	29.2	26.1	52.9
3. Some of the times	11.9	11.3	12.7	12.4	5.7	14.6	10.6	13.7	9.1	11.7	13.7	-	-	-	14.2	5.3
4. Most of the times	9.9	9.2	11.0	10.8	-	7.4	14.1	8.5	8.8	10.5	9.4	-	-	1.1	10.5	25.1
5. Every time	7.5	4.8	8.8	5.8	19.1	5.8	8.5	2.2	13.0	7.5	7.8	-	-	7.0	7.5	11.4
Item 2800 Subject A05a N★	392	163	208	330	18	97	113	87	95	173	164	-	-	46	323	18

B051B: With just 1 or 2 other people

	TOTAL	M	F	White	Black	NE	NC	S	W	Yes	No	None	Marijuana Only	Few Pills	More Pills	Any Heroin
1. Not at all	20.2	15.0	21.8	17.1	40.9	23.2	19.1	18.6	19.9	20.6	19.0	-	-	45.2	15.4	16.7
2. A few of the times	37.5	38.3	37.7	38.2	39.4	31.0	40.5	49.6	29.6	37.3	34.0	-	-	43.8	37.8	26.6
3. Some of the times	21.5	21.8	22.0	23.0	13.2	28.8	22.0	11.9	22.3	18.4	27.0	-	-	-	24.4	32.8
4. Most of the times	13.0	15.8	11.2	13.5	-	10.7	10.7	14.0	16.9	13.6	13.2	-	-	-	14.4	23.9
5. Every time	7.8	9.2	7.3	8.1	6.4	6.3	7.7	5.9	11.3	10.1	6.8	-	-	11.1	7.9	-
Item 2810 Subject A05b N★	396	166	209	334	18	97	114	88	98	175	165	-	-	47	326	18

B051C: At a party

	TOTAL	M	F	White	Black	NE	NC	S	W	Yes	No	None	Marijuana Only	Few Pills	More Pills	Any Heroin
1. Not at all	47.5	43.1	51.4	44.9	78.0	39.4	43.0	56.4	53.2	51.5	44.5	-	-	76.6	43.8	27.8
2. A few of the times	20.9	23.7	18.9	22.6	10.7	22.2	26.0	13.3	20.4	20.7	21.8	-	-	16.7	21.6	25.3
3. Some of the times	13.8	15.0	12.7	13.7	5.7	14.6	15.6	15.0	9.5	12.0	14.5	-	-	2.1	15.8	8.7
4. Most of the times	10.7	9.7	11.4	11.4	5.7	13.8	10.4	10.2	8.7	9.5	11.8	-	-	-	12.1	15.7
5. Every time	7.1	8.5	5.5	7.4	-	10.0	4.9	5.2	8.3	6.2	7.4	-	-	4.6	6.6	22.6
Item 2820 Subject A05c N★	386	158	207	325	18	95	113	84	94	171	163	-	-	43	319	18

B051D: When your date or spouse was present

	TOTAL	M	F	White	Black	NE	NC	S	W	Yes	No	None	Marijuana Only	Few Pills	More Pills	Any Heroin
1. Not at all	61.3	64.8	58.4	60.0	86.8	50.4	62.8	67.0	64.9	62.6	58.6	-	-	91.0	56.8	49.3
2. A few of the times	19.4	19.0	20.1	21.4	1.9	25.3	16.3	16.1	20.2	22.4	17.8	-	-	5.1	21.7	23.1
3. Some of the times	10.6	10.7	10.4	10.4	5.7	9.3	15.2	10.8	6.4	9.8	12.0	-	-	-	12.8	2.4
4. Most of the times	5.8	3.3	7.9	5.3	5.7	6.4	4.9	4.4	7.6	3.4	8.5	-	-	-	5.8	22.7
5. Every time	2.9	2.2	3.2	2.9	-	8.7	0.7	1.7	0.8	1.9	3.1	-	-	3.9	2.8	2.4
Item 2830 Subject A05b N★	393	163	210	331	18	96	112	88	97	174	165	-	-	47	322	18

B051E: When people over age 30 were present

	TOTAL	M	F	White	Black	NE	NC	S	W	Yes	No	None	Marijuana Only	Few Pills	More Pills	Any Heroin
1. Not at all	67.0	65.0	69.0	66.8	84.7	69.6	63.1	63.8	72.1	71.0	64.2	-	-	92.8	64.5	39.7
2. A few of the times	13.5	16.6	11.8	14.6	9.7	9.0	15.6	17.3	12.1	12.0	15.2	-	-	3.6	13.3	47.3
3. Some of the times	13.9	12.3	13.7	13.0	5.7	14.0	16.4	13.8	10.7	12.2	14.6	-	-	-	16.2	6.5
4. Most of the times	3.5	4.8	2.5	3.3	-	6.1	2.0	2.6	3.5	3.0	4.8	-	-	-	3.9	6.4
5. Every time	2.1	1.4	2.9	2.3	-	1.3	2.9	2.5	1.6	1.9	1.2	-	-	3.6	2.1	-
Item 2840 Subject A05b N★	393	163	209	331	18	95	114	88	96	174	165	-	-	47	322	18

*=less than .05 per cent.   ★=excludes respondents for whom question was inappropriate.

QUESTIONNAIRE FORM 1 1985	TOTAL	SEX		RACE		REGION				4YR COLLEGE PLANS		ILLICIT DRUG USE: LIFETIME				
		M	F	White	Black	NE	NC	S	W	Yes	No	None	Mari-juana Only	Few Pills	More Pills	Any Her-oin
N (Weighted No. of Cases):	3316	1505	1663	2415	400	783	902	1004	627	1822	1121	1307	719	444	716	29
% of Weighted Total:	100.0	45.4	50.2	72.8	12.1	23.6	27.2	30.3	18.9	55.0	33.8	39.4	21.7	13.4	21.6	0.9

B051F: During the daytime (before 4:00 p.m.)

	TOTAL	M	F	White	Black	NE	NC	S	W	Yes	No	None	Mari-juana Only	Few Pills	More Pills	Any Her-oin
1. Not at all	26.8	31.1	22.3	25.0	57.5	32.2	18.9	37.6	20.8	27.5	24.6	-	-	51.1	22.9	13.2
2. A few of the times	22.1	23.7	21.1	22.9	10.4	17.7	24.4	19.8	25.8	18.2	22.6	-	-	33.0	21.4	14.4
3. Some of the times	17.6	18.3	16.3	17.3	11.3	21.1	19.2	16.7	13.2	15.7	20.7	-	-	-	19.7	25.2
4. Most of the times	22.0	22.7	23.3	23.0	14.0	20.5	24.0	16.1	26.7	24.0	21.1	-	-	3.3	24.1	42.3
5. Every time	11.5	4.2	17.0	11.8	6.7	8.5	13.5	9.8	13.5	14.6	10.9	-	-	12.6	11.9	4.9
Item 2850 Subject A05c N★	395	164	211	333	18	97	114	88	96	174	166	-	-	47	324	18

B051G: At your home (or apartment or dorm)

	TOTAL	M	F	White	Black	NE	NC	S	W	Yes	No	None	Mari-juana Only	Few Pills	More Pills	Any Her-oin
1. Not at all	40.7	45.3	38.6	41.0	39.3	44.8	30.3	49.3	41.3	40.7	42.3	-	-	57.8	37.5	37.0
2. A few of the times	22.1	23.3	20.6	22.1	27.7	18.5	23.7	20.5	25.1	17.3	22.9	-	-	22.5	22.5	19.7
3. Some of the times	16.5	20.6	13.3	17.0	7.6	22.1	21.8	13.0	7.8	19.5	14.2	-	-	1.0	19.0	15.6
4. Most of the times	12.8	7.9	16.3	13.4	2.2	9.3	16.0	11.5	13.7	12.3	13.2	-	-	-	14.5	19.4
5. Every time	7.9	3.0	11.1	6.6	23.3	5.3	8.1	5.6	12.0	10.2	7.3	-	-	18.7	6.4	8.2
Item 2860 Subject A05c N★	392	162	209	330	18	95	114	87	97	174	165	-	-	47	323	18

B051H: At school

	TOTAL	M	F	White	Black	NE	NC	S	W	Yes	No	None	Mari-juana Only	Few Pills	More Pills	Any Her-oin
1. Not at all	33.2	35.6	29.7	29.5	72.2	32.0	28.7	38.0	35.4	38.9	28.2	-	-	70.6	27.7	15.4
2. A few of the times	25.8	28.3	24.4	27.8	8.1	30.8	22.6	23.7	26.3	19.2	28.7	-	-	21.2	26.8	27.0
3. Some of the times	18.6	18.3	18.3	17.9	11.3	17.5	21.3	17.8	17.3	17.6	19.2	-	-	2.5	21.9	5.8
4. Most of the times	15.1	11.4	19.5	17.0	2.7	12.2	17.9	15.1	14.6	17.2	16.0	-	-	-	16.0	43.7
5. Every time	7.3	6.4	8.1	7.7	5.7	7.6	9.4	5.4	6.4	7.1	7.9	-	-	5.7	7.7	8.0
Item 2880 Subject A05c N★	393	163	209	331	18	97	114	87	96	174	165	-	-	47	324	18

B051I: In a car

	TOTAL	M	F	White	Black	NE	NC	S	W	Yes	No	None	Mari-juana Only	Few Pills	More Pills	Any Her-oin
1. Not at all	47.9	35.3	57.3	45.3	74.5	49.8	42.7	44.7	55.1	52.0	45.4	-	-	74.8	43.5	41.7
2. A few of the times	23.3	27.7	20.6	25.0	14.2	23.5	22.6	25.1	22.0	15.8	29.4	-	-	23.1	23.7	22.5
3. Some of the times	19.0	26.2	13.3	19.8	11.3	16.7	26.4	15.9	15.4	22.1	15.4	-	-	-	22.1	18.8
4. Most of the times	7.0	7.9	6.6	7.1	-	6.5	5.1	11.9	5.2	6.7	9.1	-	-	-	7.5	17.1
5. Every time	2.8	3.0	2.2	2.7	-	3.4	3.1	2.3	2.4	3.3	0.7	-	-	2.1	3.1	
Item 2890 Subject A05c N★	394	164	209	332	18	97	114	87	97	174	165	-	-	47	325	18

B052: How many of the times when you used amphetamines during the last year did you use them along with each of the following drugs—that is, so that their effects overlapped?

B052A: With alcohol

	TOTAL	M	F	White	Black	NE	NC	S	W	Yes	No	None	Mari-juana Only	Few Pills	More Pills	Any Her-oin
1. Not at all	44.3	37.8	49.3	42.2	64.5	37.1	43.7	42.1	54.2	42.6	47.5	-	-	73.7	39.6	27.1
2. A few of the times	23.5	19.1	27.1	25.0	7.8	25.7	21.4	24.3	23.1	22.8	22.9	-	-	20.7	24.6	19.8
3. Some of the times	14.7	18.7	12.4	15.5	22.0	18.4	11.9	17.7	11.4	18.2	12.6	-	-	-	16.7	23.9
4. Most of the times	9.0	9.7	7.4	9.7	-	9.9	14.6	4.4	5.9	8.2	8.0	-	-	-	10.3	13.9
5. Every time	8.5	14.7	3.9	7.7	5.7	8.8	8.3	11.5	5.4	8.2	8.9	-	-	5.6	8.7	15.3
Item 2900 Subject A01h N★	395	162	213	334	18	96	113	91	96	176	166	-	-	49	322	18

B052B: With marijuana

	TOTAL	M	F	White	Black	NE	NC	S	W	Yes	No	None	Mari-juana Only	Few Pills	More Pills	Any Her-oin
1. Not at all	55.5	47.7	62.9	55.5	59.7	51.2	48.5	57.1	66.4	59.0	56.1	-	-	86.3	51.2	32.3
2. A few of the times	18.9	20.8	18.1	19.6	23.3	21.5	20.8	18.7	14.4	17.2	20.1	-	-	11.7	20.4	17.9
3. Some of the times	10.1	8.9	10.5	10.0	11.3	10.6	9.9	9.9	9.9	10.6	9.1	-	-	-	12.0	5.8
4. Most of the times	8.1	9.0	5.8	7.7	5.7	10.0	11.6	7.3	3.1	4.7	8.5	-	-	-	8.4	28.6
5. Every time	7.4	13.7	2.7	7.2	-	6.8	9.2	7.0	6.2	8.4	6.1	-	-	2.0	7.9	15.5
Item 2910 Subject A01h N★	396	163	212	334	18	96	113	91	97	176	166	-	-	49	322	18

B052C: With LSD

	TOTAL	M	F	White	Black	NE	NC	S	W	Yes	No	None	Mari-juana Only	Few Pills	More Pills	Any Her-oin
1. Not at all	95.7	94.4	97.9	97.4	89.3	93.8	95.6	94.9	98.7	95.6	97.3	-	-	100.0	96.8	63.6
2. A few of the times	1.5	1.0	2.1	1.5	-	3.9	0.6	1.8	-	0.4	2.7	-	-	-	1.1	14.0
3. Some of the times	0.5	1.2	-	-	10.7	-	1.7	-	-	1.1	-	-	-	-	-	11.1
4. Most of the times	1.8	2.5	-	0.6	-	1.9	1.2	3.3	1.3	2.3	-	-	-	-	1.6	11.3
5. Every time	0.4	0.9	-	0.5	-	0.5	0.9	-	-	0.6	-	-	-	-	0.5	-
Item 2920 Subject A01h N★	387	160	207	325	18	96	111	86	94	173	160	-	-	49	315	17

★=excludes respondents for whom question was inappropriate.

QUESTIONNAIRE FORM 1 1985	TOTAL	SEX		RACE		REGION				4YR COLLEGE PLANS		ILLICIT DRUG USE: LIFETIME				
		M	F	White	Black	NE	NC	S	W	Yes	No	None	Mari-juana Only	Few Pills	More Pills	Any Her-oin
N (Weighted No. of Cases):	3316	1505	1663	2415	400	783	902	1004	627	1822	1121	1307	719	444	716	29
% of Weighted Total:	100.0	45.4	50.2	72.8	12.1	23.6	27.2	30.3	18.9	55.0	33.8	39.4	21.7	13.4	21.6	0.9
B052D: With psychedelics other than LSD																
1. Not at all	96.2	93.0	99.7	98.0	83.7	97.1	96.0	93.1	98.4	94.5	98.7	-	-	100.0	96.7	72.5
2. A few of the times	1.8	3.9	0.3	1.5	10.7	-	2.8	3.6	0.6	3.3	0.7	-	-	-	1.0	22.8
3. Some of the times	-	-	-	-	-	-	-	-	-	-	-	-	-	-	-	-
4. Most of the times	1.4	2.4	-	0.5	-	1.9	-	3.3	1.0	2.2	-	-	-	-	1.5	4.8
5. Every time	0.6	0.6	-	-	5.7	1.1	1.2	-	-	-	0.6	-	-	-	0.7	-
Item 2930 Subject A01h N★	384	157	207	323	18	95	109	87	93	170	161	-	-	49	313	16
B053: What have been the most important reasons for your taking amphetamines without a doctor's orders? (Mark all that apply.)																
A. To experiment–to see what it's like	52.7	55.9	50.6	52.9	66.7	37.5	59.8	62.0	50.1	57.8	48.7	-	-	75.3	50.1	31.6
B. To relax or relieve tension	16.9	13.0	19.8	16.9	9.6	19.0	16.5	17.0	15.2	16.3	19.7	-	-	10.4	17.4	21.5
C. To feel good or get high	48.8	50.9	44.4	49.3	24.7	37.0	48.9	57.0	52.5	45.5	50.0	-	-	44.4	49.8	45.0
D. To seek deeper insights and understanding	2.5	3.2	1.4	1.7	12.3	2.6	3.7	1.4	1.9	3.0	1.4	-	-	-	1.9	13.2
E. To have a good time with my friends	33.7	39.2	29.3	34.5	20.7	23.8	35.3	37.6	37.6	33.8	34.1	-	-	30.7	34.1	33.9
F. To fit in with a group I like	5.6	5.0	5.7	6.1	-	6.0	5.8	6.1	4.4	3.5	8.7	-	-	3.6	5.7	3.3
G. To get away from my problems or troubles	9.8	8.0	11.5	11.1	2.2	9.2	5.7	11.1	14.0	8.1	12.5	-	-	1.4	10.4	17.3
H. Because of boredom, nothing else to do	17.7	21.1	14.1	17.0	9.2	18.4	17.4	14.6	20.1	18.7	16.3	-	-	7.0	19.0	20.8
I. Because of anger or frustration	8.1	5.4	10.0	8.9	6.8	8.4	6.5	7.9	10.1	5.6	12.0	-	-	3.2	8.5	9.8
J. To get through the day	30.0	36.6	26.3	32.7	8.9	23.5	35.0	35.2	25.6	28.7	32.9	-	-	3.6	34.0	29.1
K. To increase the effects of some other drug(s)	11.1	15.9	7.1	10.6	6.8	6.6	12.2	14.3	11.3	10.5	11.5	-	-	6.4	11.0	22.6
L. To decrease (offset) the effects of some other drug(s)	3.5	5.7	1.5	3.7	-	3.1	1.4	2.3	7.2	4.7	0.6	-	-	-	3.2	12.0
M. To stay awake	55.1	54.6	55.3	57.8	11.1	53.7	61.0	47.1	56.8	49.6	59.8	-	-	27.5	59.9	45.3
N. To get more energy	62.3	59.5	64.0	65.4	13.3	58.1	69.5	60.1	59.7	61.1	59.9	-	-	51.8	63.3	76.0
O. To help me lose weight	34.2	10.6	52.5	35.3	21.3	34.4	39.0	33.2	29.3	27.8	41.2	-	-	18.8	37.6	14.1
P. Because I am "hooked"–I feel I have to have them	0.8	0.5	0.6	0.6	-	1.1	0.5	-	1.7	0.8	0.5	-	-	-	0.7	-
Item 2940-3090 Subject A06a N★	386	160	209	330	16	91	113	87	96	174	160	-	-	48	318	18
B054: When you take amphetamines, how high do you usually get?																
1. Not at all high	12.8	15.2	11.2	10.5	42.4	19.3	12.0	13.2	7.3	10.4	10.2	-	-	35.4	9.5	2.9
2. A little high	36.7	37.5	34.8	36.1	29.8	28.4	38.3	43.2	36.8	36.0	37.8	-	-	44.6	35.3	42.8
3. Moderately high	24.9	24.1	25.2	25.9	13.7	20.5	25.0	20.5	33.1	25.1	27.0	-	-	5.8	26.9	45.0
4. Very high	5.2	8.4	2.8	5.3	-	4.9	2.6	7.0	6.8	5.0	5.1	-	-	-	6.3	-
5. I don't take them to get high	20.4	14.8	26.1	22.2	14.2	27.0	22.0	16.1	16.0	23.5	19.9	-	-	14.3	22.0	9.3
Item 3100 Subject A01e N★	380	160	203	324	16	90	110	85	95	173	157	-	-	48	313	18
B055: When you take amphetamines how long do you usually stay high?																
1. Usually don't get high	26.1	23.3	29.7	26.0	52.0	30.6	28.3	26.3	19.0	22.3	27.7	-	-	47.3	23.4	12.2
2. One to two hours	31.4	32.9	29.6	29.8	34.9	26.5	27.2	40.9	32.4	32.2	32.0	-	-	36.7	29.5	54.4
3. Three to six hours	31.2	32.2	29.0	32.3	13.1	32.3	31.5	27.0	33.5	29.8	33.0	-	-	16.0	34.4	16.9
4. Seven to 24 hours	10.8	10.2	11.7	11.2	-	10.6	13.0	5.8	12.8	14.5	7.3	-	-	-	12.1	16.6
5. More than 24 hours	0.6	1.4	-	0.7	-	-	-	-	2.3	1.3	-	-	-	-	0.7	-
Item 3110 Subject A01f N★	392	165	210	334	17	95	114	87	96	177	164	-	-	48	325	18
B056: What amphetamines have you taken during the last year without a doctor's orders? (Mark all that apply.)																
A. Benzedrine	15.5	18.0	12.7	14.9	13.2	12.7	14.6	16.5	18.4	16.8	13.6	-	-	2.5	14.6	66.0
B. Dexedrine	10.1	11.2	9.6	9.8	15.9	5.4	15.6	13.3	5.4	12.7	8.9	-	-	-	9.6	43.2
C. Methedrine	24.1	27.3	21.4	23.3	23.5	14.0	23.6	30.7	28.7	27.9	18.7	-	-	23.9	21.7	57.6
D. Ritalin	3.3	3.0	2.0	2.7	-	3.5	3.0	3.1	3.7	1.7	3.5	-	-	-	2.2	27.0
E. Preludin	3.0	2.2	2.6	2.7	-	5.6	2.3	1.4	2.8	2.3	2.5	-	-	-	2.3	19.6
F. Dexamyl	5.2	5.1	3.8	4.7	5.0	4.7	6.0	6.6	3.5	4.3	3.5	-	-	1.5	4.5	23.6
G. Methamphetamine	16.6	20.0	13.7	15.4	11.0	18.2	12.3	15.5	20.9	20.8	14.6	-	-	2.5	17.3	39.6
H. Other	27.0	34.1	21.7	25.7	24.3	31.6	20.5	35.7	22.1	25.3	28.5	-	-	24.3	27.1	31.5
I. Don't know the names of some amphetamines I have used	58.4	52.8	64.0	59.9	41.2	58.1	60.9	49.8	63.5	61.4	55.6	-	-	58.2	58.8	53.7
Item 3120-3200 Subject A01l N★	378	158	202	324	15	93	107	84	94	172	154	-	-	48	310	17

★=excludes respondents for whom question was inappropriate.

QUESTIONNAIRE FORM 1 1985	TOTAL	SEX		RACE		REGION				4YR COLLEGE PLANS		ILLICIT DRUG USE: LIFETIME				
		M	F	White	Black	NE	NC	S	W	Yes	No	None	Marijuana Only	Few Pills	More Pills	Any Heroin
N (Weighted No. of Cases):	3316	1505	1663	2415	400	783	902	1004	627	1822	1121	1307	719	444	716	29
% of Weighted Total:	100.0	45.4	50.2	72.8	12.1	23.6	27.2	30.3	18.9	55.0	33.8	39.4	21.7	13.4	21.6	0.9
B057: What methods have you used for taking amphetamines? (Mark all that apply.)																
A. By mouth	95.2	91.8	97.9	95.5	100.0	95.6	98.9	97.0	89.1	95.4	95.4	-	-	93.9	95.3	97.6
B. Injection	2.1	2.4	1.1	1.7	-	4.1	-	3.9	1.2	2.1	1.6	-	-	2.7	1.2	11.3
C. Other	15.7	26.3	7.5	15.1	-	17.5	7.5	15.2	23.9	16.3	15.5	-	-	7.6	16.1	25.6
Item 3210-3230　Subject A05d　N★	386	160	210	333	14	93	111	85	97	176	159	-	-	46	321	18
B058: Have you ever tried to stop using amphetamines and found that you couldn't stop?																
1. Yes	5.0	2.2	7.2	4.5	3.4	5.6	1.6	6.5	7.0	4.9	4.6	-	-	7.8	4.3	10.2
2. No	95.0	97.8	92.8	95.5	96.6	94.4	98.4	93.5	93.0	95.1	95.4	-	-	92.2	95.7	89.8
Item 3240　Subject A01i　N★	384	160	208	329	14	92	111	85	96	171	161	-	-	46	319	18
B059: Do you think you will be using amphetamines without a doctor's orders five years from now?																
1. I definitely will	0.6	0.7	0.4	0.5	-	1.2	0.3	0.5	0.2	0.4	0.6	0.3	0.1	0.3	1.3	4.1
2. I probably will	4.9	4.2	5.5	5.2	2.6	5.3	6.0	3.2	5.5	4.2	5.7	0.4	0.9	4.0	17.3	22.8
3. I probably will not	21.8	20.3	22.7	22.8	14.0	24.2	22.8	18.7	22.2	20.7	22.6	10.7	15.8	29.2	43.2	49.1
4. I definitely will not	72.8	74.8	71.5	71.5	83.4	69.3	71.0	77.6	72.1	74.7	71.1	88.6	83.1	66.6	38.2	23.9
Item 3250　Subject A04a　N	3174	1456	1634	2369	381	728	879	963	604	1794	1085	1280	688	427	690	26
The next questions are about QUAALUDES (Methaqualone), which are sometimes prescribed by doctors. Drugstores are not supposed to sell them without a prescription. Quaaludes are sometimes called: soapers, quads. **B060:** On how many occasions (if any) have you taken quaaludes on your own–that is, without a doctor telling you to take them . . .																
B060A: . . . in your lifetime?																
1. 0 occasions	93.4	92.8	94.1	92.7	97.9	92.3	93.8	92.0	96.5	94.9	90.9	100.0	100.0	91.0	77.9	32.4
2. 1-2	3.7	3.8	3.7	4.1	1.0	4.4	3.3	4.6	2.2	3.0	5.1	-	-	9.0	11.1	13.4
3. 3-5	1.2	1.3	1.0	1.4	0.4	1.9	1.2	1.2	0.3	0.8	1.9	-	-	4.8	15.4
4. 6-9	0.8	1.2	0.3	0.8	-	0.7	0.5	1.2	0.5	0.7	0.8	-	-	-	3.1	12.5
5. 10-19	0.5	0.4	0.5	0.5	-	0.3	0.7	0.4	0.5	0.3	0.9	-	-	-	1.8	8.1
6. 20-39	0.3	0.4	0.2	0.3	0.5	0.2	0.4	0.4	-	0.3	0.3	-	-	-	0.9	10.2
7. 40 or more	0.2	0.1	0.2	0.2	0.2	0.2	0.1	0.3	-	-	0.2	-	-	-	0.4	8.0
Item 1010　Subject A01a　N	3144	1452	1610	2360	367	714	873	949	608	1784	1072	1280	690	426	677	28
B060B: . . . during the last 12 months?																
1. 0 occasions	97.6	96.9	98.3	97.6	99.0	97.6	97.9	97.0	98.1	98.2	96.9	100.0	100.0	98.6	91.9	48.9
2. 1-2	1.7	2.3	1.2	1.8	0.3	1.9	1.4	2.2	1.3	1.5	2.3	-	-	1.4	6.2	22.4
3. 3-5	0.4	0.5	0.4	0.4	0.5	0.4	0.4	0.5	0.4	0.3	0.5	-	-	-	1.3	19.3
4. 6-9	0.1	0.2	0.1	0.2	-	-	0.2	0.1	0.2	0.1	0.2	-	-	-	0.5	3.3
5. 10-19	*	*	*	*	0.2	0.1	-	0.1	-	-	0.1	-	-	-	0.1	2.0
6. 20-39	-	-	-	-	-	-	-	-	-	-	-	-	-	-	-	-
7. 40 or more	0.1	0.1	-	*	-	-	0.1	0.1	-	-	0.1	-	-	-	0.1	4.1
Item 1020　Subject A01b　N	3141	1450	1609	2356	368	711	873	950	608	1781	1072	1280	690	424	675	28
B060C: . . . during the last 30 days?																
1. 0 occasions	99.2	98.9	99.5	99.2	99.3	99.6	98.6	99.2	99.6	99.5	98.8	100.0	100.0	100.0	97.3	75.5
2. 1-2	0.7	1.0	0.4	0.7	0.7	0.4	1.3	0.5	0.4	0.5	1.1	-	-	-	2.2	22.9
3. 3-5	0.1	*	0.1	0.1	-	-	-	0.3	-	-	0.1	-	-	-	0.3	1.6
4. 6-9	*	-	*	*	-	-	-	*	-	*	-	-	-	-	0.1	-
5. 10-19	-	-	-	-	-	-	-	-	-	-	-	-	-	-	-	-
6. 20-39	-	-	-	-	-	-	-	-	-	-	-	-	-	-	-	-
7. 40 or more	*	-	-	-	-	-	0.1	-	-	-	-	-	-	-	0.1	-
Item 1030　Subject A01c　N	3141	1450	1609	2357	368	710	873	950	609	1782	1072	1280	690	425	674	28

*=less than .05 per cent.　　★=excludes respondents for whom question was inappropriate.

QUESTIONNAIRE FORM 1 1985	TOTAL	SEX		RACE		REGION				4YR COLLEGE PLANS		ILLICIT DRUG USE: LIFETIME				
		M	F	White	Black	NE	NC	S	W	Yes	No	None	Marijuana Only	Few Pills	More Pills	Any Heroin
N (Weighted No. of Cases):	3316	1505	1663	2415	400	783	902	1004	627	1822	1121	1307	719	444	716	29
% of Weighted Total:	100.0	45.4	50.2	72.8	12.1	23.6	27.2	30.3	18.9	55.0	33.8	39.4	21.7	13.4	21.6	0.9

IF YOU HAVE NOT TAKEN QUAALUDES IN THE LAST TWELVE MONTHS, GO TO Q.B063.

THE FOLLOWING QUESTIONS REFER ONLY TO TAKING QUAALUDES WITHOUT A DOCTOR'S ORDERS. IF YOU HAVE NOT DONE THIS IN THE LAST TWELVE MONTHS, GO TO Q.B063.

B061: When you take quaaludes how high do you usually get?

	TOTAL	M	F	White	Black	NE	NC	S	W	Yes	No	None	Marijuana Only	Few Pills	More Pills	Any Heroin
1. Not at all high	5.2	2.6	6.4	3.2	-	6.2	-	7.9	4.6	1.3	7.9	-	-	16.2	2.2	7.7
2. A little high	19.8	17.0	24.7	18.1	54.8	28.7	24.2	8.3	27.0	21.1	20.1	-	-	37.0	18.6	21.6
3. Moderately high	44.4	37.3	53.7	45.6	45.2	44.8	48.6	48.6	27.9	34.4	51.0	-	-	46.8	44.6	46.3
4. Very high	29.1	43.1	11.0	31.1	-	20.4	27.3	35.1	30.5	39.6	21.0	-	-	-	32.5	24.4
5. I don't take them to get high	1.6	-	4.2	2.1	-	-	-	-	10.0	3.5	-	-	-	-	2.1	-
Item 3260 Subject A01e N★	74	42	27	55	3	18	17	28	12	33	30	-	-	3	55	14

B062: When you take quaaludes how long do you usually stay high?

	TOTAL	M	F	White	Black	NE	NC	S	W	Yes	No	None	Marijuana Only	Few Pills	More Pills	Any Heroin
1. Usually don't get high	3.9	2.6	6.4	3.2	-	6.5	-	4.6	4.6	1.3	7.9	-	-	16.2	2.2	7.7
2. One to two hours	26.2	21.6	36.1	26.4	54.8	18.6	39.7	24.6	21.0	29.1	26.4	-	-	66.9	19.9	41.1
3. Three to six hours	52.1	53.2	46.9	55.2	45.2	67.5	40.8	48.7	54.4	38.9	59.9	-	-	16.9	55.5	47.4
4. Seven to 24 hours	17.1	22.5	10.6	15.2	-	7.5	16.6	22.2	20.0	30.7	5.8	-	-	-	21.5	3.9
5. More than 24 hours	0.7	-	-	-	-	-	2.9	-	-	-	-	-	-	-	0.9	-
Item 3270 Subject A01f N★	72	42	27	55	3	17	17	27	12	33	30	-	-	3	55	14

B063: The next questions are about BARBITURATES, which doctors sometimes prescribe to help people relax or get to sleep. Drugstores are not supposed to sell them without a prescription.

Barbiturates are sometimes called: downs, downers, goofballs, yellows, reds, blues, rainbows.

They include the following drugs: Phenobarbital, Seconal, Tuinal, Nembutal, Luminal, Desbutal, Amytal.

Have you ever taken barbiturates because a doctor told you to use them?

	TOTAL	M	F	White	Black	NE	NC	S	W	Yes	No	None	Marijuana Only	Few Pills	More Pills	Any Heroin
1. No	94.8	94.2	95.5	94.2	98.7	94.5	95.6	94.6	94.5	95.0	95.0	97.4	97.1	93.6	89.0	81.9
2. Yes, but I had already tried them on my own.	0.9	0.9	0.6	0.9	-	1.2	1.3	0.4	0.9	0.8	1.0	0.2	-	0.4	3.1	12.0
3. Yes, and it was the first time I took any	4.3	4.9	3.8	4.9	1.3	4.4	3.1	5.0	4.6	4.2	4.0	2.5	2.9	6.1	7.9	6.0
Item 3280 Subject A01j N	3071	1413	1581	2325	347	695	856	931	589	1749	1044	1254	668	418	659	27

B064: On how many occasions (if any) have you taken barbiturates on your own–that is, without a doctor telling you to take them . . .

B064A: . . . in your lifetime?

	TOTAL	M	F	White	Black	NE	NC	S	W	Yes	No	None	Marijuana Only	Few Pills	More Pills	Any Heroin
1. 0 occasions	92.4	92.1	92.7	91.8	97.6	91.7	91.9	92.7	93.2	93.8	90.0	100.0	100.0	93.9	70.9	36.7
2. 1-2	3.4	3.4	3.4	3.3	1.4	2.8	3.9	3.3	3.7	2.9	4.3	-	-	6.1	11.1	21.5
3. 3-5	1.8	1.9	1.5	2.2	-	2.5	1.8	1.6	1.2	1.5	2.2	-	-	-	7.9	8.9
4. 6-9	0.8	0.9	0.8	0.9	0.5	0.7	1.2	0.6	0.9	0.6	1.2	-	-	-	3.4	11.3
5. 10-19	0.7	0.7	0.6	0.8	0.3	1.2	0.5	0.2	0.9	0.6	0.8	-	-	-	2.9	4.1
6. 20-39	0.2	0.1	0.3	0.2	-	0.2	0.4	0.3	-	0.2	0.3	-	-	-	0.8	6.1
7. 40 or more	0.7	0.8	0.7	0.7	0.2	0.9	0.3	1.3	0.1	0.3	1.3	-	-	-	2.9	11.3
Item 1040 Subject A01a N	3103	1429	1594	2337	360	705	860	941	598	1770	1056	1270	678	421	668	27

★=excludes respondents for whom question was inappropriate.

QUESTIONNAIRE FORM 1 1985	TOTAL	SEX		RACE		REGION				4YR COLLEGE PLANS		ILLICIT DRUG USE: LIFETIME				
		M	F	White	Black	NE	NC	S	W	Yes	No	None	Marijuana Only	Few Pills	More Pills	Any Heroin
N (Weighted No. of Cases):	3316	1505	1663	2415	400	783	902	1004	627	1822	1121	1307	719	444	716	29
% of Weighted Total:	100.0	45.4	50.2	72.8	12.1	23.6	27.2	30.3	18.9	55.0	33.8	39.4	21.7	13.4	21.6	0.9
B064B: ... during the last 12 months?																
1. 0 occasions	96.4	96.4	96.6	95.9	98.9	96.3	96.2	96.3	96.7	97.1	95.6	100.0	100.0	98.6	85.8	54.2
2. 1-2	1.8	1.7	1.8	2.0	0.6	1.2	1.9	1.9	2.1	1.5	2.1	-	-	1.4	6.4	26.0
3. 3-5	0.9	0.8	0.8	1.1	-	1.0	1.4	0.5	0.6	0.6	1.0	-	-	-	3.6	10.4
4. 6-9	0.2	0.3	0.2	0.2	0.4	0.4	0.3	-	0.3	0.1	0.4	-	-	-	1.0	1.8
5. 10-19	0.2	0.4	0.1	0.3	-	0.7	0.2	-	0.2	0.3	0.2	-	-	-	1.1	-
6. 20-39	0.2	0.1	0.3	0.3	-	0.2	-	0.6	-	0.1	0.4	-	-	-	0.9	4.2
7. 40 or more	0.3	0.2	0.2	0.2	-	0.2	-	0.7	0.1	0.2	0.3	-	-	-	1.0	3.4
Item 1050 Subject A01b N	3103	1429	1594	2337	360	705	860	941	598	1770	1056	1270	678	421	668	27
B064C: ... during the last 30 days?																
1. 0 occasions	98.5	98.6	98.6	98.3	99.6	98.1	98.7	98.4	98.9	98.9	98.1	100.0	100.0	99.6	93.8	88.0
2. 1-2	0.8	0.6	1.0	1.0	0.4	1.2	1.0	0.6	0.6	0.7	0.9	-	-	0.4	3.5	4.3
3. 3-5	0.3	0.4	0.1	0.3	-	0.5	0.3	0.1	0.2	0.2	0.2	-	-	-	1.2	1.4
4. 6-9	0.1	0.2	*	0.1	-	0.1	-	0.2	0.3	-	0.4	-	-	-	0.4	4.2
5. 10-19	0.2	0.3	0.2	0.2	-	0.2	-	0.6	-	0.2	0.4	-	-	-	1.1	-
6. 20-39	*	-	*	*	-	-	-	0.1	-	-	0.1	-	-	-	-	2.0
7. 40 or more	*	-	*	*	-	-	-	0.1	-	-	-	-	-	-	0.1	-
Item 1060 Subject A01c N	3103	1429	1594	2337	360	705	860	941	598	1770	1056	1270	678	421	668	27

IF YOU HAVE NOT TAKEN BARBITURATES IN THE LAST TWELVE MONTHS, GO TO Q.B072.

THE FOLLOWING QUESTIONS REFER ONLY TO TAKING BARBITURATES WITHOUT A DOCTOR'S ORDERS. IF YOU HAVE NOT DONE THIS IN THE LAST TWELVE MONTHS, GO TO Q.B072

B065: When you used barbiturates during the last year, how often did you use them in each of the following situations?

B065A: When you were alone

	TOTAL	M	F	White	Black	NE	NC	S	W	Yes	No	None	Marijuana Only	Few Pills	More Pills	Any Heroin
1. Not at all	38.8	43.3	34.8	39.5	36.2	29.7	48.8	34.7	41.5	36.1	40.8	-	-	60.7	38.2	21.5
2. A few of the times	26.0	30.6	21.3	26.1	28.8	38.7	27.3	13.2	27.2	20.9	30.9	-	-	24.6	26.0	32.0
3. Some of the times	15.5	18.5	15.2	13.3	35.0	10.4	11.4	17.5	27.2	23.7	7.3	-	-	-	13.4	38.5
4. Most of the times	13.2	6.2	20.0	14.1	-	13.1	7.1	24.6	4.0	12.7	17.5	-	-	-	16.5	-
5. Every time	6.5	1.5	8.7	6.9	-	8.0	5.4	9.9	-	6.6	3.4	-	-	14.7	5.9	8.0
Item 3290 Subject A05a N★	106	45	52	87	5	26	32	31	17	46	47	-	-	5	84	13

B065B: With just 1 or 2 other people

	TOTAL	M	F	White	Black	NE	NC	S	W	Yes	No	None	Marijuana Only	Few Pills	More Pills	Any Heroin
1. Not at all	25.2	17.5	24.6	22.3	29.0	27.3	28.1	27.5	12.3	25.7	21.5	-	-	78.9	22.9	3.7
2. A few of the times	37.0	38.9	38.5	41.4	36.0	23.7	36.6	39.7	53.7	33.0	45.8	-	-	-	42.2	25.6
3. Some of the times	20.5	26.1	17.2	20.8	35.0	28.3	24.9	12.8	13.6	19.8	19.5	-	-	-	16.1	62.0
4. Most of the times	12.5	17.5	10.0	11.9	-	12.6	10.3	17.8	6.9	16.4	8.7	-	-	-	15.6	-
5. Every time	4.8	-	9.7	3.5	-	8.0	-	2.3	13.6	5.1	4.4	-	-	21.1	3.3	8.7
Item 3300 Subject A05b N★	107	46	53	88	5	27	32	31	17	47	47	-	-	5	86	13

B065C: At a party

	TOTAL	M	F	White	Black	NE	NC	S	W	Yes	No	None	Marijuana Only	Few Pills	More Pills	Any Heroin
1. Not at all	50.6	46.6	52.3	51.8	36.2	50.2	45.0	53.6	57.0	55.8	50.7	-	-	100.0	49.5	26.9
2. A few of the times	22.1	21.5	25.7	20.1	53.6	27.9	15.7	27.6	15.2	18.6	29.5	-	-	-	23.8	24.2
3. Some of the times	11.0	16.5	6.5	12.7	10.3	12.5	12.0	10.9	6.7	12.9	4.9	-	-	-	10.4	22.2
4. Most of the times	8.7	15.4	4.4	10.6	-	9.4	11.9	5.3	7.7	10.2	4.7	-	-	-	10.2	4.4
5. Every time	7.6	-	11.0	4.8	-	-	15.4	2.6	13.5	2.4	10.2	-	-	-	6.1	22.3
Item 3310 Subject A05c N★	107	45	54	88	5	27	33	31	17	47	47	-	-	5	86	13

B065D: When your date or spouse was present

	TOTAL	M	F	White	Black	NE	NC	S	W	Yes	No	None	Marijuana Only	Few Pills	More Pills	Any Heroin
1. Not at all	62.7	60.3	65.3	66.6	71.2	43.3	67.4	66.7	76.1	66.9	61.5	-	-	100.0	59.0	64.3
2. A few of the times	19.6	25.8	17.0	17.8	28.8	30.8	14.4	19.3	13.1	13.9	27.2	-	-	-	20.4	26.1
3. Some of the times	11.5	7.3	12.3	8.8	-	14.1	10.7	12.8	6.7	11.4	6.3	-	-	-	12.9	9.6
4. Most of the times	3.4	2.7	3.1	3.3	-	4.9	3.7	1.3	4.0	2.7	5.0	-	-	-	4.2	-
5. Every time	2.8	3.8	2.3	3.4	-	6.8	3.7	-	-	5.2	-	-	-	-	3.5	-
Item 3320 Subject A05b N★	106	46	52	87	5	26	32	31	17	47	45	-	-	5	85	13

*=less than .05 per cent.   ★=excludes respondents for whom question was inappropriate.

QUESTIONNAIRE FORM 1 1985	TOTAL	SEX		RACE		REGION				4YR COLLEGE PLANS		ILLICIT DRUG USE: LIFETIME				
		M	F	White	Black	NE	NC	S	W	Yes	No	None	Marijuana Only	Few Pills	More Pills	Any Heroin
N (Weighted No. of Cases):	3316	1505	1663	2415	400	783	902	1004	627	1822	1121	1307	719	444	716	29
% of Weighted Total:	100.0	45.4	50.2	72.8	12.1	23.6	27.2	30.3	18.9	55.0	33.8	39.4	21.7	13.4	21.6	0.9
B065E: When people over age 30 were present																
1. Not at all	56.5	56.8	55.8	56.2	71.2	49.9	61.5	57.9	54.8	54.9	58.2	-	-	78.9	53.1	61.3
2. A few of the times	24.1	21.6	29.8	26.2	28.8	15.2	20.7	26.2	41.2	26.7	23.8	-	-	21.1	25.3	21.9
3. Some of the times	13.9	14.1	11.2	11.7	-	28.6	10.5	12.4	-	14.4	11.1	-	-	-	14.7	16.8
4. Most of the times	3.7	4.9	2.0	3.8	-	3.8	3.7	3.6	4.0	-	7.0	-	-	-	4.6	-
5. Every time	1.7	2.6	1.2	2.1	-	2.5	3.6	-	-	4.0	-	-	-	-	2.2	-
Item 3330 Subject A05b N★	107	46	54	88	5	27	33	31	17	47	47	-	-	5	86	13
B065F: During the daytime (before 4:00 p.m.)																
1. Not at all	45.2	50.3	37.0	44.5	74.3	48.5	60.4	32.6	33.2	35.9	46.6	-	-	78.9	41.6	44.3
2. A few of the times	26.0	25.6	30.0	28.9	25.7	22.5	26.0	27.3	28.9	21.0	35.9	-	-	-	29.7	17.4
3. Some of the times	20.5	16.1	23.1	17.8	-	10.5	13.6	34.6	24.4	30.3	12.7	-	-	-	20.4	34.1
4. Most of the times	4.9	7.9	3.1	6.0	-	16.1	-	3.2	-	6.5	4.7	-	-	-	5.5	4.2
5. Every time	3.4	-	6.8	2.8	-	2.5	-	2.3	13.6	6.3	-	-	-	21.1	2.9	-
Item 3340 Subject A05c N★	107	46	54	88	5	27	33	31	17	47	47	-	-	5	86	13
B065G: At your home (or apartment or dorm)																
1. Not at all	32.7	41.7	23.9	29.2	81.4	35.2	41.2	22.0	31.9	27.8	35.1	-	-	21.1	31.0	35.5
2. A few of the times	29.8	34.3	27.8	27.2	18.6	15.5	31.9	32.3	43.7	31.2	31.7	-	-	64.1	26.5	43.1
3. Some of the times	13.8	14.4	14.2	17.0	-	15.1	15.1	11.6	13.5	15.0	11.9	-	-	-	14.0	21.4
4. Most of the times	15.3	8.1	23.9	18.8	-	28.0	3.7	21.2	6.9	17.6	16.4	-	-	-	19.0	-
5. Every time	8.4	1.5	10.2	7.8	-	6.2	8.1	12.9	4.0	8.3	4.9	-	-	14.7	9.5	-
Item 3350 Subject A05c N★	109	46	54	88	5	27	33	32	17	47	47	-	-	5	87	13
B065H: At school																
1. Not at all	55.5	57.7	48.6	54.4	74.3	54.3	75.7	37.0	51.6	52.2	53.8	-	-	78.9	53.4	51.3
2. A few of the times	24.5	26.6	26.3	26.0	25.7	18.7	15.8	40.9	21.2	17.9	34.5	-	-	-	25.9	30.4
3. Some of the times	15.0	14.8	16.0	15.0	-	23.0	8.6	15.8	13.6	20.9	10.7	-	-	-	15.9	18.3
4. Most of the times	3.2	0.9	5.6	3.9	-	4.1	-	4.0	6.7	6.4	0.9	-	-	-	4.0	-
5. Every time	1.7	-	3.5	0.8	-	-	-	2.3	6.9	2.5	-	-	-	21.1	0.8	-
Item 3360 Subject A05c N★	107	46	54	88	5	27	33	31	17	47	47	-	-	5	86	13
B065I: In a car																
1. Not at all	58.9	53.3	62.3	60.2	71.2	55.4	49.6	68.2	65.0	59.6	62.4	-	-	78.9	56.0	64.0
2. A few of the times	16.0	20.1	14.2	17.9	18.6	10.1	21.0	13.0	21.4	7.1	26.5	-	-	-	17.9	13.7
3. Some of the times	13.6	15.3	9.8	12.3	10.3	10.3	29.4	7.3	-	12.1	6.9	-	-	-	13.6	22.4
4. Most of the times	5.7	2.7	9.2	7.0	-	15.8	-	2.5	6.7	9.0	4.1	-	-	-	7.1	-
5. Every time	5.8	8.5	4.4	2.6	-	8.5	-	9.0	6.9	12.2	-	-	-	21.1	5.3	-
Item 3380 Subject A05c N★	109	46	54	89	5	27	33	32	17	47	47	-	-	5	87	13
B066: How many of the times when you used barbiturates during the last year did you use them along with each of the following drugs– that is, so that their effects overlapped?																
B066A: With alcohol																
1. Not at all	37.1	29.0	41.0	34.6	36.2	31.0	38.6	40.0	39.0	34.4	40.2	-	-	100.0	34.9	13.4
2. A few of the times	21.3	22.7	22.0	22.9	28.8	24.9	16.2	20.8	25.9	20.0	26.4	-	-	-	25.3	8.7
3. Some of the times	20.5	24.6	18.4	22.3	35.0	27.4	25.7	12.7	13.8	25.2	13.6	-	-	-	20.4	38.3
4. Most of the times	15.3	21.6	8.6	13.2	-	8.8	16.9	20.0	14.4	14.5	15.7	-	-	-	14.3	24.6
5. Every time	5.8	2.1	10.0	6.9	-	7.9	2.6	6.5	6.9	5.7	4.0	-	-	-	5.2	15.0
Item 3390 Subject A01h N★	107	47	52	90	5	28	32	31	17	48	46	-	-	5	86	11
B066B: With marijuana																
1. Not at all	41.4	37.0	44.4	42.9	36.2	42.6	32.4	42.8	54.8	45.5	39.9	-	-	78.9	42.2	12.8
2. A few of the times	18.9	23.1	14.9	17.2	63.8	17.2	24.7	16.9	13.7	12.7	23.4	-	-	-	18.5	34.6
3. Some of the times	19.8	18.5	22.4	22.2	-	27.7	20.8	16.9	10.3	21.4	20.0	-	-	-	17.6	39.7
4. Most of the times	10.4	13.2	6.4	10.8	-	4.5	16.0	7.5	14.4	8.6	10.2	-	-	-	11.8	8.7
5. Every time	9.4	8.2	11.9	7.0	-	7.9	6.1	15.8	6.9	11.7	6.4	-	-	21.1	9.9	4.2
Item 3400 Subject A01h N★	109	47	54	90	5	28	33	31	17	48	47	-	-	5	86	13

★=excludes respondents for whom question was inappropriate.

QUESTIONNAIRE FORM 1 1985	TOTAL	SEX		RACE		REGION				4YR COLLEGE PLANS		ILLICIT DRUG USE: LIFETIME				
		M	F	White	Black	NE	NC	S	W	Yes	No	None	Marijuana Only	Few Pills	More Pills	Any Heroin
N (Weighted No. of Cases):	3316	1505	1663	2415	400	783	902	1004	627	1822	1121	1307	719	444	716	29
% of Weighted Total:	100.0	45.4	50.2	72.8	12.1	23.6	27.2	30.3	18.9	55.0	33.8	39.4	21.7	13.4	21.6	0.9
B066C: With LSD																
1. Not at all	94.0	92.5	95.9	96.1	46.4	93.3	92.6	93.0	100.0	95.1	96.6	-	-	100.0	97.5	67.5
2. A few of the times	4.9	7.5	3.3	2.6	53.6	3.8	7.4	5.8	-	4.1	3.4	-	-	-	2.0	26.7
3. Some of the times	0.7	-	-	0.9	-	2.9	-	-	-	-	-	-	-	-	-	5.9
4. Most of the times	-	-	-	-	-	-	-	-	-	-	-	-	-	-	-	-
5. Every time	0.4	-	0.7	0.4	-	-	-	1.3	-	0.8	-	-	-	-	0.5	-
Item 3410 Subject A01h N★	107	46	53	88	5	27	32	31	17	47	47	-	-	5	86	13
B066D: With psychedelics other than LSD																
1. Not at all	94.3	94.6	97.9	97.3	57.0	97.0	87.4	96.5	100.0	95.9	98.8	-	-	100.0	98.0	67.5
2. A few of the times	4.9	5.4	2.1	1.8	43.0	-	12.6	3.5	-	4.1	1.2	-	-	-	2.0	26.7
3. Some of the times	0.7	-	-	0.9	-	3.0	-	-	-	-	-	-	-	-	-	5.9
4. Most of the times	-	-	-	-	-	-	-	-	-	-	-	-	-	-	-	-
5. Every time	-	-	-	-	-	-	-	-	-	-	-	-	-	-	-	-
Item 3420 Subject A01h N★	104	45	52	86	4	26	32	30	16	46	45	-	-	5	83	13
B066E: With amphetamines																
1. Not at all	77.6	76.9	76.3	77.1	81.4	57.0	89.8	76.2	88.4	77.7	75.4	-	-	100.0	73.5	89.9
2. A few of the times	12.2	12.8	13.5	13.7	18.6	17.0	10.2	13.2	6.9	10.1	15.1	-	-	-	14.6	4.2
3. Some of the times	6.4	6.4	5.9	4.5	-	15.0	-	9.3	-	8.6	4.3	-	-	-	7.1	5.9
4. Most of the times	3.5	3.9	3.7	4.2	-	11.1	-	-	4.8	2.8	5.2	-	-	-	4.4	-
5. Every time	0.4	-	0.8	0.5	-	-	-	1.3	-	0.9	-	-	-	-	0.5	-
Item 3430 Subject A01h N★	104	45	52	85	5	25	31	31	17	46	45	-	-	5	83	13
B066F: With quaaludes																
1. Not at all	90.1	85.1	94.4	94.1	54.7	91.3	87.0	87.0	100.0	88.2	95.3	-	-	100.0	92.6	67.5
2. A few of the times	5.5	12.8	-	0.6	45.3	4.1	5.8	9.4	-	10.3	-	-	-	-	4.6	14.7
3. Some of the times	4.0	1.1	5.6	4.8	-	2.9	7.2	3.5	-	1.5	3.7	-	-	-	2.2	17.8
4. Most of the times	0.4	1.0	-	0.5	-	1.7	-	-	-	-	1.0	-	-	-	0.5	-
5. Every time	-	-	-	-	-	-	-	-	-	-	-	-	-	-	-	-
Item 3440 Subject A01h N★	107	46	53	88	5	27	33	30	17	46	47	-	-	5	86	13
B067: What are the most important reasons for your taking barbiturates without a doctor's orders? (Mark all that apply.)																
A. To experiment–to see what it's like	47.6	48.7	48.2	47.5	40.6	53.7	58.8	41.8	26.2	32.9	63.0	-	-	39.0	48.1	40.5
B. To relax or relieve tension	63.8	65.1	68.1	66.0	40.6	56.2	66.1	74.7	51.3	61.8	69.0	-	-	39.3	64.4	65.5
C. To feel good or get high	49.4	52.2	45.7	47.5	24.5	68.9	43.5	48.7	28.8	43.3	54.9	-	-	-	52.1	45.8
D. To seek deeper insights and understanding	9.8	10.7	8.6	7.8	49.3	12.0	11.3	7.9	7.1	11.3	9.2	-	-	-	6.6	24.3
E. To have a good time with my friends	21.2	30.3	14.5	19.8	14.4	24.7	20.8	23.1	12.2	23.7	18.2	-	-	-	22.2	12.9
F. To fit in with a group I like	2.3	-	2.7	0.9	-	3.8	1.9	-	5.1	1.3	1.9	-	-	-	0.9	-
G. To get away from my problems or troubles	27.4	16.3	38.7	28.1	-	33.0	15.5	41.1	14.4	32.3	24.8	-	-	-	25.9	40.0
H. Because of boredom, nothing else to do	21.6	17.6	23.0	20.4	-	41.2	17.4	12.4	14.3	15.2	24.9	-	-	-	20.9	26.2
I. Because of anger or frustration	19.2	7.5	29.9	19.4	-	17.3	15.5	24.5	19.5	20.0	21.2	-	-	-	16.0	38.8
J. To get through the day	12.2	5.0	16.4	9.9	-	15.5	12.1	15.7	-	15.6	5.7	-	-	-	11.2	13.3
K. To increase the effects of some other drug(s)	18.9	22.8	16.5	17.7	-	19.4	14.4	25.0	15.3	26.3	13.7	-	-	-	19.5	13.2
L. To decrease (offset) the effects of some other drug(s)	5.7	4.4	2.5	3.1	-	10.9	9.6	-	-	5.9	1.1	-	-	-	5.1	-
M. To get to sleep	44.3	29.8	55.0	47.1	-	46.1	34.9	49.0	50.5	43.6	47.6	-	-	46.3	40.0	65.5
N. To relieve physical pain	31.6	25.2	35.1	33.6	-	26.6	37.4	19.1	52.8	31.8	27.9	-	-	-	35.0	13.6
O. Because I am "hooked"–I have to have them	2.5	1.1	2.1	1.2	-	3.8	3.5	1.7	-	1.3	-	-	-	-	-	8.0
Item 3450-3580 Subject A06a N★	105	45	53	87	4	27	31	31	16	47	43	-	-	5	85	13
B068: When you take barbiturates how high do you usually get?																
1. Not at all high	13.9	5.1	21.6	12.6	37.1	14.4	20.9	5.5	15.5	11.6	17.4	-	-	39.0	11.1	16.8
2. A little high	23.0	25.3	19.6	24.6	-	33.3	18.6	16.9	26.2	10.0	34.0	-	-	-	26.5	11.3
3. Moderately high	37.5	46.3	31.2	35.5	20.9	34.1	37.6	46.0	25.6	30.9	46.1	-	-	-	38.1	51.3
4. Very high	6.1	6.1	5.5	7.5	-	13.6	2.6	1.8	8.7	9.3	-	-	-	-	6.6	5.9
5. I don't take them to get high	19.6	17.2	22.1	19.9	42.0	4.5	20.2	29.8	24.1	38.2	2.4	-	-	61.0	17.8	14.7
Item 3590 Subject A01e N★	103	43	52	84	5	27	31	31	15	48	41	-	-	5	84	13

★=excludes respondents for whom question was inappropriate.

QUESTIONNAIRE FORM 1 1985	TOTAL	SEX		RACE		REGION				4YR COLLEGE PLANS		ILLICIT DRUG USE: LIFETIME				
		M	F	White	Black	NE	NC	S	W	Yes	No	None	Marijuana Only	Few Pills	More Pills	Any Heroin
N (Weighted No. of Cases):	3316	1505	1663	2415	400	783	902	1004	627	1822	1121	1307	719	444	716	29
% of Weighted Total:	100.0	45.4	50.2	72.8	12.1	23.6	27.2	30.3	18.9	55.0	33.8	39.4	21.7	13.4	21.6	0.9
B069: When you take barbiturates how long do you usually stay high?																
1. Usually don't get high	27.1	17.6	36.0	28.8	37.1	20.3	30.9	31.8	22.7	35.7	23.2	-	-	100.0	24.7	8.9
2. One to two hours	26.6	33.0	19.4	26.1	54.3	40.3	27.5	18.2	17.6	19.0	28.6	-	-	-	27.2	35.4
3. Three to six hours	31.4	30.4	31.0	32.7	8.6	22.4	29.5	34.6	44.4	21.8	40.1	-	-	-	31.2	47.8
4. Seven to 24 hours	13.8	19.0	11.5	11.2	-	13.1	12.1	15.4	15.4	21.1	8.1	-	-	-	15.7	8.0
5. More than 24 hours	1.0	-	2.1	1.3	-	4.0	-	-	-	2.3	-	-	-	-	1.3	-
Item 3600 Subject A01f N ★	105	44	53	86	5	28	31	31	16	47	44	-	-	5	86	13
B070: What barbiturates have you taken during the last year without a doctor's orders? (Mark all that apply.)																
A. Phenobarbital	30.7	32.9	27.1	30.1	-	25.9	19.3	33.3	58.2	35.3	22.7	-	-	-	28.7	54.2
B. Seconal	22.8	26.8	18.2	18.8	59.4	17.3	25.5	29.0	15.6	18.2	25.0	-	-	-	17.3	64.2
C. Tuinal	10.0	14.8	5.6	7.6	75.5	12.1	12.4	6.7	7.6	7.9	9.8	-	-	-	5.8	35.4
D. Nembutal	10.7	16.6	2.3	6.7	-	8.6	16.3	12.4	-	13.3	3.0	-	-	-	11.0	7.7
E. Luminal	14.9	15.3	12.0	11.8	-	13.3	17.4	11.1	20.8	18.7	8.6	-	-	-	13.4	16.8
F. Desbutal	4.8	5.1	3.4	4.0	14.4	5.4	6.5	4.8	-	1.5	4.2	-	-	-	2.5	15.0
G. Amytal	11.3	16.8	6.4	7.0	49.3	15.3	11.8	12.3	-	12.3	6.8	-	-	-	8.9	25.4
H. Adrenocal	8.7	8.4	8.6	8.3	26.2	10.7	12.9	5.0	4.0	5.0	8.6	-	-	-	8.4	8.3
I. Other	35.6	40.1	30.0	30.7	26.2	47.0	30.3	37.4	20.8	38.1	31.1	-	-	39.5	33.0	49.1
J. Don't know the names of some that I have used	55.5	43.4	68.0	57.7	-	52.7	46.0	70.6	49.4	58.7	58.7	-	-	60.5	56.7	46.8
Item 3610-3700 Subject A01l N ★	105	45	52	86	4	29	31	31	15	48	42	-	-	5	85	13
B071: Have you ever tried to stop using barbiturates and found that you couldn't stop?																
1. Yes	3.6	2.4	5.1	4.4	-	8.2	-	1.7	6.4	2.4	4.8	-	-	-	3.8	4.0
2. No	96.4	97.6	94.9	95.6	100.0	91.8	100.0	98.3	93.6	97.6	95.2	-	-	100.0	96.2	96.0
Item 3710 Subject A01i N ★	103	43	53	85	5	27	29	31	16	46	44	-	-	5	84	13
B072: Do you think you will be using barbiturates without a doctor's prescription five years from now?																
1. I definitely will	0.5	0.5	0.5	0.4	0.7	1.2	0.2	0.5	0.2	0.5	0.5	0.4	0.2	0.9	0.7	-
2. I probably will	2.2	2.4	1.7	1.9	2.0	2.9	2.5	1.6	1.6	1.6	2.8	0.7	0.6	0.7	7.1	15.9
3. I probably will not	16.3	15.1	16.9	16.9	9.3	18.7	16.5	13.7	17.2	15.6	16.6	6.5	11.6	24.8	33.6	46.3
4. I definitely will not	81.0	82.0	80.9	80.8	88.0	77.2	80.8	84.2	81.0	82.2	80.2	92.5	87.5	73.5	58.6	37.8
Item 3720 Subject A04a N	3145	1444	1627	2358	375	715	869	957	604	1787	1081	1278	689	426	664	27
The next questions are about TRANQUILIZERS, which doctors sometimes prescribe to calm people down, quiet their nerves, or relax their muscles.																
They include the following drugs: Librium, Valium, Miltown, Equanil, Meprobamate, Serax, Atarax, Tranxene, Vistaril.																
B073: Have you ever taken tranquilizers because a doctor told you to use them?																
1. No	88.2	89.5	86.9	87.0	95.0	88.1	88.3	88.1	88.4	87.7	90.2	94.3	90.8	83.9	77.8	69.7
2. Yes, but I had already tried them on my own.	1.4	1.4	1.2	1.6	-	2.0	1.5	1.0	0.9	1.1	1.4	-	0.3	0.3	5.5	12.1
3. Yes, and it was the first time I took any	10.4	9.1	11.8	11.4	5.0	9.9	10.1	10.9	10.6	11.2	8.3	5.7	8.9	15.8	16.7	18.1
Item 3730 Subject A01j N	3142	1449	1616	2362	369	713	871	950	607	1788	1076	1280	682	437	671	27
B074: On how many occasions (if any) have you taken tranquilizers on your own–that is, without a doctor telling you to take them . . .																

★=excludes respondents for whom question was inappropriate.

QUESTIONNAIRE FORM 1 1985	TOTAL	SEX		RACE		REGION				4YR COLLEGE PLANS		ILLICIT DRUG USE: LIFETIME				
		M	F	White	Black	NE	NC	S	W	Yes	No	None	Mari-juana Only	Few Pills	More Pills	Any Her-oin
N (Weighted No. of Cases):	3316	1505	1663	2415	400	783	902	1004	627	1822	1121	1307	719	444	716	29
% of Weighted Total:	100.0	45.4	50.2	72.8	12.1	23.6	27.2	30.3	18.9	55.0	33.8	39.4	21.7	13.4	21.6	0.9
B074A: ... in your lifetime?																
1. 0 occasions	90.4	91.2	89.9	89.7	95.9	87.8	91.2	91.2	90.9	91.2	89.7	100.0	100.0	81.4	69.8	23.6
2. 1-2	5.3	4.6	5.7	5.5	2.4	5.9	4.9	5.0	5.4	4.7	5.7	-	-	18.6	11.3	33.7
3. 3-5	1.8	1.4	2.1	1.9	0.7	2.8	1.3	1.5	1.7	1.6	1.8	-	-	-	8.2	3.3
4. 6-9	1.0	1.1	0.8	1.1	0.4	1.1	1.2	0.5	1.3	1.1	0.8	-	-	-	3.9	19.3
5. 10-19	0.6	0.5	0.7	0.8	-	0.8	0.5	0.7	0.5	0.4	1.0	-	-	-	2.9	-
6. 20-39	0.4	0.6	0.3	0.4	0.5	0.8	0.6	0.2	0.2	0.5	0.5	-	-	-	1.6	11.7
7. 40 or more	0.6	0.6	0.5	0.6	-	0.7	0.4	0.9	0.1	0.5	0.6	-	-	-	2.3	8.4
Item 1070 Subject A01a N	3134	1446	1612	2358	369	714	872	943	604	1785	1077	1284	685	435	663	26
B074B: ... during the last 12 months?																
1. 0 occasions	95.1	95.1	95.2	94.5	97.6	93.1	96.0	95.4	95.6	95.3	95.0	100.0	100.0	92.5	83.1	60.8
2. 1-2	2.8	2.8	2.7	3.1	1.4	3.5	2.4	2.4	3.3	2.4	3.1	-	-	7.5	7.8	16.5
3. 3-5	0.9	0.8	1.1	1.0	0.9	1.5	0.9	0.6	0.8	1.1	0.6	-	-	-	3.8	13.3
4. 6-9	0.5	0.5	0.4	0.6	-	0.9	0.4	0.4	0.4	0.4	0.8	-	-	-	2.2	2.9
5. 10-19	0.2	0.1	0.2	0.2	-	-	0.2	0.4	-	0.2	-	-	-	-	0.8	-
6. 20-39	0.3	0.5	0.1	0.2	-	0.4	-	0.6	-	0.3	0.1	-	-	-	1.2	2.1
7. 40 or more	0.3	0.2	0.3	0.3	-	0.5	0.2	0.3	-	0.2	0.4	-	-	-	1.0	4.3
Item 1080 Subject A01b N	3130	1445	1609	2354	368	714	869	943	604	1783	1075	1284	685	433	661	26
B074C: ... during the last 30 days?																
1. 0 occasions	97.9	97.9	97.9	97.7	98.6	96.7	98.4	97.7	98.9	98.2	97.4	100.0	100.0	98.7	91.5	81.7
2. 1-2	1.3	1.3	1.3	1.4	1.4	1.8	1.1	1.6	0.7	1.1	1.6	-	-	1.3	5.0	11.6
3. 3-5	0.4	0.4	0.4	0.5	-	0.8	0.4	*	0.3	0.2	0.7	-	-	-	1.6	4.5
4. 6-9	0.1	*	0.1	0.1	-	0.2	0.1	-	-	0.1	-	-	-	-	0.2	-
5. 10-19	0.3	0.4	0.3	0.3	-	0.5	-	0.6	-	0.4	0.3	-	-	-	1.4	2.1
6. 20-39	*	-	0.1	*	-	-	-	0.1	-	-	-	-	-	-	0.2	-
7. 40 or more	*	*	-	*	-	-	0.1	-	-	-	0.1	-	-	-	0.1	-
Item 1090 Subject A01c N	3124	1441	1608	2349	368	714	868	938	604	1780	1073	1284	685	430	657	26

IF YOU HAVE NOT TAKEN TRANQUILIZERS IN THE LAST TWELVE MONTHS, GO TO Q.B082.

THE FOLLOWING QUESTIONS REFER ONLY TO TAKING TRANQUILIZERS WITHOUT A DOCTOR'S ORDERS. IF YOU HAVE NOT DONE THIS IN THE LAST TWELVE MONTHS, GO TO Q.B082.

B075: When you used tranquilizers during the last year, how often did you use them in each of the following situations?

B075A: When you were alone

	TOTAL	M	F	White	Black	NE	NC	S	W	Yes	No	None	Mari-juana Only	Few Pills	More Pills	Any Her-oin
1. Not at all	40.8	45.2	36.1	41.5	39.7	40.7	39.9	38.6	45.7	35.2	46.3	-	-	70.5	32.1	33.4
2. A few of the times	31.0	31.5	27.4	26.7	52.3	24.5	38.8	35.3	26.2	29.9	28.3	-	-	18.7	33.2	51.2
3. Some of the times	10.5	10.0	12.4	12.1	8.0	7.6	10.8	14.6	9.1	16.0	4.0	-	-	2.8	12.7	11.2
4. Most of the times	9.4	5.3	14.6	11.0	-	17.7	8.7	3.4	4.4	8.3	14.0	-	-	1.9	12.1	4.2
5. Every time	8.3	8.0	9.5	8.6	-	9.5	1.8	8.1	14.6	10.7	7.4	-	-	6.0	9.9	-
Item 3740 Subject A05a N★	147	69	70	122	9	48	33	41	26	77	53	-	-	25	107	10

B075B: With just 1 or 2 other people

	TOTAL	M	F	White	Black	NE	NC	S	W	Yes	No	None	Mari-juana Only	Few Pills	More Pills	Any Her-oin
1. Not at all	40.3	37.4	40.9	37.8	51.6	50.8	28.8	30.6	51.2	42.1	31.9	-	-	69.5	34.4	7.6
2. A few of the times	28.7	24.7	34.7	29.8	32.5	21.4	31.1	38.4	23.3	29.1	30.8	-	-	17.2	30.6	47.5
3. Some of the times	15.7	20.9	11.2	15.9	8.0	11.7	17.2	20.4	13.5	15.8	16.9	-	-	3.0	17.8	29.7
4. Most of the times	9.2	10.0	7.1	9.7	-	12.6	20.5	1.9	-	8.3	10.2	-	-	-	12.5	-
5. Every time	6.2	7.0	6.1	6.9	8.0	3.5	2.5	8.7	11.9	4.7	10.3	-	-	10.3	4.7	15.2
Item 3750 Subject A05b N★	145	68	69	121	9	47	33	40	26	75	53	-	-	24	107	10

*=less than .05 per cent.   ★=excludes respondents for whom question was inappropriate.

QUESTIONNAIRE FORM 1 1985	TOTAL	SEX		RACE		REGION				4YR COLLEGE PLANS		ILLICIT DRUG USE: LIFETIME				
		M	F	White	Black	NE	NC	S	W	Yes	No	None	Marijuana Only	Few Pills	More Pills	Any Heroin
N (Weighted No. of Cases):	3316	1505	1663	2415	400	783	902	1004	627	1822	1121	1307	719	444	716	29
% of Weighted Total:	100.0	45.4	50.2	72.8	12.1	23.6	27.2	30.3	18.9	55.0	33.8	39.4	21.7	13.4	21.6	0.9

B075C: At a party

1. Not at all	63.3	53.6	69.7	62.5	59.6	63.7	56.6	69.6	60.9	68.4	51.6	-	-	84.4	59.5	35.4
2. A few of the times	13.0	17.6	10.0	14.4	11.3	17.4	14.7	7.8	10.8	7.5	25.0	-	-	3.2	16.6	5.3
3. Some of the times	14.3	18.3	12.0	13.3	21.2	8.6	16.1	20.0	13.5	15.8	16.6	-	-	-	15.7	40.9
4. Most of the times	6.1	7.8	3.9	7.3	-	9.1	10.7	2.6	-	6.7	-	-	-	2.1	7.1	7.4
5. Every time	3.3	2.7	4.4	2.4	8.0	1.2	1.8	-	14.7	1.7	6.8	-	-	10.2	1.1	11.0
Item 3760 Subject A05c N★	147	69	70	122	9	48	33	41	26	77	53	-	-	25	107	10

B075D: When your date or spouse was present

1. Not at all	75.2	76.6	72.9	74.9	87.8	85.0	77.0	65.6	70.6	72.9	74.7	-	-	89.8	70.3	81.6
2. A few of the times	11.7	13.4	11.0	12.6	12.2	5.5	16.6	19.7	4.4	10.9	16.2	-	-	7.0	13.3	11.0
3. Some of the times	5.5	4.9	6.6	6.6	-	3.9	-	4.0	17.5	8.4	3.1	-	-	-	7.5	-
4. Most of the times	5.7	5.1	5.6	4.3	-	5.6	3.8	10.7	-	7.8	0.8	-	-	-	6.9	7.4
5. Every time	1.9	-	4.0	1.7	-	-	2.7	-	7.5	-	5.2	-	-	3.2	1.9	-
Item 3770 Subject A05b N★	141	67	69	120	8	45	30	40	26	74	52	-	-	23	104	10

B075E: When people over age 30 were present

1. Not at all	61.1	62.5	59.3	59.3	92.0	64.5	56.2	51.8	75.6	59.6	65.1	-	-	59.5	60.5	63.6
2. A few of the times	16.6	14.1	19.7	19.4	-	17.8	19.2	19.5	6.5	14.4	17.6	-	-	25.6	13.9	28.8
3. Some of the times	10.7	13.2	7.8	9.0	8.0	7.8	5.7	19.2	9.0	11.0	9.4	-	-	2.7	13.3	-
4. Most of the times	4.9	4.3	5.2	5.4	-	4.6	12.8	2.0	-	7.1	3.0	-	-	-	6.8	-
5. Every time	6.7	6.0	8.0	7.0	-	5.2	6.1	7.5	8.9	7.9	4.9	-	-	12.2	5.5	7.6
Item 3780 Subject A05b N★	147	71	70	123	9	48	33	41	26	79	53	-	-	27	105	10

B075F: During the daytime (before 4:00 p.m.)

1. Not at all	49.7	52.9	45.1	50.7	57.7	48.7	64.1	40.5	48.0	42.8	56.7	-	-	64.6	44.5	52.5
2. A few of the times	22.0	22.6	22.6	20.8	34.3	28.5	17.8	20.5	17.6	18.8	27.2	-	-	15.3	24.5	23.6
3. Some of the times	18.2	17.9	19.1	18.7	8.0	14.3	9.3	28.8	19.6	25.8	8.6	-	-	2.7	23.9	7.4
4. Most of the times	5.8	2.7	8.0	5.2	-	8.5	-	5.6	8.3	7.4	3.1	-	-	3.6	4.6	16.5
5. Every time	4.3	3.9	5.2	4.6	-	-	8.7	4.6	6.6	5.1	4.5	-	-	13.9	2.5	-
Item 3790 Subject A05c N★	147	71	70	123	9	48	33	41	26	79	53	-	-	27	105	10

B075G: At your home (or apartment or dorm)

1. Not at all	35.4	40.6	29.9	33.2	68.9	40.6	44.6	28.1	26.0	26.3	46.8	-	-	49.2	29.0	49.7
2. A few of the times	19.5	19.5	17.5	19.4	6.1	15.9	19.3	18.7	27.7	20.8	14.8	-	-	32.2	16.2	19.9
3. Some of the times	20.7	15.3	26.9	21.8	8.0	14.7	11.1	33.6	23.2	25.4	11.6	-	-	2.8	26.1	18.6
4. Most of the times	10.4	8.4	12.5	11.0	-	13.9	16.4	8.0	-	9.7	14.3	-	-	-	14.3	-
5. Every time	14.0	16.2	13.1	14.6	17.0	14.9	8.6	11.6	23.1	17.7	12.5	-	-	15.8	14.3	11.8
Item 3800 Subject A05c N★	146	69	70	122	9	47	33	41	26	77	53	-	-	26	105	10

B075H: At school

1. Not at all	67.2	73.2	59.8	65.8	100.0	62.0	79.5	56.2	78.2	63.1	72.2	-	-	82.3	62.8	60.1
2. A few of the times	15.4	12.3	19.3	15.8	-	17.1	15.7	16.3	10.8	16.3	11.7	-	-	10.8	17.2	16.0
3. Some of the times	11.7	9.6	13.8	11.6	-	10.1	4.8	19.1	11.1	14.2	9.8	-	-	-	14.4	18.6
4. Most of the times	4.1	2.4	6.3	4.9	-	10.8	-	2.8	-	5.1	3.9	-	-	-	5.7	-
5. Every time	1.6	2.5	0.8	1.9	-	-	-	5.6	-	1.3	2.5	-	-	6.9	-	5.3
Item 3810 Subject A05c N★	143	69	67	119	9	44	33	41	26	77	51	-	-	26	103	10

B075I: In a car

1. Not at all	71.9	71.1	74.0	70.8	100.0	76.0	66.4	62.9	86.4	72.0	70.1	-	-	96.8	63.7	87.3
2. A few of the times	9.7	11.6	7.4	10.4	-	5.2	15.7	10.2	9.2	7.7	15.7	-	-	3.2	12.2	5.3
3. Some of the times	11.9	8.8	15.2	14.2	-	14.2	12.2	13.8	4.4	9.7	14.2	-	-	-	16.0	7.4
4. Most of the times	3.3	3.7	1.6	3.1	-	4.7	4.0	3.3	-	4.8	-	-	-	-	3.7	-
5. Every time	3.2	4.8	1.7	1.4	-	-	1.7	9.8	-	5.8	-	-	-	-	4.4	-
Item 3830 Subject A05c N★	144	71	67	121	9	45	33	41	26	79	51	-	-	27	103	10

B076: How many of the times when you used tranquilizers during the last year did you use them along with each of the following drugs— that is, so that their effects overlapped?

★=excludes respondents for whom question was inappropriate.

QUESTIONNAIRE FORM 1 1985	TOTAL	SEX		RACE		REGION				4YR COLLEGE PLANS		ILLICIT DRUG USE: LIFETIME				
		M	F	White	Black	NE	NC	S	W	Yes	No	None	Mari-juana Only	Few Pills	More Pills	Any Heroin
N (Weighted No. of Cases):	3316	1505	1663	2415	400	783	902	1004	627	1822	1121	1307	719	444	716	29
% of Weighted Total:	100.0	45.4	50.2	72.8	12.1	23.6	27.2	30.3	18.9	55.0	33.8	39.4	21.7	13.4	21.6	0.9

B076A: With alcohol

	TOTAL	M	F	White	Black	NE	NC	S	W	Yes	No	None	Mari-juana Only	Few Pills	More Pills	Any Heroin
1. Not at all	49.7	49.5	48.9	47.8	67.5	39.8	42.4	56.2	66.6	52.9	44.2	-	-	92.2	41.9	15.6
2. A few of the times	20.1	20.7	21.8	21.8	11.3	27.4	18.1	18.0	12.6	19.0	22.4	-	-	3.3	25.3	14.8
3. Some of the times	11.2	6.4	16.1	12.0	21.2	17.7	9.6	7.8	7.1	9.3	16.0	-	-	-	11.8	37.1
4. Most of the times	15.1	21.8	6.4	13.6	-	14.1	25.7	14.1	4.4	17.3	10.6	-	-	2.1	17.7	16.0
5. Every time	4.0	1.6	6.9	4.8	-	1.0	4.2	3.9	9.2	1.5	6.9	-	-	2.4	3.3	16.5
Item 3840 Subject A01h N★	146	68	70	121	9	46	34	41	26	77	53	-	-	25	106	10

B076B: With marijuana

	TOTAL	M	F	White	Black	NE	NC	S	W	Yes	No	None	Mari-juana Only	Few Pills	More Pills	Any Heroin
1. Not at all	58.5	51.6	67.4	59.8	67.5	56.1	43.9	64.9	70.6	59.4	61.3	-	-	96.5	52.4	26.7
2. A few of the times	15.6	15.6	12.7	13.6	11.3	19.8	14.2	13.4	13.4	12.2	13.3	-	-	3.5	17.4	30.8
3. Some of the times	10.1	10.7	9.5	10.6	21.2	6.4	21.3	8.9	4.4	11.7	9.4	-	-	-	10.6	31.3
4. Most of the times	7.8	10.9	4.4	8.6	-	16.7	11.4	-	-	6.6	10.1	-	-	-	9.7	-
5. Every time	8.0	11.1	6.1	7.3	-	1.0	9.2	12.8	11.5	10.0	5.8	-	-	-	9.8	11.2
Item 3850 Subject A01h N★	144	67	70	119	9	46	32	41	26	75	53	-	-	23	106	10

B076C: With LSD

	TOTAL	M	F	White	Black	NE	NC	S	W	Yes	No	None	Mari-juana Only	Few Pills	More Pills	Any Heroin
1. Not at all	94.2	88.6	100.0	95.0	78.8	96.4	83.3	98.9	95.5	93.0	95.7	-	-	100.0	95.0	69.8
2. A few of the times	4.9	10.5	-	3.9	21.2	1.9	15.0	1.1	4.5	7.0	3.3	-	-	-	4.5	22.8
3. Some of the times	0.9	0.8	-	1.1	-	1.7	1.8	-	-	-	1.0	-	-	-	0.5	7.4
4. Most of the times	-	-	-	-	-	-	-	-	-	-	-	-	-	-	-	-
5. Every time	-	-	-	-	-	-	-	-	-	-	-	-	-	-	-	-
Item 3860 Subject A01h N★	143	67	70	119	9	46	30	41	26	75	53	-	-	23	105	10

B076D: With psychedelics other than LSD

	TOTAL	M	F	White	Black	NE	NC	S	W	Yes	No	None	Mari-juana Only	Few Pills	More Pills	Any Heroin
1. Not at all	95.2	90.8	100.0	98.6	78.8	96.4	93.6	91.9	100.0	92.5	99.2	-	-	100.0	96.4	69.8
2. A few of the times	2.3	5.0	-	-	-	-	-	8.1	-	3.8	0.8	-	-	-	2.7	4.2
3. Some of the times	1.9	2.9	-	0.6	21.2	1.7	6.4	-	-	2.6	-	-	-	-	-	26.0
4. Most of the times	0.6	1.3	-	0.7	-	1.9	-	-	-	1.2	-	-	-	-	0.8	-
5. Every time	-	-	-	-	-	-	-	-	-	-	-	-	-	-	-	-
Item 3870 Subject A01h N★	142	66	70	119	9	46	30	41	26	75	52	-	-	23	104	10

B076E: With amphetamines

	TOTAL	M	F	White	Black	NE	NC	S	W	Yes	No	None	Mari-juana Only	Few Pills	More Pills	Any Heroin
1. Not at all	89.7	88.7	90.9	90.5	100.0	81.7	98.2	89.4	93.1	89.6	90.5	-	-	100.0	87.0	88.4
2. A few of the times	3.5	3.2	4.1	3.8	-	6.4	1.8	1.1	4.5	3.2	5.0	-	-	-	4.3	4.2
3. Some of the times	6.5	7.4	5.0	5.3	-	10.8	-	9.6	2.3	7.2	3.5	-	-	-	8.2	7.4
4. Most of the times	-	-	-	-	-	-	-	-	-	-	-	-	-	-	-	-
5. Every time	0.3	0.7	-	0.4	-	1.1	-	-	-	-	1.0	-	-	-	0.5	-
Item 3880 Subject A01h N★	138	67	65	114	9	41	30	41	26	75	48	-	-	23	100	10

B076F: With quaaludes

	TOTAL	M	F	White	Black	NE	NC	S	W	Yes	No	None	Mari-juana Only	Few Pills	More Pills	Any Heroin
1. Not at all	95.1	94.7	96.1	94.4	100.0	95.1	95.8	94.2	95.5	95.0	96.2	-	-	100.0	94.9	83.4
2. A few of the times	3.7	4.6	3.2	4.1	-	2.0	4.2	4.5	4.5	5.0	2.8	-	-	-	4.6	4.2
3. Some of the times	0.9	-	0.8	1.1	-	1.8	-	1.3	-	-	-	-	-	-	-	12.4
4. Most of the times	-	-	-	-	-	-	-	-	-	-	-	-	-	-	-	-
5. Every time	0.3	0.7	-	0.4	-	1.1	-	-	-	-	0.9	-	-	-	0.5	-
Item 3890 Subject A01h N★	140	67	67	116	9	43	30	41	26	75	50	-	-	23	102	10

B076G: With barbiturates

	TOTAL	M	F	White	Black	NE	NC	S	W	Yes	No	None	Mari-juana Only	Few Pills	More Pills	Any Heroin
1. Not at all	90.0	90.0	90.1	90.5	100.0	84.1	94.8	89.9	95.2	90.0	89.5	-	-	100.0	87.6	87.6
2. A few of the times	4.4	3.5	5.7	5.3	-	10.5	2.4	1.9	-	3.0	7.8	-	-	-	6.0	-
3. Some of the times	5.3	5.7	4.2	3.8	-	4.3	2.8	8.3	4.8	7.0	1.7	-	-	-	5.9	12.4
4. Most of the times	-	-	-	-	-	-	-	-	-	-	-	-	-	-	-	-
5. Every time	0.3	0.7	-	0.4	-	1.1	-	-	-	-	1.0	-	-	-	0.5	-
Item 3900 Subject A01h N★	137	64	66	113	9	43	29	41	23	73	49	-	-	22	99	10

★=excludes respondents for whom question was inappropriate.

QUESTIONNAIRE FORM 1 1985	TOTAL	SEX		RACE		REGION				4YR COLLEGE PLANS		ILLICIT DRUG USE: LIFETIME				
		M	F	White	Black	NE	NC	S	W	Yes	No	None	Mari-juana Only	Few Pills	More Pills	Any Her-oin
N (Weighted No. of Cases):	3316	1505	1663	2415	400	783	902	1004	627	1822	1121	1307	719	444	716	29
% of Weighted Total:	100.0	45.4	50.2	72.8	12.1	23.6	27.2	30.3	18.9	55.0	33.8	39.4	21.7	13.4	21.6	0.9

B077: What have been the most important reasons for taking tranquilizers without a doctor's orders? (Mark all that apply.)

	TOTAL	M	F	White	Black	NE	NC	S	W	Yes	No	None	Mari-juana Only	Few Pills	More Pills	Any Her-oin
A. To experiment–to see what it's like	37.5	47.5	28.7	37.9	26.9	45.1	46.7	28.7	24.5	33.0	41.8	-	-	33.9	37.4	31.2
B. To relax or relieve tension	65.2	62.5	69.0	65.5	54.6	59.5	62.0	75.0	65.2	68.7	59.1	-	-	55.2	68.9	40.5
C. To feel good or get high	32.7	37.7	24.7	31.1	-	30.0	34.8	45.1	15.1	26.3	37.7	-	-	15.4	34.2	39.0
D. To seek deeper insights and understanding	7.8	7.6	5.9	2.8	29.7	6.4	8.0	12.5	2.8	8.6	5.3	-	-	-	5.8	22.8
E. To have a good time with my friends	17.1	22.4	9.4	14.8	-	10.1	30.0	15.6	17.1	16.0	18.0	-	-	11.0	16.6	15.2
F. To fit in with a group I like	2.8	2.0	0.9	1.1	-	4.2	1.9	3.4	-	2.6	-	-	-	-	1.2	-
G. To get away from my problems or troubles	20.7	14.9	25.9	21.8	-	26.6	9.8	26.2	14.2	18.9	20.0	-	-	4.1	22.4	20.7
H. Because of boredom, nothing else to do	17.5	17.1	16.9	18.8	-	18.0	25.0	8.9	20.9	16.6	18.4	-	-	7.2	16.8	26.9
I. Because of anger or frustration	17.9	11.2	23.8	17.2	-	17.7	14.0	25.3	11.6	21.7	13.1	-	-	4.1	20.2	4.2
J. To get through the day	14.9	7.2	21.3	14.3	23.8	18.0	7.9	21.4	6.9	14.5	14.1	-	-	7.2	15.9	-
K. To increase the effects of some other drug(s)	12.2	13.2	9.6	10.0	-	10.4	17.6	15.8	2.8	12.3	10.9	-	-	-	13.4	5.0
L. To decrease (offset) the effects of some other drug(s)	6.6	5.7	5.2	4.1	29.7	10.4	10.2	2.9	-	9.2	0.9	-	-	-	4.6	18.6
M. To get to sleep	48.7	38.0	56.3	49.9	23.8	53.1	48.5	50.0	37.9	46.8	48.0	-	-	26.7	52.8	42.7
N. To relieve physical pain	32.5	28.1	35.1	33.2	23.8	30.3	25.7	30.2	49.6	33.6	32.7	-	-	17.5	34.7	26.2
O. Because I am "hooked"–I have to have them	2.2	-	1.7	0.4	-	4.2	1.9	1.3	-	0.8	-	-	-	-	-	5.0
Item 3910-4040 Subject A06a N★	143	68	67	120	6	49	31	39	24	76	52	-	-	23	107	10

B078: When you take tranquilizers how high do you usually get?

	TOTAL	M	F	White	Black	NE	NC	S	W	Yes	No	None	Mari-juana Only	Few Pills	More Pills	Any Her-oin
1. Not at all high	17.6	22.2	12.7	16.5	59.2	19.9	27.0	8.9	15.4	17.4	14.0	-	-	53.3	11.1	-
2. A little high	37.5	33.6	38.8	35.4	11.1	40.1	21.6	45.2	40.3	40.1	35.8	-	-	24.9	41.6	27.4
3. Moderately high	19.8	22.7	18.7	23.1	-	13.0	21.5	20.0	31.1	12.8	27.3	-	-	22.6	36.1	
4. Very high	3.4	3.2	2.5	3.2	-	2.3	8.5	2.6	-	3.3	2.6	-	-	-	3.5	9.3
5. I don't take them to get high	21.7	18.3	27.3	21.8	29.7	24.7	21.4	23.3	13.2	26.3	20.4	-	-	21.8	21.3	27.2
Item 4050 Subject A01e N★	144	67	67	119	6	47	32	40	24	75	52	-	-	23	108	11

B079: When you take tranquilizers how long do you usually stay high?

	TOTAL	M	F	White	Black	NE	NC	S	W	Yes	No	None	Mari-juana Only	Few Pills	More Pills	Any Her-oin
1. Usually don't get high	36.8	37.6	37.0	37.4	59.2	44.3	43.4	25.6	31.0	37.3	35.7	-	-	78.7	29.1	19.9
2. One to two hours	24.7	20.1	26.7	23.4	11.1	24.7	13.5	26.6	36.1	19.8	28.4	-	-	17.2	26.2	27.2
3. Three to six hours	33.5	37.2	32.3	35.0	29.7	26.5	34.2	41.8	32.8	36.6	33.3	-	-	-	39.8	43.6
4. Seven to 24 hours	3.5	5.1	2.3	3.2	-	2.0	8.9	3.0	-	4.8	2.6	-	-	4.1	3.8	-
5. More than 24 hours	1.6	-	1.7	1.0	-	2.5	-	3.0	-	1.6	-	-	-	-	1.1	9.3
Item 4060 Subject A01f N★	134	63	65	112	6	44	31	36	24	70	51	-	-	21	101	11

B080: What tranquilizers have you taken during the last year without a doctor's orders? (Mark all that apply.)

	TOTAL	M	F	White	Black	NE	NC	S	W	Yes	No	None	Mari-juana Only	Few Pills	More Pills	Any Her-oin
A. Librium	18.6	18.8	19.0	18.5	-	19.0	19.4	20.3	14.0	16.7	22.0	-	-	-	21.8	19.6
B. Valium	77.6	70.4	85.0	81.1	15.7	81.0	82.3	76.3	67.3	80.3	80.2	-	-	49.2	85.1	73.8
C. Miltown	3.0	4.8	1.6	1.9	29.7	2.4	6.1	-	4.8	5.6	-	-	-	-	2.2	16.9
D. Equanil	6.3	6.8	6.5	4.7	-	-	3.5	13.5	9.6	8.3	4.1	-	-	-	6.4	18.5
E. Meprobamate	1.2	0.8	1.7	1.4	-	-	1.7	-	4.8	1.5	1.1	-	-	-	1.6	-
F. Serax	1.7	0.9	2.6	1.5	8.5	2.8	-	2.7	-	0.7	2.5	-	-	2.4	1.2	4.6
G. Atarax	5.2	4.4	4.9	2.8	-	2.4	3.5	9.8	4.8	6.8	2.2	-	-	-	5.9	9.3
H. Tranxene	6.0	7.1	5.7	5.2	29.7	-	11.8	6.2	9.6	8.0	4.0	-	-	4.9	3.7	30.1
I. Vistaril	7.8	4.1	12.2	9.0	-	2.4	2.2	9.0	23.1	8.4	4.1	-	-	-	8.5	18.5
J. Don't know the names of some tranquilizers I have used	37.5	45.9	31.4	35.8	46.1	27.7	31.5	47.7	46.8	35.3	34.7	-	-	43.6	36.2	41.4
Item 4070-4160 Subject A01l N★	140	64	68	117	6	45	31	40	24	75	50	-	-	23	104	11

B081: Have you ever tried to stop using tranquilizers and found that you couldn't stop?

	TOTAL	M	F	White	Black	NE	NC	S	W	Yes	No	None	Mari-juana Only	Few Pills	More Pills	Any Her-oin
1. Yes	1.8	-	2.4	1.3	-	4.6	-	1.3	-	1.4	-	-	-	-	1.0	4.6
2. No	98.2	100.0	97.6	98.7	100.0	95.4	100.0	98.7	100.0	98.6	100.0	-	-	100.0	99.0	95.4
Item 4170 Subject A01i N★	143	67	68	120	6	46	33	40	24	77	51	-	-	25	106	11

★=excludes respondents for whom question was inappropriate.

QUESTIONNAIRE FORM 1 1985	TOTAL	SEX		RACE		REGION				4YR COLLEGE PLANS		ILLICIT DRUG USE: LIFETIME				
		M	F	White	Black	NE	NC	S	W	Yes	No	None	Mari- juana Only	Few Pills	More Pills	Any Her- oin
N (Weighted No. of Cases):	3316	1505	1663	2415	400	783	902	1004	627	1822	1121	1307	719	444	716	29
% of Weighted Total:	100.0	45.4	50.2	72.8	12.1	23.6	27.2	30.3	18.9	55.0	33.8	39.4	21.7	13.4	21.6	0.9

B082: Do you think you will be using tranquilizers without a doctor's orders five years from now?

	TOTAL	M	F	White	Black	NE	NC	S	W	Yes	No	None	Mari- juana Only	Few Pills	More Pills	Any Her- oin
1. I definitely will	0.6	0.6	0.5	0.5	0.2	1.2	0.4	0.6	*	0.7	0.3	0.6	0.2	0.3	1.0	-
2. I probably will	3.0	2.2	3.5	2.7	2.6	3.7	2.8	2.5	3.3	2.3	3.7	0.9	1.0	3.3	8.0	27.0
3. I probably will not	22.0	20.2	23.3	22.6	15.3	22.6	21.9	20.1	24.3	21.4	22.0	11.7	18.7	32.4	38.4	40.2
4. I definitely will not	74.4	77.0	72.7	74.2	81.9	72.4	74.9	76.8	72.3	75.6	74.0	86.7	80.1	64.0	52.6	32.8
Item 4180 Subject A04a N	3133	1443	1619	2344	377	711	871	953	598	1779	1077	1280	683	428	655	26

The next questions are about COCAINE, which is sometimes called "coke".

B083: On how many occasions (if any) have you taken cocaine . . .

B083A: . . . in your lifetime?

	TOTAL	M	F	White	Black	NE	NC	S	W	Yes	No	None	Mari- juana Only	Few Pills	More Pills	Any Her- oin
1. 0 occasions	82.8	79.3	86.4	82.1	91.5	75.3	87.7	88.8	75.4	86.4	80.3	100.0	100.0	71.3	42.6	9.6
2. 1-2	6.6	7.6	5.7	6.6	5.7	7.4	6.9	4.9	7.8	5.9	7.0	-	-	28.7	11.6	17.8
3. 3-5	3.0	3.7	2.2	3.1	0.6	4.8	1.6	2.3	4.1	2.3	3.0	-	-	-	13.3	12.7
4. 6-9	1.6	2.0	1.2	1.9	0.1	2.5	0.9	0.8	2.6	1.4	1.7	-	-	-	7.3	-
5. 10-19	2.0	2.3	1.7	2.4	0.3	2.7	1.3	1.2	3.2	1.7	2.1	-	-	-	8.6	13.3
6. 20-39	1.7	1.7	1.6	1.7	1.1	3.6	0.7	0.4	2.9	0.9	2.8	-	-	-	7.1	16.4
7. 40 or more	2.3	3.2	1.3	2.2	0.7	3.6	0.9	1.6	4.0	1.5	3.1	-	-	-	9.5	30.1
Item 950 Subject A01a N	3163	1464	1623	2381	367	726	876	951	610	1794	1080	1283	687	435	688	26

B083B: . . . during the last 12 months?

	TOTAL	M	F	White	Black	NE	NC	S	W	Yes	No	None	Mari- juana Only	Few Pills	More Pills	Any Her- oin
1. 0 occasions	86.6	83.9	89.5	85.6	95.3	79.4	91.6	92.0	79.8	89.1	85.1	100.0	100.0	84.3	51.0	27.9
2. 1-2	5.6	6.6	4.6	6.1	2.8	7.3	5.1	4.2	6.6	5.3	5.2	-	-	15.7	15.8	5.8
3. 3-5	2.2	2.7	1.8	2.5	0.4	4.3	0.7	1.2	3.6	1.5	2.6	-	-	-	9.8	9.8
4. 6-9	1.6	1.6	1.4	1.7	0.5	1.9	0.9	0.6	3.6	1.2	1.8	-	-	-	6.8	11.7
5. 10-19	1.9	2.5	1.2	2.0	0.9	3.0	1.3	1.0	2.8	1.8	1.8	-	-	-	7.5	28.8
6. 20-39	1.0	1.1	1.0	1.3	-	2.4	0.1	0.4	1.8	0.7	1.8	-	-	-	4.4	10.0
7. 40 or more	1.1	1.6	0.5	0.9	0.2	1.7	0.4	0.7	1.8	0.5	1.7	-	-	-	4.7	6.0
Item 960 Subject A01b N	3155	1458	1621	2373	367	723	874	949	610	1789	1077	1283	687	433	683	26

B083C: . . . during the last 30 days?

	TOTAL	M	F	White	Black	NE	NC	S	W	Yes	No	None	Mari- juana Only	Few Pills	More Pills	Any Her- oin
1. 0 occasions	93.1	91.3	95.0	92.5	98.1	87.6	96.6	96.7	89.3	94.9	92.2	100.0	100.0	97.4	71.5	56.7
2. 1-2	3.8	4.8	2.8	4.3	0.9	6.5	2.1	1.8	5.8	3.0	3.7	-	-	2.6	15.2	13.2
3. 3-5	1.4	1.6	1.2	1.5	0.5	2.3	0.6	0.6	2.9	1.0	1.6	-	-	-	6.2	10.9
4. 6-9	0.8	1.1	0.6	1.0	0.6	1.9	0.6	0.2	1.0	0.5	1.3	-	-	-	3.6	5.8
5. 10-19	0.5	0.5	0.3	0.4	-	0.6	0.2	0.3	0.9	0.4	0.5	-	-	-	1.9	7.5
6. 20-39	0.2	0.2	0.2	0.2	-	0.7	-	-	0.1	*	0.4	-	-	-	0.9	-
7. 40 or more	0.2	0.4	-	0.2	-	0.3	-	0.4	-	0.2	0.2	-	-	-	0.6	6.0
Item 970 Subject A01c N	3151	1454	1621	2369	367	723	872	946	610	1788	1074	1283	687	431	680	26

IF YOU HAVE NOT TAKEN COCAINE IN THE LAST TWELVE MONTHS, GO TO Q.B091.

B084: When you used cocaine during the last year, how often did you use it in each of the following situations?

B084A: When you were alone

	TOTAL	M	F	White	Black	NE	NC	S	W	Yes	No	None	Mari- juana Only	Few Pills	More Pills	Any Her- oin
1. Not at all	75.7	71.9	80.7	78.5	60.4	74.0	76.7	75.8	77.0	79.1	69.9	-	-	94.0	74.1	42.7
2. A few of the times	13.8	16.6	10.8	11.8	30.0	12.5	18.0	12.3	14.0	12.6	15.2	-	-	4.8	14.3	34.7
3. Some of the times	8.0	9.7	5.2	7.7	3.3	10.4	3.5	9.7	6.5	6.8	10.3	-	-	-	9.0	17.1
4. Most of the times	1.6	1.6	1.3	1.0	6.3	1.1	1.0	1.5	2.5	1.5	2.0	-	-	1.2	1.7	-
5. Every time	1.0	0.2	2.0	1.0	-	2.0	0.7	0.8	-	-	2.6	-	-	-	0.9	5.5
Item 4190 Subject A05a N★	406	222	169	326	17	145	67	72	122	194	152	-	-	60	325	19

*=less than .05 per cent.   ★=excludes respondents for whom question was inappropriate.

QUESTIONNAIRE FORM 1 1985	TOTAL	SEX		RACE		REGION				4YR COLLEGE PLANS		ILLICIT DRUG USE: LIFETIME				
		M	F	White	Black	NE	NC	S	W	Yes	No	None	Marijuana Only	Few Pills	More Pills	Any Heroin
N (Weighted No. of Cases):	3316	1505	1663	2415	400	783	902	1004	627	1822	1121	1307	719	444	716	29
% of Weighted Total:	100.0	45.4	50.2	72.8	12.1	23.6	27.2	30.3	18.9	55.0	33.8	39.4	21.7	13.4	21.6	0.9
B084B: With just 1 or 2 other people																
1. Not at all	7.4	7.4	7.5	6.3	20.3	7.2	8.8	4.8	8.3	10.7	5.1	-	-	24.9	4.0	-
2. A few of the times	34.9	33.7	36.9	35.1	38.7	40.3	29.2	31.7	33.6	35.0	34.0	-	-	46.0	33.1	36.0
3. Some of the times	12.8	13.2	13.0	13.2	22.3	8.3	12.2	13.2	18.2	10.3	15.3	-	-	-	15.1	15.8
4. Most of the times	24.9	25.3	24.0	24.9	4.1	26.9	15.8	18.4	31.4	22.2	26.1	-	-	7.4	27.8	32.3
5. Every time	20.0	20.3	18.6	20.5	14.6	17.2	34.1	31.9	8.5	21.8	19.5	-	-	21.8	20.0	16.0
Item 4200 Subject A05b N★	412	226	169	329	18	147	69	72	125	196	153	-	-	60	331	19
B084C: At a party																
1. Not at all	29.6	28.4	29.2	27.8	50.8	30.9	27.3	39.6	23.5	28.4	29.2	-	-	51.4	26.2	9.3
2. A few of the times	25.5	25.2	26.4	25.2	9.1	21.8	28.8	15.9	33.3	25.2	25.2	-	-	21.8	26.3	26.2
3. Some of the times	19.5	20.8	17.7	18.2	31.0	14.9	15.2	22.3	25.3	16.9	22.4	-	-	3.5	22.0	29.2
4. Most of the times	14.0	14.3	14.5	16.1	-	22.5	12.1	6.7	9.6	17.3	11.7	-	-	5.5	15.4	20.0
5. Every time	11.5	11.3	12.3	12.7	9.0	9.9	16.6	15.4	8.3	12.2	11.6	-	-	17.8	10.1	15.3
Item 4210 Subject A05c N★	409	228	166	328	18	143	68	72	125	196	150	-	-	61	327	19
B084D: When your date or spouse was present																
1. Not at all	53.4	67.3	35.6	53.6	71.8	56.8	60.7	54.7	44.6	57.6	48.9	-	-	83.2	48.3	42.8
2. A few of the times	17.8	12.9	24.7	18.0	16.5	15.3	14.3	20.1	21.3	15.7	21.1	-	-	10.5	20.0	4.9
3. Some of the times	11.3	10.9	11.8	10.4	8.5	11.9	8.7	12.0	11.5	13.7	8.6	-	-	1.1	13.2	10.9
4. Most of the times	10.0	5.1	16.8	10.1	-	10.3	4.1	10.2	12.9	7.9	11.8	-	-	1.3	10.7	26.0
5. Every time	7.5	3.8	11.1	7.8	3.2	5.7	12.2	3.0	9.7	5.0	9.6	-	-	3.8	7.8	15.4
Item 4220 Subject A05b N★	407	225	166	325	18	143	69	72	123	195	150	-	-	60	326	19
B084E: When people over age 30 were present																
1. Not at all	67.9	66.5	69.1	67.7	72.0	65.8	65.4	71.3	69.6	72.1	61.8	-	-	90.2	65.8	29.1
2. A few of the times	15.5	14.9	15.7	15.0	19.5	17.1	15.5	8.9	17.5	14.0	17.0	-	-	4.4	16.2	42.0
3. Some of the times	8.8	9.5	8.7	8.9	5.8	7.6	9.1	13.8	7.3	8.2	10.0	-	-	2.5	9.8	13.9
4. Most of the times	5.4	5.8	5.3	5.5	2.7	7.3	4.3	4.6	4.3	2.7	9.3	-	-	-	6.0	12.1
5. Every time	2.4	3.3	1.2	2.9	-	2.2	5.7	1.4	1.2	2.9	1.9	-	-	2.9	2.2	2.9
Item 4230 Subject A05b N★	406	226	166	326	18	143	68	71	124	196	150	-	-	60	325	19
B084F: During the daytime (before 4:00 p.m.)																
1. Not at all	57.1	54.6	60.0	59.5	56.9	56.0	71.3	59.5	49.3	62.0	52.8	-	-	90.3	52.6	24.7
2. A few of the times	21.3	21.4	22.4	22.0	19.7	19.5	15.2	14.5	30.8	21.4	19.8	-	-	7.2	22.5	48.5
3. Some of the times	13.6	14.3	13.1	11.0	13.6	12.1	9.3	21.3	13.4	10.5	18.6	-	-	1.3	16.3	7.6
4. Most of the times	5.6	6.6	3.6	5.2	5.8	10.0	2.3	0.8	5.2	3.6	5.9	-	-	-	6.4	10.2
5. Every time	2.3	3.1	1.0	2.3	4.1	2.4	2.0	4.0	1.3	2.6	2.9	-	-	1.2	2.1	9.0
Item 4240 Subject A05c N★	404	225	166	325	18	143	67	71	123	195	150	-	-	60	323	19
B084G: At your home (or apartment or dorm)																
1. Not at all	55.0	51.7	60.2	56.2	67.0	54.8	66.4	54.4	49.1	57.9	52.1	-	-	76.6	51.4	41.2
2. A few of the times	22.0	24.5	19.1	20.4	14.8	20.5	19.6	23.8	24.1	21.1	22.2	-	-	7.5	24.5	28.8
3. Some of the times	9.1	10.9	7.0	10.1	1.9	6.8	2.1	9.7	15.2	8.9	8.7	-	-	1.1	10.3	13.3
4. Most of the times	8.9	7.6	9.1	7.8	16.2	10.0	7.6	8.8	8.3	6.4	11.3	-	-	4.4	9.6	11.5
5. Every time	5.1	5.3	4.6	5.5	-	7.9	4.2	3.3	3.3	5.7	5.7	-	-	10.3	4.1	5.2
Item 4250 Subject A05c N★	404	224	166	324	18	143	67	72	122	196	148	-	-	60	323	19
B084H: At school																
1. Not at all	77.6	73.5	83.4	80.0	84.8	73.0	84.2	86.2	74.4	78.2	79.0	-	-	94.7	76.1	45.8
2. A few of the times	12.9	14.1	11.0	12.3	9.4	15.8	7.9	6.2	16.2	11.9	12.6	-	-	3.2	13.7	31.4
3. Some of the times	4.9	7.4	1.2	3.4	5.8	5.4	5.2	4.6	4.4	5.8	2.8	-	-	-	5.5	11.0
4. Most of the times	2.7	2.4	3.3	1.9	-	3.5	0.8	2.3	3.1	0.5	5.1	-	-	-	2.9	8.8
5. Every time	1.9	2.6	1.0	2.3	-	2.4	1.9	0.8	1.9	3.6	0.4	-	-	2.0	1.8	2.9
Item 4260 Subject A05c N★	407	227	166	327	18	142	68	72	124	196	150	-	-	61	324	19

★=excludes respondents for whom question was inappropriate.

QUESTIONNAIRE FORM 1 1985	TOTAL	SEX		RACE		REGION				4YR COLLEGE PLANS		ILLICIT DRUG USE: LIFETIME				
		M	F	White	Black	NE	NC	S	W	Yes	No	None	Marijuana Only	Few Pills	More Pills	Any Heroin
N (Weighted No. of Cases):	3316	1505	1663	2415	400	783	902	1004	627	1822	1121	1307	719	444	716	29
% of Weighted Total:	100.0	45.4	50.2	72.8	12.1	23.6	27.2	30.3	18.9	55.0	33.8	39.4	21.7	13.4	21.6	0.9

B084I: In a car

	TOTAL	M	F	White	Black	NE	NC	S	W	Yes	No	None	Mar. Only	Few Pills	More Pills	Heroin
1. Not at all	42.4	40.6	45.9	42.9	63.6	44.8	54.8	42.7	32.7	49.2	37.6	-	-	70.8	37.9	23.7
2. A few of the times	25.6	26.1	24.4	26.6	9.4	19.3	25.6	24.7	33.3	25.2	24.3	-	-	15.5	26.8	38.6
3. Some of the times	17.2	18.2	14.5	17.2	20.6	20.6	6.4	13.4	21.3	14.0	19.2	-	-	2.0	20.3	13.3
4. Most of the times	10.6	10.0	11.9	9.1	-	12.2	2.5	13.5	11.5	6.8	15.6	-	-	1.1	11.8	21.4
5. Every time	4.2	5.2	3.2	4.2	6.3	3.1	10.6	5.8	1.2	4.7	3.3	-	-	10.6	3.1	2.9
Item 4280　Subject A05c　N★	406	226	166	327	18	143	67	72	124	196	150	-	-	60	325	19

B085: How many of the times when you used cocaine during the last year did you use it along with each of the following drugs–that is, so that their effects overlapped?

B085A: With alcohol

	TOTAL	M	F	White	Black	NE	NC	S	W	Yes	No	None	Mar. Only	Few Pills	More Pills	Heroin
1. Not at all	23.7	24.4	22.5	21.7	34.1	21.2	24.3	28.3	23.7	25.7	23.8	-	-	43.1	19.1	32.3
2. A few of the times	31.1	31.0	29.7	30.6	35.5	27.0	32.9	33.2	33.5	32.1	28.1	-	-	35.0	30.5	30.4
3. Some of the times	12.0	12.6	11.8	12.7	9.9	12.3	5.7	10.1	16.3	12.9	10.9	-	-	-	14.4	12.4
4. Most of the times	16.3	14.9	18.5	17.1	8.0	20.3	12.6	10.0	17.5	13.2	18.3	-	-	1.1	19.6	10.9
5. Every time	16.9	17.0	17.5	17.9	12.4	19.3	24.5	18.4	9.0	16.0	18.9	-	-	20.8	16.4	14.0
Item 4290　Subject A01h　N★	407	223	169	327	17	141	70	71	124	194	151	-	-	62	324	19

B085B: With marijuana

	TOTAL	M	F	White	Black	NE	NC	S	W	Yes	No	None	Mar. Only	Few Pills	More Pills	Heroin
1. Not at all	38.0	35.6	42.0	37.6	41.7	37.4	43.6	37.6	35.9	43.3	33.9	-	-	68.1	34.0	2.1
2. A few of the times	27.5	28.7	25.3	27.6	22.7	25.4	27.5	26.8	30.2	27.9	27.2	-	-	16.5	29.7	27.8
3. Some of the times	10.0	10.2	10.5	10.6	2.1	11.1	3.9	6.9	14.0	8.9	10.6	-	-	-	12.1	7.5
4. Most of the times	11.0	8.9	12.3	10.7	24.0	13.2	5.7	15.3	8.9	7.3	15.3	-	-	4.9	11.4	24.2
5. Every time	13.5	16.6	9.9	13.6	9.5	12.9	19.3	13.4	10.9	12.6	13.0	-	-	10.4	12.7	38.4
Item 4300　Subject A01h　N★	406	226	166	327	17	140	70	72	124	195	150	-	-	61	324	19

B085C: With LSD

	TOTAL	M	F	White	Black	NE	NC	S	W	Yes	No	None	Mar. Only	Few Pills	More Pills	Heroin
1. Not at all	94.5	93.4	96.3	94.7	100.0	92.0	93.0	94.5	98.1	94.2	94.7	-	-	100.0	94.4	75.7
2. A few of the times	1.9	1.7	1.8	2.1	-	3.5	1.5	0.8	0.9	1.0	2.9	-	-	-	2.1	5.7
3. Some of the times	3.1	3.8	1.9	2.7	-	3.8	3.5	4.7	1.0	4.1	2.4	-	-	-	2.8	18.6
4. Most of the times	-	-	-	-	-	-	-	-	-	-	-	-	-	-	-	-
5. Every time	0.6	1.1	-	0.4	-	0.7	1.9	-	-	0.7	-	-	-	-	0.7	-
Item 4310　Subject A01h　N★	389	212	165	316	16	135	68	70	117	190	146	-	-	61	308	18

B085D: With psychedelics other than LSD

	TOTAL	M	F	White	Black	NE	NC	S	W	Yes	No	None	Mar. Only	Few Pills	More Pills	Heroin
1. Not at all	94.5	92.8	97.0	94.8	100.0	90.9	95.4	94.5	98.0	93.1	97.8	-	-	100.0	93.7	88.3
2. A few of the times	4.2	5.9	1.8	3.6	-	7.1	0.7	5.5	2.0	5.5	0.8	-	-	-	4.8	7.6
3. Some of the times	1.0	0.6	1.2	1.3	-	2.0	1.9	-	-	0.7	1.3	-	-	-	1.1	4.0
4. Most of the times	-	-	-	-	-	-	-	-	-	-	-	-	-	-	-	-
5. Every time	0.3	0.6	-	0.4	-	-	1.9	-	-	0.7	-	-	-	-	0.4	-
Item 4320　Subject A01h　N★	390	212	166	317	16	135	68	70	117	191	146	-	-	61	308	19

B085E: With amphetamines

	TOTAL	M	F	White	Black	NE	NC	S	W	Yes	No	None	Mar. Only	Few Pills	More Pills	Heroin
1. Not at all	90.9	89.9	92.7	91.1	88.0	91.4	91.2	86.5	92.8	91.4	89.6	-	-	100.0	91.3	53.6
2. A few of the times	4.8	3.5	6.1	4.8	12.0	4.8	4.5	4.7	5.0	4.4	5.3	-	-	-	4.2	30.8
3. Some of the times	3.0	4.2	1.2	2.5	-	2.4	4.2	4.1	2.3	2.5	4.0	-	-	-	3.2	9.6
4. Most of the times	0.6	1.1	-	0.8	-	0.9	-	1.6	-	0.7	0.8	-	-	-	0.4	6.1
5. Every time	0.7	1.2	-	0.8	-	0.3	-	3.1	-	1.1	0.3	-	-	-	0.9	-
Item 4330　Subject A01h　N★	389	212	164	315	16	133	68	70	117	191	143	-	-	61	307	19

B085F: With quaaludes

	TOTAL	M	F	White	Black	NE	NC	S	W	Yes	No	None	Mar. Only	Few Pills	More Pills	Heroin
1. Not at all	98.8	99.4	98.5	98.8	100.0	97.8	100.0	97.6	100.0	99.0	99.3	-	-	100.0	98.9	93.0
2. A few of the times	0.8	0.6	1.0	1.0	-	1.0	-	2.4	-	1.0	0.7	-	-	-	0.8	2.9
3. Some of the times	0.2	-	-	0.2	-	0.6	-	-	-	-	-	-	-	-	-	4.0
4. Most of the times	0.2	-	0.5	-	-	0.6	-	-	-	-	-	-	-	-	0.3	-
5. Every time	-	-	-	-	-	-	-	-	-	-	-	-	-	-	-	-
Item 4340　Subject A01h　N★	390	212	165	317	16	135	68	70	117	191	145	-	-	61	308	19

★=excludes respondents for whom question was inappropriate.

QUESTIONNAIRE FORM 1 1985	TOTAL	SEX		RACE		REGION				4YR COLLEGE PLANS		ILLICIT DRUG USE: LIFETIME				
		M	F	White	Black	NE	NC	S	W	Yes	No	None	Mari-juana Only	Few Pills	More Pills	Any Her-oin
N (Weighted No. of Cases):	3316	1505	1663	2415	400	783	902	1004	627	1822	1121	1307	719	444	716	29
% of Weighted Total:	100.0	45.4	50.2	72.8	12.1	23.6	27.2	30.3	18.9	55.0	33.8	39.4	21.7	13.4	21.6	0.9
B085G: With barbiturates																
1. Not at all	98.9	98.7	99.6	98.8	100.0	97.8	99.3	99.0	100.0	100.0	98.5	-	-	100.0	99.0	93.0
2. A few of the times	0.7	1.3	-	0.7	-	1.7	0.7	-	-	-	1.5	-	-	-	0.7	2.7
3. Some of the times	0.2	-	-	0.2	-	0.6	-	-	-	-	-	-	-	-	-	4.2
4. Most of the times	-	-	-	-	-	-	-	-	-	-	-	-	-	-	-	-
5. Every time	0.2	-	0.4	0.2	-	-	-	1.0	-	-	-	-	-	-	0.2	-
Item 4350 Subject A01h N★	389	211	165	316	16	135	67	70	117	190	145		-	61	308	18
B085H: With tranquilizers																
1. Not at all	96.8	97.7	95.9	97.2	100.0	96.5	99.3	89.8	100.0	98.1	95.2	-	-	100.0	96.6	90.4
2. A few of the times	2.0	0.9	3.4	2.3	-	3.0	0.7	4.6	-	0.4	4.8	-	-	-	2.2	5.5
3. Some of the times	1.2	1.4	0.6	0.6	-	0.6	-	5.6	-	1.5	-	-	-	-	1.3	4.0
4. Most of the times	-	-	-	-	-	-	-	-	-	-	-	-	-	-	-	-
5. Every time	-	-	-	-	-	-	-	-	-	-	-	-	-	-	-	-
Item 4360 Subject A01h N★	390	212	166	317	16	136	68	70	117	191	146		-	61	309	19
B086: What have been the most important reasons for your taking cocaine? (Mark all that apply.)																
A. To experiment–to see what it's like	71.9	69.8	76.3	72.8	78.1	62.0	80.6	84.0	71.7	77.1	67.2	-	-	94.8	69.2	38.7
B. To relax or relieve tension	17.9	20.4	15.2	18.1	22.2	23.6	13.8	14.8	15.4	16.3	21.2	-	-	3.7	20.4	19.0
C. To feel good or get high	68.1	68.0	67.1	70.7	44.2	66.9	59.8	69.6	73.2	60.4	72.7	-	-	36.5	73.0	84.6
D. To seek deeper insights and understanding	6.9	8.4	5.0	6.0	18.9	8.9	6.9	6.6	4.6	6.3	7.6	-	-	3.0	7.5	10.4
E. To have a good time with my friends	51.3	49.9	51.7	51.2	14.9	58.4	29.8	46.2	57.9	45.3	56.1	-	-	25.6	54.8	71.2
F. To fit in with a group I like	4.5	6.2	2.2	3.7	-	5.8	5.3	1.9	4.2	4.9	4.8	-	-	7.0	4.2	3.2
G. To get away from my problems or troubles	8.5	8.2	9.3	8.2	-	8.2	7.4	9.4	9.1	6.0	11.6	-	-	1.1	9.7	13.6
H. Because of boredom, nothing else to do	15.0	18.4	11.5	14.2	6.6	13.2	15.0	12.2	18.9	11.8	18.3	-	-	2.6	16.6	32.3
I. Because of anger or frustration	4.8	5.9	3.8	4.3	-	6.4	6.0	4.5	2.5	3.6	6.7	-	-	-	6.1	-
J. To get through the day	5.8	6.9	4.4	4.8	-	5.6	-	7.1	8.4	3.7	6.5	-	-	1.1	6.3	12.8
K. To increase the effects of some other drug(s)	9.8	10.0	9.8	9.7	-	12.3	10.4	13.0	4.6	7.4	12.7	-	-	3.9	10.7	15.3
L. To decrease (offset) the effects of some other drug(s)	3.4	5.6	0.7	4.2	-	2.5	2.3	-	7.0	5.4	1.6	-	-	1.7	3.9	-
M. To stay awake	25.5	24.9	27.5	24.8	6.6	23.9	13.8	22.5	35.8	24.9	29.6	-	-	5.8	28.4	38.9
N. To get more energy	35.9	34.2	38.3	35.8	13.1	33.3	16.9	40.1	47.1	33.1	37.5	-	-	13.8	38.8	57.6
O. Because I am "hooked"–I have to have it	2.1	3.7	0.3	2.3	-	-	2.6	1.3	4.9	1.2	3.2	-	-	-	2.2	7.8
Item 4370-4510 Subject A06a N★	407	223	170	329	16	144	69	71	123	193	151		-	62	324	18
B087: When you take cocaine how high do you usually get?																
1. Not at all high	6.8	5.2	9.0	6.7	9.7	4.0	6.4	11.6	7.5	9.1	5.4	-	-	14.8	5.5	-
2. A little high	24.5	21.7	26.8	24.6	11.8	27.0	26.6	20.9	22.3	26.4	19.9	-	-	41.9	22.5	6.5
3. Moderately high	43.1	47.3	39.3	43.3	42.7	48.2	35.7	33.7	46.6	42.2	44.3	-	-	26.8	45.0	57.9
4. Very high	22.5	22.8	21.2	23.0	30.9	19.2	30.6	29.7	17.7	19.1	27.5	-	-	10.6	24.1	35.6
5. I don't take it to get high	3.1	3.0	3.6	2.4	4.9	1.6	0.7	4.1	5.8	3.3	2.8	-	-	6.0	2.8	-
Item 4520 Subject A01e N★	409	223	170	329	16	146	69	71	123	194	150		-	60	326	19
B088: When you take cocaine how long do you usually stay high?																
1. Usually don't get high	9.2	7.9	11.2	8.7	14.6	5.6	8.7	14.0	10.9	12.8	6.7	-	-	19.6	7.5	2.2
2. One to two hours	48.6	52.6	41.7	51.2	24.6	53.3	48.3	43.4	46.4	46.1	48.9	-	-	48.7	48.5	58.3
3. Three to six hours	31.8	30.1	36.6	30.7	54.2	33.3	23.4	33.0	34.0	30.9	35.2	-	-	26.8	33.3	28.4
4. Seven to 24 hours	8.5	8.4	8.5	8.8	6.6	7.1	17.3	6.8	6.3	10.2	5.4	-	-	3.3	9.4	5.6
5. More than 24 hours	1.9	1.0	2.1	0.6	-	0.7	2.3	2.9	2.5	-	3.7	-	-	1.7	1.4	5.5
Item 4530 Subject A01f N★	403	218	169	323	16	144	66	71	122	191	150		-	59	322	19
B089: Have you ever tried to stop using cocaine and found that you couldn't stop?																
1. Yes	5.3	6.9	3.2	3.7	9.6	4.9	3.3	1.3	9.3	3.8	7.9	-	-	1.5	5.4	11.0
2. No	94.7	93.1	96.8	96.3	90.4	95.1	96.7	98.7	90.7	96.2	92.1	-	-	98.5	94.6	89.0
Item 4540 Subject A01i N★	405	220	170	326	16	144	69	71	121	191	151		-	60	322	19

★=excludes respondents for whom question was inappropriate.

QUESTIONNAIRE FORM 1 1985	TOTAL	SEX		RACE		REGION				4YR COLLEGE PLANS		ILLICIT DRUG USE: LIFETIME				
		M	F	White	Black	NE	NC	S	W	Yes	No	None	Marijuana Only	Few Pills	More Pills	Any Heroin
N (Weighted No. of Cases):	3316	1505	1663	2415	400	783	902	1004	627	1822	1121	1307	719	444	716	29
% of Weighted Total:	100.0	45.4	50.2	72.8	12.1	23.6	27.2	30.3	18.9	55.0	33.8	39.4	21.7	13.4	21.6	0.9

B090: What methods have you used for taking cocaine? (Mark all that apply.)

	TOTAL	M	F	White	Black	NE	NC	S	W	Yes	No	None	Marij. Only	Few Pills	More Pills	Any Heroin
A. Sniffing or "snorting"	96.6	98.0	96.5	98.9	79.7	97.7	92.2	98.1	97.0	95.9	98.4	-	-	91.2	98.3	90.1
B. Smoking	38.6	39.3	35.8	34.5	49.7	42.7	25.7	36.8	42.1	30.4	45.1	-	-	9.9	41.5	87.9
C. Injection	2.0	1.7	1.3	1.7	-	0.6	-	6.8	1.7	1.3	1.4	-	-	-	1.5	16.5
D. By mouth	43.8	45.0	43.1	43.2	34.5	50.1	37.6	36.0	44.4	43.4	43.4	-	-	27.2	47.0	44.6
E. Other	5.3	6.1	3.8	4.9	18.9	7.9	4.7	4.1	3.4	3.7	7.9	-	-	-	5.7	12.7
Item 4550-4590 Subject A05d N★	409	225	169	330	16	145	69	73	123	194	151	-	-	62	325	19

B091: Do you think you will be using cocaine five years from now?

	TOTAL	M	F	White	Black	NE	NC	S	W	Yes	No	None	Marij. Only	Few Pills	More Pills	Any Heroin
1. I definitely will	1.5	1.6	1.3	1.5	0.6	2.1	1.7	1.5	0.9	0.9	2.3	0.3	0.3	0.7	5.1	13.4
2. I probably will	5.4	6.3	4.4	5.8	1.7	8.3	3.3	2.8	9.2	4.6	5.5	0.3	1.9	4.9	17.9	40.6
3. I probably will not	15.2	17.1	13.6	16.5	8.0	20.7	13.9	10.7	17.9	15.3	14.5	3.9	13.7	23.0	34.0	25.1
4. I definitely will not	77.8	75.0	80.8	76.2	89.7	69.0	81.2	85.1	72.0	79.2	77.6	95.5	84.1	71.4	43.1	21.0
Item 4600 Subject A04a N	3142	1452	1622	2357	371	722	869	948	603	1783	1076	1279	675	425	675	28

The next questions are about HEROIN, which is sometimes called smack, horse, skag.

B092: On how many occasions (if any) have you taken heroin . . .

B092A: . . . in your lifetime?

	TOTAL	M	F	White	Black	NE	NC	S	W	Yes	No	None	Marij. Only	Few Pills	More Pills	Any Heroin
1. 0 occasions	99.1	99.1	99.2	99.2	99.2	99.1	99.1	99.1	98.9	99.5	98.6	100.0	100.0	100.0	100.0	-
2. 1-2	0.6	0.5	0.7	0.6	0.2	0.5	0.6	0.5	1.0	0.3	1.0	-	-	-	-	66.1
3. 3-5	0.1	0.1	-	0.1	-	0.1	0.1	*	-	-	*	-	-	-	-	5.6
4. 6-9	*	0.1	-	-	-	0.2	-	-	-	-	0.1	-	-	-	-	3.7
5. 10-19	*	-	*	*	-	-	-	-	0.1	*	-	-	-	-	-	2.0
6. 20-39	*	0.1	*	*	-	-	0.1	0.1	-	-	0.1	-	-	-	-	5.0
7. 40 or more	0.2	0.2	-	0.1	0.5	0.1	0.2	0.2	-	0.1	0.1	-	-	-	-	17.5
Item 1100 Subject A01a N	3111	1440	1606	2357	358	707	863	934	606	1782	1065	1272	687	419	663	29

B092B: . . . during the last 12 months?

	TOTAL	M	F	White	Black	NE	NC	S	W	Yes	No	None	Marij. Only	Few Pills	More Pills	Any Heroin
1. 0 occasions	99.5	99.3	99.8	99.6	99.2	99.3	99.5	99.3	99.9	99.8	99.4	100.0	100.0	100.0	100.0	45.8
2. 1-2	0.3	0.4	0.1	0.2	0.2	0.6	0.2	0.3	-	0.1	0.4	-	-	-	-	30.9
3. 3-5	0.1	0.1	0.1	0.1	-	-	-	0.2	0.1	*	0.2	-	-	-	-	7.9
4. 6-9	*	*	-	-	-	-	-	*	-	-	*	-	-	-	-	1.5
5. 10-19	-	-	-	-	-	-	-	-	-	-	-	-	-	-	-	-
6. 20-39	0.1	0.1	-	-	0.5	-	0.2	-	-	0.1	-	-	-	-	-	6.6
7. 40 or more	0.1	-	-	*	-	0.1	-	0.1	-	-	-	-	-	-	-	7.2
Item 1110 Subject A01b N	3111	1439	1606	2357	358	707	863	934	606	1782	1065	1272	687	419	663	29

B092C: . . . during the last 30 days?

	TOTAL	M	F	White	Black	NE	NC	S	W	Yes	No	None	Marij. Only	Few Pills	More Pills	Any Heroin
1. 0 occasions	99.8	99.8	99.9	100.0	99.2	99.9	99.8	99.7	100.0	99.9	99.9	100.0	100.0	100.0	100.0	81.7
2. 1-2	*	*	0.1	-	0.2	-	0.1	-	-	-	0.1	-	-	-	-	4.4
3. 3-5	-	-	-	-	-	-	-	-	-	-	-	-	-	-	-	-
4. 6-9	0.1	0.1	-	-	0.5	-	0.2	-	-	0.1	-	-	-	-	-	6.6
5. 10-19	-	-	-	-	-	-	-	-	-	-	-	-	-	-	-	-
6. 20-39	-	-	-	-	-	-	-	-	-	-	-	-	-	-	-	-
7. 40 or more	0.1	-	-	*	-	0.1	-	0.1	-	-	-	-	-	-	-	7.2
Item 1120 Subject A01c N	3111	1439	1606	2357	358	707	863	934	606	1782	1065	1272	687	419	663	29

The next questions are about NARCOTICS OTHER THAN HEROIN, which are sometimes prescribed by doctors. Drugstores are not supposed to sell them without a prescription. These include:

Methadone, Codeine, Talwin, Morphine, Opium, Demerol, Laudanum, Paregoric.

*=less than .05 per cent.   ★=excludes respondents for whom question was inappropriate.

QUESTIONNAIRE FORM 1 1985	TOTAL	SEX		RACE		REGION				4YR COLLEGE PLANS		ILLICIT DRUG USE: LIFETIME				
		M	F	White	Black	NE	NC	S	W	Yes	No	None	Marijuana Only	Few Pills	More Pills	Any Heroin
N (Weighted No. of Cases):	3316	1505	1663	2415	400	783	902	1004	627	1822	1121	1307	719	444	716	29
% of Weighted Total:	100.0	45.4	50.2	72.8	12.1	23.6	27.2	30.3	18.9	55.0	33.8	39.4	21.7	13.4	21.6	0.9

B093: Have you ever taken any narcotics other than heroin because a doctor told you to use them?

	TOTAL	M	F	White	Black	NE	NC	S	W	Yes	No	None	Marijuana Only	Few Pills	More Pills	Any Heroin
1. No	81.7	83.1	80.3	79.0	92.8	78.6	84.5	83.6	78.6	80.1	84.1	88.3	86.8	72.4	69.2	80.6
2. Yes, but I had already tried them on my own.	1.9	1.8	2.0	2.1	0.5	2.4	1.8	1.2	2.8	1.8	2.0	0.1	-	1.8	7.2	12.0
3. Yes, and it was the first time I took any	16.3	15.2	17.7	18.8	6.7	19.0	13.8	15.2	18.6	18.1	13.9	11.6	13.2	25.8	23.6	7.4
Item 5020 Subject A01j N	3070	1417	1594	2338	339	696	860	922	593	1773	1040	1258	668	418	658	28

B094: On how many occasions (if any) have you taken narcotics other than heroin on your own–that is, without a doctor telling you to take them . . .

B094A: . . . in your lifetime?

	TOTAL	M	F	White	Black	NE	NC	S	W	Yes	No	None	Marijuana Only	Few Pills	More Pills	Any Heroin
1. 0 occasions	89.8	90.2	89.5	88.8	94.9	89.0	89.7	92.6	86.5	90.4	89.4	100.0	100.0	79.1	69.4	7.7
2. 1-2	5.6	4.4	6.8	6.2	3.4	6.5	6.5	3.3	7.1	5.1	6.1	-	-	20.9	11.7	32.4
3. 3-5	2.1	2.6	1.7	2.2	1.4	1.6	1.9	1.8	3.5	2.0	2.4	-	-	-	8.9	26.0
4. 6-9	1.0	1.1	1.0	1.2	0.3	1.4	0.8	0.6	1.6	1.2	0.9	-	-	-	4.2	16.6
5. 10-19	0.9	1.0	0.7	1.0	-	0.9	0.7	0.9	1.0	0.8	0.9	-	-	-	3.8	5.5
6. 20-39	0.2	0.2	0.2	0.3	-	0.2	0.2	0.2	0.2	0.2	0.1	-	-	-	0.8	3.9
7. 40 or more	0.3	0.6	0.1	0.3	-	0.4	0.2	0.5	0.1	0.4	0.3	-	-	-	1.3	7.9
Item 1130 Subject A01a N	3096	1432	1600	2345	358	699	859	940	598	1779	1059	1270	681	425	656	28

B094B: . . . during the last 12 months?

	TOTAL	M	F	White	Black	NE	NC	S	W	Yes	No	None	Marijuana Only	Few Pills	More Pills	Any Heroin
1. 0 occasions	95.2	95.1	95.3	94.6	98.1	94.2	95.6	97.0	92.9	94.8	95.8	100.0	100.0	92.2	84.3	50.0
2. 1-2	2.5	2.4	2.7	2.9	1.4	3.1	2.8	1.1	3.8	2.8	2.3	-	-	7.8	5.9	26.4
3. 3-5	1.2	1.1	1.2	1.4	0.2	1.6	0.7	0.5	2.4	1.2	1.1	-	-	-	5.1	11.0
4. 6-9	0.5	0.4	0.6	0.5	0.3	0.1	0.6	0.6	0.6	0.5	0.5	-	-	-	2.3	1.9
5. 10-19	0.4	0.7	0.1	0.4	-	0.4	0.3	0.6	0.2	0.6	-	-	-	-	1.7	4.1
6. 20-39	0.1	0.1	0.1	0.1	-	0.4	-	-	-	0.1	-	-	-	-	0.4	-
7. 40 or more	0.1	0.2	*	0.1	-	0.2	-	0.2	0.1	-	0.3	-	-	-	0.3	6.6
Item 1140 Subject A01b N	3088	1427	1598	2338	358	696	855	940	596	1777	1055	1270	681	423	651	26

B094C: . . . during the last 30 days?

	TOTAL	M	F	White	Black	NE	NC	S	W	Yes	No	None	Marijuana Only	Few Pills	More Pills	Any Heroin
1. 0 occasions	98.4	98.4	98.5	98.4	99.2	98.0	99.0	98.5	97.8	98.3	98.5	100.0	100.0	97.2	94.6	88.2
2. 1-2	1.1	1.2	1.1	1.2	0.8	1.8	0.9	0.4	1.7	1.3	1.0	-	-	2.8	3.5	1.8
3. 3-5	0.3	0.4	0.3	0.3	-	-	0.1	0.7	0.4	0.3	0.3	-	-	-	1.2	6.2
4. 6-9	0.1	-	0.1	0.1	-	-	-	0.2	0.1	0.1	0.1	-	-	-	0.4	-
5. 10-19	0.1	-	0.1	*	-	-	-	0.2	-	-	-	-	-	-	0.2	3.9
6. 20-39	*	0.1	-	0.1	-	0.2	-	-	-	-	0.1	-	-	-	0.2	-
7. 40 or more	-	-	-	-	-	-	-	-	-	-	-	-	-	-	-	-
Item 1150 Subject A01c N	3086	1427	1596	2337	358	697	855	937	596	1776	1053	1270	681	422	648	27

IF YOU HAVE NOT TAKEN NARCOTICS OTHER THAN HEROIN IN THE LAST TWELVE MONTHS, GO TO Q.B103.

THE FOLLOWING QUESTIONS REFER ONLY TO TAKING NARCOTICS OTHER THAN HEROIN WITHOUT A DOCTOR'S ORDERS. IF YOU HAVE NOT DONE THIS IN THE LAST TWELVE MONTHS, GO TO Q.B103.

B095: When you used narcotics other than heroin during the last year, how often did you use them in each of the following situations?

B095A: When you were alone

	TOTAL	M	F	White	Black	NE	NC	S	W	Yes	No	None	Marijuana Only	Few Pills	More Pills	Any Heroin
1. Not at all	38.9	30.9	45.7	39.5	100.0	26.4	52.4	43.7	34.4	38.5	36.2	-	-	57.3	32.0	50.6
2. A few of the times	28.3	39.8	18.0	25.5	-	22.6	27.2	29.9	34.2	25.0	35.0	-	-	1.7	36.7	18.5
3. Some of the times	8.2	13.2	4.1	9.2	-	4.2	8.5	15.6	6.8	8.6	5.7	-	-	-	7.9	30.9
4. Most of the times	7.9	3.2	12.3	8.3	-	18.0	5.4	3.0	3.4	6.4	11.6	-	-	9.0	8.5	-
5. Every time	16.8	12.8	19.9	17.5	-	28.8	6.5	7.8	21.2	21.6	11.4	-	-	31.9	14.9	-
Item 5030 Subject A05a N★	128	59	66	113	3	35	35	24	34	80	37	-	-	24	92	10

*=less than .05 per cent.   ★=excludes respondents for whom question was inappropriate.

QUESTIONNAIRE FORM 1 1985	TOTAL	SEX		RACE		REGION				4YR COLLEGE PLANS		ILLICIT DRUG USE: LIFETIME				
		M	F	White	Black	NE	NC	S	W	Yes	No	None	Mari- juana Only	Few Pills	More Pills	Any Her- oin
N (Weighted No. of Cases):	3316	1505	1663	2415	400	783	902	1004	627	1822	1121	1307	719	444	716	29
% of Weighted Total:	100.0	45.4	50.2	72.8	12.1	23.6	27.2	30.3	18.9	55.0	33.8	39.4	21.7	13.4	21.6	0.9

B095B: With just 1 or 2 other people

1. Not at all	34.5	22.7	45.1	34.6	-	48.6	17.8	31.1	40.7	38.9	30.7	-	-	70.2	25.5	22.7
2. A few of the times	35.4	45.9	27.0	36.5	25.8	30.1	58.5	11.5	33.2	30.2	48.4	-	-	14.6	42.5	26.1
3. Some of the times	13.3	13.3	11.5	14.4	-	8.7	6.5	21.4	18.9	9.9	13.5	-	-	-	14.6	34.5
4. Most of the times	7.5	11.1	4.5	5.9	-	8.7	-	22.4	3.9	9.5	1.6	-	-	-	9.9	5.8
5. Every time	9.3	7.0	11.9	8.6	74.2	3.9	17.2	13.6	3.3	11.5	5.8	-	-	15.2	7.6	11.0
Item 5040 Subject A05b N★	125	59	63	111	3	32	35	24	34	80	34	-	-	24	89	10

B095C: At a party

1. Not at all	63.8	55.9	72.5	62.7	100.0	67.1	64.2	44.5	73.5	70.5	59.1	-	-	92.7	61.5	11.4
2. A few of the times	16.9	19.6	15.2	19.2	-	14.2	14.1	18.4	21.4	16.4	15.9	-	-	7.3	19.2	21.8
3. Some of the times	12.4	18.8	7.1	11.4	-	9.6	14.8	30.6	-	10.0	15.7	-	-	-	15.5	15.9
4. Most of the times	2.7	3.0	2.6	3.1	-	-	6.9	1.8	1.7	2.4	4.4	-	-	-	2.0	15.9
5. Every time	4.2	2.7	2.7	3.7	-	9.1	-	4.7	3.3	0.7	5.0	-	-	-	1.8	35.0
Item 5050 Subject A05c N★	124	58	63	110	3	32	34	24	34	80	34	-	-	24	89	10

B095D: When your date or spouse was present

1. Not at all	73.7	75.8	74.8	74.5	100.0	68.8	71.3	72.0	81.7	76.6	71.4	-	-	86.0	71.6	60.0
2. A few of the times	12.6	14.2	11.7	14.3	-	12.5	16.1	2.3	16.3	11.7	17.4	-	-	5.0	15.0	11.2
3. Some of the times	6.6	9.1	4.4	4.8	-	3.7	7.1	18.9	-	7.5	4.9	-	-	-	8.7	4.7
4. Most of the times	3.6	-	6.2	3.5	-	7.0	1.7	4.5	2.0	3.5	2.1	-	-	9.0	2.6	-
5. Every time	3.5	0.9	3.0	2.9	-	7.9	3.7	2.3	-	0.6	4.2	-	-	-	2.1	24.0
Item 5060 Subject A05b N★	124	59	62	110	3	31	35	24	34	80	33	-	-	24	88	10

B095E: When people over age 30 were present

1. Not at all	66.0	60.5	71.0	66.1	100.0	76.1	67.5	60.9	59.0	64.5	64.5	-	-	85.3	60.4	55.4
2. A few of the times	16.5	22.2	11.2	17.2	-	12.3	11.9	12.2	28.5	18.6	14.3	-	-	8.8	18.5	23.2
3. Some of the times	10.2	11.4	9.9	9.3	-	9.5	11.4	22.5	-	7.7	15.6	-	-	-	13.6	9.6
4. Most of the times	1.4	2.0	-	1.1	-	2.1	1.4	-	2.0	1.5	1.9	-	-	-	2.1	-
5. Every time	5.8	4.0	7.9	6.3	-	-	7.6	4.3	10.5	7.8	3.6	-	-	5.9	5.3	11.8
Item 5070 Subject A05b N★	129	59	65	111	5	32	36	27	34	80	35	-	-	24	89	11

B095F: During the daytime (before 4:00 p.m.)

1. Not at all	41.4	41.1	41.6	39.7	85.4	44.7	42.5	43.7	35.4	35.1	54.0	-	-	55.9	36.5	24.8
2. A few of the times	23.9	27.4	22.3	27.9	-	22.7	32.5	15.9	22.6	26.0	17.5	-	-	27.7	24.5	19.8
3. Some of the times	22.7	21.5	23.6	20.8	-	18.7	12.3	25.4	34.9	24.8	18.4	-	-	4.3	29.8	15.2
4. Most of the times	7.9	7.3	7.8	8.6	-	7.2	5.8	15.0	5.1	8.9	6.7	-	-	-	7.1	35.7
5. Every time	4.1	2.7	4.6	3.0	14.6	6.8	6.9	-	2.0	5.2	3.3	-	-	12.2	2.0	4.5
Item 5080 Subject A05c N★	128	59	64	110	5	32	34	27	34	79	35	-	-	24	88	11

B095G: At your home (or apartment or dorm)

1. Not at all	34.2	32.9	33.0	32.2	100.0	32.7	48.2	43.7	13.7	26.6	41.7	-	-	32.6	31.1	36.1
2. A few of the times	22.3	26.8	18.5	23.9	-	16.5	23.5	14.5	32.7	22.5	21.0	-	-	23.7	22.2	29.1
3. Some of the times	11.5	15.0	9.2	8.8	-	12.4	3.4	23.2	9.7	11.2	11.8	-	-	-	15.5	10.1
4. Most of the times	9.5	8.9	10.6	10.4	-	11.1	10.9	2.9	11.6	12.4	4.9	-	-	5.9	10.1	17.0
5. Every time	22.6	16.4	28.7	24.7	-	27.4	13.9	15.7	32.3	27.3	20.6	-	-	37.8	21.1	7.6
Item 5090 Subject A05c N★	128	59	65	110	5	32	35	27	34	80	35	-	-	25	88	10

B095H: At school

1. Not at all	71.3	62.2	79.9	72.5	100.0	74.9	70.6	64.7	73.8	67.3	84.2	-	-	76.8	70.3	54.4
2. A few of the times	15.0	19.3	12.1	14.8	-	3.4	16.2	28.6	13.9	16.2	12.3	-	-	17.1	14.3	22.3
3. Some of the times	9.6	13.5	4.5	8.0	-	13.2	9.3	4.6	10.5	10.6	2.0	-	-	6.1	10.8	12.2
4. Most of the times	3.7	5.1	2.6	4.3	-	8.6	3.9	-	1.7	5.9	-	-	-	-	4.6	5.8
5. Every time	0.4	-	0.9	0.5	-	-	-	2.0	-	-	1.6	-	-	-	-	5.4
Item 5100 Subject A05c N★	127	59	64	110	5	32	34	27	34	79	35	-	-	24	88	10

★=excludes respondents for whom question was inappropriate.

QUESTIONNAIRE FORM 1 1985	TOTAL	SEX		RACE		REGION				4YR COLLEGE PLANS		ILLICIT DRUG USE: LIFETIME				
		M	F	White	Black	NE	NC	S	W	Yes	No	None	Mari-juana Only	Few Pills	More Pills	Any Her-oin
N (Weighted No. of Cases):	3316	1505	1663	2415	400	783	902	1004	627	1822	1121	1307	719	444	716	29
% of Weighted Total:	100.0	45.4	50.2	72.8	12.1	23.6	27.2	30.3	18.9	55.0	33.8	39.4	21.7	13.4	21.6	0.9

B095I: In a car

	TOTAL	M	F	White	Black	NE	NC	S	W	Yes	No	None	Mari-juana Only	Few Pills	More Pills	Any Her-oin
1. Not at all	72.1	65.7	78.3	72.0	74.8	72.8	66.6	62.3	84.8	79.1	65.1	-	-	87.9	67.0	66.6
2. A few of the times	13.3	15.6	11.1	14.9	-	10.9	21.2	4.1	15.2	5.6	26.5	-	-	-	16.7	21.2
3. Some of the times	6.4	6.5	6.7	7.4	-	8.2	5.3	13.5	-	6.0	4.6	-	-	-	8.6	4.7
4. Most of the times	2.1	1.7	1.4	2.4	-	5.1	-	3.6	-	0.7	3.8	-	-	-	2.1	7.4
5. Every time	6.2	10.6	2.5	3.3	25.2	3.1	6.9	16.5	-	8.7	-	-	-	12.1	5.6	-
Item 5120 Subject A05c N★	127	59	64	110	5	32	34	27	34	79	35	-	-	24	88	10

B096: How many of the times when you used narcotics other than heroin during the last year did you use them along with each of the following drugs–that is, so that their effects overlapped?

B096A: With alcohol

	TOTAL	M	F	White	Black	NE	NC	S	W	Yes	No	None	Mari-juana Only	Few Pills	More Pills	Any Her-oin
1. Not at all	55.3	54.8	57.4	53.5	85.4	39.5	60.2	47.3	72.6	64.8	42.6	-	-	89.9	47.8	21.5
2. A few of the times	18.5	16.0	21.0	21.0	-	29.1	16.8	18.6	9.2	13.1	29.6	-	-	7.1	23.0	16.9
3. Some of the times	7.4	10.0	5.7	8.7	-	8.8	5.5	6.0	8.9	7.7	8.1	-	-	-	10.2	4.7
4. Most of the times	10.2	12.2	6.4	8.3	-	18.5	2.1	22.2	-	8.5	8.9	-	-	-	12.7	18.6
5. Every time	8.7	6.9	9.5	8.6	14.6	4.0	15.3	6.0	9.3	5.9	10.8	-	-	3.0	6.3	38.2
Item 5130 Subject A01h N★	130	57	67	111	5	35	33	27	35	79	38	-	-	25	89	10

B096B: With marijuana

	TOTAL	M	F	White	Black	NE	NC	S	W	Yes	No	None	Mari-juana Only	Few Pills	More Pills	Any Her-oin
1. Not at all	55.2	48.4	63.0	54.6	60.2	63.7	41.2	36.7	74.7	62.1	48.5	-	-	78.2	52.0	11.4
2. A few of the times	16.6	19.3	12.7	17.8	-	15.3	23.7	15.7	11.8	9.7	27.0	-	-	7.1	18.4	33.6
3. Some of the times	7.8	5.0	10.9	9.1	-	11.5	3.6	8.5	7.5	7.8	7.3	-	-	-	10.2	10.5
4. Most of the times	4.1	7.8	-	4.8	-	7.7	6.7	2.0	-	3.3	3.8	-	-	-	5.2	7.4
5. Every time	16.3	19.5	13.4	13.7	39.8	1.7	24.8	37.0	6.0	17.1	13.5	-	-	14.7	14.2	37.1
Item 5140 Subject A01h N★	127	57	64	108	5	32	33	27	35	79	35	-	-	25	86	10

B096C: With LSD

	TOTAL	M	F	White	Black	NE	NC	S	W	Yes	No	None	Mari-juana Only	Few Pills	More Pills	Any Her-oin
1. Not at all	96.3	95.8	99.1	96.6	100.0	97.7	92.7	98.0	97.3	97.0	98.4	-	-	100.0	98.5	79.6
2. A few of the times	2.5	4.2	-	2.9	-	2.3	7.3	-	-	3.0	-	-	-	-	1.5	15.7
3. Some of the times	-	-	-	-	-	-	-	-	-	-	-	-	-	-	-	-
4. Most of the times	-	-	-	-	-	-	-	-	-	-	-	-	-	-	-	-
5. Every time	1.2	-	0.9	0.5	-	-	-	2.0	2.7	-	1.6	-	-	-	-	4.7
Item 5150 Subject A01h N★	128	57	64	109	5	33	33	27	35	79	35	-	-	25	86	12

B096D: With psychedelics other than LSD

	TOTAL	M	F	White	Black	NE	NC	S	W	Yes	No	None	Mari-juana Only	Few Pills	More Pills	Any Her-oin
1. Not at all	97.9	97.7	99.1	97.6	100.0	97.7	96.0	98.0	100.0	98.3	98.4	-	-	100.0	98.5	88.9
2. A few of the times	2.1	2.3	0.9	2.4	-	2.3	4.0	2.0	-	1.7	1.6	-	-	-	1.5	11.1
3. Some of the times	-	-	-	-	-	-	-	-	-	-	-	-	-	-	-	-
4. Most of the times	-	-	-	-	-	-	-	-	-	-	-	-	-	-	-	-
5. Every time	-	-	-	-	-	-	-	-	-	-	-	-	-	-	-	-
Item 5160 Subject A01h N★	127	57	64	109	5	33	33	27	34	79	35	-	-	25	86	12

B096E: With amphetamines

	TOTAL	M	F	White	Black	NE	NC	S	W	Yes	No	None	Mari-juana Only	Few Pills	More Pills	Any Her-oin
1. Not at all	92.4	92.6	94.3	91.1	100.0	81.4	92.9	100.0	95.9	94.3	93.1	-	-	100.0	92.7	71.1
2. A few of the times	4.5	5.6	1.0	5.3	-	11.9	4.0	-	1.7	4.3	-	-	-	-	3.9	20.1
3. Some of the times	2.8	0.9	4.7	3.2	-	5.2	3.1	-	2.4	1.4	5.5	-	-	-	2.9	8.8
4. Most of the times	0.4	0.8	-	0.4	-	1.5	-	-	-	-	1.4	-	-	-	0.6	-
5. Every time	-	-	-	-	-	-	-	-	-	-	-	-	-	-	-	-
Item 5170 Subject A01h N★	125	58	62	107	5	31	33	27	34	79	33	-	-	25	84	12

B096F: With quaaludes

	TOTAL	M	F	White	Black	NE	NC	S	W	Yes	No	None	Mari-juana Only	Few Pills	More Pills	Any Her-oin
1. Not at all	98.2	99.2	100.0	97.9	100.0	92.9	100.0	100.0	100.0	100.0	98.7	-	-	100.0	99.4	84.9
2. A few of the times	1.4	-	-	1.7	-	5.6	-	-	-	-	-	-	-	-	-	15.1
3. Some of the times	-	-	-	-	-	-	-	-	-	-	-	-	-	-	-	-
4. Most of the times	0.4	0.8	-	0.4	-	1.5	-	-	-	-	1.3	-	-	-	0.6	-
5. Every time	-	-	-	-	-	-	-	-	-	-	-	-	-	-	-	-
Item 5180 Subject A01h N★	126	57	63	108	5	32	33	27	34	78	35	-	-	25	85	12

★=excludes respondents for whom question was inappropriate.

	TOTAL	SEX		RACE		REGION				4YR COLLEGE PLANS		ILLICIT DRUG USE: LIFETIME				
QUESTIONNAIRE FORM 1 1985		M	F	White	Black	NE	NC	S	W	Yes	No	None	Marijuana Only	Few Pills	More Pills	Any Heroin
N (Weighted No. of Cases):	3316	1505	1663	2415	400	783	902	1004	627	1822	1121	1307	719	444	716	29
% of Weighted Total:	100.0	45.4	50.2	72.8	12.1	23.6	27.2	30.3	18.9	55.0	33.8	39.4	21.7	13.4	21.6	0.9
B096G: With barbiturates																
1. Not at all	95.3	96.6	95.9	95.1	100.0	88.1	100.0	97.4	95.6	96.8	94.5	-	-	100.0	93.9	92.9
2. A few of the times	2.9	2.6	2.4	2.8	-	4.6	-	2.6	4.4	1.9	4.2	-	-	-	4.3	-
3. Some of the times	0.9	-	1.7	1.0	-	3.4	-	-	-	1.4	-	-	-	-	1.3	-
4. Most of the times	1.0	0.8	-	1.1	-	3.9	-	-	-	-	1.3	-	-	-	0.5	7.1
5. Every time	-	-	-	-	-	-	-	-	-	-	-	-	-	-	-	-
Item 5190 Subject A01h N★	126	57	64	108	5	32	33	27	34	79	35	-	-	25	86	11
B096H: With tranquilizers																
1. Not at all	90.4	94.6	88.8	88.9	100.0	73.0	100.0	94.0	96.5	95.3	81.6	-	-	100.0	87.9	84.9
2. A few of the times	4.7	4.6	2.4	5.4	-	9.1	-	6.0	3.5	3.3	4.3	-	-	-	4.8	15.1
3. Some of the times	1.5	-	2.9	1.7	-	5.5	-	-	-	-	5.2	-	-	-	2.2	-
4. Most of the times	3.4	0.8	5.9	4.0	-	12.4	-	-	-	1.4	8.9	-	-	-	5.0	-
5. Every time	-	-	-	-	-	-	-	-	-	-	-	-	-	-	-	-
Item 5200 Subject A01h N★	129	57	67	112	5	36	33	27	33	79	37	-	-	25	88	12
B096I: With cocaine																
1. Not at all	93.2	93.3	98.5	94.0	100.0	86.7	92.7	96.5	97.3	96.5	97.1	-	-	100.0	96.3	61.2
2. A few of the times	3.4	3.1	0.6	2.9	-	7.9	4.0	1.4	-	2.2	-	-	-	-	2.5	18.4
3. Some of the times	0.4	0.9	-	0.5	-	1.6	-	-	-	-	-	-	-	-	0.6	-
4. Most of the times	1.0	0.8	-	1.1	-	3.7	-	-	-	-	1.3	-	-	-	0.5	6.5
5. Every time	2.0	1.9	0.9	1.5	-	-	3.3	2.0	2.7	1.4	1.6	-	-	-	-	13.9
Item 5210 Subject A01h N★	128	58	64	109	5	33	33	27	35	79	35	-	-	25	86	12
B096J: With heroin																
1. Not at all	98.4	100.0	98.3	98.1	100.0	96.7	96.9	100.0	100.0	100.0	97.0	-	-	100.0	100.0	81.4
2. A few of the times	0.8	-	1.7	1.0	-	-	3.1	-	-	-	3.0	-	-	-	-	9.4
3. Some of the times	-	-	-	-	-	-	-	-	-	-	-	-	-	-	-	-
4. Most of the times	-	-	-	-	-	-	-	-	-	-	-	-	-	-	-	-
5. Every time	0.8	-	-	1.0	-	3.3	-	-	-	-	-	-	-	-	-	9.2
Item 5220 Subject A01h N★	125	57	63	107	5	31	33	27	34	79	34	-	-	25	85	11
B097: What have been the most important reasons for your using narcotics other than heroin without a doctor's orders? (Mark all that apply.)																
A. To experiment–to see what it's like	46.8	52.0	42.3	46.2	74.2	38.9	69.9	50.8	27.1	45.5	43.5	-	-	33.9	48.3	59.8
B. To relax or relieve tension	38.4	42.7	35.1	39.6	-	45.1	31.3	27.7	46.8	38.6	45.0	-	-	17.5	46.0	16.6
C. To feel good or get high	44.6	55.7	35.7	42.7	74.2	44.1	51.3	62.3	25.2	43.5	47.6	-	-	27.6	48.0	50.7
D. To seek deeper insights and understanding	3.3	4.1	2.7	3.2	-	-	1.7	4.7	7.1	3.7	3.3	-	-	-	2.6	11.0
E. To have a good time with my friends	22.4	24.5	20.3	21.6	27.3	18.0	27.6	35.9	11.4	23.7	18.5	-	-	8.5	23.5	39.5
F. To fit in with a group I like	3.8	5.5	2.5	3.8	-	-	4.7	8.1	3.6	4.7	3.0	-	-	-	3.5	10.1
G. To get away from my problems or troubles	17.1	14.5	18.8	18.9	-	31.1	11.1	14.4	11.5	16.5	20.1	-	-	-	20.2	24.4
H. Because of boredom, nothing else to do	17.0	25.4	9.4	16.2	-	26.1	19.3	5.7	13.8	18.7	9.3	-	-	-	19.0	33.8
I. Because of anger or frustration	11.4	7.3	15.4	11.8	-	21.9	9.2	11.0	3.6	10.2	17.7	-	-	-	13.9	11.2
J. To get through the day	5.6	6.0	4.2	5.2	-	5.7	11.3	4.6	-	6.5	-	-	-	-	6.2	7.4
K. To increase the effects of some other drug(s)	14.9	16.0	13.4	13.0	27.3	19.6	13.6	26.2	3.5	14.4	14.2	-	-	3.3	16.4	23.2
L. To decrease (offset) the effects of some other drug(s)	3.4	5.2	2.0	2.5	-	6.0	3.8	-	2.9	3.6	4.1	-	-	-	4.1	-
M. To get to sleep	33.9	25.5	41.4	33.9	-	42.2	21.0	38.5	36.1	36.1	36.9	-	-	34.5	35.1	18.7
N. As a substitute for heroin	1.4	-	2.7	1.1	-	-	1.7	2.4	1.8	1.5	1.6	-	-	-	-	11.1
O. To relieve physical pain	45.8	47.3	45.3	46.8	25.8	46.3	35.5	27.6	69.4	53.3	38.6	-	-	53.9	46.6	17.2
P. To control coughing	19.5	12.1	26.7	21.7	-	34.3	16.6	16.5	10.0	19.9	19.5	-	-	13.8	21.2	13.4
Q. Because I am "hooked"–I have to have it	-	-	-	-	-	-	-	-	-	-	-	-	-	-	-	-
Item 5230-5370 Subject A06a N★	122	55	65	107	3	32	34	23	32	77	35	-	-	23	88	10

★=excludes respondents for whom question was inappropriate.

QUESTIONNAIRE FORM 1 1985	TOTAL	SEX		RACE		REGION				4YR COLLEGE PLANS		ILLICIT DRUG USE: LIFETIME				
		M	F	White	Black	NE	NC	S	W	Yes	No	None	Mari-juana Only	Few Pills	More Pills	Any Her-oin
N (Weighted No. of Cases):	3316	1505	1663	2415	400	783	902	1004	627	1822	1121	1307	719	444	716	29
% of Weighted Total:	100.0	45.4	50.2	72.8	12.1	23.6	27.2	30.3	18.9	55.0	33.8	39.4	21.7	13.4	21.6	0.9

B098: When you take narcotics other than heroin how high do you usually get?

1. Not at all high	12.1	17.9	7.7	11.1	25.8	7.1	14.8	8.8	16.5	12.4	7.7	-	-	10.1	14.1	-
2. A little high	28.5	28.0	30.5	29.0	-	44.0	26.0	20.3	21.0	27.4	33.4	-	-	22.8	32.9	5.4
3. Moderately high	27.7	26.7	26.1	29.9	-	26.9	30.5	33.3	21.9	22.3	35.5	-	-	4.8	28.6	72.7
4. Very high	10.4	14.0	6.3	6.4	74.2	3.0	15.9	28.5	-	11.5	6.9	-	-	8.3	10.5	14.7
5. I don't take them to get high	21.3	13.4	29.4	23.5	-	19.0	12.9	9.1	40.6	26.5	16.6	-	-	54.0	13.9	7.2
Item 5380 Subject A01e N★	126	57	65	110	3	34	34	23	34	79	35	-	-	25	90	11

B099: When you take narcotics other than heroin how long do you usually stay high?

1. Usually don't get high	25.1	23.8	26.5	27.2	25.8	22.7	19.6	13.7	41.3	30.8	9.8	-	-	57.0	18.1	6.9
2. One to two hours	30.9	32.7	31.4	31.5	47.0	34.8	40.2	12.1	31.1	25.9	45.8	-	-	23.5	35.1	15.2
3. Three to six hours	29.9	31.3	26.8	29.3	-	25.0	32.7	49.6	17.9	30.1	25.9	-	-	16.3	29.0	68.5
4. Seven to 24 hours	13.3	12.2	15.3	12.0	27.3	17.5	7.4	20.3	9.8	13.2	18.5	-	-	3.2	17.8	-
5. More than 24 hours	0.8	-	-	-	-	-	-	4.3	-	-	-	-	-	-	-	9.3
Item 5390 Subject A01f N★	128	59	64	112	3	35	34	25	34	79	36	-	-	24	92	11

B100: What narcotics other than heroin have you taken during the last year without a doctor's orders? (Mark all that apply.)

A. Methadone	13.4	10.1	12.9	13.7	-	9.4	13.9	18.9	13.4	11.1	17.5	-	-	-	13.2	38.6
B. Opium	34.7	33.7	32.4	35.2	74.2	21.4	45.0	59.1	21.6	26.6	45.7	-	-	24.7	31.4	75.0
C. Morphine	21.7	26.0	16.1	17.0	-	12.2	17.6	35.1	26.8	23.0	14.2	-	-	23.5	23.5	47.4
D. Codeine	83.8	88.4	78.6	84.3	25.8	78.7	81.3	76.1	97.5	87.4	78.2	-	-	73.5	84.2	100.0
E. Demerol	22.5	23.9	21.3	23.1	-	22.5	17.3	42.2	14.2	18.7	26.8	-	-	1.8	28.6	17.0
F. Paregoric	3.4	-	4.0	3.3	-	5.5	-	7.3	2.1	-	9.3	-	-	-	3.6	8.2
G. Talwin	3.5	-	5.2	4.0	-	2.9	-	14.6	-	-	6.3	-	-	-	3.1	12.7
H. Laudanum	3.3	2.4	2.6	3.7	-	2.9	4.0	7.3	-	1.8	4.7	-	-	-	3.4	8.2
I. Other	15.6	14.7	14.7	14.5	-	22.9	4.7	25.5	11.9	11.7	25.6	-	-	-	17.9	26.8
J. Don't know the names of some I have used	14.9	17.0	12.5	14.3	-	19.3	7.6	32.6	5.2	14.8	11.5	-	-	6.7	14.7	30.6
Item 5400-5490 Subject A01l N★	121	55	62	106	3	35	33	22	32	74	34	-	-	22	87	12

B101: Have you ever tried to stop using narcotics other than heroin and found that you couldn't stop?

1. Yes	0.8	-	1.6	1.0	-	3.1	-	-	-	1.4	-	-	-	-	1.2	-
2. No	99.2	100.0	98.4	99.0	100.0	96.9	100.0	100.0	100.0	98.6	100.0	-	-	100.0	98.8	100.0
Item 5500 Subject A01i N★	129	59	66	114	3	35	35	25	34	80	37	-	-	25	92	11

B102: What methods have you used for taking any of these narcotics other than heroin? (Mark all that apply.)

A. Sniffing or "snorting"	16.4	22.0	7.6	14.1	-	15.7	17.1	31.9	5.1	14.0	13.3	-	-	-	13.6	73.8
B. Smoking	30.4	29.7	30.0	28.4	74.2	24.0	39.1	47.7	15.5	25.6	35.5	-	-	22.5	29.1	57.6
C. Injection	3.4	3.5	-	1.9	-	3.4	-	8.1	3.3	-	5.8	-	-	-	1.8	23.0
D. By mouth	83.0	89.9	79.2	85.3	25.8	71.5	82.6	76.0	100.0	85.4	84.4	-	-	77.5	84.7	80.5
E. Other	1.3	-	2.6	1.5	-	-	-	2.2	3.4	1.5	1.5	-	-	-	-	15.0
Item 5510-5550 Subject A05d N★	127	59	65	112	3	34	34	25	34	79	36	-	-	24	92	11

B103: Do you think you will be using any narcotics other than heroin without a doctor's orders five years from now?

1. I definitely will	0.7	0.7	0.5	0.4	0.2	1.2	0.2	0.8	0.6	0.4	0.9	0.4	0.1	0.3	1.7	7.9
2. I probably will	2.3	2.9	1.6	2.3	0.9	2.1	1.7	2.0	3.7	2.0	2.1	0.2	0.9	0.6	8.1	15.7
3. I probably will not	14.6	13.5	15.4	15.7	8.6	17.4	15.2	11.4	15.2	13.5	15.8	5.1	11.0	25.1	29.3	42.4
4. I definitely will not	82.5	82.9	82.5	81.6	90.2	79.3	82.9	85.9	80.4	84.2	81.2	94.2	88.0	74.0	61.0	34.0
Item 5560 Subject A04a N	3154	1464	1627	2373	377	718	870	961	604	1797	1087	1286	689	428	659	27

B104: When (if ever) did you FIRST do each of the following things? Don't count anything you took because a doctor told you to.

★=excludes respondents for whom question was inappropriate.

	TOTAL	SEX		RACE		REGION				4YR COLLEGE PLANS		ILLICIT DRUG USE: LIFETIME				
QUESTIONNAIRE FORM 1 1985		M	F	White	Black	NE	NC	S	W	Yes	No	None	Mari- juana Only	Few Pills	More Pills	Any Her- oin
N (Weighted No. of Cases):	3316	1505	1663	2415	400	783	902	1004	627	1822	1121	1307	719	444	716	29
% of Weighted Total:	100.0	45.4	50.2	72.8	12.1	23.6	27.2	30.3	18.9	55.0	33.8	39.4	21.7	13.4	21.6	0.9
B104A: Smoke cigarettes on a daily basis																
8. Never	63.8	67.7	60.7	62.3	77.6	59.6	61.9	68.0	65.3	72.7	52.4	85.3	60.6	57.7	32.7	9.6
1. Grade 6 or below	6.2	7.4	5.0	6.5	4.0	6.1	7.1	5.6	5.7	5.6	6.3	3.8	6.9	5.1	9.2	29.8
2. Grade 7 or 8	7.9	6.9	9.1	8.0	5.0	9.5	8.5	6.0	8.2	5.3	11.9	3.2	8.1	9.7	15.4	13.8
3. Grade 9 (Freshman)	6.4	5.7	6.8	6.8	3.3	8.2	6.9	5.7	4.3	3.9	10.0	1.8	8.0	7.4	12.3	17.5
4. Grade 10 (Sophomore)	6.4	4.4	8.1	6.4	4.9	7.4	5.6	7.0	5.6	4.6	8.9	2.4	5.5	8.0	13.3	19.8
5. Grade 11 (Junior)	5.4	5.3	5.5	5.7	3.7	6.2	5.3	4.2	6.6	4.1	7.4	1.8	5.8	6.0	11.5	6.5
6. Grade 12 (Senior)	3.9	2.6	4.8	4.3	1.5	3.0	4.7	3.4	4.3	3.7	3.2	1.6	4.9	6.1	5.5	3.1
Item 5570 Subject A01g N	3000	1394	1560	2289	342	690	837	896	578	1711	1036	1210	639	417	651	26
B104B: Try an alcoholic beverage–more than just a few sips																
8. Never	7.4	7.6	6.8	5.6	17.9	4.6	5.3	11.4	7.5	7.9	7.0	17.6	0.3	1.0	0.4	-
1. Grade 6 or below	8.9	11.5	6.5	9.0	7.1	9.8	10.7	7.8	6.8	7.4	10.3	6.0	8.2	5.9	15.2	29.8
2. Grade 7 or 8	24.0	26.2	22.1	26.4	9.9	28.1	21.3	21.1	27.3	24.3	23.7	13.7	25.6	30.3	35.8	37.4
3. Grade 9 (Freshman)	22.2	20.5	24.0	24.0	12.7	26.3	22.7	18.2	22.3	22.3	21.4	16.7	24.0	26.1	27.0	12.5
4. Grade 10 (Sophomore)	19.0	17.1	20.7	18.7	20.0	16.3	18.7	19.3	22.4	19.2	18.4	17.2	23.6	21.1	16.6	9.9
5. Grade 11 (Junior)	11.6	10.5	12.5	10.4	19.3	10.2	13.4	13.0	8.2	12.0	11.6	16.7	12.1	9.8	4.1	10.4
6. Grade 12 (Senior)	7.0	6.6	7.2	5.8	13.0	4.7	7.8	9.1	5.5	6.8	7.6	12.1	6.2	5.7	1.0	-
Item 5580 Subject A01g N	2866	1349	1471	2208	310	664	802	842	558	1621	1005	1062	657	403	667	26
B104C: Try marijuana or hashish																
8. Never	46.6	43.7	49.0	44.6	52.7	41.6	47.8	55.2	37.5	51.5	41.8	100.0	-	21.0	8.1	-
1. Grade 6 or below	3.4	5.3	1.6	3.4	1.5	3.8	3.5	2.9	3.4	3.0	3.2	-	4.8	2.9	7.7	24.9
2. Grade 7 or 8	11.6	13.1	10.2	12.5	6.4	15.1	10.6	7.3	15.4	9.7	13.9	-	16.2	13.2	27.8	27.3
3. Grade 9 (Freshman)	12.2	11.9	12.5	12.6	10.5	14.9	10.5	9.4	15.9	10.8	13.9	-	19.7	18.9	23.9	24.2
4. Grade 10 (Sophomore)	12.3	12.2	12.5	12.7	12.5	14.2	11.9	10.4	13.6	10.8	13.4	-	23.7	19.8	20.0	23.7
5. Grade 11 (Junior)	8.9	9.1	8.8	9.6	8.2	7.1	10.7	8.6	9.0	8.5	9.7	-	20.0	16.6	9.9	-
6. Grade 12 (Senior)	5.0	4.7	5.3	4.7	8.2	3.2	5.0	6.3	5.3	5.7	4.0	-	15.7	7.5	2.5	-
Item 5590 Subject A01g N	3016	1400	1569	2305	346	686	838	901	591	1730	1037	1232	637	416	658	26
B104D: Try LSD																
8. Never	93.1	91.3	94.8	92.2	99.0	92.0	92.4	95.3	92.2	95.1	90.7	100.0	100.0	94.9	74.5	18.7
1. Grade 6 or below	0.1	0.2	*	*	0.5	-	0.3	0.1	-	0.1	0.1	-	-	0.3	0.1	9.6
2. Grade 7 or 8	0.6	0.5	0.7	0.7	-	0.7	0.8	0.1	0.9	0.3	1.0	-	-	0.7	1.6	15.2
3. Grade 9 (Freshman)	1.6	2.0	1.1	1.8	-	1.9	2.3	1.0	1.0	1.0	2.3	-	-	0.4	5.9	27.2
4. Grade 10 (Sophomore)	1.9	2.1	1.7	2.2	-	2.2	1.6	1.9	2.0	1.5	2.5	-	-	1.5	7.1	22.6
5. Grade 11 (Junior)	1.6	2.6	0.8	2.1	-	2.2	1.4	0.8	2.6	1.0	2.6	-	-	0.8	7.0	6.6
6. Grade 12 (Senior)	1.0	1.3	0.8	1.1	0.5	1.0	1.1	0.8	1.4	1.0	0.7	-	-	1.5	3.9	-
Item 5600 Subject A01g N	3072	1414	1613	2326	365	697	849	931	595	1762	1056	1247	673	420	651	26
B104E: Try any psychedelic other than LSD																
8. Never	94.8	93.5	95.9	93.9	99.0	91.2	95.0	96.6	95.9	95.5	93.8	100.0	100.0	96.0	79.9	19.3
1. Grade 6 or below	0.1	0.2	-	*	0.5	0.1	0.2	*	-	0.1	0.1	-	-	0.2	0.2	9.2
2. Grade 7 or 8	0.4	0.3	0.5	0.5	-	0.8	0.3	0.6	-	0.4	0.6	-	-	0.2	1.8	6.2
3. Grade 9 (Freshman)	1.5	1.6	1.3	1.6	-	2.9	1.3	0.8	1.0	1.1	1.8	-	-	1.5	5.1	29.1
4. Grade 10 (Sophomore)	1.6	1.9	1.3	1.9	0.1	2.6	1.1	1.2	1.5	1.2	2.1	-	-	0.7	6.3	25.2
5. Grade 11 (Junior)	1.0	1.4	0.6	1.2	0.2	1.6	1.3	0.1	1.2	0.9	1.0	-	-	1.1	4.0	6.7
6. Grade 12 (Senior)	0.7	0.9	0.4	0.8	0.2	0.8	0.8	0.6	0.3	0.7	0.5	-	-	0.5	2.8	4.4
Item 5610 Subject A01g N	3025	1388	1595	2286	368	685	832	927	581	1741	1035	1249	679	415	601	25
B104F: Try amphetamines																
8. Never	83.3	84.1	82.3	80.5	96.2	83.1	82.6	86.2	79.9	86.0	78.5	100.0	100.0	73.7	32.0	7.9
1. Grade 6 or below	0.5	0.6	0.3	0.5	0.5	0.3	0.7	0.6	-	0.5	0.5	-	-	0.4	1.5	14.3
2. Grade 7 or 8	2.3	2.0	2.7	2.7	0.3	2.7	1.8	2.2	2.7	1.8	3.0	-	-	1.0	11.3	6.0
3. Grade 9 (Freshman)	4.4	3.4	5.3	5.4	0.6	5.1	5.6	2.6	4.6	3.4	5.9	-	-	5.6	18.5	31.3
4. Grade 10 (Sophomore)	4.7	4.7	4.9	5.3	0.7	5.4	4.8	3.1	6.3	3.9	6.4	-	-	6.9	19.3	31.5
5. Grade 11 (Junior)	3.2	3.3	3.3	3.7	0.7	2.4	3.4	2.5	5.0	2.7	4.1	-	-	6.5	12.9	-
6. Grade 12 (Senior)	1.6	2.0	1.3	1.8	1.1	1.1	1.0	2.7	1.4	1.7	1.6	-	-	5.9	4.5	9.0
Item 5620 Subject A01g N	2854	1325	1484	2134	357	650	786	871	546	1653	976	1244	661	331	538	24

*=less than .05 per cent.

QUESTIONNAIRE FORM 1 1985	TOTAL	SEX		RACE		REGION				4YR COLLEGE PLANS		ILLICIT DRUG USE: LIFETIME				
		M	F	White	Black	NE	NC	S	W	Yes	No	None	Marijuana Only	Few Pills	More Pills	Any Heroin
N (Weighted No. of Cases):	3316	1505	1663	2415	400	783	902	1004	627	1822	1121	1307	719	444	716	29
% of Weighted Total:	100.0	45.4	50.2	72.8	12.1	23.6	27.2	30.3	18.9	55.0	33.8	39.4	21.7	13.4	21.6	0.9

B104G: Try quaaludes

	TOTAL	M	F	White	Black	NE	NC	S	W	Yes	No	None	Marijuana Only	Few Pills	More Pills	Any Heroin
8. Never	94.6	93.6	95.4	93.7	98.2	94.4	94.9	93.0	96.8	95.6	92.8	100.0	100.0	93.6	80.8	30.5
1. Grade 6 or below	0.3	0.4	0.1	0.2	0.5	0.1	0.6	0.1	0.2	0.3	0.2	-	-	0.2	0.6	12.8
2. Grade 7 or 8	0.7	0.6	0.9	0.9	-	0.8	0.4	1.3	0.2	0.5	1.1	-	-	0.5	3.0	5.6
3. Grade 9 (Freshman)	1.6	2.1	1.1	1.9	0.2	0.9	1.6	2.5	1.2	1.4	1.8	-	-	2.0	5.4	28.3
4. Grade 10 (Sophomore)	1.7	1.8	1.7	2.0	0.6	2.2	1.7	1.8	0.9	1.4	2.4	-	-	1.4	6.7	12.0
5. Grade 11 (Junior)	1.0	1.2	0.7	1.1	0.5	1.6	0.6	0.9	0.7	0.6	1.5	-	-	1.8	3.2	6.2
6. Grade 12 (Senior)	0.2	0.3	*	0.2	-	-	0.1	0.3	0.1	0.2	0.2	-	-	0.4	0.3	4.6
Item 5630 Subject A01g N	3065	1426	1596	2320	371	697	849	923	596	1755	1051	1249	680	416	641	24

B104H: Try barbiturates

	TOTAL	M	F	White	Black	NE	NC	S	W	Yes	No	None	Marijuana Only	Few Pills	More Pills	Any Heroin
8. Never	94.7	93.7	95.5	93.9	98.8	95.3	94.8	93.7	95.2	95.7	92.8	100.0	100.0	98.0	76.9	37.2
1. Grade 6 or below	0.3	0.3	0.2	0.2	0.7	0.1	0.4	0.4	-	0.3	0.2	-	-	-	0.6	15.4
2. Grade 7 or 8	0.9	0.7	1.1	1.1	-	1.1	0.2	1.4	1.1	0.5	1.6	-	-	0.5	4.1	6.4
3. Grade 9 (Freshman)	1.2	1.2	1.1	1.2	0.3	0.7	1.6	1.4	0.8	0.8	1.6	-	-	0.3	4.8	23.5
4. Grade 10 (Sophomore)	1.8	2.5	1.1	2.0	0.3	1.9	1.3	2.1	1.7	1.6	2.2	-	-	0.4	8.2	10.2
5. Grade 11 (Junior)	0.8	1.1	0.6	1.0	-	0.7	1.2	0.4	1.0	0.6	1.2	-	-	-	3.8	7.3
6. Grade 12 (Senior)	0.4	0.5	0.4	0.5	-	0.2	0.4	0.7	0.2	0.4	0.3	-	-	0.8	1.6	-
Item 5640 Subject A01g N	3011	1399	1570	2279	367	684	831	917	579	1725	1034	1249	680	404	600	22

B104I: Try tranquilizers

	TOTAL	M	F	White	Black	NE	NC	S	W	Yes	No	None	Marijuana Only	Few Pills	More Pills	Any Heroin
8. Never	93.2	93.5	93.0	92.4	98.0	91.0	94.4	93.5	93.8	93.9	92.2	100.0	100.0	89.5	75.1	28.2
1. Grade 6 or below	0.3	0.3	0.2	0.3	0.5	0.3	0.4	0.2	0.3	0.4	0.2	-	-	0.9	17.4	
2. Grade 7 or 8	0.7	0.5	0.9	0.9	-	-	0.8	0.8	1.3	0.7	0.6	-	-	1.7	2.2	10.8
3. Grade 9 (Freshman)	1.7	1.4	1.8	1.9	-	3.1	1.0	1.2	1.7	1.8	1.5	-	-	1.8	6.4	23.2
4. Grade 10 (Sophomore)	1.6	1.8	1.5	1.8	0.8	2.1	1.4	1.9	0.9	0.9	2.7	-	-	1.7	6.7	13.1
5. Grade 11 (Junior)	1.6	1.8	1.5	1.9	0.2	2.1	1.4	1.6	1.4	1.5	2.1	-	-	2.3	6.5	7.3
6. Grade 12 (Senior)	0.8	0.7	1.0	0.8	0.5	1.4	0.5	0.8	0.6	0.8	0.8	-	-	3.1	2.2	-
Item 5650 Subject A01g N	2973	1386	1546	2249	367	683	825	897	568	1694	1034	1246	678	384	589	20

B104J: Try cocaine

	TOTAL	M	F	White	Black	NE	NC	S	W	Yes	No	None	Marijuana Only	Few Pills	More Pills	Any Heroin
8. Never	83.5	79.9	86.7	82.4	92.4	77.4	88.0	89.2	75.3	86.4	81.2	100.0	100.0	72.5	43.7	9.8
1. Grade 6 or below	0.2	0.3	0.1	0.2	0.8	0.1	0.4	0.2	0.2	0.2	0.4	-	-	0.5	0.2	12.0
2. Grade 7 or 8	0.8	0.8	0.7	0.9	0.1	1.2	0.5	0.5	0.9	0.2	1.4	-	-	-	3.6	-
3. Grade 9 (Freshman)	1.9	2.6	1.2	1.9	0.9	2.4	1.5	1.3	2.6	1.2	2.6	-	-	1.6	6.8	23.6
4. Grade 10 (Sophomore)	3.8	4.6	3.2	4.0	1.1	6.2	1.7	2.1	7.0	3.0	4.6	-	-	5.4	13.2	34.2
5. Grade 11 (Junior)	5.7	6.7	4.9	6.0	2.1	7.5	4.7	3.3	8.7	4.8	6.5	-	-	7.7	21.3	13.9
6. Grade 12 (Senior)	4.1	5.1	3.2	4.6	2.6	5.2	3.2	3.4	5.3	4.1	3.3	-	-	12.3	11.2	6.5
Item 5660 Subject A01g N	3086	1426	1617	2338	371	701	856	934	594	1764	1065	1249	680	421	654	26

B104K: Try heroin

	TOTAL	M	F	White	Black	NE	NC	S	W	Yes	No	None	Marijuana Only	Few Pills	More Pills	Any Heroin
8. Never	99.3	99.3	99.3	99.4	99.5	99.4	99.3	99.5	99.0	99.6	98.9	100.0	100.0	100.0	100.0	-
1. Grade 6 or below	0.1	0.1	0.1	*	0.5	-	0.2	0.1	-	0.2	-	-	-	-	-	14.0
2. Grade 7 or 8	0.1	0.1	0.1	0.1	-	0.2	-	0.1	-	-	0.2	-	-	-	-	12.7
3. Grade 9 (Freshman)	0.2	0.1	0.3	0.2	-	-	0.4	*	0.4	0.1	0.4	-	-	-	-	27.4
4. Grade 10 (Sophomore)	0.1	0.1	0.2	0.1	-	-	-	0.1	0.6	0.1	0.2	-	-	-	-	19.5
5. Grade 11 (Junior)	0.1	*	0.1	0.1	-	-	0.1	0.1	0.1	0.1	0.1	-	-	-	-	11.9
6. Grade 12 (Senior)	0.1	0.2	-	0.1	-	0.4	-	*	-	-	0.1	-	-	-	-	14.5
Item 5670 Subject A01g N	3080	1424	1613	2336	371	703	852	932	593	1764	1063	1245	680	426	652	22

B104L: Try any narcotic other than heroin

	TOTAL	M	F	White	Black	NE	NC	S	W	Yes	No	None	Marijuana Only	Few Pills	More Pills	Any Heroin
8. Never	93.1	93.5	92.7	92.2	97.0	92.7	93.3	94.8	90.6	92.9	93.2	100.0	100.0	86.2	77.2	12.6
1. Grade 6 or below	0.2	0.3	0.2	0.3	-	0.1	0.4	0.1	0.5	0.3	0.2	-	-	0.8	0.7	-
2. Grade 7 or 8	0.8	0.9	0.6	0.8	1.3	0.9	0.7	0.7	0.8	1.0	0.5	-	-	1.1	2.3	25.5
3. Grade 9 (Freshman)	1.3	0.9	1.6	1.4	0.5	1.0	1.4	0.9	2.1	1.0	1.5	-	-	1.4	5.0	19.5
4. Grade 10 (Sophomore)	1.8	1.9	1.8	2.1	0.2	2.2	1.3	1.4	2.7	1.6	2.2	-	-	2.8	6.7	18.8
5. Grade 11 (Junior)	1.3	1.8	1.0	1.4	0.5	1.5	1.6	1.0	1.3	1.6	1.1	-	-	2.8	4.7	6.0
6. Grade 12 (Senior)	1.4	0.8	2.0	1.7	0.6	1.6	1.4	1.0	1.9	1.7	1.2	-	-	4.9	3.5	17.6
Item 5680 Subject A01g N	2966	1369	1555	2237	363	677	821	913	555	1707	1021	1242	670	387	594	17

The next questions are about your experiences in school.

*=less than .05 per cent.

QUESTIONNAIRE FORM 1 1985	TOTAL	SEX		RACE		REGION				4YR COLLEGE PLANS		ILLICIT DRUG USE: LIFETIME				
		M	F	White	Black	NE	NC	S	W	Yes	No	None	Marijuana Only	Few Pills	More Pills	Any Heroin
N (Weighted No. of Cases):	3316	1505	1663	2415	400	783	902	1004	627	1822	1121	1307	719	444	716	29
% of Weighted Total:	100.0	45.4	50.2	72.8	12.1	23.6	27.2	30.3	18.9	55.0	33.8	39.4	21.7	13.4	21.6	0.9
D001: Some people like school very much. Others don't. How do you feel about going to school?																
5. I like school very much	12.7	12.6	12.6	11.3	17.2	10.9	12.4	13.9	13.4	15.9	7.9	16.6	10.8	8.4	9.6	12.0
4. I like school quite a lot	31.4	29.4	33.1	31.9	30.0	29.0	31.2	31.2	34.5	36.0	23.0	35.8	32.8	29.5	23.3	15.8
3. I like school some	42.3	43.2	41.5	42.6	42.9	43.1	41.9	43.0	40.8	38.5	48.5	37.3	45.0	46.5	45.4	41.1
2. I don't like school very much	9.6	9.4	9.7	9.8	7.4	11.3	10.6	8.3	8.2	6.7	14.5	7.3	8.3	12.6	13.4	18.4
1. I don't like school at all	4.1	5.3	3.1	4.4	2.6	5.7	4.0	3.6	3.0	2.8	6.1	2.9	3.1	3.0	8.2	12.6
Item 7630 Subject B01,Q08 N	2917	1333	1548	2235	335	628	816	897	576	1768	1053	1220	632	388	594	21
D002: How often do you feel that the school work you are assigned is meaningful and important?																
5. Almost always	12.2	11.2	13.1	9.9	26.3	10.2	13.7	14.6	8.7	13.1	10.8	15.7	11.2	10.7	6.5	6.8
4. Often	25.6	24.2	26.5	24.2	29.4	26.1	23.9	25.8	27.3	27.5	23.0	27.2	27.4	23.8	21.2	35.9
3. Sometimes	42.3	41.3	43.7	44.5	32.7	40.0	43.6	40.9	45.3	43.5	40.4	42.2	42.4	44.7	41.8	32.3
2. Seldom	16.9	19.1	14.9	18.5	8.9	19.7	16.0	16.1	16.4	14.6	20.3	12.5	17.3	18.2	25.9	7.3
1. Never	2.9	4.2	1.8	2.9	2.8	3.9	2.8	2.6	2.2	1.3	5.4	2.4	1.8	2.6	4.6	17.6
Item 5700 Subject B01 N	2907	1329	1540	2228	333	623	816	893	575	1764	1048	1218	630	386	591	21
D003: How interesting are most of your courses to you?																
5. Very exciting and stimulating	4.4	3.6	4.9	3.5	10.4	3.3	3.7	7.0	2.3	4.5	4.1	6.0	3.3	3.6	2.7	5.5
4. Quite interesting	29.0	27.6	30.2	27.0	37.4	27.5	29.5	27.3	32.5	32.0	23.9	34.4	26.4	23.7	23.3	14.9
3. Fairly interesting	45.8	44.2	47.5	47.6	38.2	45.7	44.5	47.0	46.0	45.4	46.7	43.5	48.8	48.6	46.9	46.0
2. Slightly dull	16.3	17.8	14.9	16.9	11.3	18.2	17.5	14.2	15.5	15.3	18.0	11.9	17.5	20.3	21.2	18.9
1. Very dull	4.5	6.9	2.5	5.0	2.7	5.3	4.7	4.4	3.6	2.7	7.2	4.2	4.0	3.8	6.0	14.7
Item 5710 Subject B01 N	2899	1325	1537	2224	330	619	816	890	573	1763	1042	1217	628	383	588	21
D004: How important do you think the things you are learning in school are going to be for your later life?																
5. Very important	20.9	20.2	21.4	17.7	40.1	15.1	23.1	25.4	16.9	22.4	18.3	25.2	19.4	17.4	15.7	12.3
4. Quite important	26.9	25.3	28.3	25.8	27.6	28.3	25.2	27.5	26.9	28.3	25.1	29.4	25.2	26.7	23.0	17.5
3. Fairly important	31.7	31.4	32.0	34.3	18.8	33.5	32.8	27.6	34.6	32.8	29.3	28.2	37.2	32.3	33.5	28.2
2. Slightly important	18.3	20.3	16.6	19.8	11.7	20.3	17.2	17.1	19.5	15.5	22.8	15.0	16.5	22.1	24.7	29.4
1. Not at all important	2.2	2.8	1.7	2.4	1.8	2.7	1.8	2.4	2.1	0.9	4.6	2.3	1.6	1.4	3.0	12.6
Item 5720 Subject B01 N	2893	1321	1535	2219	329	622	814	886	571	1760	1037	1215	628	384	584	21
D005: How much competition for grades is there among students at your school?																
1. None	5.7	6.6	4.8	5.7	4.3	7.2	5.3	5.3	5.3	4.0	8.5	4.2	4.0	5.0	10.4	15.3
2. A little	20.7	21.6	20.1	20.8	19.0	23.8	21.5	18.8	19.1	18.3	24.6	17.6	19.9	21.0	27.0	40.0
3. Some	33.3	32.4	34.1	34.7	29.8	32.2	33.5	32.2	36.2	30.2	38.2	32.7	38.3	31.6	31.0	16.1
4. Quite a bit	29.4	28.8	30.2	29.7	29.3	26.2	30.1	31.3	29.1	33.6	22.8	32.1	29.8	30.9	23.5	23.4
5. A great deal	10.8	10.6	10.9	9.0	17.6	10.7	9.7	12.4	10.2	13.8	6.0	13.4	8.0	11.5	8.1	5.2
Item 5730 Subject B04 N	2883	1316	1529	2212	326	619	813	884	567	1758	1032	1210	626	385	581	21
D006: How do you think most of the students in your classes would feel if you cheated on a test?																
1. They would like it very much	2.5	2.9	1.9	1.8	5.0	2.8	2.4	2.8	1.8	1.8	3.6	1.9	1.4	1.8	4.4	26.5
2. They would like it	2.3	2.9	1.8	2.1	3.7	3.6	2.0	1.8	2.5	2.1	2.6	2.2	2.1	1.8	2.8	-
3. They would not care	79.8	81.8	78.2	80.8	76.8	79.7	78.7	80.2	81.1	78.2	82.6	75.4	85.9	82.9	81.5	57.4
4. They would dislike it	11.8	10.1	13.4	12.1	10.1	9.5	13.9	11.3	12.1	13.9	8.2	15.4	8.6	9.8	9.9	10.7
5. They would dislike it very much	3.6	2.3	4.7	3.2	4.5	4.4	3.1	4.0	2.6	3.9	2.9	5.1	2.0	3.6	1.4	5.5
Item 5740 Subject B04 N	2886	1320	1527	2217	324	617	815	882	572	1757	1032	1213	624	381	583	21

QUESTIONNAIRE FORM 1 1985	TOTAL	SEX		RACE		REGION				4YR COLLEGE PLANS		ILLICIT DRUG USE: LIFETIME				
		M	F	White	Black	NE	NC	S	W	Yes	No	None	Marijuana Only	Few Pills	More Pills	Any Heroin
N (Weighted No. of Cases):	3316	1505	1663	2415	400	783	902	1004	627	1822	1121	1307	719	444	716	29
% of Weighted Total:	100.0	45.4	50.2	72.8	12.1	23.6	27.2	30.3	18.9	55.0	33.8	39.4	21.7	13.4	21.6	0.9

D007: How do you think most of the students in your classes would feel if you intentionally did things to make your teachers angry?

	TOTAL	M	F	White	Black	NE	NC	S	W	Yes	No	None	Mari-juana Only	Few Pills	More Pills	Any Heroin
1. They would like it very much	4.0	5.0	2.9	3.2	7.2	4.3	4.2	4.5	2.4	2.3	6.2	3.2	3.9	4.2	4.8	26.5
2. They would like it	11.5	14.3	9.1	11.3	10.7	15.5	9.3	11.4	10.3	11.0	11.4	10.1	12.8	7.4	14.5	2.8
3. They would not care	42.7	45.7	40.1	42.3	49.6	43.1	44.1	41.7	41.7	41.3	45.2	41.5	44.3	47.1	40.5	42.9
4. They would dislike it	33.9	29.6	37.7	35.2	22.5	28.1	35.1	33.2	39.7	37.2	29.4	36.3	31.7	33.7	33.9	14.8
5. They would dislike it very much	8.0	5.5	10.2	8.0	10.0	9.0	7.3	9.2	5.8	8.2	7.8	9.0	7.4	7.6	6.3	13.0
Item 5750 Subject B04 N	2871	1313	1521	2206	321	613	814	878	566	1746	1028	1211	621	379	576	21

D008: How often do you find that your friends encourage you to do things which your teachers wouldn't like?

	TOTAL	M	F	White	Black	NE	NC	S	W	Yes	No	None	Mari-juana Only	Few Pills	More Pills	Any Heroin
1. Never	34.9	23.2	44.8	32.4	44.2	33.3	33.8	35.0	37.9	36.1	32.8	38.5	31.1	35.0	31.5	29.4
2. Seldom	35.2	36.0	34.7	37.1	29.2	33.7	35.2	36.1	35.5	36.4	33.4	35.9	37.7	34.5	32.9	18.7
3. Sometimes	20.2	26.8	14.5	20.9	17.6	21.3	20.7	19.9	18.8	19.7	21.0	18.4	21.3	20.7	22.4	14.7
4. Often	7.9	10.8	5.3	7.8	6.6	10.1	8.6	6.9	6.0	6.5	10.4	6.0	8.2	8.2	10.4	26.1
5. Almost always	1.8	3.2	0.7	1.8	2.2	1.6	1.7	2.1	1.9	1.3	2.4	1.3	1.6	1.6	2.7	11.2
Item 5760 Subject B04 N	2869	1310	1521	2206	321	608	812	880	569	1747	1026	1210	622	379	577	21

D009: Have you ever been in a work-study program–that is, a program where you work on a job as part of your schooling?

	TOTAL	M	F	White	Black	NE	NC	S	W	Yes	No	None	Mari-juana Only	Few Pills	More Pills	Any Heroin
1. No, not ever	79.0	81.3	77.5	80.5	72.3	82.8	79.6	77.9	75.6	85.9	67.7	82.9	77.1	80.2	73.7	65.1
2. Yes, for a half year or less	8.4	8.0	8.6	7.2	14.6	7.0	7.6	8.0	11.7	6.4	11.4	6.3	9.7	8.1	11.1	13.8
3. Yes, for about a year	9.1	7.0	10.5	9.0	7.7	5.6	10.1	10.5	9.3	5.7	14.6	7.5	10.2	7.8	10.7	21.1
4. Yes, for about two years	2.5	2.5	2.6	2.2	4.4	2.6	2.1	3.1	2.3	1.6	4.2	2.2	1.8	3.5	3.4	-
5. Yes, for more than two years	1.0	1.3	0.8	1.1	1.0	2.0	0.6	0.6	1.1	0.4	2.1	1.1	1.3	0.5	1.0	-
Item 5770 Subject B02,C01 N	2864	1309	1518	2206	319	610	808	877	569	1745	1024	1207	619	380	577	21

D010: How many times this school year have you seen a counselor individually?

	TOTAL	M	F	White	Black	NE	NC	S	W	Yes	No	None	Mari-juana Only	Few Pills	More Pills	Any Heroin
1. No times	19.7	19.2	20.1	20.1	16.0	20.4	19.8	23.8	12.7	14.3	28.4	22.4	15.8	17.8	19.6	10.0
2. 1 time	14.2	13.6	14.8	14.9	10.0	13.7	13.7	14.9	14.5	12.2	17.4	13.8	15.4	13.8	14.1	8.7
3. 2 times	19.8	20.5	19.4	20.8	16.9	18.9	20.2	20.4	19.3	19.0	20.7	18.2	21.7	22.0	19.6	21.9
4. 3 or 4 times	26.5	27.2	25.7	26.2	25.5	26.5	24.2	24.9	32.2	29.2	22.9	25.0	27.6	26.2	28.8	23.4
5. 5 - 7 times	10.7	10.6	10.9	10.1	16.0	10.8	12.4	8.5	11.6	13.5	5.9	11.3	10.7	12.1	8.9	8.1
6. 8 - 10 times	4.6	4.4	4.7	3.9	7.9	5.6	4.7	3.4	5.0	6.0	2.2	4.8	4.8	3.2	4.2	13.4
7. 11 or more times	4.5	4.5	4.5	4.0	7.6	4.1	4.9	4.2	4.6	5.8	2.5	4.5	4.0	4.9	4.7	14.5
Item 5780 Subject B05 N	2860	1306	1518	2207	315	610	808	878	564	1740	1024	1206	616	380	577	21

D011: How many times this school year have you seen a counselor as a part of a group of other students?

	TOTAL	M	F	White	Black	NE	NC	S	W	Yes	No	None	Mari-juana Only	Few Pills	More Pills	Any Heroin
1. No times	57.7	56.4	58.9	57.9	52.1	61.0	55.7	55.0	61.2	53.6	64.6	56.1	57.6	59.6	59.9	52.8
2. 1 time	14.7	13.9	15.2	15.1	12.5	13.1	15.8	15.2	14.0	14.1	14.9	15.0	14.9	14.8	14.3	7.7
3. 2 times	12.5	12.8	12.5	12.7	14.8	10.9	11.3	14.4	13.2	14.7	9.2	12.7	12.8	12.9	11.8	12.1
4. 3 or 4 times	10.7	11.5	9.8	10.5	13.4	10.2	12.6	10.5	8.7	12.3	8.4	11.1	11.6	9.0	9.6	14.5
5. 5 - 7 times	2.2	2.3	2.1	2.0	3.5	2.2	2.6	2.5	1.1	2.5	1.5	2.0	2.0	2.1	2.4	11.0
6. 8 - 10 times	0.8	1.2	0.4	0.8	0.8	0.7	1.2	0.9	0.2	0.9	0.5	1.2	-	0.2	1.2	1.9
7. 11 or more times	1.5	1.9	1.1	1.0	2.8	1.8	0.9	1.6	1.6	1.8	0.9	1.9	1.1	1.5	0.9	-
Item 5790 Subject B05 N	2859	1305	1516	2204	318	609	808	877	564	1738	1026	1208	616	378	575	21

D012: Would you have preferred to see a counselor more or less often than you have during the past year?

	TOTAL	M	F	White	Black	NE	NC	S	W	Yes	No	None	Mari-juana Only	Few Pills	More Pills	Any Heroin
5. Much more often	7.7	7.1	8.2	6.2	16.9	6.6	5.4	11.4	6.7	8.2	6.7	7.1	7.8	6.5	7.8	19.6
4. A little more often	24.5	24.0	25.0	24.7	23.2	18.6	24.9	27.1	26.2	25.9	22.7	23.4	26.8	28.1	22.3	8.5
3. About as often	49.6	50.3	49.4	52.2	38.6	53.2	51.0	43.8	53.0	53.1	43.5	52.0	48.7	50.1	48.1	27.8
2. A little less often	6.6	6.6	6.6	5.8	12.1	7.2	6.5	6.2	6.8	5.4	9.1	6.2	7.3	4.9	7.7	11.9
1. Much less often	11.5	12.0	10.8	11.1	9.2	14.4	12.1	11.5	7.3	7.4	18.0	11.2	9.4	10.5	14.0	32.2
Item 5800 Subject B05 N	2813	1277	1500	2164	314	594	797	864	558	1716	1005	1191	610	370	562	21

QUESTIONNAIRE FORM 1 1985	TOTAL	SEX		RACE		REGION				4YR COLLEGE PLANS		ILLICIT DRUG USE: LIFETIME				
		M	F	White	Black	NE	NC	S	W	Yes	No	None	Marijuana Only	Few Pills	More Pills	Any Heroin
N (Weighted No. of Cases):	3316	1505	1663	2415	400	783	902	1004	627	1822	1121	1307	719	444	716	29
% of Weighted Total:	100.0	45.4	50.2	72.8	12.1	23.6	27.2	30.3	18.9	55.0	33.8	39.4	21.7	13.4	21.6	0.9

D013: How helpful have your sessions with a counselor been to you?

5. Extremely helpful	10.5	9.0	11.7	8.1	20.9	9.2	9.1	11.7	12.3	11.8	8.7	12.0	10.9	9.1	7.8	11.7
4. Quite helpful	21.0	21.6	20.5	19.6	27.4	18.7	20.7	19.5	26.5	23.8	16.0	21.3	22.2	20.7	18.8	18.4
3. Somewhat helpful	24.6	26.6	23.1	25.8	21.4	24.9	25.4	22.5	26.6	25.1	24.9	22.5	26.9	27.9	24.9	20.9
2. A little helpful	19.0	18.2	20.0	20.2	14.4	23.0	19.3	17.5	16.6	18.6	19.8	18.4	20.5	19.1	19.8	14.4
1. Not at all helpful	10.7	11.1	10.4	11.7	5.5	10.4	10.4	11.6	10.1	10.4	10.8	9.9	9.9	8.9	14.0	24.8
8. Did not see a counselor this year	14.1	13.6	14.3	14.6	10.3	13.8	15.2	17.2	7.9	10.5	19.8	16.0	9.7	14.3	14.7	9.7
Item 5810　Subject B05　N	2891	1319	1533	2219	324	616	815	886	573	1735	1000	1205	625	387	586	22

D014: Would you have preferred more or less of each of the following types of counseling in the last year?

D014A: Choosing what courses to take

5. Much more	19.6	19.7	19.3	15.8	32.6	17.0	15.5	23.1	22.7	19.2	20.3	18.5	21.0	22.8	17.1	16.6
4. A little more	25.0	23.4	26.5	25.6	23.3	20.8	27.2	27.7	22.1	25.4	24.2	26.0	22.3	31.5	21.9	18.6
3. About right	46.1	45.3	46.9	49.9	33.9	51.0	47.6	39.6	48.8	48.5	42.2	46.8	47.0	40.4	49.4	33.8
2. A little less	3.4	3.4	3.4	2.7	6.1	4.4	3.4	3.1	2.9	2.5	4.9	3.2	3.9	1.5	4.4	2.0
1. Much less	5.9	8.2	3.9	5.9	4.1	6.8	6.4	6.4	3.5	4.5	8.3	5.4	5.8	3.9	7.1	29.1
Item 5811　Subject B05　N	2827	1284	1500	2166	317	594	800	867	566	1699	982	1184	617	379	564	22

D014B: Discussing problems with course work

5. Much more	12.3	11.0	13.1	9.6	25.0	11.4	10.0	16.6	10.2	11.0	14.0	11.7	13.7	12.9	10.6	2.8
4. A little more	24.1	24.0	24.6	23.1	27.6	19.5	22.3	26.8	27.6	24.5	23.5	22.0	25.4	25.5	26.6	28.6
3. About right	49.9	49.6	50.1	53.9	35.8	50.7	53.4	44.7	52.2	53.3	44.5	53.3	49.1	50.9	45.7	33.7
2. A little less	5.3	6.2	4.6	5.3	4.0	8.5	5.8	3.9	3.5	4.8	6.4	5.2	4.2	4.4	7.2	5.9
1. Much less	8.3	9.2	7.6	8.1	7.6	9.8	8.5	8.1	6.6	6.3	11.6	7.7	7.6	6.3	9.9	29.1
Item 5812　Subject B05　N	2797	1270	1484	2138	314	593	789	855	561	1674	980	1176	609	373	555	22

D014C: Discussing any trouble you've gotten into

5. Much more	8.0	8.2	7.5	6.2	13.2	6.6	6.7	10.5	7.3	7.0	9.7	7.2	9.4	7.3	8.1	5.4
4. A little more	10.9	10.3	11.2	9.3	16.0	12.5	8.1	11.8	11.6	8.9	12.7	8.7	11.3	14.1	12.5	6.7
3. About right	58.2	57.5	59.2	62.9	42.8	53.2	61.5	55.2	63.2	64.4	49.1	63.0	58.0	55.7	51.8	36.2
2. A little less	5.9	6.6	5.2	5.8	5.7	8.1	5.3	4.8	6.1	4.8	7.4	4.6	6.0	6.6	8.0	13.7
1. Much less	17.1	17.5	16.8	15.8	22.3	19.5	18.5	17.7	11.8	14.9	21.0	16.5	15.3	16.2	19.5	38.0
Item 5813　Subject B05　N	2730	1247	1441	2077	314	573	768	833	555	1634	957	1147	600	362	541	22

D014D: Discussing military plans

5. Much more	5.7	7.1	4.0	4.2	13.4	4.9	5.0	7.2	5.1	3.9	7.5	5.5	5.2	9.1	3.8	3.9
4. A little more	6.9	9.3	4.7	6.2	11.8	6.9	7.6	6.7	5.9	5.5	8.8	6.6	8.5	6.6	5.9	7.7
3. About right	46.1	44.7	47.8	50.9	29.4	41.7	48.7	43.8	50.6	53.0	36.6	51.0	45.4	42.7	41.3	18.3
2. A little less	5.6	7.2	4.0	5.4	5.8	6.0	5.0	5.3	6.4	5.1	5.6	4.8	6.2	4.4	6.8	2.0
1. Much less	35.7	31.8	39.6	33.3	39.6	40.5	33.7	36.9	32.0	32.6	41.5	32.1	34.8	37.1	42.2	68.0
Item 5814　Subject B05　N	2681	1248	1391	2041	309	554	767	815	544	1598	944	1120	592	357	531	22

D014E: Discussing education or training plans

5. Much more	23.7	19.8	26.9	20.8	36.1	18.1	23.2	26.8	25.8	25.8	20.0	24.3	25.3	24.6	19.6	5.4
4. A little more	31.5	30.1	32.9	32.1	32.8	31.3	32.3	31.4	30.8	34.5	25.5	31.9	31.9	33.6	30.4	16.1
3. About right	33.4	36.5	30.7	36.0	21.5	36.2	34.3	29.9	34.4	32.6	35.8	36.2	30.1	33.8	31.4	32.9
2. A little less	3.4	4.3	2.7	3.4	3.3	5.1	2.9	3.1	2.9	2.2	5.5	1.9	4.9	1.6	6.5	7.6
1. Much less	7.9	9.2	6.7	7.8	6.4	9.3	7.3	8.9	6.0	4.8	13.2	5.8	7.8	6.4	12.1	38.1
Item 5815　Subject B05　N	2792	1273	1477	2139	309	583	790	855	563	1685	966	1180	610	372	552	22

D014F: Discussing career plans or job choice

5. Much more	29.0	24.8	32.4	25.4	42.3	22.4	27.2	35.3	28.7	30.7	25.0	29.1	29.3	29.4	27.4	14.5
4. A little more	30.1	28.7	31.9	31.5	27.2	30.2	31.0	28.2	31.9	32.2	27.2	30.3	30.3	32.2	29.3	6.0
3. About right	31.7	34.9	28.8	34.3	23.0	36.8	32.4	27.1	32.2	31.0	33.8	34.2	30.9	31.8	28.4	37.8
2. A little less	2.6	2.5	2.6	2.5	2.6	3.7	2.6	2.1	2.3	1.8	3.8	1.6	3.0	1.5	4.9	-
1. Much less	6.6	9.2	4.4	6.2	4.8	6.9	6.8	7.4	4.9	4.3	10.3	4.7	6.5	5.1	10.0	41.7
Item 5816　Subject B05　N	2795	1270	1483	2141	311	588	792	853	562	1683	969	1175	613	372	554	22

QUESTIONNAIRE FORM 1 1985	TOTAL	SEX		RACE		REGION				4YR COLLEGE PLANS		ILLICIT DRUG USE: LIFETIME				
		M	F	White	Black	NE	NC	S	W	Yes	No	None	Mari-juana Only	Few Pills	More Pills	Any Her-oin
N (Weighted No. of Cases):	3316	1505	1663	2415	400	783	902	1004	627	1822	1121	1307	719	444	716	29
% of Weighted Total:	100.0	45.4	50.2	72.8	12.1	23.6	27.2	30.3	18.9	55.0	33.8	39.4	21.7	13.4	21.6	0.9
D014G: Discussing personal problems																
5. Much more	9.0	7.9	9.8	7.9	11.5	8.4	8.3	11.3	7.0	8.4	10.2	8.0	8.1	10.8	10.3	9.4
4. A little more	10.1	7.3	12.3	9.5	13.4	11.6	9.3	10.2	9.5	9.5	10.2	9.4	10.2	9.2	11.2	6.6
3. About right	51.2	53.5	49.6	55.6	35.3	48.5	51.4	47.2	57.7	57.2	42.2	57.2	48.6	52.0	44.2	23.8
2. A little less	6.7	8.1	5.4	6.3	6.9	7.4	7.1	6.0	6.7	5.9	7.6	6.2	8.1	7.6	6.2	4.8
1. Much less	23.0	23.1	23.0	20.5	33.0	24.1	23.9	23.8	19.1	19.0	29.8	19.3	25.0	20.3	28.2	55.4
Item 5817 Subject B05 N	2730	1254	1437	2087	309	576	781	831	543	1639	954	1148	597	363	543	22

These last questions concern your health.

D015: During the LAST 30 DAYS, on how many days (if any) did you have the following problems or symptoms?

D015A: Headache

	TOTAL	M	F	White	Black	NE	NC	S	W	Yes	No	None	Mari-juana Only	Few Pills	More Pills	Any Her-oin
1. None	18.6	28.3	10.3	16.7	28.1	18.6	17.0	18.3	21.6	16.9	21.4	20.6	19.0	12.8	16.9	13.5
2. One day	20.8	25.1	17.1	18.9	27.6	20.9	20.7	21.6	19.5	20.6	20.1	24.0	20.8	18.1	16.4	12.3
3. Two days	21.8	22.0	21.8	22.2	19.7	22.0	20.5	23.5	21.0	23.5	19.3	21.8	21.7	21.5	22.2	17.8
4. 3 to 5 days	20.7	14.4	25.9	22.3	15.2	19.3	24.2	19.5	18.9	20.0	22.1	19.1	22.1	26.0	19.2	21.2
5. 6 to 9 days	9.0	6.0	11.5	10.3	3.8	10.4	8.6	8.4	9.0	9.6	8.0	8.0	8.3	11.1	10.7	5.4
6. 10 to 19 days	5.8	2.3	9.0	6.6	2.7	5.2	5.5	5.9	6.8	6.1	5.7	3.9	6.3	6.2	9.1	15.8
7. 20+ days	3.2	1.8	4.5	3.1	2.8	3.6	3.5	2.8	3.2	3.2	3.4	2.5	1.8	4.3	5.5	14.0
Item 21310 Subject T N	2852	1296	1514	2187	315	600	804	877	571	1709	992	1199	623	378	567	22

D015B: Sore throat or hoarse voice

	TOTAL	M	F	White	Black	NE	NC	S	W	Yes	No	None	Mari-juana Only	Few Pills	More Pills	Any Her-oin
1. None	39.2	48.3	30.8	36.8	48.7	36.7	32.7	44.8	42.3	37.1	42.2	44.3	39.4	29.6	34.5	31.2
2. One day	16.7	17.1	16.4	16.9	15.6	17.8	17.4	16.4	15.1	17.4	15.7	16.4	16.3	20.5	15.2	10.8
3. Two days	15.7	14.2	17.0	15.7	13.0	16.5	15.9	14.8	16.0	15.7	15.8	15.1	14.7	20.1	15.6	6.0
4. 3 to 5 days	17.7	14.0	21.1	18.9	14.9	18.1	20.4	16.0	16.1	18.5	16.8	16.4	18.0	19.8	18.8	27.2
5. 6 to 9 days	6.7	4.4	8.8	7.6	4.5	6.1	8.6	5.6	6.5	7.0	6.2	5.2	7.4	6.9	9.1	13.1
6. 10 to 19 days	2.8	1.3	4.2	2.9	1.7	3.4	3.1	2.1	2.9	3.1	2.2	2.1	3.0	2.2	4.4	-
7. 20+ days	1.2	0.6	1.6	1.1	1.6	1.4	1.8	0.4	1.1	1.2	1.1	0.5	1.2	0.8	2.4	11.7
Item 21320 Subject T N	2851	1295	1515	2186	316	600	801	877	573	1710	994	1197	620	378	573	22

D015C: Trouble with sinus congestion, runny nose, or sneezing

	TOTAL	M	F	White	Black	NE	NC	S	W	Yes	No	None	Mari-juana Only	Few Pills	More Pills	Any Her-oin
1. None	25.9	29.5	22.2	23.3	33.7	25.9	23.0	27.7	27.0	23.1	30.0	28.8	25.4	19.2	24.5	19.9
2. One day	11.4	12.9	10.3	11.5	12.5	11.5	10.2	13.2	10.2	11.3	12.5	14.0	10.1	9.2	9.2	2.0
3. Two days	13.0	12.3	13.8	12.9	13.7	14.8	12.3	12.7	12.6	12.7	13.3	12.3	12.8	17.0	12.3	14.5
4. 3 to 5 days	21.9	21.3	22.5	22.4	20.6	19.7	25.2	20.3	21.8	24.4	18.6	20.7	24.3	22.2	20.1	34.2
5. 6 to 9 days	12.7	11.6	13.7	14.2	7.5	13.2	12.8	11.2	14.5	12.7	11.4	11.1	12.8	13.6	16.3	-
6. 10 to 19 days	8.9	7.8	9.7	9.5	6.7	8.2	9.5	9.2	8.2	9.7	7.2	7.5	9.7	9.8	10.7	-
7. 20+ days	6.3	4.6	7.7	6.2	5.4	6.6	7.0	5.7	5.8	6.0	7.0	5.6	4.8	9.1	6.9	29.4
Item 21330 Subject T N	2853	1297	1512	2187	318	601	803	877	572	1712	992	1201	621	378	571	22

D015D: Coughing spells

	TOTAL	M	F	White	Black	NE	NC	S	W	Yes	No	None	Mari-juana Only	Few Pills	More Pills	Any Her-oin
1. None	57.4	60.6	54.3	55.5	64.7	56.8	51.5	62.0	59.4	59.1	55.5	65.4	55.7	51.1	48.0	22.2
2. One day	13.2	14.4	12.3	13.9	9.8	11.9	15.4	13.4	11.1	11.8	14.9	10.7	14.2	16.1	16.6	2.0
3. Two days	9.4	9.2	9.5	9.4	7.7	10.0	11.8	6.9	9.0	9.2	9.4	8.2	9.4	10.6	10.4	11.7
4. 3 to 5 days	10.4	8.3	12.3	10.8	10.6	10.1	11.0	9.6	10.9	10.6	10.2	8.9	11.7	12.6	9.6	17.7
5. 6 to 9 days	4.8	4.4	5.3	5.6	3.7	5.0	5.0	4.8	4.5	4.6	5.3	4.1	5.4	3.5	6.4	19.5
6. 10 to 19 days	3.1	2.0	4.1	3.4	1.4	4.3	3.1	2.2	3.0	3.2	2.8	1.6	2.5	4.8	5.8	-
7. 20+ days	1.7	1.1	2.2	1.4	2.0	1.9	2.1	1.0	2.0	1.5	1.9	1.1	1.2	1.3	3.1	26.9
Item 21340 Subject T N	2847	1293	1510	2186	313	598	804	872	573	1710	990	1198	621	377	569	22

D015E: Chest colds

	TOTAL	M	F	White	Black	NE	NC	S	W	Yes	No	None	Mari-juana Only	Few Pills	More Pills	Any Her-oin
1. None	73.5	77.7	69.8	72.5	74.1	70.5	68.6	75.8	80.1	74.6	72.0	77.5	74.0	72.2	66.7	58.8
2. One day	8.2	8.1	8.6	8.5	8.7	7.2	8.8	9.7	6.3	7.8	9.4	6.1	8.2	10.3	11.0	20.6
3. Two days	6.4	5.2	7.3	6.4	5.3	8.9	7.0	5.1	4.8	5.8	6.9	5.8	5.7	6.5	8.5	2.7
4. 3 to 5 days	6.8	5.4	8.1	7.3	7.1	7.2	9.9	4.7	5.2	6.9	6.5	6.4	7.3	5.5	7.6	8.9
5. 6 to 9 days	2.9	2.3	3.5	3.2	2.2	4.0	3.1	2.7	2.0	2.8	3.2	2.8	3.1	2.6	3.0	-
6. 10 to 19 days	1.4	0.8	2.0	1.4	1.4	1.3	1.9	1.4	1.0	1.5	1.4	1.1	1.3	2.3	1.8	-
7. 20+ days	0.7	0.6	0.8	0.7	1.3	0.8	0.8	0.7	0.5	0.6	0.7	0.3	0.5	0.6	1.4	8.9
Item 21350 Subject T N	2824	1280	1501	2173	306	597	801	858	568	1697	980	1191	617	369	564	22

QUESTIONNAIRE FORM 1 1985	TOTAL	SEX		RACE		REGION				4YR COLLEGE PLANS		ILLICIT DRUG USE: LIFETIME				
		M	F	White	Black	NE	NC	S	W	Yes	No	None	Mari-juana Only	Few Pills	More Pills	Any Her-oin
N (Weighted No. of Cases):	3316	1505	1663	2415	400	783	902	1004	627	1822	1121	1307	719	444	716	29
% of Weighted Total:	100.0	45.4	50.2	72.8	12.1	23.6	27.2	30.3	18.9	55.0	33.8	39.4	21.7	13.4	21.6	0.9
D015F: Coughing up phlegm or blood																
1. None	84.4	85.6	83.3	83.3	90.7	83.8	82.3	86.2	85.3	83.9	85.7	88.9	84.7	81.5	78.1	54.6
2. One day	3.4	3.6	3.3	3.5	2.5	3.4	3.3	3.4	3.5	3.6	3.0	2.9	3.6	3.0	4.4	-
3. Two days	2.9	2.7	3.1	3.3	1.8	3.2	2.1	3.8	2.5	3.1	2.7	1.8	2.1	5.0	4.5	7.8
4. 3 to 5 days	4.3	3.1	5.3	4.7	1.0	4.9	5.3	2.4	5.1	4.5	4.0	2.9	5.1	4.9	6.1	5.5
5. 6 to 9 days	2.3	2.2	2.4	2.5	1.8	2.0	3.4	2.1	1.2	2.4	1.9	2.1	2.5	1.5	2.8	7.3
6. 10 to 19 days	1.3	0.9	1.7	1.4	0.9	1.4	2.3	0.9	0.7	1.4	1.3	0.6	1.2	1.7	2.6	6.0
7. 20+ days	1.3	1.8	0.9	1.2	1.3	1.4	1.3	1.2	1.6	1.2	1.5	0.8	0.9	2.3	1.6	18.8
Item 21360 Subject T N	*2830*	*1282*	*1505*	*2173*	*310*	*594*	*798*	*866*	*571*	*1700*	*986*	*1195*	*617*	*373*	*565*	*22*
D015G: Shortness of breath when you were not exercising																
1. None	84.9	89.9	80.6	84.8	86.2	84.5	83.6	85.8	85.8	86.2	84.1	90.0	85.9	80.7	77.2	58.5
2. One day	4.5	2.9	5.9	4.3	5.5	4.0	6.5	4.2	2.6	4.0	4.6	4.2	4.2	4.2	5.3	12.1
3. Two days	3.9	3.0	4.7	4.0	4.1	3.2	3.9	4.7	3.6	3.8	4.1	2.6	3.1	5.4	6.8	2.0
4. 3 to 5 days	3.0	1.9	4.0	3.4	1.2	4.8	2.8	2.4	2.4	2.8	3.3	1.5	3.5	5.3	4.2	2.8
5. 6 to 9 days	2.0	1.4	2.5	2.1	1.5	1.9	2.0	1.6	2.8	1.8	1.8	1.0	2.1	2.2	3.6	5.1
6. 10 to 19 days	0.6	0.3	1.0	0.7	0.2	0.9	0.3	0.6	0.8	0.5	0.9	0.5	0.6	0.8	0.6	10.6
7. 20+ days	1.0	0.6	1.3	0.6	1.2	0.6	0.9	0.7	2.0	0.8	1.3	0.2	0.5	1.4	2.4	8.9
Item 21370 Subject T N	*2835*	*1282*	*1509*	*2174*	*314*	*592*	*799*	*872*	*572*	*1701*	*988*	*1197*	*621*	*371*	*564*	*22*
D015H: Wheezing or gasping																
1. None	89.0	89.9	88.6	89.4	87.5	88.3	89.6	89.6	88.1	89.2	89.5	92.2	91.0	87.6	82.5	71.8
2. One day	3.6	3.3	3.6	3.4	5.8	3.5	3.4	4.2	2.9	3.8	3.1	2.9	3.3	3.2	5.5	6.1
3. Two days	2.8	2.4	3.2	2.8	2.7	2.2	2.6	3.7	2.2	2.7	3.1	1.8	2.1	4.1	4.5	-
4. 3 to 5 days	2.1	2.2	2.0	2.2	2.6	2.8	2.4	0.9	2.9	2.1	1.8	1.6	1.7	2.4	3.4	-
5. 6 to 9 days	1.1	0.8	1.4	1.3	0.1	2.2	0.7	0.3	1.8	1.2	1.1	0.6	0.8	2.1	2.0	2.8
6. 10 to 19 days	0.5	0.3	0.7	0.5	0.1	0.6	0.6	0.3	0.5	0.4	0.6	0.4	0.7	0.2	0.6	5.4
7. 20+ days	0.9	1.1	0.5	0.3	1.2	0.3	0.8	0.8	1.6	0.6	1.0	0.4	0.4	0.5	1.6	14.0
Item 21380 Subject T N	*2830*	*1283*	*1504*	*2172*	*311*	*591*	*800*	*867*	*571*	*1699*	*986*	*1191*	*620*	*371*	*565*	*22*
D015I: Trouble remembering new things																
1. None	71.6	73.9	69.5	72.9	70.6	70.4	72.0	73.0	70.0	73.3	69.5	77.1	73.5	66.9	61.1	49.2
2. One day	9.5	8.7	10.2	8.2	13.4	8.8	10.3	9.7	8.8	8.5	10.5	9.4	10.0	9.4	9.4	6.8
3. Two days	7.6	6.9	8.1	7.5	7.9	7.2	7.0	7.5	8.7	7.7	7.0	5.9	8.7	9.2	9.1	1.8
4. 3 to 5 days	5.3	4.9	5.7	5.4	4.5	6.3	4.6	5.1	5.4	4.8	6.3	4.9	4.5	5.9	6.6	9.9
5. 6 to 9 days	2.5	2.1	2.7	2.5	1.3	3.7	2.0	1.4	3.7	2.6	2.3	1.3	1.3	4.4	5.5	-
6. 10 to 19 days	1.2	0.9	1.4	1.3	0.6	0.8	1.2	0.9	1.8	0.9	1.4	0.4	0.4	1.8	3.1	5.4
7. 20+ days	2.4	2.6	2.4	2.1	1.6	2.7	2.9	2.4	1.7	2.2	3.0	1.1	1.6	2.5	5.2	26.9
Item 21390 Subject T N	*2827*	*1283*	*1502*	*2173*	*308*	*596*	*796*	*866*	*570*	*1697*	*985*	*1191*	*620*	*371*	*565*	*22*
D015J: Difficulty thinking or concentrating																
1. None	54.3	61.5	47.9	54.7	60.8	53.2	53.4	56.7	53.1	52.4	58.3	58.1	57.0	46.3	47.2	50.0
2. One day	12.3	12.2	12.6	11.6	13.5	14.4	12.2	9.7	14.2	12.4	11.0	11.8	13.1	16.8	10.8	2.0
3. Two days	12.7	10.4	14.5	12.8	10.6	11.1	13.0	13.8	12.1	13.2	11.6	12.8	11.9	12.3	14.4	1.8
4. 3 to 5 days	10.1	8.4	11.8	10.2	7.2	10.2	10.4	10.2	9.5	11.5	7.9	9.9	9.4	11.5	10.4	19.3
5. 6 to 9 days	5.4	4.0	6.6	5.4	4.1	5.6	5.4	4.1	7.2	5.6	5.7	4.0	4.8	7.0	8.0	5.3
6. 10 to 19 days	3.0	1.8	4.1	3.4	2.0	3.3	3.4	2.9	2.3	2.6	3.6	2.4	1.9	3.3	5.1	5.3
7. 20+ days	2.1	1.8	2.5	2.0	1.7	2.0	2.2	2.5	1.6	2.3	1.9	1.1	1.9	2.8	4.0	16.4
Item 21400 Subject T N	*2820*	*1277*	*1500*	*2165*	*309*	*592*	*796*	*863*	*569*	*1696*	*981*	*1189*	*617*	*372*	*562*	*22*
D015K: Trouble learning new things																
1. None	70.6	74.1	67.8	71.1	73.6	66.4	70.2	73.2	71.7	70.4	72.4	73.3	73.9	62.8	67.1	61.3
2. One day	10.5	8.8	12.2	9.8	10.7	9.9	10.6	10.0	11.9	10.7	9.9	10.5	8.7	13.1	10.4	17.1
3. Two days	8.1	7.3	8.8	8.5	5.6	9.6	7.9	7.9	7.0	8.6	6.9	7.4	9.4	9.9	7.6	-
4. 3 to 5 days	5.8	5.6	5.8	5.9	4.7	7.0	5.8	5.1	5.5	5.8	5.8	5.4	4.8	7.5	6.5	-
5. 6 to 9 days	2.6	2.4	2.7	2.5	2.9	3.8	2.8	1.7	2.3	2.8	1.9	2.0	2.0	3.3	3.9	2.4
6. 10 to 19 days	1.2	1.0	1.3	1.3	1.1	1.7	1.2	1.2	1.0	0.9	1.7	0.8	0.4	1.6	2.7	5.3
7. 20+ days	1.1	0.8	1.4	0.9	1.4	1.5	1.5	1.0	0.6	0.8	1.6	0.7	0.7	1.7	1.9	14.0
Item 21410 Subject T N	*2820*	*1275*	*1503*	*2164*	*311*	*590*	*796*	*864*	*570*	*1693*	*982*	*1190*	*619*	*371*	*559*	*22*

QUESTIONNAIRE FORM 1 1985	TOTAL	SEX		RACE		REGION				4YR COLLEGE PLANS		ILLICIT DRUG USE: LIFETIME				
		M	F	White	Black	NE	NC	S	W	Yes	No	None	Marijuana Only	Few Pills	More Pills	Any Heroin
N (Weighted No. of Cases):	3316	1505	1663	2415	400	783	902	1004	627	1822	1121	1307	719	444	716	29
% of Weighted Total:	100.0	45.4	50.2	72.8	12.1	23.6	27.2	30.3	18.9	55.0	33.8	39.4	21.7	13.4	21.6	0.9

D015L: Trouble sleeping

1. None	42.3	50.3	35.0	39.9	55.3	38.8	41.3	45.7	42.0	42.1	43.6	47.6	46.5	29.6	34.2	31.5
2. One day	14.6	14.7	14.4	14.2	12.4	13.1	14.5	14.9	15.8	14.3	14.1	15.3	13.6	18.0	11.6	13.3
3. Two days	13.6	10.8	16.2	14.2	11.3	13.5	14.0	12.9	14.1	13.9	13.0	12.1	14.7	15.3	15.3	21.5
4. 3 to 5 days	14.3	12.2	16.3	15.7	10.1	15.2	15.3	12.9	14.0	14.0	14.2	13.8	11.1	18.4	17.4	5.3
5. 6 to 9 days	7.2	6.2	8.1	7.6	3.9	10.2	7.1	6.7	5.1	7.3	7.5	5.8	7.0	9.1	9.8	-
6. 10 to 19 days	4.3	3.2	5.4	4.7	2.7	5.0	3.9	4.1	4.6	4.7	3.7	3.5	3.1	6.8	5.8	8.1
7. 20+ days	3.7	2.6	4.7	3.7	4.2	4.2	3.8	2.9	4.3	3.6	3.8	1.9	4.1	4.4	6.1	20.4
Item 21420 Subject T N	2817	1280	1495	2164	310	591	792	866	568	1690	981	1187	617	371	561	22

D015M: Trouble getting started in the morning

1. None	33.0	39.0	27.4	30.6	45.7	32.2	32.0	35.8	30.7	32.3	34.6	37.5	34.3	25.1	26.8	10.0
2. One day	11.1	11.4	10.9	9.8	18.0	9.9	10.5	11.8	12.0	9.9	13.0	10.9	13.6	9.3	10.3	9.6
3. Two days	12.9	10.1	15.4	13.3	9.6	12.3	13.4	13.4	11.8	13.6	11.3	14.8	12.7	12.1	9.7	14.9
4. 3 to 5 days	13.6	11.8	15.2	14.5	8.2	13.7	14.4	11.6	15.4	14.4	12.3	12.3	11.5	16.3	16.3	24.4
5. 6 to 9 days	9.5	7.9	10.8	10.5	5.0	12.3	9.1	8.2	9.2	9.3	9.5	8.5	9.1	11.5	11.3	7.6
6. 10 to 19 days	7.3	5.9	8.6	8.3	3.8	7.3	7.7	7.0	7.4	8.0	6.7	6.8	6.3	9.1	8.4	5.5
7. 20+ days	12.6	13.9	11.8	13.0	9.7	12.3	12.8	12.3	13.4	12.6	12.7	9.2	12.5	16.3	17.1	28.0
Item 21430 Subject T N	2821	1279	1499	2166	310	590	796	866	570	1695	979	1190	617	370	564	22

D015N: Stayed home most or all of a day because you were not feeling well

1. None	60.7	70.0	52.6	60.0	63.4	60.4	58.8	61.9	61.8	61.7	59.5	67.9	57.8	55.8	52.3	59.0
2. One day	17.5	14.2	20.6	18.2	15.2	17.7	17.6	18.7	15.4	17.0	18.1	16.2	17.8	19.5	19.6	16.3
3. Two days	12.4	9.9	14.5	12.6	11.1	14.0	12.1	12.0	11.6	12.9	11.5	9.2	13.6	14.4	16.1	9.3
4. 3 to 5 days	6.5	4.1	8.5	6.4	7.0	5.6	7.6	5.2	8.0	6.3	7.0	5.0	7.4	7.1	8.0	10.3
5. 6 to 9 days	1.8	1.0	2.5	2.0	1.3	1.3	3.0	1.0	1.8	1.6	2.1	1.3	1.8	1.2	2.8	-
6. 10 to 19 days	0.7	0.4	1.0	0.7	0.6	0.5	0.8	0.7	0.7	0.4	1.2	0.3	1.3	1.0	0.8	-
7. 20+ days	0.4	0.4	0.3	0.1	1.4	0.4	0.1	0.5	0.8	0.1	0.5	0.2	0.3	0.8	0.4	5.1
Item 21440 Subject T N	2824	1282	1499	2166	311	587	796	870	571	1697	980	1193	619	369	560	22

D016: In the LAST 12 MONTHS, how many times (if any) have you seen a doctor or other professional for each of the following?

D016A: For a routine physical check-up

1. None	48.6	48.0	49.0	48.5	45.7	42.5	46.3	51.5	53.9	44.9	55.5	51.9	44.7	47.3	46.5	36.8
2. Once	37.9	39.4	37.0	39.3	31.2	41.4	40.4	35.6	34.1	40.7	33.5	36.7	36.5	41.8	40.3	44.2
3. Twice	10.6	10.4	10.7	10.0	14.9	12.9	10.9	9.2	9.8	11.4	8.6	8.8	14.5	8.6	11.2	13.5
4. 3 to 5 times	2.1	1.7	2.4	1.7	5.1	2.2	1.9	2.5	1.7	2.3	1.6	1.9	2.7	1.9	1.6	5.5
5. 6 to 9 times	0.5	0.3	0.6	0.3	1.8	0.8	0.3	0.7	0.3	0.6	0.2	0.3	0.9	0.5	0.3	-
6. 10+ times	0.3	0.2	0.4	0.2	1.3	0.3	0.2	0.4	0.1	0.2	0.5	0.4	0.5	-	0.1	-
Item 21450 Subject T N	2811	1278	1491	2161	309	586	794	864	567	1694	973	1190	612	370	561	22

D016B: For an injury suffered in a fight, assault, or auto accident

1. None	92.6	91.6	93.5	93.2	92.3	91.0	91.5	95.0	92.2	93.2	92.3	95.2	91.5	92.2	90.5	77.6
2. Once	4.4	5.3	3.5	3.9	4.3	5.0	4.4	3.4	5.2	3.8	4.8	3.1	5.4	5.3	4.4	6.1
3. Twice	1.3	1.2	1.4	1.1	1.6	1.9	1.8	0.6	0.9	1.2	1.4	0.6	2.1	0.6	1.8	-
4. 3 to 5 times	1.0	1.2	0.8	0.9	1.0	0.9	1.7	0.6	0.9	1.0	0.9	0.5	1.0	1.0	2.1	2.0
5. 6 to 9 times	0.3	0.3	0.3	0.4	-	0.8	0.1	0.1	0.6	0.4	0.3	0.4	-	0.5	0.2	5.4
6. 10+ times	0.4	0.3	0.5	0.4	0.9	0.6	0.6	0.3	0.2	0.5	0.4	0.2	-	0.4	1.0	8.9
Item 21460 Subject T N	2811	1278	1492	2157	311	587	792	867	564	1690	975	1188	610	370	560	22

D016C: For any other accidental injury

1. None	81.2	77.4	84.5	79.1	89.5	80.6	79.8	83.3	80.5	78.6	85.4	83.5	79.6	82.2	77.7	66.1
2. Once	10.5	12.1	9.2	11.5	6.1	10.9	11.1	10.6	9.4	12.3	7.4	9.4	12.3	10.6	10.6	13.4
3. Twice	4.4	5.5	3.6	4.9	3.2	5.0	4.3	3.2	5.7	4.9	4.0	4.1	4.1	3.7	5.8	18.1
4. 3 to 5 times	2.5	3.7	1.5	2.9	0.9	2.2	2.8	2.2	3.0	2.9	1.9	1.9	2.8	2.6	3.4	2.5
5. 6 to 9 times	0.7	0.8	0.6	0.7	0.2	0.7	0.7	0.3	1.5	0.7	0.7	0.5	0.8	0.6	1.2	-
6. 10+ times	0.6	0.5	0.7	0.8	0.1	0.6	1.3	0.5	-	0.6	0.7	0.6	0.4	0.2	1.3	-
Item 21470 Subject T N	2789	1270	1478	2144	310	581	787	857	563	1680	967	1181	606	367	555	22

QUESTIONNAIRE FORM 1 1985	TOTAL	SEX		RACE		REGION				4YR COLLEGE PLANS		ILLICIT DRUG USE: LIFETIME				
		M	F	White	Black	NE	NC	S	W	Yes	No	None	Mari-juana Only	Few Pills	More Pills	Any Her-oin
N (Weighted No. of Cases):	3316	1505	1663	2415	400	783	902	1004	627	1822	1121	1307	719	444	716	29
% of Weighted Total:	100.0	45.4	50.2	72.8	12.1	23.6	27.2	30.3	18.9	55.0	33.8	39.4	21.7	13.4	21.6	0.9
D016D: For some physical illness or symptom																
1. None	62.8	70.8	56.1	61.0	71.2	64.1	63.2	61.7	62.5	60.4	67.0	66.4	63.1	56.8	59.4	53.6
2. Once	17.3	15.6	18.9	18.5	12.3	13.4	19.5	17.5	17.7	18.5	15.2	15.4	17.6	20.9	18.1	22.0
3. Twice	10.4	7.8	12.4	10.6	10.7	10.5	10.2	11.8	8.4	10.5	9.8	10.3	9.7	10.6	11.3	9.8
4. 3 to 5 times	6.6	4.8	8.2	6.9	3.5	8.6	4.8	5.4	9.1	7.6	5.1	5.0	7.2	8.9	7.6	9.5
5. 6 to 9 times	1.8	0.5	2.7	1.8	1.7	2.4	1.1	2.4	1.0	1.8	1.8	1.8	1.4	2.0	1.9	5.1
6. 10+ times	1.1	0.5	1.7	1.2	0.7	1.0	1.2	1.1	1.3	1.2	1.0	1.1	1.1	0.8	1.6	-
Item 21480 Subject T N	2796	1272	1482	2147	309	581	786	865	564	1680	972	1185	606	366	559	22
D016E: For some emotional or psychological problem or symptom																
1. None	94.7	95.6	94.1	95.0	94.2	93.4	94.7	95.4	94.8	94.1	95.6	96.5	95.4	92.7	91.7	93.1
2. Once	2.1	1.6	2.7	1.8	3.0	2.6	2.2	1.7	2.2	2.2	2.0	1.1	2.4	4.1	2.4	6.9
3. Twice	0.8	0.6	1.0	0.7	1.6	1.2	0.8	0.6	0.8	0.9	0.7	0.7	0.5	0.7	1.4	-
4. 3 to 5 times	1.0	1.1	0.8	1.0	0.6	1.4	0.8	1.0	0.6	1.1	0.7	1.1	0.4	0.9	1.5	-
5. 6 to 9 times	0.3	0.2	0.3	0.3	-	0.4	0.6	0.1	0.1	0.3	0.1	*	0.3	0.1	0.8	-
6. 10+ times	1.1	1.0	1.2	1.3	0.6	1.1	0.9	1.1	1.5	1.4	0.8	0.6	1.1	1.5	2.2	-
Item 21490 Subject T N	2796	1273	1483	2146	310	585	786	863	562	1683	970	1186	607	369	554	22
D017: In the LAST 12 MONTHS, how many times (if any) have you spent one or more nights in the hospital . . .																
D017A: Because of an injury																
1. None	95.7	95.7	96.0	96.2	94.9	95.3	95.2	95.8	96.8	96.1	95.3	96.9	96.2	94.9	94.7	84.8
2. Once	2.5	2.3	2.4	2.1	3.1	2.9	2.5	2.5	2.1	2.6	2.4	1.9	2.4	3.7	2.1	11.4
3. Twice	0.8	1.1	0.6	0.8	0.8	0.6	1.4	0.6	0.6	0.5	1.1	0.7	0.5	0.8	1.2	3.8
4. 3 to 5 times	0.4	0.4	0.5	0.3	1.1	0.4	0.4	0.5	0.4	0.3	0.7	0.3	0.3	-	1.0	-
5. 6 to 9 times	0.2	0.2	0.2	0.3	-	0.2	0.3	0.2	-	0.3	0.1	0.1	0.4	0.3	0.1	-
6. 10+ times	0.3	0.2	0.4	0.3	0.2	0.6	0.1	0.3	0.1	0.2	0.4	*	0.2	0.3	0.9	-
Item 21500 Subject T N	2797	1270	1486	2147	310	583	790	861	563	1683	971	1186	607	369	557	22
D017B: Because of some physical illness																
1. None	95.6	96.9	94.7	96.1	92.2	95.7	95.0	94.8	97.5	96.2	94.6	97.1	95.1	94.6	94.1	98.2
2. Once	2.7	1.8	3.5	2.6	4.4	2.1	3.3	3.3	1.4	2.5	3.1	2.0	2.9	3.6	3.3	1.8
3. Twice	0.7	0.4	0.9	0.5	1.9	0.7	0.7	1.0	0.5	0.6	0.8	0.3	0.8	1.0	1.2	-
4. 3 to 5 times	0.5	0.6	0.5	0.5	0.6	1.0	0.2	0.7	0.4	0.3	0.9	0.4	0.7	0.2	0.8	-
5. 6 to 9 times	0.3	0.3	0.1	0.2	0.2	0.3	0.6	0.1	-	0.3	0.2	0.1	0.3	0.3	0.4	-
6. 10+ times	0.2	0.1	0.2	0.1	0.6	0.2	0.3	0.1	0.1	0.1	0.2	0.1	0.2	0.3	0.2	-
Item 21510 Subject T N	2790	1263	1488	2142	311	581	787	861	561	1679	970	1185	600	369	558	22
D018: Overall, relative to other people your age, do you think your physical health over the past year has been . . .																
1. Much poorer than average	2.4	1.8	2.7	1.9	4.3	3.8	1.8	2.2	1.9	1.5	3.7	1.6	2.3	2.5	3.3	5.1
2. Somewhat poorer than average	7.6	4.6	10.2	7.7	5.1	7.7	6.2	8.6	7.8	7.5	7.5	7.3	7.3	5.1	9.6	27.7
3. About average	36.6	29.8	42.7	35.7	37.4	39.2	34.5	35.2	38.9	33.3	43.9	33.7	35.8	38.3	42.8	33.5
4. Somewhat better than average	31.2	33.8	28.5	32.6	28.8	29.0	33.8	32.3	28.0	33.0	27.1	31.3	32.6	34.4	27.4	24.8
5. Much better than average	22.3	30.0	15.9	22.1	24.4	20.3	23.7	21.7	23.3	24.7	17.8	26.2	22.1	19.8	16.8	8.9
Item 21520 Subject T N	2786	1262	1487	2147	299	589	782	856	560	1683	958	1180	604	366	555	22

*=less than .05 per cent.

QUESTIONNAIRE FORM 2 1985	TOTAL	SEX		RACE		REGION				4YR COLLEGE PLANS		ILLICIT DRUG USE: LIFETIME				
		M	F	White	Black	NE	NC	S	W	Yes	No	None	Mari-juana Only	Few Pills	More Pills	Any Her-oin
N (Weighted No. of Cases):	3327	1573	1651	2485	388	771	914	1017	625	1919	1172	1283	696	453	784	47
% of Weighted Total:	100.0	47.3	49.6	74.7	11.7	23.2	27.5	30.6	18.8	57.7	35.2	38.6	20.9	13.6	23.6	1.4

A01: Taking all things together, how would you say things are these days--would you say you're very happy, pretty happy, or not too happy these days?

	TOTAL	M	F	White	Black	NE	NC	S	W	Yes	No	None	Mari-juana Only	Few Pills	More Pills	Any Her-oin
3. Very happy	19.4	17.6	21.1	21.3	12.1	18.4	17.3	19.8	23.2	21.6	16.2	21.5	18.1	19.8	16.9	13.8
2. Pretty happy	70.7	73.5	68.7	71.2	70.0	69.7	74.4	70.0	67.9	70.2	72.6	70.4	72.0	69.8	71.3	69.2
1. Not too happy	9.8	8.9	10.2	7.4	17.9	11.9	8.4	10.2	9.0	8.2	11.3	8.1	9.9	10.3	11.8	17.0
Item 1190 Subject P01,Q01 N	3225	1510	1619	2426	372	740	888	991	606	1871	1131	1251	670	439	760	46

A02: The next questions ask about the kinds of things you might do. How often do you do each of the following?

A02A: Watch TV

	TOTAL	M	F	White	Black	NE	NC	S	W	Yes	No	None	Mari-juana Only	Few Pills	More Pills	Any Her-oin
5. Almost everyday	71.5	73.8	69.4	70.6	80.9	69.8	73.8	75.8	63.4	70.3	75.2	73.4	74.8	72.9	65.8	65.7
4. At least once a week	23.4	21.3	25.2	23.9	17.8	24.1	22.7	20.3	28.7	24.1	20.9	21.9	21.4	22.6	27.2	25.8
3. Once or twice a month	3.9	3.4	4.5	4.2	0.8	4.9	2.4	3.0	6.3	4.5	2.8	3.7	2.9	3.0	5.5	6.3
2. A few times a year	0.7	0.9	0.7	0.8	0.2	0.7	0.7	0.6	1.0	0.6	0.7	0.6	0.6	1.2	0.8	2.2
1. Never	0.4	0.6	0.3	0.5	0.3	0.5	0.4	0.2	0.7	0.4	0.4	0.4	0.3	0.3	0.6	-
Item 5820 Subject C07 N	3300	1560	1639	2468	383	769	904	1006	621	1903	1164	1272	692	446	780	47

A02B: Go to movies

	TOTAL	M	F	White	Black	NE	NC	S	W	Yes	No	None	Mari-juana Only	Few Pills	More Pills	Any Her-oin
5. Almost everyday	0.4	0.5	0.2	0.4	0.7	0.3	0.1	0.9	0.1	0.4	0.5	0.6	0.2	0.4	-	4.3
4. At least once a week	11.3	11.9	10.7	10.9	11.8	12.8	8.4	10.7	14.6	11.1	12.1	10.0	11.8	12.0	11.8	20.8
3. Once or twice a month	58.1	56.1	60.8	60.7	49.9	59.1	60.5	55.1	58.4	61.2	53.6	57.9	57.4	61.6	57.4	52.3
2. A few times a year	28.3	30.2	26.2	26.8	33.8	26.5	29.1	31.0	25.2	26.0	31.5	28.8	29.5	25.4	29.4	21.5
1. Never	1.8	1.4	2.1	1.2	3.7	1.2	1.8	2.2	1.7	1.4	2.3	2.7	1.2	0.5	1.4	1.1
Item 5830 Subject C07 N	3298	1561	1637	2466	384	769	903	1004	622	1901	1164	1270	692	446	780	47

A02C: Go to rock concerts

	TOTAL	M	F	White	Black	NE	NC	S	W	Yes	No	None	Mari-juana Only	Few Pills	More Pills	Any Her-oin
5. Almost everyday	0.1	0.2	-	0.1	-	-	-	0.3	0.1	0.1	0.1	-	-	-	0.2	4.3
4. At least once a week	0.4	0.5	0.2	0.4	0.3	1.2	0.3	*	0.3	0.2	0.6	-	0.4	0.1	1.2	2.5
3. Once or twice a month	4.9	6.8	3.0	5.2	2.5	5.3	5.3	3.9	5.6	4.4	5.8	1.5	4.3	3.9	11.1	16.1
2. A few times a year	52.1	53.7	51.2	57.3	32.5	54.0	52.8	51.3	50.3	55.9	47.2	39.9	57.0	60.9	63.0	61.3
1. Never	42.4	38.8	45.6	36.9	64.8	39.6	41.6	44.5	43.7	39.4	46.2	58.6	38.3	35.1	24.5	15.8
Item 5845 Subject C07 N	3316	1570	1644	2479	384	767	911	1014	624	1913	1170	1277	696	453	783	47

A02D: Ride around in a car (or motorcycle) just for fun

	TOTAL	M	F	White	Black	NE	NC	S	W	Yes	No	None	Mari-juana Only	Few Pills	More Pills	Any Her-oin
5. Almost everyday	35.2	38.5	31.1	35.1	35.5	34.8	33.8	38.2	32.8	28.2	45.6	24.7	32.1	38.4	50.2	59.8
4. At least once a week	32.9	33.2	32.3	32.9	35.6	31.3	35.0	33.3	31.2	34.6	29.5	33.8	37.2	32.8	29.2	17.4
3. Once or twice a month	15.2	15.0	16.1	16.1	11.5	15.3	16.7	13.7	15.4	17.0	13.4	18.1	14.1	13.6	13.2	6.9
2. A few times a year	9.6	7.0	12.4	9.8	8.1	9.8	9.6	8.9	10.6	11.5	7.1	13.7	9.5	8.6	4.2	5.6
1. Never	7.0	6.3	8.1	6.1	9.3	8.8	4.9	5.8	10.0	8.8	4.5	9.7	7.1	6.6	3.1	10.2
Item 5850 Subject C07 N	3317	1569	1646	2478	386	766	910	1016	625	1913	1171	1279	696	452	781	47

A02E: Participate in community affairs or volunteer work

	TOTAL	M	F	White	Black	NE	NC	S	W	Yes	No	None	Mari-juana Only	Few Pills	More Pills	Any Her-oin
5. Almost everyday	2.5	2.1	2.9	2.1	4.4	3.4	1.4	3.6	1.4	2.3	2.8	3.3	1.5	2.8	2.2	2.1
4. At least once a week	7.6	6.1	8.8	7.7	7.2	7.9	8.8	6.2	7.9	9.7	4.1	9.8	7.3	6.7	4.2	10.8
3. Once or twice a month	12.4	10.9	13.9	13.3	12.1	10.6	12.6	15.6	9.0	14.0	9.2	14.0	11.2	13.2	9.8	13.7
2. A few times a year	46.3	43.1	49.8	47.4	46.8	41.7	47.3	50.1	44.3	49.5	43.7	48.1	47.8	46.9	43.1	38.9
1. Never	31.2	37.8	24.7	29.6	29.5	36.4	29.9	24.5	37.4	24.5	40.2	24.8	32.2	30.4	40.7	34.5
Item 5860 Subject C07,O02 N	3302	1564	1636	2478	380	765	910	1007	620	1905	1168	1268	693	453	780	47

A02F: Play a musical instrument or sing

	TOTAL	M	F	White	Black	NE	NC	S	W	Yes	No	None	Mari-juana Only	Few Pills	More Pills	Any Her-oin
5. Almost everyday	29.3	23.7	35.2	28.9	35.5	29.1	30.4	29.7	27.6	34.0	21.8	34.2	26.4	30.5	23.9	29.8
4. At least once a week	8.7	7.7	9.8	8.2	13.0	6.5	8.0	9.7	10.7	10.4	5.9	9.5	10.1	6.8	7.5	7.7
3. Once or twice a month	5.2	4.3	6.3	5.2	5.6	3.8	5.7	6.5	4.3	5.3	5.6	5.2	6.3	4.8	4.7	7.1
2. A few times a year	11.6	11.2	12.0	11.4	12.7	10.1	11.0	12.2	13.7	12.4	10.2	10.3	13.2	13.0	12.0	12.8
1. Never	45.1	53.1	36.8	46.4	33.3	50.6	44.9	42.0	43.6	37.9	56.5	40.7	44.1	45.0	52.0	42.6
Item 5870 Subject C07 N	3303	1566	1636	2474	382	767	909	1005	622	1906	1167	1272	692	450	781	47

*=less than .05 per cent.

QUESTIONNAIRE FORM 2 1985	TOTAL	SEX		RACE		REGION				4YR COLLEGE PLANS		ILLICIT DRUG USE: LIFETIME				
		M	F	White	Black	NE	NC	S	W	Yes	No	None	Marijuana Only	Few Pills	More Pills	Any Heroin
N (Weighted No. of Cases):	3327	1573	1651	2485	388	771	914	1017	625	1919	1172	1283	696	453	784	47
% of Weighted Total:	100.0	47.3	49.6	74.7	11.7	23.2	27.5	30.6	18.8	57.7	35.2	38.6	20.9	13.6	23.6	1.4
A02G: Do creative writing																
5. Almost everyday	5.8	4.3	7.3	5.5	8.7	4.0	7.5	5.4	6.4	6.3	4.5	6.3	5.5	5.0	5.8	7.3
4. At least once a week	13.2	11.5	15.1	12.7	14.0	11.4	13.1	11.7	18.0	16.9	7.5	14.4	11.8	13.2	12.3	17.5
3. Once or twice a month	19.4	17.4	21.5	19.8	20.2	18.0	19.6	19.3	21.0	24.3	11.5	20.4	18.6	19.6	19.0	15.3
2. A few times a year	28.5	28.5	28.8	28.6	25.9	28.4	25.1	31.1	29.2	29.4	28.1	27.8	28.4	29.6	30.0	16.2
1. Never	33.1	38.3	27.2	33.4	31.2	38.3	34.7	32.6	25.3	23.2	48.3	31.1	35.7	32.7	32.9	43.8
Item 5880 Subject C07 N	3297	1562	1635	2471	381	765	906	1007	620	1901	1166	1275	692	446	778	47
A02H: Actively participate in sports, athletics or exercising																
5. Almost everyday	42.9	52.8	33.5	42.6	45.4	46.2	41.2	39.8	46.5	49.6	32.6	43.8	46.2	41.9	39.1	37.0
4. At least once a week	25.8	23.7	28.1	26.8	21.9	24.5	27.5	26.0	24.8	25.1	27.1	25.4	24.8	27.8	26.2	29.7
3. Once or twice a month	13.3	8.5	18.0	14.0	9.1	12.0	13.4	13.7	14.0	11.2	16.4	11.3	13.4	12.3	16.9	18.3
2. A few times a year	11.5	9.5	13.3	10.8	14.1	9.9	12.4	13.6	8.9	9.7	14.2	12.4	10.9	12.5	10.6	9.5
1. Never	6.4	5.5	7.1	5.7	9.4	7.4	5.6	6.9	5.7	4.4	9.8	7.1	4.6	5.5	7.2	5.5
Item 5890 Subject C07 N	3308	1569	1639	2477	381	767	911	1007	623	1911	1169	1272	696	450	781	47
A02I: Do art or craft work																
5. Almost everyday	11.1	11.7	10.2	10.1	11.2	11.7	10.8	9.7	12.9	10.0	11.8	10.3	10.4	8.6	14.2	14.2
4. At least once a week	9.8	9.6	10.0	10.5	7.6	10.2	8.6	8.8	12.8	10.0	8.8	9.3	7.0	12.5	11.1	17.2
3. Once or twice a month	16.3	16.0	16.5	17.3	12.0	16.1	17.3	14.9	17.2	18.4	13.1	18.1	14.9	13.2	16.9	12.4
2. A few times a year	31.2	29.7	33.3	32.7	26.8	27.9	34.2	31.4	30.4	33.8	28.6	32.1	34.3	34.9	26.2	15.4
1. Never	31.7	32.9	30.0	29.3	42.6	34.2	29.1	35.3	26.6	27.8	37.7	30.2	33.4	30.8	31.7	40.9
Item 5900 Subject C07 N	3297	1563	1633	2471	380	765	909	1004	618	1905	1165	1271	692	453	773	47
A02J: Work around the house, yard, garden, car, etc.																
5. Almost everyday	35.3	27.9	42.4	32.1	51.8	28.6	37.2	38.7	35.2	32.7	40.2	37.7	33.3	37.0	32.6	22.3
4. At least once a week	38.6	43.9	33.3	41.2	26.2	35.4	38.8	39.6	40.5	39.7	36.6	38.8	37.6	38.2	39.0	42.4
3. Once or twice a month	16.9	18.8	15.2	18.0	12.2	20.7	17.3	14.3	16.1	18.3	14.6	15.0	20.2	15.8	18.1	18.4
2. A few times a year	7.3	7.3	7.4	7.0	7.9	12.1	4.8	5.9	7.2	7.4	6.6	7.4	6.9	7.0	7.7	6.9
1. Never	2.0	2.1	1.8	1.7	1.9	3.2	2.0	1.6	1.1	1.9	1.9	1.1	2.1	2.0	2.5	10.0
Item 5910 Subject C07 N	3315	1568	1646	2482	383	768	911	1012	624	1914	1170	1281	693	451	781	47
A02K: Get together with friends, informally																
5. Almost everyday	47.2	51.8	42.5	47.9	45.1	49.6	41.5	47.8	51.5	46.3	48.4	38.3	47.2	48.2	58.9	65.2
4. At least once a week	39.9	37.8	42.1	40.7	40.1	38.0	45.8	39.0	35.1	41.9	37.6	42.4	42.5	44.0	32.7	28.7
3. Once or twice a month	9.8	7.0	12.7	9.3	9.7	8.7	10.1	9.8	10.5	9.3	10.4	14.5	8.5	6.2	5.7	0.8
2. A few times a year	2.2	2.3	2.0	1.5	3.2	2.2	1.9	2.5	2.0	1.9	2.6	3.3	1.2	0.8	1.8	4.2
1. Never	1.0	1.2	0.8	0.7	1.9	1.6	0.7	0.8	0.9	0.7	1.0	1.4	0.5	0.8	0.9	1.1
Item 5920 Subject C07,M04 N	3303	1565	1636	2470	385	766	913	1002	622	1908	1165	1272	693	446	782	47
A02L: Go shopping or window-shopping																
5. Almost everyday	3.4	1.4	5.0	2.7	4.7	4.4	2.0	3.8	3.4	2.9	4.0	2.5	3.2	3.2	4.1	12.0
4. At least once a week	36.0	24.6	47.3	34.2	40.8	36.3	34.9	37.2	35.1	38.0	33.8	37.3	33.5	37.2	36.3	29.7
3. Once or twice a month	44.9	47.6	42.8	47.0	42.8	42.8	47.9	43.1	46.0	45.9	43.6	43.6	48.4	48.0	44.2	30.3
2. A few times a year	11.7	18.7	4.7	11.7	10.5	12.0	11.8	11.3	11.8	10.7	12.8	13.0	11.6	9.0	10.8	6.6
1. Never	4.0	7.6	0.2	4.3	1.3	4.5	3.4	4.5	3.6	2.5	5.8	3.6	3.4	2.6	4.6	21.5
Item 5930 Subject C07,F01 N	3306	1567	1638	2473	382	770	909	1006	621	1913	1163	1276	692	451	779	46
A02M: Spend at least an hour of leisure time alone																
5. Almost everyday	42.0	39.8	44.5	41.2	49.0	43.0	39.6	43.8	41.2	44.4	38.7	39.6	43.6	41.3	45.5	44.0
4. At least once a week	34.4	34.8	33.9	35.1	29.5	34.3	36.2	32.4	35.0	35.5	32.3	36.9	33.4	31.2	33.0	28.1
3. Once or twice a month	12.7	12.5	12.7	13.5	8.5	11.5	14.1	11.9	13.3	12.0	13.4	11.9	14.0	16.3	10.3	14.6
2. A few times a year	5.6	6.6	4.7	5.3	5.0	5.4	4.9	6.4	5.4	4.8	6.9	6.4	5.0	5.0	5.1	3.4
1. Never	5.4	6.3	4.2	4.9	8.0	5.8	5.3	5.6	5.0	3.3	8.8	5.2	3.9	6.2	6.3	10.0
Item 5940 Subject C07 N	3306	1565	1640	2476	381	764	908	1011	622	1908	1167	1271	695	451	779	47

QUESTIONNAIRE FORM 2 1985	TOTAL	SEX		RACE		REGION				4YR COLLEGE PLANS		ILLICIT DRUG USE: LIFETIME				
		M	F	White	Black	NE	NC	S	W	Yes	No	None	Marijuana Only	Few Pills	More Pills	Any Heroin
N (Weighted No. of Cases):	3327	1573	1651	2485	388	771	914	1017	625	1919	1172	1283	696	453	784	47
% of Weighted Total:	100.0	47.3	49.6	74.7	11.7	23.2	27.5	30.6	18.8	57.7	35.2	38.6	20.9	13.6	23.6	1.4

A02N: Read books, magazines, or newspapers

	TOTAL	M	F	White	Black	NE	NC	S	W	Yes	No	None	Marijuana Only	Few Pills	More Pills	Any Heroin
5. Almost everyday	50.5	49.7	52.1	51.2	51.5	50.7	53.5	47.1	51.6	57.0	42.5	52.5	52.3	49.7	48.6	26.3
4. At least once a week	30.7	29.8	31.2	30.1	33.3	28.7	27.6	33.6	33.0	29.6	32.1	30.2	29.8	31.8	31.6	27.3
3. Once or twice a month	12.1	12.5	11.8	13.0	8.2	12.7	13.0	11.9	10.5	9.6	15.6	11.0	12.3	14.0	12.3	19.4
2. A few times a year	4.3	5.1	3.5	3.7	5.5	4.6	3.8	4.9	3.3	2.9	5.9	4.6	4.2	3.0	4.3	9.7
1. Never	2.3	2.9	1.4	1.9	1.5	3.2	2.0	2.5	1.6	0.9	3.9	1.7	1.4	1.5	3.2	17.4
Item 5950　Subject C07　N	3316	1570	1646	2480	384	769	910	1014	623	1915	1170	1277	696	453	781	47

A02O: Go to taverns, bars or nightclubs

	TOTAL	M	F	White	Black	NE	NC	S	W	Yes	No	None	Marijuana Only	Few Pills	More Pills	Any Heroin
5. Almost everyday	1.9	2.8	1.0	2.0	0.4	1.7	3.1	1.5	0.9	1.1	2.9	1.0	1.2	1.1	3.6	12.8
4. At least once a week	11.5	13.6	9.0	10.6	13.2	16.2	9.2	12.9	7.0	9.2	14.2	6.5	11.4	12.2	18.4	31.0
3. Once or twice a month	18.2	19.2	17.0	18.5	15.6	21.7	16.1	18.8	16.1	18.2	17.9	9.3	21.6	21.6	27.1	25.3
2. A few times a year	22.1	23.4	21.3	23.9	18.1	24.1	22.5	21.5	20.2	24.4	19.1	20.2	25.1	22.2	23.2	16.1
1. Never	46.2	41.0	51.7	44.9	52.7	36.3	49.1	45.3	55.8	47.2	46.0	62.9	40.7	42.8	27.7	14.8
Item 5960　Subject C07　N	3314	1567	1646	2476	386	769	907	1015	623	1914	1168	1278	693	453	781	47

A02P: Go to parties or other social affairs

	TOTAL	M	F	White	Black	NE	NC	S	W	Yes	No	None	Marijuana Only	Few Pills	More Pills	Any Heroin
5. Almost everyday	3.3	4.9	1.7	3.3	1.4	4.9	3.1	2.0	4.0	2.1	5.2	1.0	2.2	2.9	6.7	22.9
4. At least once a week	32.5	34.7	29.8	33.5	26.5	35.7	33.5	27.5	35.3	34.0	29.9	18.2	37.1	36.6	47.8	45.5
3. Once or twice a month	36.7	36.2	37.9	37.6	39.9	34.0	39.1	38.8	33.3	38.7	33.9	39.1	39.3	38.4	31.1	24.9
2. A few times a year	23.6	20.2	27.0	22.3	25.1	22.6	20.5	27.4	23.4	22.0	26.4	34.9	19.4	19.6	13.3	4.1
1. Never	3.8	4.0	3.5	3.2	7.0	2.8	3.8	4.3	4.1	3.1	4.6	6.8	2.0	2.4	1.2	2.6
Item 5970　Subject C07　N	3322	1573	1647	2483	386	768	913	1015	625	1917	1171	1281	696	453	783	47

A03: How much do you agree or disagree with each of the following statements?

A03A: In the United States, we put too much emphasis on making profits and not enough on human well-being

	TOTAL	M	F	White	Black	NE	NC	S	W	Yes	No	None	Marijuana Only	Few Pills	More Pills	Any Heroin
1. Disagree	5.9	8.4	3.4	5.5	5.4	7.6	4.2	6.0	5.9	6.6	4.5	6.4	4.9	3.0	7.1	15.9
2. Mostly disagree	9.6	11.9	7.3	10.1	6.4	9.5	8.5	10.1	10.6	10.4	9.0	10.7	11.5	8.6	7.7	-
3. Neither	19.2	21.4	16.9	20.5	11.2	18.1	20.6	16.3	22.9	18.4	20.3	18.7	18.2	19.6	19.8	32.9
4. Mostly agree	44.1	40.0	48.7	46.4	39.2	41.1	47.9	44.2	42.2	45.6	43.5	43.0	43.0	50.8	44.3	32.1
5. Agree	21.3	18.2	23.7	17.5	37.8	23.7	18.7	23.5	18.4	19.0	22.7	21.1	22.5	18.1	21.1	19.2
Item 5990　Subject F03,O03　N	3305	1570	1636	2475	382	765	909	1007	623	1908	1166	1273	694	452	778	45

A03B: People are too much concerned with material things these days

	TOTAL	M	F	White	Black	NE	NC	S	W	Yes	No	None	Marijuana Only	Few Pills	More Pills	Any Heroin
1. Disagree	3.9	5.2	2.3	3.3	6.7	5.8	2.6	4.3	2.7	3.2	4.3	2.9	4.2	3.1	5.3	4.3
2. Mostly disagree	6.4	7.9	4.8	6.9	4.8	7.1	5.8	6.0	6.9	6.5	6.0	6.3	6.5	5.9	6.6	3.5
3. Neither	11.2	16.0	6.7	11.4	7.2	12.2	13.2	8.7	11.0	10.1	13.0	9.5	11.9	13.6	11.6	25.5
4. Mostly agree	41.7	38.8	44.8	44.0	32.8	39.3	44.2	39.6	44.3	43.4	40.7	42.2	43.1	45.5	38.3	31.0
5. Agree	36.9	32.1	41.5	34.3	48.5	35.6	34.2	41.5	35.1	36.8	36.0	39.2	34.2	31.9	38.1	35.7
Item 6000　Subject F02　N	3307	1565	1641	2476	384	764	911	1010	622	1907	1169	1278	694	452	774	47

A03C: Since it helps the economy to grow, people should be encouraged to buy more

	TOTAL	M	F	White	Black	NE	NC	S	W	Yes	No	None	Marijuana Only	Few Pills	More Pills	Any Heroin
1. Disagree	15.6	14.1	17.3	14.0	25.6	15.0	14.6	17.9	14.4	12.9	19.4	15.3	15.2	16.5	16.2	16.0
2. Mostly disagree	22.3	18.7	25.3	22.9	18.9	27.4	22.1	19.4	21.1	20.9	24.6	20.1	21.9	28.7	21.3	23.1
3. Neither	32.1	29.5	35.3	33.9	22.0	29.5	34.0	31.0	34.4	35.7	27.1	33.6	31.6	28.6	32.5	34.5
4. Mostly agree	19.6	23.1	15.7	19.7	17.4	18.9	20.1	20.2	18.6	20.6	17.9	20.5	20.7	17.1	19.0	22.0
5. Agree	10.4	14.6	6.4	9.4	16.0	9.2	9.3	11.5	11.5	9.9	11.0	10.5	10.5	9.1	11.0	4.4
Item 6010　Subject F02　N	3303	1562	1640	2474	385	765	911	1013	614	1907	1167	1279	691	447	777	47

QUESTIONNAIRE FORM 2 1985	TOTAL	SEX		RACE		REGION				4YR COLLEGE PLANS		ILLICIT DRUG USE: LIFETIME				
		M	F	White	Black	NE	NC	S	W	Yes	No	None	Mari- juana Only	Few Pills	More Pills	Any Her- oin
N (Weighted No. of Cases):	3327	1573	1651	2485	388	771	914	1017	625	1919	1172	1283	696	453	784	47
% of Weighted Total:	100.0	47.3	49.6	74.7	11.7	23.2	27.5	30.6	18.8	57.7	35.2	38.6	20.9	13.6	23.6	1.4
A03D: There is nothing wrong with advertising that gets people to buy things they don't really need																
1. Disagree	31.1	28.6	33.7	30.7	35.2	32.9	27.1	32.2	32.9	30.6	32.6	33.3	28.5	29.9	31.8	19.9
2. Mostly disagree	24.8	22.8	26.9	27.0	16.3	22.3	27.4	24.3	25.2	26.9	21.9	25.7	25.9	26.4	22.4	9.2
3. Neither	16.2	16.5	15.9	16.9	10.7	15.2	20.0	14.4	14.8	16.2	16.3	14.9	14.1	17.6	18.5	29.5
4. Mostly agree	15.5	16.7	14.1	15.4	13.4	16.1	15.8	14.2	16.7	15.7	15.3	15.3	17.4	12.8	15.3	23.9
5. Agree	12.4	15.3	9.3	10.1	24.4	13.5	9.8	15.0	10.4	10.6	13.9	10.8	14.0	13.3	12.0	17.4
Item 6020 Subject F02 N	3309	1567	1641	2479	383	764	912	1011	622	1907	1171	1279	693	449	779	47
A03E: There will probably be more shortages in the future, so Americans will have to learn how to be happy with fewer "things"																
1. Disagree	10.1	13.4	6.8	9.2	13.3	12.7	8.9	9.7	9.3	9.1	10.9	8.7	10.3	8.5	12.8	19.6
2. Mostly disagree	12.9	14.6	11.6	14.2	7.6	15.8	13.7	10.7	11.7	15.2	9.5	12.4	14.6	12.9	13.3	4.3
3. Neither	16.7	15.6	17.4	17.9	8.1	17.4	17.4	15.8	16.4	18.1	15.1	17.6	16.2	15.1	14.9	26.7
4. Mostly agree	29.5	26.7	32.3	30.9	24.0	30.5	31.8	25.9	30.9	30.6	28.0	30.5	26.1	30.0	31.4	21.5
5. Agree	30.7	29.6	31.9	27.9	46.9	23.6	28.1	37.8	31.8	27.1	36.7	30.7	32.8	33.6	27.6	28.0
Item 6030 Subject F02 N	3313	1569	1643	2478	387	766	912	1013	622	1911	1171	1277	696	452	780	47
A04: Below are several ways that people have used to protest about serious social issues. How much do you approve or disapprove of these actions?																
A04A: Signing petitions																
4. Strongly approve	22.8	22.8	23.3	24.2	16.7	22.9	20.7	21.2	28.1	27.6	15.6	22.6	24.0	21.6	22.9	30.5
3. Approve	46.7	45.6	48.0	48.5	39.4	45.2	50.1	43.7	48.4	49.5	43.5	47.5	45.9	44.9	48.6	36.1
2. Disapprove	3.6	4.5	2.5	3.4	4.2	5.4	3.0	3.8	1.9	2.5	4.6	3.1	4.2	3.8	3.0	5.4
1. Strongly disapprove	0.9	1.6	0.2	0.9	0.3	1.5	1.0	0.6	0.5	0.3	1.8	0.8	0.8	0.5	1.4	1.9
8. Don't know, or it depends	26.0	25.6	26.0	23.0	39.3	24.8	25.2	30.6	21.2	20.1	34.4	26.1	25.1	29.2	24.0	26.1
Item 6040 Subject I02 N	3306	1563	1644	2478	383	764	911	1008	623	1912	1166	1272	696	453	779	47
A04B: Boycotting certain products or stores																
4. Strongly approve	12.5	14.6	10.7	12.7	12.4	14.7	11.6	10.6	14.0	16.1	7.0	12.5	14.5	11.6	11.7	6.4
3. Approve	31.6	34.1	29.1	31.8	30.1	31.8	32.2	30.0	33.1	35.7	25.9	31.5	27.6	33.6	34.5	34.9
2. Disapprove	15.1	14.8	15.0	16.0	10.2	15.4	13.6	16.7	14.5	12.6	18.5	14.2	16.3	14.7	14.5	26.6
1. Strongly disapprove	4.6	5.5	3.9	4.6	4.7	5.1	5.1	3.9	4.6	4.0	5.1	4.3	3.8	3.7	6.6	3.2
8. Don't know, or it depends	36.2	30.9	41.3	34.9	42.6	33.0	37.5	38.8	33.9	31.6	43.6	37.5	37.8	36.4	32.7	28.9
Item 6050 Subject I02 N	3291	1554	1637	2469	383	761	906	1003	621	1904	1163	1271	693	444	777	47
A04C: Lawful demonstrations																
4. Strongly approve	16.0	18.6	14.1	16.5	15.6	18.6	14.9	14.0	17.8	20.0	9.6	15.1	16.9	16.6	16.0	23.2
3. Approve	45.5	46.9	44.2	47.2	38.5	42.9	47.0	44.8	47.8	48.6	41.0	45.9	45.8	45.7	45.9	40.8
2. Disapprove	9.6	9.6	9.4	10.1	7.3	9.4	8.7	11.3	8.4	8.4	11.7	10.0	9.3	8.6	9.5	3.5
1. Strongly disapprove	3.4	3.5	3.0	2.7	6.1	3.0	3.8	3.5	3.0	2.3	4.7	3.5	3.6	3.7	2.5	5.8
8. Don't know, or it depends	25.5	21.4	29.4	23.6	32.5	26.2	25.7	26.5	23.0	20.6	33.0	25.5	24.3	25.4	26.0	26.6
Item 6060 Subject I02 N	3287	1554	1635	2472	378	761	901	1003	622	1906	1158	1265	692	449	776	47
A04D: Occupying buildings or factories																
4. Strongly approve	4.9	6.1	3.6	4.0	8.3	5.9	3.3	5.6	4.9	4.0	5.7	3.9	4.3	6.9	4.7	21.3
3. Approve	21.9	21.3	22.2	20.6	30.1	20.6	24.0	20.6	22.4	18.9	25.4	21.8	20.1	22.1	23.0	22.6
2. Disapprove	25.0	26.1	24.6	27.2	17.7	25.9	26.7	23.8	23.3	28.6	20.9	26.2	25.1	23.9	24.7	19.9
1. Strongly disapprove	9.4	11.8	7.1	9.9	5.9	9.9	8.2	11.1	8.0	10.7	7.2	10.3	10.4	8.7	8.1	3.2
8. Don't know, or it depends	38.8	34.7	42.4	38.2	37.9	37.8	37.8	38.9	41.5	37.8	40.8	37.7	40.1	38.3	39.5	33.0
Item 6070 Subject I02 N	3270	1547	1625	2454	377	755	904	997	614	1890	1154	1260	687	450	768	46
A04E: Wildcat strikes																
4. Strongly approve	3.0	4.2	1.7	2.8	3.7	4.6	1.5	3.4	2.4	2.7	2.9	2.2	2.6	3.5	3.6	10.8
3. Approve	10.4	13.2	7.7	10.6	9.5	11.7	12.6	8.1	9.2	9.4	11.7	8.5	10.8	10.2	13.6	13.1
2. Disapprove	27.9	27.7	28.1	29.6	18.9	26.7	26.0	28.8	30.7	29.7	26.5	27.7	28.3	27.2	28.9	20.1
1. Strongly disapprove	16.1	17.2	15.1	15.5	18.3	17.5	15.8	16.6	13.8	15.7	16.4	18.8	15.5	17.2	12.0	6.8
8. Don't know, or it depends	42.7	37.6	47.5	41.4	49.5	39.5	44.1	43.2	43.9	42.4	42.5	42.8	42.7	42.0	42.0	49.1
Item 6080 Subject I02 N	3259	1542	1619	2448	374	750	900	993	616	1886	1154	1258	687	444	766	45

QUESTIONNAIRE FORM 2 1985	TOTAL	SEX		RACE		REGION				4YR COLLEGE PLANS		ILLICIT DRUG USE: LIFETIME				
		M	F	White	Black	NE	NC	S	W	Yes	No	None	Mari- juana Only	Few Pills	More Pills	Any Her- oin
N (Weighted No. of Cases):	3327	1573	1651	2485	388	771	914	1017	625	1919	1172	1283	696	453	784	47
% of Weighted Total:	100.0	47.3	49.6	74.7	11.7	23.2	27.5	30.6	18.8	57.7	35.2	38.6	20.9	13.6	23.6	1.4

A04F: Blocking traffic

	TOTAL	M	F	White	Black	NE	NC	S	W	Yes	No	None	Mari- juana Only	Few Pills	More Pills	Any Her- oin
4. Strongly approve	1.8	2.6	1.0	1.5	1.9	3.0	1.1	2.0	1.4	1.5	1.8	1.3	1.0	3.5	2.0	7.4
3. Approve	3.9	4.5	3.1	3.1	4.6	4.9	3.5	4.0	3.1	3.6	3.9	2.7	4.0	3.0	5.9	4.5
2. Disapprove	39.2	36.5	42.3	39.8	39.6	36.7	38.8	40.3	41.3	41.1	37.9	40.9	41.6	38.2	35.5	35.8
1. Strongly disapprove	42.0	43.7	40.9	43.5	39.9	42.6	42.2	40.9	42.4	42.1	42.2	41.6	41.4	40.9	45.1	32.1
8. Don't know, or it depends	13.1	12.7	12.7	12.1	14.0	12.8	14.5	12.9	11.8	11.7	14.1	13.4	12.0	14.4	11.5	20.1
Item 6090 Subject I02 N	3283	1552	1631	2462	378	759	905	999	620	1898	1160	1260	692	450	775	45

A04G: Damaging things

	TOTAL	M	F	White	Black	NE	NC	S	W	Yes	No	None	Mari- juana Only	Few Pills	More Pills	Any Her- oin
4. Strongly approve	3.1	4.4	1.9	2.7	3.0	5.8	2.5	2.4	1.8	2.6	3.8	2.1	2.1	3.6	4.7	14.0
3. Approve	2.8	3.3	2.1	2.0	3.8	2.6	2.9	3.0	2.5	2.1	3.7	2.8	1.5	2.5	3.8	9.4
2. Disapprove	20.2	22.5	17.7	19.2	26.5	21.0	19.8	20.9	18.6	19.1	21.6	18.9	21.3	18.9	21.1	23.6
1. Strongly disapprove	67.3	60.7	74.4	70.3	58.4	64.6	68.4	66.5	70.4	70.8	63.0	70.6	67.7	67.7	64.3	44.0
8. Don't know, or it depends	6.6	9.1	3.9	5.7	8.3	5.9	6.6	7.2	6.7	5.5	7.8	5.6	7.4	7.3	6.1	8.9
Item 6100 Subject I02 N	3297	1565	1636	2475	380	763	910	1004	621	1910	1164	1269	694	452	777	47

A04H: Personal violence

	TOTAL	M	F	White	Black	NE	NC	S	W	Yes	No	None	Mari- juana Only	Few Pills	More Pills	Any Her- oin
4. Strongly approve	3.2	4.2	2.0	2.6	3.9	4.6	2.7	2.9	2.7	2.3	4.0	2.7	2.3	4.1	3.8	11.5
3. Approve	3.4	5.1	1.5	2.9	4.0	5.2	3.5	2.8	2.0	2.2	4.7	2.7	2.3	2.5	5.3	9.6
2. Disapprove	18.1	21.8	14.5	17.1	20.3	18.7	17.4	17.2	19.9	16.2	20.9	15.5	21.3	18.0	19.3	21.8
1. Strongly disapprove	65.9	56.5	76.0	69.3	58.4	60.1	67.7	67.2	68.3	72.5	57.8	71.3	64.7	66.5	61.1	39.1
8. Don't know, or it depends	9.4	12.4	6.0	8.1	13.4	11.4	8.8	9.8	7.1	6.8	12.5	7.7	9.4	9.0	10.6	18.0
Item 6110 Subject I02 N	3305	1566	1639	2480	380	766	912	1004	623	1911	1168	1269	695	453	781	47

A05: Do you think that you would prefer having a mate for most of your life, or would you prefer not having a mate?

	TOTAL	M	F	White	Black	NE	NC	S	W	Yes	No	None	Mari- juana Only	Few Pills	More Pills	Any Her- oin
5. Definitely prefer to have a mate	60.2	56.9	63.9	63.8	50.9	58.7	59.8	60.0	63.2	60.5	60.6	63.0	59.4	59.6	57.4	52.1
4. Probably prefer to have a mate	24.7	26.5	23.0	23.7	27.2	25.6	25.7	23.2	24.6	25.7	23.2	23.3	27.0	24.8	26.1	20.4
3. Not sure	11.4	12.1	10.5	9.5	17.6	12.9	9.6	13.4	8.9	10.4	12.6	10.9	10.8	12.0	11.3	16.5
2. Probably prefer not to have a mate	2.6	3.4	1.9	2.3	2.9	2.2	4.0	1.8	2.2	2.4	2.7	2.0	2.3	2.0	4.1	3.0
1. Definitely prefer not to have a mate	1.0	1.2	0.7	0.8	1.3	0.5	0.8	1.6	1.0	0.9	0.9	0.8	0.5	1.5	1.1	8.0
Item 6120 Subject D01 N	3308	1566	1641	2473	384	768	908	1011	621	1907	1167	1275	694	451	781	47

A06: Which do you think you are most likely to choose in the long run?

	TOTAL	M	F	White	Black	NE	NC	S	W	Yes	No	None	Mari- juana Only	Few Pills	More Pills	Any Her- oin
3. Getting married	76.4	73.2	80.3	80.1	62.4	75.7	76.7	74.4	79.9	79.2	73.6	79.9	77.9	74.6	72.2	52.4
2. I have no idea	17.0	20.6	12.9	14.7	25.5	17.0	16.9	18.7	14.6	14.5	19.3	14.9	16.7	18.7	18.3	34.1
1. Not getting married	5.7	5.7	5.5	4.2	11.4	6.6	5.9	5.2	5.1	5.8	5.6	4.5	4.8	5.3	8.3	8.4
8. Am already married	0.9	0.5	1.2	0.9	0.7	0.7	0.6	1.7	0.4	0.5	1.5	0.7	0.6	1.4	1.2	5.1
Item 6130 Subject D01 N	3263	1542	1624	2449	373	756	900	996	611	1888	1146	1260	680	448	771	46

A07: If you did get married (or are married) . . .

A07A: How likely do you think it is that you would stay married to the same person for life?

	TOTAL	M	F	White	Black	NE	NC	S	W	Yes	No	None	Mari- juana Only	Few Pills	More Pills	Any Her- oin
5. Very likely	61.7	55.9	68.1	63.7	54.1	57.4	61.3	63.7	64.1	64.4	58.9	69.3	59.9	61.3	52.6	41.1
4. Fairly likely	23.0	25.7	20.2	23.2	19.8	27.9	23.6	20.5	20.4	23.4	22.5	19.0	25.1	23.8	27.6	23.8
3. Uncertain	12.2	14.7	9.2	10.3	21.3	11.7	12.1	12.1	12.8	9.7	14.5	9.7	12.4	12.5	14.4	25.1
2. Fairly unlikely	1.9	2.4	1.4	1.7	2.6	1.8	1.9	2.1	1.7	1.7	2.2	1.4	1.8	1.8	2.5	4.2
1. Very unlikely	1.3	1.4	1.1	1.2	2.2	1.3	1.1	1.5	1.0	0.7	1.8	0.5	0.9	0.6	2.9	5.7
Item 6140 Subject D01 N	3170	1504	1568	2368	366	716	876	987	591	1817	1130	1220	669	431	747	47

A07B: How likely is it that you would want to have children?

	TOTAL	M	F	White	Black	NE	NC	S	W	Yes	No	None	Mari- juana Only	Few Pills	More Pills	Any Her- oin
5. Very likely	62.1	60.1	64.4	64.9	52.3	61.7	63.0	61.4	62.7	64.4	60.1	65.8	64.8	59.4	57.1	34.5
4. Fairly likely	19.4	21.7	17.0	17.6	22.0	20.3	18.8	18.7	20.1	19.7	18.4	18.5	17.5	19.4	22.0	25.6
3. Uncertain	11.0	12.0	9.8	10.8	14.2	13.0	9.8	11.5	9.4	9.5	12.0	10.5	10.4	11.3	11.6	21.4
2. Fairly unlikely	2.8	2.4	3.2	2.7	2.2	2.3	3.4	2.9	2.4	2.5	3.4	2.3	2.9	3.4	3.3	2.3
1. Very unlikely	3.4	2.6	4.1	3.2	4.7	2.0	2.9	3.9	4.9	3.2	3.9	2.5	2.7	5.1	4.4	4.9
8. Already have child(ren)	1.3	1.2	1.3	0.9	4.8	0.8	2.0	1.6	0.6	0.8	2.3	0.4	1.7	1.4	1.7	11.3
Item 6150 Subject D02 N	3196	1514	1585	2387	371	724	883	988	601	1835	1139	1230	674	440	753	44

QUESTIONNAIRE FORM 2 1985	TOTAL	SEX		RACE		REGION				4YR COLLEGE PLANS		ILLICIT DRUG USE: LIFETIME				
		M	F	White	Black	NE	NC	S	W	Yes	No	None	Mari- juana Only	Few Pills	More Pills	Any Her- oin
N (Weighted No. of Cases):	3327	1573	1651	2485	388	771	914	1017	625	1919	1172	1283	696	453	784	47
% of Weighted Total:	100.0	47.3	49.6	74.7	11.7	23.2	27.5	30.6	18.8	57.7	35.2	38.6	20.9	13.6	23.6	1.4

The questions in the next column ask you to imagine different kinds of married life that you might have. We want you to think about differ- ent ways you might share responsibilities for working, taking care of the home, and taking care of children. Please indicate how accept- able for you each of the different arrangements would be.

A08: Imagine you are married and have no children—how would you feel about each of the following working arrangements?

A08A: Husband works full-time, wife doesn't work

	TOTAL	M	F	White	Black	NE	NC	S	W	Yes	No	None	Mar.	Few	More	Her.
1. Not at all acceptable	27.3	14.2	39.8	23.9	41.9	31.8	24.5	26.1	27.8	29.5	23.4	27.3	29.1	26.6	25.7	21.9
2. Somewhat acceptable	31.2	28.9	33.5	31.3	31.5	27.6	34.7	29.4	33.3	32.3	30.7	31.7	31.0	32.2	30.7	26.0
3. Acceptable	33.8	45.9	22.4	37.2	23.3	31.2	35.8	36.3	30.3	31.3	37.9	33.8	33.4	32.5	34.5	47.2
4. Desirable	7.7	11.0	4.4	7.6	3.3	9.5	5.0	8.2	8.6	6.9	8.1	7.2	6.4	8.7	9.1	4.8
Item 6160 Subject C05,D04 N	3297	1564	1636	2468	381	762	910	1008	617	1903	1168	1269	693	450	778	46

A08B: Husband works full-time, wife works about half-time

1. Not at all acceptable	4.4	2.7	5.9	3.5	7.1	4.7	3.6	4.8	4.6	4.3	4.0	4.8	3.6	3.9	4.3	9.1
2. Somewhat acceptable	21.9	16.0	27.4	19.9	31.6	24.4	20.3	22.7	19.8	22.4	21.4	20.6	24.0	20.1	20.1	13.5
3. Acceptable	57.4	63.3	51.9	59.1	51.0	57.3	58.0	57.6	56.1	55.7	60.4	58.5	56.9	60.2	55.4	65.4
4. Desirable	16.3	17.9	14.8	17.4	10.3	13.6	18.1	14.9	19.5	17.6	14.2	16.1	15.6	12.2	20.1	12.0
Item 6170 Subject C05,D04 N	3301	1563	1640	2470	381	762	909	1009	621	1907	1167	1270	693	452	779	46

A08C: Both work full-time

1. Not at all acceptable	11.2	14.7	7.7	10.2	14.0	11.7	12.4	10.8	9.3	8.9	13.5	10.0	11.2	13.6	11.9	11.4
2. Somewhat acceptable	18.6	23.3	13.8	18.6	13.6	19.9	17.8	17.6	19.5	17.1	19.7	17.5	16.8	19.9	20.7	19.2
3. Acceptable	47.9	46.4	49.0	47.1	54.2	46.1	46.5	50.3	48.4	48.0	48.3	49.4	52.1	43.7	44.5	39.8
4. Desirable	22.3	15.6	29.5	24.0	18.2	22.4	23.2	21.2	22.8	25.9	18.4	23.2	19.9	22.8	22.9	29.7
Item 6180 Subject C05,D04 N	3287	1558	1632	2463	378	757	906	1005	619	1899	1161	1263	691	449	778	46

A08D: Both work about half-time

1. Not at all acceptable	39.8	43.3	36.3	37.8	49.6	41.8	37.1	43.8	34.7	36.1	45.2	37.9	41.3	40.4	41.3	31.6
2. Somewhat acceptable	32.3	29.8	35.1	34.4	26.3	28.7	35.9	31.8	32.3	33.5	31.3	33.1	34.4	33.4	29.6	27.4
3. Acceptable	20.0	20.7	19.4	20.0	18.8	21.6	20.5	17.6	21.4	21.9	16.7	21.3	18.1	15.6	21.2	31.5
4. Desirable	7.9	6.3	9.3	7.8	5.3	7.9	6.4	6.9	11.7	8.4	6.8	7.6	6.2	10.6	7.9	9.6
Item 6190 Subject C05,D04 N	3258	1550	1609	2441	372	748	903	993	614	1884	1149	1243	691	445	772	46

A08E: Husband works about half-time, wife works full-time

1. Not at all acceptable	49.2	54.2	44.2	46.9	58.1	49.5	44.7	55.7	44.8	44.8	54.8	48.8	51.4	48.5	48.3	42.6
2. Somewhat acceptable	29.6	26.5	33.0	31.4	23.6	30.0	31.1	25.6	33.4	32.7	26.2	30.7	29.8	29.4	28.6	29.1
3. Acceptable	18.1	15.8	20.4	19.4	13.8	17.4	20.6	15.4	19.8	20.3	14.6	18.5	16.3	19.1	18.7	20.2
4. Desirable	3.1	3.6	2.3	2.4	4.5	3.1	3.6	3.2	2.0	2.2	4.3	2.1	2.5	2.9	4.4	8.0
Item 6200 Subject C05,D04 N	3288	1560	1631	2466	376	761	904	1004	619	1898	1164	1264	690	451	777	46

A08F: Husband doesn't work, wife works full- time

1. Not at all acceptable	77.4	78.9	75.8	75.4	86.6	78.7	71.5	81.5	77.7	75.6	80.4	75.9	81.2	76.5	77.5	68.7
2. Somewhat acceptable	13.6	11.6	15.6	15.7	6.3	11.6	18.7	10.0	14.3	15.0	11.4	14.9	11.6	14.9	13.2	5.1
3. Acceptable	6.4	6.0	6.9	6.8	3.7	6.4	7.9	5.7	5.6	7.4	4.7	7.2	5.4	6.6	5.2	13.8
4. Desirable	2.6	3.5	1.7	2.1	3.5	3.3	2.0	2.7	2.5	2.0	3.5	2.0	1.8	2.1	4.1	12.3
Item 6210 Subject C05,D04 N	3288	1560	1629	2461	379	757	905	1008	617	1899	1162	1266	693	451	772	46

A09: Imagine you are married and have one or more pre-school children. How would you feel about each of the following working arrange- ments?

QUESTIONNAIRE FORM 2 1985	TOTAL	SEX		RACE		REGION				4YR COLLEGE PLANS		ILLICIT DRUG USE: LIFETIME				
		M	F	White	Black	NE	NC	S	W	Yes	No	None	Mari-juana Only	Few Pills	More Pills	Any Her-oin
N (Weighted No. of Cases):	3327	1573	1651	2485	388	771	914	1017	625	1919	1172	1283	696	453	784	47
% of Weighted Total:	100.0	47.3	49.6	74.7	11.7	23.2	27.5	30.6	18.8	57.7	35.2	38.6	20.9	13.6	23.6	1.4
A09A: Husband works full-time, wife doesn't work																
1. Not at all acceptable	9.5	6.2	12.6	7.6	20.4	9.3	7.2	11.8	9.2	9.4	8.4	9.0	10.4	9.3	9.0	13.9
2. Somewhat acceptable	18.1	13.0	22.2	15.8	26.3	18.2	18.4	17.7	18.1	17.7	18.1	17.7	18.0	19.8	17.9	11.5
3. Acceptable	41.3	43.6	39.4	41.2	43.9	40.3	44.4	41.0	38.6	39.3	45.8	40.9	42.8	41.9	39.9	50.9
4. Desirable	31.1	37.3	25.8	35.3	9.3	32.2	29.9	29.5	34.1	33.6	27.7	32.4	28.8	29.0	33.1	23.8
Item 6220 Subject C05,D04 N	3298	1562	1638	2471	380	762	909	1008	619	1904	1167	1271	693	451	778	46
A09B: Husband works full-time, wife works about half-time																
1. Not at all acceptable	8.7	12.0	5.6	8.6	6.2	11.9	7.5	7.6	8.2	7.9	9.6	8.7	10.3	7.0	7.7	12.7
2. Somewhat acceptable	24.4	27.7	21.6	24.1	27.4	27.1	24.6	23.9	21.4	23.1	25.4	25.7	22.4	25.6	23.9	20.7
3. Acceptable	53.3	50.4	56.0	53.4	55.0	47.9	53.9	57.0	53.0	53.4	54.5	53.1	54.0	54.9	51.9	49.2
4. Desirable	13.6	10.0	16.8	13.9	11.5	13.1	14.0	11.4	17.4	15.7	10.5	12.5	13.3	12.5	16.5	17.4
Item 6230 Subject C05,D04 N	3299	1562	1638	2472	379	763	909	1007	620	1905	1165	1272	692	451	779	46
A09C: Both work full-time																
1. Not at all acceptable	56.0	61.4	51.2	57.7	40.9	63.0	55.8	49.4	58.3	56.5	55.4	56.3	54.8	56.1	57.6	39.0
2. Somewhat acceptable	21.5	18.8	24.1	22.7	17.6	17.4	22.9	22.9	22.5	22.1	20.7	21.6	21.9	19.2	22.4	28.7
3. Acceptable	16.1	13.8	17.8	13.9	28.7	14.2	15.0	20.2	13.2	15.6	16.6	16.2	16.0	17.4	13.9	28.6
4. Desirable	6.4	6.0	6.9	5.7	12.8	5.4	6.3	7.5	6.0	5.8	7.4	6.0	7.3	7.3	6.1	3.7
Item 6240 Subject C05,D04 N	3280	1552	1632	2460	378	759	905	1000	615	1893	1160	1265	690	448	772	46
A09D: Both work about half-time																
1. Not at all acceptable	39.7	43.8	35.4	37.7	46.9	42.4	35.8	43.7	35.5	35.1	46.4	38.7	40.3	38.8	40.9	34.5
2. Somewhat acceptable	33.1	33.1	33.4	34.4	30.0	28.5	36.6	32.7	34.3	33.8	32.4	33.9	33.1	34.7	32.4	21.6
3. Acceptable	20.8	18.9	22.8	21.6	19.1	22.3	21.6	18.1	22.3	23.6	17.0	21.3	20.3	17.7	20.9	41.6
4. Desirable	6.4	4.2	8.3	6.3	4.0	6.9	6.0	5.4	7.9	7.5	4.2	6.1	6.3	8.8	5.8	2.3
Item 6250 Subject C05,D04 N	3281	1556	1627	2460	377	759	905	1001	616	1895	1159	1264	690	449	773	46
A09E: Husband works about half-time, wife works full-time																
1. Not at all acceptable	56.5	58.7	54.5	55.1	59.3	56.1	53.9	60.2	54.8	53.2	61.5	57.9	55.8	55.3	55.5	51.2
2. Somewhat acceptable	25.5	24.9	26.2	26.5	24.2	25.6	25.5	25.5	25.7	27.1	23.4	24.8	26.7	24.7	26.5	19.3
3. Acceptable	15.0	13.6	16.0	15.6	12.4	15.3	16.8	12.3	16.3	16.8	11.7	14.6	14.3	17.3	14.7	21.2
4. Desirable	3.0	2.8	3.3	2.8	4.1	3.0	3.8	2.1	3.3	2.9	3.4	2.7	3.2	2.6	3.2	8.3
Item 6260 Subject C05,D04 N	3292	1560	1633	2468	378	762	907	1005	618	1899	1165	1268	693	449	777	46
A09F: Husband doesn't work, wife works full-time																
1. Not at all acceptable	69.7	70.4	69.2	67.3	79.4	68.8	65.2	75.0	68.7	65.3	76.0	69.4	69.4	72.6	69.9	55.1
2. Somewhat acceptable	14.6	13.1	15.8	16.1	9.9	13.7	17.7	11.7	15.6	16.5	11.6	14.7	13.9	14.9	15.2	12.1
3. Acceptable	10.9	10.6	11.1	11.9	5.5	10.9	12.3	9.1	11.6	13.7	6.8	11.5	12.2	7.8	9.6	14.9
4. Desirable	4.9	5.9	4.0	4.7	5.3	6.5	4.8	4.2	4.1	4.5	5.6	4.5	4.5	4.7	5.3	17.9
Item 6270 Subject C05,D04 N	3285	1556	1631	2462	378	761	908	1002	614	1897	1162	1263	690	450	777	46
A10: Imagine you are married and have one or more pre-school children. Imagine also that the husband is working full-time and the wife does not have a job outside the home. How would you feel about each of these arrangements for the day-to-day care of the child(ren)?																
A10A: Wife does all child care																
1. Not at all acceptable	31.4	25.7	37.5	32.5	32.2	34.1	32.8	29.5	29.2	35.2	25.8	32.0	34.2	31.5	29.4	21.2
2. Somewhat acceptable	28.2	27.5	28.1	27.9	30.6	29.0	29.1	27.8	26.5	27.2	30.2	27.3	29.5	30.7	26.7	22.9
3. Acceptable	29.2	32.2	26.4	28.5	29.4	26.3	28.5	30.8	31.2	27.4	31.9	29.9	25.6	28.0	30.6	45.3
4. Desirable	11.2	14.5	7.9	11.2	7.8	10.7	9.6	11.9	13.1	10.2	12.1	10.8	10.7	9.9	13.3	10.7
Item 6280 Subject D04 N	3294	1557	1639	2464	382	760	907	1010	618	1901	1164	1270	694	451	772	46

QUESTIONNAIRE FORM 2 1985	TOTAL	SEX		RACE		REGION				4YR COLLEGE PLANS		ILLICIT DRUG USE: LIFETIME				
		M	F	White	Black	NE	NC	S	W	Yes	No	None	Mari- juana Only	Few Pills	More Pills	Any Her- oin
N (Weighted No. of Cases):	3327	1573	1651	2485	388	771	914	1017	625	1919	1172	1283	696	453	784	47
% of Weighted Total:	100.0	47.3	49.6	74.7	11.7	23.2	27.5	30.6	18.8	57.7	35.2	38.6	20.9	13.6	23.6	1.4
A10B: Wife does most of it																
1. Not at all acceptable	10.5	9.4	11.5	9.2	17.0	11.0	11.9	10.3	8.2	9.4	12.1	10.2	10.7	12.8	9.4	7.6
2. Somewhat acceptable	29.1	26.6	31.8	28.5	33.1	31.4	28.4	29.3	26.8	28.7	30.0	29.2	28.8	29.9	29.0	25.2
3. Acceptable	45.5	47.4	43.4	46.2	40.9	45.8	44.7	45.6	46.4	45.2	45.6	46.4	44.3	44.4	45.3	54.8
4. Desirable	14.9	16.7	13.3	16.1	9.0	11.7	15.0	14.8	18.7	16.7	12.3	14.2	16.2	12.9	16.3	12.4
Item 6290　Subject D04　N	3298	1562	1638	2469	380	763	909	1006	620	1905	1165	1269	694	451	777	46
A10C: Both do it equally																
1. Not at all acceptable	4.2	5.7	2.6	3.3	6.0	3.3	3.4	4.6	6.1	3.8	4.5	3.7	5.0	5.1	3.6	6.4
2. Somewhat acceptable	15.4	18.0	12.6	15.2	12.4	16.1	15.6	15.4	14.1	14.3	15.4	15.4	17.3	11.9	15.5	14.3
3. Acceptable	42.9	47.0	38.4	40.8	54.8	46.3	42.3	44.3	37.5	40.4	47.7	43.0	44.2	39.7	42.4	49.5
4. Desirable	37.5	29.3	46.4	40.7	26.7	34.3	38.8	35.7	42.3	41.6	32.4	37.8	33.4	43.3	38.5	29.8
Item 6300　Subject D04　N	3286	1559	1630	2466	376	762	906	1003	615	1894	1165	1264	692	451	773	46
A10D: Husband does most of it																
1. Not at all acceptable	44.5	42.4	46.9	43.5	47.6	42.7	42.0	47.5	45.6	43.2	45.3	45.6	44.9	43.7	43.2	52.2
2. Somewhat acceptable	39.6	41.5	37.5	41.7	33.6	42.2	41.8	36.3	38.3	41.5	36.8	38.3	42.7	39.9	38.6	28.1
3. Acceptable	13.6	14.3	13.0	13.4	13.1	12.6	13.5	14.0	14.5	13.5	15.2	13.6	11.4	12.5	16.3	18.6
4. Desirable	2.3	1.7	2.7	1.4	5.6	2.5	2.6	2.2	1.6	1.9	2.7	2.4	1.0	3.9	1.9	1.1
Item 6310　Subject D04　N	3290	1559	1633	2466	376	763	907	1002	618	1901	1161	1265	694	450	774	46
A10E: Husband does all of it																
1. Not at all acceptable	82.4	80.7	84.2	83.1	81.0	81.7	81.2	84.2	82.1	83.5	80.1	82.9	83.5	82.9	81.5	78.3
2. Somewhat acceptable	11.5	12.7	10.2	11.8	9.1	11.6	12.2	10.4	12.1	10.9	12.8	11.8	11.1	10.8	11.8	9.7
3. Acceptable	4.2	5.2	3.3	3.9	4.9	4.7	4.4	3.4	4.5	4.5	3.9	3.8	3.9	4.1	4.4	9.0
4. Desirable	1.9	1.4	2.3	1.3	4.9	2.0	2.2	2.0	1.3	1.2	3.2	1.5	1.6	2.2	2.3	3.0
Item 6320　Subject D04　N	3293	1559	1635	2466	379	763	906	1006	618	1901	1164	1267	694	451	774	46

The next section of this questionnaire is about government and public affairs.

A11: Some people think about what's going on in government very often, and others are not that interested. How much of an interest do you take in government and current events?

	TOTAL	M	F	White	Black	NE	NC	S	W	Yes	No	None	Mari- juana Only	Few Pills	More Pills	Any Her- oin
1. No interest at all	4.8	4.7	4.9	4.2	5.4	9.0	4.6	2.6	3.3	3.1	7.2	3.2	5.1	5.5	6.0	16.7
2. Very little interest	17.8	13.7	22.1	17.3	20.7	19.6	18.8	16.4	16.7	13.5	24.5	14.5	19.4	20.1	20.8	12.8
3. Some interest	49.1	44.8	52.5	49.8	44.4	48.3	51.5	46.6	50.7	47.0	52.1	48.8	49.8	51.0	46.9	55.4
4. A lot of interest	21.0	26.5	16.1	21.2	21.6	17.7	18.5	25.2	22.0	26.5	13.1	24.9	19.4	17.0	19.7	14.2
5. A very great interest	7.3	10.2	4.5	7.6	7.8	5.4	6.6	9.3	7.2	9.9	3.2	8.6	6.3	6.4	6.6	0.8
Item 6330　Subject H01,Q08　N	3298	1561	1640	2468	383	759	908	1012	620	1902	1168	1275	693	451	773	47

A12: Do you think some of the people running the government are crooked or dishonest?

	TOTAL	M	F	White	Black	NE	NC	S	W	Yes	No	None	Mari- juana Only	Few Pills	More Pills	Any Her- oin
1. Most of them are crooked or dishonest	9.7	10.3	8.9	8.9	14.2	12.2	8.2	11.1	6.7	7.6	11.0	7.6	10.1	9.8	12.2	22.1
2. Quite a few are	29.6	30.4	29.2	28.9	30.4	31.9	27.1	32.2	26.4	29.3	30.3	30.2	26.4	30.4	31.5	26.8
3. Some are	53.1	52.8	53.9	54.6	47.5	49.5	56.0	50.2	58.2	55.9	50.6	53.8	56.0	52.1	50.7	38.3
4. Hardly any are	7.1	6.4	7.4	7.5	6.0	6.2	8.3	5.9	8.2	6.8	7.7	7.8	7.4	7.1	5.1	12.9
5. None at all are crooked or dishonest	0.4	0.2	0.6	0.1	1.8	0.2	0.4	0.6	0.6	0.4	0.5	0.6	0.2	0.5	0.4	-
Item 6340　Subject H04,K01　N	3290	1556	1636	2464	379	757	907	1008	618	1896	1165	1273	689	451	773	47

A13: Do you think the government wastes much of the money we pay in taxes?

	TOTAL	M	F	White	Black	NE	NC	S	W	Yes	No	None	Mari- juana Only	Few Pills	More Pills	Any Her- oin
1. Nearly all tax money is wasted	7.1	7.5	6.9	6.7	9.7	8.7	6.8	6.0	7.5	5.6	8.7	5.6	7.8	9.5	7.5	13.7
2. A lot of tax money is wasted	48.3	48.8	48.3	49.3	42.1	49.6	48.0	47.4	48.7	49.0	48.9	46.6	47.8	46.4	53.9	36.8
3. Some tax money is wasted	36.8	36.5	37.0	36.8	37.8	35.2	37.7	37.9	35.7	37.6	35.5	39.0	35.0	38.4	32.6	43.0
4. A little tax money wasted	7.1	6.6	7.1	6.9	8.1	6.4	7.0	7.7	6.9	7.0	6.4	7.8	8.6	5.2	5.7	6.5
5. No tax money is wasted	0.7	0.6	0.7	0.3	2.3	0.2	0.6	1.0	1.2	0.7	0.6	1.0	0.9	0.6	0.3	-
Item 6350　Subject H04,K01　N	3284	1556	1630	2458	379	757	906	1003	618	1894	1161	1266	689	450	773	47

QUESTIONNAIRE FORM 2 1985	TOTAL	SEX		RACE		REGION				4YR COLLEGE PLANS		ILLICIT DRUG USE: LIFETIME				
		M	F	White	Black	NE	NC	S	W	Yes	No	None	Mari- juana Only	Few Pills	More Pills	Any Her- oin
N (Weighted No. of Cases):	3327	1573	1651	2485	388	771	914	1017	625	1919	1172	1283	696	453	784	47
% of Weighted Total:	100.0	47.3	49.6	74.7	11.7	23.2	27.5	30.6	18.8	57.7	35.2	38.6	20.9	13.6	23.6	1.4

A14: How much of the time do you think you can trust the government in Washington to do what is right?

1. Almost always	10.0	11.4	8.6	11.1	6.3	7.4	8.6	10.7	14.3	10.3	9.3	10.0	12.9	7.0	9.2	12.9
2. Often	40.0	41.3	38.5	43.1	25.7	36.9	41.8	39.7	41.6	44.4	34.4	42.8	38.9	38.8	38.7	28.7
3. Sometimes	38.8	34.9	43.3	37.3	43.1	42.2	39.4	37.8	35.7	36.4	43.8	37.1	38.3	41.2	40.0	39.9
4. Seldom	9.4	10.1	8.4	7.2	21.5	10.3	8.9	10.3	7.5	7.5	10.9	8.7	9.0	9.8	10.6	10.4
5. Never	1.7	2.3	1.2	1.3	3.4	3.2	1.3	1.5	0.9	1.4	1.6	1.4	0.9	3.2	1.6	8.1
Item 6360 Subject H04,K01 N	3289	1559	1633	2461	383	757	904	1009	619	1896	1165	1271	691	449	772	47

A15: Do you feel that the people running the government are smart people who usually know what they are doing?

1. They almost always know what they are doing	13.3	16.1	10.7	13.3	13.3	11.8	13.2	13.6	15.0	12.9	13.5	11.8	17.1	10.4	13.5	15.8
2. They usually know what they are doing	55.4	54.4	56.7	58.3	44.5	54.0	53.4	55.8	59.2	58.9	51.1	57.0	53.7	58.7	53.2	46.8
3. They sometimes know what they are doing	26.3	24.2	28.2	23.8	35.6	27.6	28.3	25.6	23.2	24.5	29.3	26.2	24.9	26.4	28.1	26.3
4. They seldom know what they are doing	3.5	3.6	3.3	3.1	6.0	4.5	3.7	4.0	1.3	2.8	4.1	4.0	3.7	1.9	3.5	1.0
5. They never know what they are doing	1.4	1.7	1.2	1.4	0.6	2.1	1.4	1.0	1.2	0.9	2.0	1.0	0.6	2.6	1.7	10.0
Item 6370 Subject H04,K01 N	3290	1558	1634	2460	383	756	905	1010	619	1899	1163	1272	690	451	771	47

A16: Would you say the government is pretty much run for a few big interests looking out for themselves, or is it run for the benefit of all the people?

1. Nearly always run for a few big interests	7.5	8.3	7.0	6.8	11.3	7.7	7.7	8.0	6.3	6.1	9.3	7.5	7.7	7.2	7.5	10.1
2. Usually run for a few big interests	19.7	20.5	18.3	19.1	20.1	22.8	19.6	17.5	19.8	17.6	22.2	19.0	18.7	17.0	23.8	18.0
3. Run some for the big interests, some for the people	48.3	44.4	52.5	48.0	49.5	46.5	47.3	51.0	47.4	49.2	47.7	48.6	49.3	50.9	45.8	35.4
4. Usually run for the benefit of all the people	20.4	22.6	18.3	22.0	14.8	18.6	21.8	19.1	22.7	22.5	17.3	21.0	20.9	19.4	18.7	31.6
5. Nearly always run for the benefit of all the people	4.1	4.2	4.0	4.0	4.4	4.3	3.6	4.5	3.9	4.6	3.5	3.9	3.3	5.5	4.2	4.9
Item 6380 Subject H04,K01 N	3282	1556	1628	2456	382	756	902	1006	619	1894	1160	1268	688	450	772	45

A17: Have you ever done, or do you plan to do, the following things?

A17A: Vote in a public election

1. I probably won't do this	3.0	3.3	2.5	2.6	2.6	4.2	2.6	2.9	2.4	1.7	4.9	2.2	3.4	2.9	3.5	12.8
2. Don't know	6.5	5.7	6.8	4.4	9.0	9.0	4.8	5.5	7.5	4.1	9.2	6.0	5.0	7.8	6.9	3.1
3. I probably will do this	83.0	81.1	85.8	85.6	80.4	81.1	82.8	83.9	84.3	87.3	77.7	84.6	82.3	83.3	83.0	66.5
4. I have already done this	7.5	9.9	4.9	7.4	8.0	5.8	9.8	7.6	5.8	6.8	8.2	7.2	9.3	6.1	6.6	17.6
Item 6390 Subject H05,I02 N	3295	1560	1639	2468	384	759	907	1010	619	1902	1166	1274	694	450	772	46

A17B: Write to public officials

1. I probably won't do this	20.8	18.5	22.7	19.9	27.2	22.3	21.4	19.4	20.6	13.9	31.8	17.3	21.1	23.6	23.3	25.9
2. Don't know	46.2	47.1	45.3	46.9	42.9	43.7	48.5	47.3	44.1	45.2	48.1	46.3	47.1	45.5	47.1	37.2
3. I probably will do this	22.1	23.4	21.2	21.5	22.8	22.4	20.8	23.5	21.4	27.3	13.6	25.1	20.6	22.6	18.7	23.0
4. I have already done this	10.8	11.0	10.8	11.8	7.1	11.6	9.3	9.9	13.8	13.7	6.5	11.3	11.1	8.4	10.9	14.0
Item 6400 Subject H05,I02 N	3290	1558	1635	2466	380	757	905	1009	620	1901	1165	1272	693	449	773	46

A17C: Give money to a political candidate or cause

1. I probably won't do this	34.2	37.7	30.6	33.4	36.6	41.2	35.6	27.8	33.7	28.1	43.4	32.4	31.1	33.6	39.5	44.3
2. Don't know	41.6	40.4	42.8	42.5	36.2	39.5	42.4	43.7	39.7	44.0	37.4	42.1	43.7	41.9	38.9	37.8
3. I probably will do this	21.1	18.9	23.6	21.1	23.1	16.4	19.2	25.2	22.9	24.4	17.1	22.8	22.2	20.1	18.8	10.3
4. I have already done this	3.1	3.0	3.0	3.0	4.1	2.8	2.8	3.3	3.6	3.6	2.0	2.7	3.0	4.5	2.8	7.6
Item 6410 Subject H05,I02 N	3288	1558	1635	2465	380	757	906	1006	620	1901	1164	1267	694	450	772	46

QUESTIONNAIRE FORM 2 1985	TOTAL	SEX		RACE		REGION				4YR COLLEGE PLANS		ILLICIT DRUG USE: LIFETIME				
		M	F	White	Black	NE	NC	S	W	Yes	No	None	Mari-juana Only	Few Pills	More Pills	Any Her-oin
N (Weighted No. of Cases):	3327	1573	1651	2485	388	771	914	1017	625	1919	1172	1283	696	453	784	47
% of Weighted Total:	100.0	47.3	49.6	74.7	11.7	23.2	27.5	30.6	18.8	57.7	35.2	38.6	20.9	13.6	23.6	1.4
A17D: Work in a political campaign																
1. I probably won't do this	47.0	50.4	43.8	48.5	37.9	54.8	51.2	37.1	47.0	39.2	58.9	43.9	45.4	45.3	53.5	58.3
2. Don't know	37.2	37.0	37.3	36.2	41.2	32.4	34.7	42.7	37.6	39.8	33.0	38.3	39.5	38.4	33.8	26.7
3. I probably will do this	10.3	7.7	12.5	9.0	16.9	8.2	8.3	14.3	9.1	13.0	5.9	11.8	9.6	9.5	8.1	11.2
4. I have already done this	5.6	4.9	6.5	6.3	4.0	4.6	5.8	5.9	6.3	8.0	2.1	6.0	5.6	6.9	4.6	3.9
Item 6420 Subject H05,I02 N	3281	1554	1632	2463	377	754	904	1003	620	1898	1163	1268	694	449	767	46
A17E: Participate in a lawful demonstration																
1. I probably won't do this	37.7	37.1	38.8	38.4	33.0	37.3	38.3	37.3	38.0	32.2	47.1	37.7	38.7	37.8	36.3	37.0
2. Don't know	45.4	45.8	44.6	45.6	46.4	44.7	45.5	47.1	43.1	46.7	42.5	46.3	44.7	45.8	45.2	38.3
3. I probably will do this	14.6	14.5	14.6	13.5	19.0	15.4	14.0	13.9	15.4	18.1	9.1	14.1	14.5	14.5	15.2	20.1
4. I have already done this	2.3	2.7	2.0	2.5	1.6	2.5	2.1	1.7	3.5	3.1	1.3	1.9	2.1	1.8	3.4	4.6
Item 6430 Subject H05,I02 N	3285	1555	1635	2465	377	756	905	1003	620	1899	1165	1264	694	450	772	46
A17F: Boycott certain products or stores																
1. I probably won't do this	42.9	39.9	45.7	44.1	38.5	41.7	43.2	45.3	39.9	37.1	52.8	42.9	42.6	42.3	42.7	52.0
2. Don't know	39.4	40.4	38.5	39.3	41.7	37.9	39.8	40.7	38.7	41.0	36.7	40.2	39.9	41.1	38.0	35.2
3. I probably will do this	13.5	14.6	12.4	12.0	17.9	16.0	13.6	10.8	14.8	16.6	8.4	13.3	13.8	12.2	13.8	12.8
4. I have already done this	4.1	5.0	3.4	4.5	2.0	4.3	3.4	3.2	6.5	5.3	2.1	3.5	3.7	4.4	5.5	-
Item 6440 Subject H05,I02 N	3284	1555	1634	2464	380	755	906	1007	616	1897	1165	1268	694	447	771	46
A18: How much do you agree or disagree with each of the following statements?																
A18A: The U.S. should begin a gradual program of disarming whether other countries do or not																
1. Disagree	37.5	50.5	24.7	38.1	32.4	37.4	32.2	41.9	38.0	38.6	36.6	37.1	39.9	31.7	38.9	38.4
2. Mostly disagree	19.2	17.7	20.7	20.3	16.2	19.9	19.5	16.5	22.2	20.0	17.8	17.7	19.1	23.8	19.7	12.5
3. Neither	18.9	13.0	25.0	18.3	23.9	18.4	20.6	18.8	17.3	16.7	22.3	20.1	17.7	19.6	17.3	32.3
4. Mostly agree	14.6	10.4	18.8	14.0	16.7	12.7	16.8	14.8	13.8	14.3	14.8	14.9	15.8	14.7	13.2	6.0
5. Agree	9.8	8.5	10.7	9.2	10.7	11.6	10.9	7.9	8.8	10.4	8.6	10.3	7.5	10.2	10.9	10.8
Item 6450 Subject H02,L03 N	3265	1549	1621	2451	374	752	901	997	615	1896	1150	1258	693	448	763	46
A18B: There may be times when the U.S. should go to war to protect the rights of other countries																
1. Disagree	22.5	19.4	25.8	20.7	32.2	26.8	23.7	20.3	19.1	20.2	26.3	18.8	23.9	22.3	27.2	24.4
2. Mostly disagree	21.7	19.6	23.4	22.2	18.8	22.2	24.2	16.8	25.1	22.6	20.3	21.3	21.9	21.6	23.1	8.6
3. Neither	19.6	17.7	21.0	20.0	18.4	17.7	19.1	21.6	19.2	19.1	19.9	19.3	20.0	21.4	17.4	35.9
4. Mostly agree	24.2	27.3	21.6	25.5	16.6	22.6	23.3	25.7	24.9	25.7	22.0	26.6	21.8	26.3	21.3	21.9
5. Agree	12.1	15.9	8.2	11.6	14.0	10.7	9.6	15.6	11.8	12.4	11.4	14.0	12.4	8.4	10.9	9.2
Item 5690 Subject H02,L03 N	3278	1553	1629	2457	381	752	903	1005	618	1892	1164	1263	694	448	769	46
A18C: The U.S. should be willing to go to war to protect its own economic interests																
1. Disagree	12.4	10.8	14.1	11.1	17.9	17.6	12.1	9.8	10.8	11.8	12.9	11.3	9.7	15.0	15.3	11.3
2. Mostly disagree	15.6	13.6	17.2	15.4	11.6	14.9	17.4	10.9	21.2	16.6	13.6	15.2	15.1	13.9	17.0	18.3
3. Neither	21.3	17.7	24.9	22.6	15.9	20.8	22.5	19.3	23.5	21.4	21.6	22.3	21.3	21.6	20.0	22.5
4. Mostly agree	29.3	31.3	27.6	31.3	24.0	28.1	29.0	30.9	28.6	30.1	28.0	28.9	32.5	27.3	28.0	26.5
5. Agree	21.4	26.7	16.2	19.7	30.7	18.6	18.9	29.1	15.9	20.1	24.0	22.3	21.3	22.1	19.7	21.3
Item 6460 Subject H02,L03 N	3275	1552	1627	2454	380	754	901	1002	617	1895	1159	1260	693	448	770	46
A18D: The only good reason for the U.S. to go to war is to defend against an attack on our own country																
1. Disagree	7.3	9.5	5.0	6.5	9.3	7.9	6.1	7.7	7.4	8.1	5.6	7.5	6.5	6.0	8.4	9.8
2. Mostly disagree	12.0	14.3	9.5	12.4	8.1	12.1	12.3	12.1	11.2	12.8	10.3	13.8	9.7	9.1	12.1	15.9
3. Neither	9.9	9.7	9.8	10.7	5.8	12.6	8.9	8.2	10.7	9.5	9.6	8.6	9.5	12.1	10.7	18.9
4. Mostly agree	30.6	26.1	35.2	31.8	26.3	29.5	30.8	30.3	32.0	30.8	31.0	28.9	32.1	33.9	30.0	24.7
5. Agree	40.3	40.3	40.5	38.6	50.4	37.9	41.8	41.6	38.7	38.7	43.4	41.2	42.3	38.9	38.7	30.7
Item 6470 Subject H02,L03 N	3273	1549	1628	2456	377	752	903	1000	618	1892	1160	1261	694	446	768	46

QUESTIONNAIRE FORM 2 1985	TOTAL	SEX		RACE		REGION				4YR COLLEGE PLANS		ILLICIT DRUG USE: LIFETIME				
		M	F	White	Black	NE	NC	S	W	Yes	No	None	Mari- juana Only	Few Pills	More Pills	Any Her- oin
N (Weighted No. of Cases):	3327	1573	1651	2485	388	771	914	1017	625	1919	1172	1283	696	453	784	47
% of Weighted Total:	100.0	47.3	49.6	74.7	11.7	23.2	27.5	30.6	18.8	57.7	35.2	38.6	20.9	13.6	23.6	1.4
A18E: The U.S. does not need to have greater military power than the Soviet Union																
1. Disagree	32.2	35.2	29.2	30.7	42.1	32.2	27.0	39.9	27.0	28.8	36.9	31.3	33.5	30.3	33.4	28.4
2. Mostly disagree	22.3	21.7	22.2	22.7	21.7	19.8	23.2	23.3	22.6	22.8	21.8	23.1	22.7	20.9	20.8	33.1
3. Neither	18.9	16.1	22.0	18.8	17.2	19.8	19.3	16.7	21.1	18.7	19.5	18.8	18.8	21.5	18.2	15.8
4. Mostly agree	15.0	15.1	15.1	16.1	10.3	14.2	18.5	12.0	16.0	16.4	12.9	16.3	13.4	16.0	14.4	9.1
5. Agree	11.5	11.9	11.4	11.7	8.7	14.1	12.0	8.1	13.3	13.3	8.9	10.5	11.6	11.3	13.1	13.6
Item 6480 Subject H02,L03 N	3263	1550	1618	2444	378	751	899	997	617	1883	1160	1251	691	448	769	46
A18F: The U.S. ought to have much more mili- tary power than any other nation in the world																
1. Disagroe	19.5	18.9	20.6	20.1	16.5	21.6	22.6	14.0	21.3	22.5	14.6	19.5	18.0	20.3	20.7	24.7
2. Mostly disagree	18.4	18.0	18.9	18.7	16.6	18.1	21.2	14.3	21.1	21.8	14.5	19.9	18.3	18.7	16.7	10.5
3. Neither	25.8	23.8	28.0	26.5	21.6	25.3	25.3	25.6	27.5	25.2	26.4	24.4	28.6	26.5	25.1	22.3
4. Mostly agree	18.1	19.3	16.3	17.5	17.5	17.8	17.0	20.6	15.9	16.1	20.0	18.7	19.3	15.8	16.8	22.4
5. Agree	18.2	20.0	16.3	17.2	27.9	17.2	13.8	25.4	14.3	14.3	24.5	17.6	15.8	18.7	20.6	20.1
Item 6490 Subject H02,L03 N	3274	1551	1627	2454	380	751	903	1000	620	1890	1162	1262	694	448	767	46
A18G: Our present foreign policy is based on our own narrow economic and power interests																
1. Disagree	5.5	7.4	3.6	5.5	5.8	8.0	4.3	4.8	5.4	5.9	4.3	6.2	4.9	3.0	5.9	7.1
2. Mostly disagree	10.8	11.7	9.7	11.0	11.0	10.8	11.2	11.2	9.9	10.5	11.1	10.2	11.3	12.9	9.9	10.0
3. Neither	44.9	39.3	50.6	47.5	32.7	43.0	46.5	44.0	46.1	43.5	48.2	43.1	45.1	43.8	48.9	51.4
4. Mostly agree	25.4	27.1	23.9	24.7	31.4	22.5	27.7	25.2	26.1	26.7	23.8	27.6	25.4	25.9	21.8	19.8
5. Agree	13.3	14.6	12.1	11.4	19.0	15.7	10.4	14.8	12.4	13.5	12.6	13.0	13.3	14.3	13.4	11.8
Item 6500 Subject H02,L03 N	3224	1530	1602	2417	375	736	896	983	609	1874	1137	1243	686	443	750	46
A18H: Servicemen should obey orders without question																
1. Disagree	14.7	12.8	16.3	12.0	24.9	18.7	12.8	13.2	14.9	16.3	10.8	14.2	13.8	16.0	15.5	15.8
2. Mostly disagree	17.6	15.0	20.3	18.2	17.3	17.6	18.8	16.1	18.6	19.6	14.9	16.0	17.1	18.0	21.0	11.1
3. Neither	22.6	19.4	25.6	23.2	16.5	18.8	26.0	21.0	24.6	21.5	23.9	22.5	25.2	21.7	20.1	28.3
4. Mostly agree	30.2	33.5	27.2	32.0	23.8	30.7	29.1	31.3	29.3	30.1	32.0	32.6	28.6	30.4	28.6	26.2
5. Agree	14.9	19.3	10.6	14.6	17.4	14.2	13.3	18.4	12.5	12.5	18.3	14.6	15.3	13.9	14.7	18.6
Item 6510 Subject L03 N	3268	1549	1626	2454	380	748	904	1001	616	1887	1162	1261	691	447	767	46
A19: This section deals with activities which may be against the rules or against the law. We hope you will answer all of these questions. However, if you find a question which you can- not answer honestly, we would prefer that you leave it blank. Remember, your answers will never be connected with your name. During the LAST 12 MONTHS, how often have you...																
A19A: Argued or had a fight with either of your parents																
1. Not at all	11.1	14.0	8.2	7.5	30.1	9.1	10.3	13.8	10.3	9.9	12.2	15.1	9.6	8.3	6.5	15.7
2. Once	9.4	11.2	7.4	7.2	16.7	9.0	9.1	11.3	7.4	8.9	9.6	11.5	10.3	7.4	6.4	9.0
3. Twice	12.1	12.6	11.9	12.7	10.3	13.3	11.1	12.8	11.1	12.0	12.9	13.2	12.6	11.2	10.8	2.6
4. 3 or 4 times	23.6	23.5	23.5	24.9	18.0	23.1	24.4	22.8	24.3	25.0	21.3	22.2	24.8	25.0	24.6	8.7
5. 5 or more times	43.8	38.7	49.1	47.7	24.8	45.4	45.2	39.3	46.9	44.2	44.0	38.0	42.8	48.1	51.7	64.0
Item 6520 Subject M03,S01 N	3292	1556	1643	2466	384	763	908	1001	619	1904	1167	1277	695	445	779	46
A19B: Hit an instructor or supervisor																
1. Not at all	96.9	94.9	99.0	96.9	98.4	95.5	97.1	97.2	98.0	97.4	96.4	98.5	97.0	96.6	95.4	82.7
2. Once	2.0	3.1	0.8	2.1	1.2	2.7	2.0	1.8	1.4	1.7	2.4	0.9	1.6	2.4	3.4	7.9
3. Twice	0.3	0.5	0.2	0.3	0.2	0.8	0.3	0.1	0.1	0.3	0.4	0.1	0.2	0.5	0.4	5.1
4. 3 or 4 times	0.4	0.8	0.1	0.5	0.2	0.9	0.2	0.5	0.1	0.4	0.5	0.3	0.9	-	0.5	-
5. 5 or more times	0.3	0.7	-	0.3	-	0.1	0.4	0.4	0.5	0.3	0.3	0.1	0.3	0.5	0.4	4.3
Item 6530 Subject M02,S01 N	3294	1558	1643	2466	384	762	907	1005	619	1911	1163	1277	696	447	778	46

	TOTAL	SEX		RACE		REGION				4YR COLLEGE PLANS		ILLICIT DRUG USE: LIFETIME				
QUESTIONNAIRE FORM 2 1985		M	F	White	Black	NE	NC	S	W	Yes	No	None	Mari- juana Only	Few Pills	More Pills	Any Her- oin
N (Weighted No. of Cases):	3327	1573	1651	2485	388	771	914	1017	625	1919	1172	1283	696	453	784	47
% of Weighted Total:	100.0	47.3	49.6	74.7	11.7	23.2	27.5	30.6	18.8	57.7	35.2	38.6	20.9	13.6	23.6	1.4

A19C: Gotten into a serious fight in school or at work

	TOTAL	M	F	White	Black	NE	NC	S	W	Yes	No	None	Marijuana Only	Few Pills	More Pills	Any Heroin
1. Not at all	81.8	76.3	87.3	81.5	83.4	74.5	83.5	84.0	84.9	85.4	77.4	89.7	83.7	77.7	71.5	55.8
2. Once	11.2	13.8	8.6	11.5	11.5	15.0	10.6	10.6	8.3	9.4	13.7	6.9	10.1	12.8	17.0	30.9
3. Twice	3.6	4.5	2.8	3.7	3.4	5.7	3.0	2.9	3.3	2.8	4.3	1.9	3.6	5.6	5.4	2.2
4. 3 or 4 times	2.2	3.3	1.2	2.2	0.9	3.5	2.2	1.3	2.0	1.6	3.0	0.9	1.2	3.4	3.9	6.7
5. 5 or more times	1.1	2.1	0.2	1.1	0.9	1.3	0.6	1.2	1.6	0.9	1.6	0.5	1.4	0.5	2.3	4.3
Item 6540 Subject B07,C01,S01 N	3296	1561	1643	2468	384	762	908	1006	619	1909	1167	1280	696	448	777	46

A19D: Taken part in a fight where a group of your friends were against another group

	TOTAL	M	F	White	Black	NE	NC	S	W	Yes	No	None	Marijuana Only	Few Pills	More Pills	Any Heroin
1. Not at all	79.4	73.9	85.1	79.5	80.8	73.1	78.9	82.1	83.3	82.1	76.2	87.7	81.4	79.0	66.7	42.5
2. Once	12.0	13.2	10.5	11.9	10.7	14.2	12.6	10.5	10.8	11.0	13.4	6.9	11.4	12.1	19.3	27.5
3. Twice	4.8	6.5	3.0	4.6	4.9	8.2	4.4	3.7	2.8	4.0	5.4	3.1	4.1	5.5	7.1	10.1
4. 3 or 4 times	2.3	3.8	1.0	2.6	2.1	2.4	2.6	2.4	1.9	1.8	3.0	1.9	1.3	1.8	4.2	6.7
5. 5 or more times	1.5	2.6	0.5	1.4	1.5	2.1	1.4	1.4	1.3	1.1	1.9	0.3	1.7	1.6	2.6	13.2
Item 6550 Subject S01 N	3292	1560	1639	2464	384	760	908	1004	619	1905	1167	1280	694	443	779	46

A19E: Hurt someone badly enough to need bandages or a doctor

	TOTAL	M	F	White	Black	NE	NC	S	W	Yes	No	None	Marijuana Only	Few Pills	More Pills	Any Heroin
1. Not at all	88.5	81.0	96.3	88.9	88.4	84.8	89.8	89.8	89.4	91.1	86.0	94.3	87.6	91.3	80.8	59.0
2. Once	6.9	11.1	2.7	6.6	8.3	9.0	6.0	6.3	6.8	5.7	7.8	3.5	8.9	4.8	10.9	19.9
3. Twice	2.2	3.7	0.7	2.2	2.0	3.9	2.0	2.0	0.9	1.8	2.6	1.1	2.3	1.8	3.8	13.8
4. 3 or 4 times	1.4	2.4	0.3	1.5	0.8	1.3	1.3	1.3	1.8	0.8	2.2	0.5	0.9	1.4	2.9	2.9
5. 5 or more times	0.9	1.8	-	0.8	0.5	1.0	0.9	0.7	1.1	0.6	1.3	0.7	0.3	0.7	1.7	4.3
Item 6560 Subject S01 N	3294	1560	1643	2467	383	764	907	1005	617	1908	1168	1280	695	445	778	46

A19F: Used a knife or gun or some other thing (like a club) to get something from a person

	TOTAL	M	F	White	Black	NE	NC	S	W	Yes	No	None	Marijuana Only	Few Pills	More Pills	Any Heroin
1. Not at all	96.5	94.7	98.7	97.1	95.4	95.6	96.6	96.8	97.2	97.7	95.4	97.9	96.6	97.5	94.5	81.1
2. Once	1.8	2.1	1.2	1.4	3.0	1.7	1.9	1.9	1.8	1.2	2.7	1.0	1.3	1.0	3.7	12.4
3. Twice	0.7	1.2	0.1	0.6	0.8	1.3	0.6	0.7	0.3	0.5	0.8	0.4	1.1	0.9	0.8	-
4. 3 or 4 times	0.3	0.7	-	0.3	0.9	0.5	0.5	0.2	-	0.2	0.3	0.2	0.7	0.2	0.3	-
5. 5 or more times	0.6	1.3	-	0.6	-	0.8	0.4	0.5	0.7	0.4	0.8	0.5	0.3	0.5	0.8	6.5
Item 6570 Subject S01 N	3295	1561	1643	2468	384	763	908	1006	618	1910	1166	1280	696	446	778	46

A19G: Taken something not belonging to you worth under $50

	TOTAL	M	F	White	Black	NE	NC	S	W	Yes	No	None	Marijuana Only	Few Pills	More Pills	Any Heroin
1. Not at all	69.9	61.4	78.5	68.8	78.3	60.3	69.6	77.9	69.0	71.3	68.5	80.8	69.4	69.9	53.5	43.0
2. Once	14.2	16.7	11.4	14.5	9.8	16.7	15.0	11.0	15.0	13.3	15.4	11.4	14.0	14.6	18.9	19.2
3. Twice	6.6	8.9	4.5	7.1	4.8	7.4	6.7	6.1	6.5	6.2	7.0	3.7	6.9	6.5	10.5	18.3
4. 3 or 4 times	4.5	6.3	2.8	4.7	3.2	7.9	4.6	2.4	3.6	4.2	5.2	2.3	4.2	4.4	8.3	8.8
5. 5 or more times	4.8	6.7	2.9	4.9	3.9	7.7	4.0	2.6	5.9	5.0	4.0	1.8	5.5	4.6	8.8	10.7
Item 6580 Subject S01 N	3286	1556	1639	2461	383	761	907	1003	615	1903	1166	1273	692	448	778	46

A19H: Taken something not belonging to you worth over $50

	TOTAL	M	F	White	Black	NE	NC	S	W	Yes	No	None	Marijuana Only	Few Pills	More Pills	Any Heroin
1. Not at all	93.0	88.1	97.9	93.4	93.8	87.9	93.1	95.4	94.9	94.8	91.5	97.4	93.4	93.8	86.4	72.6
2. Once	3.4	5.7	1.1	3.3	2.7	5.5	3.7	2.4	1.9	2.7	3.8	1.9	3.0	3.2	5.5	10.1
3. Twice	1.3	1.9	0.5	1.0	1.6	2.6	0.7	1.2	0.7	0.9	1.6	0.4	1.7	0.3	2.8	2.6
4. 3 or 4 times	0.9	1.7	0.2	0.9	1.0	1.5	1.1	0.3	1.0	0.6	0.9	0.1	0.6	1.4	2.1	8.3
5. 5 or more times	1.4	2.7	0.3	1.4	0.9	2.5	1.4	0.7	1.4	1.0	2.1	0.2	1.4	1.3	3.3	6.3
Item 6590 Subject S01 N	3285	1561	1634	2465	381	761	905	1005	615	1906	1163	1275	695	448	774	45

A19I: Taken something from a store without paying for it

	TOTAL	M	F	White	Black	NE	NC	S	W	Yes	No	None	Marijuana Only	Few Pills	More Pills	Any Heroin
1. Not at all	73.5	68.2	79.2	73.5	79.2	63.9	75.6	78.4	73.9	76.4	70.4	86.3	70.8	71.6	57.2	57.8
2. Once	11.7	12.6	10.5	11.8	9.7	13.1	11.1	10.6	12.3	10.7	12.9	7.8	12.2	14.5	15.9	12.5
3. Twice	6.1	7.5	4.3	6.3	3.2	8.6	5.9	5.3	4.7	4.7	7.8	2.7	6.9	7.4	10.0	6.9
4. 3 or 4 times	4.2	5.4	3.2	3.9	3.9	6.8	2.7	3.5	4.5	3.9	4.7	2.0	5.1	2.2	7.9	5.9
5. 5 or more times	4.5	6.2	2.8	4.5	4.1	7.5	4.6	2.2	4.7	4.3	4.2	1.2	5.1	4.2	9.0	16.9
Item 6600 Subject S01 N	3284	1551	1641	2463	382	760	906	1005	613	1904	1163	1275	692	446	777	46

QUESTIONNAIRE FORM 2 1985	TOTAL	SEX		RACE		REGION				4YR COLLEGE PLANS		ILLICIT DRUG USE: LIFETIME				
		M	F	White	Black	NE	NC	S	W	Yes	No	None	Mari- juana Only	Few Pills	More Pills	Any Her- oin
N (Weighted No. of Cases):	3327	1573	1651	2485	388	771	914	1017	625	1919	1172	1283	696	453	784	47
% of Weighted Total:	100.0	47.3	49.6	74.7	11.7	23.2	27.5	30.6	18.8	57.7	35.2	38.6	20.9	13.6	23.6	1.4
A19J: Taken a car that didn't belong to some-one in your family without permission of the owner																
1. Not at all	94.4	92.2	96.6	94.9	94.7	92.8	94.7	95.4	94.2	95.4	93.5	96.5	94.5	93.7	92.3	75.7
2. Once	3.1	3.9	2.3	3.0	3.9	3.0	3.9	2.6	2.8	3.0	3.3	2.2	3.4	3.0	4.3	7.5
3. Twice	1.0	1.4	0.5	0.8	-	2.1	0.7	0.6	0.7	0.5	1.2	0.5	0.2	1.4	2.0	2.2
4. 3 or 4 times	0.6	1.1	0.2	0.6	1.0	0.8	0.6	0.6	0.7	0.4	0.9	0.4	0.6	0.7	0.8	7.2
5. 5 or more times	0.9	1.4	0.4	0.7	0.4	1.3	0.2	0.7	1.6	0.7	1.1	0.4	1.4	1.3	0.5	7.4
Item 6610 Subject S01 N	3298	1563	1643	2471	384	764	908	1006	619	1912	1167	1280	695	448	780	46
A19K: Taken part of a car without permission of the owner																
1. Not at all	93.3	88.9	97.7	93.4	96.1	88.5	94.2	96.5	92.5	94.7	92.1	97.2	93.1	91.8	89.3	70.0
2. Once	3.4	5.1	1.5	3.2	1.8	5.7	2.8	1.9	4.0	2.9	3.8	1.7	3.6	3.7	5.6	6.5
3. Twice	1.8	3.2	0.4	1.9	1.0	3.0	1.7	0.8	2.0	1.1	2.4	0.5	1.6	2.4	3.1	15.8
4. 3 or 4 times	0.5	0.8	0.2	0.5	0.8	0.6	0.4	0.4	0.6	0.4	0.6	0.2	0.5	0.7	0.7	1.5
5. 5 or more times	1.0	1.9	0.1	0.9	0.3	2.1	0.8	0.4	0.9	0.9	1.1	0.5	1.2	1.4	1.3	6.2
Item 6620 Subject S01 N	3292	1558	1642	2466	382	762	907	1006	617	1909	1163	1279	694	446	778	46
A19L: Gone into some house or building when you weren't supposed to be there																
1. Not at all	73.8	65.5	82.0	72.9	80.7	67.4	75.4	78.2	72.2	74.4	73.6	82.1	74.7	74.1	60.4	45.4
2. Once	13.4	17.5	9.2	13.9	9.8	14.2	14.0	11.4	14.6	13.1	14.5	10.7	14.4	13.5	17.3	13.6
3. Twice	6.5	8.3	4.8	6.8	5.3	7.4	6.1	5.7	7.2	6.7	6.1	3.9	6.2	5.6	10.5	20.1
4. 3 or 4 times	3.2	3.7	2.4	3.2	1.9	5.6	2.1	2.3	3.4	3.1	3.0	1.9	2.3	3.3	5.7	9.5
5. 5 or more times	3.1	4.9	1.5	3.1	2.3	5.5	2.4	2.4	2.5	2.7	2.8	1.4	2.3	3.5	6.1	11.3
Item 6630 Subject S01 N	3287	1557	1638	2464	382	761	908	1002	616	1903	1165	1276	691	447	778	46
A19M: Set fire to someone's property on pur-pose																
1. Not at all	98.1	97.1	99.4	98.3	98.6	97.1	98.6	97.8	99.3	98.4	98.3	99.4	98.3	98.5	96.8	87.7
2. Once	1.1	1.5	0.5	1.0	1.2	1.3	0.7	1.5	0.6	0.9	1.0	0.3	1.1	0.7	2.0	5.2
3. Twice	0.3	0.6	0.1	0.2	-	0.9	0.3	0.1	-	0.2	0.5	0.1	0.3	0.1	0.9	-
4. 3 or 4 times	0.2	0.3	*	0.2	-	0.1	0.2	0.3	-	0.2	0.1	0.1	-	0.4	0.2	-
5. 5 or more times	0.3	0.5	*	0.2	0.2	0.6	0.1	0.3	0.1	0.2	0.1	0.1	0.4	0.3	0.1	7.0
Item 6640 Subject S01 N	3294	1558	1644	2469	383	763	908	1006	617	1908	1166	1278	696	448	778	46
A19N: Damaged school property on purpose																
1. Not at all	86.2	81.1	91.5	86.0	91.7	83.0	86.1	89.0	86.1	87.1	86.4	92.1	88.2	85.5	76.8	59.5
2. Once	6.7	8.5	4.8	6.8	5.3	6.7	7.1	6.1	7.3	6.7	6.6	4.3	6.4	7.9	9.8	16.7
3. Twice	3.7	5.2	2.0	3.8	1.6	5.6	3.5	2.7	3.2	3.6	3.1	2.2	3.0	2.5	7.1	11.0
4. 3 or 4 times	1.8	2.5	1.1	1.8	0.9	2.1	1.9	1.4	1.8	1.5	2.1	1.0	1.3	1.1	3.6	3.9
5. 5 or more times	1.6	2.6	0.6	1.6	0.4	2.6	1.4	0.9	1.6	1.1	1.8	0.4	1.1	2.9	2.6	8.8
Item 6650 Subject B07,S01 N	3279	1548	1639	2459	383	759	900	1004	616	1899	1161	1276	692	444	772	45
A19O: Damaged property at work on purpose																
1. Not at all	94.5	90.1	99.0	94.4	96.5	91.1	95.9	95.4	95.1	95.0	94.4	97.0	95.8	94.2	90.1	76.9
2. Once	2.7	4.8	0.7	2.8	2.2	4.2	2.1	2.0	3.1	2.4	3.1	1.4	2.0	3.5	4.9	7.5
3. Twice	1.5	2.7	0.1	1.5	1.1	2.6	1.1	1.5	0.6	1.3	1.4	0.6	0.9	1.0	3.4	6.6
4. 3 or 4 times	0.7	1.1	0.2	0.6	0.2	0.9	0.5	0.6	0.8	0.6	0.6	0.7	0.3	0.5	1.0	2.7
5. 5 or more times	0.6	1.3	-	0.7	-	1.2	0.5	0.5	0.4	0.6	0.4	0.3	1.0	0.8	0.6	6.2
Item 6660 Subject C01,S01 N	3288	1555	1643	2467	383	760	908	1004	616	1903	1167	1277	694	448	776	46
A19P: Gotten into trouble with police because of something you did																
1. Not at all	77.7	68.6	87.1	76.5	86.4	74.2	77.0	81.8	76.1	80.5	74.4	88.8	77.2	76.9	62.2	45.9
2. Once	14.1	18.2	10.1	14.5	10.6	15.2	15.3	12.2	14.3	12.7	16.8	8.7	14.7	16.7	20.8	22.4
3. Twice	4.3	6.8	1.7	4.7	2.2	6.0	3.7	3.3	4.8	4.4	3.9	1.4	5.7	2.8	8.0	14.8
4. 3 or 4 times	2.6	4.0	1.1	3.0	0.5	3.2	2.5	1.5	3.7	1.7	3.2	0.9	1.3	1.7	6.7	5.1
5. 5 or more times	1.3	2.5	0.1	1.4	0.3	1.5	1.5	1.2	1.1	0.8	1.6	0.2	1.0	1.8	2.4	11.7
Item 6670 Subject S01 N	3292	1558	1642	2468	384	761	907	1005	619	1907	1166	1277	696	448	778	46

*=less than .05 per cent.

QUESTIONNAIRE FORM 2 1985	TOTAL	SEX		RACE		REGION				4YR COLLEGE PLANS		ILLICIT DRUG USE: LIFETIME				
		M	F	White	Black	NE	NC	S	W	Yes	No	None	Mari-juana Only	Few Pills	More Pills	Any Her-oin
N (Weighted No. of Cases):	3327	1573	1651	2485	388	771	914	1017	625	1919	1172	1283	696	453	784	47
% of Weighted Total:	100.0	47.3	49.6	74.7	11.7	23.2	27.5	30.6	18.8	57.7	35.2	38.6	20.9	13.6	23.6	1.4

A20: The next questions are about some things which may have happened TO YOU. During the LAST 12 MONTHS, how often...

A20A: Has something of yours (worth under $50) been stolen?

	TOTAL	M	F	White	Black	NE	NC	S	W	Yes	No	None	Mar.	Few	More	Her.
1. Not at all	55.6	50.7	60.7	56.8	52.6	55.4	58.4	56.2	50.8	52.8	61.7	61.1	52.6	55.0	48.7	55.9
2. Once	26.9	28.2	25.3	26.3	29.3	25.7	26.0	26.9	29.8	30.3	21.6	24.6	31.3	26.2	27.9	26.7
3. Twice	10.6	12.6	8.7	10.4	8.5	11.0	9.1	10.3	12.8	10.2	10.2	8.9	10.3	10.3	14.1	13.7
4. 3 or 4 times	5.0	6.2	3.8	4.7	6.6	5.6	4.7	5.3	3.9	4.9	4.7	3.9	4.1	5.2	7.4	2.2
5. 5 or more times	1.9	2.3	1.6	1.8	3.0	2.3	1.8	1.4	2.7	1.8	1.8	1.6	1.7	3.3	1.9	1.5
Item 6680 Subject S03 N	3284	1553	1641	2464	383	760	907	1003	614	1900	1167	1275	693	446	776	46

A20B: Has something of yours (worth over $50) been stolen?

	TOTAL	M	F	White	Black	NE	NC	S	W	Yes	No	None	Mar.	Few	More	Her.
1. Not at all	85.1	81.9	88.3	86.2	79.5	82.7	88.4	84.4	84.4	85.3	85.6	90.6	81.8	83.2	80.7	79.9
2. Once	10.7	12.7	8.8	10.3	14.0	11.9	9.7	10.9	10.2	11.1	9.8	7.2	13.5	11.7	13.4	10.6
3. Twice	3.1	4.4	1.6	2.7	3.5	4.7	1.5	3.0	3.6	2.8	3.2	1.5	3.4	3.3	4.7	8.0
4. 3 or 4 times	0.9	0.7	1.0	0.7	2.6	0.4	0.2	1.4	1.6	0.7	1.2	0.7	1.0	0.9	1.1	1.5
5. 5 or more times	0.3	0.3	0.3	0.2	0.4	0.4	0.1	0.4	0.3	0.2	0.2	0.1	0.3	1.0	0.1	-
Item 6690 Subject S03 N	3282	1552	1641	2463	383	755	907	1002	618	1900	1167	1274	695	447	773	46

A20C: Has someone deliberately damaged your property (your car, clothing, etc.)?

	TOTAL	M	F	White	Black	NE	NC	S	W	Yes	No	None	Mar.	Few	More	Her.
1. Not at all	68.9	62.5	75.3	68.8	72.5	70.2	68.1	73.3	61.4	70.7	67.1	73.6	68.6	70.4	61.6	45.2
2. Once	19.4	23.3	15.7	19.9	16.7	17.3	20.6	18.7	21.3	18.7	20.1	16.6	20.5	19.4	23.2	28.5
3. Twice	7.6	9.6	5.5	7.8	5.3	9.0	8.4	4.5	9.7	6.7	8.9	6.3	7.3	6.4	10.1	14.1
4. 3 or 4 times	3.0	3.4	2.5	2.6	4.1	2.6	2.3	2.7	5.2	3.0	2.5	2.8	2.4	2.4	3.9	7.9
5. 5 or more times	1.1	1.2	1.1	0.9	1.4	0.9	0.7	0.8	2.5	0.9	1.3	0.7	1.3	1.4	1.1	4.3
Item 6700 Subject S03 N	3291	1559	1643	2470	383	761	908	1003	618	1908	1167	1278	696	448	777	46

A20D: Has someone injured you with a weapon (like a knife, gun, or club)?

	TOTAL	M	F	White	Black	NE	NC	S	W	Yes	No	None	Mar.	Few	More	Her.
1. Not at all	95.2	93.3	97.3	95.4	94.0	94.3	94.9	96.3	94.8	96.2	93.9	98.4	95.2	95.1	91.8	75.4
2. Once	3.1	4.2	2.0	3.0	4.9	3.8	3.5	2.0	3.5	2.6	3.9	0.9	2.8	2.7	6.5	5.5
3. Twice	1.1	1.7	0.5	1.1	0.7	1.3	1.5	0.9	0.7	1.0	1.2	0.4	1.6	1.2	1.2	10.6
4. 3 or 4 times	0.3	0.5	0.1	0.3	0.5	0.4	-	0.3	0.6	-	0.7	0.3	0.2	0.7	0.2	-
5. 5 or more times	0.3	0.4	0.1	0.2	-	0.2	0.1	0.6	0.4	0.2	0.2	-	0.2	0.3	0.3	8.5
Item 6710 Subject S03 N	3285	1556	1640	2469	383	760	908	1002	614	1906	1164	1275	696	445	777	46

A20E: Has someone threatened you with a weapon, but not actually injured you?

	TOTAL	M	F	White	Black	NE	NC	S	W	Yes	No	None	Mar.	Few	More	Her.
1. Not at all	83.8	78.9	89.2	85.7	74.9	81.5	86.8	83.5	82.8	86.8	80.6	90.6	84.9	81.0	75.3	58.8
2. Once	10.0	12.6	7.2	8.7	16.5	11.0	7.3	11.3	10.5	8.7	11.3	6.5	10.6	14.2	12.3	13.4
3. Twice	3.7	4.5	2.7	3.2	5.9	4.3	3.8	3.1	3.9	2.7	4.8	1.5	3.0	2.9	8.1	9.0
4. 3 or 4 times	1.4	2.2	0.5	1.2	2.3	2.2	1.2	0.9	1.5	1.2	1.7	0.7	1.2	1.1	2.5	6.6
5. 5 or more times	1.1	1.8	0.4	1.2	0.4	1.1	0.9	1.1	1.3	0.5	1.6	0.7	0.4	0.8	1.8	12.2
Item 6720 Subject S03 N	3286	1555	1643	2465	383	758	908	1002	618	1905	1165	1275	696	448	776	46

A20F: Has someone injured you on purpose without using a weapon?

	TOTAL	M	F	White	Black	NE	NC	S	W	Yes	No	None	Mar.	Few	More	Her.
1. Not at all	83.6	82.9	84.9	83.6	86.5	80.4	82.6	87.7	82.2	86.2	80.6	87.9	86.7	82.6	75.7	61.8
2. Once	9.4	9.5	8.8	9.3	7.5	10.3	10.2	7.5	10.0	8.4	10.7	7.2	7.7	10.8	12.7	19.4
3. Twice	3.5	3.5	3.3	3.6	3.4	5.3	3.2	2.4	3.3	3.0	3.8	2.6	2.6	4.2	5.1	7.0
4. 3 or 4 times	2.0	2.2	1.5	1.9	0.8	2.3	2.4	1.3	2.0	1.3	2.6	1.4	1.4	0.7	3.8	6.2
5. 5 or more times	1.6	1.8	1.5	1.6	1.8	1.8	1.6	1.2	2.4	1.1	2.3	0.9	1.6	1.6	2.6	5.6
Item 6730 Subject S03 N	3288	1559	1641	2468	383	760	907	1003	618	1907	1167	1276	696	448	776	46

QUESTIONNAIRE FORM 2 1985	TOTAL	SEX		RACE		REGION				4YR COLLEGE PLANS		ILLICIT DRUG USE: LIFETIME				
		M	F	White	Black	NE	NC	S	W	Yes	No	None	Mari- juana Only	Few Pills	More Pills	Any Her- oin
N (Weighted No. of Cases):	3327	1573	1651	2485	388	771	914	1017	625	1919	1172	1283	696	453	784	47
% of Weighted Total:	100.0	47.3	49.6	74.7	11.7	23.2	27.5	30.6	18.8	57.7	35.2	38.6	20.9	13.6	23.6	1.4
A20G: Has an unarmed person threatened you with injury, but not actually injured you?																
1. Not at all	71.8	65.1	79.1	71.1	75.5	70.4	72.6	72.5	71.3	73.3	70.2	79.6	70.9	68.5	63.3	42.4
2. Once	13.3	15.2	10.9	13.3	12.0	14.2	11.7	13.8	13.6	12.1	14.8	10.4	14.5	17.4	14.3	19.1
3. Twice	6.2	8.1	4.4	6.6	3.9	4.8	5.7	7.0	7.3	6.5	5.8	4.3	5.8	6.4	9.4	5.7
4. 3 or 4 times	4.0	5.4	2.6	4.2	4.5	4.8	4.9	2.8	3.7	3.5	4.8	3.0	3.3	4.2	6.1	11.1
5. 5 or more times	4.7	6.2	3.1	4.8	4.1	5.7	5.1	3.8	4.1	4.5	4.5	2.7	5.5	3.5	6.9	21.7
Item 6740 Subject S03 N	3288	1557	1644	2467	384	760	908	1001	618	1907	1166	1278	695	448	776	46
A21: The following questions concern ciga- rettes, alcohol, and a number of other drugs. How difficult do you think it would be for you to get each of the following types of drugs, if you wanted some?																
A21A: Marijuana (pot, grass)																
1. Probably impossible	6.0	5.0	6.7	3.9	11.9	4.5	4.8	9.2	4.3	4.6	8.1	12.9	1.4	2.6	0.7	-
2. Very difficult	3.2	2.2	3.8	1.6	6.3	2.5	2.8	4.0	3.0	3.3	2.1	5.5	1.8	2.4	0.6	3.8
3. Fairly difficult	5.4	5.0	5.7	5.9	3.9	3.8	7.6	6.3	3.1	5.5	5.2	9.0	3.9	4.1	2.0	1.0
4. Fairly easy	29.1	27.9	30.4	30.4	23.2	25.5	31.4	30.8	27.4	30.8	26.8	35.0	26.2	32.8	21.3	12.9
5. Very easy	56.3	59.8	53.3	58.1	54.7	63.7	53.4	49.8	62.2	55.8	57.8	37.5	66.8	58.1	75.4	82.3
Item 6750 Subject A03a N	3274	1552	1635	2455	382	758	903	995	618	1900	1161	1267	693	449	779	46
A21B: LSD																
1. Probably impossible	21.9	18.9	24.4	16.9	42.7	19.1	21.2	26.6	18.8	18.3	26.3	26.5	24.4	21.3	12.4	9.7
2. Very difficult	20.3	20.8	19.8	20.6	21.5	16.6	22.2	21.5	20.2	21.0	19.4	21.3	21.1	22.0	18.0	4.3
3. Fairly difficult	27.3	29.1	26.1	29.7	17.8	31.7	26.5	24.3	27.7	29.7	24.4	26.6	28.7	26.9	27.5	36.2
4. Fairly easy	23.4	22.7	24.0	25.7	11.7	24.0	21.0	22.7	27.4	24.2	22.6	21.1	21.0	21.5	30.3	27.3
5. Very easy	7.1	8.5	5.6	7.1	6.4	8.5	9.1	4.8	5.9	6.9	7.3	4.4	4.8	8.3	11.8	22.4
Item 6760 Subject A03a N	3232	1542	1603	2429	378	745	889	987	610	1871	1150	1236	688	444	777	46
A21C: Some other psychedelic (mescaline, peyote, psilocybin, PCP, etc.)																
1. Probably impossible	26.4	23.8	29.0	22.6	43.1	20.8	26.9	33.3	21.5	23.2	30.5	30.9	28.5	27.5	17.5	5.8
2. Very difficult	23.8	24.7	22.9	24.1	22.7	19.3	25.8	24.5	25.1	24.3	23.1	23.8	26.8	24.0	22.5	6.2
3. Fairly difficult	23.6	24.5	22.8	25.9	16.7	24.4	23.3	22.3	25.3	26.1	20.8	23.5	24.3	19.9	24.3	43.4
4. Fairly easy	18.8	18.6	18.8	20.3	10.1	23.8	16.4	14.8	22.6	18.8	18.5	17.5	14.6	20.7	22.7	27.3
5. Very easy	7.4	8.4	6.5	7.1	7.4	11.7	7.6	5.1	5.4	7.5	7.0	4.3	5.8	7.9	13.0	17.3
Item 6770 Subject A03a N	3219	1541	1596	2410	382	741	887	986	605	1865	1144	1235	688	439	773	46
A21D: Amphetamines (uppers, pep pills, ben- nies, speed)																
1. Probably impossible	11.1	9.8	11.8	7.2	27.6	9.1	10.0	14.6	9.4	9.1	13.5	17.3	11.4	5.3	3.4	4.5
2. Very difficult	8.6	8.3	8.6	6.9	13.9	7.7	8.4	9.0	9.2	9.9	6.3	12.3	9.9	6.6	2.9	1.9
3. Fairly difficult	14.0	16.6	11.1	14.0	15.0	15.4	13.8	12.6	14.5	16.3	9.7	15.9	18.2	11.4	8.1	13.8
4. Fairly easy	34.7	36.1	33.9	36.7	25.7	36.9	32.3	34.9	35.1	34.4	35.7	32.7	35.5	43.7	33.2	26.1
5. Very easy	31.7	29.1	34.5	35.3	17.7	30.9	35.5	28.9	31.8	30.4	34.9	21.8	25.0	32.9	52.4	53.7
Item 6780 Subject A03a N	3236	1541	1612	2429	380	742	893	991	611	1874	1152	1242	688	444	778	46
A21E: Barbiturates (downers, goofballs, reds, yellows, etc.)																
1. Probably impossible	15.6	13.4	17.4	10.8	37.1	13.0	13.9	20.5	13.4	13.2	18.0	21.1	16.6	12.3	7.7	7.7
2. Very difficult	14.0	14.7	13.2	13.0	16.7	13.7	15.9	12.2	14.4	14.6	12.9	14.6	16.6	14.5	10.8	7.6
3. Fairly difficult	19.1	21.5	16.8	20.5	14.3	21.1	18.5	17.5	20.1	21.7	14.7	19.1	24.4	16.7	15.4	15.0
4. Fairly easy	29.1	28.7	29.5	31.3	17.7	28.8	27.8	28.7	31.9	29.1	29.8	28.6	24.5	34.8	31.2	32.8
5. Very easy	22.2	21.6	23.2	24.4	14.3	23.4	24.0	21.1	20.1	21.4	24.6	16.7	17.8	21.7	35.0	36.9
Item 6790 Subject A03a N	3225	1540	1600	2420	379	742	889	984	609	1868	1149	1237	687	439	777	46
A21F: Tranquilizers																
1. Probably impossible	15.1	14.0	15.9	9.8	38.8	13.2	14.4	18.0	13.8	11.7	18.6	17.9	18.0	13.0	8.4	11.4
2. Very difficult	11.4	12.7	9.9	11.0	12.9	10.2	12.8	11.8	10.2	10.8	12.3	11.0	13.0	12.2	10.5	8.5
3. Fairly difficult	18.8	21.6	15.8	19.3	14.7	19.4	18.1	16.6	22.7	19.5	17.3	17.8	22.7	16.7	17.7	22.4
4. Fairly easy	30.4	29.9	31.5	33.2	18.8	33.4	28.4	30.4	29.6	32.5	28.5	31.3	26.3	34.1	30.6	29.9
5. Very easy	24.3	21.8	27.0	26.6	14.8	23.8	26.4	23.1	23.7	25.6	23.3	22.0	19.9	24.0	32.8	27.7
Item 6800 Subject A03a N	3223	1539	1601	2419	377	741	890	984	608	1871	1146	1242	681	441	774	45

QUESTIONNAIRE FORM 2 1985	TOTAL	SEX		RACE		REGION				4YR COLLEGE PLANS		ILLICIT DRUG USE: LIFETIME				
		M	F	White	Black	NE	NC	S	W	Yes	No	None	Marijuana Only	Few Pills	More Pills	Any Heroin
N (Weighted No. of Cases):	3327	1573	1651	2485	388	771	914	1017	625	1919	1172	1283	696	453	784	47
% of Weighted Total:	100.0	47.3	49.6	74.7	11.7	23.2	27.5	30.6	18.8	57.7	35.2	38.6	20.9	13.6	23.6	1.4
A21G: Cocaine																
1. Probably impossible	17.5	15.8	18.9	14.1	31.2	11.1	20.4	23.0	12.3	15.4	20.0	26.0	18.4	14.6	5.5	1.9
2. Very difficult	13.5	12.5	14.1	13.9	13.3	9.7	17.9	15.5	8.4	14.7	11.8	18.3	12.3	11.8	8.4	3.5
3. Fairly difficult	20.1	22.8	17.8	22.1	11.4	15.9	23.2	20.9	19.6	20.6	19.6	22.6	22.7	20.9	13.6	12.2
4. Fairly easy	25.9	24.6	27.5	27.7	21.1	29.1	23.4	23.8	29.1	28.4	22.8	21.3	28.1	31.6	27.9	34.2
5. Very easy	23.0	24.3	21.7	22.2	23.0	34.1	15.1	16.8	30.7	20.9	25.7	11.7	18.5	21.0	44.6	48.1
Item 6810 Subject A03a N	3231	1541	1606	2425	379	747	888	984	611	1874	1149	1235	690	444	776	46
A21H: Heroin (smack, horse)																
1. Probably impossible	30.8	29.8	31.4	26.8	46.1	25.3	32.6	35.8	26.9	27.1	35.5	32.1	31.7	32.0	27.7	10.9
2. Very difficult	24.1	24.7	23.7	26.0	17.2	23.8	24.5	22.5	26.7	25.8	22.4	24.1	25.2	25.3	24.1	6.0
3. Fairly difficult	24.1	25.1	23.3	26.1	14.3	27.5	23.1	21.1	26.1	25.9	21.5	22.6	23.9	22.4	27.2	37.5
4. Fairly easy	14.7	13.7	15.6	15.1	13.3	16.0	13.8	14.4	14.9	15.2	14.0	16.3	12.3	13.8	13.9	22.6
5. Very easy	6.3	6.7	6.0	6.0	9.1	7.5	6.0	6.2	5.4	6.1	6.6	4.9	6.9	6.4	7.1	23.0
Item 6820 Subject A03a N	3213	1534	1594	2412	375	741	885	979	608	1860	1147	1229	686	438	775	45
A21I: Some other narcotic (methadone, opium, codeine, paregoric, etc.)																
1. Probably impossible	24.2	22.2	25.7	19.2	44.4	21.3	23.9	29.1	20.5	19.7	30.0	27.9	28.7	24.2	14.6	6.4
2. Very difficult	19.1	20.3	17.9	20.4	15.8	17.2	21.6	18.8	18.1	20.0	18.0	21.9	17.8	21.3	14.6	9.2
3. Fairly difficult	23.6	24.2	22.9	24.3	16.5	25.9	22.1	22.0	25.5	25.7	20.9	22.7	25.3	22.7	24.9	21.6
4. Fairly easy	20.4	20.2	21.0	22.5	13.8	20.5	19.8	19.6	22.2	21.9	17.8	18.6	16.2	20.6	26.3	33.0
5. Very easy	12.7	13.1	12.5	13.6	9.6	15.1	12.5	10.6	13.6	12.7	13.3	8.9	12.0	11.2	19.6	29.8
Item 6830 Subject A03a N	3225	1540	1599	2418	379	741	888	985	611	1868	1148	1237	687	439	776	46

This section asks for your views and feelings about a number of different things.

D01: How satisfied are you with your life as a whole these days?

	TOTAL	M	F	White	Black	NE	NC	S	W	Yes	No	None	Marijuana Only	Few Pills	More Pills	Any Heroin
1. Completely dissatisfied	2.8	1.8	3.5	1.9	4.0	2.9	2.9	2.4	2.9	2.0	3.9	2.7	2.4	3.9	2.4	1.2
2. Quite dissatisfied	9.4	9.1	9.6	9.8	7.4	9.0	10.0	9.4	9.1	9.8	8.3	8.6	10.2	10.7	9.8	7.2
3. Somewhat dissatisfied	10.9	11.4	10.4	10.9	11.6	11.3	12.9	7.7	12.4	10.4	11.2	8.8	10.0	11.7	14.9	11.4
4. Neither, or mixed feelings	13.2	12.0	14.2	12.4	16.6	13.8	12.6	14.1	12.0	11.4	15.6	11.2	12.8	16.9	13.9	27.3
5. Somewhat satisfied	22.3	24.2	20.9	22.2	22.4	21.8	23.0	22.4	21.7	22.4	23.0	21.9	23.1	19.8	23.8	24.2
6. Quite satisfied	35.3	35.2	35.4	37.4	27.8	34.1	34.2	37.0	35.5	37.6	32.0	39.0	36.0	33.1	30.0	20.9
7. Completely satisfied	6.1	6.2	6.0	5.4	10.3	7.1	4.4	7.0	6.2	6.4	6.0	7.7	5.5	3.9	5.2	7.7
Item 6840 Subject P01,Q01 N	3122	1480	1591	2414	342	698	869	956	598	1887	1143	1211	654	436	740	42

D02: These next questions ask you to guess how well you might do in several different situations. How good do you think you would be...

D02A: As a husband or wife?

	TOTAL	M	F	White	Black	NE	NC	S	W	Yes	No	None	Marijuana Only	Few Pills	More Pills	Any Heroin
1. Poor	0.6	0.9	0.4	0.5	0.6	0.7	0.8	0.5	0.4	0.5	0.7	0.2	0.8	1.2	0.5	5.5
2. Not so good	2.0	2.2	1.8	1.8	1.9	3.1	2.3	1.4	1.4	2.2	1.9	1.5	1.6	2.5	2.9	5.3
3. Fairly good	9.4	10.4	8.4	8.5	12.8	8.0	9.3	10.3	9.7	7.4	12.4	8.9	7.4	8.9	11.2	31.0
4. Good	35.8	39.2	32.5	37.0	29.5	34.1	37.5	35.2	35.9	36.9	34.6	37.3	35.0	35.8	34.5	17.8
5. Very good	48.3	42.3	54.3	48.8	48.9	49.9	47.0	47.7	49.5	50.0	45.7	48.1	51.7	46.6	47.7	34.3
8. Don't know	3.9	5.1	2.6	3.3	6.2	4.3	3.1	4.9	3.1	3.1	4.7	4.0	3.6	5.1	3.1	6.1
Item 6850 Subject D01,Q01 N	3109	1477	1582	2404	341	692	870	952	595	1880	1137	1202	651	436	740	42

D02B: As a parent?

	TOTAL	M	F	White	Black	NE	NC	S	W	Yes	No	None	Marijuana Only	Few Pills	More Pills	Any Heroin
1. Poor	1.4	1.1	1.8	1.5	1.2	1.0	1.5	1.6	1.5	1.3	1.6	1.2	1.0	2.4	1.9	-
2. Not so good	2.4	2.4	2.5	2.5	1.6	1.5	2.5	2.5	3.2	2.3	2.5	1.9	2.2	3.0	3.2	2.5
3. Fairly good	9.7	11.2	8.3	9.7	9.3	9.2	10.1	10.9	7.8	8.8	11.5	10.0	7.9	9.6	10.3	18.6
4. Good	34.3	36.3	32.0	36.1	22.4	32.1	36.3	33.0	36.1	34.5	34.2	35.2	32.4	33.2	34.9	40.5
5. Very good	46.9	42.4	51.5	45.5	59.3	49.2	45.5	46.2	47.2	48.6	44.3	46.1	51.1	45.5	45.7	29.5
8. Don't know	5.2	6.6	3.8	4.7	6.2	7.0	4.0	5.8	4.2	4.5	6.0	5.5	5.4	6.2	4.0	8.9
Item 6860 Subject D02,Q01 N	3101	1473	1579	2401	338	691	866	950	594	1876	1135	1196	651	437	737	42

QUESTIONNAIRE FORM 2 1985	TOTAL	SEX		RACE		REGION				4YR COLLEGE PLANS		ILLICIT DRUG USE: LIFETIME				
		M	F	White	Black	NE	NC	S	W	Yes	No	None	Marijuana Only	Few Pills	More Pills	Any Heroin
N (Weighted No. of Cases):	3327	1573	1651	2485	388	771	914	1017	625	1919	1172	1283	696	453	784	47
% of Weighted Total:	100.0	47.3	49.6	74.7	11.7	23.2	27.5	30.6	18.8	57.7	35.2	38.6	20.9	13.6	23.6	1.4
D02C: As a worker on a job?																
1. Poor	0.1	0.2	0.1	0.1	0.2	0.1	0.2	0.2	0.2	0.1	0.2	0.1	0.3	0.2	0.1	-
2. Not so good	0.5	0.4	0.6	0.5	0.2	0.7	0.3	0.6	0.2	0.4	0.6	0.3	0.2	0.9	0.5	6.6
3. Fairly good	3.6	3.9	3.3	3.4	3.7	3.4	3.3	4.4	2.9	3.4	3.8	3.4	3.6	4.5	2.8	11.9
4. Good	32.2	32.6	31.7	33.4	25.2	33.2	33.1	32.4	29.4	31.8	33.0	33.0	30.6	34.8	31.7	30.3
5. Very good	62.3	61.2	63.5	61.8	68.1	60.8	62.2	61.4	65.6	62.9	61.5	61.7	64.5	57.4	64.2	51.2
8. Don't know	1.3	1.7	0.9	0.7	2.6	1.7	0.9	1.1	1.8	1.3	0.9	1.5	0.7	2.3	0.9	-
Item 6870 Subject C03,Q01 N	3102	1475	1578	2404	338	690	865	952	594	1875	1137	1198	653	434	737	42
D03: Some people think a lot about the social problems of the nation and the world, and about how they might be solved. Others spend little time thinking about these issues. How much do you think about such things?																
1. Never	5.5	6.5	4.4	5.1	5.6	8.4	5.0	4.6	4.5	3.8	8.3	4.1	6.2	6.5	6.0	18.1
2. Seldom	22.8	21.5	23.8	22.9	23.7	26.2	23.7	21.5	19.8	20.0	27.6	19.5	24.4	22.2	27.0	19.4
3. Sometimes	47.4	47.6	47.7	48.5	42.0	44.4	48.6	47.3	49.3	47.9	46.5	50.9	46.8	49.5	42.3	37.9
4. Quite often	20.0	19.8	20.2	19.6	23.0	17.7	18.7	21.7	21.8	23.2	15.1	21.0	19.1	19.0	19.7	19.0
5. A great deal	4.2	4.6	4.0	4.0	5.7	3.4	4.0	4.9	4.7	5.0	2.6	4.6	3.5	2.8	5.0	5.6
Item 6880 Subject J,Q08 N	3093	1466	1578	2392	338	684	863	949	597	1870	1132	1200	645	436	735	39
D04: Now we'd like you to make some ratings of how honest and moral the people are who run the following organizations. To what extent are there problems of dishonesty and immorality in the leadership of...																
D04A: Large corporations?																
1. Not at all	3.7	4.1	3.2	2.8	8.0	4.5	2.5	3.6	4.7	3.0	4.6	4.5	2.6	3.7	2.5	7.6
2. Slight	17.2	19.4	14.8	16.7	18.1	14.9	16.0	20.7	15.7	16.6	17.9	17.0	17.0	15.4	18.2	15.0
3. Moderate	36.2	34.7	37.7	38.3	25.9	35.1	38.3	35.7	35.2	38.9	33.0	38.1	34.7	37.7	35.2	21.7
4. Considerable	22.1	22.1	22.3	23.1	18.6	22.1	22.7	20.9	22.9	24.0	19.2	21.5	23.0	22.8	23.1	15.4
5. Great	5.3	6.0	4.6	5.0	6.8	7.4	4.7	4.0	5.7	4.9	5.3	4.3	6.6	6.2	4.9	10.0
8. No opinion	15.6	13.7	17.3	14.1	22.6	15.9	15.7	15.1	15.7	12.6	19.9	14.6	16.1	14.2	16.1	30.4
Item 6890 Subject K01 N	3019	1436	1538	2343	327	655	844	931	588	1820	1094	1174	636	425	707	39
D04B: Major labor unions?																
1. Not at all	4.2	5.1	3.2	3.7	6.8	3.9	3.5	5.1	3.9	3.2	6.0	4.2	3.3	5.3	3.3	5.3
2. Slight	18.2	19.8	16.5	17.4	18.9	16.6	17.2	20.0	18.8	18.7	17.6	18.5	16.7	17.5	19.6	18.6
3. Moderate	31.8	29.8	33.7	33.6	23.8	31.2	32.7	30.1	33.8	34.0	29.0	32.9	35.4	30.9	28.8	18.8
4. Considerable	20.1	21.7	18.8	20.6	17.0	21.2	22.1	19.1	17.5	20.8	18.5	19.9	16.9	22.0	22.3	23.0
5. Great	6.1	7.9	4.5	6.3	6.5	7.9	5.9	5.6	4.9	6.2	5.5	6.1	6.6	6.4	5.0	8.0
8. No opinion	19.7	15.6	23.3	18.4	27.0	19.2	18.5	20.1	21.1	17.2	23.4	18.3	20.8	18.0	21.0	26.1
Item 6900 Subject K01 N	3014	1434	1533	2343	324	651	843	931	588	1816	1092	1173	634	422	707	39
D04C: The nation's colleges and universities?																
1. Not at all	6.9	7.8	5.9	7.0	6.4	6.1	6.8	6.3	8.8	7.6	5.9	7.5	6.3	7.5	5.0	15.3
2. Slight	31.0	31.3	30.8	32.7	24.2	30.7	33.7	30.1	29.2	34.8	25.6	33.9	33.0	29.5	27.2	20.2
3. Moderate	23.1	23.4	22.8	23.6	21.8	23.2	22.4	25.1	20.8	22.0	25.0	21.2	22.9	22.9	26.9	18.5
4. Considerable	18.0	16.9	19.3	17.9	17.3	15.7	16.3	18.7	22.2	19.1	16.4	17.5	18.2	20.1	17.8	11.7
5. Great	7.2	7.8	6.5	5.7	13.6	8.8	6.6	7.6	5.6	7.2	6.9	6.4	6.0	8.4	8.5	9.5
8. No opinion	13.8	12.8	14.8	13.1	16.6	15.6	14.2	12.4	13.5	9.3	20.3	13.6	13.6	11.7	14.6	24.9
Item 6910 Subject B10,K01 N	3004	1428	1529	2333	325	651	840	927	586	1813	1086	1166	631	424	706	38
D04D: The nation's public schools?																
1. Not at all	7.4	8.7	6.0	7.2	7.7	8.5	6.9	5.8	9.3	7.2	7.9	8.3	6.7	6.2	6.5	6.6
2. Slight	28.4	29.7	27.4	30.7	21.0	27.1	32.9	28.3	23.7	31.6	22.9	31.6	28.9	28.7	24.3	12.6
3. Moderate	26.2	23.6	28.6	26.5	23.7	27.7	24.7	24.8	28.7	26.9	25.6	24.0	26.3	23.8	31.6	23.3
4. Considerable	18.8	18.3	19.6	18.2	21.1	15.0	18.5	21.2	19.7	18.4	19.9	18.6	18.3	20.6	18.5	19.6
5. Great	8.2	8.8	7.6	7.1	13.9	9.5	5.6	10.1	7.5	7.8	8.6	7.3	8.1	9.7	8.0	19.8
8. No opinion	11.0	11.0	10.9	10.4	12.6	12.2	11.4	9.7	11.1	8.0	15.1	10.1	11.6	10.9	11.1	18.1
Item 6920 Subject B10,K01 N	2992	1428	1518	2329	321	649	837	924	582	1810	1079	1165	630	420	701	38

QUESTIONNAIRE FORM 2 1985	TOTAL	SEX		RACE		REGION				4YR COLLEGE PLANS		ILLICIT DRUG USE: LIFETIME				
		M	F	White	Black	NE	NC	S	W	Yes	No	None	Mari-juana Only	Few Pills	More Pills	Any Her-oin
N (Weighted No. of Cases):	3327	1573	1651	2485	388	771	914	1017	625	1919	1172	1283	696	453	784	47
% of Weighted Total:	100.0	47.3	49.6	74.7	11.7	23.2	27.5	30.6	18.8	57.7	35.2	38.6	20.9	13.6	23.6	1.4

D04E: Churches and religious organizations?

1. Not at all	14.8	15.3	14.1	15.6	10.6	14.8	15.5	14.2	15.0	14.4	15.7	14.9	14.4	17.1	13.6	10.1
2. Slight	30.2	28.9	31.8	31.6	26.5	28.7	32.0	32.3	26.3	33.6	25.2	33.4	30.5	28.6	27.4	28.3
3. Moderate	13.7	12.3	15.0	13.6	15.7	12.2	14.1	13.0	15.9	13.7	13.4	13.9	12.6	15.4	13.7	10.8
4. Considerable	13.1	13.2	13.2	12.8	15.6	13.3	12.3	11.6	16.4	12.7	14.1	11.5	14.3	16.4	13.0	10.1
5. Great	14.6	16.9	12.5	13.7	18.1	13.6	13.1	17.6	13.1	14.0	15.2	14.6	13.4	11.5	16.2	25.3
8. No opinion	13.5	13.5	13.4	12.7	13.6	17.4	13.1	11.3	13.2	11.6	16.4	11.7	14.8	11.0	16.1	15.4
Item 6930 Subject G,K01 N	3004	1429	1529	2336	322	651	839	929	586	1811	1088	1169	633	421	705	37

D04F: The national news media (TV, magazines, news services)?

1. Not at all	4.3	4.9	3.7	3.9	6.9	6.4	3.4	4.2	3.6	3.7	5.1	4.1	3.4	4.4	4.3	14.4
2. Slight	20.4	22.6	17.9	20.6	20.6	19.2	19.7	22.3	19.6	20.2	20.4	20.1	20.6	22.3	20.2	17.0
3. Moderate	30.0	28.7	31.3	31.7	22.2	24.2	32.9	29.4	33.2	32.4	26.4	32.0	31.4	27.4	27.8	16.7
4. Considerable	23.0	22.4	23.8	22.8	23.5	24.8	22.4	22.4	22.8	24.4	21.3	22.2	23.7	25.4	22.6	17.3
5. Great	11.0	10.3	11.8	9.9	14.4	11.4	10.3	11.3	11.3	11.0	10.7	12.2	9.4	10.4	10.7	14.9
8. No opinion	11.3	11.1	11.6	11.0	12.5	14.0	11.4	10.5	9.5	8.4	16.0	9.4	11.5	10.0	14.4	19.7
Item 6940 Subject K01 N	2998	1422	1531	2332	322	647	840	928	583	1807	1086	1167	629	423	702	39

D04G: The Presidency and the administration?

1. Not at all	5.3	6.2	4.3	4.7	11.2	7.0	4.7	5.7	3.7	4.6	6.3	6.3	4.8	5.1	4.0	6.5
2. Slight	23.2	26.6	19.6	24.1	18.7	21.1	22.6	25.2	23.0	26.1	19.1	24.8	23.6	21.2	21.3	14.1
3. Moderate	29.3	28.9	29.8	31.1	19.5	29.0	30.9	27.4	30.5	31.0	27.2	29.7	29.8	29.2	30.1	15.2
4. Considerable	19.1	16.4	21.7	18.3	21.0	18.9	18.2	19.0	20.7	20.7	16.2	19.4	18.7	20.7	18.5	21.6
5. Great	8.7	9.5	8.1	8.4	11.8	9.1	8.7	8.7	8.4	7.2	10.7	6.7	9.4	8.0	11.0	19.5
8. No opinion	14.4	12.3	16.4	13.4	17.7	14.8	14.9	14.0	13.6	10.3	20.7	13.2	13.7	15.8	15.2	23.0
Item 6950 Subject H04,K01 N	2996	1426	1524	2329	321	650	839	924	584	1803	1088	1163	630	424	702	39

D04H: Congress–that is, the U.S. Senate and House of Representatives?

1. Not at all	4.3	4.7	3.6	3.6	8.7	5.8	3.5	4.6	3.1	3.6	5.2	4.2	3.7	4.2	4.4	5.2
2. Slight	20.9	24.4	17.6	20.8	20.3	18.5	22.0	21.3	21.2	23.5	16.9	22.4	19.8	20.6	20.1	10.8
3. Moderate	30.3	30.3	30.7	32.9	17.3	29.8	31.1	29.1	31.8	31.9	28.5	31.5	32.4	27.4	29.7	22.1
4. Considerable	20.6	19.1	22.0	20.8	19.4	19.9	19.8	22.0	20.3	22.3	17.6	21.5	19.3	20.6	20.0	20.7
5. Great	7.1	8.3	6.0	6.5	11.8	7.1	7.3	7.7	5.7	6.0	8.2	5.7	7.1	7.8	8.1	13.3
8. No opinion	16.9	13.2	20.2	15.4	22.4	18.9	16.4	15.3	17.9	12.7	23.6	14.6	17.7	19.4	17.7	28.0
Item 6960 Subject H04,K01 N	3002	1428	1528	2334	323	651	840	929	582	1807	1090	1165	632	425	703	39

D04I: The U.S. Supreme Court?

1. Not at all	11.6	15.2	8.1	11.4	12.8	11.7	12.0	10.0	13.4	12.7	10.1	12.8	11.5	11.1	10.1	6.8
2. Slight	26.2	26.9	25.6	27.6	20.3	26.6	27.6	26.5	23.1	29.0	21.6	26.2	29.2	28.1	22.7	26.0
3. Moderate	21.6	19.5	23.8	22.7	16.5	19.6	20.1	22.5	24.6	22.4	20.9	22.6	20.1	18.9	23.7	10.0
4. Considerable	13.7	13.3	13.9	13.2	15.6	12.4	15.0	14.2	12.4	13.6	13.6	14.2	12.4	14.6	13.1	13.0
5. Great	8.8	10.1	7.4	8.4	12.0	9.7	7.6	9.9	7.5	7.4	10.3	6.9	8.2	9.1	11.7	19.0
8. No opinion	18.2	14.9	21.2	16.6	22.8	20.1	17.5	16.9	19.1	14.8	23.5	17.2	18.6	18.2	18.7	25.2
Item 6970 Subject H04,K01 N	2987	1421	1520	2325	322	643	837	925	582	1798	1086	1159	631	424	698	37

D04J: All the courts and the justice system in general?

1. Not at all	6.2	7.8	4.6	5.6	9.9	7.4	6.6	5.4	5.5	5.7	7.3	7.6	4.5	5.9	5.3	5.4
2. Slight	25.9	27.8	24.1	27.1	22.7	25.8	28.1	25.8	23.2	28.7	21.3	27.0	28.6	26.5	22.6	15.5
3. Moderate	29.0	28.0	30.4	30.2	21.5	27.5	28.0	28.2	33.4	31.0	26.4	28.7	30.7	27.8	29.3	23.9
4. Considerable	16.5	15.9	17.1	16.5	16.5	14.8	15.6	18.3	17.0	16.7	16.1	17.2	13.3	18.3	17.2	10.3
5. Great	6.3	7.0	5.5	5.6	10.3	7.1	5.1	7.5	5.3	5.5	7.2	4.9	5.8	6.5	8.7	15.1
8. No opinion	16.0	13.6	18.3	15.0	19.1	17.3	16.7	14.8	15.5	12.4	21.6	14.7	17.1	15.0	17.0	29.7
Item 6980 Subject H04,K01 N	2983	1417	1520	2323	318	640	839	921	583	1796	1082	1158	631	424	694	38

QUESTIONNAIRE FORM 2 1985	TOTAL	SEX		RACE		REGION				4YR COLLEGE PLANS		ILLICIT DRUG USE: LIFETIME				
		M	F	White	Black	NE	NC	S	W	Yes	No	None	Mari- juana Only	Few Pills	More Pills	Any Her- oin
N (Weighted No. of Cases):	3327	1573	1651	2485	388	771	914	1017	625	1919	1172	1283	696	453	784	47
% of Weighted Total:	100.0	47.3	49.6	74.7	11.7	23.2	27.5	30.6	18.8	57.7	35.2	38.6	20.9	13.6	23.6	1.4
D04K: The police and other law enforcement agencies?																
1. Not at all	5.1	5.3	4.7	4.2	8.8	6.5	3.9	5.6	4.5	4.2	6.3	4.5	4.4	6.2	5.7	5.0
2. Slight	24.0	25.0	23.3	24.9	22.7	20.7	25.9	26.4	21.0	26.5	20.5	27.7	24.4	23.7	18.8	13.6
3. Moderate	32.5	30.8	33.9	33.7	25.1	30.7	31.3	30.0	40.4	34.2	30.4	34.2	32.6	31.5	31.8	21.4
4. Considerable	19.3	20.0	18.7	19.1	20.2	18.2	20.4	19.9	18.2	20.1	17.9	17.6	18.9	20.6	21.3	14.4
5. Great	7.9	9.1	6.7	7.6	9.5	11.5	5.8	7.7	7.3	7.3	8.4	5.4	8.5	7.4	10.7	21.9
8. No opinion	11.2	9.7	12.6	10.5	13.8	12.4	12.7	10.5	8.6	7.7	16.5	10.5	11.1	10.6	11.7	23.6
Item 6990 Subject K01 N	2986	1420	1521	2326	320	642	839	925	580	1799	1083	1155	630	425	700	38
D04L: The U.S. military?																
1. Not at all	7.4	8.7	6.0	7.2	9.0	8.1	7.3	7.8	6.2	7.0	8.2	8.1	6.5	8.3	6.3	1.5
2. Slight	24.8	25.2	24.4	26.5	16.1	25.1	25.8	25.9	21.1	26.6	22.0	25.6	24.6	25.2	24.1	17.8
3. Moderate	26.2	25.7	26.6	27.3	18.9	26.2	26.2	23.8	30.2	28.2	23.9	25.9	26.9	25.5	27.2	24.7
4. Considerable	15.8	17.8	14.2	15.6	17.4	14.0	16.3	15.5	17.8	16.5	14.5	16.1	15.1	16.6	14.6	20.4
5. Great	8.3	9.8	6.7	7.3	16.1	7.6	7.4	10.4	6.9	7.4	9.1	7.7	9.4	7.4	8.7	8.7
8. No opinion	17.5	12.9	22.0	16.2	22.5	19.0	17.1	16.6	17.8	14.3	22.4	16.5	17.5	16.9	19.0	26.7
Item 7000 Subject K01,L04 N	2988	1422	1521	2328	321	644	839	924	580	1798	1084	1156	631	425	700	37
D05: How much do you agree or disagree with each of the following statements?																
D05A: There is too much competition in this society																
1. Disagree	9.8	14.5	5.4	9.5	13.7	9.1	9.8	10.2	10.2	10.8	8.6	9.6	11.0	8.3	9.4	10.2
2. Mostly disagree	13.0	15.4	10.8	14.1	11.7	11.6	13.5	14.1	12.0	14.9	9.9	15.2	12.9	11.1	11.0	11.1
3. Neither	24.5	26.6	22.6	25.0	19.8	25.5	23.7	24.8	23.9	23.3	25.0	23.3	25.6	24.6	24.9	32.3
4. Mostly agree	34.5	27.7	40.5	34.4	33.4	32.9	36.4	31.6	38.0	34.4	35.5	34.5	31.8	38.8	35.2	32.6
5. Agree	18.2	15.8	20.7	16.9	21.4	20.8	16.7	19.3	15.9	16.5	21.0	17.5	18.7	17.2	19.6	13.7
Item 7010 Subject Q08 N	3013	1427	1540	2342	322	653	846	927	587	1817	1089	1171	634	427	704	40
D05B: Too many young people are sloppy about their grooming and clothing, and just don't care how they look																
1. Disagree	17.0	19.3	14.9	16.5	16.7	18.9	13.5	18.3	17.8	17.9	15.3	15.8	16.4	14.9	20.1	26.4
2. Mostly disagree	30.7	31.2	30.0	33.2	18.3	31.2	34.2	27.7	30.0	32.2	28.7	30.3	32.7	33.0	29.1	16.3
3. Neither	20.8	21.2	20.8	21.7	16.2	18.7	22.0	19.8	22.9	20.7	20.4	19.4	21.0	21.3	23.2	16.6
4. Mostly agree	20.2	18.2	21.7	19.6	24.1	20.8	20.3	20.1	19.4	20.0	21.0	22.1	18.3	20.4	18.1	30.8
5. Agree	11.3	10.1	12.6	9.1	24.7	10.4	10.1	14.1	10.0	9.3	14.6	12.4	11.6	10.3	9.5	9.8
Item 7020 Subject Q08 N	3011	1424	1542	2342	322	653	845	926	588	1816	1089	1170	632	426	705	40
D05C: There is too much hard rock music on the radio these days																
1. Disagree	40.1	45.6	34.8	43.2	27.1	42.5	41.3	41.0	34.2	37.3	44.3	30.7	39.7	45.2	51.0	75.1
2. Mostly disagree	22.5	20.4	24.5	24.2	16.1	23.7	24.3	19.8	23.0	24.5	19.6	22.5	24.0	23.2	22.0	9.1
3. Neither	18.1	16.1	19.8	16.8	22.8	17.7	17.9	16.6	21.3	18.2	18.0	20.7	18.9	18.1	13.0	10.3
4. Mostly agree	10.1	9.1	11.3	9.2	13.8	8.2	10.6	11.4	9.6	10.8	9.3	13.5	9.2	7.5	7.4	3.0
5. Agree	9.2	8.8	9.6	6.6	20.2	8.0	5.9	11.2	12.0	9.2	8.8	12.5	8.2	6.0	6.6	2.5
Item 7030 Subject Q08 N	3008	1423	1539	2341	319	653	844	924	587	1814	1089	1167	631	426	706	40
D05D: People should do their own thing, even if other people think it's strange																
1. Disagree	3.3	4.1	2.7	2.8	5.0	3.7	2.2	3.7	3.8	2.9	3.7	3.9	2.3	2.5	3.5	3.3
2. Mostly disagree	5.2	5.6	4.8	5.0	7.0	3.7	5.9	5.4	5.8	5.0	5.2	6.1	4.8	4.6	4.6	7.8
3. Neither	12.4	13.2	11.8	12.6	8.5	10.7	12.7	12.2	14.3	11.6	13.5	14.1	12.5	10.7	10.8	6.5
4. Mostly agree	34.7	31.9	36.9	35.2	30.5	34.2	35.5	32.9	37.1	36.8	32.9	38.2	36.2	31.7	31.4	16.1
5. Agree	44.3	45.2	43.7	44.4	49.0	47.8	43.7	45.9	39.0	43.7	44.9	37.7	44.1	50.5	49.6	66.3
Item 7040 Subject Q08 N	3002	1420	1536	2335	319	650	840	925	587	1813	1083	1165	630	425	705	39

	TOTAL	SEX		RACE		REGION				4YR COLLEGE PLANS		ILLICIT DRUG USE: LIFETIME				
QUESTIONNAIRE FORM 2 1985		M	F	White	Black	NE	NC	S	W	Yes	No	None	Mari- juana Only	Few Pills	More Pills	Any Her- oin
N (Weighted No. of Cases):	3327	1573	1651	2485	388	771	914	1017	625	1919	1172	1283	696	453	784	47
% of Weighted Total:	100.0	47.3	49.6	74.7	11.7	23.2	27.5	30.6	18.8	57.7	35.2	38.6	20.9	13.6	23.6	1.4
D05E: I get a real kick out of doing things that are a little dangerous																
1. Disagree	21.1	12.5	29.2	18.0	48.1	16.8	20.4	26.6	18.2	20.9	21.6	30.8	19.2	17.0	9.5	9.3
2. Mostly disagree	18.4	15.9	20.9	18.1	17.9	19.2	17.8	17.6	19.7	20.1	16.2	20.4	19.6	17.4	15.0	13.0
3. Neither	27.7	27.8	27.4	28.8	17.6	27.1	30.0	25.7	27.9	26.7	29.1	26.7	28.2	31.8	26.9	16.9
4. Mostly agree	21.0	26.5	15.8	23.0	8.9	22.5	20.7	18.7	23.5	22.1	18.7	15.5	22.4	20.3	28.7	32.5
5. Agree	11.8	17.4	6.7	12.1	7.5	14.4	11.0	11.3	10.7	10.2	14.4	6.6	10.6	13.4	19.8	28.4
Item 7050 Subject Q04 N	3008	1423	1539	2339	320	652	843	925	588	1815	1086	1166	631	427	706	40
D05F: I like to test myself every now and then by doing something a little risky																
1. Disagree	18.3	11.4	24.9	16.1	35.1	16.6	16.5	22.2	16.8	18.6	18.1	25.6	18.1	13.6	8.6	10.6
2. Mostly disagree	15.5	12.5	18.0	15.7	13.6	16.2	14.7	15.2	16.0	17.5	12.2	19.4	15.2	10.8	12.2	6.3
3. Neither	22.8	21.2	24.2	23.4	14.2	20.6	25.6	21.1	23.6	21.8	24.5	20.3	23.1	27.8	24.4	10.7
4. Mostly agree	28.7	33.9	23.8	30.2	21.7	28.8	29.4	26.9	30.4	30.2	26.0	24.6	29.6	30.3	34.2	37.7
5. Agree	14.8	21.0	9.1	14.5	15.5	17.7	13.7	14.6	13.3	11.9	19.2	10.1	14.1	17.5	20.5	34.7
Item 7060 Subject Q04 N	2971	1396	1530	2313	314	639	840	911	581	1792	1073	1155	623	423	697	36
D05G: I take a positive attitude toward myself																
1. Disagree	3.1	2.0	4.0	2.9	2.7	4.7	3.1	2.2	2.5	2.6	4.0	2.8	2.4	3.7	3.4	7.4
2. Mostly disagree	6.7	4.6	8.6	7.1	3.5	8.4	6.4	5.8	6.8	6.4	6.8	5.3	5.4	9.1	8.8	5.5
3. Neither	13.0	12.5	13.6	13.3	7.5	12.2	14.2	11.7	14.2	11.7	14.9	13.3	12.9	12.0	12.5	32.7
4. Mostly agree	43.1	42.7	43.5	45.5	29.7	41.1	44.8	42.2	44.5	44.5	41.5	43.3	40.5	44.3	46.4	27.2
5. Agree	34.1	38.2	30.3	31.3	56.6	33.6	31.4	38.1	32.0	34.8	32.8	35.3	38.8	30.9	28.8	27.2
Item 12550 Subject Q01 N	2978	1402	1532	2317	315	640	839	915	584	1797	1076	1157	625	425	696	38
D05H: I feel I am a person of worth, on an equal plane with others																
1. Disagree	1.7	1.8	1.5	1.3	2.9	2.0	1.6	1.8	1.2	1.1	2.4	1.7	1.2	1.5	1.6	8.1
2. Mostly disagree	4.9	3.3	6.2	5.0	4.8	5.1	5.0	4.5	5.0	4.6	5.6	3.4	4.7	8.8	5.2	7.5
3. Neither	10.6	9.8	11.1	10.4	6.9	13.1	11.7	8.1	10.1	8.7	12.9	9.8	11.5	10.0	10.6	15.8
4. Mostly agree	37.0	35.1	38.9	39.0	26.4	34.9	41.1	34.3	37.8	37.2	37.2	39.4	35.0	36.4	36.8	30.9
5. Agree	45.9	50.0	42.3	44.2	59.0	44.9	40.7	51.3	45.8	48.4	42.0	45.7	47.7	43.3	45.8	37.7
Item 12570 Subject Q01 N	2968	1397	1526	2310	314	635	838	911	583	1796	1069	1153	625	421	694	36
D05I: I am able to do things as well as most other people																
1. Disagree	1.2	1.3	1.1	1.1	2.5	1.7	1.2	1.0	0.9	1.0	1.6	0.9	1.0	1.2	1.8	3.9
2. Mostly disagree	2.5	1.9	3.2	2.1	2.2	3.4	2.0	1.9	3.2	2.6	2.4	2.5	2.0	4.0	1.9	4.7
3. Neither	7.5	7.3	7.7	7.7	4.9	8.7	9.6	5.1	6.9	6.7	8.6	5.9	7.4	6.7	10.0	20.3
4. Mostly agree	41.6	37.0	45.3	43.4	29.9	39.5	43.9	42.0	39.9	39.6	44.7	41.6	39.5	49.1	40.7	28.0
5. Agree	47.2	52.4	42.7	45.7	60.5	46.7	43.2	50.0	49.0	50.0	42.8	49.0	50.1	39.0	45.6	43.1
Item 12580 Subject Q01 N	2967	1398	1526	2310	314	637	839	910	581	1794	1069	1155	624	418	695	38
D05J: On the whole, I'm satisfied with myself																
1. Disagree	2.4	2.0	2.9	2.2	2.4	3.8	2.8	1.7	1.6	1.7	3.5	2.1	2.7	2.2	2.6	1.4
2. Mostly disagree	6.4	4.6	8.1	6.6	4.1	7.4	6.8	5.0	7.0	5.9	7.0	5.8	5.1	8.1	7.9	4.8
3. Neither	10.3	9.6	10.8	10.2	6.1	8.8	12.7	7.4	12.9	9.6	10.6	9.2	8.1	11.8	12.5	21.8
4. Mostly agree	39.8	38.7	40.5	41.7	30.0	40.5	40.4	39.5	38.7	40.4	39.6	38.8	38.5	42.4	42.2	34.6
5. Agree	41.1	45.1	37.8	39.4	57.4	39.6	37.3	46.5	39.8	42.4	39.4	44.2	45.6	35.4	34.8	37.5
Item 12620 Subject P01,Q01 N	2963	1397	1525	2311	312	633	836	912	582	1793	1066	1156	623	419	690	38
D05K: I feel I do not have much to be proud of																
1. Disagree	42.7	44.1	41.9	42.1	57.3	41.9	39.8	47.3	40.5	45.4	39.4	44.9	45.4	38.4	40.0	29.9
2. Mostly disagree	31.4	30.9	31.5	33.1	19.8	32.2	33.4	28.1	33.0	31.8	30.6	30.9	30.0	32.4	33.5	20.1
3. Neither	12.1	11.0	13.1	12.1	8.5	12.9	12.2	11.1	12.5	11.4	12.6	9.6	10.4	14.7	15.0	28.2
4. Mostly agree	8.7	8.9	8.4	8.3	8.2	8.4	9.3	8.5	8.5	7.4	10.5	9.5	8.0	8.6	8.2	15.2
5. Agree	5.1	5.0	5.1	4.4	6.2	4.6	5.3	5.0	5.5	4.0	6.9	5.1	6.2	6.0	3.4	6.6
Item 12660 Subject Q01 N	2955	1392	1523	2303	312	631	835	911	578	1784	1069	1153	621	418	688	38

	TOTAL	SEX		RACE		REGION				4YR COLLEGE PLANS		ILLICIT DRUG USE: LIFETIME				
QUESTIONNAIRE FORM 2 **1985**		M	F	White	Black	NE	NC	S	W	Yes	No	None	Mari- juana Only	Few Pills	More Pills	Any Her- oin
N (Weighted No. of Cases):	3327	1573	1651	2485	388	771	914	1017	625	1919	1172	1283	696	453	784	47
% of Weighted Total:	100.0	47.3	49.6	74.7	11.7	23.2	27.5	30.6	18.8	57.7	35.2	38.6	20.9	13.6	23.6	1.4
D05L: Sometimes I think that I am no good at all																
1. Disagree	36.3	41.4	31.7	34.4	51.9	36.0	32.0	40.4	36.4	36.9	35.8	36.9	41.3	30.4	34.6	20.6
2. Mostly disagree	22.8	23.2	22.5	23.9	17.1	21.3	24.5	21.5	24.3	23.6	22.2	23.6	22.4	22.5	22.5	13.8
3. Neither	16.6	16.0	17.1	16.7	11.1	18.9	17.0	13.2	18.8	16.3	16.5	15.0	16.2	18.0	18.5	29.8
4. Mostly agree	15.0	11.7	18.1	16.0	12.4	14.3	16.1	14.4	15.4	15.2	14.9	15.1	13.3	18.3	15.2	14.6
5. Agree	9.2	7.7	10.6	9.0	7.5	9.4	10.4	10.5	5.2	8.0	10.5	9.4	6.9	10.8	9.2	21.1
Item 12680 Subject Q01 N	2951	1393	1517	2298	311	633	831	908	580	1787	1061	1154	620	417	686	36
D05M: I feel that I can't do anything right																
1. Disagree	48.0	52.5	44.1	46.2	58.1	48.3	43.5	49.5	51.7	51.0	43.6	48.3	50.4	44.6	47.6	38.4
2. Mostly disagree	25.9	24.7	27.1	28.1	18.3	25.2	29.7	24.2	24.1	27.2	24.3	26.7	25.6	24.6	25.3	30.2
3. Neither	14.5	13.2	15.7	14.9	7.9	15.9	15.6	11.6	15.9	12.7	16.7	13.8	12.5	17.3	16.6	12.8
4. Mostly agree	7.7	6.2	8.9	7.7	9.2	8.1	7.2	9.4	5.4	6.5	9.7	7.2	8.3	8.9	7.3	8.8
5. Agree	3.9	3.4	4.2	3.2	6.5	2.4	4.1	5.3	2.9	2.7	5.7	4.0	3.1	4.6	3.2	9.9
Item 12720 Subject Q01 N	2947	1390	1516	2294	313	633	828	908	577	1782	1063	1152	621	415	687	35
D05N: I feel that my life is not very useful																
1. Disagree	57.1	60.4	54.2	56.4	67.1	55.0	53.7	61.1	58.1	61.0	51.6	58.3	60.6	52.8	55.0	38.9
2. Mostly disagree	21.7	20.3	23.1	22.7	13.8	23.9	22.8	19.2	21.8	21.1	23.0	22.1	21.3	21.7	21.5	26.0
3. Neither	11.5	10.9	11.9	12.1	5.9	12.8	13.2	8.8	11.6	9.7	14.1	10.0	9.6	15.8	13.3	16.0
4. Mostly agree	5.8	4.6	6.9	5.4	7.6	5.5	6.1	6.8	4.3	5.4	6.0	6.2	4.8	5.6	6.1	5.9
5. Agree	3.8	3.8	3.9	3.4	5.6	2.8	4.3	4.0	4.2	2.8	5.4	3.4	3.8	4.1	4.2	13.2
Item 12750 Subject Q01 N	2942	1388	1516	2291	313	631	827	908	577	1781	1061	1149	619	416	685	35
D06: How many of your friends would you estimate . . .																
D06A: Smoke cigarettes?																
1. None	13.0	12.1	13.5	11.3	21.0	9.2	10.2	13.3	20.7	14.4	10.5	21.4	10.2	8.7	4.0	7.6
2. A few	34.7	34.5	35.1	35.3	32.0	29.9	36.9	35.0	36.2	40.1	26.6	43.0	36.5	35.2	19.9	25.5
3. Some	29.6	32.3	27.2	30.1	29.3	31.0	29.1	31.9	25.1	30.3	28.5	25.6	31.7	30.4	34.3	10.7
4. Most	20.7	19.4	21.5	21.2	16.4	26.3	21.6	18.1	17.1	14.2	30.3	9.1	20.3	23.6	37.6	39.0
5. All	2.1	1.7	2.6	2.1	1.3	3.6	2.3	1.7	1.0	0.9	4.1	1.0	1.3	2.1	4.2	17.1
Item 7070 Subject A02a N	2971	1401	1528	2315	315	645	837	909	580	1795	1069	1151	626	414	705	37
D06B: Smoke marijuana (pot, grass) or hashish?																
1. None	20.5	16.6	24.4	19.6	20.7	14.0	20.8	24.3	21.6	22.7	17.0	40.0	10.0	12.5	3.8	1.1
2. A few	35.1	36.1	34.2	36.3	30.0	33.9	36.5	37.5	30.8	37.8	31.4	40.1	38.4	39.7	23.1	4.7
3. Some	24.5	25.9	23.2	25.0	28.5	24.5	24.6	25.6	26.0	23.0	26.9	15.5	31.2	29.4	30.2	38.1
4. Most	16.6	17.5	15.7	16.1	17.2	22.7	15.2	12.1	19.0	14.5	19.8	4.0	16.7	14.9	36.6	39.1
5. All	3.2	3.9	2.5	3.0	3.5	4.9	2.9	2.5	2.6	2.0	5.0	0.4	3.7	3.5	6.4	17.1
Item 7080 Subject A02a N	2965	1397	1527	2312	312	645	837	907	576	1793	1066	1148	627	414	703	37
D06C: Take LSD?																
1. None	75.6	72.9	78.3	73.8	87.2	71.5	74.8	79.8	74.9	78.4	71.8	86.2	80.7	75.9	55.4	24.5
2. A few	18.0	19.8	16.3	19.8	8.1	21.6	17.3	15.4	19.1	16.8	19.6	11.0	15.4	19.9	29.9	45.1
3. Some	4.9	5.4	4.3	5.0	3.3	5.0	6.7	3.0	5.1	3.6	6.9	2.5	2.9	3.4	11.1	17.8
4. Most	1.0	1.0	1.0	1.0	1.1	1.1	0.9	1.3	0.5	0.8	1.2	0.2	0.3	0.1	3.0	7.2
5. All	0.5	0.9	0.1	0.5	0.3	0.8	0.4	0.5	0.4	0.4	0.5	0.1	0.7	0.7	0.6	5.4
Item 7090 Subject A02a N	2956	1393	1522	2307	311	643	834	905	574	1787	1063	1143	624	413	703	37
D06D: Take other psychedelics (mescaline, peyote, PCP, etc.)?																
1. None	78.0	76.6	79.3	77.2	85.3	69.5	79.1	84.1	76.3	80.3	74.6	88.5	81.9	77.7	59.9	24.0
2. A few	16.3	16.8	15.8	17.4	9.0	20.6	15.6	12.2	19.1	15.6	17.4	9.5	15.4	18.0	26.1	49.5
3. Some	4.3	4.9	3.7	4.1	4.0	8.0	4.3	2.3	3.3	3.2	5.9	1.7	2.0	3.0	10.6	17.9
4. Most	1.1	1.1	1.0	1.0	1.3	1.5	0.7	1.0	1.1	0.8	1.6	0.3	0.3	0.9	3.0	3.1
5. All	0.3	0.5	0.2	0.3	0.3	0.4	0.3	0.4	0.2	0.1	0.6	0.1	0.4	0.4	0.4	5.4
Item 7100 Subject A02a N	2953	1390	1521	2306	311	644	833	904	572	1788	1059	1143	624	411	702	37

QUESTIONNAIRE FORM 2 1985	TOTAL	SEX		RACE		REGION				4YR COLLEGE PLANS		ILLICIT DRUG USE: LIFETIME				
		M	F	White	Black	NE	NC	S	W	Yes	No	None	Mari- juana Only	Few Pills	More Pills	Any Her- oin
N (Weighted No. of Cases):	3327	1573	1651	2485	388	771	914	1017	625	1919	1172	1283	696	453	784	47
% of Weighted Total:	100.0	47.3	49.6	74.7	11.7	23.2	27.5	30.6	18.8	57.7	35.2	38.6	20.9	13.6	23.6	1.4
D06E: Take amphetamines (uppers, pep pills, bennies, speed)?																
1. None	56.7	56.6	56.7	53.4	74.5	52.7	55.6	60.1	57.5	60.6	50.2	74.1	63.1	49.9	27.9	12.9
2. A few	29.6	31.1	28.1	31.7	19.7	32.4	29.0	28.0	29.8	29.1	30.5	20.9	29.2	39.9	38.1	43.8
3. Some	10.3	8.8	11.7	11.1	4.4	11.4	11.4	8.6	10.0	7.8	14.4	4.1	5.6	9.0	24.8	23.7
4. Most	2.9	2.8	3.0	3.2	1.2	2.7	3.5	2.7	2.3	2.1	4.1	0.8	1.8	0.8	8.3	8.2
5. All	0.5	0.7	0.4	0.5	0.3	0.8	0.4	0.6	0.3	0.4	0.8	0.1	0.4	0.4	0.8	11.4
Item 7110 Subject A02a N	*2943*	*1383*	*1519*	*2301*	*311*	*638*	*830*	*904*	*570*	*1782*	*1055*	*1139*	*624*	*410*	*697*	*37*
D06F: Take quaaludes (quads, methaqualone)?																
1. None	74.0	70.9	76.6	71.9	87.9	69.5	73.7	74.9	78.0	76.7	69.3	84.6	78.7	74.7	54.5	17.9
2. A few	20.2	22.4	18.3	22.4	8.2	23.2	19.4	20.3	17.6	19.1	22.6	12.7	18.2	22.0	31.6	57.3
3. Some	4.5	5.1	3.9	4.4	2.6	5.4	5.5	3.2	4.1	3.3	6.2	2.1	2.5	2.7	10.7	14.7
4. Most	1.1	1.0	1.1	1.0	1.0	1.7	1.1	1.1	0.1	0.7	1.5	0.5	0.3	0.2	3.0	4.6
5. All	0.3	0.4	0.1	0.2	0.3	0.2	0.2	0.5	0.2	0.1	0.4	0.1	0.4	0.4	0.1	5.4
Item 7120 Subject A02a N	*2948*	*1389*	*1517*	*2301*	*311*	*642*	*830*	*903*	*573*	*1785*	*1056*	*1138*	*624*	*411*	*702*	*37*
D06G: Take barbiturates (downers, goofballs, reds, yellows, etc.)?																
1. None	72.9	71.9	73.6	71.2	83.7	70.0	70.2	75.7	75.6	76.3	66.7	83.0	78.2	72.0	54.0	21.7
2. A few	21.4	21.7	21.1	23.3	11.8	23.4	23.2	19.5	19.5	19.5	25.2	14.2	18.7	25.0	32.0	55.6
3. Some	4.2	4.2	4.3	4.2	3.2	5.6	4.9	3.1	3.5	3.1	6.0	2.0	1.9	1.8	10.8	16.0
4. Most	1.3	1.8	0.9	1.2	0.8	0.9	1.5	1.4	1.4	1.0	1.8	0.6	0.9	0.6	3.2	1.3
5. All	0.3	0.4	0.1	0.2	0.5	0.2	0.2	0.4	0.2	0.1	0.4	0.1	0.3	0.6	-	5.4
Item 7130 Subject A02a N	*2949*	*1388*	*1519*	*2301*	*311*	*641*	*830*	*905*	*573*	*1785*	*1057*	*1141*	*623*	*411*	*701*	*37*
D06H: Take tranquilizers?																
1. None	74.2	74.0	74.2	72.2	86.1	73.2	73.6	73.7	76.8	75.5	71.3	81.8	79.7	75.2	58.2	24.3
2. A few	20.5	20.2	20.7	22.6	9.7	21.2	20.1	21.0	19.4	20.8	20.8	14.8	17.6	22.3	30.0	53.9
3. Some	4.2	4.1	4.3	4.2	3.2	4.6	5.5	3.7	2.5	2.7	6.4	2.9	2.0	1.8	9.6	9.2
4. Most	0.9	1.3	0.6	0.8	0.8	0.8	0.7	1.3	0.8	0.9	1.1	0.5	0.6	0.3	1.9	7.3
5. All	0.3	0.4	0.1	0.2	0.3	0.2	0.1	0.3	0.5	0.1	0.4	0.1	0.1	0.4	0.3	5.4
Item 7140 Subject A02a N	*2947*	*1389*	*1517*	*2302*	*311*	*641*	*831*	*901*	*573*	*1783*	*1057*	*1143*	*624*	*409*	*697*	*37*
D06I: Take cocaine?																
1. None	56.2	54.4	58.0	55.2	64.8	41.7	64.6	64.3	47.4	58.9	52.4	79.5	55.6	51.0	24.3	5.6
2. A few	27.0	27.0	26.8	28.6	22.7	32.2	25.5	24.7	26.8	26.2	28.2	17.4	33.1	35.5	31.3	37.4
3. Some	11.1	12.8	9.3	10.8	10.0	14.7	7.7	8.1	16.6	10.2	12.1	2.3	8.7	11.2	26.5	29.0
4. Most	4.6	4.5	4.8	4.4	2.0	8.4	2.1	2.3	7.8	4.0	5.4	0.8	2.0	1.0	14.6	22.6
5. All	1.2	1.3	1.0	1.0	0.5	3.0	0.1	0.7	1.4	0.7	1.9	0.1	0.5	1.3	3.3	5.4
Item 7150 Subject A02a N	*2949*	*1386*	*1521*	*2302*	*310*	*641*	*830*	*905*	*573*	*1789*	*1054*	*1142*	*624*	*411*	*699*	*37*
D06J: Take heroin (smack, horse)?																
1. None	85.5	85.1	86.1	84.9	89.8	83.8	84.4	87.1	86.8	87.5	82.5	90.1	85.4	86.0	81.0	22.1
2. A few	11.9	11.8	11.8	13.2	6.3	13.3	13.4	10.1	11.0	10.7	14.1	8.2	12.8	11.6	15.1	58.8
3. Some	1.6	1.8	1.5	1.4	1.6	2.3	1.5	1.2	1.6	1.2	2.1	1.1	0.6	0.9	3.3	11.1
4. Most	0.7	1.0	0.4	0.3	1.6	0.4	0.7	1.0	0.4	0.5	0.9	0.6	0.8	1.0	0.4	2.6
5. All	0.3	0.4	0.2	0.2	0.6	0.2	0.1	0.5	0.2	0.1	0.4	0.1	0.3	0.4	0.2	5.4
Item 7160 Subject A02a N	*2949*	*1387*	*1521*	*2302*	*310*	*642*	*830*	*904*	*573*	*1788*	*1055*	*1143*	*624*	*409*	*701*	*37*
D06K: Take other narcotics (methadone, opium, codeine, paregoric, etc.)?																
1. None	77.2	76.1	78.3	76.1	85.8	73.4	76.2	81.4	76.4	79.7	73.0	87.2	81.3	80.1	58.1	18.5
2. A few	18.2	19.2	17.4	19.6	9.9	20.6	18.8	15.2	19.4	16.9	20.6	11.1	15.1	18.6	30.7	59.9
3. Some	3.2	3.0	3.3	3.1	2.3	4.5	4.0	1.8	2.8	2.3	4.6	1.4	2.3	1.0	8.0	9.7
4. Most	1.1	1.2	0.8	1.0	1.7	0.9	0.9	1.3	1.2	0.8	1.4	0.3	1.0	-	3.0	3.1
5. All	0.3	0.5	0.2	0.3	0.3	0.6	0.1	0.4	0.2	0.2	0.4	0.1	0.3	0.4	0.2	8.8
Item 7170 Subject A02a N	*2944*	*1387*	*1515*	*2298*	*310*	*641*	*828*	*902*	*573*	*1784*	*1054*	*1138*	*624*	*409*	*699*	*37*

QUESTIONNAIRE FORM 2 1985	TOTAL	SEX		RACE		REGION				4YR COLLEGE PLANS		ILLICIT DRUG USE: LIFETIME				
		M	F	White	Black	NE	NC	S	W	Yes	No	None	Mari- juana Only	Few Pills	More Pills	Any Her- oin
N (Weighted No. of Cases):	3327	1573	1651	2485	388	771	914	1017	625	1919	1172	1283	696	453	784	47
% of Weighted Total:	100.0	47.3	49.6	74.7	11.7	23.2	27.5	30.6	18.8	57.7	35.2	38.6	20.9	13.6	23.6	1.4
D06L: Use inhalants (sniffing glue, aerosols, laughing gas, etc.)?																
1. None	78.8	75.2	82.1	78.1	85.3	76.0	78.1	80.0	81.0	79.5	77.8	86.0	79.7	77.3	68.7	34.6
2. A few	15.5	17.2	13.8	16.7	8.7	15.5	15.3	15.6	15.6	14.9	16.4	11.1	15.3	18.5	19.9	48.5
3. Some	4.2	5.4	3.1	4.0	4.4	5.5	5.5	3.1	2.6	3.9	4.4	2.2	4.1	2.6	8.3	8.9
4. Most	1.0	1.4	0.7	0.9	1.3	1.7	0.7	1.0	0.6	1.1	0.9	0.7	0.7	1.1	1.8	2.7
5. All	0.5	0.7	0.3	0.4	0.4	1.2	0.3	0.4	0.2	0.5	0.4	0.1	0.2	0.5	1.3	5.4
Item 7180 Subject A02a N	*2939*	*1384*	*1513*	*2293*	*308*	*639*	*823*	*903*	*573*	*1776*	*1055*	*1138*	*621*	*409*	*698*	*37*
D06M: Drink alcoholic beverages (liquor, beer, wine)?																
1. None	5.4	4.5	6.3	3.7	14.0	4.9	4.8	6.0	5.8	5.7	4.5	9.0	4.1	4.2	1.2	1.1
2. A few	11.4	9.4	13.2	9.1	19.6	11.0	8.5	12.9	13.6	12.3	9.8	19.6	7.9	8.8	2.7	7.4
3. Some	17.3	17.0	17.2	16.6	21.8	13.0	19.3	19.2	16.1	17.0	17.8	25.0	15.1	14.8	8.1	-
4. Most	41.3	42.5	40.5	44.1	31.2	39.4	42.5	42.1	40.5	42.8	39.1	35.9	42.9	48.5	45.6	34.9
5. All	24.7	26.6	22.8	26.5	13.3	31.8	24.9	19.8	24.0	22.1	28.7	10.5	29.9	23.8	42.4	56.6
Item 7190 Subject A02a N	*2951*	*1386*	*1524*	*2305*	*311*	*637*	*832*	*909*	*574*	*1786*	*1058*	*1148*	*623*	*411*	*697*	*36*
D06N: Get drunk at least once a week?																
1. None	17.5	14.8	20.2	13.9	32.9	17.5	14.6	18.1	20.6	19.1	14.6	27.9	13.6	13.9	6.3	4.6
2. A few	25.3	24.5	25.7	25.0	28.3	23.1	25.8	27.5	23.3	25.8	25.1	32.0	23.8	23.2	17.5	10.5
3. Some	27.4	29.5	25.4	29.5	18.8	26.8	29.8	25.1	28.1	27.8	26.5	23.6	30.0	29.6	30.2	16.3
4. Most	21.8	22.2	21.7	23.4	15.2	19.5	22.7	23.3	20.7	21.1	23.3	13.7	24.6	25.5	30.3	37.0
5. All	8.1	9.1	7.0	8.1	4.9	13.0	7.1	6.0	7.3	6.3	10.5	2.8	8.0	7.8	15.8	31.6
Item 7200 Subject A02a N	*2951*	*1385*	*1525*	*2301*	*312*	*637*	*834*	*907*	*573*	*1791*	*1053*	*1147*	*621*	*411*	*699*	*36*
Lately there has been increased attention paid to two types of drugs: PCP and amyl or butyl nitrite.																
E01: How many of your friends would you estimate . . .																
E01A: Take PCP (angel dust, crystal, peace pill, killer weed, supergrass, crystal cyclone)?																
1. None	84.1	84.8	83.6	83.7	89.9	83.8	84.4	86.7	79.9	87.3	79.4	90.7	89.0	85.2	71.0	25.4
2. A few	11.7	11.1	12.1	12.8	5.0	11.8	12.7	9.3	13.8	9.9	14.5	7.8	8.0	12.0	19.1	51.4
3. Some	3.1	2.6	3.4	2.6	4.1	2.4	2.2	3.3	4.6	2.2	4.4	1.1	1.7	1.9	7.9	12.2
4. Most	0.7	0.8	0.6	0.5	0.4	1.5	0.5	0.2	0.9	0.4	0.9	0.1	1.0	0.2	1.6	2.9
5. All	0.5	0.8	0.2	0.4	0.7	0.5	0.2	0.5	0.8	0.2	0.8	0.2	0.5	0.7	0.4	8.1
Item 7201 Subject A02a N	*2911*	*1370*	*1498*	*2276*	*303*	*625*	*824*	*896*	*565*	*1771*	*1035*	*1135*	*611*	*402*	*691*	*35*
E01B: Take amyl or butyl nitrites (poppers, snappers, Locker Room, Vaporole, Rush, Kick, Bullet)?																
1. None	84.4	82.9	85.8	83.4	92.8	84.1	83.2	87.4	81.9	86.1	81.4	92.6	89.4	84.9	68.2	30.5
2. A few	11.4	12.1	10.9	12.5	2.8	11.0	12.4	9.0	13.8	10.4	13.2	6.1	8.2	12.9	20.7	44.9
3. Some	3.2	3.6	2.7	3.2	3.6	3.4	3.1	3.0	3.4	2.5	4.4	1.2	1.9	1.2	8.2	19.0
4. Most	0.6	0.8	0.5	0.6	0.4	1.2	1.0	0.2	0.3	0.6	0.6	-	0.1	0.3	2.4	-
5. All	0.4	0.7	0.2	0.3	0.4	0.4	0.3	0.3	0.5	0.4	0.5	0.1	0.3	0.7	0.5	5.7
Item 7202 Subject A02a N	*2892*	*1361*	*1489*	*2263*	*297*	*623*	*814*	*888*	*566*	*1758*	*1031*	*1125*	*608*	*402*	*685*	*35*
E02: On how many occasions (if any) have you used PCP (angel dust, crystal, peace pill, killer weed, supergrass, crystal cyclone)?																
E02A: . . . in your lifetime?																
1. 0 occasions	95.1	93.4	96.9	95.1	98.2	92.7	96.9	96.6	92.9	96.6	93.2	99.9	98.2	97.1	86.0	40.7
2. 1-2	2.4	3.2	1.4	2.4	1.4	3.6	1.2	2.1	3.2	1.7	3.3	0.1	1.3	1.3	6.4	29.2
3. 3-5	1.0	1.3	0.8	1.1	0.2	1.8	1.0	0.7	0.9	0.8	1.6	-	-	0.5	3.2	19.2
4. 6-9	0.1	0.2	0.1	0.2	-	0.3	0.3	-	-	0.1	0.3	-	-	0.1	0.5	-
5. 10-19	0.4	0.4	0.4	0.4	0.2	0.2	0.3	0.1	1.4	0.1	0.7	-	-	-	1.7	1.5
6. 20-39	0.3	0.3	0.3	0.2	-	0.6	0.2	0.2	0.4	0.4	0.2	-	0.5	-	0.9	-
7. 40 or more	0.6	1.2	*	0.5	-	0.8	0.2	0.4	1.2	0.4	0.7	-	-	1.1	1.4	9.5
Item 1181 Subject A01a N	*2900*	*1363*	*1495*	*2272*	*295*	*621*	*823*	*891*	*565*	*1767*	*1027*	*1136*	*607*	*399*	*688*	*34*

*=less than .05 per cent.

QUESTIONNAIRE FORM 2 1985	TOTAL	SEX		RACE		REGION				4YR COLLEGE PLANS		ILLICIT DRUG USE: LIFETIME				
		M	F	White	Black	NE	NC	S	W	Yes	No	None	Mari- juana Only	Few Pills	More Pills	Any Her- oin
N (Weighted No. of Cases):	3327	1573	1651	2485	388	771	914	1017	625	1919	1172	1283	696	453	784	47
% of Weighted Total:	100.0	47.3	49.6	74.7	11.7	23.2	27.5	30.6	18.8	57.7	35.2	38.6	20.9	13.6	23.6	1.4
E02B: . . . during the last 12 months?																
1. 0 occasions	97.1	95.9	98.3	97.1	99.5	95.0	98.3	98.6	95.4	97.8	96.3	100.0	99.2	98.2	91.5	62.0
2. 1-2	1.4	1.6	1.1	1.5	0.5	2.7	0.8	0.8	1.6	0.9	1.8	-	0.3	0.1	4.0	25.1
3. 3-5	0.7	1.1	0.3	0.8	-	1.2	0.6	0.2	1.2	0.7	0.8	-	0.5	0.6	2.1	3.5
4. 6-9	0.1	0.2	*	0.1	-	0.2	0.1	-	0.1	0.1	0.2	-	-	-	0.3	3.6
5. 10-19	0.3	0.4	0.3	0.2	-	0.3	0.1	0.1	1.2	0.2	0.3	-	-	0.5	1.1	-
6. 20-39	*	0.1		*	-	0.1	0.1	-	-	-	0.1	-	-	-	0.2	-
7. 40 or more	0.3	0.7	-	0.3	-	0.5	0.1	0.3	0.5	0.3	0.5	-	-	0.5	0.8	5.8
Item 1182 Subject A01b N	2898	1361	1495	2271	295	620	823	890	565	1767	1026	1136	607	399	686	34
E02C: . . . during the last 30 days?																
1. 0 occasions	98.4	97.6	99.3	98.6	99.8	97.9	99.1	99.3	96.5	98.6	98.3	100.0	99.4	98.8	95.2	86.0
2. 1-2	0.8	1.1	0.4	0.7	0.2	0.9	0.7	0.3	1.7	0.8	0.8	-	0.6	0.1	2.3	4.7
3. 3-5	0.3	0.2	0.3	0.2	-	0.4	-	*	0.9	0.3	0.1	-	-	-	1.0	3.5
4. 6-9	0.1	0.2	-	*	-	-	0.1	-	0.4	-	0.1	-	-	0.5	0.1	-
5. 10-19	0.1	0.3	*	0.1	-	0.4	0.1	0.1	-	-	0.4	-	-	-	0.6	-
6. 20-39	*	0.1	-	*	-	-	-	-	0.2	0.1	-	-	-	-	0.1	-
7. 40 or more	0.3	0.6	-	0.3	-	0.5	-	0.3	0.4	0.2	0.4	-	-	0.5	0.6	5.8
Item 1183 Subject A01c N	2899	1362	1496	2272	296	620	823	890	566	1767	1026	1137	608	399	686	34
E03: On how many occasions (if any) have you used amyl or butyl nitrites (poppers, snappers, Locker Room, Vaporole, Rush, Kick, Bullet)?																
E03A: . . . in your lifetime?																
1. 0 occasions	92.1	88.9	95.1	91.6	96.5	90.0	92.5	94.0	90.8	93.1	90.8	99.5	96.3	91.8	78.5	44.6
2. 1-2	4.2	5.2	3.2	4.3	2.3	5.1	3.5	3.5	5.1	3.3	5.4	0.4	2.3	5.2	10.6	23.5
3. 3-5	1.5	1.8	0.9	1.6	1.1	2.1	1.1	1.1	2.0	1.4	1.3	0.1	0.6	1.1	4.3	11.5
4. 6-9	0.7	1.1	0.4	0.8	-	0.8	1.0	0.3	0.8	0.5	1.2	-	0.7	1.1	1.7	2.0
5. 10-19	0.5	1.0	0.1	0.6	-	0.4	1.1	0.2	0.4	0.6	0.4	-	0.3	0.2	1.8	3.0
6. 20-39	0.3	0.5	0.1	0.3	-	0.3	0.4	0.2	0.4	0.3	0.4	*	-	0.1	1.1	3.6
7. 40 or more	0.7	1.4	0.2	0.8	-	1.3	0.4	0.7	0.6	0.8	0.5	-	-	0.5	2.1	11.7
Item 1184 Subject A01a N	2895	1359	1494	2272	294	619	821	891	565	1767	1023	1133	608	399	686	34
E03B: . . . during the last 12 months?																
1. 0 occasions	96.0	94.2	97.9	95.6	99.0	94.5	95.7	97.5	95.8	96.6	95.1	99.8	98.1	96.7	88.9	65.9
2. 1-2	2.0	2.1	1.7	2.2	0.6	2.7	1.9	1.2	2.4	1.5	2.8	0.2	1.2	1.9	5.0	16.1
3. 3-5	0.6	0.8	0.2	0.6	0.4	0.9	0.4	0.6	0.4	0.6	0.6	0.1	0.3	0.5	1.3	9.1
4. 6-9	0.5	0.9	0.1	0.6	-	0.4	1.0	0.1	0.4	0.4	0.4	-	0.2	-	1.8	-
5. 10-19	0.4	0.9	0.1	0.4	-	0.3	0.5	0.1	1.0	0.4	0.6	-	0.1	0.8	1.0	3.0
6. 20-39	0.2	0.3	*	0.2	-	0.2	0.4	*	-	0.2	0.1	-	-	-	0.7	-
7. 40 or more	0.4	0.8	*	0.5	-	1.0	0.1	0.4	-	0.4	0.4	-	-	-	1.3	5.8
Item 1185 Subject A01b N	2891	1356	1494	2269	294	619	820	889	563	1765	1022	1132	609	399	681	34
E03C: . . . during the last 30 days?																
1. 0 occasions	98.4	97.0	99.6	98.2	99.5	97.8	98.3	98.8	98.5	98.4	98.2	99.8	99.8	99.3	95.4	73.2
2. 1-2	0.6	1.0	0.3	0.8	0.1	0.8	0.7	0.5	0.7	0.6	0.6	0.1	0.1	0.1	1.8	14.5
3. 3-5	0.4	0.7	*	0.3	0.4	0.2	0.3	0.3	0.7	0.4	0.4	0.1	0.1	0.5	0.9	3.5
4. 6-9	0.2	0.4	*	0.2	-	0.4	0.3	*	0.1	0.2	0.3	-	-	-	0.7	3.0
5. 10-19	0.1	0.2	-	0.1	-	0.1	0.2	-	-	0.1	0.1	*	-	-	0.3	-
6. 20-39	-	-	-	-	-	-	-	-	-	-	-	-	-	-	-	-
7. 40 or more	0.3	0.6	-	0.4	-	0.7	0.1	0.4	-	0.3	0.3	-	-	-	1.0	5.8
Item 1186 Subject A01c N	2890	1354	1494	2268	294	617	821	889	563	1765	1022	1133	608	399	681	34
E04: When (if ever) did you FIRST do each of the following things?																
E04A: Try PCP																
8. Never	96.2	94.7	97.5	96.1	98.4	94.0	97.6	97.1	94.8	97.1	94.9	99.8	99.3	98.1	88.0	42.2
1. Grade 6 or below	0.4	0.6	0.2	0.4	0.4	0.5	0.5	0.5	-	0.5	0.3	0.1	-	0.3	0.9	10.7
2. Grade 7 or 8	0.5	0.7	0.4	0.5	-	1.3	0.5	0.1	0.4	0.4	0.7	-	0.5	0.1	1.5	5.4
3. Grade 9 (Freshman)	0.9	1.1	0.7	0.8	1.0	0.8	0.4	1.1	1.5	0.7	1.1	0.1	0.2	0.5	2.8	11.3
4. Grade 10 (Sophomore)	0.7	0.9	0.5	0.9	-	1.6	0.2	0.4	1.2	0.3	1.4	-	-	-	2.4	15.6
5. Grade 11 (Junior)	0.8	1.4	0.2	0.8	0.2	0.7	0.8	0.4	1.4	0.6	1.0	-	-	0.8	2.4	9.7
6. Grade 12 (Senior)	0.5	0.6	0.4	0.6	-	1.3	0.1	0.3	0.7	0.4	0.7	-	-	0.2	1.9	5.1
Item 5686 Subject A01g N	2820	1313	1470	2220	285	599	805	874	543	1736	989	1129	594	385	649	30

*=less than .05 per cent.

QUESTIONNAIRE FORM 2 1985	TOTAL	SEX		RACE		REGION				4YR COLLEGE PLANS		ILLICIT DRUG USE: LIFETIME				
		M	F	White	Black	NE	NC	S	W	Yes	No	None	Mari- juana Only	Few Pills	More Pills	Any Her- oin
N (Weighted No. of Cases):	3327	1573	1651	2485	388	771	914	1017	625	1919	1172	1283	696	453	784	47
% of Weighted Total:	100.0	47.3	49.6	74.7	11.7	23.2	27.5	30.6	18.8	57.7	35.2	38.6	20.9	13.6	23.6	1.4
E04B: Try amyl or butyl nitrites																
8. Never	93.8	91.3	96.1	93.2	97.5	92.2	94.6	95.2	92.0	94.6	92.9	99.6	97.4	93.6	82.2	46.6
1. Grade 6 or below	0.2	0.4	0.1	0.2	-	0.3	0.3	0.2	0.1	0.3	0.1	0.1	-	-	0.6	6.3
2. Grade 7 or 8	0.9	1.4	0.5	0.9	1.0	0.8	0.8	0.6	1.7	1.2	0.4	-	0.2	1.4	2.2	16.1
3. Grade 9 (Freshman)	0.9	1.3	0.5	0.9	0.4	1.6	0.8	0.5	0.9	0.7	1.1	0.2	0.1	0.5	2.9	5.5
4. Grade 10 (Sophomore)	1.2	1.3	1.1	1.4	0.3	1.1	1.0	1.0	1.9	1.1	1.4	-	0.5	1.1	3.3	17.9
5. Grade 11 (Junior)	1.7	2.6	0.9	2.0	0.6	2.4	1.3	1.6	1.9	1.3	2.3	*	0.9	2.0	5.3	4.3
6. Grade 12 (Senior)	1.2	1.8	0.8	1.4	0.3	1.5	1.2	0.8	1.6	0.9	1.8	0.1	0.9	1.4	3.5	3.2
Item 5687 Subject A01g　　N	2799	1302	1458	2203	282	594	789	870	546	1722	979	1122	593	380	639	32
E05: What is your best guess about whether your parents think you drink alcoholic beverages (beer, wine, liquor)?																
1. They feel sure I don't drink	27.7	23.3	31.6	24.7	45.1	22.4	28.1	30.2	29.2	30.6	22.3	48.5	16.3	19.6	9.7	9.8
2. They think I probably don't drink	13.6	12.4	14.8	13.5	17.5	13.2	13.4	14.8	12.3	15.2	11.7	14.5	17.6	13.5	9.4	-
3. I don't know, or they differ in whether they think I do	10.0	10.1	9.7	10.0	10.2	10.1	9.6	10.2	10.0	8.6	12.5	8.9	10.9	11.2	9.3	4.5
4. They think I probably drink	17.3	17.7	17.0	18.3	11.7	17.1	19.6	14.4	18.7	17.1	17.9	10.2	23.1	20.2	22.1	25.2
5. They feel sure (or know) that I drink	31.4	36.6	27.0	33.6	15.5	37.1	29.2	30.4	29.9	28.5	35.7	17.9	32.2	35.5	49.5	60.5
Item 7510 Subject A09a　　N	2890	1356	1492	2267	293	618	820	889	563	1760	1025	1126	608	398	685	35
E06: What's your best guess about whether your parents think you smoke marijuana?																
1. They feel sure I don't	71.3	66.1	76.1	71.1	74.4	66.2	73.2	75.7	67.2	75.2	65.3	93.0	68.3	68.8	42.6	11.5
2. They think I probably don't	12.1	13.4	10.8	12.8	7.4	15.3	10.6	10.0	14.1	12.0	12.7	4.2	15.0	13.1	21.3	20.4
3. I don't know, or they differ in whether they think I do	5.8	7.0	4.8	5.9	5.5	6.1	5.8	5.3	6.4	4.6	7.7	1.2	5.5	10.5	10.4	17.4
4. They think I probably do	4.6	6.1	3.3	4.0	6.5	5.2	4.6	4.2	4.8	3.6	6.4	0.4	5.6	3.3	11.2	11.0
5. They feel sure (or know) that I do	6.1	7.4	5.0	6.2	6.2	7.2	5.8	4.8	7.5	4.6	8.0	1.1	5.6	4.4	14.4	39.8
Item 7520 Subject A09a　　N	2873	1349	1481	2255	290	617	814	880	562	1749	1020	1122	603	394	682	35
E07: Within the past three months, how often have you . . .																
E07A: Had arguments or quarrels with your parents or other older relatives?																
1. Not at all	15.3	19.5	11.5	11.7	35.6	13.1	14.8	17.3	15.2	15.0	15.6	18.9	15.1	14.7	9.2	19.2
2. Once or twice	46.7	48.5	44.9	47.0	44.3	48.6	46.6	47.9	42.8	45.2	49.4	48.5	49.0	44.5	43.7	16.8
3. Every month	14.9	13.2	16.4	16.0	8.0	14.9	13.6	13.1	19.5	16.5	12.2	13.4	16.0	14.2	17.5	11.9
4. Every week	15.9	14.1	17.4	17.7	7.7	15.7	17.9	14.1	15.8	16.3	15.3	13.6	13.6	18.9	20.0	27.5
5. Almost daily	7.3	4.7	9.7	7.5	4.4	7.6	7.1	7.5	6.8	7.0	7.5	5.7	6.2	7.7	9.5	24.7
Item 19530 Subject M03,Q09　　N	2884	1349	1492	2263	295	613	821	887	564	1756	1022	1126	607	395	680	35
E07B: Had arguments or quarrels with people in positions of authority?																
1. Not at all	54.0	45.8	61.6	51.3	65.9	47.4	53.6	58.7	54.1	53.7	54.6	62.4	56.9	51.3	39.9	26.9
2. Once or twice	35.0	39.4	30.9	36.9	27.4	38.5	35.4	33.2	33.4	35.8	34.0	30.6	33.1	39.1	41.8	38.3
3. Every month	6.4	9.1	4.0	7.0	3.7	8.8	5.8	4.8	7.3	6.7	6.0	4.3	6.5	5.4	9.6	22.1
4. Every week	3.5	4.4	2.7	3.8	1.9	4.2	4.3	2.1	3.9	2.8	4.3	2.3	2.6	3.3	6.6	5.1
5. Almost daily	1.1	1.3	0.8	1.0	1.1	1.1	0.8	1.2	1.3	1.0	1.2	0.4	0.9	0.8	2.1	7.6
Item 19540 Subject Q09　　N	2878	1351	1484	2259	294	609	820	885	563	1750	1022	1126	603	396	678	35
E07C: Been mad enough to feel like smashing something, but I didn't?																
1. Not at all	24.0	20.7	26.7	21.3	34.8	22.7	25.3	23.5	24.2	23.2	24.4	29.4	26.0	18.5	15.7	17.0
2. Once or twice	44.4	43.5	45.3	45.3	41.4	45.0	40.2	47.4	45.4	47.4	40.8	44.3	44.7	47.9	43.5	33.1
3. Every month	15.0	17.9	12.4	16.5	9.0	13.9	17.8	14.9	12.5	13.8	17.0	12.3	14.9	17.6	18.7	22.2
4. Every week	11.7	13.7	10.1	12.4	7.7	13.4	11.6	8.8	14.5	11.1	12.4	10.7	10.1	10.6	15.1	20.2
5. Almost daily	4.9	4.3	5.5	4.5	7.0	5.1	5.2	5.4	3.5	4.5	5.3	3.3	4.3	5.5	7.0	7.5
Item 19550 Subject Q09　　N	2881	1350	1488	2262	295	614	821	885	561	1755	1022	1126	606	396	680	35

*=less than .05 per cent.

QUESTIONNAIRE FORM 2 1985	TOTAL	SEX		RACE		REGION				4YR COLLEGE PLANS		ILLICIT DRUG USE: LIFETIME				
		M	F	White	Black	NE	NC	S	W	Yes	No	None	Mari-juana Only	Few Pills	More Pills	Any Her-oin
N (Weighted No. of Cases):	3327	1573	1651	2485	388	771	914	1017	625	1919	1172	1283	696	453	784	47
% of Weighted Total:	100.0	47.3	49.6	74.7	11.7	23.2	27.5	30.6	18.8	57.7	35.2	38.6	20.9	13.6	23.6	1.4

E07D: Been mad enough so you actually did smash something?

1. Not at all	71.4	61.8	80.5	70.0	79.3	69.0	73.7	70.9	71.2	75.1	65.9	79.6	73.7	69.6	58.1	41.8
2. Once or twice	20.6	26.6	15.0	21.4	16.8	19.7	19.0	22.3	21.2	18.5	23.7	15.5	19.6	22.1	29.3	22.3
3. Every month	4.6	7.0	2.3	5.1	2.0	7.4	4.5	2.8	4.6	3.7	5.7	2.9	3.8	4.3	8.0	14.3
4. Every week	2.6	3.8	1.4	2.7	1.1	2.7	2.6	2.7	2.2	2.1	3.5	1.8	2.5	3.2	2.9	16.0
5. Almost daily	0.8	0.8	0.9	0.8	0.8	1.3	0.2	1.2	0.8	0.6	1.2	0.2	0.5	0.9	1.8	5.6
Item 19560　Subject Q09　N	2866	1343	1482	2249	293	611	817	881	558	1748	1015	1125	601	395	672	35

E07E: Felt like getting into a fist fight with some-one, but didn't?

1. Not at all	45.2	33.5	56.0	44.4	50.2	39.1	46.7	46.9	46.8	48.6	39.6	55.7	44.2	40.8	31.3	28.8
2. Once or twice	37.5	43.7	31.9	37.6	35.2	40.4	34.7	38.9	36.3	35.9	40.1	33.2	39.1	45.4	40.0	23.2
3. Every month	8.7	12.4	5.3	9.4	7.6	9.3	9.8	6.5	10.1	8.1	9.7	5.4	8.1	7.4	15.0	23.2
4. Every week	5.9	7.8	4.2	6.5	2.2	8.0	6.3	5.2	4.2	5.4	6.7	4.5	5.0	4.9	8.8	23.3
5. Almost daily	2.7	2.6	2.6	2.1	4.8	3.1	2.5	2.6	2.6	1.9	3.9	1.1	3.6	1.5	4.9	1.5
Item 19570　Subject Q09　N	2871	1345	1484	2257	292	608	821	883	559	1750	1016	1125	602	391	678	35

E07F: Actually got into a fight and hit some-body?

1. Not at all	84.9	79.0	90.7	84.8	86.5	83.3	85.5	85.6	84.9	89.5	78.8	91.0	87.1	85.5	74.5	48.7
2. Once or twice	11.7	15.6	7.8	11.9	10.8	12.0	11.4	11.7	11.9	8.2	16.1	8.0	9.7	11.4	19.1	26.3
3. Every month	2.0	3.3	0.9	2.0	2.3	3.4	1.9	1.4	1.7	1.4	3.2	0.4	2.5	2.6	3.7	10.9
4. Every week	0.8	1.3	0.4	0.9	-	0.6	1.1	0.7	1.0	0.6	1.2	0.4	0.4	0.4	2.0	5.0
5. Almost daily	0.5	0.8	0.2	0.4	0.4	0.8	0.1	0.7	0.4	0.4	0.6	0.2	0.2	0.1	0.8	9.1
Item 19580　Subject Q09　N	2873	1348	1484	2256	294	609	818	885	560	1753	1015	1126	603	394	675	35

The next questions are about military service.

E08: Do you favor or oppose a military draft at the present time?

1. Strongly oppose	23.5	28.9	18.9	23.7	26.6	25.1	24.7	20.9	24.3	23.0	24.2	19.2	23.7	24.6	28.9	42.0
2. Mostly oppose	18.3	18.7	17.9	18.4	14.9	15.9	19.1	16.5	22.6	19.7	15.9	19.3	18.5	15.4	19.4	4.3
3. No opinion, or mixed	40.1	30.4	48.8	40.0	41.4	44.8	38.5	40.5	36.8	38.7	42.7	41.6	39.0	44.7	36.6	24.2
4. Mostly favor	12.5	14.0	11.0	12.6	12.1	10.5	12.6	15.2	10.2	13.3	11.4	13.7	14.5	10.5	9.7	13.0
5. Strongly favor	5.6	8.0	3.3	5.3	5.0	3.8	5.1	7.0	6.1	5.3	5.8	6.2	4.3	4.8	5.4	16.5
Item 21060　Subject L02　N	2829	1328	1461	2229	288	586	809	878	557	1730	1001	1118	595	390	658	32

E09: Do you think any military draft in the U.S. should include women as well as men?

1. No	27.0	16.3	36.9	26.5	31.4	24.1	25.5	31.3	25.3	26.7	27.3	29.0	24.4	23.9	27.1	16.3
2. Uncertain	35.2	26.8	42.3	35.3	30.9	32.5	33.9	36.1	38.4	34.0	37.7	34.6	34.0	36.7	36.1	42.7
3. Yes	37.9	56.9	20.7	38.2	37.7	43.5	40.7	32.6	36.3	39.3	34.9	36.4	41.6	39.3	36.8	41.0
Item 21070　Subject L02　N	2829	1328	1460	2231	288	586	811	876	555	1731	1001	1116	596	389	660	33

One idea for getting more high school grad-uates to serve in the military is to offer them a paid college education after three years of service in the armed forces. During the three years of military duty their pay would be fairly low, but afterward the government would pay their tuition plus $300 a month living expenses for up to four academic years.

E10: Do you think it would be a good idea for the U.S. to have such a program of paid college in return for military service?

1. Definitely not	2.1	2.3	1.7	1.7	3.7	2.4	1.3	2.2	2.7	2.2	1.6	1.5	1.7	2.3	2.6	8.9
2. Probably not	3.0	3.9	2.1	3.1	2.2	3.0	3.1	2.6	3.6	3.0	3.2	2.5	2.7	3.9	3.4	1.7
3. No opinion or uncertain	17.8	16.7	19.0	17.3	14.9	18.3	18.3	16.2	19.1	15.1	22.2	19.0	15.4	16.6	18.7	21.4
4. Yes, probably	31.1	27.7	33.7	32.2	27.0	26.5	33.9	32.4	29.7	30.6	32.4	33.4	30.3	30.2	28.4	24.6
5. Yes, definitely	46.0	49.3	43.6	45.8	52.2	49.7	43.3	46.6	44.9	49.2	40.5	43.6	49.9	46.9	46.9	43.4
Item 21080　Subject L02　N	2819	1323	1459	2223	286	582	806	874	556	1722	998	1114	591	386	659	33

QUESTIONNAIRE FORM 2 1985	TOTAL	SEX		RACE		REGION				4YR COLLEGE PLANS		ILLICIT DRUG USE: LIFETIME				
		M	F	White	Black	NE	NC	S	W	Yes	No	None	Marijuana Only	Few Pills	More Pills	Any Heroin
N (Weighted No. of Cases):	3327	1573	1651	2485	388	771	914	1017	625	1919	1172	1283	696	453	784	47
% of Weighted Total:	100.0	47.3	49.6	74.7	11.7	23.2	27.5	30.6	18.8	57.7	35.2	38.6	20.9	13.6	23.6	1.4
E11: If paid college in return for military service were available NOW, how likely is it that you would sign up for such a plan?																
1. Definitely would not	31.7	24.4	38.8	32.9	24.5	27.8	33.7	30.8	34.5	32.9	29.9	34.3	25.4	29.5	35.3	17.1
2. Probably would not	39.5	40.1	38.9	42.1	25.8	39.5	39.9	39.6	38.9	40.6	37.5	40.2	42.1	38.9	37.3	30.8
3. Probably would	21.9	26.8	17.4	19.7	34.1	25.2	21.3	22.8	18.1	20.3	25.4	19.4	22.4	25.9	22.7	38.6
4. Definitely would	6.8	8.7	4.9	5.3	15.6	7.5	5.0	6.8	8.5	6.3	7.3	6.2	10.1	5.7	4.7	13.5
Item 21090 Subject L02 N	2791	1316	1438	2199	285	574	799	870	549	1707	990	1105	589	383	647	33
E12: Some people like school very much. Others don't. How do you feel about going to school?																
5. I like school very much	12.1	10.8	13.4	9.5	24.5	9.2	12.5	14.0	11.9	13.4	9.9	17.2	9.5	9.6	7.6	5.4
4. I like school quite a lot	27.7	27.6	27.4	28.5	25.9	25.3	27.1	30.1	27.2	31.7	20.8	31.3	31.8	28.8	18.6	13.7
3. I like school some	40.9	41.8	40.3	42.0	35.3	42.9	40.7	38.8	42.4	39.1	44.8	38.3	42.4	42.7	42.8	29.9
2. I don't like school very much	13.0	12.9	13.1	13.1	11.1	14.9	13.0	11.5	13.3	11.4	15.2	9.1	12.0	13.4	20.3	17.9
1. I don't like school at all	6.3	7.0	5.7	6.9	3.1	7.6	6.8	5.6	5.2	4.3	9.2	4.0	4.4	5.4	10.6	33.1
Item 7630 Subject B01,Q08 N	2903	1363	1498	2267	303	614	820	899	570	1763	1036	1136	602	403	686	37
E13: About how many hours do you spend in an average week on all your homework including both in school and out of school?																
1. 0 hours	7.4	11.6	3.5	7.8	3.1	9.0	8.4	6.4	5.9	3.6	13.5	4.3	5.7	6.1	12.9	26.6
2. 1-4 hours	42.1	44.9	39.7	41.9	48.8	42.9	41.7	43.1	40.5	37.5	49.5	37.7	45.1	43.8	46.7	48.1
3. 5-9 hours	23.7	20.8	26.3	23.4	24.1	23.3	24.6	23.1	23.5	25.8	20.7	27.8	24.7	23.3	16.0	12.4
4. 10-14 hours	13.0	11.7	14.3	13.3	10.8	12.9	12.3	13.7	13.2	15.7	8.7	12.2	14.0	13.9	13.3	6.2
5. 15-19 hours	5.8	5.1	6.4	5.7	5.7	6.1	5.6	5.5	6.5	7.8	2.6	7.3	4.6	6.6	4.4	3.5
6. 20-24 hours	4.4	3.3	5.4	4.5	4.1	3.2	4.3	4.4	6.1	5.3	3.1	5.6	3.6	3.9	3.9	3.2
7. 25 or more hours	3.5	2.6	4.4	3.3	3.3	2.6	3.2	3.9	4.3	4.4	2.0	5.1	2.3	2.4	2.7	-
Item 7640 Subject B01 N	2892	1359	1490	2259	301	609	819	896	568	1753	1034	1133	599	402	683	37
E14: In general, how much say or influence do you feel each of the following has on HOW YOUR SCHOOL IS RUN?																
E14A: The principal																
1. Little or no influence	12.1	13.4	11.0	10.1	20.1	11.8	12.1	12.6	11.4	9.5	16.0	9.1	13.1	14.3	14.4	14.9
2. Some influence	13.4	15.0	11.8	12.3	16.9	10.6	13.0	15.7	13.5	12.6	15.0	14.2	12.8	14.5	12.5	14.6
3. Moderate influence	14.4	14.3	14.5	14.9	10.8	15.7	14.1	14.4	13.6	13.6	16.8	14.5	15.9	14.1	13.2	25.2
4. Considerable influence	25.5	25.8	25.2	27.9	16.1	24.9	27.4	21.2	30.1	26.9	22.7	26.4	22.3	24.5	27.8	16.0
5. A great deal of influence	34.5	31.4	37.5	34.7	36.0	36.9	33.4	36.0	31.3	37.4	29.5	35.8	36.0	32.6	32.1	29.3
Item 7650 Subject B10 N	2851	1335	1475	2228	295	594	808	888	561	1735	1019	1125	589	394	669	35
E14B: The teachers																
1. Little or no influence	8.3	8.7	8.0	7.4	11.3	8.8	9.0	7.5	8.0	7.0	10.5	7.5	9.2	7.3	9.4	5.1
2. Some influence	22.7	23.6	21.7	22.2	24.3	20.2	23.2	24.7	21.5	20.4	26.9	21.2	24.2	23.8	23.9	16.2
3. Moderate influence	30.4	31.7	29.1	32.6	21.4	30.3	32.3	28.7	30.4	31.6	28.7	30.2	30.1	34.7	32.2	25.8
4. Considerable influence	28.9	27.7	30.2	29.3	28.0	31.3	25.6	28.3	32.2	31.9	23.9	31.1	28.3	30.1	24.6	35.9
5. A great deal of influence	9.7	8.4	10.9	8.5	15.0	9.4	9.9	10.8	7.9	9.0	10.1	10.1	7.8	10.1	9.9	16.9
Item 7660 Subject B10 N	2844	1332	1471	2223	293	593	809	884	558	1732	1014	1122	586	391	671	35
E14C: The students																
1. Little or no influence	33.3	35.0	31.8	33.6	35.8	28.5	38.1	36.3	26.6	32.6	33.5	31.2	33.8	32.4	36.8	45.6
2. Some influence	24.4	24.3	24.8	25.2	23.7	26.6	24.8	21.8	25.7	25.7	22.9	25.2	23.0	23.0	25.7	18.2
3. Moderate influence	19.9	19.7	19.7	20.2	15.9	21.3	18.5	20.0	20.5	21.4	17.9	21.3	21.5	18.4	16.9	15.5
4. Considerable influence	13.1	12.8	13.3	12.8	10.9	14.3	9.9	13.0	16.4	12.5	13.6	13.2	11.8	17.5	11.0	12.9
5. A great deal of influence	9.3	8.1	10.5	8.1	13.6	9.3	8.8	8.8	10.8	7.8	12.1	9.1	10.0	8.8	9.6	7.8
Item 7670 Subject B10 N	2841	1330	1469	2221	291	592	807	883	560	1730	1013	1121	585	392	669	35

QUESTIONNAIRE FORM 2 1985	TOTAL	SEX		RACE		REGION				4YR COLLEGE PLANS		ILLICIT DRUG USE: LIFETIME				
		M	F	White	Black	NE	NC	S	W	Yes	No	None	Marijuana Only	Few Pills	More Pills	Any Heroin
N (Weighted No. of Cases):	3327	1573	1651	2485	388	771	914	1017	625	1919	1172	1283	696	453	784	47
% of Weighted Total:	100.0	47.3	49.6	74.7	11.7	23.2	27.5	30.6	18.8	57.7	35.2	38.6	20.9	13.6	23.6	1.4
E14D: Parents of students																
1. Little or no influence	23.3	25.6	21.6	23.4	21.6	25.5	24.5	23.3	19.4	20.1	27.6	19.0	24.4	23.2	28.5	40.8
2. Some influence	31.3	31.9	30.7	33.0	26.8	31.5	33.0	30.3	30.5	31.7	30.8	29.2	32.3	32.2	34.3	28.4
3. Moderate influence	22.5	20.8	24.0	22.8	19.8	24.2	22.0	23.5	19.8	24.6	19.7	26.0	22.2	18.5	19.6	16.1
4. Considerable influence	13.8	14.0	13.5	13.5	15.8	11.7	12.9	12.5	19.6	14.5	13.1	15.9	14.4	13.9	9.9	10.1
5. A great deal of influence	9.0	7.7	10.2	7.4	16.0	7.0	7.6	10.5	10.7	9.1	8.9	9.9	6.7	12.3	7.7	4.6
Item 7680 Subject B10 N	2837	1330	1467	2218	291	590	807	881	559	1729	1011	1120	584	393	667	35
E15: Have you had any drug education courses or lectures in school?																
1. No–GO TO Q.E19	23.9	25.8	22.1	22.8	30.3	20.8	26.1	26.2	20.5	20.5	30.2	25.2	23.1	22.6	23.2	18.0
2. No, and I wish I had– GO TO Q.E19	4.3	4.6	4.0	4.3	4.9	1.8	4.8	6.4	3.0	3.9	5.1	3.1	5.9	4.5	5.0	4.9
3. Yes	71.7	69.7	73.9	72.9	64.8	77.4	69.1	67.4	76.5	75.6	64.8	71.7	71.0	72.8	71.9	77.1
Item 7690 Subject A10a N	2703	1253	1415	2145	260	559	777	831	536	1669	942	1068	566	376	628	32
E16: Would you say that the information about drugs that you received in school classes or programs has . . .																
1. Made you less interested in trying drugs	55.6	49.1	61.0	52.7	74.6	47.3	55.4	60.0	58.8	55.5	58.1	67.5	62.6	52.9	33.2	10.4
2. Not changed your interest in trying drugs	41.6	46.9	37.2	44.7	22.4	48.8	41.3	38.2	38.7	42.1	39.1	32.2	35.1	44.3	60.9	63.7
3. Made you more interested in trying drugs	2.8	4.0	1.8	2.7	3.0	3.9	3.3	1.8	2.5	2.4	2.9	0.3	2.3	2.8	5.9	25.9
Item 7840 Subject A10a N★	1953	889	1042	1569	171	440	541	560	411	1265	617	770	408	271	457	26
E17: How many of the following drug education experiences have you had in high school? (Mark all that apply.)																
A. A special course about drugs	20.6	21.4	19.5	20.0	26.6	25.2	20.3	17.8	20.1	21.0	19.0	19.9	21.7	19.3	19.6	36.1
B. Films, lectures, or discussions in one of my regular courses	76.2	75.3	77.0	76.1	76.6	73.7	76.4	73.5	82.1	78.6	72.9	78.6	74.7	76.0	73.7	79.4
C. Films or lectures, outside of my regular courses	30.0	30.7	29.5	31.5	24.7	29.2	31.3	33.0	24.8	29.5	30.7	28.2	28.9	31.0	32.3	41.7
D. Special discussions ("rap" groups) about drugs	19.1	18.8	19.0	19.2	16.8	21.0	20.2	16.4	19.4	19.2	18.9	16.7	15.4	19.3	24.6	41.8
Item 7850-7880 Subject A10a N★	1929	869	1036	1550	169	429	535	554	412	1245	612	761	402	266	451	26
E18: Overall, how valuable were the experiences to you?																
1. Little or no value	17.3	19.5	15.6	17.8	16.8	17.2	19.0	17.6	15.0	17.1	17.5	15.1	13.8	19.4	23.0	20.1
2. Some value	43.8	46.5	41.7	46.7	26.8	44.9	47.6	39.3	44.0	43.7	44.4	42.6	41.8	44.5	47.7	51.7
3. Considerable value	24.8	22.4	26.7	24.9	20.9	25.6	23.0	24.9	26.3	25.1	24.8	23.6	30.3	23.7	24.0	6.1
4. Great value	14.0	11.5	16.0	10.7	35.5	12.4	10.5	18.2	14.7	14.2	13.3	18.7	14.2	12.4	5.4	22.1
Item 7890 Subject A10a N★	1939	876	1040	1563	168	431	538	558	412	1255	613	765	402	270	454	26
E19: During the LAST TWO WEEKS, how many times (if any) have you driven a car, truck, or motorcycle after . . .																
E19A: Drinking alcohol?																
1. None	71.0	63.4	78.2	68.3	86.9	72.0	70.3	71.5	70.5	73.4	66.9	86.4	68.9	67.2	51.8	31.0
2. Once	13.3	14.3	12.4	14.3	7.0	14.7	13.1	13.5	11.6	13.6	12.8	8.7	17.2	14.7	17.1	10.6
3. Twice	8.6	11.1	6.2	9.9	2.9	6.6	10.1	7.3	10.6	7.7	10.2	3.4	9.2	11.4	14.2	24.9
4. 3-5 times	5.0	7.8	2.4	5.6	1.8	4.7	4.4	5.6	5.3	4.2	6.6	1.1	3.8	5.9	11.4	13.7
5. 6-9 times	1.0	1.5	0.6	1.0	0.3	0.8	1.2	0.8	1.4	0.6	1.9	0.3	0.3	0.8	2.6	8.3
6. 10 or more	1.1	1.9	0.3	0.9	1.1	1.2	0.9	1.4	0.6	0.6	1.6	0.2	0.6	-	2.9	11.4
Item 1811 Subject A07a N	2824	1325	1457	2210	293	579	812	877	557	1726	1000	1115	583	388	669	36

★=excludes respondents for whom question was inappropriate.

QUESTIONNAIRE FORM 2 1985	TOTAL	SEX		RACE		REGION				4YR COLLEGE PLANS		ILLICIT DRUG USE: LIFETIME				
		M	F	White	Black	NE	NC	S	W	Yes	No	None	Mari-juana Only	Few Pills	More Pills	Any Her-oin
N (Weighted No. of Cases):	3327	1573	1651	2485	388	771	914	1017	625	1919	1172	1283	696	453	784	47
% of Weighted Total:	100.0	47.3	49.6	74.7	11.7	23.2	27.5	30.6	18.8	57.7	35.2	38.6	20.9	13.6	23.6	1.4

E19B: Having 5 or more drinks in a row?

1. None	83.4	76.0	90.1	81.7	93.1	84.4	81.9	83.1	84.9	86.5	78.2	94.1	82.3	82.4	69.4	39.1
2. Once	7.8	10.2	5.8	8.7	2.0	8.2	8.4	7.0	7.4	7.2	8.4	3.1	10.1	7.9	13.3	12.4
3. Twice	4.6	7.0	2.5	5.1	2.2	4.1	5.1	3.9	5.4	3.7	6.3	1.5	4.5	5.3	9.1	9.2
4. 3-5 times	2.6	3.9	1.2	2.8	1.2	1.8	3.0	3.3	1.5	1.7	4.0	1.1	2.8	3.1	4.0	11.7
5. 6-9 times	0.7	1.4	0.1	0.9	-	0.5	0.6	1.2	0.4	0.2	1.6	0.1	0.1	0.7	2.0	9.7
6. 10 or more	1.0	1.5	0.3	0.8	1.5	0.9	1.0	1.3	0.3	0.6	1.4	0.2	0.2	0.5	2.1	18.0
Item 1812　Subject A07a　N	2783	1296	1445	2188	281	569	800	863	550	1708	982	1097	579	380	657	36

E20: During the LAST TWO WEEKS, how many times (if any) have you been a passenger in a car . . .

E20A: When the driver had been drinking?

1. None	60.9	61.1	61.5	58.4	72.4	63.2	58.8	60.7	62.0	63.7	56.0	77.3	57.4	56.8	39.8	30.9
2. Once	17.8	16.7	18.8	19.3	10.6	14.4	18.5	17.7	20.4	18.4	17.5	12.8	22.4	19.0	22.4	11.3
3. Twice	10.7	10.6	10.3	12.0	6.0	10.7	11.7	10.3	9.6	9.9	12.2	6.1	11.2	11.7	17.0	11.7
4. 3-5 times	7.2	7.8	6.4	7.3	6.8	7.2	7.8	7.9	5.0	5.8	9.2	2.5	7.4	7.5	13.5	31.3
5. 6-9 times	1.7	2.1	1.3	1.6	1.7	1.5	1.3	1.9	2.0	1.3	2.1	0.8	0.8	1.4	4.0	5.4
6. 10 or more	1.8	1.7	1.8	1.4	2.5	3.0	1.9	1.4	0.9	0.9	3.0	0.5	0.8	3.6	3.3	9.4
Item 1815　Subject A07a　N	2806	1312	1452	2201	290	582	808	865	552	1724	989	1110	584	381	662	34

E20B: When you think the driver had 5 or more drinks?

1. None	78.5	76.3	80.7	76.3	91.3	79.2	75.7	79.8	79.8	82.5	71.8	90.5	77.7	77.3	61.5	34.4
2. Once	10.2	9.9	10.7	11.4	2.5	9.1	10.9	9.7	11.3	9.4	11.6	6.1	11.9	12.6	14.5	10.9
3. Twice	5.9	7.4	4.5	6.8	2.3	6.1	6.4	5.6	5.7	4.5	8.4	2.3	7.2	4.6	11.5	14.4
4. 3-5 times	3.3	4.0	2.5	3.6	2.0	3.7	4.3	3.1	1.9	2.4	5.0	0.8	2.5	3.6	7.5	19.6
5. 6-9 times	1.2	1.2	1.1	1.0	1.5	0.7	1.6	1.1	1.1	0.8	1.7	0.1	0.3	1.1	3.4	7.8
6. 10 or more	0.9	1.2	0.4	0.9	0.3	1.2	1.1	0.8	0.2	0.4	1.6	0.2	0.5	0.8	1.7	13.0
Item 1816　Subject A07a　N	2780	1297	1443	2185	284	573	795	863	548	1709	981	1101	577	379	654	34

E21: How often do you . . .

E21A: Eat breakfast?

1. Never	10.4	8.4	12.0	10.5	10.1	9.9	12.9	9.3	9.0	9.3	12.1	7.3	9.9	9.7	14.9	28.8
2. Seldom	27.6	24.3	30.4	26.9	31.1	31.4	27.0	26.9	25.4	26.6	28.8	23.0	27.9	36.7	29.6	32.5
3. Sometimes	17.3	15.7	18.8	16.5	23.9	15.5	15.0	19.6	19.1	16.5	18.8	17.4	16.1	14.5	19.2	27.8
4. Most days	9.3	8.1	10.4	9.2	11.5	7.7	9.1	10.2	9.9	9.1	9.9	8.6	9.6	9.5	10.1	1.6
5. Nearly every day	10.5	11.0	10.2	10.7	9.1	7.6	13.2	10.4	9.6	11.3	9.7	12.0	10.2	9.3	9.6	2.9
6. Every day	24.9	32.4	18.2	26.3	14.2	27.8	22.8	23.6	26.9	27.2	20.7	31.6	26.4	20.3	16.6	6.4
Item 20740　Subject T　N	2830	1328	1461	2222	292	587	810	875	559	1736	998	1119	582	385	672	35

E21B: Eat at least some green vegetables?

1. Never	3.4	4.0	2.7	3.0	4.9	5.6	3.5	2.9	1.9	2.6	4.9	2.5	2.7	2.3	5.1	14.5
2. Seldom	11.7	11.2	12.0	10.8	18.8	10.3	12.0	11.8	12.6	10.1	14.6	8.6	12.1	14.2	14.9	13.5
3. Sometimes	20.7	18.7	22.7	20.1	25.8	18.6	21.2	21.2	21.4	18.1	25.0	20.7	19.0	21.5	21.3	22.1
4. Most days	24.2	23.9	24.3	23.8	22.2	23.7	25.6	23.5	23.8	25.4	22.6	24.9	23.7	25.3	22.4	29.5
5. Nearly every day	20.5	19.0	21.8	21.5	18.0	19.6	21.3	22.4	17.3	22.7	17.3	20.9	23.9	18.2	18.7	13.5
6. Every day	19.5	23.2	16.5	20.8	10.3	22.2	16.5	18.3	23.0	21.2	15.6	22.3	18.6	18.4	17.6	6.8
Item 20750　Subject T　N	2822	1325	1455	2216	293	585	806	875	556	1734	991	1113	581	385	670	36

E21C: Eat at least some fruit?

1. Never	2.3	2.1	2.5	2.3	1.6	3.3	2.6	1.7	1.7	1.7	3.4	1.7	2.3	2.5	2.4	12.7
2. Seldom	10.6	10.6	10.3	10.6	13.3	11.7	11.1	11.1	8.0	8.4	14.3	7.9	11.2	11.5	13.0	19.4
3. Sometimes	24.8	23.8	25.9	24.6	29.2	22.7	24.2	27.3	23.9	21.6	30.3	22.5	23.5	26.0	29.2	26.7
4. Most days	24.5	24.0	25.0	23.9	25.7	22.0	24.0	25.9	25.9	26.1	22.1	27.0	22.9	23.9	22.1	24.0
5. Nearly every day	20.2	20.3	20.2	20.4	18.8	19.8	20.7	20.5	19.2	23.0	16.0	20.9	23.7	19.2	17.2	10.0
6. Every day	17.6	19.2	16.1	18.2	11.3	20.6	17.4	13.4	21.3	19.2	13.9	20.0	16.4	16.8	16.1	7.3
Item 20760　Subject T　N	2819	1321	1455	2219	290	585	807	872	555	1729	994	1113	578	386	670	36

	TOTAL	SEX		RACE		REGION				4YR COLLEGE PLANS		ILLICIT DRUG USE: LIFETIME				
QUESTIONNAIRE FORM 2 **1985**		M	F	White	Black	NE	NC	S	W	Yes	No	None	Mari-juana Only	Few Pills	More Pills	Any Her-oin
N (Weighted No. of Cases):	3327	1573	1651	2485	388	771	914	1017	625	1919	1172	1283	696	453	784	47
% of Weighted Total:	100.0	47.3	49.6	74.7	11.7	23.2	27.5	30.6	18.8	57.7	35.2	38.6	20.9	13.6	23.6	1.4
E21D: Exercise vigorously (jogging, swimming, calisthenics, or any other active sports)?																
1. Never	4.7	4.3	5.0	4.0	8.2	4.5	5.7	5.3	2.5	3.5	6.6	4.0	3.7	4.6	6.1	10.4
2. Seldom	15.9	12.2	19.3	15.4	20.2	14.7	16.8	16.6	14.7	13.5	20.4	14.7	15.1	16.9	18.1	20.7
3. Sometimes	25.3	19.0	31.4	26.6	21.5	22.8	25.5	28.9	21.9	23.3	28.5	26.8	24.2	25.5	24.4	16.5
4. Most days	17.3	17.5	16.8	17.5	12.6	19.5	15.0	17.1	18.5	18.1	16.3	17.3	16.8	16.8	16.9	29.1
5. Nearly every day	18.3	23.0	14.3	18.7	17.4	19.3	18.7	15.6	20.9	20.5	14.4	17.8	20.6	19.1	17.3	9.0
6. Every day	18.6	24.1	13.2	17.8	20.0	19.3	18.2	16.5	21.6	21.1	13.9	19.3	19.6	17.1	17.2	14.2
Item 20770 Subject T N	2822	1322	1458	2215	293	584	808	874	557	1732	995	1114	582	386	666	36
E21E: Get at least seven hours of sleep?																
1. Never	3.2	3.9	2.6	3.2	3.2	4.9	3.1	3.3	1.6	2.1	5.2	1.8	3.1	3.1	4.8	12.4
2. Seldom	11.2	9.8	12.3	11.2	9.8	8.3	12.7	12.1	10.6	9.9	13.0	10.0	9.4	11.2	14.3	17.8
3. Sometimes	19.5	18.5	20.3	18.9	22.5	21.4	17.8	20.7	17.9	18.2	20.6	18.4	15.4	20.8	23.6	22.1
4. Most days	24.1	23.2	25.1	24.6	19.2	23.1	25.2	22.9	25.5	25.8	21.6	22.3	26.9	26.0	24.2	21.4
5. Nearly every day	23.3	24.8	22.1	24.5	20.2	23.8	22.7	22.0	25.8	25.8	19.8	26.4	23.1	24.5	18.8	12.1
6. Every day	18.7	19.7	17.5	17.7	25.1	18.5	18.6	18.9	18.7	18.1	19.7	21.1	22.1	14.4	14.4	14.2
Item 20780 Subject T N	2820	1320	1458	2215	292	585	805	874	556	1729	996	1113	581	386	667	36
E21F: Get less sleep than you think you should?																
1. Never	8.3	8.5	8.1	7.2	15.6	10.1	6.7	8.6	8.1	7.6	9.5	9.0	11.6	4.9	5.4	16.0
2. Seldom	17.5	19.3	15.9	17.2	20.8	16.9	17.8	17.3	18.3	16.6	19.1	18.5	18.8	18.0	14.7	22.1
3. Sometimes	31.8	30.0	33.2	32.5	28.9	31.5	34.5	30.8	29.9	33.0	30.0	34.6	28.3	35.1	29.7	14.3
4. Most days	17.0	17.0	17.1	16.9	15.7	17.1	17.5	17.5	15.6	16.8	17.0	17.4	14.3	16.7	19.4	15.1
5. Nearly every day	13.6	13.5	13.6	14.1	11.1	12.7	13.0	12.8	16.4	14.5	12.5	11.9	14.7	14.0	15.2	11.1
6. Every day	11.8	11.7	12.1	12.0	7.9	11.7	10.7	13.0	11.5	11.4	11.9	8.7	12.3	11.3	15.7	21.3
Item 20790 Subject T N	2816	1320	1456	2217	290	581	805	874	556	1725	997	1112	581	385	665	36

QUESTIONNAIRE FORM 3 1985	TOTAL	SEX		RACE		REGION				4YR COLLEGE PLANS		ILLICIT DRUG USE: LIFETIME				
		M	F	White	Black	NE	NC	S	W	Yes	No	None	Mari-juana Only	Few Pills	More Pills	Any Her-oin
N (Weighted No. of Cases):	3294	1549	1638	2464	407	770	907	1006	611	1932	1148	1258	717	446	761	48
% of Weighted Total:	100.0	47.0	49.7	74.8	12.4	23.4	27.5	30.5	18.5	58.7	34.9	38.2	21.8	13.5	23.1	1.4
A01: Taking all things together, how would you say things are these days-would you say you're very happy, pretty happy, or not too happy these days?																
3. Very happy	17.4	17.1	17.7	19.1	10.3	16.6	17.3	17.8	18.1	19.2	14.4	18.4	15.1	18.3	17.8	4.2
2. Pretty happy	70.4	70.4	70.3	71.0	68.8	70.1	70.4	71.3	69.1	69.6	72.1	71.1	73.4	68.0	68.3	72.5
1. Not too happy	12.2	12.5	12.0	9.9	20.9	13.3	12.4	10.9	12.8	11.2	13.4	10.4	11.6	13.7	13.9	23.3
Item 1190 Subject P01,Q01 N	3273	1541	1626	2451	407	760	901	1002	609	1923	1144	1253	713	443	754	48
A02: Some people think a lot about the social problems of the nation and the world, and about how they might be solved. Others spend little time thinking about these issues. How much do you think about such things?																
1. Never	2.4	3.2	1.6	2.2	2.3	3.3	2.2	2.0	2.3	1.7	3.1	1.7	2.0	1.8	3.8	6.8
2. Seldom	16.4	16.6	16.0	17.3	11.9	17.4	17.3	15.4	15.5	14.4	18.9	13.2	16.7	18.0	19.9	19.1
3. Sometimes	51.3	49.1	53.6	52.2	44.7	52.4	49.4	51.5	52.7	51.0	53.4	51.8	51.7	50.3	51.1	55.8
4. Quite often	25.1	25.6	25.0	23.9	33.1	22.1	26.7	25.8	25.2	27.5	21.3	28.0	25.4	25.8	20.5	12.1
5. A great deal	4.7	5.5	3.8	4.3	8.0	4.7	4.4	5.4	4.3	5.4	3.3	5.3	4.1	4.1	4.7	6.2
Item 6880 Subject J,Q08 N	3279	1544	1629	2456	407	763	904	1002	609	1925	1145	1254	715	443	757	48
A03: The next questions ask your opinions about a number of different topics. How much do you agree or disagree with each statement below?																
A03A: Men and women should be paid the same money if they do the same work																
1. Disagree	3.4	5.7	1.2	3.1	4.0	4.2	3.3	3.7	2.0	2.4	4.6	3.1	2.9	1.7	4.8	8.3
2. Mostly disagree	1.6	2.7	0.6	1.8	1.0	1.6	3.1	0.9	0.6	1.4	2.0	1.9	2.1	0.8	1.2	-
3. Neither	1.7	2.9	0.5	1.5	1.0	1.7	1.9	1.0	2.5	1.5	2.1	1.5	2.2	1.2	1.6	2.2
4. Mostly agree	14.7	21.4	8.0	14.3	14.4	13.8	13.9	14.4	17.5	13.9	15.7	13.9	14.7	15.8	14.1	11.2
5. Agree	78.6	67.4	89.8	79.3	79.6	78.7	77.8	80.0	77.4	80.8	75.6	79.6	78.0	80.5	78.3	78.3
Item 7930 Subject D06 N	3291	1545	1637	2464	407	770	907	1003	610	1929	1148	1258	717	446	759	48
A03B: Women should be considered as seriously as men for jobs as executives or politicians																
1. Disagree	5.5	9.6	1.0	5.3	3.9	5.9	5.7	6.0	3.6	4.0	7.0	4.9	3.6	4.1	8.0	14.5
2. Mostly disagree	4.7	8.2	1.2	4.6	2.6	4.9	5.3	4.0	4.7	3.9	5.5	2.7	5.2	4.1	7.3	5.9
3. Neither	4.8	8.2	1.7	4.5	3.4	4.6	5.6	3.3	6.4	4.4	5.4	4.9	5.3	5.7	3.7	7.2
4. Mostly agree	21.7	27.7	15.9	21.3	23.8	20.1	18.7	23.8	24.7	19.9	23.9	24.6	20.2	21.8	18.5	10.3
5. Agree	63.3	46.3	80.3	64.2	66.2	64.5	64.7	62.9	60.6	67.8	58.2	62.9	65.6	64.3	62.6	62.1
Item 7940 Subject D06,H02 N	3284	1541	1635	2460	407	767	904	1003	610	1928	1146	1256	716	446	755	48
A03C: A woman should have exactly the same job opportunities as a man																
1. Disagree	7.9	14.2	1.6	6.9	11.7	9.2	7.2	9.4	5.2	5.9	9.7	8.0	5.9	6.2	9.7	10.5
2. Mostly disagree	5.5	8.6	2.1	5.3	3.9	5.0	6.3	4.7	6.4	5.2	6.5	4.8	5.0	5.5	7.6	3.5
3. Neither	5.0	8.1	2.1	5.2	2.9	2.8	7.1	4.2	5.9	4.8	5.0	5.3	4.9	5.1	4.5	2.7
4. Mostly agree	28.2	28.8	27.3	29.0	24.7	29.2	27.1	27.7	29.4	25.5	32.7	29.5	28.3	26.1	26.6	33.4
5. Agree	53.4	40.4	66.9	53.5	56.8	53.8	52.4	54.0	53.2	58.7	46.1	52.4	56.0	57.1	51.6	49.9
Item 7950 Subject D06 N	3251	1522	1623	2439	402	759	894	992	606	1911	1135	1240	713	442	745	48
A03D: A woman should have exactly the same educational opportunities as a man																
1. Disagree	1.3	1.9	0.5	1.0	2.2	0.9	1.4	1.7	1.0	1.2	1.4	1.3	0.3	0.7	2.1	2.2
2. Mostly disagree	0.7	1.1	0.1	0.5	0.9	0.8	0.8	0.2	1.1	0.4	1.0	0.3	0.8	0.2	1.4	1.2
3. Neither	1.1	1.6	0.6	0.9	0.6	1.5	1.4	1.1	0.1	0.7	1.4	1.3	1.0	0.6	1.1	1.4
4. Mostly agree	8.4	10.6	5.9	7.3	13.0	8.5	8.1	8.2	9.3	6.9	10.2	8.6	7.8	8.8	7.9	17.3
5. Agree	88.5	84.8	92.8	90.3	83.2	88.3	88.3	88.8	88.4	90.8	86.0	88.5	90.1	89.5	87.5	77.8
Item 7960 Subject D06 N	3274	1535	1631	2455	403	765	902	998	609	1920	1143	1249	715	443	756	48

MONITORING THE FUTURE

QUESTIONNAIRE FORM 3 1985	TOTAL	SEX		RACE		REGION				4YR COLLEGE PLANS		ILLICIT DRUG USE: LIFETIME				
		M	F	White	Black	NE	NC	S	W	Yes	No	None	Mari- juana Only	Few Pills	More Pills	Any Her- oin
N (Weighted No. of Cases):	3294	1549	1638	2464	407	770	907	1006	611	1932	1148	1258	717	446	761	48
% of Weighted Total:	100.0	47.0	49.7	74.8	12.4	23.4	27.5	30.5	18.5	58.7	34.9	38.2	21.8	13.5	23.1	1.4
A03E: It is usually better for everyone involved if the man is the achiever outside the home and the woman takes care of the home and family																
1. Disagree	28.6	17.2	40.1	27.3	38.2	32.1	26.4	27.0	29.8	33.0	22.9	27.7	31.2	29.8	28.1	22.2
2. Mostly disagree	18.4	14.8	22.4	19.1	17.5	15.8	19.8	18.1	20.1	19.5	16.9	19.5	19.3	17.3	17.0	6.1
3. Neither	15.8	20.2	11.5	16.9	10.3	16.0	18.1	14.2	14.5	15.7	16.3	17.2	14.3	15.8	14.8	19.2
4. Mostly agree	21.7	24.5	18.2	22.6	17.0	20.9	22.5	20.8	22.8	19.8	23.9	19.7	21.5	23.5	23.9	21.0
5. Agree	15.6	23.2	7.8	14.2	17.0	15.2	13.1	19.8	12.9	11.9	20.0	15.9	13.7	13.5	16.3	31.6
Item 7970 Subject D05 N	3278	1536	1635	2461	402	766	905	997	609	1923	1146	1253	717	444	754	48
A03F: A preschool child is likely to suffer if the mother works																
1. Disagree	17.4	13.6	21.4	14.2	37.1	16.7	17.0	20.3	14.2	17.3	16.7	17.3	18.4	17.3	16.9	19.3
2. Mostly disagree	17.9	10.9	24.0	18.3	19.4	16.6	19.8	18.3	16.0	19.2	16.7	16.5	19.3	18.7	18.8	8.1
3. Neither	15.5	14.8	16.3	17.1	9.4	17.1	15.1	13.3	17.6	16.9	13.9	15.8	15.5	18.4	14.6	7.5
4. Mostly agree	25.1	26.6	23.8	26.4	18.2	24.5	26.6	23.2	26.6	25.6	24.1	26.1	24.8	22.5	23.9	39.3
5. Agree	24.1	34.0	14.5	23.9	16.0	25.1	21.5	24.8	25.6	20.9	28.6	24.2	22.1	23.1	25.9	25.8
Item 7980 Subject D05 N	3266	1533	1625	2449	402	763	901	995	607	1919	1138	1249	714	443	750	48
A03G: A working mother can establish just as warm and secure a relationship with her children as a mother who does not work																
1. Disagree	13.5	20.3	6.6	13.6	10.6	14.1	12.2	13.6	14.5	10.9	16.7	13.4	13.7	8.9	15.4	16.0
2. Mostly disagree	16.7	22.7	11.1	18.5	7.0	16.6	18.7	15.0	16.6	18.0	14.9	16.4	14.3	21.5	15.6	27.1
3. Neither	8.1	10.6	5.8	8.4	5.1	8.9	8.3	6.7	9.2	7.9	8.5	7.9	9.0	5.8	7.8	5.8
4. Mostly agree	27.3	23.3	31.1	28.7	20.4	27.9	26.4	27.2	27.8	27.4	27.4	28.6	25.1	25.9	28.8	22.6
5. Agree	34.4	23.1	45.4	30.8	56.8	32.4	34.4	37.5	32.0	35.8	32.4	33.0	37.9	37.9	32.3	28.5
Item 7990 Subject D05 N	3288	1542	1638	2464	407	768	906	1003	610	1929	1147	1258	717	446	755	48
A04: The next questions are about pollution and the environment. How much do you agree or disagree with each statement below?																
A04A: Pollution of most types has increased in the U.S. in the last ten years																
1. Disagree	2.1	3.3	0.8	1.7	4.1	2.5	2.7	1.9	0.9	1.8	2.1	1.5	2.0	2.6	2.4	0.4
2. Mostly disagree	5.3	6.9	3.8	5.4	3.9	6.8	6.3	4.0	3.9	5.8	4.5	5.0	6.3	6.5	3.9	6.6
3. Neither	10.0	10.5	9.5	10.5	9.1	9.8	12.3	9.2	8.1	10.9	8.3	11.0	8.6	11.1	9.1	11.2
4. Mostly agree	28.4	25.0	32.0	29.6	25.7	26.7	29.4	27.8	30.2	29.8	27.5	29.0	28.2	28.8	28.3	23.3
5. Agree	54.2	54.4	53.9	52.7	57.2	54.1	49.3	57.0	56.9	51.7	57.5	53.5	54.9	51.1	56.3	58.5
Item 8000 Subject F04 N	3281	1543	1632	2459	407	766	904	1004	608	1929	1146	1254	717	446	757	48
A04B: Government should take steps to deal with our environmental problems, even if it means that most of us pay higher prices or taxes																
1. Disagree	9.1	11.4	6.7	7.2	18.0	8.7	7.7	11.8	7.1	6.5	11.7	8.0	9.1	10.5	9.8	6.0
2. Mostly disagree	10.8	9.9	11.2	9.2	15.4	11.4	10.6	11.0	9.8	10.3	11.9	10.4	9.7	8.6	12.9	12.4
3. Neither	17.2	14.2	20.5	17.9	11.0	16.1	18.4	14.2	22.0	18.3	16.1	16.5	17.4	20.1	17.3	15.1
4. Mostly agree	37.3	34.2	40.4	39.6	28.5	35.1	37.6	38.8	37.1	39.2	35.0	38.6	37.0	35.9	35.4	42.0
5. Agree	25.6	30.3	21.3	26.2	27.1	28.7	25.7	24.2	24.1	25.7	25.3	26.5	26.7	24.9	24.6	24.4
Item 8010 Subject F04,H02 N	3281	1543	1630	2456	407	766	905	1004	606	1928	1146	1252	717	446	756	48
A04C: I would prefer to pay more money for things that will last a long time, rather than have them cost less and break sooner																
1. Disagree	1.1	1.4	0.7	0.8	2.0	1.8	0.9	0.7	1.0	0.8	1.0	0.9	1.2	0.7	1.2	3.3
2. Mostly disagree	1.2	1.6	0.7	1.0	2.3	1.7	1.1	1.1	1.2	1.0	1.5	1.1	1.6	0.8	1.1	—
3. Neither	3.8	3.7	3.6	3.4	2.3	4.6	3.7	3.0	4.1	3.3	4.4	3.4	3.1	4.6	4.2	3.3
4. Mostly agree	23.0	21.2	24.8	23.6	22.7	21.3	24.3	20.3	27.6	23.4	22.5	21.9	21.4	24.7	24.3	39.9
5. Agree	70.9	72.1	70.2	71.3	70.7	70.5	70.1	74.9	66.1	71.5	70.7	72.7	72.6	69.1	69.2	53.5
Item 8020 Subject F01 N	3286	1542	1636	2461	406	767	906	1005	607	1929	1146	1254	716	446	758	48

QUESTIONNAIRE FORM 3 1985	TOTAL	SEX		RACE		REGION				4YR COLLEGE PLANS		ILLICIT DRUG USE: LIFETIME				
		M	F	White	Black	NE	NC	S	W	Yes	No	None	Mari-juana Only	Few Pills	More Pills	Any Her-oin
N (Weighted No. of Cases):	3294	1549	1638	2464	407	770	907	1006	611	1932	1148	1258	717	446	761	48
% of Weighted Total:	100.0	47.0	49.7	74.8	12.4	23.4	27.5	30.5	18.5	58.7	34.9	38.2	21.8	13.5	23.1	1.4

A04D: I would probably be willing to use a bicycle or mass transit (if available) rather than a car to get to work

1. Disagree	33.7	36.6	29.9	30.7	46.8	33.8	31.1	38.5	29.5	28.7	40.5	29.8	34.2	35.5	37.2	40.2
2. Mostly disagree	20.0	19.6	20.3	20.7	18.8	20.1	18.7	20.7	20.6	20.1	19.5	19.8	21.9	19.1	18.9	13.9
3. Neither	11.4	12.0	11.0	12.3	6.2	11.6	12.8	9.2	12.6	11.8	11.0	12.8	9.8	12.8	10.6	5.6
4. Mostly agree	20.0	17.8	22.5	21.2	14.9	20.0	20.6	18.3	21.8	23.4	15.1	21.9	18.3	18.2	19.8	26.0
5. Agree	14.9	14.0	16.3	15.2	13.3	14.5	16.7	13.2	15.5	15.9	13.8	15.8	15.7	14.4	13.5	14.3
Item 8030 Subject F07 N	3281	1542	1633	2457	406	764	904	1005	607	1927	1145	1252	717	446	756	48

A04E: I would be willing to eat less meat and more grains and vegetables, if it would help provide food for starving people

1. Disagree	11.0	18.7	3.6	11.4	8.7	12.6	12.5	9.0	10.0	9.6	12.7	8.6	11.0	10.5	14.8	11.1
2. Mostly disagree	8.7	12.2	5.0	9.0	7.2	8.2	8.8	8.5	9.5	8.5	8.9	8.1	8.3	10.1	7.8	16.0
3. Neither	13.9	17.9	10.1	14.7	7.8	15.7	17.2	11.0	11.6	13.6	14.4	14.9	13.7	11.9	14.3	12.4
4. Mostly agree	29.7	27.7	31.8	30.0	31.6	29.6	27.1	31.9	29.9	30.4	28.7	32.0	30.4	28.9	26.5	24.1
5. Agree	36.7	23.5	49.6	35.0	44.9	33.9	34.3	39.6	39.0	37.8	35.2	36.5	36.5	38.6	36.6	36.4
Item 8040 Subject F03,O03 N	3271	1536	1629	2448	405	762	904	1000	605	1926	1137	1252	713	443	753	48

A05: In the following list you will find some statements about leisure time and work. Please show whether you agree or disagree with each statement.

A05A: I like the kind of work you can forget about after the work day is over

1. Disagree	11.2	13.1	9.6	9.3	20.7	11.0	10.0	13.1	10.1	10.8	10.4	12.2	11.6	7.3	11.6	8.7
2. Mostly disagree	14.5	13.9	15.2	14.8	12.7	15.6	13.8	13.8	15.1	17.7	9.6	15.9	12.6	16.8	12.0	19.7
3. Neither	12.6	14.3	11.5	13.6	7.7	10.9	15.4	9.8	15.1	14.0	11.0	13.1	10.8	15.5	12.7	9.5
4. Mostly agree	27.2	22.8	31.7	28.5	23.9	26.6	28.9	24.8	29.5	28.6	25.6	26.4	29.5	26.6	27.2	27.4
5. Agree	34.5	35.9	32.0	33.8	34.9	35.8	31.9	38.5	30.1	28.8	43.4	32.5	35.6	33.8	36.5	34.7
Item 8050 Subject C04 N	3280	1543	1630	2454	406	763	905	1004	608	1928	1145	1254	715	446	754	48

A05B: To me, work is nothing more than making a living

1. Disagree	38.1	34.0	42.6	39.7	36.1	38.4	37.6	38.2	38.1	42.4	31.6	41.7	37.6	34.0	36.3	29.0
2. Mostly disagree	27.8	27.0	28.8	30.4	16.6	23.7	29.9	27.0	31.0	29.2	25.9	26.3	29.0	29.7	28.5	26.5
3. Neither	10.3	10.6	10.0	10.7	5.8	12.9	10.4	7.5	11.6	10.3	10.6	9.8	10.1	13.1	9.5	14.2
4. Mostly agree	12.4	14.4	10.0	11.0	14.7	13.0	11.8	12.7	11.7	10.0	16.0	11.0	12.4	11.7	13.8	16.8
5. Agree	11.5	14.0	8.6	8.1	26.9	12.0	10.3	14.6	7.6	8.1	16.0	11.2	10.9	11.5	11.9	13.5
Item 8060 Subject C06 N	3280	1543	1630	2456	406	763	906	1003	609	1926	1145	1254	713	446	756	48

A05C: I expect my work to be a very central part of my life

1. Disagree	4.2	4.6	3.8	4.0	5.3	5.3	3.0	4.4	4.3	3.5	4.9	4.3	3.5	4.4	4.1	6.3
2. Mostly disagree	7.8	6.9	8.8	8.6	4.9	8.1	9.3	6.3	7.9	8.1	8.0	7.6	6.6	12.3	7.5	5.5
3. Neither	13.3	11.7	15.0	14.8	5.5	14.6	15.6	8.2	16.4	12.7	14.5	12.7	12.5	12.5	15.6	13.3
4. Mostly agree	39.7	39.5	39.9	41.5	30.0	36.0	40.2	41.8	40.5	41.7	37.4	40.6	40.2	37.4	39.0	45.1
5. Agree	35.0	37.3	32.4	31.0	54.4	36.0	32.0	39.3	30.9	34.0	35.2	34.8	37.1	33.5	33.7	29.8
Item 8070 Subject C06 N	3271	1537	1628	2454	404	761	905	1000	605	1920	1143	1251	713	445	754	48

A05D: I want to do my best in my job, even if this sometimes means working overtime

1. Disagree	1.5	1.9	1.1	1.2	2.3	2.5	1.0	1.2	1.4	1.3	1.6	1.0	1.5	1.4	1.8	2.1
2. Mostly disagree	2.1	2.1	1.8	1.8	2.8	3.4	1.6	1.3	2.6	2.2	2.1	1.1	1.7	1.3	4.4	4.5
3. Neither	5.2	6.1	4.5	5.9	2.0	6.9	6.3	4.0	3.6	5.1	5.0	5.2	3.9	7.1	6.0	0.4
4. Mostly agree	30.9	31.0	30.9	32.7	24.7	29.9	32.6	29.9	31.2	32.3	29.7	31.5	27.8	30.9	32.8	43.0
5. Agree	60.3	58.8	61.7	58.4	68.2	57.3	58.5	63.6	61.1	59.2	61.5	61.2	65.2	59.3	55.0	50.0
Item 8080 Subject C06 N	3276	1539	1630	2453	405	762	905	1003	606	1924	1144	1251	714	446	755	48

QUESTIONNAIRE FORM 3 1985	TOTAL	SEX		RACE		REGION				4YR COLLEGE PLANS		ILLICIT DRUG USE: LIFETIME				
		M	F	White	Black	NE	NC	S	W	Yes	No	None	Mari-juana Only	Few Pills	More Pills	Any Her-oin
N (Weighted No. of Cases):	3294	1549	1638	2464	407	770	907	1006	611	1932	1148	1258	717	446	761	48
% of Weighted Total:	100.0	47.0	49.7	74.8	12.4	23.4	27.5	30.5	18.5	58.7	34.9	38.2	21.8	13.5	23.1	1.4
A05E: I would like to stay in the same job for most of my adult life																
1. Disagree	13.9	13.6	13.8	12.7	20.0	14.3	13.0	15.3	12.0	12.6	15.4	13.0	12.3	15.3	15.4	14.0
2. Mostly disagree	11.9	11.3	12.3	11.4	14.5	10.9	12.6	12.1	11.8	12.9	10.5	10.3	14.0	12.6	12.2	14.0
3. Neither	16.5	16.0	17.1	17.6	8.6	15.9	17.2	14.3	20.0	16.7	16.3	18.1	14.2	15.9	17.3	13.9
4. Mostly agree	28.7	26.9	30.9	29.1	27.8	29.4	28.7	27.9	28.9	30.2	27.1	28.0	28.1	32.5	28.5	29.0
5. Agree	29.1	32.2	25.9	29.2	29.0	29.4	28.5	30.4	27.3	27.6	30.7	30.5	31.5	23.8	26.5	29.2
Item 8090　Subject C03　N	3275	1543	1626	2450	407	765	903	998	609	1927	1142	1249	715	446	753	48
A06: If you were to get enough money to live as comfortably as you'd like for the rest of your life, would you want to work?																
1. I would want to work	75.1	73.4	77.0	73.8	79.5	72.7	74.9	77.5	74.6	76.7	72.1	79.0	75.9	76.1	68.2	65.1
2. I would not want to work	24.9	26.6	23.0	26.2	20.5	27.3	25.1	22.5	25.4	23.3	27.9	21.0	24.1	23.9	31.8	34.9
Item 8100　Subject C06　N	3221	1504	1613	2418	391	754	890	982	594	1891	1127	1235	702	434	746	46

The next questions are about living or working with people of different races. Please rate each of the statements below using the following terms:

Not at all acceptable: I'd avoid this if I possibly could.

Somewhat acceptable: I could live with this, but not be happy about it.

Acceptable: This would be O.K., or I'd be neutral about this.

Desirable: I'd really like this.

A07: How would you feel about . . .

A07A: Having close personal friends of another race?

	TOTAL	M	F	White	Black	NE	NC	S	W	Yes	No	None	Mari-juana Only	Few Pills	More Pills	Any Her-oin
1. Not at all acceptable	2.1	2.8	1.1	2.2	0.9	2.9	1.6	2.5	1.0	1.3	2.9	2.6	0.8	1.4	2.1	4.0
2. Somewhat acceptable	5.9	8.1	3.5	6.7	2.6	4.7	7.7	7.1	2.9	4.1	8.5	5.3	5.2	4.9	7.8	7.6
3. Acceptable	52.4	55.6	49.4	55.7	44.0	55.4	56.6	49.2	47.8	49.7	56.7	49.9	54.9	51.1	55.4	45.4
4. Desirable	39.6	33.5	46.0	35.4	52.4	37.0	34.1	41.2	48.4	45.0	31.8	42.2	39.1	42.6	34.8	43.0
Item 8110　Subject N01　N	3266	1535	1624	2447	402	763	897	1000	606	1918	1140	1251	713	443	749	48

A07B: Having a job with a supervisor of a different race?

	TOTAL	M	F	White	Black	NE	NC	S	W	Yes	No	None	Mari-juana Only	Few Pills	More Pills	Any Her-oin
1. Not at all acceptable	2.5	3.9	1.0	2.7	1.2	3.4	2.6	2.2	1.3	2.0	2.7	2.6	1.5	1.6	2.8	6.4
2. Somewhat acceptable	7.4	10.2	4.4	7.9	4.2	7.3	8.6	8.2	4.2	6.2	9.2	6.0	5.9	3.9	12.6	9.5
3. Acceptable	69.1	68.9	69.3	70.7	68.4	68.7	71.2	69.8	65.6	69.0	69.0	69.1	72.5	70.6	65.3	59.8
4. Desirable	21.1	17.0	25.3	18.7	26.2	20.6	17.6	19.8	28.9	22.8	19.1	22.3	20.1	23.9	19.3	24.2
Item 8120　Subject C05,N01　N	3261	1532	1623	2443	402	762	897	1000	603	1915	1140	1251	713	441	747	48

A07C: Having a family of a different race (but same level of education and income) move next door to you?

	TOTAL	M	F	White	Black	NE	NC	S	W	Yes	No	None	Mari-juana Only	Few Pills	More Pills	Any Her-oin
1. Not at all acceptable	5.8	7.2	4.0	6.2	3.6	5.9	8.4	5.7	1.8	4.3	7.7	5.6	4.3	4.6	7.2	11.8
2. Somewhat acceptable	8.3	10.4	5.9	9.1	4.4	6.4	10.0	10.1	5.1	6.4	10.9	7.9	7.6	6.5	10.4	8.3
3. Acceptable	56.3	59.1	54.0	58.0	54.0	60.3	55.1	56.0	53.3	57.0	54.5	53.4	58.0	57.8	57.7	58.5
4. Desirable	29.7	23.3	36.1	26.7	38.0	27.3	26.5	28.2	39.8	32.3	26.8	33.1	30.0	31.1	24.6	21.3
Item 8130　Subject N01　N	3261	1533	1622	2442	402	761	897	998	605	1914	1140	1249	712	442	748	48

A07D: Having your (future) children's friends be all of your race?

	TOTAL	M	F	White	Black	NE	NC	S	W	Yes	No	None	Mari-juana Only	Few Pills	More Pills	Any Her-oin
1. Not at all acceptable	18.1	16.0	20.5	16.3	24.9	17.2	14.7	20.0	21.0	19.5	15.8	19.7	17.9	17.0	16.4	23.4
2. Somewhat acceptable	18.5	18.2	19.2	18.8	18.7	17.6	17.9	17.8	21.9	20.8	15.2	20.1	18.5	19.9	14.5	21.9
3. Acceptable	44.1	45.0	43.2	45.2	39.8	46.0	45.7	40.7	44.8	43.4	45.8	41.6	47.0	43.7	45.8	37.1
4. Desirable	19.3	20.9	17.1	19.7	16.7	19.2	21.7	21.5	12.3	16.2	23.2	18.7	16.5	19.4	23.3	17.6
Item 8140　Subject N01　N	3230	1513	1610	2424	396	756	888	992	594	1898	1126	1239	706	440	740	48

QUESTIONNAIRE FORM 3 1985	TOTAL	SEX		RACE		REGION				4YR COLLEGE PLANS		ILLICIT DRUG USE: LIFETIME				
		M	F	White	Black	NE	NC	S	W	Yes	No	None	Mari- juana Only	Few Pills	More Pills	Any Her- oin
N (Weighted No. of Cases):	3294	1549	1638	2464	407	770	907	1006	611	1932	1148	1258	717	446	761	48
% of Weighted Total:	100.0	47.0	49.7	74.8	12.4	23.4	27.5	30.5	18.5	58.7	34.9	38.2	21.8	13.5	23.1	1.4

A07E: Having some of your (future) children's friends be of other races?

1. Not at all acceptable	3.1	4.4	1.6	3.5	1.7	4.2	2.9	2.9	2.3	2.5	3.6	3.0	2.7	1.8	4.2	4.4
2. Somewhat acceptable	7.6	9.6	5.6	8.3	5.4	7.2	10.2	7.6	4.5	5.4	11.3	6.7	7.6	4.7	9.8	20.4
3. Acceptable	51.0	54.4	47.5	52.4	47.9	51.6	52.0	52.2	46.9	49.9	52.6	48.8	53.9	51.5	52.5	36.7
4. Desirable	38.2	31.6	45.3	35.9	45.0	37.0	34.8	37.3	46.3	42.2	32.5	41.5	35.8	42.0	33.5	38.5
Item 8150 Subject N01 N	3250	1528	1619	2438	400	758	894	993	605	1913	1133	1247	710	442	745	48

A08: How would you feel about having a job where . . .

A08A: . . . all the employees are of your race?

1. Not at all acceptable	7.4	6.5	8.6	5.1	18.0	6.8	4.3	9.3	9.8	7.7	6.9	7.4	7.4	7.6	6.6	13.9
2. Somewhat acceptable	15.9	14.6	17.2	12.5	24.5	14.9	13.9	15.6	20.9	17.5	13.4	17.0	15.7	15.6	13.7	27.7
3. Acceptable	54.4	54.6	54.9	58.5	41.4	56.6	56.1	50.7	55.5	56.2	52.8	54.4	55.7	54.4	54.9	42.1
4. Desirable	22.2	24.3	19.3	23.9	16.1	21.7	25.8	24.4	13.9	18.5	27.0	21.2	21.2	22.4	24.9	16.4
Item 8160 Subject C05,N01 N	3257	1531	1620	2443	399	761	897	996	603	1913	1140	1245	714	443	745	48

A08B: . . . some employees are of a different race?

1. Not at all acceptable	0.9	1.5	0.3	1.0	0.5	1.0	1.1	0.7	0.8	0.8	1.0	1.1	0.5	0.5	0.5	3.3
2. Somewhat acceptable	4.5	5.8	3.1	4.2	4.9	5.1	4.7	5.1	2.6	3.5	5.0	5.0	4.1	2.8	4.9	4.8
3. Acceptable	64.7	69.0	60.4	68.6	49.0	66.9	67.6	64.0	58.6	62.3	67.8	63.2	63.2	65.3	68.3	64.7
4. Desirable	29.9	23.7	36.2	26.2	45.7	27.0	26.7	30.2	38.0	33.4	26.2	30.7	32.2	31.3	26.3	27.2
Item 8170 Subject C05,N01 N	3262	1535	1622	2444	403	762	897	998	605	1917	1140	1251	714	443	747	48

A08C: . . . most employees are of a different race?

1. Not at all acceptable	10.5	12.1	8.7	12.1	4.1	11.9	13.0	10.6	4.7	9.7	10.5	9.7	8.4	8.9	15.2	6.4
2. Somewhat acceptable	30.3	30.9	29.6	34.6	18.2	27.9	31.1	35.4	23.5	30.3	31.9	28.7	30.6	28.4	33.7	33.3
3. Acceptable	49.3	48.1	50.5	47.7	57.7	51.5	47.4	45.1	56.2	49.9	47.3	50.7	51.2	52.4	42.6	53.4
4. Desirable	10.0	8.9	11.1	5.6	20.1	8.8	8.5	8.9	15.6	10.2	10.3	10.8	9.8	10.3	8.5	6.9
Item 8180 Subject C05,N01 N	3257	1532	1620	2443	399	763	895	996	604	1912	1138	1247	713	442	748	48

A09: How would you feel about living in an area where . . .

A09A: . . . all the neighbors are of your race?

1. Not at all acceptable	4.5	4.0	5.2	2.3	11.8	3.8	2.9	4.1	8.6	4.7	4.4	4.4	5.9	4.6	2.9	7.4
2. Somewhat acceptable	10.8	10.5	10.9	7.8	21.4	8.9	9.3	11.0	15.1	12.1	8.7	12.6	9.2	11.6	7.9	18.9
3. Acceptable	53.2	52.2	54.5	55.2	45.6	56.8	51.7	49.5	56.7	54.9	51.1	53.0	55.0	51.9	52.3	48.6
4. Desirable	31.5	33.3	29.4	34.7	21.2	30.5	36.1	35.4	19.6	28.3	35.8	30.0	29.8	31.9	36.9	25.1
Item 8190 Subject N01 N	3258	1530	1622	2445	399	761	897	997	604	1916	1136	1246	714	444	746	48

A09B: . . . some of the neighbors are of other races?

1. Not at all acceptable	2.0	3.0	1.0	2.1	1.3	2.4	2.4	2.1	0.9	1.6	2.4	2.1	1.3	1.9	2.2	2.3
2. Somewhat acceptable	7.2	8.2	5.9	7.2	7.5	7.2	7.2	8.9	4.4	6.2	7.9	7.2	7.2	5.3	7.9	13.4
3. Acceptable	67.2	69.0	65.9	70.0	57.3	69.8	70.0	64.8	63.6	66.4	68.8	65.6	65.1	67.6	71.9	57.8
4. Desirable	23.6	19.8	27.1	20.7	33.9	20.6	20.5	24.2	31.2	25.8	21.0	25.1	26.5	25.3	18.0	26.5
Item 8200 Subject N01 N	3257	1529	1622	2443	399	761	897	997	602	1914	1137	1245	714	442	746	48

A09C: . . . most of the neighbors are of other races?

1. Not at all acceptable	18.3	21.2	15.3	21.8	5.8	19.8	21.5	20.2	8.1	17.6	18.9	15.8	17.2	18.2	24.3	11.4
2. Somewhat acceptable	33.0	32.7	33.5	36.6	25.8	29.6	33.8	37.9	28.1	33.3	33.2	32.4	34.1	31.4	33.8	36.9
3. Acceptable	42.0	39.8	44.0	38.1	54.2	42.7	39.7	35.8	54.8	42.6	40.9	44.1	42.4	43.2	36.3	43.0
4. Desirable	6.8	6.3	7.2	3.6	14.2	7.8	5.0	6.2	9.1	6.6	7.0	7.7	6.2	7.2	5.6	8.7
Item 8210 Subject N01 N	3254	1533	1617	2442	399	759	898	997	599	1911	1138	1244	713	442	748	46

A10: How would you feel about having your (future) children go to schools where . . .

QUESTIONNAIRE FORM 3 1985	TOTAL	SEX		RACE		REGION				4YR COLLEGE PLANS		ILLICIT DRUG USE: LIFETIME				
		M	F	White	Black	NE	NC	S	W	Yes	No	None	Mari- juana Only	Few Pills	More Pills	Any Her- oin
N (Weighted No. of Cases):	3294	1549	1638	2464	407	770	907	1006	611	1932	1148	1258	717	446	761	48
% of Weighted Total:	100.0	47.0	49.7	74.8	12.4	23.4	27.5	30.5	18.5	58.7	34.9	38.2	21.8	13.5	23.1	1.4
A10A: . . . all the children are of your race?																
1. Not at all acceptable	9.3	8.0	10.7	5.9	22.1	9.1	6.2	9.7	13.4	9.6	8.0	9.0	10.3	10.6	7.6	13.3
2. Somewhat acceptable	12.6	11.6	13.8	10.7	20.8	11.3	10.0	14.3	15.5	14.2	10.2	14.8	11.9	14.0	8.6	16.7
3. Acceptable	49.9	50.6	49.4	51.8	43.9	52.6	49.9	47.2	50.7	51.2	48.6	50.1	51.3	46.8	49.4	54.9
4. Desirable	28.2	29.7	26.1	31.7	13.1	27.0	33.9	28.8	20.4	24.9	33.2	26.1	26.5	28.6	34.4	15.1
Item 8220 Subject B03,N01 N	3249	1523	1620	2433	400	761	896	992	600	1909	1134	1245	713	435	748	46
A10B: . . . some of the children are of other races?																
1. Not at all acceptable	1.4	2.3	0.4	1.2	1.5	2.5	1.3	0.9	1.0	1.0	1.8	1.3	0.9	1.0	1.7	1.9
2. Somewhat acceptable	5.7	7.1	4.3	5.3	6.4	4.9	6.7	7.5	2.4	4.2	6.9	6.2	5.2	4.9	5.9	7.3
3. Acceptable	63.8	66.6	60.8	66.3	55.2	66.9	67.2	61.6	58.5	61.5	67.8	60.7	64.9	61.6	69.3	63.7
4. Desirable	29.1	24.0	34.5	27.1	36.8	25.7	24.8	30.0	38.1	33.3	23.5	31.8	29.1	32.4	23.1	27.1
Item 8230 Subject B03,N01 N	3252	1525	1622	2434	402	758	898	996	600	1910	1136	1249	712	435	749	45
A10C: . . . most of the children are of other races?																
1. Not at all acceptable	21.0	23.3	18.4	24.5	8.4	22.9	25.1	22.8	9.7	20.5	21.4	18.1	18.9	20.8	28.8	11.1
2. Somewhat acceptable	32.2	32.3	32.5	36.5	20.8	30.3	35.0	33.9	27.7	33.5	31.5	31.6	34.0	34.0	31.3	34.8
3. Acceptable	39.0	37.4	40.8	35.1	51.7	38.6	34.5	35.8	51.7	38.5	39.5	41.6	39.4	36.8	34.2	49.2
4. Desirable	7.7	7.0	8.3	3.9	19.2	8.2	5.4	7.4	10.9	7.6	7.7	8.7	7.8	8.4	5.7	4.8
Item 8240 Subject B03,N01 N	3241	1522	1617	2430	398	758	896	991	595	1902	1132	1242	712	434	747	46
A11: What race are your close friends?																
1. All my race	29.9	31.3	29.1	34.2	20.8	28.4	43.5	27.1	16.1	30.0	30.8	30.0	31.1	25.1	31.6	23.5
2. Almost all my race	29.8	28.3	31.1	33.1	22.2	30.3	29.7	30.5	28.1	31.2	26.9	28.8	31.3	30.2	31.3	18.6
3. Mostly my race	22.3	22.3	22.2	22.9	24.5	23.6	16.5	25.3	24.2	21.6	24.1	22.1	21.0	26.1	21.7	22.6
4. About half my race	10.7	11.2	10.2	7.3	18.6	10.8	5.8	11.3	16.8	9.9	11.2	11.2	9.8	11.7	9.6	17.1
5. Mostly other race(s)	4.1	3.9	4.1	1.5	7.7	3.5	2.1	3.7	8.3	4.0	3.7	4.2	3.8	3.4	3.5	12.1
6. Almost all other race(s)	3.3	3.1	3.2	1.0	6.2	3.4	2.3	2.3	6.5	3.2	3.2	3.7	3.0	3.5	2.3	6.1
Item 8250 Subject N03 N	3235	1519	1611	2425	400	759	892	991	593	1896	1132	1240	707	438	744	45
A12: What race are the people in your neighborhood?																
1. All my race	42.6	43.5	41.7	48.2	32.3	42.1	55.5	44.7	20.3	41.1	45.3	44.7	40.5	39.2	43.4	39.3
2. Almost all my race	27.2	26.8	27.5	30.5	20.3	24.9	27.7	25.4	32.4	28.4	26.4	25.1	30.3	28.4	28.5	26.5
3. Mostly my race	12.7	13.3	12.0	13.0	12.9	13.8	8.8	12.4	17.5	12.6	12.5	11.9	11.7	15.0	13.6	14.9
4. About half my race	8.0	6.8	9.2	5.9	14.4	10.4	3.6	9.3	9.2	6.9	8.6	7.3	8.8	7.6	8.0	7.4
5. Mostly other race(s)	5.7	5.9	5.7	1.4	12.5	5.3	2.9	5.2	11.3	6.3	4.6	6.9	4.5	6.2	3.7	7.1
6. Almost all other race(s)	3.8	3.6	3.9	1.0	7.5	3.5	1.5	3.0	9.2	4.7	2.6	4.1	4.1	3.7	2.8	4.8
Item 8260 Subject N03 N	3236	1519	1611	2426	400	760	892	989	595	1900	1132	1241	706	441	742	45
A13: What race were the students in the elementary school where you spent the most time?																
1. All my race	31.8	32.5	31.4	36.2	21.5	34.7	46.7	25.4	16.5	31.4	33.6	33.0	32.2	26.0	33.2	38.7
2. Almost all my race	27.3	28.0	27.1	32.1	10.7	27.7	30.7	21.5	31.1	27.6	27.6	27.0	24.6	29.5	30.2	19.2
3. Mostly my race	15.4	14.8	15.7	16.5	10.1	13.9	11.9	17.3	19.4	16.0	14.1	14.2	15.7	18.4	15.7	11.3
4. About half my race	14.4	12.7	15.7	11.2	28.6	12.7	4.6	24.5	14.6	13.8	14.6	13.5	17.0	16.2	11.7	16.5
5. Mostly other race(s)	6.6	6.9	6.3	2.7	19.4	7.5	3.5	7.4	9.0	6.3	6.4	7.9	5.7	6.5	5.0	7.4
6. Almost all other race(s)	4.5	5.1	3.8	1.3	9.7	3.5	2.6	3.9	9.5	4.8	3.7	4.4	4.7	3.4	4.2	7.0
Item 8270 Subject B03,N03 N	3231	1515	1612	2424	399	760	890	986	595	1897	1132	1236	706	441	742	45
A14: What race are the students in your present school (if you are in school)?																
1. All my race	14.4	16.1	13.2	16.3	10.1	11.1	27.0	12.5	3.1	13.0	15.9	15.1	14.3	13.4	14.3	12.9
2. Almost all my race	26.7	28.8	24.9	32.2	11.3	33.5	32.2	17.8	24.6	27.9	26.3	27.8	25.4	22.6	29.8	24.4
3. Mostly my race	23.2	22.3	24.3	27.0	9.9	23.3	21.9	21.6	27.8	25.1	21.2	21.9	22.4	27.6	24.7	24.5
4. About half my race	21.6	19.2	23.4	19.0	38.1	17.5	12.5	33.5	21.0	20.1	23.2	19.8	22.7	26.4	21.1	19.0
5. Mostly other race(s)	9.4	9.2	9.5	4.2	21.0	8.9	4.7	10.7	15.2	9.1	9.6	10.3	10.1	7.4	7.0	9.8
6. Almost all other race(s)	4.5	4.4	4.8	1.2	9.8	5.8	1.7	3.8	8.3	4.7	3.9	5.1	5.1	2.6	3.2	9.3
Item 8280 Subject B03,N03 N	3234	1518	1610	2423	400	760	891	988	595	1898	1130	1239	708	440	741	45

QUESTIONNAIRE FORM 3 1985	TOTAL	SEX		RACE		REGION				4YR COLLEGE PLANS		ILLICIT DRUG USE: LIFETIME				
		M	F	White	Black	NE	NC	S	W	Yes	No	None	Marijuana Only	Few Pills	More Pills	Any Heroin
N (Weighted No. of Cases):	3294	1549	1638	2464	407	770	907	1006	611	1932	1148	1258	717	446	761	48
% of Weighted Total:	100.0	47.0	49.7	74.8	12.4	23.4	27.5	30.5	18.5	58.7	34.9	38.2	21.8	13.5	23.1	1.4
A15: What race are the people that you work with on your job (if you have a job)?																
1. All my race	38.8	39.4	37.7	45.6	11.2	40.1	52.5	31.0	29.2	35.1	44.6	36.4	38.5	38.0	42.9	43.8
2. Almost all my race	23.7	22.9	25.2	27.3	11.7	25.4	21.6	23.8	24.6	25.2	21.9	25.9	20.9	26.3	22.8	12.0
3. Mostly my race	14.6	14.3	14.7	16.2	8.3	13.4	12.1	18.0	14.6	15.6	14.0	14.3	14.6	13.2	16.5	12.4
4. About half my race	9.7	9.9	9.7	7.4	24.2	8.5	7.3	13.6	8.8	9.7	9.7	8.9	11.3	11.2	8.9	11.3
5. Mostly other race(s)	7.8	8.4	6.9	2.2	27.8	6.5	3.6	9.9	12.2	8.4	5.7	8.6	8.1	8.5	5.2	3.5
6. Almost all other race(s)	5.3	5.2	5.7	1.3	16.7	6.0	2.9	3.6	10.6	6.0	4.1	5.9	6.6	2.9	3.6	16.9
Item 8290 Subject N03 N	2694	1315	1285	2041	312	631	751	791	521	1565	959	991	596	370	650	39
A16: How often do you do things (like having a conversation, eating together, playing sports) with people of other races?																
1. Not at all	8.3	8.7	7.6	9.8	3.0	8.3	14.2	5.1	4.7	6.5	11.2	7.7	8.4	5.2	10.7	7.9
2. A little	27.2	26.7	27.7	30.5	19.2	24.7	35.0	27.1	18.8	24.8	31.1	29.5	25.9	23.8	27.2	18.8
3. Some	38.0	38.2	38.4	38.9	36.6	39.1	32.3	41.8	38.8	40.0	35.6	35.8	40.2	40.7	39.0	34.8
4. A lot	26.6	26.3	26.3	20.8	41.2	27.9	18.5	26.1	37.7	28.7	22.0	27.0	25.5	30.3	23.1	38.5
Item 8300 Subject N03 N	3242	1524	1613	2432	401	761	891	992	598	1903	1134	1241	708	441	744	45
A17: Generally, how do you feel about the experiences you have had with people of other races?																
5. Very good	28.6	23.7	34.0	26.6	32.5	30.9	25.4	25.7	35.4	32.7	22.2	32.2	29.4	27.6	23.4	24.8
4. Mostly good	40.7	40.6	40.7	40.5	43.0	39.0	41.8	40.2	42.3	39.4	43.2	40.6	40.1	44.7	39.5	42.3
3. Mixed	27.7	31.2	23.7	29.4	23.6	27.2	28.3	31.9	20.4	25.8	30.6	25.2	27.7	25.9	32.5	23.7
2. Mostly bad	2.1	3.2	1.2	2.5	0.7	2.0	3.0	1.8	1.5	1.5	3.0	1.5	2.2	1.4	3.0	3.5
1. Very bad	0.9	1.3	0.4	1.0	0.3	1.0	1.5	0.5	0.5	0.6	1.1	0.4	0.7	0.4	1.6	5.6
Item 8310 Subject N03 N	3236	1521	1610	2425	401	760	888	992	595	1900	1130	1240	705	441	743	45
A18: The next questions are about some of your own plans. Are you married or engaged?																
1. Married–SKIP TO Q.A20	0.7	0.3	1.0	0.7	0.1	0.8	0.7	0.6	0.7	0.3	0.8	0.8	0.2	0.6	0.9	3.6
2. Engaged	8.4	5.2	11.2	7.7	11.9	5.5	8.6	11.8	5.9	5.2	12.9	7.0	9.1	9.3	9.3	8.0
3. Neither	90.9	94.5	87.9	91.5	88.0	93.7	90.7	87.6	93.4	94.5	86.3	92.2	90.7	90.1	89.8	88.3
Item 8320 Subject D01,R01 N	3051	1425	1531	2323	340	703	838	931	578	1819	1049	1181	665	407	701	43
A19: If it were just up to you, what would be the ideal time for you to get married?																
1. Within the next year or so	6.1	2.9	9.0	6.1	6.8	3.6	7.4	8.5	3.4	2.7	11.4	5.4	6.6	6.6	6.3	8.2
2. Two or three years from now	17.6	14.8	20.2	18.2	17.4	13.6	20.1	19.6	15.8	10.6	29.1	17.8	17.4	16.1	18.5	18.4
3. Four or five years from now	34.0	31.6	36.9	35.5	26.1	34.7	33.8	35.0	31.5	36.0	31.8	37.3	31.3	33.2	32.7	28.3
4. Over five years from now	37.5	44.9	30.6	36.3	40.9	43.3	33.7	32.3	44.5	46.5	21.9	35.5	40.3	39.8	36.6	45.1
5. I don't want to marry	4.8	5.8	3.3	3.9	8.8	4.8	5.0	4.7	4.8	4.2	5.8	4.0	4.3	4.3	5.9	-
Item 8330 Subject D01 N★	3102	1466	1540	2352	357	722	845	954	581	1839	1081	1199	676	413	718	41
A20: Have you thought at all about whether you'd like to have children or how many you'd like to have?																
3. I've thought about it a lot	38.9	25.4	52.4	38.5	44.5	33.6	40.2	43.6	35.9	38.1	40.2	38.3	39.3	45.5	36.4	35.9
2. I've thought about it a little	51.5	59.2	43.7	52.6	45.6	55.0	50.9	47.5	54.2	54.1	47.9	52.1	51.0	46.8	53.4	49.8
1. I haven't thought about it at all	9.6	15.3	4.0	8.9	9.8	11.4	8.8	8.9	9.9	7.8	11.9	9.7	9.7	7.7	10.2	14.3
Item 8340 Subject D02 N	3176	1496	1577	2389	380	753	882	955	586	1873	1102	1209	698	431	737	43
A21: All things considered, if you could have exactly the number of children you want, what number would you choose to have?																
1. None	2.8	2.8	2.6	3.0	2.2	2.9	3.3	2.0	3.2	2.7	2.9	2.7	1.7	2.7	3.8	1.1
2. One	6.1	5.2	6.9	5.8	9.9	4.7	7.5	6.8	4.6	5.7	7.2	6.6	5.6	5.0	6.7	1.9
3. Two	48.7	47.8	49.3	48.8	51.5	48.0	46.4	52.4	46.8	48.2	49.1	49.6	51.5	44.3	47.6	50.7
4. Three	19.4	21.0	18.3	20.1	16.4	21.3	20.9	18.8	15.9	20.2	18.2	18.4	18.9	26.0	17.9	21.1
5. Four	11.0	9.2	12.6	10.7	10.6	10.1	11.3	9.3	14.3	11.4	10.7	11.7	11.6	9.9	10.0	7.0
6. Five	1.8	1.5	2.0	1.5	1.9	2.0	1.8	1.4	1.9	1.7	1.7	1.8	1.5	1.7	2.1	-
7. Six or more	2.2	2.8	1.8	2.2	1.8	1.7	2.6	1.9	2.9	2.6	1.4	2.1	1.3	2.3	3.0	3.8
8. Don't know	8.1	9.7	6.4	7.9	5.6	9.3	6.2	7.4	10.5	7.5	8.8	7.1	7.8	8.0	9.0	14.4
Item 8350 Subject D02 N	3236	1524	1608	2426	399	749	890	994	603	1902	1129	1240	709	442	737	46

★=excludes respondents for whom question was inappropriate.

QUESTIONNAIRE FORM 3 1985	TOTAL	SEX		RACE		REGION				4YR COLLEGE PLANS		ILLICIT DRUG USE: LIFETIME				
		M	F	White	Black	NE	NC	S	W	Yes	No	None	Marijuana Only	Few Pills	More Pills	Any Heroin
N (Weighted No. of Cases):	3294	1549	1638	2464	407	770	907	1006	611	1932	1148	1258	717	446	761	48
% of Weighted Total:	100.0	47.0	49.7	74.8	12.4	23.4	27.5	30.5	18.5	58.7	34.9	38.2	21.8	13.5	23.1	1.4

A22: If the "population explosion" were NOT a problem, would you choose to have a larger number of children?

	TOTAL	M	F	White	Black	NE	NC	S	W	Yes	No	None	Marijuana Only	Few Pills	More Pills	Any Heroin
4. Yes, I'm sure I would want more	5.0	4.8	5.2	4.9	3.6	5.3	5.7	3.5	5.7	4.9	5.0	4.8	4.5	4.7	5.7	6.3
3. I probably would want more	10.6	9.8	11.1	9.8	12.0	10.9	10.5	10.4	10.8	10.1	11.0	10.7	10.9	9.9	10.6	2.2
2. I probably would not want more	36.3	35.0	37.0	37.6	30.9	33.7	36.1	37.0	38.8	37.8	34.6	37.5	37.6	36.8	33.2	36.5
1. I'm sure I would not want more	31.9	31.2	33.0	31.8	39.6	31.1	32.7	33.6	28.9	31.6	31.4	31.7	32.0	30.1	33.6	33.3
8. Don't know, no idea	16.2	19.1	13.6	16.0	13.9	19.0	15.0	15.4	15.8	15.5	18.0	15.4	15.1	18.5	17.0	21.8
Item 8360 Subject D02,E01 N	3258	1532	1621	2440	403	761	896	998	603	1915	1139	1247	714	443	746	48

A23: If it were just up to you, how soon after getting married would you want to have your first child?

	TOTAL	M	F	White	Black	NE	NC	S	W	Yes	No	None	Marijuana Only	Few Pills	More Pills	Any Heroin
1. I don't want to have children (or get married)	3.6	4.0	3.0	3.8	3.5	4.2	4.2	2.9	3.0	3.3	4.0	3.6	2.6	2.9	4.5	1.1
2. I wouldn't wait at all	5.8	9.4	2.3	4.9	9.6	5.4	5.6	5.8	6.8	5.2	6.4	4.2	6.2	5.9	7.3	10.0
3. I would wait one year	27.0	29.3	24.5	25.4	35.3	30.3	25.2	25.9	27.4	25.7	29.8	27.9	29.2	26.2	23.0	26.5
4. I would wait two years	29.5	25.4	33.5	30.3	22.6	26.3	27.8	31.5	32.4	31.0	26.8	30.3	28.8	31.4	28.4	25.8
5. I would wait three years	15.0	12.2	18.0	15.9	12.9	13.7	15.8	16.9	12.4	16.0	13.5	15.7	14.0	15.8	15.1	11.9
6. I would wait four or five years	7.6	5.4	9.9	7.9	5.6	7.7	7.5	7.9	7.1	7.6	7.4	6.8	7.8	7.5	8.9	14.7
7. I would wait more than five years	2.2	1.8	2.7	2.5	2.2	1.4	3.3	2.2	1.7	2.4	2.1	2.7	2.5	1.6	1.7	3.4
8. Don't know, or already have a child	9.4	12.5	6.1	9.4	8.4	11.0	10.6	7.0	9.3	8.7	10.0	8.8	8.9	8.7	11.2	6.8
Item 8370 Subject D02 N	3228	1523	1606	2424	397	749	887	992	600	1901	1130	1236	708	443	737	46

A24: Now we'd like you to make some ratings of how good or bad a job you feel each of the following organizations is doing for the country as a whole. For each one, mark the circle that best describes how you feel.

How good or bad a job is being done for the country as a whole by...

A24A: Large corporations?

	TOTAL	M	F	White	Black	NE	NC	S	W	Yes	No	None	Marijuana Only	Few Pills	More Pills	Any Heroin
1. Very poor	1.9	2.9	0.9	1.8	1.7	2.5	2.0	1.7	1.4	1.9	1.9	2.5	1.1	2.6	1.3	4.9
2. Poor	6.3	8.2	4.5	6.7	5.4	6.4	6.9	4.6	8.2	6.8	5.8	6.2	5.7	6.0	7.3	10.9
3. Fair	29.3	28.7	30.3	29.0	35.8	29.1	31.2	31.1	24.0	28.2	31.6	30.4	26.4	28.4	30.6	32.2
4. Good	34.6	34.3	34.7	35.9	27.1	32.8	32.2	36.8	36.8	35.6	33.1	34.9	40.2	31.9	30.9	34.6
5. Very good	10.3	12.1	8.2	10.1	12.4	10.0	11.3	10.6	8.5	10.3	9.9	10.2	10.3	10.0	10.0	6.6
8. No opinion	17.6	13.8	21.4	16.4	17.6	19.3	16.5	15.2	21.1	17.3	17.7	15.8	16.3	21.1	20.0	10.8
Item 8380 Subject K02 N	3238	1526	1612	2430	400	754	893	994	596	1905	1135	1243	711	440	741	48

A24B: Major labor unions?

	TOTAL	M	F	White	Black	NE	NC	S	W	Yes	No	None	Marijuana Only	Few Pills	More Pills	Any Heroin
1. Very poor	3.8	6.3	1.2	4.4	1.2	4.1	4.1	3.9	2.6	4.6	2.2	4.4	4.0	2.2	3.3	10.1
2. Poor	11.0	14.5	7.7	11.9	7.7	9.0	12.7	11.7	9.8	12.0	9.7	12.1	9.8	9.0	11.3	20.7
3. Fair	32.3	32.0	32.7	31.8	36.7	30.9	33.2	33.2	31.2	32.2	33.1	31.7	33.4	33.3	30.8	36.0
4. Good	25.6	24.6	26.4	26.0	24.2	26.2	26.3	23.8	26.8	25.1	26.1	24.3	27.9	28.1	24.7	16.0
5. Very good	7.0	7.6	6.5	6.5	10.1	10.2	5.4	6.5	6.3	6.5	7.9	7.1	6.7	7.3	6.9	8.1
8. No opinion	20.3	15.0	25.5	19.5	20.2	19.6	18.3	20.8	23.2	19.7	20.9	20.2	18.2	20.1	22.9	9.1
Item 8390 Subject K02 N	3236	1524	1610	2429	399	754	892	993	596	1905	1133	1241	710	440	740	48

A24C: The nation's colleges and universities?

	TOTAL	M	F	White	Black	NE	NC	S	W	Yes	No	None	Marijuana Only	Few Pills	More Pills	Any Heroin
1. Very poor	0.6	0.8	0.4	0.5	0.5	0.7	0.9	0.6	0.1	0.6	0.8	0.9	0.2	0.6	0.8	-
2. Poor	2.6	2.7	2.5	2.1	4.7	3.2	2.3	2.1	2.9	2.2	3.3	2.1	2.5	2.3	3.9	-
3. Fair	15.1	16.3	14.0	13.5	21.7	14.8	17.0	14.4	14.1	11.8	20.6	14.5	15.2	13.7	16.5	22.2
4. Good	43.7	43.1	44.2	45.7	36.8	44.7	43.7	44.8	40.4	44.9	42.3	45.6	40.5	45.6	42.4	39.4
5. Very good	32.4	30.9	34.2	33.2	30.1	29.2	32.4	33.5	34.6	36.3	26.1	32.2	35.9	30.6	30.6	36.3
8. No opinion	5.6	6.2	4.7	4.9	6.1	7.3	3.7	4.6	7.9	4.1	7.0	4.9	5.6	7.1	5.8	2.1
Item 8400 Subject B10,K02 N	3241	1527	1611	2432	398	755	894	993	599	1909	1132	1243	712	439	742	48

QUESTIONNAIRE FORM 3 1985	TOTAL	SEX		RACE		REGION				4YR COLLEGE PLANS		ILLICIT DRUG USE: LIFETIME				
		M	F	White	Black	NE	NC	S	W	Yes	No	None	Mari- juana Only	Few Pills	More Pills	Any Her- oin
N (Weighted No. of Cases):	3294	1549	1638	2464	407	770	907	1006	611	1932	1148	1258	717	446	761	48
% of Weighted Total:	100.0	47.0	49.7	74.8	12.4	23.4	27.5	30.5	18.5	58.7	34.9	38.2	21.8	13.5	23.1	1.4

A24D: The nation's public schools?

1. Very poor	4.3	4.6	4.0	4.6	3.2	3.7	5.6	3.5	4.7	4.3	4.3	4.0	3.6	5.5	4.6	12.7
2. Poor	13.8	14.2	13.7	13.9	12.8	17.0	13.6	11.8	13.4	15.6	11.5	11.9	13.1	12.6	18.9	14.2
3. Fair	34.9	33.4	36.5	35.4	34.8	29.9	36.1	38.6	33.5	34.3	35.6	34.2	35.1	37.7	35.5	32.3
4. Good	32.4	33.2	31.7	33.3	29.7	32.7	33.1	31.0	33.6	32.8	32.1	35.8	32.6	28.1	28.7	29.8
5. Very good	10.9	10.0	11.5	10.1	14.0	11.3	9.3	11.6	11.7	10.0	12.5	11.5	11.0	11.3	9.0	8.0
8. No opinion	3.6	4.5	2.5	2.7	5.6	5.5	2.4	3.6	3.2	2.9	4.1	2.6	4.7	4.8	3.3	3.0
Item 8410 Subject B10,K02 N	3229	1519	1610	2426	397	751	893	987	598	1907	1126	1239	711	438	739	44

A24E: Churches and religious organizations?

1. Very poor	2.6	4.0	1.2	2.8	1.8	3.3	2.9	1.9	2.2	2.3	2.9	2.5	2.0	2.0	2.8	13.1
2. Poor	5.2	5.9	4.5	5.6	2.7	6.1	5.5	4.8	4.4	5.7	4.7	4.9	4.6	4.3	6.6	8.3
3. Fair	24.7	24.2	25.1	24.6	23.4	27.4	23.6	24.8	22.7	24.0	25.7	23.3	23.1	24.6	27.8	36.5
4. Good	34.7	32.8	36.6	36.0	30.0	33.8	37.4	32.7	35.1	36.2	33.1	36.0	34.5	38.0	32.0	16.8
5. Very good	20.4	19.9	20.8	18.4	31.3	15.1	17.7	26.6	20.8	20.1	20.4	23.0	21.7	17.5	16.7	20.1
8. No opinion	12.5	13.2	11.8	12.5	10.7	14.3	12.9	9.2	14.8	11.6	13.3	10.3	14.2	13.7	14.2	5.2
Item 8420 Subject G,K02 N	3238	1523	1613	2427	401	751	896	993	598	1907	1132	1244	710	439	740	48

A24F: The national news media (TV, magazines, news services)?

1. Very poor	2.7	3.5	2.0	3.0	1.7	2.8	2.9	2.7	2.5	2.7	2.6	2.2	2.4	3.0	3.6	4.8
2. Poor	7.4	8.4	6.6	8.0	3.6	7.5	7.7	7.0	7.6	7.3	7.1	8.5	5.6	6.7	7.4	13.2
3. Fair	25.2	25.1	25.1	25.8	22.7	22.9	28.5	25.0	23.5	26.0	24.2	27.1	25.3	26.5	21.5	23.1
4. Good	36.1	33.4	39.0	37.1	33.0	37.4	37.0	34.3	36.4	37.1	36.1	35.9	34.2	35.0	39.3	41.0
5. Very good	22.7	24.0	21.5	21.2	30.8	22.9	18.0	25.7	24.6	22.8	22.7	20.6	26.1	22.7	22.8	15.1
8. No opinion	5.8	5.6	5.9	4.8	8.2	6.4	6.0	5.4	5.4	4.1	7.4	5.7	6.4	6.1	5.4	2.9
Item 8430 Subject K02 N	3235	1525	1608	2427	401	751	895	993	596	1908	1128	1239	712	439	741	47

A24G: The President and his administration?

1. Very poor	7.9	8.7	6.7	5.8	19.0	9.7	8.5	6.4	7.0	7.8	7.8	6.5	7.4	8.6	9.4	17.5
2. Poor	10.1	9.8	10.4	8.7	17.5	10.7	11.2	8.6	10.2	10.4	9.6	10.8	10.5	9.8	8.6	3.4
3. Fair	27.0	25.4	28.7	26.2	30.4	27.8	27.5	25.5	27.3	26.0	28.6	25.7	27.0	24.9	29.8	34.9
4. Good	29.3	29.4	29.2	32.3	13.1	27.5	27.9	30.4	31.7	32.0	25.9	31.0	30.4	30.3	26.3	15.8
5. Very good	16.6	20.2	13.3	19.6	4.2	15.3	16.7	18.4	15.2	16.9	16.3	18.0	15.7	13.7	16.8	22.2
8. No opinion	9.2	6.4	11.8	7.5	15.8	9.0	8.1	10.7	8.6	6.9	11.9	7.9	9.0	12.6	9.1	6.1
Item 8440 Subject H04,K02 N	3238	1523	1614	2430	398	754	896	991	598	1908	1132	1243	712	439	741	48

A24H: Congress–that is, the U.S. Senate and House of Representatives?

1. Very poor	4.4	5.6	3.0	3.5	7.5	4.3	5.4	4.6	3.0	3.7	5.7	3.7	2.8	5.1	6.3	11.2
2. Poor	9.0	11.6	6.4	8.6	11.7	10.2	8.5	8.2	9.3	9.3	8.5	9.0	9.1	9.3	8.7	3.9
3. Fair	34.0	36.2	32.0	34.3	37.0	31.4	36.1	34.1	33.6	33.3	34.7	35.0	36.5	30.8	32.1	32.7
4. Good	29.7	28.5	30.9	32.3	18.2	26.6	28.8	31.9	31.2	33.6	23.9	31.4	30.4	28.0	27.9	27.7
5. Very good	5.4	5.9	5.0	5.1	6.0	6.0	4.2	5.5	6.5	5.6	5.3	5.3	5.2	4.2	5.4	10.5
8. No opinion	17.5	12.1	22.8	16.1	19.6	21.5	17.0	15.7	16.4	14.4	22.0	15.6	16.0	22.6	19.5	14.1
Item 8450 Subject H04,K02 N	3234	1523	1610	2426	400	752	895	992	596	1906	1130	1241	712	438	739	48

A24I: The U.S. Supreme Court?

1. Very poor	2.6	3.4	1.7	2.4	3.1	2.5	3.0	2.3	2.9	2.2	3.4	2.1	1.8	3.7	3.7	4.0
2. Poor	5.8	7.1	4.7	5.6	7.4	4.8	5.6	6.8	5.6	5.1	6.6	5.3	6.5	6.3	5.7	4.2
3. Fair	29.2	31.0	27.4	29.2	31.1	29.5	31.2	28.1	27.6	28.4	30.5	29.2	28.4	25.0	32.0	33.1
4. Good	33.5	33.3	33.8	35.2	28.3	31.7	33.8	34.1	34.5	36.0	29.4	36.5	32.7	35.2	28.6	33.5
5. Very good	8.6	10.6	6.8	8.6	9.5	8.4	7.5	9.2	9.3	9.5	7.0	7.6	10.3	7.3	8.9	8.0
8. No opinion	20.3	14.7	25.7	19.1	20.6	23.1	18.9	19.4	20.1	18.7	23.0	19.3	20.4	22.4	21.2	18.2
Item 8460 Subject H04,K02 N	3223	1518	1604	2418	396	746	892	989	596	1904	1124	1236	709	437	735	48

A24J: All the courts and the justice system in general?

1. Very poor	5.6	7.2	4.0	5.9	3.9	5.7	6.5	4.7	5.4	5.5	5.9	5.3	4.0	7.3	7.0	5.0
2. Poor	14.1	15.5	12.8	14.3	12.0	15.4	11.4	15.4	14.6	14.2	14.3	13.8	15.0	16.1	13.5	11.3
3. Fair	37.3	36.7	38.5	38.0	37.9	34.5	39.3	38.8	35.6	38.8	35.7	39.7	34.9	31.7	39.8	51.5
4. Good	24.0	25.4	22.4	24.8	21.2	25.0	24.8	22.1	24.4	24.7	22.4	24.8	25.9	24.1	20.7	16.0
5. Very good	4.7	4.6	4.8	4.0	7.7	4.2	3.5	5.1	6.8	4.2	5.3	3.8	5.5	3.6	5.7	5.9
8. No opinion	14.2	10.7	17.5	13.0	17.3	15.2	14.5	13.9	13.2	12.5	16.3	12.7	14.6	17.3	14.9	10.3
Item 8470 Subject H04,K02 N	3232	1522	1608	2425	398	752	895	989	596	1904	1131	1240	710	439	738	48

QUESTIONNAIRE FORM 3 1985	TOTAL	SEX		RACE		REGION				4YR COLLEGE PLANS		ILLICIT DRUG USE: LIFETIME				
		M	F	White	Black	NE	NC	S	W	Yes	No	None	Mari-juana Only	Few Pills	More Pills	Any Her-oin
N (Weighted No. of Cases):	3294	1549	1638	2464	407	770	907	1006	611	1932	1148	1258	717	446	761	48
% of Weighted Total:	100.0	47.0	49.7	74.8	12.4	23.4	27.5	30.5	18.5	58.7	34.9	38.2	21.8	13.5	23.1	1.4

A24K: The police and other law enforcement agencies?

1. Very poor	5.6	6.9	4.3	4.9	6.3	6.3	6.0	5.1	5.1	5.2	6.1	5.0	4.9	6.4	6.6	12.8
2. Poor	12.7	12.1	13.2	12.7	14.2	14.0	13.3	11.3	12.1	11.8	14.6	10.9	13.2	13.7	14.6	16.1
3. Fair	38.9	37.6	40.6	39.2	40.7	40.3	38.0	41.7	34.1	40.2	37.1	38.0	36.3	38.9	43.4	34.9
4. Good	30.1	30.0	30.5	32.4	19.5	26.1	31.4	30.0	33.2	32.6	26.3	33.5	33.9	28.1	22.0	25.2
5. Very good	7.2	8.1	6.0	6.5	9.9	6.6	5.5	6.5	11.5	6.0	8.6	7.9	5.4	5.7	8.3	11.0
8. No opinion	5.5	5.3	5.5	4.3	9.5	6.7	5.7	5.4	4.0	4.2	7.2	4.7	6.3	7.1	5.1	-
Item 8480 Subject K02 N	3236	1524	1610	2427	399	751	894	993	598	1909	1129	1245	712	438	735	48

A24L: The U.S. military?

1. Very poor	2.3	3.4	1.1	2.7	0.4	3.2	2.3	1.4	2.8	2.7	1.9	2.0	1.5	2.2	3.3	8.0
2. Poor	3.1	3.7	2.7	3.5	1.4	3.3	3.4	1.6	4.9	4.1	1.8	3.1	3.2	3.2	3.0	4.0
3. Fair	22.0	22.7	21.9	22.3	22.4	23.5	24.5	18.0	23.1	23.3	21.0	22.5	21.2	20.7	22.6	27.5
4. Good	37.5	36.8	37.9	38.9	32.8	34.3	37.5	40.5	36.5	37.8	36.0	37.6	39.1	36.0	37.5	35.2
5. Very good	22.7	26.3	19.3	21.4	31.2	22.1	20.9	27.5	18.3	19.6	27.2	23.4	23.0	22.5	21.5	15.9
8. No opinion	12.3	7.1	17.2	11.2	11.8	13.6	11.3	11.0	14.5	12.5	12.1	11.4	12.0	15.4	12.0	9.5
Item 8490 Subject K02,L04 N	3235	1525	1609	2429	397	754	895	990	596	1904	1134	1244	710	439	738	48

A25: All things considered, do you think the armed services presently have too much or too little influence on the way this country is run?

1. Far too little	3.4	4.8	1.9	3.2	2.9	3.7	2.9	3.8	3.3	2.9	4.2	3.6	2.7	4.4	3.1	5.5
2. Too little	14.0	13.5	14.0	13.6	17.0	14.6	12.9	16.7	10.2	12.3	16.3	13.4	14.3	16.5	13.7	9.4
3. About right	61.5	60.4	63.1	62.5	60.2	59.0	60.4	62.4	64.6	61.0	63.0	63.7	61.8	57.4	60.1	57.6
4. Too much	16.4	15.6	17.0	16.1	15.9	17.6	18.0	14.1	16.4	18.0	13.3	14.9	17.5	16.0	17.7	19.2
5. Far too much	4.7	5.6	4.0	4.6	3.9	5.0	5.8	3.0	5.5	5.8	3.2	4.3	3.6	5.7	5.4	8.2
Item 8500 Subject K03,L04 N	3192	1513	1579	2395	393	746	880	983	583	1871	1127	1229	690	438	732	46

A26: Do you think the U.S. spends too much or too little on the armed services?

1. Far too little	3.1	5.0	1.2	3.3	2.5	3.7	3.1	3.5	1.8	2.7	3.9	3.1	2.7	4.0	3.1	7.2
2. Too little	15.1	17.2	13.1	15.1	17.1	13.9	14.3	18.7	11.8	14.7	16.1	15.6	15.8	14.1	14.8	4.9
3. About right	36.6	35.1	38.1	37.5	32.3	31.3	34.4	41.4	38.8	34.1	40.9	38.0	35.4	34.1	36.9	44.2
4. Too much	30.6	26.8	34.1	30.2	30.0	34.1	33.0	26.6	29.1	31.7	28.1	30.4	31.6	29.8	29.3	29.5
5. Far too much	14.6	15.9	13.4	13.9	18.0	17.1	15.2	9.9	18.5	16.8	11.1	13.0	14.5	18.0	15.8	14.1
Item 8510 Subject K03,L04 N	3212	1524	1588	2412	393	751	884	982	595	1887	1128	1238	694	438	742	46

A27: Next are some questions which ask about your experiences and attitudes concerning particular drugs. First we want your answers about some drugs that can be bought at a drugstore without a doctor's prescription—sometimes called over-the-counter or non-prescription drugs.

DURING THE LAST 12 MONTHS, on how many occasions have you...

A27A: . . . used non-prescription drugs which are supposed to relieve pain (such as aspirin, Anacin, Bufferin, or Excedrin)?

1. 0 occasions	8.5	11.8	5.3	5.7	20.4	6.8	8.3	8.7	10.8	7.2	9.3	10.3	7.8	6.8	6.0	14.5
2. 1-2	16.7	20.0	13.7	14.7	25.8	18.6	17.1	15.3	15.9	15.6	17.9	20.8	17.5	15.8	9.4	16.3
3. 3-5	17.7	18.9	16.5	17.0	21.0	17.1	18.3	18.2	16.8	17.1	19.1	21.2	16.9	15.3	14.7	19.0
4. 6-9	14.1	15.5	13.1	14.3	12.7	12.6	12.7	15.3	16.2	15.3	12.5	13.3	12.7	14.6	14.6	5.9
5. 10-19	17.5	15.3	19.3	19.0	10.7	15.9	16.9	19.0	17.8	17.9	17.7	16.6	16.5	19.2	19.3	14.2
6. 20-39	10.7	8.1	13.4	12.5	4.0	11.5	10.4	10.0	11.5	11.6	9.8	8.2	11.4	12.7	13.7	8.4
7. 40 or more	14.7	10.5	18.7	16.8	5.4	17.5	16.2	13.4	10.9	15.4	13.8	9.7	13.2	17.5	22.3	21.6
Item 8520 Subject A01b N	3266	1541	1629	2452	403	761	902	998	604	1921	1139	1257	716	446	755	46

QUESTIONNAIRE FORM 3 1985	TOTAL	SEX		RACE		REGION				4YR COLLEGE PLANS		ILLICIT DRUG USE: LIFETIME				
		M	F	White	Black	NE	NC	S	W	Yes	No	None	Mari-juana Only	Few Pills	More Pills	Any Her-oin
N (Weighted No. of Cases):	3294	1549	1638	2464	407	770	907	1006	611	1932	1148	1258	717	446	761	48
% of Weighted Total:	100.0	47.0	49.7	74.8	12.4	23.4	27.5	30.5	18.5	58.7	34.9	38.2	21.8	13.5	23.1	1.4

A27B: ... used non-prescription drugs that are supposed to help people get to sleep (such as Sleep-Eze, Sominex, or Nytol)?

	TOTAL	M	F	White	Black	NE	NC	S	W	Yes	No	None	Mari-juana Only	Few Pills	More Pills	Any Her-oin
1. 0 occasions	88.0	88.5	87.9	87.8	88.7	89.7	86.8	87.4	88.7	88.3	87.3	93.6	93.4	82.5	79.5	56.6
2. 1-2	6.6	6.7	6.5	6.7	8.0	5.8	7.1	7.0	6.4	6.7	6.6	4.3	4.3	11.0	9.4	19.4
3. 3-5	2.5	2.3	2.7	2.7	1.0	2.4	3.5	1.9	2.2	2.3	3.1	0.7	1.0	2.5	6.0	8.6
4. 6-9	1.2	1.0	1.2	1.1	0.4	0.7	0.9	1.6	1.5	1.1	1.3	0.6	0.5	1.9	2.3	4.6
5. 10-19	0.9	0.8	1.0	0.9	1.0	0.7	1.1	1.0	0.8	0.9	1.0	0.5	0.7	0.8	1.4	6.1
6. 20-39	0.3	0.2	0.3	0.3	0.3	0.3	0.1	0.5	*	0.2	0.5	-	0.1	0.9	0.3	-
7. 40 or more	0.5	0.6	0.5	0.5	0.5	0.5	0.6	0.6	0.4	0.6	0.3	0.3	-	0.5	1.1	4.7
Item 8530 Subject A01b N	3257	1536	1624	2447	399	758	900	993	605	1917	1136	1255	714	446	750	46

A27C: ... used non-prescription drugs that are supposed to help people stay awake (such as No-Doz, Wake, or Vivarin)?

	TOTAL	M	F	White	Black	NE	NC	S	W	Yes	No	None	Mari-juana Only	Few Pills	More Pills	Any Her-oin
1. 0 occasions	80.6	80.9	81.1	79.3	89.7	82.9	80.5	81.1	77.2	80.6	80.4	92.2	86.2	76.3	61.6	43.7
2. 1-2	7.7	7.2	7.9	8.2	6.0	5.9	8.7	7.4	8.8	8.2	6.8	4.1	6.1	11.2	12.5	15.4
3. 3-5	4.0	4.5	3.2	4.1	1.7	4.1	3.2	4.5	4.2	3.6	4.8	1.9	3.2	4.0	7.8	6.9
4. 6-9	2.7	3.0	2.3	3.0	0.4	2.3	2.6	2.3	4.2	2.8	2.5	0.8	2.1	3.1	6.1	6.3
5. 10-19	2.1	1.6	2.5	2.3	0.9	2.4	2.4	1.8	1.8	1.8	2.6	0.5	1.3	0.8	5.3	10.7
6. 20-39	1.4	1.2	1.6	1.5	0.8	1.2	1.0	1.8	1.8	1.6	1.3	0.3	0.8	3.0	3.0	2.4
7. 40 or more	1.5	1.5	1.3	1.5	0.6	1.3	1.7	1.1	2.0	1.4	1.6	0.3	0.4	1.6	3.7	14.6
Item 8540 Subject A01b N	3256	1537	1622	2446	398	760	899	993	604	1914	1137	1253	712	446	754	46

A27D: ... used non-prescription drugs that are supposed to calm people down–keep them from being nervous or in a bad mood (such as Cope, Compoz, Devarex, or Miles Nervine)?

	TOTAL	M	F	White	Black	NE	NC	S	W	Yes	No	None	Mari-juana Only	Few Pills	More Pills	Any Her-oin
1. 0 occasions	94.4	94.7	94.7	95.1	93.9	96.1	93.3	93.3	95.6	95.8	92.3	98.1	98.0	91.7	89.1	64.3
2. 1-2	2.7	2.3	2.9	2.4	3.0	1.8	3.6	2.7	2.4	1.6	4.0	0.9	1.2	4.3	4.6	14.3
3. 3-5	0.6	0.9	0.4	0.6	0.6	0.1	0.5	1.1	0.6	0.4	1.1	0.1	0.2	1.3	1.1	6.1
4. 6-9	0.8	0.7	0.5	0.7	0.5	0.6	1.1	0.7	0.6	0.5	1.2	0.2	0.2	1.1	1.5	4.5
5. 10-19	0.6	0.4	0.7	0.5	0.7	0.7	0.5	0.9	0.3	0.7	0.4	0.1	0.2	0.2	2.1	2.1
6. 20-39	0.3	0.2	0.3	0.2	0.9	0.3	0.3	0.4	0.2	0.5	0.1	0.3	-	0.2	0.3	4.2
7. 40 or more	0.7	0.8	0.5	0.6	0.3	0.4	0.8	1.0	0.4	0.5	0.9	0.3	0.2	1.2	1.2	4.6
Item 8550 Subject A01b N	3255	1535	1623	2447	396	759	900	993	603	1913	1137	1254	710	446	754	46

A28: Individuals differ in whether or not they disapprove of people doing certain things. Do YOU disapprove of people (who are 18 or older) doing each of the following?

A28A: Smoking one or more packs of cigarettes per day

	TOTAL	M	F	White	Black	NE	NC	S	W	Yes	No	None	Mari-juana Only	Few Pills	More Pills	Any Her-oin
1. Don't disapprove	27.7	28.4	26.5	29.6	18.6	30.8	31.7	25.7	21.1	21.1	37.6	14.9	26.4	30.9	46.4	53.1
2. Disapprove	34.8	32.7	37.0	34.6	33.8	34.2	34.1	35.2	36.1	37.8	30.9	39.5	36.3	31.4	28.5	33.3
3. Strongly disapprove	37.5	38.9	36.5	35.8	47.6	35.0	34.2	39.2	42.8	41.1	31.5	45.6	37.3	37.7	25.2	13.7
Item 8560 Subject A11a N	3264	1540	1627	2449	403	762	902	997	603	1921	1138	1256	716	446	754	45

A28B: Trying marijuana (pot, grass) once or twice

	TOTAL	M	F	White	Black	NE	NC	S	W	Yes	No	None	Mari-juana Only	Few Pills	More Pills	Any Her-oin
1. Don't disapprove	48.6	48.9	48.0	51.6	37.6	59.0	50.3	38.5	49.6	47.1	50.8	16.5	64.2	59.3	79.3	80.1
2. Disapprove	24.3	24.1	24.5	24.0	22.6	22.9	24.7	23.8	26.0	26.0	21.6	30.5	23.5	25.2	14.4	12.9
3. Strongly disapprove	27.1	27.0	27.5	24.4	39.8	18.0	25.0	37.7	24.4	26.9	27.6	53.0	12.3	15.5	6.3	7.0
Item 8570 Subject A11a N	3263	1541	1626	2451	401	763	901	996	603	1919	1139	1257	714	446	755	46

A28C: Smoking marijuana occasionally

	TOTAL	M	F	White	Black	NE	NC	S	W	Yes	No	None	Mari-juana Only	Few Pills	More Pills	Any Her-oin
1. Don't disapprove	34.2	35.4	32.9	36.3	26.9	43.2	35.5	26.2	34.1	31.9	37.4	7.3	42.5	40.5	65.6	72.1
2. Disapprove	26.7	27.4	26.2	26.0	27.7	29.2	24.6	25.1	29.2	27.6	25.5	24.1	33.6	29.1	23.1	16.1
3. Strongly disapprove	39.1	37.2	40.8	37.7	45.4	27.6	39.9	48.7	36.7	40.5	37.2	68.5	23.9	30.4	11.3	11.8
Item 8580 Subject A11a N	3260	1537	1627	2450	399	761	901	994	603	1920	1135	1253	716	446	753	46

*=less than .05 per cent.

QUESTIONNAIRE FORM 3 1985	TOTAL	SEX		RACE		REGION				4YR COLLEGE PLANS		ILLICIT DRUG USE: LIFETIME				
		M	F	White	Black	NE	NC	S	W	Yes	No	None	Mari-juana Only	Few Pills	More Pills	Any Her-oin
N (Weighted No. of Cases):	3294	1549	1638	2464	407	770	907	1006	611	1932	1148	1258	717	446	761	48
% of Weighted Total:	100.0	47.0	49.7	74.8	12.4	23.4	27.5	30.5	18.5	58.7	34.9	38.2	21.8	13.5	23.1	1.4
A28D: Smoking marijuana regularly																
1. Don't disapprove	14.5	18.5	10.3	14.7	13.0	16.8	16.1	11.5	14.2	10.6	19.9	2.8	12.5	12.8	34.0	54.5
2. Disapprove	24.4	24.2	24.6	24.3	24.8	31.2	22.1	21.1	24.6	24.9	23.4	12.1	33.0	31.1	32.9	20.4
3. Strongly disapprove	61.1	57.2	65.0	61.0	62.3	52.0	61.8	67.4	61.2	64.6	56.7	85.1	54.5	56.1	33.1	25.0
Item 8590 Subject A11a N	3254	1536	1624	2447	402	757	901	995	602	1918	1132	1254	715	446	749	46
A28E: Trying LSD once or twice																
1. Don't disapprove	10.5	12.5	8.3	11.4	6.2	13.6	12.1	7.5	9.1	9.8	11.4	3.2	8.0	10.8	23.0	47.7
2. Disapprove	17.5	17.8	17.5	18.2	13.6	21.2	17.6	16.2	14.9	16.8	19.0	13.3	16.7	19.5	23.2	24.4
3. Strongly disapprove	72.0	69.7	74.2	70.4	80.1	65.2	70.3	76.3	76.1	73.4	69.6	83.5	75.4	69.7	53.8	27.9
Item 8600 Subject A11a N	3259	1537	1628	2451	401	762	901	992	604	1919	1135	1257	716	445	753	44
A28F: Taking LSD regularly																
1. Don't disapprove	3.0	4.4	1.7	2.6	4.7	3.5	3.2	2.8	2.6	2.2	4.1	1.5	3.3	3.3	4.6	6.9
2. Disapprove	9.7	11.7	7.5	9.4	9.9	12.7	8.6	9.6	8.0	7.9	12.2	5.8	7.4	9.7	16.0	44.7
3. Strongly disapprove	87.2	84.0	90.7	88.0	85.3	83.9	88.2	87.6	89.4	89.9	83.8	92.7	89.3	87.0	79.4	48.4
Item 8610 Subject A11a N	3263	1541	1627	2452	401	762	902	996	603	1921	1138	1256	716	446	754	46
A28G: Trying heroin (smack, horse) once or twice																
1. Don't disapprove	6.0	7.4	4.6	6.0	7.1	7.8	6.9	4.7	4.8	5.3	7.1	2.5	6.6	6.5	8.8	43.9
2. Disapprove	13.7	13.3	14.2	14.2	11.4	15.8	12.6	14.1	12.1	13.7	13.9	12.0	11.3	14.0	17.4	24.0
3. Strongly disapprove	80.3	79.3	81.2	79.8	81.5	76.4	80.5	81.3	83.2	81.0	79.0	85.6	82.1	79.4	73.8	32.1
Item 8620 Subject A11a N	3261	1539	1627	2450	401	760	902	995	604	1919	1138	1257	715	446	753	46
A28H: Taking heroin occasionally																
1. Don't disapprove	3.2	4.4	1.9	2.8	5.1	3.2	3.3	3.1	3.0	2.7	3.7	1.6	3.9	4.3	3.5	17.2
2. Disapprove	9.5	10.3	8.5	9.0	10.5	12.7	7.9	9.9	7.2	8.0	11.8	7.3	7.8	10.2	12.6	34.1
3. Strongly disapprove	87.3	85.3	89.6	88.2	84.3	84.1	88.8	87.0	89.8	89.3	84.5	91.2	88.3	85.5	83.9	48.7
Item 8630 Subject A11a N	3259	1538	1625	2450	398	763	900	992	604	1919	1137	1255	716	445	752	46
A28I: Taking heroin regularly																
1. Don't disapprove	2.4	3.7	1.3	2.0	4.9	2.2	2.2	2.9	2.3	1.9	3.2	1.4	3.4	3.0	2.3	9.8
2. Disapprove	6.9	7.9	5.7	5.8	9.7	8.8	6.3	7.0	5.3	5.3	8.7	5.6	5.5	7.0	8.3	26.6
3. Strongly disapprove	90.6	88.4	93.0	92.1	85.5	88.9	91.5	90.1	92.4	92.8	88.1	93.0	91.1	90.0	89.4	63.6
Item 8640 Subject A11a N	3238	1526	1618	2434	399	757	892	986	602	1904	1129	1243	711	443	750	46
A28J: Trying a barbiturate (downer, goofball, red, yellow, etc.) once or twice																
1. Don't disapprove	15.1	16.2	14.0	16.7	9.0	19.2	18.2	10.8	12.3	13.7	17.5	3.7	11.5	16.9	34.8	43.5
2. Disapprove	21.7	22.1	21.2	23.2	15.2	23.7	18.2	23.3	21.9	21.9	21.3	17.1	20.9	22.7	28.4	37.2
3. Strongly disapprove	63.2	61.7	64.8	60.1	75.8	57.2	63.6	65.9	65.8	64.4	61.2	79.3	67.6	60.4	36.7	19.3
Item 8650 Subject A11a N	3265	1541	1628	2453	402	763	902	996	604	1921	1139	1257	717	446	755	46
A28K: Taking barbiturates regularly																
1. Don't disapprove	4.5	6.3	2.3	3.9	5.7	5.1	4.8	4.4	3.2	3.1	6.2	1.8	4.4	4.9	7.3	24.3
2. Disapprove	20.7	22.1	19.4	20.3	23.2	24.0	18.2	21.5	19.0	18.9	23.9	11.9	19.8	22.3	33.9	45.7
3. Strongly disapprove	74.8	71.7	78.3	75.9	71.1	70.8	77.0	74.1	77.8	78.0	69.8	86.3	75.8	72.9	58.9	30.0
Item 8660 Subject A11a N	3253	1535	1622	2447	401	757	902	994	601	1917	1133	1252	715	444	752	46
A28L: Trying an amphetamine (upper, pep pill, bennie, speed) once or twice																
1. Don't disapprove	25.1	25.3	25.1	27.8	14.4	30.3	28.3	19.2	23.7	23.5	27.9	6.6	17.5	31.7	57.4	59.3
2. Disapprove	25.3	24.1	26.4	26.5	18.4	27.2	24.7	25.2	24.0	25.2	25.5	20.8	31.7	28.5	25.0	24.4
3. Strongly disapprove	49.6	50.6	48.5	45.7	67.2	42.5	47.0	55.6	52.4	51.3	46.5	72.6	50.8	39.8	17.6	16.3
Item 8670 Subject A11a N	3261	1539	1627	2450	402	761	901	996	603	1920	1137	1257	716	445	754	46

QUESTIONNAIRE FORM 3 1985	TOTAL	SEX		RACE		REGION				4YR COLLEGE PLANS		ILLICIT DRUG USE: LIFETIME				
		M	F	White	Black	NE	NC	S	W	Yes	No	None	Marijuana Only	Few Pills	More Pills	Any Heroin
N (Weighted No. of Cases):	3294	1549	1638	2464	407	770	907	1006	611	1932	1148	1258	717	446	761	48
% of Weighted Total:	100.0	47.0	49.7	74.8	12.4	23.4	27.5	30.5	18.5	58.7	34.9	38.2	21.8	13.5	23.1	1.4
A28M: Taking amphetamines regularly																
1. Don't disapprove	6.7	8.6	4.8	6.9	6.3	7.3	7.9	6.0	5.4	5.1	9.3	2.1	4.7	6.7	14.7	31.1
2. Disapprove	21.5	22.1	20.7	21.6	18.4	25.4	20.5	20.8	19.2	19.2	24.5	10.6	20.8	24.3	37.7	32.9
3. Strongly disapprove	71.9	69.3	74.5	71.5	75.4	67.4	71.7	73.3	75.5	75.7	66.2	87.3	74.5	69.0	47.6	36.0
Item 8680 Subject A11a N	3246	1529	1623	2439	401	755	898	995	599	1915	1127	1248	716	443	749	46
A28N: Trying cocaine once or twice																
1. Don't disapprove	20.7	22.8	18.3	22.4	12.2	30.0	19.1	13.2	24.0	18.7	23.0	4.8	13.7	23.1	50.7	62.7
2. Disapprove	17.5	18.1	17.3	17.1	18.3	18.9	13.6	19.2	18.7	18.4	16.8	13.6	21.9	24.3	15.8	12.7
3. Strongly disapprove	61.7	59.2	64.4	60.5	69.5	51.1	67.2	67.5	57.3	62.9	60.2	81.6	64.4	52.7	33.5	24.6
Item 8690 Subject A11a N	3259	1539	1624	2449	401	759	902	995	603	1918	1136	1256	716	444	754	46
A28O: Taking cocaine regularly																
1. Don't disapprove	6.2	8.3	3.9	5.9	6.1	7.6	6.6	4.7	6.1	4.2	8.8	1.7	4.6	4.1	13.9	42.5
2. Disapprove	14.1	16.1	11.9	14.1	12.0	19.8	11.2	11.4	15.5	12.3	16.1	6.2	10.9	18.3	27.1	19.0
3. Strongly disapprove	79.8	75.6	84.2	80.0	81.9	72.6	82.2	83.9	78.4	83.4	75.0	92.2	84.5	77.6	59.0	38.5
Item 8700 Subject A11a N	3238	1531	1614	2442	393	753	900	989	596	1909	1129	1245	710	445	751	46
A28P: Trying one or two drinks of an alcoholic beverage (beer, wine, liquor)																
1. Don't disapprove	79.7	79.6	79.7	83.7	61.4	87.4	81.3	72.9	78.7	80.0	79.7	65.0	86.9	86.8	92.5	91.6
2. Disapprove	12.4	10.7	14.2	10.5	22.6	8.4	10.9	16.8	12.6	13.0	11.9	20.1	9.5	9.3	4.7	2.8
3. Strongly disapprove	7.9	9.6	6.1	5.7	16.0	4.1	7.8	10.3	8.7	7.0	8.4	14.9	3.7	3.8	2.8	5.6
Item 8710 Subject A11a N	3253	1535	1624	2443	402	759	896	997	601	1916	1135	1252	716	444	751	46
A28Q: Taking one or two drinks nearly every day																
1. Don't disapprove	29.1	36.6	21.4	31.6	17.4	32.8	31.2	26.7	25.1	26.2	34.3	17.8	31.8	30.4	42.0	65.4
2. Disapprove	40.0	38.0	42.4	40.8	37.4	41.2	38.8	41.2	38.5	41.9	37.3	40.4	41.7	44.3	36.4	20.7
3. Strongly disapprove	30.9	25.4	36.2	27.7	45.2	26.0	30.0	32.1	36.4	31.9	28.4	41.8	26.5	25.3	21.5	13.9
Item 8720 Subject A11a N	3242	1532	1617	2440	397	754	899	988	601	1916	1126	1246	711	444	751	46
A28R: Taking four or five drinks nearly every day																
1. Don't disapprove	8.0	12.3	3.4	8.4	5.9	8.2	9.1	7.8	6.5	5.7	11.8	3.6	9.6	7.9	12.9	20.6
2. Disapprove	27.0	32.4	21.8	28.2	20.9	28.7	28.2	27.3	22.5	24.4	31.1	20.9	28.9	28.5	32.9	36.8
3. Strongly disapprove	65.0	55.3	74.8	63.4	73.2	63.1	62.7	64.9	71.0	70.0	57.0	75.4	61.5	63.5	54.1	42.6
Item 8730 Subject A11a N	3256	1538	1624	2449	402	760	902	994	601	1922	1136	1254	716	445	752	46
A28S: Having five or more drinks once or twice each weekend																
1. Don't disapprove	39.6	47.5	31.6	43.8	17.4	45.1	45.9	34.0	32.5	35.0	47.4	19.9	44.8	42.7	64.0	62.8
2. Disapprove	25.6	23.7	27.8	26.0	25.5	27.2	23.6	25.8	26.5	27.4	22.2	28.4	28.0	27.6	18.6	12.8
3. Strongly disapprove	34.8	28.8	40.6	30.2	57.1	27.7	30.6	40.2	41.0	37.5	30.4	51.7	27.2	29.7	17.4	24.3
Item 8740 Subject A11a N	3259	1540	1624	2448	402	758	901	996	603	1920	1136	1254	716	445	753	46
A29: During the LAST 12 MONTHS, how often have you been around people who were taking each of the following to get high or for "kicks"?																
A29A: Marijuana (pot, grass) or hashish																
1. Not at all	26.5	24.9	28.1	25.8	25.7	20.5	27.2	33.2	22.2	26.6	25.1	52.0	10.8	16.4	6.2	8.2
2. Once or twice	22.6	22.1	23.5	22.8	23.8	20.3	20.7	24.7	24.8	24.9	21.0	25.9	28.2	25.5	11.0	13.3
3. Occasionally	26.7	27.0	25.5	26.8	27.9	29.4	27.4	23.5	27.4	27.6	25.6	16.4	36.3	35.5	29.4	24.4
4. Often	24.2	26.0	22.9	24.6	22.7	29.8	24.8	18.6	25.6	20.9	28.2	5.7	24.8	22.5	53.3	54.1
Item 20590 Subject A02b N	3252	1537	1624	2449	399	760	899	991	602	1918	1135	1252	716	445	754	46

QUESTIONNAIRE FORM 3 1985	TOTAL	SEX		RACE		REGION				4YR COLLEGE PLANS		ILLICIT DRUG USE: LIFETIME				
		M	F	White	Black	NE	NC	S	W	Yes	No	None	Mari- juana Only	Few Pills	More Pills	Any Her- oin
N (Weighted No. of Cases):	3294	1549	1638	2464	407	770	907	1006	611	1932	1148	1258	717	446	761	48
% of Weighted Total:	100.0	47.0	49.7	74.8	12.4	23.4	27.5	30.5	18.5	58.7	34.9	38.2	21.8	13.5	23.1	1.4
A29B: LSD																
1. Not at all	86.8	85.7	88.1	85.9	94.0	82.9	84.4	92.4	86.0	87.6	86.2	94.8	93.5	87.1	69.6	40.7
2. Once or twice	8.6	9.0	8.2	9.2	3.8	10.9	10.1	4.7	10.0	8.2	9.1	2.8	5.3	10.3	18.6	37.2
3. Occasionally	3.2	3.4	2.9	3.5	2.0	4.2	4.2	2.3	2.1	2.9	3.5	1.9	0.7	1.9	8.8	6.8
4. Often	1.3	1.9	0.8	1.4	0.1	1.9	1.3	0.6	1.9	1.2	1.2	0.5	0.5	0.7	3.1	15.3
Item 20600 Subject A02b N	*3216*	*1516*	*1615*	*2428*	*391*	*753*	*886*	*982*	*595*	*1902*	*1124*	*1245*	*708*	*439*	*741*	*45*
A29C: Other psychedelics (mescaline, peyote, PCP, etc.)																
1. Not at all	87.5	85.6	89.3	87.0	93.2	77.8	88.2	94.3	87.4	88.3	87.1	94.4	92.9	88.5	72.6	54.2
2. Once or twice	7.5	8.3	6.8	8.0	3.3	11.8	7.4	3.6	8.9	7.5	7.5	2.8	5.6	9.5	15.5	21.3
3. Occasionally	3.6	4.5	2.7	3.6	2.8	7.3	3.4	1.8	2.2	3.1	4.1	2.3	1.0	1.6	8.6	13.2
4. Often	1.4	1.6	1.1	1.3	0.7	3.0	1.0	0.3	1.5	1.0	1.3	0.6	0.5	0.5	3.2	11.3
Item 20610 Subject A02b N	*3247*	*1537*	*1620*	*2447*	*398*	*758*	*896*	*990*	*603*	*1913*	*1136*	*1251*	*714*	*445*	*753*	*46*
A29D: Amphetamines (uppers, pep pills, bennies, speed)																
1. Not at all	59.0	59.9	57.8	54.8	78.4	57.6	53.1	64.2	60.8	61.5	54.0	79.7	63.4	53.6	24.7	30.5
2. Once or twice	21.3	21.6	21.4	23.2	14.2	23.1	19.7	21.8	20.7	21.3	22.0	13.9	26.5	28.8	25.1	13.8
3. Occasionally	13.2	12.7	13.5	14.8	4.6	12.9	17.2	9.9	12.9	11.6	15.9	4.7	8.0	14.7	30.6	24.7
4. Often	6.5	5.7	7.3	7.3	2.8	6.3	10.0	4.1	5.6	5.6	8.1	1.7	2.2	3.0	19.6	31.0
Item 20620 Subject A02b N	*3246*	*1534*	*1623*	*2445*	*398*	*758*	*898*	*989*	*601*	*1915*	*1133*	*1251*	*716*	*445*	*750*	*46*
A29E: Barbiturates (downers, goofballs, reds, yellows, etc.)																
1. Not at all	81.1	80.1	82.4	79.5	90.6	80.0	77.8	84.2	82.4	83.4	77.3	91.5	87.5	82.2	60.8	26.6
2. Once or twice	11.9	12.4	11.4	13.0	6.7	14.0	12.5	10.6	10.5	11.0	13.8	5.2	10.7	12.9	22.1	40.6
3. Occasionally	5.2	5.7	4.4	5.7	1.4	4.3	7.0	3.9	6.1	4.4	6.4	2.9	1.4	3.8	13.0	15.1
4. Often	1.7	1.7	1.8	1.8	1.3	1.7	2.8	1.3	0.9	1.1	2.5	0.5	0.4	1.2	4.2	17.7
Item 20630 Subject A02b N	*3247*	*1538*	*1621*	*2448*	*398*	*757*	*897*	*990*	*603*	*1913*	*1136*	*1250*	*716*	*445*	*752*	*46*
A29F: Tranquilizers (Librium, Valium, Miltown)																
1. Not at all	76.6	78.7	74.7	74.4	88.5	74.9	76.1	78.6	76.3	77.2	75.5	84.6	84.2	74.7	59.3	37.7
2. Once or twice	15.1	13.5	16.4	16.4	8.3	15.3	14.4	14.1	17.6	14.9	16.6	10.7	12.8	15.8	23.7	29.7
3. Occasionally	6.1	5.6	6.7	6.9	2.1	7.1	7.8	5.1	3.8	5.9	5.8	3.6	3.0	6.6	12.5	15.9
4. Often	2.2	2.2	2.2	2.3	1.1	2.7	1.6	2.1	2.3	2.0	2.0	1.2	0.1	2.9	4.6	16.7
Item 20640 Subject A02b N	*3242*	*1535*	*1620*	*2446*	*398*	*758*	*894*	*988*	*601*	*1916*	*1129*	*1250*	*715*	*445*	*750*	*45*
A29G: Cocaine ("coke")																
1. Not at all	61.7	61.1	62.6	62.2	65.3	48.7	71.1	70.6	49.6	62.5	61.2	83.1	64.7	53.8	30.3	31.9
2. Once or twice	19.8	20.1	19.7	19.9	22.8	23.1	16.4	18.1	23.6	20.5	19.4	10.6	24.6	30.6	24.0	20.9
3. Occasionally	11.3	12.2	10.2	10.9	7.5	16.9	7.3	7.6	16.2	10.9	11.3	4.7	6.8	11.8	25.5	13.6
4. Often	7.1	6.6	7.4	7.0	4.4	11.3	5.2	3.6	10.6	6.1	8.1	1.6	3.8	3.7	20.1	33.6
Item 20650 Subject A02b N	*3251*	*1538*	*1624*	*2450*	*399*	*759*	*899*	*990*	*603*	*1917*	*1136*	*1251*	*716*	*445*	*754*	*46*
A29H: Heroin (smack, horse)																
1. Not at all	94.5	94.0	95.3	94.9	95.9	93.6	94.1	96.2	93.5	95.0	94.5	96.0	97.6	93.9	91.8	58.1
2. Once or twice	3.6	3.9	3.0	3.4	2.2	4.4	3.5	2.4	4.5	3.4	3.3	2.4	1.8	4.7	5.6	20.2
3. Occasionally	1.4	1.5	1.3	1.3	1.5	1.5	1.9	1.1	1.1	1.2	1.7	1.1	0.3	1.0	1.9	18.8
4. Often	0.5	0.6	0.4	0.5	0.4	0.4	0.5	0.3	0.9	0.4	0.5	0.5	0.3	0.3	0.6	2.9
Item 20660 Subject A02b N	*3237*	*1536*	*1612*	*2441*	*396*	*758*	*894*	*987*	*598*	*1911*	*1130*	*1245*	*715*	*444*	*750*	*46*
A29I: Other narcotics (methadone, opium, codeine, paregoric, etc.)																
1. Not at all	81.6	80.7	82.4	80.4	90.0	81.2	79.0	86.6	77.6	82.6	80.1	92.7	89.0	81.1	58.7	38.9
2. Once or twice	12.1	13.0	11.1	12.9	6.3	12.0	12.4	9.1	16.7	11.6	13.0	5.1	8.8	14.5	24.8	26.9
3. Occasionally	4.5	4.2	4.8	4.8	2.6	4.9	6.7	2.9	3.3	4.4	4.5	1.5	1.8	2.9	11.9	19.3
4. Often	1.8	2.0	1.8	1.9	1.1	1.9	1.9	1.4	2.4	1.4	2.4	0.7	0.4	1.5	4.5	14.9
Item 20670 Subject A02b N	*3243*	*1538*	*1616*	*2447*	*396*	*757*	*897*	*988*	*601*	*1915*	*1132*	*1249*	*716*	*443*	*751*	*46*

QUESTIONNAIRE FORM 3 1985	TOTAL	SEX		RACE		REGION				4YR COLLEGE PLANS		ILLICIT DRUG USE: LIFETIME				
		M	F	White	Black	NE	NC	S	W	Yes	No	None	Mari- juana Only	Few Pills	More Pills	Any Her- oin
N (Weighted No. of Cases):	3294	1549	1638	2464	407	770	907	1006	611	1932	1148	1258	717	446	761	48
% of Weighted Total:	100.0	47.0	49.7	74.8	12.4	23.4	27.5	30.5	18.5	58.7	34.9	38.2	21.8	13.5	23.1	1.4

A29J: Alcoholic beverages (beer, wine, liquor)

	TOTAL	M	F	White	Black	NE	NC	S	W	Yes	No	None	Mari.	Few	More	Any
1. Not at all	6.0	5.9	5.8	4.5	11.4	5.8	6.0	6.7	4.9	5.2	6.3	12.5	1.6	2.1	1.4	0.4
2. Once or twice	9.8	9.1	10.5	8.3	16.4	7.7	9.6	11.3	10.4	10.5	8.5	16.3	6.6	8.0	2.7	8.7
3. Occasionally	24.7	24.2	25.6	23.7	28.2	24.6	23.1	27.0	23.7	25.2	24.6	35.0	20.4	23.7	13.7	9.7
4. Often	59.5	60.7	58.1	63.5	44.0	62.0	61.3	55.0	61.0	59.1	60.6	36.3	71.4	66.3	82.2	81.1
Item 20680 Subject A02b N	3250	1538	1625	2451	399	756	900	991	603	1919	1136	1254	716	445	752	46

This section asks for your views and feelings about a number of different things.

D01: How satisfied are you with your life as a whole these days?

	TOTAL	M	F	White	Black	NE	NC	S	W	Yes	No	None	Mari.	Few	More	Any
1. Completely dissatisfied	2.5	2.8	2.4	2.3	2.9	2.8	2.3	1.7	3.9	2.1	3.1	1.7	2.7	2.5	3.2	2.4
2. Quite dissatisfied	9.2	9.0	9.4	9.7	8.0	11.3	9.9	7.3	8.8	9.2	9.5	9.1	10.0	8.4	9.1	4.1
3. Somewhat dissatisfied	10.9	8.9	12.3	10.7	13.4	10.1	12.3	10.9	9.6	11.1	11.1	9.2	10.2	11.9	13.5	15.1
4. Neither, or mixed feelings	13.2	13.2	13.3	12.6	13.4	13.4	13.7	12.5	13.3	11.7	16.4	11.7	12.8	14.8	14.8	16.4
5. Somewhat satisfied	25.1	26.0	24.6	25.5	24.4	25.0	23.3	27.2	24.6	25.3	23.9	23.6	26.3	24.9	27.0	26.5
6. Quite satisfied	33.4	34.3	32.5	34.4	29.2	31.0	32.5	35.4	34.4	35.2	30.6	36.5	34.1	33.2	28.9	30.4
7. Completely satisfied	5.7	5.9	5.4	4.8	8.8	6.4	6.0	5.0	5.4	5.5	5.4	8.3	3.9	4.4	3.6	5.0
Item 6840 Subject P01,Q01 N	3096	1451	1574	2364	370	682	871	954	589	1898	1102	1198	683	418	717	44

D02: These questions are about your health during the last MONTH.

D02A: Have you been bothered by shortness of breath when you were not exercising or working hard?

	TOTAL	M	F	White	Black	NE	NC	S	W	Yes	No	None	Mari.	Few	More	Any
1. Never	72.0	76.5	68.2	72.0	70.4	69.6	70.6	74.0	73.9	75.7	66.1	78.7	72.4	69.4	64.3	48.7
2. Seldom	17.4	16.4	18.3	17.6	18.0	18.7	18.8	15.9	16.4	15.3	20.5	13.8	19.2	19.8	19.7	33.2
3. Sometimes	9.1	6.4	11.3	9.0	10.2	9.6	9.5	9.2	7.5	7.7	11.6	6.7	7.7	8.7	13.2	16.6
4. Often	1.5	0.7	2.2	1.3	1.4	2.1	1.0	0.9	2.3	1.3	1.7	0.8	0.7	2.1	2.8	1.6
Item 8850 Subject T N	3091	1449	1575	2368	369	680	870	952	588	1900	1101	1198	683	416	712	44

D02B: Have you been bothered by your heart beating hard?

	TOTAL	M	F	White	Black	NE	NC	S	W	Yes	No	None	Mari.	Few	More	Any
1. Never	74.1	77.7	70.5	73.6	72.8	74.2	72.0	75.0	75.4	75.5	71.4	79.1	76.2	70.6	67.0	53.7
2. Seldom	16.5	14.7	18.2	16.8	16.0	17.7	17.2	16.5	13.9	16.4	16.8	13.8	16.6	19.2	18.4	31.7
3. Sometimes	8.1	6.5	9.7	8.2	9.8	6.2	9.2	8.0	8.8	7.0	10.1	6.2	6.7	8.8	12.5	5.6
4. Often	1.4	1.1	1.6	1.4	1.4	1.9	1.6	0.5	1.9	1.1	1.8	0.9	0.4	1.4	2.1	9.0
Item 8860 Subject T N	3087	1446	1572	2362	368	680	869	948	589	1900	1098	1194	682	416	712	44

D02C: Have you had spells of dizziness?

	TOTAL	M	F	White	Black	NE	NC	S	W	Yes	No	None	Mari.	Few	More	Any
1. Never	59.8	69.2	51.1	59.8	65.3	63.6	57.4	59.1	60.0	60.4	58.6	64.4	63.9	58.1	50.2	38.8
2. Seldom	24.7	20.8	28.4	25.1	19.2	23.0	25.6	25.3	24.3	25.2	23.6	24.9	21.4	27.4	26.1	31.9
3. Sometimes	12.5	8.1	16.3	12.1	13.6	10.1	13.9	13.0	12.2	12.0	13.8	9.1	12.5	11.1	18.3	22.6
4. Often	3.1	1.9	4.1	3.0	2.0	3.4	3.1	2.6	3.5	2.4	4.0	1.7	2.2	3.4	5.4	6.7
Item 8870 Subject T N	3081	1440	1571	2358	368	680	868	945	588	1897	1095	1187	683	416	712	44

D02D: Have your hands trembled enough to bother you?

	TOTAL	M	F	White	Black	NE	NC	S	W	Yes	No	None	Mari.	Few	More	Any
1. Never	79.3	84.4	74.0	78.8	79.7	79.3	77.3	78.8	82.8	80.0	77.8	83.0	84.8	79.4	69.7	55.6
2. Seldom	13.0	10.1	15.8	13.2	12.7	13.6	13.1	13.7	10.9	12.9	13.2	11.8	11.3	13.3	15.4	21.5
3. Sometimes	5.8	4.0	7.7	5.9	6.2	5.2	7.5	5.1	5.3	5.5	6.5	3.9	3.2	5.8	10.7	17.9
4. Often	1.9	1.4	2.5	2.1	1.4	1.8	2.1	2.4	1.0	1.6	2.5	1.3	0.7	1.4	4.2	5.1
Item 8880 Subject T N	3083	1444	1570	2359	368	680	867	948	588	1899	1094	1192	682	414	713	44

D02E: Have you been troubled by your hands sweating so that they felt damp and clammy?

	TOTAL	M	F	White	Black	NE	NC	S	W	Yes	No	None	Mari.	Few	More	Any
1. Never	66.2	68.6	63.7	64.6	75.2	70.6	61.6	66.5	67.4	67.8	63.1	70.2	64.9	67.0	62.4	47.2
2. Seldom	22.0	21.2	22.8	23.1	14.9	17.4	25.8	22.3	21.3	21.2	23.7	20.2	23.2	22.5	21.7	39.8
3. Sometimes	8.5	6.9	10.1	9.0	5.6	9.1	8.6	7.7	8.9	8.6	8.3	7.0	8.3	8.9	11.3	7.9
4. Often	3.3	3.3	3.4	3.3	4.2	2.9	4.0	3.4	2.4	2.4	4.9	2.7	3.5	1.6	4.6	5.0
Item 8890 Subject T N	3083	1443	1571	2361	367	681	867	947	588	1899	1094	1193	681	415	712	44

QUESTIONNAIRE FORM 3 1985	TOTAL	SEX		RACE		REGION				4YR COLLEGE PLANS		ILLICIT DRUG USE: LIFETIME				
		M	F	White	Black	NE	NC	S	W	Yes	No	None	Mari-juana Only	Few Pills	More Pills	Any Her-oin
N (Weighted No. of Cases):	3294	1549	1638	2464	407	770	907	1006	611	1932	1148	1258	717	446	761	48
% of Weighted Total:	100.0	47.0	49.7	74.8	12.4	23.4	27.5	30.5	18.5	58.7	34.9	38.2	21.8	13.5	23.1	1.4
D02F: Have there been times when you couldn't take care of things because you just couldn't get going?																
1. Never	53.2	59.0	47.0	53.2	54.0	55.7	52.7	53.2	51.0	52.5	53.9	60.3	51.7	49.4	45.8	39.1
2. Seldom	27.3	25.3	29.7	28.0	23.9	24.4	27.6	28.2	29.0	28.2	26.4	25.7	29.8	28.9	26.7	33.8
3. Sometimes	15.8	12.9	18.7	15.6	18.0	16.8	15.8	15.6	14.8	16.1	15.5	12.5	15.4	16.7	20.4	23.2
4. Often	3.7	2.7	4.7	3.2	4.1	3.2	3.9	3.0	5.2	3.3	4.3	1.5	3.0	5.0	7.1	3.9
Item 8900 Subject T N	3082	1443	1570	2361	367	679	868	948	587	1901	1093	1191	681	415	713	44
D03: At any time during the LAST 12 MONTHS, have you felt in your own mind that you should REDUCE or STOP your use of . . .																
D03A: Alcohol?																
1. Yes	35.5	36.5	34.6	35.5	37.9	30.6	38.3	36.7	34.8	34.0	38.7	27.3	43.9	37.1	38.7	42.5
2. No	50.2	49.6	50.6	53.3	30.1	62.4	47.9	44.9	48.3	51.2	48.8	43.3	50.2	54.8	56.7	49.9
8. Haven't used in last 12 months	14.3	13.9	14.8	11.3	32.0	7.0	13.8	18.3	16.9	14.8	12.5	29.3	5.9	8.1	4.5	7.6
Item 8910 Subject A01i N	2652	1266	1328	2098	271	575	772	793	512	1637	920	952	609	356	671	37
D03B: Cigarettes?																
1. Yes	24.7	23.0	26.0	25.6	19.6	28.0	27.9	22.5	19.8	19.8	32.6	8.1	30.5	25.9	45.2	50.2
2. No	14.4	13.9	14.6	14.1	15.1	14.4	15.5	14.3	12.7	12.1	18.1	9.1	15.9	15.6	18.8	28.7
8. Haven't used in last 12 months	60.9	63.1	59.4	60.3	65.3	57.6	56.6	63.2	67.6	68.1	49.3	82.8	53.6	58.5	36.0	21.1
Item 8920 Subject A01i N	3001	1402	1530	2312	348	662	852	912	575	1847	1050	1160	676	395	693	40
D03C: Marijuana?																
1. Yes	22.2	25.5	19.2	22.2	23.4	25.0	21.8	19.3	24.3	19.8	25.6	-	34.8	31.4	43.7	43.2
2. No	17.8	16.2	19.0	18.8	13.2	23.8	19.4	12.8	16.4	16.8	19.8	-	27.8	21.2	36.3	41.7
8. Haven't used in last 12 months	59.9	58.3	61.8	59.1	63.5	51.3	58.8	67.9	59.2	63.4	54.6	100.0	37.3	47.4	20.1	15.1
Item 8930 Subject A01i N	2672	1246	1364	2081	284	598	764	804	506	1681	907	1089	562	339	625	34
D03D: Psychedelics (LSD, etc.)?																
1. Yes	2.1	2.5	1.5	2.2	0.3	3.4	2.8	0.8	1.7	1.7	2.7	-	-	0.3	7.3	32.8
2. No	2.2	2.7	1.7	2.4	1.9	3.1	2.9	1.6	1.0	1.9	2.9	-	-	0.3	7.9	27.0
8. Haven't used in last 12 months	95.7	94.8	96.8	95.4	97.8	93.5	94.2	97.6	97.3	96.4	94.3	100.0	100.0	99.4	84.8	40.2
Item 8940 Subject A01i N	2729	1259	1407	2142	289	597	791	814	529	1719	920	1091	621	357	601	33
D03E: Amphetamines (uppers)?																
1. Yes	4.7	4.8	4.5	4.9	1.3	5.2	5.7	3.9	3.9	3.8	6.5	-	-	3.0	20.8	20.1
2. No	5.8	5.0	6.6	6.3	3.1	6.9	7.9	3.8	4.5	5.4	6.5	-	-	2.8	24.2	50.0
8. Haven't used in last 12 months	89.5	90.2	88.9	88.8	95.6	87.9	86.4	92.3	91.5	90.8	86.9	100.0	100.0	94.2	55.0	29.8
Item 8950 Subject A01i N	2569	1219	1304	2017	279	585	738	760	486	1645	846	1085	618	310	497	34
D03F: Tranquilizers?																
1. Yes	1.4	1.6	1.0	1.4	0.3	1.4	1.6	1.4	1.0	1.2	1.7	-	-	1.0	4.8	14.7
2. No	2.3	2.0	2.4	2.2	1.8	2.7	2.7	2.2	1.1	2.0	2.3	-	-	2.3	7.3	29.8
8. Haven't used in last 12 months	96.4	96.3	96.6	96.4	97.9	95.8	95.6	96.4	98.0	96.8	96.0	100.0	100.0	96.7	87.9	55.5
Item 9005 Subject A01i N	2666	1234	1377	2088	284	587	766	792	522	1686	897	1086	620	342	561	32
D03G: Barbiturates/Quaaludes (downers)?																
1. Yes	1.6	2.1	0.9	1.7	0.5	1.3	2.6	1.2	1.2	1.4	2.0	-	-	0.6	5.1	30.3
2. No	1.9	2.3	1.4	1.8	2.4	2.2	2.5	2.1	0.5	1.0	3.4	-	-	0.6	6.7	28.2
8. Haven't used in last 12 months	96.4	95.6	97.7	96.5	97.1	96.5	94.9	96.6	98.3	97.6	94.6	100.0	100.0	98.8	88.1	41.5
Item 8970 Subject A01i N	2698	1260	1381	2124	286	590	781	804	523	1695	915	1090	620	349	579	35
D03H: Cocaine?																
1. Yes	4.5	5.1	3.8	4.4	2.7	6.0	3.0	3.4	6.7	4.2	4.8	-	-	5.2	14.7	29.6
2. No	7.2	7.0	7.2	7.5	4.3	11.5	6.4	4.0	8.5	5.8	10.0	-	-	6.5	25.1	40.8
8. Haven't used in last 12 months	88.3	87.9	89.0	88.1	93.0	82.5	90.5	92.6	84.8	90.0	85.2	100.0	100.0	88.3	60.2	29.6
Item 8980 Subject A01i N	2745	1274	1411	2157	285	608	794	823	520	1734	919	1091	620	340	632	38

QUESTIONNAIRE FORM 3 1985	TOTAL	SEX		RACE		REGION				4YR COLLEGE PLANS		ILLICIT DRUG USE: LIFETIME				
		M	F	White	Black	NE	NC	S	W	Yes	No	None	Marijuana Only	Few Pills	More Pills	Any Heroin
N (Weighted No. of Cases):	3294	1549	1638	2464	407	770	907	1006	611	1932	1148	1258	717	446	761	48
% of Weighted Total:	100.0	47.0	49.7	74.8	12.4	23.4	27.5	30.5	18.5	58.7	34.9	38.2	21.8	13.5	23.1	1.4
D03I: Heroin?																
1. Yes	0.4	0.3	0.2	0.2	0.4	0.2	0.7	0.4	0.1	0.3	0.5	-	-	-	-	26.9
2. No	0.4	0.5	0.4	0.3	1.0	0.6	0.6	0.3	-	0.2	0.5	-	-	-	-	31.0
8. Haven't used in last 12 months	99.2	99.2	99.4	99.5	98.6	99.2	98.7	99.3	99.9	99.5	99.0	100.0	100.0	100.0	100.0	42.2
Item 8990 Subject A01i N	2759	1281	1416	2173	286	612	796	819	533	1738	933	1090	621	366	627	30
D03J: Other narcotics?																
1. Yes	1.3	1.4	1.0	1.2	0.7	2.0	1.1	0.8	1.5	1.3	0.9	-	-	-	4.2	29.9
2. No	1.9	2.0	1.8	2.1	1.0	1.9	2.7	1.4	1.6	1.4	2.9	-	-	0.6	6.8	30.6
8. Haven't used in last 12 months	96.8	96.5	97.1	96.6	98.2	96.2	96.2	97.8	96.9	97.3	96.2	100.0	100.0	99.4	89.0	39.4
Item 9000 Subject A01i N	2647	1221	1368	2078	278	584	759	794	510	1684	875	1089	618	339	547	29
D04: How likely is it that you will use marijuana in the next 12 months?																
1. Definitely will-GO TO Q.D05	11.1	13.1	9.4	12.1	5.9	16.2	12.6	7.6	8.8	9.5	14.1	1.6	6.7	9.8	32.6	49.7
2. Probably will-GO TO Q.D05	13.6	12.8	14.4	13.9	10.2	15.4	12.2	11.6	17.0	13.8	13.4	1.1	23.8	17.6	24.3	20.1
3. Probably will not	19.3	18.0	20.5	20.7	16.2	22.6	21.8	15.8	17.4	20.3	17.2	9.3	30.7	29.0	21.5	13.5
4. Definitely will not	55.9	56.1	55.7	53.3	67.7	45.7	53.3	65.0	56.7	56.4	55.3	88.0	38.8	43.5	21.6	16.7
Item 9010 Subject A04a N	2801	1291	1446	2189	299	607	803	865	526	1728	982	1155	615	364	607	34

Here are some reasons people give for not using marijuana, or for stopping use. If you have never used marijuana, or if you have stopped using it, please tell us which reasons are true for you. (Mark all that apply.)

	TOTAL	M	F	White	Black	NE	NC	S	W	Yes	No	None	Mari-juana Only	Few Pills	More Pills	Any Heroin
A. Concerned about possible psychological damage	68.1	68.6	68.6	69.2	65.6	66.0	70.7	69.9	63.2	71.0	62.1	74.0	64.5	64.8	54.5	66.8
B. Concerned about possible physical damage	66.9	67.4	67.5	67.7	65.3	63.6	68.1	67.7	67.0	71.9	58.1	72.4	63.2	65.4	52.4	50.2
C. Concerned about getting arrested	38.3	45.1	32.5	38.5	36.6	36.1	38.9	41.5	34.2	36.9	40.8	38.7	40.9	39.3	33.5	27.0
D. Concerned about becoming addicted to marijuana	45.1	46.4	44.2	42.7	59.1	38.9	48.4	49.3	39.3	45.1	44.8	51.3	41.9	38.5	33.3	18.8
E. It's against my beliefs	51.9	50.5	53.1	53.4	39.6	44.4	52.5	55.5	52.3	55.4	45.7	66.3	33.8	44.1	30.4	39.7
F. Concerned about loss of energy or ambition	35.2	37.7	33.6	34.7	35.5	28.8	33.8	37.8	39.3	36.1	34.1	35.7	31.2	34.0	41.7	24.1
G. Concerned about possible loss of control of myself	50.3	47.2	53.5	50.4	52.2	45.5	54.4	50.7	48.2	51.6	48.3	55.3	43.9	48.5	44.4	24.1
H. It might lead to stronger drugs	49.1	49.3	49.0	48.8	55.3	44.3	50.7	54.1	43.0	49.8	48.2	53.9	47.8	47.7	34.6	25.2
I. Not enjoyable, I didn't like it	34.0	33.4	34.8	32.6	38.1	33.8	34.0	31.0	39.1	32.0	37.6	22.4	55.8	39.4	42.9	18.8
J. My parents would disapprove	59.1	59.1	59.4	59.7	57.1	53.8	63.3	61.3	54.2	60.3	57.2	63.6	54.9	59.1	47.7	22.8
K. My husband/wife (or boyfriend/girlfriend) would disapprove	31.2	30.3	32.3	30.8	32.2	21.5	32.7	37.0	28.5	28.7	36.6	31.7	31.0	29.8	30.9	8.3
L. I don't like being with the people who use it	41.9	40.6	43.6	42.8	35.4	34.5	41.6	47.5	40.2	42.1	40.9	52.7	28.0	35.2	28.2	8.3
M. My friends don't use it	34.1	32.8	35.6	35.9	26.6	29.1	32.6	38.5	33.7	38.0	26.4	42.4	20.7	33.0	23.8	-
N. I might have a bad trip	23.9	23.3	24.7	23.3	27.2	19.6	27.6	24.3	22.2	22.6	26.7	23.5	26.0	22.7	25.3	8.3
O. Too expensive	22.2	25.7	19.1	23.4	19.1	17.1	26.3	22.1	21.5	20.4	25.3	21.0	21.9	25.6	24.8	15.8
P. Not available	6.6	7.8	5.7	6.8	6.4	6.3	7.6	7.0	4.9	5.8	7.8	7.1	5.8	4.8	7.5	18.8
Q. Don't feel like getting high	61.4	59.8	63.7	61.9	55.3	62.2	63.2	57.3	64.9	61.0	62.5	63.4	61.0	59.6	56.4	61.2
Item 9020-9180 Subject A06a N★	2039	925	1066	1570	240	397	580	675	387	1303	674	1080	409	264	257	8

D05A: Has your use of alcohol ever caused any of the following problems for you?

Responses to this set of questions are not included because of complexities in the presentation and interpretation of the data.

Item 9190-9350 Subject A07b N

★=excludes respondents for whom question was inappropriate.

QUESTIONNAIRE FORM 3 1985	TOTAL	SEX		RACE		REGION				4YR COLLEGE PLANS		ILLICIT DRUG USE: LIFETIME				
		M	F	White	Black	NE	NC	S	W	Yes	No	None	Mari- juana Only	Few Pills	More Pills	Any Her- oin
N (Weighted No. of Cases):	3294	1549	1638	2464	407	770	907	1006	611	1932	1148	1258	717	446	761	48
% of Weighted Total:	100.0	47.0	49.7	74.8	12.4	23.4	27.5	30.5	18.5	58.7	34.9	38.2	21.8	13.5	23.1	1.4

D05M: Has your use of marijuana ever caused any of the following problems for you? (Mark all that apply.)

Responses to this set of questions are not included because of complexities in the presentation and interpretation of the data.

Item 9360-9520   Subject A07b   N

D05O: Has your use of other drugs ever caused any of the following problems for you? (Mark all that apply.)

Responses to this set of questions are not included because of complexities in the presentation and interpretation of the data.

Item 9530-9690   Subject A07b   N

E01: Do you agree or disagree that most efforts to prevent (or clean up) pollution . . .

E01A: . . . are just too expensive

	TOTAL	M	F	White	Black	NE	NC	S	W	Yes	No	None	Mari- juana Only	Few Pills	More Pills	Any Her- oin
1. Disagree	21.3	24.2	18.6	20.3	29.0	25.6	18.6	22.1	18.9	21.3	21.8	20.5	20.9	23.3	21.9	19.0
2. Mostly disagree	22.7	22.1	23.2	24.0	14.1	25.8	21.1	21.6	23.2	25.1	18.5	23.7	21.2	23.7	21.9	21.6
3. Neither	35.9	30.7	40.9	36.5	32.0	32.7	38.5	33.3	39.8	36.0	36.0	34.5	37.5	35.6	37.7	34.8
4. Mostly agree	13.9	15.4	12.7	14.1	13.6	11.0	16.2	15.0	12.2	12.3	16.4	15.6	14.9	9.4	12.0	20.2
5. Agree	6.2	7.6	4.6	5.2	11.4	4.9	5.6	8.0	5.9	5.3	7.3	5.7	5.5	7.9	6.5	4.4

Item 9700   Subject F04   N   2911   1356   1488   2254   331   628   828   891   563   1803   1017   1149   649   385   658   36

E01B: . . . cost more jobs than it's worth

	TOTAL	M	F	White	Black	NE	NC	S	W	Yes	No	None	Mari- juana Only	Few Pills	More Pills	Any Her- oin
1. Disagree	23.8	25.9	22.1	23.8	25.1	27.9	22.6	23.6	21.1	25.2	21.5	23.5	26.0	25.4	21.0	33.6
2. Mostly disagree	25.8	25.7	25.8	27.4	16.0	27.4	27.6	22.8	25.9	28.4	22.0	29.3	22.4	24.1	25.4	7.5
3. Neither	35.1	31.9	38.2	35.6	30.1	31.7	36.0	34.8	37.8	33.5	37.0	33.5	35.2	37.9	35.6	38.0
4. Mostly agree	10.9	11.3	10.3	9.5	20.0	9.6	9.2	13.4	11.0	9.6	13.5	9.4	13.1	8.4	12.1	16.4
5. Agree	4.5	5.2	3.6	3.7	8.8	3.3	4.5	5.3	4.3	3.4	6.0	4.3	3.3	4.2	5.9	4.5

Item 9710   Subject F04   N   2887   1341   1478   2235   328   621   825   886   556   1786   1011   1145   642   381   652   35

E01C: . . . are proposed by people who usually don't know what they are talking about

	TOTAL	M	F	White	Black	NE	NC	S	W	Yes	No	None	Mari- juana Only	Few Pills	More Pills	Any Her- oin
1. Disagree	17.5	18.0	17.1	16.8	22.1	19.4	16.0	16.3	19.3	19.0	14.8	16.8	19.8	19.4	15.7	10.4
2. Mostly disagree	22.3	21.4	23.3	24.4	13.4	24.4	22.9	21.7	20.3	23.9	19.0	23.4	22.5	20.6	21.5	18.9
3. Neither	36.6	33.0	40.1	36.5	33.2	34.2	37.2	36.4	38.7	36.6	37.6	36.2	35.1	36.2	39.2	33.6
4. Mostly agree	15.5	16.4	14.3	14.9	18.9	14.1	15.7	16.0	16.1	13.9	18.8	15.6	15.7	15.6	14.1	28.9
5. Agree	8.1	11.1	5.3	7.3	12.5	7.9	8.3	9.5	5.6	6.7	9.9	7.9	7.0	8.2	9.4	8.1

Item 9720   Subject F04   N   2865   1336   1464   2225   324   614   818   883   549   1783   995   1139   641   376   642   36

E01D: . . . will not be enough anyhow

	TOTAL	M	F	White	Black	NE	NC	S	W	Yes	No	None	Mari- juana Only	Few Pills	More Pills	Any Her- oin
1. Disagree	16.5	17.5	15.4	15.9	19.9	19.3	16.2	16.0	14.4	17.1	15.7	18.2	17.0	13.2	15.1	14.4
2. Mostly disagree	22.9	24.6	21.8	24.6	20.0	23.7	22.2	23.8	21.9	25.5	18.5	23.8	22.6	25.1	20.9	13.6
3. Neither	34.5	30.2	38.2	33.9	32.2	33.0	35.4	31.8	39.0	33.3	36.8	34.0	32.4	36.3	36.3	33.3
4. Mostly agree	18.9	19.0	18.6	18.8	17.0	17.8	17.6	20.5	19.7	18.3	19.8	17.5	22.0	18.1	18.6	22.3
5. Agree	7.2	8.7	6.0	6.8	11.0	6.3	8.6	7.9	5.0	5.9	9.1	6.4	6.0	7.3	9.1	16.4

Item 9730   Subject F04   N   2850   1339   1448   2216   319   611   815   875   549   1771   991   1133   634   376   642   34

QUESTIONNAIRE FORM 3 1985	TOTAL	SEX		RACE		REGION				4YR COLLEGE PLANS		ILLICIT DRUG USE: LIFETIME				
		M	F	White	Black	NE	NC	S	W	Yes	No	None	Marijuana Only	Few Pills	More Pills	Any Heroin
N (Weighted No. of Cases):	3294	1549	1638	2464	407	770	907	1006	611	1932	1148	1258	717	446	761	48
% of Weighted Total:	100.0	47.0	49.7	74.8	12.4	23.4	27.5	30.5	18.5	58.7	34.9	38.2	21.8	13.5	23.1	1.4

E01E: ... are useless because this society won't last long enough for such efforts to do any good

1. Disagree	35.2	35.6	35.0	36.9	30.8	35.5	35.7	35.1	34.0	39.3	28.2	37.2	35.1	37.8	32.0	14.0
2. Mostly disagree	21.4	22.0	21.1	22.4	15.7	21.0	21.6	21.7	21.1	22.7	19.0	20.7	23.3	20.7	20.0	32.7
3. Neither	29.1	27.5	30.5	28.9	25.5	29.7	28.9	27.5	31.2	26.9	33.1	28.1	26.7	27.0	35.5	25.0
4. Mostly agree	9.2	8.7	9.3	8.0	15.5	8.1	9.6	9.5	9.2	7.3	12.7	9.1	10.7	7.9	7.5	13.5
5. Agree	5.2	6.3	4.1	3.8	12.5	5.8	4.1	6.2	4.4	3.9	7.0	4.9	4.3	6.5	5.0	14.8
Item 9740 Subject F04 N	2853	1332	1457	2216	323	608	817	880	549	1778	989	1136	636	380	634	36

E02: There has been talk about shortages of energy, food, and raw materials in this country. Do you think that in the coming years we will have plenty to meet our needs, a sufficient amount, or will we have to consume less?

1. Plenty to meet our needs	17.4	25.0	10.5	17.7	19.6	15.9	18.7	18.9	14.9	16.9	18.2	17.8	17.5	16.0	17.2	25.8
2. A sufficient amount	54.2	51.0	57.1	54.6	49.8	53.4	55.2	53.2	55.4	54.5	53.6	53.1	56.9	56.7	51.9	60.7
3. Will have to consume less	28.3	24.0	32.4	27.7	30.6	30.8	26.1	28.0	29.7	28.5	28.2	29.1	25.6	27.3	30.9	13.5
Item 9750 Subject F05 N	2759	1265	1434	2169	292	574	804	841	540	1730	945	1096	622	365	614	34

E03: The questions in this section deal with population problems. How much do you agree or disagree with each statement?

E03A: Our government should help other countries to control their population

1. Disagree	21.1	27.1	15.9	20.2	24.8	21.2	20.9	21.8	20.3	18.9	24.9	21.4	21.7	19.0	20.7	32.8
2. Mostly disagree	19.1	18.2	20.3	20.4	16.7	20.8	19.9	17.7	18.3	20.6	16.2	18.7	21.8	17.1	18.0	23.6
3. Neither	24.3	22.0	26.4	24.1	21.3	23.3	24.2	22.1	29.0	23.8	24.3	24.8	21.6	28.4	24.5	11.5
4. Mostly agree	22.5	20.5	24.6	22.9	19.8	22.4	23.6	23.8	19.2	25.0	19.6	23.1	23.2	19.9	22.4	23.7
5. Agree	12.9	12.2	12.9	12.4	17.4	12.4	11.3	14.7	13.1	11.8	14.9	12.0	11.7	15.5	14.4	8.4
Item 9760 Subject E01,H02 N	2873	1333	1477	2231	322	603	821	883	566	1793	994	1141	648	378	638	36

E03B: Governments should avoid making policy about population and let the individual decide

1. Disagree	11.4	11.6	11.0	10.6	15.6	8.9	11.7	12.7	11.8	10.3	13.3	11.5	13.6	8.6	10.4	13.8
2. Mostly disagree	20.3	19.6	21.3	21.9	16.7	20.7	19.6	21.4	19.5	22.5	17.1	20.2	20.7	22.6	19.9	14.4
3. Neither	28.5	28.9	28.3	28.3	23.1	29.1	29.5	25.9	30.5	27.1	30.5	27.7	28.2	26.7	31.1	26.6
4. Mostly agree	23.3	20.7	25.6	23.8	22.0	23.2	24.2	22.8	22.7	25.0	20.4	24.9	20.1	24.0	22.6	25.1
5. Agree	16.5	19.2	13.8	15.3	22.6	18.2	15.1	17.2	15.5	15.1	18.6	15.8	17.3	18.2	16.0	20.2
Item 9770 Subject E01,H02 N	2856	1328	1465	2221	317	600	820	877	559	1781	988	1136	641	375	636	37

E03C: I feel strongly enough about preventing overpopulation that I'd be willing to limit my family to two children

1. Disagree	17.6	18.3	16.6	16.8	21.1	18.3	18.3	17.1	16.8	16.7	18.8	16.5	18.3	17.7	17.9	29.0
2. Mostly disagree	12.4	13.5	11.7	12.7	12.1	13.0	12.0	11.9	13.3	12.6	12.3	13.2	11.7	11.6	11.7	17.4
3. Neither	26.0	25.8	26.4	25.8	26.7	30.2	25.1	23.5	26.7	26.3	25.9	27.1	24.6	26.4	25.1	19.1
4. Mostly agree	21.1	19.5	22.6	22.1	14.9	17.9	23.0	22.0	20.5	22.5	18.8	21.3	21.2	19.3	21.8	28.5
5. Agree	22.8	22.9	22.7	22.6	25.3	20.6	21.6	25.6	22.6	21.8	24.2	21.8	24.2	24.9	23.4	6.0
Item 9780 Subject E01 N	2849	1323	1464	2214	320	598	812	878	561	1779	986	1135	638	376	634	36

E03D: To prevent overpopulation, I might decide not to have any children of my own

1. Disagree	54.9	52.8	56.9	56.2	46.1	54.1	53.5	56.7	54.9	56.8	51.6	52.9	56.2	57.6	55.9	70.4
2. Mostly disagree	16.3	17.0	15.9	16.8	15.2	13.8	18.4	15.6	17.0	16.6	15.9	18.4	17.1	14.9	13.1	8.4
3. Neither	18.1	19.4	16.6	17.5	21.9	20.6	18.3	17.3	16.5	17.0	19.6	18.0	16.9	17.3	19.9	14.9
4. Mostly agree	4.9	4.6	5.2	4.4	7.6	5.3	4.1	4.9	5.8	4.5	6.0	4.8	5.0	5.0	4.7	2.7
5. Agree	5.8	6.2	5.4	5.1	9.1	6.1	5.7	5.5	5.8	5.1	6.9	5.9	4.9	5.2	6.3	3.6
Item 9790 Subject E01 N	2843	1321	1460	2209	319	596	814	876	557	1776	982	1131	638	374	633	36

MONITORING THE FUTURE

QUESTIONNAIRE FORM 3 1985	TOTAL	SEX		RACE		REGION				4YR COLLEGE PLANS		ILLICIT DRUG USE: LIFETIME				
		M	F	White	Black	NE	NC	S	W	Yes	No	None	Marijuana Only	Few Pills	More Pills	Any Heroin
N (Weighted No. of Cases):	3294	1549	1638	2464	407	770	907	1006	611	1932	1148	1258	717	446	761	48
% of Weighted Total:	100.0	47.0	49.7	74.8	12.4	23.4	27.5	30.5	18.5	58.7	34.9	38.2	21.8	13.5	23.1	1.4

E03E: High schools should offer instruction in birth control methods

1. Disagree	6.4	8.1	4.5	5.4	12.1	4.6	6.2	7.9	6.1	5.7	7.4	8.1	5.9	6.4	3.3	8.4
2. Mostly disagree	4.6	5.6	3.9	4.1	6.2	5.5	3.3	5.8	3.8	4.7	4.3	5.9	3.9	2.9	3.4	11.5
3. Neither	15.7	18.4	13.1	15.0	17.2	17.5	16.9	13.8	15.1	14.8	17.0	18.4	14.0	13.7	14.0	10.0
4. Mostly agree	24.5	25.7	23.1	25.8	16.7	24.0	26.1	24.0	23.3	24.3	25.1	26.2	26.2	18.9	22.0	30.7
5. Agree	48.9	42.2	55.4	49.7	47.8	48.3	47.5	48.6	51.8	50.6	46.1	41.4	50.0	58.0	57.2	39.4
Item 9800 Subject E02 N	2848	1323	1463	2214	319	596	815	876	560	1778	984	1132	639	374	635	36

E03F: I personally consider most methods of birth control to be immoral

1. Disagree	45.7	41.3	49.7	49.1	33.0	45.0	48.5	44.0	44.9	49.1	40.3	38.9	50.4	48.6	51.4	48.2
2. Mostly disagree	18.4	19.2	17.7	19.6	15.0	18.0	18.1	19.5	17.6	18.1	19.3	18.0	20.4	20.9	15.9	14.7
3. Neither	22.2	24.1	20.6	20.5	25.1	24.1	21.6	20.7	23.3	21.0	23.6	26.2	18.3	16.7	22.1	25.5
4. Mostly agree	6.8	7.4	6.2	5.8	11.2	7.1	5.5	7.4	7.3	6.4	7.2	8.0	6.6	5.5	5.3	7.6
5. Agree	7.0	8.1	5.8	5.0	15.7	5.8	6.3	8.4	6.9	5.3	9.6	8.8	4.3	8.1	5.3	4.1
Item 9810 Subject E02 N	2831	1316	1454	2203	316	590	811	873	557	1770	976	1124	634	373	632	37

E03G: The government should make birth control information and services available without cost to anyone who wants them

1. Disagree	7.5	8.1	7.0	7.3	9.1	5.1	8.2	8.4	8.0	6.2	9.1	8.5	7.1	7.1	6.3	9.0
2. Mostly disagree	7.4	7.5	7.2	7.4	5.4	6.9	6.8	7.9	8.1	8.0	6.2	9.0	6.2	7.1	5.9	6.8
3. Neither	17.1	18.1	16.2	16.7	18.6	19.2	15.7	16.9	17.1	16.3	18.3	18.2	16.9	13.9	16.8	21.0
4. Mostly agree	23.6	24.6	23.1	25.0	16.6	21.3	28.0	22.4	21.8	23.9	23.3	24.6	23.7	21.3	23.4	17.3
5. Agree	44.3	41.6	46.5	43.5	50.3	47.5	41.4	44.5	45.0	45.6	43.1	39.7	46.1	50.5	47.6	45.9
Item 9820 Subject E02,H02 N	2843	1321	1460	2210	319	595	814	877	557	1774	983	1127	641	374	633	36

E04: Did you have a unit on sex education when you were in high school?

1. No, and I'm glad I didn't	8.3	10.4	6.4	7.8	9.9	5.5	6.4	11.7	9.1	7.0	10.2	8.7	7.4	6.1	8.7	18.3
2. No, and I wish I had	21.9	22.1	22.1	21.5	31.1	15.9	16.2	34.8	16.7	20.7	24.0	22.9	22.2	23.8	18.3	23.3
3. Yes, and it was very worthwhile	25.9	22.6	28.6	23.4	33.8	33.2	25.2	20.7	26.9	24.8	27.5	26.2	28.5	25.9	23.2	28.0
4. Yes, and it was somewhat worthwhile	34.5	34.2	34.9	37.1	23.0	36.4	41.7	25.1	36.7	37.4	29.6	34.0	33.9	34.6	37.3	20.8
5. Yes, but it was not worthwhile at all	9.4	10.8	8.1	10.3	2.1	8.9	10.6	7.8	10.6	10.0	8.7	8.1	8.0	9.7	12.4	9.5
Item 9860 Subject B01,E02 N	2815	1307	1445	2186	315	602	806	856	551	1757	966	1110	634	373	631	35

E05: Did you ever study about birth control methods in high school?

1. No, and I'm glad I didn't	11.1	15.2	7.4	11.0	10.8	9.8	9.5	14.4	9.7	9.4	13.5	12.8	9.0	9.9	10.0	22.7
2. No, and I wish I had	27.3	25.2	29.8	27.4	30.5	21.2	23.6	36.3	25.5	27.5	27.4	26.4	28.1	29.8	26.6	18.8
3. Yes, and it was very worthwhile	25.9	22.4	29.1	23.8	34.6	29.8	25.8	21.5	28.5	25.4	26.9	23.8	29.9	27.2	24.9	30.7
4. Yes, and it was somewhat worthwhile	29.7	30.2	29.0	31.5	21.4	33.1	33.6	22.7	31.0	31.8	26.0	30.9	28.2	27.2	31.5	23.3
5. Yes, but it was not worthwhile at all	6.0	7.0	4.8	6.2	2.6	6.1	7.4	5.0	5.3	6.0	6.1	6.1	4.8	6.0	6.9	4.5
Item 9870 Subject B01,E02 N	2798	1297	1438	2170	312	597	805	850	546	1749	958	1102	631	372	628	35

E06: How important is each of the following for being looked up to or having high status in your school?

E06A: Coming from the right family

1. No importance	16.1	17.2	15.3	15.0	20.9	20.7	13.1	13.4	19.8	16.2	15.9	14.5	16.3	16.9	17.9	13.8
2. Little importance	16.8	16.2	17.5	18.9	10.6	18.3	15.4	17.7	16.1	18.9	13.4	17.5	16.8	15.6	16.8	14.9
3. Moderate importance	30.0	26.9	32.9	32.3	18.2	28.0	34.6	30.1	25.4	30.4	29.3	30.8	27.8	30.5	32.0	23.7
4. Great importance	18.8	20.4	17.3	18.0	23.2	15.8	19.8	19.5	19.6	17.7	21.5	18.9	19.5	18.9	17.2	35.0
5. Very great importance	18.2	19.3	17.0	15.9	27.1	17.2	17.1	19.4	19.2	16.9	20.0	18.2	19.7	18.2	16.1	12.6
Item 13580 Subject B04 N	2793	1299	1433	2176	309	585	807	852	550	1760	949	1106	632	368	620	36

QUESTIONNAIRE FORM 3 1985	TOTAL	SEX		RACE		REGION				4YR COLLEGE PLANS		ILLICIT DRUG USE: LIFETIME				
		M	F	White	Black	NE	NC	S	W	Yes	No	None	Marijuana Only	Few Pills	More Pills	Any Heroin
N (Weighted No. of Cases):	3294	1549	1638	2464	407	770	907	1006	611	1932	1148	1258	717	446	761	48
% of Weighted Total:	100.0	47.0	49.7	74.8	12.4	23.4	27.5	30.5	18.5	58.7	34.9	38.2	21.8	13.5	23.1	1.4

E06B: Being a leader in student activities

1. No importance	10.3	10.8	9.6	9.5	9.9	10.7	9.8	9.8	11.3	7.0	15.7	8.1	9.6	11.7	13.1	16.9
2. Little importance	14.4	14.9	14.0	14.5	13.9	18.7	12.0	13.0	15.7	13.5	15.9	13.2	16.9	14.3	14.4	8.2
3. Moderate importance	34.5	34.0	35.0	35.9	28.4	35.6	36.2	31.3	36.0	36.9	30.5	33.6	33.1	37.2	36.9	32.9
4. Great importance	26.5	26.3	27.0	27.0	29.7	22.6	26.7	29.7	25.4	28.5	23.7	29.3	26.3	21.6	23.4	35.4
5. Very great importance	14.3	14.0	14.4	13.1	18.1	12.5	15.4	16.2	11.5	14.2	14.3	15.8	14.0	15.3	12.1	6.6
Item 13590　Subject B04,M05　N	2788	1298	1428	2175	307	583	805	850	550	1756	947	1104	630	368	617	36

E06C: Having a nice car

1. No importance	16.3	15.7	16.9	14.2	24.9	22.1	15.4	16.5	11.4	16.1	16.0	16.5	16.8	18.2	14.1	7.9
2. Little importance	20.1	16.6	23.4	20.7	19.5	22.1	20.7	19.7	18.0	21.2	18.3	21.4	18.9	21.2	18.3	19.4
3. Moderate importance	33.6	34.0	33.4	36.3	21.3	31.9	36.7	32.5	32.5	35.1	30.8	33.1	36.7	29.1	34.6	32.5
4. Great importance	17.2	19.4	15.0	17.0	17.4	12.5	16.8	16.9	23.3	16.7	18.7	18.5	16.2	16.6	16.3	25.4
5. Very great importance	12.7	14.3	11.3	11.8	16.9	11.4	10.5	14.4	14.9	10.8	16.2	10.5	11.5	14.9	16.6	14.8
Item 13600　Subject B04,F01　N	2775	1287	1425	2164	304	579	803	849	545	1751	938	1098	627	368	615	34

E06D: Getting good grades

1. No importance	4.9	4.9	4.9	4.6	4.1	5.0	4.0	5.4	5.4	4.4	5.3	4.7	3.5	5.2	5.5	12.2
2. Little importance	11.6	11.4	11.8	12.7	4.3	11.4	10.8	9.5	16.2	10.8	13.0	10.0	11.0	14.3	13.2	15.1
3. Moderate importance	34.4	33.7	35.4	39.3	14.8	35.6	37.5	31.7	32.9	34.8	33.9	32.0	36.5	33.4	37.1	43.8
4. Great importance	28.4	29.8	27.1	28.2	31.8	28.3	28.7	28.5	27.8	29.6	27.0	30.2	28.6	26.8	27.1	13.5
5. Very great importance	20.7	20.3	20.8	15.2	45.0	19.8	19.0	25.0	17.7	20.3	20.9	23.0	20.3	20.4	17.0	15.4
Item 13610　Subject B04　N	2781	1288	1431	2172	306	581	806	845	549	1753	941	1103	629	366	616	35

E06E: Being a good athlete

1. No importance	10.1	8.3	11.7	8.9	12.7	11.5	8.8	11.5	8.2	7.4	14.7	10.2	8.6	10.3	10.2	9.9
2. Little importance	13.2	11.3	14.8	13.2	12.9	15.6	10.8	15.6	10.6	11.6	16.6	12.8	11.5	14.7	14.1	15.4
3. Moderate importance	27.8	25.8	29.8	28.3	26.5	28.1	27.7	27.7	27.6	27.9	27.0	27.6	26.6	26.2	31.5	25.1
4. Great importance	28.3	31.2	25.6	29.1	24.5	27.2	29.0	26.7	31.1	31.8	22.7	28.9	31.2	27.8	25.6	27.7
5. Very great importance	20.6	23.4	18.1	20.5	23.5	17.7	23.7	18.5	22.5	21.4	19.1	20.6	22.1	21.0	18.6	21.9
Item 13620　Subject B04　N	2768	1290	1417	2159	306	578	798	847	544	1743	940	1095	626	367	612	35

E06F: Knowing a lot about intellectual matters

1. No importance	11.2	10.2	12.2	11.7	6.5	11.8	10.1	11.6	11.5	9.4	14.0	10.0	9.3	12.0	14.1	14.3
2. Little importance	25.7	23.2	28.3	28.4	13.4	24.8	28.0	24.1	25.8	25.1	27.5	25.5	28.8	28.1	22.6	26.1
3. Moderate importance	37.9	39.0	36.7	39.3	32.5	37.0	38.0	38.5	37.9	39.9	35.0	39.5	35.5	39.0	37.7	32.0
4. Great importance	16.8	18.9	14.7	14.6	27.1	17.2	15.0	18.1	16.8	18.1	14.0	17.2	18.9	13.4	15.4	13.8
5. Very great importance	8.4	8.7	8.1	6.0	20.6	9.2	8.8	7.6	7.9	7.5	9.6	7.8	7.4	7.5	10.3	13.8
Item 13630　Subject B04　N	2780	1293	1424	2167	308	581	802	850	548	1750	943	1101	627	368	616	35

E06G: Planning to go to college

1. No importance	11.1	13.1	8.9	11.2	6.6	13.1	11.4	11.0	8.6	5.6	20.4	10.0	8.8	11.3	14.0	21.3
2. Little importance	14.3	13.6	14.8	15.2	11.2	15.7	14.3	12.8	15.1	12.2	17.6	13.5	13.9	16.5	14.8	9.3
3. Moderate importance	30.8	31.6	30.5	33.7	21.7	25.9	34.8	30.3	31.1	30.1	32.4	29.8	32.2	29.1	33.2	30.9
4. Great importance	23.9	23.2	24.8	23.7	25.9	23.1	21.8	24.8	26.6	28.3	16.8	25.2	23.7	24.7	21.9	26.2
5. Very great importance	19.9	18.4	21.0	16.1	34.7	22.3	17.7	21.0	18.6	23.7	12.7	21.5	21.4	18.4	16.1	12.3
Item 13640　Subject B04　N	2782	1292	1427	2168	308	582	803	850	547	1750	947	1102	627	368	617	35

E07: How about using drugs (other than marijuana or alcohol)–does that cause a student to be looked up to or looked down on?

E07A: Among the majority of students in my school, such drug use is . . .

1. Looked down on a lot	22.5	24.0	20.8	21.6	22.0	17.1	24.3	26.8	18.8	23.3	20.2	26.7	24.7	20.0	14.7	5.4
2. Looked down on some	22.2	21.6	22.9	23.6	17.6	23.3	22.0	23.1	19.8	23.4	20.9	26.3	20.6	20.7	18.2	17.5
3. Neither, or mixed	45.8	44.8	47.2	46.4	40.7	51.8	44.1	39.7	51.4	44.7	48.7	39.3	44.7	47.9	56.9	53.7
4. Looked up to some	7.8	7.7	7.7	6.9	16.1	5.8	6.9	9.5	8.3	7.1	8.4	6.3	8.4	9.3	8.4	15.1
5. Looked up to a lot	1.8	1.8	1.5	1.5	3.6	1.9	2.7	0.9	1.7	1.6	1.7	1.4	1.6	2.1	1.7	8.3
Item 13650　Subject A12b　N	2764	1286	1416	2166	305	574	801	847	542	1737	939	1096	622	369	613	35

QUESTIONNAIRE FORM 3 1985	TOTAL	SEX		RACE		REGION				4YR COLLEGE PLANS		ILLICIT DRUG USE: LIFETIME				
		M	F	White	Black	NE	NC	S	W	Yes	No	None	Mari-juana Only	Few Pills	More Pills	Any Her-oin
N (Weighted No. of Cases):	3294	1549	1638	2464	407	770	907	1006	611	1932	1148	1258	717	446	761	48
% of Weighted Total:	100.0	47.0	49.7	74.8	12.4	23.4	27.5	30.5	18.5	58.7	34.9	38.2	21.8	13.5	23.1	1.4

E07B: Among my own group of friends, such drug use is . . .

1. Looked down on a lot	38.5	34.4	42.4	39.7	36.2	31.8	38.3	45.5	34.8	42.5	31.0	58.5	33.6	31.3	13.1	10.2
2. Looked down on some	18.0	19.7	16.8	18.5	16.7	17.1	17.3	18.9	18.4	18.1	17.7	17.8	20.4	17.7	16.9	11.2
3. Neither, or mixed	34.2	35.1	32.8	33.1	35.0	39.4	34.7	29.2	35.8	32.0	38.6	20.6	36.7	42.7	49.4	51.9
4. Looked up to some	6.8	7.4	6.3	6.0	10.7	8.2	6.3	5.4	8.4	5.5	8.9	2.5	7.3	6.8	14.5	6.4
5. Looked up to a lot	2.5	3.4	1.7	2.7	1.4	3.5	3.3	1.0	2.7	1.9	3.8	0.6	1.9	1.6	6.1	20.3
Item 13660 Subject A12b N	2767	1286	1419	2168	305	574	802	846	544	1742	939	1097	625	370	611	35

E07C: My own feelings about such drug use is that . . .

1. I look down on it a lot	52.1	51.1	53.3	52.5	55.4	46.3	52.0	57.9	49.5	55.1	46.3	76.9	44.7	44.1	22.4	7.8
2. I look down on it some	17.1	16.1	18.2	17.9	14.5	17.4	15.5	16.9	19.4	18.0	15.7	11.0	22.4	19.9	21.0	22.3
3. Neither, or mixed	27.0	28.5	25.2	26.1	24.7	31.7	27.3	22.8	28.3	23.9	32.9	11.3	30.0	33.4	46.9	49.6
4. I look up to it some	2.9	3.2	2.7	2.6	4.3	3.3	3.5	2.0	2.7	2.5	3.6	0.5	2.2	2.6	8.0	2.8
5. I look up to it a lot	0.9	1.1	0.5	0.9	1.0	1.3	1.7	0.4	0.1	0.5	1.5	0.3	0.7	0.1	1.8	17.5
Item 13670 Subject A11c N	2764	1284	1418	2165	305	574	800	847	544	1743	935	1097	623	369	611	35

E08: The next questions are about some things which may have happened TO YOU while you were at school (inside or outside or in a schoolbus).

During the LAST 12 MONTHS, how often ...

E08A: Has something of yours (worth under $50) been stolen?

1. Not at all	64.0	62.8	65.6	63.8	66.5	61.4	66.7	65.6	60.2	61.3	68.3	67.6	63.2	65.0	58.4	52.2
2. Once	23.1	22.4	23.6	23.8	19.6	24.9	21.7	23.1	23.4	24.9	20.6	21.3	21.6	25.0	26.8	24.0
3. Twice	9.0	10.0	8.1	8.6	8.4	9.1	7.7	7.9	12.3	9.9	7.5	7.7	10.7	4.9	11.7	14.2
4. 3 or 4 times	2.7	3.3	2.0	2.5	4.0	3.0	2.8	2.2	2.9	3.2	1.5	2.4	3.4	2.9	2.1	3.2
5. 5 or more times	1.3	1.6	0.7	1.3	1.6	1.6	1.1	1.2	1.3	0.8	2.1	1.1	1.1	2.1	1.0	6.4
Item 9871 Subject B07,S03 N	2840	1315	1459	2210	315	596	813	877	555	1779	967	1119	634	383	632	40

E08B: Has something of yours (worth over $50) been stolen?

1. Not at all	87.9	86.1	89.9	89.4	83.7	86.5	90.1	88.8	84.6	88.0	87.7	90.4	84.8	91.8	85.4	75.2
2. Once	8.7	9.7	7.8	8.2	8.2	9.3	7.5	8.0	10.7	8.6	9.1	7.4	9.4	6.9	10.8	18.3
3. Twice	2.0	2.1	1.8	1.3	4.8	2.7	1.4	1.9	2.2	2.2	1.3	1.3	3.0	0.6	2.6	0.5
4. 3 or 4 times	0.9	1.4	0.3	0.6	2.3	0.9	0.5	0.8	1.7	0.7	1.2	0.4	2.4	0.4	0.4	-
5. 5 or more times	0.6	0.8	0.1	0.5	1.0	0.6	0.6	0.5	0.8	0.5	0.6	0.5	0.4	0.3	0.8	5.9
Item 9872 Subject B07,S03 N	2843	1319	1458	2213	315	600	814	874	554	1780	967	1119	635	382	635	40

E08C: Has someone deliberately damaged your property (your car, clothing, etc.)?

1. Not at all	73.1	65.8	79.9	73.4	72.0	76.3	72.0	75.6	67.2	75.4	69.2	75.5	73.7	70.9	70.5	65.1
2. Once	18.2	23.1	14.0	18.5	17.0	15.7	19.2	17.3	20.7	17.1	20.0	17.7	18.1	18.6	19.0	19.0
3. Twice	5.8	7.1	4.4	5.4	6.3	5.3	5.3	5.3	7.8	4.7	7.6	5.0	4.8	7.0	6.9	6.7
4. 3 or 4 times	1.9	2.3	1.5	1.8	2.5	1.0	2.7	1.0	3.3	1.9	2.0	0.6	2.3	2.9	2.9	3.3
5. 5 or more times	1.1	1.7	0.3	0.9	2.3	1.7	0.8	0.9	1.1	0.9	1.2	1.2	1.2	0.5	0.7	5.8
Item 9873 Subject B07,S03 N	2837	1319	1451	2208	312	594	813	874	555	1778	963	1119	631	381	634	40

E08D: Has someone injured you with a weapon (like a knife, gun, or club)?

1. Not at all	94.1	91.2	97.4	94.6	91.1	92.1	94.2	94.7	95.2	96.4	90.5	96.7	94.4	96.6	90.3	64.0
2. Once	3.6	5.6	1.5	3.2	5.6	3.8	3.3	3.6	4.0	2.1	6.4	2.2	3.7	2.7	5.7	16.8
3. Twice	1.5	2.0	0.7	1.4	2.4	2.2	1.4	1.3	0.9	0.7	2.4	0.7	1.2	0.4	3.0	8.4
4. 3 or 4 times	0.3	0.4	0.3	0.4	0.4	1.0	0.2	0.2	-	0.3	0.3	0.3	0.1	-	0.3	7.5
5. 5 or more times	0.5	0.8	-	0.5	0.6	0.8	0.9	0.3	-	0.5	0.4	0.2	0.6	0.3	0.8	3.3
Item 9874 Subject B07,S03 N	2830	1311	1452	2203	313	593	812	872	553	1776	958	1111	631	383	633	40

QUESTIONNAIRE FORM 3 1985	TOTAL	SEX		RACE		REGION				4YR COLLEGE PLANS		ILLICIT DRUG USE: LIFETIME				
		M	F	White	Black	NE	NC	S	W	Yes	No	None	Mari- juana Only	Few Pills	More Pills	Any Her- oin
N (Weighted No. of Cases):	3294	1549	1638	2464	407	770	907	1006	611	1932	1148	1258	717	446	761	48
% of Weighted Total:	100.0	47.0	49.7	74.8	12.4	23.4	27.5	30.5	18.5	58.7	34.9	38.2	21.8	13.5	23.1	1.4

E08E: Has someone threatened you with a weapon, but not actually injured you?

1. Not at all	86.5	80.5	92.4	88.4	77.4	85.4	87.2	87.3	85.2	88.2	83.9	90.8	87.5	86.0	79.9	66.1
2. Once	8.6	11.6	5.6	7.0	14.0	7.8	6.5	9.0	11.9	7.8	10.0	5.7	8.3	9.1	12.9	15.3
3. Twice	2.4	3.5	1.2	2.2	4.6	2.6	2.8	2.4	1.6	2.0	2.8	1.9	2.0	2.0	3.6	6.1
4. 3 or 4 times	1.5	2.7	0.4	1.5	2.1	2.5	2.3	0.6	0.6	1.2	1.9	1.1	1.0	1.9	2.3	1.5
5. 5 or more times	1.1	1.7	0.4	1.0	1.9	1.7	1.2	0.8	0.7	0.8	1.3	0.6	1.2	1.0	1.3	11.0
Item 9875 Subject B07,S03 N	2831	1309	1455	2204	312	595	813	872	551	1776	961	1114	632	382	630	40

E08F: Has someone injured you on purpose without using a weapon?

1. Not at all	85.8	81.6	90.0	86.4	81.8	82.3	85.4	88.8	85.6	87.8	82.4	90.7	88.1	83.4	79.0	53.4
2. Once	8.7	11.5	5.9	7.7	12.5	10.3	7.6	8.1	9.5	7.8	10.2	6.8	6.5	10.7	11.5	30.1
3. Twice	2.9	3.6	2.3	3.3	2.5	4.2	3.6	1.8	2.3	2.4	4.0	1.3	3.0	3.9	4.4	8.2
4. 3 or 4 times	1.5	2.0	1.1	1.4	2.3	1.2	1.8	1.0	2.0	1.3	1.8	0.6	1.2	2.0	2.6	8.2
5. 5 or more times	1.1	1.2	0.8	1.2	0.9	2.0	1.5	0.3	0.6	0.7	1.6	0.6	1.2	-	2.5	-
Item 9876 Subject B07,S03 N	2827	1310	1451	2202	313	593	812	870	552	1774	959	1112	630	379	634	40

E08G: Has an unarmed person threatened you with injury, but not actually injured you?

1. Not at all	75.4	67.5	82.8	75.5	74.8	73.8	75.0	78.3	73.0	75.9	74.5	81.8	75.4	74.3	66.8	55.1
2. Once	13.0	16.4	9.7	12.0	14.9	12.7	11.5	13.4	14.9	14.0	11.3	10.6	14.4	14.4	14.6	11.7
3. Twice	5.0	6.6	3.6	5.3	4.2	6.1	5.0	4.3	4.9	4.8	5.4	3.8	3.9	4.1	8.3	8.6
4. 3 or 4 times	3.8	5.4	2.3	4.1	2.9	4.1	4.2	2.7	4.5	3.3	4.4	2.4	4.1	4.6	4.6	13.0
5. 5 or more times	2.8	4.1	1.6	3.0	3.2	3.3	4.3	1.3	2.6	2.0	4.3	1.4	2.1	2.5	5.8	11.7
Item 9877 Subject B07,S03 N	2819	1304	1449	2198	311	593	810	866	550	1772	952	1111	628	381	628	39

E09: Looking toward the future, how important would it be for you to have each of the following things?

E09A: At least one car

1. Not important	3.8	5.0	2.5	3.1	6.5	3.2	3.7	4.3	3.8	2.9	4.5	3.7	3.5	1.1	5.3	4.3
2. Somewhat important	15.2	15.3	15.4	14.6	20.6	15.5	15.3	15.7	14.1	15.9	13.5	19.1	14.0	13.5	10.7	18.8
3. Quite important	35.4	32.7	37.7	36.2	32.2	40.3	34.1	33.5	34.7	35.4	36.9	36.8	34.7	36.2	33.5	25.0
4. Extremely important	45.6	47.0	44.4	46.1	40.7	41.0	46.8	46.5	47.3	45.7	45.1	40.4	47.8	49.2	50.5	52.0
Item 13835 Subject F01 N	2801	1293	1443	2181	308	594	803	858	546	1762	944	1111	622	380	616	40

E09B: At least two cars

1. Not important	41.0	34.5	47.3	40.9	44.5	46.4	37.4	42.4	38.2	40.2	42.1	45.7	37.3	39.3	37.5	36.2
2. Somewhat important	32.0	33.5	30.5	32.8	28.0	30.8	33.2	32.0	31.8	32.7	31.6	32.0	34.4	33.6	29.4	27.7
3. Quite important	17.8	20.0	15.6	18.0	18.2	15.6	19.4	17.0	19.2	19.0	16.1	16.2	19.8	18.2	17.8	29.5
4. Extremely important	9.1	12.0	6.6	8.3	9.2	7.2	10.0	8.6	10.8	8.2	10.2	6.1	8.5	8.9	15.3	6.6
Item 13840 Subject F01 N	2793	1294	1434	2176	306	589	801	858	545	1759	940	1106	620	378	619	38

E09C: A large (full-sized) car

1. Not important	62.0	54.6	69.0	62.9	59.3	61.0	58.9	63.9	64.8	61.3	63.2	62.4	61.2	65.3	61.4	56.4
2. Somewhat important	23.3	26.3	20.6	23.8	18.5	24.9	25.3	20.5	22.9	23.5	22.8	23.4	25.6	23.4	20.3	26.2
3. Quite important	9.9	12.3	7.5	9.4	14.4	9.9	9.6	11.0	8.6	10.2	9.5	9.4	10.0	7.4	11.6	9.9
4. Extremely important	4.9	6.8	2.9	3.9	7.7	4.2	6.3	4.7	3.8	5.0	4.5	4.7	3.2	3.9	6.7	7.5
Item 13850 Subject F01 N	2777	1283	1429	2166	304	583	801	854	540	1753	934	1102	618	376	609	39

E09D: A new car every two or three years

1. Not important	60.7	52.1	68.8	60.0	65.9	61.3	56.8	61.2	64.9	58.6	63.2	66.0	60.7	58.6	54.0	41.0
2. Somewhat important	24.3	27.4	21.6	25.7	18.8	23.7	26.7	24.7	21.0	25.6	22.8	22.7	25.4	25.4	24.7	35.4
3. Quite important	8.7	11.7	5.7	8.7	9.2	8.6	9.6	8.5	7.8	9.5	7.8	6.8	9.6	8.4	11.0	12.2
4. Extremely important	6.3	8.9	4.0	5.6	6.1	6.4	6.9	5.6	6.3	6.3	6.2	4.5	4.2	7.6	10.3	11.4
Item 13860 Subject F01 N	2784	1284	1435	2169	306	584	799	857	544	1754	934	1105	622	372	614	39

QUESTIONNAIRE FORM 3 1985	TOTAL	SEX		RACE		REGION				4YR COLLEGE PLANS		ILLICIT DRUG USE: LIFETIME				
		M	F	White	Black	NE	NC	S	W	Yes	No	None	Mari-juana Only	Few Pills	More Pills	Any Heroin
N (Weighted No. of Cases):	3294	1549	1638	2464	407	770	907	1006	611	1932	1148	1258	717	446	761	48
% of Weighted Total:	100.0	47.0	49.7	74.8	12.4	23.4	27.5	30.5	18.5	58.7	34.9	38.2	21.8	13.5	23.1	1.4
E09E: Clothes in the latest style																
1. Not important	15.5	21.6	10.0	15.5	9.1	17.6	15.6	15.0	13.9	13.2	19.0	19.8	11.3	11.1	13.5	27.8
2. Somewhat important	33.4	33.1	33.9	35.0	23.1	30.8	34.5	35.2	31.8	32.9	35.1	36.6	32.9	34.2	29.2	20.9
3. Quite important	31.4	29.1	33.3	32.4	34.1	31.8	30.6	30.2	34.0	33.3	28.4	28.9	36.3	32.2	31.9	23.1
4. Extremely important	19.7	16.2	22.8	17.2	33.7	19.8	19.3	19.6	20.3	20.6	17.5	14.8	19.4	22.5	25.5	28.3
Item 13870 Subject F01 N	2786	1290	1431	2172	303	586	799	857	544	1760	934	1101	622	378	614	38
E09F: A house of my own (instead of an apartment or condominium)																
1. Not important	14.4	11.4	16.7	14.1	14.6	15.2	13.6	14.7	13.9	13.7	15.0	15.2	12.3	13.7	14.4	16.8
2. Somewhat important	25.0	21.6	28.1	26.6	19.6	23.0	26.1	26.0	23.8	24.2	27.3	25.4	27.4	22.6	23.6	27.5
3. Quite important	30.2	33.0	27.8	31.6	25.4	33.4	29.5	29.9	28.2	30.5	30.8	31.0	28.8	28.4	31.7	29.5
4. Extremely important	30.4	34.1	27.4	27.7	40.5	28.3	30.7	29.3	34.1	31.6	26.9	28.4	31.5	35.2	30.3	26.2
Item 13880 Subject F01 N	2790	1289	1436	2183	304	587	802	860	541	1759	936	1105	622	377	614	39
E09G: Lots of space around my house, a big yard																
1. Not important	14.9	12.6	16.6	13.5	18.2	13.1	14.3	15.5	16.7	14.4	15.8	13.9	12.6	17.9	15.8	18.2
2. Somewhat important	27.6	25.4	29.2	28.4	25.8	26.1	27.7	28.4	28.1	26.7	29.6	28.0	28.7	25.5	27.2	32.0
3. Quite important	31.2	32.4	30.3	32.9	26.3	33.7	31.5	30.6	29.0	32.1	30.2	33.2	32.8	28.8	29.0	19.9
4. Extremely important	26.2	29.6	23.9	25.2	29.7	27.0	26.5	25.5	26.1	26.8	24.4	24.9	26.0	27.7	27.9	29.9
Item 13890 Subject F01 N	2790	1292	1433	2176	304	587	803	858	541	1755	940	1104	619	377	618	39
E09H: A well-kept garden and lawn																
1. Not important	14.0	13.7	13.8	13.7	15.0	17.3	13.0	12.8	13.7	13.2	15.2	11.9	12.0	16.9	16.1	19.6
2. Somewhat important	29.7	28.7	30.4	30.6	24.3	30.7	31.8	30.9	23.5	29.7	29.9	30.8	29.5	26.1	29.7	45.0
3. Quite important	34.5	33.3	36.1	36.1	28.9	34.2	32.1	35.2	37.1	35.5	33.6	36.3	35.1	35.4	31.7	21.5
4. Extremely important	21.9	24.3	19.8	19.6	31.7	17.7	23.1	21.1	25.7	21.6	21.3	20.9	23.4	21.7	22.5	14.0
Item 13900 Subject F01 N	2776	1279	1432	2168	301	584	798	852	541	1750	932	1098	619	375	613	39
E09I: Major labor-saving appliances (washer, drier, dishwasher, etc.)																
1. Not important	7.8	8.8	6.5	7.3	10.0	9.2	8.3	6.4	8.0	5.8	11.1	6.7	7.1	7.9	9.3	10.8
2. Somewhat important	27.0	27.3	26.6	27.0	22.9	28.6	26.5	27.8	24.6	25.3	29.9	27.3	26.6	28.7	25.3	37.2
3. Quite important	37.4	37.5	37.7	38.9	31.6	36.7	37.2	38.1	37.3	39.3	34.4	41.2	39.9	31.2	33.5	21.7
4. Extremely important	27.8	26.4	29.2	26.8	35.5	25.5	27.9	27.7	30.1	29.6	24.5	24.8	26.5	32.2	31.8	30.3
Item 13910 Subject F01 N	2784	1291	1429	2171	304	583	802	856	543	1754	936	1102	619	375	616	39
E09J: A high-quality stereo																
1. Not important	14.1	9.9	17.9	13.3	19.3	11.2	14.4	16.5	12.9	12.6	16.1	18.4	11.8	12.4	9.0	9.5
2. Somewhat important	30.3	24.3	35.6	29.9	30.4	30.0	30.0	31.7	28.7	30.3	30.7	32.7	33.6	30.9	23.5	18.1
3. Quite important	30.9	34.5	28.0	32.5	24.9	33.7	29.6	31.0	29.8	32.1	29.2	30.4	30.9	32.4	31.3	34.1
4. Extremely important	24.7	31.3	18.6	24.2	25.4	25.1	26.0	20.7	28.7	25.1	24.0	18.5	23.7	24.3	36.2	38.3
Item 13920 Subject F01 N	2781	1289	1427	2169	304	581	802	855	543	1754	932	1102	619	375	614	39
E09K: A vacation house																
1. Not important	51.8	45.1	58.2	52.9	51.7	44.7	53.9	55.3	50.5	49.7	56.0	56.8	47.0	51.9	48.5	34.1
2. Somewhat important	26.5	29.5	23.6	27.1	20.1	29.0	25.2	25.1	27.8	27.9	23.0	25.4	29.7	25.5	25.2	36.2
3. Quite important	11.4	12.5	10.0	11.1	12.0	14.8	10.8	9.8	11.1	12.2	10.3	9.4	14.1	12.7	11.7	11.0
4. Extremely important	10.4	12.9	8.2	8.9	16.3	11.5	10.1	9.8	10.5	10.3	10.7	8.5	9.3	9.9	14.6	18.6
Item 13930 Subject F01 N	2778	1288	1425	2167	303	580	802	855	541	1751	933	1102	617	375	613	39
E09L: A motor-powered, recreational vehicle (powerboat, snowmobile)																
1. Not important	49.0	35.5	61.4	47.2	63.6	47.0	45.9	54.9	46.2	50.3	45.8	55.3	46.9	47.3	41.2	37.5
2. Somewhat important	26.0	29.3	22.8	27.1	16.7	25.7	25.9	26.1	26.4	26.2	25.8	24.6	27.7	27.2	25.6	25.9
3. Quite important	13.3	17.8	9.2	14.1	9.3	16.5	15.0	9.5	13.4	12.3	15.4	11.0	14.7	14.6	15.8	13.7
4. Extremely important	11.7	17.4	6.6	11.6	10.3	10.8	13.2	9.5	14.0	11.2	13.1	9.1	10.6	10.9	17.4	23.0
Item 13940 Subject F01 N	2777	1285	1427	2164	304	579	802	856	540	1749	933	1100	619	375	611	39

QUESTIONNAIRE FORM 3 1985	TOTAL	SEX		RACE		REGION				4YR COLLEGE PLANS		ILLICIT DRUG USE: LIFETIME				
		M	F	White	Black	NE	NC	S	W	Yes	No	None	Mari-juana Only	Few Pills	More Pills	Any Her-oin
N (Weighted No. of Cases):	3294	1549	1638	2464	407	770	907	1006	611	1932	1148	1258	717	446	761	48
% of Weighted Total:	100.0	47.0	49.7	74.8	12.4	23.4	27.5	30.5	18.5	58.7	34.9	38.2	21.8	13.5	23.1	1.4

E10: When (if ever) did you FIRST do each of the following things? Don't count anything you took because a doctor told you to.

E10A: Smoke cigarettes on a daily basis

	TOTAL	M	F	White	Black	NE	NC	S	W	Yes	No	None	Mari-juana Only	Few Pills	More Pills	Any Her-oin
8. Never	67.9	72.0	64.3	66.0	78.1	60.9	63.2	73.1	74.6	75.9	53.8	91.0	61.9	60.7	38.0	17.6
1. Grade 6 or below	4.1	4.2	4.0	4.2	3.5	4.9	4.0	4.3	2.9	3.0	6.0	1.7	3.4	6.3	6.8	21.1
2. Grade 7 or 8	8.2	6.3	9.7	9.1	4.1	10.5	11.7	5.2	4.9	5.6	12.9	1.5	8.2	8.5	19.4	19.5
3. Grade 9 (Freshman)	6.7	6.3	7.2	7.0	5.0	9.2	6.5	5.8	5.9	4.6	10.3	2.7	9.0	6.5	11.7	14.4
4. Grade 10 (Sophomore)	5.2	3.5	6.6	5.4	3.6	6.4	4.8	5.6	3.7	3.6	7.9	0.6	6.0	6.5	11.3	18.8
5. Grade 11 (Junior)	5.2	5.0	5.4	5.6	2.1	5.1	5.7	4.4	5.6	5.0	5.7	1.5	7.6	7.1	8.2	8.5
6. Grade 12 (Senior)	2.8	2.7	2.8	2.7	3.7	3.0	4.0	1.6	2.5	2.3	3.6	0.9	3.8	4.5	4.6	-
Item 5570 Subject A01g N	2476	1126	1291	1944	272	516	738	759	463	1547	842	1013	529	317	559	35

E10B: Try an alcoholic beverage - more than just a few sips

	TOTAL	M	F	White	Black	NE	NC	S	W	Yes	No	None	Mari-juana Only	Few Pills	More Pills	Any Her-oin
8. Never	9.0	9.3	8.5	7.2	18.8	4.8	9.7	11.0	9.3	9.0	8.0	21.1	1.2	1.0	2.2	-
1. Grade 6 or below	10.5	11.9	9.2	10.3	11.4	13.0	9.8	9.4	10.6	9.6	11.9	6.6	9.5	12.6	15.8	24.4
2. Grade 7 or 8	21.7	24.1	19.3	23.5	12.3	25.6	21.2	18.8	22.8	20.7	24.3	10.7	21.9	25.3	35.0	38.1
3. Grade 9 (Freshman)	23.2	23.8	23.2	24.1	17.5	25.4	25.2	20.5	22.2	23.4	23.6	17.9	27.3	25.0	27.2	26.3
4. Grade 10 (Sophomore)	17.8	16.6	18.8	18.6	15.1	17.9	17.5	18.9	16.3	19.5	14.3	16.6	23.1	20.2	14.2	5.0
5. Grade 11 (Junior)	12.1	8.8	15.1	11.2	15.7	10.1	10.4	13.9	14.5	12.5	11.5	17.3	12.6	11.7	4.9	2.8
6. Grade 12 (Senior)	5.6	5.4	5.9	5.1	9.2	3.3	6.3	7.5	4.2	5.3	6.4	9.9	4.4	4.0	0.7	3.5
Item 5580 Subject A01g N	2515	1145	1317	2000	238	539	735	750	490	1590	836	939	573	347	592	38

E10C: Try marijuana or hashish

	TOTAL	M	F	White	Black	NE	NC	S	W	Yes	No	None	Mari-juana Only	Few Pills	More Pills	Any Her-oin
8. Never	47.3	45.9	48.4	45.9	53.3	39.5	44.4	58.4	42.4	50.1	42.4	100.0	-	27.9	8.8	4.2
1. Grade 6 or below	3.4	4.4	2.5	3.0	6.2	3.5	3.1	2.4	5.1	2.3	4.8	-	3.8	3.1	8.3	19.4
2. Grade 7 or 8	12.0	13.6	10.5	12.5	7.1	14.8	10.6	7.3	18.2	10.3	15.5	-	17.6	14.0	25.8	26.2
3. Grade 9 (Freshman)	12.4	12.9	11.9	12.8	10.9	14.1	14.5	10.1	11.0	11.4	14.2	-	19.1	17.9	25.4	21.8
4. Grade 10 (Sophomore)	11.4	11.3	11.4	11.8	10.6	15.3	10.8	9.8	10.8	11.6	11.1	-	19.1	19.2	20.5	20.6
5. Grade 11 (Junior)	8.0	6.9	9.1	8.2	7.4	8.4	9.3	6.4	8.3	7.9	7.9	-	22.8	9.3	8.3	7.7
6. Grade 12 (Senior)	5.5	5.0	6.2	5.8	4.5	4.3	7.3	5.6	4.1	6.3	4.1	-	17.6	8.5	2.9	-
Item 5590 Subject A01g N	2606	1185	1368	2058	261	552	756	795	503	1645	871	1068	545	344	587	38

E10D: Try LSD

	TOTAL	M	F	White	Black	NE	NC	S	W	Yes	No	None	Mari-juana Only	Few Pills	More Pills	Any Her-oin
8. Never	95.2	94.3	96.2	94.6	98.8	95.1	92.6	97.1	95.9	95.9	93.7	100.0	100.0	98.3	82.8	29.8
1. Grade 6 or below	0.1	-	*	*	0.3	0.2	-	-	0.1	*	-	-	-	-	0.3	-
2. Grade 7 or 8	0.4	0.8	0.1	0.5	-	0.3	0.4	0.5	0.4	0.2	0.8	-	-	-	1.3	10.0
3. Grade 9 (Freshman)	1.3	1.6	1.0	1.3	-	1.9	1.9	0.7	0.9	0.9	1.9	-	-	0.3	4.2	28.4
4. Grade 10 (Sophomore)	1.2	1.1	1.4	1.4	0.3	1.0	2.4	0.3	1.2	1.1	1.6	-	-	0.3	4.9	10.1
5. Grade 11 (Junior)	1.1	1.1	1.0	1.4	-	0.6	1.5	1.3	0.8	1.0	1.4	-	-	0.3	4.7	5.6
6. Grade 12 (Senior)	0.7	1.1	0.4	0.7	0.5	0.9	1.0	0.2	0.7	0.8	0.6	-	-	0.8	1.8	16.1
Item 5600 Subject A01g N	2684	1227	1395	2096	292	560	770	828	525	1704	887	1089	602	359	576	35

E10E: Try any psychedelic other than LSD

	TOTAL	M	F	White	Black	NE	NC	S	W	Yes	No	None	Mari-juana Only	Few Pills	More Pills	Any Her-oin
8. Never	96.9	95.8	97.8	96.4	99.1	94.1	97.0	98.8	96.6	97.4	96.3	100.0	100.0	99.0	88.7	38.7
1. Grade 6 or below	0.2	0.3	-	*	0.3	0.4	-	0.3	-	0.1	0.3	-	-	-	0.2	13.5
2. Grade 7 or 8	0.3	0.5	0.1	0.4	-	0.5	0.1	0.3	0.5	0.3	0.4	-	-	-	1.6	-
3. Grade 9 (Freshman)	1.0	1.2	0.8	1.1	-	1.4	1.6	-	1.1	0.6	1.5	-	-	-	3.9	15.6
4. Grade 10 (Sophomore)	0.8	0.9	0.7	1.0	-	2.1	0.4	0.2	1.1	0.7	0.9	-	-	0.7	2.8	13.9
5. Grade 11 (Junior)	0.3	0.5	0.1	0.4	-	0.6	0.2	0.3	0.1	0.3	0.3	-	-	0.2	1.0	5.9
6. Grade 12 (Senior)	0.5	0.8	0.4	0.6	0.5	0.9	0.7	0.1	0.6	0.7	0.3	-	-	-	1.9	12.4
Item 5610 Subject A01g N	2658	1209	1386	2074	295	552	760	830	516	1696	869	1090	605	357	551	29

E10F: Try amphetamines

	TOTAL	M	F	White	Black	NE	NC	S	W	Yes	No	None	Mari-juana Only	Few Pills	More Pills	Any Her-oin
8. Never	84.8	85.9	84.0	82.7	97.4	82.7	81.6	88.3	86.2	87.0	80.1	100.0	100.0	74.1	32.2	15.6
1. Grade 6 or below	0.4	0.6	0.1	0.3	0.4	0.9	-	0.6	-	0.1	0.8	-	-	-	1.1	14.2
2. Grade 7 or 8	2.4	2.4	2.4	2.9	0.3	3.1	3.0	0.9	3.3	1.8	3.9	-	-	3.4	11.9	7.7
3. Grade 9 (Freshman)	4.9	4.4	5.2	5.6	0.6	4.5	6.6	4.3	3.8	3.7	7.3	-	-	4.3	23.6	32.3
4. Grade 10 (Sophomore)	3.4	2.7	4.0	3.8	0.4	5.4	3.8	2.4	2.3	3.2	3.9	-	-	7.9	14.5	15.1
5. Grade 11 (Junior)	2.5	2.4	2.7	2.9	-	1.8	3.2	1.9	3.2	2.8	2.0	-	-	5.1	11.5	1.7
6. Grade 12 (Senior)	1.6	1.7	1.6	1.8	1.0	1.7	1.7	1.6	1.2	1.3	2.1	-	-	5.3	5.2	13.3
Item 5620 Subject A01g N	2374	1110	1214	1842	275	523	673	732	446	1532	759	1084	600	226	403	34

*=less than .05 per cent.

QUESTIONNAIRE FORM 3 1985	TOTAL	SEX M	SEX F	RACE White	RACE Black	NE	NC	S	W	4YR COLLEGE PLANS Yes	No	None	Marijuana Only	Few Pills	More Pills	Any Heroin
N (Weighted No. of Cases):	3294	1549	1638	2464	407	770	907	1006	611	1932	1148	1258	717	446	761	48
% of Weighted Total:	100.0	47.0	49.7	74.8	12.4	23.4	27.5	30.5	18.5	58.7	34.9	38.2	21.8	13.5	23.1	1.4

E10G: Try quaaludes

8. Never	95.6	95.2	96.2	95.0	98.8	95.0	95.4	95.2	97.5	96.4	94.1	100.0	100.0	96.2	85.6	43.4
1. Grade 6 or below	0.2	0.3	0.1	0.2	0.7	0.6	-	0.3	-	0.2	0.1	-	-	0.3	0.5	2.2
2. Grade 7 or 8	0.9	0.8	1.0	1.0	-	0.7	0.5	1.3	1.1	0.5	1.7	-	-	1.4	2.6	14.3
3. Grade 9 (Freshman)	1.3	1.4	1.0	1.5	-	0.7	1.2	2.1	0.5	0.7	2.2	-	-	0.7	5.0	7.2
4. Grade 10 (Sophomore)	1.4	1.3	1.4	1.6	0.3	2.4	1.9	0.7	0.5	1.3	1.5	-	-	1.2	4.5	17.5
5. Grade 11 (Junior)	0.4	0.5	0.3	0.5	0.1	0.3	0.7	0.2	0.4	0.5	0.3	-	-	0.2	1.4	4.8
6. Grade 12 (Senior)	0.2	0.4	0.1	0.3	-	0.3	0.3	0.3	-	0.3	0.1	-	-	-	0.5	10.6
Item 5630 Subject A01g N	2684	1231	1391	2098	293	564	767	834	518	1703	892	1089	605	357	571	35

E10H: Try barbiturates

8. Never	95.2	94.5	96.2	95.0	97.6	93.6	94.4	96.2	96.4	96.4	93.0	100.0	100.0	96.5	83.3	26.0
1. Grade 6 or below	0.4	0.4	0.4	0.3	0.3	1.1	-	0.4	0.4	0.2	0.6	-	-	0.6	0.7	14.7
2. Grade 7 or 8	1.0	1.0	0.8	1.1	-	0.9	1.0	0.6	1.5	0.4	2.2	-	-	0.1	3.6	16.8
3. Grade 9 (Freshman)	1.2	1.5	0.8	1.4	0.4	1.3	1.9	1.0	0.6	0.9	1.9	-	-	0.8	5.3	6.4
4. Grade 10 (Sophomore)	1.2	1.5	1.1	1.4	0.6	2.0	1.5	1.0	0.5	1.1	1.4	-	-	1.5	3.5	22.0
5. Grade 11 (Junior)	0.6	0.8	0.3	0.6	-	0.8	0.8	0.4	0.5	0.7	0.4	-	-	-	3.0	2.9
6. Grade 12 (Senior)	0.3	0.3	0.4	0.2	1.0	0.3	0.4	0.5	0.1	0.3	0.5	-	-	0.4	0.7	11.2
Item 5640 Subject A01g N	2610	1197	1350	2029	291	554	742	805	509	1664	853	1089	605	342	511	38

E10I: Try tranquilizers

8. Never	94.9	94.6	95.3	94.3	99.3	94.8	93.8	95.6	95.8	95.6	93.6	100.0	100.0	93.2	81.5	48.6
1. Grade 6 or below	0.3	0.5	0.2	0.2	0.4	0.4	-	0.5	0.4	0.1	0.8	-	-	0.7	0.8	7.8
2. Grade 7 or 8	0.8	0.8	0.8	0.8	-	1.8	0.4	0.5	0.6	0.6	1.1	-	-	-	2.9	15.1
3. Grade 9 (Freshman)	1.1	1.1	1.0	1.3	-	0.3	1.4	1.4	1.0	0.9	1.4	-	-	0.5	4.9	6.9
4. Grade 10 (Sophomore)	1.1	1.5	0.8	1.4	-	0.9	2.0	0.8	0.8	0.9	1.8	-	-	1.3	4.0	16.3
5. Grade 11 (Junior)	0.9	0.9	1.0	1.0	0.1	1.2	1.4	0.1	1.1	1.1	0.7	-	-	1.8	3.6	1.8
6. Grade 12 (Senior)	0.8	0.6	1.0	1.0	0.3	0.7	0.9	1.1	0.4	0.8	0.7	-	-	2.5	2.4	3.6
Item 5650 Subject A01g N	2537	1174	1309	1974	280	524	728	782	502	1622	828	1086	605	303	480	37

E10J: Try cocaine

8. Never	85.6	83.5	87.8	85.1	93.0	80.5	89.2	91.0	76.9	87.5	82.3	100.0	100.0	77.3	52.3	15.6
1. Grade 6 or below	0.3	0.5	0.1	0.2	1.1	1.0	0.1	0.1	-	0.2	0.1	-	-	0.3	1.0	2.8
2. Grade 7 or 8	0.6	0.7	0.4	0.5	0.2	0.5	0.3	0.5	1.0	0.4	0.7	-	-	0.9	1.8	3.2
3. Grade 9 (Freshman)	2.3	3.3	1.4	2.4	-	2.8	1.5	1.1	4.6	0.9	4.8	-	-	0.2	8.7	26.9
4. Grade 10 (Sophomore)	2.9	2.9	2.8	3.1	1.2	4.5	2.7	1.5	3.8	2.4	3.9	-	-	3.5	10.1	20.3
5. Grade 11 (Junior)	4.0	4.1	3.9	4.1	2.0	4.6	2.3	3.1	7.3	4.1	3.8	-	-	6.9	13.5	16.7
6. Grade 12 (Senior)	4.4	5.1	3.6	4.5	2.6	5.9	3.7	2.8	6.3	4.4	4.5	-	-	11.0	12.5	14.6
Item 5660 Subject A01g N	2673	1224	1387	2089	290	560	773	827	513	1701	877	1089	603	345	575	36

E10K: Try heroin

8. Never	99.0	98.9	99.3	99.2	99.2	98.9	98.5	99.3	99.4	99.5	98.3	100.0	100.0	100.0	100.0	-
1. Grade 6 or below	0.1	-	0.1	-	0.4	0.7	-	-	-	-	-	-	-	-	-	6.7
2. Grade 7 or 8	0.1	0.3	-	*	-	-	-	0.3	0.2	-	0.4	-	-	-	-	15.1
3. Grade 9 (Freshman)	0.2	0.2	0.1	0.1	0.5	-	0.2	0.2	0.2	-	0.5	-	-	-	-	16.4
4. Grade 10 (Sophomore)	0.3	0.2	0.2	0.2	-	0.4	0.4	0.1	0.2	0.1	0.5	-	-	-	-	28.4
5. Grade 11 (Junior)	0.2	0.2	0.1	0.2	-	-	0.6	-	-	0.3	-	-	-	-	-	17.4
6. Grade 12 (Senior)	0.1	0.2	0.1	0.2	-	0.1	0.3	0.1	-	0.1	0.3	-	-	-	-	16.0
Item 5670 Subject A01g N	2704	1240	1400	2110	291	569	781	829	525	1708	900	1087	606	362	599	25

E10L: Try any narcotic other than heroin

8. Never	96.6	96.1	97.1	96.2	98.9	95.4	95.7	98.1	96.8	97.1	95.8	100.0	100.0	98.2	87.2	36.3
1. Grade 6 or below	0.2	0.1	0.2	0.1	0.4	0.9	0.2	-	-	0.2	-	-	-	0.5	0.4	8.2
2. Grade 7 or 8	0.3	0.5	0.1	0.4	-	0.5	0.1	0.3	0.4	0.3	0.2	-	-	0.3	0.9	6.3
3. Grade 9 (Freshman)	0.9	1.2	0.7	1.0	-	1.1	1.0	0.4	1.3	0.6	1.6	-	-	0.1	3.7	16.4
4. Grade 10 (Sophomore)	0.9	0.9	0.9	0.9	0.7	1.6	1.0	0.4	0.6	0.9	1.0	-	-	0.4	3.5	12.3
5. Grade 11 (Junior)	0.7	0.8	0.5	0.9	-	0.6	1.1	0.4	0.6	0.7	0.6	-	-	0.2	2.5	14.4
6. Grade 12 (Senior)	0.4	0.4	0.5	0.6	-	-	0.9	0.5	0.2	0.3	0.8	-	-	0.2	1.8	6.1
Item 5680 Subject A01g N	2553	1175	1319	1974	287	534	728	795	496	1629	833	1090	607	330	468	33

*=less than .05 per cent.

QUESTIONNAIRE FORM 3 1985	TOTAL	SEX		RACE		REGION				4YR COLLEGE PLANS		ILLICIT DRUG USE: LIFETIME				
		M	F	White	Black	NE	NC	S	W	Yes	No	None	Mari-juana Only	Few Pills	More Pills	Any Her-oin
N (Weighted No. of Cases):	3294	1549	1638	2464	407	770	907	1006	611	1932	1148	1258	717	446	761	48
% of Weighted Total:	100.0	47.0	49.7	74.8	12.4	23.4	27.5	30.5	18.5	58.7	34.9	38.2	21.8	13.5	23.1	1.4

E10M: Try inhalants

8. Never	91.1	88.6	93.3	90.1	99.5	88.9	90.3	93.6	90.7	92.1	89.7	99.3	94.5	85.9	76.8	46.8
1. Grade 6 or below	1.2	1.6	0.8	1.3	0.4	1.6	1.4	1.0	0.9	0.9	1.5	0.2	0.8	1.7	3.1	4.9
2. Grade 7 or 8	2.2	2.9	1.7	2.3	-	2.6	1.5	1.7	3.8	1.5	3.3	0.2	0.8	5.2	5.3	9.6
3. Grade 9 (Freshman)	1.4	1.8	1.0	1.6	0.2	2.2	1.7	0.5	1.6	1.0	1.9	0.1	0.7	1.3	3.9	20.0
4. Grade 10 (Sophomore)	1.3	1.1	1.6	1.4	-	2.3	1.6	0.9	0.7	1.3	1.5	*	0.6	1.7	4.2	7.9
5. Grade 11 (Junior)	1.7	2.5	1.0	2.1	-	1.4	3.0	1.0	1.4	2.0	1.4	-	1.7	3.0	4.4	4.1
6. Grade 12 (Senior)	1.0	1.5	0.5	1.2	-	1.1	0.5	1.4	0.9	1.2	0.6	0.2	0.9	1.2	2.2	6.7
Item 5685 Subject A01g N	2535	1148	1326	1977	276	517	731	793	493	1605	835	1053	566	334	525	32

*=less than .05 per cent.

MONITORING THE FUTURE

QUESTIONNAIRE FORM 4 1985	TOTAL	SEX		RACE		REGION				4YR COLLEGE PLANS		ILLICIT DRUG USE: LIFETIME				
		M	F	White	Black	NE	NC	S	W	Yes	No	None	Mari-juana Only	Few Pills	More Pills	Any Her-oin
N (Weighted No. of Cases):	3279	1565	1610	2464	390	772	892	1004	612	1853	1170	1312	662	442	746	24
% of Weighted Total:	100.0	47.7	49.1	75.1	11.9	23.5	27.2	30.6	18.7	56.5	35.7	40.0	20.2	13.5	22.8	0.7

A01: Taking all things together, how would you say things are these days-would you say you're very happy, pretty happy, or not too happy these days?

3. Very happy	18.7	18.3	19.1	20.5	12.5	18.8	17.9	19.0	19.0	21.1	15.5	20.6	18.0	15.6	18.8	4.2
2. Pretty happy	68.6	70.5	67.3	70.3	64.3	68.5	69.8	67.2	69.4	68.1	70.4	66.8	69.6	73.3	68.2	77.5
1. Not too happy	12.7	11.2	13.6	9.2	23.2	12.6	12.3	13.8	11.6	10.8	14.1	12.6	12.4	11.1	13.0	18.3
Item 1190 Subject P01,Q01 N	3274	1560	1610	2459	390	769	890	1004	611	1851	1170	1308	662	442	744	24

A02: Looking ahead to the next five years, do you think that things in this country will get better or worse?

1. Get much better	4.0	4.9	3.0	3.4	3.4	3.7	3.3	4.7	4.4	4.4	2.2	5.0	3.3	3.4	3.0	-
2. Get somewhat better	34.5	39.2	29.7	35.2	34.3	34.7	35.4	32.6	35.9	37.3	30.1	36.2	35.1	30.5	32.1	34.1
3. Stay about the same	32.3	30.2	34.2	34.9	20.5	33.4	32.6	32.5	30.0	31.7	34.4	31.4	33.0	35.7	33.0	24.9
4. Get somewhat worse	25.2	21.5	29.1	23.5	33.2	24.4	24.8	26.0	25.3	23.7	27.9	22.8	25.3	26.7	28.1	34.3
5. Get much worse	4.1	4.1	3.9	3.0	8.6	3.8	4.0	4.2	4.4	2.8	5.4	4.6	3.3	3.7	3.7	6.8
Item 9940 Subject I01 N	3274	1562	1608	2461	390	770	889	1004	611	1852	1169	1309	662	441	744	24

A03: Looking ahead to the next five years, do you think that things in the rest of the world will get better or worse?

1. Get much better	2.3	2.4	2.0	1.5	4.3	2.2	1.8	2.8	2.3	2.4	1.7	2.6	1.8	2.8	1.3	-
2. Get somewhat better	21.9	21.5	22.1	21.1	24.9	24.1	21.3	19.2	24.6	23.0	20.1	23.0	23.1	18.1	21.4	12.1
3. Stay about the same	31.0	30.8	31.1	33.3	23.5	32.4	34.7	30.1	25.6	30.4	32.8	31.6	34.4	28.8	28.2	35.2
4. Get somewhat worse	36.4	36.5	36.9	36.8	34.0	33.7	34.9	38.2	39.2	37.1	36.2	33.3	33.2	43.5	41.0	39.9
5. Get much worse	8.3	8.7	7.9	7.2	13.3	7.6	7.2	9.8	8.4	7.1	9.2	9.5	7.5	6.8	8.0	12.8
Item 9950 Subject I01 N	3268	1561	1603	2456	390	768	889	1002	610	1848	1166	1307	662	439	744	24

A04: How do you think your own life will go in the next five years–do you think it will get better or worse?

1. Get much better	43.3	41.4	44.8	41.3	54.4	46.3	41.0	44.1	41.6	43.6	41.2	42.0	41.8	42.8	46.1	46.8
2. Get somewhat better	45.1	46.0	44.7	46.8	37.3	43.7	44.2	45.1	48.2	45.6	45.9	47.5	47.8	44.5	41.1	38.5
3. Stay about the same	9.1	9.4	8.6	9.7	5.4	8.0	11.8	8.7	7.4	9.0	9.4	8.3	8.3	9.9	10.0	5.2
4. Get somewhat worse	2.1	2.5	1.7	2.1	1.8	1.5	2.8	1.8	2.2	1.6	2.9	2.0	1.6	2.0	2.5	9.5
5. Get much worse	0.4	0.7	0.2	0.1	1.1	0.5	0.2	0.3	0.7	0.2	0.6	0.3	0.5	0.8	0.3	-
Item 9960 Subject I01 N	3271	1560	1607	2458	388	768	889	1003	611	1851	1166	1311	660	441	742	24

A05: Some people think a lot about the social problems of the nation and the world, and about how they might be solved. Others spend little time thinking about these issues. How much do you think about such things?

1. Never	2.2	2.4	1.9	2.1	1.9	3.0	2.7	1.6	1.4	1.3	3.2	1.7	2.2	2.7	2.4	10.6
2. Seldom	18.0	19.0	17.2	19.0	14.4	16.7	21.3	15.8	18.3	15.5	21.7	16.1	18.1	22.5	19.0	23.6
3. Sometimes	50.3	49.9	50.1	51.1	47.5	53.5	48.5	52.0	46.0	49.6	50.6	50.8	53.1	47.5	48.5	47.5
4. Quite often	24.7	23.7	25.9	23.9	27.6	22.6	22.4	25.5	29.3	28.0	20.6	26.4	21.4	23.8	24.9	13.8
5. A great deal	4.9	5.0	4.9	3.8	8.5	4.2	5.1	5.1	5.0	5.6	3.9	5.0	5.2	3.6	5.2	4.5
Item 6880 Subject J,Q08 N	3275	1562	1609	2461	390	769	890	1004	612	1851	1170	1311	662	442	743	24

A06: These questions are about pollution and the environment. Please mark the circle that shows how much you agree or disagree with each statement below.

A06A: In general, pollution has increased in the U.S. in the last ten years

1. Disagree	3.6	4.7	2.4	2.7	8.2	4.2	3.9	3.9	2.0	3.4	3.5	3.7	3.6	3.7	3.2	-
2. Mostly disagree	7.6	8.5	6.7	8.4	6.8	7.1	8.4	9.3	4.4	8.9	5.1	8.2	7.3	8.7	6.6	2.1
3. Neither	7.0	8.0	6.4	7.4	5.0	5.5	9.3	6.7	6.2	7.1	7.0	6.9	5.9	9.6	6.5	19.2
4. Mostly agree	35.0	31.4	38.6	35.8	32.1	34.6	37.5	32.3	36.5	36.6	34.5	34.7	38.2	34.2	33.7	23.4
5. Agree	46.7	47.5	45.9	45.6	47.9	48.6	40.9	47.8	50.9	44.0	50.0	46.5	44.9	43.8	49.9	55.3
Item 9970 Subject F04 N	3269	1558	1607	2457	389	769	888	1001	611	1851	1167	1308	662	441	742	24

QUESTIONNAIRE FORM 4 1985	TOTAL	SEX		RACE		REGION				4YR COLLEGE PLANS		ILLICIT DRUG USE: LIFETIME				
		M	F	White	Black	NE	NC	S	W	Yes	No	None	Mari-juana Only	Few Pills	More Pills	Any Her-oin
N (Weighted No. of Cases):	3279	1565	1610	2464	390	772	892	1004	612	1853	1170	1312	662	442	746	24
% of Weighted Total:	100.0	47.7	49.1	75.1	11.9	23.5	27.2	30.6	18.7	56.5	35.7	40.0	20.2	13.5	22.8	0.7
A06B: The dangers of pollution are not really as great as government, the media, and environmental groups would like us to believe																
1.　Disagree	39.2	38.9	39.7	39.5	38.7	40.4	36.9	39.5	40.7	41.7	36.2	39.9	40.4	37.6	37.8	45.3
2.　Mostly disagree	25.9	24.9	26.9	28.2	18.5	24.7	28.6	24.8	25.0	28.5	23.7	27.0	23.6	25.5	26.9	29.7
3.　Neither	11.3	10.1	12.1	10.9	10.4	11.9	11.9	9.3	12.8	10.2	12.2	9.7	12.4	11.3	13.0	9.7
4.　Mostly agree	15.7	16.7	14.8	15.1	20.9	13.2	14.8	19.0	14.6	13.7	18.3	16.0	14.3	18.4	14.2	9.5
5.　Agree	8.0	9.4	6.5	6.3	11.4	9.8	7.8	7.3	7.0	5.9	9.6	7.4	9.3	7.1	8.2	5.8
Item 9980　Subject F04　N	*3258*	*1550*	*1604*	*2451*	*387*	*763*	*887*	*1001*	*607*	*1847*	*1164*	*1305*	*659*	*439*	*738*	*24*
A06C: America needs growth to survive, and that is going to require some increase in pollution																
1.　Disagree	36.0	34.4	37.9	35.7	40.3	39.9	33.4	35.7	35.2	37.8	34.1	36.6	36.0	35.3	36.4	32.3
2.　Mostly disagree	21.8	22.7	21.1	23.7	13.8	23.2	22.6	20.4	20.8	23.6	20.2	20.4	23.7	22.4	22.8	13.9
3.　Neither	12.1	11.6	12.4	12.5	8.4	11.2	12.8	11.0	13.8	12.1	11.5	12.4	11.7	12.5	10.8	18.8
4.　Mostly agree	18.6	19.3	17.8	19.2	18.3	16.8	22.0	17.0	18.4	17.7	19.8	17.1	18.1	21.3	19.7	21.0
5.　Agree	11.6	12.0	10.9	8.8	19.2	9.0	9.1	15.9	11.8	8.9	14.5	13.5	10.5	8.6	10.2	14.0
Item 9990　Subject F04　N	*3248*	*1552*	*1596*	*2446*	*386*	*765*	*886*	*992*	*606*	*1839*	*1160*	*1297*	*658*	*439*	*739*	*24*
A06D: People will have to change their buying habits and way of life to correct our environmental problems																
1.　Disagree	13.5	15.5	11.3	12.0	18.1	16.0	12.3	14.5	10.7	12.0	15.0	12.7	12.5	13.6	15.1	19.9
2.　Mostly disagree	14.5	15.7	13.6	15.9	11.2	12.5	16.9	13.6	15.3	16.2	12.4	12.7	15.9	14.4	16.2	20.4
3.　Neither	16.9	16.6	17.5	17.5	14.5	15.9	15.4	18.4	16.7	16.8	17.0	15.2	17.4	20.0	17.8	14.7
4.　Mostly agree	30.6	28.9	32.1	32.0	27.6	29.1	31.4	30.5	31.7	31.3	30.2	33.4	28.8	28.1	30.1	12.8
5.　Agree	24.4	23.3	25.6	22.6	28.5	25.0	22.0	26.5	23.9	23.7	25.5	26.0	25.5	23.9	20.9	32.2
Item 10000　Subject F04　N	*3251*	*1552*	*1596*	*2444*	*386*	*766*	*882*	*995*	*609*	*1840*	*1160*	*1303*	*657*	*437*	*736*	*24*
A06E: Government should take action to solve our environmental problems even if it means that some of the products we now use would have to be changed or banned																
1.　Disagree	5.9	7.6	4.1	5.2	7.8	6.6	4.9	7.0	4.7	4.6	7.1	4.9	5.5	6.2	7.3	3.4
2.　Mostly disagree	8.9	10.2	7.4	9.0	11.2	6.4	10.7	9.1	8.8	8.4	9.3	8.3	7.9	11.5	9.3	-
3.　Neither	13.1	13.9	12.3	13.2	13.3	11.0	15.7	11.7	14.4	12.6	13.8	12.8	12.7	11.1	14.5	39.2
4.　Mostly agree	34.2	30.3	38.0	35.8	29.8	35.6	34.4	32.2	35.2	35.0	34.1	33.1	36.4	32.3	35.9	22.6
5.　Agree	37.9	37.9	38.2	36.8	37.9	40.4	34.3	39.9	36.8	39.5	35.7	40.9	37.5	38.9	33.0	34.9
Item 10010　Subject F04,H02　N	*3264*	*1554*	*1608*	*2457*	*387*	*767*	*889*	*998*	*610*	*1846*	*1167*	*1308*	*659*	*440*	*741*	*24*
A06F: Government should place higher taxes on products which cause pollution in their manufacture or disposal, so that companies will be encouraged to find better ways to produce them																
1.　Disagree	13.7	15.1	12.7	11.6	21.9	14.9	12.5	14.6	12.5	11.6	16.0	13.7	12.5	13.3	14.4	24.5
2.　Mostly disagree	12.1	13.2	10.9	12.1	13.7	13.5	10.5	11.1	14.0	12.2	11.9	11.1	13.7	12.8	11.9	3.5
3.　Neither	13.8	13.2	14.6	14.8	10.5	12.5	17.6	13.7	10.1	12.8	15.1	13.0	14.4	14.7	15.2	17.3
4.　Mostly agree	27.4	23.5	30.8	28.7	24.2	26.0	27.4	27.7	28.7	29.1	25.1	29.9	27.4	23.1	25.7	9.0
5.　Agree	33.0	35.1	31.1	32.7	29.7	33.0	31.9	32.8	34.7	34.4	31.8	32.3	32.0	36.1	32.8	45.8
Item 10020　Subject F04,H02　N	*3259*	*1554*	*1605*	*2453*	*386*	*767*	*884*	*999*	*609*	*1845*	*1164*	*1305*	*660*	*439*	*738*	*24*
A06G: I wish that government would ban throw-away bottles and beverage cans																
1.　Disagree	30.3	30.2	30.8	30.4	33.1	26.8	26.1	34.2	34.2	30.4	29.8	27.9	29.6	35.6	31.2	41.6
2.　Mostly disagree	14.7	14.4	15.2	15.2	13.9	13.8	14.8	15.9	13.9	14.8	14.9	13.1	16.7	15.8	15.8	6.5
3.　Neither	24.9	22.6	27.5	26.2	19.4	24.7	25.3	23.5	27.0	26.9	22.9	26.5	24.8	23.1	25.0	28.1
4.　Mostly agree	12.7	13.5	11.5	12.5	13.9	13.5	13.4	12.5	11.0	12.3	13.1	14.0	12.1	10.5	11.8	11.4
5.　Agree	17.4	19.2	15.1	15.8	19.6	21.2	20.4	13.9	13.9	15.6	19.4	18.5	16.9	15.0	16.2	12.4
Item 10030　Subject F04,H02　N	*3244*	*1547*	*1595*	*2442*	*385*	*760*	*881*	*997*	*605*	*1839*	*1157*	*1301*	*655*	*438*	*733*	*24*

QUESTIONNAIRE FORM 4 1985	TOTAL	SEX		RACE		REGION				4YR COLLEGE PLANS		ILLICIT DRUG USE: LIFETIME				
		M	F	White	Black	NE	NC	S	W	Yes	No	None	Mari- juana Only	Few Pills	More Pills	Any Her- oin
N (Weighted No. of Cases):	3279	1565	1610	2464	390	772	892	1004	612	1853	1170	1312	662	442	746	24
% of Weighted Total:	100.0	47.7	49.1	75.1	11.9	23.5	27.2	30.6	18.7	56.5	35.7	40.0	20.2	13.5	22.8	0.7
A06H: T.V. commercials stimulate people to buy a lot of things they don't really need																
1. Disagree	5.8	7.3	4.1	5.1	8.0	6.3	5.8	6.5	4.0	5.6	5.5	5.4	6.9	5.9	4.6	11.0
2. Mostly disagree	6.9	8.8	5.1	7.6	4.5	6.5	8.8	5.7	6.5	7.4	5.6	6.4	5.7	6.9	8.3	2.4
3. Neither	7.6	9.3	6.1	8.1	5.4	7.3	9.0	5.9	8.5	8.1	6.9	7.2	9.6	6.6	7.9	7.4
4. Mostly agree	27.9	29.4	26.5	29.1	28.0	27.6	29.3	27.2	27.6	28.4	27.4	26.0	30.2	28.4	28.7	40.2
5. Agree	51.8	45.2	58.3	50.1	54.1	52.3	47.0	54.8	53.5	50.4	54.6	55.0	47.6	52.3	50.6	38.9
Item 10040 Subject F02 N	3260	1555	1602	2454	386	766	885	999	610	1843	1166	1306	660	439	739	24
A06I: T.V. commercials do a lot of good by showing new products that we might not know about otherwise																
1. Disagree	5.8	6.2	5.5	5.5	6.2	6.6	5.1	5.0	7.1	6.0	5.3	5.5	5.5	6.0	6.1	6.3
2. Mostly disagree	8.8	9.0	8.6	10.0	4.0	10.0	9.6	6.7	9.7	10.6	6.8	8.3	11.4	8.8	7.8	2.1
3. Neither	16.0	16.6	15.3	17.7	10.8	18.3	17.1	12.5	17.2	17.4	13.9	14.6	16.0	12.6	19.3	25.4
4. Mostly agree	36.6	36.2	37.2	38.2	31.0	34.8	37.7	36.4	37.8	37.1	36.9	36.9	37.7	39.2	35.4	35.9
5. Agree	32.8	32.0	33.4	28.6	48.0	30.4	30.5	39.4	28.1	28.8	37.1	34.7	29.4	33.3	31.4	30.3
Item 10050 Subject F02 N	3246	1552	1592	2444	383	756	885	996	609	1846	1153	1299	661	438	730	24
A06J: My family and I often buy things we don't really need; we could get along with much less																
1. Disagree	13.9	12.2	15.4	11.9	20.5	14.6	13.5	13.5	14.5	12.6	15.7	14.6	13.5	14.6	12.9	10.5
2. Mostly disagree	14.4	16.6	12.2	13.9	13.0	17.4	14.7	11.0	15.7	13.8	13.8	14.7	12.5	17.5	13.4	16.2
3. Neither	13.4	15.8	11.0	14.3	11.9	13.5	16.4	12.1	10.9	13.5	13.3	11.5	17.5	13.7	13.3	15.6
4. Mostly agree	28.1	29.5	26.9	30.1	23.0	25.7	29.2	27.7	30.0	30.3	25.1	28.9	27.0	26.7	28.0	21.8
5. Agree	30.2	25.9	34.5	29.7	31.6	28.8	26.2	35.7	29.0	29.7	32.1	30.2	29.5	27.5	32.4	35.9
Item 10060 Subject F01 N	3255	1554	1599	2451	385	763	887	997	607	1842	1163	1301	657	439	739	24
A06K: By the year 2000, engineers and scientists will probably have invented devices that will solve our pollution problems																
1. Disagree	11.9	13.5	10.2	11.2	13.1	13.5	12.7	9.7	12.4	11.6	12.3	12.3	11.4	11.5	11.4	21.7
2. Mostly disagree	19.1	20.1	18.7	20.5	13.0	18.6	17.7	19.0	22.2	21.2	17.2	19.5	20.7	19.2	18.3	5.0
3. Neither	22.6	18.6	26.3	23.4	19.7	21.6	26.3	20.7	21.8	21.8	24.1	21.7	21.2	25.8	23.2	28.6
4. Mostly agree	30.7	31.0	30.4	32.0	26.3	30.2	29.6	32.6	29.9	32.4	28.0	30.9	28.9	28.3	33.8	27.3
5. Agree	15.6	16.7	14.4	12.8	27.3	16.2	13.8	18.1	13.7	13.0	18.5	15.5	17.8	15.2	13.3	17.4
Item 10070 Subject F04 N	3258	1554	1604	2450	387	764	888	996	610	1849	1161	1303	662	439	739	24
A07: In your own actions–the things you buy and the things you do–how much of an effort do you make to conserve energy and protect the environment?																
1. None	7.0	6.2	8.1	6.8	8.4	8.9	7.3	6.7	4.9	6.6	7.9	5.4	5.7	6.8	10.9	16.9
2. A little	28.1	27.0	29.1	28.2	28.6	27.6	28.0	28.6	28.3	28.5	26.7	25.5	29.8	29.4	30.7	16.6
3. Some	52.2	54.4	50.3	53.5	45.3	52.2	53.1	50.4	53.7	52.5	52.8	54.2	52.4	54.5	48.1	52.4
4. Quite a bit	12.6	12.4	12.5	11.5	17.7	11.3	11.5	14.3	13.1	12.4	12.6	14.9	12.2	9.4	10.4	14.1
Item 10080 Subject F04 N	3162	1484	1580	2391	368	741	863	971	587	1804	1125	1269	638	428	715	22
The next questions are about work.																
A08: Different people may look for different things in their work. Below is a list of some of these things. Please read each one, then indicate how important this thing is for you.																
A08A: A job where you can see the results of what you do																
1. Not important	0.6	1.0	0.3	0.4	1.0	0.9	0.4	0.8	0.4	0.5	0.8	0.6	0.1	1.1	0.9	—
2. A little important	6.0	7.2	5.1	6.5	4.6	7.5	8.1	4.2	4.3	5.7	7.0	6.1	4.2	6.9	6.5	16.0
3. Pretty important	35.1	37.0	33.5	37.9	21.3	32.0	37.5	33.7	37.7	36.0	35.8	36.2	32.9	33.8	37.6	33.8
4. Very important	58.2	54.9	61.1	55.2	73.1	59.7	54.0	61.3	57.5	57.8	56.4	57.1	62.8	58.2	55.0	50.2
Item 10090 Subject C04 N	3251	1551	1596	2450	383	764	883	995	608	1842	1161	1298	657	440	739	24

QUESTIONNAIRE FORM 4 1985	TOTAL	SEX		RACE		REGION				4YR COLLEGE PLANS		ILLICIT DRUG USE: LIFETIME				
		M	F	White	Black	NE	NC	S	W	Yes	No	None	Mari-juana Only	Few Pills	More Pills	Any Her-oin
N (Weighted No. of Cases):	3279	1565	1610	2464	390	772	892	1004	612	1853	1170	1312	662	442	746	24
% of Weighted Total:	100.0	47.7	49.1	75.1	11.9	23.5	27.2	30.6	18.7	56.5	35.7	40.0	20.2	13.5	22.8	0.7

A08B: A job that has high status and prestige

	TOTAL	M	F	White	Black	NE	NC	S	W	Yes	No	None	Mari-juana Only	Few Pills	More Pills	Any Her-oin
1. Not important	6.8	7.2	6.7	7.6	3.7	8.6	6.6	6.2	5.9	7.5	6.2	7.5	5.7	6.8	6.8	-
2. A little important	23.7	22.7	25.2	26.7	13.0	23.4	25.9	21.0	25.1	23.6	24.5	24.3	23.8	28.4	20.6	11.1
3. Pretty important	38.0	39.1	36.2	39.0	30.6	35.9	41.3	37.5	36.7	37.6	39.0	37.3	39.0	37.9	37.8	64.7
4. Very important	31.5	31.1	31.9	26.7	52.8	32.1	26.2	35.3	32.3	31.2	30.3	30.9	31.4	27.0	34.8	24.2
Item 10100 Subject C04 N	3239	1545	1591	2445	380	764	881	989	605	1836	1159	1291	657	440	737	24

A08C: A job which is interesting to do

	TOTAL	M	F	White	Black	NE	NC	S	W	Yes	No	None	Mari-juana Only	Few Pills	More Pills	Any Her-oin
1. Not important	0.4	0.6	0.3	0.3	0.7	0.1	0.8	0.5	0.4	0.4	0.6	0.1	0.5	0.7	0.6	-
2. A little important	1.4	1.4	1.0	1.1	1.2	1.9	1.3	1.4	0.7	0.9	1.5	1.5	1.1	1.6	1.2	-
3. Pretty important	11.6	13.1	9.8	10.3	18.8	9.9	12.4	12.8	10.8	10.5	13.0	11.7	11.1	11.2	10.4	18.8
4. Very important	86.6	85.0	89.0	88.2	79.3	88.2	85.6	85.3	88.1	88.2	84.9	86.7	87.4	86.5	87.8	81.2
Item 10110 Subject C04 N	3227	1543	1583	2436	377	757	880	986	605	1828	1157	1285	652	440	734	24

A08D: A job where the chances for advancement and promotion are good

	TOTAL	M	F	White	Black	NE	NC	S	W	Yes	No	None	Mari-juana Only	Few Pills	More Pills	Any Her-oin
1. Not important	1.3	1.3	1.3	1.3	0.8	0.8	1.6	1.2	1.5	1.4	1.4	1.2	1.7	1.9	0.6	5.4
2. A little important	5.6	5.4	5.8	6.5	1.4	5.2	6.5	5.0	5.9	6.6	4.7	6.5	5.1	4.3	5.5	2.1
3. Pretty important	25.7	24.7	26.6	27.2	19.5	25.9	27.6	23.3	26.6	25.9	25.1	28.9	25.5	24.1	22.5	31.5
4. Very important	67.4	68.6	66.3	65.0	78.3	68.0	64.3	70.5	66.1	66.1	68.7	63.4	67.8	69.7	71.4	61.0
Item 10120 Subject C04 N	3252	1551	1598	2450	385	764	885	997	606	1840	1162	1299	656	441	739	24

A08E: A job that gives you an opportunity to be directly helpful to others

	TOTAL	M	F	White	Black	NE	NC	S	W	Yes	No	None	Mari-juana Only	Few Pills	More Pills	Any Her-oin
1. Not important	2.0	3.0	0.9	2.2	0.7	2.3	2.7	1.5	1.4	1.8	2.4	1.6	1.6	2.6	2.8	2.2
2. A little important	14.8	21.5	8.0	15.6	9.7	16.5	15.1	13.3	14.5	14.2	15.8	12.4	14.8	14.1	20.1	19.1
3. Pretty important	37.0	40.7	33.4	38.5	29.2	36.0	36.6	36.2	40.2	37.6	36.2	35.9	37.4	38.5	36.8	61.7
4. Very important	46.2	34.7	57.7	43.7	60.4	45.2	45.6	49.0	43.9	46.4	45.6	50.1	46.3	44.9	40.3	16.9
Item 10130 Subject C04,O01 N	3250	1547	1600	2449	384	763	883	997	607	1839	1163	1300	654	441	739	24

A08F: A job which provides you with a chance to earn a good deal of money

	TOTAL	M	F	White	Black	NE	NC	S	W	Yes	No	None	Mari-juana Only	Few Pills	More Pills	Any Her-oin
1. Not important	2.0	1.7	2.5	2.3	0.7	1.9	2.8	1.8	1.4	2.6	1.4	3.0	1.3	0.8	1.4	-
2. A little important	7.4	6.9	7.7	8.4	3.4	7.4	8.8	6.1	7.4	8.6	6.0	7.7	8.1	10.3	4.8	4.0
3. Pretty important	30.6	27.1	34.5	33.3	20.6	29.0	33.0	27.8	33.5	34.6	25.9	33.2	30.3	27.2	29.1	24.6
4. Very important	60.0	64.3	55.3	55.9	75.3	61.8	55.4	64.3	57.6	54.2	66.7	56.1	60.2	61.7	64.6	71.4
Item 10140 Subject C04,F01 N	3252	1549	1600	2451	386	763	885	996	608	1842	1162	1300	657	440	738	24

A08G: A job where you have the chance to be creative

	TOTAL	M	F	White	Black	NE	NC	S	W	Yes	No	None	Mari-juana Only	Few Pills	More Pills	Any Her-oin
1. Not important	5.1	6.5	3.8	5.6	4.4	5.7	6.1	5.0	3.3	4.1	6.2	5.1	4.6	5.2	5.7	-
2. A little important	22.2	22.4	22.0	23.0	19.1	20.2	24.2	23.4	19.8	20.7	25.5	21.5	19.6	26.6	23.3	25.9
3. Pretty important	35.7	36.2	35.6	36.1	36.2	33.3	36.1	36.1	37.7	37.7	33.7	36.2	38.6	35.2	32.5	54.6
4. Very important	36.9	34.9	38.6	35.3	40.3	40.8	33.6	35.6	39.2	37.5	34.6	37.2	37.3	33.0	38.6	19.5
Item 10150 Subject C04 N	3248	1546	1599	2446	386	764	883	994	607	1839	1160	1298	657	440	737	24

A08H: A job where the skills you learn will not go out of date

	TOTAL	M	F	White	Black	NE	NC	S	W	Yes	No	None	Mari-juana Only	Few Pills	More Pills	Any Her-oin
1. Not important	3.1	2.9	3.1	2.9	4.9	2.5	3.6	3.1	3.0	3.3	2.8	3.5	3.1	2.4	2.6	5.4
2. A little important	9.0	9.1	9.1	9.8	5.7	10.5	8.3	8.2	9.6	10.4	7.5	9.3	7.7	9.4	9.8	5.6
3. Pretty important	32.5	31.8	32.9	33.6	27.2	30.9	34.0	31.5	34.0	32.5	33.5	30.9	35.2	32.2	32.3	32.1
4. Very important	55.4	56.2	54.9	53.7	62.2	56.0	54.1	57.3	53.4	53.8	56.2	56.3	54.0	55.9	55.3	56.9
Item 10160 Subject C04 N	3247	1550	1593	2449	382	763	885	993	606	1840	1160	1297	655	441	738	24

A08I: A job that gives you a chance to make friends

	TOTAL	M	F	White	Black	NE	NC	S	W	Yes	No	None	Mari-juana Only	Few Pills	More Pills	Any Her-oin
1. Not important	2.0	2.7	1.1	1.5	4.1	2.8	1.3	2.1	1.7	1.8	2.1	2.2	1.3	0.7	2.5	-
2. A little important	10.3	12.1	8.3	9.8	14.2	10.3	11.8	10.1	8.5	9.6	10.7	9.3	10.7	12.4	10.1	5.2
3. Pretty important	34.9	40.4	29.2	36.3	29.2	33.6	36.4	33.9	35.8	34.7	35.5	33.8	37.5	34.3	35.5	53.6
4. Very important	52.9	44.8	61.4	52.5	52.5	53.2	50.6	53.9	54.0	53.8	51.6	54.6	50.5	52.5	51.9	41.2
Item 10170 Subject C04,M04 N	3253	1549	1600	2451	385	764	884	997	608	1842	1162	1299	657	441	739	24

QUESTIONNAIRE FORM 4 1985	TOTAL	SEX		RACE		REGION				4YR COLLEGE PLANS		ILLICIT DRUG USE: LIFETIME				
		M	F	White	Black	NE	NC	S	W	Yes	No	None	Marijuana Only	Few Pills	More Pills	Any Heroin
N (Weighted No. of Cases):	3279	1565	1610	2464	390	772	892	1004	612	1853	1170	1312	662	442	746	24
% of Weighted Total:	100.0	47.7	49.1	75.1	11.9	23.5	27.2	30.6	18.7	56.5	35.7	40.0	20.2	13.5	22.8	0.7

A08J: A job which uses your skills and abilities–lets you do the things you can do best

1. Not important	0.6	0.9	0.1	0.4	0.7	1.1	0.6	0.3	0.2	0.5	0.5	0.6	0.5	0.2	0.6	-
2. A little important	3.8	4.4	3.1	25.2	4.3	5.0	4.3	3.4	2.1	3.1	4.9	3.7	3.6	4.7	3.6	13.6
3. Pretty important	24.2	27.7	20.9	25.2	21.3	22.9	24.1	24.4	25.7	23.4	25.9	23.1	26.0	20.9	26.2	40.8
4. Very important	71.4	67.0	75.9	70.6	73.6	71.0	70.9	71.8	72.1	73.0	68.6	72.7	69.9	74.2	69.6	45.6
Item 10180 Subject C04 N	3247	1547	1597	2445	386	764	881	995	608	1838	1160	1299	656	438	737	24

A08K: A job that is worthwhile to society

1. Not important	3.3	4.3	2.2	3.2	3.2	5.1	2.5	3.1	2.4	2.5	3.8	2.4	2.7	4.2	4.2	8.6
2. A little important	14.7	19.1	10.4	15.4	10.3	16.0	14.8	12.2	17.2	13.1	17.9	13.3	12.4	15.5	19.0	11.7
3. Pretty important	37.0	37.8	36.1	38.7	28.8	37.7	38.9	35.1	36.8	36.6	37.7	35.0	36.6	42.1	37.7	44.9
4. Very important	45.0	38.8	51.3	42.7	57.7	41.2	43.8	49.6	43.7	47.8	40.6	49.3	48.3	38.1	39.0	34.8
Item 10190 Subject C04,O01 N	3236	1543	1593	2437	384	758	880	992	606	1836	1154	1294	654	440	731	24

A08L: A job where you have more than two weeks vacation

1. Not important	17.9	14.5	21.5	18.7	17.4	17.4	20.4	19.3	12.8	17.6	19.0	19.5	18.5	15.4	16.5	17.9
2. A little important	33.9	30.0	37.9	35.2	29.3	33.3	34.3	33.1	35.3	34.5	32.9	34.8	33.1	32.5	33.6	25.4
3. Pretty important	26.4	28.7	24.0	26.4	27.5	26.0	28.0	25.2	26.8	26.1	27.1	26.0	26.1	31.3	26.0	18.9
4. Very important	21.7	26.8	16.6	19.7	25.8	23.3	17.3	22.4	25.1	21.7	21.0	19.7	22.3	20.8	23.9	37.9
Item 10200 Subject C04 N	3245	1549	1594	2447	383	763	883	993	607	1839	1160	1296	655	440	738	24

A08M: A job where you get a chance to participate in decision making

1. Not important	3.8	4.6	2.9	3.7	3.4	5.8	3.8	3.2	2.3	2.8	5.1	4.4	2.7	4.1	3.1	11.2
2. A little important	19.2	20.1	18.4	20.4	13.9	19.3	21.4	19.0	16.2	16.7	23.4	19.9	17.2	21.7	18.6	5.2
3. Pretty important	45.4	45.5	45.2	47.0	39.4	42.1	46.8	45.7	46.8	46.1	45.2	45.5	49.0	43.4	44.0	50.9
4. Very important	31.6	29.9	33.5	28.9	43.4	32.8	27.9	32.1	34.6	34.3	26.3	30.2	31.1	30.8	34.4	32.7
Item 10210 Subject C04 N	3245	1547	1595	2445	384	762	883	994	607	1838	1158	1296	656	441	737	23

A08N: A job which leaves a lot of time for other things in your life

1. Not important	2.0	1.5	2.4	1.7	3.4	2.6	1.8	2.4	0.7	1.9	1.7	2.5	1.8	1.7	1.2	-
2. A little important	15.8	12.2	19.4	16.6	15.3	13.7	18.4	16.6	13.2	15.8	16.2	16.8	17.3	13.6	13.8	18.5
3. Pretty important	40.5	39.7	41.3	43.0	33.0	39.7	41.2	39.4	42.2	41.5	40.0	39.7	40.7	41.0	42.6	45.4
4. Very important	41.8	46.6	36.9	38.6	48.3	44.1	38.6	41.5	44.0	40.8	42.1	41.0	40.2	43.7	42.4	36.1
Item 10220 Subject C04 N	3231	1539	1591	2434	382	760	879	990	602	1829	1158	1289	654	439	734	24

A08O: A job which allows you to establish roots in a community and not have to move from place to place

1. Not important	10.3	10.6	9.9	10.0	11.1	11.4	12.1	8.5	9.0	10.9	8.7	9.0	8.5	11.8	12.4	7.9
2. A little important	18.9	17.2	20.8	18.5	22.6	20.1	16.9	18.8	20.6	19.4	18.2	17.9	20.6	20.4	19.3	11.8
3. Pretty important	32.1	32.4	31.9	32.9	29.0	33.6	33.8	29.9	31.5	34.2	31.2	33.3	34.0	27.9	31.4	44.7
4. Very important	38.7	39.8	37.4	38.6	37.4	34.9	37.1	42.7	38.9	35.5	41.9	39.9	36.9	39.9	36.9	35.6
Item 10230 Subject C04 N	3248	1549	1596	2446	384	764	883	996	604	1840	1159	1297	657	437	739	24

A08P: A job which leaves you mostly free of supervision by others

1. Not important	7.3	6.4	8.1	7.0	9.1	6.8	7.0	8.8	6.2	7.2	6.9	7.1	8.6	8.4	5.9	3.1
2. A little important	26.8	25.0	28.9	27.8	26.1	24.0	29.9	26.6	26.2	27.0	26.1	28.6	28.3	25.4	22.9	22.9
3. Pretty important	40.3	40.7	40.1	41.2	40.6	42.0	39.3	40.1	39.6	40.7	41.2	40.9	40.0	41.0	40.0	40.2
4. Very important	25.6	27.9	22.8	24.1	24.2	27.2	23.8	24.5	28.0	25.2	25.7	23.5	23.1	26.7	28.8	33.7
Item 10240 Subject C04 N	3250	1550	1597	2448	385	763	885	997	605	1840	1162	1299	657	440	739	24

QUESTIONNAIRE FORM 4 1985	TOTAL	SEX		RACE		REGION				4YR COLLEGE PLANS		ILLICIT DRUG USE: LIFETIME				
		M	F	White	Black	NE	NC	S	W	Yes	No	None	Mari- juana Only	Few Pills	More Pills	Any Her- oin
N (Weighted No. of Cases):	3279	1565	1610	2464	390	772	892	1004	612	1853	1170	1312	662	442	746	24
% of Weighted Total:	100.0	47.7	49.1	75.1	11.9	23.5	27.2	30.6	18.7	56.5	35.7	40.0	20.2	13.5	22.8	0.7
A08Q: A job that offers a reasonably predictable, secure future																
1. Not important	1.4	1.3	1.5	1.5	0.6	1.5	1.2	0.9	2.4	1.7	1.0	1.3	1.4	1.0	1.9	-
2. A little important	5.1	5.9	4.3	5.1	3.7	6.2	5.3	4.2	5.2	5.9	3.9	5.4	4.7	3.8	5.2	7.8
3. Pretty important	27.6	28.7	26.8	30.0	20.4	28.8	29.0	24.4	29.5	29.3	25.5	26.9	29.2	29.6	26.6	42.5
4. Very important	65.8	64.1	67.4	63.5	75.3	63.5	64.6	70.5	62.9	63.1	69.6	66.3	64.7	65.7	66.3	49.7
Item 10250　Subject C04　N	3243	1546	1595	2444	385	760	885	994	604	1837	1158	1298	656	440	735	23
A08R: A job where you can learn new things, learn new skills																
1. Not important	1.6	2.3	0.8	1.6	2.1	2.0	1.8	1.1	1.9	1.7	1.3	1.3	1.6	1.9	1.9	5.6
2. A little important	11.4	12.9	10.4	13.1	5.1	12.0	13.3	10.2	9.9	12.8	9.8	10.8	12.0	12.6	12.3	10.7
3. Pretty important	39.4	41.3	37.6	42.7	26.4	39.1	40.4	38.8	39.3	42.3	37.0	37.3	39.9	40.4	41.2	56.7
4. Very important	47.6	43.4	51.1	42.7	66.4	47.0	44.5	50.0	48.8	43.2	52.0	50.6	46.6	45.1	44.7	27.0
Item 10260　Subject B02,C04　N	3246	1547	1597	2447	384	760	885	994	607	1841	1158	1299	656	440	737	23
A08S: A job where you do not have to pretend to be a type of person that you are not																
1. Not important	5.3	6.4	3.9	5.0	7.7	5.8	5.8	4.5	5.4	4.0	7.1	5.2	5.1	5.9	5.5	-
2. A little important	5.4	6.7	3.8	4.9	7.3	6.2	5.0	5.3	4.8	4.4	6.0	5.1	5.2	6.9	4.8	7.2
3. Pretty important	19.0	24.3	13.5	19.4	15.6	19.1	20.7	16.8	20.0	19.4	18.6	18.0	20.7	18.0	18.9	44.2
4. Very important	70.3	62.5	78.7	70.8	69.4	68.9	68.5	73.4	69.8	72.2	68.2	71.7	69.0	69.2	70.8	48.6
Item 10270　Subject C04　N	3242	1544	1596	2445	383	759	885	991	607	1839	1159	1295	655	441	736	23
A08T: A job that most people look up to and respect																
1. Not important	4.9	6.2	3.7	5.0	5.1	4.8	5.4	4.7	4.5	4.8	4.7	4.8	3.7	5.8	5.0	3.3
2. A little important	16.0	16.5	15.4	17.8	9.2	18.4	16.3	13.9	15.9	15.6	17.0	15.2	16.7	14.2	18.5	15.0
3. Pretty important	36.7	36.9	36.6	38.9	26.1	36.1	39.3	33.9	38.1	37.5	37.1	36.1	36.5	42.1	35.1	50.0
4. Very important	42.4	40.4	44.3	38.3	59.6	40.7	38.9	47.5	41.4	42.1	41.3	44.0	43.1	37.8	41.4	31.7
Item 10280　Subject C04　N	3242	1545	1595	2444	384	760	884	993	605	1838	1156	1296	655	440	736	23
A08U: A job that permits contact with a lot of people																
1. Not important	8.1	10.1	5.7	7.9	8.4	8.9	7.2	9.0	6.6	6.3	10.4	7.0	7.6	7.9	10.2	11.0
2. A little important	22.4	28.4	16.4	23.1	20.1	21.1	24.2	22.0	22.0	19.8	26.2	22.6	23.4	24.7	19.9	21.6
3. Pretty important	35.3	35.5	35.3	36.0	36.4	34.5	34.8	36.8	34.6	37.2	33.4	34.6	35.7	32.4	37.3	46.7
4. Very important	34.3	26.0	42.6	32.9	35.2	35.5	33.8	32.3	36.7	36.7	30.0	35.8	33.2	35.0	32.5	20.7
Item 10290　Subject C04,M05　N	3235	1539	1593	2437	383	757	883	990	604	1835	1154	1296	651	438	734	23
A08V: A job with an easy pace that lets you work slowly																
1. Not important	25.9	26.9	25.4	26.3	27.3	25.7	26.5	24.7	27.2	28.8	21.2	25.7	29.4	22.3	24.9	25.8
2. A little important	38.4	36.1	40.6	40.3	31.1	34.9	40.9	38.0	40.1	38.5	40.2	38.8	36.1	41.0	40.5	23.9
3. Pretty important	25.0	25.1	25.0	24.1	27.4	27.3	21.4	27.2	24.0	22.7	27.5	24.5	25.4	28.9	22.7	40.3
4. Very important	10.7	11.9	9.0	9.3	14.3	12.1	11.3	10.2	8.7	10.0	11.1	11.0	9.1	7.7	11.8	9.9
Item 10300　Subject C04　N	3236	1541	1595	2439	384	758	883	992	604	1836	1155	1295	655	439	735	23
A08W: A job where most problems are quite difficult and challenging																
1. Not important	15.1	14.9	15.6	15.4	15.4	17.2	15.6	14.6	12.9	13.7	17.8	14.0	14.5	16.5	17.2	11.7
2. A little important	34.6	31.9	37.0	35.4	32.0	31.0	38.5	34.4	33.5	31.7	39.3	35.1	32.3	34.4	35.9	38.8
3. Pretty important	37.5	39.5	35.8	37.4	35.0	41.6	33.7	35.4	41.3	40.1	33.8	37.1	40.7	36.9	36.1	42.1
4. Very important	12.8	13.7	11.6	11.8	17.5	10.2	12.2	15.7	12.3	14.4	9.1	13.8	12.5	12.2	10.8	7.5
Item 10310　Subject C04　N	3241	1545	1595	2443	385	758	885	993	605	1837	1158	1296	656	441	735	23

QUESTIONNAIRE FORM 4 1985	TOTAL	SEX		RACE		REGION				4YR COLLEGE PLANS		ILLICIT DRUG USE: LIFETIME				
		M	F	White	Black	NE	NC	S	W	Yes	No	None	Marijuana Only	Few Pills	More Pills	Any Heroin
N (Weighted No. of Cases):	3279	1565	1610	2464	390	772	892	1004	612	1853	1170	1312	662	442	746	24
% of Weighted Total:	100.0	47.7	49.1	75.1	11.9	23.5	27.2	30.6	18.7	56.5	35.7	40.0	20.2	13.5	22.8	0.7

A09: What kind of work do you think you will be doing when you are 30 years old? Mark the one that comes closest to what you expect to be doing.

	TOTAL	M	F	White	Black	NE	NC	S	W	Yes	No	None	Marijuana Only	Few Pills	More Pills	Any Heroin
01. Laborer (car washer, sanitary worker, farm laborer)	0.3	0.5	-	0.1	1.0	0.1	0.4	0.2	0.2	0.1	0.5	0.2	0.4	-	0.1	9.5
02. Service worker (cook, waiter, barber, janitor, gas station attendant, practical nurse, beautician)	2.7	0.6	4.3	2.6	5.0	2.1	4.4	2.5	1.3	1.0	5.4	2.4	3.2	3.8	2.4	-
03. Operative or semi-skilled worker (garage worker, taxicab, bus or truck driver, assembly line worker, welder)	2.2	4.0	0.3	2.2	2.6	2.2	2.7	2.7	0.8	0.3	5.2	2.4	1.9	2.6	2.1	4.3
04. Sales clerk in a retail store (shoe salesperson, department store clerk, drug store clerk)	1.2	0.6	1.7	0.9	3.0	0.9	0.8	1.5	1.8	0.5	2.0	1.2	0.7	1.1	1.4	2.1
05. Clerical or office worker (bank teller, bookkeeper, secretary, typist, postal clerk or carrier, ticket agent)	9.7	1.8	17.3	9.3	13.3	10.0	10.8	10.5	6.5	4.9	17.1	10.0	6.7	9.8	11.3	12.3
06. Protective service (police officer, fireman, detective)	3.3	5.3	1.3	3.5	2.0	3.9	2.9	1.9	5.1	2.4	4.8	3.0	4.7	4.1	2.3	-
07. Military service	4.1	6.5	1.7	3.4	10.2	2.2	3.4	5.4	5.4	2.8	5.6	3.9	4.0	5.1	4.1	-
08. Craftsman or skilled worker (carpenter, electrician, brick layer, mechanic, machinist, tool and die maker, telephone installer)	8.9	17.5	0.6	9.3	7.3	10.7	9.5	8.1	6.9	3.2	17.0	7.8	8.6	9.0	10.0	17.8
09. Farm owner, farm manager	0.9	1.4	0.4	1.0	-	0.5	1.5	0.8	0.7	0.6	1.5	1.3	0.5	0.4	1.0	3.3
10. Owner of small business (restaurant owner, shop owner)	6.4	6.6	6.1	6.5	5.9	6.4	5.7	6.5	7.4	5.3	8.5	4.6	6.9	7.7	8.4	-
11. Sales representative (insurance agent, real estate broker, bond salesman)	1.7	2.3	1.1	1.7	1.1	1.7	1.0	2.0	2.4	2.3	0.9	1.0	1.5	3.4	1.9	2.7
12. Manager or administrator (office manager, sales manager, school administrator, government official)	8.9	7.7	10.1	8.0	10.4	9.8	7.8	8.4	10.2	11.3	5.6	8.8	10.8	9.5	7.2	4.9
13. Professional without doctoral degree (registered nurse, librarian, engineer, architect, social worker, technician, accountant, actor, artist, musician)	28.6	27.1	30.6	29.4	24.5	31.2	27.4	27.7	28.7	37.9	14.5	31.9	27.5	23.0	28.4	19.8
14. Professional with doctoral degree or equivalent (lawyer, physician, dentist, scientist, college professor)	13.4	12.8	14.3	14.1	10.0	11.1	12.2	14.9	15.8	21.3	1.7	13.7	15.9	11.5	12.7	6.4
15. Full-time homemaker or housewife	2.1	0.1	4.0	2.4	0.8	2.2	2.5	1.8	1.8	0.9	4.2	2.7	1.4	2.7	1.2	-
16. Don't know-GO TO Q.A13	5.6	5.1	6.1	5.6	2.8	5.2	6.9	5.1	4.8	5.4	5.6	5.1	5.4	6.3	5.5	16.9
Item 10320 Subject C03 N	3092	1469	1535	2359	353	728	851	932	580	1784	1095	1238	633	421	705	20

A10: How likely do you think it is that you will actually get to do this kind of work?

	TOTAL	M	F	White	Black	NE	NC	S	W	Yes	No	None	Marijuana Only	Few Pills	More Pills	Any Heroin
1. Not very likely	0.5	0.7	0.3	0.4	0.1	1.0	0.4	0.2	0.4	0.3	0.6	0.9	0.2	0.2	0.3	-
2. Somewhat likely	6.4	6.9	5.9	5.6	8.8	4.9	6.7	6.6	7.5	5.4	7.4	6.6	6.1	6.0	7.7	3.1
3. Fairly likely	22.4	23.4	21.0	22.1	22.7	21.4	26.5	20.5	20.7	21.3	24.4	22.0	24.8	20.6	21.3	25.0
4. Very likely	47.0	45.6	48.1	48.4	43.6	48.1	44.2	50.3	44.2	52.8	39.2	47.3	48.1	46.0	46.3	35.4
5. Certain	16.7	14.9	18.7	16.1	19.6	16.4	14.5	16.8	20.2	16.4	16.5	17.4	15.7	19.8	15.3	9.2
6. I already do this kind of work	7.1	8.4	6.0	7.4	5.1	8.3	7.7	5.6	7.1	3.8	11.9	6.4	5.0	7.3	9.2	27.3
Item 10330 Subject C03 N★	3004	1436	1473	2265	369	706	808	921	570	1718	1068	1207	613	405	681	17

A11: How certain are you that this kind of work is a good choice for you?

	TOTAL	M	F	White	Black	NE	NC	S	W	Yes	No	None	Marijuana Only	Few Pills	More Pills	Any Heroin
1. Not at all certain	2.6	2.2	2.8	2.6	2.3	3.5	2.3	2.5	2.2	2.5	2.6	2.6	2.5	1.8	2.8	6.9
2. Somewhat certain	7.6	7.3	7.4	6.7	10.0	7.5	8.0	7.5	7.4	6.7	8.1	7.2	7.4	5.2	9.1	10.6
3. Fairly certain	31.2	31.7	31.3	33.5	22.3	27.8	33.1	31.3	32.6	33.0	29.9	29.4	29.2	35.5	34.4	14.2
4. Very certain	41.0	42.3	39.5	40.8	42.7	43.4	38.7	41.6	40.1	42.5	39.2	44.0	43.6	38.6	35.2	55.4
5. Completely certain	17.6	16.4	19.0	16.4	22.7	17.8	17.9	17.1	17.7	15.3	20.1	16.8	17.3	18.9	18.4	12.9
Item 10340 Subject C03 N★	3023	1445	1481	2277	370	710	813	926	574	1721	1081	1214	618	406	687	17

★=excludes respondents for whom question was inappropriate.

QUESTIONNAIRE FORM 4 1985	TOTAL	SEX		RACE		REGION				4YR COLLEGE PLANS		ILLICIT DRUG USE: LIFETIME				
		M	F	White	Black	NE	NC	S	W	Yes	No	None	Marijuana Only	Few Pills	More Pills	Any Heroin
N (Weighted No. of Cases):	3279	1565	1610	2464	390	772	892	1004	612	1853	1170	1312	662	442	746	24
% of Weighted Total:	100.0	47.7	49.1	75.1	11.9	23.5	27.2	30.6	18.7	56.5	35.7	40.0	20.2	13.5	22.8	0.7

A12: How satisfying do you think this kind of work will be for you?

1. Not very satisfying	0.6	0.4	0.6	0.5	1.1	0.7	0.4	0.8	0.7	0.3	1.0	0.5	0.6	0.2	1.0	-
2. Somewhat satisfying	4.6	5.1	3.8	4.3	6.2	4.9	4.9	4.2	4.5	2.9	6.8	3.9	4.4	3.9	6.3	-
3. Quite satisfying	24.7	25.7	23.5	25.7	18.6	23.9	29.4	23.6	20.4	22.8	28.6	24.8	22.6	24.2	26.4	23.0
4. Very satisfying	43.5	44.4	43.0	43.5	46.4	40.4	40.2	45.7	48.4	45.9	40.2	45.8	42.9	45.7	38.7	51.8
5. Extremely satisfying	26.6	24.3	29.1	26.1	27.7	30.1	25.0	25.7	26.0	28.1	23.4	25.1	29.5	26.1	27.5	25.3
Item 10350 Subject C03,P02 N★	3022	1445	1482	2277	370	711	813	925	573	1722	1080	1214	618	406	687	17

A13: To what extent do you think the things listed below will prevent you from getting the kind of work you would like to have?

A13A: Your religion

1. Not at all	90.3	89.3	91.9	92.1	84.8	90.9	89.9	88.8	92.3	91.1	91.0	89.7	89.4	92.1	92.4	85.2
2. Somewhat	4.3	4.2	4.1	3.9	4.9	3.9	4.4	4.8	3.6	4.6	3.2	4.7	3.4	4.5	3.5	9.3
3. A lot	1.7	1.6	1.4	0.9	3.4	2.2	1.4	1.9	1.2	1.2	1.7	2.0	1.7	1.1	1.0	-
8. Don't know	3.8	4.9	2.6	3.1	7.0	2.9	4.3	4.5	2.9	3.1	4.1	3.6	5.5	2.4	3.2	5.6
Item 10360 Subject C03,G N	3172	1516	1556	2396	371	741	867	975	589	1798	1135	1268	643	432	716	24

A13B: Your sex

1. Not at all	77.8	90.4	65.7	78.9	74.3	78.1	76.2	78.0	79.4	75.2	81.3	76.3	79.7	77.2	80.2	80.3
2. Somewhat	16.6	6.5	27.0	16.6	16.4	15.9	17.5	17.2	15.2	19.5	13.3	18.1	14.6	18.3	14.2	10.4
3. A lot	3.7	1.9	4.7	3.0	5.3	4.0	3.5	3.7	3.7	3.4	3.7	3.2	3.0	4.1	4.5	3.7
8. Don't know	1.9	1.1	2.6	1.5	4.0	2.1	2.8	1.0	1.7	1.9	1.8	2.3	2.6	0.4	1.0	5.6
Item 10370 Subject C03,D06 N	3175	1517	1556	2395	374	741	867	977	589	1802	1135	1270	643	432	716	24

A13C: Your race

1. Not at all	84.4	84.4	85.3	93.9	44.4	84.0	86.3	82.0	85.9	84.3	86.5	83.6	83.2	84.7	88.8	83.8
2. Somewhat	9.2	9.0	9.1	3.7	32.8	9.1	8.6	10.1	8.6	10.0	7.2	8.7	10.6	10.0	7.2	7.4
3. A lot	3.4	3.5	2.8	1.2	11.8	3.9	2.7	3.8	2.9	2.7	3.6	3.7	3.4	3.2	2.1	3.2
8. Don't know	3.1	3.1	2.8	1.2	11.0	2.9	2.4	4.1	2.6	3.0	2.8	4.0	2.8	2.1	1.9	5.6
Item 10380 Subject C03,N02 N	3171	1517	1555	2395	374	740	867	974	590	1799	1135	1270	643	431	715	24

A13D: Your family background

1. Not at all	88.8	87.9	90.3	91.8	83.1	88.3	88.9	89.2	88.8	89.5	88.9	88.9	89.2	88.0	90.2	79.7
2. Somewhat	6.2	6.9	5.4	5.6	5.2	7.2	7.2	5.1	5.1	5.7	6.4	5.4	6.3	7.1	6.7	7.2
3. A lot	2.2	1.9	2.0	1.2	5.1	2.0	1.3	2.9	2.4	2.0	2.1	2.3	1.7	2.4	1.0	9.4
8. Don't know	2.8	3.3	2.3	1.4	6.6	2.5	2.6	2.8	3.6	2.8	2.6	3.4	2.7	2.5	2.1	3.7
Item 10390 Subject C03 N	3172	1515	1556	2394	373	741	866	977	588	1802	1134	1267	643	432	716	24

A13E: Your political views

1. Not at all	83.0	83.7	83.5	87.2	73.3	82.4	83.5	81.9	84.7	83.5	84.1	83.1	83.8	81.8	84.5	87.0
2. Somewhat	8.6	8.7	8.1	7.4	12.2	9.2	7.5	9.3	8.1	9.5	6.5	7.1	9.9	10.5	7.9	7.4
3. A lot	2.0	2.2	1.6	1.0	2.7	2.2	3.1	1.6	1.0	1.6	2.4	1.5	1.6	2.4	2.5	5.6
8. Don't know	6.4	5.4	6.9	4.4	11.8	6.3	5.8	7.2	6.3	5.4	7.0	8.3	4.7	5.3	5.1	-
Item 10400 Subject C03,H01 N	3172	1514	1557	2394	373	740	867	976	589	1800	1134	1268	642	433	716	24

A13F: Your education

1. Not at all	47.5	48.3	47.3	48.3	48.9	48.7	41.5	52.0	47.4	52.2	41.4	52.8	44.9	44.9	41.1	51.2
2. Somewhat	25.5	25.1	26.0	26.6	21.0	22.9	29.5	22.0	28.5	20.6	32.8	23.0	28.2	24.3	29.3	14.6
3. A lot	23.6	23.3	23.3	22.2	24.9	25.2	24.8	23.2	20.5	24.0	22.3	20.9	22.9	27.1	26.5	34.2
8. Don't know	3.5	3.3	3.3	2.9	5.2	3.2	4.3	2.8	3.6	3.2	3.5	3.4	4.0	3.7	3.1	-
Item 10410 Subject B09,C03 N	3177	1518	1559	2397	374	741	867	977	592	1802	1135	1271	644	431	717	24

A13G: Lack of vocational training

1. Not at all	52.3	53.0	52.0	53.6	50.4	54.0	48.2	54.6	52.1	55.0	48.7	54.2	52.6	51.2	49.9	43.2
2. Somewhat	27.1	27.2	26.8	27.2	24.8	27.4	26.9	26.3	28.4	25.0	29.9	25.5	27.8	28.5	28.9	20.2
3. A lot	12.2	11.9	12.3	11.5	13.9	11.1	15.7	11.4	9.9	10.6	14.5	11.1	11.7	12.2	14.1	27.8
8. Don't know	8.4	8.0	8.9	7.8	10.9	7.5	9.3	7.6	9.6	9.5	6.9	9.2	7.9	8.1	7.1	8.8
Item 10420 Subject C03 N	3165	1515	1548	2390	374	735	867	977	586	1791	1135	1264	643	433	712	24

QUESTIONNAIRE FORM 4 1985	TOTAL	SEX		RACE		REGION				4YR COLLEGE PLANS		ILLICIT DRUG USE: LIFETIME				
		M	F	White	Black	NE	NC	S	W	Yes	No	None	Mari- juana Only	Few Pills	More Pills	Any Her- oin
N (Weighted No. of Cases):	3279	1565	1610	2464	390	772	892	1004	612	1853	1170	1312	662	442	746	24
% of Weighted Total:	100.0	47.7	49.1	75.1	11.9	23.5	27.2	30.6	18.7	56.5	35.7	40.0	20.2	13.5	22.8	0.7
A13H: Lack of ability																
1. Not at all	58.9	60.7	57.3	60.2	57.1	59.3	55.5	59.4	62.6	60.6	56.9	59.8	57.5	62.1	56.1	53.8
2. Somewhat	15.4	14.6	15.9	15.0	15.3	15.8	15.5	14.9	15.4	13.6	17.5	15.0	17.8	13.5	15.8	12.2
3. A lot	21.4	21.2	22.2	21.0	23.0	20.9	23.4	21.5	19.1	22.1	20.7	20.0	21.7	21.6	23.8	33.9
8. Don't know	4.3	3.6	4.7	3.8	4.5	4.0	5.5	4.2	3.0	3.7	4.8	5.2	3.0	2.9	4.2	-
Item 10430 Subject C03 N	*3166*	*1515*	*1550*	*2390*	*375*	*739*	*862*	*978*	*588*	*1795*	*1133*	*1265*	*645*	*431*	*713*	*24*
A13I: Not knowing the right people																
1. Not at all	43.7	41.9	45.5	45.0	44.0	41.2	43.6	46.7	42.1	41.7	46.8	42.7	44.7	44.3	44.2	41.3
2. Somewhat	40.2	42.0	38.7	40.5	36.0	43.4	38.6	38.7	41.0	42.8	36.7	41.7	39.7	41.3	37.9	31.3
3. A lot	10.1	11.1	9.1	9.4	10.8	10.7	11.4	8.3	10.7	10.1	10.0	8.8	9.4	9.8	13.4	21.8
8. Don't know	5.9	5.1	6.7	5.1	9.2	4.7	6.4	6.2	6.2	5.5	6.6	6.9	6.2	4.6	4.5	5.6
Item 10440 Subject C03 N	*3169*	*1516*	*1555*	*2393*	*374*	*738*	*867*	*974*	*590*	*1800*	*1134*	*1266*	*643*	*432*	*717*	*24*
A13J: Not wanting to work hard																
1. Not at all	60.8	60.4	61.7	60.5	63.1	60.1	58.4	61.0	64.5	61.3	60.6	64.6	58.9	59.6	56.6	63.7
2. Somewhat	9.8	10.7	8.5	10.6	6.9	11.1	11.6	8.1	8.1	9.8	9.2	8.2	7.9	11.6	12.8	2.5
3. A lot	27.7	27.0	28.4	27.5	27.3	27.5	28.4	28.4	25.6	27.8	27.9	25.5	32.0	26.6	28.8	30.6
8. Don't know	1.8	1.9	1.4	1.5	2.7	1.3	1.5	2.4	1.8	1.2	2.4	1.7	1.2	2.2	1.8	3.2
Item 10450 Subject C03 N	*3168*	*1515*	*1553*	*2392*	*372*	*740*	*866*	*974*	*588*	*1799*	*1135*	*1263*	*644*	*432*	*717*	*24*
A13K: Not wanting to conform																
1. Not at all	51.8	50.1	53.5	52.4	52.7	49.3	50.7	53.3	54.1	49.6	54.9	52.8	51.4	50.5	50.9	44.5
2. Somewhat	22.5	23.2	21.5	23.6	17.0	23.7	23.2	21.1	22.5	25.7	18.2	23.3	22.4	20.8	22.4	26.0
3. A lot	14.9	16.4	14.0	13.8	19.3	13.7	14.7	16.5	14.1	15.0	15.0	12.7	17.2	16.8	15.6	22.4
8. Don't know	10.8	10.3	10.9	10.3	11.0	13.4	11.4	9.1	9.3	9.7	11.8	11.3	9.0	11.9	11.1	7.1
Item 10460 Subject C03,Q08 N	*3154*	*1506*	*1548*	*2384*	*370*	*736*	*862*	*970*	*587*	*1793*	*1128*	*1256*	*643*	*431*	*713*	*24*
A14: If you were to get enough money to live as comfortably as you'd like for the rest of your life, would you want to work?																
1. I would want to work	79.4	77.1	81.7	78.7	81.4	78.4	77.7	78.5	84.3	81.8	76.3	82.7	80.5	75.9	75.7	49.7
2. I would not want to work	20.6	22.9	18.3	21.3	18.6	21.6	22.3	21.5	15.7	18.2	23.7	17.3	19.5	24.1	24.3	50.3
Item 8100 Subject C06 N	*3239*	*1546*	*1596*	*2445*	*382*	*758*	*882*	*992*	*607*	*1838*	*1160*	*1297*	*654*	*436*	*739*	*24*
A15: How much do you agree or disagree with each statement below?																
A15A: One sees so few good or happy marriages that one questions it as a way of life																
1. Disagree	27.6	26.4	28.9	29.9	19.0	29.0	28.3	26.0	27.3	30.5	25.1	29.1	28.2	28.2	25.1	16.7
2. Mostly disagree	19.9	19.2	20.9	22.2	12.7	18.4	21.3	17.1	24.3	22.8	15.8	20.1	21.6	18.4	18.9	30.3
3. Neither	20.2	23.8	16.6	19.9	20.3	19.3	21.9	19.3	20.2	18.1	23.2	19.0	21.4	21.6	20.0	34.3
4. Mostly agree	20.5	19.5	21.5	19.1	26.1	19.2	20.9	21.4	20.2	19.7	21.1	19.8	18.5	20.8	23.0	1.8
5. Agree	11.8	11.1	12.2	8.8	21.9	14.0	7.6	16.2	8.0	8.9	14.8	11.9	10.3	11.0	13.0	16.9
Item 10470 Subject D03 N	*3235*	*1545*	*1595*	*2446*	*380*	*758*	*883*	*989*	*606*	*1838*	*1160*	*1293*	*656*	*440*	*739*	*24*
A15B: It is usually a good idea for a couple to live together before getting married in order to find out whether they really get along																
1. Disagree	25.5	20.5	30.7	26.6	21.5	18.3	26.5	32.1	22.1	25.9	25.4	35.8	18.9	21.3	16.2	13.8
2. Mostly disagree	13.0	11.3	14.3	13.1	10.1	11.2	15.2	12.6	12.4	13.9	11.9	13.8	13.4	12.7	12.0	-
3. Neither	16.0	17.3	14.8	16.9	10.3	17.3	16.0	14.7	16.2	17.7	14.2	15.7	17.7	17.5	13.4	29.6
4. Mostly agree	22.8	24.2	21.4	22.6	25.8	27.2	22.2	19.9	22.6	22.9	22.5	19.5	24.3	22.2	26.8	38.1
5. Agree	22.9	26.7	18.7	20.7	32.3	25.9	20.1	20.6	26.7	19.5	26.0	15.1	25.7	26.3	31.6	18.5
Item 10480 Subject D03 N	*3244*	*1550*	*1599*	*2450*	*382*	*761*	*884*	*993*	*607*	*1840*	*1162*	*1299*	*656*	*440*	*739*	*24*

QUESTIONNAIRE FORM 4 1985	TOTAL	SEX		RACE		REGION				4YR COLLEGE PLANS		ILLICIT DRUG USE: LIFETIME				
		M	F	White	Black	NE	NC	S	W	Yes	No	None	Mari-juana Only	Few Pills	More Pills	Any Her-oin
N (Weighted No. of Cases):	3279	1565	1610	2464	390	772	892	1004	612	1853	1170	1312	662	442	746	24
% of Weighted Total:	100.0	47.7	49.1	75.1	11.9	23.5	27.2	30.6	18.7	56.5	35.7	40.0	20.2	13.5	22.8	0.7

A15C: Having a close intimate relationship with only one partner is too restrictive for the average person

1. Disagree	40.9	34.6	47.7	43.4	33.9	38.9	42.9	42.7	37.6	41.3	40.7	47.2	38.4	37.5	35.6	32.4
2. Mostly disagree	24.2	25.9	23.2	26.1	18.8	24.5	23.8	21.9	28.4	27.5	20.9	22.0	25.2	27.0	25.4	19.2
3. Neither	13.2	14.6	11.8	12.6	12.7	15.8	14.0	11.9	11.0	13.1	13.8	11.7	15.3	11.4	15.5	16.8
4. Mostly agree	13.6	15.0	11.5	11.6	19.8	13.2	12.6	14.0	14.9	12.0	14.6	11.1	13.3	15.4	16.9	21.0
5. Agree	8.1	10.0	5.8	6.2	14.9	7.7	6.8	9.5	8.1	6.1	10.0	8.0	7.8	8.8	6.6	10.7
Item 10490 Subject D03 N	3241	1551	1595	2450	381	759	880	994	607	1839	1161	1295	657	440	739	24

A15D: Having a job takes away from a woman's relationship with her husband

1. Disagree	48.2	36.3	60.3	47.6	55.5	51.0	45.3	48.4	48.3	50.8	45.0	47.5	51.1	45.7	49.6	35.0
2. Mostly disagree	24.7	26.4	23.4	26.4	17.4	23.6	25.2	25.3	24.1	25.5	24.6	25.7	23.1	24.2	24.6	18.8
3. Neither	13.3	18.4	7.8	13.2	9.4	12.7	13.4	12.1	15.7	12.2	14.5	13.2	13.0	12.4	13.8	22.0
4. Mostly agree	9.0	12.3	5.5	8.6	11.6	8.1	10.7	8.4	8.4	7.9	9.9	8.5	7.9	12.9	8.1	8.0
5. Agree	4.9	6.6	2.9	4.2	6.2	4.5	5.3	5.7	3.5	3.6	6.0	5.1	4.9	4.8	3.9	16.2
Item 10500 Subject D05 N	3236	1546	1595	2446	379	757	883	992	605	1838	1158	1297	654	440	736	24

A15E: Having a job gives a wife more of a chance to develop herself as a person

1. Disagree	3.4	4.4	2.5	3.2	4.0	4.4	2.2	4.0	3.1	3.4	3.1	4.0	3.7	3.2	1.7	-
2. Mostly disagree	2.6	3.9	1.1	2.4	2.3	2.3	2.6	2.6	2.8	1.9	3.3	1.8	4.1	2.2	2.6	8.8
3. Neither	9.3	14.7	4.0	9.7	5.7	11.3	9.7	7.8	9.0	8.6	9.8	7.8	10.3	10.2	10.7	17.4
4. Mostly agree	30.0	38.2	22.7	31.5	25.0	28.0	32.4	27.6	33.0	29.2	31.1	31.2	29.5	29.1	29.7	31.4
5. Agree	54.6	38.9	69.7	53.1	63.0	54.0	53.1	58.0	52.2	56.8	52.7	55.2	52.5	55.2	55.3	42.4
Item 10510 Subject D05 N	3238	1547	1596	2446	381	760	881	991	607	1841	1158	1295	656	439	739	24

A15F: Being a father and raising children is one of the most fulfilling experiences a man can have

1. Disagree	3.7	4.4	3.0	3.9	3.4	4.5	2.9	4.1	3.4	3.8	3.8	2.4	4.2	5.9	4.3	12.8
2. Mostly disagree	3.9	4.8	3.0	3.8	3.3	4.3	4.1	3.5	3.8	3.4	3.8	3.7	3.5	3.2	4.1	18.1
3. Neither	20.1	18.1	21.8	21.3	13.2	20.8	22.1	17.6	20.4	20.0	19.6	17.1	21.0	18.6	25.3	24.6
4. Mostly agree	33.1	33.3	33.5	35.7	27.6	30.8	36.1	31.1	34.9	34.4	32.8	33.4	35.7	32.8	31.9	13.6
5. Agree	39.2	39.5	38.7	35.3	52.5	39.7	34.8	43.2	38.3	38.3	40.0	43.3	35.6	39.5	34.4	31.0
Item 10520 Subject D05 N	3221	1542	1585	2434	380	754	879	984	603	1831	1152	1287	653	438	736	24

A15G: Most mothers should spend more time with their children than they do now

1. Disagree	5.7	5.1	6.3	5.8	6.3	8.7	4.0	5.0	5.4	6.5	4.9	5.4	5.6	5.9	6.2	5.6
2. Mostly disagree	10.4	9.9	11.2	11.4	5.6	10.5	12.8	7.9	10.9	11.1	10.2	8.8	11.1	12.3	11.1	14.0
3. Neither	25.5	28.5	22.3	27.9	16.0	28.1	28.9	20.1	26.0	28.1	21.4	24.2	25.0	22.3	30.0	36.3
4. Mostly agree	29.9	30.9	29.5	30.3	27.2	27.7	28.4	30.0	34.5	30.2	30.4	30.8	31.5	29.4	28.9	11.7
5. Agree	28.6	25.7	30.7	24.7	44.8	25.1	25.9	37.0	23.2	24.2	33.1	30.7	26.7	30.1	23.9	32.4
Item 10530 Subject D05 N	3233	1547	1593	2441	382	757	882	990	604	1835	1157	1295	656	438	735	24

A15H: If a wife works, her husband should take a greater part in housework and child-care

1. Disagree	4.9	6.2	3.3	4.5	5.2	5.2	3.5	5.8	5.2	3.8	6.2	4.6	4.9	5.0	5.1	17.9
2. Mostly disagree	5.5	5.8	5.2	5.6	5.3	3.4	6.2	6.2	6.1	5.2	5.8	5.7	6.0	4.6	5.7	10.8
3. Neither	14.7	16.3	13.2	14.9	13.0	15.9	15.7	13.7	13.6	14.6	15.4	13.4	14.7	14.6	16.2	20.4
4. Mostly agree	35.0	38.9	31.8	36.6	26.1	36.6	36.3	32.3	35.6	36.3	33.7	34.6	35.4	36.0	36.7	26.5
5. Agree	39.8	32.8	46.5	38.4	50.4	38.8	38.3	42.1	39.4	40.2	38.8	41.7	39.0	39.8	36.3	24.4
Item 10540 Subject D05 N	3235	1547	1595	2445	383	760	879	993	604	1835	1160	1295	655	438	739	24

QUESTIONNAIRE FORM 4 1985	TOTAL	SEX		RACE		REGION				4YR COLLEGE PLANS		ILLICIT DRUG USE: LIFETIME				
		M	F	White	Black	NE	NC	S	W	Yes	No	None	Mari-juana Only	Few Pills	More Pills	Any Her-oin
N (Weighted No. of Cases):	3279	1565	1610	2464	390	772	892	1004	612	1853	1170	1312	662	442	746	24
% of Weighted Total:	100.0	47.7	49.1	75.1	11.9	23.5	27.2	30.6	18.7	56.5	35.7	40.0	20.2	13.5	22.8	0.7

A16: How much TV do you estimate you watch on an average weekday?

	TOTAL	M	F	White	Black	NE	NC	S	W	Yes	No	None	Mari-juana Only	Few Pills	More Pills	Any Her-oin
1. None	3.9	3.8	4.0	4.4	1.4	5.0	3.1	2.9	5.4	4.7	2.9	3.9	3.7	3.6	4.6	1.8
2. Half-hour or less	13.6	14.3	13.3	14.9	6.6	13.0	13.5	10.4	19.5	16.2	9.6	12.8	15.5	13.6	13.3	25.0
3. About one hour	19.8	19.4	20.1	22.5	7.0	19.2	22.2	17.2	21.3	22.0	17.3	17.5	18.3	19.1	25.2	20.8
4. About two hours	22.1	23.1	21.3	22.6	17.4	21.9	20.9	22.3	24.0	22.3	22.5	21.8	23.3	22.8	21.2	21.0
5. About three hours	17.3	17.8	17.4	17.2	20.2	16.3	16.8	18.8	16.9	16.0	20.0	18.5	16.8	17.6	17.1	10.1
6. About four hours	11.5	11.9	11.0	10.5	16.5	13.9	11.4	13.3	5.9	9.8	14.0	11.9	12.5	11.2	10.3	8.9
7. Five hours or more	11.7	9.8	12.9	7.9	30.8	10.6	12.1	15.2	6.9	8.9	13.7	13.7	9.9	12.0	8.5	12.5
Item 10550 Subject C07 N	3229	1541	1592	2441	381	760	882	985	602	1835	1154	1292	652	440	735	24

A17: In the past year, how many books have you read just because you wanted to–that is, without their being assigned?

	TOTAL	M	F	White	Black	NE	NC	S	W	Yes	No	None	Mari-juana Only	Few Pills	More Pills	Any Her-oin
1. None	19.3	26.5	12.0	19.4	15.0	23.1	19.5	17.9	16.2	14.1	25.9	17.3	19.3	19.6	22.2	24.2
2. One	13.4	13.1	13.6	13.1	15.8	11.3	15.5	12.8	14.1	11.6	14.6	12.2	13.2	16.1	13.6	13.3
3. Two to five	37.3	36.0	38.7	36.2	44.2	34.3	34.9	39.1	41.5	38.6	35.9	36.8	41.4	38.1	33.7	43.9
4. Six to ten	12.0	10.0	14.2	12.5	10.6	13.7	12.0	11.5	10.9	14.4	9.5	12.0	11.6	12.4	12.8	6.9
5. Ten or more	18.0	14.4	21.5	18.8	14.4	17.6	18.1	18.6	17.3	21.3	14.1	21.6	14.5	13.7	17.6	11.7
Item 10560 Subject C07 N	3263	1557	1608	2457	386	769	887	997	610	1849	1167	1309	661	441	742	24

A18: Some people think about what's going on in government very often, and others are not that interested. How much of an interest do you take in government and current events?

	TOTAL	M	F	White	Black	NE	NC	S	W	Yes	No	None	Mari-juana Only	Few Pills	More Pills	Any Her-oin
1. No interest at all	5.0	4.7	5.1	4.7	5.1	5.7	6.3	4.0	4.0	2.8	8.4	4.7	3.0	7.6	5.9	9.3
2. Very little interest	18.5	14.8	22.3	17.7	21.9	21.3	19.9	18.2	13.1	14.5	23.2	18.3	20.5	17.8	17.0	13.1
3. Some interest	47.5	46.3	48.7	48.4	43.6	45.8	46.7	48.0	50.4	47.1	49.1	46.6	47.3	49.2	48.8	64.3
4. A lot of interest	20.8	23.4	18.1	21.9	18.5	19.7	19.3	21.0	24.2	25.3	14.4	21.9	20.1	16.9	21.9	10.2
5. A very great interest	8.1	10.8	5.8	7.3	10.9	7.5	7.8	8.8	8.3	10.3	4.9	8.4	9.1	8.5	6.4	3.2
Item 6330 Subject H01,Q08 N	3250	1553	1604	2456	381	766	888	990	606	1845	1165	1309	659	439	741	24

A19: Some people think that there ought to be changes in the amount of influence and power that certain organizations have in our society. Do you think the following organizations should have more influence, less influence, or about the same amount of influence as they have now?

A19A: Large corporations?

	TOTAL	M	F	White	Black	NE	NC	S	W	Yes	No	None	Mari-juana Only	Few Pills	More Pills	Any Her-oin
1. Much less	5.4	7.1	3.9	5.7	3.2	7.0	5.6	3.9	5.4	6.3	4.4	5.4	5.0	5.7	5.5	16.4
2. Less	27.1	29.6	24.9	29.4	18.2	30.2	26.3	24.9	27.9	32.4	20.0	28.9	26.5	23.2	28.6	24.1
3. Same as now	39.0	38.6	39.6	41.3	27.9	34.9	41.8	37.2	43.2	37.8	41.9	35.9	38.1	43.2	42.4	44.6
4. More	10.3	9.4	10.9	7.8	22.6	9.2	8.3	13.3	9.8	8.1	12.4	11.1	10.6	11.1	8.0	4.3
5. Much more	3.5	3.7	3.2	2.2	10.1	2.1	3.4	5.7	2.1	2.6	4.3	3.9	5.1	2.0	1.3	—
8. No opinion	14.6	11.6	17.4	13.6	17.9	16.6	14.7	14.9	11.6	12.8	17.0	14.8	14.7	14.8	14.3	10.6
Item 10570 Subject K03 N	3227	1542	1596	2437	381	757	881	986	604	1834	1157	1301	654	441	732	24

A19B: Major labor unions?

	TOTAL	M	F	White	Black	NE	NC	S	W	Yes	No	None	Mari-juana Only	Few Pills	More Pills	Any Her-oin
1. Much less	8.6	12.7	4.8	9.9	2.1	7.9	8.7	9.1	8.6	11.1	5.6	9.1	9.2	8.3	7.8	4.1
2. Less	20.0	23.4	16.9	22.6	9.7	17.7	21.7	20.4	19.6	22.8	16.7	20.9	19.2	20.5	18.9	13.9
3. Same as now	29.8	28.5	31.1	31.6	23.1	30.6	30.4	27.1	32.1	29.8	30.7	28.9	28.9	32.2	31.4	32.2
4. More	19.9	17.8	22.1	17.4	30.8	20.4	18.4	20.2	21.1	18.1	21.7	18.3	22.0	20.2	20.5	25.2
5. Much more	6.6	6.9	6.0	4.1	17.3	8.2	5.2	6.7	6.6	4.7	8.6	6.5	8.1	4.9	6.1	13.0
8. No opinion	15.1	10.6	19.2	14.4	17.1	15.2	15.5	16.4	12.0	13.5	16.7	16.3	12.6	13.9	15.3	11.6
Item 10580 Subject K03 N	3222	1541	1593	2435	380	756	880	984	602	1830	1159	1301	654	439	731	24

A19C: Churches and religious organizations?

	TOTAL	M	F	White	Black	NE	NC	S	W	Yes	No	None	Mari-juana Only	Few Pills	More Pills	Any Her-oin
1. Much less	7.6	10.2	5.3	7.9	3.5	8.7	7.5	5.2	10.4	8.2	7.1	5.8	7.9	7.4	10.0	20.4
2. Less	11.4	11.4	11.6	12.7	4.6	11.7	12.0	8.0	15.6	12.9	10.1	9.7	12.2	12.4	13.4	20.4
3. Same as now	33.0	33.2	32.6	35.6	20.1	38.8	34.2	26.1	35.3	34.5	30.2	30.9	35.0	35.9	34.2	35.5
4. More	21.9	21.2	23.1	22.7	23.2	18.1	23.8	24.7	19.7	22.2	22.5	24.2	21.2	19.2	20.3	8.4
5. Much more	15.4	13.5	16.8	11.3	37.3	9.9	11.9	25.9	10.4	13.8	17.0	19.8	15.2	14.1	8.6	7.3
8. No opinion	10.6	10.4	10.6	9.9	11.3	12.7	10.7	10.1	8.5	8.3	13.1	9.6	8.6	10.9	13.4	7.9
Item 10590 Subject G,K03 N	3225	1546	1593	2438	381	757	881	984	603	1832	1160	1304	653	441	730	24

QUESTIONNAIRE FORM 4 1985	TOTAL	SEX		RACE		REGION				4YR COLLEGE PLANS		ILLICIT DRUG USE: LIFETIME				
		M	F	White	Black	NE	NC	S	W	Yes	No	None	Marijuana Only	Few Pills	More Pills	Any Heroin
N (Weighted No. of Cases):	3279	1565	1610	2464	390	772	892	1004	612	1853	1170	1312	662	442	746	24
% of Weighted Total:	100.0	47.7	49.1	75.1	11.9	23.5	27.2	30.6	18.7	56.5	35.7	40.0	20.2	13.5	22.8	0.7

A19D: The national news media (TV, magazines, news services)?

1. Much less	9.2	10.2	8.3	9.1	7.8	9.4	7.1	10.2	10.3	11.1	6.3	8.7	7.3	9.9	11.5	11.8
2. Less	25.3	25.7	25.5	27.9	16.2	26.6	26.0	24.1	24.8	27.3	22.9	27.1	25.5	25.8	23.0	10.2
3. Same as now	40.3	40.9	39.5	42.5	31.1	39.9	41.9	38.7	41.3	40.0	40.6	38.2	43.3	41.0	41.2	31.3
4. More	12.5	11.2	13.6	11.3	17.8	11.6	11.0	13.4	14.2	11.8	13.9	12.8	12.3	12.5	11.3	41.7
5. Much more	5.7	5.4	5.9	2.9	18.5	4.8	6.5	6.9	4.0	5.4	5.7	6.9	5.4	3.0	4.8	2.2
8. No opinion	6.9	6.7	7.1	6.4	8.5	7.6	7.5	6.8	5.4	4.4	10.6	6.3	6.2	7.8	8.3	2.8
Item 10600 Subject K03 N	3219	1541	1592	2437	378	752	882	981	604	1833	1157	1300	652	439	731	24

A19E: The Presidency and the administration?

1. Much less	4.0	4.4	3.5	3.1	9.1	4.0	4.1	4.5	2.8	3.2	4.8	3.4	3.9	3.3	5.0	11.8
2. Less	11.6	10.1	12.9	10.9	14.5	13.4	12.4	9.2	12.3	11.2	12.0	10.9	10.2	11.7	14.1	16.0
3. Same as now	40.6	39.8	41.5	43.0	32.7	43.9	41.6	39.7	36.4	43.6	37.0	39.4	44.0	41.0	40.0	44.8
4. More	21.4	24.0	19.3	23.6	11.8	18.3	20.0	22.3	25.7	23.8	18.6	22.8	20.6	23.2	19.0	19.4
5. Much more	11.3	12.7	10.0	10.1	16.6	9.3	10.6	13.7	11.1	10.6	12.4	12.4	12.0	9.4	10.1	-
8. No opinion	11.1	9.0	12.9	9.2	15.4	11.1	11.3	10.6	11.7	7.6	15.3	11.2	9.3	11.3	11.9	7.9
Item 10610 Subject H04,K03 N	3222	1543	1592	2437	379	755	880	981	604	1833	1156	1299	655	440	731	24

A19F: The Congress–that is, the U.S. Senate and House of Representatives?

1. Much less	3.2	4.5	1.9	2.9	3.8	4.4	2.5	2.9	3.0	2.3	4.6	2.5	2.4	4.6	4.1	9.8
2. Less	9.7	10.3	9.1	9.6	8.4	10.4	10.6	8.9	8.9	8.8	11.2	8.9	8.6	10.1	11.8	9.2
3. Same as now	42.0	41.8	42.2	44.4	32.9	45.1	41.1	40.3	42.1	43.9	38.8	41.0	43.5	43.3	41.8	37.2
4. More	24.6	25.6	24.1	26.0	22.9	19.3	24.5	27.5	26.5	27.5	21.1	26.8	28.5	22.3	19.8	23.4
5. Much more	8.5	9.6	7.4	6.8	17.0	9.0	8.0	9.4	7.4	8.2	8.4	8.7	8.2	8.4	8.4	5.7
8. No opinion	12.0	8.4	15.4	10.2	15.1	11.8	13.3	11.0	12.1	9.3	15.9	12.1	8.7	11.2	14.1	14.7
Item 10620 Subject H04,K03 N	3220	1542	1591	2437	377	752	881	983	604	1831	1156	1302	651	440	730	23

A19G: The U.S. Supreme Court?

1. Much less	2.1	2.9	1.4	2.1	1.9	3.0	1.7	2.3	1.3	1.3	3.0	1.7	1.3	2.1	3.2	10.1
2. Less	5.9	5.2	6.6	5.9	3.4	5.5	6.2	5.6	6.3	5.7	5.9	5.1	4.7	9.2	6.4	13.4
3. Same as now	44.4	44.0	44.8	46.0	37.6	48.8	43.8	42.8	42.4	47.0	40.9	44.2	46.9	42.5	44.9	31.6
4. More	25.3	27.5	23.0	26.2	24.3	21.4	24.5	26.7	28.9	27.2	23.3	25.7	27.0	25.2	23.0	31.4
5. Much more	10.4	11.9	9.1	8.7	19.6	9.2	10.3	11.5	10.4	9.9	10.6	11.4	10.8	10.0	8.6	4.4
8. No opinion	11.9	8.4	15.1	11.1	13.2	12.2	13.5	11.0	10.7	8.9	16.2	11.9	9.4	11.0	13.9	9.0
Item 10630 Subject H04,K03 N	3215	1540	1589	2429	380	757	878	980	600	1829	1153	1299	653	432	734	23

A19H: All the courts and the justice system in general?

1. Much less	1.8	2.6	1.1	1.6	2.4	2.2	2.0	1.9	1.0	1.0	2.9	1.4	1.5	1.4	2.8	9.8
2. Less	5.6	6.1	5.1	5.8	3.6	5.6	6.8	4.5	5.8	4.8	6.3	4.2	5.6	8.2	6.4	15.0
3. Same as now	42.9	43.2	42.3	43.9	38.6	45.7	43.4	41.0	41.7	44.4	41.4	41.3	44.5	41.8	45.2	45.8
4. More	26.7	26.9	26.9	27.7	24.0	24.2	26.5	28.0	28.0	30.5	21.5	29.0	27.5	26.2	23.3	14.7
5. Much more	10.7	11.6	10.0	9.5	16.2	9.8	7.9	13.0	12.1	10.3	11.3	11.5	10.7	10.4	9.2	5.7
8. No opinion	12.3	9.6	14.6	11.5	15.2	12.5	13.4	11.6	11.4	9.0	16.6	12.6	10.2	11.9	13.1	9.0
Item 10640 Subject H04,K03 N	3213	1538	1588	2430	379	750	878	981	603	1828	1154	1298	653	438	728	23

A19I: The police and other law enforcement agencies?

1. Much less	2.7	4.0	1.5	2.6	3.1	3.2	2.5	2.8	2.4	1.8	4.4	1.2	3.0	3.4	4.1	26.2
2. Less	7.4	9.1	5.7	7.4	7.3	7.0	8.0	6.2	8.8	7.0	7.9	4.6	6.9	8.7	11.9	20.0
3. Same as now	29.4	30.9	27.9	31.0	22.6	31.7	34.1	24.4	27.9	31.6	26.1	28.4	32.1	28.2	30.0	36.0
4. More	32.5	31.6	33.4	33.8	24.6	29.3	30.8	35.1	34.6	35.1	29.4	34.1	32.8	33.4	29.7	7.7
5. Much more	20.2	18.4	22.4	18.7	32.9	19.4	17.2	24.4	18.7	18.6	22.3	24.3	18.3	19.7	15.4	2.6
8. No opinion	7.8	6.2	9.0	6.4	9.5	9.4	7.4	7.1	7.6	5.9	9.8	7.4	6.9	6.6	9.0	7.6
Item 10650 Subject K03 N	3222	1544	1591	2435	381	755	881	983	602	1831	1158	1302	654	438	731	23

QUESTIONNAIRE FORM 4 1985	TOTAL	SEX		RACE		REGION				4YR COLLEGE PLANS		ILLICIT DRUG USE: LIFETIME				
		M	F	White	Black	NE	NC	S	W	Yes	No	None	Mari- juana Only	Few Pills	More Pills	Any Her- oin
N (Weighted No. of Cases):	3279	1565	1610	2464	390	772	892	1004	612	1853	1170	1312	662	442	746	24
% of Weighted Total:	100.0	47.7	49.1	75.1	11.9	23.5	27.2	30.6	18.7	56.5	35.7	40.0	20.2	13.5	22.8	0.7

A19J: The U.S. military?

1. Much less	5.3	6.2	4.5	5.4	3.3	6.7	5.9	3.3	5.9	5.7	5.1	4.7	3.8	5.8	7.1	9.8
2. Less	10.3	10.8	9.8	10.9	8.2	11.4	9.7	8.0	13.6	12.9	7.1	9.6	10.3	13.0	10.1	10.1
3. Same as now	38.8	37.3	40.1	40.1	30.9	39.4	43.7	34.6	37.5	40.7	36.8	39.1	42.0	38.5	36.2	42.0
4. More	20.2	21.5	19.7	21.1	22.1	19.1	17.7	23.6	19.8	20.3	20.5	21.2	19.6	18.3	20.6	19.2
5. Much more	13.6	16.6	10.5	12.3	21.2	11.2	10.8	19.2	11.8	10.3	16.9	13.0	14.0	14.6	13.4	8.0
8. No opinion	11.7	7.6	15.4	10.3	14.4	12.2	12.1	11.3	11.3	10.1	13.7	12.5	10.3	9.7	12.6	11.0
Item 10660 Subject K03,L04 N	3221	1544	1591	2436	381	755	881	982	603	1832	1156	1301	655	438	731	23

The next questions ask your views about drugs.

A20: Do you think that people (who are 18 or older) should be prohibited by law from doing each of the following?

A20A: Smoking marijuana (pot, grass) in private

1. No	40.4	42.8	37.6	38.9	41.9	43.9	38.6	36.7	44.5	38.4	41.7	22.8	43.1	44.4	66.4	71.6
2. Not sure	14.9	13.4	16.4	15.5	15.8	15.7	13.8	15.7	14.4	15.4	14.9	13.9	19.3	16.4	11.9	5.3
3. Yes	44.7	43.8	46.0	45.6	42.4	40.4	47.6	47.6	41.0	46.2	43.4	63.3	37.6	39.2	21.7	23.0
Item 10780 Subject A13a N	3254	1556	1608	2456	387	768	886	996	605	1845	1168	1307	660	439	746	24

A20B: Smoking marijuana in public places

1. No	14.0	17.0	10.4	11.9	16.8	17.1	12.3	13.0	14.2	10.0	17.7	10.1	15.0	14.1	18.7	34.2
2. Not sure	7.8	8.7	6.8	8.4	4.4	8.7	9.0	6.5	7.0	6.9	8.7	2.6	7.3	7.7	16.9	11.3
3. Yes	78.2	74.3	82.8	79.7	78.8	74.2	78.6	80.5	78.8	83.1	73.7	87.2	77.7	78.2	64.4	54.5
Item 10790 Subject A13a N	3254	1556	1607	2458	384	768	888	993	605	1848	1166	1307	660	439	746	24

A20C: Taking LSD in private

1. No	20.2	22.0	17.9	16.9	31.7	24.1	19.0	19.9	17.7	16.3	24.0	15.8	19.8	22.9	25.1	56.9
2. Not sure	9.2	9.9	8.1	8.0	13.3	8.1	8.7	9.7	10.2	8.1	9.5	7.6	9.8	7.5	11.9	7.2
3. Yes	70.6	68.1	74.0	75.0	55.0	67.8	72.3	70.4	72.1	75.6	66.4	76.6	70.5	69.6	63.0	36.0
Item 10800 Subject A13a N	3248	1555	1603	2453	383	767	887	991	603	1843	1165	1303	660	438	746	24

A20D: Taking LSD in public places

1. No	11.9	14.1	8.8	9.7	16.7	12.9	11.1	11.8	11.8	8.0	15.8	9.9	13.7	13.1	11.2	44.0
2. Not sure	3.4	4.7	2.0	3.1	2.9	4.0	3.3	3.5	2.3	2.9	3.2	1.9	2.2	2.6	6.9	8.8
3. Yes	84.8	81.2	89.1	87.2	80.4	83.1	85.6	84.7	85.8	89.1	81.1	88.2	84.1	84.3	81.9	47.2
Item 10810 Subject A13a N	3241	1553	1600	2452	381	765	885	988	603	1842	1160	1303	660	437	741	24

A20E: Taking amphetamines (uppers) or barbiturates (downers) in private

1. No	27.5	29.0	25.3	25.2	33.2	31.0	27.6	25.0	27.0	23.3	31.7	17.9	23.8	31.6	44.4	60.0
2. Not sure	16.3	15.8	16.6	16.1	16.3	17.0	14.9	15.4	18.6	16.3	16.0	12.6	19.2	19.1	18.1	10.6
3. Yes	56.3	55.1	58.1	58.7	50.5	52.0	57.5	59.6	54.3	60.5	52.3	69.5	57.0	49.3	37.4	29.3
Item 10820 Subject A13a N	3249	1553	1606	2456	383	767	887	992	603	1845	1164	1306	657	439	744	24

A20F: Taking amphetamines or barbiturates in public places

1. No	13.7	15.8	11.0	11.9	17.1	14.4	13.8	12.5	14.7	9.9	17.6	10.1	12.9	13.2	19.8	40.4
2. Not sure	8.0	9.0	6.9	8.2	5.6	8.7	8.6	6.7	8.2	7.2	8.9	3.8	7.1	9.0	15.4	13.1
3. Yes	78.3	75.2	82.1	79.8	77.3	76.9	77.6	80.8	77.0	82.9	73.5	86.0	80.0	77.8	64.8	46.5
Item 10830 Subject A13a N	3247	1553	1604	2454	384	767	887	992	602	1843	1163	1305	656	439	744	24

A20G: Taking heroin (smack, horse) in private

1. No	19.2	21.0	16.8	15.8	30.8	20.3	18.1	19.8	18.5	14.9	23.4	15.4	20.7	23.4	21.1	51.1
2. Not sure	7.5	7.1	7.6	6.2	12.8	6.9	7.9	7.7	7.3	6.6	8.2	6.6	7.5	7.4	8.0	12.9
3. Yes	73.3	71.8	75.5	78.0	56.4	72.8	74.0	72.5	74.3	78.5	68.5	78.0	71.8	69.2	70.9	36.0
Item 10840 Subject A13a N	3246	1552	1605	2454	383	765	886	991	604	1846	1162	1304	657	439	744	24

QUESTIONNAIRE FORM 4 1985	TOTAL	SEX		RACE		REGION				4YR COLLEGE PLANS		ILLICIT DRUG USE: LIFETIME				
		M	F	White	Black	NE	NC	S	W	Yes	No	None	Marijuana Only	Few Pills	More Pills	Any Heroin
N (Weighted No. of Cases):	3279	1565	1610	2464	390	772	892	1004	612	1853	1170	1312	662	442	746	24
% of Weighted Total:	100.0	47.7	49.1	75.1	11.9	23.5	27.2	30.6	18.7	56.5	35.7	40.0	20.2	13.5	22.8	0.7

A20H: Taking heroin in public places

1. No	11.2	13.6	8.2	9.0	16.3	11.0	10.8	11.3	11.7	7.5	14.9	9.8	13.9	13.7	8.3	41.1
2. Not sure	3.0	3.5	2.4	2.6	3.0	3.8	3.1	3.2	1.6	2.6	3.0	1.8	2.0	1.7	6.1	5.1
3. Yes	85.8	82.9	89.4	88.4	80.7	85.1	86.0	85.6	86.7	90.0	82.0	88.4	84.1	84.5	85.7	53.8
Item 10850 Subject A13a N	3247	1552	1605	2457	383	766	886	991	604	1845	1163	1307	657	438	744	24

A20I: Getting drunk in private

1. No	65.8	69.3	62.6	68.9	51.0	70.0	66.0	61.1	67.8	67.1	65.5	52.1	70.1	73.8	81.9	68.4
2. Not sure	14.4	12.1	16.5	14.0	15.9	13.6	14.0	15.7	13.6	14.8	13.7	20.4	14.3	8.5	7.7	-
3. Yes	19.8	18.7	20.8	17.1	33.2	16.4	19.9	23.2	18.5	18.1	20.8	27.4	15.6	17.7	10.4	31.6
Item 10860 Subject A13a N	3248	1551	1607	2458	383	765	887	990	605	1845	1164	1307	658	437	746	24

A20J: Getting drunk in public places

1. No	26.1	28.0	23.7	26.8	19.0	27.9	31.3	19.8	26.4	24.0	27.8	16.5	28.5	25.9	40.5	50.5
2. Not sure	20.9	22.5	19.1	22.5	11.3	20.8	23.4	16.5	24.4	21.9	20.0	16.5	24.5	26.4	22.3	11.3
3. Yes	53.1	49.4	57.2	50.7	69.7	51.3	45.3	63.7	49.2	54.1	52.2	67.0	47.0	47.7	37.2	38.2
Item 10870 Subject A13a N	3246	1552	1606	2456	381	764	887	991	604	1844	1163	1307	656	439	745	24

A20K: Smoking tobacco in certain specified public places

1. No	41.2	39.9	42.1	42.3	36.5	42.5	42.8	41.8	36.0	38.8	44.7	33.2	41.1	44.1	53.1	60.7
2. Not sure	16.1	16.5	15.7	15.3	19.3	15.1	16.3	17.0	15.5	14.1	18.2	19.5	17.5	14.6	9.5	5.3
3. Yes	42.8	43.6	42.2	42.4	44.2	42.4	41.0	41.2	48.5	47.1	37.0	47.3	41.4	41.3	37.4	34.0
Item 10760 Subject A13a N	3246	1549	1608	2453	384	766	887	989	605	1844	1163	1305	657	439	744	24

A21: In particular, there has been a great deal of public debate about whether marijuana use should be legal. Which of the following policies would you favor?

1. Using marijuana should be entirely legal	16.6	18.9	14.1	16.9	14.1	15.0	17.0	15.5	20.1	14.9	18.6	7.1	15.8	16.5	32.2	66.3
2. It should be a minor violation –like a parking ticket– but not a crime	25.7	26.0	25.7	24.3	29.2	32.2	26.0	18.5	28.8	26.5	24.5	14.9	30.6	33.1	36.8	14.5
3. It should be a crime	40.8	39.6	42.2	42.2	35.4	36.8	40.5	46.8	36.3	42.9	38.4	63.0	30.4	32.7	17.0	6.9
4. Don't know	16.9	15.5	18.0	16.6	21.3	16.0	16.5	19.1	14.8	15.7	18.5	14.9	23.2	17.7	14.0	12.3
Item 10880 Subject A13b N	3236	1551	1601	2447	383	766	884	987	598	1838	1164	1300	655	438	745	24

A22: If it were legal for people to USE marijuana, should it also be legal to SELL marijuana?

1. No	32.6	31.4	33.8	33.0	30.6	31.1	34.5	31.2	33.7	30.9	35.1	45.0	28.8	26.4	18.5	-
2. Yes, but only to adults	43.2	46.7	40.1	44.0	41.8	44.2	42.3	42.4	44.8	45.7	40.0	31.6	45.5	49.5	58.1	61.6
3. Yes, to anyone	11.2	10.3	11.8	10.2	12.7	13.4	8.2	12.2	11.0	11.1	10.4	9.9	12.4	11.9	10.9	18.8
4. Don't know	13.1	11.6	14.4	12.9	14.9	11.3	15.0	14.2	10.5	12.3	14.5	13.5	13.3	12.2	12.5	19.6
Item 10890 Subject A13b N	3237	1551	1603	2450	383	767	884	984	602	1838	1166	1300	657	438	744	24

A23: If marijuana were legal to use and legally available, which of the following would you be most likely to do?

1. Not use it, even if it were legal and available	63.0	61.3	64.7	61.8	71.7	58.8	63.6	68.6	58.3	64.4	60.9	90.0	55.7	53.3	28.9	12.8
2. Try it	7.5	7.6	7.4	7.6	5.5	8.2	7.7	6.4	8.2	8.4	6.3	5.2	11.3	12.0	5.9	3.7
3. Use it about as often as I do now	17.7	18.9	16.7	19.3	7.5	20.7	17.8	11.9	23.1	16.9	18.8	0.5	17.8	23.0	44.7	41.6
4. Use it more often than I do now	3.7	3.6	3.6	4.0	2.5	4.6	4.2	3.9	1.6	3.0	4.9	0.2	4.8	2.4	8.5	28.9
5. Use it less than I do now	1.6	2.1	1.1	1.6	2.0	1.8	0.9	1.4	2.6	1.5	1.6	0.2	1.5	2.3	3.6	7.8
6. Don't know	6.5	6.5	6.5	5.8	10.8	5.9	5.8	7.8	6.2	5.8	7.4	3.9	8.9	7.0	8.4	5.3
Item 10900 Subject A13b N	3232	1547	1605	2453	379	761	884	982	604	1841	1165	1304	658	434	743	24

This section asks for your views and feelings about a number of different things.

QUESTIONNAIRE FORM 4 1985	TOTAL	SEX		RACE		REGION				4YR COLLEGE PLANS		ILLICIT DRUG USE: LIFETIME				
		M	F	White	Black	NE	NC	S	W	Yes	No	None	Marijuana Only	Few Pills	More Pills	Any Heroin
N (Weighted No. of Cases):	3279	1565	1610	2464	390	772	892	1004	612	1853	1170	1312	662	442	746	24
% of Weighted Total:	100.0	47.7	49.1	75.1	11.9	23.5	27.2	30.6	18.7	56.5	35.7	40.0	20.2	13.5	22.8	0.7

D01: How satisfied are you with your life as a whole these days?

1. Completely dissatisfied	1.8	1.3	2.1	1.5	2.0	1.5	2.1	1.8	1.7	1.6	1.8	2.1	2.3	1.0	1.4	-
2. Quite dissatisfied	9.2	9.1	9.4	8.9	8.8	11.3	8.6	9.0	8.1	9.1	9.0	9.3	7.1	8.6	11.2	10.8
3. Somewhat dissatisfied	11.9	11.6	12.1	11.1	15.1	12.2	12.0	12.2	10.9	11.9	12.0	11.9	12.1	9.1	14.1	11.8
4. Neither, or mixed feelings	13.5	11.3	15.1	13.1	13.7	13.2	15.1	11.6	14.4	11.6	16.4	11.7	14.4	15.0	14.2	24.6
5. Somewhat satisfied	24.0	25.6	22.7	24.0	26.0	24.0	23.0	24.1	25.1	23.5	23.9	22.7	22.0	27.9	24.7	24.2
6. Quite satisfied	33.4	35.3	31.7	35.5	26.2	30.4	33.9	35.1	33.3	36.1	30.5	35.1	36.7	31.5	29.6	25.0
7. Completely satisfied	6.3	5.8	6.9	5.9	8.2	7.3	5.4	6.1	6.6	6.3	6.3	7.2	5.3	6.9	4.8	3.6
Item 6840　Subject P01,Q01　N	3049	1444	1551	2369	345	683	847	938	581	1802	1122	1240	620	413	699	21

D02: FOR THOSE WHO HAVE A JOB: All things considered, how satisfied are you with your present job?

1. Completely dissatisfied	4.6	4.6	4.6	4.2	5.8	5.1	4.6	5.0	3.5	3.5	6.2	3.4	5.0	4.2	5.4	20.2
2. Quite dissatisfied	9.7	8.6	10.7	9.8	10.1	9.1	10.3	9.5	9.7	9.1	10.3	9.1	9.7	11.6	9.3	21.6
3. Somewhat dissatisfied	13.5	13.6	13.3	13.4	14.4	15.1	13.4	12.6	12.9	13.1	13.7	12.3	11.7	15.4	16.2	6.1
4. Neither, or mixed feelings	15.8	16.9	14.5	15.4	19.7	16.5	15.8	15.7	15.0	14.6	17.7	15.3	18.5	14.2	16.2	5.1
5. Somewhat satisfied	27.7	29.4	25.9	27.6	30.0	25.5	26.6	27.1	32.5	28.4	26.8	27.7	29.9	27.8	25.4	29.0
6. Quite satisfied	24.4	23.1	25.9	25.5	12.6	24.4	24.2	24.8	24.2	26.6	21.6	27.4	20.4	22.1	24.8	11.6
7. Completely satisfied	4.4	3.8	5.1	4.2	7.4	4.3	5.0	5.3	2.2	4.6	3.8	4.6	4.9	4.7	2.7	6.4
Item 10910　Subject C01,P02　N★	1916	960	917	1566	155	478	540	515	383	1105	730	739	384	276	468	20

D03A: Which best describes your recent employment experience?

1. I have a paid job now.	62.0	62.6	61.3	64.6	47.0	68.8	62.4	54.4	65.4	61.4	63.3	58.3	64.2	63.0	67.0	89.3
2. No paid job now, but I had one during the past 3 months.	9.2	10.1	8.4	8.5	11.5	9.4	8.8	8.7	10.7	8.3	10.5	8.3	7.5	10.3	11.2	8.5
3. No paid job in the past 3 months –GO TO QUESTION D10	20.2	20.9	19.7	20.0	23.5	15.5	21.0	24.3	18.3	21.6	18.1	22.1	21.2	19.6	16.6	-
4. Never had a paid job–GO TO QUESTION D10	8.5	6.5	10.7	6.8	18.0	6.4	7.8	12.6	5.6	8.6	8.0	11.2	7.0	7.1	5.2	2.2
Item 21530　Subject C01　N	2732	1316	1367	2166	282	621	763	817	530	1627	995	1104	555	380	619	19

The next questions are about your present or most recent paid job. (If you presently hold more than one paid job, answer for the more important one.)

D03B: On the average, how many hours per week do (did) you work on this particular job?

1. 5 or less hours	7.5	7.3	7.6	6.5	14.3	6.1	5.9	8.1	10.7	8.3	6.6	10.4	5.5	6.4	5.2	6.2
2. 6 to 10 hours	13.0	12.4	13.8	12.2	14.5	12.4	13.1	11.4	15.7	15.0	9.6	15.1	14.3	10.6	10.2	9.4
3. 11 to 15 hours	14.7	13.2	16.2	15.5	9.5	14.9	16.5	15.3	11.1	15.8	12.8	15.2	14.5	15.8	13.9	9.8
4. 16 to 20 hours	22.4	20.7	24.5	23.1	17.8	23.6	23.7	19.9	22.5	23.1	22.0	22.5	26.7	21.6	20.1	13.7
5. 21 to 25 hours	17.3	15.7	19.0	17.6	14.7	17.8	16.9	17.7	16.8	16.5	18.4	14.4	15.1	21.4	21.1	21.5
6. 26 to 30 hours	11.6	13.2	9.9	11.6	14.1	12.9	11.2	12.0	10.4	10.6	12.8	10.2	10.6	13.5	13.0	23.4
7. 31 to 35 hours	6.5	7.7	5.2	6.5	7.5	4.6	6.4	7.8	7.1	5.0	9.2	4.7	6.9	5.7	9.1	8.2
8. 36 or more hours	6.9	9.9	3.8	6.9	7.6	7.7	6.4	7.7	5.7	5.6	8.6	7.5	6.4	4.9	7.5	7.8
Item 21540　Subject C01　N★	2134	1043	1046	1711	201	506	601	588	439	1237	811	806	441	302	527	21

D04: About how old is (was) your supervisor?

1. Age 20 or younger	2.8	3.5	2.0	2.3	5.2	2.1	2.8	2.7	3.6	3.0	2.3	3.3	2.4	2.4	2.1	5.9
2. 21 to 25	14.6	13.3	16.2	14.5	17.0	11.9	15.7	16.5	13.6	16.3	12.5	11.5	18.0	14.7	15.8	12.6
3. 26 to 30	23.6	22.8	24.7	23.4	27.3	24.7	24.8	21.8	23.3	23.7	24.0	25.6	24.6	21.5	21.5	13.2
4. 31 or older	59.0	60.5	57.1	59.7	50.5	61.2	56.8	59.1	59.5	57.0	61.2	59.6	55.0	61.4	60.6	68.3
Item 21550　Subject C01,M02　N★	2099	1031	1027	1679	203	489	586	594	430	1205	800	795	429	306	514	20

★=excludes respondents for whom question was inappropriate.

QUESTIONNAIRE FORM 4 1985	TOTAL	SEX		RACE		REGION				4YR COLLEGE PLANS		ILLICIT DRUG USE: LIFETIME				
		M	F	White	Black	NE	NC	S	W	Yes	No	None	Mari-juana Only	Few Pills	More Pills	Any Her-oin
N (Weighted No. of Cases):	3279	1565	1610	2464	390	772	892	1004	612	1853	1170	1312	662	442	746	24
% of Weighted Total:	100.0	47.7	49.1	75.1	11.9	23.5	27.2	30.6	18.7	56.5	35.7	40.0	20.2	13.5	22.8	0.7
D05: How many of the other workers are within 2 or 3 years of your own age?																
1. None	19.4	19.7	18.5	19.5	15.3	17.7	18.8	20.4	20.8	15.8	24.3	21.5	19.7	17.0	17.4	12.3
2. A few	28.2	27.9	28.8	28.0	27.2	25.0	26.2	30.0	32.2	29.2	25.9	29.7	29.9	28.6	24.3	41.9
3. About half	15.6	15.1	15.6	14.7	21.4	19.3	14.9	14.6	13.5	14.7	16.9	14.8	13.9	16.5	17.1	10.7
4. Most	14.4	14.6	14.4	14.6	13.5	16.7	15.6	12.4	12.7	16.6	11.3	12.6	15.5	15.3	15.7	11.1
5. Nearly all	15.9	15.0	17.0	16.4	18.7	14.9	16.1	15.9	16.5	17.9	13.0	16.1	15.5	17.3	15.0	18.1
6. All	6.6	7.7	5.7	6.8	3.8	6.4	8.4	6.7	4.4	5.7	8.5	5.3	5.5	5.3	10.5	5.9
Item 21560 Subject C01 N ★	2101	1036	1024	1683	202	488	589	595	429	1207	801	796	428	305	518	20
D06: To what extent does (did) this job . . .																
D06A: Use your skills and abilities–let you do the things you do best?																
1. Not at all	20.6	23.9	17.5	20.2	21.1	22.8	19.3	19.9	20.8	21.9	18.9	19.6	19.5	19.1	24.8	12.9
2. A little	30.2	28.9	31.3	31.5	26.5	33.8	31.4	27.7	28.0	30.8	28.7	28.9	28.2	32.2	33.4	14.3
3. Some extent	24.8	23.9	26.0	24.2	25.5	22.9	20.7	25.8	31.3	25.4	24.4	25.6	28.7	24.2	20.4	34.1
4. Considerable extent	14.0	13.6	14.1	15.3	9.9	9.7	17.1	16.4	11.5	13.3	15.6	15.4	10.7	15.1	13.7	17.2
5. A great extent	10.4	9.7	11.2	8.8	17.1	10.7	11.6	10.3	8.4	8.7	12.4	10.6	12.9	9.3	7.8	21.3
Item 21570 Subject C01 N ★	2085	1020	1024	1675	198	487	583	585	430	1201	794	792	418	304	516	20
D06B: Teach you new skills that will be useful in your future work?																
1. Not at all	25.8	29.6	22.4	26.3	25.8	29.7	27.7	22.1	23.7	27.4	23.4	23.1	25.8	23.4	30.3	41.6
2. A little	24.8	22.8	26.9	25.4	20.1	26.0	21.9	25.6	26.2	26.0	23.1	24.4	28.0	23.1	24.3	18.4
3. Some extent	21.7	20.0	23.1	21.6	19.6	17.8	21.5	21.8	25.9	21.8	21.5	23.3	19.2	23.7	20.7	13.9
4. Considerable extent	16.5	16.6	16.5	17.0	13.8	15.7	16.8	18.0	15.1	15.5	18.7	16.2	17.4	18.4	15.1	11.1
5. A great extent	11.3	11.1	11.2	9.7	20.8	10.8	12.1	12.5	9.1	9.4	13.4	13.0	9.7	11.4	9.5	14.9
Item 21580 Subject C01 N ★	2080	1016	1023	1671	197	481	582	585	432	1194	795	788	421	304	512	20
D06C: Make good use of special skills you learned in technical, vocational, business, or professional studies?																
1. Not at all	56.0	55.6	56.8	58.7	41.3	61.3	56.1	50.5	57.6	61.8	49.0	53.8	57.7	51.8	61.9	58.1
2. A little	16.4	16.8	16.1	15.8	16.6	14.5	14.4	18.0	19.2	15.5	17.5	14.5	17.8	21.8	15.5	4.5
3. Some extent	11.3	11.4	11.1	10.6	16.8	9.9	9.3	13.4	12.9	9.5	13.4	12.7	10.3	11.8	9.3	10.6
4. Considerable extent	8.1	8.9	7.1	8.1	7.6	6.2	10.3	9.3	5.5	6.5	10.3	9.7	5.7	9.0	6.2	15.6
5. A great extent	8.2	7.4	8.8	6.7	17.6	8.1	9.9	8.9	4.8	6.7	9.9	9.3	8.5	5.6	7.1	11.2
Item 21590 Subject C01 N ★	2066	1007	1019	1657	197	478	578	581	430	1186	790	785	415	302	510	20
D06D: Let you get to know people with social backgrounds very different from yours?																
1. Not at all	18.4	18.2	18.5	19.2	16.0	19.6	20.1	17.1	16.6	17.9	18.8	19.1	20.9	14.8	17.3	34.9
2. A little	23.1	23.2	23.5	23.4	21.1	20.4	25.4	23.0	22.1	21.7	25.0	22.4	24.5	24.8	23.1	7.7
3. Some extent	22.7	23.8	21.6	23.3	20.4	27.6	19.6	20.5	24.6	23.8	21.5	21.3	20.8	21.6	25.8	34.5
4. Considerable extent	18.0	19.3	16.4	18.0	16.6	16.5	18.9	17.9	18.5	18.3	17.9	19.4	17.6	21.0	15.2	10.6
5. A great extent	17.8	15.4	20.1	16.1	25.8	15.9	16.1	21.6	17.0	18.4	16.8	17.8	16.1	17.8	18.6	12.3
Item 21600 Subject C01,M05 N ★	2067	1010	1017	1659	196	479	581	580	428	1189	789	784	416	303	511	20
D06E: Let you get to know people over age 30?																
1. Not at all	12.0	13.1	10.9	11.3	16.5	11.8	11.0	12.4	13.2	13.8	9.9	9.2	18.4	9.1	12.9	11.4
2. A little	18.7	20.5	17.3	18.7	18.0	15.1	21.1	20.1	17.7	18.3	19.0	21.2	18.2	17.6	16.6	18.4
3. Some extent	19.9	19.9	19.8	20.5	18.4	22.4	19.1	18.9	19.4	20.7	18.7	20.8	17.9	21.2	19.5	18.5
4. Considerable extent	22.3	22.7	21.7	23.5	15.3	23.8	23.6	21.0	20.7	20.4	25.5	21.4	20.1	22.6	25.7	21.0
5. A great extent	27.1	23.8	30.4	26.0	31.9	26.9	25.2	27.6	28.9	26.8	26.9	27.4	25.6	29.5	25.4	30.7
Item 21610 Subject C01,M02 N ★	2061	1008	1012	1653	197	476	577	581	428	1185	786	784	415	303	506	20
D06F: Cause you stress and tension?																
1. Not at all	24.8	29.3	20.6	24.9	25.5	23.3	24.8	27.2	23.4	26.8	22.2	28.0	23.5	31.7	17.3	29.2
2. A little	32.7	32.8	32.6	32.6	30.8	34.2	31.0	31.7	34.8	33.8	31.3	33.5	37.4	21.7	35.0	12.3
3. Some extent	21.6	19.6	23.8	22.0	21.1	19.1	20.8	23.0	23.4	20.1	23.4	19.1	22.7	26.4	22.6	16.3
4. Considerable extent	11.3	10.6	11.6	11.4	11.4	12.2	12.5	8.4	12.8	12.0	10.1	11.1	9.7	10.9	12.3	20.5
5. A great extent	9.5	7.7	11.4	9.1	11.2	11.2	10.9	9.7	5.6	7.2	13.0	8.3	6.7	9.3	12.9	21.6
Item 21620 Subject C01 N ★	2052	1002	1009	1646	195	476	574	578	425	1183	780	780	414	300	505	20

★=excludes respondents for whom question was inappropriate.

QUESTIONNAIRE FORM 4 1985	TOTAL	SEX		RACE		REGION				4YR COLLEGE PLANS		ILLICIT DRUG USE: LIFETIME				
		M	F	White	Black	NE	NC	S	W	Yes	No	None	Marijuana Only	Few Pills	More Pills	Any Heroin
N (Weighted No. of Cases):	3279	1565	1610	2464	390	772	892	1004	612	1853	1170	1312	662	442	746	24
% of Weighted Total:	100.0	47.7	49.1	75.1	11.9	23.5	27.2	30.6	18.7	56.5	35.7	40.0	20.2	13.5	22.8	0.7

D06G: Interfere with your education?

1. Not at all	47.7	44.9	50.4	48.0	49.5	48.5	48.2	47.0	47.2	48.1	48.3	52.1	46.3	42.6	45.7	45.0
2. A little	27.2	28.1	26.5	27.3	26.2	28.2	24.9	29.2	26.5	28.2	25.1	24.9	32.3	31.1	24.0	11.6
3. Some extent	13.9	13.8	13.9	15.0	11.9	12.5	15.3	12.9	14.7	13.6	14.1	13.6	11.3	15.7	15.4	19.9
4. Considerable extent	6.5	8.1	4.9	6.1	4.8	6.2	6.9	6.1	6.8	5.8	6.8	5.2	6.2	5.8	8.5	23.5
5. A great extent	4.7	5.2	4.3	3.6	7.6	4.6	4.7	4.8	4.9	4.1	5.8	4.3	3.8	4.8	6.3	-
Item 21630 Subject C01 N★	2059	1007	1011	1650	197	474	577	580	428	1186	784	783	414	301	507	20

D06H: Interfere with your social life?

1. Not at all	23.9	22.8	24.9	22.8	32.1	27.2	22.8	23.9	21.6	22.5	25.9	28.7	22.7	22.3	17.2	38.6
2. A little	31.1	31.6	31.0	32.0	27.9	31.0	29.2	30.7	34.4	32.1	30.0	29.4	38.0	33.9	28.0	13.0
3. Some extent	21.8	21.5	22.2	22.8	16.5	16.5	23.7	22.5	24.4	23.9	19.8	21.5	18.4	20.1	25.9	26.7
4. Considerable extent	13.3	14.4	12.3	13.2	10.0	14.0	15.4	11.1	12.9	13.6	12.1	11.9	12.7	13.2	16.2	10.6
5. A great extent	9.9	9.7	9.6	9.1	13.4	11.4	8.9	11.8	6.8	7.9	12.3	8.6	8.2	10.4	12.7	11.2
Item 21640 Subject C01 N★	2051	1000	1010	1648	192	475	574	579	422	1185	778	782	413	299	504	20

D06I: Interfere with your family life?

1. Not at all	45.4	43.0	47.7	44.5	54.2	51.2	42.1	46.2	42.4	45.1	46.6	47.2	45.3	42.5	45.0	47.1
2. A little	26.2	28.2	24.2	27.8	16.6	24.0	28.4	24.5	28.0	26.5	26.7	25.8	28.9	27.3	24.5	10.2
3. Some extent	16.8	17.0	16.9	16.7	16.9	13.9	16.2	17.0	20.8	17.5	15.6	16.2	14.7	21.2	17.1	16.8
4. Considerable extent	7.4	8.3	6.7	7.2	7.8	6.6	8.4	7.6	6.6	7.1	6.7	7.4	7.0	5.9	7.5	17.0
5. A great extent	4.1	3.5	4.5	3.8	4.5	4.3	5.0	4.6	2.1	3.7	4.5	3.4	4.0	3.2	5.9	8.9
Item 21650 Subject C01 N★	2051	1000	1010	1646	194	473	577	576	424	1187	776	780	414	301	502	20

D07: To what extent is (was) this job . . .

D07A: An interesting job to do?

1. Not at all	18.6	20.6	16.6	19.3	17.2	20.4	19.8	16.2	18.1	18.0	19.2	16.8	16.6	16.8	23.1	25.4
2. A little	23.1	23.2	23.4	23.2	21.5	25.8	21.7	21.0	25.1	24.3	21.8	20.3	27.7	19.5	26.4	20.0
3. Some extent	27.8	27.2	27.8	28.1	21.2	25.5	25.9	29.4	30.4	28.0	27.5	28.4	26.6	32.4	25.5	21.8
4. Considerable extent	18.3	17.7	18.8	18.8	17.4	15.7	18.4	21.1	17.2	17.9	18.8	20.9	16.0	18.2	16.5	17.9
5. A great extent	12.2	11.2	13.4	10.7	22.7	12.6	14.2	12.3	9.2	11.8	12.7	13.7	13.1	13.0	8.4	14.9
Item 21660 Subject C01 N★	2049	997	1011	1644	194	473	573	579	424	1183	777	785	411	299	501	20

D07B: A job you COULD be happy doing for most of your life?

1. Not at all	66.2	65.7	67.4	67.5	60.7	70.2	64.7	62.9	68.4	71.9	57.9	61.7	68.9	65.6	73.0	45.6
2. A little	12.5	12.8	11.9	12.8	12.0	11.4	11.5	12.9	14.3	10.4	15.2	14.0	10.0	15.4	10.1	17.2
3. Some extent	9.3	7.9	10.5	8.8	9.9	7.1	10.7	10.2	8.9	8.2	11.3	9.7	11.5	8.2	7.4	16.0
4. Considerable extent	6.6	8.6	4.3	6.3	7.5	5.0	7.3	7.6	6.2	5.6	8.4	8.3	5.3	5.3	5.3	10.0
5. A great extent	5.3	4.9	5.9	4.5	9.9	6.4	5.8	6.4	2.2	3.9	7.2	6.4	4.2	5.5	4.2	11.2
Item 21670 Subject C01 N★	2042	994	1008	1639	193	471	569	578	425	1182	772	782	410	299	499	20

D07C: The type of work you EXPECT to be doing for most of your life?

1. Not at all	75.3	75.4	75.9	76.7	72.9	76.1	72.4	73.8	80.6	82.0	65.7	72.4	80.2	75.7	77.7	52.4
2. A little	7.2	6.9	7.1	7.0	6.7	7.2	7.1	7.8	6.7	6.7	8.2	7.8	7.3	9.1	5.7	-
3. Some extent	7.4	6.5	8.3	7.0	7.7	7.3	8.7	7.9	5.3	4.5	12.0	9.3	5.1	4.7	7.2	17.2
4. Considerable extent	5.0	6.3	3.8	4.8	5.8	3.5	6.6	5.3	4.1	4.1	6.1	5.7	4.0	5.1	4.5	12.7
5. A great extent	5.0	5.0	4.9	4.6	6.9	5.8	5.3	5.2	3.3	2.8	8.0	4.7	3.3	5.4	4.9	17.6
Item 21680 Subject C01 N★	2040	995	1005	1638	192	468	570	577	424	1184	768	780	410	299	498	20

D07D: A good stepping-stone toward the kind of work you want in the long run?

1. Not at all	55.1	56.0	54.6	55.9	50.5	59.6	54.7	51.7	55.3	59.9	47.9	53.1	56.5	54.0	58.3	48.3
2. A little	18.6	18.8	18.2	18.5	20.3	16.5	16.9	22.3	18.2	18.8	18.5	18.4	20.6	19.2	17.3	21.4
3. Some extent	9.0	8.1	9.8	8.5	10.2	7.6	10.7	8.2	9.5	7.1	12.2	10.9	8.2	6.9	8.2	12.8
4. Considerable extent	8.5	8.8	8.1	8.8	5.2	7.9	8.2	9.7	8.1	7.9	9.7	8.8	6.7	10.4	8.2	6.3
5. A great extent	8.8	8.3	9.2	8.3	13.8	8.4	9.5	8.1	9.0	6.4	11.7	8.9	7.9	9.6	8.1	11.2
Item 21690 Subject C01 N★	2032	987	1005	1633	191	464	571	575	422	1181	765	778	409	297	495	20

★=excludes respondents for whom question was inappropriate.

QUESTIONNAIRE FORM 4 1985	TOTAL	SEX		RACE		REGION				4YR COLLEGE PLANS		ILLICIT DRUG USE: LIFETIME				
		M	F	White	Black	NE	NC	S	W	Yes	No	None	Mari- juana Only	Few Pills	More Pills	Any Her- oin
N (Weighted No. of Cases):	3279	1565	1610	2464	390	772	892	1004	612	1853	1170	1312	662	442	746	24
% of Weighted Total:	100.0	47.7	49.1	75.1	11.9	23.5	27.2	30.6	18.7	56.5	35.7	40.0	20.2	13.5	22.8	0.7

D07E: The kind of work people do just for the money?

1. Not at all	20.7	19.1	22.6	21.3	16.9	22.3	19.5	21.0	20.1	20.6	22.2	22.5	21.7	21.6	17.3	17.3
2. A little	17.6	16.9	18.0	17.4	19.1	15.2	16.0	20.3	18.4	15.8	18.5	16.6	21.8	17.4	15.4	6.2
3. Some extent	18.2	15.6	20.5	17.6	18.3	14.8	19.7	18.7	19.0	17.1	20.4	19.8	15.5	18.2	17.8	23.4
4. Considerable extent	15.2	18.5	11.7	15.6	13.4	16.3	14.4	13.7	17.3	15.8	14.9	16.9	14.4	13.2	14.6	20.6
5. A great extent	28.3	29.9	27.2	28.2	32.3	31.3	30.3	26.2	25.2	30.7	23.9	24.2	26.6	29.6	34.9	32.5
Item 21700 Subject C01 N★	2028	990	999	1631	190	464	568	574	422	1179	761	777	408	292	497	20

D08: To what extent did any high school teacher or counselor help you get this job?

1. Not at all	82.2	83.0	81.2	84.1	68.0	85.3	79.5	80.2	85.1	86.6	75.4	80.7	83.3	80.2	85.5	69.9
2. A little	4.0	4.6	3.5	3.7	6.5	3.5	4.2	4.4	4.1	3.1	5.7	4.8	3.7	5.6	1.8	6.4
3. Some extent	3.3	3.1	3.4	3.1	3.4	2.6	3.7	2.8	4.2	2.5	4.7	3.1	3.1	4.0	3.4	10.4
4. Considerable extent	4.5	4.7	4.4	3.9	9.0	2.7	5.4	6.1	3.2	3.0	6.5	5.2	3.2	4.0	4.8	9.3
5. A great extent	5.9	4.5	7.5	5.2	13.1	6.0	7.2	6.5	3.3	4.8	7.6	6.3	6.8	6.1	4.6	4.0
Item 21710 Subject C01,M02 N★	2001	982	980	1610	189	455	565	567	415	1163	750	766	408	293	483	20

D09: Is (was) this job part of a work-study program?

1. Yes	16.4	13.9	18.5	15.0	26.9	12.1	14.6	21.7	16.1	11.3	23.9	15.2	16.5	18.7	16.2	11.4
2. No	83.6	86.1	81.5	85.0	73.1	87.9	85.4	78.3	83.9	88.7	76.1	84.8	83.5	81.3	83.8	88.6
Item 21720 Subject C01 N★	1987	956	994	1605	182	460	552	564	411	1160	743	761	404	289	485	18

D10: People have different opinions about world problems. How much do you agree or disagree with each of the following statements?

D10A: I feel that I can do very little to change the way the world is today

1. Disagree	9.3	10.0	8.7	8.2	13.6	9.7	8.8	9.9	8.9	10.6	7.3	10.3	8.9	9.6	7.7	4.7
2. Mostly disagree	20.3	17.9	22.8	20.4	20.3	18.7	18.2	20.5	24.9	23.7	15.2	22.8	19.4	17.8	18.0	8.1
3. Neither	24.3	24.9	23.7	24.8	23.1	25.1	26.4	23.1	22.5	22.4	27.2	24.2	25.2	24.2	24.9	25.9
4. Mostly agree	29.2	28.7	29.9	30.8	24.4	28.1	30.2	29.6	28.4	30.0	27.8	29.0	29.1	29.1	30.7	20.9
5. Agree	16.8	18.6	14.9	15.8	18.6	18.4	16.4	16.9	15.3	13.4	22.6	13.7	17.5	19.3	18.7	40.3
Item 10920 Subject I02,J N	2876	1355	1473	2247	315	609	807	904	556	1720	1038	1188	573	400	642	21

D10B: It does little good to clean up air and water pollution because this society will not last long enough for it to matter

1. Disagree	40.4	41.3	40.0	41.4	33.4	40.9	38.0	40.2	43.4	45.8	31.6	43.4	40.8	40.2	35.2	25.0
2. Mostly disagree	28.0	25.9	29.8	30.2	21.0	26.8	29.1	27.5	28.3	28.5	27.5	26.7	32.0	24.4	29.8	10.2
3. Neither	17.6	17.4	17.5	16.9	16.3	18.8	21.0	14.8	15.9	14.1	22.7	15.7	14.3	20.1	22.1	38.5
4. Mostly agree	8.2	8.7	7.5	7.0	15.7	7.6	7.5	9.5	7.9	8.0	9.0	8.4	8.1	8.2	7.6	9.5
5. Agree	5.9	6.7	5.2	4.4	13.6	5.9	4.4	8.0	4.5	3.6	9.2	5.8	4.7	7.0	5.3	16.7
Item 10930 Subject F05,J N	2859	1349	1461	2235	312	602	803	899	555	1707	1038	1183	569	397	636	22

D10C: When things get tough enough, we'll put our minds to it and find a technological solution

1. Disagree	6.5	7.8	5.3	6.1	8.6	7.7	6.8	5.5	6.7	6.7	6.6	6.9	5.7	5.6	7.6	9.4
2. Mostly disagree	10.4	10.9	10.2	10.9	7.4	11.4	12.3	8.4	9.9	11.8	8.3	9.7	11.9	10.2	10.8	15.1
3. Neither	24.0	20.5	27.2	24.6	19.8	21.7	28.1	21.1	25.1	22.0	26.8	21.3	21.8	24.1	29.3	22.6
4. Mostly agree	38.1	36.6	39.1	39.7	33.3	37.8	36.7	39.6	37.7	38.7	37.0	40.4	39.2	37.3	34.9	29.2
5. Agree	21.0	24.2	18.2	18.7	30.9	21.4	16.1	25.4	20.6	20.7	21.3	21.6	21.4	22.7	17.4	23.7
Item 10940 Subject I01,J N	2833	1344	1440	2216	310	595	789	899	550	1701	1021	1172	563	397	627	21

★=excludes respondents for whom question was inappropriate.

QUESTIONNAIRE FORM 4 1985	TOTAL	SEX		RACE		REGION				4YR COLLEGE PLANS		ILLICIT DRUG USE: LIFETIME				
		M	F	White	Black	NE	NC	S	W	Yes	No	None	Mari-juana Only	Few Pills	More Pills	Any Her-oin
N (Weighted No. of Cases):	3279	1565	1610	2464	390	772	892	1004	612	1853	1170	1312	662	442	746	24
% of Weighted Total:	100.0	47.7	49.1	75.1	11.9	23.5	27.2	30.6	18.7	56.5	35.7	40.0	20.2	13.5	22.8	0.7
D10D: When I think about all the terrible things that have been happening, it is hard for me to hold out much hope for the world																
1. Disagree	18.2	18.8	17.8	18.4	16.8	19.3	14.2	19.4	21.2	21.2	13.8	18.2	20.6	18.2	16.0	4.3
2. Mostly disagree	28.5	28.8	28.2	30.6	19.4	29.4	28.3	26.7	30.5	32.4	22.6	30.8	28.3	27.6	26.0	22.4
3. Neither	27.0	27.6	26.5	28.0	18.9	27.7	30.7	23.8	26.2	23.1	33.4	25.1	24.9	28.5	31.3	23.8
4. Mostly agree	18.8	17.9	19.5	17.4	28.6	15.8	20.0	21.0	16.7	17.5	20.5	19.0	17.7	18.7	19.5	26.8
5. Agree	7.5	7.0	8.0	5.6	16.3	7.8	6.8	9.1	5.4	5.9	9.7	6.9	8.5	6.9	7.2	22.6
Item 10950 Subject J N	2818	1335	1434	2202	309	594	785	890	548	1693	1013	1170	560	395	622	18
D10E: I often wonder if there is any real purpose to my life in light of the world situation																
1. Disagree	28.7	29.4	28.7	29.2	26.8	29.0	27.2	27.1	33.3	33.3	21.5	30.7	29.4	28.1	25.6	24.9
2. Mostly disagree	20.2	19.4	20.6	21.3	15.7	19.4	20.6	19.3	22.1	22.5	17.3	21.0	21.3	19.7	18.4	12.7
3. Neither	27.8	28.2	27.1	28.5	25.4	30.1	30.0	29.1	20.1	24.7	33.7	25.3	28.3	28.7	31.3	20.5
4. Mostly agree	16.1	16.5	15.8	15.3	17.4	14.8	16.6	15.2	18.0	14.1	18.5	16.3	13.7	17.0	17.6	23.9
5. Agree	7.2	6.6	7.7	5.7	14.7	6.7	5.6	9.3	6.5	5.4	9.0	6.7	7.3	6.5	7.1	17.9
Item 10960 Subject J N	2811	1334	1430	2199	308	588	782	892	549	1689	1011	1162	558	396	622	21
D10F: My guess is that this country will be caught up in a major world upheaval in the next 10 years																
1. Disagree	14.7	15.9	13.6	15.0	13.7	16.2	12.4	16.7	13.3	16.0	12.5	14.8	17.7	13.8	12.3	10.2
2. Mostly disagree	18.1	19.6	16.7	19.6	13.8	17.4	21.1	16.6	17.3	19.2	17.1	20.4	16.3	15.8	17.6	6.4
3. Neither	34.4	31.4	37.2	34.6	34.6	34.1	36.5	33.2	33.5	31.7	39.2	34.5	34.3	33.3	35.1	42.2
4. Mostly agree	21.6	21.6	21.6	20.9	20.9	21.9	19.5	21.3	24.8	22.7	19.6	19.4	21.9	24.2	24.9	13.3
5. Agree	11.1	11.5	10.9	9.9	17.1	10.5	10.5	12.1	11.1	10.5	11.6	11.0	9.8	12.9	10.1	27.9
Item 10970 Subject J N	2800	1328	1425	2188	309	587	781	888	543	1680	1010	1160	554	396	617	20
D10G: Nuclear or biological annihilation will probably be the fate of all mankind, within my lifetime																
1. Disagree	21.6	25.3	18.6	22.5	19.4	21.1	20.8	21.8	22.9	25.0	16.2	23.5	22.7	20.1	17.8	3.6
2. Mostly disagree	18.5	20.8	16.5	19.9	11.9	18.5	19.8	16.4	19.9	21.0	14.8	19.5	18.9	16.7	18.3	11.2
3. Neither	31.4	26.8	35.4	31.8	30.8	32.1	31.6	33.3	27.3	28.6	36.2	30.7	31.5	33.3	30.9	28.3
4. Mostly agree	17.1	14.9	19.0	16.1	19.5	16.3	18.6	16.0	17.5	15.6	19.7	15.9	16.3	17.1	20.1	28.7
5. Agree	11.5	12.3	10.6	9.7	18.4	12.0	9.2	12.5	12.5	9.8	13.2	10.3	10.5	12.8	12.9	28.1
Item 10980 Subject J N	2797	1331	1420	2192	306	588	784	888	538	1686	1004	1155	557	396	617	21
D10H: The human race has come through tough times before, and will do so again																
1. Disagree	4.8	5.7	3.8	4.1	9.5	5.6	4.9	5.0	3.5	3.9	6.0	4.0	4.4	4.5	6.1	15.5
2. Mostly disagree	7.1	8.6	5.9	6.6	8.8	6.5	7.9	6.6	7.8	6.9	7.4	7.4	6.5	6.4	7.8	6.2
3. Neither	22.6	21.0	24.1	22.7	22.3	20.6	27.4	20.7	21.3	20.1	26.7	22.0	21.8	23.4	22.7	39.5
4. Mostly agree	35.8	31.5	39.7	37.4	27.2	35.4	34.7	36.1	37.2	36.9	34.6	35.4	38.0	34.0	37.8	10.8
5. Agree	29.7	33.2	26.5	29.2	32.2	31.9	25.2	31.7	30.3	32.2	25.3	31.2	29.4	31.7	25.6	28.0
Item 10990 Subject J N	2811	1336	1428	2200	308	587	787	892	545	1692	1011	1163	559	397	622	21
The next questions are about alcohol use–this time asking separately about beer, wine, and hard liquor.																
D11: On how many occasions (if any) have you had a beer to drink . . .																
D11A: . . . in your lifetime?																
1. 0 occasions	11.8	9.8	13.7	9.1	28.7	7.8	10.0	15.8	12.1	12.3	10.3	25.0	2.7	4.0	1.9	-
2. 1-2	12.6	9.5	15.3	11.3	22.1	9.4	14.5	14.1	11.1	12.8	12.1	21.6	8.3	6.7	3.9	-
3. 3-5	8.8	7.2	10.4	8.2	11.1	6.6	8.3	10.9	8.8	8.7	9.3	13.1	6.9	8.6	3.6	-
4. 6-9	7.5	5.8	9.1	7.3	7.4	8.3	6.6	6.6	9.4	7.8	7.1	8.0	8.6	8.6	5.6	-
5. 10-19	11.2	10.5	12.3	11.9	7.1	12.5	11.9	10.0	11.0	11.4	10.7	9.7	18.2	14.8	6.4	3.0
6. 20-39	12.2	11.8	12.3	13.0	10.6	13.5	12.9	11.8	10.1	12.1	12.6	7.5	19.0	16.2	11.6	10.0
7. 40 or more	35.9	45.4	26.9	39.3	12.9	41.9	35.8	30.7	37.4	34.9	37.9	15.1	36.2	41.1	67.0	87.0
Item 11000 Subject A01a N	2703	1274	1389	2154	269	579	760	839	525	1647	956	1080	548	385	626	20

QUESTIONNAIRE FORM 4 1985	TOTAL	SEX		RACE		REGION				4YR COLLEGE PLANS		ILLICIT DRUG USE: LIFETIME				
		M	F	White	Black	NE	NC	S	W	Yes	No	None	Mari-juana Only	Few Pills	More Pills	Any Her-oin
N (Weighted No. of Cases):	3279	1565	1610	2464	390	772	892	1004	612	1853	1170	1312	662	442	746	24
% of Weighted Total:	100.0	47.7	49.1	75.1	11.9	23.5	27.2	30.6	18.7	56.5	35.7	40.0	20.2	13.5	22.8	0.7

D11B: . . . during the last 12 months?

	TOTAL	M	F	White	Black	NE	NC	S	W	Yes	No	None	Mari-juana Only	Few Pills	More Pills	Any Her-oin
1. 0 occasions	25.5	19.8	30.9	21.5	50.5	19.3	24.8	30.8	24.9	26.1	24.5	44.5	12.7	15.1	10.1	6.1
2. 1-2	14.2	11.3	16.9	13.9	17.0	14.2	12.6	14.7	15.6	14.8	12.4	19.4	13.0	16.1	5.9	-
3. 3-5	11.2	11.0	11.3	11.6	8.5	10.3	12.1	10.6	11.6	10.9	11.9	11.0	14.2	12.7	8.4	-
4. 6-9	9.4	8.9	9.7	10.0	7.4	12.0	9.7	8.2	8.0	9.0	10.0	7.4	14.3	10.6	8.5	7.4
5. 10-19	13.6	15.4	12.0	14.8	7.5	14.8	13.7	14.0	11.6	13.5	14.1	8.0	20.1	16.3	15.8	11.4
6. 20-39	11.1	13.6	8.7	11.6	4.9	10.4	12.0	9.4	13.2	11.6	10.3	4.8	13.0	16.4	17.5	4.4
7. 40 or more	15.0	19.9	10.5	16.7	4.1	19.0	15.0	12.2	15.2	14.2	16.8	4.8	12.7	12.8	33.9	70.7
Item 11010 Subject A01b N	2681	1268	1373	2144	259	577	756	827	521	1636	950	1067	545	382	626	20

D11C: . . . during the last 30 days?

	TOTAL	M	F	White	Black	NE	NC	S	W	Yes	No	None	Mari-juana Only	Few Pills	More Pills	Any Her-oin
1. 0 occasions	43.3	35.5	50.6	39.4	65.7	35.6	42.6	49.0	43.6	44.9	40.2	66.1	31.3	34.9	20.2	19.2
2. 1-2	20.9	20.7	21.0	21.8	18.0	24.4	20.9	19.5	19.2	20.8	20.9	17.6	28.9	26.0	16.8	4.4
3. 3-5	13.3	15.9	11.2	14.4	7.9	13.3	14.3	11.4	15.1	13.5	13.4	8.1	17.8	13.4	18.9	2.6
4. 6-9	10.3	12.1	8.3	10.7	5.4	11.5	10.8	8.5	11.1	9.5	11.7	4.4	10.6	16.5	16.3	14.0
5. 10-19	8.1	10.1	6.3	9.2	1.7	10.1	6.8	7.6	8.4	7.7	8.8	2.7	9.1	6.8	17.3	9.6
6. 20-39	2.5	3.2	1.8	2.8	-	3.2	2.4	2.4	2.1	2.3	3.0	0.3	0.9	1.4	7.2	35.8
7. 40 or more	1.6	2.6	0.8	1.6	1.4	1.9	2.2	1.7	0.4	1.4	1.9	0.8	1.4	1.0	3.3	14.5
Item 11020 Subject A01c N	2686	1269	1376	2146	261	579	754	830	522	1635	955	1069	543	385	628	20

D12: Think back over the LAST TWO WEEKS. How many times have you had five or more 12-ounce cans of beer (or the equivalent) in a row?

	TOTAL	M	F	White	Black	NE	NC	S	W	Yes	No	None	Mari-juana Only	Few Pills	More Pills	Any Her-oin
1. None	68.0	57.4	77.6	64.8	87.1	64.5	65.8	73.4	66.2	70.2	64.5	86.9	64.0	59.1	44.2	21.4
2. Once	10.8	13.1	8.7	12.2	3.3	8.6	12.7	9.2	13.1	10.8	11.0	5.7	14.7	15.7	13.3	7.3
3. Twice	8.1	10.8	5.8	8.6	3.7	9.7	9.9	5.3	8.4	7.5	9.3	3.7	8.7	12.7	13.1	8.7
4. Three to five times	7.8	10.6	5.2	8.6	3.5	10.4	6.5	7.3	7.5	7.2	8.6	2.5	7.8	8.9	16.5	15.3
5. Six to nine times	3.1	4.4	1.9	3.4	1.4	3.4	2.8	3.0	3.1	2.5	3.9	0.7	3.0	2.0	7.4	28.9
6. Ten or more times	2.2	3.7	0.9	2.3	1.1	3.4	2.2	1.8	1.7	1.7	2.7	0.5	1.7	1.5	5.4	18.5
Item 11030 Subject A01d N	2642	1226	1378	2107	262	556	743	825	517	1619	927	1065	542	368	608	18

D13: On how many occasions (if any) have you had wine to drink . . .

D13A: . . . in your lifetime?

	TOTAL	M	F	White	Black	NE	NC	S	W	Yes	No	None	Mari-juana Only	Few Pills	More Pills	Any Her-oin
1. 0 occasions	14.1	15.9	12.5	11.9	31.6	7.7	13.8	20.0	12.2	13.0	15.4	24.5	8.8	7.7	5.2	3.0
2. 1-2	16.7	16.4	16.8	15.9	22.5	14.4	17.7	18.5	14.8	14.8	20.3	23.5	16.5	14.5	6.6	2.2
3. 3-5	17.1	18.3	16.0	17.5	12.4	17.8	16.6	16.4	18.0	18.3	14.9	19.4	17.8	19.1	11.2	7.8
4. 6-9	15.1	14.7	15.6	15.4	13.1	13.1	16.4	15.2	15.2	14.1	16.4	13.1	17.2	16.4	15.1	18.9
5. 10-19	16.1	15.0	17.3	17.0	11.1	17.2	16.9	14.1	17.1	17.9	13.3	10.2	19.6	22.4	20.4	7.7
6. 20-39	10.0	9.0	10.9	11.0	4.3	13.9	9.3	7.5	11.0	10.4	9.8	5.6	12.7	9.1	16.4	17.4
7. 40 or more	10.8	10.8	10.9	11.4	4.9	15.8	9.3	8.3	11.7	11.4	10.0	3.8	7.6	10.9	25.1	42.9
Item 11040 Subject A01a N	2722	1290	1391	2169	272	579	766	849	528	1649	967	1086	549	391	634	20

D13B: . . . during the last 12 months?

	TOTAL	M	F	White	Black	NE	NC	S	W	Yes	No	None	Mari-juana Only	Few Pills	More Pills	Any Her-oin
1. 0 occasions	32.6	34.9	30.2	30.0	53.9	26.0	31.2	39.8	30.2	29.6	36.7	45.5	28.5	29.1	17.0	13.0
2. 1-2	26.6	25.9	27.4	27.0	22.1	26.9	29.4	24.2	26.1	27.7	25.0	30.9	26.6	26.4	19.9	12.4
3. 3-5	15.2	16.3	14.3	15.7	10.2	14.2	16.3	14.9	15.1	15.3	14.5	11.4	18.2	17.1	17.2	-
4. 6-9	10.6	9.0	12.1	11.5	7.4	12.3	11.6	8.3	11.1	11.3	10.3	6.9	13.7	12.5	13.3	18.4
5. 10-19	8.2	7.4	9.0	8.9	3.2	11.4	7.3	6.4	8.8	8.8	7.2	3.1	7.8	9.9	16.5	12.8
6. 20-39	3.8	2.9	4.5	3.6	1.7	4.2	2.9	3.4	5.1	4.0	3.5	1.8	4.2	3.5	6.7	12.7
7. 40 or more	3.1	3.6	2.4	3.3	1.5	4.9	1.4	3.0	3.7	3.2	2.8	0.4	1.1	1.7	9.5	30.7
Item 11050 Subject A01b N	2681	1268	1372	2137	266	572	754	835	519	1628	950	1070	542	382	627	20

D13C: . . . during the last 30 days?

	TOTAL	M	F	White	Black	NE	NC	S	W	Yes	No	None	Mari-juana Only	Few Pills	More Pills	Any Her-oin
1. 0 occasions	64.0	65.8	62.6	62.4	78.8	56.1	65.9	69.3	61.6	62.7	65.4	76.3	60.0	64.6	47.1	29.1
2. 1-2	22.3	21.3	23.0	23.2	14.8	25.8	23.7	18.1	23.0	22.8	22.0	17.2	26.7	23.2	26.5	16.9
3. 3-5	7.5	6.9	8.2	8.2	2.9	10.5	6.7	6.4	7.3	8.3	6.4	4.1	8.9	7.4	12.2	12.5
4. 6-9	3.5	3.1	3.9	3.5	1.8	3.6	2.1	3.2	6.2	3.9	3.1	1.5	2.8	3.9	6.9	27.0
5. 10-19	1.5	1.4	1.4	1.6	1.1	1.9	1.2	1.7	1.0	1.2	2.1	0.6	1.2	0.7	3.5	8.2
6. 20-39	0.6	0.7	0.6	0.6	0.5	0.8	0.3	0.8	0.6	0.8	0.4	0.1	0.3	0.2	2.2	-
7. 40 or more	0.5	0.7	0.2	0.6	0.1	1.2	0.1	0.5	0.3	0.4	0.5	0.1	0.1	0.1	1.5	6.4
Item 11060 Subject A01c N	2672	1262	1370	2134	262	571	755	831	516	1625	948	1066	539	383	625	20

QUESTIONNAIRE FORM 4 1985	TOTAL	SEX		RACE		REGION				4YR COLLEGE PLANS		ILLICIT DRUG USE: LIFETIME				
		M	F	White	Black	NE	NC	S	W	Yes	No	None	Mari-juana Only	Few Pills	More Pills	Any Her-oin
N (Weighted No. of Cases):	3279	1565	1610	2464	390	772	892	1004	612	1853	1170	1312	662	442	746	24
% of Weighted Total:	100.0	47.7	49.1	75.1	11.9	23.5	27.2	30.6	18.7	56.5	35.7	40.0	20.2	13.5	22.8	0.7

D14: Think back over the LAST TWO WEEKS. How many times have you had five or more 4-ounce glasses of wine in a row (or the equivalent, which is about three-fourths of a bottle)?

1. None	87.2	87.1	87.5	86.9	91.7	84.3	87.7	89.1	86.7	88.1	86.1	95.3	86.5	87.4	75.1	51.8
2. Once	6.1	5.8	6.4	6.3	4.2	7.7	6.7	4.9	5.6	6.1	5.9	3.3	7.5	5.8	10.0	8.7
3. Twice	2.8	2.7	2.9	2.9	1.9	2.5	2.4	2.7	3.8	3.0	2.7	0.5	3.5	2.7	6.0	2.6
4. Three to five times	2.2	1.9	2.5	2.5	0.5	2.7	2.5	1.5	2.5	1.9	2.9	0.6	2.0	3.1	4.7	5.0
5. Six to nine times	1.2	1.9	0.7	1.0	1.5	2.2	0.4	1.2	1.4	0.7	1.9	0.3	0.4	0.9	3.4	13.0
6. Ten or more times	0.4	0.6	0.2	0.4	0.3	0.5	0.2	0.6	*	0.2	0.4	0.1	0.1	0.1	0.8	18.9
Item 11070 Subject A01d N	2664	1252	1372	2118	269	556	751	834	522	1618	944	1079	540	377	611	15

These next questions are about hard liquor. (Hard liquor includes whiskey, Scotch, bourbon, gin, vodka, rum, etc., or mixed drinks made with liquor.)

D15: On how many occasions (if any) have you had liquor to drink . . .

D15A: . . . in your lifetime?

1. 0 occasions	20.3	19.0	21.5	16.5	48.0	15.4	18.8	25.9	18.8	20.3	19.6	38.7	10.4	6.9	4.4	7.4
2. 1-2	14.1	13.2	15.2	14.1	17.1	11.3	16.0	15.1	12.8	15.2	12.3	19.5	14.9	15.1	4.3	-
3. 3-5	11.2	11.7	10.6	11.2	10.7	10.3	10.9	11.9	11.5	10.9	11.9	13.3	14.3	11.1	5.5	4.9
4. 6-9	11.1	11.0	11.4	11.9	9.7	11.8	12.4	10.3	9.8	11.1	11.2	10.1	14.0	13.7	8.3	13.0
5. 10-19	16.0	16.1	15.9	17.6	4.9	18.3	14.6	15.2	16.8	16.4	15.4	9.7	21.0	21.0	19.6	6.9
6. 20-39	12.2	13.2	11.3	13.2	5.5	14.0	12.7	10.1	12.8	12.5	12.2	5.2	14.6	18.1	19.0	9.1
7. 40 or more	15.0	15.8	14.0	15.5	4.0	18.9	14.5	11.4	17.4	13.7	17.4	3.6	10.7	14.0	39.0	58.7
Item 11080 Subject A01a N	2682	1263	1378	2142	265	558	757	842	525	1632	946	1075	546	385	613	20

D15B: . . . during the last 12 months?

1. 0 occasions	35.8	33.9	37.6	31.4	69.2	29.7	33.7	43.4	33.0	35.4	35.5	56.3	27.2	26.8	12.9	11.8
2. 1-2	17.2	18.3	16.3	18.2	10.8	15.1	19.9	15.9	17.8	17.2	16.7	19.2	21.3	18.8	9.8	13.5
3. 3-5	14.6	13.6	15.7	15.8	8.1	18.8	14.9	11.4	14.7	15.0	14.8	10.9	17.9	16.4	16.6	3.0
4. 6-9	11.3	13.5	9.2	12.4	5.0	13.6	11.0	11.4	9.0	11.7	10.6	6.9	15.4	13.7	14.3	3.9
5. 10-19	10.5	9.1	11.6	11.1	3.8	10.4	11.1	8.8	12.3	10.2	10.7	4.5	10.6	12.4	19.9	8.7
6. 20-39	5.5	5.6	5.2	5.7	0.9	6.5	4.5	4.0	8.2	5.6	5.7	1.0	4.4	9.6	11.9	13.2
7. 40 or more	5.2	6.0	4.5	5.5	2.2	6.0	5.0	5.1	5.0	4.9	5.9	1.4	3.1	2.3	14.6	45.9
Item 11090 Subject A01b N	2660	1253	1367	2122	262	555	748	835	522	1623	936	1067	541	380	610	20

D15C: . . . during the last 30 days?

1. 0 occasions	60.0	59.7	60.5	57.2	81.0	57.9	59.9	63.0	57.9	60.4	59.0	78.5	55.4	57.3	34.0	24.9
2. 1-2	21.4	22.0	20.8	23.2	10.0	22.7	22.5	19.7	20.9	22.2	19.8	14.8	28.1	21.6	26.9	15.6
3. 3-5	9.2	9.1	9.4	9.9	4.3	8.9	9.1	8.8	10.5	8.3	11.2	4.3	9.0	12.4	16.5	3.9
4. 6-9	5.3	5.3	5.1	5.7	2.3	5.9	4.9	4.9	5.7	5.2	5.5	1.6	4.2	5.5	12.1	18.1
5. 10-19	2.7	2.0	3.3	2.7	1.9	2.9	2.8	2.0	3.4	2.5	3.1	0.6	2.5	2.3	6.7	12.7
6. 20-39	0.9	1.0	0.7	1.0	-	0.8	0.4	1.1	1.4	1.0	0.6	-	0.5	0.7	2.2	22.6
7. 40 or more	0.6	0.9	0.2	0.4	0.4	0.9	0.5	0.6	0.3	0.5	0.7	0.2	0.4	0.1	1.6	2.2
Item 11100 Subject A01c N	2656	1252	1364	2120	261	554	747	833	522	1621	934	1063	541	380	609	20

D16: Think back over the LAST TWO WEEKS. How many times have you had five or more mixed drinks or shot-glasses of hard liquor in a row?

1. None	80.4	79.1	81.8	78.9	92.6	76.2	80.7	83.0	80.2	81.7	78.0	92.9	80.9	77.2	59.5	40.4
2. Once	8.2	8.8	7.6	9.2	2.2	10.3	8.9	7.7	5.7	8.0	8.7	3.8	8.0	10.7	14.4	4.3
3. Twice	5.8	6.3	5.4	6.4	2.4	6.5	6.1	4.6	6.6	5.4	6.5	2.2	6.6	6.9	11.5	8.4
4. Three to five times	3.6	3.7	3.5	3.7	2.1	3.4	3.3	2.8	5.7	3.2	4.7	0.7	2.9	4.1	9.7	11.0
5. Six to nine times	1.1	0.9	1.2	1.1	0.1	1.7	0.5	0.9	1.5	1.1	1.1	0.1	0.8	0.9	2.8	17.9
6. Ten or more times	0.9	1.3	0.5	0.7	0.7	1.8	0.5	1.0	0.3	0.6	0.9	0.3	0.7	0.3	2.1	18.1
Item 11110 Subject A01d N	2576	1193	1346	2064	253	520	727	814	514	1588	890	1064	521	368	566	16

These next questions ask for your opinions about the military services in the United States.

E01: To what extent do you think the following opportunities are available to people who work in the military services?

*=less than .05 per cent.

QUESTIONNAIRE FORM 4 1985	TOTAL	SEX		RACE		REGION				4YR COLLEGE PLANS		ILLICIT DRUG USE: LIFETIME				
		M	F	White	Black	NE	NC	S	W	Yes	No	None	Mari- juana Only	Few Pills	More Pills	Any Her- oin
N (Weighted No. of Cases):	3279	1565	1610	2464	390	772	892	1004	612	1853	1170	1312	662	442	746	24
% of Weighted Total:	100.0	47.7	49.1	75.1	11.9	23.5	27.2	30.6	18.7	56.5	35.7	40.0	20.2	13.5	22.8	0.7
E01A: A chance to get ahead																
1. To a very little extent	8.7	12.3	5.2	7.8	9.5	10.5	7.6	7.7	9.8	8.3	9.5	8.6	8.2	8.3	9.8	3.0
2. To a little extent	11.6	14.1	9.2	12.2	6.9	12.9	12.1	9.4	12.9	11.6	11.4	11.1	10.6	15.3	11.0	4.8
3. To some extent	42.0	40.6	43.2	44.1	32.0	38.4	44.4	42.9	40.9	44.8	37.5	41.5	45.5	39.1	41.3	62.0
4. To a great extent	24.8	20.8	28.6	24.4	28.9	23.4	24.4	24.9	26.5	24.6	25.3	24.6	23.8	26.1	24.4	25.8
5. To a very great extent	13.0	12.2	13.8	11.5	22.7	14.7	11.5	15.0	9.9	10.8	16.4	14.2	11.9	11.1	13.5	4.4
Item 11120 Subject L04 N	2726	1297	1381	2137	302	563	760	868	536	1648	973	1133	547	381	599	17
E01B: A chance to get more education																
1. To a very little extent	4.7	7.3	2.3	4.4	4.2	5.9	5.1	3.7	4.5	4.6	5.0	5.6	4.5	2.5	5.0	-
2. To a little extent	8.7	10.4	7.2	8.9	7.8	8.6	7.3	9.4	9.6	8.5	8.7	7.4	10.6	9.8	8.7	3.0
3. To some extent	30.8	33.6	28.1	31.3	24.4	28.5	30.2	30.5	34.5	33.4	25.9	29.5	31.1	31.6	32.0	39.4
4. To a great extent	36.6	31.9	41.0	37.9	33.0	37.8	38.8	34.7	35.5	37.3	36.8	37.3	36.2	36.4	35.5	41.1
5. To a very great extent	19.2	16.8	21.4	17.5	30.7	19.3	18.6	21.8	15.8	16.3	23.6	20.2	17.6	19.7	18.7	16.5
Item 11130 Subject B10,L04 N	2715	1293	1375	2129	302	558	757	867	534	1649	963	1132	546	377	595	17
E01C: A chance to advance to a more responsible position																
1. To a very little extent	4.7	7.0	2.4	4.5	3.5	6.8	4.5	3.3	4.9	3.8	6.3	5.2	3.6	2.8	5.9	-
2. To a little extent	7.6	9.7	5.5	7.8	7.8	7.4	7.6	7.1	8.6	7.7	6.7	6.8	7.1	11.8	6.6	15.6
3. To some extent	28.3	29.0	27.6	29.5	21.5	27.5	29.3	28.4	27.4	30.4	25.1	27.2	30.7	26.3	28.9	23.5
4. To a great extent	39.6	37.3	42.0	40.8	32.7	36.9	41.7	37.6	43.0	40.6	38.2	38.5	41.0	39.0	40.9	56.5
5. To a very great extent	19.8	17.0	22.4	17.4	34.5	21.4	16.9	23.7	16.2	17.5	23.6	22.3	17.6	20.1	17.6	4.4
Item 11140 Subject L04 N	2715	1293	1374	2128	303	560	757	866	532	1644	966	1133	546	375	596	17
E01D: A chance to have a personally more fulfilling job																
1. To a very little extent	7.5	11.1	4.2	7.8	6.2	8.4	7.4	6.1	9.1	7.8	7.2	7.3	8.6	4.7	8.9	12.1
2. To a little extent	12.6	14.8	10.6	13.0	9.6	12.9	13.6	10.6	14.3	13.6	11.0	12.6	12.5	14.2	12.1	8.0
3. To some extent	36.3	35.8	37.1	38.1	23.6	33.6	38.3	35.1	38.5	40.6	29.7	34.9	39.0	36.6	36.5	43.0
4. To a great extent	28.7	25.6	31.6	28.8	30.3	27.7	30.1	30.4	25.3	26.6	32.4	29.3	25.0	30.3	29.2	32.4
5. To a very great extent	14.8	12.8	16.6	12.3	30.2	17.5	10.6	17.9	12.9	11.3	19.6	15.9	14.9	14.2	13.3	4.4
Item 11150 Subject C05,L04 N	2709	1291	1370	2125	300	559	754	861	534	1643	963	1128	546	373	597	17
E01E: A chance to get their ideas heard																
1. To a very little extent	17.3	23.4	11.7	18.6	9.3	20.5	16.3	12.2	23.6	20.1	13.2	16.8	17.6	14.4	20.3	19.7
2. To a little extent	23.8	25.4	22.2	25.2	16.2	22.9	23.7	24.2	24.1	26.9	18.6	22.9	22.3	28.0	24.1	18.5
3. To some extent	32.6	29.5	35.9	33.0	29.0	28.0	36.8	32.7	31.6	32.4	32.8	33.2	34.0	28.9	32.9	39.0
4. To a great extent	17.1	14.1	19.9	16.4	24.6	16.6	16.6	20.2	13.6	13.9	22.2	17.5	17.7	18.0	15.0	18.4
5. To a very great extent	9.2	7.7	10.4	6.9	20.9	12.1	6.6	10.8	7.1	6.7	13.2	9.7	8.5	10.7	7.7	4.4
Item 11160 Subject L04 N	2707	1290	1370	2124	300	559	755	861	532	1642	961	1128	546	372	595	17
E02: To what extent is it likely that a person in the military can get things changed and set right if he is being treated unjustly by a superior?																
1. To a very little extent	20.8	25.6	16.2	20.6	19.4	20.1	21.2	20.0	22.3	23.2	17.1	20.9	18.8	19.1	23.3	25.8
2. To a little extent	28.9	27.2	30.3	30.4	20.5	29.4	28.9	25.7	33.6	31.6	24.6	28.6	29.5	29.5	30.1	10.7
3. To some extent	37.0	33.0	41.0	37.1	38.7	36.8	37.3	39.7	32.3	34.9	40.9	37.0	40.6	35.5	34.3	38.5
4. To a great extent	10.0	10.4	9.6	9.3	15.6	10.3	10.5	10.2	8.5	8.0	12.8	10.3	7.6	13.0	9.0	3.8
5. To a very great extent	3.4	3.9	2.9	2.6	5.7	3.4	2.2	4.5	3.3	2.4	4.5	3.2	3.4	2.9	3.2	21.3
Item 11170 Subject L04 N	2662	1279	1336	2091	298	547	741	848	526	1612	945	1113	529	366	591	16
E03: To what extent do you think there is any discrimination against women who are in the armed services?																
1. To a very little extent	14.7	18.0	11.5	13.6	20.9	14.9	14.4	14.9	14.3	12.4	18.5	15.0	15.1	11.9	14.6	13.2
2. To a little extent	27.4	29.3	25.7	28.7	21.6	27.7	29.9	26.4	25.2	27.9	26.3	28.9	27.7	28.6	22.7	44.0
3. To some extent	39.3	36.6	42.1	40.1	38.1	38.8	41.1	40.6	35.3	39.3	40.0	40.1	41.8	35.5	39.2	7.9
4. To a great extent	13.8	11.5	15.5	13.4	12.9	14.7	10.5	12.7	19.1	15.2	10.9	11.3	11.0	19.0	18.0	13.7
5. To a very great extent	4.9	4.6	5.2	4.1	6.5	3.9	4.2	5.4	6.0	5.2	4.3	4.7	4.3	5.0	5.5	21.2
Item 11180 Subject D06,L04 N	2662	1270	1344	2094	294	545	739	850	527	1612	944	1114	533	364	588	16

QUESTIONNAIRE FORM 4 1985	TOTAL	SEX		RACE		REGION				4YR COLLEGE PLANS		ILLICIT DRUG USE: LIFETIME				
		M	F	White	Black	NE	NC	S	W	Yes	No	None	Marijuana Only	Few Pills	More Pills	Any Heroin
N (Weighted No. of Cases):	3279	1565	1610	2464	390	772	892	1004	612	1853	1170	1312	662	442	746	24
% of Weighted Total:	100.0	47.7	49.1	75.1	11.9	23.5	27.2	30.6	18.7	56.5	35.7	40.0	20.2	13.5	22.8	0.7
E04: To what extent do you think there is any discrimination against black people who are in the armed services?																
1. To a very little extent	32.9	36.5	29.1	33.5	33.2	29.9	31.5	36.1	32.7	31.9	35.1	33.2	36.8	30.0	30.2	22.1
2. To a little extent	28.7	28.9	28.6	29.7	19.6	32.0	29.4	24.3	31.0	30.4	25.9	29.1	29.5	28.4	28.2	27.1
3. To some extent	29.4	25.5	33.1	29.7	30.6	28.0	29.9	31.6	26.6	29.4	28.8	27.8	26.9	31.6	33.7	23.9
4. To a great extent	6.3	6.0	6.6	5.1	11.3	6.8	6.1	5.3	7.7	6.2	6.5	6.9	5.1	7.8	4.7	13.8
5. To a very great extent	2.8	3.0	2.6	2.0	5.3	3.3	3.0	2.7	2.0	2.1	3.7	3.0	1.7	2.1	3.2	13.1
Item 11190 Subject L04,N02 N	2637	1268	1322	2076	291	546	733	834	525	1597	935	1104	529	358	583	16
E05: Do you personally feel that you would receive more just and fair treatment as a civilian or as a member of the military service?																
1. Much more fair in the military service	5.1	6.3	3.9	3.9	13.5	3.8	4.2	7.0	4.8	3.4	7.1	5.6	4.4	5.4	4.7	-
2. More fair in the military service	10.9	11.9	9.8	11.0	11.0	9.8	10.6	12.0	10.8	9.9	12.8	10.5	9.1	13.5	12.0	3.8
3. About the same	46.5	43.2	49.8	47.3	46.4	48.8	47.1	46.4	43.5	46.4	46.3	46.5	50.3	43.7	45.8	39.9
4. More fair as a civilian	14.5	16.6	12.4	15.5	6.8	14.7	14.0	13.6	16.4	16.1	12.4	14.0	16.0	15.9	12.9	13.8
5. Much more fair as a civilian	10.7	14.0	7.7	11.4	5.3	9.9	10.1	9.6	14.3	13.0	7.3	10.3	10.5	11.8	10.5	27.0
6. Question not appropriate for me	12.2	7.9	16.4	10.8	17.1	13.1	14.0	11.5	10.2	11.2	14.0	13.2	9.6	9.6	14.1	15.5
Item 11200 Subject L04 N	2633	1254	1334	2073	291	535	731	842	525	1603	931	1096	531	360	584	16
E06: If YOU felt that it was necessary for the U.S. to fight in some future war, how likely is it that you would volunteer for military service in that war?																
1. I'm sure that I would volunteer	14.2	23.3	5.8	14.8	11.7	12.4	14.6	15.6	13.3	12.5	17.3	15.1	12.2	13.0	14.5	31.1
2. I would very likely volunteer	7.5	11.4	4.0	8.0	5.1	8.7	7.7	7.0	7.0	7.5	7.4	7.2	7.2	8.2	7.8	14.5
3. I would probably volunteer	16.4	20.9	11.7	16.8	12.0	15.0	16.3	18.0	15.2	17.0	14.7	15.6	17.9	18.9	15.1	5.2
4. I would probably NOT volunteer	17.1	14.3	19.7	16.9	18.9	16.4	17.5	17.8	16.3	17.1	17.7	16.1	20.8	18.6	15.1	2.7
5. I would very likely NOT volunteer	7.9	5.5	10.4	8.1	6.4	7.2	7.9	6.8	10.4	9.1	6.1	7.9	9.2	6.7	7.7	-
6. I would definitely NOT volunteer	15.0	9.5	20.1	14.0	23.1	19.1	14.0	14.2	13.3	15.0	15.1	16.4	12.8	13.8	15.3	4.8
7. In my opinion, there is no such thing as a "necessary" war	21.9	15.0	28.3	21.3	22.8	21.3	22.0	20.5	24.4	21.8	21.8	21.7	19.9	20.7	24.4	41.6
Item 11220 Subject L03 N	2641	1256	1342	2082	290	532	738	844	527	1610	929	1113	533	359	574	16
E07: How closely do your ideas agree with your PARENTS' ideas about . . .																
Our ideas are . . .																
E07A: What you should do with your life.																
1. Very similar	27.5	25.8	28.9	27.1	32.6	31.0	23.6	29.2	26.8	30.8	21.6	30.8	25.9	23.7	26.4	10.8
2. Mostly similar	44.4	43.9	45.1	47.1	32.6	42.7	47.7	42.0	45.1	48.0	39.2	44.7	48.4	45.7	39.7	29.0
3. Mostly different	11.9	12.9	11.1	11.2	16.1	11.4	12.2	12.1	11.7	9.6	16.3	10.1	10.8	15.7	14.1	7.0
4. Very different	7.1	7.1	6.8	6.2	9.5	6.3	7.3	7.4	6.9	4.4	11.1	5.3	6.6	8.3	8.9	43.4
8. Don't know	9.2	10.3	8.1	8.5	9.3	8.6	9.1	9.3	9.5	7.2	11.9	9.1	8.4	6.6	11.0	9.8
Item 11230 Subject M03 N	2713	1281	1388	2123	299	550	761	861	541	1651	955	1130	551	365	600	18
E07B: What you do in your leisure time																
1. Very similar	9.8	8.5	10.8	9.1	13.7	10.1	7.8	12.1	8.3	9.2	9.8	13.3	6.8	7.6	7.3	-
2. Mostly similar	32.4	30.0	34.9	33.9	27.5	30.8	33.4	32.8	31.7	34.3	28.9	33.0	37.3	35.5	24.6	16.0
3. Mostly different	29.1	29.5	28.6	30.4	21.1	27.0	31.5	25.3	33.7	30.2	28.0	28.6	28.0	29.0	32.2	23.5
4. Very different	22.4	24.5	20.2	20.9	26.8	24.9	21.2	22.7	21.1	20.0	27.3	18.2	21.5	22.0	30.4	53.4
8. Don't know	6.4	7.6	5.5	5.7	10.9	7.2	6.0	7.1	5.1	6.3	6.0	6.9	6.4	5.9	5.5	7.1
Item 11240 Subject C08,M03 N	2694	1272	1380	2114	294	544	755	857	538	1642	947	1121	548	361	599	17
E07C: How you dress–what clothes you wear																
1. Very similar	23.3	18.7	27.8	23.5	29.0	22.6	21.9	25.9	21.6	23.8	21.9	25.5	23.6	21.6	20.7	10.2
2. Mostly similar	42.9	43.1	42.8	45.4	31.2	42.9	45.1	40.7	43.4	45.2	39.7	40.5	47.5	44.4	42.3	38.4
3. Mostly different	16.2	18.1	14.2	15.4	16.9	17.6	16.6	15.0	16.3	15.6	17.1	16.6	14.3	16.9	17.6	9.9
4. Very different	12.5	13.0	12.0	11.0	17.5	10.2	12.4	14.3	12.3	11.2	15.1	13.0	10.7	10.6	13.3	34.4
8. Don't know	5.0	7.0	3.2	4.7	5.4	6.6	4.0	4.1	6.4	4.2	6.2	4.4	4.0	6.5	6.1	7.1
Item 11250 Subject M03 N	2697	1273	1381	2111	294	546	756	856	539	1645	947	1124	548	360	601	17

QUESTIONNAIRE FORM 4 1985	TOTAL	SEX		RACE		REGION				4YR COLLEGE PLANS		ILLICIT DRUG USE: LIFETIME				
		M	F	White	Black	NE	NC	S	W	Yes	No	None	Marijuana Only	Few Pills	More Pills	Any Heroin
N (Weighted No. of Cases):	3279	1565	1610	2464	390	772	892	1004	612	1853	1170	1312	662	442	746	24
% of Weighted Total:	100.0	47.7	49.1	75.1	11.9	23.5	27.2	30.6	18.7	56.5	35.7	40.0	20.2	13.5	22.8	0.7
E07D: How you spend your money																
1. Very similar	11.3	9.0	13.4	10.0	20.3	11.5	9.3	14.4	8.8	11.3	10.5	15.5	9.6	9.0	6.7	-
2. Mostly similar	33.0	30.3	35.5	34.6	20.8	33.5	33.8	30.8	34.6	37.0	26.8	36.4	36.6	30.5	25.1	8.5
3. Mostly different	26.3	27.8	24.9	27.1	23.3	23.5	29.3	24.3	28.2	26.6	25.2	23.4	25.0	28.3	31.5	4.8
4. Very different	24.1	26.2	22.0	22.9	30.9	25.6	23.6	24.8	22.3	20.4	31.1	19.8	23.5	25.3	31.4	79.6
8. Don't know	5.4	6.6	4.2	5.4	4.7	5.9	4.0	5.7	6.2	4.7	6.4	4.9	5.2	6.9	5.2	7.1
Item 11260 Subject M03 N	2692	1272	1377	2111	292	543	756	855	539	1643	948	1123	548	358	600	17
E07E: What things are O.K. to do when you are on a date																
1. Very similar	15.8	13.0	17.9	14.6	20.4	13.0	12.9	19.4	16.7	16.3	14.8	19.8	11.5	13.3	14.2	12.2
2. Mostly similar	30.3	27.6	33.1	31.2	26.4	28.0	30.0	31.8	30.5	31.4	28.0	32.9	31.1	31.0	24.0	7.6
3. Mostly different	19.3	20.7	18.1	19.9	16.5	17.0	21.8	18.1	19.9	19.3	19.3	16.1	21.3	24.6	20.6	26.1
4. Very different	21.3	22.8	19.8	21.7	21.2	24.2	22.5	19.3	19.7	19.3	25.3	16.1	21.4	20.2	30.4	41.1
8. Don't know	13.4	15.9	11.1	12.6	15.5	17.8	12.7	11.4	13.3	13.6	12.6	15.0	14.6	10.9	10.8	13.0
Item 11270 Subject M03 N	2692	1272	1377	2108	293	545	754	855	538	1645	944	1118	550	360	599	17
E07F: Whether it is O.K. to drink																
1. Very similar	25.1	22.5	28.0	23.6	39.0	20.5	22.9	30.0	25.1	26.0	22.8	36.9	18.6	18.2	13.9	10.3
2. Mostly similar	33.4	32.7	33.9	35.2	19.7	36.8	33.4	32.2	32.0	35.3	30.2	32.0	33.1	34.7	36.4	28.8
3. Mostly different	17.5	18.3	16.8	19.3	8.8	15.5	19.6	15.6	19.6	18.5	16.9	11.8	22.8	23.5	19.6	6.6
4. Very different	18.1	19.3	16.7	17.7	18.3	19.1	19.4	17.0	16.9	15.1	23.1	11.8	20.1	19.3	26.0	47.0
8. Don't know	5.9	7.3	4.6	4.2	14.2	8.0	4.7	5.3	6.4	5.0	6.9	7.5	5.4	4.3	4.1	7.4
Item 11280 Subject M03 N	2756	1298	1410	2159	297	563	777	865	551	1673	966	1131	556	371	626	22
E07G: Whether it is O.K. to use marijuana																
1. Very similar	50.9	49.2	52.9	52.4	52.6	44.7	53.0	56.0	46.3	52.2	49.0	76.2	39.6	42.0	21.9	11.5
2. Mostly similar	13.4	12.0	14.7	13.5	11.2	13.5	12.0	12.7	16.1	14.3	12.5	8.8	20.3	14.8	15.7	1.9
3. Mostly different	6.8	7.1	6.4	6.9	4.7	7.1	6.8	6.0	7.6	6.3	7.2	2.1	8.5	11.0	11.6	2.7
4. Very different	21.6	22.1	20.6	21.4	18.5	25.8	22.0	18.3	21.7	20.4	23.5	6.0	24.2	23.8	43.9	70.7
8. Don't know	7.4	9.5	5.4	5.8	12.9	8.9	6.1	7.0	8.3	6.7	7.7	6.9	7.5	8.4	7.0	13.3
Item 11290 Subject M03 N	2747	1296	1403	2153	295	560	777	860	550	1668	962	1127	554	371	624	22
E07H: Whether it is O.K. to use other drugs																
1. Very similar	59.2	58.0	61.0	61.7	58.1	54.9	59.9	65.1	53.5	62.8	54.3	79.5	59.8	52.0	28.7	-
2. Mostly similar	12.2	10.8	13.7	12.0	8.4	13.6	11.2	10.4	15.0	13.0	11.4	8.1	17.0	15.9	14.3	-
3. Mostly different	4.2	4.7	3.4	4.1	4.1	3.5	5.5	3.1	4.6	4.3	5.3	0.9	2.7	6.0	9.9	11.5
4. Very different	17.2	17.8	16.1	16.2	16.5	19.3	16.8	14.1	20.3	14.4	21.0	4.8	13.5	18.3	39.1	81.2
8. Don't know	7.2	8.7	5.7	6.0	12.9	8.8	6.6	7.3	6.5	6.5	8.0	6.6	6.9	7.8	8.1	7.4
Item 11300 Subject M03 N	2739	1292	1400	2148	293	561	774	856	548	1664	960	1123	555	368	622	22
E07I: What values are important in life																
1. Very similar	36.7	36.2	37.5	35.6	49.3	35.7	32.9	41.8	34.7	38.0	33.6	45.0	37.0	32.7	25.2	10.1
2. Mostly similar	41.3	40.3	42.0	43.5	24.7	41.0	43.8	37.8	43.7	43.8	38.1	36.2	46.0	43.1	45.0	36.5
3. Mostly different	10.5	11.0	10.2	10.6	9.0	8.9	11.8	9.0	12.7	9.0	13.3	8.5	9.2	12.9	13.5	17.4
4. Very different	6.1	6.2	5.6	5.8	8.7	7.0	6.7	6.5	3.5	4.9	7.7	4.2	4.8	6.0	9.8	28.7
8. Don't know	5.5	6.3	4.7	4.6	8.3	7.4	4.7	4.9	5.4	4.3	7.3	6.1	3.0	5.4	6.5	7.4
Item 11310 Subject M03 N	2742	1287	1407	2147	296	555	775	863	548	1668	958	1129	555	368	617	22
E07J: The value of education																
1. Very similar	55.9	54.9	57.1	55.0	64.8	55.3	51.7	60.9	54.3	63.0	43.7	60.8	57.3	50.3	49.6	28.1
2. Mostly similar	30.9	28.5	32.8	32.4	22.9	29.5	33.5	27.9	33.3	28.0	36.0	27.1	32.1	35.6	34.4	25.6
3. Mostly different	5.8	6.6	5.1	5.9	4.4	5.4	7.2	4.8	5.8	4.5	8.3	5.4	5.3	5.4	6.5	26.4
4. Very different	4.1	4.9	3.2	4.0	4.2	5.0	4.6	3.7	3.2	1.9	7.6	3.0	2.9	5.6	5.6	14.4
8. Don't know	3.4	5.1	1.8	2.7	3.6	4.7	3.1	2.7	3.4	2.6	4.4	3.7	2.5	3.0	3.8	5.4
Item 11320 Subject B09,M03 N	2737	1285	1404	2143	297	553	776	862	546	1665	957	1126	553 *	367	617	22

QUESTIONNAIRE FORM 4 1985	TOTAL	SEX		RACE		REGION				4YR COLLEGE PLANS		ILLICIT DRUG USE: LIFETIME				
		M	F	White	Black	NE	NC	S	W	Yes	No	None	Mari-juana Only	Few Pills	More Pills	Any Heroin
N (Weighted No. of Cases):	3279	1565	1610	2464	390	772	892	1004	612	1853	1170	1312	662	442	746	24
% of Weighted Total:	100.0	47.7	49.1	75.1	11.9	23.5	27.2	30.6	18.7	56.5	35.7	40.0	20.2	13.5	22.8	0.7

E07K: What are appropriate roles for women

1. Very similar	32.2	26.1	38.1	31.7	38.7	33.0	28.1	35.8	31.3	34.2	28.5	35.5	31.6	30.1	28.3	9.8
2. Mostly similar	38.0	38.9	37.2	41.0	24.3	31.9	40.3	38.6	39.8	39.2	36.2	35.5	42.0	41.2	37.9	15.7
3. Mostly different	10.0	10.7	9.1	9.3	10.7	11.5	10.5	7.4	11.6	9.1	11.3	9.2	8.6	9.7	12.6	8.1
4. Very different	5.7	4.9	6.0	4.8	8.4	6.8	6.4	4.7	5.0	4.1	8.4	5.1	5.9	6.1	5.5	23.0
8. Don't know	14.2	19.4	9.6	13.2	18.0	16.8	14.7	13.4	12.3	13.3	15.6	14.7	11.9	12.9	15.8	43.4
Item 11330 Subject D05,M03 N	2728	1280	1400	2135	294	553	774	857	544	1662	953	1123	553	369	612	22

E07L: Conservation and pollution issues

1. Very similar	21.8	22.7	21.1	21.9	22.3	22.4	19.3	24.4	20.9	23.5	18.1	25.9	17.7	19.0	20.1	21.0
2. Mostly similar	30.9	33.4	28.8	32.8	23.8	29.2	32.6	30.6	30.6	32.4	29.0	31.0	34.7	31.3	27.2	7.2
3. Mostly different	7.2	8.8	5.7	7.0	8.2	6.9	6.9	6.7	8.7	6.5	8.8	6.5	8.2	5.1	8.7	14.4
4. Very different	3.7	4.1	3.2	2.9	7.3	5.0	4.2	3.5	1.9	2.4	5.9	2.5	4.3	4.5	4.1	14.4
8. Don't know	36.4	31.0	41.1	35.4	38.4	36.5	37.0	34.8	37.9	35.2	38.1	34.1	35.1	40.1	39.9	43.1
Item 11340 Subject F04,M03 N	2726	1278	1400	2138	290	552	772	858	545	1660	952	1125	550	369	612	22

E07M: Racial issues

1. Very similar	31.3	31.6	30.8	30.0	44.6	32.5	25.5	35.2	32.2	33.7	26.6	35.9	31.7	26.3	26.6	36.2
2. Mostly similar	32.1	32.7	31.9	34.3	24.4	30.8	31.9	34.0	30.7	34.1	29.7	30.0	34.2	36.6	31.4	21.3
3. Mostly different	8.6	9.5	7.7	8.8	6.8	7.2	11.5	6.4	9.5	9.0	8.0	8.2	8.9	7.0	9.6	7.7
4. Very different	6.0	5.2	6.8	5.7	3.9	6.0	7.4	5.1	5.5	5.1	7.7	5.5	4.9	7.7	7.0	6.1
8. Don't know	21.9	21.0	22.8	21.2	20.2	23.5	23.7	19.3	22.0	18.1	28.1	20.5	20.3	22.5	25.4	28.7
Item 11350 Subject M03,N02 N	2722	1280	1395	2137	289	554	769	856	544	1659	950	1122	551	368	611	22

E07N: Religion

1. Very similar	38.5	38.0	39.2	37.5	49.5	35.7	36.0	44.2	36.0	40.0	35.2	44.6	37.8	35.4	30.8	20.4
2. Mostly similar	30.7	29.6	31.8	32.8	22.9	28.8	33.1	32.2	27.0	31.1	30.5	29.3	33.2	32.1	31.3	18.1
3. Mostly different	10.2	10.6	9.8	10.1	7.9	10.6	10.6	7.5	13.5	11.5	8.4	7.6	13.0	9.8	12.6	14.4
4. Very different	7.3	8.3	6.3	7.2	7.3	8.5	7.1	6.3	8.1	7.0	7.9	5.6	6.5	7.8	9.9	16.4
8. Don't know	13.2	13.5	12.9	12.4	12.3	16.4	13.2	9.9	15.4	10.4	18.0	12.9	9.5	15.0	15.4	30.6
Item 11360 Subject G,M03 N	2728	1281	1398	2138	292	553	770	859	546	1661	952	1124	552	369	612	22

E07O: Politics

1. Very similar	19.3	20.3	18.7	19.4	25.7	15.3	18.1	25.3	15.8	20.5	16.2	22.8	20.8	14.5	15.0	12.0
2. Mostly similar	32.6	34.1	31.3	34.1	23.5	34.6	29.6	32.8	34.4	36.8	26.3	34.6	32.6	32.1	29.8	20.4
3. Mostly different	9.2	10.0	8.4	9.5	7.8	10.4	8.7	8.7	9.6	9.3	9.7	8.5	9.4	10.0	9.8	9.5
4. Very different	5.6	7.3	3.8	5.1	7.6	5.3	6.9	4.6	5.4	4.9	6.8	4.7	4.3	7.3	7.1	14.1
8. Don't know	33.3	28.3	37.7	32.0	35.4	34.4	36.8	28.6	34.6	28.6	41.1	29.4	32.8	36.1	38.3	44.1
Item 11370 Subject H01,M03 N	2730	1281	1401	2142	291	555	771	858	546	1662	952	1124	552	369	613	22

E08: How do you think your CLOSE FRIENDS feel (or would feel) about YOU doing each of the following things?

E08A: Smoking one or more packs of cigarettes per day

1. Not disapprove	26.3	28.3	24.2	27.1	19.2	31.5	30.6	24.2	18.2	20.2	37.3	16.8	19.5	27.8	47.3	76.5
2. Disapprove	34.1	35.0	33.4	35.2	33.0	34.6	34.7	35.5	30.6	35.3	31.4	33.6	38.5	36.2	30.7	21.2
3. Strongly disapprove	39.6	36.7	42.5	37.7	47.8	33.9	34.7	40.3	51.1	44.4	31.3	49.6	42.0	36.0	22.0	2.3
Item 11470 Subject A12b N	2688	1262	1379	2116	284	547	759	846	536	1645	932	1104	550	361	600	22

E08B: Trying marijuana (pot, grass) once or twice

1. Not disapprove	45.3	45.6	45.1	46.7	35.2	52.9	45.7	36.3	51.4	44.9	46.2	20.0	53.9	57.6	75.4	84.6
2. Disapprove	23.3	26.3	20.7	23.3	27.8	21.4	23.8	26.5	19.6	23.7	22.4	28.5	27.5	18.5	14.2	11.5
3. Strongly disapprove	31.3	28.2	34.3	30.0	37.0	25.7	30.5	37.2	29.0	31.4	31.4	51.6	18.7	23.9	10.3	3.9
Item 11480 Subject A12b N	2687	1260	1379	2112	286	544	759	847	537	1645	932	1104	547	362	602	22

QUESTIONNAIRE FORM 4 1985	TOTAL	SEX		RACE		REGION				4YR COLLEGE PLANS		ILLICIT DRUG USE: LIFETIME				
		M	F	White	Black	NE	NC	S	W	Yes	No	None	Mari-juana Only	Few Pills	More Pills	Any Her-oin
N (Weighted No. of Cases):	3279	1565	1610	2464	390	772	892	1004	612	1853	1170	1312	662	442	746	24
% of Weighted Total:	100.0	47.7	49.1	75.1	11.9	23.5	27.2	30.6	18.7	56.5	35.7	40.0	20.2	13.5	22.8	0.7
E08C: Smoking marijuana occasionally																
1. Not disapprove	35.8	36.5	34.6	36.7	28.5	43.0	35.9	29.2	38.7	34.0	39.2	13.0	38.8	45.3	68.0	90.4
2. Disapprove	25.1	27.9	22.7	24.8	30.6	24.2	26.2	25.1	24.6	25.6	23.3	26.1	33.6	22.9	17.1	5.7
3. Strongly disapprove	39.1	35.6	42.6	38.5	40.9	32.8	37.9	45.7	36.7	40.4	37.5	60.9	27.5	31.8	14.8	3.9
Item 11490 Subject A12b N	2679	1260	1371	2108	282	546	758	838	537	1639	930	1101	547	359	600	22
E08D: Smoking marijuana regularly																
1. Not disapprove	19.0	22.5	15.5	18.7	18.6	23.5	21.0	14.8	18.3	15.2	24.9	7.4	15.9	16.2	43.1	78.0
2. Disapprove	27.7	29.3	26.0	27.8	29.4	29.5	26.6	27.6	27.4	27.0	28.3	21.4	32.0	36.2	30.5	18.1
3. Strongly disapprove	53.3	48.1	58.5	53.5	52.0	47.0	52.4	57.6	54.2	57.8	46.8	71.3	52.1	47.6	26.4	3.9
Item 11500 Subject A12b N	2671	1256	1368	2104	280	545	754	836	536	1638	925	1098	545	360	596	22
E08E: Trying LSD once or twice																
1. Not disapprove	11.4	13.9	8.9	11.6	8.7	13.9	11.7	9.3	11.9	10.3	12.3	5.5	8.4	11.1	23.5	64.2
2. Disapprove	22.3	23.1	21.3	22.4	24.0	24.2	23.9	21.3	19.4	20.7	24.8	19.6	22.1	22.4	27.3	22.6
3. Strongly disapprove	66.3	63.0	69.8	66.0	67.3	61.9	64.4	69.4	68.6	69.0	62.9	74.8	69.5	66.5	49.2	13.2
Item 11510 Subject A12b N	2669	1254	1366	2100	281	546	754	835	534	1636	924	1098	542	360	596	22
E08F: Trying an amphetamine (upper, pep pill, bennie, speed) once or twice																
1. Not disapprove	23.0	23.0	22.7	24.4	12.0	27.4	24.8	18.0	24.0	21.9	24.1	10.4	13.8	24.2	52.7	74.5
2. Disapprove	23.2	24.4	22.0	23.7	24.0	24.7	24.6	22.1	21.6	21.2	26.3	21.3	26.4	25.6	22.8	10.8
3. Strongly disapprove	53.7	52.5	55.3	51.9	64.0	47.9	50.6	59.9	54.3	56.9	49.6	68.3	59.8	50.2	24.5	14.7
Item 11520 Subject A12b N	2664	1249	1367	2099	279	542	752	836	535	1631	926	1096	543	358	595	21
E08G: Taking one or two drinks nearly every day																
1. Not disapprove	24.6	30.7	18.9	25.1	18.4	29.1	26.0	24.0	18.9	20.9	29.8	15.9	19.4	29.3	41.4	63.7
2. Disapprove	34.1	38.0	30.5	35.7	30.5	34.9	34.3	34.0	33.3	34.6	34.0	32.5	38.1	34.7	33.3	33.5
3. Strongly disapprove	41.3	31.3	50.7	39.2	51.1	36.0	39.7	42.0	47.7	44.6	36.3	51.7	42.6	36.0	25.4	2.8
Item 11530 Subject A12b N	2665	1248	1369	2097	282	541	752	837	536	1637	921	1098	543	361	595	21
E08H: Taking four or five drinks nearly every day																
1. Not disapprove	11.8	17.5	6.3	11.3	12.3	11.6	13.2	11.7	10.3	8.7	16.1	7.5	10.4	11.1	20.1	51.4
2. Disapprove	26.9	31.0	22.9	27.7	25.6	28.8	28.3	28.6	20.1	24.2	31.4	24.0	21.6	32.0	34.2	21.9
3. Strongly disapprove	61.3	51.5	70.7	61.0	62.1	59.5	58.5	59.7	69.7	67.1	52.6	68.5	68.0	56.9	45.7	26.7
Item 11540 Subject A12b N	2663	1248	1366	2097	280	542	753	835	533	1634	922	1096	542	359	594	21
E08I: Having five or more drinks once or twice each weekend																
1. Not disapprove	44.1	50.2	38.3	47.7	21.1	48.0	51.1	37.7	40.4	42.7	46.6	27.3	44.9	48.8	69.7	92.7
2. Disapprove	24.0	24.6	23.6	23.5	27.9	24.1	21.2	26.1	24.7	25.2	22.1	25.5	30.8	25.1	15.7	-
3. Strongly disapprove	31.8	25.2	38.1	28.7	51.0	27.9	27.7	36.2	34.9	32.2	31.3	47.2	24.2	26.1	14.6	7.3
Item 11550 Subject A12b N	2655	1245	1362	2091	281	540	751	834	531	1629	920	1092	539	359	593	21
E08J: Driving a car after having 1-2 drinks																
1. Not disapprove	35.4	40.9	30.3	38.7	18.4	32.9	44.3	32.9	29.3	35.0	36.3	21.3	37.1	37.8	56.4	82.8
2. Disapprove	30.3	29.6	30.8	30.8	29.6	33.1	26.4	32.6	29.3	29.8	31.1	31.7	32.9	31.2	26.7	4.0
3. Strongly disapprove	34.3	29.5	38.9	30.5	52.0	34.0	29.4	34.4	41.4	35.2	32.5	47.0	30.0	31.0	16.9	13.2
Item 11551 Subject A12b N	2666	1249	1368	2096	282	541	752	838	535	1634	922	1096	542	361	596	21
E08K: Driving a car after having 5 or more drinks																
1. Not disapprove	7.9	12.8	3.4	8.0	8.2	7.2	9.8	8.2	5.7	6.3	10.5	4.4	8.5	5.6	13.1	54.1
2. Disapprove	23.7	27.9	19.9	24.9	19.1	21.2	28.4	24.8	17.9	21.8	26.4	20.3	22.8	27.8	28.6	21.6
3. Strongly disapprove	68.4	59.3	76.7	67.0	72.8	71.6	61.9	67.1	76.4	71.9	63.1	75.3	68.7	66.7	58.3	24.4
Item 11552 Subject A12b N	2663	1249	1365	2094	281	540	753	834	535	1636	920	1095	542	359	596	21

	TOTAL	SEX		RACE		REGION				4YR COLLEGE PLANS		ILLICIT DRUG USE: LIFETIME				
QUESTIONNAIRE FORM 4 1985		M	F	White	Black	NE	NC	S	W	Yes	No	None	Mari- juana Only	Few Pills	More Pills	Any Her- oin
N (Weighted No. of Cases):	3279	1565	1610	2464	390	772	892	1004	612	1853	1170	1312	662	442	746	24
% of Weighted Total:	100.0	47.7	49.1	75.1	11.9	23.5	27.2	30.6	18.7	56.5	35.7	40.0	20.2	13.5	22.8	0.7

E09: In some communities parents who are particularly concerned with drug or alcohol abuse among young people have formed groups of concerned parents to deal with these problems. In these groups parents try to become more informed and sometimes to set some common guidelines for young peoples' behavior. In general, what do you think of the idea of having parents get together in groups such as these?

	TOTAL	M	F	White	Black	NE	NC	S	W	Yes	No	None	Mari-juana Only	Few Pills	More Pills	Any Heroin
1. A bad idea	5.1	7.7	2.8	5.1	6.6	5.0	5.8	5.4	3.8	3.5	7.9	4.9	4.0	5.6	5.5	19.1
2. More bad than good	6.1	8.3	4.1	6.3	3.7	4.6	5.6	8.3	5.0	5.8	6.6	3.2	6.3	8.1	9.9	25.6
3. Don't know or can't say	25.7	27.5	23.9	26.4	23.1	28.8	28.2	23.1	23.1	24.5	27.9	21.0	24.6	26.1	34.5	41.6
4. More good than bad	22.6	21.2	24.2	23.8	18.1	21.4	23.0	21.0	25.7	24.2	19.7	22.7	21.4	25.3	23.2	8.4
5. A good idea	40.4	35.4	45.1	38.5	48.6	40.2	37.4	42.1	42.4	41.9	37.9	48.2	43.7	35.0	26.9	5.3
Item 21730 Subject A16a N	2614	1220	1349	2062	275	522	741	822	530	1609	901	1093	526	350	577	18

E10: To the best of your knowledge, how many of your close friends have parents who are involved in such parent groups?

	TOTAL	M	F	White	Black	NE	NC	S	W	Yes	No	None	Mari-juana Only	Few Pills	More Pills	Any Heroin
1. None	70.0	67.2	72.3	70.1	63.4	70.5	72.4	67.7	69.7	69.2	72.3	70.5	68.0	70.5	69.6	84.9
2. A few	20.1	22.0	18.5	20.7	19.2	21.0	19.0	21.2	18.9	21.3	17.3	19.5	21.0	21.2	20.3	15.1
3. Some	9.4	10.1	8.7	8.8	16.6	8.6	8.4	10.4	10.1	8.9	10.0	9.8	9.9	7.9	9.4	-
4. Most or all	0.5	0.6	0.5	0.5	0.7	-	0.2	0.7	1.2	0.6	0.5	0.3	1.0	0.5	0.7	-
Item 21740 Subject A16a N	2599	1212	1342	2046	274	523	728	817	531	1602	895	1083	528	349	569	20

E11: Has either (or both) of your own parents been involved in such a group?

	TOTAL	M	F	White	Black	NE	NC	S	W	Yes	No	None	Mari-juana Only	Few Pills	More Pills	Any Heroin
1. No–GO TO QUESTION E14.	91.7	91.5	92.0	92.1	86.8	94.0	91.3	91.8	89.8	92.5	91.3	93.7	91.5	90.3	89.4	91.4
2. Yes, in the past, but not now	5.7	6.4	5.1	5.0	12.1	4.4	5.7	5.9	6.7	5.0	6.2	4.3	6.0	6.6	7.4	8.6
3. Yes, now	2.6	2.1	2.9	2.8	1.1	1.6	2.9	2.3	3.4	2.5	2.5	2.0	2.5	3.1	3.2	-
Item 21750 Subject A16a N	2558	1186	1330	2017	265	514	717	808	519	1589	867	1076	521	337	555	20

E12: Has the involvement of your parent(s) in such a group had any impact on your own feelings about drug or alcohol use?

	TOTAL	M	F	White	Black	NE	NC	S	W	Yes	No	None	Mari-juana Only	Few Pills	More Pills	Any Heroin
1. Made me much less likely to use drugs or alcohol	26.7	26.0	28.2	22.3	48.7	22.0	28.4	27.4	27.0	27.8	23.0	42.6	34.9	4.3	10.2	43.2
2. Made me somewhat less likely to use drugs or alcohol	16.4	16.3	16.1	18.2	10.8	17.3	20.9	16.4	10.1	17.1	17.4	10.4	9.9	33.2	23.1	-
3. No impact either way	53.0	51.3	54.5	55.6	36.6	57.5	48.1	51.2	58.9	53.7	52.2	44.6	52.1	57.0	60.5	56.8
4. Made me somewhat more likely to use drugs or alcohol	2.7	4.5	0.8	2.6	4.0	-	1.9	4.2	3.2	1.1	5.1	2.3	3.1	2.4	3.3	-
5. Made me much more likely to use drugs or alcohol	1.2	2.0	0.4	1.3	-	3.2	0.8	0.8	0.8	0.3	2.4	-	-	3.1	2.9	-
Item 21760 Subject A16a N★	308	156	141	216	54	48	87	103	70	155	127	106	66	43	78	3

E13: What about your relationship with your parents? Has their involvement in the parent group made your relationship better or worse?

	TOTAL	M	F	White	Black	NE	NC	S	W	Yes	No	None	Mari-juana Only	Few Pills	More Pills	Any Heroin
1. Much worse	6.5	11.0	1.9	6.3	3.3	10.1	4.2	4.6	9.4	5.1	8.0	7.1	3.3	9.3	7.7	-
2. Somewhat worse	11.0	14.5	6.9	9.8	11.7	20.2	10.4	9.0	7.9	6.9	16.6	7.2	13.7	14.3	12.8	-
3. No effect, don't know	49.2	42.9	55.6	51.8	40.2	34.8	45.2	53.7	58.4	52.0	47.8	48.5	50.5	46.7	50.0	56.8
4. Somewhat better	20.4	17.5	23.8	20.3	22.1	20.0	27.5	17.9	15.2	24.6	15.6	22.4	20.2	22.2	15.6	-
5. Much better	13.0	14.1	11.8	11.7	22.6	14.8	12.8	14.8	9.2	11.5	11.9	14.7	12.3	7.4	13.9	43.2
Item 21770 Subject A16a N★	314	159	146	218	57	51	89	105	70	158	128	108	68	47	77	3

★=excludes respondents for whom question was inappropriate.

QUESTIONNAIRE FORM 4 1985	TOTAL	SEX		RACE		REGION				4YR COLLEGE PLANS		ILLICIT DRUG USE: LIFETIME				
		M	F	White	Black	NE	NC	S	W	Yes	No	None	Mari-juana Only	Few Pills	More Pills	Any Her-oin
N (Weighted No. of Cases):	3279	1565	1610	2464	390	772	892	1004	612	1853	1170	1312	662	442	746	24
% of Weighted Total:	100.0	47.7	49.1	75.1	11.9	23.5	27.2	30.6	18.7	56.5	35.7	40.0	20.2	13.5	22.8	0.7

E14: In some communities young people themselves have formed groups aimed at avoiding drug use, such as Youth for Drug-Free Alternatives. How many of your close friends have been members of such a group?

	TOTAL	M	F	White	Black	NE	NC	S	W	Yes	No	None	Mari-juana Only	Few Pills	More Pills	Any Her-oin
1. None	77.5	77.4	77.8	77.2	75.9	80.5	76.3	75.7	79.1	78.7	76.1	80.7	75.8	74.6	74.4	82.0
2. A few	14.9	15.0	14.6	15.1	16.1	13.4	15.8	16.1	13.2	14.4	15.6	12.3	16.0	16.1	17.8	15.9
3. Some	6.8	6.6	6.7	6.7	7.4	5.6	6.8	7.3	7.0	6.1	7.5	6.2	7.8	8.3	6.5	2.1
4. Most or all	0.9	1.0	0.8	1.0	0.7	0.5	1.1	1.0	0.7	0.8	0.8	0.8	0.3	1.1	1.4	-
Item 21780 Subject A16a N	2605	1213	1347	2052	275	522	731	822	530	1607	897	1084	530	350	572	20

E15: Have you ever participated in such a group?

	TOTAL	M	F	White	Black	NE	NC	S	W	Yes	No	None	Mari-juana Only	Few Pills	More Pills	Any Her-oin
3. Yes, now	3.7	3.4	3.9	3.9	3.9	3.1	5.0	3.6	2.9	4.1	3.1	3.5	3.8	2.2	4.6	10.3
2. Yes, in the past, but not now	5.4	5.3	5.5	5.6	7.3	3.7	5.7	6.4	5.3	4.9	5.8	4.1	5.2	7.9	6.6	4.7
1. No	90.8	91.3	90.7	90.5	88.7	93.2	89.3	90.0	91.9	91.0	91.0	92.4	91.0	90.0	88.8	85.1
Item 21790 Subject A16a N	2564	1190	1329	2026	266	522	716	805	521	1585	878	1070	519	343	564	19

QUESTIONNAIRE FORM 5 1985	TOTAL	SEX		RACE		REGION				4YR COLLEGE PLANS		ILLICIT DRUG USE: LIFETIME				
		M	F	White	Black	NE	NC	S	W	Yes	No	None	Mari-juana Only	Few Pills	More Pills	Any Her-oin
N (Weighted No. of Cases):	3286	1584	1601	2463	410	782	901	997	604	1920	1159	1252	655	479	794	45
% of Weighted Total:	100.0	48.2	48.7	75.0	12.5	23.8	27.4	30.4	18.4	58.4	35.3	38.1	19.9	14.6	24.2	1.4

A01: Taking all things together, how would you say things are these days–would you say you're very happy, pretty happy, or not too happy these days?

	TOTAL	M	F	White	Black	NE	NC	S	W	Yes	No	None	Mari-juana Only	Few Pills	More Pills	Any Her-oin
3. Very happy	18.1	16.2	19.8	19.4	10.9	18.9	19.1	17.5	16.8	20.0	14.2	21.0	17.3	16.6	14.6	13.9
2. Pretty happy	69.5	72.5	67.0	70.0	71.2	67.6	68.2	69.4	73.9	68.7	72.4	67.7	73.3	73.3	68.1	64.7
1. Not too happy	12.4	11.4	13.1	10.6	17.9	13.5	12.8	13.1	9.3	11.4	13.4	11.2	9.4	10.1	17.3	21.4
Item 1190 Subject P01,Q01 N	3272	1579	1596	2456	409	778	898	995	602	1915	1154	1248	652	479	792	43

A02: Some people think a lot about the social problems of the nation and the world, and about how they might be solved. Others spend little time thinking about these issues. How much do you think about such things?

	TOTAL	M	F	White	Black	NE	NC	S	W	Yes	No	None	Mari-juana Only	Few Pills	More Pills	Any Her-oin
1. Never	1.8	2.1	1.5	1.9	1.0	2.7	1.8	1.2	1.4	1.5	1.8	1.4	1.9	1.1	2.2	9.9
2. Seldom	15.3	14.9	15.2	16.4	11.9	14.9	15.3	14.4	17.1	13.4	17.9	13.7	15.9	15.2	16.2	28.9
3. Sometimes	54.2	52.1	56.5	55.1	50.0	56.8	55.1	53.1	51.3	52.9	57.2	52.7	59.1	54.2	54.5	31.3
4. Quite often	24.2	26.3	22.1	22.6	31.7	20.6	24.2	25.2	27.1	26.7	20.1	27.2	19.6	26.0	21.9	20.3
5. A great deal	4.6	4.6	4.7	4.0	5.4	5.0	3.6	6.1	3.2	5.5	3.1	5.0	3.6	3.5	5.1	9.6
Item 6880 Subject J,Q08 N	3280	1582	1600	2461	409	780	901	995	604	1918	1157	1250	653	479	794	45

A03: Of all the problems facing the nation today, how often do you worry about each of the following?

A03A: Chance of nuclear war

	TOTAL	M	F	White	Black	NE	NC	S	W	Yes	No	None	Mari-juana Only	Few Pills	More Pills	Any Her-oin
1. Never	9.0	9.5	8.4	8.8	9.1	8.2	8.7	9.6	9.3	7.7	11.2	9.1	8.6	8.6	8.6	10.8
2. Seldom	26.5	27.3	25.2	27.4	21.0	25.7	27.0	24.6	30.0	27.0	25.6	25.2	26.8	30.3	25.7	34.9
3. Sometimes	39.9	37.9	42.7	40.7	37.1	41.6	43.0	38.2	35.9	41.0	39.1	42.4	42.0	34.0	39.8	21.7
4. Often	24.6	25.3	23.7	23.1	32.8	24.5	21.4	27.6	24.9	24.3	24.1	23.3	22.6	27.1	25.9	32.5
Item 11660 Subject J N	3271	1578	1595	2458	406	780	896	992	604	1917	1156	1247	651	477	793	45

A03B: Population growth

	TOTAL	M	F	White	Black	NE	NC	S	W	Yes	No	None	Mari-juana Only	Few Pills	More Pills	Any Her-oin
1. Never	31.7	32.9	30.3	33.5	26.6	35.9	32.5	30.1	27.5	31.3	32.9	29.0	34.3	31.4	34.3	26.2
2. Seldom	42.6	41.1	44.7	43.3	39.6	42.4	42.0	42.9	43.2	43.7	40.8	43.7	42.7	43.7	40.8	37.3
3. Sometimes	19.8	19.7	19.7	18.4	25.0	16.1	20.4	21.3	21.5	19.6	20.4	20.6	17.6	20.3	19.8	16.8
4. Often	5.9	6.3	5.3	4.8	8.8	5.6	5.1	5.8	7.9	5.4	5.9	6.7	5.4	4.6	5.1	19.6
Item 11670 Subject E01,J N	3270	1576	1597	2457	407	780	894	992	604	1918	1155	1249	652	478	789	45

A03C: Crime and violence

	TOTAL	M	F	White	Black	NE	NC	S	W	Yes	No	None	Mari-juana Only	Few Pills	More Pills	Any Her-oin
1. Never	2.3	3.3	1.2	2.1	1.7	2.3	1.8	3.0	1.7	2.1	2.7	2.4	1.6	1.8	2.5	12.7
2. Seldom	15.5	20.1	10.9	17.0	9.3	17.7	16.5	13.4	14.3	14.7	15.9	13.1	17.9	16.3	15.9	23.7
3. Sometimes	42.6	45.0	40.4	45.2	29.7	42.6	46.8	39.2	42.2	43.8	41.6	43.2	43.6	43.4	41.2	26.6
4. Often	39.7	31.6	47.6	35.7	59.2	37.4	34.9	44.4	41.8	39.5	39.8	41.3	36.9	38.5	40.4	37.0
Item 11680 Subject J N	3262	1573	1592	2453	406	779	891	990	602	1916	1150	1244	650	477	790	45

A03D: Pollution

	TOTAL	M	F	White	Black	NE	NC	S	W	Yes	No	None	Mari-juana Only	Few Pills	More Pills	Any Her-oin
1. Never	13.2	13.8	12.8	12.8	15.4	12.1	13.3	14.5	12.3	12.8	14.7	11.6	13.7	14.0	14.4	11.9
2. Seldom	39.9	38.7	41.0	39.9	45.8	39.6	43.3	38.8	37.2	39.2	40.4	38.2	41.4	40.4	41.5	26.2
3. Sometimes	34.0	33.0	34.9	34.9	26.7	35.1	32.4	33.2	36.2	35.3	32.6	35.8	33.0	33.8	32.1	49.9
4. Often	12.9	14.5	11.3	12.4	12.1	13.2	11.1	13.5	14.3	12.7	12.3	14.4	11.9	11.9	11.9	12.0
Item 11690 Subject F04,J N	3256	1570	1590	2447	403	774	893	986	603	1909	1151	1242	649	477	787	45

A03E: Energy shortages

	TOTAL	M	F	White	Black	NE	NC	S	W	Yes	No	None	Mari-juana Only	Few Pills	More Pills	Any Her-oin
1. Never	24.8	22.7	27.0	25.7	24.8	24.8	25.6	24.3	24.6	23.1	28.2	20.5	28.2	25.3	27.9	29.8
2. Seldom	41.5	40.9	42.7	43.0	34.8	40.8	44.3	38.8	42.7	44.0	37.6	43.5	41.5	39.1	40.8	41.8
3. Sometimes	27.1	29.0	24.7	26.2	28.1	28.7	24.9	28.7	25.8	27.0	26.6	28.8	24.9	29.1	25.2	20.3
4. Often	6.6	7.4	5.5	5.1	12.4	5.7	5.2	8.2	6.9	5.9	7.6	7.1	5.4	6.5	6.0	8.1
Item 11700 Subject F05,J N	3261	1573	1592	2457	397	778	895	987	601	1913	1150	1247	649	475	789	45

QUESTIONNAIRE FORM 5 1985	TOTAL	SEX M	SEX F	RACE White	RACE Black	REGION NE	NC	S	W	4YR COLLEGE PLANS Yes	No	ILLICIT DRUG USE: LIFETIME None	Marijuana Only	Few Pills	More Pills	Any Heroin
N (Weighted No. of Cases):	3286	1584	1601	2463	410	782	901	997	604	1920	1159	1252	655	479	794	45
% of Weighted Total:	100.0	48.2	48.7	75.0	12.5	23.8	27.4	30.4	18.4	58.4	35.3	38.1	19.9	14.6	24.2	1.4
A03F: Race relations																
1. Never	23.9	26.1	22.2	27.2	10.2	24.9	26.8	21.3	22.7	21.1	29.1	21.2	24.7	23.4	27.5	27.9
2. Seldom	32.7	35.4	29.9	36.1	20.4	34.8	34.2	29.2	33.5	33.8	30.8	32.0	30.9	36.8	35.0	18.4
3. Sometimes	27.0	25.3	28.5	25.1	31.4	25.6	26.6	27.5	28.7	26.9	27.3	30.0	28.3	22.7	23.2	20.5
4. Often	16.4	13.1	19.5	11.7	38.0	14.7	12.4	22.0	15.2	18.2	12.8	16.7	16.1	17.1	14.3	33.2
Item 11710 Subject J,N02 N	3259	1570	1593	2449	404	777	895	984	604	1912	1150	1243	650	474	790	45
A03G: Hunger and poverty																
1. Never	6.7	10.8	2.6	7.4	3.8	7.2	6.9	6.0	6.8	6.0	8.0	5.5	7.5	5.8	8.0	11.3
2. Seldom	23.6	31.5	16.0	26.3	13.2	24.6	24.6	21.3	24.6	22.5	26.1	22.0	25.4	24.3	25.1	20.9
3. Sometimes	41.7	40.4	43.2	41.6	40.6	43.4	42.7	39.7	41.4	42.1	40.4	41.4	41.0	46.7	40.3	40.1
4. Often	28.0	17.4	38.2	24.7	42.5	24.8	25.8	33.0	27.2	29.4	25.4	31.2	26.0	23.2	26.6	27.8
Item 11720 Subject F03,J N	3255	1569	1589	2451	400	779	893	983	600	1912	1146	1243	651	475	783	45
A03H: Using open land for housing or industry																
1. Never	39.4	36.5	42.5	39.9	40.2	42.4	41.9	38.6	33.1	40.1	37.4	37.0	38.6	41.3	42.5	37.2
2. Seldom	30.2	29.5	31.2	30.0	31.8	26.1	31.7	31.7	30.9	31.1	29.1	32.7	30.5	29.7	26.7	31.4
3. Sometimes	19.6	20.6	18.1	19.3	18.0	19.5	17.0	19.4	23.9	19.3	20.2	18.1	21.2	22.8	17.9	24.6
4. Often	10.8	13.5	8.3	10.9	10.0	12.0	9.4	10.3	12.1	9.4	13.3	12.2	9.6	6.3	12.9	6.9
Item 11730 Subject F05,J N	3263	1573	1593	2456	402	778	895	988	602	1915	1151	1244	650	477	791	45
A03I: Urban decay																
1. Never	46.4	44.4	48.4	47.7	47.7	45.2	46.4	48.6	44.3	44.1	50.2	42.7	51.0	48.4	46.9	53.2
2. Seldom	35.7	35.9	35.6	35.8	34.2	31.7	38.5	34.8	38.1	36.9	33.6	37.4	33.1	33.2	36.6	30.5
3. Sometimes	13.9	14.5	13.1	12.5	14.8	16.5	12.7	13.3	13.3	15.1	12.1	16.6	12.1	12.8	12.2	8.1
4. Often	4.0	5.1	3.0	4.0	3.3	6.5	2.5	3.4	4.2	3.9	4.1	3.3	3.8	5.6	4.2	8.2
Item 11740 Subject J N	3241	1560	1585	2438	401	774	889	979	599	1905	1140	1234	646	474	785	45
A03J: Economic problems																
1. Never	9.2	9.4	8.5	9.7	7.2	10.8	8.6	8.3	9.5	7.8	11.3	6.8	10.1	8.2	11.7	19.3
2. Seldom	30.3	29.6	31.4	31.9	25.4	34.1	29.6	28.4	29.5	29.0	32.5	29.4	31.3	29.0	30.8	35.4
3. Sometimes	41.0	41.7	40.7	40.2	47.7	38.0	41.6	42.3	42.3	41.6	40.0	41.1	41.1	44.5	40.9	20.4
4. Often	19.4	19.3	19.5	18.2	19.7	17.1	20.2	21.0	18.7	21.7	16.2	22.6	17.6	18.3	16.6	25.0
Item 11750 Subject J N	3261	1574	1589	2454	403	778	897	986	599	1913	1150	1245	650	476	789	45
A03K: Drug abuse																
1. Never	9.0	12.9	5.3	8.6	10.0	10.8	8.8	7.9	9.1	7.9	10.2	9.1	9.0	7.7	8.6	21.9
2. Seldom	21.8	26.8	16.8	23.1	15.5	21.6	24.2	18.5	23.9	22.2	21.9	20.6	23.5	22.5	22.5	15.0
3. Sometimes	36.6	35.0	38.4	38.6	31.4	35.1	38.9	35.2	37.5	38.4	34.3	36.4	39.0	38.1	35.5	17.9
4. Often	32.5	25.3	39.4	29.6	43.1	32.5	28.1	38.4	29.6	31.4	33.5	34.0	28.4	31.7	33.3	45.2
Item 11760 Subject J N	3274	1580	1597	2460	406	779	899	992	604	1919	1157	1249	653	478	792	45
A04: How well do you think your experiences and training (at home, school, work, etc.) have prepared you to be a good...																
A04A: Husband or wife																
1. Poorly	3.0	3.3	2.7	2.9	1.7	3.9	3.3	1.5	3.7	3.2	2.4	2.4	2.1	3.2	3.9	14.1
2. Not so well	4.1	4.9	3.1	3.8	3.8	5.0	3.7	3.3	5.0	4.2	3.6	3.3	3.2	6.8	4.1	8.8
3. Fairly well	20.8	24.4	17.5	21.6	15.6	20.4	21.4	21.2	19.8	19.5	22.5	19.8	20.9	19.9	23.6	14.5
4. Well	41.5	42.2	40.6	42.4	38.1	42.5	43.3	38.5	42.2	39.9	43.8	39.8	42.5	39.9	43.2	49.3
5. Very well	30.6	25.2	36.0	29.2	40.7	28.2	28.2	35.4	29.4	33.1	27.8	34.7	31.3	30.3	25.1	13.2
Item 11770 Subject D01 N	3190	1544	1550	2412	391	752	882	970	587	1884	1114	1223	633	463	776	42
A04B: Parent																
1. Poorly	2.2	2.9	1.4	2.1	1.9	1.3	2.7	1.9	2.7	2.2	2.2	1.8	1.8	3.0	2.0	11.2
2. Not so well	5.5	7.2	3.8	5.6	4.5	5.1	6.5	4.5	6.1	4.9	6.4	3.8	5.4	5.3	8.1	9.8
3. Fairly well	20.6	23.7	17.9	22.0	12.5	22.5	19.5	20.6	19.8	20.6	20.3	20.3	18.1	21.2	23.0	32.3
4. Well	38.2	40.3	36.2	39.9	33.2	39.2	38.4	35.4	41.1	37.3	39.4	37.8	42.0	35.9	38.4	21.3
5. Very well	33.6	25.9	40.7	30.4	48.0	31.9	32.9	37.5	30.3	35.0	31.8	36.3	32.6	34.6	28.4	25.4
Item 11780 Subject D02 N	3220	1552	1571	2427	397	761	886	977	595	1901	1127	1230	643	468	781	42

QUESTIONNAIRE FORM 5 1985	TOTAL	SEX		RACE		REGION				4YR COLLEGE PLANS		ILLICIT DRUG USE: LIFETIME				
		M	F	White	Black	NE	NC	S	W	Yes	No	None	Mari- juana Only	Few Pills	More Pills	Any Her- oin
N (Weighted No. of Cases):	3286	1584	1601	2463	410	782	901	997	604	1920	1159	1252	655	479	794	45
% of Weighted Total:	100.0	48.2	48.7	75.0	12.5	23.8	27.4	30.4	18.4	58.4	35.3	38.1	19.9	14.6	24.2	1.4
A04C: Worker on a job																
1. Poorly	1.5	2.1	0.9	1.5	1.0	1.5	1.6	1.0	2.2	1.6	1.3	1.1	0.9	1.7	2.0	12.2
2. Not so well	2.1	2.2	1.7	2.1	2.0	2.5	2.3	1.6	2.1	2.0	2.0	2.3	1.5	1.9	2.4	2.3
3. Fairly well	12.6	12.3	13.0	12.7	9.2	12.9	12.5	12.1	13.0	12.8	12.5	11.7	11.8	11.6	15.1	9.7
4. Well	40.9	39.1	42.8	42.3	32.9	40.8	40.9	40.7	41.6	40.4	42.4	40.9	43.3	40.7	40.4	30.0
5. Very well	42.9	44.2	41.6	41.5	54.8	42.2	42.7	44.6	41.2	43.3	41.8	44.0	42.6	44.1	40.1	45.7
Item 11790 Subject C01 N	3249	1569	1584	2453	396	771	899	983	597	1905	1145	1237	645	474	792	44
A05: Apart from the particular kind of work you want to do, how would you rate each of the following settings as a place to work?																
A05A: Working in a large corporation																
1. Not at all acceptable	4.3	4.4	4.1	4.5	2.7	4.8	4.8	3.8	3.5	4.4	4.5	4.8	3.7	3.1	3.8	14.0
2. Somewhat acceptable	19.8	18.9	20.9	21.4	13.6	21.7	18.6	19.2	20.4	17.7	23.0	20.2	17.8	18.4	22.7	9.0
3. Acceptable	47.4	47.7	46.9	47.2	49.7	47.4	45.8	48.8	47.7	45.8	50.8	49.1	45.5	47.9	46.6	34.8
4. Desirable	28.5	29.1	28.1	26.9	33.9	26.1	30.9	28.2	28.3	32.2	21.8	25.9	33.0	30.5	27.0	42.3
Item 11800 Subject C05 N	3265	1577	1593	2457	405	778	898	989	600	1916	1153	1244	653	477	790	45
A05B: Working in a small business																
1. Not at all acceptable	3.4	3.4	3.2	2.2	7.1	3.8	3.0	4.0	2.5	2.7	4.2	2.4	3.2	4.0	3.9	11.0
2. Somewhat acceptable	23.7	24.2	22.9	21.7	31.6	23.8	22.6	24.5	23.7	23.8	23.0	20.6	26.9	23.2	25.2	28.1
3. Acceptable	53.5	53.5	54.1	54.2	54.2	53.3	54.4	53.7	51.9	53.7	53.0	55.1	53.0	53.3	53.1	45.0
4. Desirable	19.5	18.9	19.9	21.9	7.1	19.1	20.0	17.8	21.9	19.8	19.8	21.8	16.9	19.5	17.7	15.8
Item 11810 Subject C05 N	3259	1572	1591	2455	402	778	896	987	598	1911	1151	1245	653	477	785	45
A05C: Working in a government agency																
1. Not at all acceptable	16.0	15.2	16.8	16.6	11.7	17.1	17.4	14.5	15.0	13.1	20.1	15.9	17.1	14.0	15.7	22.5
2. Somewhat acceptable	29.8	30.2	29.7	31.8	19.3	29.6	31.2	27.3	31.9	29.8	30.8	30.0	29.4	30.2	29.6	39.1
3. Acceptable	35.4	35.6	34.3	35.4	36.5	34.9	33.4	37.2	36.0	38.0	31.1	36.6	35.0	35.0	34.6	15.5
4. Desirable	18.8	18.9	19.1	16.3	32.5	18.3	18.0	21.0	17.2	19.1	18.0	17.6	18.5	20.8	20.0	22.9
Item 11820 Subject C05,H05 N	3258	1571	1592	2453	401	776	893	990	599	1910	1152	1243	650	477	788	45
A05D: Working in the military service																
1. Not at all acceptable	44.2	38.3	51.0	47.6	26.9	46.4	45.5	39.3	47.6	46.8	42.5	44.2	43.8	41.7	45.8	52.3
2. Somewhat acceptable	28.6	28.6	28.1	28.2	28.9	28.5	28.1	29.5	28.0	27.3	29.2	27.9	28.6	33.2	27.7	24.6
3. Acceptable	17.1	19.8	14.3	16.1	23.3	16.8	16.4	18.9	15.4	17.9	15.5	17.7	16.8	16.1	17.5	3.3
4. Desirable	10.1	13.3	6.6	8.1	20.9	8.3	9.9	12.4	9.1	8.0	12.8	10.2	10.8	9.0	9.1	19.7
Item 11830 Subject C05,L04 N	3257	1571	1591	2453	402	778	893	989	598	1913	1150	1245	649	476	788	45
A05E: Working in a school or university																
1. Not at all acceptable	25.8	31.4	20.4	27.4	19.9	30.0	23.9	25.2	24.0	19.4	35.5	21.0	27.1	24.9	31.6	41.4
2. Somewhat acceptable	35.7	37.1	34.1	35.3	36.1	33.3	35.6	36.9	36.9	35.1	36.5	34.0	36.9	41.2	35.1	23.4
3. Acceptable	27.1	22.2	31.9	26.0	30.3	26.8	27.1	28.3	25.8	30.6	21.5	31.5	26.8	22.7	23.2	20.5
4. Desirable	11.4	9.3	13.7	11.3	13.8	9.9	13.4	9.7	13.4	14.9	6.4	13.5	9.3	11.2	10.1	14.7
Item 11840 Subject B10,C05 N	3257	1573	1587	2454	400	778	893	987	599	1910	1151	1242	651	476	789	43
A05F: Working in a police department or police agency																
1. Not at all acceptable	26.6	25.8	27.2	25.3	32.4	28.3	24.9	27.2	25.9	27.6	25.3	26.2	27.2	23.1	28.3	37.5
2. Somewhat acceptable	36.0	36.9	35.6	36.6	33.9	35.4	36.8	36.7	34.3	36.8	34.1	35.2	38.2	39.8	33.5	32.9
3. Acceptable	26.1	24.9	26.9	26.8	21.5	26.3	27.6	25.2	24.9	24.9	27.8	28.6	23.7	23.1	25.8	14.8
4. Desirable	11.4	12.4	10.4	11.2	12.3	10.0	10.7	11.0	14.9	10.6	12.8	10.0	10.9	14.0	12.4	14.9
Item 11850 Subject C05 N	3258	1571	1591	2455	400	778	895	985	600	1912	1151	1242	651	476	789	45
A05G: Working in a social service organization																
1. Not at all acceptable	23.9	35.2	12.2	25.3	15.3	26.7	23.8	21.8	23.6	22.5	25.3	21.3	29.0	23.4	23.2	43.8
2. Somewhat acceptable	36.7	40.8	32.8	35.6	38.7	38.2	34.2	36.4	39.1	35.4	38.6	36.9	37.0	35.7	37.6	19.2
3. Acceptable	27.0	19.5	34.3	26.7	28.1	26.9	25.7	29.6	25.0	28.4	24.7	29.6	21.6	29.4	26.4	12.8
4. Desirable	12.4	4.4	20.7	12.3	17.9	8.2	16.3	12.2	12.3	13.7	11.5	12.2	12.4	11.6	12.8	24.2
Item 11860 Subject C05,O01 N	3248	1572	1581	2446	399	775	892	983	597	1912	1144	1239	646	476	786	45

QUESTIONNAIRE FORM 5 1985	TOTAL	SEX		RACE		REGION				4YR COLLEGE PLANS		ILLICIT DRUG USE: LIFETIME				
		M	F	White	Black	NE	NC	S	W	Yes	No	None	Marijuana Only	Few Pills	More Pills	Any Heroin
N (Weighted No. of Cases):	3286	1584	1601	2463	410	782	901	997	604	1920	1159	1252	655	479	794	45
% of Weighted Total:	100.0	48.2	48.7	75.0	12.5	23.8	27.4	30.4	18.4	58.4	35.3	38.1	19.9	14.6	24.2	1.4

A05H: Working with a small group of partners

	TOTAL	M	F	White	Black	NE	NC	S	W	Yes	No	None	Marijuana Only	Few Pills	More Pills	Any Heroin
1. Not at all acceptable	10.1	10.1	9.8	8.9	14.2	10.1	9.5	11.4	8.9	8.7	11.9	8.4	10.7	8.7	12.1	16.5
2. Somewhat acceptable	28.4	28.5	28.0	26.3	36.5	29.3	26.0	31.9	24.9	27.2	30.1	27.2	28.1	29.8	29.1	30.7
3. Acceptable	42.0	41.4	43.0	43.6	36.5	41.3	45.7	37.4	44.8	41.8	42.9	45.3	41.3	41.3	39.6	27.4
4. Desirable	19.5	20.1	19.1	21.3	12.9	19.3	18.8	19.2	21.4	22.3	15.0	19.1	20.0	20.1	19.3	25.4
Item 11870 Subject C05 N	3259	1574	1590	2456	401	777	897	985	601	1915	1149	1244	651	476	789	45

A05I: Working on your own (self-employed)

	TOTAL	M	F	White	Black	NE	NC	S	W	Yes	No	None	Marijuana Only	Few Pills	More Pills	Any Heroin
1. Not at all acceptable	7.8	6.0	9.6	7.3	8.3	8.7	8.4	7.5	6.4	6.8	9.4	7.1	7.9	8.4	8.4	8.1
2. Somewhat acceptable	14.7	13.5	15.9	15.4	12.1	13.1	16.0	14.1	15.8	15.3	13.4	15.3	16.4	14.6	13.6	2.5
3. Acceptable	31.7	29.1	34.3	32.5	30.4	28.4	35.1	31.3	31.7	32.8	30.4	34.7	34.3	31.7	25.0	21.9
4. Desirable	45.7	51.4	40.1	44.9	49.2	49.8	40.4	47.0	46.1	45.0	46.7	42.9	41.5	45.3	53.0	67.5
Item 11880 Subject C05 N	3263	1576	1591	2458	403	777	897	988	601	1917	1150	1245	650	477	790	45

A06: If you were to get enough money to live as comfortably as you'd like for the rest of your life, would you want to work?

	TOTAL	M	F	White	Black	NE	NC	S	W	Yes	No	None	Marijuana Only	Few Pills	More Pills	Any Heroin
1. I would want to work	79.7	76.5	82.7	78.3	82.6	74.9	81.4	81.7	80.1	80.3	78.2	83.6	79.7	79.9	74.1	65.6
2. I would not want to work	20.3	23.5	17.3	21.7	17.4	25.1	18.6	18.3	19.9	19.7	21.8	16.4	20.3	20.1	25.9	34.4
Item 8100 Subject C06 N	3238	1558	1589	2440	400	771	889	980	598	1901	1142	1236	647	476	781	44

A07: The next questions are about race relations. How much have you gotten to know people of other races...

A07A: In school?

	TOTAL	M	F	White	Black	NE	NC	S	W	Yes	No	None	Marijuana Only	Few Pills	More Pills	Any Heroin
1. Not at all	9.1	9.4	8.6	10.5	2.2	8.5	16.2	5.7	4.7	8.1	11.3	9.1	8.3	8.7	9.8	13.3
2. A little	19.7	19.9	19.7	22.5	10.2	20.1	23.9	16.1	18.8	20.4	19.6	20.4	17.5	21.9	20.0	15.6
3. Some	27.2	27.1	27.2	28.5	20.8	24.8	24.7	28.5	32.2	25.3	30.3	26.8	27.0	27.4	28.9	22.8
4. A lot	41.3	40.3	42.4	35.4	64.9	44.6	30.5	47.3	43.0	43.6	36.5	40.1	45.7	39.7	39.2	37.4
8. Does not apply to me	2.7	3.3	2.1	3.0	1.8	2.0	4.7	2.4	1.2	2.6	2.4	3.6	1.6	2.2	2.1	11.0
Item 11890 Subject B03,N03 N	3257	1569	1593	2451	405	778	895	987	596	1908	1156	1242	650	477	787	45

A07B: In your neighborhood?

	TOTAL	M	F	White	Black	NE	NC	S	W	Yes	No	None	Marijuana Only	Few Pills	More Pills	Any Heroin
1. Not at all	31.8	31.4	32.3	36.8	13.5	28.1	39.9	30.6	26.5	33.0	31.0	31.9	29.8	34.1	32.9	25.5
2. A little	23.2	24.1	22.8	23.4	18.1	25.3	19.8	22.2	27.3	22.6	23.9	23.5	24.0	22.0	24.0	13.7
3. Some	20.1	19.0	20.5	18.4	26.5	19.9	16.6	20.1	25.6	20.1	20.5	19.7	20.8	21.2	19.0	19.4
4. A lot	14.4	15.1	13.5	9.1	36.1	17.6	9.3	16.5	14.2	13.3	14.4	14.3	14.2	12.8	13.9	22.4
8. Does not apply to me	10.5	10.4	10.9	12.2	5.8	9.0	14.4	10.6	6.5	10.9	10.2	10.5	11.1	10.0	10.2	19.0
Item 11900 Subject N03 N	3253	1569	1591	2452	404	776	898	986	593	1909	1151	1245	644	478	787	45

A07C: In church?

	TOTAL	M	F	White	Black	NE	NC	S	W	Yes	No	None	Marijuana Only	Few Pills	More Pills	Any Heroin
1. Not at all	35.2	37.5	32.9	38.6	23.5	39.7	38.6	33.3	27.3	34.7	36.4	32.2	35.6	37.1	38.7	39.3
2. A little	20.8	21.2	20.5	21.4	17.4	19.2	20.8	20.4	23.8	21.1	21.1	22.5	18.8	22.3	19.7	8.7
3. Some	15.1	14.0	15.8	12.9	21.6	13.3	14.3	16.6	16.3	15.0	14.3	15.7	17.9	16.5	11.1	7.2
4. A lot	8.8	7.3	10.3	5.4	22.4	6.7	7.2	11.4	9.6	9.2	7.9	11.6	7.5	6.4	5.8	22.7
8. Does not apply to me	20.0	20.1	20.4	21.7	15.1	21.0	19.0	18.3	23.1	20.1	20.3	18.1	20.2	17.7	24.6	22.0
Item 11910 Subject G,N03 N	3248	1567	1587	2445	402	775	894	983	596	1911	1146	1240	645	477	787	45

A07D: On sports teams?

	TOTAL	M	F	White	Black	NE	NC	S	W	Yes	No	None	Marijuana Only	Few Pills	More Pills	Any Heroin
1. Not at all	19.0	16.1	21.4	20.3	9.8	18.6	24.9	16.1	15.4	16.0	24.5	20.4	17.0	15.2	20.6	17.1
2. A little	15.9	15.9	16.1	17.2	9.4	14.5	19.2	14.2	15.6	17.1	14.2	17.6	14.3	19.5	13.1	10.8
3. Some	20.1	22.4	17.8	21.5	16.4	21.9	18.9	19.6	20.6	20.0	20.2	18.3	21.5	20.4	21.7	22.0
4. A lot	27.3	33.6	21.3	22.6	50.1	27.8	19.0	32.6	30.4	30.1	22.2	27.2	31.2	29.9	22.0	28.6
8. Does not apply to me	17.7	12.0	23.5	18.3	14.3	17.2	18.0	17.5	18.0	16.9	18.9	16.5	15.9	15.0	22.6	21.6
Item 11920 Subject N03 N	3247	1569	1588	2445	402	775	893	984	595	1909	1147	1241	645	477	786	45

QUESTIONNAIRE FORM 5 1985	TOTAL	SEX		RACE		REGION				4YR COLLEGE PLANS		ILLICIT DRUG USE: LIFETIME				
		M	F	White	Black	NE	NC	S	W	Yes	No	None	Marijuana Only	Few Pills	More Pills	Any Heroin
N (Weighted No. of Cases):	3286	1584	1601	2463	410	782	901	997	604	1920	1159	1252	655	479	794	45
% of Weighted Total:	100.0	48.2	48.7	75.0	12.5	23.8	27.4	30.4	18.4	58.4	35.3	38.1	19.9	14.6	24.2	1.4

A07E: In clubs?

1. Not at all	25.7	28.6	22.6	28.8	14.0	27.1	31.3	22.5	20.6	22.4	31.5	24.0	23.6	24.9	31.0	26.0
2. A little	18.7	18.8	18.8	20.6	11.4	17.8	19.0	17.9	20.7	20.2	16.9	18.9	19.9	22.9	15.3	16.1
3. Some	20.7	18.4	22.9	19.6	22.2	20.9	16.1	25.5	19.6	22.4	17.8	22.1	21.2	20.8	18.0	13.8
4. A lot	15.2	13.6	16.7	10.9	32.4	14.8	10.6	19.0	16.5	17.2	11.5	16.2	16.5	14.2	12.8	20.0
8. Does not apply to me	19.7	20.6	19.0	20.1	20.0	19.5	23.1	15.1	22.6	17.7	22.4	18.8	18.8	17.1	23.0	24.1
Item 11930 Subject N03 N	3249	1569	1588	2448	402	776	896	982	596	1911	1148	1244	645	476	785	45

A07F: On a job?

1. Not at all	16.4	17.7	15.2	18.6	7.5	18.1	21.1	12.2	14.2	16.5	16.6	18.2	15.3	15.2	15.8	18.2
2. A little	15.6	16.3	15.0	17.6	7.1	17.7	16.7	13.4	15.0	15.3	16.2	15.2	15.3	15.7	16.5	15.3
3. Some	22.6	22.9	21.8	23.0	21.6	23.7	20.7	22.1	25.1	22.8	22.4	21.0	24.7	23.0	23.1	25.3
4. A lot	32.2	32.3	32.2	27.7	47.3	32.4	24.7	37.8	34.0	30.5	34.0	28.8	31.1	35.0	35.9	31.8
8. Does not apply to me	13.1	10.8	15.8	13.1	16.5	8.1	16.8	14.6	11.7	14.8	10.8	16.8	13.6	11.2	8.7	9.4
Item 11940 Subject C01,N03 N	3255	1572	1590	2450	405	776	897	984	598	1913	1150	1243	649	477	787	45

A08: Thinking about the country as a whole, would you say relations between white people and black people have been getting better, getting worse, or staying pretty much the same?

1. Better	28.3	32.5	24.5	29.1	24.8	28.3	25.5	27.1	34.4	29.2	27.1	28.1	31.8	25.2	28.3	19.1
2. A little better	47.5	44.8	49.6	46.9	52.1	47.8	48.9	46.7	46.1	48.8	45.7	46.1	47.6	51.1	48.0	39.1
3. Same	19.2	17.4	21.4	19.4	17.3	19.2	20.2	20.0	16.5	17.7	21.7	21.0	15.5	19.3	18.8	34.1
4. A little worse	3.5	3.3	3.6	3.1	4.8	3.4	3.5	4.2	2.3	3.4	3.3	3.7	3.1	3.2	3.4	0.8
5. Worse	1.5	2.0	0.9	1.5	1.0	1.3	1.8	2.0	0.7	0.9	2.2	1.2	1.9	1.2	1.5	6.9
Item 11950 Subject N02 N	3261	1575	1594	2454	407	774	898	989	600	1910	1154	1248	652	477	786	45

The next questions are about driving.

A09: Do you have a driver's license?

1. Yes	86.5	89.8	83.1	90.0	71.0	76.9	90.9	90.0	86.5	88.3	84.1	85.4	88.9	89.0	85.5	80.6
2. No, but I soon will– GO TO Q.A13	11.1	8.5	13.8	8.3	23.9	19.9	7.3	8.0	10.8	9.8	12.7	11.4	9.5	9.3	13.0	12.9
3. No–GO TO Q.A13	2.4	1.7	3.1	1.7	5.0	3.2	1.8	2.0	2.7	1.8	3.3	3.2	1.6	1.7	1.5	6.5
Item 11960 Subject F07 N	3149	1528	1541	2429	357	743	878	949	579	1874	1101	1200	634	458	772	45

A10: Do you own a car?

1. Yes	53.1	60.1	45.3	55.5	31.3	46.4	47.7	58.0	61.0	49.5	58.9	48.1	49.0	53.0	63.3	69.8
2. No, but I expect to own one in another year or two	29.7	26.7	32.8	27.1	54.8	31.0	32.9	26.5	28.5	28.2	32.1	29.1	31.2	34.4	27.0	27.1
3. No	17.2	13.2	21.8	17.4	13.9	22.6	19.4	15.5	10.5	22.3	9.0	22.9	19.8	12.6	9.7	3.0
Item 11970 Subject F07 N★	2729	1373	1284	2188	253	573	800	854	502	1658	927	1027	564	407	661	36

A11: Are you able to use someone else's car when you want to?

1. Yes, whenever I wish	33.0	32.5	33.8	33.3	25.8	28.4	34.3	36.4	30.4	31.8	34.2	35.1	27.9	34.3	34.6	25.1
2. Yes, most of the time	44.8	42.5	47.0	45.5	42.6	46.4	47.3	40.6	45.9	47.4	41.4	43.9	50.0	44.4	42.0	45.2
3. Sometimes	15.3	18.2	12.0	15.1	20.1	16.5	12.5	16.7	15.9	14.8	16.2	15.6	14.3	14.0	15.3	23.3
4. Rarely	4.7	4.7	4.7	4.3	7.3	6.2	4.1	4.3	4.3	3.8	5.6	3.4	5.3	6.2	5.0	6.4
5. Never	2.3	2.0	2.5	1.8	4.2	2.4	1.7	2.0	3.5	2.1	2.5	1.9	2.6	1.1	3.1	-
Item 11980 Subject F07 N★	2724	1369	1283	2183	253	571	799	853	502	1654	926	1026	563	407	658	36

A12: Do you make an effort to cut down on driving, in order to save gasoline?

1. Not at all	22.4	25.2	19.4	22.8	19.0	30.2	18.4	20.9	22.6	23.0	20.9	15.9	27.2	25.4	26.9	27.3
2. Not very much	32.4	32.2	33.0	33.4	28.1	34.5	32.8	31.4	31.0	33.8	29.8	33.2	30.8	33.2	32.3	35.6
3. Yes, to some extent	36.0	34.0	37.4	35.1	40.9	25.6	40.1	37.4	38.9	34.8	38.4	38.5	35.7	35.4	32.2	32.1
4. Yes, quite a bit	5.6	5.3	6.1	5.4	5.8	4.7	6.1	6.0	5.0	5.2	6.5	7.7	3.0	3.9	5.3	3.9
8. Don't know	3.6	3.3	4.1	3.3	6.2	5.0	2.6	4.4	2.4	3.3	4.3	4.7	3.4	2.0	3.3	1.0
Item 11990 Subject F07 N★	2724	1371	1281	2184	253	573	799	854	498	1656	924	1027	564	407	657	36

★=excludes respondents for whom question was inappropriate.

	TOTAL	SEX		RACE		REGION				4YR COLLEGE PLANS		ILLICIT DRUG USE: LIFETIME				
QUESTIONNAIRE FORM 5 **1985**		M	F	White	Black	NE	NC	S	W	Yes	No	None	Mari-juana Only	Few Pills	More Pills	Any Her-oin
N (Weighted No. of Cases):	3286	1584	1601	2463	410	782	901	997	604	1920	1159	1252	655	479	794	45
% of Weighted Total:	100.0	48.2	48.7	75.0	12.5	23.8	27.4	30.4	18.4	58.4	35.3	38.1	19.9	14.6	24.2	1.4
A13: Do you make an effort to cut down on the amount of electricity you use in order to save energy?																
1. Not at all	9.9	12.4	7.7	10.5	7.7	13.7	8.5	9.1	8.3	10.2	9.0	8.4	9.1	10.5	11.5	31.7
2. Not very much	29.3	28.8	29.8	31.8	19.4	30.3	30.2	28.9	27.2	30.0	29.0	26.2	29.6	33.1	31.9	23.9
3. Yes, to some extent	45.0	42.8	46.8	44.8	45.5	42.5	46.9	43.8	47.2	43.6	47.6	46.8	46.4	42.0	43.3	40.5
4. Yes, quite a bit	14.4	14.5	14.3	11.6	24.6	12.2	12.9	16.7	15.8	15.3	12.1	16.9	13.2	13.7	12.0	3.9
8. Don't know	1.4	1.5	1.5	1.2	2.8	1.2	1.5	1.5	1.4	0.9	2.3	1.7	1.7	0.7	1.3	-
Item 12000 Subject F05 N	3263	1577	1596	2457	408	775	899	990	599	1913	1156	1249	653	478	787	44
A14: In the house or apartment where you live, is an effort made to reduce heat during the winter, in order to save energy?																
1. Not at all	7.0	7.3	6.8	6.2	10.7	8.6	6.1	7.2	6.2	6.6	8.1	6.3	5.5	7.6	8.5	18.7
2. Not very much	16.2	16.6	15.5	15.0	20.0	16.7	15.1	16.9	16.0	14.5	18.2	15.8	16.5	18.0	15.4	8.0
3. Yes, to some extent	39.4	41.0	37.7	40.1	38.3	36.3	38.0	43.0	39.4	38.9	39.5	37.6	42.3	38.1	40.3	32.0
4. Yes, quite a bit	35.3	33.5	37.5	37.0	28.8	35.2	39.2	31.1	36.9	38.6	31.4	37.5	33.6	34.8	34.7	38.9
8. Don't know	2.1	1.6	2.5	1.6	2.2	3.3	1.6	1.9	1.5	1.3	2.9	2.8	2.0	1.6	1.2	2.3
Item 12010 Subject F05 N	3265	1577	1597	2457	408	776	899	991	600	1914	1155	1249	653	478	786	44
A15: How do you feel about each of the following?																
A15A: How much do you enjoy shopping for things like clothes, records, sporting goods, and books?																
1. Not at all	1.7	3.1	0.3	1.8	0.3	2.2	1.7	1.5	1.5	1.8	1.6	2.0	0.9	1.1	2.0	8.8
2. Not very much	8.1	12.5	3.6	8.3	6.2	6.5	9.2	8.1	8.5	7.0	9.2	8.6	7.5	7.9	7.6	17.1
3. Pretty much	30.6	43.4	17.9	32.4	20.2	32.2	32.8	26.1	32.7	29.5	31.9	29.7	32.5	34.0	29.1	26.6
4. Very much	59.6	40.9	78.2	57.5	73.3	59.1	56.3	64.2	57.3	61.7	57.2	59.8	59.1	56.9	61.3	47.6
Item 12020 Subject F01 N	3267	1577	1599	2459	408	777	899	991	600	1914	1156	1249	653	478	788	44
A15B: How much do you care about having the latest fashion in your clothes, records, leisure activities, and so on?																
1. Not at all	6.6	10.0	3.0	7.0	1.8	6.2	7.0	5.9	7.9	6.2	7.7	6.9	5.8	6.3	7.1	8.4
2. Not very much	24.4	28.6	20.0	25.4	15.0	24.8	26.6	20.6	26.9	24.0	25.2	26.7	20.1	24.1	23.4	40.1
3. Pretty much	40.0	38.7	41.8	41.5	32.1	40.1	39.4	38.9	42.4	40.6	38.0	39.9	44.8	41.4	36.5	31.3
4. Very much	29.0	22.7	35.2	26.1	51.1	29.0	27.1	34.6	22.8	29.3	29.1	26.5	29.3	28.2	33.1	20.2
Item 12030 Subject F01 N	3261	1574	1596	2456	407	775	899	987	600	1912	1155	1246	653	477	788	44
A15C: How much do you care about whether your family has most of the things your friends and neighbors have?																
1. Not at all	22.5	21.6	23.4	21.4	27.6	24.8	21.1	21.5	23.5	20.6	25.2	22.4	21.3	22.2	23.5	34.3
2. Not very much	50.1	50.7	49.8	51.3	45.5	48.2	50.7	49.6	52.6	50.2	50.7	50.4	49.2	48.9	51.3	53.8
3. Pretty much	20.5	21.0	19.8	21.3	17.6	20.3	23.4	20.0	17.1	22.7	17.6	21.6	22.9	21.7	16.5	7.8
4. Very much	6.9	6.7	7.0	6.0	9.2	6.7	4.8	8.9	6.8	6.6	6.5	5.6	6.6	7.2	8.6	4.1
Item 12040 Subject F01 N	3257	1573	1593	2452	406	775	898	985	599	1911	1152	1247	649	477	786	44
A16: When you are older, do you expect to own more possessions than your parents do now, or about the same, or less? I expect to own . . .																
1. Much less than my parents	1.7	2.2	1.1	1.5	2.6	1.4	2.0	1.6	1.7	1.5	2.0	1.6	1.8	1.4	1.7	4.4
2. Somewhat less than my parents	6.3	6.0	6.5	6.9	3.6	5.9	8.0	4.9	6.4	5.3	7.6	6.2	5.6	5.4	7.2	9.9
3. About as much as my parents	33.0	28.9	36.4	34.6	23.3	29.2	36.7	31.4	35.0	30.1	37.5	34.0	33.3	35.3	29.4	32.1
4. Somewhat more than my parents	38.7	38.0	39.8	38.8	42.0	41.2	37.5	41.3	33.3	40.3	36.7	39.7	39.8	39.2	37.4	23.6
5. Much more than my parents	20.3	24.9	16.2	18.2	28.5	22.3	15.8	20.9	23.6	22.7	16.2	18.6	19.5	18.8	24.2	30.0
Item 12050 Subject F01 N	3258	1573	1594	2452	406	772	896	991	599	1908	1154	1248	651	475	786	44

QUESTIONNAIRE FORM 5 1985	TOTAL	SEX		RACE		REGION				4YR COLLEGE PLANS		ILLICIT DRUG USE: LIFETIME				
		M	F	White	Black	NE	NC	S	W	Yes	No	None	Mari-juana Only	Few Pills	More Pills	Any Her-oin
N (Weighted No. of Cases):	3286	1584	1601	2463	410	782	901	997	604	1920	1159	1252	655	479	794	45
% of Weighted Total:	100.0	48.2	48.7	75.0	12.5	23.8	27.4	30.4	18.4	58.4	35.3	38.1	19.9	14.6	24.2	1.4

A17: Compared with your parents, what is the smallest amount that you could be content or satisfied to own?

The least I could be content to own is . . .

	TOTAL	M	F	White	Black	NE	NC	S	W	Yes	No	None	Mari-juana Only	Few Pills	More Pills	Any Her-oin
1. Much less than my parents	9.0	8.6	9.3	10.0	6.9	8.9	11.0	8.1	7.3	9.3	8.6	9.3	8.5	10.8	7.7	9.9
2. Somewhat less than my parents	27.7	25.1	30.2	30.4	13.7	22.6	32.4	25.9	30.0	29.3	26.3	28.4	25.5	28.3	28.5	23.2
3. About as much as my parents	43.4	42.0	44.8	43.4	43.8	45.2	40.1	46.0	41.7	41.8	45.1	44.4	44.7	40.9	42.0	45.7
4. Somewhat more than my parents	14.6	17.6	11.6	12.2	24.8	17.0	13.3	13.9	14.3	14.4	14.5	13.0	16.0	14.0	16.2	11.7
5. Much more than my parents	5.4	6.8	4.1	4.1	10.8	6.2	3.3	6.0	6.7	5.2	5.5	4.9	5.3	6.0	5.5	9.5
Item 12060　Subject F01　　N	3238	1567	1581	2439	402	765	892	984	598	1900	1148	1238	649	470	784	44

A18: These next questions ask your opinions about a number of different topics. How much do you agree or disagree with each statement below?

A18A: We ought to worry about our own country and let the rest of the world take care of itself

	TOTAL	M	F	White	Black	NE	NC	S	W	Yes	No	None	Mari-juana Only	Few Pills	More Pills	Any Her-oin
1. Disagree	26.5	24.4	28.5	24.3	34.8	24.8	25.3	28.5	27.2	28.1	22.4	28.5	25.2	26.7	23.9	27.6
2. Mostly disagree	27.0	25.9	28.3	27.9	21.9	26.1	27.8	26.7	27.3	30.5	21.4	26.2	30.6	28.8	25.0	16.1
3. Neither	14.3	13.5	14.7	14.4	11.2	14.9	14.2	12.8	16.1	13.9	15.0	13.7	16.1	13.4	13.9	17.8
4. Mostly agree	21.1	21.4	20.9	22.4	19.6	22.3	21.2	21.1	19.4	19.3	25.2	21.5	17.1	20.2	24.6	17.2
5. Agree	11.1	14.9	7.6	10.9	12.5	11.9	11.5	10.9	10.0	8.2	16.0	10.1	11.1	10.9	12.6	21.3
Item 12070　Subject O03　　N	3261	1578	1591	2452	408	777	897	986	601	1913	1154	1247	653	475	789	45

A18B: It would be better if we all felt more like citizens of the world than of any particular country

	TOTAL	M	F	White	Black	NE	NC	S	W	Yes	No	None	Mari-juana Only	Few Pills	More Pills	Any Her-oin
1. Disagree	10.3	13.8	6.5	11.2	5.5	13.1	8.9	9.8	9.5	10.4	10.2	9.4	10.5	10.9	10.8	16.9
2. Mostly disagree	11.1	12.9	8.9	11.7	8.5	10.2	11.6	10.9	11.7	10.7	11.3	10.5	10.6	11.3	11.7	10.3
3. Neither	19.6	19.4	20.1	20.8	11.6	20.7	22.8	15.4	20.3	18.7	21.5	20.3	18.8	19.2	19.1	25.3
4. Mostly agree	29.0	26.3	31.8	29.5	27.3	28.1	28.1	31.3	28.0	30.8	27.3	30.5	30.6	28.8	26.8	17.1
5. Agree	30.1	27.6	32.8	26.7	47.2	27.9	28.7	32.7	30.5	29.4	29.7	29.3	29.6	29.8	31.6	30.4
Item 12080　Subject O03　　N	3259	1576	1592	2452	408	775	897	988	599	1913	1154	1246	652	474	788	45

A18C: I find it hard to be sympathetic toward starving people in foreign lands, when there is so much trouble in our own country

	TOTAL	M	F	White	Black	NE	NC	S	W	Yes	No	None	Mari-juana Only	Few Pills	More Pills	Any Her-oin
1. Disagree	38.2	26.7	49.5	36.0	51.8	34.6	35.7	44.0	36.8	39.6	34.5	40.1	37.8	39.1	36.4	21.4
2. Mostly disagree	23.3	21.9	24.7	24.3	19.3	22.9	24.1	22.0	24.6	25.1	21.5	25.2	23.3	22.4	21.2	21.4
3. Neither	13.1	17.6	8.8	13.9	7.4	14.1	13.8	10.9	14.4	12.5	14.7	13.3	14.3	13.7	11.2	14.2
4. Mostly agree	15.1	19.1	10.9	15.6	12.5	16.6	17.4	12.4	14.4	14.7	15.6	12.8	16.4	16.3	16.6	14.3
5. Agree	10.3	14.7	6.0	10.2	9.1	11.7	8.9	10.7	9.8	8.1	13.7	8.6	8.2	8.5	14.7	28.7
Item 12090　Subject F03,O03　　N	3258	1575	1591	2450	407	776	896	985	601	1912	1154	1246	653	475	789	44

A18D: Maybe some minority groups do get unfair treatment, but that's no business of mine

	TOTAL	M	F	White	Black	NE	NC	S	W	Yes	No	None	Mari-juana Only	Few Pills	More Pills	Any Her-oin
1. Disagree	40.6	32.1	48.8	36.8	56.1	43.6	35.7	41.1	43.0	46.1	31.8	41.5	44.0	39.8	38.0	34.6
2. Mostly disagree	28.3	29.5	27.3	30.9	19.8	28.4	31.8	24.8	28.8	28.8	28.1	27.8	28.9	30.2	27.8	26.8
3. Neither	17.7	21.0	14.6	19.6	9.0	15.5	19.5	18.5	16.6	15.4	20.5	16.8	15.2	19.1	20.3	20.4
4. Mostly agree	7.9	9.7	6.2	7.6	8.5	6.9	8.9	8.4	6.9	6.3	10.8	8.3	6.3	5.7	9.5	4.4
5. Agree	5.5	7.7	3.1	5.0	6.6	5.6	4.2	7.2	4.7	3.3	8.7	5.7	5.6	5.1	4.5	13.8
Item 12100　Subject N02,O03　　N	3252	1571	1589	2448	402	774	895	984	599	1905	1154	1245	651	473	785	45

A18E: I get very upset when I see other people treated unfairly

	TOTAL	M	F	White	Black	NE	NC	S	W	Yes	No	None	Mari-juana Only	Few Pills	More Pills	Any Her-oin
1. Disagree	3.4	4.2	2.4	3.3	3.6	3.5	3.1	4.0	2.7	2.7	4.1	3.0	3.6	2.7	3.6	14.1
2. Mostly disagree	5.1	6.3	3.6	5.5	1.9	7.2	4.0	4.4	5.1	4.1	6.7	3.9	3.7	4.2	7.7	10.8
3. Neither	8.2	13.2	3.5	9.1	5.0	9.9	8.7	6.4	8.2	7.0	9.2	7.8	6.6	10.7	8.4	13.4
4. Mostly agree	31.7	35.7	28.2	34.3	24.6	29.4	33.6	30.4	34.0	31.9	32.6	30.8	34.2	33.2	31.6	15.7
5. Agree	51.7	40.6	62.3	47.8	64.9	50.1	50.6	54.8	50.1	54.3	47.4	54.4	51.8	49.1	48.7	46.0
Item 12110　Subject O03　　N	3254	1572	1590	2452	405	772	894	988	600	1910	1153	1246	649	476	786	45

QUESTIONNAIRE FORM 5 1985	TOTAL	SEX M	F	RACE White	Black	REGION NE	NC	S	W	4YR COLLEGE PLANS Yes	No	ILLICIT DRUG USE: LIFETIME None	Marijuana Only	Few Pills	More Pills	Any Heroin
N (Weighted No. of Cases):	3286	1584	1601	2463	410	782	901	997	604	1920	1159	1252	655	479	794	45
% of Weighted Total:	100.0	48.2	48.7	75.0	12.5	23.8	27.4	30.4	18.4	58.4	35.3	38.1	19.9	14.6	24.2	1.4
A18F: I would agree to a good plan to make a better life for the poor, even if it cost me money																
1. Disagree	7.1	10.3	3.8	7.8	3.4	9.0	5.0	7.5	6.9	5.7	9.1	6.0	5.8	7.7	8.6	21.0
2. Mostly disagree	9.8	13.1	6.7	10.8	5.0	11.0	9.8	8.8	10.3	10.4	9.2	7.5	9.8	11.6	12.0	15.0
3. Neither	23.5	25.5	21.6	25.5	14.9	23.1	26.6	20.0	25.1	22.2	25.5	23.0	21.3	23.6	26.4	26.3
4. Mostly agree	36.6	32.0	41.5	37.8	33.9	35.3	37.6	37.3	35.7	39.5	32.9	36.9	40.5	37.5	33.4	18.4
5. Agree	23.0	19.1	26.5	18.1	42.8	21.6	21.0	26.5	21.9	22.2	23.3	26.6	22.6	19.6	19.5	19.3
Item 12120 Subject O03 N	3255	1573	1591	2448	407	772	894	988	601	1909	1156	1245	653	475	786	45
A18G: It's not really my problem if others are in trouble and need help																
1. Disagree	40.9	32.8	48.9	38.9	49.4	42.5	38.5	44.6	36.4	42.9	37.7	43.4	41.7	40.3	37.2	42.7
2. Mostly disagree	34.7	35.7	34.2	36.8	26.4	31.9	39.8	30.7	37.4	36.6	32.7	33.5	36.8	35.9	35.7	21.7
3. Neither	14.2	17.3	11.1	14.7	12.1	15.3	13.5	14.2	14.0	12.1	16.8	14.0	12.4	14.8	15.1	13.8
4. Mostly agree	7.4	9.8	4.8	7.2	7.8	7.4	6.7	7.0	8.8	6.1	9.4	6.6	6.4	7.2	8.4	14.6
5. Agree	2.8	4.4	1.0	2.4	4.3	2.9	1.5	3.6	3.3	2.3	3.4	2.4	2.7	1.8	3.6	7.2
Item 12130 Subject O03 N	3241	1565	1585	2441	403	764	892	984	600	1900	1151	1238	652	470	786	43
A18H: Americans could change their eating habits to provide more food for the hungry people in other parts of the world, and at the same time be healthier themselves																
1. Disagree	10.3	14.6	5.9	11.0	6.3	12.1	9.8	9.1	10.6	9.2	12.0	7.0	10.2	13.3	13.0	26.3
2. Mostly disagree	11.9	16.3	7.8	12.8	8.7	11.3	12.8	10.3	13.7	11.3	12.9	11.7	11.5	13.8	11.1	17.5
3. Neither	18.3	20.0	16.5	18.4	16.7	19.1	17.6	17.2	20.1	18.2	18.0	17.3	21.8	15.4	17.9	23.9
4. Mostly agree	29.2	27.5	31.0	29.2	31.9	29.0	31.3	28.6	27.5	30.6	28.2	30.9	30.0	28.2	27.8	8.2
5. Agree	30.4	21.6	38.9	28.6	36.4	28.5	28.6	34.9	28.1	30.6	28.9	33.1	26.6	29.2	30.2	24.1
Item 12140 Subject F03,O03 N	3250	1574	1587	2445	405	769	895	985	600	1906	1155	1243	653	473	785	45
A18I: My family and I often buy things we really don't need; we could get along with much less																
1. Disagree	13.0	15.2	11.0	11.2	22.4	14.3	11.6	13.3	13.3	11.0	16.5	11.9	13.7	11.4	15.1	15.7
2. Mostly disagree	16.3	17.7	14.5	16.7	15.3	19.4	15.6	14.9	15.4	15.8	17.2	17.5	17.6	11.7	15.6	18.0
3. Neither	17.0	20.8	13.5	17.4	13.6	17.8	19.9	14.8	15.3	17.5	15.1	17.6	16.2	17.9	16.5	16.5
4. Mostly agree	28.3	25.3	31.6	29.8	22.9	23.7	31.4	27.4	31.2	29.8	26.3	29.2	27.2	31.8	26.6	14.5
5. Agree	25.4	21.1	29.5	24.9	25.8	24.8	21.4	29.7	24.9	25.8	24.9	23.8	25.4	25.6	27.1	35.4
Item 10060 Subject F01 N	3246	1568	1586	2447	403	768	895	983	600	1905	1152	1244	649	472	784	45
A18J: Most people will have fuller and happier lives if they choose legal marriage rather than staying single, or just living with someone																
1. Disagree	23.9	20.9	27.0	23.3	28.3	30.0	21.0	22.7	22.5	23.6	24.0	20.0	23.3	24.1	30.3	36.9
2. Mostly disagree	15.0	15.6	14.6	15.2	14.8	14.1	17.0	15.0	13.4	14.9	15.3	12.5	14.8	15.9	18.8	6.9
3. Neither	26.4	26.9	25.7	25.8	28.1	27.7	28.1	23.8	26.6	26.4	26.2	26.0	30.5	26.7	22.9	30.3
4. Mostly agree	15.5	17.8	13.3	16.8	10.8	12.8	16.3	16.8	15.8	17.0	13.3	16.9	14.7	16.3	13.8	14.9
5. Agree	19.1	18.8	19.4	18.9	18.0	15.5	17.6	21.7	21.7	18.1	21.2	24.6	16.7	17.0	14.2	10.9
Item 12150 Subject D03 N	3244	1567	1587	2442	406	764	894	985	600	1905	1151	1243	652	468	787	45
A18K: Parents should encourage just as much independence in their daughters as in their sons																
1. Disagree	5.0	7.9	2.1	4.1	7.0	5.2	3.3	6.3	5.3	4.5	5.6	5.3	4.8	3.8	4.7	19.9
2. Mostly disagree	6.5	11.3	1.8	6.3	4.7	7.1	4.7	6.3	8.7	7.2	5.7	6.5	7.1	7.2	5.7	8.7
3. Neither	8.9	14.7	3.1	9.1	5.8	9.2	9.7	6.9	10.6	8.4	9.0	8.5	9.1	8.9	8.7	12.2
4. Mostly agree	23.7	28.2	19.1	23.6	24.3	23.7	27.0	19.6	25.4	21.7	26.5	24.8	23.0	24.1	22.9	12.1
5. Agree	55.8	37.9	73.8	56.8	58.3	54.8	55.2	60.8	50.0	58.2	53.2	54.9	56.0	56.0	58.0	47.1
Item 12160 Subject D05 N	3253	1569	1592	2447	407	769	896	986	602	1906	1155	1246	652	473	788	45

QUESTIONNAIRE FORM 5 1985	TOTAL	SEX		RACE		REGION				4YR COLLEGE PLANS		ILLICIT DRUG USE: LIFETIME				
		M	F	White	Black	NE	NC	S	W	Yes	No	None	Mari- juana Only	Few Pills	More Pills	Any Her- oin
N (Weighted No. of Cases):	3286	1584	1601	2463	410	782	901	997	604	1920	1159	1252	655	479	794	45
% of Weighted Total:	100.0	48.2	48.7	75.0	12.5	23.8	27.4	30.4	18.4	58.4	35.3	38.1	19.9	14.6	24.2	1.4

A18L: Being a mother and raising children is one of the most fulfilling experiences a woman can have

	TOTAL	M	F	White	Black	NE	NC	S	W	Yes	No	None	Mari.	Few	More	Any
1. Disagree	5.8	4.3	7.2	6.0	4.2	8.8	5.5	3.9	5.4	5.5	6.5	5.7	4.1	5.1	7.2	11.0
2. Mostly disagree	6.4	4.9	7.8	6.4	6.2	6.4	6.9	5.8	6.6	7.5	4.0	5.5	6.9	7.7	7.0	3.7
3. Neither	29.4	41.1	18.1	31.4	21.5	30.6	31.1	26.0	31.1	31.8	25.2	27.7	31.9	30.5	30.5	26.3
4. Mostly agree	26.7	23.5	29.9	26.9	25.3	25.4	28.3	25.8	27.2	25.4	29.4	27.4	25.6	29.6	24.8	20.7
5. Agree	31.7	26.1	37.0	29.3	42.7	28.8	28.2	38.5	29.7	29.8	34.9	33.7	31.4	27.1	30.4	38.4
Item 12170 Subject D05 N	3202	1529	1583	2408	403	755	884	971	592	1888	1130	1222	645	467	778	42

A18M: Most fathers should spend more time with their children than they do now

	TOTAL	M	F	White	Black	NE	NC	S	W	Yes	No	None	Mari.	Few	More	Any
1. Disagree	1.5	1.7	1.2	1.4	1.3	2.0	1.2	1.8	0.8	1.4	1.5	1.3	1.2	1.0	1.8	12.7
2. Mostly disagree	3.1	3.7	2.3	3.1	2.1	3.3	3.8	2.3	3.0	2.7	3.6	2.1	3.6	3.7	3.5	4.0
3. Neither	16.9	19.2	14.8	18.8	6.6	20.5	17.7	13.7	15.5	17.9	15.5	14.8	20.2	18.2	17.4	12.7
4. Mostly agree	35.5	36.9	34.6	36.1	34.4	35.8	37.4	30.5	40.7	36.1	34.4	37.2	34.6	37.5	32.8	26.0
5. Agree	43.0	38.5	47.2	40.5	55.6	38.4	39.9	51.8	38.8	41.9	45.0	44.5	40.3	39.6	44.4	44.7
Item 12180 Subject D05 N	3237	1560	1588	2437	404	764	890	985	597	1900	1149	1239	653	467	787	43

A18N: The husband should make all the important decisions in the family

	TOTAL	M	F	White	Black	NE	NC	S	W	Yes	No	None	Mari.	Few	More	Any
1. Disagree	43.2	23.8	62.0	43.8	45.2	44.4	43.0	44.0	40.5	46.8	37.7	42.2	43.4	45.5	44.5	29.9
2. Mostly disagree	20.3	21.9	19.2	21.2	18.9	19.7	22.2	17.9	22.0	21.3	18.5	20.2	20.2	20.6	20.9	8.0
3. Neither	16.6	23.7	9.3	16.7	12.3	14.7	17.5	16.6	17.8	15.0	18.5	17.0	15.1	16.1	16.7	21.1
4. Mostly agree	11.8	17.3	6.7	10.6	15.1	11.7	10.3	12.7	12.8	10.2	14.4	12.4	13.2	11.1	9.8	17.8
5. Agree	8.1	13.3	2.8	7.8	8.6	9.5	7.1	8.8	6.9	6.6	10.9	8.2	8.1	6.7	8.1	23.1
Item 12190 Subject D05 N	3247	1566	1591	2444	407	768	893	986	601	1904	1154	1246	652	469	788	44

A19: Some people think about what's going on in government very often, and others are not that interested. How much of an interest do you take in government and current events?

	TOTAL	M	F	White	Black	NE	NC	S	W	Yes	No	None	Mari.	Few	More	Any
1. No interest at all	4.4	4.3	4.2	4.4	3.9	6.2	4.5	2.9	4.0	2.9	6.2	3.3	3.9	3.3	5.9	21.5
2. Very little interest	18.3	13.5	22.6	18.7	17.7	21.8	18.8	15.9	16.8	14.5	23.3	16.1	20.1	21.0	18.4	16.8
3. Some interest	49.9	48.2	52.0	49.2	52.2	48.1	51.1	50.4	49.5	47.7	54.6	50.5	48.8	50.5	50.2	32.5
4. A lot of interest	19.6	23.0	16.1	19.7	20.2	16.4	18.3	22.4	21.1	24.0	12.7	20.4	20.7	16.9	19.5	17.1
5. A very great interest	7.9	10.9	5.1	8.0	6.1	7.5	7.2	8.4	8.5	10.9	3.2	9.7	6.5	8.3	6.0	12.1
Item 6330 Subject H01,Q08 N	3248	1568	1591	2447	406	773	891	986	598	1905	1150	1243	651	473	785	45

A20: If you have at least an average income in the future, how likely is it that you will contribute money to the following organizations? If you have already contributed, mark the last circle only. Are you likely to contribute to...

A20A: The United Fund or other community charities?

	TOTAL	M	F	White	Black	NE	NC	S	W	Yes	No	None	Mari.	Few	More	Any
1. Definitely not	5.1	7.0	2.7	4.9	3.8	5.7	5.7	3.3	6.2	4.2	6.5	3.7	4.2	5.9	5.9	30.5
2. Probably not	17.4	20.4	14.4	19.4	10.0	20.7	16.9	14.4	19.0	15.9	19.4	14.2	20.2	15.9	21.2	15.7
3. Don't know	46.1	47.3	44.9	48.4	35.4	49.2	46.5	43.2	46.3	45.8	46.7	48.2	43.9	44.9	46.8	36.0
4. Probably will	23.4	18.7	28.5	20.4	37.6	16.7	23.6	28.9	22.6	25.5	20.1	25.1	25.0	24.9	18.3	14.7
5. Definitely will	2.9	2.6	3.3	2.2	7.0	3.4	2.3	3.8	1.9	3.2	2.4	3.2	2.6	3.4	2.6	3.2
6. Already have	5.1	4.1	6.1	4.7	6.2	4.4	5.1	6.4	4.0	5.5	4.8	5.7	4.2	5.1	5.2	
Item 12200 Subject O02 N	3231	1563	1582	2435	402	760	890	984	596	1900	1150	1244	650	470	779	40

A20B: International relief organizations (CARE, UNICEF, etc.)?

	TOTAL	M	F	White	Black	NE	NC	S	W	Yes	No	None	Mari.	Few	More	Any
1. Definitely not	5.1	7.8	2.4	5.3	3.5	5.9	4.9	4.6	5.5	4.3	6.5	3.6	5.6	5.8	5.7	26.1
2. Probably not	13.8	17.7	10.2	15.6	6.5	15.4	14.3	10.4	16.7	12.7	15.5	12.4	14.5	13.6	15.6	12.1
3. Don't know	31.4	35.6	27.1	33.0	24.1	32.5	30.7	29.6	34.1	29.5	34.2	31.8	33.3	27.4	31.8	25.6
4. Probably will	33.8	28.1	39.3	32.5	37.7	30.1	32.4	38.6	32.8	35.8	31.2	35.8	31.4	36.4	32.2	21.2
5. Definitely will	7.8	4.9	10.7	5.4	20.7	7.0	8.0	9.3	6.1	7.8	7.0	8.4	7.5	7.6	6.6	12.8
6. Already have	8.1	5.9	10.3	8.1	7.4	9.1	9.7	7.7	4.8	10.0	5.6	8.1	7.7	9.3	8.1	2.1
Item 12210 Subject O02 N	3235	1566	1584	2439	402	763	889	984	598	1902	1151	1244	651	472	777	42

QUESTIONNAIRE FORM 5 1985	TOTAL	SEX		RACE		REGION				4YR COLLEGE PLANS		ILLICIT DRUG USE: LIFETIME				
		M	F	White	Black	NE	NC	S	W	Yes	No	None	Mari-juana Only	Few Pills	More Pills	Any Her-oin
N (Weighted No. of Cases):	3286	1584	1601	2463	410	782	901	997	604	1920	1159	1252	655	479	794	45
% of Weighted Total:	100.0	48.2	48.7	75.0	12.5	23.8	27.4	30.4	18.4	58.4	35.3	38.1	19.9	14.6	24.2	1.4

A20C: Minority group organizations (NAACP, SCLC, etc.)?

	TOTAL	M	F	White	Black	NE	NC	S	W	Yes	No	None	Mari-juana Only	Few Pills	More Pills	Any Her-oin
1. Definitely not	11.3	15.5	7.1	12.6	3.7	11.5	10.9	11.3	11.5	10.4	12.7	9.3	10.2	10.1	14.6	36.6
2. Probably not	26.8	27.7	25.9	31.7	5.6	28.6	27.7	24.7	26.3	28.4	24.9	24.3	27.9	31.9	28.2	10.7
3. Don't know	41.2	37.6	44.9	44.3	25.1	40.3	42.5	39.4	43.4	41.0	42.2	45.1	35.8	37.5	42.5	40.8
4. Probably will	14.5	13.1	15.8	10.1	30.1	15.0	14.3	14.6	14.1	13.5	15.7	15.1	17.0	13.2	11.4	10.0
5. Definitely will	4.8	4.6	5.0	0.9	28.4	3.1	3.7	8.2	3.1	5.3	3.4	4.8	7.0	5.8	2.5	1.8
6. Already have	1.4	1.5	1.3	0.4	7.1	1.4	0.9	1.7	1.6	1.3	1.2	1.4	2.1	1.5	0.8	-
Item 12220 Subject N02,O02　N	3229	1562	1581	2437	400	762	890	983	593	1895	1153	1242	651	471	774	42

A20D: Church or religious organizations?

	TOTAL	M	F	White	Black	NE	NC	S	W	Yes	No	None	Mari-juana Only	Few Pills	More Pills	Any Her-oin
1. Definitely not	5.7	7.4	4.2	6.1	1.6	8.0	5.1	3.1	7.8	5.0	6.8	4.2	5.4	6.6	6.7	26.8
2. Probably not	10.0	10.7	9.3	11.3	4.2	12.5	7.9	6.5	15.7	9.3	11.4	6.9	9.7	11.1	14.6	9.3
3. Don't know	16.2	18.3	14.3	16.8	11.0	21.4	15.5	12.6	16.8	14.5	18.3	14.5	17.4	13.2	19.6	23.9
4. Probably will	25.6	25.5	25.3	25.0	27.0	22.3	26.7	27.9	24.6	23.8	28.4	24.3	27.2	25.0	26.7	17.5
5. Definitely will	15.1	13.4	16.8	13.7	26.6	12.3	15.9	19.5	10.3	17.8	11.2	18.6	13.4	15.6	10.9	9.7
6. Already have	27.3	24.7	30.0	27.1	29.5	23.5	28.9	30.4	24.8	29.5	24.0	31.6	26.9	28.4	21.5	12.8
Item 12230 Subject G,O02　N	3220	1553	1582	2430	396	764	886	972	598	1892	1149	1234	648	472	775	42

A20E: Political parties or organizations?

	TOTAL	M	F	White	Black	NE	NC	S	W	Yes	No	None	Mari-juana Only	Few Pills	More Pills	Any Her-oin
1. Definitely not	19.2	19.7	18.7	19.0	16.5	22.3	20.0	15.3	20.2	16.4	23.9	16.0	20.7	18.6	22.5	37.8
2. Probably not	27.5	24.5	30.4	28.8	24.2	26.0	28.9	27.1	25.2	26.5	29.3	27.5	27.8	23.2	30.8	12.0
3. Don't know	34.4	34.6	34.1	34.0	35.0	35.1	32.7	34.6	36.1	34.4	34.0	34.0	35.5	38.5	31.5	38.6
4. Probably will	13.5	14.8	12.4	12.9	18.8	10.3	12.7	17.2	12.9	15.9	9.8	15.6	11.5	14.4	10.9	7.2
5. Definitely will	3.2	3.7	2.7	2.9	3.9	2.8	2.6	3.7	4.0	4.2	1.6	4.3	2.0	2.7	3.0	-
6. Already have	2.2	2.8	1.7	2.4	1.7	1.6	3.1	2.2	1.6	2.6	1.4	2.6	2.4	2.5	1.3	4.4
Item 12240 Subject H05,O02　N	3220	1558	1577	2431	401	756	890	979	595	1894	1147	1239	649	471	772	42

A20F: Citizen lobbies (Common Cause, Public Citizen, etc.)?

	TOTAL	M	F	White	Black	NE	NC	S	W	Yes	No	None	Mari-juana Only	Few Pills	More Pills	Any Her-oin
1. Definitely not	11.8	14.1	9.2	12.1	7.6	12.3	12.2	10.1	13.2	10.4	14.3	10.0	13.8	8.9	13.4	36.7
2. Probably not	26.1	25.4	27.4	28.0	20.1	26.2	28.7	23.0	27.2	26.7	25.1	24.0	27.1	29.3	27.9	19.4
3. Don't know	45.5	44.6	46.4	46.0	44.2	44.6	45.7	46.7	44.6	46.8	43.7	48.3	47.1	43.1	41.9	36.7
4. Probably will	13.7	12.9	14.2	11.8	21.1	14.3	10.7	15.9	13.7	13.0	14.3	14.2	9.8	15.5	14.5	4.2
5. Definitely will	2.0	2.1	1.8	1.3	5.4	1.7	1.9	2.9	1.0	2.2	1.7	2.2	1.5	2.4	1.7	1.8
6. Already have	0.9	1.0	1.0	0.8	1.7	0.8	0.8	1.5	0.3	0.9	1.0	1.3	0.6	0.8	0.6	1.2
Item 12250 Subject H05,I02,O02　N	3224	1563	1577	2434	401	757	888	982	597	1898	1147	1239	651	469	776	42

A20G: Charities to help fight diseases (Cancer, Heart Disease, etc.)?

	TOTAL	M	F	White	Black	NE	NC	S	W	Yes	No	None	Mari-juana Only	Few Pills	More Pills	Any Her-oin
1. Definitely not	2.4	4.1	0.7	2.1	3.0	2.4	2.3	2.0	3.2	1.7	3.6	1.6	1.8	2.6	3.2	16.8
2. Probably not	4.0	5.4	2.7	4.2	2.3	3.7	4.2	2.6	6.4	3.8	4.4	2.8	4.6	5.8	4.2	11.3
3. Don't know	16.0	20.7	11.1	17.0	13.5	17.6	16.9	11.8	19.6	14.3	18.1	15.7	17.2	13.5	16.8	17.0
4. Probably will	37.8	37.5	38.3	39.2	30.6	36.0	37.3	39.2	38.6	40.3	35.5	40.0	35.7	36.7	37.6	26.3
5. Definitely will	26.8	21.8	32.0	24.3	39.6	26.7	26.1	29.9	22.8	27.4	25.8	26.7	28.7	26.0	26.2	22.4
6. Already have	13.0	10.5	15.2	13.2	10.6	13.6	13.3	14.4	9.4	12.6	12.7	13.1	12.1	15.4	12.0	6.2
Item 12260 Subject O02　N	3225	1563	1578	2430	402	757	890	979	599	1897	1147	1240	648	472	776	42

A20H: Organizations concerned with population problems (Planned Parenthood, ZPG, etc.)?

	TOTAL	M	F	White	Black	NE	NC	S	W	Yes	No	None	Mari-juana Only	Few Pills	More Pills	Any Her-oin
1. Definitely not	9.8	12.8	6.8	10.6	7.5	11.8	10.4	8.7	8.2	9.2	10.8	9.0	9.9	7.1	11.4	34.0
2. Probably not	21.5	24.5	18.7	22.7	11.7	22.3	19.1	22.0	23.3	22.8	19.1	21.9	23.4	22.0	20.1	8.8
3. Don't know	41.5	42.8	40.4	42.2	39.0	39.7	41.7	43.1	41.0	41.9	41.6	44.8	41.8	38.9	38.3	27.4
4. Probably will	19.8	15.2	24.0	17.8	31.5	18.7	20.8	19.9	20.3	19.2	20.3	18.3	18.3	21.2	22.1	20.1
5. Definitely will	6.2	3.8	8.5	5.3	10.0	6.3	6.5	5.7	6.6	5.9	7.1	4.9	5.5	9.3	6.8	8.2
6. Already have	1.2	0.8	1.6	1.4	0.4	1.2	1.5	0.6	1.5	1.2	1.1	1.0	1.1	1.5	1.3	1.6
Item 12270 Subject E01,O02　N	3233	1566	1582	2441	403	760	892	983	598	1900	1152	1244	650	473	776	42

QUESTIONNAIRE FORM 5 1985	TOTAL	SEX		RACE		REGION				4YR COLLEGE PLANS		ILLICIT DRUG USE: LIFETIME				
		M	F	White	Black	NE	NC	S	W	Yes	No	None	Mari- juana Only	Few Pills	More Pills	Any Her- oin
N (Weighted No. of Cases):	3286	1584	1601	2463	410	782	901	997	604	1920	1159	1252	655	479	794	45
% of Weighted Total:	100.0	48.2	48.7	75.0	12.5	23.8	27.4	30.4	18.4	58.4	35.3	38.1	19.9	14.6	24.2	1.4

A20I: Organizations concerned with environmental problems (Sierra Club, Friends of Earth, etc.)?

1. Definitely not	9.9	11.6	8.3	10.2	8.7	10.5	9.7	9.6	9.8	8.4	12.6	7.1	12.3	9.1	12.4	20.7
2. Probably not	20.3	19.3	21.4	21.8	15.2	19.5	22.7	21.0	16.6	20.8	19.5	20.2	19.3	22.1	19.9	13.4
3. Don't know	42.2	39.4	44.8	42.4	40.9	39.7	44.5	41.8	42.8	42.0	42.8	45.5	42.9	40.0	39.0	26.5
4. Probably will	19.6	19.6	19.7	18.5	25.2	21.0	16.3	20.4	21.7	20.5	18.1	19.3	16.7	22.8	20.9	25.1
5. Definitely will	6.4	8.2	4.6	5.7	8.7	7.6	5.6	5.7	7.4	6.8	5.5	5.8	7.6	4.6	6.9	14.3
6. Already have	1.5	1.9	1.2	1.4	1.4	1.8	1.3	1.4	1.7	1.5	1.5	2.1	1.1	1.4	0.9	-
Item 12280 Subject F04,O02　　N	3230	1562	1583	2437	401	760	889	982	598	1899	1151	1243	649	469	780	42

Now we have a different kind of question.

A21: How satisfied are you with your life as a whole these days?

1. Completely dissatisfied	2.0	1.6	2.2	1.5	3.8	2.2	1.6	2.2	1.8	1.5	2.1	2.1	0.5	2.6	2.2	5.3
2. Quite dissatisfied	7.1	6.1	8.3	7.4	5.8	10.2	5.2	6.4	7.4	7.2	7.8	6.6	7.5	6.8	8.2	5.7
3. Somewhat dissatisfied	8.6	8.8	8.7	8.7	5.8	8.7	9.2	7.8	9.1	8.9	8.6	6.9	7.4	9.3	12.0	9.7
4. Neither, or mixed feelings	13.4	12.2	14.5	13.4	14.0	11.8	14.8	14.5	11.7	12.3	14.4	11.6	12.0	12.0	17.9	18.1
5. Somewhat satisfied	25.7	27.3	24.5	25.8	30.4	26.6	23.4	26.4	26.7	24.9	27.0	26.0	26.1	27.6	24.1	27.8
6. Quite satisfied	36.0	37.0	34.8	37.0	29.9	34.2	39.2	34.3	36.3	38.7	32.5	38.4	39.8	35.9	30.0	23.3
7. Completely satisfied	7.2	7.1	7.0	6.3	10.4	6.4	6.5	8.4	7.0	6.6	7.5	8.4	6.6	5.8	5.6	10.1
Item 6840 Subject P01,Q01　　N	3253	1578	1589	2452	405	767	894	990	602	1912	1150	1250	652	477	791	44

A22: These questions are about whether you think women are discriminated against in each of the following areas. To what extent are women discriminated against...

A22A: In getting a college education?

1. Not at all	45.9	52.5	39.1	46.4	43.0	53.3	41.8	46.1	42.1	45.5	45.8	40.7	48.1	48.9	50.0	51.8
2. Very little	29.8	25.4	34.6	32.7	20.4	27.2	32.2	27.4	33.6	31.0	29.1	30.0	29.8	30.0	31.1	15.0
3. Some	12.3	8.6	15.8	11.5	13.5	9.7	14.6	11.8	12.6	13.7	10.5	14.3	10.1	12.2	10.5	19.1
4. A good deal	3.1	2.2	3.7	2.2	6.6	2.3	3.3	3.5	3.0	3.0	3.0	3.5	3.2	3.6	1.5	3.9
5. A great deal	1.8	1.6	2.0	0.8	6.6	1.0	1.2	2.9	2.0	1.2	2.3	2.3	2.6	0.8	0.9	2.3
8. Don't know	7.2	9.6	4.8	6.4	9.9	6.5	6.9	8.2	6.7	5.7	9.2	9.1	6.2	4.6	6.0	7.8
Item 12290 Subject D06　　N	3244	1576	1583	2448	405	763	894	986	601	1911	1148	1247	651	473	790	45

A22B: In gaining positions of leadership over men and women?

1. Not at all	6.6	10.2	3.2	6.3	6.6	8.2	5.9	6.3	6.4	6.1	7.1	6.5	6.2	5.0	7.0	26.3
2. Very little	13.6	16.0	11.1	14.4	8.4	16.0	12.8	13.2	12.3	13.1	14.5	12.6	14.6	15.2	13.4	9.7
3. Some	34.8	35.1	34.8	36.8	26.2	34.9	36.0	33.6	34.9	34.9	34.3	34.6	33.8	38.8	35.1	22.0
4. A good deal	27.2	23.1	31.5	27.5	26.1	26.2	26.9	27.5	28.2	29.5	25.1	27.9	27.8	26.0	27.0	18.7
5. A great deal	12.9	8.8	16.6	10.3	25.9	10.9	13.3	13.9	13.5	12.7	12.6	13.1	13.4	12.0	12.2	18.1
8. Don't know	4.8	6.8	2.8	4.7	6.8	3.9	5.1	5.4	4.7	3.6	6.5	5.3	4.3	2.8	5.3	5.1
Item 12300 Subject D06　　N	3246	1578	1583	2449	404	764	893	986	602	1911	1149	1247	651	475	790	45

A22C: In obtaining executive positions in business?

1. Not at all	9.1	12.2	5.8	8.6	8.4	10.8	7.9	9.0	8.8	7.9	10.6	8.1	8.6	9.1	9.6	28.6
2. Very little	16.4	17.7	15.1	17.1	10.9	19.8	15.5	15.5	15.2	15.6	18.0	16.3	15.6	16.1	17.2	21.6
3. Some	31.6	32.3	31.3	33.9	24.6	30.8	32.0	31.6	31.8	32.3	31.1	30.3	31.1	37.1	32.1	7.8
4. A good deal	24.4	20.7	27.8	23.7	28.4	21.3	24.7	25.1	27.1	25.5	23.3	24.8	24.3	22.1	25.3	22.9
5. A great deal	11.6	7.5	15.9	9.6	20.3	10.9	11.8	12.1	11.3	12.7	9.6	12.7	13.0	10.6	9.5	11.8
8. Don't know	6.9	9.6	4.1	7.0	7.5	6.4	8.1	6.8	6.0	6.0	7.4	7.7	7.4	5.1	6.3	7.3
Item 12310 Subject D06　　N	3240	1576	1581	2447	403	763	892	984	602	1910	1146	1247	653	474	789	45

A22D: In obtaining top jobs in the professions?

1. Not at all	10.9	14.7	7.2	10.1	11.5	13.7	9.0	10.0	11.6	10.3	11.3	9.9	10.6	10.0	11.8	26.4
2. Very little	19.0	19.9	18.0	20.8	11.5	19.9	18.6	17.7	20.3	18.1	21.0	16.2	19.7	22.9	20.1	22.4
3. Some	30.2	29.9	30.6	31.2	25.1	29.8	30.6	31.6	27.8	31.3	28.7	31.0	29.4	30.4	30.8	11.5
4. A good deal	21.1	17.2	24.9	21.0	24.2	18.8	23.2	21.0	21.4	21.6	20.6	23.1	21.8	22.1	17.7	15.8
5. A great deal	11.6	8.4	14.9	9.4	21.2	10.8	11.1	13.0	11.1	12.0	10.4	11.7	11.7	8.9	12.3	21.0
8. Don't know	7.2	9.9	4.4	7.5	6.6	7.1	7.5	6.6	7.8	6.6	8.1	8.1	6.8	5.7	7.2	2.9
Item 12320 Subject D06　　N	3234	1570	1581	2443	402	758	893	981	601	1905	1145	1246	650	472	788	45

QUESTIONNAIRE FORM 5 1985	TOTAL	SEX		RACE		REGION				4YR COLLEGE PLANS		ILLICIT DRUG USE: LIFETIME				
		M	F	White	Black	NE	NC	S	W	Yes	No	None	Mari-juana Only	Few Pills	More Pills	Any Her-oin
N (Weighted No. of Cases):	3286	1584	1601	2463	410	782	901	997	604	1920	1159	1252	655	479	794	45
% of Weighted Total:	100.0	48.2	48.7	75.0	12.5	23.8	27.4	30.4	18.4	58.4	35.3	38.1	19.9	14.6	24.2	1.4
A22E: In getting skilled labor jobs?																
1. Not at all	11.9	14.6	9.0	11.3	10.4	13.3	12.1	11.0	11.1	11.5	11.9	11.2	12.0	8.7	14.0	23.2
2. Very little	19.3	18.9	20.0	20.4	16.5	23.3	16.8	19.1	18.0	20.4	18.5	17.7	21.4	22.7	18.8	11.7
3. Some	32.4	32.0	32.6	33.8	26.1	30.3	36.4	29.4	33.8	32.4	32.5	31.7	31.7	34.3	33.4	18.6
4. A good deal	17.7	15.6	19.6	17.3	18.4	17.2	16.5	18.8	18.3	18.0	17.1	18.3	15.5	18.4	18.1	15.9
5. A great deal	8.4	7.3	9.5	6.8	18.6	6.4	6.9	11.7	7.9	7.8	9.4	7.8	10.2	7.2	8.2	19.1
8. Don't know	10.4	11.5	9.3	10.4	10.0	9.5	11.3	10.0	10.9	9.9	10.7	13.4	9.1	8.7	7.5	11.4
Item 12330 Subject D06 N	3230	1571	1578	2440	401	759	893	980	598	1903	1145	1241	650	472	789	45
A22F: In getting elected to political office?																
1. Not at all	6.9	10.7	3.0	7.2	4.1	7.5	6.8	6.4	6.8	6.1	7.1	7.4	5.7	5.3	6.9	20.6
2. Very little	11.8	15.5	8.1	12.0	9.2	15.7	10.0	10.9	11.0	11.8	11.9	12.3	10.7	12.7	10.7	14.5
3. Some	24.8	27.2	22.7	25.9	20.5	23.6	26.3	25.0	23.7	26.3	23.2	25.4	25.1	24.1	25.2	14.1
4. A good deal	24.8	20.4	28.7	25.7	20.2	22.1	25.9	25.1	26.3	26.6	22.3	24.8	24.7	27.8	24.4	7.4
5. A great deal	26.1	18.8	33.7	24.2	39.0	26.5	25.4	26.5	26.2	25.2	27.9	23.9	27.6	27.7	27.8	29.0
8. Don't know	5.6	7.4	3.7	5.0	7.0	4.6	5.6	6.0	6.1	4.0	7.6	6.3	6.2	2.5	4.9	14.3
Item 12340 Subject D06,H02 N	3238	1576	1578	2447	401	764	893	982	598	1911	1145	1245	652	472	790	45
A22G: In getting equal pay for equal work?																
1. Not at all	14.5	19.9	9.4	14.3	12.9	14.9	13.3	16.2	13.2	13.3	15.8	14.6	13.7	13.7	14.9	28.3
2. Very little	18.5	22.5	14.1	19.6	13.5	21.7	16.1	18.9	17.3	19.7	17.2	17.2	21.1	18.0	19.1	17.4
3. Some	24.9	23.2	26.9	26.0	20.9	24.0	25.2	23.6	27.5	25.9	23.4	24.4	25.3	25.8	25.3	19.7
4. A good deal	18.6	15.1	22.1	18.8	17.6	15.9	22.8	16.7	19.0	19.7	17.2	20.5	14.9	21.1	17.6	8.0
5. A great deal	17.7	11.4	23.9	15.8	27.1	17.3	17.4	18.5	17.3	16.5	19.3	17.8	18.7	17.7	16.6	14.4
8. Don't know	5.8	7.9	3.6	5.5	8.1	6.3	5.3	6.1	5.7	4.9	7.1	5.5	6.4	3.8	6.6	12.2
Item 12350 Subject D06 N	3244	1578	1583	2448	404	764	893	985	601	1912	1148	1247	653	476	790	45
A23: The next questions ask for your opinions on the effects of using certain drugs and other substances. First, how much do you think people risk harming themselves (physically or in other ways), if they...																
A23A: Smoke one or more packs of cigarettes per day																
1. No risk	1.9	2.3	1.3	1.1	3.3	1.8	2.1	1.5	2.3	1.1	2.5	1.8	1.3	2.1	1.7	9.1
2. Slight risk	6.1	7.2	5.0	5.9	5.0	6.9	5.5	6.9	4.8	3.6	10.0	4.3	5.1	5.5	9.2	13.7
3. Moderate risk	24.0	23.2	24.5	24.6	22.2	24.5	24.5	23.3	22.6	22.0	27.9	19.9	24.5	24.1	29.6	27.9
4. Great risk	66.5	65.6	68.0	67.5	65.0	65.1	66.4	66.5	68.5	71.9	57.9	71.4	68.6	66.9	58.8	49.3
5. Can't say, drug unfamiliar	1.6	1.8	1.2	0.8	4.6	1.8	1.0	1.8	1.8	1.3	1.7	2.6	0.4	1.3	0.7	-
Item 12360 Subject A14a N	3250	1575	1589	2451	405	767	893	988	602	1910	1151	1248	654	475	790	45
A23B: Try marijuana (pot, grass) once or twice																
1. No risk	32.6	36.9	28.7	35.0	21.5	43.5	30.4	23.1	37.6	31.0	34.9	10.9	39.6	38.7	55.4	67.0
2. Slight risk	35.1	30.8	39.1	35.6	35.2	32.5	36.5	35.6	35.7	37.6	31.4	34.2	41.3	38.6	31.2	14.6
3. Moderate risk	14.7	13.5	16.1	14.8	16.9	9.7	16.0	17.9	13.7	14.9	14.2	22.2	11.4	10.9	8.2	10.3
4. Great risk	14.8	15.7	13.8	12.8	21.4	11.4	15.2	19.9	10.3	14.1	16.4	27.2	6.8	10.5	4.8	7.7
5. Can't say, drug unfamiliar	2.8	3.1	2.3	1.9	5.1	3.0	1.9	3.5	2.7	2.4	3.1	5.6	1.0	1.3	0.4	0.4
Item 12370 Subject A14a N	3244	1571	1587	2449	402	769	893	987	596	1907	1148	1245	653	477	787	45
A23C: Smoke marijuana occasionally																
1. No risk	8.4	11.2	5.5	8.3	7.8	10.0	7.5	5.1	13.0	7.0	10.1	2.1	7.7	8.5	17.0	34.1
2. Slight risk	26.1	27.2	24.9	27.7	19.3	33.0	25.2	21.9	25.6	26.2	25.8	10.7	32.9	31.8	40.9	37.3
3. Moderate risk	38.3	33.8	43.0	39.3	36.3	35.1	40.7	37.3	40.4	41.0	34.3	39.6	42.0	43.9	31.5	18.8
4. Great risk	24.5	24.7	24.5	23.0	31.1	19.0	24.8	32.4	18.4	23.6	26.8	42.3	16.7	14.8	9.9	9.8
5. Can't say, drug unfamiliar	2.7	3.0	2.1	1.7	5.5	2.8	1.9	3.3	2.7	2.2	3.0	5.4	0.7	1.0	0.7	-
Item 12380 Subject A14a N	3248	1575	1588	2451	405	770	892	985	602	1911	1149	1247	652	476	792	45

QUESTIONNAIRE FORM 5 1985	TOTAL	SEX		RACE		REGION				4YR COLLEGE PLANS		ILLICIT DRUG USE: LIFETIME				
		M	F	White	Black	NE	NC	S	W	Yes	No	None	Mari-juana Only	Few Pills	More Pills	Any Her-oin
N (Weighted No. of Cases):	3286	1584	1601	2463	410	782	901	997	604	1920	1159	1252	655	479	794	45
% of Weighted Total:	100.0	48.2	48.7	75.0	12.5	23.8	27.4	30.4	18.4	58.4	35.3	38.1	19.9	14.6	24.2	1.4
A23D: Smoke marijuana regularly																
1. No risk	2.6	3.7	1.3	2.0	4.6	2.8	2.5	2.0	3.3	2.0	3.5	1.7	1.2	1.9	4.5	15.0
2. Slight risk	5.8	7.5	3.9	5.7	6.4	6.3	5.4	4.5	7.8	4.4	7.4	1.4	3.8	5.2	13.6	26.6
3. Moderate risk	18.8	20.6	17.3	19.8	15.0	24.2	16.0	16.3	20.4	18.6	19.1	7.6	20.4	23.8	31.9	17.8
4. Great risk	70.4	65.4	75.6	70.9	69.6	63.8	74.1	74.5	66.7	73.1	67.4	84.4	73.8	68.0	49.6	37.3
5. Can't say, drug unfamiliar	2.4	2.8	1.8	1.6	4.4	2.9	2.0	2.7	1.8	2.0	2.6	4.8	0.9	1.0	0.3	3.4
Item 12390 Subject A14a N	3243	1575	1583	2449	403	767	891	983	602	1910	1146	1246	651	474	790	45
A23E: Try LSD once or twice																
1. No risk	4.4	5.6	3.3	3.8	6.6	5.1	4.4	3.0	5.8	3.2	6.0	2.0	2.7	4.0	8.0	31.4
2. Slight risk	16.6	14.8	18.4	17.9	9.6	18.5	17.8	13.7	17.1	16.7	17.2	12.2	14.5	17.9	24.3	26.4
3. Moderate risk	25.3	22.9	27.4	26.9	19.6	23.9	28.7	22.4	26.6	25.8	23.1	24.5	24.7	25.6	28.0	15.8
4. Great risk	43.5	45.4	42.0	42.6	48.4	41.0	40.4	49.3	41.9	45.5	42.2	50.4	45.6	41.7	32.6	20.7
5. Can't say, drug unfamiliar	10.3	11.3	9.0	8.9	15.7	11.5	8.7	11.6	8.6	8.8	11.6	10.8	12.5	10.8	7.1	5.7
Item 12400 Subject A14a N	3243	1573	1587	2449	403	768	891	983	601	1908	1148	1247	653	473	789	45
A23F: Take LSD regularly																
1. No risk	1.6	2.2	1.1	0.8	4.1	1.4	1.2	1.6	2.4	1.2	2.2	1.5	1.1	1.6	1.6	8.3
2. Slight risk	0.9	1.2	0.4	0.8	0.3	1.4	1.0	0.6	0.5	0.8	0.9	0.4	0.7	0.5	1.2	12.6
3. Moderate risk	5.1	5.7	4.2	4.8	4.5	6.1	5.1	4.7	4.2	4.3	6.1	3.1	2.8	5.7	9.2	11.0
4. Great risk	82.9	80.0	86.3	85.2	76.0	80.3	84.5	82.3	84.7	85.7	79.7	84.9	83.1	82.1	81.5	65.7
5. Can't say, drug unfamiliar	9.6	11.0	8.1	8.3	15.1	10.7	8.2	10.8	8.2	8.1	11.1	10.1	12.3	10.1	6.5	2.3
Item 12410 Subject A14a N	3235	1570	1582	2441	405	765	890	980	600	1904	1143	1244	647	474	792	44
A23G: Try heroin (smack, horse) once or twice																
1. No risk	3.0	3.8	2.2	2.2	4.3	3.1	2.8	2.9	3.5	2.6	3.5	1.7	1.9	3.2	4.0	36.5
2. Slight risk	13.0	11.2	14.4	13.5	10.9	15.5	13.3	11.1	12.4	12.8	14.0	10.8	12.3	15.5	15.0	20.5
3. Moderate risk	25.2	22.6	27.4	27.0	19.5	23.4	28.1	22.7	27.4	26.0	23.4	26.7	22.2	25.2	26.2	19.0
4. Great risk	47.3	50.3	45.2	47.5	48.3	45.7	45.5	50.3	47.4	48.9	45.9	49.6	48.6	45.9	44.9	21.7
5. Can't say, drug unfamiliar	11.5	12.1	10.8	9.8	16.9	12.4	10.4	13.0	9.4	9.7	13.2	11.2	14.9	10.2	9.9	2.3
Item 12420 Subject A14a N	3244	1574	1587	2451	404	768	891	983	601	1909	1147	1245	652	475	791	45
A23H: Take heroin occasionally																
1. No risk	1.5	1.9	1.1	0.8	3.7	1.2	1.3	1.3	2.5	1.2	1.9	1.5	1.3	1.6	1.2	8.6
2. Slight risk	1.8	1.9	1.6	1.6	2.1	2.0	1.6	1.7	2.1	1.9	1.7	1.0	1.2	1.9	2.3	18.7
3. Moderate risk	16.5	12.9	19.6	17.4	14.4	18.5	17.0	16.0	14.3	16.5	16.8	16.3	15.2	16.2	18.1	25.3
4. Great risk	69.8	71.8	68.4	71.5	64.0	67.3	71.1	68.7	72.6	71.7	67.5	71.5	68.3	70.9	69.4	45.1
5. Can't say, drug unfamiliar	10.4	11.4	9.3	8.8	15.8	11.1	8.9	12.3	8.4	8.7	12.1	9.7	14.0	9.4	8.9	2.3
Item 12430 Subject A14a N	3247	1574	1589	2451	404	768	892	985	601	1910	1149	1248	652	475	792	45
A23I: Take heroin regularly																
1. No risk	1.5	2.1	0.9	0.8	3.8	1.4	1.0	1.4	2.5	1.3	1.7	1.2	1.4	1.6	1.5	9.2
2. Slight risk	0.5	0.4	0.5	0.3	0.5	0.2	0.4	0.6	0.7	0.5	0.4	0.5	0.3	0.1	0.2	9.2
3. Moderate risk	1.7	2.1	1.2	1.6	1.6	2.3	1.8	1.5	1.1	1.3	2.1	1.4	0.5	2.7	1.9	8.4
4. Great risk	86.0	84.3	88.1	88.6	78.0	84.9	87.5	84.4	87.7	88.4	83.6	86.9	84.2	86.2	87.7	69.6
5. Can't say, drug unfamiliar	10.3	11.1	9.4	8.7	16.0	11.1	9.2	12.1	8.0	8.6	12.2	10.0	13.6	9.3	8.6	3.6
Item 12440 Subject A14a N	3232	1567	1581	2442	402	765	888	980	600	1907	1139	1246	649	471	788	42
A23J: Try barbiturates (downers, goofballs, reds, yellows, etc.) once or twice																
1. No risk	9.8	11.5	8.2	10.0	7.4	13.3	8.1	7.1	12.4	8.2	12.5	3.1	6.3	10.6	21.6	33.3
2. Slight risk	25.2	23.5	26.6	27.6	14.5	24.8	28.3	22.0	26.2	25.3	25.3	19.0	22.7	28.1	35.6	23.1
3. Moderate risk	28.6	26.4	30.7	29.7	25.1	30.7	28.3	28.3	26.7	30.0	26.5	30.8	28.8	28.4	25.7	23.2
4. Great risk	26.1	27.7	24.9	24.7	31.2	20.2	25.9	30.7	26.3	27.0	25.1	35.5	29.1	22.8	10.6	20.4
5. Can't say, drug unfamiliar	10.4	10.9	9.7	8.0	21.9	11.0	9.5	11.9	8.4	9.5	10.5	11.5	13.1	10.1	6.5	-
Item 12450 Subject A14a N	3246	1575	1587	2451	403	767	892	985	602	1910	1149	1246	653	475	791	45

QUESTIONNAIRE FORM 5 1985	TOTAL	SEX		RACE		REGION				4YR COLLEGE PLANS		ILLICIT DRUG USE: LIFETIME				
		M	F	White	Black	NE	NC	S	W	Yes	No	None	Mari-juana Only	Few Pills	More Pills	Any Heroin
N (Weighted No. of Cases):	3286	1584	1601	2463	410	782	901	997	604	1920	1159	1252	655	479	794	45
% of Weighted Total:	100.0	48.2	48.7	75.0	12.5	23.8	27.4	30.4	18.4	58.4	35.3	38.1	19.9	14.6	24.2	1.4
A23K: Take barbiturates regularly																
1. No risk	2.1	2.9	1.3	1.1	4.3	2.6	1.8	1.3	3.0	1.3	3.0	1.5	1.5	2.2	2.6	14.6
2. Slight risk	3.7	4.6	2.7	4.0	1.8	5.5	3.3	2.7	3.5	2.9	4.7	1.5	1.8	2.1	8.6	19.0
3. Moderate risk	15.7	17.6	13.9	17.4	9.2	20.5	15.7	13.3	13.3	13.5	18.8	9.1	12.3	17.9	27.5	20.8
4. Great risk	68.3	64.0	72.7	69.6	62.3	61.4	69.6	70.4	71.6	73.1	62.3	76.4	71.8	68.0	54.8	45.5
5. Can't say, drug unfamiliar	10.3	11.0	9.4	8.0	22.5	9.9	9.6	12.2	8.6	9.1	11.1	11.6	12.6	9.8	6.5	-
Item 12460 Subject A14a N	3230	1563	1583	2447	397	764	887	982	596	1904	1144	1245	643	475	787	45
A23L: Try amphetamines (uppers, pep pills, bennies, speed) once or twice																
1. No risk	13.6	15.6	11.7	14.7	6.9	16.7	13.8	10.1	15.3	11.8	16.4	4.0	8.5	14.0	31.6	43.9
2. Slight risk	26.4	24.8	28.0	28.8	17.6	27.4	29.0	22.8	27.3	27.3	25.6	19.4	26.3	31.7	35.2	26.3
3. Moderate risk	26.8	24.0	29.8	27.3	25.3	25.7	27.4	27.2	26.7	28.2	24.4	31.1	26.4	27.4	20.8	16.0
4. Great risk	25.2	26.8	23.5	23.3	34.3	22.2	23.0	30.5	23.5	26.0	24.5	35.7	27.9	19.5	9.9	13.8
5. Can't say, drug unfamiliar	7.9	8.7	6.8	5.9	15.8	8.0	6.8	9.4	7.1	6.6	9.0	9.9	10.8	7.4	2.5	-
Item 12470 Subject A14a N	3239	1570	1586	2446	403	764	890	985	600	1908	1145	1247	650	475	786	45
A23M: Take amphetamines regularly																
1. No risk	2.5	3.2	1.9	1.8	4.3	3.0	2.4	1.7	3.2	1.5	3.7	1.3	1.6	2.3	4.0	20.3
2. Slight risk	5.5	6.9	4.1	6.1	2.3	6.3	4.9	4.6	6.9	4.7	6.6	1.8	2.6	3.6	14.7	6.1
3. Moderate risk	16.4	17.6	15.6	18.0	10.6	19.7	19.7	13.1	12.5	14.7	19.2	8.8	10.9	22.9	28.7	29.6
4. Great risk	67.2	62.6	71.5	68.0	64.7	62.1	66.0	70.3	70.6	72.4	60.7	77.3	73.6	64.0	49.9	38.6
5. Can't say, drug unfamiliar	8.4	9.7	6.9	6.2	18.0	8.9	7.1	10.2	6.8	6.8	9.8	10.8	11.3	7.2	2.8	5.4
Item 12480 Subject A14a N	3235	1569	1584	2448	397	766	891	976	601	1909	1141	1244	651	475	788	45
A23N: Try cocaine once or twice																
1. No risk	11.7	15.1	8.3	12.1	6.9	17.0	8.3	8.1	16.2	10.1	14.1	3.1	5.7	12.3	28.3	46.5
2. Slight risk	22.5	21.7	23.3	23.9	17.9	26.6	22.5	16.4	27.2	22.8	21.6	13.8	22.4	29.9	32.1	31.1
3. Moderate risk	25.9	22.2	29.5	26.4	26.3	24.1	27.1	27.5	23.9	27.1	24.2	29.5	26.5	25.0	20.7	11.6
4. Great risk	34.0	34.8	33.6	32.9	40.6	27.2	36.2	41.0	28.0	35.1	33.2	46.4	37.0	29.0	16.4	9.5
5. Can't say, drug unfamiliar	5.8	6.2	5.3	4.8	8.3	5.1	5.9	7.1	4.7	4.8	6.9	7.2	8.4	3.9	2.6	1.3
Item 12490 Subject A14a N	3236	1570	1586	2449	404	763	892	983	598	1908	1145	1247	651	472	789	44
A23O: Take cocaine regularly																
1. No risk	2.6	3.4	1.8	1.8	4.3	3.8	1.6	2.1	3.2	2.0	3.2	1.5	1.5	1.6	4.7	16.5
2. Slight risk	2.9	4.3	1.4	3.0	0.7	4.5	1.5	1.8	4.4	2.2	3.9	0.3	1.7	1.1	7.9	17.0
3. Moderate risk	10.0	13.0	6.8	10.6	9.7	14.9	9.0	7.4	9.6	8.0	12.2	4.1	7.1	13.0	19.1	23.7
4. Great risk	79.0	73.0	85.3	80.1	76.5	72.0	81.8	82.1	78.4	83.4	73.7	87.1	81.7	80.5	66.0	41.5
5. Can't say, drug unfamiliar	5.6	6.2	4.7	4.5	8.8	4.8	6.1	6.5	4.4	4.4	7.0	7.0	8.0	3.8	2.3	1.2
Item 12500 Subject A14a N	3235	1570	1584	2447	401	765	890	983	597	1907	1145	1243	648	474	791	45
A23P: Try one or two drinks of an alcoholic beverage (beer, wine, liquor)																
1. No risk	49.2	54.6	44.1	53.1	29.1	57.9	48.9	39.3	54.6	50.1	47.5	30.2	55.3	57.8	68.3	71.4
2. Slight risk	35.6	30.6	40.6	34.6	45.3	29.5	37.1	40.9	32.5	36.9	33.9	45.1	34.2	32.4	24.7	19.0
3. Moderate risk	9.1	8.3	10.1	8.1	14.2	7.4	8.8	11.2	8.6	8.5	10.4	14.6	8.1	6.3	3.7	5.0
4. Great risk	5.0	5.3	4.4	3.7	8.7	3.7	4.5	7.6	3.1	3.7	6.6	8.0	2.1	2.8	3.1	4.5
5. Can't say, drug unfamiliar	1.1	1.2	0.9	0.5	2.7	1.6	0.7	1.1	1.3	0.7	1.6	2.2	0.3	0.7	0.2	-
Item 12510 Subject A14a N	3237	1571	1583	2448	403	767	890	982	598	1906	1145	1240	653	475	790	45
A23Q: Take one or two drinks nearly every day																
1. No risk	8.8	13.1	4.6	8.8	7.7	11.1	7.9	7.9	8.8	7.4	10.7	5.6	6.8	8.5	14.3	34.3
2. Slight risk	23.8	26.9	21.2	24.8	18.6	24.8	23.1	24.2	23.0	22.2	25.4	17.8	25.8	30.4	27.1	24.4
3. Moderate risk	41.7	39.0	44.3	42.2	45.7	43.8	42.7	40.8	39.2	43.3	40.1	41.8	45.0	41.8	40.9	20.0
4. Great risk	24.4	19.8	29.0	23.6	25.4	18.5	25.5	25.9	27.7	26.3	22.2	32.6	21.9	18.4	17.5	17.9
5. Can't say, drug unfamiliar	1.2	1.3	0.8	0.6	2.6	1.9	0.7	1.1	1.2	0.7	1.5	2.2	0.5	0.9	0.1	3.4
Item 12520 Subject A14a N	3241	1571	1587	2449	404	767	891	983	600	1908	1149	1246	651	476	789	45

QUESTIONNAIRE FORM 5 1985	TOTAL	SEX		RACE		REGION				4YR COLLEGE PLANS		ILLICIT DRUG USE: LIFETIME				
		M	F	White	Black	NE	NC	S	W	Yes	No	None	Mari- juana Only	Few Pills	More Pills	Any Her- oin
N (Weighted No. of Cases):	3286	1584	1601	2463	410	782	901	997	604	1920	1159	1252	655	479	794	45
% of Weighted Total:	100.0	48.2	48.7	75.0	12.5	23.8	27.4	30.4	18.4	58.4	35.3	38.1	19.9	14.6	24.2	1.4
A23R: Take four or five drinks nearly every day																
1. No risk	3.3	4.8	1.7	2.6	4.2	3.5	3.5	2.7	3.6	2.2	4.8	2.0	1.8	3.2	5.5	18.3
2. Slight risk	5.7	8.5	3.1	6.1	3.0	6.9	4.4	4.9	7.7	4.8	7.3	3.7	4.6	6.4	8.7	19.5
3. Moderate risk	19.8	23.3	16.8	21.1	15.8	19.9	20.5	21.8	15.5	17.9	22.2	16.8	20.6	22.0	22.4	19.8
4. Great risk	69.8	62.0	77.3	69.4	74.1	68.0	70.6	69.0	72.0	74.2	63.9	74.9	72.4	67.2	63.2	42.4
5. Can't say, drug unfamiliar	1.4	1.4	1.1	0.7	2.9	1.7	1.0	1.6	1.2	0.9	1.8	2.5	0.5	1.2	0.2	-
Item 12530 Subject A14a N	3245	1575	1587	2451	404	767	892	983	602	1910	1149	1246	652	476	791	45
A23S: Have five or more drinks once or twice each weekend																
1. No risk	9.1	13.7	4.8	9.3	7.2	13.1	8.2	7.0	8.6	7.4	11.2	4.3	7.2	9.3	16.7	35.4
2. Slight risk	16.6	20.5	12.9	17.8	12.7	18.5	15.9	14.1	19.1	16.6	16.6	9.6	17.9	22.5	22.7	20.2
3. Moderate risk	29.9	28.9	31.4	32.7	19.3	29.3	31.4	28.7	30.6	31.5	28.0	26.0	32.6	32.4	33.4	24.3
4. Great risk	43.0	35.5	49.8	39.5	57.4	37.0	43.7	48.8	40.3	43.7	42.5	57.8	41.7	34.5	27.0	20.1
5. Can't say, drug unfamiliar	1.4	1.4	1.1	0.6	3.4	2.0	0.9	1.4	1.5	0.9	1.7	2.4	0.5	1.2	0.2	-
Item 12540 Subject A14a N	3246	1575	1588	2451	405	768	892	984	602	1910	1150	1247	652	476	791	45

This section asks for your views and feelings about a number of different things.

D01: Do you agree or disagree with each of the following?

	TOTAL	M	F	White	Black	NE	NC	S	W	Yes	No	None	Mari- juana Only	Few Pills	More Pills	Any Her- oin
D01A: I take a positive attitude toward myself																
1. Disagree	2.5	2.0	2.9	2.2	3.3	2.5	2.9	2.9	1.3	1.9	3.4	2.1	2.0	2.3	3.5	2.9
2. Mostly disagree	5.8	4.5	7.1	6.3	1.5	6.7	6.3	4.6	5.8	5.3	6.8	5.5	5.5	4.5	7.3	9.5
3. Neither	8.2	8.0	8.3	8.8	2.7	9.8	9.1	6.6	7.3	7.8	8.4	8.0	7.4	6.1	10.1	12.1
4. Mostly agree	46.9	43.5	50.2	49.7	32.2	42.6	48.7	47.5	48.5	47.6	46.7	44.0	48.2	53.5	47.6	28.7
5. Agree	36.7	42.0	31.5	33.0	60.4	38.4	33.0	38.4	37.1	37.4	34.7	40.4	36.9	33.5	31.5	46.8
Item 12550 Subject Q01 N	3091	1492	1540	2384	364	722	860	924	586	1892	1120	1193	623	454	750	39
D01B: Good luck is more important than hard work for success																
1. Disagree	36.1	33.4	39.0	34.9	43.6	33.7	35.3	39.1	35.5	36.1	36.0	37.5	36.1	32.8	35.8	43.5
2. Mostly disagree	38.6	36.1	41.4	42.0	25.4	40.2	40.1	36.9	37.2	41.4	34.6	38.9	39.4	40.1	37.4	21.5
3. Neither	14.7	17.2	11.9	15.3	8.9	16.4	15.4	12.0	15.7	13.7	15.5	12.0	16.3	18.6	15.4	11.6
4. Mostly agree	7.5	9.6	5.5	6.2	12.7	7.3	6.3	8.2	8.7	6.4	9.4	7.8	5.9	6.7	8.6	15.1
5. Agree	3.1	3.6	2.3	1.5	9.4	2.5	2.9	3.8	2.9	2.3	4.4	3.7	2.3	1.8	2.7	8.4
Item 12560 Subject Q02 N	3087	1490	1538	2380	364	719	859	924	585	1888	1119	1193	623	455	745	39
D01C: I feel I am a person of worth, on an equal plane with others																
1. Disagree	1.7	1.8	1.7	1.6	2.0	1.6	1.5	2.3	1.3	1.1	2.4	1.9	1.0	1.0	2.2	2.9
2. Mostly disagree	3.4	2.4	4.1	3.4	2.0	2.6	3.1	4.3	3.6	3.3	3.5	2.5	4.4	1.7	5.2	5.2
3. Neither	9.0	9.0	9.0	9.0	5.2	8.7	9.7	6.7	11.8	7.8	11.0	8.2	9.2	8.3	10.9	6.1
4. Mostly agree	42.1	41.7	42.7	43.9	34.9	44.2	45.9	37.6	40.8	41.1	43.7	41.7	42.1	46.5	40.5	35.3
5. Agree	43.8	45.2	42.5	42.2	55.9	42.9	39.8	49.1	42.5	46.7	39.5	45.6	43.3	42.5	41.3	50.5
Item 12570 Subject Q01 N	3076	1485	1533	2372	362	719	855	920	582	1884	1113	1191	621	453	740	39
D01D: I am able to do things as well as most other people																
1. Disagree	1.1	1.1	1.2	1.0	1.6	0.8	1.3	1.5	0.6	0.6	1.9	1.3	1.0	0.6	1.0	5.7
2. Mostly disagree	2.2	1.2	3.1	2.2	2.4	2.4	2.2	1.4	3.3	2.0	2.3	1.8	1.7	2.2	2.8	2.4
3. Neither	5.3	5.1	5.3	5.3	4.5	5.6	5.1	4.3	6.6	4.9	6.0	4.4	6.0	5.3	5.9	8.1
4. Mostly agree	44.1	40.8	47.4	46.3	33.8	43.8	48.8	42.1	40.8	43.3	45.8	43.1	45.8	45.6	45.0	30.6
5. Agree	47.3	51.9	43.0	45.2	57.7	47.4	42.6	50.7	48.8	49.2	44.1	49.3	45.5	46.2	45.3	53.3
Item 12580 Subject Q01 N	3076	1486	1532	2375	359	717	857	919	583	1885	1112	1189	622	453	741	38

QUESTIONNAIRE FORM 5 1985	TOTAL	SEX		RACE		REGION				4YR COLLEGE PLANS		ILLICIT DRUG USE: LIFETIME				
		M	F	White	Black	NE	NC	S	W	Yes	No	None	Marijuana Only	Few Pills	More Pills	Any Heroin
N (Weighted No. of Cases):	3286	1584	1601	2463	410	782	901	997	604	1920	1159	1252	655	479	794	45
% of Weighted Total:	100.0	48.2	48.7	75.0	12.5	23.8	27.4	30.4	18.4	58.4	35.3	38.1	19.9	14.6	24.2	1.4
D01E: Every time I try to get ahead, something or somebody stops me																
1. Disagree	15.7	15.2	16.1	15.4	19.0	19.1	13.8	14.7	15.9	16.9	13.3	15.4	18.9	14.0	14.4	14.5
2. Mostly disagree	33.9	32.4	35.8	35.6	23.7	32.1	36.0	32.4	35.5	38.6	26.7	35.6	34.4	33.6	31.8	22.2
3. Neither	23.9	25.3	22.5	24.8	19.4	26.1	24.0	21.0	25.8	23.1	25.0	23.5	20.8	29.8	24.6	14.8
4. Mostly agree	18.3	18.2	18.0	17.4	23.9	15.2	19.2	21.6	15.6	15.5	22.9	17.3	18.0	16.0	20.8	27.7
5. Agree	8.2	8.8	7.6	6.8	14.0	7.4	7.1	10.3	7.2	5.8	12.1	8.2	7.9	6.5	8.4	20.9
Item 12590 Subject Q02 N	3069	1479	1533	2369	360	716	852	918	583	1878	1113	1189	620	453	737	38
D01F: Planning only makes a person unhappy since plans hardly ever work out anyway																
1. Disagree	30.2	26.0	34.4	30.1	31.7	27.2	30.3	31.3	32.0	33.4	24.5	33.7	32.0	27.9	25.4	13.5
2. Mostly disagree	32.7	32.0	33.8	35.0	23.5	32.0	34.6	31.4	33.0	35.3	29.0	35.3	29.9	31.7	31.7	33.8
3. Neither	17.0	19.9	14.4	17.7	13.8	19.7	17.1	16.0	15.0	15.3	19.4	14.3	18.4	19.0	18.6	16.3
4. Mostly agree	13.3	15.6	10.9	12.4	16.5	13.7	12.4	12.7	15.3	11.0	17.4	10.7	11.5	15.5	17.7	18.2
5. Agree	6.7	6.6	6.6	4.8	14.5	7.4	5.5	8.6	4.7	5.1	9.7	6.0	8.2	5.9	6.6	18.3
Item 12600 Subject Q02 N	3067	1478	1532	2365	361	714	853	919	581	1873	1115	1192	621	449	736	37
D01G: People who accept their condition in life are happier than those who try to change things																
1. Disagree	18.7	18.0	19.4	18.2	24.0	19.0	17.4	21.3	16.1	21.1	15.0	20.0	17.4	16.5	19.3	20.5
2. Mostly disagree	21.8	22.1	21.6	23.5	17.0	23.8	22.5	20.0	21.3	24.1	17.9	22.6	22.4	19.1	22.5	19.2
3. Neither	22.5	24.5	20.6	22.6	17.8	21.4	23.6	20.8	25.0	22.5	22.4	22.6	22.2	24.9	21.1	18.7
4. Mostly agree	21.8	21.6	21.9	22.6	18.5	20.0	23.5	20.6	23.2	19.6	25.8	20.8	22.2	24.3	21.1	18.6
5. Agree	15.2	13.8	16.1	13.1	22.8	15.7	13.0	17.3	14.4	12.8	18.9	14.0	15.8	15.2	16.0	23.0
Item 12610 Subject Q02 N	3055	1470	1529	2355	360	710	849	917	579	1869	1107	1187	620	450	728	38
D01H: On the whole, I'm satisfied with myself																
1. Disagree	3.6	2.9	4.3	2.9	5.9	4.1	3.0	4.4	2.6	3.1	4.4	3.1	2.1	2.2	6.3	5.5
2. Mostly disagree	7.1	6.9	7.2	7.4	4.9	8.0	7.3	6.8	6.4	6.5	8.1	6.1	7.8	5.4	9.4	10.1
3. Neither	9.1	9.5	8.8	9.2	7.4	10.4	8.8	8.5	9.1	8.8	9.5	6.9	9.4	9.3	12.4	18.9
4. Mostly agree	38.7	38.2	39.4	40.9	32.3	34.5	39.2	39.8	41.6	40.1	36.9	38.9	37.6	41.9	38.4	30.5
5. Agree	41.4	42.5	40.3	39.7	49.6	43.0	41.7	40.5	40.3	41.6	41.1	45.0	43.2	41.2	33.5	35.1
Item 12620 Subject P01,Q01 N	3056	1473	1526	2356	360	711	851	916	577	1866	1112	1187	619	450	729	39
D01I: People like me don't have much of a chance to be successful in life																
1. Disagree	60.8	57.2	64.7	60.9	64.3	60.8	59.8	63.3	58.5	67.2	50.7	61.1	65.4	65.6	54.3	49.0
2. Mostly disagree	23.3	24.5	22.4	24.9	16.7	21.7	24.1	22.5	25.4	21.8	25.9	24.7	20.9	18.4	26.3	21.8
3. Neither	9.6	11.2	7.9	9.3	7.8	11.0	11.2	6.2	10.6	7.3	13.1	8.3	8.6	11.2	11.9	6.9
4. Mostly agree	3.8	4.3	3.0	3.2	5.9	3.8	3.4	4.4	3.3	2.3	6.1	3.6	2.8	3.3	4.6	8.8
5. Agree	2.5	2.8	2.0	1.6	5.3	2.6	1.5	3.7	2.2	1.5	4.2	2.2	2.3	1.5	2.8	13.4
Item 12630 Subject Q02 N	3064	1479	1528	2366	357	714	853	917	580	1873	1113	1191	619	451	732	39
D01J: When I make plans, I am almost certain that I can make them work																
1. Disagree	2.4	2.5	2.3	2.0	6.0	2.3	2.7	2.9	1.3	1.7	3.5	2.0	2.8	1.7	2.9	5.5
2. Mostly disagree	6.1	5.7	6.5	6.1	5.6	7.6	5.9	5.8	5.2	5.1	7.6	5.4	5.1	5.7	8.4	9.0
3. Neither	15.6	16.7	14.7	16.4	9.6	16.0	17.5	13.6	15.4	15.5	15.3	13.8	16.1	16.6	18.1	9.8
4. Mostly agree	46.0	43.9	47.9	47.9	37.6	44.9	46.0	47.1	45.6	47.6	43.5	47.7	44.6	48.6	43.9	38.5
5. Agree	29.9	31.2	28.6	27.5	41.2	29.1	27.9	30.6	32.6	30.1	30.0	31.2	31.4	27.5	26.8	37.2
Item 12640 Subject Q02 N	3067	1481	1529	2367	361	716	855	917	580	1875	1113	1190	620	453	732	39
D01K: A lot of times I feel lonely																
1. Disagree	17.8	19.7	15.7	17.1	21.7	21.0	16.1	16.2	18.7	17.6	17.4	18.7	19.5	16.6	14.5	35.8
2. Mostly disagree	30.1	29.2	31.0	32.4	21.9	28.8	31.9	29.7	29.5	32.4	26.8	31.1	31.5	30.8	27.3	22.7
3. Neither	18.0	21.1	14.9	18.8	11.2	18.0	19.5	14.6	20.9	18.5	16.9	17.6	16.9	20.6	18.1	10.8
4. Mostly agree	21.6	18.8	24.8	21.2	23.8	21.3	21.7	24.1	17.9	21.0	22.8	20.5	19.8	19.5	26.7	11.6
5. Agree	12.6	11.3	13.7	10.6	21.4	10.9	10.8	15.3	13.1	10.5	16.1	12.2	12.3	12.4	13.4	19.0
Item 12650 Subject Q03 N	3014	1454	1504	2333	352	692	847	903	572	1839	1088	1174	609	447	715	37

	TOTAL	SEX		RACE		REGION				4YR COLLEGE PLANS		ILLICIT DRUG USE: LIFETIME				
QUESTIONNAIRE FORM 5 **1985**		M	F	White	Black	NE	NC	S	W	Yes	No	None	Mari-juana Only	Few Pills	More Pills	Any Her-oin
N (Weighted No. of Cases):	3286	1584	1601	2463	410	782	901	997	604	1920	1159	1252	655	479	794	45
% of Weighted Total:	100.0	48.2	48.7	75.0	12.5	23.8	27.4	30.4	18.4	58.4	35.3	38.1	19.9	14.6	24.2	1.4
D01L: I feel I do not have much to be proud of																
1. Disagree	43.0	42.5	43.6	41.5	55.6	44.3	40.4	45.3	41.6	47.1	36.4	46.9	44.4	42.7	36.2	32.9
2. Mostly disagree	31.4	32.8	30.0	33.5	21.9	30.9	34.4	28.6	32.1	31.4	32.0	30.8	33.3	31.2	32.2	22.7
3. Neither	10.4	11.0	9.7	10.5	6.6	10.1	11.0	9.9	10.4	8.9	12.8	9.5	9.7	11.9	11.4	8.9
4. Mostly agree	9.9	8.9	10.9	9.7	7.8	10.8	9.0	10.1	9.9	9.3	10.0	8.8	8.3	9.0	13.2	12.6
5. Agree	5.3	4.7	5.8	4.8	8.0	3.9	5.1	6.1	6.0	3.2	8.7	4.0	4.4	5.3	7.0	22.9
Item 12660　Subject Q01　　N	3009	1450	1503	2328	352	691	847	900	571	1837	1085	1172	607	446	715	36
D01M: There is always someone I can turn to if I need help																
1. Disagree	4.1	4.5	3.7	3.7	5.5	4.6	2.9	4.8	3.9	3.4	5.2	3.4	3.5	3.8	5.4	13.9
2. Mostly disagree	5.8	6.8	4.6	5.8	5.8	6.7	5.9	4.8	6.2	5.6	6.2	5.6	5.7	4.8	6.9	9.2
3. Neither	6.5	8.8	4.0	6.5	4.4	6.1	7.6	6.4	5.6	6.4	6.3	5.8	7.1	5.7	7.4	10.0
4. Mostly agree	27.9	30.1	26.1	29.0	22.2	27.7	28.7	26.6	28.9	29.1	26.5	27.1	26.6	32.3	27.4	24.7
5. Agree	55.7	49.7	61.5	55.1	62.1	54.9	54.8	57.4	55.4	55.5	55.9	58.0	57.1	53.4	52.8	42.3
Item 12670　Subject Q03　　N	2999	1444	1501	2323	351	686	843	900	569	1832	1081	1172	607	443	710	36
D01N: Sometimes I think that I am no good at all																
1. Disagree	31.8	35.4	28.4	29.6	52.4	30.7	32.2	33.8	29.3	33.6	28.6	34.9	32.6	30.5	26.7	21.1
2. Mostly disagree	26.1	25.1	26.8	28.1	17.1	26.5	25.6	25.7	27.0	27.3	24.5	25.6	25.0	26.8	27.9	23.8
3. Neither	16.9	18.4	15.6	17.5	7.8	18.6	17.4	14.5	18.0	16.7	17.4	16.2	17.2	19.2	16.2	30.3
4. Mostly agree	14.6	11.7	17.4	15.4	11.1	13.5	16.9	14.5	12.9	14.2	15.3	14.5	13.6	16.4	15.4	6.4
5. Agree	10.5	9.3	11.7	9.4	11.6	10.6	7.9	11.6	12.7	8.2	14.2	8.9	11.6	7.1	13.8	18.3
Item 12680　Subject Q01　　N	2995	1441	1499	2318	350	685	844	897	568	1831	1078	1170	607	442	709	36
D01O: I often feel left out of things																
1. Disagree	19.8	20.5	19.3	18.5	30.9	22.4	18.5	20.7	17.3	20.1	18.9	21.5	20.8	19.8	16.1	22.0
2. Mostly disagree	28.7	30.0	27.4	30.2	21.1	25.9	31.3	27.1	31.1	31.8	24.4	28.1	32.2	28.4	27.7	19.1
3. Neither	19.0	20.8	17.4	19.9	12.3	20.6	17.5	17.9	20.9	18.9	18.9	17.5	18.9	21.5	19.9	14.9
4. Mostly agree	20.4	18.8	21.8	20.2	21.0	19.0	22.1	19.7	20.7	19.3	21.9	20.4	17.8	21.2	22.7	14.4
5. Agree	12.1	9.9	14.1	11.2	14.7	12.1	10.6	14.7	10.1	10.0	15.9	12.5	10.2	9.2	13.5	29.6
Item 12690　Subject Q03　　N	2990	1438	1497	2314	349	684	844	898	564	1827	1077	1165	602	442	713	36
D01P: I believe a person is master of his/her own fate																
1. Disagree	4.6	4.3	4.7	4.3	4.4	4.9	4.5	5.1	3.5	3.9	5.5	4.7	5.5	3.8	3.3	17.7
2. Mostly disagree	6.2	5.6	6.8	6.5	4.4	7.5	4.4	7.4	5.5	6.1	6.4	5.9	5.6	6.7	7.1	4.0
3. Neither	18.9	16.7	20.9	20.3	12.3	18.4	18.7	18.8	20.1	18.2	20.4	21.5	16.5	16.9	18.4	14.0
4. Mostly agree	34.9	34.1	36.2	36.9	25.3	36.5	39.3	31.0	32.7	36.0	33.9	34.8	35.1	35.8	35.5	20.3
5. Agree	35.4	39.3	31.4	32.1	53.6	32.8	33.1	37.7	38.2	35.8	33.8	33.2	37.3	36.8	35.6	44.0
Item 12700　Subject Q02　　N	2989	1439	1494	2315	349	687	840	897	565	1827	1076	1168	600	443	711	36
D01Q: There is usually someone I can talk to, if I need to																
1. Disagree	3.2	3.6	2.9	2.7	4.5	3.3	2.0	4.1	3.6	2.6	4.2	2.8	2.5	2.7	3.9	18.8
2. Mostly disagree	4.4	5.5	3.5	4.4	4.1	5.2	4.2	3.9	4.7	4.5	4.3	3.5	4.2	4.7	5.7	13.3
3. Neither	5.2	7.2	3.1	5.1	4.0	4.4	6.1	5.6	4.3	5.2	5.2	5.2	3.5	3.9	7.3	8.3
4. Mostly agree	27.4	30.3	24.6	28.5	21.3	28.3	27.3	26.2	28.2	27.7	27.3	26.2	26.4	30.5	28.3	20.4
5. Agree	59.7	53.5	66.0	59.3	66.1	58.6	60.5	60.2	59.2	60.1	58.9	62.3	63.3	58.1	54.8	39.2
Item 12710　Subject Q03　　N	2981	1435	1494	2307	349	683	838	897	562	1821	1074	1164	601	439	710	36
D01R: I feel that I can't do anything right																
1. Disagree	43.6	45.1	42.2	42.9	51.5	45.8	40.4	44.1	45.0	46.8	38.3	45.2	45.6	44.3	39.0	38.8
2. Mostly disagree	27.9	26.5	29.2	29.6	20.5	25.0	30.5	27.6	28.2	29.2	26.4	28.9	26.6	28.5	28.4	16.7
3. Neither	15.1	15.0	15.1	15.4	9.5	15.8	16.5	15.1	12.1	14.4	16.1	14.0	13.6	16.7	17.0	16.9
4. Mostly agree	8.7	8.5	9.1	8.1	12.7	9.9	8.5	8.0	8.6	7.0	11.5	7.2	9.4	7.7	10.7	11.9
5. Agree	4.6	4.9	4.4	4.0	5.8	3.5	4.0	5.2	6.1	2.7	7.7	4.7	4.7	2.8	4.9	15.7
Item 12720　Subject Q01　　N	2966	1432	1483	2295	347	681	834	892	559	1814	1068	1160	598	435	707	36

QUESTIONNAIRE FORM 5 1985	TOTAL	SEX		RACE		REGION				4YR COLLEGE PLANS		ILLICIT DRUG USE: LIFETIME				
		M	F	White	Black	NE	NC	S	W	Yes	No	None	Marijuana Only	Few Pills	More Pills	Any Heroin
N (Weighted No. of Cases):	3286	1584	1601	2463	410	782	901	997	604	1920	1159	1252	655	479	794	45
% of Weighted Total:	100.0	48.2	48.7	75.0	12.5	23.8	27.4	30.4	18.4	58.4	35.3	38.1	19.9	14.6	24.2	1.4

D01S: I often wish I had more good friends

1. Disagree	18.6	16.2	21.0	18.1	23.4	24.7	17.6	16.9	15.7	17.9	19.9	16.9	18.0	20.0	21.2	20.7
2. Mostly disagree	15.1	14.3	15.8	16.1	12.1	15.3	16.1	13.0	16.9	16.5	12.8	14.6	15.7	15.6	15.6	11.4
3. Neither	18.4	21.9	15.0	18.9	14.5	18.7	19.4	17.4	17.9	18.6	17.8	19.3	19.9	19.4	14.3	21.5
4. Mostly agree	25.3	24.3	26.3	26.1	19.7	23.6	25.1	27.2	24.4	25.7	24.8	26.1	22.0	25.0	27.4	22.3
5. Agree	22.6	23.3	21.9	20.8	30.2	17.8	21.7	25.5	25.1	21.3	24.6	23.1	24.4	19.9	21.5	24.0
Item 12730 Subject Q03 N	2964	1427	1486	2298	345	679	836	891	558	1811	1068	1156	598	434	707	36

D01T: Planning ahead makes things turn out better

1. Disagree	3.8	3.6	3.9	2.7	8.9	5.0	2.3	4.3	3.6	2.6	5.7	3.2	5.3	2.0	4.0	17.0
2. Mostly disagree	7.0	6.7	7.1	7.2	6.7	8.8	8.6	5.1	5.7	6.2	8.6	5.0	8.1	7.2	9.3	3.2
3. Neither	17.3	16.0	18.6	17.9	11.1	18.6	17.4	16.2	17.0	16.2	19.1	14.6	16.1	18.8	21.4	21.5
4. Mostly agree	40.1	40.0	40.0	42.9	32.6	38.8	41.6	40.2	39.0	43.3	35.0	43.3	37.2	41.9	37.0	34.4
5. Agree	31.9	33.7	30.4	29.3	40.7	28.8	30.1	34.1	34.8	31.7	31.6	34.0	33.4	30.1	28.4	23.9
Item 12740 Subject Q02 N	2962	1427	1484	2297	345	679	833	893	556	1812	1065	1154	599	437	705	35

D01U: I feel that my life is not very useful

1. Disagree	49.8	48.9	50.9	48.6	60.1	53.2	47.7	51.1	46.5	52.2	45.5	51.7	54.1	48.7	45.0	25.2
2. Mostly disagree	28.2	29.3	27.4	30.5	18.9	25.5	29.7	27.8	29.9	29.3	27.1	29.3	27.5	30.3	26.6	17.5
3. Neither	11.8	12.7	10.6	11.5	9.0	11.0	11.9	11.4	13.0	10.5	13.9	11.0	10.5	12.6	13.7	14.4
4. Mostly agree	6.4	5.2	7.2	6.4	5.8	5.8	8.2	5.3	6.1	4.9	8.6	5.1	4.6	4.5	10.0	22.8
5. Agree	3.9	3.8	3.8	2.9	6.2	4.4	2.6	4.5	4.4	3.0	4.9	2.8	3.2	4.0	4.7	20.1
Item 12750 Subject Q01 N	2952	1424	1477	2286	344	678	832	887	554	1803	1064	1153	596	434	702	36

D01V: I usually have a few friends around that I can get together with

1. Disagree	4.9	4.9	4.8	4.4	6.3	6.0	4.0	5.3	4.2	3.9	6.2	5.0	3.4	4.3	5.9	14.1
2. Mostly disagree	5.7	5.7	5.7	5.3	6.2	6.1	7.0	4.9	4.7	5.7	5.8	6.0	5.9	3.4	6.4	5.7
3. Neither	7.0	8.2	5.6	6.8	5.8	5.8	7.9	7.6	5.9	5.9	8.5	7.3	6.6	5.5	7.3	14.3
4. Mostly agree	35.0	34.0	36.0	36.4	29.9	34.2	33.7	36.2	36.1	34.7	36.0	35.9	32.2	38.1	34.5	30.2
5. Agree	47.4	47.2	47.9	47.0	51.8	47.8	47.4	46.0	49.1	49.7	43.6	45.8	51.9	48.7	46.0	35.6
Item 12760 Subject Q03 N	2958	1426	1481	2289	344	675	835	890	558	1812	1061	1155	600	434	703	36

D01W: I am eager to leave home and live on my own–independent from my parents

1. Disagree	8.3	8.2	8.4	6.9	11.2	10.4	6.6	8.3	8.5	6.6	11.1	9.5	7.5	7.2	7.8	4.9
2. Mostly disagree	10.5	11.6	9.6	10.8	9.6	9.7	10.8	12.3	7.9	10.6	10.3	11.2	9.5	12.3	9.5	1.5
3. Neither	19.5	21.5	17.5	20.3	9.8	18.8	22.5	16.0	21.6	20.5	17.4	22.6	19.9	16.4	15.9	18.6
4. Mostly agree	30.0	29.0	30.9	30.7	29.9	32.0	28.1	30.8	29.2	30.8	29.3	30.7	32.4	30.6	26.6	31.4
5. Agree	31.7	29.7	33.6	31.2	39.4	29.1	32.0	32.5	32.9	31.5	31.9	26.0	30.7	33.4	40.1	43.5
Item 13950 Subject I03,Q01 N	2948	1421	1476	2281	343	674	830	889	555	1806	1057	1151	600	432	701	36

D01X: I feel hesitant about taking a full-time job and becoming part of the "adult world"

1. Disagree	31.7	33.3	30.3	30.0	38.4	36.9	28.4	29.5	34.0	28.7	36.7	26.9	31.3	34.7	38.3	36.7
2. Mostly disagree	21.9	21.1	22.9	22.9	19.0	22.4	22.0	22.1	21.1	23.2	20.0	22.7	21.2	23.7	20.6	21.8
3. Neither	14.7	16.5	12.8	15.1	9.6	14.2	16.3	13.9	14.2	15.6	13.2	16.5	15.7	9.5	13.9	12.3
4. Mostly agree	20.5	18.1	22.7	21.3	18.5	16.3	21.6	23.0	20.0	22.3	17.8	22.7	20.7	21.9	16.9	10.8
5. Agree	11.1	11.0	11.3	10.7	14.5	10.2	11.7	11.5	10.7	10.2	12.3	11.3	11.0	10.3	10.4	18.3
Item 13960 Subject I03,Q01 N	2940	1415	1475	2276	344	669	829	890	552	1798	1059	1148	600	432	697	36

The next two questions ask your views about different lifestyles that have been in the news lately.

	TOTAL	SEX		RACE		REGION				4YR COLLEGE PLANS		ILLICIT DRUG USE: LIFETIME				
QUESTIONNAIRE FORM 5 1985		M	F	White	Black	NE	NC	S	W	Yes	No	None	Mari-juana Only	Few Pills	More Pills	Any Her-oin
N (Weighted No. of Cases):	3286	1584	1601	2463	410	782	901	997	604	1920	1159	1252	655	479	794	45
% of Weighted Total:	100.0	48.2	48.7	75.0	12.5	23.8	27.4	30.4	18.4	58.4	35.3	38.1	19.9	14.6	24.2	1.4
D02: A man and a woman who live together without being married are . . . (Mark ONE circle.)																
1. Experimenting with a worthwhile alternative lifestyle	24.0	24.6	23.3	24.2	22.1	29.2	24.0	19.4	25.3	23.0	25.6	20.9	24.7	24.2	27.4	45.3
2. Doing their own thing and not affecting anyone else	50.1	50.6	49.7	51.1	50.1	53.5	49.4	47.3	51.8	50.2	50.8	42.5	53.7	56.8	56.0	39.2
3. Living in a way that could be destructive to society	6.0	6.7	5.3	5.6	7.4	3.7	5.9	7.7	6.2	6.1	5.4	8.5	5.3	4.6	3.3	3.0
4. Violating a basic principle of human morality	13.0	10.8	15.2	13.1	12.6	6.3	14.2	18.1	11.2	13.8	11.7	20.3	9.2	9.0	7.1	11.0
8. None of the above	6.8	7.3	6.5	6.0	7.8	7.4	6.5	7.6	5.4	6.8	6.5	7.8	7.1	5.4	6.1	1.6
Item 12770 Subject D03 N	2918	1395	1474	2260	338	664	818	882	555	1790	1046	1140	593	431	690	36
D03: A man and a woman who decide to have and raise a child out of wedlock are . . .																
1. Experimenting with a worthwhile alternative lifestyle	8.5	8.8	8.1	8.1	11.6	10.9	7.7	7.4	8.7	8.1	8.7	6.7	10.1	8.0	10.1	15.1
2. Doing their own thing and not affecting anyone else	36.8	36.3	37.1	35.9	42.3	43.9	36.4	30.8	38.5	33.8	42.1	30.6	38.9	41.1	42.5	38.5
3. Living in a way that could be destructive to society	17.2	18.2	16.4	18.7	11.8	12.7	19.4	18.3	17.6	18.6	14.5	19.4	16.8	16.5	13.9	20.1
4. Violating a basic principle of human morality	24.0	23.4	24.7	24.7	19.1	17.4	23.6	29.5	24.1	25.7	22.1	31.2	19.1	19.6	19.9	13.0
8. None of the above	13.4	13.3	13.7	12.6	15.2	15.1	12.9	14.0	11.2	13.9	12.6	12.0	15.0	14.9	13.6	13.3
Item 12775 Subject D03 N	2892	1379	1464	2246	331	660	812	869	551	1777	1036	1128	586	428	685	36
D04: These next questions ask how you feel about your present financial situation and your future financial security.																
D04A: I feel that I have enough money to get along pretty well																
1. Never	11.4	10.6	12.2	9.2	20.6	12.4	11.0	10.4	12.2	10.2	13.4	10.6	11.9	10.6	12.8	15.9
2. Seldom	19.0	19.3	19.1	19.1	19.1	18.6	20.0	18.8	18.6	16.0	24.9	17.0	20.9	15.6	22.6	33.4
3. Sometimes	34.7	32.1	36.8	35.3	35.7	30.9	35.6	37.0	34.3	35.2	34.2	35.5	34.9	35.3	32.7	19.5
4. Often	25.7	26.6	24.7	27.1	16.9	27.4	24.8	24.0	27.6	28.0	21.5	27.4	24.3	30.9	21.6	10.9
5. Always	9.2	11.3	7.2	9.3	7.8	10.8	8.6	9.8	7.3	10.6	6.1	9.5	8.0	7.6	10.3	20.3
Item 12990 Subject C02 N	2902	1389	1461	2248	332	656	816	876	554	1782	1036	1129	592	431	686	35
D04B: I get very concerned about how I am going to be able to pay my next bills																
1. Never	26.4	25.4	27.3	25.4	34.4	26.8	26.3	26.3	26.1	28.1	23.7	28.2	26.8	27.2	21.9	34.3
2. Seldom	25.9	25.0	27.0	26.7	21.5	24.8	27.8	25.3	25.3	27.3	23.5	26.2	28.6	24.7	24.1	14.0
3. Sometimes	25.9	27.1	24.7	26.2	22.9	24.4	25.9	24.6	29.5	26.0	25.9	26.0	24.9	28.8	24.7	24.6
4. Often	14.9	14.9	14.6	15.3	11.9	16.1	13.1	16.6	13.3	13.1	17.8	13.5	13.1	13.8	19.6	11.9
5. Always	7.0	7.5	6.4	6.4	9.3	7.9	6.9	7.2	5.8	5.5	9.2	6.1	6.7	5.4	9.6	15.1
Item 13000 Subject C02 N	2864	1374	1439	2219	330	644	805	864	551	1759	1026	1115	585	421	678	36
D04C: I worry whether I will have any job at all in a few months																
1. Never	38.5	41.0	36.6	39.7	34.3	44.7	35.7	34.9	41.3	41.9	32.4	37.4	44.2	38.0	36.8	30.2
2. Seldom	24.1	21.7	26.3	25.0	19.4	23.2	25.2	24.7	22.6	24.6	23.6	23.7	21.8	27.0	24.4	24.8
3. Sometimes	19.6	19.5	19.8	19.4	20.6	17.3	20.1	21.1	19.5	18.6	22.0	21.7	16.6	17.9	19.8	20.3
4. Often	11.6	12.0	11.1	11.1	12.4	10.1	12.8	12.2	10.7	10.0	14.1	11.6	11.7	12.8	11.0	14.2
5. Always	6.1	5.7	6.2	4.9	13.2	4.7	6.2	7.2	5.8	4.8	7.9	5.5	5.7	4.3	8.0	10.4
Item 13010 Subject C02 N	2868	1373	1444	2222	329	643	808	864	553	1760	1027	1117	584	424	679	35
D04D: I feel sure that I could go out and get a new job (with decent pay) whenever I want one																
1. Never	9.3	7.8	10.7	8.1	18.3	7.9	11.8	9.3	7.2	8.2	10.9	10.5	10.0	5.6	8.5	15.2
2. Seldom	21.4	20.1	22.3	21.4	19.8	15.8	24.4	23.0	21.1	19.9	24.3	19.6	21.4	21.9	24.3	5.0
3. Sometimes	33.8	30.0	38.0	35.0	27.0	34.3	34.8	32.5	34.0	34.2	33.7	36.0	34.8	31.6	31.3	42.0
4. Often	21.8	24.3	19.3	23.1	16.1	23.4	20.9	21.4	22.1	23.7	18.3	23.0	21.4	24.1	19.5	11.8
5. Always	13.6	17.7	9.7	12.4	18.9	18.6	8.2	13.8	15.6	14.1	12.7	11.0	12.3	16.8	16.5	26.0
Item 13020 Subject C02 N	2852	1368	1434	2212	327	636	806	862	548	1749	1024	1115	581	419	675	35

QUESTIONNAIRE FORM 5 1985	TOTAL	SEX		RACE		REGION				4YR COLLEGE PLANS		ILLICIT DRUG USE: LIFETIME				
		M	F	White	Black	NE	NC	S	W	Yes	No	None	Mari-juana Only	Few Pills	More Pills	Any Her-oin
N (Weighted No. of Cases):	3286	1584	1601	2463	410	782	901	997	604	1920	1159	1252	655	479	794	45
% of Weighted Total:	100.0	48.2	48.7	75.0	12.5	23.8	27.4	30.4	18.4	58.4	35.3	38.1	19.9	14.6	24.2	1.4

FOR THOSE WHO HAVE A JOB:

D04E: I feel sure I that can keep working steadily with my present employer as long as I want to

	TOTAL	M	F	White	Black	NE	NC	S	W	Yes	No	None	Marijuana Only	Few Pills	More Pills	Any Heroin
1. Never	4.5	4.9	3.8	3.8	9.0	3.7	5.5	5.6	2.5	3.6	5.8	4.0	6.6	2.5	3.5	12.2
2. Seldom	4.7	4.2	4.7	4.2	9.3	4.9	4.0	5.0	4.9	3.7	6.1	4.3	4.4	4.5	4.6	13.5
3. Sometimes	13.7	13.7	13.4	13.1	14.5	13.4	13.0	14.7	13.5	11.9	16.3	13.3	12.6	12.0	15.6	18.9
4. Often	29.2	27.7	31.0	29.6	27.4	29.1	31.3	27.0	29.4	31.8	24.9	30.8	25.7	30.2	29.5	25.1
5. Always	48.0	49.5	47.1	49.3	39.8	48.8	46.2	47.7	49.8	48.9	47.0	47.5	50.7	50.8	46.8	30.3
Item 13030 Subject C02 N★	1925	987	897	1552	179	464	538	544	379	1154	710	713	394	290	478	29

D04F: I worry about getting fired or laid-off from my job

	TOTAL	M	F	White	Black	NE	NC	S	W	Yes	No	None	Marijuana Only	Few Pills	More Pills	Any Heroin
1. Never	56.9	55.1	59.0	58.6	46.7	61.2	54.5	56.2	55.7	59.5	52.8	58.6	55.8	57.8	55.6	41.7
2. Seldom	23.6	22.5	25.0	24.1	23.0	20.8	24.9	25.3	22.6	24.7	22.0	21.6	26.4	23.6	25.4	7.3
3. Sometimes	12.2	13.4	10.7	11.3	15.6	12.7	13.2	11.2	11.3	10.8	14.5	14.0	11.5	9.6	10.6	31.7
4. Often	4.2	4.3	3.9	3.1	9.6	2.6	2.7	5.2	7.1	2.9	6.1	3.0	4.5	5.1	4.0	14.5
5. Always	3.2	4.7	1.3	2.8	5.1	2.6	4.7	2.0	3.3	2.1	4.6	2.8	1.8	3.9	4.3	4.8
Item 13040 Subject C02 N★	1918	982	896	1546	177	463	535	541	378	1149	708	711	392	289	478	28

D05: Please think about all the money you earned during the past year, including last summer.

About how much of your past year's earnings have gone into:

D05A: Savings for your future education

	TOTAL	M	F	White	Black	NE	NC	S	W	Yes	No	None	Marijuana Only	Few Pills	More Pills	Any Heroin
1. None	52.3	54.5	50.1	52.2	54.8	52.5	48.0	53.8	55.9	45.2	65.7	44.8	52.1	54.6	63.3	52.4
2. A little	18.5	16.1	20.8	19.0	13.8	16.0	20.7	18.3	18.6	19.7	16.5	20.3	21.3	15.1	15.6	15.9
3. Some	11.5	11.1	11.8	11.1	11.9	12.1	11.8	12.3	9.0	12.8	8.5	13.0	10.3	12.3	10.1	6.1
4. About half	7.7	8.6	6.8	7.3	9.1	8.4	7.0	6.9	9.0	9.7	4.3	8.8	7.3	8.8	4.3	17.9
5. Most	6.0	6.3	5.9	6.4	6.0	7.6	7.3	4.9	4.2	7.9	2.7	8.1	4.4	6.6	3.8	6.8
6. Almost all	3.0	2.4	3.6	3.3	1.6	2.8	4.2	2.5	2.4	3.9	1.3	4.0	3.7	1.5	2.0	1.0
7. All	1.0	1.0	0.9	0.7	2.7	0.7	1.0	1.2	0.9	0.8	0.9	1.0	1.0	1.0	0.8	-
Item 20830 Subject C02 N	2764	1351	1360	2172	290	623	787	819	535	1704	981	1074	561	414	655	35

D05B: Savings or payments for a car or car expenses

	TOTAL	M	F	White	Black	NE	NC	S	W	Yes	No	None	Marijuana Only	Few Pills	More Pills	Any Heroin
1. None	47.5	38.8	56.2	44.8	65.4	49.8	48.8	47.7	42.5	50.8	42.5	52.3	47.8	47.0	40.9	31.1
2. A little	17.5	18.3	16.8	18.3	10.3	17.7	18.0	17.7	16.2	18.2	15.9	17.9	20.4	14.7	15.9	14.0
3. Some	13.5	15.4	11.6	14.1	9.0	11.6	12.3	14.4	16.2	13.1	14.7	13.0	11.6	10.3	17.1	30.6
4. About half	9.4	11.6	7.0	10.2	6.4	8.2	9.5	9.1	11.3	8.0	11.8	7.6	8.0	13.8	11.0	13.1
5. Most	6.7	9.1	4.3	7.1	3.3	7.8	6.5	5.5	7.5	6.0	7.9	5.6	7.6	6.3	8.4	2.0
6. Almost all	4.1	5.2	3.0	4.3	4.3	3.7	3.6	3.8	5.5	3.3	5.1	2.9	3.6	5.7	5.2	-
7. All	1.3	1.6	0.9	1.2	1.2	1.1	1.3	1.8	0.7	0.7	2.1	0.8	0.9	2.2	1.6	9.2
Item 20840 Subject C02 N	2749	1344	1354	2164	288	622	784	813	530	1697	977	1066	562	412	650	34

D05C: Other savings for long-range purposes

	TOTAL	M	F	White	Black	NE	NC	S	W	Yes	No	None	Marijuana Only	Few Pills	More Pills	Any Heroin
1. None	47.9	46.5	49.1	47.7	54.1	47.6	46.8	48.8	48.3	47.4	49.7	44.4	48.3	48.5	53.6	35.5
2. A little	23.1	23.4	22.9	23.6	17.6	22.8	21.7	24.2	24.1	24.8	20.2	25.0	22.2	22.1	22.1	22.2
3. Some	12.8	13.1	12.6	13.0	11.3	13.1	14.5	12.0	11.1	11.6	14.9	14.3	11.3	12.5	10.6	24.9
4. About half	6.6	7.5	5.7	6.2	6.8	7.5	5.9	5.5	8.4	6.7	6.4	6.8	6.2	6.7	6.8	6.0
5. Most	4.9	4.6	5.2	5.1	4.6	4.7	6.4	4.4	3.8	5.2	4.3	5.4	5.1	4.9	3.5	10.3
6. Almost all	3.3	2.9	3.6	3.3	3.7	2.9	3.4	4.0	2.6	3.3	3.3	2.8	5.4	3.4	2.3	1.1
7. All	1.4	1.9	0.9	1.1	2.0	1.5	1.3	1.1	1.7	1.0	1.3	1.4	1.4	1.8	1.1	-
Item 20850 Subject C02 N	2748	1342	1353	2156	289	624	779	813	532	1697	974	1063	562	415	652	33

★=excludes respondents for whom question was inappropriate.

QUESTIONNAIRE FORM 5 1985	TOTAL	SEX		RACE		REGION				4YR COLLEGE PLANS		ILLICIT DRUG USE: LIFETIME				
		M	F	White	Black	NE	NC	S	W	Yes	No	None	Marijuana Only	Few Pills	More Pills	Any Heroin
N (Weighted No. of Cases):	3286	1584	1601	2463	410	782	901	997	604	1920	1159	1252	655	479	794	45
% of Weighted Total:	100.0	48.2	48.7	75.0	12.5	23.8	27.4	30.4	18.4	58.4	35.3	38.1	19.9	14.6	24.2	1.4

D05D: Spending on your own needs and activities – things such as clothing, stereo, TV, records, other possessions, movies, eating out, other recreation, hobbies, gifts for others, and other personal expenses

	TOTAL	M	F	White	Black	NE	NC	S	W	Yes	No	None	Mar.	Few	More	Her.
1. None	5.3	5.8	4.7	3.9	10.6	5.3	4.8	6.6	4.1	3.9	7.9	5.8	4.7	5.1	4.9	12.1
2. A little	18.2	19.3	17.4	19.1	12.7	17.1	18.9	19.3	17.1	19.4	16.5	22.0	17.9	14.5	14.3	22.4
3. Some	18.2	19.1	17.1	18.5	17.3	17.4	19.8	16.1	20.1	19.0	16.9	17.7	16.7	22.7	17.2	15.5
4. About half	16.1	17.5	14.7	16.9	10.9	14.0	17.9	16.4	15.3	14.8	18.3	14.7	18.6	16.0	15.4	21.2
5. Most	18.3	17.6	19.1	18.8	17.4	21.5	16.7	16.8	19.2	18.9	17.3	18.5	17.1	21.4	18.2	9.7
6. Almost all	15.0	12.1	18.0	14.9	15.0	16.4	13.6	16.5	13.1	15.8	13.8	14.2	15.5	11.7	18.6	13.5
7. All	8.8	8.7	9.0	7.9	16.0	8.3	8.3	8.3	11.1	8.1	9.4	7.1	9.7	8.6	11.4	5.8
Item 20860 Subject C02 N	2749	1340	1356	2162	287	622	783	810	533	1697	976	1062	559	417	651	35

D05E: Helping to pay family living expenses (groceries, housing, etc.)

	TOTAL	M	F	White	Black	NE	NC	S	W	Yes	No	None	Mar.	Few	More	Her.
1. None	56.6	54.5	59.5	61.3	30.7	54.8	60.7	53.8	57.1	62.1	47.5	57.4	56.4	56.8	56.1	49.2
2. A little	25.3	27.6	22.8	24.5	31.2	27.1	23.9	24.5	26.5	23.8	28.3	23.5	24.7	28.2	26.5	28.0
3. Some	9.3	8.7	10.0	8.0	15.5	9.2	8.8	11.5	7.1	7.8	12.3	10.5	7.9	7.7	10.1	7.1
4. About half	3.3	3.6	2.7	2.8	5.5	3.0	2.9	3.6	3.6	2.5	4.5	2.7	4.4	2.9	3.0	10.1
5. Most	2.5	2.5	2.2	1.7	7.1	2.2	1.6	3.0	3.3	1.9	3.1	2.4	3.7	1.8	1.8	3.4
6. Almost all	1.9	1.8	2.0	1.0	6.6	2.7	1.3	2.1	1.9	1.4	3.1	2.1	2.0	2.0	1.7	2.2
7. All	1.0	1.2	0.8	0.6	3.4	1.0	0.9	1.5	0.6	0.6	1.3	1.4	0.9	0.7	0.8	-
Item 20870 Subject C02 N	2748	1341	1355	2161	287	624	783	808	533	1699	972	1060	561	415	652	35

The next questions ask about characteristics which some people associate with the use of particular drugs. We want to know what you think.

E01: Do YOU think that people who smoke marijuana several times a week tend to be . . .

E01A: More creative than average

	TOTAL	M	F	White	Black	NE	NC	S	W	Yes	No	None	Mar.	Few	More	Her.
1. No	62.8	60.3	65.7	65.2	54.3	61.3	67.1	61.0	61.3	67.3	55.4	69.4	63.6	66.3	51.5	22.7
2. Yes	14.6	18.4	10.8	13.8	17.7	15.6	12.6	14.8	16.4	11.9	18.6	6.8	14.1	10.9	28.8	44.9
3. Not sure, no opinion	22.5	21.3	23.5	21.0	28.0	23.2	20.3	24.1	22.3	20.7	26.0	23.9	22.2	22.7	19.8	32.4
Item 13060 Subject A11c N	2852	1364	1441	2207	331	635	803	868	547	1765	1002	1110	573	424	681	37

E01B: Less sensible than average

	TOTAL	M	F	White	Black	NE	NC	S	W	Yes	No	None	Mar.	Few	More	Her.
1. No	23.0	26.7	19.7	21.8	27.7	27.6	22.3	21.1	21.7	21.4	25.6	13.1	22.3	24.6	37.6	38.9
2. Yes	60.0	56.8	62.7	62.6	50.2	55.8	63.1	58.6	62.8	62.7	55.9	67.6	60.5	60.4	47.8	48.3
3. Not sure, no opinion	17.0	16.4	17.6	15.6	22.0	16.7	14.6	20.3	15.5	15.9	18.5	19.3	17.2	15.0	14.6	12.8
Item 13070 Subject A11c N	2845	1358	1437	2203	331	635	798	868	544	1763	999	1105	572	424	680	37

E01C: More interesting people than average

	TOTAL	M	F	White	Black	NE	NC	S	W	Yes	No	None	Mar.	Few	More	Her.
1. No	63.9	60.2	67.7	66.4	55.4	65.8	66.1	62.3	60.9	66.7	59.1	68.5	65.4	67.9	54.5	32.1
2. Yes	16.0	19.7	12.3	14.4	21.0	16.2	14.0	15.8	19.0	14.2	19.4	8.6	14.7	14.4	28.2	54.3
3. Not sure, no opinion	20.1	20.1	20.0	19.2	23.6	18.0	19.9	22.0	20.1	19.1	21.4	22.9	19.9	17.7	17.3	13.6
Item 13080 Subject A11c N	2839	1359	1430	2199	331	633	798	863	545	1764	992	1105	570	421	680	37

E01D: Less hard-working than average

	TOTAL	M	F	White	Black	NE	NC	S	W	Yes	No	None	Mar.	Few	More	Her.
1. No	24.6	25.1	24.3	23.5	29.9	25.6	27.1	21.5	24.9	21.4	30.1	15.1	25.2	27.8	36.9	37.7
2. Yes	57.2	56.5	57.7	59.2	46.7	57.6	54.2	57.8	60.2	60.6	51.5	62.1	56.9	56.5	50.2	52.5
3. Not sure, no opinion	18.2	18.4	17.9	17.3	23.4	16.8	18.6	20.8	14.9	18.0	18.4	22.7	17.9	15.7	12.9	9.8
Item 13090 Subject A11c N	2839	1360	1429	2198	329	633	801	860	545	1762	995	1104	569	423	680	36

E01E: More independent than average

	TOTAL	M	F	White	Black	NE	NC	S	W	Yes	No	None	Mar.	Few	More	Her.
1. No	52.1	48.0	56.4	52.4	55.8	51.9	52.8	51.2	53.1	53.5	50.2	52.9	52.5	57.7	47.6	46.7
2. Yes	27.1	32.4	21.6	27.6	18.9	30.3	27.2	23.6	28.6	26.7	27.8	20.6	27.6	25.9	37.1	43.5
3. Not sure, no opinion	20.8	19.6	22.0	20.0	25.4	17.9	20.0	25.3	18.3	19.8	21.9	26.5	19.9	16.4	15.3	9.8
Item 13100 Subject A11c N	2832	1352	1430	2191	329	629	798	860	545	1759	990	1103	567	423	678	36

QUESTIONNAIRE FORM 5 1985	TOTAL	SEX		RACE		REGION				4YR COLLEGE PLANS		ILLICIT DRUG USE: LIFETIME				
		M	F	White	Black	NE	NC	S	W	Yes	No	None	Mari- juana Only	Few Pills	More Pills	Any Her- oin
N (Weighted No. of Cases):	3286	1584	1601	2463	410	782	901	997	604	1920	1159	1252	655	479	794	45
% of Weighted Total:	100.0	48.2	48.7	75.0	12.5	23.8	27.4	30.4	18.4	58.4	35.3	38.1	19.9	14.6	24.2	1.4
E01F: More emotionally unstable than average																
1. No	21.0	24.3	18.1	21.2	20.4	23.9	21.4	18.7	20.8	18.5	25.4	12.1	22.6	20.8	33.3	39.5
2. Yes	60.5	56.4	64.6	61.1	56.9	55.9	61.4	61.8	62.7	64.1	54.5	66.2	60.6	64.1	50.5	46.9
3. Not sure, no opinion	18.4	19.3	17.3	17.7	22.7	20.2	17.3	19.6	16.5	17.4	20.0	21.8	16.7	15.1	16.2	13.6
Item 13110 Subject A11c N	2825	1349	1426	2187	327	625	799	860	540	1754	991	1103	564	422	674	36
E01G: More concerned about other people than average																
1. No	70.2	68.2	72.4	72.1	59.6	68.6	72.1	69.9	69.9	73.7	64.8	70.8	72.8	71.9	66.6	66.9
2. Yes	8.7	9.5	7.6	8.0	12.4	10.5	8.5	6.4	10.3	6.6	11.7	4.2	7.4	11.1	14.8	22.4
3. Not sure, no opinion	21.1	22.3	20.0	19.9	28.0	20.9	19.4	23.7	19.8	19.7	23.5	25.1	19.8	17.0	18.6	10.7
Item 13120 Subject A11c N	2832	1352	1430	2192	329	629	799	861	543	1760	990	1105	564	421	680	36
E01H: More weak-willed than average																
1. No	24.3	27.7	21.5	24.1	25.9	27.4	25.4	21.4	23.7	21.8	28.0	14.0	22.5	28.1	39.4	46.1
2. Yes	55.0	52.4	56.9	55.5	50.7	51.5	54.9	55.6	58.0	59.1	48.5	61.5	56.8	54.9	43.0	46.4
3. Not sure, no opinion	20.7	19.9	21.6	20.4	23.5	21.1	19.7	22.9	18.3	19.0	23.5	24.4	20.7	17.0	17.6	7.5
Item 13130 Subject A11c N	2828	1348	1428	2189	328	625	799	861	544	1757	989	1102	565	422	677	37
E01I: More criminal than average																
1. No	26.1	27.5	24.9	26.5	26.1	32.0	26.4	22.4	25.0	23.8	30.0	14.8	25.8	30.7	40.5	54.5
2. Yes	51.8	51.7	51.7	52.7	48.3	44.2	54.0	54.0	53.6	54.1	48.4	58.7	52.0	51.3	41.4	35.6
3. Not sure, no opinion	22.1	20.8	23.3	20.8	25.6	23.8	19.7	23.6	21.4	22.1	21.6	26.5	22.2	18.1	18.1	9.8
Item 13140 Subject A11c N	2827	1349	1429	2190	326	622	801	860	545	1759	987	1102	562	424	678	36

The next questions are similar, but ask about illegal drugs other than marijuana–like psychedelics, barbiturates, narcotics, and amphetamines.

E02: Do YOU think that people who use illegal drugs (other than marijuana) several times a week tend to be . . .

	TOTAL	M	F	White	Black	NE	NC	S	W	Yes	No	None	Mari- juana Only	Few Pills	More Pills	Any Her- oin
E02A: More creative than average																
1. No	62.2	57.7	66.9	64.2	52.5	60.3	63.0	61.9	63.5	65.2	57.4	67.3	58.9	65.9	55.7	45.1
2. Yes	11.5	13.5	9.2	10.8	16.2	13.3	10.7	10.8	11.8	9.8	14.0	7.0	9.9	11.0	19.1	29.2
3. Not sure, no opinion	26.3	28.8	23.9	25.0	31.3	26.4	26.3	27.3	24.7	25.1	28.6	25.8	31.2	23.1	25.1	25.7
Item 13330 Subject A11c N	2801	1335	1415	2170	323	619	797	842	544	1747	971	1088	561	420	670	36
E02B: Less sensible than average																
1. No	15.1	16.0	14.3	13.7	19.6	16.2	16.7	12.8	15.1	11.7	20.5	11.8	11.0	14.8	23.7	22.3
2. Yes	62.0	57.8	65.8	64.9	49.8	60.1	61.5	63.0	63.1	67.7	52.8	66.5	61.9	65.0	53.9	52.7
3. Not sure, no opinion	22.9	26.2	19.9	21.4	30.6	23.6	21.8	24.3	21.8	20.6	26.6	21.7	27.1	20.2	22.3	24.9
Item 13340 Subject A11c N	2798	1331	1416	2165	323	616	795	842	546	1746	969	1089	557	418	670	37
E02C: More interesting people than average																
1. No	63.7	58.6	68.8	66.3	54.6	62.1	65.7	62.9	64.1	66.9	58.4	67.6	61.5	68.0	58.5	37.9
2. Yes	10.7	13.6	7.8	9.0	15.9	12.0	8.4	10.7	12.8	9.0	14.0	6.4	8.6	10.3	18.1	32.3
3. Not sure, no opinion	25.5	27.8	23.4	24.6	29.4	25.8	26.0	26.4	23.2	24.1	27.7	26.0	29.9	21.7	23.4	29.7
Item 13350 Subject A11c N	2793	1330	1412	2165	319	615	794	840	545	1744	966	1088	556	419	668	37
E02D: Less hard-working than average																
1. No	16.1	15.9	16.1	15.1	22.1	16.6	16.5	16.4	14.6	13.0	21.5	12.3	12.5	16.6	24.2	29.0
2. Yes	58.8	56.9	60.9	61.1	46.3	59.0	58.3	55.9	63.7	63.3	50.9	62.0	59.6	63.7	51.2	47.3
3. Not sure, no opinion	25.1	27.2	23.0	23.8	31.6	24.4	25.1	27.7	21.6	23.7	27.6	25.6	27.9	19.7	24.6	23.7
Item 13360 Subject A11c N	2792	1329	1412	2161	322	615	794	840	542	1743	966	1084	557	419	669	37

QUESTIONNAIRE FORM 5 1985	TOTAL	SEX		RACE		REGION				4YR COLLEGE PLANS		ILLICIT DRUG USE: LIFETIME				
		M	F	White	Black	NE	NC	S	W	Yes	No	None	Mari- juana Only	Few Pills	More Pills	Any Her- oin
N (Weighted No. of Cases):	3286	1584	1601	2463	410	782	901	997	604	1920	1159	1252	655	479	794	45
% of Weighted Total:	100.0	48.2	48.7	75.0	12.5	23.8	27.4	30.4	18.4	58.4	35.3	38.1	19.9	14.6	24.2	1.4
E02E: More independent than average																
1. No	52.1	46.2	57.8	52.9	51.8	48.0	53.2	52.2	55.2	54.5	47.8	53.5	49.8	55.8	50.4	42.8
2. Yes	20.8	24.2	17.4	20.9	16.2	24.7	18.8	19.1	21.7	19.6	22.9	19.0	20.1	19.8	24.2	30.2
3. Not sure, no opinion	27.1	29.6	24.8	26.2	32.1	27.3	28.0	28.8	23.1	26.0	29.3	27.6	30.1	24.4	25.4	27.0
Item 13370 Subject A11c N	2785	1321	1412	2152	323	614	791	837	542	1736	965	1084	555	417	666	37
E02F: More emotionally unstable than average																
1. No	13.0	13.5	12.5	12.5	13.0	16.4	12.5	10.4	14.1	9.6	19.0	9.5	10.5	12.0	19.8	35.3
2. Yes	64.4	59.7	68.8	66.3	58.4	59.8	65.6	65.9	65.4	69.7	55.3	68.1	64.5	68.3	58.0	41.0
3. Not sure, no opinion	22.6	26.8	18.8	21.2	28.5	23.8	21.9	23.6	20.5	20.7	25.7	22.4	25.0	19.8	22.3	23.7
Item 13380 Subject A11c N	2789	1326	1410	2158	322	611	792	841	545	1740	966	1084	557	420	665	37
E02G: More concerned about other people than average																
1. No	66.7	62.9	70.5	69.1	56.6	65.0	67.9	66.0	68.1	69.9	61.4	68.8	65.3	68.2	64.8	53.7
2. Yes	6.6	7.7	5.3	5.5	11.2	6.7	6.3	6.0	7.8	4.9	9.3	4.5	6.2	7.0	9.3	18.9
3. Not sure, no opinion	26.7	29.4	24.1	25.4	32.2	28.2	25.8	28.0	24.1	25.2	29.3	26.7	28.5	24.9	25.9	27.4
Item 13390 Subject A11c N	2782	1323	1409	2153	323	608	791	841	543	1738	961	1082	557	417	664	36
E02H: More weak-willed than average																
1. No	14.6	15.1	14.1	14.7	14.0	18.8	15.2	12.2	12.8	11.7	19.4	11.0	12.3	15.1	21.6	25.3
2. Yes	58.4	54.9	61.7	59.7	53.7	52.3	59.0	60.1	61.9	63.6	50.0	62.3	59.4	59.5	51.3	48.0
3. Not sure, no opinion	27.0	30.0	24.1	25.6	32.3	28.9	25.8	27.7	25.3	24.7	30.7	26.7	28.3	25.4	27.1	26.7
Item 13400 Subject A11c N	2787	1324	1412	2158	321	610	791	843	544	1738	966	1083	560	417	664	37
E02I: More criminal than average																
1. No	14.4	14.0	14.8	14.3	15.0	16.1	15.9	13.3	12.0	12.5	17.3	12.7	10.4	13.9	20.6	19.4
2. Yes	59.8	59.3	60.3	61.2	56.3	54.9	60.4	61.2	62.1	62.9	54.3	62.3	61.0	62.9	53.1	57.0
3. Not sure, no opinion	25.8	26.7	24.9	24.5	28.7	28.9	23.7	25.5	25.9	24.6	28.3	25.0	28.6	23.2	26.3	23.7
Item 13410 Subject A11c N	2789	1326	1412	2156	323	611	790	843	545	1741	964	1085	558	420	664	37

The next few questions ask how YOU view cigarette smoking.

E03: In my opinion, when a guy my age is smoking a cigarette, it makes him look . . .

E03A: Cool, calm, in-control

	TOTAL	M	F	White	Black	NE	NC	S	W	Yes	No	None	Mari- juana Only	Few Pills	More Pills	Any Her- oin
1. Disagree	62.9	62.9	63.0	63.2	60.9	57.8	64.2	64.6	64.1	67.7	55.0	75.0	60.3	56.2	51.3	43.4
2. Mostly disagree	12.2	12.8	11.8	12.4	10.3	13.1	11.7	11.8	12.4	12.4	11.5	9.8	14.3	15.8	12.5	9.1
3. Neither	18.1	17.4	18.8	18.7	16.0	20.3	18.3	17.1	17.0	15.2	23.3	10.0	18.1	21.0	29.1	24.0
4. Mostly agree	4.5	3.7	5.1	3.9	6.9	5.7	3.9	3.5	5.3	3.7	5.6	2.9	5.3	3.2	6.0	20.6
5. Agree	2.3	3.2	1.3	1.8	5.9	3.0	1.9	2.9	1.2	1.0	4.6	2.2	2.0	3.9	1.2	2.9
Item 20880 Subject A11c N	2769	1319	1399	2152	313	604	797	833	535	1722	967	1074	552	418	664	36

E03B: Insecure

	TOTAL	M	F	White	Black	NE	NC	S	W	Yes	No	None	Mari- juana Only	Few Pills	More Pills	Any Her- oin
1. Disagree	14.5	15.8	13.1	13.2	15.3	19.6	13.3	12.5	13.6	11.7	19.5	10.6	15.2	11.6	21.3	24.8
2. Mostly disagree	9.0	7.2	10.6	9.1	10.9	8.7	9.1	9.3	8.6	8.4	10.0	7.3	9.3	11.5	10.1	3.6
3. Neither	30.8	29.7	31.6	31.7	25.1	32.6	31.7	29.2	29.9	28.8	34.2	23.3	34.7	34.8	37.0	41.8
4. Mostly agree	21.8	21.9	22.0	22.8	19.5	18.8	21.5	24.4	21.4	24.8	17.3	24.7	21.4	21.9	17.2	22.2
5. Agree	24.0	25.4	22.7	23.2	29.1	20.3	24.4	24.5	26.6	26.4	18.9	34.1	19.4	20.3	14.4	7.5
Item 20890 Subject A11c N	2764	1311	1401	2147	313	602	792	835	535	1722	962	1072	555	413	662	36

E03C: Rugged, tough, independent

	TOTAL	M	F	White	Black	NE	NC	S	W	Yes	No	None	Mari- juana Only	Few Pills	More Pills	Any Her- oin
1. Disagree	52.3	52.2	52.3	52.7	50.3	52.7	52.2	52.0	52.5	55.7	46.7	63.2	48.5	43.3	44.6	39.1
2. Mostly disagree	14.7	15.9	13.9	15.3	11.8	11.9	14.7	15.4	16.9	15.6	13.0	13.7	16.8	17.5	13.8	5.4
3. Neither	21.4	21.2	21.7	21.8	18.8	23.1	22.0	21.1	19.4	19.1	25.6	13.5	22.3	26.0	29.7	33.8
4. Mostly agree	8.2	6.5	9.8	7.8	11.4	8.6	9.2	6.9	8.0	7.4	9.1	6.2	10.1	8.4	9.3	17.4
5. Agree	3.4	4.3	2.3	2.4	7.7	3.6	2.0	4.6	3.1	2.1	5.6	3.4	2.4	4.8	2.6	4.4
Item 20900 Subject A11c N	2753	1306	1396	2137	312	600	792	827	534	1714	959	1069	548	415	660	36

QUESTIONNAIRE FORM 5 1985	TOTAL	SEX		RACE		REGION				4YR COLLEGE PLANS		ILLICIT DRUG USE: LIFETIME				
		M	F	White	Black	NE	NC	S	W	Yes	No	None	Mari- juana Only	Few Pills	More Pills	Any Her- oin
N (Weighted No. of Cases):	3286	1584	1601	2463	410	782	901	997	604	1920	1159	1252	655	479	794	45
% of Weighted Total:	100.0	48.2	48.7	75.0	12.5	23.8	27.4	30.4	18.4	58.4	35.3	38.1	19.9	14.6	24.2	1.4

E03D: Conforming

1. Disagree	28.4	30.0	26.7	26.8	33.6	28.1	29.1	28.1	28.4	25.5	32.3	29.8	28.3	25.2	28.1	34.8
2. Mostly disagree	9.1	9.5	8.8	9.3	11.3	10.1	9.1	9.1	7.8	8.9	9.6	7.9	10.6	9.8	9.6	2.7
3. Neither	38.9	37.7	40.4	39.6	33.1	37.0	42.3	37.9	37.4	37.3	42.5	33.5	39.7	41.5	45.6	35.0
4. Mostly agree	11.8	11.0	12.2	12.0	10.1	11.5	9.6	12.6	13.9	13.5	8.8	12.0	12.1	14.5	9.3	15.2
5. Agree	11.9	11.7	11.9	12.3	11.9	13.2	9.8	12.4	12.4	14.8	6.8	16.8	9.3	9.0	7.5	12.3
Item 20910 Subject A11c N	2721	1295	1374	2113	305	601	782	811	526	1699	942	1053	544	411	651	36

E03E: Mature, sophisticated

1. Disagree	60.2	56.9	63.4	60.8	58.6	56.8	61.7	61.2	60.5	64.4	53.2	72.1	58.4	52.2	49.8	33.5
2. Mostly disagree	13.6	16.2	11.0	14.2	12.9	13.6	13.4	12.9	14.9	14.0	12.8	12.3	14.4	18.5	11.9	11.8
3. Neither	19.9	19.5	20.6	19.8	17.8	22.8	20.2	19.0	17.8	16.9	25.2	10.2	20.8	23.5	31.7	38.6
4. Mostly agree	3.8	3.8	3.6	3.5	4.3	3.6	3.7	3.3	5.0	3.2	4.6	3.0	3.5	3.8	5.0	8.1
5. Agree	2.4	3.6	1.3	1.7	6.4	3.1	1.1	3.7	1.7	1.5	4.2	2.4	2.9	2.0	1.7	7.9
Item 20920 Subject A11c N	2744	1300	1393	2131	309	602	786	824	532	1712	953	1064	548	412	659	36

E03F: Like he's TRYING to appear mature and sophisticated

1. Disagree	13.7	14.2	12.8	11.8	17.3	16.6	13.0	13.0	12.4	10.1	19.0	11.6	13.9	11.3	18.2	15.7
2. Mostly disagree	5.8	6.4	5.2	5.9	5.1	4.8	6.1	5.2	7.3	5.6	6.5	2.9	7.9	7.1	7.9	5.9
3. Neither	18.1	18.1	18.2	19.0	12.8	22.9	18.2	15.8	16.5	16.2	21.6	10.9	17.6	21.6	27.4	35.4
4. Mostly agree	19.8	19.5	20.5	20.8	17.2	19.1	20.1	19.8	20.3	21.1	17.8	20.9	21.4	19.3	16.9	16.9
5. Agree	42.6	41.8	43.4	42.5	47.6	36.7	42.6	46.2	43.5	47.1	35.1	53.8	39.2	40.8	29.5	26.1
Item 20930 Subject A11c N	2761	1313	1397	2144	311	599	791	835	537	1721	958	1071	555	419	658	34

E04: In my opinion, when a girl my age is smoking a cigarette, it makes her look . . .

E04A: Cool, calm, in-control

1. Disagree	68.4	69.0	67.9	68.5	65.6	62.8	68.1	69.9	72.4	73.0	60.7	79.5	67.4	62.9	56.8	39.0
2. Mostly disagree	9.8	9.9	9.9	10.3	8.7	9.7	11.2	9.1	8.9	9.8	9.4	8.7	12.0	10.0	9.5	10.3
3. Neither	16.6	16.0	17.1	16.7	15.5	20.8	16.0	16.1	13.7	13.5	22.0	7.8	16.7	21.3	27.0	25.7
4. Mostly agree	3.3	2.8	3.7	2.9	4.8	4.0	3.2	2.6	3.6	2.5	4.7	1.8	1.7	4.0	5.5	16.9
5. Agree	2.0	2.3	1.5	1.5	5.4	2.6	1.6	2.3	1.3	1.2	3.2	2.1	2.1	1.8	1.2	8.0
Item 20940 Subject A11c N	2717	1279	1388	2109	308	587	776	821	532	1707	930	1054	546	411	647	35

E04B: Insecure

1. Disagree	16.4	18.4	14.7	14.2	21.9	20.2	13.6	15.6	17.7	13.1	22.7	12.9	17.0	15.0	21.9	26.3
2. Mostly disagree	7.2	6.3	8.1	7.3	8.0	6.6	8.0	7.6	6.1	5.9	9.7	5.1	7.8	7.3	9.7	8.9
3. Neither	26.1	25.4	26.1	26.8	22.0	29.9	27.9	24.3	21.8	24.2	29.2	20.1	27.9	30.0	31.7	26.8
4. Mostly agree	19.4	18.1	20.7	20.5	15.6	18.5	19.3	20.4	18.8	20.8	16.7	19.6	20.0	24.3	15.2	24.1
5. Agree	30.9	31.8	30.5	31.1	32.6	24.7	31.2	32.0	35.6	36.1	21.7	42.3	27.4	23.4	21.4	13.9
Item 20950 Subject A11c N	2722	1281	1392	2114	308	588	778	823	534	1707	934	1054	549	410	650	35

E04C: Independent and liberated

1. Disagree	55.8	55.0	56.5	56.1	56.9	51.5	55.8	58.0	57.1	59.6	49.5	67.8	53.4	45.7	45.9	34.3
2. Mostly disagree	13.9	15.4	12.9	14.8	9.5	13.9	14.2	14.0	13.5	14.5	12.8	11.1	16.3	13.7	8.9	8.9
3. Neither	20.5	19.8	21.1	20.4	20.2	23.6	21.5	18.4	19.1	18.1	24.9	12.4	20.9	25.5	29.4	28.9
4. Mostly agree	6.6	6.0	7.0	6.1	7.2	8.0	6.7	5.4	6.7	5.5	8.7	5.3	5.9	7.9	7.6	19.8
5. Agree	3.2	3.8	2.4	2.6	6.2	3.0	1.9	4.2	3.7	2.4	4.1	3.3	2.8	2.6	3.4	8.0
Item 20960 Subject A11c N	2707	1270	1388	2103	305	583	777	816	532	1699	929	1051	542	409	647	35

E04D: Conforming

1. Disagree	33.0	36.0	30.2	30.6	41.7	33.4	32.1	34.0	32.3	30.0	38.5	33.2	34.7	30.3	33.0	31.2
2. Mostly disagree	8.6	9.5	7.9	8.4	11.8	9.2	9.2	8.3	7.4	7.2	10.7	7.1	9.2	9.3	9.8	5.7
3. Neither	34.9	31.6	38.0	36.3	27.0	32.8	38.7	34.1	33.1	33.8	37.8	31.4	33.1	37.7	40.7	37.9
4. Mostly agree	9.9	9.4	10.4	10.2	9.1	12.0	8.5	9.5	10.3	11.9	6.2	9.9	10.5	12.8	7.4	15.0
5. Agree	13.5	13.5	13.6	14.4	10.3	12.5	11.5	14.1	16.9	17.1	6.9	18.5	12.5	9.9	9.1	10.2
Item 20970 Subject A11c N	2687	1268	1369	2087	304	585	771	809	521	1694	914	1036	542	406	643	35

	TOTAL	SEX		RACE		REGION				4YR COLLEGE PLANS		ILLICIT DRUG USE: LIFETIME				
QUESTIONNAIRE FORM 5 **1985**		M	F	White	Black	NE	NC	S	W	Yes	No	None	Mari- juana Only	Few Pills	More Pills	Any Her- oin
N (Weighted No. of Cases):	3286	1584	1601	2463	410	782	901	997	604	1920	1159	1252	655	479	794	45
% of Weighted Total:	100.0	48.2	48.7	75.0	12.5	23.8	27.4	30.4	18.4	58.4	35.3	38.1	19.9	14.6	24.2	1.4
E04E: Mature, sophisticated																
1. Disagree	64.6	63.8	65.5	65.3	63.0	58.3	65.3	66.3	67.9	68.3	58.8	75.7	66.3	57.0	52.2	37.0
2. Mostly disagree	11.7	12.4	11.0	12.3	9.3	12.2	11.5	11.2	12.1	11.6	11.1	9.7	12.2	14.2	13.1	10.5
3. Neither	17.2	16.5	18.0	17.3	13.0	22.4	17.4	15.6	13.7	15.0	21.2	9.1	15.3	21.2	28.0	33.4
4. Mostly agree	4.3	4.6	3.8	3.7	8.4	5.3	4.3	3.9	3.9	3.6	5.8	3.4	4.7	5.3	4.3	10.7
5. Agree	2.2	2.7	1.7	1.5	6.3	1.8	1.5	3.0	2.4	1.6	3.1	2.1	1.6	2.4	2.4	8.3
Item 20980 Subject A11c N	2706	1273	1385	2100	307	580	776	820	530	1702	925	1048	542	408	650	34
E04F: Like she's TRYING to appear mature and sophisticated																
1. Disagree	15.0	15.8	14.0	12.4	21.0	16.5	14.4	14.8	14.4	10.8	22.1	12.8	16.2	13.5	18.7	10.2
2. Mostly disagree	5.3	5.7	4.9	5.4	4.7	5.1	4.4	5.2	6.8	4.6	6.4	2.6	5.3	7.7	7.5	7.3
3. Neither	15.5	15.4	15.2	16.0	10.2	19.4	16.0	13.9	13.0	13.2	19.8	9.2	14.7	16.2	24.2	40.7
4. Mostly agree	18.3	17.2	19.5	19.5	15.7	18.6	18.5	18.0	18.1	19.2	16.7	18.7	17.4	21.3	16.8	13.2
5. Agree	46.0	45.8	46.4	46.7	48.4	40.4	46.7	48.1	47.6	52.1	35.0	56.7	46.3	41.3	32.8	28.6
Item 20990 Subject A11c N	2712	1276	1386	2104	305	574	779	821	537	1706	924	1054	547	410	643	35
E05: Do you agree or disagree..																
E05A: Smokers know how to enjoy life more than nonsmokers																
1. Disagree	74.7	72.4	77.0	75.1	73.5	72.0	76.6	74.5	75.1	78.4	68.4	83.1	74.6	72.1	63.9	58.2
2. Mostly disagree	9.1	9.5	8.6	9.2	9.4	9.5	8.3	10.2	8.2	8.2	10.6	7.1	10.6	10.6	10.1	7.4
3. Neither	13.2	13.9	12.4	13.3	11.6	16.0	12.5	12.3	12.4	10.9	17.4	8.3	12.3	12.3	21.5	32.9
4. Mostly agree	1.4	1.7	1.1	1.2	2.6	1.4	1.6	1.3	1.3	1.4	1.5	0.1	1.4	3.1	2.6	-
5. Agree	1.6	2.5	0.9	1.2	2.9	1.1	1.0	1.8	2.9	1.1	2.2	1.5	1.2	1.9	2.0	1.5
Item 21000 Subject A11c N	2753	1305	1397	2135	314	591	783	840	539	1721	950	1072	552	417	651	36
E05B: I prefer to date people who don't smoke																
1. Disagree	9.8	8.7	10.6	9.3	12.0	12.4	9.8	8.8	8.5	6.4	15.4	5.1	10.1	8.6	17.0	20.5
2. Mostly disagree	3.4	2.7	4.0	3.6	3.0	3.2	4.3	3.3	2.4	2.6	5.0	1.0	3.0	3.5	7.2	11.1
3. Neither	17.4	16.1	18.4	17.7	12.5	20.4	17.8	15.1	16.9	13.3	24.5	10.2	17.7	16.4	28.4	34.6
4. Mostly agree	10.6	11.2	10.0	11.0	10.3	11.2	10.5	11.0	9.6	10.8	9.7	10.1	10.6	13.6	10.2	4.7
5. Agree	58.8	61.3	57.0	58.4	62.1	52.8	57.5	61.8	62.7	66.8	45.4	73.7	58.6	58.0	37.1	29.1
Item 21010 Subject A11c N	2751	1305	1396	2135	314	591	784	839	538	1720	948	1074	553	413	650	35
E05C: The harmful effects of cigarettes have been exaggerated																
1. Disagree	51.2	49.6	53.0	53.3	45.7	52.6	52.5	48.1	52.4	56.5	41.7	61.1	49.7	46.2	40.2	41.7
2. Mostly disagree	18.4	18.3	18.5	19.6	10.5	18.6	18.1	19.9	16.4	19.1	17.4	15.0	21.3	20.5	20.5	20.4
3. Neither	15.3	16.4	14.2	14.7	16.9	16.4	16.3	13.8	15.1	12.4	20.6	11.2	16.0	19.6	18.5	15.8
4. Mostly agree	8.3	8.3	8.2	8.2	9.3	8.2	7.2	9.6	8.0	6.9	10.9	5.5	8.1	7.9	13.1	10.7
5. Agree	6.8	7.3	6.2	4.2	17.6	4.1	5.9	8.6	8.2	5.1	9.4	7.2	4.9	5.8	7.7	11.4
Item 21020 Subject A11c N	2741	1299	1392	2128	313	589	781	833	538	1716	944	1070	548	416	647	35
E05D: I think that becoming a smoker reflects poor judgment																
1. Disagree	13.2	12.9	12.9	12.0	18.1	14.8	13.1	13.6	10.8	9.1	20.8	8.7	11.7	12.3	21.1	22.6
2. Mostly disagree	8.5	8.6	8.7	8.8	6.4	10.4	8.4	6.8	9.3	8.1	9.3	4.7	9.4	10.9	12.1	19.0
3. Neither	21.7	19.8	23.4	21.8	20.6	23.3	23.4	19.1	21.6	19.6	25.4	18.4	22.3	24.1	24.4	35.3
4. Mostly agree	16.4	15.8	16.9	17.1	15.1	15.0	16.4	17.2	16.7	17.2	14.6	17.1	17.2	16.1	15.9	4.4
5. Agree	40.2	43.0	38.1	40.4	39.9	36.5	38.7	43.3	41.6	46.1	29.9	51.1	39.4	36.6	26.6	18.7
Item 21030 Subject A11c N	2748	1304	1394	2136	312	591	782	837	538	1717	950	1071	552	416	649	36
E05E: I personally don't mind being around people who are smoking																
1. Disagree	36.1	36.5	35.8	35.1	40.6	31.7	35.1	37.7	39.7	40.5	28.9	49.5	30.9	30.0	24.2	13.6
2. Mostly disagree	14.9	14.8	15.1	15.6	13.4	16.1	15.6	14.0	14.2	17.7	10.3	16.5	17.4	16.0	10.3	7.4
3. Neither	14.1	16.9	11.2	14.4	11.2	14.3	15.8	13.1	12.8	12.9	16.0	13.0	14.4	13.4	14.8	21.8
4. Mostly agree	16.2	15.3	17.2	16.4	17.6	16.6	15.2	15.6	18.0	15.8	16.6	12.2	19.1	17.6	18.7	24.7
5. Agree	18.7	16.4	20.7	18.5	17.1	21.2	18.3	19.6	15.3	13.0	28.2	8.8	18.2	23.1	31.8	32.4
Item 21040 Subject A11c N	2749	1302	1396	2133	313	587	783	837	541	1715	950	1071	555	413	648	36

QUESTIONNAIRE FORM 5 1985	TOTAL	SEX		RACE		REGION				4YR COLLEGE PLANS		ILLICIT DRUG USE: LIFETIME				
		M	F	White	Black	NE	NC	S	W	Yes	No	None	Mari-juana Only	Few Pills	More Pills	Any Her-oin
N (Weighted No. of Cases):	3286	1584	1601	2463	410	782	901	997	604	1920	1159	1252	655	479	794	45
% of Weighted Total:	100.0	48.2	48.7	75.0	12.5	23.8	27.4	30.4	18.4	58.4	35.3	38.1	19.9	14.6	24.2	1.4
E05F: Smoking is a dirty habit																
1. Disagree	10.2	9.9	10.3	9.6	14.8	12.7	9.2	11.0	7.8	7.2	15.8	7.4	10.1	8.3	15.0	26.7
2. Mostly disagree	5.9	4.9	7.0	5.8	6.3	3.7	6.2	5.8	7.9	5.1	7.4	3.0	6.2	9.5	8.0	5.3
3. Neither	16.6	17.7	15.5	16.4	16.1	19.0	19.2	14.0	14.1	13.9	21.2	12.3	19.7	18.0	19.9	20.2
4. Mostly agree	15.5	15.2	15.8	15.9	12.8	16.0	15.4	14.7	16.5	17.4	11.8	14.6	15.7	15.9	16.5	23.1
5. Agree	51.8	52.3	51.4	52.2	49.9	48.6	50.0	54.5	53.7	56.3	43.8	62.7	48.2	48.3	40.6	24.7
Item 21050 Subject A11c N	2743	1300	1393	2128	314	586	781	838	538	1714	947	1071	553	412	646	36
E06: The next questions ask how you feel about the amount of supervision that you received from your parents (or guardians) during your high school years. For each of the following areas, do you feel that you received about the right amount of supervision, too little, or too much?																
E06A: What kinds of parties, dances or other events you could go to																
1. Far too little supervision	11.0	13.2	8.8	9.2	15.9	11.9	10.8	9.1	13.2	8.9	14.7	7.7	9.1	9.4	17.2	35.0
2. Too little	7.5	8.7	6.4	6.2	11.5	6.7	6.6	8.7	7.8	6.4	8.9	5.9	8.4	7.2	9.9	1.5
3. About right	65.4	62.5	68.1	68.0	56.5	62.4	65.8	67.2	65.2	69.4	59.1	72.6	67.7	64.9	53.4	50.9
4. Too much supervision	11.1	10.1	12.0	11.7	9.5	12.5	12.0	10.0	10.1	11.4	10.5	10.5	9.6	11.9	13.3	1.0
5. Far too much	5.0	5.4	4.7	4.9	6.6	6.5	4.8	5.1	3.7	3.9	6.8	3.4	5.3	6.6	6.3	11.6
Item 21800 Subject M03 N	2767	1316	1397	2144	312	585	789	849	543	1718	960	1077	555	419	649	38
E06B: How late you stayed out on dates																
1. Far too little supervision	6.6	8.4	4.7	5.2	11.7	8.6	5.8	5.7	6.9	5.4	8.6	4.7	5.1	6.0	9.4	35.7
2. Too little	7.0	8.1	5.9	6.5	7.7	6.0	8.1	6.8	6.4	6.2	7.6	5.9	6.7	6.2	8.6	10.3
3. About right	59.6	59.8	59.5	60.8	57.0	59.0	57.8	61.6	60.0	61.7	56.4	64.2	63.2	56.8	53.1	30.9
4. Too much supervision	18.1	14.1	21.9	19.1	13.7	18.3	19.3	16.0	19.4	19.6	16.1	18.3	16.2	19.1	19.1	10.2
5. Far too much	8.7	9.6	7.9	8.4	10.0	8.1	9.0	9.8	7.2	7.2	11.3	6.8	8.8	11.8	9.7	12.9
Item 21810 Subject M03 N	2757	1311	1394	2138	314	583	790	845	539	1714	954	1070	556	418	649	37
E06C: The way you dressed																
1. Far too little supervision	5.6	7.7	3.5	4.8	9.8	5.4	4.4	6.2	6.6	4.9	6.4	4.3	4.4	5.5	7.8	25.6
2. Too little	4.4	5.2	3.8	3.4	7.0	4.7	4.1	5.1	3.5	3.8	5.6	3.4	4.8	4.1	5.7	7.9
3. About right	79.7	75.8	83.4	81.1	74.2	79.3	80.9	79.4	78.8	81.0	77.6	82.9	84.0	78.8	73.2	50.1
4. Too much supervision	6.8	6.7	6.8	7.3	4.6	7.3	6.5	6.2	7.5	7.5	5.6	7.0	3.9	7.2	8.5	7.6
5. Far too much	3.5	4.6	2.6	3.4	4.5	3.4	4.0	3.1	3.5	2.7	4.8	2.5	3.0	4.5	4.9	8.9
Item 21820 Subject M03 N	2757	1310	1393	2136	311	583	788	845	540	1711	957	1077	550	417	647	37
E06D: What you did with your money																
1. Far too little supervision	5.2	6.8	3.5	4.4	8.1	5.9	5.1	4.8	5.5	4.4	6.6	3.4	4.0	5.2	8.8	16.0
2. Too little	11.1	11.5	10.8	11.1	9.5	10.5	12.5	10.2	11.0	11.4	10.3	9.4	12.0	10.1	13.5	11.7
3. About right	61.9	61.1	62.9	63.3	60.1	59.0	62.5	64.4	60.4	63.8	58.6	69.2	63.7	60.6	50.3	38.2
4. Too much supervision	15.7	13.9	17.4	15.5	15.3	16.7	14.2	15.4	17.5	15.7	16.4	14.1	14.4	17.1	18.6	22.5
5. Far too much	6.0	6.8	5.4	5.7	7.1	7.8	5.7	5.3	5.6	4.7	8.1	4.0	5.9	6.9	8.8	11.6
Item 21830 Subject M03 N	2750	1306	1393	2135	307	581	788	843	538	1708	956	1077	549	418	643	37
E06E: How often you went out in the evening																
1. Far too little supervision	5.1	6.4	3.8	4.1	9.7	6.7	4.4	4.6	5.2	3.6	7.8	3.3	4.3	3.6	8.5	19.8
2. Too little	6.7	7.9	5.7	5.6	10.3	7.8	5.6	6.5	7.6	5.6	8.0	5.4	5.5	7.5	8.4	23.1
3. About right	60.1	60.0	60.4	62.1	55.2	59.9	59.8	62.5	56.8	62.6	56.1	68.2	63.5	52.7	50.7	27.5
4. Too much supervision	19.9	18.7	20.9	20.4	17.2	16.4	21.4	18.2	23.9	20.6	18.7	16.7	18.9	25.6	22.5	14.1
5. Far too much	8.2	7.1	9.3	7.7	7.6	9.2	8.9	8.1	6.5	7.6	9.4	6.4	7.7	10.6	10.0	15.5
Item 21840 Subject M03 N	2745	1306	1387	2132	307	578	788	841	538	1708	953	1072	550	416	643	37
E06F: How much time you spent on homework																
1. Far too little supervision	8.2	9.6	6.6	8.2	8.4	7.7	8.7	7.6	9.0	7.1	10.2	5.0	6.6	8.1	14.6	20.1
2. Too little	18.9	20.8	17.3	19.2	18.8	18.8	18.4	17.2	22.3	18.3	20.3	17.8	20.4	17.5	20.8	19.5
3. About right	55.9	51.5	60.0	56.5	50.4	52.9	59.4	57.0	52.1	57.8	52.2	61.5	56.2	53.7	48.2	39.5
4. Too much supervision	11.1	12.0	10.6	10.4	15.2	13.0	8.5	11.5	12.4	11.8	9.9	11.2	10.2	13.6	10.1	8.8
5. Far too much	5.9	6.1	5.5	5.6	7.2	7.6	4.9	6.7	4.2	5.0	7.4	4.5	6.5	7.2	6.3	12.2
Item 21850 Subject M03 N	2743	1303	1389	2134	308	579	787	839	538	1705	953	1072	550	415	642	36

	TOTAL	SEX		RACE		REGION				4YR COLLEGE PLANS		ILLICIT DRUG USE: LIFETIME				
QUESTIONNAIRE FORM 5 **1985**		M	F	White	Black	NE	NC	S	W	Yes	No	None	Mari- juana Only	Few Pills	More Pills	Any Her- oin
N (Weighted No. of Cases):	3286	1584	1601	2463	410	782	901	997	604	1920	1159	1252	655	479	794	45
% of Weighted Total:	100.0	48.2	48.7	75.0	12.5	23.8	27.4	30.4	18.4	58.4	35.3	38.1	19.9	14.6	24.2	1.4
E06G: What courses you took in school																
1. Far too little supervision	6.4	7.0	5.8	6.0	7.5	5.9	6.1	6.9	6.8	5.2	8.4	4.9	3.8	4.9	11.8	16.8
2. Too little	11.5	10.3	12.4	10.8	14.2	10.9	12.5	9.4	14.0	11.3	11.2	8.3	11.8	14.5	14.5	17.6
3. About right	70.4	69.6	71.3	72.3	63.6	70.3	72.1	71.1	67.1	71.6	68.7	75.9	72.1	71.2	61.3	33.5
4. Too much supervision	7.5	8.0	7.3	7.1	10.8	6.7	6.1	8.7	8.8	8.2	6.8	8.0	7.6	5.0	8.1	10.2
5. Far too much	4.1	5.1	3.2	3.8	3.9	6.3	3.2	3.9	3.3	3.7	4.9	2.9	4.8	4.4	4.3	21.9
Item 21860 Subject M03 N	2743	1304	1388	2134	305	576	787	839	540	1705	953	1069	551	416	644	36
E06H: The hours you could work during the school year																
1. Far too little supervision	5.6	6.7	4.4	4.7	8.8	4.7	5.4	6.0	6.4	4.3	7.9	3.5	4.4	4.8	9.2	31.3
2. Too little	8.4	9.0	7.6	7.5	10.8	10.5	7.0	8.3	8.3	7.5	9.8	7.6	8.6	6.3	10.9	2.9
3. About right	73.0	69.8	76.6	75.0	66.5	71.5	75.8	72.7	71.0	74.6	70.5	77.7	75.6	72.2	65.9	40.1
4. Too much supervision	8.5	8.5	8.4	8.4	10.1	9.0	7.5	8.4	9.6	10.0	6.1	8.0	6.9	10.4	9.3	7.4
5. Far too much	4.5	6.0	3.1	4.4	3.8	4.3	4.3	4.7	4.6	3.6	5.8	3.2	4.5	6.3	4.7	18.3
Item 21870 Subject M03 N	2711	1291	1370	2109	302	577	773	829	532	1683	945	1052	548	407	641	37
E06I: How much TV you watched																
1. Far too little supervision	9.5	10.0	8.8	8.1	13.9	11.4	8.5	8.6	10.4	7.9	12.0	7.1	7.8	11.1	12.9	28.2
2. Too little	12.7	13.9	11.0	12.0	17.4	12.3	12.8	13.4	11.8	12.5	12.7	11.6	14.1	12.0	13.2	14.0
3. About right	66.9	63.5	70.8	70.6	50.7	65.4	68.0	67.7	65.6	68.8	64.2	70.0	67.9	65.6	64.2	38.6
4. Too much supervision	6.6	6.6	6.6	5.6	10.7	6.3	6.6	5.9	8.0	7.3	5.6	7.5	5.6	8.0	4.7	6.3
5. Far too much	4.3	5.9	2.8	3.6	7.3	4.6	4.2	4.3	4.2	3.5	5.5	3.7	4.6	3.3	5.0	12.9
Item 21880 Subject M03 N	2732	1298	1382	2126	304	576	786	832	538	1700	948	1064	550	416	640	36
E06J: What kinds of TV programs you watched																
1. Far too little supervision	11.2	12.7	9.3	9.3	17.4	13.1	8.7	11.6	12.2	9.1	14.6	8.5	10.6	10.8	14.9	38.4
2. Too little	8.0	7.8	8.3	7.0	14.8	7.4	8.3	8.7	7.2	7.7	8.3	7.0	8.1	8.5	9.3	5.7
3. About right	71.5	69.0	74.5	74.7	58.9	70.9	74.5	70.1	70.1	74.4	67.3	73.5	73.1	71.2	69.0	42.3
4. Too much supervision	5.7	6.3	5.2	5.5	4.7	5.7	5.7	5.7	5.9	5.9	5.4	7.4	4.7	6.4	3.2	6.7
5. Far too much	3.5	4.2	2.8	3.5	4.3	2.9	2.8	4.0	4.5	2.9	4.4	3.6	3.4	3.0	3.5	6.9
Item 21890 Subject M03 N	2730	1298	1380	2126	303	576	786	833	536	1699	947	1062	550	414	641	37
E07: Over the LAST 12 MONTHS, about how often have you gone to parties?																
1. Not at all–GO TO Q.9	13.8	13.9	13.2	11.6	20.8	13.1	11.7	16.2	13.8	11.9	17.0	22.9	9.7	9.8	4.8	5.2
2. Once a month or less	34.1	30.1	38.4	35.4	27.6	30.5	33.6	37.5	33.4	34.5	33.6	44.4	30.8	30.3	23.5	19.5
3. 2 or 3 times a month	25.9	26.3	25.5	26.0	27.0	26.0	27.6	25.7	23.5	28.7	20.8	20.8	29.3	29.3	30.0	9.8
4. About once a week	15.2	16.2	14.2	15.5	13.9	15.3	16.5	12.5	17.3	15.3	15.4	8.9	18.8	19.2	19.3	29.5
5. 2 or 3 times a week	8.1	9.8	6.6	8.7	6.3	9.6	8.1	5.8	10.2	7.4	9.1	1.6	9.2	8.7	16.7	17.9
6. Over 3 times a week	2.9	3.8	2.0	2.8	4.4	5.5	2.5	2.3	1.8	2.2	4.1	1.4	2.2	2.7	5.7	18.1
Item 21900 Subject C07 N	2654	1242	1367	2081	288	561	755	811	526	1661	918	1033	538	406	622	32
E08: Now think about the parties you went to in the last 12 months. How often...																
E08A: Were people over age 30 present at least some of the time?																
1. Never	39.3	38.5	40.2	38.6	45.0	40.0	40.5	37.6	39.1	38.4	41.6	39.0	42.7	41.2	35.6	37.8
2. Seldom	29.6	31.9	27.4	31.7	18.8	29.0	31.4	27.9	30.3	31.5	26.1	26.6	30.9	32.0	31.8	33.0
3. Sometimes	19.8	19.3	20.2	19.2	22.2	20.2	18.5	20.9	19.5	18.7	21.8	19.5	17.6	17.8	23.2	15.0
4. Most times	7.0	6.0	7.7	6.7	6.6	7.9	5.9	6.8	7.9	7.6	5.7	8.7	5.2	6.0	6.4	7.7
5. Always	4.4	4.2	4.5	3.9	7.5	2.9	3.7	6.8	3.3	3.9	4.8	6.2	3.6	2.9	3.1	6.5
Item 21910 Subject C07,M02 N★	2364	1123	1201	1885	242	503	696	702	463	1498	790	833	493	373	609	34
E08B: Did someone get high on alcohol?																
1. Never	10.3	8.7	11.7	8.6	15.6	6.4	11.5	12.2	9.6	10.3	10.3	20.6	3.5	5.2	4.5	9.4
2. Seldom	4.9	4.7	4.9	4.1	8.5	4.2	4.2	6.0	5.1	5.4	3.9	9.4	3.1	3.4	1.2	7.6
3. Sometimes	14.3	12.2	16.2	13.3	18.2	14.6	12.8	17.1	12.1	13.9	15.1	18.4	13.0	12.5	11.0	15.2
4. Most times	25.5	24.7	26.0	27.4	21.2	28.0	28.9	24.1	20.1	25.2	26.3	22.7	31.0	29.5	23.0	5.7
5. Always	45.0	49.7	41.2	46.5	36.4	46.8	42.7	40.7	53.1	45.2	44.4	28.9	49.4	49.3	60.2	62.1
Item 21920 Subject A02b,C07 N★	2366	1127	1199	1883	244	502	697	703	464	1497	791	831	491	376	612	35

★=excludes respondents for whom question was inappropriate.

QUESTIONNAIRE FORM 5 1985	TOTAL	SEX		RACE		REGION				4YR COLLEGE PLANS		ILLICIT DRUG USE: LIFETIME				
		M	F	White	Black	NE	NC	S	W	Yes	No	None	Mari-juana Only	Few Pills	More Pills	Any Her-oin
N (Weighted No. of Cases):	3286	1584	1601	2463	410	782	901	997	604	1920	1159	1252	655	479	794	45
% of Weighted Total:	100.0	48.2	48.7	75.0	12.5	23.8	27.4	30.4	18.4	58.4	35.3	38.1	19.9	14.6	24.2	1.4
E08C: Did most people get high on alcohol?																
1. Never	13.0	10.9	15.0	11.2	18.4	8.8	13.0	15.2	14.1	13.8	11.6	26.1	4.6	8.1	5.2	9.4
2. Seldom	8.1	6.8	9.0	7.3	13.2	7.6	6.9	11.1	6.2	8.8	7.4	13.2	6.2	6.6	4.0	4.4
3. Sometimes	19.5	19.9	19.0	19.2	24.4	20.4	20.7	22.3	12.4	20.3	17.9	22.8	21.7	19.8	13.5	13.1
4. Most times	31.3	31.0	31.7	34.2	19.0	33.2	34.6	27.6	30.0	31.3	31.9	22.6	38.8	39.0	33.2	16.8
5. Always	28.1	31.3	25.2	28.2	25.0	30.0	24.9	23.8	37.4	25.8	31.2	15.3	28.8	26.5	44.1	56.4
Item 21930 Subject A02b,C07 N★	2361	1126	1196	1881	243	501	697	700	463	1496	788	829	492	373	611	35
E08D: Did you get high on alcohol?																
1. Never	28.2	23.3	32.8	23.5	53.8	21.7	28.2	34.1	26.5	31.2	23.4	55.4	15.8	15.4	9.7	16.8
2. Seldom	12.8	10.5	14.8	13.0	13.2	9.4	12.7	16.0	11.7	12.9	12.7	14.5	15.9	15.6	6.2	7.8
3. Sometimes	25.5	25.1	26.0	27.5	16.9	25.0	28.5	26.0	21.1	25.1	25.8	18.8	30.8	28.7	29.7	13.2
4. Most times	20.0	22.6	17.6	21.9	9.5	25.9	19.6	14.7	22.0	20.3	20.1	7.7	25.0	28.6	27.5	16.8
5. Always	13.5	18.4	8.8	14.1	6.6	18.0	11.0	9.1	18.8	10.5	18.1	3.6	12.6	11.7	26.9	45.4
Item 21940 Subject A05c,C07 N★	2345	1113	1192	1869	239	497	690	696	462	1486	782	825	484	373	607	35
E08E: Did you feel pressure to drink alcohol?																
1. Never	61.1	52.0	69.5	59.3	65.6	61.2	59.2	62.9	61.1	59.4	64.3	63.0	59.9	58.5	61.3	57.9
2. Seldom	19.2	22.8	16.0	21.0	10.5	20.3	19.5	18.1	19.4	21.1	16.0	17.5	19.4	22.3	20.5	7.1
3. Sometimes	12.7	15.6	9.9	12.9	15.4	13.5	13.7	11.9	11.7	12.3	13.4	12.9	11.3	12.8	13.2	22.3
4. Most times	3.7	5.0	2.6	4.0	3.1	2.8	4.9	3.6	3.1	3.8	3.2	3.0	5.0	4.6	2.9	3.0
5. Always	3.3	4.6	1.9	2.8	5.5	2.2	2.8	3.6	4.8	3.4	3.0	3.6	4.5	1.9	2.2	9.6
Item 21950 Subject A02b,C07 N★	2355	1122	1194	1876	242	497	695	700	463	1489	788	828	491	373	607	34
E08F: Did you feel pressure to drink enough to get high?																
1. Never	69.9	62.6	77.0	69.5	71.1	69.4	68.7	72.2	68.9	69.2	71.6	75.7	66.2	70.8	65.4	62.2
2. Seldom	16.5	18.8	14.6	17.6	11.6	17.5	16.6	15.0	17.4	17.7	14.2	14.0	16.3	17.1	19.8	17.7
3. Sometimes	8.5	10.8	5.9	8.0	9.8	9.2	10.2	7.1	7.2	8.4	8.6	6.8	11.0	8.3	9.1	4.4
4. Most times	2.7	3.9	1.5	2.8	3.5	1.9	2.8	2.8	3.4	2.5	3.0	1.5	3.8	2.3	3.2	8.7
5. Always	2.4	3.8	1.0	2.0	4.1	2.1	1.7	2.9	3.1	2.3	2.6	2.0	2.8	1.6	2.6	7.0
Item 21960 Subject A02b,C07 N★	2358	1124	1196	1880	242	497	696	701	464	1494	787	828	493	373	609	35
E08G: Did someone get high on marijuana?																
1. Never	31.3	29.7	32.9	31.7	23.6	23.2	33.6	36.9	28.2	32.0	31.2	57.7	18.2	22.6	13.1	6.4
2. Seldom	13.2	12.5	13.4	13.8	12.2	14.7	14.3	12.6	10.5	14.3	11.5	16.0	13.7	17.2	6.2	10.9
3. Sometimes	22.4	23.8	21.2	22.9	20.3	24.5	23.1	21.2	21.2	24.3	19.3	14.7	30.4	28.6	23.6	12.9
4. Most times	16.0	15.8	16.0	16.1	18.2	18.5	14.7	14.9	16.8	15.2	16.3	5.5	21.8	17.8	24.1	16.5
5. Always	17.1	18.2	16.5	15.5	25.7	19.1	14.4	14.2	23.4	14.2	21.7	6.0	15.9	13.8	33.1	53.3
Item 21970 Subject A02b,C07 N★	2349	1120	1192	1873	240	497	691	696	465	1490	784	823	491	372	608	35
E08H: Did most people get high on marijuana?																
1. Never	39.4	38.2	40.7	41.2	24.1	32.9	42.0	46.0	32.3	42.9	34.5	67.4	27.9	33.1	16.6	6.4
2. Seldom	19.9	20.1	19.6	20.5	15.2	19.6	20.1	18.9	21.3	23.2	14.3	16.6	25.3	25.4	17.1	12.4
3. Sometimes	19.0	19.1	18.7	19.1	20.9	19.3	17.5	17.6	22.9	17.3	21.5	9.6	25.1	21.0	24.9	29.0
4. Most times	10.7	10.5	10.7	10.2	17.0	14.3	12.1	8.6	8.0	8.9	13.4	3.0	11.6	12.4	19.2	14.1
5. Always	11.1	12.1	10.3	8.9	22.8	14.0	8.4	8.8	15.5	7.7	16.3	3.5	10.0	8.2	22.2	38.1
Item 21980 Subject A02b,C07 N★	2354	1121	1193	1876	240	499	693	698	465	1491	785	823	492	374	608	35
E08I: Did you get high on marijuana?																
1. Never	62.2	59.9	64.8	61.8	67.1	51.0	63.2	71.8	58.4	66.1	55.9	98.2	52.7	56.2	26.5	21.8
2. Seldom	15.4	14.8	15.7	16.4	12.6	19.5	16.8	10.9	15.9	15.3	15.0	0.7	26.9	25.4	21.0	6.7
3. Sometimes	9.8	9.4	10.1	9.7	7.6	11.0	9.3	9.0	10.4	9.4	10.8	0.8	11.6	10.0	19.5	22.6
4. Most times	6.2	6.8	5.8	6.1	6.7	8.3	6.0	4.5	6.8	4.6	8.9	-	5.3	5.7	14.9	21.3
5. Always	6.4	9.2	3.6	6.0	6.1	10.3	4.7	3.8	8.6	4.6	9.4	0.3	3.4	2.7	18.2	27.6
Item 21990 Subject A05c,C07 N★	2356	1124	1193	1876	243	495	698	698	465	1494	785	829	491	372	607	35

★=excludes respondents for whom question was inappropriate.

QUESTIONNAIRE FORM 5 1985	TOTAL	SEX		RACE		REGION				4YR COLLEGE PLANS		ILLICIT DRUG USE: LIFETIME				
		M	F	White	Black	NE	NC	S	W	Yes	No	None	Mari-juana Only	Few Pills	More Pills	Any Her-oin
N (Weighted No. of Cases):	3286	1584	1601	2463	410	782	901	997	604	1920	1159	1252	655	479	794	45
% of Weighted Total:	100.0	48.2	48.7	75.0	12.5	23.8	27.4	30.4	18.4	58.4	35.3	38.1	19.9	14.6	24.2	1.4

E08J: Did you feel pressure to use marijuana?

	TOTAL	M	F	White	Black	NE	NC	S	W	Yes	No	None	MJ Only	Few Pills	More Pills	Heroin
1. Never	82.6	78.7	86.5	83.6	75.9	81.0	82.3	86.0	79.8	83.7	81.0	91.8	77.9	80.9	75.3	72.9
2. Seldom	9.6	11.7	7.7	9.7	6.9	11.4	10.1	6.5	11.4	9.5	9.2	3.6	13.0	10.3	14.1	18.9
3. Sometimes	4.9	5.8	3.9	4.2	11.1	4.8	5.0	4.3	5.7	4.5	6.0	2.1	5.1	6.7	7.5	3.0
4. Most times	1.3	1.7	0.8	1.1	3.0	1.0	1.8	1.1	1.2	1.1	1.4	1.6	1.0	1.1	1.5	-
5. Always	1.6	2.1	1.1	1.4	3.1	1.8	0.8	2.0	1.9	1.3	2.4	0.9	3.0	0.9	1.6	5.1
Item 22000 Subject A02b,C07 N★	2353	1122	1193	1874	243	494	698	697	464	1492	785	827	491	371	607	35

E08K: Did someone get high on other drugs?

	TOTAL	M	F	White	Black	NE	NC	S	W	Yes	No	None	MJ Only	Few Pills	More Pills	Heroin
1. Never	52.9	52.4	53.2	53.8	53.8	51.0	57.1	56.9	42.6	53.2	52.8	72.2	51.7	55.2	27.7	19.1
2. Seldom	18.3	18.3	18.1	19.2	14.0	17.3	19.2	18.8	17.2	20.5	13.7	15.3	19.2	17.3	21.7	23.7
3. Sometimes	19.0	19.2	18.9	18.2	19.2	20.2	16.9	16.3	24.6	18.0	20.4	9.0	19.7	21.0	30.4	31.6
4. Most times	4.8	4.0	5.8	4.6	5.8	6.1	3.8	3.5	7.0	4.0	6.8	2.2	4.5	4.6	9.0	4.6
5. Always	5.0	6.1	4.0	4.2	7.1	5.4	2.9	4.4	8.7	4.3	6.3	1.4	4.8	1.9	11.1	20.9
Item 22010 Subject A02b,C07 N★	2338	1112	1187	1861	241	493	692	691	462	1484	778	820	488	369	606	35

E08L: Did most people get high on other drugs?

	TOTAL	M	F	White	Black	NE	NC	S	W	Yes	No	None	MJ Only	Few Pills	More Pills	Heroin
1. Never	58.8	58.5	59.0	60.7	50.4	54.3	64.9	62.9	48.5	61.6	54.5	75.8	60.5	58.8	35.6	33.2
2. Seldom	20.3	19.9	20.7	20.9	16.4	20.9	20.1	18.0	23.3	21.3	17.6	13.8	20.0	23.3	27.4	22.9
3. Sometimes	14.1	13.3	14.8	12.4	21.7	16.7	10.9	13.5	16.9	12.3	17.3	7.5	12.3	13.6	24.3	23.0
4. Most times	3.3	3.5	3.3	3.0	7.4	4.0	2.3	3.1	4.6	2.6	4.8	1.8	3.2	2.7	5.7	10.2
5. Always	3.5	4.8	2.2	3.0	4.1	4.1	1.8	2.5	6.8	2.2	5.7	1.1	4.0	1.6	7.1	10.7
Item 22020 Subject A02b,C07 N★	2324	1101	1186	1852	243	487	688	688	460	1477	772	818	489	365	599	34

E08M: Did you get high on other drugs?

	TOTAL	M	F	White	Black	NE	NC	S	W	Yes	No	None	MJ Only	Few Pills	More Pills	Heroin
1. Never	84.8	82.6	87.1	85.4	85.9	78.6	88.2	88.1	81.2	87.9	79.6	98.2	93.8	91.0	57.9	36.9
2. Seldom	6.0	6.4	5.5	5.7	3.9	6.6	5.7	4.8	7.3	5.1	7.6	0.6	2.2	4.1	17.2	12.7
3. Sometimes	6.3	7.1	5.7	6.0	6.8	10.1	4.7	5.5	6.0	5.4	7.8	0.9	2.3	2.8	17.6	34.7
4. Most times	1.3	1.4	0.8	1.1	2.6	2.3	0.8	0.5	2.0	0.7	2.0	-	0.4	1.4	3.3	6.6
5. Always	1.7	2.5	0.8	1.7	0.9	2.4	0.5	1.1	3.5	0.9	3.0	0.4	1.3	0.7	4.0	9.1
Item 22030 Subject A05c,C07 N★	2331	1102	1191	1859	243	484	694	692	461	1478	778	823	490	365	598	34

E08N: Did you feel pressure to use other drugs?

	TOTAL	M	F	White	Black	NE	NC	S	W	Yes	No	None	MJ Only	Few Pills	More Pills	Heroin
1. Never	90.7	88.3	93.1	91.9	85.2	89.6	91.8	91.8	88.5	91.4	89.3	94.6	92.8	89.4	84.9	76.1
2. Seldom	4.4	5.1	3.7	3.9	6.3	5.0	3.9	3.3	6.0	4.3	4.6	2.3	3.3	4.6	7.8	9.7
3. Sometimes	2.7	3.3	2.2	2.5	4.1	3.7	2.3	2.2	3.2	2.7	2.6	1.2	1.9	4.8	4.3	6.2
4. Most times	1.0	1.2	0.7	0.8	1.0	0.7	1.1	1.3	0.6	0.7	1.7	0.9	0.5	0.6	1.6	2.9
5. Always	1.2	2.1	0.4	0.8	3.4	1.0	0.9	1.4	1.7	0.8	1.8	1.0	1.4	0.6	1.5	5.2
Item 22040 Subject A02b,C07 N★	2327	1099	1190	1858	242	486	692	691	458	1476	776	823	487	366	596	34

E09: Now think about how you would LIKE parties to be. At the parties you go to, how often...

E09A: Would you like people over age 30 to be present at least some of the time?

	TOTAL	M	F	White	Black	NE	NC	S	W	Yes	No	None	MJ Only	Few Pills	More Pills	Heroin
1. Never	42.3	43.3	41.4	40.9	54.3	39.3	43.5	41.7	44.8	42.4	41.7	36.5	49.2	43.6	44.4	49.0
2. Seldom	24.0	25.3	23.1	25.3	17.1	25.5	23.6	25.6	20.8	25.8	21.6	25.4	28.2	23.1	20.0	6.6
3. Sometimes	24.0	22.6	25.4	24.8	16.3	26.6	24.0	22.0	24.3	23.3	25.3	27.3	15.4	23.4	26.9	22.1
4. Most times	6.3	5.8	6.7	6.2	6.6	6.7	5.8	6.5	6.5	5.5	7.2	6.8	5.1	7.5	5.5	8.9
5. Always	3.3	3.0	3.5	2.8	5.7	1.9	3.1	4.3	3.6	2.9	4.2	4.1	2.1	2.4	3.1	13.4
Item 22050 Subject C08,M02 N	2649	1254	1348	2076	289	550	769	806	524	1653	914	1040	530	398	622	36

E09B: Would you like to get high on alcohol?

	TOTAL	M	F	White	Black	NE	NC	S	W	Yes	No	None	MJ Only	Few Pills	More Pills	Heroin
1. Never	36.3	31.7	40.4	31.4	60.7	29.3	34.8	42.8	35.9	37.1	35.4	61.6	24.8	23.2	12.4	24.3
2. Seldom	16.4	15.7	17.0	16.9	14.5	14.9	17.4	17.2	15.3	16.7	15.6	15.5	16.7	21.0	14.8	19.5
3. Sometimes	26.0	25.8	26.5	28.1	16.4	27.6	27.4	25.1	23.9	26.0	25.9	16.1	31.0	31.2	36.1	10.9
4. Most times	12.5	14.4	10.9	14.1	5.0	15.0	13.2	8.9	14.4	13.4	11.6	5.0	19.1	16.5	16.9	14.4
5. Always	8.7	12.5	5.2	9.5	3.4	13.1	7.1	6.0	10.4	6.7	11.5	1.8	8.4	8.0	19.8	30.9
Item 22060 Subject A05c,C08 N	2640	1247	1347	2069	286	547	767	806	520	1645	911	1038	527	400	619	35

★=excludes respondents for whom question was inappropriate.

QUESTIONNAIRE FORM 5 1985	TOTAL	SEX		RACE		REGION				4YR COLLEGE PLANS		ILLICIT DRUG USE: LIFETIME				
		M	F	White	Black	NE	NC	S	W	Yes	No	None	Marijuana Only	Few Pills	More Pills	Any Heroin
N (Weighted No. of Cases):	3286	1584	1601	2463	410	782	901	997	604	1920	1159	1252	655	479	794	45
% of Weighted Total:	100.0	48.2	48.7	75.0	12.5	23.8	27.4	30.4	18.4	58.4	35.3	38.1	19.9	14.6	24.2	1.4

E09C: Would you like other people to get high on alcohol?

	TOTAL	M	F	White	Black	NE	NC	S	W	Yes	No	None	Marijuana Only	Few Pills	More Pills	Any Heroin
1. Never	35.1	30.1	39.5	30.1	59.3	27.9	33.8	42.0	33.8	35.0	35.7	57.9	24.4	22.1	14.4	23.0
2. Seldom	17.3	15.6	18.8	17.5	16.4	15.0	19.6	17.4	16.4	18.4	15.5	18.1	17.6	19.2	14.8	17.3
3. Sometimes	28.1	28.8	27.7	30.8	15.7	31.2	28.1	26.6	27.1	28.3	27.7	17.3	34.8	32.9	38.5	12.5
4. Most times	12.1	14.3	10.1	13.7	4.2	15.7	12.4	8.3	13.6	12.8	10.9	4.9	17.0	18.4	15.5	16.7
5. Always	7.5	11.2	3.9	7.9	4.4	10.3	6.1	5.7	9.2	5.5	10.2	1.8	6.2	7.4	16.8	30.5
Item 22070　Subject A11d,C08　N	2632	1244	1341	2062	288	547	767	798	520	1642	911	1036	528	395	616	35

E09D: Would you like to use marijuana?

	TOTAL	M	F	White	Black	NE	NC	S	W	Yes	No	None	Marijuana Only	Few Pills	More Pills	Any Heroin
1. Never	67.2	64.5	69.7	67.2	70.7	54.4	69.5	77.1	62.1	70.2	62.3	95.8	61.2	59.3	31.3	24.6
2. Seldom	12.6	13.0	12.0	12.6	11.4	17.6	11.4	7.5	17.2	12.2	13.3	2.5	18.4	21.1	19.4	17.1
3. Sometimes	10.0	8.5	11.5	10.1	9.0	14.0	9.9	7.2	10.0	9.1	11.5	0.9	12.4	12.5	21.6	12.8
4. Most times	4.8	6.1	3.7	4.9	4.5	5.3	5.0	4.3	4.6	4.9	4.6	0.6	4.5	4.0	11.7	13.7
5. Always	5.4	7.9	3.1	5.4	4.4	8.8	4.2	4.0	6.0	3.6	8.3	0.2	3.5	3.1	15.9	31.9
Item 22080　Subject A05c,C08　N	2645	1254	1345	2075	288	549	770	805	521	1653	910	1039	530	397	619	36

E09E: Would you like other people to use marijuana?

	TOTAL	M	F	White	Black	NE	NC	S	W	Yes	No	None	Marijuana Only	Few Pills	More Pills	Any Heroin
1. Never	63.8	60.8	66.6	63.4	68.5	51.1	66.9	73.8	57.2	66.4	59.5	92.1	57.5	53.3	30.1	19.4
2. Seldom	14.9	14.3	15.3	15.1	11.2	19.0	14.6	9.5	19.4	15.2	14.6	5.1	19.9	22.8	22.1	24.6
3. Sometimes	12.5	12.1	13.0	13.3	10.3	17.5	11.8	9.2	13.3	11.8	13.6	1.6	15.0	17.1	25.8	17.1
4. Most times	3.8	5.1	2.6	3.5	4.8	3.6	3.0	4.0	5.0	3.4	4.6	0.6	3.4	3.9	9.0	10.1
5. Always	5.0	7.6	2.4	4.7	5.2	8.7	3.7	3.5	5.1	3.2	7.7	0.6	4.3	2.9	13.0	28.8
Item 22090　Subject A11d,C08　N	2621	1242	1333	2058	285	544	762	798	518	1641	902	1034	528	393	610	34

E09F: Would you like to use other drugs?

	TOTAL	M	F	White	Black	NE	NC	S	W	Yes	No	None	Marijuana Only	Few Pills	More Pills	Any Heroin
1. Never	85.7	82.5	88.5	85.8	87.5	79.4	88.5	89.7	82.0	88.1	81.9	97.8	92.8	89.3	59.9	34.4
2. Seldom	5.9	6.7	5.1	5.9	4.4	7.4	4.7	4.5	8.1	5.6	6.3	0.8	3.4	5.9	16.1	15.7
3. Sometimes	5.0	5.9	4.2	4.8	5.6	7.6	4.9	2.7	5.7	3.6	6.8	0.7	2.0	3.7	14.3	21.0
4. Most times	1.6	2.2	1.2	1.8	0.7	2.3	1.1	1.5	2.0	1.3	2.2	0.4	0.8	0.3	4.6	13.5
5. Always	1.8	2.7	1.0	1.7	1.8	3.3	0.8	1.6	2.2	1.3	2.8	0.3	1.0	0.7	5.1	15.4
Item 22100　Subject A05c,C08　N	2645	1251	1347	2076	287	549	768	807	522	1653	911	1039	529	397	622	36

E09G: Would you like other people to use other drugs?

	TOTAL	M	F	White	Black	NE	NC	S	W	Yes	No	None	Marijuana Only	Few Pills	More Pills	Any Heroin
1. Never	83.2	79.7	86.2	83.4	84.8	78.3	86.9	87.1	76.7	86.2	78.8	96.1	88.8	83.9	58.9	25.2
2. Seldom	7.3	7.3	7.4	7.5	4.5	7.3	6.2	5.9	11.1	6.5	8.7	2.0	4.8	8.7	16.7	29.6
3. Sometimes	6.0	7.6	4.6	5.8	7.4	8.2	5.3	3.7	8.2	4.8	7.6	0.8	4.0	6.2	15.7	14.2
4. Most times	1.6	2.1	1.1	1.5	1.6	3.1	0.8	1.6	1.0	1.3	2.1	0.6	0.9	0.3	4.0	13.6
5. Always	2.0	3.3	0.6	1.8	1.7	3.2	0.8	1.7	2.9	1.3	2.8	0.5	1.5	0.9	4.7	17.4
Item 22110　Subject A11d,C08　N	2624	1239	1337	2056	287	543	763	798	520	1640	905	1036	522	396	613	33

E10: If you had ever used marijuana or hashish, do you think that you would have said so in this questionnaire?

	TOTAL	M	F	White	Black	NE	NC	S	W	Yes	No	None	Marijuana Only	Few Pills	More Pills	Any Heroin
1. No	6.4	8.1	4.7	4.8	11.9	7.4	7.0	6.3	4.9	4.8	9.1	8.4	5.1	4.8	4.6	11.0
2. Not sure	7.0	7.4	6.5	6.9	8.3	3.6	9.1	9.0	4.1	6.8	7.4	11.4	3.2	5.2	3.9	12.2
3. Yes	55.6	54.9	57.0	55.6	56.0	56.7	53.7	56.9	55.3	58.3	51.9	77.3	43.8	47.2	37.6	17.3
4. I did say so	31.0	29.6	31.8	32.6	23.8	32.3	30.2	27.8	35.6	30.2	31.7	2.9	47.9	42.9	54.0	59.5
Item 20800　Subject A15a　N	2624	1239	1337	2058	286	545	767	800	512	1637	906	1016	525	397	626	36

E11: If you had ever used amphetamines (without a doctor's orders), do you think that you would have said so in this questionnaire?

	TOTAL	M	F	White	Black	NE	NC	S	W	Yes	No	None	Marijuana Only	Few Pills	More Pills	Any Heroin
1. No	9.1	12.2	5.9	6.8	19.4	11.2	9.2	8.6	7.6	6.0	13.8	8.8	10.6	9.0	7.6	13.8
2. Not sure	8.0	8.6	7.4	8.0	7.2	5.5	9.8	8.6	7.0	8.3	7.8	11.3	5.1	6.5	6.1	7.8
3. Yes	67.5	65.5	70.3	68.3	66.5	67.9	67.0	66.8	69.0	71.7	61.5	77.2	76.6	72.7	43.4	26.7
4. I did say so	15.3	13.7	16.5	16.9	6.8	15.3	13.9	16.0	16.3	14.0	16.9	2.7	7.6	11.8	42.9	51.7
Item 20810　Subject A15a　N	2619	1236	1335	2056	283	543	771	797	508	1633	904	1015	522	398	624	36

	TOTAL	SEX		RACE		REGION				4YR COLLEGE PLANS		ILLICIT DRUG USE: LIFETIME				
QUESTIONNAIRE FORM 5 1985		M	F	White	Black	NE	NC	S	W	Yes	No	None	Mari-juana Only	Few Pills	More Pills	Any Her-oin
N (Weighted No. of Cases):	3286	1584	1601	2463	410	782	901	997	604	1920	1159	1252	655	479	794	45
% of Weighted Total:	100.0	48.2	48.7	75.0	12.5	23.8	27.4	30.4	18.4	58.4	35.3	38.1	19.9	14.6	24.2	1.4

E12: If you had ever used heroin, do you think that you would have said so in this questionnaire?

1. No	10.4	13.6	7.1	7.8	20.3	11.1	9.9	9.7	11.6	7.3	15.5	9.5	10.0	10.8	11.2	16.6
2. Not sure	9.6	10.2	9.2	10.1	7.4	7.9	10.8	10.3	8.3	10.0	9.3	12.5	6.7	8.6	7.6	11.5
3. Yes	72.4	69.5	75.9	74.3	66.1	73.9	72.6	72.0	71.1	75.7	67.2	75.4	76.1	73.5	67.5	15.9
4. I did say so	7.6	6.8	7.8	7.8	6.2	7.1	6.6	7.9	9.1	6.9	8.0	2.6	7.2	7.2	13.7	56.0
Item 20820 Subject A15a N	2622	1238	1337	2056	287	541	770	800	511	1637	905	1017	524	397	624	36

Cross-Time Index of Questionnaire Items, 1975-1985

Introduction to the Indexing Conventions

Beginning with the 1982 volume, the cross-time index of question locations is organized first by subject area (see Table 3 for complete listing). Within each subject area, questions are listed in numerical sequence according to item reference number, which is the unique numerical identifier assigned to each question in the study.

The Question Index may be used in two major ways:

1. **Locating a Question Across Years.** Having located a question of interest in the Descriptive Results section, the reader may determine in what other years that same question has appeared by simply looking it up by subject area and item reference number. The Index will show all years in which that item has appeared and also show its location each year (by questionnaire form, section, and item number). All items will retain their unique reference numbers in future years as well, and thus may be located in exactly the same way in subsequent volumes in this series.

EXAMPLE: A reader interested in a particular item about the nation needing more long-range planning would note that it has been classified under subject area I01 ("Expectations concerning social change") and that it has been assigned item reference number 1200. The index entry for item 1200 shows that this item has appeared in Section A of questionnaire Form 1 in all annual surveys in the series. Its question number was 4A in 1975 and 2A thereafter.

2. **Locating Questions by Subject Area.** Given an interest in some particular subject area, one can quickly scan the Index to locate all questions dealing with that area. Table 3 lists all the subject areas into which items are classified, along with the alphanumeric code assigned to each area.

EXAMPLE: A reader interested in items dealing with religion should first locate the relevant code in Table 3: Code G, "Religion." The second step is to scan that section of the item index, noting for every item its item reference number and page location in this volume. The reader may or may not find the abbreviated description of the item (given in the third column of the index and further described below) helpful in deciding whether to look up a particular item in the Descriptive Results section. Some of these descriptions are rather clear as to their meaning, but others are less so.

Definition of the Column Headings

The definitions of column headings, and the conventions used for the entries in each column, are given below under the numbers indicated in the following key.

①**Item Reference Number.** A unique identification number is assigned to each question for the duration of this research and reporting series. It appears below that question in the Descriptive Results section, as well as in this index and the indices of all other volumes in this series.

②**Page Location.** The second column of the Question Index gives the page number of the present volume on which a verbatim statement of the question may be found along with this year's descriptive results.

③**Item Description (Abbreviated).** This is a brief mnemonic description — up to 16 characters in length — that attempts to characterize the content of the question. Originally developed for question identification on OSIRIS computer files, it may in many cases allow one to determine the relevance of the question to one's own interest and thus reduce the number of irrelevant questions that must be looked up in the Descriptive Results section.

④**Questionnaire Location by Year.** An entry is provided for every year in which an item appeared in one of the study's questionnaire forms. The six (or fewer) characters comprising the entry indicate the form in which the question appeared, the section of that form, and the question number. Take as an example the questionnaire location 1A004A. This location code indicates that the question appeared in Form 1, Section A, and was labeled as Question 4a.

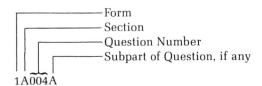

Occasionally an entry will be enclosed in parentheses. This indicates that there was a change (usually minor) in the wording of the question and/or the answer alternatives in subsequent years.

A form number (ranging from 1 to 5) is usually shown in the first character location. However, two substitute characters will replace the form number at times:

+ A plus sign indicates that the item appeared in all five forms that year and that it appeared in the same location on all forms.
* An asterisk indicates that the item appeared in four forms (Forms 2 through 5) and in the same location on all forms.

⑤ **Subject Area.** Table 3 shows the subject content areas that have been distinguished here and gives the alphanumeric code assigned to each of them. Every question item in the index has been classified into (and listed under) one or more of the subject areas, and the index (beginning with the 1982 volume) has been organized by subject area.

Figure 2

Guide to Cross-Time Index

| ① | ② | ③ | ④ |

Item Reference Number	Page Loc. in this Volume	ITEM DESCRIPTION (ABBREVIATED)	QUESTIONNAIRE LOCATION BY YEAR (FORM, SECTION, AND QUESTION NUMBER)								
			1975	1976	1977	1978	1979	1980	1981	1982/83	1984/85

⑤ —— A01a: DRUGS. Number of uses in lifetime

Item Ref.	Page	Description	1975	1976	1977	1978	1979	1980	1981	1982/83	1984/85
760	25	EVR SMK CIG,REGL	1A018 *B01	+B01	+B01	+B01	+B01	+B01	+B01	+B01	+B01
790	25	EVER DRINK	1A026 *B03	*B03	*B03	*B03	*B03	*B03	*B03	*B03	*B03
810	41	#X DRNK/LIFETIME	1A028A	1B007A	1B007A	1B007A	1B007A	1B007A	1B007A	1B007A	1B007A
	25		*B04A	*B04A	*B04A	*B04A	*B04A	*B04A	*B04A	*B04A	*B04A
860	26	#XMJ+HS/LIFETIME	1A044A *B07A	*B07A	*B07A	*B07A	*B07A	*B07A	*B07A	*B07A	*B07A
890	50	#X LSD/LIFETIME	1A057A	1B029A	1B029A	1B029A	1B029A	1B029A	1B029A	1B033A	1B033A
	27		*B08A	*B08A	*B08A	*B08A	*B08A	*B08A	*B08A	*B08A	*B08A
920	53	#X PSYD/LIFETIME	1A071A	1B038A	1B038A	1B038A	1B038A	1B038A	1B038A	1B042A	1B042A
	27		*B09A	*B09A	*B09A	*B09A	*B09A	*B09A	*B09A	*B09A	*B09A
950	70	#X COKE/LIFETIME	1A144A	1B076A	1B076A	1B076A	1B076A	1B076A	1B076A	1B083A	1B083A
	28		*B10A	*B10A	*B10A	*B10A	*B10A	*B10A	*B10A	*B10A	*B10A
980	56	#X AMPH/LIFETIME	1A087A	1B043A	1B043A	1B043A	1B043A	1B043A	(1B043A)	1B050A	1B050A
	28		*B11A	*B11A	*B11A	*B11A	*B11A	*B11A	(*B11A)	*B11A	*B11A
1010	60	#X QUAD/LIFETIME	1A102A	1B053A	1B053A	1B053A	1B053A	1B053A	1B053A	1B060A	1B060A
	29		*B12A	*B12A	*B12A	*B12A	*B12A	*B12A	*B12A	*B12A	*B12A
1040	61	#X BRBT/LIFETIME	1A116A	1B057A	1B057A	1B057A	1B057A	1B057A	1B057A	1B064A	1B064A
	30		*B13A	*B13A	*B13A	*B13A	*B13A	*B13A	*B13A	*B13A	*B13A
1070	66	#X TRQL/LIFETIME	1A131A	1B067A	1B067A	1B067A	1B067A	1B067A	1B067A	1B074A	1B074A
	30		*B14A	*B14A	*B14A	*B14A	*B14A	*B14A	*B14A	*B14A	*B14A
1100	74	#X "H"/LIFETIME	1A158A	1B085A	1B085A	1B085A	1B085A	1B085A	1B085A	1B092A	1B092A
	31		*B15A	*B15A	*B15A	*B15A	*B15A	*B15A	*B15A	*B15A	*B15A
1130	75	#X NARC/LIFETIME	1A173A	1B095A	1B095A	1B095A	1B095A	1B095A	1B095A	1B094A	1B094A
	31		*B16A	*B16A	*B16A	*B16A	*B16A	*B16A	*B16A	*B16A	*B16A
1160	32	#X INHL/LIFETIME		*B17A	*B17A	*B17A	*B17A	*B17A	*B17A	*B17A	*B17A
1181	111	#X PCP/LIFETIME								2E02A	2E02A
1184	112	#X PPRS/LIFETIME								2E03A	2E03A
2040	45	#X HASH/LIFETIM		1B018A							1B018A
2070	46	#X MARJ/LIFETIME		1B							1B019A
11000	164	#X BEER/LIFETIME									
11040	165	#X WINE/LIFETIME									
11080	166	#X LIQR/LIFETIME									
21180	49	MJ/HSH EVR DLY									
	49										

Table 3

Subject Area Key
(Referenced by letter in the Question Index)

A. **Drugs.** Drug use and related attitudes and beliefs, drug availabilty and exposure, surrounding conditions and social meaning of drug use.
Views of significant others regarding drugs.

A01 Use of Drugs
    A01a — . . . in lifetime
    A01b — . . . in the last 12 months
    A01c — . . . in the last 30 days
    A01d —Quantity used
    A01e —How high? (How often?)
    A01f —How long high?
    A01g —Incidence of first use
    A01h —Use with other drugs
    A01i —Try to stop?
    A01j — . . . on doctor's orders?
    A01k —Bad trip?
    A01l —Kinds of drugs

A02 Exposure to Drug Use
    A02a —Friends' use of drugs
    A02b —Exposure to users

A03 Availability of Drugs

A04 Expected Future Use

A05 Conditions of Use
    A05a —Alone
    A05b —With others
    A05c —Settings
    A05d —Mode of drug administration

A06 Reasons for Use, Abstention, and
Stopping

A07 Problems with Drugs

A08 Sources of Help regarding Drugs

A09 Parental Awareness of Use

A10 Drug Education

A11 Own Attitudes regarding Drugs and
Drug Users
    A11a —For adults
    A11b —For own children
    A11c —Perception of drug users

A12 Others' Attitudes regarding Drugs and
Drug Users

    A12a —Parents
    A12b —Friends and students
    A12c —Perception of drug users

A13 Legal Issues regarding Drugs
    A13a —Preferred legality for adults
    A13b —Own response to legalization
    A13c —Knowledge of marijuana laws

A14 Risk of Drug Harm
    A14a —To self
    A14b —To others

B. **Education.**

B01 High school: scholastic status,
objectives, experiences

B02 Combining work and school: attitudes,
experiences

B03 Interracial contact at school

B04 Student norms

B05 Counseling

B06 Absenteeism and truancy

B07 Delinquency and victimization at school

B08 Opinions regarding competency testing

B09 Post high school: status, plans,
characteristics

B10 Attitudes regarding educational
institutions

C. **Work and Leisure.**

C01 Present or recent work experience

C02 Income sources; financial security

C03 Vocational plans, aspiration,
expectations

C04 Preferences regarding job characteristics

Table 3 (continued)

C05 Desirability of different working arrangements and settings

C06 Work ethic/success orientation

C07 Leisure time: extent, activities

C08 Attitudes toward leisure time

D. Sex Roles and Family.

D01 Dating and marriage: status, attitudes, expectations

D02 Parenthood: status, attitudes, expectations

D03 Values surrounding marriage and family

D04 Preferences regarding marital/familial arrangements

D05 Sex role attitudes

·D06 Opinions regarding sex discrimination

E. Population Concerns.

E01 Overpopulation

E02 Birth control

F. Conservation, Materialism, Equity, etc.

F01 Personal materialism

F02 Societal materialism and advertising

F03 Concern with world hunger and poverty

F04 Ecological concerns

F05 Concern with conservation of resources

F06 Preferences regarding dwelling type and urbanicity

F07 Driving and use of mass transit

G. Religion. Religious preferences, activities, views.

H. Politics.

H01 Political interest and preferences

H02 Attitudes toward governmental policies and practices

H03 Views about the role of citizens in government. (See also I02: Attitudes regarding activism)

H04 Confidence in government

H05 Voting, political activism

I. Social Change.

I01 Expectations concerning societal change

I02 Attitudes regarding activism

I03 Reactions to personal and social change

J. Social Problems. Interest and concerns.

K. Major Social Institutions

K01 Trust (See also C05: Institutions as work settings)

K02 Satisfaction with performance

K03 Preferred influence

L. Military.

L01 Plans for military service

L02 Attitudes toward a draft

L03 Views about the use of military force

L04 Attitudes toward the military as an institution and occupation

M. Interpersonal Relationships.

M01 Dating

M02 Cross-age relationships with adults outside the family (See also B05)

M03 Agreement/disagreement with parents

Table 3 (continued)

M04   Friendships (See also Q03: Loneliness)

M05   Community at large

N. Race Relations.

N01   Preferred interracial contact

N02   Attitudes about discrimination

N03   Actual interracial contacts

O. Concern for Others.

O01   Attitudes regarding social service, charitable activism

O02   Involvement in community, altruistic activities

O03   Concern with the problems of others

P. Happiness.

P01   Happiness; satisfaction with life and self

P02   Satisfaction with specific life domains

Q. Other Personality Variables.

Q01   Attitudes about self, self-esteem

Q02   Locus of control

Q03   Loneliness

Q04   Risk taking

Q05   Trust in others

Q06   (Changed to Subject Area T.)

Q07   Importance placed on various life goals

Q08   Social, political, cultural orientation

Q09   Hostility

R. Background.

R01   Age, sex, race, and marital status

R02   Family characteristics

R03   Living arrangements and household characteristics

S. Deviance and Victimization.

S01   Delinquent behaviors

S02   Driving violations and accidents

S03   Victimization experiences

T. Health Habits and Symptoms.

Item Refer- ence Number	Page Loc. in this Volume	ITEM DESCRIPTION (ABBREVIATED)	QUESTIONNAIRE LOCATION BY YEAR (FORM, SECTION, AND QUESTION NUMBER)								
			1975	1976	1977	1978	1979	1980	1981	1982/83	1984/85

A01a: DRUGS. Number of uses in lifetime

Item Ref.	Page	ITEM DESCRIPTION	1975	1976	1977	1978	1979	1980	1981	1982/83	1984/85
760	25	EVR SMK CIG,REGL	1A018	+B01	+B01	+B01	+B01	+B01	+B01	+B01	+B01
			*B01								
790	25	EVER DRINK	1A026	*B03	*B03	*B03	*B03	*B03	*B03	*B03	*B03
			*B03								
810	41	#X DRNK/LIFETIME	1A028A	1B007A	1B007A	1B007A	1B007A	1B007A	1B007A	1B007A	1B007A
	25		*B04A	*B04A	*B04A	*B04A	*B04A	*B04A	*B04A	*B04A	*B04A
860	26	#XMJ+HS/LIFETIME	1A044A	*B07A	*B07A	*B07A	*B07A	*B07A	*B07A	*B07A	*B07A
			*B07A								
890	50	#X LSD/LIFETIME	1A057A	1B029A	1B029A	1B029A	1B029A	1B029A	1B029A	1B033A	1B033A
	27		*B08A	*B08A	*B08A	*B08A	*B08A	*B08A	*B08A	*B08A	*B08A
920	53	#X PSYD/LIFETIME	1A071A	1B038A	1B038A	1B038A	1B038A	1B038A	1B038A	1B042A	1B042A
	27		*B09A	*B09A	*B09A	*B09A	*B09A	*B09A	*B09A	*B09A	*B09A
950	70	#X COKE/LIFETIME	1A144A	1B076A	1B076A	1B076A	1B076A	1B076A	1B076A	1B083A	1B083A
	28		*B10A	*B10A	*B10A	*B10A	*B10A	*B10A	*B10A	*B10A	*B10A
980	56	#X AMPH/LIFETIME	1A087A	1B043A	1B043A	1B043A	1B043A	1B043A	(1B043A)	1B050A	1B050A
	28		*B11A	*B11A	*B11A	*B11A	*B11A	*B11A	(*B11A)	*B11A	*B11A
1010	60	#X QUAD/LIFETIME	1A102A	1B053A	1B053A	1B053A	1B053A	1B053A	1B053A	1B060A	1B060A
	29		*B12A	*B12A	*B12A	*B12A	*B12A	*B12A	*B12A	*B12A	*B12A
1040	61	#X BRBT/LIFETIME	1A116A	1B057A	1B057A	1B057A	1B057A	1B057A	1B057A	1B064A	1B064A
	30		*B13A	*B13A	*B13A	*B13A	*B13A	*B13A	*B13A	*B13A	*B13A
1070	66	#X TRQL/LIFETIME	1A131A	1B067A	1B067A	1B067A	1B067A	1B067A	1B067A	1B074A	1B074A
	30		*B14A	*B14A	*B14A	*B14A	*B14A	*B14A	*B14A	*B14A	*B14A
1100	74	#X "H"/LIFETIME	1A158A	1B085A	1B085A	1B085A	1B085A	1B085A	1B085A	1B092A	1B092A
	31		*B15A	*B15A	*B15A	*B15A	*B15A	*B15A	*B15A	*B15A	*B15A
1130	75	#X NARC/LIFETIME	1A173A	1B095A	1B095A	1B095A	1B095A	1B095A	1B095A	1B094A	1B094A
	31		*B16A	*B16A	*B16A	*B16A	*B16A	*B16A	*B16A	*B16A	*B16A
1160	32	#X INHL/LIFETIME		*B17A	*B17A	*B17A	*B17A	*B17A	*B17A	*B17A	*B17A
1181	111	#X PCP/LIFETIME					2E02A	2E02A	2E02A	2E02A	2E02A
1184	112	#X PPRS/LIFETIME					2E03A	2E03A	2E03A	2E03A	2E03A
2040	45	#X HASH/LIFETIM		1B018A	1B018A	1B018A	1B018A	1B018A	1B018A	1B018A	1B018A
2070	46	#X MARJ/LIFETIME		1B019A	1B019A	1B019A	1B019A	1B019A	1B019A	1B019A	1B019A
11000	164	#X BEER/LIFETIME		4D04A	4D04A	4D04A	4D04A	4D04A	4D04A	4D11A	4D11A
11040	165	#X WINE/LIFETIME		4D06A	4D06A	4D06A	4D06A	4D06A	4D06A	4D13A	4D13A
11080	166	#X LIQR/LIFETIME		4D08A	4D08A	4D08A	4D08A	4D08A	4D08A	4D15A	4D15A
21180	49	MJ/HSH EVR DLY								1B028	1B028
21200	49	RECENT DAILY MJ								1B030	1B030
21210	49	#X DAILY MJ/LFT								1B031	1B031
21220	54	#X DIETPILL/LFT								1B046A	1B046A
21250	55	#X STA-AWAK/LFT								1B047A	1B047A
21280	55	#X LOOKALIK/LFT								1B048A	1B048A

A01b: DRUGS. Number of uses in last 12 months

Item Ref.	Page	ITEM DESCRIPTION	1975	1976	1977	1978	1979	1980	1981	1982/83	1984/85
820	42	#X DRNK/LAST12MO	1A028B	1B007B	1B007B	1B007B	1B007B	1B007B	1B007B	1B007B	1B007B
	25		*B04B	*B04B	*B04B	*B04B	*B04B	*B04B	*B04B	*B04B	*B04B
870	26	#XMJ+HS/LAST12MO	1A044B	*B07B	*B07B	*B07B	*B07B	*B07B	*B07B	*B07B	*B07B
			*B07B								
900	50	#X LSD/LAST 12MO	1A057B	1B029B	1B029B	1B029B	1B029B	1B029B	1B029B	1B033B	1B033B
	27		*B08B	*B08B	*B08B	*B08B	*B08B	*B08B	*B08B	*B08B	*B08B
930	53	#X PSYD/LAST12MO	1A071B	1B038B	1B038B	1B038B	1B038B	1B038B	1B038B	1B042B	1B042B
	27		*B09B	*B09B	*B09B	*B09B	*B09B	*B09B	*B09B	*B09B	*B09B
960	70	#X COKE/LAST12MO	1A144B	1B076B	1B076B	1B076B	1B076B	1B076B	1B076B	1B083B	1B083B
	28		*B10B	*B10B	*B10B	*B10B	*B10B	*B10B	*B10B	*B10B	*B10B
990	56	#X AMPH/LAST12MO	1A087B	1B043B	1B043B	1B043B	1B043B	1B043B	(1B043B)	1B050B	1B050B
	29		*B11B	*B11B	*B11B	*B11B	*B11B	*B11B	(*B11B)	*B11B	*B11B
1020	60	#X QUAD/LAST12MO	1A102B	1B053B	1B053B	1B053B	1B053B	1B053B	1B053B	1B060B	1B060B
	29		*B12B	*B12B	*B12B	*B12B	*B12B	*B12B	*B12B	*B12B	*B12B
1050	62	#X BRBT/LAST12MO	1A116B	1B057B	1B057B	1B057B	1B057B	1B057B	1B057B	1B064B	1B064B
	30		*B13B	*B13B	*B13B	*B13B	*B13B	*B13B	*B13B	*B13B	*B13B
1080	66	#X TRQL/LAST12MO	1A131B	1B067B	1B067B	1B067B	1B067B	1B067B	1B067B	1B074B	1B074B
	30		*B14B	*B14B	*B14B	*B14B	*B14B	*B14B	*B14B	*B14B	*B14B
1110	74	#X "H"/LAST 12MO	1A158B	1B085B	1B085B	1B085B	1B085B	1B085B	1B085B	1B092B	1B092B
	31		*B15B	*B15B	*B15B	*B15B	*B15B	*B15B	*B15B	*B15B	*B15B

(continued)

Item Reference Number	Page Loc. in this Volume	ITEM DESCRIPTION (ABBREVIATED)	QUESTIONNAIRE LOCATION BY YEAR (FORM, SECTION, AND QUESTION NUMBER)								
			1975	1976	1977	1978	1979	1980	1981	1982/83	1984/85

A01b: DRUGS. Number of uses in last 12 months *(continued)*

Item Reference Number	Page Loc. in this Volume	ITEM DESCRIPTION (ABBREVIATED)	1975	1976	1977	1978	1979	1980	1981	1982/83	1984/85
1140	75	#X NARC/LAST12MO	1A173B	1B095B	1B095B	1B095B	1B095B	1B095B	1B095B	1B094B	1B094B
	31		*B16B	*B16B	*B16B	*B16B	*B16B	*B16B	*B16B	*B16B	*B16B
1170	32	#X INHL/LAST12MO		*B17B	*B17B	*B17B	*B17B	*B17B	*B17B	*B17B	*B17B
1182	112	#X PCP/LAST12MO					2E02B	2E02B	2E02B	2E02B	2E02B
1185	112	#X PPRS/LAST12MO					2E03B	2E03B	2E03B	2E03B	2E03B
2050	45	#X HASH/LAST12M		1B018B	1B018B	1B018B	1B018B	1B018B	1B018B	1B018B	1B018B
2080	46	#X MARJ/LAST12MO		1B019B	1B019B	1B019B	1B019B	1B019B	1B019B	1B019B	1B019B
8520	128	12MO,#OCC PAINRF	3A48A	3A27A	3A27A	3A27A	3A27A	3A27A	3A27A	3A27A	3A27A
8530	129	12MO,#OCC SLP PL	3A48B	3A27B	3A27B	3A27B	3A27B	3A27B	3A27B	3A27B	3A27B
8540	129	12MO,#OCC AWK PL	3A48C	3A27C	3A27C	3A27C	3A27C	3A27C	3A27C	3A27C	3A27C
8550	129	12MO,#OCC CALM P	3A48D	3A27D	3A27D	3A27D	3A27D	3A27D	3A27D	3A27D	3A27D
11010	165	#X BEER/LAST12MO		4D04B	4D04B	4D04B	4D04B	4D04B	4D04B	4D11B	4D11B
11050	165	#X WINE/LAST12MO		4D06B	4D06B	4D06B	4D06B	4D06B	4D06B	4D13B	4D13B
11090	166	#X LIQR/LAST12MO		4D08B	4D08B	4D08B	4D08B	4D08B	4D08B	4D15B	4D15B
21230	54	#X DIETPILL/12M								1B046B	1B046B
21260	55	#X STA-AWAK/12M								1B047B	1B047B
21290	56	#X LOOKALIK/12M								1B048B	1B048B

A01c: DRUGS. Number of uses in last 30 days

Item Reference Number	Page Loc. in this Volume	ITEM DESCRIPTION (ABBREVIATED)	1975	1976	1977	1978	1979	1980	1981	1982/83	1984/85
780	41	#CIGS SMKD/30DAY	1A020	1B003	1B003	1B003	1B003	1B003	1B003	1B003	1B003
	25		*B02	*B02	*B02	*B02	*B02	*B02	*B02	*B02	*B02
830	42	#X DRNK/LAST30DA	1A028C	1B007C	1B007C	1B007C	1B007C	1B007C	1B007C	1B007C	1B007C
	25		*B04C	*B04C	*B04C	*B04C	*B04C	*B04C	*B04C	*B04C	*B04C
880	27	#XMJ+HS/LAST30DA	1A044C	*B07C	*B07C	*B07C	*B07C	*B07C	*B07C	*B07C	*B07C
			*B07C								
910	50	#X LSD/LAST 30DA	1A057C	1B029C	1B029C	1B029C	1B029C	1B029C	1B029C	1B033C	1B033C
	27		*B08C	*B08C	*B08C	*B08C	*B08C	*B08C	*B08C	*B08C	*B08C
940	53	#X PSYD/LAST30DA	1A071C	1B038C	1B038C	1B038C	1B038C	1B038C	1B038C	1B042C	1B042C
	28		*B09C	*B09C	*B09C	*B09C	*B09C	*B09C	*B09C	*B09C	*B09C
970	70	#X COKE/LAST30DA	1A144C	1B076C	1B076C	1B076C	1B076C	1B076C	1B076C	1B083C	1B083C
	28		*B10C	*B10C	*B10C	*B10C	*B10C	*B10C	*B10C	*B10C	*B10C
1000	57	#X AMPH/LAST30DA	1A087C	1B043C	1B043C	1B043C	1B043C	1B043C	(1B043C)	1B050C	1B050C
	29		*B11C	*B11C	*B11C	*B11C	*B11C	*B11C	(*B11C)	*B11C	*B11C
1030	60	#X QUAD/LAST30DA	1A102C	1B053C	1B053C	1B053C	1B053C	1B053C	1B053C	1B060C	1B060C
	29		*B12C	*B12C	*B12C	*B12C	*B12C	*B12C	*B12C	*B12C	*B12C
1060	62	#X BRBT/LAST30DA	1A116C	1B057C	1B057C	1B057C	1B057C	1B057C	1B057C	1B064C	1B064C
	30		*B13C	*B13C	*B13C	*B13C	*B13C	*B13C	*B13C	*B13C	*B13C
1090	66	#X TRQL/LAST30DA	1A131C	1B067C	1B067C	1B067C	1B067C	1B067C	1B067C	1B074C	1B074C
	30		*B14C	*B14C	*B14C	*B14C	*B14C	*B14C	*B14C	*B14C	*B14C
1120	74	#X "H"/LAST 30DA	1A158C	1B085C	1B085C	1B085C	1B085C	1B085C	1B085C	1B092C	1B092C
	31		*B15C	*B15C	*B15C	*B15C	*B15C	*B15C	*B15C	*B15C	*B15C
1150	75	#X NARC/LAST30DA	1A173C	1B095C	1B095C	1B095C	1B095C	1B095C	1B095C	1B094C	1B094C
	32		*B16C	*B16C	*B16C	*B16C	*B16C	*B16C	*B16C	*B16C	*B16C
1180	32	#X INHL/LAST30DA		*B17C	*B17C	*B17C	*B17C	*B17C	*B17C	*B17C	*B17C
1183	112	#X PCP/LAST30DA					2E02C	2E02C	2E02C	2E02C	2E02C
1186	112	#X PPRS/LAST30DA					2E03C	2E03C	2E03C	2E03C	2E03C
2060	45	#X HASH/LAST30D		1B018C	1B018C	1B018C	1B018C	1B018C	1B018C	1B018C	1B018C
2090	46	#X MARJ/LAST30DA		1B019C	1B019C	1B019C	1B019C	1B019C	1B019C	1B019C	1B019C
11020	165	#X BEER/LAST30DA		4D04C	4D04C	4D04C	4D04C	4D04C	4D04C	4D11C	4D11C
11060	165	#X WINE/LAST30DA		4D06C	4D06C	4D06C	4D06C	4D06C	4D06C	4D13C	4D13C
11100	166	#X LIQR/LAST30DA		4D08C	4D08C	4D08C	4D08C	4D08C	4D08C	4D15C	4D15C
21240	54	#X DIETPILL/30D								1B046C	1B046C
21270	55	#X STA-AWAK/30D								1B047C	1B047C
21300	56	#X LOOKALIK/30D								1B048C	1B048C

A01d: DRUGS. Quantity used

Item Reference Number	Page Loc. in this Volume	ITEM DESCRIPTION (ABBREVIATED)	1975	1976	1977	1978	1979	1980	1981	1982/83	1984/85
850	44	5+DRK ROW/LST 2W	1A035	1B012	1B012	1B012	1B012	1B012	1B012	1B012	1B012
	26		*B06	*B06	*B06	*B06	*B06	*B06	*B06	*B06	*B06
1990	44	#X/2W,3-4 DR RW	1A036	1B013	1B013	1B013	1B013	1B013	1B013	1B013	1B013
2000	44	#X/2WK,2 DRK RW	1A037	1B014	1B014	1B014	1B014	1B014	1B014	1B014	1B014
2010	45	#X/2WK,JST 1DRK	1A038	1B015	1B015	1B015	1B015	1B015	1B015	1B015	1B015
		(continued)									

Item Reference Number	Page Loc. in this Volume	ITEM DESCRIPTION (ABBREVIATED)	QUESTIONNAIRE LOCATION BY YEAR (FORM, SECTION, AND QUESTION NUMBER)								
			1975	1976	1977	1978	1979	1980	1981	1982/83	1984/85

A01d: DRUGS. Quantity used *(continued)*

Item Reference Number	Page Loc.	ITEM DESCRIPTION	1975	1976	1977	1978	1979	1980	1981	1982/83	1984/85
2360	48	JOINT/DA LST MO		1B025	1B025	1B025	1B025	1B025	1B025	1B025	1B025
2370	48	OZS.MJ LST MO/6		1B026	1B026	1B026	1B026	1B026	1B026	1B026	1B026
11030	165	5+BR/LST2WK,10+X		4D05	4D05	4D05	4D05	4D05	4D05	4D12	4D12
11070	166	#X 20OZ+ WN/2 WK		4D07	4D07	4D07	4D07	4D07	4D07	4D14	4D14
11110	166	#X 5+LIQ/LST 2WK		4D09	4D09	4D09	4D09	4D09	4D09	4D16	4D16
21100		#CANS COLA/DAY							5E10		
21110		#CUPS COFFEE/DAY							5E11		
21120		#CUPS TEA/DAY							5E12		
21130		#12OZ CAF DRK/DA								5E08	
21140		#12OZ OTH DRK/DA								5E09	
21150		#CUPS COFFEE/DA								5E10	
21160		#CUPS OF TEA/DAY								5E11	
21170		#CUPS DECAFF/DAY								5E12	

A01e: DRUGS. How high, how often high

Item Reference Number	Page Loc.	ITEM DESCRIPTION	1975	1976	1977	1978	1979	1980	1981	1982/83	1984/85
840	26	#X DRK ENF FL HI	*B05	*B05	*B05	*B05	*B05	*B05	*B05	*B05	*B05
1970	44	#X DRK ENF FL 4	1A033	1B010	1B010	1B010	1B010	1B010	1B010	1B010	1B010
2340	48	MJ/HSH,VRY HIGH	1A050	1B023	1B023	1B023	1B023	1B023	1B023	1B023	1B023
2650	52	LSD,GET VERY HI	1A063	1B033	1B033	1B033	1B033	1B033	1B033	1B037	1B037
2700	53	PSYD,GT VERY HI	1A077	1B039	1B039	1B039	1B039	1B039	1B039	1B043	1B043
3100	59	AMPH,GT VERY HI	1A093	1B047	1B047	1B047	1B047	1B047	1B047	1B054	1B054
3260	61	QUAD GT VERY HI	1A108	1B054	1B054	1B054	1B054	1B054	1B054	1B061	1B061
3590	64	BARB,GT VERY HI	1A122	1B061	1B061	1B061	1B061	1B061	1B061	1B068	1B068
4050	69	TRNQ,GT VERY HI	1A137	1B071	1B071	1B071	1B071	1B071	1B071	1B078	1B078
4520	73	COK,GET VERY HI	1A150	1B080	1B080	1B080	1B080	1B080	1B080	1B087	1B087
4930		HER,GT VERY HI	1A164	1B089	1B089	1B089	1B089	1B089	1B089		
5380	79	NARC,GT VERY HI	1A179	1B099	1B099	1B099	1B099	1B099	1B099	1B098	1B098

A01f: DRUGS. How long high

Item Reference Number	Page Loc.	ITEM DESCRIPTION	1975	1976	1977	1978	1979	1980	1981	1982/83	1984/85
1980	44	DRK AL,HI24+HR	1A034	1B011	1B011	1B011	1B011	1B011	1B011	1B011	1B011
2350	48	MJ/HSH,HI 24+HR	1A051	1B024	1B024	1B024	1B024	1B024	1B024	1B024	1B024
2660	52	LSD,HIGH 24+ HR	1A064	1B034	1B034	1B034	1B034	1B034	1B034	1B038	1B038
2710	54	PSYD,HI 24+ HRS	1A078	1B040	1B040	1B040	1B040	1B040	1B040	1B044	1B044
3110	59	AMPH,HI 24+ HRS	1A094	1B048	1B048	1B048	1B048	1B048	1B048	1B055	1B055
3270	61	QUAD,HI 24+ HRS	1A109	1B055	1B055	1B055	1B055	1B055	1B055	1B062	1B062
3600	65	BARB,HI 24+ HRS	1A123	1B062	1B062	1B062	1B062	1B062	1B062	1B069	1B069
4060	69	TRNQ,HI 24+ HRS	1A138	1B072	1B072	1B072	1B072	1B072	1B072	1B079	1B079
4530	73	COK,HIGH 24+ HR	1A151	1B081	1B081	1B081	1B081	1B081	1B081	1B088	1B088
4940		HER,HI 24+ HRS	1A165	1B090	1B090	1B090	1B090	1B090	1B090		
5390	79	NARC,HI 24+ HRS	1A180	1B100	1B100	1B100	1B100	1B100	1B100	1B099	1B099

A01g: DRUGS. Incidence of first use

Item Reference Number	Page Loc.	ITEM DESCRIPTION	1975	1976	1977	1978	1979	1980	1981	1982/83	1984/85
1680	40	SMK CIG DLY/12G	1A019	1B002	(1B002)	1B002	1B002	1B002	1B002	1B002	1B002
5570	80	GR 1ST SMOK DLY	1A019	1B105A	1B105A	1B105A	1B105A	1B105A	1B105A	1B104A	1B104A
	143				3E12A	3E12A	3E12A	3E12A	3E12A	3E10A	3E10A
5580	80	GR 1ST TRY ALC	1A027	1B105B	1B105B	1B105B	1B105B	1B105B	1B105B	1B104B	1B104B
	143				3E12B	3E12B	3E12B	3E12B	3E12B	3E10B	3E10B
5590	80	GR 1ST TRY MJ	1A043	1B105C	1B105C	1B105C	1B105C	1B105C	1B105C	1B104C	1B104C
	143				3E12C	3E12C	3E12C	3E12C	3E12C	3E10C	3E10C
5600	80	GR 1ST TRY LSD	1A056	1B105D	1B105D	1B105D	1B105D	1B105D	1B105D	1B104D	1B104D
	143				3E12D	3E12D	3E12D	3E12D	3E12D	3E10D	3E10D
5610	80	GR 1ST TRY PSY	1A070	1B105E	1B105E	1B105E	1B105E	1B105E	1B105E	1B104E	1B104E
	143				3E12E	3E12E	3E12E	3E12E	3E12E	3E10E	3E10E
5620	80	GR 1ST TRY AMP	1A086	1B105F	1B105F	1B105F	1B105F	1B105F	1B105F	1B104F	1B104F
	143				3E12F	3E12F	3E12F	3E12F	3E12F	3E10F	3E10F
5630	81	GR 1ST TRY QUA	1A101	1B105G	1B105G	1B105G	1B105G	1B105G	1B105G	1B104G	1B104G
	144				3E12G	3E12G	3E12G	3E12G	3E12G	3E10G	3E10G
5640	81	GR 1ST TRY BRB	1A115	1B105H	1B105H	1B105H	1B105H	1B105H	1B105H	1B104H	1B104H
	144				3E12H	3E12H	3E12H	3E12H	3E12H	3E10H	3E10H
5650	81	GR 1ST TRY TRN	1A130	1B105I	1B105I	1B105I	1B105I	1B105I	1B105I	1B104I	1B104I
		(continued)									

Item Reference Number	Page Loc. in this Volume	ITEM DESCRIPTION (ABBREVIATED)	QUESTIONNAIRE LOCATION BY YEAR (FORM, SECTION, AND QUESTION NUMBER)								
			1975	1976	1977	1978	1979	1980	1981	1982/83	1984/85

A01g: DRUGS. Incidence of first use *(continued)*

Item Reference Number	Page Loc. in this Volume	ITEM DESCRIPTION (ABBREVIATED)	1975	1976	1977	1978	1979	1980	1981	1982/83	1984/85
	144				3E12I	3E12I	3E12I	3E12I	3E12I	3E10I	3E10I
5660	81	GR 1ST TRY COK	1A143	1B105J	1B105J	1B105J	1B105J	1B105J	1B105J	1B104J	1B104J
	144				3E12J	3E12J	3E12J	3E12J	3E12J	3E10J	3E10J
5670	81	GR 1ST TRY HER	1A157	1B105K	1B105K	1B105K	1B105K	1B105K	1B105K	1B104K	1B104K
	144				3E12K	3E12K	3E12K	3E12K	3E12K	3E10K	3E10K
5680	81	GR 1ST TRY NRC	1A172	1B105L	1B105L	1B105L	1B105L	1B105L	1B105L	1B104L	1B104L
	144					3E12L	3E12L	3E12L	3E12L	3E10L	3E10L
5685	145	GR 1ST TRY INHAL				3E12M	3E12M	3E12M	3E12M	3E10M	3E10M
5686	112	GR 1ST TRY PCP						2E04A	2E04A	2E04A	2E04A
5687	113	GR 1ST TRY PPRS						2E04B	2E04B	2E04B	2E04B
21190	49	GR 1ST DAILY MJ								1B029	1B029

A01h: DRUGS. Use with other drugs

Item Reference Number	Page Loc. in this Volume	ITEM DESCRIPTION (ABBREVIATED)	1975	1976	1977	1978	1979	1980	1981	1982/83	1984/85
2200	47	#X OVL MJ+ ALC		1B021	1B021	1B021	1B021	1B021	1B021	1B021	1B021
2500	51	#X OVL LSD+ ALC		1B031A	1B031A	1B031A	1B031A	1B031A	1B031A	1B035A	1B035A
2510	52	#X OVL LSD+ MJ		1B031B	1B031B	1B031B	1B031B	1B031B	1B031B	1B035B	1B035B
2900	58	#X OVL AMPH+ALC		1B045A	1B045A	1B045A	1B045A	1B045A	1B045A	1B052A	1B052A
2910	58	#X OVL AMPH+MJ		1B045B	1B045B	1B045B	1B045B	1B045B	1B045B	1B052B	1B052B
2920	58	#X OVL AMPH+LSD		1B045C	1B045C	1B045C	1B045C	1B045C	1B045C	1B052C	1B052C
2930	59	#X OVL AMPH+PSY		1B045D	1B045D	1B045D	1B045D	1B045D	1B045D	1B052D	1B052D
3390	63	#X OVL BARB+ALC		1B059A	1B059A	1B059A	1B059A	1B059A	1B059A	1B066A	1B066A
3400	63	#X OVL BARB+MJ		1B059B	1B059B	1B059B	1B059B	1B059B	1B059B	1B066B	1B066B
3410	64	#X OVL BARB+LSD		1B059C	1B059C	1B059C	1B059C	1B059C	1B059C	1B066C	1B066C
3420	64	#X OVL BARB+PSY		1B059D	1B059D	1B059D	1B059D	1B059D	1B059D	1B066D	1B066D
3430	64	#X OVL BARB+AMP		1B059E	1B059E	1B059E	1B059E	1B059E	1B059E	1B066E	1B066E
3440	64	#X OVL BARB+QUA		1B059F	1B059F	1B059F	1B059F	1B059F	1B059F	1B066F	1B066F
3840	68	#X OVL TRQL+ALC		1B069A	1B069A	1B069A	1B069A	1B069A	1B069A	1B076A	1B076A
3850	68	#X OVL TRQL+MJ		1B069B	1B069B	1B069B	1B069B	1B069B	1B069B	1B076B	1B076B
3860	68	#X OVL TRQL+LSD		1B069C	1B069C	1B069C	1B069C	1B069C	1B069C	1B076C	1B076C
3870	68	#X OVL TRQL+PSY		1B069D	1B069D	1B069D	1B069D	1B069D	1B069D	1B076D	1B076D
3880	68	#X OVL TRQL+AMP		1B069E	1B069E	1B069E	1B069E	1B069E	1B069E	1B076E	1B076E
3890	68	#X OVL TRQL+QUA		1B069F	1B069F	1B069F	1B069F	1B069F	1B069F	1B076F	1B076F
3900	68	#X OVL TRQL+BRB		1B069G	1B069G	1B069G	1B069G	1B069G	1B069G	1B076G	1B076G
4290	72	#X OVL COKE+ALC		1B078A	1B078A	1B078A	1B078A	1B078A	1B078A	1B085A	1B085A
4300	72	#X OVL COKE+MJ		1B078B	1B078B	1B078B	1B078B	1B078B	1B078B	1B085B	1B085B
4310	72	#X OVL COKE+LSD		1B078C	1B078C	1B078C	1B078C	1B078C	1B078C	1B085C	1B085C
4320	72	#X OVL COKE+PSY		1B078D	1B078D	1B078D	1B078D	1B078D	1B078D	1B085D	1B085D
4330	72	#X OVL COKE+AMP		1B078E	1B078E	1B078E	1B078E	1B078E	1B078E	1B085E	1B085E
4340	72	#X OVL COKE+QUA		1B078F	1B078F	1B078F	1B078F	1B078F	1B078F	1B085F	1B085F
4350	73	#X OVL COKE+BRB		1B078G	1B078G	1B078G	1B078G	1B078G	1B078G	1B085G	1B085G
4360	73	#X OVL COKE+TRN		1B078H	1B078H	1B078H	1B078H	1B078H	1B078H	1B085H	1B085H
4710		#X OVL HER +ALC		1B087A	1B087A	1B087A	1B087A	1B087A	1B087A		
4720		#X OVL HER +MJ		1B087B	1B087B	1B087B	1B087B	1B087B	1B087B		
4730		#X OVL HER +LSD		1B087C	1B087C	1B087C	1B087C	1B087C	1B087C		
4740		#X OVL HER +PSY		1B087D	1B087D	1B087D	1B087D	1B087D	1B087D		
4750		#X OVL HER +AMP		1B087E	1B087E	1B087E	1B087E	1B087E	1B087E		
4760		#X OVL HER +QUA		1B087F	1B087F	1B087F	1B087F	1B087F	1B087F		
4770		#X OVL HER +BRB		1B087G	1B087G	1B087G	1B087G	1B087G	1B087G		
4780		#X OVL HER +TRN		1B087H	1B087H	1B087H	1B087H	1B087H	1B087H		
4790		#X OVL HER +COK		1B087I	1B087I	1B087I	1B087I	1B087I	1B087I		
5130	77	#X OVL NARC+ALC		1B097A	1B097A	1B097A	1B097A	1B097A	1B097A	1B096A	1B096A
5140	77	#X OVL NARC+MJ		1B097B	1B097B	1B097B	1B097B	1B097B	1B097B	1B096B	1B096B
5150	77	#X OVL NARC+LSD		1B097C	1B097C	1B097C	1B097C	1B097C	1B097C	1B096C	1B096C
5160	77	#X OVL NARC+PSY		1B097D	1B097D	1B097D	1B097D	1B097D	1B097D	1B096D	1B096D
5170	77	#X OVL NARC+AMP		1B097E	1B097E	1B097E	1B097E	1B097E	1B097E	1B096E	1B096E
5180	77	#X OVL NARC+QUA		1B097F	1B097F	1B097F	1B097F	1B097F	1B097F	1B096F	1B096F
5190	78	#X OVL NARC+BRB		1B097G	1B097G	1B097G	1B097G	1B097G	1B097G	1B096G	1B096G
5200	78	#X OVL NARC+TRN		1B097H	1B097H	1B097H	1B097H	1B097H	1B097H	1B096H	1B096H
5210	78	#X OVL NARC+COK		1B097I	1B097I	1B097I	1B097I	1B097I	1B097I	1B096I	1B096I
5220	78	#X OVL NARC+HER		1B097J	1B097J	1B097J	1B097J	1B097J	1B097J	1B096J	1B096J

Item Reference Number	Page Loc. in this Volume	ITEM DESCRIPTION (ABBREVIATED)	QUESTIONNAIRE LOCATION BY YEAR (FORM, SECTION, AND QUESTION NUMBER)								
			1975	1976	1977	1978	1979	1980	1981	1982/83	1984/85
A01i: DRUGS. Tried to stop											
1690	41	*TRY STP SMK&FL	1A021	1B004	1B004	1B004	1B004	1B004	1B004	1B004	1B004
1700	41	*WNT STP SMK NW	1A022	1B005	1B005	1B005	1B005	1B005	1B005	1B005	1B005
2020	45	*TRY STP ALC&FL	1A039	1B016	1B016	1B016	1B016	1B016	1B016	1B016	1B016
2380	49	*TRY STP MJ &FL	1A052	1B027	1B027	1B027	1B027	1B027	1B027	1B027	1B027
2680	52	*TRY STP LSD&FL	1A066	1B036	1B036	1B036	1B036	1B036	1B036	1B040	1B040
3240	60	*TRY STP AMP&FL	1A096	1B051	1B051	1B051	1B051	1B051	1B051	1B058	1B058
3710	65	TRY STP BARB&FL	1A125	1B064	1B064	1B064	1B064	1B064	1B064	1B071	1B071
4170	69	*TRY STP TRQ&FL	1A139	1B074	1B074	1B074	1B074	1B074	1B074	1B081	1B081
4540	73	*TRY STP COK&FL	1A152	1B082	1B082	1B082	1B082	1B082	1B082	1B089	1B089
4950		TRY STP HER& FL	1A166	1B091	1B091	1B091	1B091	1B091	1B091		
5500	79	TRY STP NARC&FL	1A182	1B102	1B102	1B102	1B102	1B102	1B102	1B101	1B101
8910	134	12MO REDUCE ALCL		3D03A	3D03A	3D03A	3D03A	3D03A	3D03A	3D03A	3D03A
8920	134	12MO REDUCE CIG		3D03B	3D03B	3D03B	3D03B	3D03B	3D03B	3D03B	3D03B
8930	134	12MO REDUCE MARJ		3D03C	3D03C	3D03C	3D03C	3D03C	3D03C	3D03C	3D03C
8940	134	12MO REDUCE PSYC		3D03D	3D03D	3D03D	3D03D	3D03D	3D03D	3D03D	3D03D
8950	134	12MO REDUCE AMPH		3D03E	3D03E	3D03E	3D03E	3D03E	3D03E	3D03E	3D03E
8960		12MO REDUCE QUAL		3D03F	3D03F	3D03F					
8970	134	12MO REDUCE BARB		3D03G	3D03G	(3D03G)	3D03G	3D03G	3D03G	3D03G	3D03G
8980	134	12MO REDUCE COKE		3D03H	3D03H	3D03H	3D03H	3D03H	3D03H	3D03H	3D03H
8990	135	12MO REDUCE HRN		3D03I	3D03I	3D03I	3D03I	3D03I	3D03I	3D03I	3D03I
9000	135	12MO REDUCE NARC		3D03J	3D03J	3D03J	3D03J	3D03J	3D03J	3D03J	3D03J
9005	134	12MO REDUCE TRQL					3D03F	3D03F	3D03F	3D03F	3D03F
A01j: DRUGS. Use on doctor's orders											
2790	56	DR TOLD TK AMPH	1A085	1B042	1B042	1B042	1B042	1B042	1B042	1B049	1B049
3280	61	DR TOLD TK BARB	1A114	1B056	1B056	1B056	1B056	1B056	1B056	1B063	1B063
3730	65	DR TOLD TK TRNQ	1A129	1B066	1B066	1B066	1B066	1B066	1B066	1B073	1B073
5020	75	DR TOLD TK NARC	1A171	1B094	1B094	1B094	1B094	1B094	1B094	1B093	1B093
A01k: DRUGS. Bad trip											
2670	52	1+ BAD TRIP LSD	1A065	1B035	1B035	1B035	1B035	1B035	1B035	1B039	1B039
A01l: DRUGS. Specific kinds of drugs											
2720	54	TKN YR,MESCALIN	1A079A	1B041A	1B041A	1B041A	1B041A	1B041A	1B041A	1B045A	1B045A
2730	54	TKN YR,PEYOTE	1A079B	1B041B	1B041B	1B041B	1B041B	1B041B	1B041B	1B045B	1B045B
2740	54	TKN YR,PSILOCYB	1A079C	1B041C	1B041C	1B041C	1B041C	1B041C	1B041C	1B045C	1B045C
2750	54	TKN YR,PCP		1B041D	1B041D	1B041D	1B041D	1B041D	1B041D	1B045D	1B045D
2760	54	TKN YR,CNCT THC	1A079D	1B041E	1B041E	1B041E	1B041E	1B041E	1B041E	1B045E	1B045E
2770	54	TKN YR,OTH PSYD	1A079E	1B041F	1B041F	1B041F	1B041F	1B041F	1B041F	1B045F	1B045F
2780	54	TKN YR,DK NAME	1A079F	1B041G	1B041G	1B041G	1B041G	1B041G	1B041G	1B045G	1B045G
3120	59	TKN YR,BENZDRIN	1A095A	1B049A	1B049A	1B049A	1B049A	1B049A	1B049A	1B056A	1B056A
3130	59	TKN YR,DEXEDRIN	1A095B	1B049B	1B049B	1B049B	1B049B	1B049B	1B049B	1B056B	1B056B
3140	59	TKN YR,METHDRIN	1A095C	1B049C	1B049C	1B049C	1B049C	1B049C	1B049C	1B056C	1B056C
3150	59	TKN YR,RITALIN	1A095D	1B049D	1B049D	1B049D	1B049D	1B049D	1B049D	1B056D	1B056D
3160	59	TKN YR,PRELUDIN	1A095E	1B049E	1B049E	1B049E	1B049E	1B049E	1B049E	1B056E	1B056E
3170	59	TKN YR,DEXAMYL	1A095F	1B049F	1B049F	1B049F	1B049F	1B049F	1B049F	1B056F	1B056F
3180	59	TKN YR,METHAMPH	1A095G	1B049G	1B049G	1B049G	1B049G	1B049G	1B049G	1B056G	1B056G
3190	59	TKN YR,OTH AMPH	1A095H	1B049H	1B049H	1B049H	1B049H	1B049H	1B049H	1B056H	1B056H
3200	59	TKN YR,DNT KN N	1A095I	1B049I	1B049I	1B049I	1B049I	1B049I	1B049I	1B056I	1B056I
3610	65	TKN YR,PHNOBARB	1A124A	1B063A	1B063A	1B063A	1B063A	1B063A	1B063A	1B070A	1B070A
3620	65	TKN YR,SECONAL	1A124B	1B063B	1B063B	1B063B	1B063B	1B063B	1B063B	1B070B	1B070B
3630	65	TKN YR,TUINAL	1A124C	1B063C	1B063C	1B063C	1B063C	1B063C	1B063C	1B070C	1B070C
3640	65	TKN YR,NEMBUTAL	1A124D	1B063D	1B063D	1B063D	1B063D	1B063D	1B063D	1B070D	1B070D
3650	65	TKN YR,LUMINAL	1A124E	1B063E	1B063E	1B063E	1B063E	1B063E	1B063E	1B070E	1B070E
3660	65	TKN YR,DESBUTAL	1A124F	1B063F	1B063F	1B063F	1B063F	1B063F	1B063F	1B070F	1B070F
3670	65	TKN YR,AMYTAL	1A124G	1B063G	1B063G	1B063G	1B063G	1B063G	1B063G	1B070G	1B070G
3680	65	TKN YR,ADRNOCAL	1A124H	1B063H	1B063H	1B063H	1B063H	1B063H	1B063H	1B070H	1B070H
3690	65	TKN YR,OTH BRBT	1A124I	1B063I	1B063I	1B063I	1B063I	1B063I	1B063I	1B070I	1B070I
3700	65	TKN YR,DNT KNOW	1A124J	1B063J	1B063J	1B063J	1B063J	1B063J	1B063J	1B070J	1B070J
4070	69	TKN YR,LIBRIUM		1B073A	1B073A	1B073A	1B073A	1B073A	1B073A	1B080A	1B080A
		(continued)									

Item Reference Number	Page Loc. in this Volume	ITEM DESCRIPTION (ABBREVIATED)	QUESTIONNAIRE LOCATION BY YEAR (FORM, SECTION, AND QUESTION NUMBER)								
			1975	1976	1977	1978	1979	1980	1981	1982/83	1984/85

A01I: DRUGS. Specific kinds of drugs *(continued)*

4080	69	TKN YR,VALIUM		1B073B	1B073B	1B073B	1B073B	1B073B	1B073B	1B080B	1B080B
4090	69	TKN YR,MILTOWN		1B073C	1B073C	1B073C	1B073C	1B073C	1B073C	1B080C	1B080C
4100	69	TKN YR,EQUANIL		1B073D	1B073D	1B073D	1B073D	1B073D	1B073D	1B080D	1B080D
4110	69	TKN YR,MEPRBMTE		1B073E	1B073E	1B073E	1B073E	1B073E	1B073E	1B080E	1B080E
4120	69	TKN YR,SERAX		1B073F	1B073F	1B073F	1B073F	1B073F	1B073F	1B080F	1B080F
4130	69	TKN YR,ATARAX		1B073G	1B073G	1B073G	1B073G	1B073G	1B073G	1B080G	1B080G
4140	69	TKN YR,TRANXENE		1B073H	1B073H	1B073H	1B073H	1B073H	1B073H	1B080H	1B080H
4150	69	TKN YR,VISTARIL		1B073I	1B073I	1B073I	1B073I	1B073I	1B073I	1B080I	1B080I
4160	69	TKN YR,DNT KNW		1B073J	1B073J	1B073J	1B073J	1B073J	1B073J	1B080J	1B080J
5400	79	NARC TKN MTHDNE	1A181A	1B101A	1B101A	1B101A	1B101A	1B101A	1B101A	1B100A	1B100A
5410	79	NARC TKN OPIUM	1A181B	1B101B	1B101B	1B101B	1B101B	1B101B	1B101B	1B100B	1B100B
5420	79	NARC TKN MRPHNE	1A181C	1B101C	1B101C	1B101C	1B101C	1B101C	1B101C	1B100C	1B100C
5430	79	NARC TKN CODEIN	1A181D	1B101D	1B101D	1B101D	1B101D	1B101D	1B101D	1B100D	1B100D
5440	79	NARC TKN DEMROL	1A181E	1B101E	1B101E	1B101E	1B101E	1B101E	1B101E	1B100E	1B100E
5450	79	NARC TKN PARGRC	1A181F	1B101F	1B101F	1B101F	1B101F	1B101F	1B101F	1B100F	1B100F
5460	79	NARC TKN TALWIN	1A181G	1B101G	1B101G	1B101G	1B101G	1B101G	1B101G	1B100G	1B100G
5470	79	NARC TKN LDANUM	1A181H	1B101H	1B101H	1B101H	1B101H	1B101H	1B101H	1B100H	1B100H
5480	79	NARC TKN OTHER	1A181I	1B101I	1B101I	1B101I	1B101I	1B101I	1B101I	1B100I	1B100I
5490	79	NARC TKN DNT KN	1A181J	1B101J	1B101J	1B101J	1B101J	1B101J	1B101J	1B100J	1B100J

A02a: DRUGS. Friends' use

7070	109	ALL FRD SMK CIGS	2A41A	2D06A	2D06A	2D06A	2D06A	2D06A	2D06A	2D06A	2D06A
7080	109	ALL FRD SMK MARJ	2A41B	2D06B	2D06B	2D06B	2D06B	2D06B	2D06B	2D06B	2D06B
7090	109	ALL FRD TAKE LSD	2A41C	2D06C	2D06C	2D06C	2D06C	2D06C	2D06C	2D06C	2D06C
7100	109	ALL FRD TK PSYDL	2A41D	2D06D	2D06D	2D06D	2D06D	2D06D	2D06D	2D06D	2D06D
7110	110	ALL FRD TK AMPH	2A41E	2D06E	2D06E	2D06E	2D06E	2D06E	2D06E	2D06E	2D06E
7120	110	ALL FRD TK QUALD	2A41F	2D06F	2D06F	2D06F	2D06F	2D06F	2D06F	2D06F	2D06F
7130	110	ALL FRD TK BARBT	2A41G	2D06G	2D06G	2D06G	2D06G	2D06G	2D06G	2D06G	2D06G
7140	110	ALL FRD TK TRNQL	2A41H	2D06H	2D06H	2D06H	2D06H	2D06H	2D06H	2D06H	2D06H
7150	110	ALL FRD TK COKE	2A41I	2D06I	2D06I	2D06I	2D06I	2D06I	2D06I	2D06I	2D06I
7160	110	ALL FRD TK HERON	2A41J	2D06J	2D06J	2D06J	2D06J	2D06J	2D06J	2D06J	2D06J
7170	110	ALL FRD TK NARC	2A41K	2D06K	2D06K	2D06K	2D06K	2D06K	2D06K	2D06K	2D06K
7180	111	ALL FRD TK INHL	2A41L	2D06L	2D06L	2D06L	2D06L	2D06L	2D06L	2D06L	2D06L
7190	111	ALL FRD DRK ALCL	2A41M	2D06M	2D06M	2D06M	2D06M	2D06M	2D06M	2D06M	2D06M
7200	111	ALL FRD GT DRUNK	2A41N	2D06N	2D06N	2D06N	2D06N	2D06N	2D06N	2D06N	2D06N
7201	111	# FRNDS TAKE PCP					2E01A	2E01A	2E01A	2E01A	2E01A
7202	111	# FRNDS TK PPRS					2E01B	2E01B	2E01B	2E01B	2E01B

A02b: DRUGS. Exposure to users

8750		OFT W PL TK MARJ	3A55A	5E07A	5E08A	5E08A					
8760		OFT W PL TK LSD	3A55B	5E07B	5E08B	5E08B					
8770		OFT W PL TK PSYC	3A55C	5E07C	5E08C	5E08C					
8780		OFT W PL TK QUAL		5E07D	5E08D	5E08D					
8790		OFT W PL TK BARB	3A55E	5E07E	5E08E	5E08E					
8800		OFT W PL TK TRQL	3A55F	5E07F	5E08F	5E08F					
8810		OFT W PL TK COKE	3A55G	5E07G	5E08G	5E08G					
8820		OFT W PL TK HRN	3A55H	5E07H	5E08H	5E08H					
8830		OFT W PL TK NARC	3A55I	5E07I	5E08I	5E08I					
8835		OFT W PL TK INHL		5E07J	5E08J	5E08J					
8840		OFT W PL TK ALCL	3A55K	5E07K	5E08K	5E08K					
20590	131	12MO NR OTH MARJ		3A29A	3A29A	3A29A	3A29A	3A29A	3A29A	3A29A	3A29A
20600	132	12MO NR OTH LSD		3A29B	3A29B	3A29B	3A29B	3A29B	3A29B	3A29B	3A29B
20610	132	12MO NR OTH PSYC		3A29C	3A29C	3A29C	3A29C	3A29C	3A29C	3A29C	3A29C
20620	132	12MO NR OTH AMPH		3A29D	3A29D	3A29D	3A29D	3A29D	3A29D	3A29D	3A29D
20630	132	12MO NR OTH BARB		3A29E	3A29E	3A29E	3A29E	3A29E	3A29E	3A29E	3A29E
20640	132	12MO NR OTH TRQL		3A29F	3A29F	3A29F	3A29F	3A29F	3A29F	3A29F	3A29F
20650	132	12MO NR OTH COKE		3A29G	3A29G	3A29G	3A29G	3A29G	3A29G	3A29G	3A29G
20660	132	12MO NR OTH HRN		3A29H	3A29H	3A29H	3A29H	3A29H	3A29H	3A29H	3A29H
20670	132	12MO NR OTH NARC		3A29I	3A29I	3A29I	3A29I	3A29I	3A29I	3A29I	3A29I
20680	133	12MO NR OTH ALCL		3A29J	3A29J	3A29J	3A29J	3A29J	3A29J	3A29J	3A29J
21920	200	PARTY-ONE HI ALC									5E08B

(continued)

Item Reference Number	Page Loc. in this Volume	ITEM DESCRIPTION (ABBREVIATED)	QUESTIONNAIRE LOCATION BY YEAR (FORM, SECTION, AND QUESTION NUMBER)								
			1975	1976	1977	1978	1979	1980	1981	1982/83	1984/85

A02b: DRUGS. Exposure to users *(continued)*

Item Reference Number	Page Loc. in this Volume	ITEM DESCRIPTION (ABBREVIATED)	1975	1976	1977	1978	1979	1980	1981	1982/83	1984/85
21930	201	PARTY-OTH HI ALC									5E08C
21950	201	PARTY-PRESS ALCL									5E08E
21960	201	PARTY-PRS HI ALC									5E08F
21970	201	PARTY-ONE HI MJ									5E08G
21980	201	PARTY-OTH HI MJ									5E08H
22000	202	PARTY-PRESS MJ									5E08J
22010	202	PARTY-ONE HI OTD									5E08K
22020	202	PARTY-OTH HI OTD									5E08L
22040	202	PARTY-PRESS OTDG									5E08N

A03a: DRUGS. Availability

Item Reference Number	Page Loc. in this Volume	ITEM DESCRIPTION (ABBREVIATED)	1975	1976	1977	1978	1979	1980	1981	1982/83	1984/85
6750	103	EASY GT MARIJUAN	2A40A	2A21A	2A21A	2A21A	2A21A	2A21A	2A21A	2A21A	2A21A
6760	103	EASY GT LSD	2A40B	2A21B	2A21B	2A21B	2A21B	2A21B	2A21B	2A21B	2A21B
6770	103	EASY GT PSYDELIC	2A40C	2A21C	2A21C	2A21C	2A21C	2A21C	2A21C	2A21C	2A21C
6780	103	EASY GT AMPHTMNS	2A40D	2A21D	2A21D	2A21D	2A21D	2A21D	2A21D	2A21D	2A21D
6790	103	EASY GT BBTUATES	2A40F	2A21E	2A21E	2A21E	2A21E	2A21E	2A21E	2A21E	2A21E
6800	103	EASY GT TRANQLIZ	2A40G	2A21F	2A21F	2A21F	2A21F	2A21F	2A21F	2A21F	2A21F
6810	104	EASY GT COCAINE	2A40H	2A21G	2A21G	2A21G	2A21G	2A21G	2A21G	2A21G	2A21G
6820	104	EASY GT HEROIN	2A40I	2A21H	2A21H	2A21H	2A21H	2A21H	2A21H	2A21H	2A21H
6830	104	EASY GT NARCOTIC	2A40J	2A21I	2A21I	2A21I	2A21I	2A21I	2A21I	2A21I	2A21I

A04a: DRUGS. Expected future use

Item Reference Number	Page Loc. in this Volume	ITEM DESCRIPTION (ABBREVIATED)	1975	1976	1977	1978	1979	1980	1981	1982/83	1984/85
1710	41	NO SMK IN 5 YR	1A023	1B006	1B006	1B006	1B006	1B006	1B006	1B006	1B006
2030	45	NO ALC IN 5 YR	1A040	1B017	1B017	1B017	1B017	1B017	1B017	1B017	1B017
2390	49	NO MJ/HSH IN5YR	1A053	1B028	1B028	1B028	1B028	1B028	1B028	1B032	1B032
2690	53	NO LSD IN 5 YRS	1A067	1B037	1B037	1B037	1B037	1B037	1B037	1B041	1B041
3250	60	NO AMPH IN 5YR	1A097	1B052	1B052	1B052	1B052	1B052	1B052	1B059	1B059
3720	65	NO BARB IN 5YR	1A126	1B065	1B065	1B065	1B065	1B065	1B065	1B072	1B072
4180	70	NO TRNQ IN 5YR	1A140	1B075	1B075	1B075	1B075	1B075	1B075	1B082	1B082
4600	74	NO COKE IN 5YR	1A154	1B084	1B084	1B084	1B084	1B084	1B084	1B091	1B091
5010		NO HER IN 5 YR	1A168	1B093	1B093	1B093	1B093	1B093	1B093		
5560	79	NO NARC IN 5YR	1A184	1B104	1B104	1B104	1B104	1B104	1B104	1B103	1B103
9010	135	NXT 12MOS USE MJ			3D04	3D04	3D04	3D04	3D04	3D04	3D04

A05a: DRUGS. Use alone

Item Reference Number	Page Loc. in this Volume	ITEM DESCRIPTION (ABBREVIATED)	1975	1976	1977	1978	1979	1980	1981	1982/83	1984/85
1720	42	#X/YR ALC ALONE		1B008A	1B008A	1B008A	1B008A	1B008A	1B008A	1B008A	1B008A
2100	46	#X/YR MJ ALONE	1A045	1B020A	1B020A	1B020A	1B020A	1B020A	1B020A	1B020A	1B020A
2400	50	#X/YR LSD ALONE		1B030A	1B030A	1B030A	1B030A	1B030A	1B030A	1B034A	1B034A
2800	57	#X/YR AMPH ALNE		1B044A	1B044A	1B044A	1B044A	1B044A	1B044A	1B051A	1B051A
3290	62	#X/YR BRBT ALNE		1B058A	1B058A	1B058A	1B058A	1B058A	1B058A	1B065A	1B065A
3740	66	#X/YR TRQL ALNE		1B068A	1B068A	1B068A	1B068A	1B068A	1B068A	1B075A	1B075A
4190	70	#X/YR COKE ALNE		1B077A	1B077A	1B077A	1B077A	1B077A	1B077A	1B084A	1B084A
4610		#X/YR HER ALONE		1B086A	1B086A	1B086A	1B086A	1B086A	1B086A		
5030	75	#X/YR NARC ALNE		1B096A	1B096A	1B096A	1B096A	1B096A	1B096A	1B095A	1B095A

A05b: DRUGS. Use with others

Item Reference Number	Page Loc. in this Volume	ITEM DESCRIPTION (ABBREVIATED)	1975	1976	1977	1978	1979	1980	1981	1982/83	1984/85
1730	42	#X/YR ALC-2 PPL		1B008B	1B008B	1B008B	1B008B	1B008B	1B008B	1B008B	1B008B
1750	42	#X/YR ALC-DT/SP		1B008D	1B008D	1B008D	1B008D	1B008D	1B008D	1B008D	1B008D
1760	43	#X/YR ALC-ADLTS		1B008E	1B008E	1B008E	1B008E	1B008E	1B008E	1B008E	1B008E
2110	46	#X/YR MJ-2 PPL		1B020B	1B020B	1B020B	1B020B	1B020B	1B020B	1B020B	1B020B
2130	47	#X/YR MJ-DT/SP		1B020D	1B020D	1B020D	1B020D	1B020D	1B020D	1B020D	1B020D
2140	47	#X/YR MJ-ADLTS		1B020E	1B020E	1B020E	1B020E	1B020E	1B020E	1B020E	1B020E
2410	50	#X/YR LSD-2 PPL		1B030B	1B030B	1B030B	1B030B	1B030B	1B030B	1B034B	1B034B
2430	51	#X/YR LSD-DT/SP		1B030D	1B030D	1B030D	1B030D	1B030D	1B030D	1B034D	1B034D
2440	51	#X/YR LSD-ADLTS		1B030E	1B030E	1B030E	1B030E	1B030E	1B030E	1B034E	1B034E
2810	57	#X/YR AMPH-2PPL		1B044B	1B044B	1B044B	1B044B	1B044B	1B044B	1B051B	1B051B
2830	57	#X/YR AMPH-DT/S		1B044D	1B044D	1B044D	1B044D	1B044D	1B044D	1B051D	1B051D
2840	57	#X/YR AMPH-ADLT		1B044E	1B044E	1B044E	1B044E	1B044E	1B044E	1B051E	1B051E
3300	62	#X/YR BRBT-2PPL		1B058B	1B058B	1B058B	1B058B	1B058B	1B058B	1B065B	1B065B
		(continued)									

Item Reference Number	Page Loc. in this Volume	ITEM DESCRIPTION (ABBREVIATED)	QUESTIONNAIRE LOCATION BY YEAR (FORM, SECTION, AND QUESTION NUMBER)								
			1975	1976	1977	1978	1979	1980	1981	1982/83	1984/85

A05b: DRUGS. Use with others (continued)

3320	62	#X/YR BRBT-DT/S		1B058D	1B058D	1B058D	1B058D	1B058D	1B058D	1B065D	1B065D
3330	63	#X/YR BRBT-ADLT		1B058E	1B058E	1B058E	1B058E	1B058E	1B058E	1B065E	1B065E
3750	66	#X/YR TRQL-2PPL		1B068B	1B068B	1B068B	1B068B	1B068B	1B068B	1B075B	1B075B
3770	67	#X/YR TRQL-DT/S		1B068D	1B068D	1B068D	1B068D	1B068D	1B068D	1B075D	1B075D
3780	67	#X/YR TRQL-ADLT		1B068E	1B068E	1B068E	1B068E	1B068E	1B068E	1B075E	1B075E
4200	71	#X/YR COKE-2PPL		1B077B	1B077B	1B077B	1B077B	1B077B	1B077B	1B084B	1B084B
4220	71	#X/YR COKE-DT/S		1B077D	1B077D	1B077D	1B077D	1B077D	1B077D	1B084D	1B084D
4230	71	#X/YR COKE-ADLT		1B077E	1B077E	1B077E	1B077E	1B077E	1B077E	1B084E	1B084E
4620		#X/YR HER-2 PPL		1B086B	1B086B	1B086B	1B086B	1B086B	1B086B		
4640		#X/YR HER-DA/SP		1B086D	1B086D	1B086D	1B086D	1B086D	1B086D		
4650		#X/YR HER-ADULT		1B086E	1B086E	1B086E	1B086E	1B086E	1B086E		
5040	76	#X/YR NARC-2PPL		1B096B	1B096B	1B096B	1B096B	1B096B	1B096B	1B095B	1B095B
5060	76	#X/YR NARC-DT/S		1B096D	1B096D	1B096D	1B096D	1B096D	1B096D	1B095D	1B095D
5070	76	#X/YR NARC-ADLT		1B096E	1B096E	1B096E	1B096E	1B096E	1B096E	1B095E	1B095E

A05c: DRUGS. Settings of use

1740	42	#X/YR ALC@PARTY		1B008C	1B008C	1B008C	1B008C	1B008C	1B008C	1B008C	1B008C
1770	43	#X/YR ALC-DATIM		1B008F	1B008F	1B008F	1B008F	1B008F	1B008F	1B008F	1B008F
1780	43	#X/YR ALC@HOME		1B008G	1B008G	1B008G	1B008G	1B008G	1B008G	1B008G	1B008G
1790	43	#X/YR ALC@SCHL		1B008H	1B008H	1B008H	1B008H	1B008H	1B008H	1B008H	1B008H
1810	43	#X/YR ALCIN CAR		1B008I	1B008I	1B008I	1B008I	1B008I	1B008I	1B008I	1B008I
2120	46	#X/YR MJ@PARTY		1B020C	1B020C	1B020C	1B020C	1B020C	1B020C	1B020C	1B020C
2150	47	#X/YR MJ-DATIME		1B020F	1B020F	1B020F	1B020F	1B020F	1B020F	1B020F	1B020F
2160	47	#X/YR MJ@HOME		1B020G	1B020G	1B020G	1B020G	1B020G	1B020G	1B020G	1B020G
2170	47	#X/YR MJ@SCHL		1B020H	1B020H	1B020H	1B020H	1B020H	1B020H	1B020H	1B020H
2190	47	#X/YR MJIN CAR		1B020I	1B020I	1B020I	1B020I	1B020I	1B020I	1B020I	1B020I
2420	50	#X/YR LSD@PARTY		1B030C	1B030C	1B030C	1B030C	1B030C	1B030C	1B034C	1B034C
2450	51	#X/YR LSD-DATIM		1B030F	1B030F	1B030F	1B030F	1B030F	1B030F	1B034F	1B034F
2460	51	#X/YR LSD@HOME		1B030G	1B030G	1B030G	1B030G	1B030G	1B030G	1B034G	1B034G
2470	51	#X/YR LSD@SCHL		1B030H	1B030H	1B030H	1B030H	1B030H	1B030H	1B034H	1B034H
2490	51	#X/YR LSDIN CAR		1B030I	1B030I	1B030I	1B030I	1B030I	1B030I	1B034I	1B034I
2820	57	#X/YR AMPH@PRTY		1B044C	1B044C	1B044C	1B044C	1B044C	1B044C	1B051C	1B051C
2850	58	#X/YR AMPH-DATM		1B044F	1B044F	1B044F	1B044F	1B044F	1B044F	1B051F	1B051F
2860	58	#X/YR AMPH@HOME		1B044G	1B044G	1B044G	1B044G	1B044G	1B044G	1B051G	1B051G
2880	58	#X/YR AMPH@SCHL		1B044H	1B044H	1B044H	1B044H	1B044H	1B044H	1B051H	1B051H
2890	58	#X/YR AMPH@CAR		1B044I	1B044I	1B044I	1B044I	1B044I	1B044I	1B051I	1B051I
3310	62	#X/YR BRBT@PRTY		1B058C	1B058C	1B058C	1B058C	1B058C	1B058C	1B065C	1B065C
3340	63	#X/YR BRBT-DATM		1B058F	1B058F	1B058F	1B058F	1B058F	1B058F	1B065F	1B065F
3350	63	#X/YR BRBT@HOME		1B058G	1B058G	1B058G	1B058G	1B058G	1B058G	1B065G	1B065G
3360	63	#X/YR BRBT@SCHL		1B058H	1B058H	1B058H	1B058H	1B058H	1B058H	1B065H	1B065H
3380	63	#X/YR BRBT@CAR		1B058I	1B058I	1B058I	1B058I	1B058I	1B058I	1B065I	1B065I
3760	67	#X/YR TRQL@PRTY		1B068C	1B068C	1B068C	1B068C	1B068C	1B068C	1B075C	1B075C
3790	67	#X/YR TRQL-DATM		1B068F	1B068F	1B068F	1B068F	1B068F	1B068F	1B075F	1B075F
3800	67	#X/YR TRQL@HOME		1B068G	1B068G	1B068G	1B068G	1B068G	1B068G	1B075G	1B075G
3810	67	#X/YR TRQL@SCHL		1B068H	1B068H	1B068H	1B068H	1B068H	1B068H	1B075H	1B075H
3830	67	#X/YR TRQL@CAR		1B068I	1B068I	1B068I	1B068I	1B068I	1B068I	1B075I	1B075I
4210	71	#X/YR COKE@PRTY		1B077C	1B077C	1B077C	1B077C	1B077C	1B077C	1B084C	1B084C
4240	71	#X/YR COKE-DATM		1B077F	1B077F	1B077F	1B077F	1B077F	1B077F	1B084F	1B084F
4250	71	#X/YR COKE@HOME		1B077G	1B077G	1B077G	1B077G	1B077G	1B077G	1B084G	1B084G
4260	71	#X/YR COKE@SCHL		1B077H	1B077H	1B077H	1B077H	1B077H	1B077H	1B084H	1B084H
4280	72	#X/YR COKE@CAR		1B077I	1B077I	1B077I	1B077I	1B077I	1B077I	1B084I	1B084I
4630		#X/YR HER@PARTY		1B086C	1B086C	1B086C	1B086C	1B086C	1B086C		
4660		#X/YR HER-DATIM		1B086F	1B086F	1B086F	1B086F	1B086F	1B086F		
4670		#X/YR HER@HOME		1B086G	1B086G	1B086G	1B086G	1B086G	1B086G		
4680		#X/YR HER@SCHL		1B086H	1B086H	1B086H	1B086H	1B086H	1B086H		
4700		#X/YR HER@CAR		1B086I	1B086I	1B086I	1B086I	1B086I	1B086I		
5050	76	#X/YR NARC@PRTY		1B096C	1B096C	1B096C	1B096C	1B096C	1B096C	1B095C	1B095C
5080	76	#X/YR NARC-DATM		1B096F	1B096F	1B096F	1B096F	1B096F	1B096F	1B095F	1B095F
5090	76	#X/YR NARC@HOME		1B096G	1B096G	1B096G	1B096G	1B096G	1B096G	1B095G	1B095G
5100	76	#X/YR NARC@SCHL		1B096H	1B096H	1B096H	1B096H	1B096H	1B096H	1B095H	1B095H
5120	77	#X/YR NARC @CAR		1B096I	1B096I	1B096I	1B096I	1B096I	1B096I	1B095I	1B095I
21940	201	PARTY-YOU HI ALC									5E08D
		(continued)									

Item Reference Number	Page Loc. in this Volume	ITEM DESCRIPTION (ABBREVIATED)	QUESTIONNAIRE LOCATION BY YEAR (FORM, SECTION, AND QUESTION NUMBER)								
			1975	1976	1977	1978	1979	1980	1981	1982/83	1984/85

A05c: DRUGS. Settings of use (continued)

Item Reference Number	Page Loc.	ITEM DESCRIPTION	1975	1976	1977	1978	1979	1980	1981	1982/83	1984/85
21990	201	PARTY-YOU HI MJ									5E08I
22030	202	PARTY-YOU HI OTD									5E08M
22060	202	PRF PTY-U HI ALC									5E09B
22080	203	PRF PTY-U USE MJ									5E09D
22100	203	PR PTY-U USE OTD									5E09F

A05d: DRUGS. Mode of administration

Item Reference Number	Page Loc.	ITEM DESCRIPTION	1975	1976	1977	1978	1979	1980	1981	1982/83	1984/85
3210	60	MTHD AMPH-MOUTH		1B050A	1B050A	1B050A	1B050A	1B050A	1B050A	1B057A	1B057A
3220	60	MTHD AMPH-INJCT		1B050B	1B050B	1B050B	1B050B	1B050B	1B050B	1B057B	1B057B
3230	60	MTHD AMPH-OTHER		1B050C	1B050C	1B050C	1B050C	1B050C	1B050C	1B057C	1B057C
4550	74	MTHD COKE SNORT	1A153A	1B083A	1B083A	1B083A	1B083A	1B083A	1B083A	1B090A	1B090A
4560	74	MTHD COKE-SMOKE	1A153B	1B083B	1B083B	1B083B	1B083B	1B083B	1B083B	1B090B	1B090B
4570	74	MTHD COKE-INJCT	1A153C	1B083C	1B083C	1B083C	1B083C	1B083C	1B083C	1B090C	1B090C
4580	74	MTHD COKE-MOUTH	1A153D	1B083D	1B083D	1B083D	1B083D	1B083D	1B083D	1B090D	1B090D
4590	74	MTHD COKE-OTHER	1A153E	1B083E	1B083E	1B083E	1B083E	1B083E	1B083E	1B090E	1B090E
4960		METHD HRN SNORT	1A167A	1B092A	1B092A	1B092A	1B092A	1B092A	1B092A		
4970		METHD HRN-SMOKE	1A167B	1B092B	1B092B	1B092B	1B092B	1B092B	1B092B		
4980		METHD HRN-INJCT	1A167C	1B092C	1B092C	1B092C	1B092C	1B092C	1B092C		
4990		METHD HRN-MOUTH	1A167D	1B092D	1B092D	1B092D	1B092D	1B092D	1B092D		
5000		METHD HRN-OTHER	1A167E	1B092E	1B092E	1B092E	1B092E	1B092E	1B092E		
5510	79	METH NARC SNORT	1A183A	1B103A	1B103A	1B103A	1B103A	1B103A	1B103A	1B102A	1B102A
5520	79	METH NARC SMOKE	1A183B	1B103B	1B103B	1B103B	1B103B	1B103B	1B103B	1B102B	1B102B
5530	79	METH NARC INJCT	1A183C	1B103C	1B103C	1B103C	1B103C	1B103C	1B103C	1B102C	1B102C
5540	79	METH NARC MOUTH	1A183D	1B103D	1B103D	1B103D	1B103D	1B103D	1B103D	1B102D	1B102D
5550	79	METH NARC OTHER	1A183E	1B103E	1B103E	1B103E	1B103E	1B103E	1B103E	1B102E	1B102E

A06a: DRUGS. Reasons for use, abstention, and stopping

Item Reference Number	Page Loc.	ITEM DESCRIPTION	1975	1976	1977	1978	1979	1980	1981	1982/83	1984/85
1820	43	ALC EXPERIMENT		1B009A	1B009A	1B009A	1B009A	1B009A	1B009A	1B009A	1B009A
1830	43	ALC RELAX	1A032A	1B009B	1B009B	1B009B	1B009B	1B009B	1B009B	1B009B	1B009B
1840	43	ALC GET HIGH	1A032B	1B009C	1B009C	1B009C	1B009C	1B009C	1B009C	1B009C	1B009C
1850	43	ALC SEEK INSGHT	1A032C	1B009D	1B009D	1B009D	1B009D	1B009D	1B009D	1B009D	1B009D
1860	43	ALC GD TM FRNDS	1A032D	1B009E	1B009E	1B009E	1B009E	1B009E	1B009E	1B009E	1B009E
1870	43	ALC FIT IN GRP	1A032E	1B009F	1B009F	1B009F	1B009F	1B009F	1B009F	1B009F	1B009F
1880	43	ALC GET AWY PRB	1A032F	1B009G	1B009G	1B009G	1B009G	1B009G	1B009G	1B009G	1B009G
1890	43	ALC BOREDOM	1A032G	1B009H	1B009H	1B009H	1B009H	1B009H	1B009H	1B009H	1B009H
1900	43	ALC ANGR&FRSTRN	1A032H	1B009I	1B009I	1B009I	1B009I	1B009I	1B009I	1B009I	1B009I
1910	43	ALC GT THRU DAY	1A032J	1B009J	1B009J	1B009J	1B009J	1B009J	1B009J	1B009J	1B009J
1920	43	ALC INCRS EF DR	1A032K	1B009K	1B009K	1B009K	1B009K	1B009K	1B009K	1B009K	1B009K
1930	43	ALC DECRS EF DR	1A032L	1B009L	1B009L	1B009L	1B009L	1B009L	1B009L	1B009L	1B009L
1940	43	ALC GET SLEEP		1B009M	1B009M	1B009M	1B009M	1B009M	1B009M	1B009M	1B009M
1950	43	ALC TASTES GOOD	1A032N	1B009N	1B009N	1B009N	1B009N	1B009N	1B009N	1B009N	1B009N
1960	43	ALC I AM HOOKED	1A032M	1B009O	1B009O	1B009O	1B009O	1B009O	1B009O	1B009O	1B009O
2210	48	MJ EXPERIMENT	1A049A	1B022A	1B022A	1B022A	1B022A	1B022A	1B022A	1B022A	1B022A
2220	48	MJ RELAX	1A049B	1B022B	1B022B	1B022B	1B022B	1B022B	1B022B	1B022B	1B022B
2230	48	MJ GET HIGH	1A049C	1B022C	1B022C	1B022C	1B022C	1B022C	1B022C	1B022C	1B022C
2240	48	MJ SEEK INSIGHT	1A049D	1B022D	1B022D	1B022D	1B022D	1B022D	1B022D	1B022D	1B022D
2250	48	MJ GD TM FRNDS	1A049E	1B022E	1B022E	1B022E	1B022E	1B022E	1B022E	1B022E	1B022E
2260	48	MJ FIT IN GRP	1A049F	1B022F	1B022F	1B022F	1B022F	1B022F	1B022F	1B022F	1B022F
2270	48	MJ GET AWY PRB	1A049G	1B022G	1B022G	1B022G	1B022G	1B022G	1B022G	1B022G	1B022G
2280	48	MJ BOREDOM	1A049H	1B022H	1B022H	1B022H	1B022H	1B022H	1B022H	1B022H	1B022H
2290	48	MJ ANGR&FRUSTRN	1A049I	1B022I	1B022I	1B022I	1B022I	1B022I	1B022I	1B022I	1B022I
2300	48	MJ GET THRU DAY	1A049K	1B022J	1B022J	1B022J	1B022J	1B022J	1B022J	1B022J	1B022J
2310	48	MJ INCRS EF DRG	1A049L	1B022K	1B022K	1B022K	1B022K	1B022K	1B022K	1B022K	1B022K
2320	48	MJ DECRS EF DRG	1A049M	1B022L	1B022L	1B022L	1B022L	1B022L	1B022L	1B022L	1B022L
2330	48	MJ I AM HOOKED		1B022M	1B022M	1B022M	1B022M	1B022M	1B022M	1B022M	1B022M
2520	52	LSD EXPERIMENT	1A062A	1B032A	1B032A	1B032A	1B032A	1B032A	1B032A	1B036A	1B036A
2530	52	LSD RELAX	1A062B	1B032B	1B032B	1B032B	1B032B	1B032B	1B032B	1B036B	1B036B
2540	52	LSD GET HIGH	1A062C	1B032C	1B032C	1B032C	1B032C	1B032C	1B032C	1B036C	1B036C
2550	52	LSD SEEK INSGHT	1A062D	1B032D	1B032D	1B032D	1B032D	1B032D	1B032D	1B036D	1B036D
2560	52	LSD GD TM FRNDS	1A062E	1B032E	1B032E	1B032E	1B032E	1B032E	1B032E	1B036E	1B036E
2570	52	LSD FIT IN GRP	1A062F	1B032F	1B032F	1B032F	1B032F	1B032F	1B032F	1B036F	1B036F

(continued)

Item Refer- ence Number	Page Loc. in this Volume	ITEM DESCRIPTION (ABBREVIATED)	QUESTIONNAIRE LOCATION BY YEAR (FORM, SECTION, AND QUESTION NUMBER)								
			1975	1976	1977	1978	1979	1980	1981	1982/83	1984/85

A06a: DRUGS. Reasons for use, abstention, and stopping *(continued)*

2580	52	LSD GT AWY PRB	1A062G	1B032G	1B032G	1B032G	1B032G	1B032G	1B032G	1B036G	1B036G
2590	52	LSD BOREDOM	1A062H	1B032H	1B032H	1B032H	1B032H	1B032H	1B032H	1B036H	1B036H
2600	52	LSD ANGR&FRSTRN	1A062I	1B032I	1B032I	1B032I	1B032I	1B032I	1B032I	1B036I	1B036I
2610	52	LSD GT THRU DAY	1A062K	1B032J	1B032J	1B032J	1B032J	1B032J	1B032J	1B036J	1B036J
2620	52	LSD INCRS EF DR	1A062L	1B032K	1B032K	1B032K	1B032K	1B032K	1B032K	1B036K	1B036K
2630	52	LSD DCRS EF DRG	1A062M	1B032L	1B032L	1B032L	1B032L	1B032L	1B032L	1B036L	1B036L
2640	52	LSD I AM HOOKED		1B032M	1B032M	1B032M	1B032M	1B032M	1B032M	1B036M	1B036M
2940	59	AMPH EXPERIMENT	1A092A	1B046A	1B046A	1B046A	1B046A	1B046A	1B046A	1B053A	1B053A
2950	59	AMPH RELAX	1A092B	1B046B	1B046B	1B046B	1B046B	1B046B	1B046B	1B053B	1B053B
2960	59	AMPH GET HIGH	1A092C	1B046C	1B046C	1B046C	1B046C	1B046C	1B046C	1B053C	1B053C
2970	59	AMPH SK INSIGHT	1A092D	1B046D	1B046D	1B046D	1B046D	1B046D	1B046D	1B053D	1B053D
2980	59	AMPH GD TM FRND	1A092E	1B046E	1B046E	1B046E	1B046E	1B046E	1B046E	1B053E	1B053E
2990	59	AMPH FIT IN GRP	1A092F	1B046F	1B046F	1B046F	1B046F	1B046F	1B046F	1B053F	1B053F
3000	59	AMPH GT AWY PRB	1A092G	1B046G	1B046G	1B046G	1B046G	1B046G	1B046G	1B053G	1B053G
3010	59	AMPH BOREDOM	1A092H	1B046H	1B046H	1B046H	1B046H	1B046H	1B046H	1B053H	1B053H
3020	59	AMPH ANGR&FRSTN	1A092I	1B046I	1B046I	1B046I	1B046I	1B046I	1B046I	1B053I	1B053I
3030	59	AMPH GT THRU DA	1A092K	1B046J	1B046J	1B046J	1B046J	1B046J	1B046J	1B053J	1B053J
3040	59	AMPH INCR EF DR	1A092L	1B046K	1B046K	1B046K	1B046K	1B046K	1B046K	1B053K	1B053K
3050	59	AMPH DCRS EF DR	1A092M	1B046L	1B046L	1B046L	1B046L	1B046L	1B046L	1B053L	1B053L
3060	59	AMPH STAY AWAKE	1A092N	1B046M	1B046M	1B046M	1B046M	1B046M	1B046M	1B053M	1B053M
3070	59	AMPH GET>ENERGY	1A092O	1B046N	1B046N	1B046N	1B046N	1B046N	1B046N	1B053N	1B053N
3080	59	AMPH LOSE WGHT	1A092P	1B046O	1B046O	1B046O	1B046O	1B046O	1B046O	1B053O	1B053O
3090	59	AMPH I AM HOOKD	1A092Q	1B046P	1B046P	1B046P	1B046P	1B046P	1B046P	1B053P	1B053P
3450	64	BARB EXPERIMENT	1A121A	1B060A	1B060A	1B060A	1B060A	1B060A	1B060A	1B067A	1B067A
3460	64	BARB RELAX	1A121B	1B060B	1B060B	1B060B	1B060B	1B060B	1B060B	1B067B	1B067B
3470	64	BARB GET HIGH	1A121C	1B060C	1B060C	1B060C	1B060C	1B060C	1B060C	1B067C	1B067C
3480	64	BARB SK INSIGHT	1A121D	1B060D	1B060D	1B060D	1B060D	1B060D	1B060D	1B067D	1B067D
3490	64	BARB GD TM FRND	1A121E	1B060E	1B060E	1B060E	1B060E	1B060E	1B060E	1B067E	1B067E
3500	64	BARB FIT IN GRP	1A121F	1B060F	1B060F	1B060F	1B060F	1B060F	1B060F	1B067F	1B067F
3510	64	BARB GT AWY PRB	1A121G	1B060G	1B060G	1B060G	1B060G	1B060G	1B060G	1B067G	1B067G
3520	64	BARB BOREDOM	1A121H	1B060H	1B060H	1B060H	1B060H	1B060H	1B060H	1B067H	1B067H
3530	64	BARB ANGR&FRSTN	1A121I	1B060I	1B060I	1B060I	1B060I	1B060I	1B060I	1B067I	1B067I
3540	64	BARB GT THRU DA	1A121K	1B060J	1B060J	1B060J	1B060J	1B060J	1B060J	1B067J	1B067J
3550	64	BARB INCR EF DR	1A121L	1B060K	1B060K	1B060K	1B060K	1B060K	1B060K	1B067K	1B067K
3560	64	BARB DCRS EF DR	1A121M	1B060L	1B060L	1B060L	1B060L	1B060L	1B060L	1B067L	1B067L
3570	64	BARB GET SLEEP	1A121N	1B060M	1B060M	1B060M	1B060M	1B060M	1B060M	1B067M	1B067M
3575	64	BARB RLV PHYS PN				1B060N	1B060N	1B060N	1B060N	1B067N	1B067N
3580	64	BARB I AM HOOKD	1A121O	1B060N	1B060N	1B060O	1B060O	1B060O	1B060O	1B067O	1B067O
3910	69	TRNQ EXPERIMENT	1A136A	1B070A	1B070A	1B070A	1B070A	1B070A	1B070A	1B077A	1B077A
3920	69	TRNQ RELAX	1A136B	1B070B	1B070B	1B070B	1B070B	1B070B	1B070B	1B077B	1B077B
3930	69	TRNQ GET HIGH	1A136C	1B070C	1B070C	1B070C	1B070C	1B070C	1B070C	1B077C	1B077C
3940	69	TRNQ SK INSIGHT	1A136D	1B070D	1B070D	1B070D	1B070D	1B070D	1B070D	1B077D	1B077D
3950	69	TRNQ GD TM FRND	1A136E	1B070E	1B070E	1B070E	1B070E	1B070E	1B070E	1B077E	1B077E
3960	69	TRNQ FIT IN GRP	1A136F	1B070F	1B070F	1B070F	1B070F	1B070F	1B070F	1B077F	1B077F
3970	69	TRNQ GT AWY PRB	1A136G	1B070G	1B070G	1B070G	1B070G	1B070G	1B070G	1B077G	1B077G
3980	69	TRNQ BOREDOM	1A136H	1B070H	1B070H	1B070H	1B070H	1B070H	1B070H	1B077H	1B077H
3990	69	TRNQ ANGR&FRSTN	1A136I	1B070I	1B070I	1B070I	1B070I	1B070I	1B070I	1B077I	1B077I
4000	69	TRNQ GT THRU DA	1A136K	1B070J	1B070J	1B070J	1B070J	1B070J	1B070J	1B077J	1B077J
4010	69	TRNQ INCR EF DR	1A136L	1B070K	1B070K	1B070K	1B070K	1B070K	1B070K	1B077K	1B077K
4020	69	TRNQ DCRS EF DR	1A136M	1B070L	1B070L	1B070L	1B070L	1B070L	1B070L	1B077L	1B077L
4030	69	TRNQ GET SLEEP	1A136N	1B070M	1B070M	1B070M	1B070M	1B070M	1B070M	1B077M	1B077M
4035	69	TRNQ RLV PHYS PN				1B070N	1B070N	1B070N	1B070N	1B077N	1B077N
4040	69	TRNQ I AM HOOKD	1A136O	1B070N	1B070N	1B070O	1B070O	1B070O	1B070O	1B077O	1B077O
4370	73	COKE EXPERIMENT	1A149A	1B079A	1B079A	1B079A	1B079A	1B079A	1B079A	1B086A	1B086A
4380	73	COKE RELAX	1A149B	1B079B	1B079B	1B079B	1B079B	1B079B	1B079B	1B086B	1B086B
4390	73	COKE GET HIGH	1A149C	1B079C	1B079C	1B079C	1B079C	1B079C	1B079C	1B086C	1B086C
4400	73	COKE SK INSIGHT	1A149D	1B079D	1B079D	1B079D	1B079D	1B079D	1B079D	1B086D	1B086D
4410	73	COKE GD TM FRND	1A149E	1B079E	1B079E	1B079E	1B079E	1B079E	1B079E	1B086E	1B086E
4420	73	COKE FIT IN GRP	1A149F	1B079F	1B079F	1B079F	1B079F	1B079F	1B079F	1B086F	1B086F
4430	73	COKE GT AWY PRB	1A149G	1B079G	1B079G	1B079G	1B079G	1B079G	1B079G	1B086G	1B086G
4440	73	COKE BOREDOM	1A149H	1B079H	1B079H	1B079H	1B079H	1B079H	1B079H	1B086H	1B086H
4450	73	COKE ANGR&FRSTN	1A149I	1B079I	1B079I	1B079I	1B079I	1B079I	1B079I	1B086I	1B086I
4460	73	COKE GT THRU DA	1A149K	1B079J	1B079J	1B079J	1B079J	1B079J	1B079J	1B086J	1B086J
		(continued)									

Item Reference Number	Page Loc. in this Volume	ITEM DESCRIPTION (ABBREVIATED)	QUESTIONNAIRE LOCATION BY YEAR (FORM, SECTION, AND QUESTION NUMBER)								
			1975	1976	1977	1978	1979	1980	1981	1982/83	1984/85

A06a: DRUGS. Reasons for use, abstention, and stopping *(continued)*

Item Reference Number	Page Loc. in this Volume	ITEM DESCRIPTION (ABBREVIATED)	1975	1976	1977	1978	1979	1980	1981	1982/83	1984/85
4470	73	COKE INCR EF DR	1A149L	1B079K	1B079K	1B079K	1B079K	1B079K	1B079K	1B086K	1B086K
4480	73	COKE DCRS EF DR	1A149M	1B079L	1B079L	1B079L	1B079L	1B079L	1B079L	1B086L	1B086L
4490	73	COKE STAY AWAKE		1B079M	1B079M	1B079M	1B079M	1B079M	1B079M	1B086M	1B086M
4500	73	COKE GET>ENERGY	1A149N	1B079N	1B079N	1B079N	1B079N	1B079N	1B079N	1B086N	1B086N
4510	73	COKE I AM HOOKD	1A149O	1B079O	1B079O	1B079O	1B079O	1B079O	1B079O	1B086O	1B086O
4800		HERIN EXPERIMENT	1A163A	1B088A	1B088A	1B088A	1B088A	1B088A	1B088A		
4810		HERIN RELAX	1A163B	1B088B	1B088B	1B088B	1B088B	1B088B	1B088B		
4820		HERIN GET HIGH	1A163C	1B088C	1B088C	1B088C	1B088C	1B088C	1B088C		
4830		HERIN SK INSIGT	1A163D	1B088D	1B088D	1B088D	1B088D	1B088D	1B088D		
4840		HERIN GD TM FRN	1A163E	1B088E	1B088E	1B088E	1B088E	1B088E	1B088E		
4850		HERIN FT IN GRP	1A163F	1B088F	1B088F	1B088F	1B088F	1B088F	1B088F		
4860		HERIN GT AWY PB	1A163G	1B088G	1B088G	1B088G	1B088G	1B088G	1B088G		
4870		HERIN BOREDOM	1A163H	1B088H	1B088H	1B088H	1B088H	1B088H	1B088H		
4880		HERIN ANGR&FRST	1A163I	1B088I	1B088I	1B088I	1B088I	1B088I	1B088I		
4890		HERIN GT THR DA	1A163K	1B088J	1B088J	1B088J	1B088J	1B088J	1B088J		
4900		HERIN INC EF DG	1A163L	1B088K	1B088K	1B088K	1B088K	1B088K	1B088K		
4910		HERIN DEC EF DG	1A163M	1B088L	1B088L	1B088L	1B088L	1B088L	1B088L		
4920		HERIN I AM HOOK	1A163N	1B088M	1B088M	1B088M	1B088M	1B088M	1B088M		
5230	78	NARC EXPERIMENT	1A178A	1B098A	1B098A	1B098A	1B098A	1B098A	1B098A	1B097A	1B097A
5240	78	NARC RELAX	1A178B	1B098B	1B098B	1B098B	1B098B	1B098B	1B098B	1B097B	1B097B
5250	78	NARC GET HIGH	1A178C	1B098C	1B098C	1B098C	1B098C	1B098C	1B098C	1B097C	1B097C
5260	78	NARC SK INSIGTS	1A178D	1B098D	1B098D	1B098D	1B098D	1B098D	1B098D	1B097D	1B097D
5270	78	NARC GD TM FRND	1A178E	1B098E	1B098E	1B098E	1B098E	1B098E	1B098E	1B097E	1B097E
5280	78	NARC FIT IN GRP	1A178F	1B098F	1B098F	1B098F	1B098F	1B098F	1B098F	1B097F	1B097F
5290	78	NARC GT AWY PBM	1A178G	1B098G	1B098G	1B098G	1B098G	1B098G	1B098G	1B097G	1B097G
5300	78	NARC BOREDOM	1A178H	1B098H	1B098H	1B098H	1B098H	1B098H	1B098H	1B097H	1B097H
5310	78	NARC ANGR&FRSTN	1A178I	1B098I	1B098I	1B098I	1B098I	1B098I	1B098I	1B097I	1B097I
5320	78	NARC GT THRU DA	1A178K	1B098J	1B098J	1B098J	1B098J	1B098J	1B098J	1B097J	1B097J
5330	78	NARC INC EF DG	1A178L	1B098K	1B098K	1B098K	1B098K	1B098K	1B098K	1B097K	1B097K
5340	78	NARC DEC EF DG	1A178M	1B098L	1B098L	1B098L	1B098L	1B098L	1B098L	1B097L	1B097L
5350	78	NARC GET SLEEP		1B098M	1B098M	1B098M	1B098M	1B098M	1B098M	1B097M	1B097M
5360	78	NARC SBST HERIN	1A178O	1B098N	1B098N	1B098N	1B098N	1B098N	1B098N	1B097N	1B097N
5363	78	NARC RLV PHYS PN				1B098O	1B098O	1B098O	1B098O	1B097O	1B097O
5366	78	NARC RLV COUGHNG				1B098P	1B098P	1B098P	1B098P	1B097P	1B097P
5370	78	NARC I AM HOOKD	1A178N	1B098O	1B098O	1B098Q	1B098Q	1B098Q	1B098Q	1B097Q	1B097Q
9020	135	CNCRN PSYCH DAMG		(3D04A)	(3D04A)	3D04A	3D04A	3D04A	3D04A	3D04A	3D04A
9030	135	CNCRN PHYSCL DMG		(3D04B)	(3D04B)	3D04B	3D04B	3D04B	3D04B	3D04B	3D04B
9040	135	CNCRN GT ARRESTD		(3D04C)	(3D04C)	3D04C	3D04C	3D04C	3D04C	3D04C	3D04C
9050	135	CNCRN BECOM ADCT		(3D04D)	(3D04D)	3D04D	3D04D	3D04D	3D04D	3D04D	3D04D
9060	135	AGST MY BELIEFS		(3D04E)	(3D04E)	3D04E	3D04E	3D04E	3D04E	3D04E	3D04E
9070	135	CNCRN LEGY&AMBTN		(3D04F)	(3D04F)	3D04F	3D04F	3D04F	3D04F	3D04F	3D04F
9080	135	CNCRN LOSS CNTRL		(3D04G)	(3D04G)	3D04G	3D04G	3D04G	3D04G	3D04G	3D04G
9090	135	MJ ->STRNGR DRGS		(3D04H)	(3D04H)	3D04H	3D04H	3D04H	3D04H	3D04H	3D04H
9100	135	MJ NOT ENJOYABLE		(3D04I)	(3D04I)	3D04I	3D04I	3D04I	3D04I	3D04I	3D04I
9110	135	PRNTS DISAPPROVE		(3D04J)	(3D04J)	3D04J	3D04J	3D04J	3D04J	3D04J	3D04J
9120	135	HS/WF DISAPPROVE		(3D04K)	(3D04K)	3D04K	3D04K	3D04K	3D04K	3D04K	3D04K
9130	135	DONT LIKE USERS		(3D04L)	(3D04L)	3D04L	3D04L	3D04L	3D04L	3D04L	3D04L
9140	135	FRNDS DNT USE IT		(3D04M)	(3D04M)	3D04M	3D04M	3D04M	3D04M	3D04M	3D04M
9150	135	PSSBLY BAD TRIP		(3D04N)	(3D04N)	3D04N	3D04N	3D04N	3D04N	3D04N	3D04N
9160	135	TOO EXPENSIVE			3D04O	3D04O	3D04O	3D04O	3D04O	3D04O	3D04O
9170	135	NOT AVAILABLE			3D04P	3D04P	3D04P	3D04P	3D04P	3D04P	3D04P
9180	135	NOT WNT GET HIGH			3D04Q	3D04Q	3D04Q	3D04Q	3D04Q	3D04Q	3D04Q

A07a: DRUGS. Tickets, accidents after use

Item Reference Number	Page Loc. in this Volume	ITEM DESCRIPTION (ABBREVIATED)	1975	1976	1977	1978	1979	1980	1981	1982/83	1984/85
660	22	#TCKTS AFT DRNK		+C29A	+C29A	+C29A	+C29A	+C29A	+C29A	+C29A	+C29A
670	23	#TCKTS AFT MARJ		+C29B	+C29B	+C29B	+C29B	+C29B	+C29B	+C29B	+C29B
680	23	#TCKTS AFT OTDG		+C29C	+C29C	+C29C	+C29C	+C29C	+C29C	+C29C	+C29C
700	23	#ACDTS AFT DRNK		+C31A	+C31A	+C31A	+C31A	+C31A	+C31A	+C31A	+C31A
710	23	#ACDTS AFT MARJ		+C31B	+C31B	+C31B	+C31B	+C31B	+C31B	+C31B	+C31B
720	23	#ACDTS AFT OTDG		+C31C	+C31C	+C31C	+C31C	+C31C	+C31C	+C31C	+C31C
1811	116	#X/2W DRIVE+ALCL									2E19A
1812	117	#X/2W DRIVE+5DRK									2E19B
		(continued)									

Item Reference Number	Page Loc. in this Volume	ITEM DESCRIPTION (ABBREVIATED)	QUESTIONNAIRE LOCATION BY YEAR (FORM, SECTION, AND QUESTION NUMBER)								
			1975	1976	1977	1978	1979	1980	1981	1982/83	1984/85

A07a: DRUGS. Tickets, accidents after use (continued)

Item Reference Number	Page Loc. in this Volume	ITEM DESCRIPTION (ABBREVIATED)	1975	1976	1977	1978	1979	1980	1981	1982/83	1984/85
1815	117	#X/2W RIDE+ALCL									2E20A
1816	117	#X/2W RIDE+5DRK									2E20B

A07b: DRUGS. Problems after use

Item Reference Number	Page Loc. in this Volume	ITEM DESCRIPTION (ABBREVIATED)	1975	1976	1977	1978	1979	1980	1981	1982/83	1984/85
9190	135	AL CS BEHV REGRT		3D05A	3D05A	3D05A	3D05A	3D05A	3D05A	3D05A	3D05A
9200	135	AL HURT REL PRNT		3D05A	3D05A	3D05A	3D05A	3D05A	3D05A	3D05A	3D05A
9210	135	AL HURT REL SPSE		3D05A	3D05A	3D05A	3D05A	3D05A	3D05A	3D05A	3D05A
9220	135	AL HURT REL FRND		3D05A	3D05A	3D05A	3D05A	3D05A	3D05A	3D05A	3D05A
9230	135	AL HURT REL TCHR		3D05A	3D05A	3D05A	3D05A	3D05A	3D05A	3D05A	3D05A
9240	135	AL INV PL BD INF		3D05A	3D05A	3D05A	3D05A	3D05A	3D05A	3D05A	3D05A
9250	135	AL HURT PERF JOB		3D05A	3D05A	3D05A	3D05A	3D05A	3D05A	3D05A	3D05A
9260	135	AL CAUS <INTERSTD		3D05A	3D05A	3D05A	3D05A	3D05A	3D05A	3D05A	3D05A
9270	135	AL CS <STABL EMTN		3D05A	3D05A	3D05A	3D05A	3D05A	3D05A	3D05A	3D05A
9280	135	AL CS HAV <ENERGY		3D05A	3D05A	3D05A	3D05A	3D05A	3D05A	3D05A	3D05A
9290	135	AL INTF THNK CLR		3D05A	3D05A	3D05A	3D05A	3D05A	3D05A	3D05A	3D05A
9300	135	AL BD PSYCH EFCT		3D05A	3D05A	3D05A	3D05A	3D05A	3D05A	3D05A	3D05A
9310	135	AL CS HEALTH BAD		3D05A	3D05A	3D05A	3D05A	3D05A	3D05A	3D05A	3D05A
9320	135	AL CS DRIV UNSAF		3D05A	3D05A	3D05A	3D05A	3D05A	3D05A	3D05A	3D05A
9330	135	AL GT TRBL W POL		3D05A	3D05A	3D05A	3D05A	3D05A	3D05A	3D05A	3D05A
9340	135	AL CS NO PROBLEM			3D05A	3D05A	3D05A	3D05A	3D05A	3D05A	3D05A
9350	135	AL NEVER USED DG			3D05A	3D05A	3D05A	3D05A	3D05A	3D05A	3D05A
9360	136	MJ CS BEHV REGRT		3D05M	3D05M	3D05M	3D05M	3D05M	3D05M	3D05M	3D05M
9370	136	MJ HURT REL PRNT		3D05M	3D05M	3D05M	3D05M	3D05M	3D05M	3D05M	3D05M
9380	136	MJ HURT REL SPSE		3D05M	3D05M	3D05M	3D05M	3D05M	3D05M	3D05M	3D05M
9390	136	MJ HURT REL FRND		3D05M	3D05M	3D05M	3D05M	3D05M	3D05M	3D05M	3D05M
9400	136	MJ HURT REL TCHR		3D05M	3D05M	3D05M	3D05M	3D05M	3D05M	3D05M	3D05M
9410	136	MJ INV PL BD INF		3D05M	3D05M	3D05M	3D05M	3D05M	3D05M	3D05M	3D05M
9420	136	MJ HURT PERF JOB		3D05M	3D05M	3D05M	3D05M	3D05M	3D05M	3D05M	3D05M
9430	136	MJ CAUS <INTERSTD		3D05M	3D05M	3D05M	3D05M	3D05M	3D05M	3D05M	3D05M
9440	136	MJ CS <STABL EMTN		3D05M	3D05M	3D05M	3D05M	3D05M	3D05M	3D05M	3D05M
9450	136	MJ CS HAV <ENERGY		3D05M	3D05M	3D05M	3D05M	3D05M	3D05M	3D05M	3D05M
9460	136	MJ INTF THNK CLR		3D05M	3D05M	3D05M	3D05M	3D05M	3D05M	3D05M	3D05M
9470	136	MJ BD PSYCH EFCT		3D05M	3D05M	3D05M	3D05M	3D05M	3D05M	3D05M	3D05M
9480	136	MJ CS HEALTH BAD		3D05M	3D05M	3D05M	3D05M	3D05M	3D05M	3D05M	3D05M
9490	136	MJ CS DRIV UNSAF		3D05M	3D05M	3D05M	3D05M	3D05M	3D05M	3D05M	3D05M
9500	136	MJ GT TRBL W POL		3D05M	3D05M	3D05M	3D05M	3D05M	3D05M	3D05M	3D05M
9510	136	MJ CS NO PROBLEM			3D05M	3D05M	3D05M	3D05M	3D05M	3D05M	3D05M
9520	136	MJ NEVER USED DG			3D05M	3D05M	3D05M	3D05M	3D05M	3D05M	3D05M
9530	136	OT CS BEHV REGRT		3D05O	3D05O	3D05O	3D05O	3D05O	3D05O	3D05O	3D05O
9540	136	OT HURT REL PRNT		3D05O	3D05O	3D05O	3D05O	3D05O	3D05O	3D05O	3D05O
9550	136	OT HURT REL SPSE		3D05O	3D05O	3D05O	3D05O	3D05O	3D05O	3D05O	3D05O
9560	136	OT HURT REL FRND		3D05O	3D05O	3D05O	3D05O	3D05O	3D05O	3D05O	3D05O
9570	136	OT HURT REL TCHR		3D05O	3D05O	3D05O	3D05O	3D05O	3D05O	3D05O	3D05O
9580	136	OT INV PL BD INF		3D05O	3D05O	3D05O	3D05O	3D05O	3D05O	3D05O	3D05O
9590	136	OT HURT PERF JOB		3D05O	3D05O	3D05O	3D05O	3D05O	3D05O	3D05O	3D05O
9600	136	OT CAUS <INTERSTD		3D05O	3D05O	3D05O	3D05O	3D05O	3D05O	3D05O	3D05O
9610	136	OT CS <STABL EMTN		3D05O	3D05O	3D05O	3D05O	3D05O	3D05O	3D05O	3D05O
9620	136	OT CS HAV <ENERGY		3D05O	3D05O	3D05O	3D05O	3D05O	3D05O	3D05O	3D05O
9630	136	OT INTF THNK CLR		3D05O	3D05O	3D05O	3D05O	3D05O	3D05O	3D05O	3D05O
9640	136	OT BD PSYCH EFCT		3D05O	3D05O	3D05O	3D05O	3D05O	3D05O	3D05O	3D05O
9650	136	OT CS HEALTH BAD		3D05O	3D05O	3D05O	3D05O	3D05O	3D05O	3D05O	3D05O
9660	136	OT CS DRIV UNSAF		3D05O	3D05O	3D05O	3D05O	3D05O	3D05O	3D05O	3D05O
9670	136	OT GT TRBL W POL		3D05O	3D05O	3D05O	3D05O	3D05O	3D05O	3D05O	3D05O
9680	136	OT CS NO PROBLEM			3D05O	3D05O	3D05O	3D05O	3D05O	3D05O	3D05O
9690	136	OT NEVER USED DG			3D05O	3D05O	3D05O	3D05O	3D05O	3D05O	3D05O

A08a: DRUGS. Sources of help

Item Reference Number	Page Loc. in this Volume	ITEM DESCRIPTION (ABBREVIATED)	1975	1976	1977	1978	1979	1980	1981	1982/83	1984/85
7540		TRN FA/MO DRG HP			2E05A		2E07A				
7550		TRN SR/BR DRG HP			2E05B		2E07B				
7560		TRN RLTVS DRG HP			2E05C		2E07C				
7570		TRN FRND DRG HP			2E05D		2E07D				
		(continued)									

Item Reference Number	Page Loc. in this Volume	ITEM DESCRIPTION (ABBREVIATED)	QUESTIONNAIRE LOCATION BY YEAR (FORM, SECTION, AND QUESTION NUMBER)								
			1975	1976	1977	1978	1979	1980	1981	1982/83	1984/85

A08a: DRUGS. Sources of help *(continued)*

7580		TRN DOCTR DRG HP			2E05E		2E07E				
7590		TRN CLINC DRG HP			2E05F		2E07F				
7600		TRN CNSLR DRG HP			2E05G		2E07G				
7610		TRN TCHR DRG HP			2E05H		2E07H				
7620		TRN MNSTR DRG HP			2E05I		2E07I				

A09a: DRUGS. Parental awareness of use

7510	113	PRNT THK U DRINK			2E02	2E01	2E04	2E05	2E05	2E05	2E05
7520	113	PRNT THK U SM MJ			2E03	2E02	2E05	2E06	2E06	2E06	2E06
7530		PRNT THK USE DRG			2E04	2E03	2E06	2E07	2E07		

A10a: DRUGS. Education

7690	116	HAD DRUG EDUCATN		2E05	2E09	2E09	2E11	2E12	2E12	2E15	2E15
7840	116	DG ED,>DG INTRST		2E06	2E10	2E10	2E12	2E13	2E13	2E16	2E16
7850	116	DG ED,SPC COURSE		2E07A	2E11A	2E11A	2E13A	2E14A	2E14A	2E17A	2E17A
7860	116	DG ED,IN REG CRS		2E07B	2E11B	2E11B	2E13B	2E14B	2E14B	2E17B	2E17B
7870	116	DG ED,NT REG CRS		2E07C	2E11C	2E11C	2E13C	2E14C	2E14C	2E17C	2E17C
7880	116	DG ED,SPC DISCUS		2E07D	2E11D	2E11D	2E13D	2E14D	2E14D	2E17D	2E17D
7890	116	DG ED,GRT VALUE		2E08	2E12	2E12	2E14	2E15	2E15	2E18	2E18

A11a: DRUGS. Own attitudes about use by adults

8560	129	DAP SMK 1PCK CIG	(3A53A)	3A28A	3A28A	3A28A	3A28A	3A28A	3A28A	3A28A	3A28A
8570	129	DAP TRY MRJ 1-2T	(3A53B)	3A28B	3A28B	3A28B	3A28B	3A28B	3A28B	3A28B	3A28B
8580	129	DAP SMK MRJ OCCS	(3A53C)	3A28C	3A28C	3A28C	3A28C	3A28C	3A28C	3A28C	3A28C
8590	130	DAP SMK MRJ REGL	(3A53D)	3A28D	3A28D	3A28D	3A28D	3A28D	3A28D	3A28D	3A28D
8600	130	DAP TRY LSD 1-2T	(3A53E)	3A28E	3A28E	3A28E	3A28E	3A28E	3A28E	3A28E	3A28E
8610	130	DAP TKG LSD REGL	(3A53F)	3A28F	3A28F	3A28F	3A28F	3A28F	3A28F	3A28F	3A28F
8620	130	DAP TRY HRN 1-2T	(3A53G)	3A28G	3A28G	3A28G	3A28G	3A28G	3A28G	3A28G	3A28G
8630	130	DAP TKG HRN OCCS	(3A53H)	3A28H	3A28H	3A28H	3A28H	3A28H	3A28H	3A28H	3A28H
8640	130	DAP TKG HRN REGL	(3A53I)	3A28I	3A28I	3A28I	3A28I	3A28I	3A28I	3A28I	3A28I
8650	130	DAP TRY BRB 1-2T	(3A53J)	3A28J	3A28J	3A28J	3A28J	3A28J	3A28J	3A28J	3A28J
8660	130	DAP TKG BRB REGL	(3A53K)	3A28K	3A28K	3A28K	3A28K	3A28K	3A28K	3A28K	3A28K
8670	130	DAP TRY AMP 1-2T	(3A53L)	3A28L	3A28L	3A28L	3A28L	3A28L	3A28L	3A28L	3A28L
8680	131	DAP TKG AMP REGL	(3A53M)	3A28M	3A28M	3A28M	3A28M	3A28M	3A28M	3A28M	3A28M
8690	131	DAP TRY COC 1-2T	(3A53N)	3A28N	3A28N	3A28N	3A28N	3A28N	3A28N	3A28N	3A28N
8700	131	DAP TKG COC REGL	(3A53O)	3A28O	3A28O	3A28O	3A28O	3A28O	3A28O	3A28O	3A28O
8710	131	DAP TRY DRK ALCL	(3A53P)	3A28P	3A28P	3A28P	3A28P	3A28P	3A28P	3A28P	3A28P
8720	131	DAP 1-2 DRK/DAY	(3A53Q)	3A28Q	3A28Q	3A28Q	3A28Q	3A28Q	3A28Q	3A28Q	3A28Q
8730	131	DAP 4-5 DRK/DAY	(3A53R)	3A28R	3A28R	3A28R	3A28R	3A28R	3A28R	3A28R	3A28R
8740	131	DAP 5+ DRK WKNDS	(3A53S)	3A28S	3A28S	3A28S	3A28S	3A28S	3A28S	3A28S	3A28S

A11b: DRUGS. Own attitudes about use by own children

7210		FBD CHLD CIG RGL			2E01A						
7220		FBD CHLD MJ OCCS			2E01B						
7230		FBD CHLD MJ RGLY			2E01C						
7240		FBD CHLD LSD OCC			2E01D						
7250		FBD CHLD AMPH OC			2E01E						
7260		FBD CHLD BARB OC			2E01F						
7270		FBD CHLD COKE OC			2E01G						
7280		FBD CHLD HRN OCC			2E01H						
7290		FBD CHLD DRNK OC			2E01I						
7300		FBD CHLD DRNK RG			2E01J						
7310		FBD CHLD DRUNKOC			2E01K						

A11c: DRUGS. Own perceptions of users

13060	194	I/MJ USR,>CREATV			5E01A	5E01A	5E01A	5E01A	5E01A	5E01A	5E01A
13070	194	I/MJ USR,<SENSBL			5E01B	5E01B	5E01B	5E01B	5E01B	5E01B	5E01B
13080	194	I/MJ USR,>INTRST			5E01C	5E01C	5E01C	5E01C	5E01C	5E01C	5E01C
		(continued)									

Item Reference Number	Page Loc. in this Volume	ITEM DESCRIPTION (ABBREVIATED)	QUESTIONNAIRE LOCATION BY YEAR (FORM, SECTION, AND QUESTION NUMBER)								
			1975	1976	1977	1978	1979	1980	1981	1982/83	1984/85

A11c: DRUGS. Own perceptions of users *(continued)*

Item Reference Number	Page Loc.	ITEM DESCRIPTION	1975	1976	1977	1978	1979	1980	1981	1982/83	1984/85
13090	194	I/MJ USR,<HRDWKG			5E01D	5E01D	5E01D	5E01D	5E01D	5E01D	5E01D
13100	194	I/MJ USR,>INDPND			5E01E	5E01E	5E01E	5E01E	5E01E	5E01E	5E01E
13110	195	I/MJ USR,>UNSTBL			5E01F	5E01F	5E01F	5E01F	5E01F	5E01F	5E01F
13120	195	I/MJ USR,>CNCRND			5E01G	5E01G	5E01G	5E01G	5E01G	5E01G	5E01G
13130	195	I/MJ USR,>WKWLD			5E01H	5E01H	5E01H	5E01H	5E01H	5E01H	5E01H
13140	195	I/MJ USR,>CRMNL			5E01I	5E01I	5E01I	5E01I	5E01I	5E01I	5E01I
13330	195	I/DG USR,>CREATV			5E03A	5E03A		5E03A		5E03A	5E02A
13340	195	I/DG USR,<SENSBL			5E03B	5E03B		5E03B		5E03B	5E02B
13350	195	I/DG USR,>INTRST			5E03C	5E03C		5E03C		5E03C	5E02C
13360	195	I/DG USR,<HRDWKG			5E03D	5E03D		5E03D		5E03D	5E02D
13370	196	I/DG USR,>INDPND			5E03E	5E03E		5E03E		5E03E	5E02E
13380	196	I/DG USR,>UNSTBL			5E03F	5E03F		5E03F		5E03F	5E02F
13390	196	I/DG USR,>CNCRND			5E03G	5E03G		5E03G		5E03G	5E02G
13400	196	I/DG USR,>WKWLD			5E03H	5E03H		5E03H		5E03H	5E02H
13410	196	I/DG USR,>CRMNL			5E03I	5E03I		5E03I		5E03I	5E02I
13670	140	DRG USE+,MY FLGS			5E07C	5E07C	5E05C	5E07C		3E07C	3E07C
20880	196	GUY SMK COOL							5E03A	5E05A	5E03A
20890	196	GUY SMK INSECURE							5E03B	5E05B	5E03B
20900	196	GUY SMK INDPNDNT							5E03C	5E05C	5E03C
20910	197	GUY SMK CONFORMG							5E03D	5E05D	5E03D
20920	197	GUY SMK MATURE							5E03E	5E05E	5E03E
20930	197	GUY SM TRY MATUR							5E03F	5E05F	5E03F
20940	197	GIRL SMK COOL							5E04A	5E06A	5E04A
20950	197	GRL SMK INSECURE							5E04B	5E06B	5E04B
20960	197	GRL SMK INDPNDNT							5E04C	5E06C	5E04C
20970	197	GRL SMK CONFORMG							5E04D	5E06D	5E04D
20980	198	GRL SMK MATURE							5E04E	5E06E	5E04E
20990	198	GRL SM TRY MATUR							5E04F	5E06F	5E04F
21000	198	SMKRS ENJOY LIFE							5E05A	5E07A	5E05A
21010	198	PRFR DATE N-SMKR							5E05B	5E07B	5E05B
21020	198	HARMFUL CIG EXAG							5E05C	5E07C	5E05C
21030	198	SMKR POOR JDGMNT							5E05D	5E07D	5E05D
21040	198	DONT MIND SMOKNG							5E05E	5E07E	5E05E
21050	199	SMKG DIRTY HABIT							5E05F	5E07F	5E05F

A11d: DRUGS. Own attitudes about use by people of high school age

Item Reference Number	Page Loc.	ITEM DESCRIPTION	1975	1976	1977	1978	1979	1980	1981	1982/83	1984/85
22070	203	PR PTY-OTH HI AL									5E09C
22090	203	PR PTY-OT USE MJ									5E09E
22110	203	PR PTY-OT USE OT									5E09G

A12a: DRUGS. Parents' attitudes about use

Item Reference Number	Page Loc.	ITEM DESCRIPTION	1975	1976	1977	1978	1979	1980	1981	1982/83	1984/85
11380		PRNT DAP CIGS	4A35A	4E09A	4E09A	4E08A	4E08A				
11390		PRNT DAP TRY MRJ	4A35B	4E09B	4E09B	4E08B	4E08B				
11400		PRNT DAP MJ OCC	4A35C	4E09C	4E09C	4E08C	4E08C				
11410		PRNT DAP MJ REG	4A35D	4E09D	4E09D	4E08D	4E08D				
11420		PRNT DAP TRY LSD	4A35E	4E09E	4E09E	4E08E	4E08E				
11430		PRNT DAP TRY AMP	4A35F	4E09F	4E09F	4E08F	4E08F				
11440		PRNT DAP 1-2DR/D	4A35G	4E09G	4E09G	4E08G	4E08G				
11450		PRNT DAP 4-5DR/D	4A35H	4E09H	4E09H	4E08H	4E08H				
11460		PRNT DAP 5+DR/WE	4A35I	4E09I	4E09I	4E08I	4E08I				

A12b: DRUGS. Friends' and students' attitudes about use

Item Reference Number	Page Loc.	ITEM DESCRIPTION	1975	1976	1977	1978	1979	1980	1981	1982/83	1984/85
11470	170	FRD DAP CIGS			4E10A		4E09A	4E08A	4E08A	4E08A	4E08A
11480	170	FRD DAP TRY MARJ			4E10B		4E09B	4E08B	4E08B	4E08B	4E08B
11490	171	FRD DAP MJ OCC			4E10C		4E09C	4E08C	4E08C	4E08C	4E08C
11500	171	FRD DAP MJ REG			4E10D		4E09D	4E08D	4E08D	4E08D	4E08D
11510	171	FRD DAP TRY LSD			4E10E		4E09E	4E08E	4E08E	4E08E	4E08E
11520	171	FRD DAP TRY AMP			4E10F		4E09F	4E08F	4E08F	4E08F	4E08F
11530	171	FRD DAP 1-2DR/DA			4E10G		4E09G	4E08G	4E08G	4E08G	4E08G
11540	171	FRD DAP 4-5DR/DA			4E10H		4E09H	4E08H	4E08H	4E08H	4E08H
		(continued)									

Item Reference Number	Page Loc. in this Volume	ITEM DESCRIPTION (ABBREVIATED)	QUESTIONNAIRE LOCATION BY YEAR (FORM, SECTION, AND QUESTION NUMBER)								
			1975	1976	1977	1978	1979	1980	1981	1982/83	1984/85

A12b: DRUGS. Friends' and students' attitudes about use (continued)

Item Reference Number	Page Loc. in this Volume	ITEM DESCRIPTION (ABBREVIATED)	1975	1976	1977	1978	1979	1980	1981	1982/83	1984/85
11550	171	FRD DAP 5+DR/WKD			4E10I		4E09I	4E08I	4E08I	4E08I	4E08I
11551	171	FRD DAP DRIV+2DR									4E08J
11552	171	FRD DAP DRIV+5DR									4E08K
13650	139	DRG USE+,MAJ STD		5E06A	5E07A	5E07A	5E05A	5E07A		3E07A	3E07A
13660	140	DRG USE+,MY FRND		5E06B	5E07B	5E07B	5E05B	5E07B		3E07B	3E07B

A12c: DRUGS. Others' perceptions of users

Item Reference Number	Page Loc. in this Volume	ITEM DESCRIPTION (ABBREVIATED)	1975	1976	1977	1978	1979	1980	1981	1982/83	1984/85
12780		PSN TKG MJ/AMBTS		5D02A							
12790		PSN TKG MJ/-SOCL		5D02B							
12800		PSN TKG MJ/CNFMG		5D02C							
12810		PSN TKG MJ/CRMNL		5D02D							
12820		PSN TKG MJ/-STBL		5D02E							
12830		PSN TKG MJ/INTRS		5D02F							
12840		PSN TKG MJ/RBLS		5D02G							
12850		PSN TKG MJ/SNSBL		5D02H							
12860		PSN TKG MJ/SX PR		5D02I							
12870		PSN TKG MJ/WKWLD		5D02J							
12890		PSN TKG DG/AMBTS		5D03A							
12900		PSN TKG DG/-SOCL		5D03B							
12910		PSN TKG DG/CNFMG		5D03C							
12920		PSN TKG DG/CRMNL		5D03D							
12930		PSN TKG DG/-STBL		5D03E							
12940		PSN TKG DG/INTRS		5D03F							
12950		PSN TKG DG/RBLS		5D03G							
12960		PSN TKG DG/SNSBL		5D03H							
12970		PSN TKG DG/SX PR		5D03I							
12980		PSN TKG DG/WKWLD		5D03J							
13190		PPL/MJUSR>CREATV			5E02A	5E02A		5E02A	5E02A	5E02A	
13200		PPL/MJUSR<SENSBL			5E02B	5E02B		5E02B	5E02B	5E02B	
13210		PPL/MJUSR>INTRST			5E02C	5E02C		5E02C	5E02C	5E02C	
13220		PPL/MJUSR<HRDWKG			5E02D	5E02D		5E02D	5E02D	5E02D	
13230		PPL/MJUSR>INDPND			5E02E	5E02E		5E02E	5E02E	5E02E	
13240		PPL/MJUSR>UNSTBL			5E02F	5E02F		5E02F	5E02F	5E02F	
13250		PPL/MJUSR>CNCRND			5E02G	5E02G		5E02G	5E02G	5E02G	
13260		PPL/MJUSR>WKWLD			5E02H	5E02H		5E02H	5E02H	5E02H	
13270		PPL/MJUSR>CRMNL			5E02I	5E02I		5E02I	5E02I	5E02I	
13490		PPL/DGUSR>CREATV			5E04A	5E04A		5E04A		5E04A	
13500		PPL/DGUSR<SENSBL			5E04B	5E04B		5E04B		5E04B	
13510		PPL/DGUSR>INTRST			5E04C	5E04C		5E04C		5E04C	
13520		PPL/DGUSR<HRDWKG			5E04D	5E04D		5E04D		5E04D	
13530		PPL/DGUSR>INDPND			5E04E	5E04E		5E04E		5E04E	
13540		PPL/DGUSR>UNSTBL			5E04F	5E04F		5E04F		5E04F	
13550		PPL/DGUSR>CNCRND			5E04G	5E04G		5E04G		5E04G	
13560		PPL/DGUSR>WKWLD			5E04H	5E04H		5E04H		5E04H	
13570		PPL/DGUSR>CRMNL			5E04I	5E04I		5E04I		5E04I	

A13a: DRUGS. Preferred legality for adults

Item Reference Number	Page Loc. in this Volume	ITEM DESCRIPTION (ABBREVIATED)	1975	1976	1977	1978	1979	1980	1981	1982/83	1984/85
10760	159	LAW 4 SMK TOBPUB			4A20K	4A20K	4A20K	4A20K	4A20K	4A20K	4A20K
10770		ILGL AD SMK CIG		4A20A							
10780	158	ILGL AD MRJ PRIV		4A20B	4A20A	4A20A	4A20A	4A20A	4A20A	4A20A	4A20A
10790	158	ILGL AD MRJ PUBL		4A20C	4A20B	4A20B	4A20B	4A20B	4A20B	4A20B	4A20B
10800	158	ILGL AD LSD PRIV		4A20D	4A20C	4A20C	4A20C	4A20C	4A20C	4A20C	4A20C
10810	158	ILGL AD LSD PUBL		4A20E	4A20D	4A20D	4A20D	4A20D	4A20D	4A20D	4A20D
10820	158	ILGL AD AMP PRIV		4A20F	4A20E	4A20E	4A20E	4A20E	4A20E	4A20E	4A20E
10830	158	ILGL AD AMP PUBL		4A20G	4A20F	4A20F	4A20F	4A20F	4A20F	4A20F	4A20F
10840	158	ILGL AD HRN PRIV		4A20H	4A20G	4A20G	4A20G	4A20G	4A20G	4A20G	4A20G
10850	159	ILGL AD HRN PUBL		4A20I	4A20H	4A20H	4A20H	4A20H	4A20H	4A20H	4A20H
10860	159	ILGL AD DRNK PRV		4A20J	4A20I	4A20I	4A20I	4A20I	4A20I	4A20I	4A20I
10870	159	ILGL AD DRNK PBL		4A20K	4A20J	4A20J	4A20J	4A20J	4A20J	4A20J	4A20J

Item Reference Number	Page Loc. in this Volume	ITEM DESCRIPTION (ABBREVIATED)	QUESTIONNAIRE LOCATION BY YEAR (FORM, SECTION, AND QUESTION NUMBER)								
			1975	1976	1977	1978	1979	1980	1981	1982/83	1984/85

A13b: DRUGS. Own response to legalization

Item Reference Number	Page Loc. in this Volume	ITEM DESCRIPTION (ABBREVIATED)	1975	1976	1977	1978	1979	1980	1981	1982/83	1984/85
10880	159	CRIME 2 USE MARJ	4A32	4A21	4A21	4A21	4A21	4A21	4A21	4A21	4A21
10890	159	LEGAL 2 SELL MRJ	4A33	4A22	4A22	4A22	4A22	4A22	4A22	4A22	4A22
10900	159	USE <MJ IF LEGAL	4A34	4A23	4A23	4A23	4A23	4A23	4A23	4A23	4A23

A13c: DRUGS. Knowledge of marijuana laws

Item Reference Number	Page Loc. in this Volume	ITEM DESCRIPTION (ABBREVIATED)	1975	1976	1977	1978	1979	1980	1981	1982/83	1984/85
13050		R'S STATE LAW/MJ		5D04	5D05	5D05	5D05	5D05			

A14a: DRUGS. Risk of harm to self

Item Reference Number	Page Loc. in this Volume	ITEM DESCRIPTION (ABBREVIATED)	1975	1976	1977	1978	1979	1980	1981	1982/83	1984/85
12360	185	RSK OF CIG1+PK/D	5A41A	5A23A	5A23A	5A23A	5A23A	5A23A	5A23A	5A23A	5A23A
12370	185	RSK OF MJ 1-2 X	5A41B	5A23B	5A23B	5A23B	5A23B	5A23B	5A23B	5A23B	5A23B
12380	185	RSK OF MJ OCSNLY	5A41C	5A23C	5A23C	5A23C	5A23C	5A23C	5A23C	5A23C	5A23C
12390	186	RSK OF MJ REGLY	5A41D	5A23D	5A23D	5A23D	5A23D	5A23D	5A23D	5A23D	5A23D
12400	186	RSK OF LSD 1-2 X	5A41E	5A23E	5A23E	5A23E	5A23E	5A23E	5A23E	5A23E	5A23E
12410	186	RSK OF LSD REGLY	5A41F	5A23F	5A23F	5A23F	5A23F	5A23F	5A23F	5A23F	5A23F
12420	186	RSK OF 'H' 1-2 X	5A41G	5A23G	5A23G	5A23G	5A23G	5A23G	5A23G	5A23G	5A23G
12430	186	RSK OF 'H' OCSNL	5A41H	5A23H	5A23H	5A23H	5A23H	5A23H	5A23H	5A23H	5A23H
12440	186	RSK OF 'H' REGLY	5A41I	5A23I	5A23I	5A23I	5A23I	5A23I	5A23I	5A23I	5A23I
12450	186	RSK OF BARB 1-2X	5A41J	5A23J	5A23J	5A23J	5A23J	5A23J	5A23J	5A23J	5A23J
12460	187	RSK OF BARB REGY	5A41K	5A23K	5A23K	5A23K	5A23K	5A23K	5A23K	5A23K	5A23K
12470	187	RSK OF AMPH 1-2X	5A41L	5A23L	5A23L	5A23L	5A23L	5A23L	5A23L	5A23L	5A23L
12480	187	RSK OF AMPH REG	5A41M	5A23M	5A23M	5A23M	5A23M	5A23M	5A23M	5A23M	5A23M
12490	187	RSK OF COKE 1-2X	5A41N	5A23N	5A23N	5A23N	5A23N	5A23N	5A23N	5A23N	5A23N
12500	187	RSK OF COKE REG	5A41O	5A23O	5A23O	5A23O	5A23O	5A23O	5A23O	5A23O	5A23O
12510	187	RSK OF 1-2 DRINK	5A41P	5A23P	5A23P	5A23P	5A23P	5A23P	5A23P	5A23P	5A23P
12520	187	RSK OF 1-2 DR/DA	5A41Q	5A23Q	5A23Q	5A23Q	5A23Q	5A23Q	5A23Q	5A23Q	5A23Q
12530	188	RSK OF 4-5 DR/DA	5A41R	5A23R	5A23R	5A23R	5A23R	5A23R	5A23R	5A23R	5A23R
12540	188	RSK OF 5+DR/WKND	5A41S	5A23S	5A23S	5A23S	5A23S	5A23S	5A23S	5A23S	5A23S

A14b: DRUGS. Risk of harm to others

Item Reference Number	Page Loc. in this Volume	ITEM DESCRIPTION (ABBREVIATED)	1975	1976	1977	1978	1979	1980	1981	1982/83	1984/85
7320		RSK/OT CIG1+PK/D		2E01A							
7330		RSK/OT MJ 1-2 X		2E01B							
7340		RSK/OT MJ OCSNLY		2E01C							
7350		RSK/OT MJ REGLY		2E01D							
7360		RSK/OT LSD 1-2 X		2E01E							
7370		RSK/OT LSD REGLY		2E01F							
7380		RSK/OT 'H' 1-2 X		2E01G							
7390		RSK/OT 'H' OCSNL		2E01H							
7400		RSK/OT 'H' REGLY		2E01I							
7410		RSK/OT BARB 1-2X		2E01J							
7420		RSK/OT BARB REGY		2E01K							
7430		RSK/OT AMPH 1-2X		2E01L							
7440		RSK/OT AMPH REG		2E01M							
7450		RSK/OT COKE 1-2X		2E01N							
7460		RSK/OT COKE REG		2E01O							
7470		RSK/OT 1-2 DRINK		2E01P							
7480		RSK/OT 1-2 DR/DA		2E01Q							
7490		RSK/OT 4-5 DR/DA		2E01R							
7500		RSK/OT 5+DR/WKND		2E01S							

A15a: DRUGS. Admitting use in questionnaire

Item Reference Number	Page Loc. in this Volume	ITEM DESCRIPTION (ABBREVIATED)	1975	1976	1977	1978	1979	1980	1981	1982/83	1984/85
20800	203	WLD ADMT USE MJ					5E09	5E09	5E14	5E13	5E10
20810	203	WLD ADMT USE AMP					5E10	5E10	5E15	5E14	5E11
20820	204	WLD ADMT USE HER					5E11	5E11	5E16	5E15	5E12

A16a: DRUGS. Parent groups

Item Reference Number	Page Loc. in this Volume	ITEM DESCRIPTION (ABBREVIATED)	1975	1976	1977	1978	1979	1980	1981	1982/83	1984/85
21730	172	IDEA PARENTS GRP								4E09†	4E09
21740	172	#FRNDS PRNTS GRP								4E10†	4E10
21750	172	OWN PRNTS IN GRP								4E11†	4E11
		(continued)									

† This question appears in 1983 but does not appear in 1982.

Item Reference Number	Page Loc. in this Volume	ITEM DESCRIPTION (ABBREVIATED)	QUESTIONNAIRE LOCATION BY YEAR (FORM, SECTION, AND QUESTION NUMBER)								
			1975	1976	1977	1978	1979	1980	1981	1982/83	1984/85

A16a: DRUGS. Parent groups (continued)

Item	Page	Description	1975	1976	1977	1978	1979	1980	1981	1982/83	1984/85
21760	172	GP IMPCT OWN FLG								4E12†	4E12
21770	172	GP CHG RELP PRNT								4E13†	4E13
21780	173	#FRNDS ANTIDG GP								4E14†	4E14
21790	173	EVR IN ANTIDG GP								4E15†	4E15

B01: EDUCATION. High school: scholastic status, objectives, experiences

Item	Page	Description	1975	1976	1977	1978	1979	1980	1981	1982/83	1984/85
390	19	WHEN R XPCT GRAD		+C14	+C14	+C14	+C14	+C14	+C14	+C14	+C14
400	19	R'S HS PROGRAM		+C15	+C15	+C15	+C15	+C15	+C15	+C15	+C15
410	19	RT SF SCH AB>AVG		+C16	+C16	+C16	+C16	+C16	+C16	+C16	+C16
420	19	RT SF INTELL>AVG		+C17	+C17	+C17	+C17	+C17	+C17	+C17	+C17
470	20	R HS GRADE/D=1		+C20	+C20	+C20	+C20	+C20	+C20	+C20	+C20
1310	35	SAT EDUC EXPRNCS	1A009E	1A006E	1A006E	1A006E	1A006E	1A006E	1A006E	1A006E	1A006E
1660	40	GO SCH ENJY XPR	1A013I	1A011I	1A011I	1A011I	1A011I	1A011I	1A011I	1A011I	1A011I
1670	40	DO WL SC IMP/JB	1A013H	1A011J	1A011J	1A011J	1A011J	1A011J	1A011J	1A011J	1A011J
5700	82	*SC WRK NVR MNG		1D002	1D002	1D002	1D002	1D002	1D002	1D002	1D002
5710	82	*MST COUR V DUL		1D003	1D003	1D003	1D003	1D003	1D003	1D003	1D003
5720	82	*LRN SCH NT IMP		1D004	1D004	1D004	1D004	1D004	1D004	1D004	1D004
7630	82	R LIKES SCHOOL		1D001	1D001	1D001	1D001	1D001	1D001	1D001	1D001
	115		2E02	2E06	2E06	2E08	2E09	2E09		2E12	2E12
			3E08	3E07	3E07	3E07	3E07	3E07			
			4E10	5E05	5E05	5E03	5E05				
			5E04								
7640	115	HRS/WK SPND HMWK		2E03	2E07	2E07	2E09	2E10	2E10	2E13	2E13
9860	138	HAD SEX ED IN HS		3E09	3E08	3E08	3E08	3E08	3E08	3E04	3E04
9870	138	STUDY BC IN HS		3E10	3E09	3E09	3E09	3E09	3E09	3E05	3E05

B02: EDUCATION. Combining work and school: attitudes, experiences

Item	Page	Description	1975	1976	1977	1978	1979	1980	1981	1982/83	1984/85
5770	83	R IN WK-STDY PG		1D009	1D009	1D009	1D009	1D009	1D009	1D009	1D009
10260	151	JOB IMPC LRNING	4A08R	4A08R	4A08R	4A08R	4A08R	4A08R	4A08R	4A08R	4A08R

B03: EDUCATION. Interracial contact at school

Item	Page	Description	1975	1976	1977	1978	1979	1980	1981	1982/83	1984/85
8220	124	DES AL CHL SM RC	3A19L	3A10A	3A10A	3A10A	3A10A	3A10A	3A10A	3A10A	3A10A
8230	124	DES SM CHL OT RC	3A19M	3A10B	3A10B	3A10B	3A10B	3A10B	3A10B	3A10B	3A10B
8240	124	DES MS CHL OT RC	3A19N	3A10C	3A10C	3A10C	3A10C	3A10C	3A10C	3A10C	3A10C
8270	124	ELEMSCH AL OT RC	3A21	3A13	3A13	3A13	3A13	3A13	3A13	3A13	3A13
8280	124	HISCH AL OT RC	3A20	3A14	3A14	3A14	3A14	3A14	3A14	3A14	3A14
11890	177	RCL CNTCT SCHOOL		5A07A	5A07A	5A07A	5A07A	5A07A	5A07A	5A07A	5A07A

B04: EDUCATION. Student norms

Item	Page	Description	1975	1976	1977	1978	1979	1980	1981	1982/83	1984/85
5730	82	LOT CMPTN GRADE		1D005	1D005	1D005	1D005	1D005	1D005	1D005	1D005
5740	82	STDTS DSLK CHTG		1D006	1D006	1D006	1D006	1D006	1D006	1D006	1D006
5750	83	ST -LK PROV TCH		1D007	1D007	1D007	1D007	1D007	1D007	1D007	1D007
5760	83	FRD NCG/TCH -LK		1D008	1D008	1D008	1D008	1D008	1D008	1D008	1D008
13580	138	STS SCH RT FAMLY		5E05A	5E06A	5E06A	5E04A	5E06A		3E06A	3E06A
13590	139	STS SCH LDS STU		5E05B	5E06B	5E06B	5E04B	5E06B		3E06B	3E06B
13600	139	STS SCH NIC CAR		5E05C	5E06C	5E06C	5E04C	5E06C		3E06C	3E06C
13610	139	STS SCH HI GRDE		5E05D	5E06D	5E06D	5E04D	5E06D		3E06D	3E06D
13620	139	STS SCH GD ATHLT		5E05E	5E06E	5E06E	5E04E	5E06E		3E06E	3E06E
13630	139	STS SCH INTLCTL		5E05F	5E06F	5E06F	5E04F	5E06F		3E06F	3E06F
13640	139	STS SCH PLN CLG		5E05G	5E06G	5E06G	5E04G	5E06G		3E06G	3E06G

B05: EDUCATION. Counseling

Item	Page	Description	1975	1976	1977	1978	1979	1980	1981	1982/83	1984/85
5780	83	#X/YR COUNS IND		1D010	1D010	1D010	1D010	1D010	1D010	1D010	1D010
5790	83	#X/YR COUNS GRP		1D011	1D011	1D011	1D011	1D011	1D011	1D011	1D011
5800	83	R LK C COUNS MR		1D012	1D012	1D012	1D012	1D012	1D012	1D012	1D012
5810	84	CSLNG VRY HLPFL		(1D013)	1D013	1D013	1D013	1D013	1D013	1D013	1D013
5811	84	CNSL COURSES					1D014A	1D014A	1D014A	1D014A	1D014A
5812	84	CNSL CL PROB					1D014B	1D014B	1D014B	1D014B	1D014B
		(continued)									

† This question appears in 1983 but does not appear in 1982.

Item Reference Number	Page Loc. in this Volume	ITEM DESCRIPTION (ABBREVIATED)	QUESTIONNAIRE LOCATION BY YEAR (FORM, SECTION, AND QUESTION NUMBER)								
			1975	1976	1977	1978	1979	1980	1981	1982/83	1984/85

B05: EDUCATION. Counseling *(continued)*

5813	84	CNSL TRBL R IN					1D014C	1D014C	1D014C	1D014C	1D014C
5814	84	CNSL MILTRY PLN					1D014D	1D014D	1D014D	1D014D	1D014D
5815	84	CNSL EDUC PLANS					1D014E	1D014E	1D014E	1D014E	1D014E
5816	84	CNSL CAREER PLN					1D014F	1D014F	1D014F	1D014F	1D014F
5817	85	CNSL PRNL PROB					1D014G	1D014G	1D014G	1D014G	1D014G

B06: EDUCATION. Absenteeism and truancy

430	19	#DA/4W SC MS ILL		+C18A	+C18A	+C18A	+C18A	+C18A	+C18A	+C18A	+C18A
440	20	#DA/4W SC MS CUT		+C18B	+C18B	+C18B	+C18B	+C18B	+C18B	+C18B	+C18B
450	20	#DA/4W SC MS OTH		+C18C	+C18C	+C18C	+C18C	+C18C	+C18C	+C18C	+C18C
460	20	#DA/4W SKP CLASS		+C19	+C19	+C19	+C19	+C19	+C19	+C19	+C19

B07: EDUCATION. Delinquency and victimization at school

6540	100	FRQ FGT WRK/SCHL	2A39C	2A19C	2A19C	2A19C	2A19C	2A19C	2A19C	2A19C	2A19C
6650	101	FRQ DMG SCH PPTY	2A39N	2A19N	2A19N	2A19N	2A19N	2A19N	2A19N	2A19N	2A19N
9871	140	SM1 SCL ROB <$50		4E11A	3E10A	3E10A	5E06A	5E08A	5E13A	3E08A	3E08A
9872	140	SM1 SCL ROB >$50		4E11B	3E10B	3E10B	5E06B	5E08B	5E13B	3E08B	3E08B
9873	140	SM1 SCL DMG PRTY		4E11C	3E10C	3E10C	5E06C	5E08C	5E13C	3E08C	3E08C
9874	140	SM1 SCL IN U W/W		4E11D	3E10D	3E10D	5E06D	5E08D	5E13D	3E08D	3E08D
9875	141	SM1 SCL TH U W/W		4E11E	3E10E	3E10E	5E06E	5E08E	5E13E	3E08E	3E08E
9876	141	SM1 SCL IN U -WP		4E11F	3E10F	3E10F	5E06F	5E08F	5E13F	3E08F	3E08F
9877	141	SM1 SCL TH U W/I		4E11G	3E10G	3E10G	5E06G	5EO8G	5E13G	3E08G	3E08G

B08: EDUCATION. Opinions regarding competency testing

7900		16YR+,TEST->DIPL				2E13A	(2E13A)	5E07A	2E16A	2E16A	2E19A	
7910		14YR+,TEST->DIPL				2E13B	(2E13B)	5E07B	2E16B	2E16B	2E19B	
7920		ALL STD H.S.TEST				2E13C	(2E13C)	5E07C	2E16C	2E16C	2E19C	

B09: EDUCATION. Post high school: status, plans, characteristics

480	20	R WL DO VOC/TEC		+C21A	+C21A	+C21A	+C21A	+C21A	+C21A	+C21A	+C21A
490	20	R WL DO ARMD FC		+C21B	+C21B	+C21B	+C21B	+C21B	+C21B	+C21B	+C21B
500	21	R WL DO 2YR CLG		+C21C	+C21C	+C21C	+C21C	+C21C	+C21C	+C21C	+C21C
510	21	R WL DO 4YR CLG		+C21D	+C21D	+C21D	+C21D	+C21D	+C21D	+C21D	+C21D
520	21	R WL DO GRD/PRF		+C21E	+C21E	+C21E	+C21E	+C21E	+C21E	+C21E	+C21E
530	21	R WNTDO VOC/TEC		+C22A	+C22A	+C22A	+C22A	+C22A	+C22A	+C22A	+C22A
540	21	R WNTDO ARMD FC		+C22B	+C22B	+C22B	+C22B	+C22B	+C22B	+C22B	+C22B
550	21	R WNTDO 2YR CLG		+C22C	+C22C	+C22C	+C22C	+C22C	+C22C	+C22C	+C22C
560	21	R WNTDO 4YR CLG		+C22D	+C22D	+C22D	+C22D	+C22D	+C22D	+C22D	+C22D
570	21	R WNTDO GRD/PRF		+C22E	+C22E	+C22E	+C22E	+C22E	+C22E	+C22E	+C22E
580	21	R WNTDO NONE		+C22F	+C22F	+C22F	+C22F	+C22F	+C22F	+C22F	+C22F
10410	153	JOB OBSTC EDUCTN		4A13F	4A13F	4A13F	4A13F	4A13F	4A13F	4A13F	4A13F
11320	169	P'IDEA OF EDUC	4A27J	4E08J	4E08J	4E07J	4E07J	4E07J	4E07J	4E07J	4E07J

B10: EDUCATION. Attitudes regarding educational institutions

6910	105	DHNSTY COLL&UNIV	2A20C	2D04C	2D04C	2D04C	2D04C	2D04C	2D04C	2D04C	2D04C
6920	105	DHNSTY PBLC SCHL	2A20D	2D04D	2D04D	2D04D	2D04D	2D04D	2D04D	2D04D	2D04D
7650	115	PRCL INFL SCL RN		2E04A	2E08A	2E08A	2E10A	2E11A	2E11A	2E14A	2E14A
7660	115	TCHR INFL SCL RN		2E04B	2E08B	2E08B	2E10B	2E11B	2E11B	2E14B	2E14B
7670	115	STDS INFL SCL RN		2E04C	2E08C	2E08C	2E10C	2E11C	2E11C	2E14C	2E14C
7680	116	PRTS INFL SCL RN		2E04D	2E08D	2E08D	2E10D	2E11D	2E11D	2E14D	2E14D
8400	126	GD JB COLLG&UNIV	3A27C	3A24C	3A24C	3A24C	3A24C	3A24C	3A24C	3A24C	3A24C
8410	127	GD JB PBLC SCHOL	3A27D	3A24D	3A24D	3A24D	3A24D	3A24D	3A24D	3A24D	3A24D
11130	167	MLTRY MORE ED		4E01B	4E01B	4E01B	4E01B	4E01B	4E01B	4E01B	4E01B
11840	176	PLC WRK SCH/UNIV	5A09E	5A05E	5A05E	5A05E	5A05E	5A05E	5A05E	5A05E	5A05E

Item Reference Number	Page Loc. in this Volume	ITEM DESCRIPTION (ABBREVIATED)	QUESTIONNAIRE LOCATION BY YEAR (FORM, SECTION, AND QUESTION NUMBER)								
			1975	1976	1977	1978	1979	1980	1981	1982/83	1984/85

C01: WORK and LEISURE. Present or recent work experience

Item Reference Number	Page Loc.	ITEM DESCRIPTION	1975	1976	1977	1978	1979	1980	1981	1982/83	1984/85
590	21	HRS/W WRK SCHYR		+C23	+C23	+C23	+C23	+C23	+C23	+C23	+C23
1270	34	SAT PRESENT JOB	1A009A	1A006A	1A006A	1A006A	1A006A	1A006A	1A006A	1A006A	1A006A
5770	83	R IN WK-STDY PG		1D009	1D009	1D009	1D009	1D009	1D009	1D009	1D009
6540	100	FRQ FGT WRK/SCHL	2A39C	2A19C	2A19C	2A19C	2A19C	2A19C	2A19C	2A19C	2A19C
6660	101	FRQ DMG WK PRPTY	2A39O	2A19O	2A19O	2A19O	2A19O	2A19O	2A19O	2A19O	2A19O
10910	160	CMP SATFD W/JOB		4D02	4D02	4D02	4D02	4D02	4D02	4D02	4D02
11790	176	XPRC MK R GD WKR		5A04C	5A04C	5A04C	5A04C	5A04C	5A04C	5A04C	5A04C
11940	178	RCL CNTCT JOB		5A07F	5A07F	5A07F	5A07F	5A07F	5A07F	5A07F	5A07F
21530	160	RCNT EMPLYMT EXP								4D03A	4D03A
21540	160	JOB-#HRS/WEEK								4D03B	4D03B
21550	160	JOB-SUPERVSR AGE								4D04	4D04
21560	161	JOB-#WKRS OWN AG								4D05	4D05
21570	161	JOB-USE BEST SKL								4D06A	4D06A
21580	161	JOB-TEACH SKILLS								4D06B	4D06B
21590	161	JOB-USE LRND SKL								4D06C	4D06C
21600	161	JOB-DIF SOC BKGD								4D06D	4D06D
21610	161	JOB-OVER AGE 30								4D06E	4D06E
21620	161	JOB->STRESS								4D06F	4D06F
21630	162	JOB-INTRFR W ED								4D06G	4D06G
21640	162	JOB-INTRFR W SOC								4D06H	4D06H
21650	162	JOB-INTRFR W FAM								4D06I	4D06I
21660	162	JOB-INTERESTING								4D07A	4D07A
21670	162	JOB-HAPPY FR LIF								4D07B	4D07B
21680	162	JOB-EXPCT FR LIF								4D07C	4D07C
21690	162	JOB-STEP STONE								4D07D	4D07D
21700	163	JOB-DO JST FOR $								4D07E	4D07E
21710	163	JOB-TCHR HELP GT								4D08	4D08
21720	163	JOB-WORK STUDY								4D09	4D09

C02: WORK and LEISURE. Income sources; financial security

Item Reference Number	Page Loc.	ITEM DESCRIPTION	1975	1976	1977	1978	1979	1980	1981	1982/83	1984/85
600	21	R$/AVG WEEK JOB		+C24A	+C24A	+C24A	+C24A	+C24A	(+C24A)	+C24A	+C24A
610	22	R$/AVG WEEK OTH		+C24B	+C24B	+C24B	+C24B	+C24B	(+C24B)	+C24B	+C24B
12990	192	I HAVE ENOUGH $			5D04A	5D04A	5D04A	5D04A	5D02A	5D04A	5D04A
13000	192	I LACK $FR BILL			5D04B	5D04B	5D04B	5D04B	5D02B	5D04B	5D04B
13010	192	I WRY@-FINDG JOB			5D04C	5D04C	5D04C	5D04C	5D02C	5D04C	5D04C
13020	192	I CAN FIND JOB			5D04D	5D04D	5D04D	5D04D	5D02D	5D04D	5D04D
13030	193	I CAN KEEP MYJOB			5D04E	5D04E	5D04E	5D04E	5D02E	5D04E	5D04E
13040	193	I WRY@LOSS MYJOB			5D04F	5D04F	5D04F	5D04F	5D02F	5D04F	5D04F
20830	193	%$SAVE FUTR EDUC							5D03A	5D05A	5D05A
20840	193	%$SAVE/SPEND CAR							5D03B	5D05B	5D05B
20850	193	%$SAVE OTHER							5D03C	5D05C	5D05C
20860	194	%$SPEND ON SELF							5D03D	5D05D	5D05D
20870	194	%$SPEND HELP FAM							5D03E	5D05E	5D05E

C03: WORK and LEISURE. Vocational plans, aspirations, expectations

Item Reference Number	Page Loc.	ITEM DESCRIPTION	1975	1976	1977	1978	1979	1980	1981	1982/83	1984/85
480	20	R WL DO VOC/TEC		+C21A	+C21A	+C21A	+C21A	+C21A	+C21A	+C21A	+C21A
530	21	R WNTDO VOC/TEC		+C22A	+C22A	+C22A	+C22A	+C22A	+C22A	+C22A	+C22A
6870	105	HOW GD AS WORKER	2A19C	2D02C	2D02C	2D02C	2D02C	2D02C	2D02C	2D02C	2D02C
8090	122	SAME JOB MST LIF	3A08I	3A05E	3A05E	3A05E	3A05E	3A05E	3A05E	3A05E	3A05E
10320	152	KIND OF WORK @30	4A09	4A09	4A09	4A09	4A09	4A09	4A09	4A09	4A09
10330	152	R SURE GT THS WK		4A10	4A10	4A10	4A10	4A10	4A10	4A10	4A10
10340	152	R SURE WK GD CHC		4A11	4A11	4A11	4A11	4A11	4A11	4A11	4A11
10350	153	R THNK WK BE SAT		4A12	4A12	4A12	4A12	4A12	4A12	4A12	4A12
10360	153	JOB OBSTC RELGN		4A13A	4A13A	4A13A	4A13A	4A13A	4A13A	4A13A	4A13A
10370	153	JOB OBSTC SEX		4A13B	4A13B	4A13B	4A13B	4A13B	4A13B	4A13B	4A13B
10380	153	JOB OBSTC RACE		4A13C	4A13C	4A13C	4A13C	4A13C	4A13C	4A13C	4A13C
10390	153	JOB OBSTC BKGRND		4A13D	4A13D	4A13D	4A13D	4A13D	4A13D	4A13D	4A13D
10400	153	JOB OBSTC POL VW		4A13E	4A13E	4A13E	4A13E	4A13E	4A13E	4A13E	4A13E
10410	153	JOB OBSTC EDUCTN		4A13F	4A13F	4A13F	4A13F	4A13F	4A13F	4A13F	4A13F
10420	153	JOB OBSTC -VOC T		4A13G	4A13G	4A13G	4A13G	4A13G	4A13G	4A13G	4A13G
10430	154	JOB OBSTC -ABLTY		4A13H	4A13H	4A13H	4A13H	4A13H	4A13H	4A13H	4A13H
		(continued)									

Item Reference Number	Page Loc. in this Volume	ITEM DESCRIPTION (ABBREVIATED)	QUESTIONNAIRE LOCATION BY YEAR (FORM, SECTION, AND QUESTION NUMBER)								
			1975	1976	1977	1978	1979	1980	1981	1982/83	1984/85

C03: WORK and LEISURE. Vocational plans, aspirations, expectations *(continued)*

10440	154	JOB OBSTC - PULL		4A13I	4A13I	4A13I	4A13I	4A13I	4A13I	4A13I	4A13I
10450	154	JOB OBSTC -WK HD		4A13J	4A13J	4A13J	4A13J	4A13J	4A13J	4A13J	4A13J
10460	154	JOB OBSTC -CONFM		4A13K	4A13K	4A13K	4A13K	4A13K	4A13K	4A13K	4A13K

C04: WORK and LEISURE. Preferences regarding job characteristics

1460	37	IMP STEADY WORK		1A007F	1A007F	1A007F	1A007F	1A007F	1A007F	1A007F	1A007F
8050	121	LIK WRK CAN FRGT	3A08D	3A05A	3A05A	3A05A	3A05A	3A05A	3A05A	3A05A	3A05A
10090	148	JOB IMPC SE RSLT	4A08A	4A08A	4A08A	4A08A	4A08A	4A08A	4A08A	4A08A	4A08A
10100	149	JOB IMPC STATUS	4A08B	4A08B	4A08B	4A08B	4A08B	4A08B	4A08B	4A08B	4A08B
10110	149	JOB IMPC INTRSTG	4A08C	4A08C	4A08C	4A08C	4A08C	4A08C	4A08C	4A08C	4A08C
10120	149	JOB IMPC ADVNCMT	4A08D	4A08D	4A08D	4A08D	4A08D	4A08D	4A08D	4A08D	4A08D
10130	149	JOB IMPC HLP OTH	4A08E	4A08E	4A08E	4A08E	4A08E	4A08E	4A08E	4A08E	4A08E
10140	149	JOB IMPC EARN $	4A08F	4A08F	4A08F	4A08F	4A08F	4A08F	4A08F	4A08F	4A08F
10150	149	JOB IMPC CREATVY	4A08G	4A08G	4A08G	4A08G	4A08G	4A08G	4A08G	4A08G	4A08G
10160	149	JOB IMPC UTILITY	4A08H	4A08H	4A08H	4A08H	4A08H	4A08H	4A08H	4A08H	4A08H
10170	149	JOB IMPC MK FRND	4A08I	4A08I	4A08I	4A08I	4A08I	4A08I	4A08I	4A08I	4A08I
10180	150	JOB IMPC USE SKL	4A08J	4A08J	4A08J	4A08J	4A08J	4A08J	4A08J	4A08J	4A08J
10190	150	JOB IMPC WRTHWLE	4A08K	4A08K	4A08K	4A08K	4A08K	4A08K	4A08K	4A08K	4A08K
10200	150	JOB IMPC VACATN	4A08L	4A08L	4A08L	4A08L	4A08L	4A08L	4A08L	4A08L	4A08L
10210	150	JOB IMPC MK DCSN	4A08M	4A08M	4A08M	4A08M	4A08M	4A08M	4A08M	4A08M	4A08M
10220	150	JOB IMPC FRE TIM		4A08N	4A08N	4A08N	4A08N	4A08N	4A08N	4A08N	4A08N
10230	150	JOB IMPC NO MVNG	4A08O	4A08O	4A08O	4A08O	4A08O	4A08O	4A08O	4A08O	4A08O
10240	150	JOB IMPC NO SPRV	4A08P	4A08P	4A08P	4A08P	4A08P	4A08P	4A08P	4A08P	4A08P
10250	151	JOB IMPC SECURTY	4A08Q	4A08Q	4A08Q	4A08Q	4A08Q	4A08Q	4A08Q	4A08Q	4A08Q
10260	151	JOB IMPC LRNING	4A08R	4A08R	4A08R	4A08R	4A08R	4A08R	4A08R	4A08R	4A08R
10270	151	JOB IMPC BE SELF	4A08S	4A08S	4A08S	4A08S	4A08S	4A08S	4A08S	4A08S	4A08S
10280	151	JOB IMPC RESPECT	4A08T	4A08T	4A08T	4A08T	4A08T	4A08T	4A08T	4A08T	4A08T
10290	151	JOB IMPC CNTC PL	4A08U	4A08U	4A08U	4A08U	4A08U	4A08U	4A08U	4A08U	4A08U
10300	151	JOB IMPC EZ PACE		4A08V	4A08V	4A08V	4A08V	4A08V	4A08V	4A08V	4A08V
10310	151	JOB IMPC HRD PRB		4A08W	4A08W	4A08W	4A08W	4A08W	4A08W	4A08W	4A08W

C05: WORK and LEISURE. Desirability of different working arrangements and settings

6160	94	-CHL,HB WK1.,W=0	2A15A	2A08A	2A08A	2A08A	2A08A	2A08A	2A08A	2A08A	2A08A
6170	94	-CHL,HB WK1.,W.5	2A15B	2A08B	2A08B	2A08B	2A08B	2A08B	2A08B	2A08B	2A08B
6180	94	-CHL,HB&WF WK 1.	2A15C	2A08C	2A08C	2A08C	2A08C	2A08C	2A08C	2A08C	2A08C
6190	94	-CHL,HB&WF WK .5	2A15D	2A08D	2A08D	2A08D	2A08D	2A08D	2A08D	2A08D	2A08D
6200	94	-CHL,W WK 1.,H.5	2A15E	2A08E	2A08E	2A08E	2A08E	2A08E	2A08E	2A08E	2A08E
6210	94	-CHL,W WK 1.,H=0	2A15F	2A08F	2A08F	2A08F	2A08F	2A08F	2A08F	2A08F	2A08F
6220	95	PSCH,HB WK1.,W=0	2A16A	2A09A	2A09A	2A09A	2A09A	2A09A	2A09A	2A09A	2A09A
6230	95	PSCH,HB WK1.,W.5	2A16B	2A09B	2A09B	2A09B	2A09B	2A09B	2A09B	2A09B	2A09B
6240	95	PSCH,HB&WF WK 1.	2A16C	2A09C	2A09C	2A09C	2A09C	2A09C	2A09C	2A09C	2A09C
6250	95	PSCH,HB&WF WK .5	2A16D	2A09D	2A09D	2A09D	2A09D	2A09D	2A09D	2A09D	2A09D
6260	95	PSCH,WF WK1.,H.5	2A16E	2A09E	2A09E	2A09E	2A09E	2A09E	2A09E	2A09E	2A09E
6270	95	PSCH,WF WK1.,H=0	2A16F	2A09F	2A09F	2A09F	2A09F	2A09F	2A09F	2A09F	2A09F
8120	122	DES SUPVR DIF RC	3A19B	3A07B	3A07B	3A07B	3A07B	3A07B	3A07B	3A07B	3A07B
8160	123	DES AL WKS SM RC	3A19F	3A08A	3A08A	3A08A	3A08A	3A08A	3A08A	3A08A	3A08A
8170	123	DES SO WKS DF RC	3A19G	3A08B	3A08B	3A08B	3A08B	3A08B	3A08B	3A08B	3A08B
8180	123	DES MS WKS DF RC	3A19H	3A08C	3A08C	3A08C	3A08C	3A08C	3A08C	3A08C	3A08C
11150	167	MLTRY >FLFLLG JB		4E01D	4E01D	4E01D	4E01D	4E01D	4E01D	4E01D	4E01D
11800	176	PLC WRK LG CORPN	5A09A	5A05A	5A05A	5A05A	5A05A	5A05A	5A05A	5A05A	5A05A
11810	176	PLC WRK SM BSNSS	5A09B	5A05B	5A05B	5A05B	5A05B	5A05B	5A05B	5A05B	5A05B
11820	176	PLC WRK GVT AGCY	5A09C	5A05C	5A05C	5A05C	5A05C	5A05C	5A05C	5A05C	5A05C
11830	176	PLC WRK MLTY SVC	5A09D	5A05D	5A05D	5A05D	5A05D	5A05D	5A05D	5A05D	5A05D
11840	176	PLC WRK SCH/UNIV	5A09E	5A05E	5A05E	5A05E	5A05E	5A05E	5A05E	5A05E	5A05E
11850	176	PLC WRK PLC DEPT	5A09F	5A05F	5A05F	5A05F	5A05F	5A05F	5A05F	5A05F	5A05F
11860	176	PLC WRK SOC SVCS	5A09G	5A05G	5A05G	5A05G	5A05G	5A05G	5A05G	5A05G	5A05G
11870	177	PLC WRK SML GRP	5A09H	5A05H	5A05H	5A05H	5A05H	5A05H	5A05H	5A05H	5A05H
11880	177	PLC WRK SLF EMPL	5A09I	5A05I	5A05I	5A05I	5A05I	5A05I	5A05I	5A05I	5A05I

Item Reference Number	Page Loc. in this Volume	ITEM DESCRIPTION (ABBREVIATED)	QUESTIONNAIRE LOCATION BY YEAR (FORM, SECTION, AND QUESTION NUMBER)								
			1975	1976	1977	1978	1979	1980	1981	1982/83	1984/85

C06: WORK and LEISURE. Work ethic/success orientation

Item Reference Number	Page Loc. in this Volume	ITEM DESCRIPTION	1975	1976	1977	1978	1979	1980	1981	1982/83	1984/85
1410	36	IMP B SUCCSS WK		1A007A	1A007A	1A007A	1A007A	1A007A	1A007A	1A007A	1A007A
8060	121	WRK=ONLY MK LVNG	3A08E	3A05B	3A05B	3A05B	3A05B	3A05B	3A05B	3A05B	3A05B
8070	121	WRK CNTRL PRT LF	3A08G	3A05C	3A05C	3A05C	3A05C	3A05C	3A05C	3A05C	3A05C
8080	121	OVTM 2DO BST JOB	3A08H	3A05D	3A05D	3A05D	3A05D	3A05D	3A05D	3A05D	3A05D
8100	122	ENUF$,NT WNT WRK	3A10	3A06	3A06	3A06	3A06	3A06	3A06	3A06	3A06
	154		4A09A	4A14	4A14	4A14	4A14	4A14	4A14	4A14	4A14
	177		5A11	5A06	5A06	5A06	5A06	5A06	5A06	5A06	5A06

C07: WORK and LEISURE. Leisure time: extent, activities

Item Reference Number	Page Loc. in this Volume	ITEM DESCRIPTION	1975	1976	1977	1978	1979	1980	1981	1982/83	1984/85
620	22	#X/AV WK GO OUT		+C25	+C25	+C25	+C25	+C25	+C25	+C25	+C25
630	22	#X DATE 3+/WK		+C26	+C26	+C26	+C26	+C26	+C26	+C26	+C26
5820	89	DALY WATCH TV		2A02A	2A02A	2A02A	2A02A	2A02A	2A02A	2A02A	2A02A
5830	89	DALY GO TO MOVIE		2A02B	2A02B	2A02B	2A02B	2A02B	2A02B	2A02B	2A02B
5840		DALY ART,MSC,PLA		2A02C	2A02C	2A02C	2A02C	2A02C	2A02C	2A02C	
5845	89	DALY ROCK CONCRT									2A02C
5850	89	DALY RIDE FORFUN			2A02D	2A02D	2A02D	2A02D	2A02D	2A02D	2A02D
5860	89	DALY CMNTY AFFRS		2A02E	2A02E	2A02E	2A02E	2A02E	2A02E	2A02E	2A02E
5870	89	DALY PLA MSC,SNG		2A02F	2A02F	2A02F	2A02F	2A02F	2A02F	2A02F	2A02F
5880	90	DALY CREAT WRTNG		2A02G	2A02G	2A02G	2A02G	2A02G	2A02G	2A02G	2A02G
5890	90	DALY ACTV SPORTS		2A02H	2A02H	2A02H	2A02H	2A02H	2A02H	2A02H	2A02H
5900	90	DALY ART/CRAFTS		2A02I	2A02I	2A02I	2A02I	2A02I	2A02I	2A02I	2A02I
5910	90	DALY WRK HSE,CAR		2A02J	2A02J	2A02J	2A02J	2A02J	2A02J	2A02J	2A02J
5920	90	DALY VIST W/FRDS		2A02K	2A02K	2A02K	2A02K	2A02K	2A02K	2A02K	2A02K
5930	90	DALY GO SHOPPING		2A02L	2A02L	2A02L	2A02L	2A02L	2A02L	2A02L	2A02L
5940	90	DALY ALONE LEISR		(2A02M)	2A02M	2A02M	2A02M	2A02M	2A02M	2A02M	2A02M
5950	91	DALY READ BK,MAG		2A02N	2A02N	2A02N	2A02N	2A02N	2A02N	2A02N	2A02N
5960	91	DALY GO TO BARS		2A02O	2A02O	2A02O	2A02O	2A02O	2A02O	2A02O	2A02O
5970	91	DALY GO TO PARTY		2A02P	2A02P	2A02P	2A02P	2A02P	2A02P	2A02P	2A02P
5980		DALY GO CHURCH		2A02D							
10550	156	#HRS TV/DAY/5+		4A16	4A16	4A16	4A16	4A16	4A16	4A16	4A16
10560	156	#BKS LAST YR/10+		4A17	4A17	4A17	4A17	4A17	4A17	4A17	4A17
21900	200	#X/LAST12M PARTY									5E07
21910	200	PARTY-PPL OVR 30									5E08A
21920	200	PARTY-ONE HI ALC									5E08B
21930	201	PARTY-OTH HI ALC									5E08C
21940	201	PARTY-YOU HI ALC									5E08D
21950	201	PARTY-PRESS ALCL									5E08E
21960	201	PARTY-PRS HI ALC									5E08F
21970	201	PARTY-ONE HI MJ									5E08G
21980	201	PARTY-OTH HI MJ									5E08H
21990	201	PARTY-YOU HI MJ									5E08I
22000	202	PARTY-PRESS MJ									5E08J
22010	202	PARTY-ONE HI OTD									5E08K
22020	202	PARTY-OTH HI OTD									5E08L
22030	202	PARTY-YOU HI OTD									5E08M
22040	202	PARTY-PRESS OTDG									5E08N

C08: WORK and LEISURE. Attitudes toward leisure time

Item Reference Number	Page Loc. in this Volume	ITEM DESCRIPTION	1975	1976	1977	1978	1979	1980	1981	1982/83	1984/85
1370	36	SAT SPD LEISR	1A009K	1A006K	1A006K	1A006K	1A006K	1A006K	1A006K	1A006K	1A006K
1440	37	IMP TM RCRN&HBY		1A007D	1A007D	1A007D	1A007D	1A007D	1A007D	1A007D	1A007D
9880		DK DO W LEISR TM			3E11A		3E11A	3E11A	3E11A		
9890		TM QUIK/LEIS HRS			3E11B		3E11B	3E11B	3E11B		
9900		WASTE LEIS TIME			3E11C		3E11C	3E11C	3E11C		
9910		ENUF TIME FR THG			3E11D		3E11D	3E11D	3E11D		
11240	168	P'IDEA OF LSR TM	4A27B	4E08B	4E08B	4E07B	4E07B	4E07B	4E07B	4E07B	4E07B
22050	202	PRFR PTY-PPL >30									5E09A
22060	202	PRF PTY-U HI ALC									5E09B
22070	203	PR PTY-OTH HI AL									5E09C
22080	203	PRF PTY-U USE MJ									5E09D
22090	203	PR PTY-OT USE MJ									5E09E
22100	203	PR PTY-U USE OTD									5E09F
22110	203	PR PTY-OT USE OT									5E09G

Item Reference Number	Page Loc. in this Volume	ITEM DESCRIPTION (ABBREVIATED)	QUESTIONNAIRE LOCATION BY YEAR (FORM, SECTION, AND QUESTION NUMBER)								
			1975	1976	1977	1978	1979	1980	1981	1982/83	1984/85

D01: SEX ROLES and FAMILY. Dating and marriage: status, attitudes, expectations

60	16	R NOT MARRIED		+C06	+C06	+C06	+C06	+C06	+C06	+C06	+C06
6120	93	DFNTLY PRFR MATE	2A10	2A05	2A05	2A05	2A05	2A05	2A05	2A05	2A05
6130	93	THINK WILL MARRY	2A11	2A06	2A06	2A06	2A06	2A06	2A06	2A06	2A06
6140	93	LIKLY STAY MARRD	2A12A	2A07A	2A07A	2A07A	2A07A	2A07A	2A07A	2A07A	2A07A
6850	104	HOW GD AS SPOUSE	2A19A	2D02A	2D02A	2D02A	2D02A	2D02A	2D02A	2D02A	2D02A
8320	125	MARRD OR ENGAGED	3A41	3A18	3A18	3A18	3A18	3A18	3A18	3A18	3A18
8330	125	WHN WANT GT MARR	3A42	3A19	3A19	3A19	3A19	3A19	3A19	3A19	3A19
11770	175	XPRC MK R GD SPS		5A04A	5A04A	5A04A	5A04A	5A04A	5A04A	5A04A	5A04A

D02: SEX ROLES and FAMILY. Parenthood: status, attitudes, expectations

6150	93	LIKLY HAVE KIDS	2A12B	2A07B	2A07B	2A07B	2A07B	2A07B	2A07B	2A07B	2A07B
6860	104	HOW GD AS PARENT	2A19B	2D02B	2D02B	2D02B	2D02B	2D02B	2D02B	2D02B	2D02B
8340	125	THGT LOT HAV CHL	3A43	3A20	3A20	3A20	3A20	3A20	3A20	3A20	3A20
8350	125	# CHLDN WANT(6+)	3A44	3A21	3A21	3A21	3A21	3A21	3A21	3A21	3A21
8360	126	IF -POP, MR CHLD	3A45	3A22	3A22	3A22	3A22	3A22	3A22	3A22	3A22
8370	126	WHN 1ST CHL(5+Y)	3A46	3A23	3A23	3A23	3A23	3A23	3A23	3A23	3A23
11780	175	XPRC MK R GD PRT		5A04B	5A04B	5A04B	5A04B	5A04B	5A04B	5A04B	5A04B

D03: SEX ROLES and FAMILY. Values surrounding marriage and family

1420	37	IMP GD MRRG&FAM		1A007B	1A007B	1A007B	1A007B	1A007B	1A007B	1A007B	1A007B
10470	154	FEW GD MAR, ? IT	4A11A	4A15A	4A15A	4A15A	4A15A	4A15A	4A15A	4A15A	4A15A
10480	154	GD LIV TG BF MRG	4A11B	4A15B	4A15B	4A15B	4A15B	4A15B	4A15B	4A15B	4A15B
10490	155	1 PRTNR=RSTRCTVE	4A11C	4A15C	4A15C	4A15C	4A15C	4A15C	4A15C	4A15C	4A15C
12150	181	FULLR LVS IF MRY	5A12A	5A18J	5A18J	5A18J	5A18J	5A18J	5A18J	5A18J	5A18J
12770	192	LV TGTH=BD MRLTY		5D05	5D02	5D02	5D02	5D02		5D02	5D02
12775	192	FAM-MAR=BD MRLTY		5D06	5D03	5D03	5D03	5D03		5D03	5D03

D04: SEX ROLES and FAMILY. Preferences regarding marital/familial arrangements

6160	94	-CHL,HB WK1.,W=0	2A15A	2A08A	2A08A	2A08A	2A08A	2A08A	2A08A	2A08A	2A08A
6170	94	-CHL,HB WK1.,W.5	2A15B	2A08B	2A08B	2A08B	2A08B	2A08B	2A08B	2A08B	2A08B
6180	94	-CHL,HB&WF WK 1.	2A15C	2A08C	2A08C	2A08C	2A08C	2A08C	2A08C	2A08C	2A08C
6190	94	-CHL,HB&WF WK .5	2A15D	2A08D	2A08D	2A08D	2A08D	2A08D	2A08D	2A08D	2A08D
6200	94	-CHL,W WK 1.,H.5	2A15E	2A08E	2A08E	2A08E	2A08E	2A08E	2A08E	2A08E	2A08E
6210	94	-CHL,W WK 1.,H=0	2A15F	2A08F	2A08F	2A08F	2A08F	2A08F	2A08F	2A08F	2A08F
6220	95	PSCH,HB WK1.,W=0	2A16A	2A09A	2A09A	2A09A	2A09A	2A09A	2A09A	2A09A	2A09A
6230	95	PSCH,HB WK1.,W.5	2A16B	2A09B	2A09B	2A09B	2A09B	2A09B	2A09B	2A09B	2A09B
6240	95	PSCH,HB&WF WK 1.	2A16C	2A09C	2A09C	2A09C	2A09C	2A09C	2A09C	2A09C	2A09C
6250	95	PSCH,HB&WF WK .5	2A16D	2A09D	2A09D	2A09D	2A09D	2A09D	2A09D	2A09D	2A09D
6260	95	PSCH,WF WK1.,H.5	2A16E	2A09E	2A09E	2A09E	2A09E	2A09E	2A09E	2A09E	2A09E
6270	95	PSCH,WF WK1.,H=0	2A16F	2A09F	2A09F	2A09F	2A09F	2A09F	2A09F	2A09F	2A09F
6280	95	H WK,W -WK,W CCR	2A17A	2A10A	2A10A	2A10A	2A10A	2A10A	2A10A	2A10A	2A10A
6290	96	H WK,W -WK,W>CCR	2A17B	2A10B	2A10B	2A10B	2A10B	2A10B	2A10B	2A10B	2A10B
6300	96	H WK,W -WK,=CHCR	2A17C	2A10C	2A10C	2A10C	2A10C	2A10C	2A10C	2A10C	2A10C
6310	96	H WK,W -WK,H>CCR	2A17D	2A10D	2A10D	2A10D	2A10D	2A10D	2A10D	2A10D	2A10D
6320	96	H WK,W -WK,H CCR	2A17E	2A10E	2A10E	2A10E	2A10E	2A10E	2A10E	2A10E	2A10E
11560		H&W WK,WF AL HWK			4E11A	4E10A	4E10A	4E10A	4E10A		
11570		H&W WK,WF MS HWK			4E11B	4E10B	4E10B	4E10B	4E10B		
11580		H&W WK,DO = HWRK			4E11C	4E10C	4E10C	4E10C	4E10C		
11590		H&W WK,HB MS HWK			4E11D	4E10D	4E10D	4E10D	4E10D		
11600		H&W WK,HB AL HWK			4E11E	4E10E	4E10E	4E10E	4E10E		
11610		H&W WK+CH,W CHCR			4E12A	4E11A	4E11A	4E11A	4E11A		
11620		H&W WK+CH,W>CHCR			4E12B	4E11B	4E11B	4E11B	4E11B		
11630		H&W WK+CH,=CHCAR			4E12C	4E11C	4E11C	4E11C	4E11C		
11640		H&W WK+CH,H>CHCR			4E12D	4E11D	4E11D	4E11D	4E11D		
11650		H&W WK+CH,H CHCR			4E12E	4E11E	4E11E	4E11E	4E11E		
13150		FAM+REL GD/CHILD		5E01A							
13160		FAM+REL GD/PARNT		5E01B							
13170		FAM+REL GD/GRPNT		5E01C							
13180		FAM+REL,R LIK/PT		5E01D							
13280		FAM+CPL GD/CHILD		5E02A							

(continued)

Item Reference Number	Page Loc. in this Volume	ITEM DESCRIPTION (ABBREVIATED)	QUESTIONNAIRE LOCATION BY YEAR (FORM, SECTION, AND QUESTION NUMBER)								
			1975	1976	1977	1978	1979	1980	1981	1982/83	1984/85

D04: SEX ROLES and FAMILY. Preferences regarding marital/familial arrangements *(continued)*

13290		FAM+CPL GD/PARNT		5E02B							
13300		FAM+CPL GD/CPLS		5E02C							
13310		FAM+CPL,LIK/PRNT		5E02D							
13320		FAM+CPL,LIK/-CHD		5E02E							
13420		CPL+OTH +CHD MAR		5E03A							
13430		CPL+OTH +CHD DVC		5E03B							
13440		CPL+OTH +MAR CPL		5E03C							
13450		CPL+OTH +DIV PRT		5E03D							
13460		CPL+OTH +UNMARRD		5E03E							
13470		CPL+OTH,LK,MR PT		5E03F							
13480		CPL+OTH,LK,DVC P		5E03G							

D05: SEX ROLES and FAMILY. Sex role attitudes

7970	120	MN=ACHV/WMN=HOME	3A17H	3A03E	3A03E	3A03E	3A03E	3A03E	3A03E	3A03E	3A03E
7980	120	CHL SUFF W WK MO	3A17I	3A03F	3A03F	3A03F	3A03F	3A03F	3A03F	3A03F	3A03F
7990	120	WK MO AS WRM REL	3A17J	3A03G	3A03G	3A03G	3A03G	3A03G	3A03G	3A03G	3A03G
10500	155	JB INTFR REL HBD	4A11E	4A15D	4A15D	4A15D	4A15D	4A15D	4A15D	4A15D	4A15D
10510	155	JB DVLP WF PERSN	4A11G	4A15E	4A15E	4A15E	4A15E	4A15E	4A15E	4A15E	4A15E
10520	155	RS CHLD + FR MAN	4A11H	4A15F	4A15F	4A15F	4A15F	4A15F	4A15F	4A15F	4A15F
10530	155	MO SH B W CHL>TM	4A11I	4A15G	4A15G	4A15G	4A15G	4A15G	4A15G	4A15G	4A15G
10540	155	WF WK,HBD SHD>HW	4A11K	4A15H	4A15H	4A15H	4A15H	4A15H	4A15H	4A15H	4A15H
11330	170	P'IDEA OF SX RLS	4A27K	4E08K	4E08K	4E07K	4E07K	4E07K	4E07K	4E07K	4E07K
12160	181	ENCRG=INDP DT/SN	5A12B	5A18K	5A18K	5A18K	5A18K	5A18K	5A18K	5A18K	5A18K
12170	182	BNG MOTH V FULFL	5A12D	5A18L	5A18L	5A18L	5A18L	5A18L	5A18L	5A18L	5A18L
12180	182	FTHR>TIME W CHLD	5A12G	5A18M	5A18M	5A18M	5A18M	5A18M	5A18M	5A18M	5A18M
12190	182	HSB MAK IMP DCSN	5A12H	5A18N	5A18N	5A18N	5A18N	5A18N	5A18N	5A18N	5A18N

D06: SEX ROLES and FAMILY. Opinions regarding sex discrimination

7930	119	MEN&WOMN/=$,=WRK	3A17A	3A03A	3A03A	3A03A	3A03A	3A03A	3A03A	3A03A	3A03A
7940	119	CNSDR WMN/HI JOB	3A17B	3A03B	3A03B	3A03B	3A03B	3A03B	3A03B	3A03B	3A03B
7950	119	WMN SHD =JOB OPP	3A17C	3A03C	3A03C	3A03C	3A03C	3A03C	3A03C	3A03C	3A03C
7960	119	WMN SHD =ED OPP	3A17D	3A03D	3A03D	3A03D	3A03D	3A03D	3A03D	3A03D	3A03D
10370	153	JOB OBSTC SEX		4A13B	4A13B	4A13B	4A13B	4A13B	4A13B	4A13B	4A13B
11180	167	MLTRY DSCRM WOMN		4E03	4E03	4E03	4E03	4E03	4E03	4E03	4E03
12290	184	DSCM WN COLLG ED	5A21A	5A22A	5A22A	5A22A	5A22A	5A22A	5A22A	5A22A	5A22A
12300	184	DSCM WN LDRSHP	5A21B	5A22B	5A22B	5A22B	5A22B	5A22B	5A22B	5A22B	5A22B
12310	184	DSCM WN EXEC/BSN	5A21C	5A22C	5A22C	5A22C	5A22C	5A22C	5A22C	5A22C	5A22C
12320	184	DSCM WN TOP/PRFN	5A21D	5A22D	5A22D	5A22D	5A22D	5A22D	5A22D	5A22D	5A22D
12330	185	DSCM WN SKL LABR	5A21E	5A22E	5A22E	5A22E	5A22E	5A22E	5A22E	5A22E	5A22E
12340	185	DSCM WN PLTCL OF	5A21F	5A22F	5A22F	5A22F	5A22F	5A22F	5A22F	5A22F	5A22F
12350	185	DSCM WN =PAY =WK	5A21G	5A22G	5A22G	5A22G	5A22G	5A22G	5A22G	5A22G	5A22G

E01: POPULATION CONCERNS. Overpopulation

8360	126	IF -POP, MR CHLD	3A45	3A22	3A22	3A22	3A22	3A22	3A22	3A22	3A22
9760	137	GOV HP PRB POPL	3A32N	3E04A	3E04A	3E04A	3E04A	3E04A	3E04A	3E03A	3E03A
9770	137	GOV NO POP PLCY	3A32A	3E04B	3E04B	3E04B	3E04B	3E04B	3E04B	3E03B	3E03B
9780	137	STR OVPOP,LMT FM	3A32B	3E04C	3E04C	3E04C	3E04C	3E04C	3E04C	3E03C	3E03C
9790	137	PRV OVPOP,NO CHL	3A32C	3E04D	3E04D	3E04D	3E04D	3E04D	3E04D	3E03D	3E03D
9830		US POP SZ LRGER	3A34	3E06	3E05	3E05	3E05	3E05	3E05		
9840		GVNG FOOD O CNTY	3A33	3E05							
9850		WRLD POP SZ LRGR	3A35	3E07	3E06	3E06	3E06	3E06	3E06		
11670	174	WR/NT POP GROWTH	5A04B	5A03B	5A03B	5A03B	5A03B	5A03B	5A03B	5A03B	5A03B
12270	183	CTB TO POP PRBMS	5A20H	5A20H	5A20H	5A20H	5A20H	5A20H	5A20H	5A20H	5A20H

E02: POPULATION CONCERNS. Birth control

9800	138	HISCH INS BRTH C	3A32E	3E04E	3E04E	3E04E	3E04E	3E04E	3E04E	3E03E	3E03E
9810	138	BRTH CNT IMMORAL	3A32I	3E04F	3E04F	3E04F	3E04F	3E04F	3E04F	3E03F	3E03F
9820	138	GOV BRTHC NO CST	3A32M	3E04G	3E04G	3E04G	3E04G	3E04G	3E04G	3E03G	3E03G
9860	138	HAD SEX ED IN HS		3E09	3E08	3E08	3E08	3E08	3E08	3E04	3E04
9870	138	STUDY BC IN HS		3E10	3E09	3E09	3E09	3E09	3E09	3E05	3E05

Item Reference Number	Page Loc. in this Volume	ITEM DESCRIPTION (ABBREVIATED)	QUESTIONNAIRE LOCATION BY YEAR (FORM, SECTION, AND QUESTION NUMBER)								
			1975	1976	1977	1978	1979	1980	1981	1982/83	1984/85

F01: CONSERVATION, MATERIALISM, EQUITY, ETC. Personal materialism

Item Reference Number	Page Loc. in this Volume	ITEM DESCRIPTION (ABBREVIATED)	1975	1976	1977	1978	1979	1980	1981	1982/83	1984/85
1350	35	SAT STD OF LVG	1A009I	1A006I	1A006I	1A006I	1A006I	1A006I	1A006I	1A006I	1A006I
1430	37	IMP LOTS OF $		1A007C	1A007C	1A007C	1A007C	1A007C	1A007C	1A007C	1A007C
5930	90	DALY GO SHOPPING		2A02L	2A02L	2A02L	2A02L	2A02L	2A02L	2A02L	2A02L
7700		NOW OWN HAIR DRY		2E09A							
7710		NOW OWN WT/S SKI		2E09B							
7720		NOW OWN CAMERA		2E09C							
7730		NOW OWN WATCH		2E09D							
7740		NOW OWN HKG BKPK		2E09E							
7750		NOW OWN CK RADIO		2E09F							
7760		NOW OWN EL SHAVR		2E09G							
7770		NOW OWN TENIS RQ		2E09H							
7780		NOW OWN TV SET		2E09I							
7790		NOW OWN BICYCLE		2E09J							
7800		NOW OWN CAR		2E09K							
7810		NOW OWN TAPE REC		2E09L							
7820		NOW OWN ELT CALC		2E09M							
7830		NOW OWN BT/SNMBL		2E09N							
8020	120	MR$FR LASTG THG	3A31E	3A04C	3A04C	3A04C	3A04C	3A04C	3A04C	3A04C	3A04C
10060	148	FAM BUYS THG -ND	4A22L	4A06J	4A06J	4A06J	4A06J	4A06J	4A06J	4A06J	4A06J
	181				5A18I	5A18I	5A18I	5A18I	5A18I	5A18I	5A18I
10140	149	JOB IMPC EARN $	4A08F	4A08F	4A08F	4A08F	4A08F	4A08F	4A08F	4A08F	4A08F
12020	179	ENJOY SHOPPING	5A35A	5A15A	5A15A	5A15A	5A15A	5A15A	5A15A	5A15A	5A15A
12030	179	CARE LATST FASHN	5A35B	5A15B	5A15B	5A15B	5A15B	5A15B	5A15B	5A15B	5A15B
12040	179	CR FAM HV NBR HV	5A35C	5A15C	5A15C	5A15C	5A15C	5A15C	5A15C	5A15C	5A15C
12050	179	XPCT 2 OWN>PRNTS	5A36	5A16	5A16	5A16	5A16	5A16	5A16	5A16	5A16
12060	180	LST CNT OWN>PRNT	5A37	5A17	5A17	5A17	5A17	5A17	5A17	5A17	5A17
13600	139	STS SCH NIC CAR		5E05C	5E06C	5E06C	5E04C	5E06C		3E06C	3E06C
13700		BY SOON HAIR DRY		2E10A							
13710		BY SOON WT/S SKI		2E10B							
13720		BY SOON CAMERA		2E10C							
13730		BY SOON WATCH		2E10D							
13740		BY SOON HKG BKPK		2E10E							
13750		BY SOON CK RADIO		2E10F							
13760		BY SOON EL SHAVR		2E10G							
13770		BY SOON TENIS RQ		2E10H							
13780		BY SOON TV SET		2E10I							
13790		BY SOON BICYCLE		2E10J							
13800		BY SOON CAR		2E10K							
13810		BY SOON TAPE REC		2E10L							
13820		BY SOON ELT CALC		2E10M							
13830		BY SOON BT/SNMBL		2E10N							
13835	141	IMP HAV 1 CAR		3E12A		3E11A	3E10A	3E10A	3E10A	3E09A	3E09A
13840	141	IMP HAV 2 CARS		3E12B		3E11B	3E10B	3E10B	3E10B	3E09B	3E09B
13850	141	IMP HAV LARG CAR		3E12C		3E11C	3E10C	3E10C	3E10C	3E09C	3E09C
13860	141	IMP HAV NW CR OF		3E12D		3E11D	3E10D	3E10D	3E10D	3E09D	3E09D
13870	142	IMP HAV NW CLTHS		3E12E		3E11E	3E10E	3E10E	3E10E	3E09E	3E09E
13880	142	IMP HAV OWN HSE		3E12F		3E11F	3E10F	3E10F	3E10F	3E09F	3E09F
13890	142	IMP HAV BIG YARD		3E12G		3E11G	3E10G	3E10G	3E10G	3E09G	3E09G
13900	142	IMP HAV NEAT LWN		3E12H		3E11H	3E10H	3E10H	3E10H	3E09H	3E09H
13910	142	IMP HAV APPLINCS		3E12I		3E11I	3E10I	3E10I	3E10I	3E09I	3E09I
13920	142	IMP HAV G STEREO		3E12J		3E11J	3E10J	3E10J	3E10J	3E09J	3E09J
13930	142	IMP HAV VAC HSE		3E12K		3E11K	3E10K	3E10K	3E10K	3E09K	3E09K
13940	142	IMP HAV REC VEH		3E12L		3E11L	3E10L	3E10L	3E10L	3E09L	3E09L

F02: CONSERVATION, MATERIALISM, EQUITY, ETC. Societal materialism and advertising

Item Reference Number	Page Loc. in this Volume	ITEM DESCRIPTION (ABBREVIATED)	1975	1976	1977	1978	1979	1980	1981	1982/83	1984/85
6000	91	2MUCH CNCRN MTRL	2A23K	2A03B	2A03B	2A03B	2A03B	2A03B	2A03B	2A03B	2A03B
6010	91	ENCOURG PPL BUY>	2A23L	2A03C	2A03C	2A03C	2A03C	2A03C	2A03C	2A03C	2A03C
6020	92	-WRNG ADVERTISNG	2A23M	2A03D	2A03D	2A03D	2A03D	2A03D	2A03D	2A03D	2A03D
6030	92	MOR SHORTGS FUTR	2A23N	2A03E	2A03E	2A03E	2A03E	2A03E	2A03E	2A03E	2A03E
10040	148	TV COMM CRT NDS	4A22H	4A06H	4A06H	4A06H	4A06H	4A06H	4A06H	4A06H	4A06H
10050	148	TV COMMRCLS GOOD	4A22I	4A06I	4A06I	4A06I	4A06I	4A06I	4A06I	4A06I	4A06I

Item Reference Number	Page Loc. in this Volume	ITEM DESCRIPTION (ABBREVIATED)	QUESTIONNAIRE LOCATION BY YEAR (FORM, SECTION, AND QUESTION NUMBER)								
			1975	1976	1977	1978	1979	1980	1981	1982/83	1984/85

F03: CONSERVATION, MATERIALISM, EQUITY, ETC. Concern with world hunger and poverty

Item Reference Number	Page Loc. in this Volume	ITEM DESCRIPTION	1975	1976	1977	1978	1979	1980	1981	1982/83	1984/85
5990	91	US 2 MUCH PROFIT	2A23J	2A03A	2A03A	2A03A	2A03A	2A03A	2A03A	2A03A	2A03A
8040	121	EAT DIF->FD STRV	3A31G	3A04E	3A04E	3A04E	3A04E	3A04E	3A04E	3A04E	3A04E
11720	175	WR/NT HNGR&PVRTY	5A04G	5A03G	5A03G	5A03G	5A03G	5A03G	5A03G	5A03G	5A03G
12090	180	-SYMP TWD STARVG	5A19E	5A18C	5A18C	5A18C	5A18C	5A18C	5A18C	5A18C	5A18C
12140	181	RB CHNG ETG HABT		5A18H	5A18H	5A18H	5A18H	5A18H	5A18H	5A18H	5A18H
16440		SAT EAT<BEEF>GRN				2E05B					
19470		EAT<FD,>OWN CITY					5E08A				
19480		EAT<FD,>NRBY STT					5E08B				
19490		EAT<FD,>DIF REGN					5E08C				
19500		EAT<FD,>ASIAN CN					5E08D				

F04: CONSERVATION, MATERIALISM, EQUITY, ETC. Ecological concerns

Item Reference Number	Page Loc. in this Volume	ITEM DESCRIPTION	1975	1976	1977	1978	1979	1980	1981	1982/83	1984/85
1640	40	US NEEDS GROWTH	1A013E	1A011G	1A011G	1A011G	1A011G	1A011G	1A011G	1A011G	1A011G
8000	120	POLLUT INCREASED	3A31A	3A04A	3A04A	3A04A	3A04A	3A04A	3A04A	3A04A	3A04A
8010	120	GOVT DEAL ENV PR	3A31D	3A04B	3A04B	3A04B	3A04B	3A04B	3A04B	3A04B	3A04B
9700	136	PRVNT POL TOO >$		3E02A	3E02A	3E02A	3E02A	3E02A	3E02A	3E01A	3E01A
9710	136	PRVNT POL CST JB		3E02B	3E02B	3E02B	3E02B	3E02B	3E02B	3E01B	3E01B
9720	136	PRVNT POL PPL DK		3E02C	3E02C	3E02C	3E02C	3E02C	3E02C	3E01C	3E01C
9730	136	PRVNT POL -ENUF		3E02D	3E02D	3E02D	3E02D	3E02D	3E01D	3E01D	3E01D
9740	137	PRVNT POL USELSS		3E02E	3E02E	3E02E	3E02E	3E02E	3E02E	3E01E	3E01E
9970	146	PLLTN INCR IN US	4A22A	4A06A	4A06A	4A06A	4A06A	4A06A	4A06A	4A06A	4A06A
9980	147	PLLTN NT SO DANG	4A22B	4A06B	4A06B	4A06B	4A06B	4A06B	4A06B	4A06B	4A06B
9990	147	PLLTN NEC 4 GRTH	4A22C	4A06C	4A06C	4A06C	4A06C	4A06C	4A06C	4A06C	4A06C
10000	147	INDVL RESP 4 ENV	4A22D	4A06D	4A06D	4A06D	4A06D	4A06D	4A06D	4A06D	4A06D
10010	147	GOVT RESP 4 ENV	4A22E	4A06E	4A06E	4A06E	4A06E	4A06E	4A06E	4A06E	4A06E
10020	147	GOVT TAX PLLTRS	4A22F	4A06F	4A06F	4A06F	4A06F	4A06F	4A06F	4A06F	4A06F
10030	147	GOVT BAN DSPSBLE	4A22G	4A06G	4A06G	4A06G	4A06G	4A06G	4A06G	4A06G	4A06G
10070	148	POL SLVD BY 2000	4A22M	4A06K	4A06K	4A06K	4A06K	4A06K	4A06K	4A06K	4A06K
10080	148	R EFRT 2 HLP ENV	4A23	4A07	4A07	4A07	4A07	4A07	4A07	4A07	4A07
11340	170	P'IDEA OF ECLOGY	4A27L	4E08L	4E08L	4E07L	4E07L	4E07L	4E07L	4E07L	4E07L
11690	174	WR/NT POLLUTION	5A04D	5A03D	5A03D	5A03D	5A03D	5A03D	5A03D	5A03D	5A03D
12280	184	CTB TO ENVIR PBM	5A20I	5A20I	5A20I	5A20I	5A20I	5A20I	5A20I	5A20I	5A20I
16450		SAT TAX FR ECLGY				2E05C					

F05: CONSERVATION, MATERIALISM, EQUITY, ETC. Concern with conservation of resources

Item Reference Number	Page Loc. in this Volume	ITEM DESCRIPTION	1975	1976	1977	1978	1979	1980	1981	1982/83	1984/85
9750	137	FUTR,HAV2 CNSUM<		3E03	3E03	3E03	3E03	3E03	3E03	3E02	3E02
10930	163	SOCTY WONT LAST	4A28B	4D03B	4D03B	4D03B	4D03B	4D03B	4D03B	4D10B	4D10B
11700	174	WR/NT ENRGY SHRT	5A04E	5A03E	5A03E	5A03E	5A03E	5A03E	5A03E	5A03E	5A03E
11730	175	WR/NT USE OPN LD	5A04H	5A03H	5A03H	5A03H	5A03H	5A03H	5A03H	5A03H	5A03H
12000	179	R CUT ELECTRICTY		5A13	5A13	5A13	5A13	5A13	5A13	5A13	5A13
12010	179	RDCE HEAT R'S HM		5A14	5A14	5A14	5A14	5A14	5A14	5A14	5A14

F06: CONSERVATION, MATERIALISM, EQUITY, ETC. Preferences regarding dwelling type and urbanicity

Item Reference Number	Page Loc. in this Volume	ITEM DESCRIPTION	1975	1976	1977	1978	1979	1980	1981	1982/83	1984/85
17860		DESRD LVG RURAL				4E09A		4E09A	4E09A	4E09A‡	
17870		DESRD LVG SM TWN				4E09B		4E09B	4E09B	4E09B‡	
17880		DESRD LVG SM CTY				4E09C		4E09C	4E09C	4E09C‡	
17890		DESRD LVG SUBURB				4E09D		4E09D	4E09D	4E09D‡	
17900		DESRD LVG LG CTY				4E09E		4E09E	4E09E	4E09E‡	
17910		DSRD HSG 1 FAMLY				4E09F		4E09F	4E09F	4E09F‡	
17920		DSRD HSG 2 FAMLY				4E09G		4E09G	4E09G	4E09G‡	
17930		DSRD HSG CNDMINM				4E09H		4E09H	4E09H	4E09H‡	
17940		DSRD HSG APT BLD				4E09I		4E09I	4E09I	4E09I‡	
17950		DSRD HSG HI RISE				4E09J		4E09J	4E09J	4E09J‡	

F07: CONSERVATION, MATERIALISM, EQUITY, ETC. Driving and use of mass transit

Item Reference Number	Page Loc. in this Volume	ITEM DESCRIPTION	1975	1976	1977	1978	1979	1980	1981	1982/83	1984/85
640	22	DRIVE>200 MI/WK		+C27	+C27	+C27	+C27	+C27	+C27	+C27	+C27
8030	121	USE BYC/MAS TRAN	3A31F	3A04D	3A04D	3A04D	3A04D	3A04D	3A04D	3A04D	3A04D
11960	178	DNT HV DRVR LCNS	5A22	5A09	5A09	5A09	5A09	5A09	5A09	5A09	5A09
11970	178	DONT OWN CAR	5A23	5A10	5A10	5A10	5A10	5A10	5A10	5A10	5A10

(continued)

‡ This question appears in 1982 but does not appear in 1983.

Item Reference Number	Page Loc. in this Volume	ITEM DESCRIPTION (ABBREVIATED)	QUESTIONNAIRE LOCATION BY YEAR (FORM, SECTION, AND QUESTION NUMBER)								
			1975	1976	1977	1978	1979	1980	1981	1982/83	1984/85

F07: CONSERVATION, MATERIALISM, EQUITY, ETC. Driving and use of mass transit (continued)

Item Reference Number	Page Loc. in this Volume	ITEM DESCRIPTION	1975	1976	1977	1978	1979	1980	1981	1982/83	1984/85
11980	178	NEVR USE OTHS CR	5A24	5A11	5A11	5A11	5A11	5A11	5A11	5A11	5A11
11990	178	R CUT DRIVING		5A12	5A12	5A12	5A12	5A12	5A12	5A12	5A12
16430		SAT EVB CAR POOL				2E05A					

G: RELIGION. Religious preferences, activities, views

Item Reference Number	Page Loc. in this Volume	ITEM DESCRIPTION	1975	1976	1977	1978	1979	1980	1981	1982/83	1984/85
360	18	R'S RELGS PRFNC		+C13A	+C13A	+C13A	+C13A	+C13A	(+C13A)	+C13A	+C13A
370	18	R'ATTND REL SVC		+C13B	+C13B	+C13B	+C13B	+C13B	+C13B	+C13B	+C13B
380	19	RLGN IMP R'S LF		+C13C	+C13C	+C13C	+C13C	+C13C	+C13C	+C13C	+C13C
5980		DALY GO CHURCH		2A02D							
6930	106	DHNSTY CHURCHES	2A20E	2D04E	2D04E	2D04E	2D04E	2D04E	2D04E	2D04E	2D04E
8420	127	GD JB CHURCHES	3A27E	3A24E	3A24E	3A24E	3A24E	3A24E	3A24E	3A24E	3A24E
10360	153	JOB OBSTC RELGN		4A13A	4A13A	4A13A	4A13A	4A13A	4A13A	4A13A	4A13A
10590	156	>INFLC CHURCHES	4A14C	4A19C	4A19C	4A19C	4A19C	4A19C	4A19C	4A19C	4A19C
11360	170	P'IDEA OF RLGION	4A27N	4E08N	4E08N	4E07N	4E07N	4E07N	4E07N	4E07N	4E07N
11910	177	RCL CNTCT CHURCH		5A07C	5A07C	5A07C	5A07C	5A07C	5A07C	5A07C	5A07C
12230	183	CTB TO RELGS ORG	5A20D	5A20D	5A20D	5A20D	5A20D	5A20D	5A20D	5A20D	5A20D

H01: POLITICS. Political interest and preferences

Item Reference Number	Page Loc. in this Volume	ITEM DESCRIPTION	1975	1976	1977	1978	1979	1980	1981	1982/83	1984/85
340	18	R'S POLTL PRFNC		+C11	+C11	+C11	+C11	+C11	+C11	+C11	+C11
350	18	R'POL BLF RADCL		+C12	+C12	+C12	+C12	+C12	+C12	+C12	+C12
6330	96	INTEREST IN GOVT	2A31	2A11	2A11	2A11	2A11	2A11	2A11	2A11	2A11
	156		4A29	3E01	3E01	3E01	3E01	3E01	3E01	4A18	4A18
	182		5A40	4A18	4A18	4A18	4A18	4A18	4A18	5A19	5A19
				5A19	5A19	5A19	5A19	5A19	5A19		
10400	153	JOB OBSTC POL VW		4A13E	4A13E	4A13E	4A13E	4A13E	4A13E	4A13E	4A13E
11370	170	P'IDEA OF PLTICS	4A27O	4E08O	4E08O	4E07O	4E07O	4E07O	4E07O	4E07O	4E07O

H02: POLITICS. Attitudes toward governmental policies and practices

Item Reference Number	Page Loc. in this Volume	ITEM DESCRIPTION	1975	1976	1977	1978	1979	1980	1981	1982/83	1984/85
1390	36	SAT GOVT OPRTNG		1A006M	1A006M	1A006M	1A006M	1A006M	1A006M	1A006M	1A006M
5690	98	US GO WAR FR OTH	2A38B	2A18B	2A18B	2A18B	2A18B	2A18B	2A18B	2A18B	2A18B
6450	98	US SHD DISARM	2A38A	2A18A	2A18A	2A18A	2A18A	2A18A	2A18A	2A18A	2A18A
6460	98	US WAR PRTCT ECN	2A38C	2A18C	2A18C	2A18C	2A18C	2A18C	2A18C	2A18C	2A18C
6470	98	US ONLY WAR DFNS	2A38D	2A18D	2A18D	2A18D	2A18D	2A18D	2A18D	2A18D	2A18D
6480	99	-US MIL PWR>USSR	2A38E	2A18E	2A18E	2A18E	2A18E	2A18E	2A18E	2A18E	2A18E
6490	99	US NEED>PWR OTHS	2A38F	2A18F	2A18F	2A18F	2A18F	2A18F	2A18F	2A18F	2A18F
6500	99	US FRN PLCY NRRW	2A38G	2A18G	2A18G	2A18G	2A18G	2A18G	2A18G	2A18G	2A18G
7940	119	CNSDR WMN/HI JOB	3A17B	3A03B	3A03B	3A03B	3A03B	3A03B	3A03B	3A03B	3A03B
8010	120	GOVT DEAL ENV PR	3A31D	3A04B	3A04B	3A04B	3A04B	3A04B	3A04B	3A04B	3A04B
9760	137	GOV HP PRB POPL	3A32N	3E04A	3E04A	3E04A	3E04A	3E04A	3E04A	3E03A	3E03A
9770	137	GOV NO POP PLCY	3A32A	3E04B	3E04B	3E04B	3E04B	3E04B	3E04B	3E03B	3E03B
9820	138	GOV BRTHC NO CST	3A32M	3E04G	3E04G	3E04G	3E04G	3E04G	3E04G	3E03G	3E03G
10010	147	GOVT RESP 4 ENV	4A22E	4A06E	4A06E	4A06E	4A06E	4A06E	4A06E	4A06E	4A06E
10020	147	GOVT TAX PLLTRS	4A22F	4A06F	4A06F	4A06F	4A06F	4A06F	4A06F	4A06F	4A06F
10030	147	GOVT BAN DSPSBLE	4A22G	4A06G	4A06G	4A06G	4A06G	4A06G	4A06G	4A06G	4A06G
11210		-MLTRY COUP U.S.		4E06	4E06						
12340	185	DSCM WN PLTCL OF	5A21F	5A22F	5A22F	5A22F	5A22F	5A22F	5A22F	5A22F	5A22F

H03: POLITICS. Views about the role of citizens in government (See also I02: Attitudes regarding activism)

Item Reference Number	Page Loc. in this Volume	ITEM DESCRIPTION	1975	1976	1977	1978	1979	1980	1981	1982/83	1984/85
1580	39	-OBY LW=-GD CTZN		1A011A	1A011A	1A011A	1A011A	1A011A	1A011A	1A011A	1A011A
1590	39	GD CTZN ALG GOVT		1A011B	1A011B	1A011B	1A011B	1A011B	1A011B	1A011B	1A011B
1600	39	GD CTZN CHG GOVT	1A013B	1A011C	1A011C	1A011C	1A011C	1A011C	1A011C	1A011C	1A011C
1620	39	CTZN GRP HV EFCT		1A011E	1A011E	1A011E	1A011E	1A011E	1A011E	1A011E	1A011E

H04: POLITICS. Confidence in government

Item Reference Number	Page Loc. in this Volume	ITEM DESCRIPTION	1975	1976	1977	1978	1979	1980	1981	1982/83	1984/85
1630	39	OUR SYST ST BS	1A013C	1A011F	1A011F	1A011F	1A011F	1A011F	1A011F	1A011F	1A011F
6340	96	GOVT PPL -DSHNST	2A32	2A12	2A12	2A12	2A12	2A12	2A12	2A12	2A12
6350	96	GOVT DSNT WASTE$	2A33	2A13	2A13	2A13	2A13	2A13	2A13	2A13	2A13
6360	97	NEVER TRUST GOVT	2A34	2A14	2A14	2A14	2A14	2A14	2A14	2A14	2A14
		(continued)									

Item Refer- ence Number	Page Loc. in this Volume	ITEM DESCRIPTION (ABBREVIATED)	1975	1976	1977	1978	1979	1980	1981	1982/83	1984/85

H04: POLITICS. Confidence in government (continued)

Item	Page	Description	1975	1976	1977	1978	1979	1980	1981	1982/83	1984/85
6370	97	GVT PPL DK DOING	2A35	2A15	2A15	2A15	2A15	2A15	2A15	2A15	2A15
6380	97	GOVT RUN FOR PPL	2A36	2A16	2A16	2A16	2A16	2A16	2A16	2A16	2A16
6950	106	DHNSTY PRES&ADMN	2A20G	2D04G	2D04G	2D04G	2D04G	2D04G	2D04G	2D04G	2D04G
6960	106	DHNSTY CONGRESS	2A20H	2D04H	2D04H	2D04H	2D04H	2D04H	2D04H	2D04H	2D04H
6970	106	DHNSTY SUPRM CRT	2A20I	2D04I	2D04I	2D04I	2D04I	2D04I	2D04I	2D04I	2D04I
6980	106	DHNSTY JUSTC SYS	2A20J	2D04J	2D04J	2D04J	2D04J	2D04J	2D04J	2D04J	2D04J
8440	127	GD JB PRES&ADMN	3A27G	3A24G	3A24G	3A24G	3A24G	3A24G	3A24G	3A24G	3A24G
8450	127	GD JB CONGRESS	3A27H	3A24H	3A24H	3A24H	3A24H	3A24H	3A24H	3A24H	3A24H
8460	127	GD JB SUPRM CRT	3A27I	3A24I	3A24I	3A24I	3A24I	3A24I	3A24I	3A24I	3A24I
8470	127	GD JB JUSTC SYST	3A27J	3A24J	3A24J	3A24J	3A24J	3A24J	3A24J	3A24J	3A24J
10610	157	>INFLC PRES&ADMN	4A14E	4A19E	4A19E	4A19E	4A19E	4A19E	4A19E	4A19E	4A19E
10620	157	>INFLC CONGRESS	4A14F	4A19F	4A19F	4A19F	4A19F	4A19F	4A19F	4A19F	4A19F
10630	157	>INFLC SUPRM CRT	4A14G	4A19G	4A19G	4A19G	4A19G	4A19G	4A19G	4A19G	4A19G
10640	157	>INFLC JUSTC SYS	4A14H	4A19H	4A19H	4A19H	4A19H	4A19H	4A19H	4A19H	4A19H

H05: POLITICS. Voting, political activism

Item	Page	Description	1975	1976	1977	1978	1979	1980	1981	1982/83	1984/85
1610	39	VOTE->MAJ IMPCT		1A011D	1A011D	1A011D	1A011D	1A011D	1A011D	1A011D	1A011D
6390	97	DO OR PLN VOTE	2A37A	2A17A	2A17A	2A17A	2A17A	2A17A	2A17A	2A17A	2A17A
6400	97	DO OR PLN WRITE	2A37B	2A17B	2A17B	2A17B	2A17B	2A17B	2A17B	2A17B	2A17B
6410	97	DO OR PLN GIVE $	2A37C	2A17C	2A17C	2A17C	2A17C	2A17C	2A17C	2A17C	2A17C
6420	98	DO OR PLN WK CPG	2A37D	2A17D	2A17D	2A17D	2A17D	2A17D	2A17D	2A17D	2A17D
6430	98	DO OR PLN DEMNST	2A37E	2A17E	2A17E	2A17E	2A17E	2A17E	2A17E	2A17E	2A17E
6440	98	DO OR PLN BOYCOT	2A37F	2A17F	2A17F	2A17F	2A17F	2A17F	2A17F	2A17F	2A17F
9920		R WL VOTE IN '76		3E11							
11820	176	PLC WRK GVT AGCY	5A09C	5A05C	5A05C	5A05C	5A05C	5A05C	5A05C	5A05C	5A05C
12240	183	CTB TO PLTCL PTY	5A20E	5A20E	5A20E	5A20E	5A20E	5A20E	5A20E	5A20E	5A20E
12250	183	CTB TO CTZN LBBY	5A20F	5A20F	5A20F	5A20F	5A20F	5A20F	5A20F	5A20F	5A20F
16340		EFCTV VOTING				2E04C					

I01: SOCIAL CHANGE. Expectations concerning societal change

Item	Page	Description	1975	1976	1977	1978	1979	1980	1981	1982/83	1984/85
1200	33	US NEEDS PLANNG	1A004A	1A002A	1A002A	1A002A	1A002A	1A002A	1A002A	1A002A	1A002A
1230	33	X AHEAD TOUGHER	1A004G	1A002D	1A002D	1A002D	1A002D	1A002D	1A002D	1A002D	1A002D
9940	146	FUTR CNTRY WORSE	+A01	4A02	4A02	4A02	4A02	4A02	4A02	4A02	4A02
9950	146	FUTR WORLD WORSE	+A02	4A03	4A03	4A03	4A03	4A03	4A03	4A03	4A03
9960	146	FUTR R LIFE WRSE	+A03	4A04	4A04	4A04	4A04	4A04	4A04	4A04	4A04
10940	163	THG TUF,TCHN SLV	4A28C	4D03C	4D03C	4D03C	4D03C	4D03C	4D03C	4D10C	4D10C

I02: SOCIAL CHANGE. Attitudes regarding activism

Item	Page	Description	1975	1976	1977	1978	1979	1980	1981	1982/83	1984/85
1610	39	VOTE->MAJ IMPCT		1A011D	1A011D	1A011D	1A011D	1A011D	1A011D	1A011D	1A011D
1620	39	CTZN GRP HV EFCT		1A011E	1A011E	1A011E	1A011E	1A011E	1A011E	1A011E	1A011E
1650	40	LV THNGS TO GOD	1A004C	1A011H	1A011H	1A011H	1A011H	1A011H	1A011H	1A011H	1A011H
6040	92	APRV PETITIONS	2A21A	2A04A	2A04A	2A04A	2A04A	2A04A	2A04A	2A04A	2A04A
6050	92	APRV BOYCOTT	2A21B	2A04B	2A04B	2A04B	2A04B	2A04B	2A04B	2A04B	2A04B
6060	92	APRV LWFL DMSTN	2A21C	2A04C	2A04C	2A04C	2A04C	2A04C	2A04C	2A04C	2A04C
6070	92	APRV OCCUPY BLDG	2A21D	2A04D	2A04D	2A04D	2A04D	2A04D	2A04D	2A04D	2A04D
6080	92	APRV WLDCAT STRK	2A21E	2A04E	2A04E	2A04E	2A04E	2A04E	2A04E	2A04E	2A04E
6090	93	APRV BLK TRAFFIC	2A21F	2A04F	2A04F	2A04F	2A04F	2A04F	2A04F	2A04F	2A04F
6100	93	APRV DAMAG THING	2A21G	2A04G	2A04G	2A04G	2A04G	2A04G	2A04G	2A04G	2A04G
6110	93	APRV PSNL VIOLNC	2A21H	2A04H	2A04H	2A04H	2A04H	2A04H	2A04H	2A04H	2A04H
6390	97	DO OR PLN VOTE	2A37A	2A17A	2A17A	2A17A	2A17A	2A17A	2A17A	2A17A	2A17A
6400	97	DO OR PLN WRITE	2A37B	2A17B	2A17B	2A17B	2A17B	2A17B	2A17B	2A17B	2A17B
6410	97	DO OR PLN GIVE $	2A37C	2A17C	2A17C	2A17C	2A17C	2A17C	2A17C	2A17C	2A17C
6420	98	DO OR PLN WK CPG	2A37D	2A17D	2A17D	2A17D	2A17D	2A17D	2A17D	2A17D	2A17D
6430	98	DO OR PLN DEMNST	2A37E	2A17E	2A17E	2A17E	2A17E	2A17E	2A17E	2A17E	2A17E
6440	98	DO OR PLN BOYCOT	2A37F	2A17F	2A17F	2A17F	2A17F	2A17F	2A17F	2A17F	2A17F
10920	163	I CNT CHNG WORLD	4A28A	4D03A	4D03A	4D03A	4D03A	4D03A	4D03A	4D10A	4D10A
12250	183	CTB TO CTZN LBBY	5A20F	5A20F	5A20F	5A20F	5A20F	5A20F	5A20F	5A20F	5A20F
16320		EFCTV WRIT OFCLS				2E04A					
16330		EFCTV WRK PL CPN				2E04B					
16340		EFCTV VOTING				2E04C					
		(continued)									

Item Reference Number	Page Loc. in this Volume	ITEM DESCRIPTION (ABBREVIATED)	QUESTIONNAIRE LOCATION BY YEAR (FORM, SECTION, AND QUESTION NUMBER)								
			1975	1976	1977	1978	1979	1980	1981	1982/83	1984/85

I02: SOCIAL CHANGE. Attitudes regarding activism *(continued)*

Item Ref	Page	Description	1975	1976	1977	1978	1979	1980	1981	1982/83	1984/85
16350		EFCTV PETITIONS				2E04D					
16360		EFCTV BOYCOTT				2E04E					
16370		EFCTV LWFL DMSTN				2E04F					
16380		EFCTV OCPY BLDGS				2E04G					
16390		EFCTV WLDCT STRK				2E04H					
16400		EFCTV BLK TRAFIC				2E04I					
16410		EFCTV DAMAG THNG				2E04J					
16420		EFCTV PSNL VLNC				2E04K					

I03: SOCIAL CHANGE. Reactions to personal and social change

Item Ref	Page	Description	1975	1976	1977	1978	1979	1980	1981	1982/83	1984/85
1210	33	ENJOY FAST PACE	1A004B	1A002B	1A002B	1A002B	1A002B	1A002B	1A002B	1A002B	1A002B
1220	33	THG CHG 2 QUICK	1A004D	1A002C	1A002C	1A002C	1A002C	1A002C	1A002C	1A002C	1A002C
13950	191	EAGR TO LEAV HOM						5D01W	5D01W	5D01W	5D01W
13960	191	HEST PRT ADLT WL						5D01X	5D01X	5D01X	5D01X

J: SOCIAL PROBLEMS. Interest and concerns

Item Ref	Page	Description	1975	1976	1977	1978	1979	1980	1981	1982/83	1984/85
1230	33	X AHEAD TOUGHER	1A004G	1A002D	1A002D	1A002D	1A002D	1A002D	1A002D	1A002D	1A002D
6880	105	THK ABT SOC ISSU	*A06	2D03	2D03	2D03	2D03	2D03	2D03	2D03	2D03
	119			3A02	3A02	3A02	3A02	3A02	3A02	3A02	3A02
	146			4A05	4A05	4A05	4A05	4A05	4A05	4A05	4A05
	174			5A02	5A02	5A02	5A02	5A02	5A02	5A02	5A02
10920	163	I CNT CHNG WORLD	4A28A	4D03A	4D03A	4D03A	4D03A	4D03A	4D03A	4D10A	4D10A
10930	163	SOCTY WONT LAST	4A28B	4D03B	4D03B	4D03B	4D03B	4D03B	4D03B	4D10B	4D10B
10940	163	THG TUF,TCHN SLV	4A28C	4D03C	4D03C	4D03C	4D03C	4D03C	4D03C	4D10C	4D10C
10950	164	NO HOPE 4 WORLD	4A28D	4D03D	4D03D	4D03D	4D03D	4D03D	4D03D	4D10D	4D10D
10960	164	WNDR PURPS 2 LIF	4A28E	4D03E	4D03E	4D03E	4D03E	4D03E	4D03E	4D10E	4D10E
10970	164	WRLD UPHVL 10 YR	4A28F	4D03F	4D03F	4D03F	4D03F	4D03F	4D03F	4D10F	4D10F
10980	164	ANNHLTN IN LFTM	4A28G	4D03G	4D03G	4D03G	4D03G	4D03G	4D03G	4D10G	4D10G
10990	164	HMN RCE RSILIENT	4A28H	4D03H	4D03H	4D03H	4D03H	4D03H	4D03H	4D10H	4D10H
11660	174	WR/NT NUCLER WAR	5A04A	5A03A	5A03A	5A03A	5A03A	5A03A	5A03A	5A03A	5A03A
11670	174	WR/NT POP GROWTH	5A04B	5A03B	5A03B	5A03B	5A03B	5A03B	5A03B	5A03B	5A03B
11680	174	WR/NT CRIME&VLNC	5A04C	5A03C	5A03C	5A03C	5A03C	5A03C	5A03C	5A03C	5A03C
11690	174	WR/NT POLLUTION	5A04D	5A03D	5A03D	5A03D	5A03D	5A03D	5A03D	5A03D	5A03D
11700	174	WR/NT ENRGY SHRT	5A04E	5A03E	5A03E	5A03E	5A03E	5A03E	5A03E	5A03E	5A03E
11710	175	WR/NT RACE RELTN	5A04F	5A03F	5A03F	5A03F	5A03F	5A03F	5A03F	5A03F	5A03F
11720	175	WR/NT HNGR&PVRTY	5A04G	5A03G	5A03G	5A03G	5A03G	5A03G	5A03G	5A03G	5A03G
11730	175	WR/NT USE OPN LD	5A04H	5A03H	5A03H	5A03H	5A03H	5A03H	5A03H	5A03H	5A03H
11740	175	WR/NT URBN DECAY	5A04I	5A03I	5A03I	5A03I	5A03I	5A03I	5A03I	5A03I	5A03I
11750	175	WR/NT ECON PRBLM	5A04J	5A03J	5A03J	5A03J	5A03J	5A03J	5A03J	5A03J	5A03J
11760	175	WR/NT DRUG ABUSE	5A04K	5A03K	5A03K	5A03K	5A03K	5A03K	5A03K	5A03K	5A03K

K01: MAJOR SOCIAL INSTITUTIONS. Trust (See also C05: Institutions as work settings)

Item Ref	Page	Description	1975	1976	1977	1978	1979	1980	1981	1982/83	1984/85
6340	96	GOVT PPL -DSHNST	2A32	2A12	2A12	2A12	2A12	2A12	2A12	2A12	2A12
6350	96	GOVT DSNT WASTE$	2A33	2A13	2A13	2A13	2A13	2A13	2A13	2A13	2A13
6360	97	NEVER TRUST GOVT	2A34	2A14	2A14	2A14	2A14	2A14	2A14	2A14	2A14
6370	97	GVT PPL DK DOING	2A35	2A15	2A15	2A15	2A15	2A15	2A15	2A15	2A15
6380	97	GOVT RUN FOR PPL	2A36	2A16	2A16	2A16	2A16	2A16	2A16	2A16	2A16
6890	105	DHNSTY LARG CORP	2A20A	2D04A	2D04A	2D04A	2D04A	2D04A	2D04A	2D04A	2D04A
6900	105	DHNSTY LBR UNION	2A20B	2D04B	2D04B	2D04B	2D04B	2D04B	2D04B	2D04B	2D04B
6910	105	DHNSTY COLL&UNIV	2A20C	2D04C	2D04C	2D04C	2D04C	2D04C	2D04C	2D04C	2D04C
6920	105	DHNSTY PBLC SCHL	2A20D	2D04D	2D04D	2D04D	2D04D	2D04D	2D04D	2D04D	2D04D
6930	106	DHNSTY CHURCHES	2A20E	2D04E	2D04E	2D04E	2D04E	2D04E	2D04E	2D04E	2D04E
6940	106	DHNSTY NEWS MDIA	2A20F	2D04F	2D04F	2D04F	2D04F	2D04F	2D04F	2D04F	2D04F
6950	106	DHNSTY PRES&ADMN	2A20G	2D04G	2D04G	2D04G	2D04G	2D04G	2D04G	2D04G	2D04G
6960	106	DHNSTY CONGRESS	2A20H	2D04H	2D04H	2D04H	2D04H	2D04H	2D04H	2D04H	2D04H
6970	106	DHNSTY SUPRM CRT	2A20I	2D04I	2D04I	2D04I	2D04I	2D04I	2D04I	2D04I	2D04I
6980	106	DHNSTY JUSTC SYS	2A20J	2D04J	2D04J	2D04J	2D04J	2D04J	2D04J	2D04J	2D04J
6990	107	DHNSTY POLICE	2A20K	2D04K	2D04K	2D04K	2D04K	2D04K	2D04K	2D04K	2D04K
7000	107	DHNSTY MILITARY	2A20L	2D04L	2D04L	2D04L	2D04L	2D04L	2D04L	2D04L	2D04L

Item Reference Number	Page Loc. in this Volume	ITEM DESCRIPTION (ABBREVIATED)	QUESTIONNAIRE LOCATION BY YEAR (FORM, SECTION, AND QUESTION NUMBER)								
			1975	1976	1977	1978	1979	1980	1981	1982/83	1984/85

K02: MAJOR SOCIAL INSTITUTIONS. Satisfaction with performance

Item Reference Number	Page Loc. in this Volume	ITEM DESCRIPTION (ABBREVIATED)	1975	1976	1977	1978	1979	1980	1981	1982/83	1984/85
1390	36	SAT GOVT OPRTNG		1A006M	1A006M	1A006M	1A006M	1A006M	1A006M	1A006M	1A006M
8380	126	GD JB LARG CORPS	3A27A	3A24A	3A24A	3A24A	3A24A	3A24A	3A24A	3A24A	3A24A
8390	126	GD JB LBR UNIONS	3A27B	3A24B	3A24B	3A24B	3A24B	3A24B	3A24B	3A24B	3A24B
8400	126	GD JB COLLG&UNIV	3A27C	3A24C	3A24C	3A24C	3A24C	3A24C	3A24C	3A24C	3A24C
8410	127	GD JB PBLC SCHOL	3A27D	3A24D	3A24D	3A24D	3A24D	3A24D	3A24D	3A24D	3A24D
8420	127	GD JB CHURCHES	3A27E	3A24E	3A24E	3A24E	3A24E	3A24E	3A24E	3A24E	3A24E
8430	127	GD JB NEWS MEDIA	3A27F	3A24F	3A24F	3A24F	3A24F	3A24F	3A24F	3A24F	3A24F
8440	127	GD JB PRES&ADMIN	3A27G	3A24G	3A24G	3A24G	3A24G	3A24G	3A24G	3A24G	3A24G
8450	127	GD JB CONGRESS	3A27H	3A24H	3A24H	3A24H	3A24H	3A24H	3A24H	3A24H	3A24H
8460	127	GD JB SUPRM CRT	3A27I	3A24I	3A24I	3A24I	3A24I	3A24I	3A24I	3A24I	3A24I
8470	127	GD JB JUSTC SYST	3A27J	3A24J	3A24J	3A24J	3A24J	3A24J	3A24J	3A24J	3A24J
8480	128	GD JB POLICE	3A27K	3A24K	3A24K	3A24K	3A24K	3A24K	3A24K	3A24K	3A24K
8490	128	GD JB MILITARY	3A27L	3A24L	3A24L	3A24L	3A24L	3A24L	3A24L	3A24L	3A24L

K03: MAJOR SOCIAL INSTITUTIONS. Preferred influence

Item Reference Number	Page Loc. in this Volume	ITEM DESCRIPTION (ABBREVIATED)	1975	1976	1977	1978	1979	1980	1981	1982/83	1984/85
8500	128	MIL TOO MCH INFL	3A28	3A25	3A25	3A25	3A25	3A25	3A25	3A25	3A25
8510	128	US TOO MCH$MILT	3A29	3A26	3A26	3A26	3A26	3A26	3A26	3A26	3A26
10570	156	>INFLC LARG CORP	4A14A	4A19A	4A19A	4A19A	4A19A	4A19A	4A19A	4A19A	4A19A
10580	156	>INFLC LBR UNION	4A14B	4A19B	4A19B	4A19B	4A19B	4A19B	4A19B	4A19B	4A19B
10590	156	>INFLC CHURCHES	4A14C	4A19C	4A19C	4A19C	4A19C	4A19C	4A19C	4A19C	4A19C
10600	157	>INFLC NEWS MDIA	4A14D	4A19D	4A19D	4A19D	4A19D	4A19D	4A19D	4A19D	4A19D
10610	157	>INFLC PRES&ADMN	4A14E	4A19E	4A19E	4A19E	4A19E	4A19E	4A19E	4A19E	4A19E
10620	157	>INFLC CONGRESS	4A14F	4A19F	4A19F	4A19F	4A19F	4A19F	4A19F	4A19F	4A19F
10630	157	>INFLC SUPRM CRT	4A14G	4A19G	4A19G	4A19G	4A19G	4A19G	4A19G	4A19G	4A19G
10640	157	>INFLC JUSTC SYS	4A14H	4A19H	4A19H	4A19H	4A19H	4A19H	4A19H	4A19H	4A19H
10650	157	>INFLC POLICE	4A14I	4A19I	4A19I	4A19I	4A19I	4A19I	4A19I	4A19I	4A19I
10660	158	>INFLC MILITARY	4A14J	4A19J	4A19J	4A19J	4A19J	4A19J	4A19J	4A19J	4A19J

L01: MILITARY. Plans for military service

Item Reference Number	Page Loc. in this Volume	ITEM DESCRIPTION (ABBREVIATED)	1975	1976	1977	1978	1979	1980	1981	1982/83	1984/85
490	20	R WL DO ARMD FC		+C21B	+C21B	+C21B	+C21B	+C21B	+C21B	+C21B	+C21B
540	21	R WNTDO ARMD FC		+C22B	+C22B	+C22B	+C22B	+C22B	+C22B	+C22B	+C22B
730	24	R'S BRANCH SERV		+C32	+C32	+C32	+C32	+C32	+C32	+C32	+C32
740	24	R XPCTS B OFFCR		+C33	+C33	+C33	+C33	+C33	+C33	+C33	+C33
750	24	R XPCTS MLTR CR		+C34	+C34	+C34	+C34	+C34	+C34	+C34	+C34

L02: MILITARY. Attitudes toward a draft

Item Reference Number	Page Loc. in this Volume	ITEM DESCRIPTION (ABBREVIATED)	1975	1976	1977	1978	1979	1980	1981	1982/83	1984/85
21060	114	FAVOR MLTY DRAFT							5E06	2E08	2E08
21070	114	DRAFT INCL WOMEN							5E07	2E09	2E09

L03: MILITARY. Views about the use of military force

Item Reference Number	Page Loc. in this Volume	ITEM DESCRIPTION (ABBREVIATED)	1975	1976	1977	1978	1979	1980	1981	1982/83	1984/85
5690	98	US GO WAR FR OTH	2A38B	2A18B	2A18B	2A18B	2A18B	2A18B	2A18B	2A18B	2A18B
6450	98	US SHD DISARM	2A38A	2A18A	2A18A	2A18A	2A18A	2A18A	2A18A	2A18A	2A18A
6460	98	US WAR PRTCT ECN	2A38C	2A18C	2A18C	2A18C	2A18C	2A18C	2A18C	2A18C	2A18C
6470	98	US ONLY WAR DFNS	2A38D	2A18D	2A18D	2A18D	2A18D	2A18D	2A18D	2A18D	2A18D
6480	99	-US MIL PWR>USSR	2A38E	2A18E	2A18E	2A18E	2A18E	2A18E	2A18E	2A18E	2A18E
6490	99	US NEED>PWR OTHS	2A38F	2A18F	2A18F	2A18F	2A18F	2A18F	2A18F	2A18F	2A18F
6500	99	US FRN PLCY NRRW	2A38G	2A18G	2A18G	2A18G	2A18G	2A18G	2A18G	2A18G	2A18G
6510	99	SRVCMEN SHD OBEY	2A38H	2A18H	2A18H	2A18H	2A18H	2A18H	2A18H	2A18H	2A18H
11210		-MLTRY COUP U.S.		4E06	4E06						
11220	168	NT VOL 4 NEC WAR		4E07	4E07	4E06	4E06	4E06	4E06	4E06	4E06

L04: MILITARY. Attitudes toward the military as an institution and occupation

Item Reference Number	Page Loc. in this Volume	ITEM DESCRIPTION (ABBREVIATED)	1975	1976	1977	1978	1979	1980	1981	1982/83	1984/85
7000	107	DHNSTY MILITARY	2A20L	2D04L	2D04L	2D04L	2D04L	2D04L	2D04L	2D04L	2D04L
8490	128	GD JB MILITARY	3A27L	3A24L	3A24L	3A24L	3A24L	3A24L	3A24L	3A24L	3A24L
8500	128	MIL TOO MCH INFL	3A28	3A25	3A25	3A25	3A25	3A25	3A25	3A25	3A25
8510	128	US TOO MCH$MILT	3A29	3A26	3A26	3A26	3A26	3A26	3A26	3A26	3A26
10660	158	>INFLC MILITARY	4A14J	4A19J	4A19J	4A19J	4A19J	4A19J	4A19J	4A19J	4A19J
11120	167	MLTRY GET AHEAD		4E01A	4E01A	4E01A	4E01A	4E01A	4E01A	4E01A	4E01A
		(continued)									

Item Reference Number	Page Loc. in this Volume	ITEM DESCRIPTION (ABBREVIATED)	QUESTIONNAIRE LOCATION BY YEAR (FORM, SECTION, AND QUESTION NUMBER)								
			1975	1976	1977	1978	1979	1980	1981	1982/83	1984/85

L04: MILITARY. Attitudes toward the military as an institution and occupation (continued)

11130	167	MLTRY MORE ED		4E01B	4E01B	4E01B	4E01B	4E01B	4E01B	4E01B	4E01B
11140	167	MLTRY ADVNC RESP		4E01C	4E01C	4E01C	4E01C	4E01C	4E01C	4E01C	4E01C
11150	167	MLTRY >FLFLLG JB		4E01D	4E01D	4E01D	4E01D	4E01D	4E01D	4E01D	4E01D
11160	167	MLTRY IDEAS HERD		4E01E	4E01E	4E01E	4E01E	4E01E	4E01E	4E01E	4E01E
11170	167	EXTNT MLTRY JSTC		4E02	4E02	4E02	4E02	4E02	4E02	4E02	4E02
11180	167	MLTRY DSCRM WOMN		4E03	4E03	4E03	4E03	4E03	4E03	4E03	4E03
11190	168	MLTRY DSCRM BLKS		4E04	4E04	4E04	4E04	4E04	4E04	4E04	4E04
11200	168	>FAIR MLTRY CVLN		4E05	4E05	4E05	4E05	4E05	4E05	4E05	4E05
11830	176	PLC WRK MLTY SVC	5A09D	5A05D	5A05D	5A05D	5A05D	5A05D	5A05D	5A05D	5A05D
21080	114	MLTRY PAY CLG GD							5E08	2E10	2E10
21090	115	R WD DO MLTY/CLG							5E09	2E11	2E11

M01: INTERPERSONAL RELATIONSHIPS. Dating

620	22	#X/AV WK GO OUT		+C25	+C25	+C25	+C25	+C25	|C25	+C25	+C25
630	22	#X DATE 3+/WK		+C26	+C26	+C26	+C26	+C26	+C26	+C26	+C26

M02: INTERPERSONAL RELATIONSHIPS. Cross-age relationships with adults outside the family (See also B05)

1240	33	TM SPT ADLT MST	1A006	1A003	1A003	1A003	1A003	1A003	1A003	1A003	1A003
1250	34	LK MR TM ADLT	1A007	1A004	1A004	1A004	1A004	1A004	1A004	1A004	1A004
1260	34	LK MR TM YG CHD	1A008	1A005	1A005	1A005	1A005	1A005	1A005	1A005	1A005
6530	99	FRQ HIT SUPRVISR	2A39B	2A19B	2A19B	2A19B	2A19B	2A19B	2A19B	2A19B	2A19B
21550	160	JOB-SUPERVSR AGE								4D04	4D04
21610	161	JOB-OVER AGE 30								4D06E	4D06E
21710	163	JOB-TCHR HELP GT								4D08	4D08
21910	200	PARTY-PPL OVR 30									5E08A
22050	202	PRFR PTY-PPL >30									5E09A

M03: INTERPERSONAL RELATIONSHIPS. Agreement/disagreement with parents

1330	35	SAT GT ALNG PRNT	1A009G	1A006G	1A006G	1A006G	1A006G	1A006G	1A006G	1A006G	1A006G
1500	38	IMP LIV CLS PRNT		1A007J	1A007J	1A007J	1A007J	1A007J	1A007J	1A007J	1A007J
6520	99	FRQ FIGHT PARNTS	2A39A	2A19A	2A19A	2A19A	2A19A	2A19A	2A19A	2A19A	2A19A
11230	168	P'IDEA OF DO LIF	4A27A	4E08A	4E08A	4E07A	4E07A	4E07A	4E07A	4E07A	4E07A
11240	168	P'IDEA OF LSR TM	4A27B	4E08B	4E08B	4E07B	4E07B	4E07B	4E07B	4E07B	4E07B
11250	168	P'IDEA OF CLTHES	4A27C	4E08C	4E08C	4E07C	4E07C	4E07C	4E07C	4E07C	4E07C
11260	169	P'IDEA OF SPND $	4A27D	4E08D	4E08D	4E07D	4E07D	4E07D	4E07D	4E07D	4E07D
11270	169	P'IDEA OF DATE	4A27E	4E08E	4E08E	4E07E	4E07E	4E07E	4E07E	4E07E	4E07E
11280	169	P'IDEA OF OK DRK	4A27F	4E08F	4E08F	4E07F	4E07F	4E07F	4E07F	4E07F	4E07F
11290	169	P'IDEA OF OK MRJ	4A27G	4E08G	4E08G	4E07G	4E07G	4E07G	4E07G	4E07G	4E07G
11300	169	P'IDEA OF OK DRG	4A27H	4E08H	4E08H	4E07H	4E07H	4E07H	4E07H	4E07H	4E07H
11310	169	P'IDEA OF VALUES	4A27I	4E08I	4E08I	4E07I	4E07I	4E07I	4E07I	4E07I	4E07I
11320	169	P'IDEA OF EDUC	4A27J	4E08J	4E08J	4E07J	4E07J	4E07J	4E07J	4E07J	4E07J
11330	170	P'IDEA OF SX RLS	4A27K	4E08K	4E08K	4E07K	4E07K	4E07K	4E07K	4E07K	4E07K
11340	170	P'IDEA OF ECLOGY	4A27L	4E08L	4E08L	4E07L	4E07L	4E07L	4E07L	4E07L	4E07L
11350	170	P'IDEA OF RCL IS	4A27M	4E08M	4E08M	4E07M	4E07M	4E07M	4E07M	4E07M	4E07M
11360	170	P'IDEA OF RLGION	4A27N	4E08N	4E08N	4E07N	4E07N	4E07N	4E07N	4E07N	4E07N
11370	170	P'IDEA OF PLTICS	4A27O	4E08O	4E08O	4E07O	4E07O	4E07O	4E07O	4E07O	4E07O
13150		FAM+REL GD/CHILD		5E01A							
13160		FAM+REL GD/PARNT		5E01B							
13170		FAM+REL GD/GRPNT		5E01C							
13180		FAM+REL,R LIK/PT		5E01D							
19530	113	3MO/DLY ARG PRNT						2E08A	2E08A	2E07A	2E07A
21800	199	PRNT SUPRV PARTY									5E06A
21810	199	PRNT SUPRV DATES									5E06B
21820	199	PRNT SUPRV DRESS									5E06C
21830	199	PRNT SUPRV MONEY									5E06D
21840	199	PRNT SUPRV EVENG									5E06E
21850	199	PRNT SUPRV HOMWK									5E06F
21860	200	PRN SUPRV COURSE									5E06G
21870	200	PRNT SUPRV WORK									5E06H
21880	200	PRN SUPR TV QNTY									5E06I
21890	200	PRN SUPR TV QLTY									5E06J

Item Reference Number	Page Loc. in this Volume	ITEM DESCRIPTION (ABBREVIATED)	QUESTIONNAIRE LOCATION BY YEAR (FORM, SECTION, AND QUESTION NUMBER)								
			1975	1976	1977	1978	1979	1980	1981	1982/83	1984/85

M04: INTERPERSONAL RELATIONSHIPS. Friendships (See also Q03: Loneliness)

1320	35	SAT OWN FRIENDS	1A009F	1A006F	1A006F	1A006F	1A006F	1A006F	1A006F	1A006F	1A006F
1450	37	IMP STRG FRDSHP		1A007E	1A007E	1A007E	1A007E	1A007E	1A007E	1A007E	1A007E
5920	90	DALY VIST W/FRDS		2A02K	2A02K	2A02K	2A02K	2A02K	2A02K	2A02K	2A02K
10170	149	JOB IMPC MK FRND	4A08I	4A08I	4A08I	4A08I	4A08I	4A08I	4A08I	4A08I	4A08I

M05: INTERPERSONAL RELATIONSHIPS. Community at large

1480	37	IMP LDR COMUNTY		1A007H	1A007H	1A007H	1A007H	1A007H	1A007H	1A007H	1A007H
10290	151	JOB IMPC CNTC PL	4A08U	4A08U	4A08U	4A08U	4A08U	4A08U	4A08U	4A08U	4A08U
13590	139	STS SCH LDS STU		5E05B	5E06B	5E06B	5E04B	5E06B		3E06B	3E06B
21600	161	JOB-DIF SOC BKGD								4D06D	4D06D
21730	172	IDEA PARENTS GRP								4E09†	4E09
21740	172	#FRNDS PRNTS GRP								4E10†	4E10
21750	172	OWN PRNTS IN GRP								4E11†	4E11
21760	172	GP IMPCT OWN FLG								4E12†	4E12
21770	172	GP CHG RELP PRNT								4E13†	4E13
21780	173	#FRNDS ANTIDG GP								4E14†	4E14
21790	173	EVR IN ANTIDG GP								4E15†	4E15

N01: RACE RELATIONS. Preferred interracial contact

8110	122	DES FRND OTH RC	3A19A	3A07A	3A07A	3A07A	3A07A	3A07A	3A07A	3A07A	3A07A
8120	122	DES SUPVR DIF RC	3A19B	3A07B	3A07B	3A07B	3A07B	3A07B	3A07B	3A07B	3A07B
8130	122	DES FAM NX DF RC	3A19C	3A07C	3A07C	3A07C	3A07C	3A07C	3A07C	3A07C	3A07C
8140	122	DES CHL FD SM RC	3A19D	3A07D	3A07D	3A07D	3A07D	3A07D	3A07D	3A07D	3A07D
8150	123	DES CHL FD OT RC	3A19E	3A07E	3A07E	3A07E	3A07E	3A07E	3A07E	3A07E	3A07E
8160	123	DES AL WKS SM RC	3A19F	3A08A	3A08A	3A08A	3A08A	3A08A	3A08A	3A08A	3A08A
8170	123	DES SO WKS DF RC	3A19G	3A08B	3A08B	3A08B	3A08B	3A08B	3A08B	3A08B	3A08B
8180	123	DES MS WKS DF RC	3A19H	3A08C	3A08C	3A08C	3A08C	3A08C	3A08C	3A08C	3A08C
8190	123	DES AL NGB SM RC	3A19I	3A09A	3A09A	3A09A	3A09A	3A09A	3A09A	3A09A	3A09A
8200	123	DES SO NGB OT RC	3A19J	3A09B	3A09B	3A09B	3A09B	3A09B	3A09B	3A09B	3A09B
8210	123	DES MS NGB OT RC	3A19K	3A09C	3A09C	3A09C	3A09C	3A09C	3A09C	3A09C	3A09C
8220	124	DES AL CHL SM RC	3A19L	3A10A	3A10A	3A10A	3A10A	3A10A	3A10A	3A10A	3A10A
8230	124	DES SM CHL OT RC	3A19M	3A10B	3A10B	3A10B	3A10B	3A10B	3A10B	3A10B	3A10B
8240	124	DES MS CHL OT RC	3A19N	3A10C	3A10C	3A10C	3A10C	3A10C	3A10C	3A10C	3A10C

N02: RACE RELATIONS. Attitudes about discrimination

1520	38	IMP CRRCT INEQL		1A007L	1A007L	1A007L	1A007L	1A007L	1A007L	1A007L	1A007L
10380	153	JOB OBSTC RACE		4A13C	4A13C	4A13C	4A13C	4A13C	4A13C	4A13C	4A13C
11190	168	MLTRY DSCRM BLKS		4E04	4E04	4E04	4E04	4E04	4E04	4E04	4E04
11350	170	P'IDEA OF RCL IS	4A27M	4E08M	4E08M	4E07M	4E07M	4E07M	4E07M	4E07M	4E07M
11710	175	WR/NT RACE RELTN	5A04F	5A03F	5A03F	5A03F	5A03F	5A03F	5A03F	5A03F	5A03F
11950	178	B/W RLTNS WRSE	5A15	5A08	5A08	5A08	5A08	5A08	5A08	5A08	5A08
12100	180	MNRTY NT MY BSNS	5A19F	5A18D	5A18D	5A18D	5A18D	5A18D	5A18D	5A18D	5A18D
12220	183	CTB TO MNRTY GRP	5A20C	5A20C	5A20C	5A20C	5A20C	5A20C	5A20C	5A20C	5A20C

N03: RACE RELATIONS. Actual interracial contacts

8250	124	FRNDS AL OT RC	3A22	3A11	3A11	3A11	3A11	3A11	3A11	3A11	3A11
8260	124	NGBHD AL OT RC	3A23	3A12	3A12	3A12	3A12	3A12	3A12	3A12	3A12
8270	124	ELEMSCH AL OT RC	3A21	3A13	3A13	3A13	3A13	3A13	3A13	3A13	3A13
8280	124	HISCH AL OT RC	3A20	3A14	3A14	3A14	3A14	3A14	3A14	3A14	3A14
8290	125	WRKRS AL OT RC		3A15	3A15	3A15	3A15	3A15	3A15	3A15	3A15
8300	125	DO LOT THG OT RC	3A24	3A16	3A16	3A16	3A16	3A16	3A16	3A16	3A16
8310	125	VRY GD EXP OT RC	3A25	3A17	3A17	3A17	3A17	3A17	3A17	3A17	3A17
11890	177	RCL CNTCT SCHOOL		5A07A	5A07A	5A07A	5A07A	5A07A	5A07A	5A07A	5A07A
11900	177	RCL CNTCT NGHBHD		5A07B	5A07B	5A07B	5A07B	5A07B	5A07B	5A07B	5A07B
11910	177	RCL CNTCT CHURCH		5A07C	5A07C	5A07C	5A07C	5A07C	5A07C	5A07C	5A07C
11920	177	RCL CNTCT SPORTS		5A07D	5A07D	5A07D	5A07D	5A07D	5A07D	5A07D	5A07D
11930	178	RCL CNTCT CLUBS		5A07E	5A07E	5A07E	5A07E	5A07E	5A07E	5A07E	5A07E
11940	178	RCL CNTCT JOB		5A07F	5A07F	5A07F	5A07F	5A07F	5A07F	5A07F	5A07F

† This question appears in 1983 but does not appear in 1982.

Item Reference Number	Page Loc. in this Volume	ITEM DESCRIPTION (ABBREVIATED)	QUESTIONNAIRE LOCATION BY YEAR (FORM, SECTION, AND QUESTION NUMBER)								
			1975	1976	1977	1978	1979	1980	1981	1982/83	1984/85

O01: CONCERN FOR OTHERS. Attitudes regarding social service, charitable activism

Item Ref.	Page	Description	1975	1976	1977	1978	1979	1980	1981	1982/83	1984/85
1470	37	IMP CNTRBTN SOC		1A007G	1A007G	1A007G	1A007G	1A007G	1A007G	1A007G	1A007G
1520	38	IMP CRRCT INEQL		1A007L	1A007L	1A007L	1A007L	1A007L	1A007L	1A007L	1A007L
10130	149	JOB IMPC HLP OTH	4A08E	4A08E	4A08E	4A08E	4A08E	4A08E	4A08E	4A08E	4A08E
10190	150	JOB IMPC WRTHWLE	4A08K	4A08K	4A08K	4A08K	4A08K	4A08K	4A08K	4A08K	4A08K
11860	176	PLC WRK SOC SVCS	5A09G	5A05G	5A05G	5A05G	5A05G	5A05G	5A05G	5A05G	5A05G

O02: CONCERN FOR OTHERS. Involvement in community, altruistic activities

Item Ref.	Page	Description	1975	1976	1977	1978	1979	1980	1981	1982/83	1984/85
5860	89	DALY CMNTY AFFRS		2A02E	2A02E	2A02E	2A02E	2A02E	2A02E	2A02E	2A02E
12200	182	CTB TO UNTD FUND	5A20A	5A20A	5A20A	5A20A	5A20A	5A20A	5A20A	5A20A	5A20A
12210	182	CTB TO INTL RELF	5A20B	5A20B	5A20B	5A20B	5A20B	5A20B	5A20B	5A20B	5A20B
12220	183	CTB TO MNRTY GRP	5A20C	5A20C	5A20C	5A20C	5A20C	5A20C	5A20C	5A20C	5A20C
12230	183	CTB TO RELGS ORG	5A20D	5A20D	5A20D	5A20D	5A20D	5A20D	5A20D	5A20D	5A20D
12240	183	CTB TO PLTCL PTY	5A20E	5A20E	5A20E	5A20E	5A20E	5A20E	5A20E	5A20E	5A20E
12250	183	CTB TO CTZN LBBY	5A20F	5A20F	5A20F	5A20F	5A20F	5A20F	5A20F	5A20F	5A20F
12260	183	CTB TO VS DISEAS	5A20G	5A20G	5A20G	5A20G	5A20G	5A20G	5A20G	5A20G	5A20G
12270	183	CTB TO POP PRBMS	5A20H	5A20H	5A20H	5A20H	5A20H	5A20H	5A20H	5A20H	5A20H
12280	184	CTB TO ENVIR PBM	5A20I	5A20I	5A20I	5A20I	5A20I	5A20I	5A20I	5A20I	5A20I

O03: CONCERN FOR OTHERS. Concern with the problems of others

Item Ref.	Page	Description	1975	1976	1977	1978	1979	1980	1981	1982/83	1984/85
5990	91	US 2 MUCH PROFIT	2A23J	2A03A	2A03A	2A03A	2A03A	2A03A	2A03A	2A03A	2A03A
8040	121	EAT DIF->FD STRV	3A31G	3A04E	3A04E	3A04E	3A04E	3A04E	3A04E	3A04E	3A04E
9840		GVNG FOOD O CNTY	3A33	3E05							
12070	180	WRRY ABT OW CTRY	5A19A	5A18A	5A18A	5A18A	5A18A	5A18A	5A18A	5A18A	5A18A
12080	180	BTTR IF CTZ WRLD	5A19C	5A18B	5A18B	5A18B	5A18B	5A18B	5A18B	5A18B	5A18B
12090	180	-SYMP TWD STARVG	5A19E	5A18C	5A18C	5A18C	5A18C	5A18C	5A18C	5A18C	5A18C
12100	180	MNRTY NT MY BSNS	5A19F	5A18D	5A18D	5A18D	5A18D	5A18D	5A18D	5A18D	5A18D
12110	180	UPST PL TR -FAIR	5A19G	5A18E	5A18E	5A18E	5A18E	5A18E	5A18E	5A18E	5A18E
12120	181	HELP POOR W MY $	5A19I	5A18F	5A18F	5A18F	5A18F	5A18F	5A18F	5A18F	5A18F
12130	181	-MY PRB OT ND HP	5A19K	5A18G	5A18G	5A18G	5A18G	5A18G	5A18G	5A18G	5A18G
12140	181	RB CHNG ETG HABT		5A18H	5A18H	5A18H	5A18H	5A18H	5A18H	5A18H	5A18H
16430		SAT EVB CAR POOL				2E05A					
16440		SAT EAT <BEEF>GRN				2E05B					
19470		EAT <FD,>OWN CITY					5E08A				
19480		EAT <FD,>NRBY STT					5E08B				
19490		EAT <FD,>DIF REGN					5E08C				
19500		EAT <FD,>ASIAN CN					5E08D				

P01: HAPPINESS. Happiness; satisfaction with life and self

Item Ref.	Page	Description	1975	1976	1977	1978	1979	1980	1981	1982/83	1984/85
1190	33	VRY HPY THS DAYS		1A001	1A001	1A001	1A001	1A001	1A001	1A001	1A001
	89			2A01	2A01	2A01	2A01	2A01	2A01	2A01	2A01
	119			3A01	3A01	3A01	3A01	3A01	3A01	3A01	3A01
	146			4A01	4A01	4A01	4A01	4A01	4A01	4A01	4A01
	174			5A01	5A01	5A01	5A01	5A01	5A01	5A01	5A01
1340	35	SAT YOURSELF	1A009H	1A006H	1A006H	1A006H	1A006H	1A006H	1A006H	1A006H	1A006H
1380	36	SAT LIFE AS WHLE	1A009L	1A006L	1A006L	1A006L	1A006L	1A006L	1A006L	1A006L	1A006L
6840	104	CMP SATFD W/LIFE		2D01	2D01	2D01	2D01	2D01	2D01	2D01	2D01
	133			3D01	3D01	3D01	3D01	3D01	3D01	3D01	3D01
	160			4D01	4D01	4D01	4D01	4D01	4D01	4D01	4D01
	184			5A21	5A21	5A21	5A21	5A21	5A21	5A21	5A21
12620	108	SATISFD W MYSELF	5A39H	5D01H	5D01H	5D01H	5D01H	5D01H	5D01H	5D01H	2D05J
	189										5D01H

P02: HAPPINESS. Satisfaction with specific life domains

Item Ref.	Page	Description	1975	1976	1977	1978	1979	1980	1981	1982/83	1984/85
1270	34	SAT PRESENT JOB	1A009A	1A006A	1A006A	1A006A	1A006A	1A006A	1A006A	1A006A	1A006A
1280	34	SAT NEIGHBORHOD	1A009B	1A006B	1A006B	1A006B	1A006B	1A006B	1A006B	1A006B	1A006B
1290	34	SAT PRSNL SAFTY	1A009C	1A006C	1A006C	1A006C	1A006C	1A006C	1A006C	1A006C	1A006C
1300	35	SAT OWN PROP SF	1A009D	1A006D	1A006D	1A006D	1A006D	1A006D	1A006D	1A006D	1A006D
1310	35	SAT EDUC EXPRNCS	1A009E	1A006E	1A006E	1A006E	1A006E	1A006E	1A006E	1A006E	1A006E
1320	35	SAT OWN FRIENDS	1A009F	1A006F	1A006F	1A006F	1A006F	1A006F	1A006F	1A006F	1A006F

(continued)

Item Reference Number	Page Loc. in this Volume	ITEM DESCRIPTION (ABBREVIATED)	QUESTIONNAIRE LOCATION BY YEAR (FORM, SECTION, AND QUESTION NUMBER)								
			1975	1976	1977	1978	1979	1980	1981	1982/83	1984/85

P02: HAPPINESS. Satisfaction with specific life domains (continued)

1330	35	SAT GT ALNG PRNT	1A009G	1A006G	1A006G	1A006G	1A006G	1A006G	1A006G	1A006G	1A006G
1350	35	SAT STD OF LVG	1A009I	1A006I	1A006I	1A006I	1A006I	1A006I	1A006I	1A006I	1A006I
1360	36	SAT TIME FR THGS	1A009J	1A006J	1A006J	1A006J	1A006J	1A006J	1A006J	1A006J	1A006J
1370	36	SAT SPD LEISR	1A009K	1A006K	1A006K	1A006K	1A006K	1A006K	1A006K	1A006K	1A006K
1400	36	SAT AMT OF FUN		1A006N	1A006N	1A006N	1A006N	1A006N	1A006N	1A006N	1A006N
10350	153	R THNK WK BE SAT		4A12	4A12	4A12	4A12	4A12	4A12	4A12	4A12
10910	160	CMP SATFD W/JOB		4D02	4D02	4D02	4D02	4D02	4D02	4D02	4D02

Q01: OTHER PERSONALITY VARIABLES. Attitudes about self, self-esteem

1190	33	VRY HPY THS DAYS		1A001	1A001	1A001	1A001	1A001	1A001	1A001	1A001
	89			2A01	2A01	2A01	2A01	2A01	2A01	2A01	2A01
	119			3A01	3A01	3A01	3A01	3A01	3A01	3A01	3A01
	146			4A01	4A01	4A01	4A01	4A01	4A01	4A01	4A01
	174			5A01	5A01	5A01	5A01	5A01	5A01	5A01	5A01
1340	35	SAT YOURSELF	1A009H	1A006H	1A006H	1A006H	1A006H	1A006H	1A006H	1A006H	1A006H
1400	36	SAT AMT OF FUN		1A006N	1A006N	1A006N	1A006N	1A006N	1A006N	1A006N	1A006N
6840	104	CMP SATFD W/LIFE		2D01	2D01	2D01	2D01	2D01	2D01	2D01	2D01
	133			3D01	3D01	3D01	3D01	3D01	3D01	3D01	3D01
	160			4D01	4D01	4D01	4D01	4D01	4D01	4D01	4D01
	184			5A21	5A21	5A21	5A21	5A21	5A21	5A21	5A21
6850	104	HOW GD AS SPOUSE	2A19A	2D02A	2D02A	2D02A	2D02A	2D02A	2D02A	2D02A	2D02A
6860	104	HOW GD AS PARENT	2A19B	2D02B	2D02B	2D02B	2D02B	2D02B	2D02B	2D02B	2D02B
6870	105	HOW GD AS WORKER	2A19C	2D02C	2D02C	2D02C	2D02C	2D02C	2D02C	2D02C	2D02C
12550	108	POS ATT TWD SELF	5A39A	5D01A	5D01A	5D01A	5D01A	5D01A	5D01A	5D01A	2D05G
	188										5D01A
12570	108	AM PRSN OF WORTH	5A39C	5D01C	5D01C	5D01C	5D01C	5D01C	5D01C	5D01C	2D05H
	188										5D01C
12580	108	DO WELL AS OTHRS	5A39D	5D01D	5D01D	5D01D	5D01D	5D01D	5D01D	5D01D	2D05I
	188										5D01D
12620	108	SATISFD W MYSELF	5A39H	5D01H	5D01H	5D01H	5D01H	5D01H	5D01H	5D01H	2D05J
	189										5D01H
12660	108	-MUCH TO B PROUD			5D01L	5D01L	5D01L	5D01L	5D01L	5D01L	2D05K
	190										5D01L
12680	109	I AM NO GOOD			5D01N	5D01N	5D01N	5D01N	5D01N	5D01N	2D05L
	190										5D01N
12720	109	I DO WRONG THING			5D01R	5D01R	5D01R	5D01R	5D01R	5D01R	2D05M
	190										5D01R
12750	109	MY LIFE NT USEFL			5D01U	5D01U	5D01U	5D01U	5D01U	5D01U	2D05N
	191										5D01U
13950	191	EAGR TO LEAV HOM						5D01W	5D01W	5D01W	5D01W
13960	191	HEST PRT ADLT WL						5D01X	5D01X	5D01X	5D01X

Q02: OTHER PERSONALITY VARIABLES. Locus of control

1210	33	ENJOY FAST PACE	1A004B	1A002B	1A002B	1A002B	1A002B	1A002B	1A002B	1A002B	1A002B
1220	33	THG CHG 2 QUICK	1A004D	1A002C	1A002C	1A002C	1A002C	1A002C	1A002C	1A002C	1A002C
12560	188	LUCK>IMP HRD WRK	5A39B	5D01B	5D01B	5D01B	5D01B	5D01B	5D01B	5D01B	5D01B
12590	189	TRY GT AHD,STOPD	5A39E	5D01E	5D01E	5D01E	5D01E	5D01E	5D01E	5D01E	5D01E
12600	189	PLNNG MKS UNHPPY	5A39F	5D01F	5D01F	5D01F	5D01F	5D01F	5D01F	5D01F	5D01F
12610	189	ACPT LIFE->HAPPR	5A39G	5D01G	5D01G	5D01G	5D01G	5D01G	5D01G	5D01G	5D01G
12630	189	PPL LK ME -CHANC	5A39I	5D01I	5D01I	5D01I	5D01I	5D01I	5D01I	5D01I	5D01I
12640	189	MY PLANS DO WORK			5D01J	5D01J	5D01J	5D01J	5D01J	5D01J	5D01J
12700	190	PPL MASTER FATE			5D01P	5D01P	5D01P	5D01P	5D01P	5D01P	5D01P
12740	191	PLANS->BTR RSLTS			5D01T	5D01T	5D01T	5D01T	5D01T	5D01T	5D01T

Q03: OTHER PERSONALITY VARIABLES. Loneliness

12650	189	OFTN FEEL LONELY			5D01K	5D01K	5D01K	5D01K	5D01K	5D01K	5D01K
12670	190	ALWYS SM1 HELP R			5D01M	5D01M	5D01M	5D01M	5D01M	5D01M	5D01M
12690	190	OFTN FL LEFT OUT			5D01O	5D01O	5D01O	5D01O	5D01O	5D01O	5D01O
12710	190	USLY SM1 TALK TO			5D01Q	5D01Q	5D01Q	5D01Q	5D01Q	5D01Q	5D01Q
12730	191	OFT WSH MOR FRND			5D01S	5D01S	5D01S	5D01S	5D01S	5D01S	5D01S
12760	191	USLY FRDS BE WTH			5D01V	5D01V	5D01V	5D01V	5D01V	5D01V	5D01V

Item Reference Number	Page Loc. in this Volume	ITEM DESCRIPTION (ABBREVIATED)	QUESTIONNAIRE LOCATION BY YEAR (FORM, SECTION, AND QUESTION NUMBER)								
			1975	1976	1977	1978	1979	1980	1981	1982/83	1984/85

Q04: OTHER PERSONALITY VARIABLES. Risk taking

Item Reference Number	Page Loc.	ITEM DESCRIPTION	1975	1976	1977	1978	1979	1980	1981	1982/83	1984/85
7050	108	KICK DO DANGR TH		2D05E	2D05E	2D05E	2D05E	2D05E	2D05E	2D05E	2D05E
7060	108	LIKE RISK SOME X		2D05F	2D05F	2D05F	2D05F	2D05F	2D05F	2D05F	2D05F

Q05: OTHER PERSONALITY VARIABLES. Trust in others

Item Reference Number	Page Loc.	ITEM DESCRIPTION	1975	1976	1977	1978	1979	1980	1981	1982/83	1984/85
1550	38	PPL CAN B TRSTD	1A010	1A008	1A008	1A008	1A008	1A008	1A008	1A008	1A008
1560	38	PPL TRY B HLPFL	1A011	1A009	1A009	1A009	1A009	1A009	1A009	1A009	1A009
1570	38	PPL TRY BE FAIR	1A012	1A010	1A010	1A010	1A010	1A010	1A010	1A010	1A010

Q06: OTHER PERSONALITY VARIABLES. See Subject Area T: HEALTH HABITS AND SYMPTOMS

Q07: OTHER PERSONALITY VARIABLES. Importance placed on various life goals

Item Reference Number	Page Loc.	ITEM DESCRIPTION	1975	1976	1977	1978	1979	1980	1981	1982/83	1984/85
1410	36	IMP B SUCCSS WK		1A007A	1A007A	1A007A	1A007A	1A007A	1A007A	1A007A	1A007A
1420	37	IMP GD MRRG&FAM		1A007B	1A007B	1A007B	1A007B	1A007B	1A007B	1A007B	1A007B
1430	37	IMP LOTS OF $		1A007C	1A007C	1A007C	1A007C	1A007C	1A007C	1A007C	1A007C
1440	37	IMP TM RCRN&HBY		1A007D	1A007D	1A007D	1A007D	1A007D	1A007D	1A007D	1A007D
1450	37	IMP STRG FRDSHP		1A007E	1A007E	1A007E	1A007E	1A007E	1A007E	1A007E	1A007E
1460	37	IMP STEADY WORK		1A007F	1A007F	1A007F	1A007F	1A007F	1A007F	1A007F	1A007F
1470	37	IMP CNTRBTN SOC		1A007G	1A007G	1A007G	1A007G	1A007G	1A007G	1A007G	1A007G
1480	37	IMP LDR COMUNTY		1A007H	1A007H	1A007H	1A007H	1A007H	1A007H	1A007H	1A007H
1490	37	IMP CHLD BTR OPP		1A007I	1A007I	1A007I	1A007I	1A007I	1A007I	1A007I	1A007I
1500	38	IMP LIV CLS PRNT		1A007J	1A007J	1A007J	1A007J	1A007J	1A007J	1A007J	1A007J
1510	38	IMP GT AWY AREA		1A007K	1A007K	1A007K	1A007K	1A007K	1A007K	1A007K	1A007K
1520	38	IMP CRRCT INEQL		1A007L	1A007L	1A007L	1A007L	1A007L	1A007L	1A007L	1A007L
1530	38	IMP NEW XPRNCE		1A007M	1A007M	1A007M	1A007M	1A007M	1A007M	1A007M	1A007M
1540	38	IMP FND PRPS LF		1A007N	1A007N	1A007N	1A007N	1A007N	1A007N	1A007N	1A007N

Q08: OTHER PERSONALITY VARIABLES. Social, political, cultural orientation

Item Reference Number	Page Loc.	ITEM DESCRIPTION	1975	1976	1977	1978	1979	1980	1981	1982/83	1984/85
6330	96	INTEREST IN GOVT	2A31	2A11	2A11	2A11	2A11	2A11	2A11	2A11	2A11
	156		4A29	3E01	3E01	3E01	3E01	3E01	3E01	4A18	4A18
	182		5A40	4A18	4A18	4A18	4A18	4A18	4A18	5A19	5A19
				5A19	5A19	5A19	5A19	5A19	5A19		
6880	105	THK ABT SOC ISSU	*A06	2D03	2D03	2D03	2D03	2D03	2D03	2D03	2D03
	119			3A02	3A02	3A02	3A02	3A02	3A02	3A02	3A02
	146			4A05	4A05	4A05	4A05	4A05	4A05	4A05	4A05
	174			5A02	5A02	5A02	5A02	5A02	5A02	5A02	5A02
7010	107	2MCH COMPTN SCTY	2A23C	2D05A	2D05A	2D05A	2D05A	2D05A	2D05A	2D05A	2D05A
7020	107	2MANY YNG SLOPPY	2A23H	2D05B	2D05B	2D05B	2D05B	2D05B	2D05B	2D05B	2D05B
7030	107	2MUCH HARD ROCK	2A23I	2D05C	2D05C	2D05C	2D05C	2D05C	2D05C	2D05C	2D05C
7040	107	SHD DO OWN THING	2A23A	2D05D	2D05D	2D05D	2D05D	2D05D	2D05D	2D05D	2D05D
7630	82	R LIKES SCHOOL		1D001	1D001	1D001	1D001	1D001	1D001	1D001	1D001
	115			2E02	2E06	2E06	2E08	2E09	2E09	2E12	2E12
				3E08	3E07	3E07	3E07	3E07	3E07		
				4E10	5E05	5E05	5E03	5E05			
				5E04							
10460	154	JOB OBSTC -CONFM		4A13K	4A13K	4A13K	4A13K	4A13K	4A13K	4A13K	4A13K
17570		PPL SHD CONFORM					5E02A				
17580		PPL SHD LV HRMNY					5E02B				
17590		PPL SHD B FRANK					5E02C				
17600		PPL SHD THK FREE					5E02D				
17610		PPL SHD B INDPNT					5E02E				

Q09: OTHER PERSONALITY VARIABLES. Hostility

Item Reference Number	Page Loc.	ITEM DESCRIPTION	1975	1976	1977	1978	1979	1980	1981	1982/83	1984/85
19530	113	3MO/DLY ARG PRNT						2E08A	2E08A	2E07A	2E07A
19540	113	3MO/DLY ARG AUTH						2E08B	2E08B	2E07B	2E07B
19550	113	3MO/DLY MAD						2E08C	2E08C	2E07C	2E07C
19560	114	3MO/DLY MAD,SMSH						2E08D	2E08D	2E07D	2E07D
19570	114	3MO/DLY WANT FGT						2E08E	2E08E	2E07E	2E07E
19580	114	3MO/DLY DID FGHT						2E08F	2E08F	2E07F	2E07F

Item Reference Number	Page Loc. in this Volume	ITEM DESCRIPTION (ABBREVIATED)	QUESTIONNAIRE LOCATION BY YEAR (FORM, SECTION, AND QUESTION NUMBER)								
			1975	1976	1977	1978	1979	1980	1981	1982/83	1984/85

R01: BACKGROUND. Age, sex, race, and marital status

10	16	R'S BIRTH YEAR		+C01	+C01	+C01	+C01	+C01	+C01	+C01	+C01
20	16	R'S BIRTH MONTH		+C02	+C02	+C02	+C02	+C02	+C02	+C02	+C02
30	16	R'S SEX		+C03	+C03	+C03	+C03	+C03	+C03	+C03	+C03
40	16	R'S RACE		+C04	+C04	+C04	+C04	+C04	+C04	+C04	+C04
60	16	R NOT MARRIED		+C06	+C06	+C06	+C06	+C06	+C06	+C06	+C06
8320	125	MARRD OR ENGAGED	3A41	3A18	3A18	3A18	3A18	3A18	3A18	3A18	3A18

R02: BACKGROUND. Family characteristics

75	17	# OLDER BR/SIS									+C07A
76	17	# YOUNGER BR/SR									+C07B
310	17	FATHR EDUC LEVEL		+C08	+C08	+C08	+C08	+C08	+C08	+C08	+C08
320	17	MOTHR EDUC LEVEL		+C09	+C09	+C09	+C09	+C09	+C09	+C09	+C09
330	18	MOTH PD JB R YNG		+C10	+C10	+C10	+C10	+C10	+C10	+C10	+C10

R03: BACKGROUND. Living arrangements and household characteristics

50	16	R SPD >TIM R-URB		+C05	+C05	+C05	+C05	+C05	+C05	+C05	+C05
80	17	R'S HSHLD ALONE		+C07A	+C07A	+C07A	+C07A	+C07A	+C07A	+C07A	+C07Ca
90	17	R'S HSHLD FATHER		+C07B	+C07B	+C07B	+C07B	+C07B	+C07B	+C07B	+C07Cb
100	17	R'S HSHLD MOTHER		+C07C	+C07C	+C07C	+C07C	+C07C	+C07C	+C07C	+C07Cc
110	17	R'S HSHLD BR/SR		+C07D	+C07D	+C07D	+C07D	+C07D	+C07D	+C07D	+C07Cd
120	17	R'S HSHLD GRPRNT		+C07E	+C07E	+C07E	+C07E	+C07E	+C07E	+C07E	+C07Ce
130	17	R'S HSHLD SPOUSE		+C07F	+C07F	+C07F	+C07F	+C07F	+C07F	+C07F	+C07Cf
140	17	R'S HSHLD CHLDRN		+C07G	+C07G	+C07G	+C07G	+C07G	+C07G	+C07G	+C07Cg
150	17	R'S HSHLD RELTVS		+C07H	+C07H	+C07H	+C07H	+C07H	+C07H	+C07H	+C07Ch
160	17	R'S HSHLD NONRLT		+C07I	+C07I	+C07I	+C07I	+C07I	+C07I	+C07I	+C07Ci

S01: DEVIANCE AND VICTIMIZATION. Delinquent behaviors

6520	99	FRQ FIGHT PARNTS	2A39A	2A19A	2A19A	2A19A	2A19A	2A19A	2A19A	2A19A	2A19A
6530	99	FRQ HIT SUPRVISR	2A39B	2A19B	2A19B	2A19B	2A19B	2A19B	2A19B	2A19B	2A19B
6540	100	FRQ FGT WRK/SCHL	2A39C	2A19C	2A19C	2A19C	2A19C	2A19C	2A19C	2A19C	2A19C
6550	100	FRQ GANG FIGHT	2A39D	2A19D	2A19D	2A19D	2A19D	2A19D	2A19D	2A19D	2A19D
6560	100	FRQ HURT SM1 BAD	2A39E	2A19E	2A19E	2A19E	2A19E	2A19E	2A19E	2A19E	2A19E
6570	100	FRQ THREAT WEAPN	2A39F	2A19F	2A19F	2A19F	2A19F	2A19F	2A19F	2A19F	2A19F
6580	100	FRQ STEAL <$50	2A39G	2A19G	2A19G	2A19G	2A19G	2A19G	2A19G	2A19G	2A19G
6590	100	FRQ STEAL >$50	2A39H	2A19H	2A19H	2A19H	2A19H	2A19H	2A19H	2A19H	2A19H
6600	100	FRQ SHOPLIFT	2A39I	2A19I	2A19I	2A19I	2A19I	2A19I	2A19I	2A19I	2A19I
6610	101	FRQ CAR THEFT	2A39J	2A19J	2A19J	2A19J	2A19J	2A19J	2A19J	2A19J	2A19J
6620	101	FRQ STEAL CAR PT	2A39K	2A19K	2A19K	2A19K	2A19K	2A19K	2A19K	2A19K	2A19K
6630	101	FRQ TRESPAS BLDG	2A39L	2A19L	2A19L	2A19L	2A19L	2A19L	2A19L	2A19L	2A19L
6640	101	FRQ ARSON	2A39M	2A19M	2A19M	2A19M	2A19M	2A19M	2A19M	2A19M	2A19M
6650	101	FRQ DMG SCH PPTY	2A39N	2A19N	2A19N	2A19N	2A19N	2A19N	2A19N	2A19N	2A19N
6660	101	FRQ DMG WK PRPTY	2A39O	2A19O	2A19O	2A19O	2A19O	2A19O	2A19O	2A19O	2A19O
6670	101	FRQ TRUBL POLICE	2A39P	2A19P	2A19P	2A19P	2A19P	2A19P	2A19P	2A19P	2A19P

S02: DEVIANCE AND VICTIMIZATION. Driving violations and accidents

650	22	#X/12MO R TCKTD		+C28	+C28	+C28	+C28	+C28	+C28	+C28	+C28
660	22	#TCKTS AFT DRNK		+C29A	+C29A	+C29A	+C29A	+C29A	+C29A	+C29A	+C29A
670	23	#TCKTS AFT MARJ		+C29B	+C29B	+C29B	+C29B	+C29B	+C29B	+C29B	+C29B
680	23	#TCKTS AFT OTDG		+C29C	+C29C	+C29C	+C29C	+C29C	+C29C	+C29C	+C29C
690	23	#ACCIDNTS/12 MO		+C30	+C30	+C30	+C30	+C30	+C30	+C30	+C30
700	23	#ACDTS AFT DRNK		+C31A	+C31A	+C31A	+C31A	+C31A	+C31A	+C31A	+C31A
710	23	#ACDTS AFT MARJ		+C31B	+C31B	+C31B	+C31B	+C31B	+C31B	+C31B	+C31B
720	23	#ACDTS AFT OTDG		+C31C	+C31C	+C31C	+C31C	+C31C	+C31C	+C31C	+C31C

S03: DEVIANCE AND VICTIMIZATION. Victimization experiences

6680	102	SM1 ROB YRS <$50		2A20A	2A20A	2A20A	2A20A	2A20A	2A20A	2A20A	2A20A
6690	102	SM1 ROB YRS >$50		2A20B	2A20B	2A20B	2A20B	2A20B	2A20B	2A20B	2A20B
6700	102	SM1 DMG YR PRPTY		2A20C	2A20C	2A20C	2A20C	2A20C	2A20C	2A20C	2A20C
		(continued)									

QUESTIONNAIRE LOCATION BY YEAR (FORM, SECTION, AND QUESTION NUMBER)

S03: DEVIANCE AND VICTIMIZATION. Victimization experiences *(continued)*

Item Reference Number	Page Loc. in this Volume	ITEM DESCRIPTION (ABBREVIATED)	1975	1976	1977	1978	1979	1980	1981	1982/83	1984/85
6710	102	SM1 INJR U W/WPN	2A20D	2A20D	2A20D	2A20D	2A20D	2A20D	2A20D	2A20D	2A20D
6720	102	SM1 THRTN U W/WP	2A20E	2A20E	2A20E	2A20E	2A20E	2A20E	2A20E	2A20E	2A20E
6730	102	SM1 INJR YU -WPN	2A20F	2A20F	2A20F	2A20F	2A20F	2A20F	2A20F	2A20F	2A20F
6740	103	SM1 THRT U W/INJ	2A20G	2A20G	2A20G	2A20G	2A20G	2A20G	2A20G	2A20G	2A20G
9871	140	SM1 SCL ROB <$50		4E11A	3E10A	3E10A	5E06A	5E08A	5E13A	3E08A	3E08A
9872	140	SM1 SCL ROB >$50		4E11B	3E10B	3E10B	5E06B	5E08B	5E13B	3E08B	3E08B
9873	140	SM1 SCL DMG PRTY		4E11C	3E10C	3E10C	5E06C	5E08C	5E13C	3E08C	3E08C
9874	140	SM1 SCL IN U W/W		4E11D	3E10D	3E10D	5E06D	5E08D	5E13D	3E08D	3E08D
9875	141	SM1 SCL TH U W/W		4E11E	3E10E	3E10E	5E06E	5E08E	5E13E	3E08E	3E08E
9876	141	SM1 SCL IN U -WP		4E11F	3E10F	3E10F	5E06F	5E08F	5E13F	3E08F	3E08F
9877	141	SM1 SCL TH U W/I		4E11G	3E10G	3E10G	5E06G	5EO8G	5E13G	3E08G	3E08G

T: HEALTH HABITS AND SYMPTOMS

Item Reference Number	Page Loc. in this Volume	ITEM DESCRIPTION (ABBREVIATED)	1975	1976	1977	1978	1979	1980	1981	1982/83	1984/85
8850	133	OFTN SHRTNS BRTH	(3D02A)	3D02A	3D02A	3D02A	3D02A	3D02A	3D02A	3D02A	3D02A
8860	133	OFTN HEART BEATG	(3D02B)	3D02B	3D02B	3D02B	3D02B	3D02B	3D02B	3D02B	3D02B
8870	133	OFTN SPLLS DZZNS	(3D02C)	3D02C	3D02C	3D02C	3D02C	3D02C	3D02C	3D02C	3D02C
8880	133	OFTN HNDS TRMBLE	(3D02D)	3D02D	3D02D	3D02D	3D02D	3D02D	3D02D	3D02D	3D02D
8890	133	OFTN HNDS SWEATG	(3D02E)	3D02E	3D02E	3D02E	3D02E	3D02E	3D02E	3D02E	3D02E
8900	134	OFTN CDNT GT GNG	(3D02F)	3D02F	3D02F	3D02F	3D02F	3D02F	3D02F	3D02F	3D02F
20690		ATTN TO NUTRITON					2E15A				
20700		MIN CHOLESTEROL					2E15B				
20710		AVOID ADDITIVES					2E15C				
20720		TRY GET EXERCISE					2E15D				
20730		CNTRL OWN HEALTH					2E16				
20740	117	OFTN EAT BRKFST					2E17A	2E17A	2E17A	2E20A	2E21A
20750	117	OFTN EAT GN VEG					2E17B	2E17B	2E17B	2E20B	2E21B
20760	117	OFTN EAT FRUIT					2E17C	2E17C	2E17C	2E20C	2E21C
20770	118	OFTN EXERCISE					2E17D	2E17D	2E17D	2E20D	2E21D
20780	118	OFTN 7HRS SLEEP					2E17E	2E17E	2E17E	2E20E	2E21E
20790	118	OFTN SLEEP <SHLD					2E17F	2E17F	2E17F	2E20F	2E21F
21310	85	#DA HEADACHE								1D015A	1D015A
21320	85	#DA SORE THROAT								1D015B	1D015B
21330	85	#DA SINUS CONG								1D015C	1D015C
21340	85	#DA COUGHING								1D015D	1D015D
21350	85	#DA CHEST COLD								1D015E	1D015E
21360	86	#DA COUGH PHLM								1D015F	1D015F
21370	86	#DA SHORT BRTH								1D015G	1D015G
21380	86	#DA WHEEZING								1D015H	1D015H
21390	86	#DA TRBL REMEM								1D015I	1D015I
21400	86	#DA DFCT THINK								1D015J	1D015J
21410	86	#DA TRBL LEARN								1D015K	1D015K
21420	87	#DA TRBL SLEEP								1D015L	1D015L
21430	87	#DA TRBL START								1D015M	1D015M
21440	87	#DA STAY HOME								1D015N	1D015N
21450	87	#X/12M DOC-CHEK								1D016A	1D016A
21460	87	#X/12M DOC-FGHT								1D016B	1D016B
21470	87	#X/12M DOC-INJ								1D016C	1D016C
21480	88	#X/12M DOC-ILL								1D016D	1D016D
21490	88	#X/12M DOC-PSY								1D016E	1D016E
21500	88	#X/12M HSP-INJ								1D017A	1D017A
21510	88	#X/12M HSP-ILL								1D017B	1D017B
21520	88	RLTV PHY HEALTH								1D018	1D018

Appendix A
Sampling Error Estimates and Tables

All of the percentages reported in this volume are really *estimates* of the response percentages that would have been obtained if, instead of using a sample survey, we had asked all high schools throughout the United States to participate, and in all schools that agreed to participate we had invited the whole senior class to fill out the questionnaires. The question naturally arises: How accurate are the present percentage estimates based on a limited number of schools and seniors? For any particular percentage resulting from a sample survey we cannot know exactly how much error has resulted from sampling, but we can make reasonably good estimates of "confidence intervals" — ranges within which the "true" population value is very likely to fall. The word "true" in this context is defined quite narrowly; it refers only to the value that would be found if we had set out to survey the total population — all high school seniors in the United States. Thus this concept of "true" population value does *not* take account of biases that might occur due to refusals, distortion of responses, faulty question wording, and other factors. Each of these sources of possible error is discussed in the "Representativeness and Validity" section of the Introduction to this volume. The reader is urged to review this material and take it into account along with the sampling error estimates included in this appendix.

The estimation of confidence intervals in surveys involving complex samples can be a highly complicated combination of statistical science plus informed judgment. It is an area in which there is no single "right answer" or "best approach." We suspect that many of those using this volume will not be especially interested in *how* we have chosen to solve the problems involved in estimating confidence intervals, so long as we provide guidelines that can be applied in a

fairly simple and straightforward manner. This appendix is designed to accomplish that. Appendix B provides a more extensive discussion of how we obtained the confidence intervals shown here, and it also provides guidelines for computing specific confidence intervals for a wider range of possible applications than can be covered in the tables provided in this appendix.

A very rough example of a confidence interval can be stated in these terms: For percentages based on the total sample (all five questionnaire forms), the "true" values are rarely more than 1.5 percent higher or lower than the percentage estimates reported in this volume. How rarely? The chances are much lower than 1 in 20. Indeed, many of the percentages reported for the total sample are accurate to within one percent.

Of course, most of the data reported here are based on items included only in one or another of the five questionnaire forms. Since such percentages are based on only one-fifth of the total sample, they are somewhat less accurate. The loss in accuracy is less than might be imagined, however, for reasons spelled out in Appendix B. For present purposes, it is enough to say that percentages based on 3,000 or more seniors responding to one questionnaire form are rarely (less than 1 in 20) farther than 2.4 percent away from the "true" value.

We have thus far provided two very rough illustrations of confidence intervals — a range of ± 1.5 percent for percentages based on the total sample, and a range of ± 2.4 percent for percentages based on the number of seniors responding to one questionnaire form. While these two intervals provide some notion of the overall range of accuracy of the sample, they fall short of our needs in a number of respects. We need to be able to assign confidence intervals for subgroups such as males, females, those who plan to complete college, and so forth, all of which involve smaller numbers of cases and thus some reduction in accuracy. We also need to take account of the fact that, other things equal, confidence intervals grow smaller when one moves from the middle of the scale (percentages near 50 percent) to the extremes (e.g., 4 percent or 96 percent). Further, we need to provide guidelines for evaluating the *difference* between two percentages; for example, we may wish to know whether the difference between male and female percentages in response to a particular question is large enough so that it is not likely to be merely the result of sampling error. Another type of difference of considerable interest is that between percentages from two different years; for example, we may wish to know whether an increase in the percentage of daily marijuana users from one year to the next is large enough to be considered a statistically significant change.

Each of the requirements mentioned above is taken into account in the tables of confidence intervals which follow.

Confidence Intervals for Single Percentages

Table A-1 provides confidence intervals for single percentages that are reasonably good approximations for most *variables* and for most *subgroups* (as well as for the total sample). The table entries slightly underestimate the confidence intervals for regional subgroups and for blacks. These underestimates can be corrected reasonably well by multiplying the entries in Table A-1 by a factor of 1.1 for data based on a single form and by a factor of 1.33 for data based on all five forms. A more serious problem is that the table entries substantially underestimate the confidence intervals for certain variables which tend to be somewhat homogeneous within schools, as well as other factors likely to show clustering according to geographical area or socioeconomic level. A discussion of some of these variables is provided at the end of this appendix.

Table A-1 accommodates various numbers of cases (presented as different columns in the table), and various percentages (presented as different rows in the table). The table entries, when added to and subtracted from the observed percentage, establish the 95 percent confidence interval (calculated as 1.96 sampling errors). Thus, for example, to determine the accuracy of a result of 67.4 percent based on a sample of 1,632 cases, one should first look for the closest values in the table (in this case, about 70 percent and a number of cases approximately equal to 1,500); next determine the values to be added to and subtracted from the observed percentage (in this case the values

would be + 2.8 percent and − 2.9 percent); and then compute the confidence interval around the observed percentage of 67.4 percent (in this case an interval ranging from 64.5 percent to 70.2 percent). This procedure yields an interval such that, for most variables, the chances are 95 in 100 that if all high school seniors in the country had been asked to participate in the survey the resulting percentage would fall within the interval.

Confidence Intervals for Differences between Two Percentages

Table A-2 provides confidence intervals for differences between certain percentages. Specifically, the table can be used for *comparisons* between males and females, between those who do and do not plan to complete four years of college, and between those falling into different categories of the five-level index of drug usage. The above comparisons are appropriate for data from any single year (e.g., male seniors in 1976 compared with female seniors in 1976, or the "marijuana only" seniors in 1977 compared with the "no illicit drugs" seniors in 1977). Table A-2 is also useful in assessing *one-year* trends for any of the above subgroups as well as for the total sample. For example, one may be interested in a confidence interval (or significance level) for the difference between the percentage of female seniors in 1977 who used marijuana and the percentage of female seniors in 1978 who did so. The values in Table A-2 are appropriate for confidence intervals across adjacent years (e.g., 1976 compared with 1977), provided the same subgroup (e.g., females) is being considered both years. The confidence intervals for comparisons across non-adjacent years (e.g., 1976 compared with 1978), are slightly larger.

With appropriate corrections, the entries in Table A-2 can be used for trends covering more than one year and for trends or comparisons involving regional subgroups and blacks. Each of these applications requires some upward adjustment of the table entries; guidelines for such adjustments are provided in the notes accompanying Table A-2.

For information on the derivation of Table A-2 and for guidelines to be used in computing confidence intervals not covered in that table, the reader is referred to Appendix B.

In order to find the appropriate confidence interval in Table A-2, one must first locate that portion of the table which deals with percentage values closest to the two percentages being compared (for example, if one wished to compare a value of 28.1 percent with one of 35.4 percent, the "p = 30 percent or 70 percent" portion of the table would be closest). The next step is to locate the specific table entry which corresponds most closely to the numbers of cases involved in the two percentages being compared (e.g., if those numbers were 1,478 and 1,563 for 28.1 percent and 35.4 percent, the correct table entry would be 3.9 percent). That table entry, when added to and subtracted from the difference between the two percentages, yields the 95 percent confidence interval for the difference. (In the above illustration that would be 7.3 percent ± 3.9 percent or an interval from 3.4 percent to 11.2 percent.) The chances are only 1 in 20 that the "true" difference between two percentages lies outside of this interval.

Another use of Table A-2 is to test whether a difference between two percentages is "statistically significant." If the table entry is smaller than the difference between the two percentages (as is true in the above illustration), then the difference is statistically significant at the 95 percent level (sometimes indicated as p<.05).

Some Cautions

The tables provided here are based on averages of large numbers of sampling errors computed across a wide range of the variables which appear in this volume, as well as across all of the subgroups for which data are reported here. We are confident that the values in the tables are reasonably accurate for most purposes, but we must repeat the caution that the tables slightly underestimate confidence intervals for the following groups and comparisons:

> Blacks
> Regions (Northeast, North Central, South, West)
> Comparisons among regions
> Comparisons across non-adjacent years (e.g., 1976 vs. 1978)

A more important problem is that the tables substantially underestimate the confidence intervals for certain variables that, for various reasons, show greater than average homogeneity within schools. After an extensive, but by no means exhaustive, sampling of the kinds of variables which might show such clustering by school, we can provide the following examples of the kinds of variables for which Tables A-1 and A-2 substantially underestimate the confidence intervals.

Variables Related to Educational Background and Aspirations.
The questionnaire items dealing with father's education, mother's education, high school curriculum (college preparatory versus all other), and plans for completing four years of college, all show an appreciable amount of clustering by school. Accordingly, for such variables the confidence intervals provided in the tables should be doubled.

Other items dealing with plans for technical/vocational schooling, a two-year college program, or graduate/professional study, also require adjustment. The confidence intervals in the tables should be multiplied by a factor of 1.5 in order to be applicable to these variables.

It seems clear that the common factor underlying these particular variables is the tendency for family socioeconomic level to be somewhat homogeneous within school districts — some schools serve wealthier populations than others. That makes the form of sampling we use somewhat less efficient for measuring those variables (like those listed above) which are closely associated with family socioeconomic level. Therefore, we urge the reader to treat with caution any variables which are likely to be strongly linked to socioeconomic factors. In the absence of more specific computations of sampling errors, a good rule of thumb for dealing with such variables would be to double the confidence intervals provided in Tables A-1 and A-2.

Variables Related to Geographic Location.
Another category of variables which are somewhat homogeneous within schools and school districts consists of those things which reflect differences in region and/or urbanicity. An obvious example is a background question asking where the respondent grew up; the response category "on a farm" shows a very high degree of clustering within schools. One would have to more than double the confidence intervals in the tables to deal with such a measure. Similarly high clustering was found for some responses about religious preference; for example, those whose preference is Baptist are located primarily in the South (and probably heavily in rural areas), whereas those whose preference is Jewish are located primarily in the Northeast (especially in larger cities). The confidence intervals in Tables A-1 and A-2 should be multiplied by a factor as large as 3 in order to be applicable to such variables.

Other variables which show some greater than average homogeneity within schools include such ideologically related dimensions as frequency of attending religious services, importance of religion, and political preference. Still other variables showing high homogeneity, probably because of their association with urbanicity, include driving (percentage who usually do not drive at all), working (percentage with no job), and household composition (percentage with father not living in the home). For each of the variables mentioned in this paragraph, the confidence intervals shown in Tables A-1 and A-2 should be multiplied by a factor of about 1.5.

Variables Involving Use of Alcohol and Marijuana.
Extensive work has been done to compute

sampling errors and confidence intervals for the drug use measures included in this volume (see Johnston, Bachman, and O'Malley, 1977, 1979, especially Appendix B). Most drug use variables show sampling errors which lie within the range of those provided in Tables A-1 and A-2. Usage levels for alcohol and marijuana, however, show some degree of homogeneity within schools, thus requiring that the table levels be adjusted. For items dealing with alcohol use, the entries in Table A-1 should be multiplied by a factor of 1.6; for items dealing with marijuana use, the correction factor is 1.35.

As noted earlier, this appendix has presented guidelines for using the tables of confidence intervals provided herein. Those readers interested in learning more about the rationale underlying such tables, the procedures used to derive the particular tables presented here, and guidelines for further computations of confidence intervals may consult Appendix B of this volume.

Notes to Table A-1

Caution: The entries in this table systematically underestimate confidence intervals for regional subgroups and for blacks. In order to correct these underestimates, the table entries should be multiplied by a factor of 1.10 for data from a single form and by a factor of 1.33 for data based on five forms. Further cautions and corrections are required for some specific variables which relate to educational background and aspirations, geographic location, and the use of alcohol and marijuana (see discussion in the final sections of Appendix A).

The values in this table, when added to and subtracted from an observed percentage, establish the 95 percent confidence interval around that percentage, incorporating a design effect. Table values were calculated using the following formula (adapted from Hays, 1973, p. 379):

$$\text{lower limit} = p - \frac{2N'p + (1.96)^2 - 1.96\sqrt{4N'p\,(1-p) + (1.96)^2}}{2[N' + (1.96)^2]}$$

$$\text{upper limit} = \frac{2N'p + (1.96)^2 + 1.96\sqrt{4N'p\,(1-p) + (1.96)^2}}{2[N' + (1.96)^2]} - p$$

where p = the percentage, and N' is the "effective N," N' = N/(1.3 + .00015N). (See Appendix B for a discussion of the concept of "effective N.")

Table A-1

Confidence Intervals (95% Level) around Percentage Values

Number of Cases

	100	200	300	400	500	700	1000	1500	2000	2500	3000	3500	4000	5000	7000	10000	15000	20000
99%+	0.9	0.8	0.7	0.7	0.6	0.6	0.5	0.5	0.4	0.4	0.4	0.4	0.3	0.3	0.3	0.3	0.3	0.2
--	5.6	3.2	2.4	1.9	1.7	1.3	1.1	0.8	0.7	0.6	0.6	0.6	0.5	0.5	0.4	0.4	0.3	0.3
97%+	2.1	1.8	1.6	1.4	1.3	1.2	1.0	0.9	0.8	0.8	0.7	0.7	0.6	0.6	0.6	0.5	0.5	0.5
−	6.6	4.1	3.2	2.6	2.3	1.9	1.6	1.3	1.1	1.0	0.9	0.9	0.8	0.8	0.7	0.6	0.6	0.5
95%+	3.1	2.5	2.2	2.0	1.8	1.6	1.4	1.2	1.1	1.0	0.9	0.9	0.9	0.8	0.7	0.7	0.6	0.6
−	7.4	4.7	3.7	3.1	2.7	2.3	1.9	1.5	1.4	1.2	1.1	1.1	1.0	0.9	0.8	0.8	0.7	0.7
90%+	4.9	3.8	3.3	2.9	2.7	2.3	2.0	1.7	1.5	1.4	1.3	1.3	1.2	1.1	1.0	0.9	0.9	0.8
−	8.8	5.8	4.6	4.0	3.5	2.9	2.5	2.0	1.8	1.6	1.5	1.4	1.4	1.3	1.1	1.0	0.9	0.9
85%+	6.6	4.8	4.1	3.6	3.3	2.9	2.5	2.1	1.9	1.7	1.6	1.5	1.5	1.4	1.2	1.1	1.0	1.0
−	9.7	6.6	5.3	4.5	4.0	3.4	2.9	2.4	2.1	1.9	1.8	1.7	1.6	1.5	1.3	1.2	1.1	1.1
80%+	7.4	5.6	4.7	4.2	3.8	3.3	2.8	2.4	2.1	2.0	1.8	1.7	1.7	1.5	1.4	1.3	1.2	1.1
−	10.3	7.1	5.7	4.9	4.4	3.7	3.1	2.6	2.3	2.1	2.0	1.8	1.8	1.6	1.5	1.3	1.2	1.2
70%+	9.1	6.8	5.6	5.0	4.5	3.9	3.3	2.8	2.5	2.3	2.1	2.0	1.9	1.8	1.6	1.5	1.4	1.3
−	11.1	7.7	6.3	5.5	4.9	4.2	3.5	2.9	2.6	2.4	2.2	2.1	2.0	1.8	1.7	1.5	1.4	1.3
50%+	11.0	7.9	6.5	5.7	5.1	4.4	3.7	3.1	2.8	2.5	2.4	2.2	2.1	2.0	1.8	1.6	1.5	1.4
−	11.0	7.9	6.5	5.7	5.1	4.4	3.7	3.1	2.8	2.5	2.4	2.2	2.1	2.0	1.8	1.6	1.5	1.4
30%+	11.1	7.7	6.3	5.5	4.9	4.2	3.5	2.9	2.6	2.4	2.2	2.1	2.0	1.8	1.7	1.5	1.4	1.3
−	9.1	6.8	5.6	5.0	4.5	3.9	3.3	2.8	2.5	2.3	2.1	2.0	1.9	1.8	1.6	1.5	1.4	1.3
20%+	10.3	7.1	5.7	4.9	4.4	3.7	3.1	2.6	2.3	2.1	2.0	1.8	1.8	1.6	1.5	1.3	1.2	1.2
−	7.4	5.6	4.7	4.2	3.8	3.3	2.8	2.4	2.1	2.0	1.6	1.7	1.7	1.5	1.4	1.3	1.2	1.1
15%+	9.7	6.6	5.3	4.5	4.0	3.4	2.9	2.4	2.1	1.9	1.8	1.7	1.6	1.5	1.3	1.2	1.1	1.1
−	6.3	4.8	4.1	3.6	3.3	2.9	2.5	2.1	1.9	1.7	1.6	1.5	1.5	1.4	1.2	1.1	1.0	1.0
10%+	8.8	5.8	4.6	4.0	3.5	2.9	2.5	2.0	1.8	1.6	1.5	1.4	1.4	1.3	1.1	1.0	0.9	0.9
−	4.9	3.8	3.3	2.9	2.7	2.3	2.0	1.7	1.5	1.4	1.3	1.3	1.2	1.1	1.0	0.9	0.9	0.8
5%+	7.4	4.7	3.7	3.1	2.7	2.3	1.9	1.5	1.4	1.2	1.1	1.1	1.0	0.9	0.8	0.8	0.7	0.7
−	3.1	2.5	2.2	2.0	1.8	1.6	1.4	1.2	1.1	1.0	0.9	0.9	0.9	0.8	0.7	0.7	0.6	0.6
3%+	6.6	4.1	3.2	2.6	2.3	1.9	1.6	1.3	1.1	1.0	0.9	0.9	0.8	0.8	0.7	0.6	0.6	0.5
−	2.1	1.8	1.6	1.4	1.3	1.2	1.0	0.9	0.8	0.8	0.7	0.7	0.6	0.6	0.6	0.5	0.5	0.5
1%+	5.6	3.2	2.4	1.9	1.7	1.3	1.1	0.8	0.7	0.6	0.6	0.6	0.5	0.5	0.4	0.4	0.3	0.3
−	0.9	0.8	0.7	0.7	0.6	0.6	0.5	0.5	0.4	0.4	0.4	0.4	0.3	0.3	0.3	0.3	0.3	0.2

Notes to Table A-2

The entries in this table (which appear on the next two pages) are appropriate for *comparisons* between (a) males and females, (b) those who do and do not plan four years of college, and (c) those falling into different categories of the five-level index of drug usage. The table entries are also appropriate for *one-year trends* for the total sample and any of the subgroups except region. Most other trends and subgroup comparisons require that the table entries be multiplied by an adjustment factor, given below.

Outline of Steps to Follow (see text of appendix for illustrations)

1. Locate the portion of the table with "p" values closest to the two percentages being compared.

2. Locate the specific entry closest to the weighted Ns for the two percentages.

3. Multiply that entry by any necessary adjustment factor (see below).

4. That table value (or adjusted table value), when added to and subtracted from the difference between the two percentages, yields the 95 percent confidence interval for the difference.

5. Also, if the table value (or adjusted table value) is smaller than the difference between the two percentages, then the difference may be described as "statistically significant at the 95 percent level."

	Adjustment Factor (to be multiplied by table entry)
Adjustment Factors	
For comparisons between blacks and whites	
based on single form data	*
based on five form data	1.25
For comparisons between any two regions	
based on single form data	1.15
based on five form data	1.50
For one-year trends involving any region	
based on single form data	*
based on five form data	1.25
For trends over two or more years involving any region	
based on single form data	*
based on five form data	1.35
For trends over two or more years involving all other groups	
based on single form data	*
based on five form data	1.15

*indicates that no adjustment is necessary for category shown

NOTE: The table entries were calculated using the following formula: $1.96\sqrt{p(1-p)\left(\frac{1}{N'_1}+\frac{1}{N'_2}\right)}$

where $N'_1 = N_1/DEFF$, and $N'_2 = N_2/DEFF$, $DEFF = 1.3 + .000075\left[\frac{N_1 N_2}{N_1 + N_2}\right]$

Table A-2

Confidence Intervals (95% Confidence Level) for Differences Between Two Percentages

p = 1% or 99%

$N_1 =$	100	200	300	400	500	700	1000	1500	2000	3000	4000	5000	7000	10000	15000	20000
$N_2 = 100$	3.2															
200	2.7	2.2														
300	2.6	2.0	1.8													
400	2.5	1.9	1.7	1.6												
500	2.4	1.9	1.6	1.5	1.4											
700	2.4	1.8	1.6	1.4	1.3	1.2										
1000	2.3	1.7	1.5	1.3	1.2	1.1	1.0									
1500	2.3	1.7	1.4	1.3	1.2	1.0	0.9	0.8								
2000	2.3	1.7	1.4	1.2	1.1	1.0	0.9	0.8	0.7							
3000	2.3	1.6	1.4	1.2	1.1	1.0	0.8	0.7	0.7	0.6						
4000	2.3	1.6	1.4	1.2	1.1	0.9	0.8	0.7	0.7	0.6	0.6					
5000	2.3	1.6	1.3	1.2	1.1	0.9	0.8	0.7	0.6	0.6	0.5	0.5				
7000	2.3	1.6	1.3	1.2	1.1	0.9	0.8	0.7	0.6	0.5	0.5	0.5	0.4			
10000	2.2	1.6	1.3	1.2	1.0	0.9	0.8	0.7	0.6	0.5	0.5	0.5	0.4	0.4		
15000	2.2	1.6	1.3	1.2	1.0	0.9	0.8	0.6	0.6	0.5	0.5	0.4	0.4	0.4	0.4	
20000	2.2	1.6	1.3	1.1	1.0	0.9	0.8	0.6	0.6	0.5	0.5	0.4	0.4	0.4	0.3	0.3

p = 3% or 97%

$N_1 =$	100	200	300	400	500	700	1000	1500	2000	3000	4000	5000	7000	10000	15000	20000
$N_2 = 100$	5.4															
200	4.7	3.8														
300	4.4	3.5	3.1													
400	4.3	3.3	2.9	2.7												
500	4.2	3.2	2.8	2.6	2.4											
700	4.1	3.1	2.7	2.4	2.3	2.1										
1000	4.0	3.0	2.5	2.3	2.1	1.9	1.8									
1500	4.0	2.9	2.4	2.2	2.0	1.8	1.6	1.5								
2000	3.9	2.9	2.4	2.1	1.9	1.7	1.5	1.4	1.3							
3000	3.9	2.8	2.3	2.1	1.9	1.7	1.5	1.3	1.2	1.1						
4000	3.9	2.8	2.3	2.0	1.9	1.6	1.4	1.2	1.1	1.0	0.9					
5000	3.9	2.8	2.3	2.0	1.8	1.6	1.4	1.2	1.1	1.0	0.9	0.9				
7000	3.9	2.8	2.3	2.0	1.8	1.6	1.4	1.2	1.0	0.9	0.9	0.8	0.8			
10000	3.9	2.8	2.3	2.0	1.8	1.5	1.3	1.1	1.0	0.9	0.8	0.8	0.7	0.7		
15000	3.8	2.7	2.3	2.0	1.8	1.5	1.3	1.1	1.0	0.9	0.8	0.7	0.7	0.6	0.6	
20000	3.8	2.7	2.3	2.0	1.8	1.5	1.3	1.1	1.0	0.9	0.8	0.7	0.7	0.6	0.6	0.6

Table A-2 (continued)

$N_1 = $	100	200	300	400	500	700	1000	1500	2000	3000	4000	5000	7000	10000	15000	20000
$N_2 = 100$	6.9															
200	6.0	4.9														
300	5.6	4.5	4.0													
400	5.5	4.3	3.8	3.5												
500	5.4	4.1	3.6	3.3	3.1											
700	5.2	3.9	3.4	3.1	2.9	2.7										
1000	5.1	3.8	3.2	2.9	2.7	2.5	2.2									
1500	5.1	3.7	3.1	2.8	2.6	2.3	2.1	1.9								
2000	5.0	3.6	3.1	2.7	2.5	2.2	2.0	1.7	1.6							
3000	5.0	3.6	3.0	2.6	2.4	2.1	1.9	1.6	1.5	1.4						
4000	5.0	3.6	3.0	2.6	2.4	2.1	1.8	1.6	1.4	1.3	1.2					
5000	4.9	3.6	2.9	2.6	2.3	2.0	1.8	1.5	1.4	1.2	1.2	1.1				
7000	4.9	3.5	2.9	2.6	2.3	2.0	1.7	1.5	1.3	1.2	1.1	1.0	1.0			
10000	4.9	3.5	2.9	2.5	2.3	2.0	1.7	1.4	1.3	1.1	1.1	1.0	0.9	0.9		
15000	4.9	3.5	2.9	2.5	2.3	2.0	1.7	1.4	1.3	1.1	1.0	1.0	0.9	0.8	0.8	
20000	4.9	3.5	2.9	2.5	2.3	1.9	1.7	1.4	1.3	1.1	1.0	0.9	0.9	0.8	0.7	0.7

$p = 5\%$ or 95%

$N_1 = $	100	200	300	400	500	700	1000	1500	2000	3000	4000	5000	7000	10000	15000	20000
$N_1 = 100$	9.5															
200	8.2	6.7														
300	7.8	6.2	5.5													
400	7.5	5.9	5.2	4.8												
500	7.4	5.7	4.9	4.6	4.3											
700	7.2	5.4	4.7	4.3	4.0	3.7										
1000	7.1	5.2	4.5	4.0	3.7	3.4	3.1									
1500	7.0	5.1	4.3	3.8	3.5	3.2	2.8	2.6								
2000	6.9	5.0	4.2	3.7	3.4	3.0	2.7	2.4	2.2							
3000	6.9	4.9	4.1	3.6	3.3	2.9	2.6	2.2	2.1	1.9						
4000	6.8	4.9	4.1	3.6	3.3	2.8	2.5	2.2	2.0	1.8	1.7					
5000	6.8	4.9	4.0	3.6	3.2	2.8	2.4	2.1	1.9	1.7	1.6	1.5				
7000	6.8	4.9	4.0	3.5	3.2	2.8	2.4	2.0	1.8	1.6	1.5	1.4	1.3			
10000	6.8	4.8	4.0	3.5	3.2	2.7	2.3	2.0	1.8	1.6	1.4	1.4	1.3	1.2		
15000	6.8	4.8	4.0	3.5	3.1	2.7	2.3	2.0	1.8	1.5	1.4	1.3	1.2	1.1	1.1	
20000	6.8	4.8	4.0	3.5	3.1	2.7	2.3	1.9	1.7	1.5	1.4	1.3	1.2	1.1	1.0	1.0

$p = 10\%$ or 90%

Table A-2 (continued)

$N_1 = 100$	200	300	400	500	700	1000	1500	2000	3000	4000	5000	7000	10000	15000	20000
$N_2 = 100$ 11.3															
200 9.8	8.0														
300 9.3	7.3	6.6													
400 9.0	7.0	6.2	5.7						p = 15% or 85%						
500 8.8	6.7	5.9	5.4	5.1											
700 8.6	6.5	5.6	5.1	4.8	4.4										
1000 8.4	6.2	5.3	4.8	4.5	4.0	3.7									
1500 8.3	6.1	5.1	4.6	4.2	3.8	3.4	3.0								
2000 8.2	6.0	5.0	4.5	4.1	3.6	3.2	2.9	2.7							
3000 8.2	5.9	4.9	4.3	3.9	3.5	3.0	2.7	2.5	2.2						
4000 8.1	5.8	4.9	4.3	3.9	3.4	2.9	2.6	2.3	2.1	2.0					
5000 8.1	5.8	4.8	4.2	3.8	3.3	2.9	2.5	2.3	2.0	1.9	1.8				
7000 8.1	5.8	4.8	4.2	3.8	3.3	2.8	2.4	2.2	1.9	1.8	1.7	1.6			
10000 8.1	5.8	4.8	4.2	3.8	3.2	2.8	2.4	2.1	1.9	1.7	1.6	1.5	1.4		
15000 8.1	5.7	4.7	4.1	3.7	3.2	2.7	2.3	2.1	1.8	1.7	1.6	1.4	1.3	1.3	
20000 8.0	5.7	4.7	4.1	3.7	3.2	2.7	2.3	2.1	1.8	1.6	1.5	1.4	1.3	1.2	1.2

$N_1 = 100$	200	300	400	500	700	1000	1500	2000	3000	4000	5000	7000	10000	15000	20000
$N_2 = 100$ 12.7															
200 11.0	9.0														
300 10.4	8.2	7.4													
400 10.0	7.8	6.9	6.4						p = 20% or 80%						
500 9.8	7.5	6.6	6.1	5.7											
700 9.6	7.2	6.2	5.7	5.3	4.9										
1000 9.4	7.0	6.0	5.4	5.0	4.5	4.1									
1500 9.3	6.8	5.7	5.1	4.7	4.2	3.8	3.4								
2000 9.2	6.7	5.6	5.0	4.6	3.6	3.2	3.0								
3000 9.1	6.6	5.5	4.9	4.4	3.9	3.4	3.0	2.8	2.5						
4000 9.1	6.5	5.4	4.8	4.3	3.8	3.3	2.9	2.6	2.4	2.2					
5000 9.1	6.5	5.4	4.7	4.3	3.7	3.2	2.8	2.6	2.3	2.1	2.0				
7000 9.1	6.5	5.4	4.7	4.2	3.7	3.2	2.7	2.5	2.2	2.0	1.9	1.8			
10000 9.0	6.5	5.3	4.7	4.2	3.6	3.1	2.7	2.4	2.1	1.9	1.8	1.7	1.6		
15000 9.0	6.4	5.3	4.6	4.2	3.6	3.1	2.6	2.3	2.0	1.9	1.7	1.6	1.5	1.4	
20000 9.0	6.4	5.3	4.6	4.2	3.6	3.1	2.6	2.3	2.0	1.8	1.7	1.6	1.5	1.4	1.3

Table A-2 (continued)

p = 30% or 70%

$N_2 \backslash N_1$	100	200	300	400	500	700	1000	1500	2000	3000	4000	5000	7000	10000	15000	20000
100	14.5															
200	12.6	10.3														
300	11.9	9.4	8.4													
400	11.5	8.9	7.9	7.3												
500	11.3	8.6	7.6	7.0	6.6											
700	11.0	8.3	7.2	6.5	6.1	5.6										
1000	10.8	8.0	6.8	6.2	5.7	5.2	4.7									
1500	10.6	7.8	6.6	5.9	5.4	4.8	4.3	3.9								
2000	10.6	7.7	6.4	5.7	5.2	4.6	4.1	3.7	3.4							
3000	10.5	7.6	6.3	5.6	5.1	4.4	3.9	3.4	3.2	2.9						
4000	10.4	7.5	6.2	5.5	5.0	4.3	3.8	3.3	3.0	2.7	2.5					
5000	10.4	7.5	6.2	5.4	4.9	4.3	3.7	3.2	2.9	2.6	2.4	2.3				
7000	10.4	7.4	6.1	5.4	4.9	4.2	3.6	3.1	2.5	2.3	2.2	2.1				
10000	10.4	7.4	6.1	5.3	4.8	4.2	3.6	3.0	2.7	2.4	2.2	2.1	1.9	1.8		
15000	10.3	7.4	6.1	5.3	4.8	4.1	3.5	3.0	2.7	2.3	2.1	2.0	1.8	1.7	1.6	
20000	10.3	7.4	6.1	5.3	4.8	4.1	3.5	3.0	2.6	2.3	2.1	2.0	1.8	1.7	1.6	1.5

p = 35% or 65%

$N_2 \backslash N_1$	100	200	300	400	500	700	1000	1500	2000	3000	4000	5000	7000	10000	15000	20000
100	15.8															
200	13.7	11.2														
300	13.0	10.3	9.2													
400	12.6	9.8	8.6	8.0												
500	12.3	9.4	8.2	7.6	7.2											
700	12.0	9.0	7.8	7.1	6.7	6.1										
1000	11.8	8.7	7.5	6.7	6.2	5.6	5.1									
1500	11.6	8.5	7.2	6.4	5.9	5.3	4.7	4.3								
2000	11.5	8.4	7.0	6.2	5.7	5.1	4.5	4.0	3.7							
3000	11.4	8.2	6.9	6.1	5.5	4.8	4.3	3.7	3.4	3.1						
4000	11.4	8.2	6.8	6.0	5.4	4.7	4.1	3.6	3.3	3.0	2.8					
5000	11.3	8.1	6.7	5.9	5.4	4.7	4.1	3.5	3.2	2.8	2.7	2.5				
7000	11.3	8.1	6.7	5.9	5.3	4.6	4.0	3.4	3.1	2.7	2.5	2.4	2.2			
10000	11.3	8.1	6.7	5.8	5.3	4.5	3.9	3.3	3.0	2.6	2.4	2.3	2.1	2.0		
15000	11.3	8.0	6.6	5.8	5.2	4.5	3.8	3.3	2.9	2.5	2.3	2.2	2.0	1.9	1.8	
20000	11.3	8.0	6.6	5.8	5.2	4.5	3.8	3.2	2.9	2.5	2.3	2.1	2.0	1.8	1.7	1.6

Appendix B
Procedures Used to Derive Design Effects and Sampling Errors

Appendix A provided a very brief and relatively nontechnical explanation of sampling error estimates, accompanied by two tables of confidence intervals which can be used to ascertain the accuracy of most percentages reported in this volume. The present appendix is intended to provide some background concerning the strategy and rationale involved in computing these confidence intervals. It also offers guidance for those wishing to make sampling computations beyond those contained in Appendix A.

This appendix, like the first, is intended to be readable and usable by the nonstatistician. For that reason, we take the time to outline (albeit briefly) a number of relatively elementary factors involved in estimating confidence intervals.

Factors Influencing the Size of Confidence Intervals

The most straightforward types of samples, from a statistical standpoint at least, are simple random samples. In such samples the confidence limits for a proportion are influenced by the size of the sample or subgroups being considered and also by the size of the proportion. For example, the 95 percent confidence interval for a proportion p based on a simple random sample of N cases is approximated by:
$p \pm 1.96 \sqrt{p(1-p)/N}$. In a complex probability sample such as the present one, there are a number of other factors which influence the size of confidence limits. This section lists all of the factors which have been taken into account in calculating confidence intervals for use with the data in this volume, beginning with the most simple factors and then proceeding to the more complex.

Number of Cases (N). Other things equal, the larger a sample (or subgroup within a sample), the smaller or more precise will be the confidence interval for a percentage based on that sample. One of the factors determining the size of the confidence interval is $1/\sqrt{N}$. Thus, for example, if all other things were equal, a sample of 400 would have confidence intervals half as large (or twice as precise) as a sample of 100, because $1/\sqrt{400}$ is half as large as $1/\sqrt{100}$.

Size of Percentage. Other things equal, percentage values around 50 percent have larger confidence intervals than higher or lower percentage values. This is because another of the factors determining the size of the confidence interval is $\sqrt{p(1-p)}$ where p is a proportion ranging from 0 to 1.0 (or, to put it in percentage terms, the factor is $\sqrt{x\%(100-x\%)}$). Thus, for example, a proportion of either .1 or .9 (a percentage of either 10 percent or 90 percent) will have a confidence interval only three-fifths as large as the confidence interval around a proportion of .5 (or 50 percent), because $\sqrt{.1(1-.1)}$ is three-fifths as large as $\sqrt{.5(1-.5)}$.

Design Effects in Complex Samples. Under conditions of simple random sampling, a confidence interval can be determined solely on the basis of the number of cases and the percentage value involved. More complex samples such as the one used in the present study make use of stratification and clustering and often differential weighting of respondent scores, and these all influence sampling error. While stratification tends to heighten the precision of a sample, the effects of clustering and weighting reduce precision (compared with a simple random sample of the same size). Therefore, it is not appropriate to apply the standard, simple random sampling formulas to such complex samples in order to obtain estimates of sampling errors, because they would almost always underestimate the actual sampling errors.

Methods exist for correcting for this underestimation, however. Kish (1965, p. 258) defines a correction term called the design effect (DEFF), where:

$$DEFF = \frac{\text{actual sampling variance}}{\substack{\text{expected sampling variance} \\ \text{from a simple random sample} \\ \text{with same number of elements}}}$$

Thus, if the actual sampling variance in a complex sample is four times as large as the expected sampling variance from a simple random sample with the same number of cases, the DEFF is 4.0. Since confidence intervals are proportionate to the square root of variance, the confidence intervals for such a sample would be twice as large (because the square root of 4 is 2) as the confidence interval for a simple random sample with the same number of cases. A fairly simple and straightforward way of applying the concept of design effect may be to note that an increase in design effect has the same impact on precision as a reduction in the number of cases in a simple random sample. For example, a sample of 16,000 cases with a design effect of 4.0 would have the same degree of precision (the same size confidence intervals around various percentages) as a simple random sample of 4,000.

In principle, every different statistic resulting from a complex sample can have its own design effect, and different statistics in the same sample may have quite different design effects. However, it is not feasible to compute every design effect, nor would it be feasible to report every one. Thus, in practice, design effects are averaged across a number of statistics and these average values are used to estimate the design effects for other statistics based on the same sample. Sometimes a single design effect is applied to all statistics of a given type (e.g., percentages) for a given sample. In the present study, however, a rather extensive exploration of design effects revealed a number of systematic differences. These systematic differences have to do with the particular measures being examined, the subgroups involved, and the question of whether a trend over time is being considered. The most consistent difference involves the number of cases in the group or subgroup for which the design effect is computed.

The Relationship between Subgroup Size and Design Effects. Kish et al. (1976) have observed that design effects tend to be smaller for subgroups than for total samples; moreover, the smaller the subgroup the smaller the design effect is likely to be. The ex-

planation for this widespread phenomenon is that the average number of cases in each sampling cluster is an important factor in determining the size of the design effect, and as subgroup size decreases so does this average number of cases per cluster. This point is illustrated by several subgroups treated in the present volume — males, females, those planning four years of college, and those not planning four years of college. All (or virtually all) of the schools in the sample have both male and female students, as well as some students who plan four years of college and others who do not. Thus, each of these four subgroups is spread more or less evenly across the full number of clusters (schools). Since each of these subgroups includes roughly half of the total sample, the average number of cases per cluster is about half as large as for the total sample, and this leads to a smaller design effect than is found for the total sample. Other subgroups involving different patterns of drug use are also distributed more or less evenly across all clusters and thus are subject to the same phenomenon of smaller design effects because of the smaller number of cases per cluster.

One very important exception to the pattern of smaller design effects for subgroups·involves the four geographic region subgroups presented in this volume. These subgroups do not cut across all clusters; instead, regions have been described as "segregated" subgroups, in contrast to the "cross-class" subgroups discussed above. For such segregated subgroups the average number of cases per cluster is about the same as is found in the total sample, and thus the design effects are not lower than those for the total sample (Kish et al., 1976). Another subgroup which is in some respects similar to regional subgroups is the category of blacks. Black respondents are not found equally across high schools throughout the United States. There are, of course, regional differences in proportions of blacks, and these contribute substantially to this lack of equal distribution. In addition, there are patterns of segregation in housing which continue to be reflected in the unequal distribution of blacks in high schools. The net effect of these several factors is that the black subgroup in our sample is "partially segregated" in a sampling sense as well as in the more usual usage of that word. For that reason, the design effects for blacks are somewhat larger than for other subgroups of approximately similar size.

Because the subgroups consisting of blacks and the four regional groups all have larger design effects than other subgroups of the same size, it is necessary to adjust the confidence intervals for these subgroups as indicated in Appendix A. (At a later point in the present appendix we will say more about these adjustment factors.)

One other kind of "subgroup" must be noted in this discussion of the relationship between subgroup size and design effects. One-fifth of the total sample filled out each of the five separate questionnaire forms, and thus the respondents to each of these forms may be viewed as a "cross-class" subgroup of the total sample. The average cluster size for a single form is exactly 20 percent of the average cluster size for the total sample. That means, of course, that the single form samples (which are the basis for the large majority of the data presented in this volume) are distinctly more "efficient" than the sample based on all five forms. Accordingly, single form data have much smaller design effects (as displayed later in this appendix).

Design Effects for Comparisons between Subgroups. We noted above that a number of subgroups treated in this volume can be described as "cross-class" subgroups, meaning that members of the subgroup are distributed more or less evenly across sampling clusters. For these kinds of subgroups, it turns out that *comparisons* are relatively efficient, from a sampling standpoint. The technical explanation for this phenomenon is that there is a higher degree of covariance between such subgroup pairs than would be the case in a comparison of independent subgroups. Now let us offer a fairly nontechnical illustration to indicate why this is so. Suppose that a researcher interested in use of marijuana during the senior year of high school obtained data from five high schools concerning female seniors' marijuana use and data from five other high schools concerning male seniors' marijuana use. Suppose that the percentage values for marijuana use during senior year were as follows:

Female seniors (five schools): 60%, 20%, 65%, 30%, 50%

Male seniors (five other schools): 40%, 80%, 25%, 70%, 60%

Even though there is a difference of ten percentage points between males and females (if the five schools in each case are averaged), there is still so much variability among schools that one would not conclude with very much confidence that females in general are less likely than males to use marijuana during the senior year of high school. Suppose, on the other hand, that the researcher had obtained data from a total of only five schools and had obtained data concerning both male and female seniors in each school as follows:

	Females	Males
School A	60%	70%
School B	20%	25%
School C	65%	80%
School D	30%	40%
School E	50%	60%

The same group of percentages, this time based on five pairings of males and females rather than independent observations, are much more strongly suggestive of systematic differences between the sexes.

A process analogous to that illustrated above is involved when "cross-class" subgroups are compared, and the increased accuracy or sampling efficiency is reflected in relatively small sampling errors and design effects.

Design Effects for Trends. Thus far this discussion of factors influencing design effects and confidence intervals has focused only on groups and subgroups within a single year. But one of the central purposes of the Monitoring the Future project is to monitor trends over time; indeed, the study procedures have been standardized across years insofar as possible in order to provide the opportunity for sensitive measurement of change. One of the factors designed to produce an added degree of consistency from one year to the next is the use of each school for two data collections, which means that for any two successive years half of the sample of schools is the same. This, plus the fact that the other half of the school sample in a given year is from the same primary sampling units as the half sample it replaced, means that there is a good deal of consistency in the sampling and clustering of the sample from one year to the next. As a result, when cross-year comparisons are made (say, between 1976 and 1977), the design effects are appreciably smaller (i.e., the efficiency is greater) than if completely independent samples of schools had been drawn each year. In other words, the 1976 and 1977 samples are not independent; on the contrary, there is a considerable degree of covariance between them. A similar level of covariance occurs between any pair of adjacent-year samples (e.g., 1977 and 1978), because about half of the schools in both samples were the same. This covariance, or partial "matching," reduces the design effect for differences observed between adjacent years, compared to what they would have been with totally independent samples.

It follows from the discussion above that a trend over an interval greater than one year (e.g., a comparison between 1976 and 1978 which involves totally non-overlapping school samples) is likely to have a design effect which is larger than that for a comparison between adjacent-year samples.

Variables with Unusually Large Design Effects. Kish et al. (1976) stress the importance of computing sampling errors for many kinds of variables, and they point out that they have found "very wide ranges in values of sampling errors (standard errors and design effects) between diverse variables within the same survey" (p. 21). Our own experience has been that, among most variables, the variation in sampling errors and design effects seems more random than consistent, and thus we are reasonably comfortable with the use of averaging procedures (described below) in order to derive a set of general purpose tables. There are some important exceptions to the above generalization, however. Variables which are likely to be grouped according to geographical area (region and/or urbanicity), as well as variables that may differ systematically from one school to another, show much higher than usual amounts of homogeneity within sample clusters. It follows necessarily that such variables also have much higher than usual design effects. The variables in the Monitoring the Future study which seem most likely to show such high design effects tend to be grouped into the questionnaire segment dealing with background factors and educational aspirations (Section C of all questionnaire forms). These variables were excluded from the process of computing overall design effects and the confidence intervals provided in Tables A-1 and A-2. Appendix A provides a further discussion of some of these variables and offers some suggestions for adjusting the confidence interval tables to deal with them.

Procedures Used in Deriving Design Effects and Tables of Confidence Intervals

Having taken some pains to review the several factors which can influence design effects and confidence intervals, it is now a fairly simple matter for us to summarize the steps followed to compute the tables of confidence intervals shown in Appendix A. We were heavily influenced in this effort by the work of Kish and his colleagues (Kish, 1965; Kish et al., 1976) in two ways. First, we followed their recommendation that sampling errors be computed and averaged across a goodly number of variables and subgroups. Second, we paid particular attention to their observation that design effects tend to be smaller for subgroups than for total samples (a point discussed earlier in this appendix).

Confidence Intervals for Single Percentages. Our procedure was to compute sampling errors and design effects for most of the variables which are common to all five forms (those in the C sections of all questionnaires, and those in the B sections of Forms 2 through 5), and for every twentieth variable in the A, D, and E sections of Forms 2 through 5. (Form 1 was omitted because most of this form is comprised of drug-related items, and such items involve high proportions of missing data because respondents are instructed to skip over many questions which are not applicable to them). Design effects were computed for each of the subgroups reported in this volume, as well as for the total sample. Design effects for each subgroup and for the total were averaged across variables for the C sec-

tion material (all five forms), the B section material (drug use measures, all five forms), and the sampling of variables from the A, D, and E sections (single form data). As noted earlier, the variables which showed unusually high levels of homogeneity within sample clusters were excluded from the C section variables when they were averaged. The 1977 data were used for this analysis. Later replication using 1976 data provided nearly identical values.

The averaging process consisted of taking a mean of the *square roots* of the design effects. Kish and his colleagues (1976) refer to the design effect as DEFF, and to the square root of the design effect as DEFT; thus, $\sqrt{DEFF} = DEFT$. We will find it useful to use this terminology in what follows. The rationale for computing means of DEFT rather than DEFF is that the former value is directly proportionate to the size of confidence intervals. A further reason for doing so is that the values of DEFT approximate a normal distribution much more closely than the values of DEFF, which are skewed upward. (A comparison of mean DEFTs and median DEFTs showed them to be quite similar, something which certainly is not true of mean and median DEFFs).

Bearing in mind that design effects tend to be smaller for subgroups than for total samples, and bearing in mind also that confidence intervals are directly proportionate to DEFT and to $\sqrt{N}$, we plotted the mean DEFT values for the total sample and for all subgroups, in each case relating DEFT to $\sqrt{N}$. The results are shown in Figure B-1. Note that distinctions are made between "cross-class" and "segregated" subgroups, and between mean DEFTs based on five forms and those based on single forms (the $\sqrt{N}$ values for the latter are, of course, much smaller).*

Setting aside the "segregated" subgroups (regions and blacks) for the moment, it is clear that the rest of the mean DEFTs in Figure B-1 show a very clear and consistent pattern: the higher the value $\sqrt{N}$ the higher the mean DEFT. It turns out that these mean DEFT values are very closely approximated by the function $DEFT = \sqrt{1.3 + .00015N}$, as shown by the solid line in the figure. (The function can also be stated as $DEFF = 1.3 + .00015N$.) The particular parameters in that function were derived empirically, but the basic function (i.e., $DEFT = \sqrt{a + bN}$) was adapted directly from the work of Kish et al. (1976).

Given the above function that fitted the mean DEFT values for the total sample and the "cross-class" subgroups, we returned to the problem of assigning DEFT values for the "segregated" subgroups. The simplest solution was to select two adjustment factors which could be multiplied by the confidence interval values in Table A-1. These adjustment factors are shown by the dashed lines in Figure B-1; they cor-

* The five form data consisted of C section material, excluding those variables related to region, urbanicity, and/or socioeconomic level.

Figure B-1
Design Effects for Single Percentages

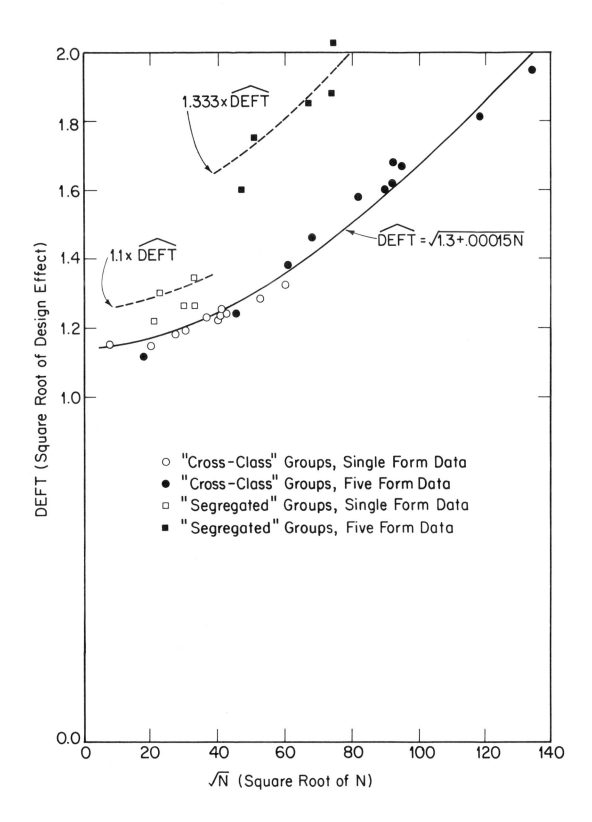

respond to multiplying the "standard" DEFT (solid line) by a factor of 1.1 for single form data and by a factor of 1.33 for five form data. These adjustments, which were selected on empirical grounds, yield design effects for the "segregated" subgroups which are approximately equal to the design effects for the total sample (treating single form and five form data separately, of course). This is reassuring, since Kish et al. (1976) have reported that "segregated" subgroups can in general be expected to show design effects approximately equivalent to the design effects for the total sample.

After the data in Figure B-1 were plotted and the form of the main function (indicated by the solid line) was determined, DEFT values for drug use measures (material in Section B of all forms) were checked. It was found that the DEFTs for only two drug categories, alcohol and marijuana, exceeded the values indicated by the function; accordingly, adjustment factors were developed for these two drugs (1.6 and 1.35, respectively).

Confidence Intervals for Differences between Two Percentages. Our procedure here was directly parallel to that followed in determining confidence intervals for single percentages. DEFT values for the differences between 1977 and 1976 percentages were computed using virtually the same set of items as used earlier. Also computed were mean DEFT values for comparisons in the same year between subgroups such as males and females, those who did and did not plan to complete four years of college, blacks and whites, pairings of regions, and pairings of drug use groups. It was found that, for any given level of N, the mean DEFT values for subgroup comparisons were quite similar to the mean DEFT values for one-year trends; accordingly, all of these mean DEFTs were included in Figure B-2, which plots mean DEFTs for differences between percentages. In this figure, as in Figure B-1, the strong relationship was evident between mean DEFTs and the numbers of cases in the two groups being compared. This relationship can be very closely approximated by the function DEFT = $\sqrt{1.3 + .000075N}$ (which can also be stated DEFF = $1.3 + .000075N$), where $N = 2N_1N_2/N_1 + N_2$.

It was expected on grounds of sampling theory that as we found earlier, the function which fit most differences between percentages would not fit differences involving regions and differences involving blacks. In fact, the data indicated that some adjustment is necessary for black-white comparisons using data from all five forms, and also for comparisons as well as trends involving any region. We have not tried to show those adjustments in Figure B-2, but the several values involved are shown in the guidelines to Table A-2.

It was also expected on the grounds of sampling theory that trends across an interval of two or more

years would show somewhat higher values of DEFT than one-year trends. It turned out that this was true only for data from all five forms; data based on one form only did not show significantly higher values. The adjustment factors for trends involving five forms over two or more years are shown in Table A-2.

Use of Weighted Numbers of Cases in Entering Confidence Interval Tables. We should mention in passing that the recommendations for using the tables in Appendix A indicate that *weighted* N values should be used. The computer program which generated our design effect statistics makes use of weights in calculating percentages and actual sampling variances. But in computing the DEFF ratio, defined as the actual sampling variance divided by the expected sampling variance from a simple random sample with the same number of elements, the program makes use of the *unweighted* numbers of cases to determine "the same number of elements." Since the mean weights used in the 1975, 1976, and 1977 data tables are slightly lower than 1.0, this means that when entering the tables in Appendix A with weighted data from those years, one is being very slightly "conservative" (slightly reduced risk of a Type 1 error, slightly increased risk of a Type 2 error). It is important to realize that if one took the trouble to make corrections for this "conservatism," the correction would rarely be as great as multiplying the Table A-1 and Table A-2 entries by a factor of .95; and in the large majority of cases the correction would involve multiplying by a factor of about .98. We find such discrepancies to be trivially small, particularly when compared with what Kish et al. (1976, p. 12) describe as the "heroic simplifications" required in some of the steps leading to general purpose tables of design effects and confidence intervals.

Before the 1978 data tables were produced we had come to realize the advantages in having weighted values which averaged 1.0; accordingly, beginning with the 1978 data, the weighted N values in the tables do approximate the actual numbers of cases quite closely. But it was impractical to redo the 1975 through 1977 data tables to incorporate this refinement. Another alternative would have been to employ slightly different versions of Tables A-1 and A-2, containing slightly different confidence intervals for each of those three years; however, we felt that such an approach could introduce confusion when cross-year comparisons were made. Thus, we opted for the solution which seems to us to be most simple and manageable, even though it involves the slight degree of "conservatism" noted above. For readers who find this solution undesirable, we have included Tables B-1 and B-2, which present weighted and unweighted Ns for the various subgroups for each year. Table B-1 contains Ns for all five forms (except for 1975 which shows Ns for Forms 2 through 5), and Table B-2 con-

Figure B-2
Design Effects for Differences Between Percentages

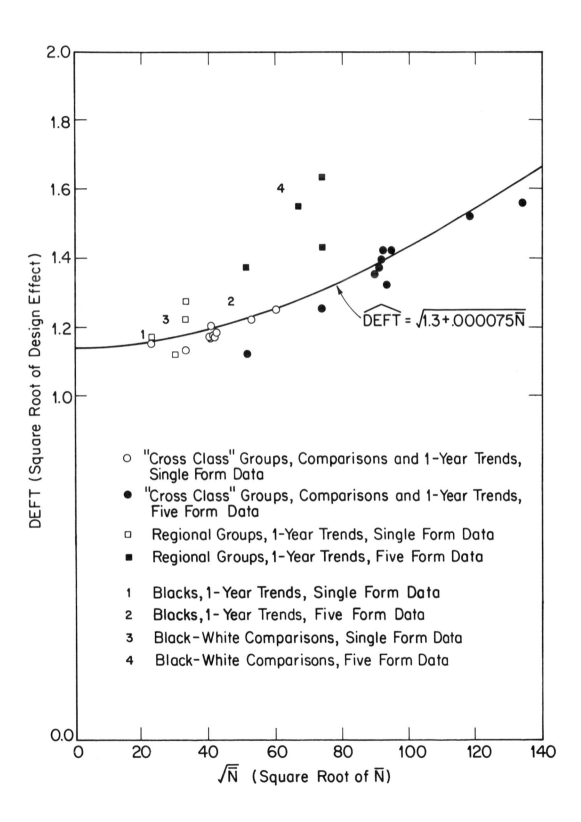

tains approximate Ns for a single form. Thus, readers who wish to avoid the slight "conservatism" (and also to be more precise for subgroups in 1978 and later whose average weight is not exactly 1.0) may determine the unweighted Ns. Some correction for missing data should be made in this case; this can be accom-

plished by calculating the percentage of missing data (using the weighted Ns from the data table and the weighted N from Table B-1 or B-2) and adjusting the unweighted N accordingly. These adjusted unweighted Ns can then be used in Appendix A.

TABLE B-1

Sample Sizes (Unweighted and Weighted) in Subgroups by Year

Number of Cases

	Class of 1975*		Class of 1976		Class of 1977		Class of 1978		Class of 1979		Class of 1980		Class of 1981		Class of 1982		Class of 1983		Class of 1984		Class of 1985	
	Unwtd	Wtd	Unwtd	Wtd	Unwtd	Wtd	Unwtd	Wtd	Unwtd	Wtd	Unwtd	Wtd	Unwtd	Wtd	Unwtd	Wtd	Unwtd	Wtd	Unwtd	Wtd	Unwtd	Wtd
Total Sample	12627	12108	16678	15138	18436	15830	18924	18916	16662	16662	16524	16524	18267	18267	18348	18348	16947	16947	16499	16499	16502	16502
Sex:																						
Male	5799	5571	7999	7241	8449	7358	8603	8779	7889	7778	7935	7744	8775	8725	8979	8828	8106	8074	7653	7800	7620	7776
Female	6371	6100	7924	7257	9188	7850	9416	9266	8139	8232	7874	8078	8752	8865	8610	8788	8160	8227	8144	8029	8287	8164
Race:																						
White	**	**	12933	11796	13818	12240	14663	14847	13432	13299	12894	12846	13625	13985	13753	13887	12697	12806	12223	12337	12162	12291
Black	**	**	1806	1716	2500	1938	2205	2096	1617	1742	1939	2098	2495	2265	2203	2080	2191	2067	2281	2244	2195	1995
Region:																						
Northeast	3014	2695	4034	3570	4760	3959	4841	4607	3926	4016	4281	3877	4269	4290	4719	4741	4130	4056	3658	3387	3615	3878
North Central	3951	3832	5098	4687	5697	4758	5576	5411	5385	4874	4340	4873	5069	5484	5223	5383	4245	4784	4018	4612	4612	4516
South	3366	3857	4177	4597	4908	4820	5566	6292	4713	5055	4667	5049	5513	5600	5191	5551	5522	5434	5726	5568	5263	5028
West	2296	1724	3369	2284	3071	2294	2941	2605	2638	2717	3236	2726	3416	2893	3215	2672	3050	2673	3097	2932	3012	3079
College Plans:																						
Complete 4 yrs	**	**	7963	6994	8933	7407	9264	8844	8571	8203	9191	8658	10256	9878	9851	9360	9342	9062	9114	9103	9592	9448
None or under 4 yrs	**	**	7179	6877	7764	7048	7857	8413	6715	7063	5995	6578	6486	7008	6971	7507	6214	6555	6002	6124	5588	5770
Illicit Drug Use:																						
None	4329	4400	6532	6091	6672	5878	6400	6595	5426	5654	5322	5591	5954	6148	6157	6328	6001	6082	6124	6199	6401	6412
Marijuana Only	2044	1894	3950	3457	4955	4050	5354	5214	4756	4610	4480	4357	4313	4179	4127	4040	3657	3599	3585	3529	3541	3449
Few Pills	1163	1113	1942	1736	2173	1813	2329	2304	2171	2168	2150	2104	2297	2306	2449	2439	2308	2315	2198	2196	2228	2264
More Pills	2157	1989	3427	2987	3857	3266	3906	3885	3622	3543	3873	3760	4972	4925	4896	4839	4333	4306	3946	3936	3737	3802
Any Heroin	231	216	319	268	321	280	289	302	193	186	186	180	183	189	212	210	210	206	206	207	196	193

*The number of cases shown for 1975 is based on Forms 2 through 5 only, because the data from Form 1 are intentionally not included in tabulations based on drug and demographic items which appeared in all forms.

**Missing data problems were severe for race and college plans in 1975; accordingly, these data have been excluded from all tables in the 1975 report.

TABLE B-2
Sample Sizes (Unweighted and Weighted) in Subgroups by Year
for Questions on a Single Form*

Number of Cases

	Class of 1975		Class of 1976		Class of 1977		Class of 1978		Class of 1979		Class of 1980		Class of 1981		Class of 1982		Class of 1983		Class of 1984		Class of 1985	
	Unwtd	Wtd	Unwtd	Wtd	Unwtd	Wtd	Unwtd	Wtd	Unwtd	Wtd	Unwtd	Wtd	Unwtd	Wtd	Unwtd	Wtd	Unwtd	Wtd	Unwtd	Wtd	Unwtd	Wtd
Total Sample	3157	3027	3336	3028	3687	3166	3785	3783	3332	3332	3305	3305	3653	3653	3670	3670	3389	3389	3300	3300	3300	3300
Sex:																						
Male	1450	1393	1600	1488	1690	1472	1721	1756	1578	1556	1587	1549	1755	1745	1796	1766	1621	1615	1531	1560	1524	1555
Female	1593	1525	1585	1451	1838	1570	1883	1853	1628	1646	1575	1616	1750	1773	1722	1758	1632	1645	1629	1606	1657	1633
Race:																						
White	**	**	2587	2359	2764	2448	2933	2969	2686	2660	2579	2569	2725	2797	2751	2777	2540	2561	2445	2467	2432	2458
Black	**	**	361	343	500	388	441	419	323	348	388	420	499	453	441	416	438	413	456	449	439	399
Region:																						
Northeast	754	674	807	714	952	792	968	921	785	803	856	775	854	858	944	948	826	811	732	677	723	776
North Central	988	958	1020	937	1139	952	1115	1082	1077	975	868	975	1014	1097	1045	1077	849	957	804	804	922	903
South	842	964	835	919	982	964	1113	1258	943	1011	933	1010	1103	1120	1038	1110	1104	1087	1145	1114	1053	1006
West	574	431	674	457	614	459	588	521	528	543	647	545	683	579	643	534	610	535	619	586	602	616
College Plans:																						
Complete 4 yrs	**	**	1593	1399	1787	1481	1853	1769	1714	1641	1838	1732	2051	1976	1970	1872	1868	1812	1823	1821	1918	1890
None or under 4 yrs	**	**	1436	1375	1553	1410	1571	1683	1343	1413	1199	1316	1297	1402	1394	1501	1243	1311	1200	1225	1118	1154
Illicit Drug Use																						
None	1082	1100	1306	1218	1334	1176	1280	1319	1085	1131	1064	1118	1191	1230	1231	1266	1200	1216	1225	1240	1280	1282
Marijuana Only	511	474	790	691	991	810	1071	1043	951	922	896	871	863	836	825	808	731	720	717	706	708	690
Few Pills	291	278	388	347	435	363	466	461	434	434	430	421	459	461	490	488	462	463	440	439	446	453
More Pills	539	497	685	597	771	653	781	777	724	709	775	752	994	985	979	968	867	861	789	787	747	760
Any Heroin	58	54	64	54	64	56	58	60	39	37	37	36	37	38	42	42	42	41	41	41	39	39

*The Ns given here are very close approximations of the N in the given subgroup for any of the five different questionnaire forms used in the year.

**Missing data problems were severe for race and college plans in 1975; accordingly, these data have been excluded from all tables in the 1975 report.

Further Applications of these Design Effects and Sampling Errors

One of the reasons for providing the above review of the factors influencing design effects and confidence intervals, and the procedures used in computing our confidence interval tables, is to provide sufficient background and data to permit the interested reader to go beyond the material provided in Appendix A. In this section we consider two specific extensions, the calculation of levels of "statistical significance" higher than 95 percent and the computation of means and their confidence intervals.

Calculating Confidence Intervals for Higher Levels of Statistical Significance. The entries contained in Tables A-1 and A-2 provide the 95 percent confidence level (also referred to as the .05 level of significance). These entries were computed by multiplying the standard error (square root of sample variance) by a factor of 1.96. The 99 percent confidence interval (.01 level of significance) uses a factor of 2.58 standard errors, and the 99.9 percent confidence interval (.001 level of significance) uses a factor of 3.29 standard errors. To convert the entries in Tables A-1 and A-2 to these higher levels, it is necessary only to multiply the entries by the appropriate constant shown below (keeping in mind that any other adjustments required in the tables must also be applied):

Confidence Interval	Significance Level	Multiply entries in Tables A-1 and A-2 by the following:
99%	.01	2.58/1.96= 1.32
99.9%	.001	3.29/1.96= 1.68

Computing Means and Their Confidence Intervals. Many of the questionnaire items included in this volume have ordinal response scales (e.g., agree, agree mostly, neither, disagree mostly, disagree), and it is often the case that a survey analyst will be willing to treat such scales as if they involved equal intervals. In such cases, means and standard deviations are more "efficient" in their use of information than are dichotomies which yield a single percentage or a pair of percentages (e.g., those who respond "agree" or "agree mostly," versus all others). It is a relatively straightforward matter to compute means and standard deviations for the total sample or any of the subgroups treated in this volume. The problem, then, is to be able to specify confidence intervals for the means, or for the differences between pairs of means. In the case of simple random samples, one needs only the means, standard deviations (or variances), and numbers of cases in order to compute confidence intervals. But in complex samples such as the present one,

it is also necessary to take account of design effects. If an estimate of design effect is available, one of the simplest procedures to follow is to divide the actual numbers of cases by the design effect (thereby "depreciating" the actual number to its equivalent value in simple random sample terms) and then employ the standard statistical procedures which have been developed for application to simple random samples. Thus, for example, if the design effect (DEFF) for a sample of 18,000 were 4.0, then one could divide the 18,000 by 4.0 and the result, 4,500, could be entered as the value of "N" in statistical tables and formulas designed for use with simple random samples. To take another example, if one were comparing means based on two subgroups, each involving about 9,000 cases, and if DEFF (for both subgroups) was 2.0, then one could compute the significance of the difference between the two means as if the N for each group were 4,500 (i.e., 9,000 divided by 2.0).

In short, the strategy involves dividing the actual number of cases by the appropriate DEFF in order to get a "simple random sampling equivalent N" or, more simply, an "effective N" for use in statistical procedures designed for random samples.

Design Effects for Use in Computing "Effective Ns." In order to employ the strategy outlined above, one must have estimates of design effects which are judged to be appropriate for one's purposes. In the case of means based on the percentages reported in this volume, we are confident (based on personal communications with Kish) that it is appropriate to use the same DEFF values as were used in developing Tables A-1 and A-2. For other, more complex statistics, we cannot make the same assertion, although it is generally the case that design effects for such statistics are not larger than those for means and percentages (Kish and Frankel, 1970; Frankel, 1971).

In Table B-3 we provide guidelines for computing DEFF values for single percentages (or means) and for differences between two percentages (or means). For reasons discussed elsewhere in this appendix, we must provide for different (and somewhat higher) DEFFs for "segregated" subgroups (regional subgroups and sometimes also blacks), and for trends over two or more years (in contrast to one-year trends). And in all instances, of course, the DEFF values are very much influenced by the average size of sampling clusters, which is always dependent on the number of cases (N). Accordingly, all of the design effect formulas in Table B-3 require computations which take account of N. (It should also be noted that the formulas in Table B-3 correspond exactly to the values of design effects and adjustment factors used in Tables A-1 and A-2 in Appendix A.

A Concluding Note. In their very useful paper dealing with sampling errors for fertility surveys, Kish

Table B-3
Guidelines for Computing Design Effects (DEFFs) for Percentages
and Means Derived from Monitoring the Future Samples

DEFINITIONS

$$\text{DEFF (design effect} = \frac{\text{(estimated sampling variance}}{\text{expected sampling variance from simple}}$$
$$\text{random sample with same number of elements}$$

N = number of respondents on whom a single percentage or mean is based

$\overline{N}$ = $2N_1N_2/(N_1 + N_2)$, for use in comparisons of two percentages or means, based on two groups of sizes N_1 and N_2.

DESIGN EFFECT FORMULAS

1. For single percentages or means involving . . .
   a. regional subgroups or blacks
      DEFF for single form data ....(1.3 + .00015N) (1.21)
      DEFF for five form data ....(1.3 + .00015N) (1.78)

   b. all other subgroups or total sample
      DEFF for single form or five form data ....1.3 + .00015N

2. For comparisons between . . .
   a. any two regions
      DEFF for single form data ....$(1.3 + .000075\overline{N})$ (1.32)
      DEFF for five form data ....$(1.3 + .000075\overline{N})$ (2.25)

   b. blacks and whites
      DEFF for single form data..$1.3 + .000075\overline{N}$
      DEFF for five form data ....$(1.3 + .000075\overline{N})$ (1.56)

   c. genders, college plans groups, or any two "drug use" subgroups
      DEFF for single form or five form data ....$1.3 + .000075\overline{N}$

3. For one-year trends involving . . .
   a. any region
      DEFF for single form data...$1.3 + .000075\overline{N}$
      DEFF for five form data ....$(1.3 + .000075\overline{N})$ (1.56)
   b. all other subgroups or total sample
      DEFF for single form or five form data ....$1.3 + .000075\overline{N}$

4. For trends over two or more years involving . . .
   a. any region
      DEFF for single form data...$1.3 + .000075\overline{N}$
      DEFF for five form data ....$(1.3 + .000075\overline{N})$ (1.82)
   b. all other subgroups or total sample
      DEFF for single form data...$1.3 + .000075\overline{N}$
      DEFF for five form data ....$(1.3 + .000075\overline{N})$ (1.32)

et al. (1976) commented that some of the methods they used "... emerged after several false starts." They went on to say that the volume and diversity of the data they were dealing with "... presented new challenges and opportunities." And they added, "Our methods are subject to further developments and modifications, and we invite participation and suggestions" (p. 10). Our own attempts to apply the methods of Kish and his colleagues to the data reported in this volume have been challenged by the diversity of the data, have involved several false starts, and we hope are subject to further developments and modifications. We invite readers to offer their suggestions, and we also encourage readers to inquire about further work that we and/or others may carry out during the coming months and years.

Appendix C
Questionnaire Covers, Instructions, and Sample Page

monitoring **the future**

a continuing study of the lifestyles and values of youth

This questionnaire is part of a nationwide study of high school seniors, conducted each year by the University of Michigan's Institute for Social Research. The questions ask your opinions about a number of things — the way things are now and the way you think they ought to be in the future. In a sense, many of your answers on this questionnaire will count as "votes" on a wide range of important issues.

If this study is to be helpful, it is important that you answer each question as thoughtfully and frankly as possible. All your answers will be kept strictly confidential, and will never be seen by anyone who knows you.

This study is completely voluntary. If there is any question that you or your parents would find objectionable for any reason, just leave it blank.

In a few months, we would like to mail each of you a summary of the nationwide results from this study. Also, in about a year we would like to mail another questionnaire to some of you, asking about how your plans have worked out and what's happening in your lives.

In order to include you in these mailings, we ask for your name and address on a special form at the end of this questionnaire. This form is to be torn out and handed in separately. Once the address form and the questionnaire have been separated, there is no way they can be matched again, except by using a special computer tape at the University of Michigan. The only purpose for that tape is to match a follow-up questionnaire with this one.

Other seniors have said that these questionnaires are very interesting and that they enjoy filling them out. We hope you will too. Be sure to read the instructions on the other side of this cover page before you begin to answer. Thank you very much for being an important part of this project.

INSTITUTE FOR SOCIAL RESEARCH
THE UNIVERSITY OF MICHIGAN
ANN ARBOR, MICHIGAN

271

INSTRUCTIONS

1. This is not a test, so there are no right or wrong answers; we would
    like you to work fairly quickly, so that you can finish.

2. All of the questions should be answered by marking one of the answer spaces.
    If you don't always find an answer that fits exactly, use the one that comes
    closest. If any question does not apply to you, or you are not sure of what it
    means, just leave it blank.

3. Your answers will be read automatically by a machine called an optical mark
    reader. Please follow these instructions carefully:

      • Use only the black lead pencil you have been given.

      • Make heavy black marks inside the circles.   These kinds of markings
                                                                   will work: ●   ◕   ◑
      • Erase cleanly any answer you wish to change.

      • Make no other markings or comments on the   These kinds of markings
        answer pages, since they interfere with the   will NOT work: ⊙   ✿   ○
        automatic reading. (If you want to add a
        comment about any question, please use the
        space provided below.)

- -

(THIS SPACE FOR WRITTEN COMMENTS)

WHY YOUR NAME AND ADDRESS?

As we told you earlier, we'd like to send you a summary of the nationwide results of the present study, and in about a year we want to mail a shorter questionnaire to some of you. In order to include you in these follow-ups, we would like to have an address where information will be sure to reach you during the coming year.

HOW IS CONFIDENTIALITY PROTECTED?

● The information on this page will be used ONLY for mailing, and will always be kept separate from your answers. A special Grant of Confidentiality from the U.S. government protects all information gathered in this research project.

● The questionnaire and address pages will be collected separately, sealed immediately in separate envelopes, and sent to two different cities for processing.

● Once a questionnaire and address page have been separated, there is no way they can be matched, except by using a special computer tape at the University of Michigan. That tape contains the two DIFFERENT numbers that appear on the back of this address page and on the back of the questionnaire. These numbers will be used ONLY to match a follow-up questionnaire with this one.

Before filling out this address page, please separate it from the rest of the questionnaire by FOLDING ALONG THE PERFORATED LINE AND TEARING CAREFULLY.

Please **PRINT** your name and the address where you can most likely be reached during the coming year.

Mr.
Miss_ _
Ms.   FIRST NAME   INITIAL   LAST NAME
Mrs.

STREET _

CITY _

STATE _ ZIP _ _ _ _ _ _ _ _ _ _

TELEPHONE NO.   (   ) — _ _ _ _ _ _ _ _ _ _ _ _ _ _ _ _ _ _
                      AREA

In case we should have trouble getting mail to you, if you move, please **PRINT** the name and address of one other person (with a different address than your own) who will know where to reach you in the future. (Examples of such a person: aunt or uncle, older sister or brother, or close friend.)

Mr.
Miss_ _
Ms.   FIRST NAME   INITIAL   LAST NAME
Mrs.

STREET _

CITY _

STATE _ ZIP _ _ _ _ _ _ _ _ _ _

TELEPHONE NO.   (   ) — _ _ _ _ _ _ _ _ _ _ _ _ _ _ _ _ _ _
                      AREA

THANK YOU AGAIN FOR YOUR HELP

PART A

* BEFORE BEGINNING BE SURE YOU HAVE
READ THE INSTRUCTIONS ON THE COVER.

1. Taking all things together, how would you say things are these days--would you say you're very happy, pretty happy, or not too happy these days?

   ○ Very happy
   ○ Pretty happy
   ○ Not too happy

2. Some people think a lot about the social problems of the nation and the world, and about how they might be solved. Others spend little time thinking about these issues. How much do you think about such things?

   ① Never
   ② Seldom
   ③ Sometimes
   ④ Quite often
   ⑤ A great deal

3. Of all the problems facing the nation today, how often do you worry about each of the following? (Mark one circle for each line.)

	Never Seldom Sometimes Often
a. Chance of nuclear war	①②③④
b. Population growth	①②③④
c. Crime and violence	①②③④
d. Pollution	①②③④
e. Energy shortages	①②③④
f. Race relations	①②③④
g. Hunger and poverty	①②③④
h. Using open land for housing or industry	①②③④
i. Urban decay	①②③④
j. Economic problems	①②③④
k. Drug abuse	①②③④

4. How well do you think your experiences and training (at home, school, work, etc.) have prepared you to be a good. . .

	Poorly Not So Well Fairly Well Well Very Well
a. ...husband or wife?	①②③④⑤
b. ...parent?	①②③④⑤
c. ...worker on a job?	①②③④⑤

5. Apart from the particular kind of work you want to do, how would you rate each of the following settings as a place to work? (Mark one circle for each line.)

	Not At All Acceptable Somewhat Acceptable Acceptable Desirable
a. Working in a large corporation	①②③④
b. Working in a small business	①②③④
c. Working in a government agency	①②③④
d. Working in the military service	①②③④
e. Working in a school or university	①②③④
f. Working in a police department or police agency	①②③④
g. Working in a social service organization	①②③④
h. Working with a small group of partners	①②③④
i. Working on your own (self-employed)	①②③④

6. If you were to get enough money to live as comfortably as you'd like for the rest of your life, would you want to work?

   ① I would want to work
   ② I would not want to work

References

Adelson, J. "What Generation Gap?" *New York Times Magazine*, January 18, 1970, pp. 1–11.

Adelson, J. "Adolescence and the Generation Gap." *Psychology Today*, February 1979, pp. 33–37.

Bachman, J.G., and Johnston, L.D. "The Monitoring the Future Project Design and Procedures," (Occasional Paper #1). Institute for Social Research, The University of Michigan, Ann Arbor, 1978.

Bachman, J.D., and Johnston, L.D. "The Freshmen, 1979." *Psychology Today*, September 1979, pp. 79–87.

Bachman, J.G.; Johnston, L.D.; and O'Malley, P.M. "Smoking, Drinking, and Drug Use Among American High School Students: Correlates and Trends, 1975-1979." *American Journal of Public Health* 71 (1981):59–69.

Bachman, J.G., and O'Malley, P.M. "When Four Months Equal a Year: Inconsistencies in Students' Reports of Drug Use." *Public Opinion Quarterly* 45 (1981):536–548.

Bachman, J.G., and O'Malley, P.M. "Yea-saying, Nay-saying, and Going to Extremes: Are Black-White Differences in Survey Results Due to Response Styles?" *Public Opinion Quarterly*, 48 (1984):409–427.

Bachman, J.G.; O'Malley, P.M.; and Johnston, J. Youth in Transition, Volume VI: *Adolescence to Adulthood — A Study of Change and Stability in the Lives of Young Men*. Ann Arbor: Institute for Social Research, The University of Michigan, 1978.

Dearman, N.B., and Plisko, V.W. *The Condition of Education*. (National Center for Education Statistics). Washington, D.C.: U.S. Government Printing Office, 1982.

Frankel, M.R. *Inference from Survey Samples: An Empirical Investigation*. Ann Arbor: Institute for Social Research, The University of Michigan, 1971.

Hays, W.L. *Statistics for the Social Sciences* (2nd ed.). New York: Holt, Rinehart, & Winston, 1973.

Johnston, L.D. *Drugs and American Youth*. Ann Arbor: Institute for Social Research, The University of Michigan, 1973.

Johnston, L.D.; Bachman, J.G.; and O'Malley, P.M. *Drug Use Among American High School Students, 1975-1977* (National Institute on Drug Abuse). Washington, D.C.: U.S. Government Printing Office, 1977.

Johnston, L.D.; Bachman, J.G.; and O'Malley, P.M. *Drugs and the Class of 1978: Behaviors, Attitudes, and Recent National Trends* (National Institute on Drug Abuse). Washington, D.C.: U.S. Government Printing Office, 1979(a).

Johnston, L.D.; Bachman, J.G.; and O'Malley, P.M. *1979 Highlights: Drugs and the Nation's High School Students, Five Year National Trends* (National Institute on Drug Abuse). Washington, D.C.: U.S. Government Printing Office, 1979(b).

Johnston, L.D.; Bachman, J.G.; and O'Malley, P.M. *Highlights from Student Drug Use in America: 1975-1980* (National Institute on Drug Abuse). Washington, D.C.: U.S. Government Printing Office, 1981.

Johnston, L.D.; Bachman, J.G.; and O'Malley, P.M. *Student Drug Use in America, 1975-1981*. (National Institute on Drug Abuse). Washington, D.C.: U.S. Government Printing Office, 1982.

Johnston, L.D.; Bachman, J.G.; and O'Malley, P.M. *Student Drug Use, Attitudes and Beliefs: National Trends 1975-1982*. (National Institute on Drug Abuse). Washington, D.C.: U.S. Government Printing Office, 1983.

Johnston, L.D.; O'Malley, P.M.; and Bachman. J.G. *Highlights from Drugs and American High School Students, 1975-1983*. (National Institute on Drug Abuse). Washington, D.C.: U.S. Government Printing Office, 1984.

Johnston, L.D.; O'Malley, P.M.; and Bachman, J.G. *Drugs and American High School Students, 1975-1983*. (National Institute on Drug Abuse). Washington, D.C.: U.S. Government Printing Office, 1984.

Johnston, L.D.; O'Malley, P.M.; and Bachman, J.G. *Drug Use Among American High School Students, College Students, and Other Young Adults, National Trends Through 1985*. (National Institute on Drug Abuse). Washington, D.C.: U.S. Government Printing Office, 1986.

Kish, L. *Survey Sampling*. New York: John Wiley & Sons, 1965.

Kish, L., and Frankel, M.R. "Balanced Repeated Replication for Standard Errors." *Journal of the American Statistical Association* 65 (1970):1071–1094.

Kish, L.; Groves, R.M.; and Krotki, K.P. *Sampling Errors for Fertility Surveys* (Occasional Papers Series No. 17). Voorburg, The Netherlands: International Statistical Institute, 1976.

U.S. Bureau of the Census, *Current Population Reports*. Series P-20, No. 319, School enrollment — social and economic characteristics of students, October 1976. Washington, D.C.: U.S. Government Printing Office, 1978.